ENCYCLOPEDIA OF INVESTMENTS

SECOND EDITION

Jack P. Friedman is the Julio S. Laguarta Professor of Real Estate in the Real Estate Center, and in the Department of Finance, at Texas A&M University. His main areas of interest are portfolio management, investment analysis, taxation, and appraisal of real estate. He has written 11 books and more than 100 articles, contributing frequently to The Appraisal Journal, Real Estate Review, Real Estate Finance, *and other journals. He is a consultant to large banks and government agencies, is on the editorial board of five journals, and is a fellow in the prestigious Homer Hoyt Institute. He received his BBA from Wake Forest University, MBA from Pace University, and Ph.D. from Georgia State University. A Certified Public Accountant, Dr. Friedman also holds professional designations from the Society of Real Estate Appraisers and American Society of Appraisers.*

ENCYCLOPEDIA OF INVESTMENTS

SECOND EDITION

Editor-in-Chief
JACK P. FRIEDMAN
Laguarta Professor of Real Estate
Real Estate Center
Department of Finance
Texas A&M University

WG&L
WARREN, GORHAM & LAMONT
Boston • New York

WARREN, GORHAM & LAMONT, INC.
210 South Street, Boston, Massachusetts 02111

ISBN 0-7913-0365-9

Library of Congress Catalog Card No. 89-50553

PRINTED IN THE UNITED STATES OF AMERICA

CONTRIBUTING AUTHORS

Richard A. Bagg
Director of Auctions, Auctions by Bowers and Merena, Inc., Wolfeboro, N.H.
Coins

Michele Beiny
Vice-President, The Antique Porcelain Company of New York, Inc.
Porcelain

Rotraut Beiny
President, The Antique Porcelain Company of New York, Inc.
Porcelain

Richard J. Blum
Vice-President, First National Bank of Chicago
Bank Certificates of Deposit

Marshall E. Blume
Howard Butcher Professor of Finance, The Wharton School, University of Pennsylvania, Philadelphia
Modern Portfolio Theory

John C. Bogle
Chairman, Vanguard Group of Investment Companies, Valley Forge, Pa.
Mutual Funds

Q. David Bowers
Chairman, Bowers & Merena Galleries, and Auctions by Bowers and Merena, Inc., Wolfeboro, N.H.
Coins

Perry L. Burns
Executive Vice-President, Shearson Lehman Hutton, Inc., New York
Zero Coupon Bonds

Archie Cherkezian
President, William Cherkezian & Son, Inc., New York; Editor, *The Oriental Rug Magazine*
Rugs

Thomas C. Coleman
Vice-President and Director, Department of Economic Analysis and Planning, Chicago Board of Trade
Futures: Financial, Agricultural, Currency

J. Patrick Cooney
Assistant Vice-President, Fine Arts Management Services, Citibank, New York
Paintings

Glenn E. Crellin
Division Vice-President for Economics and Research, National Association of Realtors, Washington, D.C.
Real Estate: Single-Family Rental

D. Larry Crumbley
Shelton Taxation Professor, Texas A&M University; Editor, *The Handbook of Estate Planning*
Estate Planning for Investors

Gary Darrow
Owner, Darrow's Fun Antiques, New York
Collectibles

Ted E. Davis
Senior Vice-President, First City National Bank of Houston
Bank-Managed Accounts

Alvaro Meneses-Diaz
Vice-President, MTB Banking Corporation, New York
Metals: Gold, Silver, Platinum, Palladium

Jan L. Dillow
Vice-President, Shearson Lehman Hutton, Inc., New York
Zero Coupon Bonds

Joseph J. Dini
Vice-President, OPF Group Ltd., Burlington, Mass. and Woodcliff Lake, N.J.
Equipment Leasing

Thomas H. Dinsmore
President, Davis/Dinsmore Management Company, New York
Convertible Securities

Jeremy G. Duffield
Senior Vice-President, Vanguard Group of Investment Companies, Valley Forge, Pa.
Mutual Funds

Gene L. Dunbar
Vice-President and Senior Trust Officer, NBC Bank of San Antonio
Real Estate: Farms and Ranches

Alice Levi Duncan
Director of Sculpture and Works of Art, Christie's, New York
Sculpture

Henry Engler
Vice-President, Capital Markets Group of Chemical Bank, New York
U.S. Treasury and Agency Securities

Paul H. Epstein
Partner, Proskauer Rose Goetz & Mendelsohn, New York
Theatrical Productions

Kim Ford
Certified Public Accountant, Gerald L. Hill and Company, San Antonio
Real Estate: Farms and Ranches

Katherine A. Foulser
Manager, Roulac Real Estate Consulting Group of Deloitte Haskins & Sells, New York
Real Estate: Limited Partnerships

Irving D. Friedman
Private investor, retired attorney and stockbroker, New York
Corporate Bonds

Thomas G. Gillis
Senior Vice-President of Financial Institutions, Structured Finance Debt Rating Services Division, Standard & Poor's Corporation, New York
Mortgage-Backed Securities

Jay L. Gottlieb
Advisory Economist, Department of Economic Analysis and Planning, Chicago Board of Trade
Futures: Financial, Agricultural, Currency

Donald S. Grubbs, Jr.
President, Grubbs and Company, Inc., Silver Spring, Md.
Individual Retirement Plans
Pension Plan Investments

James E. Hamer
Former Trust Officer, The Northern Trust Company, Chicago
Real Estate: Farms and Ranches

John A. Hays
Assistant Vice-President of American Decorative Arts, Christie's New York
Furniture

Roger G. Ibbotson
Professor in Practice of Finance, Yale University School of Management, New Haven, Conn.
Historical Returns on Principal Investments

Priscilla Juvelis
Dealer in rare books and manuscripts, Boston
Books

Eugene M. Krader
Managing Editor of Tax, Warren, Gorham & Lamont, Inc., New York
Tax Considerations for Collector-Investors

David S. Krause
Chief Financial Officer, Precision Plus, Inc., Walworth, Wis.
Sports Memorabilia

George W. Kutner
Assistant Professor of Finance, Marquette University, Milwaukee, Wis.
Sports Memorabilia

Nancy J. Kyle
Vice-President, Morgan Guaranty Trust Company, New York
Foreign Equities

Charles W. Lard
President, Alternative Investment Management Company, Hartford, Conn.
Preferred Stocks

Harris Lawless
President, Harris Lawless & Associates, Freedom, Cal.
Real Estate: Multifamily Rental

Adrian F. Lee
Vice-President, International Capital Markets Research and New Product Development, J.P. Morgan Investment Management, Inc., New York
Diversification Through International Money Markets

Jeffrey R. Leeds
Managing Director, Capital Markets Group of Chemical Bank, New York
U.S. Treasury and Agency Securities

Terrence L. Love, Sr.
Chairman, Land Development Analysts, Inc., Atlanta
Real Estate: Undeveloped Land

James M.D. Maloney
Executive Vice-President, Arabians Ltd., China Spring, Tex.
Horses

Richard Mark
Associate Professor of Accounting, University of Texas at Arlington
Oil and Gas

Antoinette Leonard Matlins
Author, lecturer, and advisor on gemstones, S. Woodstock, Vt.
Gemstones

Edward E. Milam
Professor of Accounting, University of Mississippi
Estate Planning for Investors

Gretchen S. Morrison
Economist, First National Bank of Chicago
Bank Certificates of Deposit

Gordon J. Munro
Former Vice-President, Pensions Department, New York Life Insurance Company
Life Insurance: Guaranteed Interest Contracts

John B. Nicholson
President, Berryhill Associates, Washington, D.C.
Real Estate: Investment Trusts

David Nochimson
Member of the law firm of Ziffren, Brittenham & Branca, Los Angeles
Motion Pictures

David L. Renz
Vice-President and Director of Financial Services, The Prudential Asset Management Co., Inc., Florham Park, N.J.
Life Insurance: Separate Accounts

Peter M. Rexford
Founder of the first Rare Stamp and Coin Division for a New York Stock Exchange Member Firm; writer of a nationally syndicated newspaper column on stamps and coins
Stamps

Keith B. Romney
Founder of Keith Romney Associates, Condominium, Timesharing, and Fractional Ownership Consultants, Salt Lake City, Utah
Real Estate: Condominiums, Cooperatives, Time-shares, Fractionals

Mark Rosen
Institutional Bond Trader, Ehrlich Bober & Co., Inc., New York
Municipal Securities

Stephen E. Roulac
Partner in Charge of Roulac Real Estate Consulting Group of Deloitte Haskins & Sells, New York, Los Angeles, and San Francisco; author, editor, and lecturer on real estate
Real Estate: Limited Partnerships

Jack H. Rubens
Assistant Professor, Department of Finance, Cleveland State University
Role of Tangibles in an Investment Portfolio

Robert S. Rubinstein
Vice-President and Actuary, Integrity Life Insurance Company, New York
Annuities

George M. Schofield
President, George M. Schofield Co., St. Helena, Cal.
Wines

Joseph A. Schrank
Vice-President, Alternative Investment Management Company, Hartford, Conn.
Preferred Stocks

John R. Schumann
Former Vice-President and Attorney, Trust Department, The Northern Trust Company, Chicago
Real Estate: Farms and Ranches

Maria Crawford Scott
Editor of the *AAII Journal*, a publication of the American Association of Individual Investors, Chicago
The Financial Planning Industry

Patricia D. Segall
Senior Analyst, IDD Information Services, Inc., New York
Commercial Paper

Allan M. Shapiro
Member of the New York Bar
Theatrical Productions

Laurence B. Siegel
Managing Director, Ibbotson Associates, Inc., Chicago
Historical Returns on Principal Investments

David J. Skinner
Stock and Bond Broker, Edward D. Jones & Co., College Station, Tex.
Common Stocks

David G. Sparks
Vice-President, Lewis, Foote & Company, Philadelphia
Venture Capital

Joan C. Terwilliger
Assistant Secretary, Morgan Guaranty Trust Company, New York
Bank-Managed Accounts

John R. Thomas
Vice-President, Morgan Guaranty Trust Company, New York
Bank-Managed Accounts

Gary L. Trennepohl
Chairman of the Department of Finance, Texas A&M University, College Station, Tex.; Faculty Member, Chicago Board Options Exchange
Options: Puts and Calls

Paul Vandekar
President, Earle D. Vandekar of Knightsbridge, Inc., New York
Porcelain

Luis Vigdor
Executive Vice-President, MTB Banking Corporation, New York
Metals: Gold, Silver, Platinum, Palladium

Marvin B. Waring
Managing Director, Ibbotson Associates, Inc., Chicago
Historical Returns on Principal Investments

Alden W. Watson
Associate, Proskauer Rose Goetz & Mendelsohn, New York
Theatrical Productions

James R. Webb
Professor and Chairman, Department of Finance, J. Nance College of Business, Cleveland State University
Role of Tangibles in an Investment Portfolio

Ted R. Whitmer
Real Estate Appraiser, The Ted Whitmer Co., Houston
Real Estate: Commercial and Industrial

Fred Williams
Staff Reporter, *Pensions and Investment Age*, The Newspaper of Corporate and Institutional Investing, Dallas
Oil and Gas

Charles E. Wooley
Author and Consultant, Methuen, Mass.
Collectibles

Jonathan L. Wooley
Corporate Vice-President and Actuary, New York Life Insurance Company
Life Insurance: Guaranteed Interest Contracts

Allan E. Young
Professor of Finance in the School of Management, Syracuse University
Warrants and Rights

PREFACE

THE PURPOSE of the *Encyclopedia* is to present—in a clear and concise fashion—accurate, unbiased information on a wide array of investments. Relatively few people have extensive formal education in investments, and even those who work in the investment field generally specialize in only one or two broad areas. In addition, for those who want general information about many types of investments, the *Encyclopedia* can be of special value. The reader can obtain a great deal of information about new areas of investments because the articles offer complete overviews of forty-eight investment opportunities. The investment professional as well as others who want to learn more about certain types of investments will find these articles to be concise, thoroughly researched, and up-to-date.

The main body of the *Encyclopedia* presents forty-eight separate articles on a wide range of different investment opportunities, from Annuities to Zero Coupon Bonds. The authors are recognized experts who were carefully chosen for their expertise and eminence in their fields. For uniformity and logical flow, each article follows a common organization, which is arranged according to these major headings:

- Basic Characteristics
- Attractive Features
- Potential Risks
- Tax Consequences
- Representative Types of Investors
- Important Factors in Buying and Selling
- Glossary
- Suggested Reading

The discussion under Basic Characteristics presents an overview of the investment, including its varieties and quality grades. The reader will learn why it is an investment and not a consumable good. Its potential for appreciation, cash flow, other financial benefits, and leverage opportunities are described under Attractive Features. In addition, as with all investments, there are potential risks that must be understood. Tax consequences, especially those that are unique to the investment, are covered in each article as well.

The age, family situation, income, wealth, risk tolerance, or temperament of an investor will determine the suitability of a given investment, and some investments are more appropriate for an institution than an individual. Investor suitability is discussed under Representative Types of Investors. Successful investing requires the ability to buy and sell in the same market, and thus requires understanding of both the retail and wholesale markets. Important Factors in Buying and Selling covers such matters, along with liquidity and other concerns when selling.

Because a knowledge of basic terminology is essential for effective communication, each article includes a Glossary of key terms. In addition, the suggested reading list notes important books and periodicals for those who seek more printed information. Finally, where appropriate, a list of dealers and brokers is provided in order to acquaint the reader with some names associated with the field.

At the end of the *Encyclopedia* a separate part, entitled "Investment Strategy," provides a unifying framework for assembling and assessing a portfolio. The article on "Modern Portfolio Theory" illustrates the powers of diversification, with its potential to simultaneously increase returns and reduce risk. "Historical Returns on Principal Investments" is a meticulously compiled, unbiased source of long-term information on returns and risk for major types of investments. "Role of Tangibles in an Investment Portfolio" offers insights in constructing a mixed-asset portfolio, and "Diversification Through International Money Markets" discusses the advantages of global investment.

The two articles on tax planning are essential because after-tax income is an important yardstick in assessing the appropriateness of an investment. In this regard, "Income Tax Considerations for Investor-Collectors" consolidates the rules that apply to a large class of assets, while "Estate Planning for Investors" discusses how to pass an estate to the next generation with a minimal tax bite. Finally, "The Financial Planning Industry" describes the credentials that may be possessed by financial planners.

Regardless of whether the reader seeks general information or precise information about a specific area, the *Encyclopedia*'s structure and presentation allows pleasurable and efficient reading. I hope it will be highly rewarding to its readers.

ACKNOWLEDGMENTS

I would like to express sincere appreciation to all involved with the *Encyclopedia*. Obviously, it would not have been possible without the expertise of over eighty contributors, each of whom generously shared vast knowledge about an investment.

Eugene Simonoff, Executive Vice-President and Publisher of Warren, Gorham & Lamont, is credited with the vision and action that first brought the plans off the drawing board into print. John Boyd, Vice-President, was instrumental in developing the coverage and structure of this edition. The *Encyclopedia* could not have been published without the tireless efforts of Lee Jackson, Senior Editor, whose technical and personal skills are reflected throughout. I thank Keith Stout for creating the design for the text, and Arlene Reisberg who painstakingly copyedited the entire manuscript. I am also deeply grateful to Lucy Morgan and Suzanne Barnhill for preparing extensive amounts of correspondence and many of the manuscripts. I thank Marshall Blume, Editor-in-Chief of the first edition, especially for broadening the array of investment vehicles from that originally proposed, and my esteemed colleague, Jack Harris, for his valued opinions in matters too numerous to describe.

Encouragement for this second edition was provided by many, including writers and editors of *Business Week*, *Money*, *Fortune*, and other highly respected business periodicals in which they praised the first edition as the most valuable investment book of the year and as essential for every investor's library. Texas A&M University's College of Business, and particularly the Real Estate Center, provided the facilities and atmosphere conducive to this project. For this, I am especially grateful to Director Rick Floyd, Department Chairman Gary Trennepohl, Dean Benton Cocanougher, and President William Mobley. Most important, I thank my parents, wife, and children for their love and encouragement.

JACK P. FRIEDMAN
November 1989

CONTENTS

ENCYCLOPEDIA OF INVESTMENTS

SECOND EDITION

ANNUITIES

Robert S. Rubinstein

BASIC CHARACTERISTICS

Definition

Literally speaking, the word "annuity" means a series of payments made at regular intervals (annually, monthly, or quarterly) over a defined period (e.g., for a number of years, for life, or in perpetuity). It has been said that the concept of the annuity is life insurance in reverse. Life insurance represents a risk-pooling arrangement whereby many individuals contribute so that substantial funds may be paid on behalf of those who die in any given year. The life annuity contract also embodies a pooling arrangement. However, in the case of the annuity, those who live long benefit at the expense of those who die early. While life insurance protects the purchaser against dying too soon, annuities protect against living too long—that is, the hazard of outliving one's income.

Although differing in function, life insurance and annuities have certain characteristics in common. Both are insurance arrangements involving risk pooling. Both deal with probabilities of survival. More important, in the case of whole life insurance and most deferred annuities, both include an investment element and provide significant cash surrender values in addition to protection against a major hazard.

All annuities can be characterized as either immediate annuities or deferred annuities.

Immediate Annuities

An immediate annuity contract provides for a single-sum payment, or premium, to be made to the insurance company. In return, the company agrees to make to the annuitant

Robert S. Rubinstein, FSA, MAAA is Vice-President and Actuary with Integrity Life Insurance Company.

(or contract owner, if different) a periodic series of payments beginning within a year of the commencement date of the contract. A life annuity provides for payments to be made as long as one or more persons are alive. A life annuity can also contain a minimum payment period. For example, a life-ten-year-certain annuity provides for periodic payments during the lifetime of one or more individuals, and guarantees that a minimum of ten years' payments will be made either to the annuitant(s) or to a named beneficiary if the annuitant is deceased.

Deferred Annuities

A deferred annuity contract can be broken into two main parts: provisions applicable to the accumulation period and provisions governing settlements. Unlike an immediate annuity, which is intended only to produce a given income from a certain sum of money, a deferred annuity is a vehicle intended to accumulate funds and also to achieve an income at retirement or some other later date.

The typical contract will provide for either a single payment or a series of payments. If a series of payments is contemplated under the contract, the owner usually has discretion over the amount and timing within certain prescribed limits. Such a contract is said to be flexible premium-paying.

During the accumulation period, the premiums, less any applicable charges, are invested in a manner described in the contract. A *fixed deferred annuity* provides for investment in the company's general account. A variable deferred annuity provides for investment in one or more variable annuity funds, known as separate accounts.

Settlement Options. When a deferred annuity contract matures, the holder generally is entitled to select from several settlement options, including single-sum immediate cash payout, life annuity, or annuity certain (not depending on the annuitant's survival). If the contract holder elects annuitization, for example, the account balance, less any applicable state premium taxes, would be applied to purchase a life annuity or annuity certain at current settlement rates. Since the insurance company usually has recovered its sales expenses by this time, the current rates are often more favorable than rates applicable to new money used to purchase an immediate annuity. In addition, the contract will stipulate a set of minimum guaranteed settlement rates. These rates are based on conservative interest assumptions; therefore, they presently provide less income than do the current rates. It should be noted that it is the existence of these guarantees that causes the contract to be classified by the Internal Revenue Service (IRS), Securities and Exchange Commission (SEC), and other regulatory bodies as an annuity. For example, an individual may invest in a mutual fund directly, without an annuity wrapper, or open up an individual retirement account (IRA) or Keogh account (HR-10) with a bank. Owing to the absence of any annuity rate guarantees, and indeed any provision for annuitizing whatsoever, these alternative investments should not be confused with the annuity contract. While other financial institutions offer many of the same investment features during the accumulation period, only the insurance company can offer a life annuity income option.

Tax Qualification. Many annuities are purchased under special tax-favored arrangements that have been authorized by Congress. These annuities are termed "tax-qualified." These tax-favored arrangements include corporate pension, profit-sharing and thrift plans, 401(k) plans, individual retirement annuities, HR-10 plans, tax-sheltered annuities, and certain public employee deferred compensation plans. Annuities not purchased under one of the tax-favored arrangements are referred to as non-tax-qualified. Non-tax-qualified annuities also contain significant tax advantages.

Primary Determinants of Value

If an immediate guaranteed lifetime income is desired, it is a simple matter to compare the annuity income offered by the XYZ Company to that of other companies and select the company that pays the highest amount. In addition, the investor should compute the percentage of the purchase price (return) paid out each year and compare this to the yield currently obtainable on other conservative investments. In doing this, the investor should require a significantly higher return on the annuity than on a long-term investment since, unlike other investments, the investor cannot recover the principal. Also, the investor should consider his health, need for inflation protection, and personal tax situation.

In the case of a deferred annuity, a comparison even among other like annuities can be extremely complicated due to variations in expense charges, interest guarantees, investment flexibility, and so on. The following are the important factors to consider when choosing among competing deferred annuities and when comparing deferred annuities to other investments, such as bank certificates of deposit and mutual funds.

Sales and Administrative Charges. A variety of charges exist, and many products have several types of charges.

Front-End Load. This is a percentage charge that is deducted from each payment before the payment is credited to the holder's account. In the 1960s, many annuity contracts had loads of 15 percent and higher. In the 1970s, as competition increased, front-end loads were reduced below 10 percent. Today, the vast majority of annuities do not have front-end loads, except possibly to cover state premium taxes.

Contingent Withdrawal or Surrender Charge. Under most annuities, a contingent withdrawal, or surrender, charge is levied for some or all withdrawals. Companies that are licensed in New York State, for example, are limited by law to a charge equal to 7 percent of the accumulated contract value. The typical no-front-end-load, single-premium annuity contains charges that grade down rapidly, such as 7 percent in year 1, 6 percent in year 2, etc., down to no charge in year 8. However, some companies levy a permanent surrender charge, which is not waived except on annuitization, that is, unless the holder converts the accumulated value into a life annuity or an annuity certain.

Periodic payment annuity surrender charges do not grade down nearly as quickly, since the company is continually incurring additional sales and administrative expenses when each new payment is made. The SEC has effectively limited aggregate variable annuity surrender charges to 9 percent of payments (excluding account appreciation). Many companies have even more liberal charges. Nationwide's Spectrum policy, for example, has a 5 percent surrender charge, which may not exceed 5 percent of payments made during the last ninety-six months. Thus, a holder who left payments in for eight years would thereafter never incur a surrender charge with regard to these payments.

Many companies offer the right to withdraw up to 10 percent of the annuity's value without charge, either immediately or after a set number of years. This feature can be used to withdraw funds for an emergency or for a child's education, for example.

The surrender charge assists the insurer to recover unamortized acquisition expense. In the case of fixed annuities, it also helps protect the insurer from having to liquidate large amounts of investments below amortized value to pay contract holders who surrender during periods when other new investments are yielding more than the annuity. Such a situation is referred to as financial disintermediation. The surrender charge serves both to deter surrenders and to reimburse the insurer for a portion of the resultant loss.

Annual Administrative Charges. Many single-payment fixed annuities do not have any explicit charges other than those stated above. However, some single-payment and most periodic-payment annuities contain an administrative charge. The typical charge is from $15 to $30 per year, up to an annual maximum of 2 percent of account value. The charge usually is made whether or not premiums are paid in a given year. Some companies have a smaller annual charge along with a per-payment processing fee of up to one dollar.

Premium Taxes. About 20 percent of the states impose a premium tax on the insurer, ranging from 0.20 to 2.35 percent, with respect to payments under some or all types of annuity contracts. Companies differ in the manner in which they pass along this expense to the contract holder. Some companies do not have a direct tax charge, but absorb this expense in their general pricing. Other companies do charge for the tax, either as the payments are remitted or on annuitization (but not if a partial or full cash surrender is made).

Asset Charge—Interest Holdback. Under variable contracts (and some fixed contracts), the insurer deducts a daily charge from the unit value (i.e., price) of the account in order to cover investment expenses and mortality and expense guarantees. This charge typically equates to an annual charge of 1.25 to 2 percent. In other words, if the account's investment performance were such that a 10 percent investment gain (net realized and unrealized capital gains and losses after any charges for federal income taxes) were realized for a year, a company with 1.5 percent asset charge would pass on an 8.5 percent gain to the contract holder.

In comparing the asset charges of a contract that uses an insurance company separate account with one that invests in an outside mutual fund, the investor should add the mutual fund's underlying asset charge to the charge levied by the insurance company. For example, one company's contract specifies an asset charge of only 1.3 percent, but when this is added to the charges of the underlying mutual funds, the total charge is as high as 2.24 percent. It is this total charge on which the investor should focus.

Underwriters of fixed annuities finance the investment expenses and the cost of providing mortality and expense guarantees through the difference between the interest rate earned and the rate credited to the contract. The amount of interest held back is generally not stipulated in the contract, nor is such an amount set in advance. However, the insurance laws of the vast majority of states require companies to credit interest in an equitable manner. For example, a company must be able to demonstrate that it is not favoring new business over existing business. Companies using the investment year (or new money) method of allocating investment income may, however, credit higher rates to new contract holders than to existing holders if the expectation is for a higher rate of investment return on assets underlying the new contracts than for those underlying the old.

In comparing the charges of competing annuities, the prospective annuitant should evaluate his intentions regarding the purpose and future use of the annuity. Does he intend to use the contract as a long-term retirement vehicle? If so, it may be worth while to select a contract with a relatively higher early surrender charge, if the contract appears favorable in other respects. Is there a need to draw on the account value within a few years? Then, a contract free-corridor provision, permitting free withdrawals up to a certain percentage of the premium(s) or account value, is an important feature.

Interest Rate. Along with the contract charges, the interest rate credited on payments allocated to the fixed account is of utmost importance to the buyer, particularly if the fixed account is the only investment option available under the contract. The relative importance of the interest assumption is even greater than many investors expect, due to the nature of compounding. For example, an individual investing a level amount annually over a twenty-year period and earning an effective annual rate of 10 percent would achieve an account value that is 5.8 percent higher than if the effective rate were 9.5 percent. In other words, 0.5 percent additional interest each year is equivalent to a 5.8 percent load after twenty years. Generally, differences in interest rates paid far outweigh differences in load or surrender charges as a factor in determining final retirement account values over a period of years.

In addition to the amount of interest currently credited to new contracts, the investor should also consider the duration of the current interest guarantees. For fixed annuities, this usually ranges anywhere from three months to ten years, with one year and five years being very common. There also may or may not be significant later-year guarantees.

Portfolio vs. New-Money Basis. Another consideration is whether the company credits interest on a portfolio or new-money basis. On the portfolio basis, every like contract holder, regardless of the contract issue date, receives the same interest rate. Under the new-money method, different rates are usually credited to different pockets of monies, depending on when they were contributed. For example, a company might credit 9 percent on contributions remitted after December 31, 1989 and 8.5 percent on contributions remitted earlier. Under a modified new-money method that at least one company uses, each contract holder receives a single rate, but this rate may differ among contract holders, depending on the issue class to which the contract belongs. Companies that use a new-money approach are usually better able to increase rates on existing contracts when new-money rates increase than are companies that use a portfolio approach. However, the converse is also true: Companies on a new-money basis are more likely to lower rates on existing contracts when new-money rates decrease. Hence, an investor who believes future interest rates will increase or who wishes to obtain protection against future interest rate increases even at the risk of sharp sudden declines might prefer a company that uses a new-money basis. An investor who seeks to receive a more stable interest rate over time might prefer a company that uses a portfolio approach.

It may be helpful for the investor to know the historical rates credited on existing classes of business. For example, a prospective purchaser of a single-premium deferred annuity that offers a yearly renewable one-year interest guarantee should inquire as to the recent renewal rates of contracts issued one or more years ago.

Investment Policy. The investment policy of the fixed account is also of concern to the investor. The contract itself may state merely that the assets are invested in the company's general account, but the selling agent may be able to provide the purchaser with a statement of the company's investment policy. Core investments generally consist of good-quality (BAA quality or higher) publicly traded bonds, direct placements, and mortgages. Short-term money market instruments are also used. Some companies invest a portion of their general account funds in high yield (junk) bonds, equity real estate, and other types of investments that provide a higher expected rate of return to the insurer. Traditionally, companies invested in issues that mature in fifteen years or more. Since only a small fraction of these investments were repaid each year, companies were unable to pass along the full benefit of higher new money rates where such rates existed. Since the late 1970s, rapid fluctuations of yields on fixed investments resulted in many companies shortening their maturities. When companies do choose to invest long-term, they are increasingly turning to inflation-adaptive instruments that provide for periodic renegotiation of the interest rate. While these companies cannot usually afford to offer significant long-term interest guarantees, they do have the ability to adjust rates fairly often, either up or down. This provides the purchaser with some protection against future rampant interest rate rises.

Finally, the prospective annuitant who is not interested in short-term or long-term rate guarantees, but whose chief objective is to receive a return reflective of current short-term rates with minimal risk of loss of principal, can invest in a variable annuity with a money market account.

Investment Flexibility. The investor should consider the range of investment opportunities available under the contract. Fixed contracts offer only one account, while one variable annuity has as many as nine. Any restrictions regarding transferability of past accumulations and changing future payment allocations between accounts should also be considered. Many contracts have no restrictions whatsoever.

Investment Performance. In the case of variable annuities, investors should examine the prior investment performance coupled with the investment objectives of the account. This information can be obtained from the prospectus or annual statement of the separate account.

Settlement Rates. Since the investor under a deferred annuity may wish to annuitize at a later time, he should consider both the range of settlements offered and the quality of the current and guaranteed rates (as compared with those offered by other companies) before selecting an annuity. The current settlement rates, although not contained in the contract, largely influence the amount of income the annuitant will be able to purchase at retirement. Settlement rates vary greatly, and a product's attractiveness in the accumulation phase is often not indicative of the quality of its settlement options.

Company's Best Rating. A highly respected independent company, A.M. Best Company, publishes *Best's Insurance Reports: Life—Health,* which assigns a letter rating to all life insurance companies, ranging from C (fair) to A+ (excellent). This rating indicates Best's opinion of the long-term ability of the company to discharge its responsibilities to contract holders. Two of the criteria used are particularly important to annuity contract holders: net resources adequate to absorb unusual shocks, and soundness of investments.

Types of Life Insurance Annuities

The annuity, as defined earlier, encompasses a wide range of products. The following is a description of each major type.

Fixed Immediate Annuity. As mentioned earlier, this is an arrangement whereby the company, in return for a single premium, agrees to pay the annuitant (who is usually the owner) a specific number of dollars each month, quarter, or year, for life. The simplest form is the straight life annuity, under which the income ceases with the last regular payment prior to the annuitant's death.

Refund Annuity. This provides that, should the annuitant die before total payments have equaled or exceeded the premium, the difference shall be payable to the beneficiary named in the contract. The cash refund annuity provides for this payment in a single sum, whereas the installment refund annuity provides for a continuation of the annuity's periodic payments until the premium has been recovered.

Period Certain Annuity. This provides that, should the annuitant die before the stated period (e.g., ten years from the date of issue), the payments will be payable to the beneficiary until the period has elapsed. The beneficiary may also choose to receive the commuted value of the remaining payments (based on the commutation interest rate contained in the contract) in lieu of a stream of payments.

Joint and Survivor Annuity. This provides for payments during the joint lifetime of two annuitants and during the lifetime of the survivor. The buyer can elect that a lower income be payable to the survivor rather than to the joint annuitants. For example, a contract could provide for payment to the survivor equal to 50 percent of the initial payment.

Payments under all types of annuities, except for the joint and survivor, are usually level. However, a few companies sell fixed annuities with increasing payments.

Rates for these various annuities differ, depending on the amount of risk the insurance company is asked to assume. Therefore, the amount of income that can be obtained from a fixed premium is, for example, higher for a straight life annuity than for a refund annuity, and higher for a male than for a female of the same age (due to the female's longer life expectancy). One company's sample rates are shown in Table 1.

Variable Immediate Annuity. The preceding discussion applies to this product also, except that here, the company agrees to pay the annuitant a set number of annuity units,

TABLE 1. Typical Annuity Rate Structure—December 1988

		Monthly Life Income per $1,000 of Premium	
Type of Annuity	Age	Males	Females
Straight life	75	$11.65	$10.48
Straight life	80	13.60	12.46
Installment refund	75	10.55	9.89
Straight life—joint and survivor (100 percent of initial income paid to survivor)	75 (male) 72 (female)	$8.60	

not dollars. The dollar value of an annuity unit is linked to the investment performance of a separate account, which is usually invested in common stocks. The initial amount of income is based on the insurer's mortality and expense assumptions and an assumed interest rate mandated by state law. This rate is 5 percent for most states. Subsequent payments increase if the account's unit value increases at an annual rate higher than 5 percent and otherwise decrease. For example, if the unit value grows at a 9 percent annual rate, the payments increase at about a 4 percent annual rate. Thus, unlike the case of a fixed immediate annuity, the purchaser bears all the investment risk. However, as in the case of a fixed immediate annuity, the company bears the mortality and expense risk.

Variable immediate annuities have not been well received since they were introduced in the 1960s. One reason is that the initial payment is much lower than that of a fixed annuity (which might be based on an assumed long-term invested earnings rate of 8.5 percent or more today). Also, although this product offers potential for future increases in payments, many annuitants dislike receiving payments that fluctuate greatly from month to month, depending upon the investment performance of the separate account. Many individuals who will accept variable accumulations before retirement will not accept variable payouts after retirement. This is because most annuitants prefer to receive predictable amounts of regular income and are usually unwilling to assume much risk over a period as short as the life expectancy remaining at retirement.

Annuity Certain. Under this type of annuity, the purchaser pays a single premium to the company and, in turn, receives a regular fixed payment (principal and interest) for a specified number of years. No life contingencies are involved.

Fixed Deferred Annuity. Under this contract, a relatively low rate of interest (e.g., 4 percent) is typically guaranteed throughout the accumulation period; the company periodically credits additional interest, based on either its past or projected investment experience with respect to the underlying assets. In recent years, companies have begun to guarantee initial interest rates that are significantly higher than the long-term guaranteed rate. For example, a contract might guarantee 8.5 percent for the first policy year and provide for a declaration of a new rate before each subsequent policy year, but specify that such new rate shall never be less than the minimum guarantee of 4 percent.

Variable Deferred Annuity. Under this contract, the premiums are invested in one or more separate accounts. Unlike a life insurance company's general account, which is required by state laws to be invested primarily in bonds and mortgages, separate accounts are generally invested in common stocks. Separate accounts can also be invested in other instruments, such as long-term bonds, money market instruments, and real estate. The accumulated value of the contract changes daily to reflect the market value of these underlying funds and the deductions and charges that are described in the prospectus. There is no minimum investment guarantee (except, perhaps, on death of the annuitant); hence, account values can fluctuate widely.

The traditional variable deferred annuity, first widely marketed in the early 1970s, used one or two (rarely more) separate accounts managed by the insurance company. An important variation of the traditional product is the investment wrap around annuity. In one type of arrangement, the purchaser of an insurer's variable annuity can choose among several of the various mutual funds managed by an investment management company that is otherwise unaffiliated with the insurance company. Merrill Lynch, Dreyfus, and Putnam are among the firms that have affiliated with insurance companies to offer such a product. This second generation variable annuity permits the insurance company to offer a much wider range of investment alternatives than it could economically offer if it had to set up its own separate accounts. As a result, variable annuities offering as many as ten or more mutual fund separate accounts are now being offered. The types of funds offered can include equity growth, equity income, global equity, high yield, managed funds, and U.S. government guaranteed funds.

Some variable annuities include a fixed account that is contained in the insurer's general account. Under this combination annuity, the insurer declares one or more rates of interest applicable to the fixed account money and the insurer bears the risk of capital loss with respect to this account.

Group Deferred Annuity. Under this contract, the purchaser pays the insurer a single premium, on behalf of each annuitant, that purchases life income benefits that are scheduled to commence at later dates, usually at the annuitants' scheduled retirements. Such contracts usually do not have cash surrender values before retirement, although, if an annuitant dies before retirement, the contract may specify that the premium, with or without interest, will be refunded. After the income commences, the contract functions as an individual immediate annuity with respect to the annuitant. Such annuities are typically purchased to fund accrued benefits for participants of a terminating pension plan. The rates will be partially based on the insurer's expectation of the participants' mortality experience.

Group Deposit Administration (DA) Contract. The DA contract is used to provide unallocated funding (i.e., preretirement funds are not allocated to individual participants) for company pension plans that provide predetermined retirement benefits (defined benefit plans). Contributions are generally allocated to the insurance company's general account and are credited with a guaranteed amount of interest (e.g., 5 percent) plus additional interest, included in the annually declared dividend, which is determined by the investment year (new-money) method. The insurance company also guarantees a set of annuity settlement rates for accumulations that derive from contributions received during an initial period, such as five years. (The guaranteed rates are periodically reestablished thereafter.) The insurance company's current rates apply if they produce a higher income. In addition to investment experience, expenses and postretirement mortality rate experience, to the extent that they are more favorable than was assumed by the insurer in pricing, are gradually passing through to the plan trustee in the form of dividends.

With a group DA contract, unlike an individual fixed deferred annuity, a market value adjustment is charged if the purchaser withdraws funds prematurely when the book value of the contract's reserves exceeds market value (such as when new interest rates are higher than the average rate earned on the account). In addition to general account funding, companies also offer funding through separate accounts, in which diverse pension plan clients share ratably in a fund's performance or, for very large cases ($10 million or more of assets), individually managed accounts.

Annual administrative charges grade down with the size of the fund (as a percentage of the fund), with a typical contractual annual minimum of $2,000. For example, the fee could be 0.50 percent of the first $2 million of mean funds grading down to 0.04 percent of the portion of mean funds that exceed $50 million. Additional fees are charged for certain services the insurer performs, such as keeping individual employee records, processing withdrawals, processing retirements, and paying retirement benefits.

Immediate Participation Guarantee (IPG) Contracts. Many pension plan administrators, particularly the larger ones (such as $100,000 or more in annual premiums), are not interested in complete insurance company guarantees followed by gradual participation through dividends. Instead, they prefer immediate full participation with only residual guarantees. Under the IPG contract, as long as the unallocated (i.e., preretirement) funds are maintained at a certain level (e.g., not less than 10 percent of those allocated to retired lives), the total funds, including those allocated to retired lives, will be credited with the full investment results, charged with the full expenses incurred, and charged or credited with the postretirement mortality results actually experienced.

In another variation, sometimes referred to as a direct experience DA contract, the insurer provides full guarantees with respect to the retired lives only.

ATTRACTIVE FEATURES

Lifetime Income Option

The annuity is the only vehicle that can offer the investor a guaranteed lifetime income, either immediately or at some future date.

Investment Flexibility

Some variable annuities, particularly those that allocate contributions to one or more mutual funds or separate accounts, offer an uncommon degree of investment flexibility. Contributions may be allocated in any way among many funds, and past accumulations may be transferred among funds without charge or tax consequences. While invested money often may be transferred between various no-load mutual funds without charge, the annuity vehicle is unique in permitting interaccount transfers without the owner incurring current income tax on the gain (i.e., the excess of the accumulated amount over the amount invested). This flexibility permits the annuitant to choose the most appropriate investment at any given time, thereby maximizing investment growth. For example, if an annuitant contributed $10,000 to a common stock account, and with appreciation this had grown to $15,000, the $15,000 could be transferred to another fund within the annuity, such as a money market fund, without the $5,000 gain being subject to current income tax. However, if the same $10,000 had been invested in a common stock mutual fund, appreciated to $15,000, and the shares were sold and transferred to, say, a bank certificate of deposit (CD), the gain would be subject to tax for the year of transfer. Although many contracts are extremely flexible, the annuitant should note any restrictions that a particular contract imposes on transferability between funds.

The IRS permits tax-free exchanges of one annuity contract for another. This enables an annuitant to take advantage of another company's product should, for example, its interest rate be higher than it is under the current product.

Tax Deferral of Income

Deferred annuities defer current taxes on investment earnings, which compound tax-deferred until actually withdrawn or received as income. Without the diminishing effect of taxation, capital can compound and build up at a much faster rate. This is an extremely attractive feature that, for the man-in-the-street (nonqualified) market, is unique to the annuity. (For further discussion, see *Tax Consequences*, later in this article.)

Investment, Mortality, and Expense Guarantees

Interest. As noted earlier, most single-premium contracts offer either a one-year or five-year initial interest guarantee. Many flexible premium products offer significant guarantees that often apply to future as well as current contributions. Insurance companies are alone in offering interest guarantees with respect to future contributions.

Money Back Guarantee. Many no-front-end-load annuity contracts guarantee that the company will return the full premium to the owner on termination. Thus, an individual has the option of switching out of a fixed annuity to another vehicle a month or two after issue, only forfeiting interest earned to that date.

Minimum Death Benefit. Many deferred variable annuities specify that on death of the annuitant, the beneficiary will receive an amount equal to either the total contributions less withdrawals or the fund value, whichever is greater. In other words, in the event of the annuitant's death, the company bears the risk of fund depreciation.

Expense Guarantee. Under individual contracts, expense loadings, termination charges, administrative charges, and asset charges are usually guaranteed for the contract's lifetime. Thus, the insurer bears the risk that the administrative and investment expenses will exceed the amounts anticipated at issue. The insurer often includes a risk charge in the asset charge to cover this.

Annuity Rate Guarantee/Betterment of Rates Provision. Most individual deferred contracts contain lifetime fixed annuity rate guarantees that can be significant if interest rates ever drop to the levels that existed before the 1970s or if mortality improves significantly. The contracts state that current declared rates, as modified by the company from time to time, will apply should those be more favorable than the guaranteed rates.

POTENTIAL RISKS

Through selection of the particular contract, the buyer has considerable discretion regarding the amount of risk he wants to assume. The company's rates, of course, reflect the amount of risk it is being asked to assume. Over the years, there has been a trend away from traditional insurance company guarantees to fewer and weaker guarantees. The payoff to the consumer is a less expensive product with the potential for higher yields if the insurer's experience should prove favorable. The following risks are assumed in varying degrees by the buyer and the company, depending on the product selected.

Possible Principal Risk—Market Volatility

Although fixed deferred annuities are considered to be one of the safest investment vehicles around, variable annuities involve market risks comparable to those inherent in mutual fund investments. The investment policies of the funds (stated in the prospectus) can be either virtually none, as in the money market fund; or some, as in a fixed-income bond fund; or considerable, as in a high-growth stock fund. The historical account unit or share values shown in the prospectus or its supplement can serve as a barometer of past volatility.

Income Variability

As discussed previously, many companies have moved away from offering high, long-term interest guarantees and have changed to shorter-term or inflation-adaptive investment strategies. While such companies offer little income protection if market interest rates should decline markedly, they may offer more inflationary protection than the traditional products do.

A feature found in some single-premium contracts, known as a bailout provision, can help cushion a buyer's fear that the company will keep future rates significantly below market levels. This provision states that should the current declared rate ever fall below a contractual minimum, which is often within 1 and 2 percent of the initial rate, the contract can be surrendered without charge.

Liquidity Problems

A buyer of an immediate annuity sacrifices all liquidity, since the contract does not have any cash surrender values. A buyer of a deferred annuity should be aware that, while he generally can liquidate the contract for its cash value at any time, there may be significant contractual penalties for doing so.[1] Even if the contract does not stipulate early withdrawal penalties, it may have front-end charges that render it a poor investment if surrendered in the first few years.

TAX CONSEQUENCES

Annuitants and individuals contemplating the purchase of an annuity should be aware of the tax ramifications related to the various types of products. The investor who uses the annuity vehicle shrewdly can obtain significant tax advantages, some of which are not available with respect to any other type of investment. The rules governing the income taxation of amounts received under annuity contracts are contained in Section 72 of the Internal Revenue Code (the Code).

Deferred Annuities

Tax Deferral—Non-Tax-Qualified Contracts. The major tax advantage of a non-tax-qualified deferred annuity contract during the accumulation period is that the contract holder avoids the payment of federal, state, and local income taxes on the earnings credited to the contract until they are withdrawn, presumably at retirement when the holder

[1] Under certain tax-qualified plans, such as individual retirement annuities, HR-10 plans, and 401(k) plans, there are also substantial penalties imposed by the IRS for premature distributions before age 59½. Under nonqualified plans, interest or other investment earnings withdrawn before age 59½ are subject to a 10 percent IRS penalty. Also, New York State requires companies licensed in that state to reserve the right in their contracts to withhold payments of fixed annuity cash values for up to six months to protect the company from having to take substantial capital losses during periods of extremely heavy surrenders. Companies almost never invoke this right, however.

may be in a lower tax bracket. Amounts withdrawn during the accumulation period are treated as earnings first and principal last. The IRS imposes a 10 percent penalty tax on withdrawals of earnings made before age 59½, unless the owner dies or is disabled.

The advantage of tax deferral to the contract holder is twofold. First, by timing his withdrawals of the contract earnings to occur during a period when his marginal tax rate is less than the marginal rate in effect at the time the earnings were accrued, the percentage tax bite can be lessened. In other words, the investor can determine the best time to pay tax on the earnings. Second, money that normally would be paid in taxes is automatically reinvested, producing additional tax-deferred earnings thereon.

If an annuity purchased after February 28, 1986 is held by a nonnatural person (e.g., corporation or trust), then the contract is not treated as an annuity for tax purposes, and the income earned in the contract is currently taxable.

Table 2 provides an example of an investment with and without a tax deferral of earnings.

Under an immediate annuity or a settlement option, a constant pro rata portion of each payment is considered to be taxable earnings. The rules pertaining to immediate annuity taxation apply to a settlement option elected under a deferred annuity, except that the investment in the contract would equal the original cost basis less any amounts withdrawn that were not included in taxable income. For example, if a $15,000 contract were purchased, and $5,000 of principal had been withdrawn earlier, the $5,000 would not have been taxable. When the annuity payment period begins, the investment in the contract would be $15,000 − 5,000 = $10,000 regardless of the contract's value at that time.

Tax Deferral—Tax-Qualified Contract. Holders of this contract not only enjoy the benefit of tax-deferral on contractual earnings as described previously for non-tax-qualified contracts, but, in addition, forgo current income taxation on the contributions.

TABLE 2. Effect of Tax Deferral on $10,000 Lump-Sum Annuity Investment

Without Tax Deferral	With Tax Deferral
$10,000 investment Earnings: 9 percent/ year, compounded annually	$10,000 investment Earnings: 9 percent/year compounded annually
Tax in 33 percent bracket = 3 percent of annual income	
$17,908 account value in ten years at 6 percent interest (after annual taxes)	$23,674 account value in ten years (before taxes)*
	$19,116 cash after 33 percent tax on earnings at end of ten years
$32,071 account value in twenty years (after annual taxes)	$56,044 account value in twenty years (before taxes)*
	$40,698 cash after 33 percent tax on earnings at end of twenty years*

*Assumes no front-end load or withdrawal charge applies. Also, excludes effects of any annual administrative or asset charges. The investor should carefully consider the impact of any applicable charges contained in the annuity contract.

TABLE 3. Effect of Tax Deferral on $100 Monthly Annuity Investment

Without Tax Shelter	With Tax Shelter
$100 earnings	$100 earnings
33 tax (based on 33 percent bracket)	0 tax
$ 67 invested	$100 invested
Earnings: 9 percent/year compounded annually	Earnings: 9 percent/year
Tax = 3 percent	Tax = 0 percent
6 percent after-tax earnings	9 percent after-tax earnings
$30,391 account value in twenty years (after taxes)	$63,911 account value in twenty years (before taxes)*
	$42,820 cash after 33 percent tax*
	$46,016 cash after 28 percent tax*

*Assumes that no front-end load or withdrawal charge applies. Also, excludes effects of any annual administrative or asset charges. The investor should carefully consider the impact of any applicable charges contained in the annuity contract.

Withdrawals, however, are fully taxable when taken[2]—either as a lump sum or in the form of annuity payments. Table 3 illustrates the tax benefit that might be experienced by a public school teacher who contributed $100 per month to a tax-sheltered annuity.

It should be noted that the amount of money accumulated under this contract would greatly exceed the amount accumulated in a non-tax-sheltered investment even if the same yield were earned and the tax bracket did not change.

Taxation of Death Benefit Under Non-Tax-Qualified Contract. If the annuitant dies before his deferred annuity contract matures, and a contingent annuitant was not designated at the time of sale, any contract earnings that have not been previously withdrawn are taxed as ordinary income to the beneficiary. However, the beneficiary will not be fully taxed on those earnings in the year of death if he elects, within sixty days after the annuitant's death, to apply the death benefit under a life income or annuity certain option. In that case, the periodic payments will be taxable to the beneficiary under the regular immediate annuity rules, based on the decedent's investment in the contract and the beneficiary's expected return. The entire value of the annuity is includable in the gross estate for estate tax purposes.

In addition, if the owner of the annuity contract dies prior to maturity, the proceeds must be distributed within five years unless a spousal owner's beneficiary had been designated. In that case, the contract can continue with the owner's beneficiary as the new owner.

---

2 Usually, distributions are taxed as ordinary income. However, a favorable five-year-averaging method may be elevated by 401(k) and pension plan participants in certain limited instances.

Taxation of Death Benefit Under Tax-Qualified Contract. Generally, the entire death benefit is taxable to the beneficiary as ordinary income and is also subject to estate taxes. However, in several of the tax-qualified markets, a more favorable tax treatment is available. For example, in the case of an individual retirement annuity, distribution is not required until the date the annuitant would have attained age 70½ as long as the beneficiary is the annuitant's spouse.

Tax Penalties for Early Withdrawals. To discourage use of qualified plans for purposes other than to provide retirement income, the IRS generally imposes a 10 percent penalty tax on distributions prior to age 59½. Exemptions from the tax are made for employees in a plan who have reached age 55, separated from service and satisfied the plan's early retirement requirements, and for certain hardship withdrawals. Generally, payments must start in the year the annuitant attains age 70½.

Tax-Free Exchange of Annuity Contracts. Contract holders should take advantage of Section 1035(a) of the Code when desiring to transfer the cash value of one annuity contract for another contract to obtain, for example, a higher yield. Section 1035(a) provides for a tax-free exchange of one annuity contract for another as long as the contracts are payable to the same person(s). Where contracts of different insurers are used, the holder must assign the existing contract in exchange for the new one rather than simply surrender the existing contract and allocate the proceeds to the new contract.

Immediate Annuities

A pro rata share of each payment received under an immediate annuity (or an annuity settlement under a deferred annuity) is considered to be interest and is thus subject to ordinary income taxation. This contrasts with the nonqualified deferred annuity, in which distributions are received tax-free until the premiums have been recovered. The percentage of each payment that is deemed to be principal is called the exclusion ratio; it is obtained by dividing the expected return by the contract's cost basis (generally, the premium cost in the case of a non-qualified immediate annuity). The expected return of a life annuity is generally equal to the annual payment times the annuitant's life expectancy in years, based on IRS tables; for an annuity certain, it is simply the total amount of guaranteed payments. For example, if a seventy-year-old male purchased a straight life annuity with $50,000 of after-tax dollars and received an income of $6,600 per year, his exclusion ratio would be 47.3 percent, obtained as follows:

$$\begin{aligned}&\text{Premium} \div (\text{annual income} \times \text{life expectancy})\\&= 50{,}000 \div (6{,}600 \times 16.0)\\&= 50{,}000 \div 105{,}600\\&= 47.3\%\end{aligned}$$

Thus, if the annuitant were in a 28 percent marginal tax bracket, his tax would be only 14.76 percent of each payment (28% × 52.7%). (52.7% = 100% − 47.3%.)

Under prior law, once the exclusion ratio was determined for a particular contract, it generally remained the same even if the annuitant outlived his life expectancy. Under present law, applicable to distributions after December 31, 1986, once the annuitant recovers all of his principal, there can no longer be any excludable annuity payment (i.e., 100 percent of the annuity payments are then taxable).

Investors in their seventies and eighties who are considering whether to purchase a life annuity or an interest-bearing investment, such as a taxable CD, should consider the relative tax effects of the two investments, noting that 100 percent of the interest earned under a CD is taxable. Of course, the investor should also note that the full principal is left intact under a CD but entirely lost under an immediate annuity, except for any refund feature that may allow for recovery of a portion of the principal upon the annuitant's death.

Payments under immediate annuities purchased with pretax dollars, such as qualified annuities bought under pension plans, are fully taxable. When a deferred annuity contract begins to pay out a regular income, an exclusion ratio applies only to the portion of the premiums that represents after-tax dollars. For example, assume an annuity purchased with a $10,000 premium had grown in value to $15,000 and no prior withdrawals had been made. If the $15,000 were applied toward a life income option, the exclusion ratio would be two-thirds of the ratio calculated according to the method previously described.

REPRESENTATIVE TYPES OF INVESTORS

Investors fall into two broad categories: purchasers of non-tax-qualified contracts and purchasers of tax-qualified contracts.

Non-Tax-Qualified Contracts

The typical purchaser of a deferred annuity is an individual, usually age 45 or older, who has a need for a tax-deferred accumulation vehicle that will be used to supplement his pension and Social Security income at retirement. Many purchasers are in relatively high marginal tax brackets (28 percent and up) and thus have a particularly strong need to defer taxes on investment earnings.

The typical purchaser of an immediate annuity is an individual in the 65- to 90-year range who desires a guaranteed lifetime income. Such an investor is not concerned with preserving his principal in the event of death. Due to the safe high-yield investments available today, many investors are not finding this an attractive contract until they are into their seventies and thus are able to receive an income of 15 to 20 percent of the principal.

Other types of buyers include casualty insurance companies, which purchase annuities to fund long-term claim settlements due to accidents that (for example) result in permanent disability; and charitable and other nonprofit institutions that issue, in return for gifts, immediate life annuities on the lives of donors.

Tax-Qualified Contracts

Tax-qualified contracts are purchased either to fund retirement benefits or to defer income to a later date when the individual presumably would be in a lower tax bracket. A number of different individuals and groups are eligible to purchase tax-qualified annuities.

Pension, Thrift, and Profit-Sharing Plans. Larger plans (typically, those with an annual premium of $25,000 or more) can fund their plans through a group deposit administration contract or a group immediate participation guarantee contract. Smaller plans can use specially designed small-group contracts or individual annuity contracts.

Tax-Sheltered Annuity (TSA). The Code allows employees of educational institutions and certain other nonprofit organizations to exclude a portion of their salary from current taxation through the purchase of an annuity contract. The maximum amount that can be contributed is generally 20 percent if includable compensation (total compensation less the employee's TSA compensation), multiplied by the number of years of service with the employer, less total contributions made in prior years by the employer into a TSA or qualified pension plan on the employee's behalf. Contributions, however, cannot exceed $9,500 per year as adjusted for cost of living increases. There are also special provisions that may allow employees to make "catch-up" contributions to compensate for smaller contributions made in previous years.

Individual Retirement Annuity. All individuals under age 70½ who have earned income can contribute up to $2,000 (or the amount of earned income, if less) during a taxable year to an individual retirement account (IRA). An individual retirement annuity is one of several instruments that can be used to fund an IRA. If there is a nonemployed spouse, an additional amount can be contributed on the spouse's behalf as long as the total contributions for both spouses do not exceed $2,250 and no more than $2,000 is contributed on behalf of either spouse. If neither the individual nor spouse is covered by another qualified plan, then the contribution is deductible.

If either the individual or the spouse is covered by another qualified plan, then the IRA contributions are only deductible if the adjusted gross income (AGI) is below certain limits. The deduction is phased out for married couples filing joint returns between $40,000 and $50,000 AGI and for single persons between $25,000 and $35,000 AGI (before IRA deductions).

Simplified Employee Pension (SEP). The Code allows employers to establish SEPs, under which employers can make contributions toward their employees' retirement income without becoming involved in more complex retirement plans. Under a SEP, the employer makes contributions directly to IRAs established on the employees' behalf. The maximum employer contribution on behalf of each employee is the lesser of $30,000 or 15 percent of the employee's total annual compensation. The employee can also make the regular IRA contribution described in the preceding paragraph, either to the SEP plan, if it permits this, or to a separate IRA.

Tax-Qualified Retirement Plans

Corporations, partnerships, and sole proprietorships may establish tax-qualified retirement plans for the working owners and their employees which provide for contributions to be made to annuities and certain other funding vehicles that are tax deductible.

The annual limit for contributions on behalf of an employee to a defined contribution plan is the lesser of 25 percent of compensation or earned income, or $30,000. Salary reduction contributions made under a cash or deferred arrangement (401(k) program) are limited in any year to $7,313, as adjusted for cost-of-living increases. The employer may not consider compensation or earned income in excess of $200,000 in calculating contributions to the plan. Generally, voluntary nondeductible contributions are limited to 10 percent of salary.

Special limits on contributions apply to anyone who participates in more than one tax-qualified retirement plan or who controls another trade or business. There is also an overall limit on the total amount of contributions and benefits under all tax-favored retirement programs in which a person participates.

Public Employee Deferred Compensation Plan (PEDC). The Code provides for PEDC plans on a tax-qualified basis. Employees and independent contractors performing services for a qualified employer may voluntarily elect to defer a portion of their compensation, by way of a salary reduction agreement, to some later date. Qualified employers may be a state, including political subdivisions or agencies of a state, or tax-exempt rural electric cooperatives as defined under Section 501(c)(12) of the Code, as well as their affiliates (Section 501(c)(6) organizations). With the exception of a catch-up rule, the normal maximum limitation is 33⅓ percent of income not to exceed $7,500.

Rollover Individual Retirement Annuity. Under the conditions and limitations of the Code, a person receiving a cash lump-sum distribution from a tax-qualified retirement plan or a distribution from an IRA or the spouse of an employee receiving a lump-sum death benefit from the employee's tax qualified retirement plan may purchase a rollover individual retirement annuity with all or part of the money in order to further defer taxes on the distribution. The contract must be purchased within sixty days after the distribution is made. Generally, a lump-sum distribution is a payment of all or a portion of amounts in the person's account that were received in a distribution that occurred during one of the individual's tax years (generally a calendar year), that became payable as a result of separation of service, attainment of age 59½, disability, or termination of plan.

For example, consider a forty-five-year-old male who has terminated service with the XYZ Corporation and has a vested benefit of $50,000 under the corporation's qualified plan. Assume he has the right to take a cash settlement. If he needs $10,000 now (which would be subject to ordinary income tax), he could invest the $40,000 balance in a rollover individual retirement annuity and defer taxes until it is withdrawn. However, the normal IRA restrictions would apply. Hence, withdrawals before age 59½ would be subject to the 10 percent penalty tax (in addition to ordinary taxation), and distribution would have to commence by age 70½.

IMPORTANT FACTORS IN BUYING

On the market today are large numbers of annuity products with a variety of charges, interest rates, investment alternatives, and other features. The reader has already been given a survey of features offered and their relative importance. A discussion of how to get into the market follows. (A list of selected companies is included here.) A potential buyer generally cannot purchase from the company directly, but most companies will assign an agent or broker to the client if requested. The buyer should consult *Best's Retirement Income Guide* for comprehensive surveys of available individual annuity products.

Comparison of the Individual Deferred Annuity and Alternative Investments

As mentioned throughout this article, the investor who is contemplating purchasing an annuity should also examine alternative investments, such as bank CDs, money market funds, common stock mutual funds, and individual common stocks and bonds. The investor in the non-tax-qualified market has a full range of alternative products available, while investors in tax-qualified markets have a more limited selection of products from which to choose. In comparing the annuity to alternative investments, the investor should determine whether the additional benefits provided by the annuity contract (e.g., personalized service from an agent or broker, investment and mortality guarantees, unusual investment flexibility) are worth the charges that the annuity imposes (e.g., front-end loads, termination charges, premium taxes in some states, annual administrative fees, and asset charges). For example, in comparing a non-tax-qualified, no-front-end-load wraparound mutual fund annuity with a direct investment in one or more mutual funds, the investor should determine if the asset charges levied by the insurance company (over and above the mutual fund charges) and the early withdrawal charge are worth the benefits derived from such annuity features as tax deferral, investment flexibility, guaranteed settlement rates, and the minimum death benefit.

IRAs vs. Bank CD

A common example is the individual who wishes to invest in an IRA and is faced with the choice of funding through either an annuity offered by an insurance company or a bank CD. Unlike annuities, bank CDs do not contain loads, withdrawal charges (except before the CD's expiration date, which is generally from one to five years), or annual adminstrative fees. However, the annuity offers a wide range of features not offered by the bank.

For instance, an annuity offers the option of obtaining, at a later date, an income for the investor that cannot be outlived. Although the purchaser of a bank IRA eventually could use all or a portion of the account's value to purchase a life income from an insurance company, he would not have the benefit of a minimum rate guarantee nor the opportunity to purchase life income at rates more favorable than those available to brand new purchasers.

Many annuities offer one or more investment accounts in addition to an interest-bearing account. Many annuities provide significant interest guarantees with respect to future payments, while a CD only guarantees interest on the current payment.

Furthermore, most periodic-payment annuities accept very low payments, such as $20, and credit the contractual interest rate from the date of receipt. Banks, on the other hand, often require substantial minimum payments ($500 and up) to earn their highest rates.

Withdrawal charges under no-front-end-load annuities are generally stiffer than those of CDs, which waive all charges at the expiry date of the interest guarantee. However, CD withdrawal penalties before the expiry date (which involve significant interest forfeitures) are often comparable to those of the annuities. In addition, the investor who requires a relatively small amount of emergency cash may be able to avoid a withdrawal charge under an annuity contract that contains a free corridor, but could not avoid a penalty under a CD (except at the expiry date).

Finally, the purchaser of an annuity receives the personal services of an agent or broker, often including an individualized projection (based on the purchaser's actual age, sex, and contribution level) of account growth and retirement income under a range of settlement options. The agent or broker, through his or her training and experience, is often able to furnish quality advice in such areas as tax and estate planning. While assistance can also be obtained from a designated individual at a local bank branch office, that individual may not be equipped or have the time to offer the range of services offered by an agent or broker.

Channels of Distribution

Career Agents. These are licensed selling agents who generally sell products offered by one company only, although at times they will place business in another company if that company's rate is much better or if the desired product is not offered by their own company. The career agents' job is to service as well as to sell the company's products. As servicers, they are often able to obtain the company's prompt attention to a customer's problem due to the traditionally strong relationship between career agent and company.

Insurance Brokers. These are licensed salespersons who market products offered by several companies. Such brokers are often better able to shop around for a superior rate than are career agents.

Stock Brokerage Houses. As part of a drive to provide total financial services to their clients, many brokerage houses market insurance company products, including annuities.

Bank and Savings and Loan (S&L) Sales Representatives. Unlike agents and brokers, who are compensated virtually entirely on a commission basis, these individuals are salaried (often with some incentive compensation). Like career agents, they generally emphasize only a single company's product. Sales are made to individuals at local bank and S&L branches.

Individual Immediate Annuities

These are primarily marketed through career agents and insurance brokers. The buyer should shop around, since rates vary widely. Competitiveness of a company's deferred annuity or insurance products is often not indicative of the competitiveness of its immediate annuity rates. Commissions are in the 2 to 3 percent range.

The following is a list of some of the major underwriters of individual immediate annuities. Most of these companies write in both non-tax-qualified and tax-qualified markets and are licensed to sell in the majority of states.

- Bankers Life and Casualty Company, Chicago, Ill.
- CNA Insurance Company, Chicago, Ill.
- Equitable Life Assurance Society of the United States, New York, N.Y.
- Great West Life Assurance Company, Winnepeg, MB, Canada
- Integrity Life Insurance Company, Phoenix, Ariz.
- John Hancock Mutual Life Insurance, Boston, Mass.
- Lincoln National Life Insurance Company, Fort Wayne, Ind.
- Manufacturers Life Insurance Company, Toronto, Ontario, Canada
- Metropolitan Life Insurance Company, New York, N.Y.
- New England Mutual Life, Boston, Mass.
- Phoenix Mutual Life Insurance Company, Hartford, Conn.

- Prudential Insurance Company, Newark, N.J.
- Traveler's Insurance Company, Hartford, Conn.

Individual Single-Premium Deferred Annuities

These are heavily marketed by career agents, insurance brokers, and stock brokers. Commissions range from 2 to 5 percent of the premium. Products are extremely competitive.

The following is a selection of major underwriters. Most companies write in both qualified and nonqualified markets and are licensed to sell in a majority of states.

- Anchor National Life Insurance Company, Phoenix, Ariz.
- Banker Life and Casualty Company, Chicago. Ill.
- CNA Insurance Company, Chicago, Ill.
- Equitable Variable Life Insurance Company, New York, N.Y.
- Executive Life Insurance Company, Beverly Hills, Cal.
- Great American Life Insurance Company, Los Angeles, Cal.
- Great-West Life Assurance Company, Winnipeg, MB, Canada.
- Integrity Life Insurance Company, Phoenix, Ariz.
- Investors Life Insurance Company of North America, Philadelphia, Pa.
- John Alden Life Insurance Company, Coral Gables, Fla.
- Kemper Investors Life Insurance Company, Chicago, Ill.
- Keystone Provident Life Insurance Company, Boston, Mass.
- Manufacturers Life Insurance Company, Toronto, Ontario, Canada M4W1E5.
- Metropolitan Life Insurance Company, New York, N.Y.
- Presidential Life Insurance Company, Nyack, N.J.
- Tandem Insurance Group, Chicago, Ill.
- United Pacific Life Insurance Company, Philadelphia, Pa.

Individual Periodic-Payment Deferred Annuities

Most of this business is sold through career agents, although insurance brokers are also active. (Stockholders are not active in this business.) Since the periodic-payment market is not as competitive as the single-payment market (particularly for non-tax-qualified business), an investor who has enough funds to meet the single-payment minimum (e.g., $5,000) may do better to purchase such a product and invest ongoing payments in a periodic-payment annuity. Commissions vary considerably, from 3 to 12 percent of first year payments and from 1 to 5 percent of renewal year payments. The following is a list of some of the leading companies actively selling this product. Most of these companies write in both non-tax-qualified and tax-qualified markets and are licensed to sell in the majority of states.

- Connecticut Mutual Life Insurance Company, Hartford, Conn.
- Equitable Life Assurance Society of the United States, New York, N.Y.

- Great-West Life Assurance Company. Winnipeg, Canada. R3C3A5.
- Hartford Life Insurance Company, Hartford, Conn.
- Integrity Life Insurance Company, Phoenix, Ariz.
- Lincoln National Life Insurance Company, Fort Wayne, Ind.
- Metropolitan Life Insurance Company, New York, N.Y.
- Nationwide Life Insurance Company, Columbus, Ohio
- Prudential Insurance Company, Newark, N.J.
- Teachers Insurance and Annuity Association (tax-sheltered annuities only), New York, N.Y.
- Traveler's Insurance Company, Hartford, Conn.
- Variable Annuity Life Insurance Company, Houston, Tex.
- Washington National Insurance Company, Evanston, Ill.

Group Annuities

Insurance companies generally market large group products through salaried company representatives who are trained pension consultants. Smaller group products are often marketed by company agents.

A few of the companies active in this business are Aetna Life and Annuity Company, Connecticut General Life Insurance, The Equitable Life Assurance Society of the United States, Metropolitan Life Insurance Company, and Prudential Insurance Company.

GLOSSARY

accumulation period—The period under a deferred annuity contract from (1) the date the annuity is purchased until (2) the annuitant's retirement date, the date the annuity contract is surrendered for its cash value, or the annuitant's death, whichever occurs first.

asset charge—An annual percentage charge that is deducted daily from the assets of a separate account and is reflected in the account's unit value.

bailout provision—A provision, sometimes found in single-premium deferred annuity contracts, that enables the owner to surrender the contract without charge if the current interest rate offered drops below a specified rate set in the contract.

deferred annuity—An annuity that provides for both an accumulation period and a retirement (income-paying) period.

fixed deferred annuity—A deferred annuity that guarantees a minimum accumulation interest rate and provides for dividends or excess interest.

fixed immediate annuity—An annuity that begins to pay, generally within one year of purchase, a regular income for life.

front-end load—A percentage charge that the insurer deducts from an annuity payment to offset sales and administrative expenses.

general account—The account to which the insurer allocates assets to fund fixed annuities. Investments consist primarily of bonds, notes, and mortgages.

non-tax-qualified annuities—A "man-in-the-street" annuity that is not purchased under a special tax-favored program. Income accumulates on a tax-deferred basis, but annuity contributions are not tax-deductible to the annuitant.

separate account—A separate investment account to which the insurer allocates assets to fund variable annuities. The investment experience of such an account is kept separate from the insurer's other assets.

settlement options—Life income, fixed period payment, interest-bearing or other options available at the retirement date to the annuitant under a deferred annuity.

tax-qualified annuity—An annuity purchased under a special tax-favored arrangement. Income accumulates on a tax-deferred basis and contributions are not usually included in the annuitant's current income.

variable deferred annuity—A deferred annuity that provides for investment of contributions in one or more separate accounts.

variable immediate annuity—An income-paying annuity providing for regular payments varying in dollar amount depending on the investment experience of a separate account.

SUGGESTED READING

The following is a list of selected publications that contain information of interest to potential buyers of annuities.

BOOKS AND ANNUALS

Best's Retirement Income Guide. Published by A.M. Best Company, Oldwick, N.J. A comprehensive survey, updated and published semiannually, of the three basic types of individual annuity plans: single-premium deferred annuities, flexible-premium retirement annuities, and single-premium immediate annuities. The emphasis within the Guide is to provide a comparison of these contracts offered by the approximately eighty-five contributing life insurance companies.

Best's Settlement Options Manual. Published by A.M. Best Company, Oldwick, N.J. An annual publication giving complete rates and procedures used by most of the larger insurance companies upon settlement of life insurance or annuity proceeds under the various options.

Note: Two statistical studies by A.M. Best, released annually, rank the leading life insurance companies on amounts of prior year's business for individual and group annuity premiums, and major benefits paid, respectively. These studies are published in *Best's Insurance Management Report* and *Best's Review*.

Tax Facts. Published by National Underwriter Company, Cincinnati, Ohio. An annual publication that reflects selected pertinent legislation, regulations, rulings, and court decisions affecting life, health, estate, business, and annuity plans.

Insurance Contracts Profiles. Published by Evaluation Associates, Inc., Westport, Conn. This publication surveys group deposit administration contracts, immediate participation guarantee contracts, and other types of unallocated group funding contracts, and contains comparative information regarding fund charges, investment alternatives, and contractual features.

ARTICLES AND PUBLICATIONS

Campbell, Paul A. *The Variable Annuity.* Hartford: Connecticut General Life Insurance Company, 1969. This publication contains a comprehensive discussion of the variable annuity; it covers history, inflation responsiveness, technical designs, and government regulation.

Fabian, Douglas; and Meriwether, Diane. "Securing Your Future With a Variable Annuity." Published by *Dick Fabian's Telephone Switch Newsletter*, Huntington Beach, Cal., 1988. This publication discusses the pros and cons of variable annuity investing and provides competitive information on thirty-eight products.

Medical College of Georgia. *Tax-Sheltered Annuities: A Comparative Analysis.* Augusta, Georgia, 1980.

Morehart, Thomas B. "Evaluating the Tax-Sheltered Annuity vs. The Taxed Investment," *CLU Journal*, Jan. 1979, pp. 23–30.

These two publications discuss tax-sheltered annuity products—what they are, how various products compare with each other, and advantanges and disadvantages as compared to a fully taxed investment.

BANK CERTIFICATES OF DEPOSIT

Richard J. Blum
Gretchen S. Morrison

BASIC CHARACTERISTICS

Definition and Origin

Certificates of deposit, commonly known as CDs, are a key tool employed by large banks as a means of liability management, and when introduced, CDs were one of the major sources of bank funds. A CD is a financial instrument that evidences the placement of a sum of money with a bank for a specific period at an agreed-on rate of interest. It is normally quoted and sold on an interest-bearing basis and may be in either negotiable or non-negotiable form. CDs are issued by banks of all sizes and have provided these institutions with the funds with which to augment their loan and investment portfolios.

In 1961, Citibank (First National City Bank of New York, at that time), issued the first CD to attract corporate investment funds. The large cash balances that corporations had previously left with banks were declining as sophisticated cash managers invested their cash reserves in Treasury bills and commercial paper. The introduction of CDs was the attempt by banks to reattract some of those dollars. Since that time, federal regulations on the creation of financial instruments have been relaxed. As a result, CDs have evolved from a rather simple beginning and are now available in a variety of forms. These different forms have been developed to make the CD attractive to a wide range of investors.

The major determinant of a CD's value, regardless of the form of issuance, is the creditworthiness of the issuer. The value of a CD issued in negotiable form, however, is also

Richard J. Blum is a Vice-President and Gretchen S. Morrison is an Economist at the First National Bank of Chicago.

dependent on its worth in the secondary market. This in turn is influenced by the CD's maturity and its rate of interest relative to prevailing market rates of interest on CDs with similar maturities.

A CD should not be confused with a time deposit or commercial paper issued by a bank holding company. A time deposit is an insured bank deposit not evidenced by a negotiable instrument. Bank commercial paper is not a bank deposit, but a noninsured negotiable debt instrument issued by a bank holding company or one of its nonbank subsidiaries.

Regulatory Impact

Regulation Q of the Federal Reserve Board (the Board) governs the rate of interest that banks may pay on CDs. In August 1970, the Board suspended the rate ceiling on CDs of $100,000 or more that were issued for less than ninety days. In 1973, the exemption was extended to CDs in amounts of $100,000 or more for all maturities. Banks, therefore, may pay whatever market rate is required to attract these large deposits. On amounts less than $100,000, Regulation Q has been relaxed to the extent that virtually no limitations are imposed on the rate banks may pay on smaller CDs.

CDs are effectively divided into those that total $100,000 or more and those that total less than $100,000. CDs totaling $100,000 or more may have fixed or variable rates. Most of these CDs are in negotiable form, and those of major banks may be traded in the secondary market. Smaller CDs in amounts less than $100,000 are nonnegotiable and thus cannot be traded in the secondary market.

Insurance on demand and savings accounts, as well as on CDs and other time accounts, is provided by the Federal Deposit Insurance Corporation (FDIC). Currently, each depositor's accounts are insured in the aggregate for $100,000. While this insurance is important for the small individual investor, it is virtually meaningless for corporate and other large depositors.

Types of CDs

The most basic division of CDs is into fixed rate and variable rate categories. The large, fixed rate CD is the oldest and most common type, and was used by banks to compete against other fixed rate short-term instruments, such as Treasury bills and commercial paper. The variable rate CD was designed by banks in a variety of forms to attract investors who wanted some protection against highly volatile interest rate movements. By giving investors some protection against interest rate movements, banks were able to extend the maturities of their CDs and thus take advantage at that time of lower bank reserve requirements on longer-term CDs.

For the smaller investor purchasing CDs under $100,000, almost all issues have a fixed rate of interest with maturities ranging from thirty days to ten or fifteen years. The minimum deposit is generally $1,000, and the CDs are handled in book-entry form. That is, the individual does not actually receive an engraved certificate evidencing the deposit, but rather is sent quarterly statements by the issuing bank showing CD amount, maturity date, and interest rate. Periodic interest is then automatically credited to the customer's account.

Fixed Rate Negotiable CDs. Fixed rate CDs are issued for a specific amount at a specific rate for a specific number of days. The rate is quoted on an interest-bearing basis, and the time factor employed in the interest calculation uses actual number of days on the basis of a 360-day year. The formula for the interest calculation is as follows:

$$I = PRT$$

where I = Interest

P = Principal amount deposited

R = Rate of interest expressed as a percentage

T = Time expressed as the exact number of days from date of deposit to maturity divided by 360

For example, interest on a $1 million CD for 180 days at 12 percent equals:

$$\$1 \text{ million} \times .12 \times (180/360) = \$60{,}000.$$

Face amount. Large negotiable CDs are issued for any amount, starting at $100,000. Standard issue size is $1 million, but trades of $5 million are considered round-lot trades by money center banks. Single transactions can exceed $100 million. Investors who may have to sell a CD in the secondary market prior to maturity should request $5 million denominations at the time of issuance. Negotiable CDs can be issued in either bearer or registered form. The CDs issued in registered form can be negotiated on proper endorsement of that instrument.

Maturities. Maturities of negotiable CDs range from 7 days to 10 years. Most CDs, however, are issued for maturities ranging from 14 to 180 days. Investors will pick specific dates within this period in order to provide cash for tax, dividend, and other known payments. In addition, shorter-term CDs have less market risk should they have to be sold in the secondary market.

Purchase and Redemption. Large negotiable CDs are usually issued at the main office of the issuing bank. Major money center banks, however, will also issue the CD through an agent bank in New York. Payment for CDs is made by the buyer in immediately available funds, and principal and interest are repaid in immediately available funds. Payment is normally effected by charging the buyer's account at the bank issuing the CD or by instructing the buyer's safekeeping agent to pay immediately available funds to the issuer on delivery of the CD to the specified agent. CD trades are usually settled on a cash basis (same day), but regular settlement (next day) and skip-day settlement (two days forward) can also be arranged.

Maturing CDs must be presented to the issuing bank or a designated agent in order to receive payment of principal and interest. CDs that pay semiannual interest must also be presented in similar fashion for the investor to receive interest payments. Regulation Q does not allow banks to pay additional interest on CDs that are presented after the maturity date.

Discount CD. The discount CD was developed in the late 1970s to provide investors with an instrument whose yield would be easily compared to other discount paper, such as Treasury bills. This instrument, like a bill, is sold to investors at a cost that is less than its stated maturity value. The difference between cost and maturity value is the investor's interest. The rate of return on this instrument can be quoted on either a bank discount basis or its simple-interest equivalent. For example, a discount CD issued for $1 million for 180 days at a bank discount rate of 12 percent will cost an investor $940,000. The earnings of $60,000 over the 180-day period translate into an annual simple-interest equivalent yield of 12.77 percent.

$$\$1 \text{ million} - (\$1 \text{ million} \times .12 \times \frac{180}{360}) = \$940{,}000$$

$$\frac{\$60{,}000}{\$940{,}000} \div \frac{180}{360} = 12.77\%$$

This instrument created an accounting headache for banks, which were required to calculate reserves on it as if it were a deposit whose size rose over the life of the CD by the amount of the original discount. It never really gained acceptance and is seldom issued.

Variable Rate CDs. This instrument was created because of the increased volatility of short-term interest rates and the former difference in reserve requirements between deposits of 180 days or more and those of 179 days or less.[1] Investors who were reluctant to invest funds for six months because of the risk of rising interest rates wanted the ability to increase their return if in fact interest rates did go higher. Banks that would pay lower reserve requirements if they could attract 180-day or longer money and that needed to fund variable rate assets began to offer investors a variable rate CD. The instrument normally takes on the following form: The coupon is set at a specified spread over one of several base rates, which is reset periodically. The most commonly used base rates are LIBOR, prime rate, Federal Reserve funds, CD composite, commercial paper composite rate, and Treasury bills. The payment schedule is then determined, and is usually monthy, quarterly, or semiannually. Normally reset dates and interest payments coincide.

A typical variable rate CD is a six-month instrument whose rate is 10 to 25 basis points over the thirty-day secondary-CD rate as determined by the Federal Reserve Bank of New York. Interest is paid every thirty days. On the payment date, the new rate is determined for the next thirty days. A wide variety of bases, spreads, and payment schedules can be used, depending on market conditions. Variable rate CDs are normally sold directly to dealers, who then place them with investors. Dealers normally agree with the issuing bank to buy back the CD from the investor at par on coupon change dates, and at a bid price between payment dates, thus creating a secondary market for the instrument. In the absence of such a buy-back agreement, the price of the security in the secondary market would become much more volatile. An optional variable rate CD has also been issued where the various spreads and bases are determined at the time of issuance, but where the maturities within the agreed-on term are chosen by the buyer. At the end of the first maturity, the investor chooses the next maturity and its associated base and spread. This process is repeated and continues until maturity.

---

[1] Prior to October 30, 1980, the reserve requirements imposed on CDs under Regulation D of the Federal Reserve Board were determined by the maturity of the CD. Beginning November 2, 1978, reserves on deposits having maturities in the less than 180-day range were 8 percent, while reserves on deposits maturing in the 180-day to four-year range were 4.50 percent. A bank paying a 12 percent simple-interest rate on a CD due in less than 180 days had an effective cost of 13.04 percent (12 percent/0.92). The effective cost on a 12 percent CD due in 180 days or more was only 12.57 percent (12 percent/0.955). Thus, banks could afford to pay a higher simple-interest rate (up to 12.46 percent) for money due in 180 days or more than they could afford to pay for money due in 179 days or less and still achieve a cost saving.

Domestic, Euro, and Yankee CDs. The instruments discussed so far have been domestic CDs, issued by U.S. banks within the United States. This is the oldest CD market, but since its peak in 1982, it is no longer the largest or most active. The introduction of Eurodollar (Euro) CDs in 1966 spawned an instrument that caught up with the domestic market in the early 1980s and now dwarfs it (see Figures 1 and 2).

Euro CDs. In 1966, Citibank introduced the first Euro CD. Like a domestic CD, a Euro CD is a dollar-denominated negotiable instrument evidencing the placement of a sum of money with a bank, issued for a specific time and paying a stated rate of interest. The distinction is that Euro CDs are issued by a bank outside the United States, which can be an offshore branch of a U.S. bank or a foreign bank; instruments issued by the latter are known as foreign Euro CDs.

"Euro" simply indicates a deposit made outside the domestic market, so that Euro CDs can be issued in Singapore or the Caribbean, although London is the undisputed center of the Euro markets. Because Euro instruments are offshore, they escape many of the regulations that cover their domestic counterparts, specifically interest rate ceiling (although these no longer restrict domestic CDs) and reserve requirements. As a result, Euro CDs bear a higher level of interest (5 to 10 basis points) than comparable domestics.

The vast majority of Euro CDs are fixed rate, rather than variable, have maturities ranging from one to twelve months, and pay interest at maturity. Euro CDs are not restricted to U.S. dollars and can be issued in other currencies, such as Australian or Canadian dollars. However, at least 99 percent of current outstandings are denominated in U.S. currency. The predominant issuers are branches of U.S. and Japanese banks, although continental European and British banks also have a presence.

Sales of Euro CDs are made for settlement two days forward. At that time, payment is made by a transfer of funds in New York, while the actual instrument is issued and kept in London. It should be noted that although the entity issuing a Euro instrument is located outside the United States, the associated dollars always remain in the United States. Euro CDs are always evidenced by a bearer instrument (see Figure 3) and are not a book-entry or registered instrument, as domestic CDs can be. Like domestics, delivery of the Euro instrument is made against payment. This can present a problem for Euro CDs because the time zone differences between New York and London prohibit simultaneous delivery and payment. To solve this problem, the First Chicago Clearing Centre (FCCC) was established to act as agent and safekeeper for the CDs. FCCC assures members payment and delivery on any transaction done with another member.

Yankee. A negotiable CD issued in the United States by a branch of a foreign bank is known as a Yankee CD. Major issuers are the Japanese, followed by Canadian and European banks, who use the proceeds to finance loans made to U.S. and foreign corporations operating in the United States. When they were introduced in the early 1970s, Yankee CDs had to offer considerably higher yields than domestics because they did not have an established investor base, and investors were wary of unfamiliar names. For similar reasons, foreign issuers rely more heavily on dealers to help place their paper. Although foreign instruments are more accepted now, Yankee CDs suffer from lack of liquidity. So investors who buy them are generally yield buyers; they accept the limited liquidity and perceived sovereign risk in return for a higher yield.

FIGURE 1. Outstanding Domestic CDs of Large Commercial Banks
Source: *Federal Reserve Bulletin*

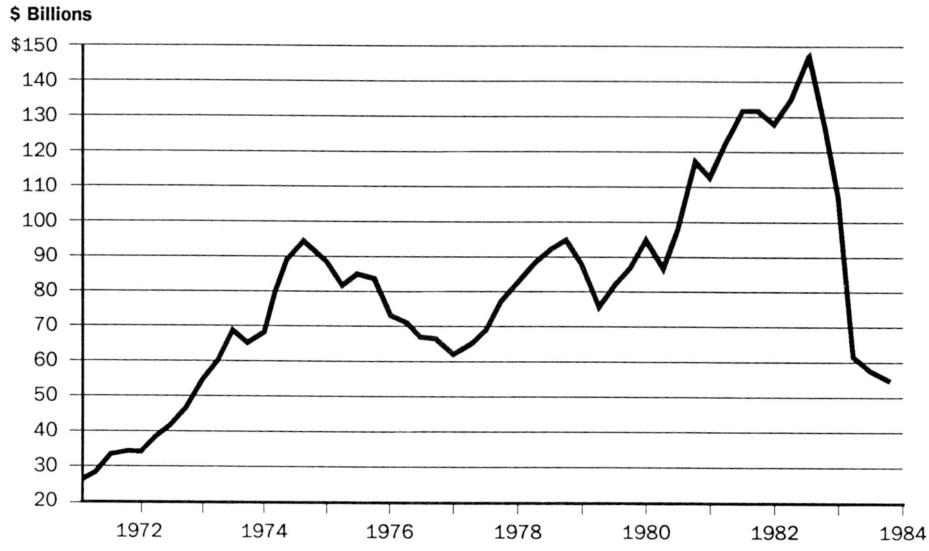

FIGURE 2. Outstanding Eurodollar CDs
Source: Bank of England

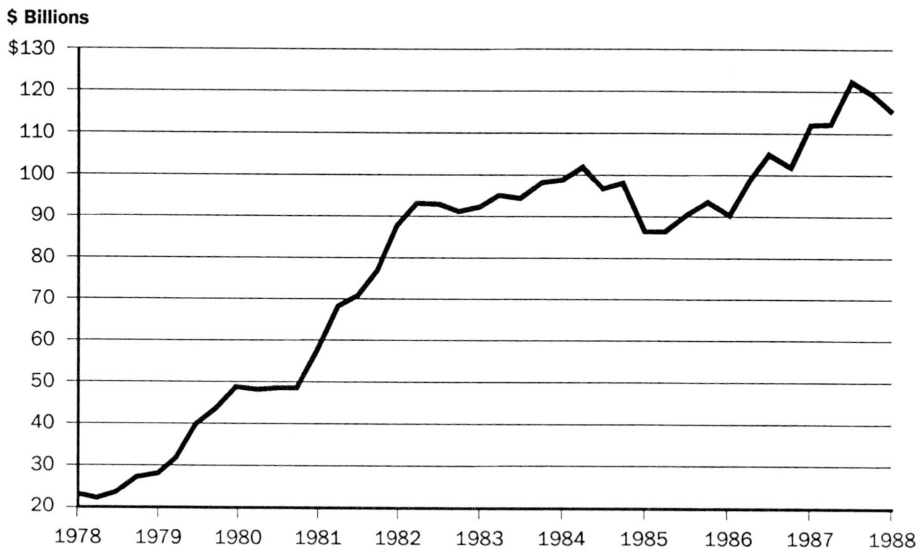

FIGURE 3. A Specimen of a Negotiable Euro CD for $500,000

Source: The First National Bank of Chicago

The Primary and Secondary Markets

The Primary Market. A CD issued by a bank directly to the initial investor is called a primary CD. Most banks prefer to issue large negotiable CDs directly to the primary investor. Banks who issue directly to the investor have better knowledge of who owns their liabilities and an increased likelihood of rolling over the CD at maturity. The rate at which a bank offers its CD directly to an investor for a specific maturity is called its primary rate. The common maturities for which banks will quote a primary CD rate are 14 to 29 days, 30 to 59 days, 60 to 89 days, 90 to 179 days, 180 to 269 days, 270 to 359 days, and one year or longer. The rates for these different maturities make up what is called a bank's primary CD scale. Banks may be willing to negotiate rates above the primary scale on large blocks of money. At money center banks, rates on a block of money above $5 million may be negotiated, depending on market conditions. The primary CD scales will vary from one bank to another, depending on market conditions, the size and creditworthiness of the bank, the bank's current need for funds, and the bank's outlook for interest rates.

The Secondary Market. A CD sold by an investor or dealer to some other dealer or investor is called a secondary CD. The secondary market came into existence for two reasons: First, primary CD holders needed liquidity and hence a market in which to sell their CDs prior to maturity; second, banks needed another distribution network through which they could quickly sell a larger volume of CDs than their own primary network was willing to purchase. This market is composed of approximately seventy bank and nonbank dealers who stand ready to make a market in the CDs of the fifty largest U.S. banks and certain foreign agency banks. Today, these dealers enhance the liquidity of the CD market, and trading volume can exceed $1 billion a day. (See the list of dealers at the end of this article.)

Role of Dealers and Brokers. Dealers in the secondary market quote bid and offered rates for CDs by the month, which is broken down into "early" and "late." Early refers to an instrument maturing in the first fifteen days of the month; late refers to anything maturing after the fifteenth. Thus, dealers have bids or offers for early June CDs or late August CDs as opposed to the traditional thirty-, sixty-, or ninety-day rate scale used by banks in the primary market. The spread between the bid and offered side of the market is normally 3 basis points in the short end (six months or under), but this spread can narrow or widen, depending on market conditions. Trades with dealers are done on a net basis with no commission added.

The minimum denomination of a CD traded in the secondary market is $1 million. Round lots are considered to be $5 million blocks. Settlement for CDs bought or sold in the secondary market is normally made on a regular basis, but cash trades can also be arranged. Settlement for CDs is in immediately available funds, and delivery must be made to a bank in New York or the dealer's New York office. Dealers must make a bid on CDs, but, since they cannot sell CDs short, they may not have an offering rate. Dealers who underwrite a bank offering of CDs will usually charge the issuing bank a commission ranging from 2 to 10 basis points; the average for major money center banks is 5 basis points.

Brokers in CDs add liquidity to the secondary market by accepting bids and offers for CDs from a list of approved dealers. The dealer specifies the amount, the selling or buying rate, the maturity range, and the tier in which the bank's name falls. These bids and offers, which are good for a certain period, are communicated by various means to other dealers who can sell or buy the specified securities at the broker's bid or offer price. Dealers use brokers to execute trades in a confidential manner, since the dealer who consummates a trade through the broker does not know who the dealer is on the other side of the transaction. The price of buying or selling through a broker is either paid by the dealer who agrees to execute a trade shown to him by the broker or is split by both buyer and seller; the fee ranges from 1/2 to 2 basis points.

Yield-Basis Pricing. Fixed rate CDs are sold in the secondary market on a yield basis. This yield is used to compute a dollar price and establishes the amount paid for the principal of a CD. To this amount must be added the amount of interest accrued since the date of issuance. The formula for the price of a secondary CD is as follows:

$$X = \frac{P \times (360 + R_i T_1)}{(R_S T_3 + 360)} - \frac{(PRT_2)}{360}$$

where

X = Price of the CD in the secondary market

P = Principal of the deposit

R_i = Initial rate of the deposit expressed as a decimal

T_1 = Original term of the CD in days

T_2 = Days from issuance date to sale date

T_3 = Days from sale date to maturity date

R_S = Rate at which the CD is sold expressed as a decimal

TABLE 1. Return on $1 Million CDs Sold in Secondary Market Prior to Maturity

	Example 1	Example 2	Example 3	Example 4
Original term of CD (days)	180	180	360	360
Remaining term of CD (days)	90	90	180	180
Interest rate on CD	12%	12%	12%	12%
Secondary market bid for CD	11%	13%	11%	13%
Principal received	$1,001,630.17	$996,634.38	$1,001,611.37	$991,643.19
Accrued interest	$30,000.00	$30,000.00	$60,000.00	$60,000.00
Total proceeds	$1,031,630.17	$1,026,634.38	$1,061,611.37	$1,051,643.19
Per annum yield for period held	12.65%	10.65%	12.32%	10.33%
Gain or (loss)	$1,630.17	($3,365.62)	$1,611.37	($8,356.81)

Source: Authors' data

For example, a $1 million CD issued for 180 days at a rate of 12 percent, which is sold at 11 percent after ninety days, will cost an investor $1,001,630.17. To this amount must be added $30,000 in accrued interest so that the CD costs the investor $1,031,630.17. (See Table 1 for other examples.)

$$X = \frac{\$1{,}000{,}000 \times [360 + (.12 \times 180)]}{(.11 \times 90) + 360} - \frac{\$1{,}000{,}000 \times (.12 \times 90)}{360}$$

$$= \$1{,}031{,}630.17 - 30{,}000.00$$

$$= \$1{,}001{,}630.17$$

In the secondary market, banks are tiered according to how their CDs trade relative to conditions, but currently, the first tier of banks consists of the ten largest domestic banks, often referred to as Tops.

In addition to credit quality, the required yield on a bank's CDs is influenced by the supply of its paper already present in the market. Any bank that has a lot of paper outstanding will be required to pay a higher interest rate, or "pay up," when it tries to issue more. Conversely, any top bank that issues CDs less frequently will be able to pay a lower rate of interest, because its paper has scarcity value to investors. Even among the top banks, there are subtle differences in perceived credit quality and amount of available top paper.

In the second tier are certain large regional banks. Other regional banks and large foreign banks fall into the third tier. CDs of banks in the second tier often trade 5 to 15 basis points in yield above first-tier banks, although there are some particularly well regarded regional and foreign banks whose CDs trade at yields equal to those of top banks. CDs of third-tier banks trade 5 to 15 basis points in yield above second-tier banks. In periods of tight money and increasing interest rates, the spread between the rates paid by top banks and those paid by lower-tier banks expands, while in periods of easier money and declining interest rates, this spread contracts.

The tiering process also affects the rate at which banks can issue CDs in the primary market. Large investors who need the liquidity provided by the secondary market will exact the credit-risk premium at the time of purchase by requiring the issuing bank in a lower tier to pay a higher rate. Small, local-bank CDs may be excellent credit risks but, because they are not known outside their local markets, are not traded in the secondary market. Sophisticated investors may demand a liquidity premium because these local-bank CDs are less liquid. However, because these smaller banks may not compete in their local market with larger banks, or do not attempt to obtain funds from large investors, many can issue CDs at rates equal to or lower than those paid by large money center banks.

ATTRACTIVE FEATURES

Safety and Current Return

The CD provides investors with safety of principal and attractive current return. As the creditworthiness of the approximately 15,000 banks in the United States obviously varies, investors must give some consideration to the financial conditions of the issuer. The FDIC has not been forced to contend with the potential financial panic that could arise from a major bank failure owing to their practice of merging weak or failing banks with stronger partners. In addition, the FDIC insurance of $100,000 on all accounts, including CDs, has acted to build the confidence of smaller investors and avoid the bank runs that were all too prevalent during the 1930s. Even in the case of First Republic Bank of Texas, a bank of $26.8 billion in assets that was declared insolvent in August 1988, the FDIC opted to honor *all* deposits made, not just up to the $100,000 limit.

When yields on CDs are compared with those of other money market instruments at various maturities, the rankings from lowest to highest yield are generally the following: Treasury bills, U.S. government agency securities, CDs, bankers' acceptances, commercial paper, and Euro deposits.

Liquidity and Convenience

The liquidity of major bank CDs is provided by the large secondary market, and trades of $25 million to $50 million are quite common. Although CDs are not as liquid as Treasury bills, investors in major bank CDs should have little problem selling them prior to maturity. As recent financial history has shown, short-term interest rates can be highly volatile, and some principal can be lost by an investor who sells a CD prior to maturity in a falling secondary market (rising interest rates). Equally possible, however, is the gain that investors may receive if they sell a CD in a rising secondary market (falling interest rates). (See Examples 1 and 3 in Table 1.) Investors who wish to speculate on short-term interest rate movements will find the CD to be an excellent medium for this purpose.

A CD can also be used as collateral against a loan. The rate on a loan using CDs as collateral is determined by the lending institution. Regulation Q, however, requires that a bank lending money to customers who use their own CD as collateral must charge a minimum of one percent above the rate of interest being paid on the CD. Regulation Q does not apply if a bank loans against the CD of some other bank. A bank is allowed to prepay a CD if asked by a customer, but it has no obligation to prepay it. There may be a prepayment penalty in the form of forfeited interest as well.

Buying a CD is a very convenient transaction to execute, particularly if the customer already has other banking relationships with the issuing bank. The investor merely has to call the institution, obtain the necessary rate quotations, and decide the amount and maturity he wishes to purchase. The bank will charge the customer's account, issue the CD, hold it in safekeeping, and credit the proceeds at maturity back to the customer's account. No visits to the bank are necessary. The statement and safekeeping receipt plus the advice of debit and credit to the investor's account give accurate data for budget and tax purposes.

POTENTIAL RISKS

Credit Risks

The large negotiable CD, like all investments, is subject to a number of risks. An investor should consider the credit and market risks before buying a CD. These two risks influence the rate at which the CD is issued in the primary market and have a continued effect on the rate at which the CD can be sold in the secondary market. These risks may exist individually or collectively and may change in magnitude, depending on market conditions.

Investors should examine the creditworthiness of the banks with which they place CDs. One method of analyzing a bank's credit standing is to observe the tier in which a bank's CD trades in the secondary market. This tiering process is heavily influenced by a bank's credit standing in the national market. Another method of analyzing a bank's credit rating is to review the bond and commercial paper ratings of the holding company that owns the bank. Moody's Investor's Service, Inc. and Standard & Poor's Corporation both rate long-term bond debt and short-term commercial paper. Bank ratings published by Keefe, Bruyette & Woods, Inc., and others, enable the investor to make a comparison among individual banks. Only after he has made a credit analysis of the issuing bank can the investor determine the rate that should be received from that bank, given the rates posted by other banks in the market.

Market Risks

Sale in a Rising-Interest Rate Environment. When evaluating market risk, the investor should consider the effects that a substantial increase in interest rates will have on the value of CDs that have to be sold prior to maturity. In a rising-rate environment, an accidental or deliberate mismatch of fixed assets and liabilities, with asset maturity greater than liability maturity, can be very costly either in terms of actual losses or in foregone opportunities. Inaccurate cash-flow projections could force investors to sell the CDs prior to maturity to raise necessary cash. Investors who forecast declining interest rates and buy CDs expecting to sell them at a profit prior to maturity may later find that interest rates are in fact rising, and would thus be forced to sell to reduce their losses. Examples 2 and 4 in Table 1 indicate the change in value of a 12 percent CD being sold in the secondary market at a 13 percent rate. It should also be noted from Table 1 that the longer the remaining term on the CD, the greater the potential loss in principal given the same one percent increase in interest rates. As interest rates have become more volatile in recent years, the market risk on longer CDs has increased appreciably.

FIGURE 4. Rates and Spread Between Three-Month CDs and Three-Month Treasury Bills

Source: Bank of America

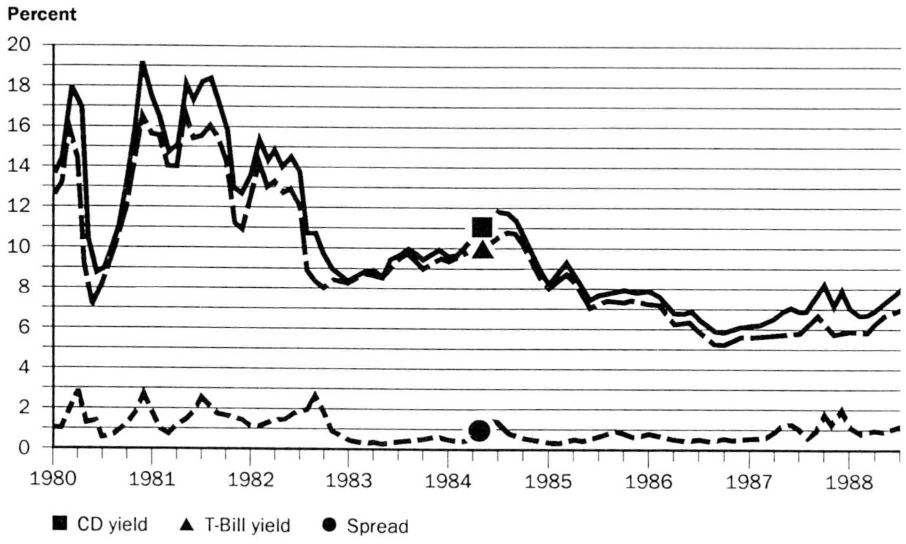

Analyzing the CD-Treasury Bill Spread. Another method of evaluating market risk is to look at the yield spread between CDs and Treasury bills. Figure 4 shows the tight relationship between the yields of secondary CDs and Treasury bills. The spread on three-month CDs and three-month Treasury bills has averaged 94 basis points from January 1980 to June 1988. This spread has been as low as 22 basis points and as high as 274 basis points during this eight-and-a-half-year period. While a large portion of the spread change represents a change in investors' perception of credit risk, another portion represents a change in the investors' perception of the market risk of CDs.

During periods of tight money, the spread between Treasury bills and CDs widens as banks bid up the price for funds and investors seek increased marketability in Treasury bills. As interst rates decline, this spread narrows. Dealers are also not as willing to take on large blocks of CDs at the bid price when interest rates are rising as they are when interest rates are falling because of the increased risk of losses in a rising-rate environment. Investors who purchase the CDs of smaller banks (below the top fifty banks in the country) cannot be guaranteed marketability of the instrument in the secondary market at any time unless the local issuing bank, as agent, can arrange to find a buyer.

TAX CONSEQUENCES

The following discussion is generally true regarding the tax implications for CD holders; however, investors should seek the advice of tax counsel to determine their individual tax standing.

The federal tax consequences of owning CDs are as follows. Large corporations (annual gross receipts greater than $5 million) are generally required to use an accrual method of tax accounting for interest earned on CDs. Small corporations, farming corporations, and personal service corporations engaged principally in health, law, engineering, architecture, accounting, actuarial science, performing arts, and consulting can use a cash method of tax accounting for interest earned on CDs.

If a corporation or an individual acquires at a discount in the secondary market a CD issued before July 18, 1984 that has a term in excess of one year and holds it to maturity, the gain is taxed as a long-term capital gain. Because the present tax rate on ordinary income and capital gains is the same, this characterization of the gain is significant only if a corporation has capital losses because capital losses are deductible only against capital gains.

If a corporation or an individual acquires at a discount in the secondary market a CD issued after July 18, 1984 that has a term in excess of one year and either sells it, gives it to another, or holds it to maturity, the gain is treated as ordinary interest income. It will also be characterized as investment interest income for purposes of the limitation on investment interest expense applicable to individuals. However, neither an issuer nor its agent is required to send a Form 1099 to report to an individual and the Internal Revenue Service (IRS) the amount of market discount that might be taxable to an individual.

Any interest expense incurred to purchase or carry a new market discount CD is deferred and becomes deductible only when the market discount is recognized in taxable income. A debt is incurred to purchase or carry a new market discount CD when the debt is collateralized by the CD. However, unsecured debt or debt secured by other collateral may or may not be incurred to purchase or carry a market discount CD, depending on all the facts and circumstances.

If a corporation or an individual acquires a CD with a term of less than one year in the secondary market, the gain is taxed at the short-term capital gains rate.

A CD that is issued with a discount (i.e., a "zero coupon" CD) and with a term greater than one year, is an original issue discount (OID) CD. If the OID is above 25 basis points over the entire term of the CD, which it would almost always be, it must be accrued in income on a constant yield basis for both accrual and cash basis taxpayers. Individual taxpayers and the IRS will receive a Form 1099-OID from the issuer or its agent showing the amount of OID accruable each year for tax purposes.

Individuals who suffer a premature withdrawal penalty are allowed to deduct this penalty from gross income. Individuals are required to supply their names and taxpayer identification numbers to the CD issuer or its agent. If a taxpayer does not supply that number, the interest income earned on the CD will be subject to 20 percent backup withholding. Nonresident aliens who submit an appropriate form to the CD issuer or its agent will be able to avoid backup withholding without being required to supply a taxpayer identification number. Finally, individuals and the IRS will receive a Form 1099 that shows the amount of interest income or OID they earned each calendar year on the CD.

Many states use the same federal income tax rules described here to subject interest income and OID on CDs to state income taxation. However, tax-exempt entities are generally not affected by either federal or state income taxes.

REPRESENTATIVE TYPES OF INVESTORS

Large CDs are purchased by a wide range of investors. Financial institutions are the largest purchasers, followed in importance by corporations and government bodies. Foreign banks and governments are also large buyers, as are nonprofit organizations and wealthy individuals.

Financial institutions are particularly large buyers of CDs. Banks, acting in the capacity of trustee, and money market mutual funds are substantial buyers. Bank trust departments find that CDs provide attractive yields to pension funds, profit-sharing funds, and other entities for which the bank acts as trustee.

Corporations find CDs an attractive instrument in which to invest their surplus funds. The funds are invested to mature on dates when the corporation has a known cash outflow. Maturities are chosen to coincide with tax, dividend, supplier payment, payroll, and other known payment dates. The portfolio management guidelines vary among corporations. Some corporations buy CDs to hold to maturity, while others actively trade their entire portfolio.

State and local government units invest large sums of tax receipts in CDs. Government units usually receive tax payments at regular times during the year. This inflow of tax revenue must be used to pay expenses throughout the year. As a result, the government unit will take the tax receipts and invest a certain portion in CDs that mature during periods when tax revenues are not being received. Banks may have to secure the funds these entities place in CDs by pledging U.S. government or suitable municipal securities as collateral against the deposit. State and local laws determine which deposits must be secured and what constitutes suitable collateral.

Foreign banks and governments have become large buyers of U.S. CDs over the past fifteen years. During this period, the United States has run substantial deficits in its balance of payments. Some of the dollars accumulated by nations that have run large surpluses, particularly OPEC nations and Japan, have been deposited with major money center banks in the form of CDs. Foreign banks have found it convenient to keep a certain portion of their dollar reserves in the form of CDs as well. Wealthy individuals and nonprofit organizations, such as foundations and college endowment funds, are also significant purchasers of bank CDs.

IMPORTANT FACTORS IN BUYING AND SELLING

Knowledge of current market conditions and correct assessment of future trends in interest rates are key factors in the successful management of a short-term portfolio. Consequently, the investor must select those banks and dealers whose sales representatives give an accurate picture of current market conditions and include the outlook for the near term as well. While the prediction of interest rate movements is hardly a science, certain institutions have a better track record than others. The investor must feel confident in dealing with the various sales representatives and feel that they are interested in dealing at market prices over the long term rather than exploiting any short-term advantages. The sales representative should know where his bank or dealer firm is competitive (on the market) and where it is noncompetitive (off the market). An accurate picture of market conditions for all short-term instruments should be given to the investor by the sales representative so that the investor can weigh the option of alternative investment strategies.

Shopping the Markets

Large buyers of CDs must compare rates available from banks in the primary market with rates available from dealers in the secondary market. Buyers must also compare the amounts and maturities banks are willing to write in the primary market with those available in the secondary market. Only after such comparisons have been made can the investor make the appropriate investment decision. Rates in the secondary market normally will be about 5 basis points higher than the rates quoted in the primary market. However, secondary dealers may not have the bank names and maturity dates desired by the investor.

Buying in the Primary Market

An investor who has a large block of money to place may find that by the time he executes a number of trades in the secondary market this has moved the market to lower rate levels. By buying directly from a bank in the primary market, the investor may be able to execute the order in the size necessary and for the exact maturity date desired without moving the market. Certainly on large placements, investors normally should be able to negotiate a primary rate competitive with those in the secondary market. Only after obtaining the necessary market information can the investor decide where to execute transactions and thus maximize return. Sellers of CDs should evaluate the bids of a number of dealers with respect to rate and size before executing the transaction. Given the volatility of markets in recent years, the investor must make decisions quickly in order to execute transactions at the quoted rates. Investors who have large portfolios and desire to trade actively in the market need a large number of bank and dealer contacts to effect a wide range of portfolio transactions at competitive prices.

Avoiding Fails and Errors

Investors should confirm all details of a transaction with the bank or dealer at the time the transaction is consummated. This confirmation process eliminates errors and misunderstandings. The investor must also give his safekeeping agent equally clear instructions with respect to all aspects of the transaction. Lack of clear instructions can result in fails, incorrect accounting entries, and time-consuming negotiations over compensation. An investor who gives clear instructions to all parties involved in a transaction has the right to expect the transaction to be completed correctly and in a timely fashion.

Setting Credit and Market Risk Standards

The investor is responsible for setting risk standards for the portfolio. In setting credit risk standards, the investor must determine which bank names are acceptable and the amount of each bank name to hold. In setting market risk standards, the investor must evaluate the accuracy of cash-flow projections and interest rate forecasts. The potential profit and loss impact of meeting unforeseen needs through forced portfolio liquidation is an important ingredient in this evaluation process. The investor should never forget that the placement of money for any term is an implicit, if not explicit, speculation on the movement of interest rates.

Only after setting the credit and market risk standards can the investor set goals for portfolio performance that can be monitored effectively. The portfolio manager can achieve potentially higher rates of return only by increasing the market and credit risks within the portfolio. Portfolio managers who are willing to accept higher market risk must be able to shift their portfolios quickly between short and long maturities as their interest rate forecast changes or as market circumstances dictate. Investors who wish to minimize market risk should confine their portfolios to shorter-term maturities.

CUSTODIAL CARE

Negotiable CDs should be held by a bank acting in its capacity as a safekeeping agent. By holding CDs at a bank, the investor avoids the financial risk of loss or theft and obtains the convenience of easy payment and accurate record keeping. Major banks have a specific department to pay for securities on delivery, hold them in safekeeping, and collect principal and interest on proper maturity and payment dates. Issuing banks normally do not assess a charge for holding CDs that they have sold directly to their customers. If a CD is lost, the holder normally must post an indemnification bond before the issuing bank will pay off the instrument.

By having a bank hold the certificate, the holder is assured of timely receipt of principal and interest. Because the bank credits the buyer's account on payment dates, the buyer can reinvest the proceeds on the same day and thus avoid the loss of interest that arises from failure to present the certificate on the due date or coupon payment date. Banks will not pay any CD unless it is in their own or their agent's possession, and Regulation Q does not allow banks to pay interest on CDs after maturity. Most banks will contact CD holders prior to maturity date in an attempt to roll over the CD. However, there is no legal obligation to do so, and many notifications are sent out by mail. Thus, it is important that all buyers of CDs maintain proper maturity records so that they maximize their returns by ensuring that the proceeds of a maturing CD are invested as soon as they are available. In most instances, the rollover and associated payment and safekeeping arrangements can be accomplished through a single phone call or letter.

GLOSSARY

basis point—One one-hundredth of a percent. Usually referred to as an 01, its mathematical value is .0001. On a $1 million security, the value of a basis point for 360 days, 180 days, and 90 days is $100, $50, and $25, respectively.

book-entry securities—Securities that are not represented by an engraved piece of paper but are maintained in computerized records. Most nonnegotiable CDs are in book-entry form.

broker—One who brings buyers and sellers together for a commission, paid by either the party that agrees to execute the trade or by both buyer and seller. A broker does not take a position in the instrument.

dealer—A financial institution that stands willing to buy or sell a security at a stated price or yield. A dealer acts as a principal, buying and selling for his own account.

Euro CDs—CDs issued by a U.S. bank branch or foreign bank located outside the United States. Almost all Euro CDs are issued in London.

Eurodollars—U.S. dollars deposited in a U.S. bank branch or foreign bank located outside the United States.

LIBOR—The London Interbank Offered Rate on Eurodollar deposits traded between banks.

make a market—To quote both a bid and offer price for a security.

prime rate—The rate at which banks lend to their best customers.

reserve requirements—The amount, expressed as a percentage of a particular type of deposit, that banks must hold in the form of cash or a deposit at the Federal Reserve Bank as determined by Federal Reserve Regulation D.

rollover—The reinvestment of the principal or proceeds of a maturing security in the same type of security.

scale—A dealer's list of rates he is willing to pay on CDs of varying maturities. Scales change from day to day and even from minute to minute.

spread—A rate, usually expressed in basis points, that measures the difference between the bid and offer price of a security, or that measures the difference in yield between two securities. It is also used to measure the additional rate added to some base yield to give a final yield on a variable rate security.

Treasury—A negotiable security, either a bill, note, or bond, issued by the U.S. Treasury.

variable rate CD—A CD that has a rate of return that is reset at specific intervals, or roll dates, over its term. The rate is composed of a fixed spread and a stated base rate; the base rate is reset on the roll dates and can be LIBOR, prime rate, or the rate on any number of standard short-term securities. Interest is paid either at maturity or at certain specified intervals.

Yankee CD—A CD issued in the domestic market by a branch of a foreign bank.

yield—Rate of discount that makes the present value of a security equal to its current market price. An annual simple-interest yield does not take into account any effects of compounding and is effectively the annualized return on a security divided by its cost.

DOMESTIC AND EURO CD DEALERS

American National Bank and Trust Co., St. Paul, Minn.

Ashwell & Co., Chicago, Ill.

Banco Popular de Puerto Rico, San Juan, P.R.

Bank of America NT & SA, San Francisco, Cal.

Bank of Boston, Mass.

Bank of New York, N.Y.

Bank One of Columbus, NA, Ohio

Bankers Trust Co., New York, N.Y.

Bear, Stearns & Co., New York, N.Y.

Capital Markets Corp., Denver, Colo.

Carroll McEntee & McGinley, Inc., New York, N.Y.

Carty & Company, Inc., Memphis, Tenn.

Chemical Bank, New York, N.Y.

Centerre Bank NA, St. Louis, Mo.

Central Bank of the South, Birmingham, Ala.

Chase Manhattan Bank, NA, New York, N.Y.

Citicorp Investment Bank, New York, N.Y.

Citizens & Southern National Bank, Atlanta, Ga.

Commerce Bank of Kansas City, NA, Mo.

Continental Illinois National Bank and Trust Co. of Chicago, Ill.

Craigie Incorporated, Richmond, Va.

Cranston Securities Co., Columbus, Ohio

Cronin & Co., Inc., Minneapolis, Minn.

Dean Witter Reynolds, Inc., New York, N.Y.

Discount Corp. of New York, N.Y.

Dorsey & Co., Inc., New Orleans, La.

Drexel Burnham Lambert, GSI, New York, N.Y.

Exchange National Bank of Chicago, Chicago, Ill.

FBS Capital Markets Group, Minneapolis, Minn.

First Boston Corp., New York, N.Y.

First Interstate Capital Markets, Inc., New York, N.Y.

First National Bank of Chicago, Ill.

Fleet National Bank, Warren, R.I.

Goldman, Sachs & Co., New York, N.Y.

Irving Securities, Inc., New York, N.Y.

Kidder, Peabody & Co., Inc., New York, N.Y.

Marcus, Stowell & Beye, Ft. Lauderdale, Fla.

Manufacturers Hanover Trust Co., New York, N.Y.

Mark Twain Bank, NA, St. Louis, Mo.

Marquette Bank Minneapolis NA, Minneapolis, Minn.

Mellon Bank, NA, Pittsburgh, Pa.

Merrill Lynch Money Markets, Inc., New York, N.Y.

Midland-Montagu Government Securities Inc., San Francisco, Cal.

J.P. Morgan Securities, Inc., New York, N.Y.

Morgan Stanley & Co., Inc., New York, N.Y.

Moseley Securities Corp., New York, N.Y.

National City Bank, Cleveland, Ohio

Nikko Securities International, New York, N.Y.

Nomura Securities International, New York, N.Y.

Northern Trust Co., Chicago, Ill.

Paine Webber Inc., New York, N.Y.

Piper, Jaffray & Hopwood, Inc., Minneapolis, Minn.

Prudential-Bache Securities, Inc., New York, N.Y.

Rauscher Pierce Refsnes, Inc., Dallas, Tex.

L.F. Rothschild, Unterberg, Towbin, Inc., New York, N.Y.

Salomon Brothers, Inc., New York, N.Y.

Scott & Stringfellow, Inc., Lynchburg, Va.

Security Pacific National Bank — Security Trading, Los Angeles, Cal.

Shearson Lehman Commercial Paper, Inc., New York, N.Y.

Smith Barney, Harris Upham & Co., Inc., New York, N.Y.

State Street Bank and Trust Co., Boston, Mass.

Swiss Bank Corp. — New York, New York, N.Y.

Texas Commerce Bank, Houston, Tex.

Thomson McKinnon Securities, Inc., New York, N.Y.

Trust Co. Bank, Atlanta, Ga.

Tucker, Anthony & R.L. Day, Inc., New York, N.Y.

UMIC, Inc., Memphis, Tenn.

United Missouri Bank of Kansas City, Mo.

Wachovia Bank & Trust Company, NA, Winston Salem, N.C.

A. Webster Dougherty & Co., Inc., Philadelphia, Pa.

Yamaichi International (America), Inc., New York, N.Y.

TRADE ORGANIZATIONS

American Bankers' Association, Washington, D.C.

Association of Primary Dealers in U.S. Government Securities, New York, N.Y.

LEADING BROKERS

Cantor, Fitzgerald Securities Corp., New York, N.Y.

Fulton Prebon (USA), Inc., New York, N.Y.

Fundamental Money Markets, New York, N.Y.

Garvin Guy Butler, New York, N.Y.

Hilliard Farber & Co., New York, N.Y.

Mabon Nugent & Co., New York, N.Y.

Tullet and Tokyo Forex, Inc., New York, N.Y.

SUGGESTED READING

DAILY PERIODICALS

American Banker

The New York Times

Wall Street Journal

WEEKLY PERIODICALS

Bondweek, published by Institutional Investor, Inc., New York, N.Y.

MONTHLY PERIODICALS

Federal Reserve Bulletin, Federal Reserve Board, Washington, D.C.

REFERENCE BOOKS

Darst, David M. *The Complete Bond Book.* New York: McGraw-Hill, 1975.

The First Boston Corporation. *Handbook of Securities of the United States Government and Federal Agencies and Related Money Market Instruments*, 32nd ed. New York: 1986.

Stigum, Marcia. *The Money Market*, rev. ed. Homewood: Dow Jones-Irwin, 1983.

———, in collaboration with John Mann. *Money Market Yield Calculations: Yields, Break-Evens, and Arbitrage*, rev. ed. Homewood: Dow Jones-Irwin, 1988.

BANK-MANAGED ACCOUNTS

John R. Thomas
Joan C. Terwilliger
Ted E. Davis

BASIC CHARACTERISTICS

Bank-managed accounts are trust funds that take three general forms: commingled, or pooled, funds, for the exclusive use of the bank's employee benefit clients; common trust funds, available to the trusts of estates and individuals; and individually invested accounts, portfolios set up for a single investor (individual or corporate) and owned exclusively by the investor. These funds are generally not registered as mutual funds under the Investment Company Act of 1940. Unlike mutual funds, they have no board of directors, no prospectus, and generally no management fee.

General Attributes

A commingled or common fund is established by a trust company solely for the use of its clients and may not legally be used by persons outside the established trust relationship. In this respect, these funds differ from mutual funds through which investors at large may pool their resources. (As of early 1989, banks are not permitted to sell registered mutual funds; they can be offered to the public only by investment companies or brokerage houses.) Banks can manage mutual funds so long as they do not offer them to clients.

An individually invested account, set up for an individual or an organization, consists of a number of different securities and may be balanced between fixed income and equities,

John R. Thomas is a Vice-President and Joan C. Terwilliger is a former Assistant Secretary at Morgan Guaranty Trust Company of New York; they prepared this article in its original form for the first edition. Ted E. Davis is Senior Vice-President at First City National Bank of Houston; he revised and updated this article

or may be concentrated in one or the other depending on how conservatively the portfolio is to be invested.

The technique known as commingling involves the pooling of securities to create a fund of a certain type or classification of security. The commingling technique applies to both commingled funds and common trust funds, although only an Employee Retirement Income Security Act of 1974 (ERISA) client's fund is formally designated a commingled fund. In its broadest sense, the idea of commingling or pooling securities can be compared with the mutual fund concept; in each instance, participants share in the total return of a fund represented by dividends and/or interest and appreciation.

Pricing of Pooled Funds. Pooled funds are valued at the end of every month or more frequently, and the assigned unit (share) value is adjusted accordingly. (Mutual funds are valued on a daily basis; special valuations for pooled funds may occur when warranted by extraordinary market conditions.) Within the fund, public market securities are priced on the basis of market closing trades (last price), or in the case of narrowly traded securities, on a mean price (between bid and asked); private placements are priced on a matrix (valuation model) created from a composite of similar public issues and discounted for liquidity restrictions peculiar to the type of investment and its marketability. Because of the difficulty of valuation, private placements are not normally found in bank-pooled funds. (See further discussion of pricing under *Acquiring and Retiring Pooled Fund Shares,* later in this article.)

The Pooling Concept

The efficiency of asset management may be greatly enhanced by the use of the pooled vehicle. The element of timing is often crucial to the execution of security trades. The pooled-fund manager has immediate access to each holding in the fund and easy reference to the weighted effect of each security on the portfolio's total performance. The individually invested account manager, although he may have direct access to account holdings, must take the time to consider each account profile to determine the advisability of a purchase or sale. Furthermore, the pooling of securities makes it possible for individual trusts, through participation in the funds, to share in attractive investments of a number of companies, even though the market supply (shares or issues outstanding) may be limited. Thus, the investor can participate in a composite fund of securities consisting of many small to medium-sized companies in which it would have been impractical to invest directly on behalf of individual trusts.

The degree to which assets are invested on a pooled basis depends on the participating client and his trustee. For example, when a trust is established for an individual and his beneficiary, parameters are set for the degree of emphasis to be placed on current and future income, growth and capital appreciation, tax-free return, and risk tolerance. Should a decision then be made to use a common fund vehicle, a selection is made from the various equity, convertible, fixed-income, and tax-exempt funds to satisfy the needs of the client and the beneficiary.

Common Stock Investing. In planning a comprehensive equity portfolio, the account manager may elect to review each industry with an in-house or outside research group to determine which of the various sectors and subsectors of the economy should be emphasized and which should be eliminated from consideration. From the industries that remain, a selection of stocks is made on the basis of their short- or long-term attractiveness, as well as risk tolerance and anticipated total return (dividend payment plus appreciation). Within an industry, the portfolio may concentrate on a particular aspect of the sector or subsector, such as the area of the public served (e.g., regional banks versus money center banks) or the types of goods sold (e.g., specialty retailing versus mass marketing).

In rapidly declining or ascending markets in which the herd instinct seems to have overpowered the fundamental analytical approach to stock selection, the choice of specific companies may take precedence over industry considerations.

The turnover, or trading in and out, of securities is generally based on long-range considerations of a fundamental nature, using a two- to three-year time horizon. However, in an overvalued situation, a stock may be sold and then repurchased at a later date when its price is judged to be more in line with researched criteria peculiar to its industry or to the company itself.

Another form of equity ownership is real estate. During the 1960s and early 1970s it was necessary for a tax-exempt trust to use an indirect ownership vehicle such as a real estate investment trust to avoid the tax consequences of outright ownership in real estate. Since then, changes in the law have resolved this conflict and direct owner participation is actively sought. Real estate investments are generally packaged and marketed as a joint effort by the developer and institutional buyer, with the advice and assistance of legal counsel. Initial returns from equity real estate investments are a form of fixed income insofar as a contractual rate of interest is paid; the equity feature generally becomes more important after construction and remodeling has taken place, and the investor receives an incremental return by participating in a percentage of the rents collected.

Fixed-Income Investing. The fixed component of a portfolio may be structured with varying maturities to meet the basic needs of an individual and his beneficiary, to service the actuarial needs of the corporation and its employees, or to satisfy the cash flow requirements of an institution or foundation. Good credit quality is also an important consideration; it can be determined in some instances by referring to Moody's and Standard & Poor's (S&P) investment services. In-house credit committees also perform a crucial function in monitoring existing investments and establishing credit quality estimates for private placement issues, as opposed to public market issues of bonds. Highest quality issues, such as Treasury bonds and notes, Treasury bills, securities of government agencies, of the Federal National Mortgage Association (FNMA or Fannie Mae), and Federal Home Loan (FHL) bonds, may represent a small percentage of a well-diversified portfolio or a greater percentage of a safety-of-principal portfolio consisting of short-term investments.

Most pooled funds hold a minimum issue size of $100,000; this is considered to be a round lot and is easy to trade. Treasury issues under $1 million are considered odd lots. Smaller pieces of an issue could present a liquidity problem as they are more difficult and costly to trade. Conversely, a private placement has no issue-size consideration. Since trading is of no consequence in a private placement, each participant is allocated a pro rata share of the institutional purchase and receives a proportionate share of the amortization (payback of principal and interest).

In some cases a portfolio will be a hybrid of individual public market bonds, represented by government, corporate, and finance bonds, but will have its private placement component represented by units of specialized pooled funds. Qualified pensions and institutions may find it advantageous to purchase and hold private placements through the medium of the commingled or pooled fund. This commingling increases the efficiency of servicing an issue for amortization and for the execution of consent agreements related to changes in the borrower's financial restructuring; it also affords the investor an attractive way of spreading risk among a larger number of issues.

Variety of Investments

Commingled Funds. The commingled concept for the investment of pension, profit-sharing, and thrift fund assets has evolved from the establishment of the basic common stock and bond funds to the creation of a profusion of funds aimed at designated areas of investment opportunity.

Common Stock Funds. Portfolios usually are invested in a diverse group of large capitalization (more than $1 billion in market value) common stocks with fifty or more issues held in a fund. Investments are made in a broad class of industry sectors so that the fund is not adversely affected by economic events that would impact one sector. It is usual to break the portfolios down into subsectors, such as capital goods, energy, consumer, utility, and transportation.

The funds will usually be 80 or 90 percent invested in common stocks with the remainder invested in money market securities. Unless the fund's objective includes a market-timing function, it would be rare to find a cash reserve ratio higher than 20 percent. Equities owned in a common stock fund with a general objective of capital appreciation will usually provide some income returns through dividends. If the fund has an objective of providing a generous income return, the equity portfolio will consist of more high-yielding stocks, with earnings growth secondary.

Intermediate capitalization stocks ($500 to $1 billion in market value) will be used for their prospects for more rapid growth in sales and earnings, especially if the companies can acquire others in the same business. Small capitalization companies (under $500 million) may also be used for their higher potential rewards. The risk in small companies is higher owing to the need for new capital to finance growth, as well as a thinner layer of management. Common stock funds will spread this risk by owning a large number of small companies. Another approach is to form a separate fund solely to invest in smaller-growth companies.

International equities are classified as stocks of foreign companies traded on foreign exchanges. Country weightings in an international equity fund are of significant value to that fund's performance, and these weightings are periodically changed to reflect world financial, political, and economic conditions. Past experience has shown that the market volatility of an equity portfolio can be lowered by a representative holding of international equities.

Equity real estate is synonymous with direct ownership of real estate, which has equity features such as the outright ownership of office buildings and shopping centers. Securities of this type are purchased privately under agreement with the borrower with the assistance of separate legal counsel for the lender and for the borrower.

Opportunity equities represent a further refinement of the pooled fund process. Companies classified under this heading may be considered undervalued relative to their financial condition, book value, replacement cost, or economic value.

Convertibles. Convertible issues are originated by the borrower as either public market or private placement securities. They can be of a fixed-income or a preferred-stock nature. Convertibles tend to lower the volatility of a portfolio because they decline less in down markets, but they also appreciate more slowly as markets rise.

Fixed-Income Funds. Money market funds are used by bank trustees as temporary interest-earning vehicles for money that is earmarked for more permanent investments, or for money to be distributed to employees in the form of retirement benefits, profit sharing, or thrift fund payments. Included in a money market fund would be such instruments as negotiable certificates of deposit, banker's acceptances, commercial paper, and Treasury bills. Issues of this type are traded through primary dealers in U.S. government securities, including money center banks located throughout the United States and including certain broker/dealers.

Temporary investments excluded, a bond portfolio may consist of varying amounts of intermediate- and long-term maturities tailored to the risk factor of the portfolio and the future requirements of these funds. Maturity structure can fluctuate depending on the forecast of interest rates, market opportunities, and adjustments for yield curve fluctuations. Since the early 1980s, constantly changing interest rates and response to inflationary pressures have led to more active trading of public market bond issues.

International fixed-income securities may be denominated in U.S. dollars or in foreign currencies; dollar securities may be issued in the United States or in the country of origin, nondollar securities are issued in the respective country of origin. International credit instruments of foreign obligors have been used selectively by bank trustees since the latter part of the 1970s.

Common Trust Funds. The common trust vehicle for the pooling of personal trust assets was originally formed to give individual trusts the advantage of diversified investing. This broadening of participation in equity and fixed-income markets permitted individual trusts to have representative holdings in a greater number of issues without the expense involved in odd-lot trading of small holdings. Types of common trust funds may be classified basically as equity, fixed income, convertible, and tax-exempt.

Common Trust Equity Fund. This may include common stocks of domestic, multinational, and foreign-based companies, or it may be a specialized fund consisting mainly of emerging growth companies and small companies of superior growth potential.

Convertible Common Trust Fund. This kind of fund invests in fixed-income and preferred issues that are convertible into common stock. A representative holding in this type of fund tends to lower a portfolio's volatility.

Fixed-Income Fund. A fixed-income fund for the common trust investor may include not only public issues of U.S. companies but also private placements, government bonds, and dollar-denominated international bonds. Other refinements of fixed-income funds may be available to the common trust, such as a specialized intermediate fund, which invests in short- and intermediate-term maturities of public, private, government, and international issues.

Tax-Exempt Common Fund. Securities that are issued by municipal, state, and governmental entities are purchased by this type of fund. The interest paid on these issues is exempt from federal income taxes. Certain refinements have been instituted by bank trustees to give the personal trust the opportunity to invest in an intermediate tax-exempt fund and a similar fund for trust beneficiaries residing in a particular state, such as New York, New Jersey, or Florida.

Individually Invested Accounts. An individually managed trust account contains a selection of individual stock and bond issues. A hypothetical trust of less than $1 million in size would not have a diversification as broad as that of a larger trust; that is, the number of issues would be less in a small trust. On the other hand, the allocation of assets between equity and fixed income for any size trust depends to a large extent on the account profile, growth orientation, yield emphasis, payout requirements, and other factors. The minimum account size generally ranges from $250 thousand to $1 million, although some banks may have a lower minimum. Minimum fees are usually charged, however.

Private placement securities do not usually play a role in the lesser-sized trust as the servicing of them for amortization, interest payments, consent agreements, and the like is too costly and cumbersome.

ATTRACTIVE FEATURES

Current Cash Return

To achieve a high current return, the investor may enjoy the advantages of a wide variety of securities.

The Fixed-Income Market. Money market instruments, such as banker's acceptances and commercial paper, as well as U.S. government and agency securities such as Treasury bills, Fannie Maes, Government National Mortgage Association (GNMA or Ginnie Mae) pass-through securities and FHLs, pay relatively high interest rates and can be bought for short-term maturity. Investment managers offer pooled money market funds similar to those that are available through brokers. The basic purpose of bank-managed money market funds is to provide a liquid vehicle that will earn interest for short-term money but will make those funds available to the investor on a daily basis. The interest rates on these funds are tied to current money market rates, and the funds' attractiveness to the investor is enhanced by a yield that changes daily, taking advantages of sharply rising rates. Many banks use outside-managed money funds and automatically invest client cash into these daily on a sweep basis. These funds can invest in certificates of deposit (CDs) or commercial paper or can be solely in short Treasury instruments.

The Convertible Market. Convertibles are attractive from the standpoint of both yield and risk. Convertible bonds and preferred stocks provide a good current rate of return from interest and/or dividends. In a declining stock market, convertibles have a stabilizing influence owing to their fixed-income component. They also lend a degree of stability to a portfolio during periods of rising interest rates.

The Equity Market. This market has thousands of publicly traded stocks, but only relatively few—namely, public utility stocks—pay dividends and yield the investor a return competitive with money market investments. However, a high cash dividend may not always justify the use of a stock in a portfolio. Some companies may seem to maintain a good payout ratio (dividend as a percentage of total earnings), but may be highly leveraged with frequent issuing of new debt securities or may increase the float (shares outstanding) of their stock by issuing new shares more often than the accepted norm, resulting in a dilution of current shares outstanding. A high dividend payout also leaves little cash for investing in the company's basic business.

Deferred Return

Bank investment managers offer several avenues of investment to the individual or corporate investor who is not dependent on current income. Classified among deferred-return investments would be drilling and exploration programs for oil and gas, the purchasing of gold, and dealing in collectibles, such as paintings. Investing in this type of deferred-income vehicle requires a good deal of expertise and is done with the assistance of professionals in the particular field.

There are investment banks and brokerage houses that specialize in structuring direct oil and gas drilling investments for the individual taxable client, and passive oil and gas programs for the tax-exempt pension fund institution and foundation. In order to achieve tax-deferred status for this type of venture, annual income must be reinvested for a minimum of three years. Insurance is essential to cover liability for possible blowouts of oil wells and other such disasters. While the active, direct investor participates in acreage acquisitions, exploratory drilling, and well development, the passive investor makes loans for these activities and for the purchase of oil and gas reserves, all with royalty interests.

A means of partially deferring returns is the real estate equity investment. In a project involving the development or expansion of an office building, shopping center, hotel, or other commercial property, the initial cash flow is generally lower in the early years compared to regular mortgage return, but once the expansion or development has been completed, the investor benefits from the guaranteed return to the investor plus an incremental participating return in the rents collected.

The principle of deferred return also may be carried through to common stock investing by looking to companies in early stages of development that initially plow back their earnings into operations and expansion and that are regarded as potential candidates for growth of total return. These companies are usually private, and some banks use them in a venture capital pool, which may be offered to clients or held for the bank's own investments.

Capital Gains

The discipline of selling fully valued or overpriced securities is a difficult art to master. At the peak of the market cycle in 1972, investors could look back on a prolonged period of price/earnings (P/E) ratios ranging from 10 to 20 for the well-established, mature company, and ratios of 30 to 50 for the young and fast-growing company. In the market environment of that period, the investor was easily lulled into a false sense of security. As inflation started to climb after the 1973 Arab-Israeli war boosted oil prices fourfold, and interest rates started to climb, many investors fled stocks for such asset-based investments as gold, art, and land. The resulting selling pressure caused equity prices to collapse in 1973 and 1974 with the Dow Jones average plunging to its lowest level since 1962. Many high-price earnings stocks fell 50 to 80 percent in market value.

The selling of securities to realize profits is a necessary component of overall investment strategy. However, capital gains must be viewed not only from an investment perspective but also with an eye to the taxable consequences. Persons in high-income brackets may choose to avoid excessive taxes by balancing gains with realized losses. This may be accomplished by forward planning; for example, a municipal bond holding may be sold and the proceeds reinvested in a higher-quality municipal issue of similar coupon and maturity; however, it should be kept in mind that losses realized within thirty days of the sale and repurchase of an identical security (wash sale) are generally disallowed for tax purposes.

A capital gain or loss can be experienced by a pooled-fund participant in one of two ways: Within the fund itself, a security may be sold, resulting in a realized profit; or the participating trust may sell shares or units held in a common trust fund at a higher price than was paid for them. In the first instance, the investor is taxed on the pro rata share of the realized gain from the sale of the security within the fund; in the second, a tax is levied on the gain realized from the sale of the units or shares of the common fund per se.

The capital gains tax is not relevant to the management of tax-exempt trusts, as there are no tax levies on these funds. Benefit payments to retired participants in a pension fund are taxed as ordinary income, but the tax rate is lower than that incurred during an active salaried employment.

Safety of Principal

Erosion of principal may occur in both stock and bond markets as these markets respond to the political, social, and economic forces that surround them. If an individual or corporation determines that a percentage of assets to be invested must not be exposed to market risk, there are several possible investment alternatives.

Bond Immunization. Immunization is not a new idea, but it finally came into its own in the 1970s as an answer to market volatility. It is based on an actuarial analysis of determining bullet years for cash requirements. It is a useful tool for a corporation that wishes to set aside a portion of its pension assets in a relatively risk-free portfolio of fixed income securities with varying maturities. The maturities are tailored to the years in which retirements have been projected to occur. These projections are made by the plan actuary. It should be remembered that actuarial forecasts can only be estimates of forward cash requirements; this is why only a portion of overall funds are placed in an immunized portfolio. The concept can be applied to individual accounts when projected outflow is relatively certain, as in the case of annual gifts or donations.

Short-Term Government Securities. A portfolio of short-term U.S. government and government agency securities is another means of providing safety of principal. These securities possess the high-quality, risk-free characteristics desired, although the return on investment is subject to fluctuating interest rates.

Hedge Against Inflation

There is no sure way for the investor to meet the challenge of inflation. The theory that common stocks are one of the best hedges against inflation has been subscribed to by numerous investment managers. During the 1972 to 1982 period, inflation rose to new highs, peaking in 1981 at 12 percent annual rate. During this time, common stock prices did not keep up with inflation in regard to total return. Corporate profits were bloated with inflationary inventory gains, and investors were unwilling to put a high P/E ratio on these earnings. Since 1981 inflation has waned, with a low point reached in 1986 of less than 2 percent as measured by the consumer price index. Oil prices hit $10 per barrel in mid-1986, down from $35 to 1980.

During the 1982 to 1987 bull market investors placed a higher P/E multiple on earnings with the result that P/E ratios hit a post-1972 high in mid-1987. However, rising inflationary forces and sharply higher interest rates caused equity prices to erode, and with Treasury bonds reaching 10 percent in October 1987, the markets panicked and lost 25 percent of their value during that month, one of the worst declines since 1929.

Much of this reaction to inflation has been guided by the threshold of pain that can be withstood by the individual or corporate client. For the client who has a low risk tolerance or short-term investment goals, the more comfortable investment would be the short-term money market or municipal market instruments. With the aid of the histogramming technique, the fixed-income manager will use his expertise to play the yield curve by rotating invested funds among short-term (up to one year), medium-term (average maturity five to ten years), and longer-term (exceeding ten years) maturities in anticipation of market trends.

The real estate equity type of investment is another tool increasingly being recognized by institutional investors. The immediate return from equity real estate has been in the range of 9 to 11 percent during the initial term. This rate is offered by the property owner-developer who, in effect, takes on the investor as a partner, offering an acceptable return during the primary years of the investment. Once the commercial property has been fully developed and rented, the investor receives an incremental return from a percentage of rentals and rent renewals that should increase over the years, effectively giving the investor a hedge against inflation. However, owing to intensive overbuilding in many sections of the country, real estate properties may not be generating enough cash flow to service debt and costs. In that case, real estate funds will offer poor returns and may suffer losses if not geographically diversified.

POTENTIAL RISKS

Instability of Principal and Income

Stability is, first and foremost, a function of the quality of the issuer. It cannot be measured statistically. However, in the case of stocks and bonds, a judgment may be made by evaluating the corporation's ability to pay, as well as its historical soundness and capacity to perform under adverse conditions.

To determine the measure of a company's solvency and its future earnings capability, both qualitative and quantitative analysis is performed by in-house research groups, supplemented by outside broker research. This technical analysis is designed to give the investor a perspective of probability to guide him from the known quantity of past market performance into the anticipated future performance. Analytical information supplied for each company includes its expected return, earnings comparisons, market-related data such as price range and capitalization, historical and anticipated growth rates for earnings per share and dividends, return on equity, payout ratios (percentage of total earnings paid out in dividends), and comparisons of earnings-per-share estimates with brokerage house forecasts.

An important guide to fixed-income investing is a company's credit rating. Moody's and S&P's services supply and update these ratings on a regular basis. As an additional safeguard, banks have established in-house credit committees to monitor and anticipate changes in credit ratings affecting corporations and municipal bond investments. An existing bond portfolio can suffer unrealized (paper) losses when interest rate forecasts and new issue rates are increasing. Bond managers have taken the precaution of shortening the maturity structure in their portfolios during periods of high inflation when interest rates tend to increase at an unusually rapid pace.

Market Volatility

To avoid wide swings in the market performance of an account, the equity manager will diversify his holdings in terms of both risk (or beta) of individual securities and of industry weighting; the fixed-income manager will diversify by maturity and by credit instrument.

For the individually invested account, this is accomplished by broad selection of blue chip and well-established growth companies, perhaps with a sprinkling of smaller companies dealing in unique products or services. This stock selection is complemented by several issues of good-quality municipal (for taxable account) and corporate bonds of varying maturity, and/or several money market issues to meet liquidity needs. The percentage of distribution between equities and fixed income will favor equities for a higher level of risk and will favor fixed income when the risk tolerance is low.

Convertible preferreds and bonds can be used to smooth volatility, as they tend to decline less in down markets but also increase at a slower pace in up markets.

International investments also can play an important role in smoothing performance fluctuations and reducing volatility. Investment management firms may have branch offices overseas that have developed expertise in international investing, or they may rely on foreign investment firms that have U.S. branches. Foreign markets operate quite differently than those in the United States, and they have far fewer issues available. There is also less active trading of international securities on foreign markets.

A portfolio of commingled or common trust funds can be similarly tailored to the objectives of the client by weighting the account's participation in a selection of different types of pooled funds, each of which has an assigned level of risk and expected return.

Illiquidity

The short-term investor, who needs to earn interest on his money but who must have the flexibility of cashing in a holding on a moment's notice, must turn to money market instruments such as Treasury bills, other government and government agency securities, banker's acceptances, and commercial paper. These money market instruments are usually purchased for a maturity of less than one year. Money market funds consisting of such instruments are offered by brokerage houses for the individual client and by bank and insurance company pension trustees for the corporate client.

Investments in stocks and bonds have varying degrees of liquidity. Round lots of stocks (100 shares) and bonds ($100,000 principal amount) are generally considered to be more liquid than odd lots (smaller denominations). Liquidity may also be a function of shares outstanding (issued) or the amount of bonds outstanding, which is called float. Private placements are generally considered to be illiquid types of investment as they are not traded on any public exchange. Investor perception of the relative attractiveness of a company may influence the trading of its debt or equity securities.

The assets held in pooled funds are generally priced at the end of every month, at which time a prospective investor may purchase units or shares, and a participant may sell his interest in the fund. There are rare occasions when a fund of highly specialized investments, such as real estate, will not be in a position to take on new investors or to redeem units for existing holders without prior notice. A fund of short-term money market investments is open for purchase and sale transactions on a daily basis.

For purposes of investment planning, the liquidity needs of the individual or corporation should be established, monitored, and provided for as an integral part of the investment package.

TAX CONSEQUENCES

Income tax treatment for the personal trust, estate, or advisory account is multifaceted and complicated. A bank trustee or investment advisor will have the support of in-house or outside tax experts to provide him with the tax liability background on which to build a trust's portfolio. A trust that is being invested in individual securities may be structured with tax-exempt bonds and low-income equities, including preferred and common stocks that are partially tax-exempt, so that the grantor or beneficiary who is already in a relatively high tax bracket can avoid further increased liability. On the other hand, in a case where the taxability is of nominal concern, the portfolio may contain high-yielding stocks and fixed-income securities that do not have tax-exempt features.

A personal trust or estate includes in the computation of its taxable income the distribution received from a common trust fund during the fund's fiscal year. Similarly, the common trust fund's capital gains and losses, although not distributed to the participating trust or estate, are includable in the computation of the trust's or estate's taxable income. The amount of undistributed capital gains and losses allocable to the trust or estate participating in a common trust fund is determined in the same fashion as the income distribution (i.e., on a pro rata basis). The tax bases for a participating account in a common trust fund are regularly adjusted for realized gains and losses. In a manner similar to mutual fund accounting, the distribution of gains and the debiting of losses for the fund's participants are eliminated in favor of the tax-basis adjustment. This avoids the possibility of duplicating the tax liability for gains and the tax credit for losses realized in the common trust fund. For income tax purposes, the treatment of the common trust fund is similar to that of a partnership: The common trust fund does not pay tax on its capital gains; rather, the participating trusts or estates bear the direct tax responsibility.

Tax planning for the individual trust or estate also may include investments in oil and gas drilling, real estate, and other enterprises that are considered to have tax-sheltering or tax-deferring advantages. This is a highly specialized field of investment in which there are varying degrees of risk and uncertain rewards. They should be entered into with caution and pursued only with advice and counsel from experienced investment managers knowledgeable about this type of vehicle.

ACQUIRING AND RETIRING POOLED FUND SHARES

Participation in pooled funds is no longer a function of an account's size, but rather of the desire to diversify assets efficiently and inexpensively. The individual or corporation will find that the trustee can construct a portfolio of units or shares in a selected group of pooled funds so that specific needs of cash flow and growth can be appropriately met.

Common Trust Fund Investors

Common trust funds, as established by law, are for the exclusive use of the individual clients of the sponsoring trust company. A cotrustee must agree to the use of these pooled funds before investments in them are made. Most individual trust agreements have interpretive general language or specific authorization that permits the assets of a trust to be invested in a common trust fund. However, certain states do not permit the use of these funds, and the state of residency of the client governs.

Commingled Fund Investors

Investments in commingled funds are made on behalf of a trust or fund for which the trust company acts as sole trustee or as investment manager. The trust must be a tax-exempt pension trust, profit-sharing trust, or other type of retirement trust, and it must be part of a plan or group of plans qualified and exempt from tax under the Internal Revenue Code. The authorization for participation in a commingled fund must be specifically contained in the trust agreement, which may have general language including all available pooled funds or specific language for one or more funds selected by the sponsoring company. A corporation or institution may elect to have a group of managers, each of whom is considered to have expertise in a specific type of investment such as fixed-income, real estate, equity, and convertibles.

Mechanics and Pricing

The mechanics of acquiring or retiring units or shares for the participant's account is the responsibility of the bank trustee, who purchases (from clients wishing to redeem their holdings) and sells (to other clients) units or shares of the pooled fund based on the composite of individually priced securities within the fund. The price range of a share of a pooled fund varies considerably by the type of fund and its longevity. For example, a bond fund established in the 1950s would have a lower coupon rate associated with the individual holdings and therefore a lower unit price; a more recent bond fund would be priced close to par, either above or below, depending on interest rate fluctuations. Conversely, a special situations (small companies) stock fund, which has reaped the rewards of a wise selection of securities in its universe, may have increased in price several times per share over a ten- or fifteen-year period.

CUSTODIAL CARE

The custody and servicing of securities is provided by most investment management firms as a supportive service for in-house accounts, or an independent service for outside companies and individuals seeking professional caretaking facilities.

In many instances the custodian will interface with the Depository Trust Company (DTC), which is owned by its participating members. The DTC has a fully automated system that accepts securities on a book-entry basis. Security transactions normally are cleared through DTC within the required five-day settlement period, providing evidence of ownership to the participating members without the physical movement of the securities from seller to buyer. The Federal Reserve System operates in much the same fashion by providing a book-entry system for transactions in Treasury bills and government bonds.

Additional safekeeping facilities for securities and other valuables are provided in the vaults of trust companies. Specifications for the construction of these vaults are contained in the burglary prevention manual issued by the National Bureau of Casualty and Surety Underwriters. Most trust companies conform to the highest class-ten rating for the required specifications. The custodian does not assume liability as an insurer but does carry an on-premises blanket bond insurance to cover the usual risks of security loss, dishonesty of employees, burglary, robbery, destruction, or disappearance. It will also carry insurance to cover securities in transit by its own messengers. Most custodians will take the precaution of making duplicate records (on microfilm) that are transported daily to a safe storage area far removed from trust company vaults, so that a client's account can be reconstructed if original records are destroyed. The records of trust company custodians are examined by separate internal auditors and by outside certified public accountants. They are also subject to annual examination by the state banking department and by the Federal Reserve Banks.

Securities that are left in safekeeping are registered in the name of a nominee partnership provided by the trust company to assure prompt negotiability in the event of sale or transfer. Most banks have a fully automated custodial system that provides for the crediting of interest and dividend payments to each account on the payment date. This information is supplied in advance so that the money can be invested on the payment date.

The custodian will supply the client with the following updated information:

- Stock dividends, splits, and distributions
- Dividend omissions
- Dividend reinvestment plans
- Subscription offerings
- Purchase and exchange offers
- Tender offers for preferred stocks and bonds
- Calls on preferred stocks and bonds
- Conversion of preferred stock and bond issues
- Company name changes
- Modification to bond indentures
- Government subscription and exchange offerings

Additional safeguards provided by custodial trusts include an armed security force, alarm control systems, television surveillance, controlled access to the premises, smoke- and fire-alarm devices, certificate number control, and polygraph examinations for all secured-area employees.

GLOSSARY

amortization—The return or payback of principal on a fixed-income security in periodic installments to the lender.

average life—The length of time between the initial issuing of a bond and the final payback of principal by the borrower prior to the bond's stated maturity.

beta—A measure of market risk. The stock market as a whole has a beta of 1.0. Greater than 1.0 indicates higher volatility; less than 1.0 indicates lower volatility.

commingled fund—Broadly, a trust fund in which the equities of a number of investors are combined for common management; a pooled fund. Formally, a fund to which participation is legally limited to a bank's pension or employee benefits clients.

common trust fund—A pooled fund available to individual investors.

current return—Yield received by the investor from cash payments in the forms of interest on bonds and dividends on stock.

histogramming—A technique performed by a group of fixed income professionals who give individual predictions of interest rate levels for U.S. government securities of varying maturities, namely, three months and twelve months hence. From these predictions, a yield curve is plotted and a consensus forecast reached.

immunization—The investment of a fixed-income portfolio using an actuarial type of analysis in the purchase of bullet maturities, each of which is targeted for future cash requirements.

individually invested account—A trust account for an individual or corporation in which all holdings are owned by the investor.

liquidity—The degree to which a security is easily traded; generally speaking, stocks with a greater number of shares outstanding are more marketable, as are short-term public market bonds such as U.S. government and government agency securities.

odd lots—Denominations of a principal amount of a bond that are not multiples of $100,000, or of shares of stock not in multiples of 100.

payout ratio—The dividend paid to stockholders as a percentage of that company's total assets.

pooled fund—See *commingled fund; common trust fund.*

private placement—A security purchased by the lender directly from the borrower.

total return—A composite of the yield from dividends and income plus the appreciation of increase of an asset's market value.

wash sale—The sale and repurchase of an identical amount of the same security.

SUGGESTED READING

Bernstein, P. *Financial Statement Analysis*, 4th ed. Homewood, Ill.: Irwin, 1988.

———, ed. *The Theory and Practice of Bond Portfolio Management*, Vols. I and II. New York: Institutional Investor Books, 1980.

Carosso, Vincent P. *Investment Banking in America*. Cambridge: Harvard University Press, 1970.

Cohen, Jerome B. *Investment Analysis and Portfolio Management*, 3rd ed. Homewood, Ill.: Dow Jones-Irwin, 1977.

———, Zinbarg, Edward D., and Zeikel, Arthur. *Investment Analysis and Portfolio Management*, 5th ed. Homewood, Ill.: Irwin, 1987.

Cutler, Steven E. *Trust Investments*, Park Ridge: Bank Administration Institute, 1979.

Fabozzi, Frank J., and Pollack, Irving M. *Handbook of Fixed Income Securities*, 2nd ed. Homewood, Ill.: Dow Jones-Irwin, 1987.

Malkiel, Burton, G. A *Random Walk Down Wall Street*, 4th ed. New York: Norton, 1985.

Munn, Glenn G. *Encyclopedia of Banking and Finance*. Boston: Bankers Publishing Co., 1973.

Soldofsky, Robert M. *Institutional Holdings of Common Stock 1900–2000—History, Projection, and Interpretation*. University of Michigan, 1971.

BOOKS

John F. Fleming
Priscilla Juvelis

BASIC CHARACTERISTICS

Determinants of Value

Rare books—including manuscripts, limited editions, finely printed and illustrated, and finely bound books—form a group of collectibles that offer a variety of returns for the investor. One collects books, as one collects stamps or coins, because of their intellectual value and their historical association as well as for their beauty. For example, a first edition of John Milton's *Poems* (1645) is valuable because of the light it sheds on early printing and spelling and on other facets of the printing trade of the time. In addition, the literary scholar looks to the first printing of a literary work (along with the manuscript, if it is available) as a primary source for the text. Moreover, this same first edition of Milton's *Poems* has intrinsic value based on its rarity, since in all probability there are no more than three dozen copies extant of this famous work. A copy of Toulouse-Lautrec's *Histoire Naturelle* in a Legrain binding is desired as much for the images by one of the great painters as it is for the binding.

Relative Nature of Rarity. Simply because only a few copies exist does not necessarily make a book valuable, although it may indeed be rare. Thus, a rare book by a minor and nearly forgotten author may have very modest value. On the other hand, rarity is a

---

The late John F. Fleming was a New York consultant and dealer in rare books and manuscripts; he prepared this article in its original form for the first edition. Priscilla Juvelis is a dealer in rare books and manuscripts in Boston and had been an associate of John Fleming; she revised and updated this article.

relative matter, as demonstrated in the case of the most notable single volume in English literature—the *First Folio* (1623) of Shakespeare's work. This book exists in approximately 180 copies, scattered throughout the world; many of them are in a single collection in the Folger Library in Washington, D.C. By usual book-collecting standards, this is not really a rare book; however, it is such a literary monument in terms of authorship and content that it is widely sought after and expensive; as a result, it is indeed considered a major rare book. Of course, a truly rare book is Edgar Allan Poe's *Tamerlane.* His first book is the "black tulip" of American literature. A copy recently discovered brought the number of known copies to twelve. The price realized at auction in June 1987 was $198,000. One hadn't appeared for sale since 1975, when it realized $123,000.

Physical Condition. The price that a particular copy of a rare book can command relative to other copies is determined by its condition. It is well-known among more sophisticated collectors, and often learned sadly by neophytes, that most collectors cannot really afford to buy less than the best copy available of a particular book. The price of an excellent copy of a work is often many times higher in the marketplace than that of a mediocre or poor one. One month after a spendid Shakespeare *Folio* fetched $775,000 in Paris, a similar but not nearly so well-preserved copy was sold for a mere $175,000 in London.

Points of Issue. The serious collector wants his copy of a rare book to be of the earliest printing. In the course of printing a first edition, an important mistake may be noticed in the earliest copies. The presses are stopped, a correction is made, and the remainder of the edition is known as a second issue. These are less desirable and less valuable. An example is Nathaniel Hawthorne's *Twice Told Tales* (1837), in which the leaf of contents lists the fifth story as beginning on page 78, an error that is corrected to page 77 in the second issue. Another example is Poe's *Tales of the Grotesque and Arabesque* (1840), where, in the first issue, page 213 is wrongly numbered.

Publishers' advertisements sometimes make a point of establishing priority, but they are not too dependable. In the famous case of Hawthorne's *The Scarlet Letter* (1850), the advertisements are usually dated 1850 in the first edition and 1849 in the second. It is suspected that the book's sudden success found the publishers unprepared and that, lacking a further supply of advertisements, they substituted earlier ones that they happened to have on hand. A myriad of variations in printing has been noted by bibliographers in almost every subject. This is why many collectors specialize in one author or one subject until they attain the technical bibliographical knowledge needed to go further afield.

To acquire and understand this knowledge is no easy task. The following is a sample of a bibliographical description taken from the bibliographical bible of English literature from the fifteenth to seventeenth centuries.[1]

> D.[ONNE], J.[OHN] Poems, by J.D. With Elegies on the Authors Death. London: Printed by M.[iles] F.[lesher] for John Marriot, and are to be sold at his shop in St. Dunstans Church-yard in Fleet-Street, 1633. First Edition, quarto. Collation: A^4 (the first, blank and genuine); A^2, B-Fff^4 (the last, blank and genuine); 210 leaves.

[1] Emma Unger and William A. Jackson, *The Carl H. Pforzheimer Library of English Literature. 1475–1700*, Vol. I. Privately printed, 1940. Excerpt from page 287.

Contents: blank, Sig[A]; title, recto [A2]; verso blank; Epistle, recto A3-recto[A4]; The printer to the understanders, recto A-recto A2; Hexastichon Biblipolae, signed 'Jo. (MAR.'[RIOT]), verso A2; text, pp. 1–406; blank, pp. [407–8]. (P. 161 is numbered 145, 164–5 are 148–9, 168 is 152, 194–5 are 164–5, 198–9 are 168–9, and 250 is 205).

Provenance. Another determinant of value in rare books is provenance, or former ownership. Volumes from great rare-book libraries of the past—those of Vendel, Esmerian, Streeter, Goodwin, Holford, Hoe, Heber, Kern, Pforzheimer, and Houghton—are identifiable through their book plates or other markings. Such books are much sought after, since the great collectors usually bought or commissioned purchases of the best copies available. As collectors gain experience, they become aware of the niceties and points of condition of a rare book and seek some indication of the previous owners.

Other Attributes of Rarity

Rare books is really a collective term for a number of different kinds of book collectibles. Some books are rare in the traditional sense of scarcity because they were published many, many years ago. Other books were published in limited editions; these derive their value not necessarily from age or priority but because few copies were printed, usually on special papers bound in a special way, and often containing signatures of authors, illustrators, printers, or others associated with the particular edition of the book. There is also the class of fine books or "Press" books, frequently a series of unconnected literary or other books composed and printed by a particular press, such as Nonesuch Press, Doves Press, and Ashendine Press. Another category is that of beautifully printed books illustrated with original graphics by a major artist, such as Picasso, Braque, or Matisse. This is known as a livre d'artiste, or an artist's book. All of these categories, which have found eager collectors through the years, have included many books of increasing financial value determined by the marketplace.

ATTRACTIVE FEATURES

Aesthetic and Historical Interest

Rare books, unlike negotiable financial instruments that merely represent value, are notable for inherent value. Scholars, indeed, have argued that a book's importance lies only in its intellectual message, not in its physical form, and, consequently, that collecting rare books for their scarcity, design, and the collector's notorious penchant for physical possession is futile and absurd. However, as an investment, books enjoy an increasingly large market among collectors seeking objects of lasting monetary worth that at the same time further their desires to identify with a notable author. Thus, among the most sought-after books is any first edition of John Milton or William Shakespeare, two of the greatest authors in the history of English literature. Just as sought after are the books containing original graphic art, such as Matisse's *Jazz*, which realized $49,000 in 1984 and around $150,000 in 1988.

Return on Investment

The investor in rare books usually (but certainly not always) makes a profit over time. However, even assuming pristine condition and legitimate and intelligent advice in purchasing, there is no guarantee that, for example, the copy of Fielding's *Tom Jones* (published in six volumes in 1749) that was bought in the 1920s for $1,500 will be worth appreciably more thirty years later. It so happens that this particular book, although one of the greatest and most renowned novels in the English language, has actually maintained, in average condition, pretty much the same value in the marketplace over the last forty to fifty years. Of course, the greatest book ever published, which is also the first book ever published, is the Gutenberg Bible (1455). Estelle Doheny's copy brought $5,390,000 when it was sold in October 1987. This particular copy had been sold to the Countess Doheny in 1950 for $70,093.75—and her copy is Volume I only ; Volume II did not survive!

Hedge Against Inflation

Interesting anomalies notwithstanding, rare books in all categories are usually an excellent hedge against inflation. As they are acquired by libraries and other institutions that seldom put them on the market again, the books become more scarce, and consequently values increase. Price resistance per se is rarely a controlling factor in the market; a book is worth what collectors are willing to pay for it, and a recent auction price or other market indicator is the sole determinant of monetary value.

Intangible Benefits

Perhaps the most meaningful—but hardest to measure in terms of return on investment—benefits derived from collecting rare books are the aesthetic, intellectual, and psychological pleasures derived from associating with great objects. Beyond this is the sheer fun and pleasure of collecting, of coming suddenly on something one has looked for and finding it all at once available. The collector sophisticated enough or lucky enough to come on a particularly good value as well is all the more ahead. However, the collector who restricts his search to potential bargains may easily lose in the long run. It is not wise in book investments, as in any commercial venture, to put price before all other criteria.

SUCCESSFUL RARE-BOOK INVESTMENTS

Shakespeare's *First Folio*

The sales record of the *First Folio* presents a very good case for the potential investor to analyze. There are approximately 180 copies known, of which about twenty are in their original state. It is thought that 600 copies of the original edition were published, and the survival of 180 copies shows it was appreciated and sought after more than any other book of its time. For more than a century, no monetary value was placed on it. The first known auction of the Shakespeare *First Folio* was in 1687, but the records of that auction and the *First Folio's* price are lost. The earliest complete auction record appears in 1756, when a copy was sold for three guineas. Ten years later, another copy sold for the same price. For some time, three guineas was the highest price obtainable, and during the same period, other copies changed hands for much less. In about 1760, the celebrated actor, David Garrick, purchased one for £1.16.

Although the price ebbed, its upward movement was never seriously checked. In 1787, Dr. Richard Wright's copy fetched £10 at auction. A big jump came in 1790, when the Duke of Roxburghe paid £35.14 at auction. It was then called the most expensive book in the English language. The same copy was reauctioned in 1812 for £100, another record price. When the Duke of Roxburghe's library was sold at Sotheby's in 1812, his copy of the *First Folio,* which he had purchased twenty-two years earlier, advanced almost 300 percent, from twenty guineas to £100. The sale of this collection caused a sensation; it is still written and talked about today.

Upon entering the twentieth century, the pace quickens. In 1905, Mr. Bernard Buchanan George, who had purchased his *First Folio* in July 1899 for £1,700, sold it along with the second, third, and fourth editions for £10,000 ($50,000). This was the greatest advance in any six years and proved quite a successful financial investment. In March 1907, the Van Antwerp copy brought £3,600; in 1911 the Hoe copy brought £13,000. For the next twenty years, several defective copies were sold for sums in the neighborhood of £8,000. Then, in 1933, in the depths of the Depression, the marvelous copy belonging to Lord Rosebery was sold for the enormous sum of £14,500 ($72,500). It was sold again at auction in 1945 for $50,000.

The Rosebery-Hogan copy was held in one collection from 1945 to 1980, when it was sold in Paris on May 20. The book-collecting world was stunned when this copy realized the enormous sum of $775,000, thus becoming the most expensive literary book in the world. The new owner, somewhat concerned about the price he had paid, asked his banker what today's relative value would be of 50,000 1945 dollars. He was informed that 50,000 1945 dollars had the purchasing power of $750,000 today.

Experience has shown that great collected books are the last commodity to feel a depression, just as they are the last to show financial gain in affluent times. The prices paid at auction for the *First Folio* are due to the excitement generated by the sale combined with the supreme egos of certain collectors and dealers who compete against each other. It was Peter Wilson, the former head and guiding genius of Sotheby's of London who once said, "If you take the theater out of the auction you have nothing."

Although few books have enjoyed the notoriety or financial success of the *First Folio*, this recapitulation of its auction history is important because it illustrates the general appreciation, over time, that rare books enjoy. It also shows some of the unexplainable vagaries of the marketplace.

The Houghton Collection

A recent collection of superb copies of celebrated books to appear on the market is that of Arthur A. Houghton, Jr. His collection of books and manuscripts of English literature from the sixteenth to the nineteenth centuries was unsurpassed in condition and quality. The collection was dispensed of in two sales at Christie's of London in 1979 and 1980. A sample of Houghton's costs on most of the items compared to the auction price received should be a revelation to the would-be collector.

Table 1 shows in dollars what a few of the books cost Houghton, the dates of purchase, and what they fetched at the Houghton auctions.

Books for which Houghton paid an approximate $290,000, bought over a period of forty years, fetched $1,865,583. It would be interesting to calculate their investment value. Of course, the value to Houghton of his added fame and the joys he experienced in pursuit of the game of book collecting must be immeasurable. Mr. Houghton's experience may be one of fortunate excess; however, it is seldom that a basic investment in rare books is not recoupable over time, whether or not the investor makes a profit. The investor who has bought wisely with respect to current value and condition need not be overly concerned with safety of the investment principal.

TABLE 1. Selected Purchase and Retail Prices—Houghton Collection

Date of Purchase	Title	Price Paid by Houghton	Auction Price
1932	Shakespeare, *Works* (1632)	$ 4,750	$ 10,800
1932	Shakespeare, *Works* (1623)	75,000	192,000
1933	Spenser, *Faerie Queene* (1590-1596) Shakespeare, *Poems* (1640)	15,000	53,400
1933	Oppian, *Halientica* (1478)	369	6,300
1934	Caxton, *Chronicles of England* (1480)	6,220	139,500
1935	Machiavelli, *Prince* (1640)	45	1,056
1935	Purchase, *His Pilgrimes* (1624-1625) (5 vols.)	480	14,400
1935	Ariosto, *Orlando Furioso* (1591)	985	14,625
1935	Evelyn, *Sylva* (1664) (presentation copy)	675	5,850
1935	Holinshed's *Chronicle* (1577)	975	4,950
1935	*Common Prayer Book* (1549)	16,610	112,500
1935	Donne, *Poems* (1633)	285	3,600
1935	Ford, *Broken Heart* (1633)	858	5,400
1935	Herbert, *The Temple* (1633)	4,100	15,750
1935	Milton, *Paradise Lost* (1667)	19,000	91,200
1936	Schedel, *Chronicle* (1493)	585	24,000
1936	Herrick, *A.L.S to His Uncle*	775	24,000
1941	Milton, *On Education* (1644)	850	13,200
1941	Shadwell, *Psyche* (1675)	245	6,240
1941	Blake, *Songs of Innocence & E.* (1795)	6,610	157,000
1941	Congreve, *Incognita* (1692)	500	16,875
1941	Lovelace, *Lucasta* (1649)	1,300	16,875
1941	Herrick, *Hesperides* (1648)	1,950	24,750
1941	Gascoigne, *Hundred Flowers* (1573)	2,550	54,000
1941	Gascoigne, *Poesies* (1575)	950	37,500
1941	Gascoigne, *Whole Works* (1587)	1,450	33,750
1941	Campion, *1st etc. Book of Ayres* (1610)	680	40,500
1941	Daniel, *Delia* (1592)	5,850	45,000
1941	Daniel, *Works* (1601)	850	5,850
1942	Sidney, *Astrophel & Stella* (1591) Sidney, *Pembrokes Arcadia* (1590)	5,000	74,400
1945	Brontë, *Poems* (1846)	1,800	7,875
1950	Sidney, *Sonnets* (ms.)	5,990	36,000

continued

TABLE 1. *(continued)*

Date of Purchase	Title	Price Paid by Houghton	Auction Price
1956	B.R. *Orpheus* (1595)		$ 48,000
	Barnes, *Divine Centurie* (1595)		22,500
	Bastard, *Chresteleres* (1598)		13,500
	Breton, *Workes of Young Wyt* (1577)		42,750
	Breton, *A Divine Poem* (1601)		
	Breton, *Longing of a Blessed Heart* (1601)		49,500
	Breton, *Honour of Valour* (1605)		
	Edwards, *Paradis* (1600)		13,500
	Godwyn, *Dolorous Lovers* (1520)		38,250
	Homer, *Georgicks* (Trans. by Chapman, Presentation) (1618)		21,375
	Howard, *Songs* (1557) (Shakespeare's copy)		54,000
	James, I., *Essayes* (1584)		29,250
	O.J., *Lamentations of Troy* (1594)		12,375
	Phillis & Flora, *Contention* (1598)		5,850
	Raynolds, *Primerese* (1596)		50,400
	Smith, *Cloris* (1592)		16,800
	Pettie, G., *Petite Palace* (1576)		36,000
	Watson, *Passionate Century* (1582)		48,000
	Withal Short Dictionary (1553)		28,000
	Lot	$ 42,500	$ 576,437
1961	Sidney, *Countess of Pembroke* (ms.)	$ 20,000	$ 48,000
Totals		$290,742	$1,865,583

Source: Author's data

New Areas in Collecting

As an alternative to buying books of universally acknowledged value, the investor may benefit by foresight with respect to some up-and-coming areas for collecting.

Livres d'artiste in Fine Bindings. One of the most recent collecting areas to rise in price is that of the finely bound book illustrated with original graphics by a major artist. For example, a copy of *Couleurs* by Remy de Groumont, illustrated with original etchings by Laboureur and bound by Paul Bonet, sold for $4,000 in 1974. In 1982, the same copy sold for $20,000. Toulouse-Lautrec's *Histoire Naturelle* sold for around $8,000 in 1974. A similar copy sold for $16,176 in 1982. In 1984, another copy sold for $85,000.

Detective Fiction. Another rise in prices can be seen in the area of detective fiction. For example, Dashiell Hammett's *The Thin Man* in a dust jacket brought $350 in the

1981 Goldstone sale. In 1984, a copy brought $1,200; in 1986, a copy fetched $1,600. Prices for Raymond Chandler's first editions and firsts of Sherlock Holmes are steady risers as well.

Modern First Editions. Since the Goodwin sale in 1977, prices have steadily risen in this area as well. James Joyce is the best example of the demand creating rising prices. *Ulysses* was printed in an issue of 1,000 copies only: 100 signed copies; 150 on arches paper, and 750 on whatman paper. The Goodwin copy inscribed brought $10,000 in 1977. The Gilvarry copy inscribed fetched $35,000 in 1986.

POTENTIAL RISKS

Inferior Copies

One basic risk in the collecting of rare books is the possibility of purchasing a specimen of a particular book that is inferior in some way, is not a complete copy, or is otherwise damaged; this, of course, will lower the value. It is extremely important to purchase in a knowledgeable fashion.

Market Volatility

This second basic risk is not excessive, but it is nonetheless real. For example, when the songwriter Jerome Kern sold his library in 1929, he sold it at the height of an inflationary and optimistic economic period. The prices paid for some of his books have never been equaled in fifty years of continued inflation and rising values.

Illiquidity

Books are not the ideal investment for those who require relative liquidity. Long-term investment value, for the serious collector, must be accompanied by an appreciation of the pleasures of ownership.

TAX CONSEQUENCES

The tax benefits available to book collectors, as to collectors of any other appreciating art object, are limited. The taxpayer cannot depreciate an object that appreciates in value. However, it is possible to donate to a qualified charitable source books that have increased in value many times through the years as determined by current appraisal. The investor should obtain a qualified appraisal of the materials before they are donated, so that the IRS will be inclined to accept the amount that he claims the donated books are worth. The donor is then entitled to a tax deduction for the current fair market value of the books, which more often than not is far above the purchase cost or basis. Separate rules apply to those who are recognized as investors by the IRS. (See article on "Tax Considerations for Collector-Investors," elsewhere in this volume.) For complete guidance in these matters, readers are urged to consult a professional tax advisor.

REPRESENTATIVE TYPES OF INVESTORS

As there is no typical reader, there is really no typical collector. For centuries, books have been collected by kings and scholars for whatever reason may have motivated them. As a pure investment, books require too much knowledge of bibliography and the market itself for one to consider collecting them on a casual or impulse basis. Yet, for the collector who holds an active interest and curiosity in a particular area, rare books offer a unique source of intellectual satisfaction and potential gain.

Of course, in addition to individual collectors, libraries and other scholarly institutions hold a substantial number of the world's rare books.

IMPORTANT FACTORS IN BUYING AND SELLING

Need for Knowledge and Interest

It is important for the potential collector to know at the outset that books, like most collectibles, require a good deal of background knowledge on market values, special characteristics of an edition or issue, and a general understanding of bibliographical techniques. In addition, the book collector should have some interest in a particular subject, writer, or genre.

Choosing a Dealer

A serious beginner will gravitate to a dealer whose taste and acumen he trusts to give him, through early purchases, an intelligent understanding of both intrinsic and extrinsic value. A reliable dealer is of invaluable help in monitoring the marketplace and providing information of previous auctions, sale records, and catalogs.

CUSTODIAL CARE

The scientific care and preservation of rare books is a relatively recent concern of the bibliographic world. Besides fire, only extreme heat or extreme dampness historically have ruined these surprisingly hardy productions.

The northern hemisphere, in which most of the world's rare books originated, has always enjoyed a relatively moderate climate that did little damage to printed books or even manuscripts, particularly if they received even minimal care. Prior to the nineteenth century, paper was made from pure linen fibers, which proved to be a durable surface for print. Indeed, one can find books dating from the 1500s that appear as fresh and bright as if they were printed yesterday. In the nineteenth century, wood pulp and chemicals were introduced into the making of paper, and, as this trend has continued to the present day, the life of book paper has become increasingly limited.

It is only in the last fifty years that scientific care has been applied to old and rare books and manuscripts. Methods for neutralizing paper acidity are a real concern for rare-book librarians, dealers, and collectors. Leather preservation, although less immediately crucial, remains a problem in both early and modern fine bindings. There are restoratio specialists who address these and similar problems. Leather-bound volumes should be stored in an atmosphere that is neither too hot, too cold, too dry, nor too humid. Twice a year, the leather should be lightly treated—not soaked—with any one of a number of leather dressings, such as British Museum Dressing, Lexol, or one of the preservative preparations that a dealer or bookbinder can provide. The basic aim is to keep the leather from drying out. On the other hand, if too much of a liquid preparation is used, the leather fibers may part and/or the solution may pass through the covers onto the leaves themselves. (The restorers listed at the end of this article are the best resource for maintenance information.)

GLOSSARY

as issued—The original condition of a volume, especially when an anomalous feature occurred that had not been anticipated, such as an inverted or transposed folio.

association copy— A copy that either belonged to the author or to a person whose relationship with the author (or the book's contents) bears an interesting association.

autograph—In rare-book parlance, a manuscript that the author has signed or handwritten.

boards— Sides of hard-cover books that are not bound in leather, pasteboard or cardboard.

broadside or broadsheet—Printing done on only one side of a sheet of paper.

collation—The description of the physical makeup of a book using bibliographic criteria.

editio princeps—The Latin phrase used by antiquarians for "first edition."

edition and impression—An "edition" represents all copies of a book printed from one set of type or plates; an "impression" is each printing of that edition. One edition may go through many impressions.

errata—When errors are discovered after printing, often a separate sheet is added after binding to list these mistakes for the reader.

ex-library—Any book that has been in a lending library.

foxed, foxing—Paper stained or discolored, usually from age.

leaf—Sheet of paper containing a front and back page — the single production unit.

provenance—Ownership history of a book traced in a variety of ways, which often provides an interesting sidelight to owning a particular copy of a rare book.

re-backed—A book that has been given a new spine or strip along the back to secure the front and back covers.

sophisticated—A euphemistic term for a book that has had pages added or replaced from other copies.

variants—A copy of a particular edition that is noticeably different from other copies because of misprint, changes made during printing, or other factors.

LEADING ANTIQUARIAN BOOKSELLERS AND RESTORERS

BOOKSELLERS

Argosy Book Store, Inc., New York, N.Y. Out-of-print, early maps and prints, Americana, rare medical books, first editions.

J.N. Bartfield, New York, N.Y. Paintings, bindings, sets, rare books, color plate books.

Brattle Book Shop, Boston, Mass. Used and rare books.

Martin Breslauer, Inc., New York, N.Y. Autographs, early illustrated books, fine bindings, incunabula, manuscripts.

James Cummins, Bookseller, New York, N.Y. Literature, sporting books, press books.

Dawson's Book Shop, Los Angeles, Cal. Western Americana, books about books, miniature books, mountaineering, Oriental art.

Anthony Garnett—Fine Books, St. Louis, Mo. Fine printing, first editions, press books, English literature.

Edwin V. Glaser, Rare Books, Sausalito, Cal. Early science and medicine, history of ideas, rare books in many fields.

Goodspeed's Book Shop, Inc., Boston, Mass. Autographs, Americana, genealogies, first editions, prints.

Lathrop C. Harper, Inc., New York, N.Y. Incunabula, illuminated manuscripts, illustrated books, early science and medicine, all fine books before 1800.

Heritage Bookshop, Inc., Los Angeles, Cal. Rare books, Californiana, press books, manuscripts, first editions.

Jonathan A. Hill, Bookseller, New York, N.Y. Science and medicine, bibliography, voyages, travels and exploration, press books and fine printing, printing and printing history.

Joseph the Provider—Books, Santa Barbara, Cal. Modern literature, manuscripts, letters, signed and associated copies, first editions.

Priscilla Juvelis, Inc., Boston, Mass. Livres d'artiste, fine bindings, illustrated books, first editions.

H.P. Kraus, New York, N.Y. Incunabula, history of science, cartography, Americana, medieval manuscripts.

George S. MacManus Co., Philadelphia, Pa. English and American literature, Pennsylvania, local history, rare Americana, Western Americana.

Martayan Lan, Inc., New York, N.Y. Americana, history of science, early illustrated books, maps and prints.

Howard S. Mott, Inc., Sheffield, Mass. Autograph letters and manuscripts, Caribbean (esp. Lesser Antilles), Americana, rare books, first editions.

Pepper & Stern—Rare books, Sharon, Mass.; Santa Barbara, Cal. English and American literature, detective fiction, rare cinema material, autographs.

The Printer's Devil, Arlington, Mass.; Boston, Mass. Medicine: books, prints, instruments; appraisals; rare books; history of medicine; early and rare medicine.

Kenneth W. Rendell, Inc., Newton, Mass. Autograph letters, manuscripts, ancient writing, medieval manuscripts, appraisals.

Paul C. Richards—Autographs, Templeton, Mass. Autographed material, signed photographs, association and inscribed books, stocks and bonds, documents.

B. & L. Rootenberg—Rare Books, Sherman Oaks, Cal. Rare books and manuscripts, science and medicine, literary classics, first editions.

Leona Rostenberg & Madeleine B. Stein — Rare Books, New York, N.Y. Renaissance, political theory, ephemera.

William Salloch, Ossining, N.Y. Rare books and manuscripts, incunabula classics, Renaissance, Middle Ages.

Justin G. Schiller, Ltd., New York, N.Y. Early children's literature, illustrated books, original drawings, decorative arts, history of education.

Dorothy Sloan, Austin, Tex. Americana, Texana, Latin Americana, Southwest U.S., women's history.

C.A. Stonehill, Inc., New Haven, Conn. English literature and history, incunabula, manuscripts, appraisals.

W. Thomas Taylor, Austin, Tex. American literature, typography, incunabula, press books, English literature.

Trebizond Rare Books, New York, N.Y. English, continental, and American literature, voyages and travels, Americana.

E. Wharton & Co., Oakton, Va. First editions (nineteenth- and twentieth-century American and British literature); autograph and manuscript material, Edith Wharton and other women writers.

Ursus Books Ltd., New York, N.Y. Art and architecture, illustrated books, decorative prints, natural history.

Irving Zucker—Art Books, New York, N.Y. Typography and printing, old and rare books, modern French illustrated, fine and applied arts, color plate books.

SPECIALISTS IN BOOK AND MANUSCRIPT RESTORATION

Peter Geraty, Easthampton, N.Y.

Caroline Horton, New York, N.Y.

Sky Meadow Bindery, Inc., Suffern, N.Y.

Laura Young, New York, N.Y.

SUGGESTED READING

The most comprehensive single source for general and author bibliographies is *The New Cambridge Bibliography of English Literature*, 4 vols. plus an index, published by Cambridge University, England, 1973–1976. This invaluable reference source lists numerous individual author bibliographies as well as critical and bibliographical essays on particular topics and authors.

Individual author bibliographies and topics other than literature are far too numerous to list here. The would-be collector should know, however, that almost any conceivable subject —from aeronautics to insects—has some published bibliographic listings. The quickest source to these may be found by inquiring at the reference desk of any large university or municipal library. Antiquarian book dealers, of course, will be able to refer the collector to the standard bibliographic references relating to any topics of interest.

Some particularly useful bibliographic references for collectors follow.

Blanck, J.N. *Bibliography of American Literature*, 6 vols. New Haven: Yale University Press for the Bibliographical Society of America, 1955–1963.

Bowers, Fredson. *Principles of Bibliographical Description*. Princeton: Princeton University Press, 1949. Reprinted by Russell and Russell, New York, 1962.

Connolly, Cyril. *The Modern Movement*. New York, 1965.

Garvey, Elinor. *The Artist & the Book*. Boston, 1960.

The Grolier Club of New York. *100 Books Famous in English Literature*. New York, 1902. Reprinted by Kraus, Millwood, N.Y.

Hayward, John. *English Poetry, A Descriptive Catalogue: First and Early Editions of Works of the English Poets From Chaucer to the Present Day*. National Book League, 1947, rev. 1950. Reprinted by Greenwood Press, Westport, Conn.

McKerrow, Ronald B. *An Introduction to Bibliography for Literary Students*. Cambridge: Oxford University Press, 1927.

Pollard, A.W., and Redgrave, G.R. *A Short-Title Catalogue of Books Printed in England, Scotland and Ireland and of English Books Printed Abroad, 1475–1640*. London: The Bibliographical Society, and Cambridge: Oxford University Press, 1962. Second edition (Vol. 2), 1976.

Queen, Ellery. *Queen's Quorum*. Boston, 1951.

Sadleir, Michael. *19th Century Fiction*. 2 vols. Los Angeles: London and University of California Press, 1951.

Shawyer, N.M. *A Catalogue of the Collection of 18th Century Printed Books and Manuscripts Formed by Lord Rothschild*. London: privately printed, 1954.

Unger, Emma V., and Jackson, William A. *The Carl H. Pforzheimer Library of English Literature, 1475–1700*. 3 vols. New York: privately printed, 1940.

Wing, David. *Short-Title Catalogue of Books Printed in England, Scotland, Ireland, Wales and British America, and of English Books Printed in Other Countries, 1641–1700*. Second edition, 2 vols. New York: Index Society, Columbia University Press, and Modern Language Association, 1972 and 1981.

COINS

Q. David Bowers
Richard A. Bagg

BASIC CHARACTERISTICS

Coins, once the domain of the historian and student, have become popular as an investment medium. Pension funds, trusts, profit-sharing plans, investment advisors, and many individuals have purchased coins for their investment potential.

Indeed, the track record of selected coins, when viewed over the perspective of several decades, is nothing less than spectacular. Using figures published annually in R. S. Yeoman's *A Guide Book of United States Coins*, the performance of a coin can be charted easily. (See *Price Performance Tables* 1–8 in this article.) An Uncirculated (or new condition) 1801 ten-dollar gold piece was listed at $100 in 1950. In 1960, its price rose to $290 which increased to $1,200 by 1970. This coin was priced at $8,000 in 1980, which grew to $15,000 by 1988. (See Table 3.) Is such growth indicative of a one-of-a-kind situation, or is it representative of coins in general? Actually, hundreds of different U.S. coins have performed nearly as well or even better in past years. An 1834 Uncirculated quarter climbed from $5 in 1950 to $1,100 in 1988. A study of fifteen classic U.S. coins—scarce, early issues in higher-condition grades—shows that a group valued at $1,010 in 1950 was valued at $118,250 thirty-eight years later. (See Table 3.)

This discussion is concerned primarily with U.S. coins, as they are of greatest concern to the typical investor. However, over 2,500 years, countless varieties of coins have been

---

Q. David Bowers is Chairman of the Board of Bowers and Merena Galleries, Inc., and Auctions by Bowers and Merena, Inc., Wolfeboro, N.H. Richard A. Bagg, Ph.D., is Director of Auctions at Auctions by Bowers and Merena, Inc.

FIGURE 1. Some Popular Coins

The Colonial coinage of Massachusetts is one of the most fascinating series in early American numismatics. Illustrated is an example of the famous Pine Tree shilling struck in silver.

1896 Morgan dollar. This majestic silver dollar is one of the most popularly collected crown-sized coins in the world. Minted from 1878 to 1921, several hundred million were manufactured.

1907 high relief double eagle is said to be America's most beautiful coin. These impressive gold coins have traditionally been favorites with collectors.

issued by hundreds of different authorities, ranging from countries to cities, states, and private individuals.

Historical Background

Briefly defined, "coins" are metallic objects, usually round and flat, that serve as a medium of exchange. In modern times, coins have been struck at special government institutions called mints, which use high-speed presses to stamp them out from designs on engraved dies. The location at which a coin was minted can sometimes affect its value and make it desirable to a collector.

In past years, there have been seven different mints in the United States. The Philadelphia Mint, established in 1792 and first operated on a production basis in 1793, is the main mint today. Over the years, the institution has moved to several different buildings and locations within Philadelphia, each one larger than the last. With only a few exceptions, coins struck at the Philadelphia Mint have no mintmark or mint letter.

In 1838, three additional mints were established. The New Orleans Mint operated until 1909 and issued coins bearing "O" mintmarks. The Dahlonega (Georgia) and Charlotte (North Carolina) Mints each operated from 1838 to 1861, struck gold coins only, and issued coins with "D" and "C" mintmarks, respectively.

The San Francisco Mint, still in operation today, commenced business in 1854. Its coins bear "S" mintmarks. From 1870 to 1893, the Carson City (Nevada) Mint produced coins, mainly silver, with "CC" mintmarks, using metal from the nearby Comstock Lode.

In 1906, the Denver Mint, still in operation today, commenced business. Its coins bear "D" mintmarks.

ATTRACTIVE FEATURES

Inherent Interest

Coin collecting is an interesting pursuit. As coin prices have increased over the years, many coin collectors have found that their favorite hobby has also been their best investment. Coins literally carry imprints of history. Rulers, nations, wars, monetary crises, exploration and discovery, and countless other situations have been depicted on or memorialized by coins. Imagine where a worn 1890 nickel has been and what it has seen: It may have traveled to the 1893 Columbian Exposition in Chicago, been in and out of penny arcades, furnished admission to Charlie Chaplin movies, and so on. Carson City silver dollars of the 1880s, fairly easily obtained today, are large and heavy reminders of the rip-roaring days of silver mining, when the West was truly wild.

The coin collector can share experiences with others by belonging to organizations, attending conventions, engaging in research, and becoming otherwise involved. There are countless books and periodicals to read, museums to visit, and facts to learn. After a hard day on the job, many people find solace and comfort by quietly studying metallic reminders of years ago.

Convenience

Coins are small and can be stored easily. A bank safe-deposit box can store hundreds of thousands of dollars worth of rare coins. Because of their size and light weight, individual coins can be moved from place to place without attracting attention. They can be safely and easily sent through the mail by registering and insuring them at the post office. Indeed, it may come as a surprise that most commercial coin transactions are handled this way. Coin buyers will travel to Los Angeles, New York, or some other location to bid in an auction and then will have their purchases shipped home by mail, simply because that is the safest way. By means of insured, registered mail, the U.S. Postal Service enables a patron to insure a valuable article (up to specified limits) and then sign for it on receipt. In addition, the Postal Service itself maintains strong internal safeguards whereby each person handling the article within the system must sign for it as it is transferred. When the Hope Diamond was sent from New York to Washington, D.C. a few years ago, a number of methods were considered to ensure its safety, including armored truck, special messenger, and mail. It was finally decided to send it by registered mail through the post office. It arrived safely.

Application of Standard Descriptions

Coin nomenclature is universal, and a very valuable coin can be described briefly. For example, the description "1894-S dime, MS-65"[1] refers to a Choice Uncirculated example of the 1894-S dime of which two dozen pieces were made and only about a dozen of which are known today. With such a brief description, a dealer in Boston can offer a piece to another dealer in Los Angeles, give a price, and in a moment's notice a decision can be reached. There is no need for complicated and involved description or procedures. Reference books exist on almost all areas of U.S. and world coinage, so the coin buyer has a wealth of information available for research and study.

Active Market

Thousands of dealers worldwide must constantly replenish their stock to supply hundreds of thousands, if not millions, of customers. Most dealers find that buying coins, not selling them, is their greatest problem. Important collections of choice coins have always been in demand and will no doubt always continue to be so.

Demonstrated Track Record

In recent decades, coin prices have trended upwards as charted at ten-year intervals. (See *Price Performance Tables* in this article.) As in any market, there have been cycles and fluctuations, and not all coins have gone up in value. For example, a roll of forty 1950-D nickels in Uncirculated grade sold for $1,200 in 1965 but, in 1988, was worth only about $300. For every U.S. coin that went down in price during that year, 100 or more went up. For example, $1,000 invested in a typical group of U.S. coins in 1948 would have increased in value to over $100,000 thirty-nine years later (as reported in Q. David Bowers' *High Profits From Rare Coin Investment*). During the same approximate period, the Dow-Jones Industrial average went from 177.30 (the last day of trading figures used in 1948) to about 2,000 in late 1987. Stated another way, a $1,000 investment in the Dow-Jones averages, not including reinvestment of dividends, would have yielded slightly more than $11,000 during the same time interval.

At the same time, an investment in a savings account at 5 percent interest (although such interest was not readily available in the United States during the late 1940s and

[1] "MS-65" defines the grade of the coin. The grading system is discusssed in greater detail later in this article.

1950s), with interest compounded quarterly, would have risen from $1,000 to the $6,700 range by late 1987.

Also during the same period, inflation caused the purchasing power of the dollar to decline very sharply. According to U.S. government statistics, $1,000 in 1948 (if kept in cash) would have declined in purchasing power to about $200 today.

Privacy

Coins may be collected privately. Buyers may be anonymous if they wish, and their neighbors will have no idea that their coin collections, safely stored in safe-deposit boxes, may be worth several times the price of their houses. What a buyer owns in the way of coins is no one else's business. At the same time, too much privacy is not advisable. When buying coins, a collector should always insist on a written bill of sale and a receipt. Some very "clever" buyers of Krugerrands, who thought they were outwitting the government and everyone else by paying cash for Krugerrands that were believed to contain one ounce of gold each, did not ask for a record. A year or two later, they tried to sell the pieces only to find that they were made of gold-plated base metal and were worth nothing. When the original sellers of the pieces are approached, chances are they will either be out of business or will deny that they sold those coins. It is very important that the buyer insist on written statements for each and every piece bought.

POTENTIAL RISKS

As previously suggested, all is not roses in coin collecting and investing. There are some problem areas, and it is wise to make note of them, as brochures and advertisements offering coins for sale do not always mention them.

Authenticity

There are many clever forgeries of coins, and many people are victimized each year. Thus, it is important to insist on a written receipt when buying coins, since it is protection if a coin should later be proved spurious. Dealers who are members of the Professional Numismatists Guild and the International Association of Professional Numismatists guarantee the authenticity of every coin they sell. If a coin is later determined to be counterfeit, the buyer's money will be refunded in full—an important protection. Although buying a counterfeit coin from a member of one of these organizations is unlikely, mistakes do happen. If an investor buys coins from a dealer who is not established in the rare-coin field, the chance of getting forgeries increases dramatically. During a trip to several European countries, hundreds of U.S. gold coins at various banks and bullion exchanges were examined. Although the pieces bore price tags indicating that they were indeed rare and authentic, less than half of them were genuine. It pays to be careful.

Grading

Under the official American Numismatic Association (ANA) Grading System, a coin is assigned a grade indicating its state of wear. (See *Determining Value*, later in this article.) Before buying, an investor should be sure the coins are graded properly, for a small difference in grade can make a big difference in price. Nearly all dealers offer a return period when coins are ordered, usually from fourteen to thirty days after receipt. The buyer should use this time to verify that the coins are indeed as described, taking them to other collectors and dealers or submitting them to the ANA Grading Service, which, for a fee, will give a grading opinion. Once the time limit has expired, it may be too late to return a coin because of a grading problem. A buyer who pays $6,500 for an MS-65 1886-0 silver dollar and later finds that it is only an MS-60 (and worth only $350) may be out of luck unless this is discovered soon after the coin is purchased.

A number of grading services have sealed coins in plastic containers, or "slabs," marked with a grade to protect the consumer. As of 1988, the most reliable of these seem to be the Professional Coin Grading Service (PCGS) and the Numismatic Guaranty Corporation of America (NGC). However, even though these slabs are marked with precise grades (e.g., MS-63 or MS-65), these grades are not always consistently applied. These two services, in part, help to eliminate wide fluctuations in grading, which took place as recently as 1987.

TAX CONSEQUENCES

In many areas, there is no property tax to be paid when coins are held. Taxes are due only when the coins are sold at a profit. The Internal Revenue Service has ruled that, under certain conditions, rare coins can be exchanged for other rare coins in a tax-free transaction, thus making it possible to upgrade a collection without a tax penalty. (See article on "Tax Considerations for Collector-Investors," elsewhere in this volume.) For advice in these matters, investors are urged to consult a professional tax advisor.

IMPORTANT FACTORS IN BUYING AND SELLING

Determining Value

What determines a coin's value? Most people would think that age is the most important factor. Actually, age has very little to do with the value of a coin or its desirability to a collector. It is perhaps surprising to learn that a 2,000-year-old copper coin of ancient Rome can be purchased for $5 or $10, while certain rare varieties of Lincoln cents can cost $1,000 each or more. Among the factors that determine a coin's value are the following:

Condition (Basic Grades). The condition, or state of wear, of a coin is exceedingly important. With very few exceptions, the closer to new or Uncirculated grade a coin is, the more it is worth. Coins are divided into the following basic grades, as enumerated by the official ANA Grading System.

Uncirculated or mint state (MS). An Uncirculated piece is like new and represents a piece that has not been in hand-to-hand circulation as a medium of exchange. However, when coins emerge from high-speed mechanical presses, they are dumped together with other coins into bins, run through mechanical sorters, put into bags, and shipped from bank to bank. Even Uncirculated coins will show some nicks and contact marks. Accordingly, Uncirculated pieces are divided into several subgrades. The ANA Scale runs from condition 1, or a piece that is worn nearly smooth, to condition 70, which is perfect. Uncirculated coins, also known as mint state, fall into the 60 to 70 range. The ANA Grading System notes that an MS-60, or Typical Uncirculated coin, is one that shows numerous light surface marks and blemishes but does not show actual wear. The coin may be brilliant (as bright as when first minted) or it may have acquired toning. MS-65, or Choice

Uncirculated, refers to a piece that has only a few scattered nicks and marks. Generally, MS-65 is the grade that collectors who can afford the finest aspire to own. MS-70, or Perfect Uncirculated, is a theoretical condition that does not exist for many issues more than a few decades old, simply because of the minting and handling processes described earlier. Additional Uncirculated grades are the intermediate grades of MS-67, or Gem Uncirculated, and MS-63, or Select Uncirculated.

Almost Uncirculated (AU). Once a coin has seen very light wear, it may be known as Almost Uncirculated. The ANA Grading System recognizes two divisions: AU-50 and AU-55.

Extremely Fine (EF). This grade, which includes Extremely Fine-40 and Choice Extremely Fine-45 (EF-45), designates a piece that shows more wear than AU but still has nearly all of the design details sharp.

Very Fine (VF). This piece shows even more wear than Extremely Fine and is designated as VF-20 or VF-30, depending on the characteristics within the grade.

Fine (F). A Fine piece is extensively worn, but most of the major lettering is still readable. F-12 and F-15 are the numerical equivalents.

Very Good (VG). A Very Good piece is considerably worn and has some of the lettering gone, particularly on the higher spots. It is numerically designated as VG-8.

Good (G). This coin is worn almost smooth. Most of the major letters and the date are clear, but many other design details are gone. It is abbreviated as G-4.

Poor, Fair, and About Good (P, F, and AG). These coins are so worn that they are only of value if they are of exceedingly rare varieties (1 to 3 on numerical grading scale).

Each of the preceding grades has specific detailed definitions, which are listed in *The Official ANA Grading Guide.* This guide must be consulted to accurately determine a coin's condition.

Sometimes, a small difference in grade can make a vast difference in price. For example, the 1989 edition of *A Guide Book of United States Coins* listed an 1886-O (New Orleans Mint) silver dollar at the following grades and values: VF-20, $14; EF-40, $18; AU-50, $50; MS-60, $350; and MS-65, $6,500. In other words, an MS-60 was listed at seven times the price of an AU-50 piece. Even more dramatic is the difference between MS-60 at $350 and MS-65 at $6,500. Obviously, it is crucial to know how to grade coins properly and accurately, or to buy from someone who does. If one were to purchase an MS-65 coin at $6,500 and find that the piece was really only MS-60, more than 90 percent of the investment would be lost immediately. There are many abuses in this area.

In addition to the grades mentioned above, a special grade called Proof designates coins made especially for collectors. They are struck from mirror-like dies with a high degree of polish created by specially prepared metallic coining blanks. These coins are produced in limited quantities on slow-speed, hand-fed presses, and have sold at a premium to collectors over the years. Although there are some exceptions, prior to 1968, most Proof coins were struck at the Philadelphia Mint. Since that time, the San Francisco Mint has been the issuer. Proof coins, which are graded according to the amount of nicks and marks they have, can be classified as Proof-60 (with numerous marks), Choice Proof-65 (with just a few marks), and Perfect Proof-70. Most early Proofs are collected in Proof-65 grade, with

Proof-70 examples unknown. Generally, a Proof coin is worth more than an Uncirculated example of the same issue, but there are some exceptions.

Rarity. Rarity is a prime determinant of a coin's value. If all other factors are equal, a coin of which 100 specimens are known will be worth considerably more than a coin of which there are a million examples. Most of the world's price records for rare coins are held by pieces that are extremely rare. For example, only seven pieces are known of the 1787 Brasher Doubloon, which, at $725,000 (realized in the sale of the Garrett Collection by Bowers & Ruddy Galleries in 1979) was the highest price ever recorded at auction for a rare coin of any type. Only fifteen examples are known of the 1804 silver dollar, a specimen of which sold for $400,000 in 1980, $500,000 in 1985, and $990,000 in 1989. An Uncirculated 1894-S dime (just twenty-four were minted and only about a dozen are known to exist today) would bring $75,000 or more if offered today. An 1876-CC twenty-cent piece in Uncirculated grade, of which about two dozen are known, is valued in the $50,000 range.

Rarity depends on several things. The original mintage is an important factor. Generally, the more pieces that were minted, the more that are apt to survive today. As an example of this, 1,476,490 Liberty-head nickels were made in 1885. In 1911, 39,559,372 nickels of the same design were produced. As might be expected, the 1885 is a scarcer coin. An Uncirculated MS-60 example of the 1885 coin lists in catalogues for $1,200, while the 1911 in the same grade brings just $100. Coins were sometimes hoarded, with the result that the mintage figures are not particularly meaningful. This is especially true for silver dollars. From 1878 onward, the government produced hundreds of millions of silver dollars in response to political pressures from the West. The market for silver was poor, so the government was persuaded to buy quantities of silver that it did not want and to coin them into silver dollars. Millions of these remained in Treasury vaults until the early 1960s, when they were released at face value. Included in the release were pieces dated in the 1870s, 1880s, and 1890s. There were 228,000 1885-CC silver dollars minted, and when an inventory of the Treasury holdings was taken in the 1960s, it was discovered that over half of these still remained in existence in the original bags of issue. Therefore, an Uncirculated 1885-CC dollar is common today. On the other hand, 350,000 1889-CC dollars were minted, but most of these were put into circulation or melted many years ago; consequently, perhaps no more than 5,000 to 10,000 exist today in Uncirculated grade. So although the mintage of an 1889-CC dollar is higher than it is for an 1885-CC, the 1889-CC sells for dozens of times more on today's market.

Coins can have different degrees of rarity in different grades. For example, a 1919-D half-dollar in worn condition, described as G-4, is not particularly hard to find. The catalog listing is $10. However, an Uncirculated or MS-60 piece is very rare and is listed at $2,000. With the exception of coins that were hoarded by collectors or were not released by the government, most coin issues are scarcer in Uncirculated grade than in worn conditions.

Demand. Demand is one of the most important determinants of a coin's value. Unless someone wants a coin, it is worth only its face value, or the value of its metallic content.

Different series among American coins are collected with varying degrees of interest. Coins that are very popular (and, hence, in great demand) usually bring more than coins that are not. For example, scarce issues among one-cent pieces, nickels, dimes, quarters, half-dollars, and silver dollars tend to sell for high figures, while scarce issues in obscure series sell for less.

A 1914-D Lincoln cent, a coin of which 1,193,000 were minted, lists at $350 in Extremely Fine (EF-40) grade. There are many thousands of these in existence. However, because tens of thousands of people want to obtain one of each date and mintmark variety of these Lincoln cents, the $350 price is easily sustained. On the other hand, there may be a streetcar token of Kingston, Pennsylvania, of which just five examples are known. It too can be Extremely Fine, but because there is very little demand from collectors for rare varieties of Kingston streetcar tokens, the piece may be worth only a few dollars, even though it is thousands of times more rare than the 1914-D Lincoln cent. Demand is everything.

Demand and popularity tend to change over time. Sometimes, a particular type of rare coin will be in strong demand for a few years. As soon as the tastes of collectors change, the focus will be on something else. The astute investor will study patterns of demand and will try to preduct future changes.

Age. As noted earlier, age is not an important determinant of a coin's value. The public often considers an old coin automatically to be valuable but, for the collector, such considerations as condition, demand, and rarity are much more important.

Metallic Content. The metallic or meltdown value of a coin can be important, particularly for pieces struck in precious metals. A $20 U.S. gold piece of the year 1928 is not particularly rare, for millions of them were minted, but it is quite valuable. Like other $20 or double-eagle pieces, it contains nearly a full ounce of gold, and its value is therefore related to the world market value for gold. Generally, a $20 piece will sell for more than its gold content. For example, if gold is selling for $600 per ounce, an Extremely Fine $20 gold piece of a common date may bring $700. If gold sells for $900, then the coin will bring $1,000. If gold sells for $300, then the coin will bring about $375.

The more common a gold coin is, the more responsive it is to bullion price movements. Among American gold coins, there are certain common issues of the denominations $5, $10, and $20. On a worldwide scale, such pieces as the Canadian Maple Leaf, the Austrian 100-corona, and the Mexican 50-peso piece, all of gold, are responsive to metallic price fluctuations. Certain other denominations of U.S. gold coins (e.g., $1, $2.50, $3, and $4) are sufficiently rare that they are not affected measurably by changes in the price of gold. For example, an 1861-D (Dahlonega, Georgia, Mint) one-dollar gold piece in Uncirculated MS-60 grade lists at $28,000, although if gold were selling at $600 an ounce, the piece would have a meltdown value of about $15.

Certain silver coins (bags of worn silver dollars and bags of common American silver coins from the 1930s, 1940s, 1950s, and early 1960s) are often traded in bulk, based on the fluctuating value of silver. For investment purposes, bulk gold and silver coins are not particularly related to the rare coin market. The rise and fall of gold and silver bullion is much more of a determinant of the value of a common-date $20 gold piece than is the demand by collectors. Accordingly, investment in such pieces should be guided by the buyer's belief in the future of the metals market, not by coin-collecting considerations.

Other Considerations. There are a number of other considerations that help determine a coin's value. The design may be appealing, and the coin may sell more for this reason. Or a coin might have some romantic or historical connection—with the Civil War, for example—and it may sell more for this reason. Sometimes, the quality or status of a collection will add to a particular coin's value. The fabulous Garrett Collection was formed during the period 1865 until about 1940 by the family that managed the Baltimore and Ohio Railroad, and it contained many of the finest examples of great American rarities. When it was sold at public auction in a series of sales from 1979 to 1981, many pieces sold for much more than other pieces of the same variety would have sold for, because collectors wanted to own pieces that were once in the Garrett Collection.

Selecting a Dealer

The Professional Numismatists Guild, the leading organization of rare-coin dealers, has as its members most of the long-established leading firms, and close to 200 dealers. In addition, thousands of other people buy and sell coins in their spare time as part of a business involving stamps or antiques. There is an active market at all times. (See *Selected Dealers*, later in this article.)

When selecting a rare-coin dealer or professional numismatist (as they are called), it is important to check carefully and verify credentials. There are no licensing requirements to become a rare-coin dealer, and anyone who has enough money to print business cards or fancy brochures can proclaim to be "the world's best coin dealer." There have been many problems in this regard, particularly in times of intense coin-market activity. Sometimes, the dealers with the most lavish brochures and the highest advertising budgets are of questionable reputation and financial strength.

A dealer who belongs to the Professional Numismatists Guild or to the International Association of Professional Numismatists is pledged to a strict code of ethics, and the buyer has certain protections should any problems arise. However, there are many reputable dealers who do not belong to these groups for various reasons, including length of time in business, insufficient capital, or simply no desire to belong. In any event, the buyer should check around, compare grades and prices, and make a decision. It is easy to avoid mistakes at the outset, but it is not easy to correct them once they have been made. "Investigate before investing" is an axiom appropriate to all areas of investment activity. It is surprising how gullible some coin buyers can be. If someone were to put up a sign in a store window saying "IBM stock at half market price" or "$100 bills for $75 each," few people would be buyers. But if someone puts up a sign saying, "The greatest coin dealer offers coins at half price," customers will come flocking in.

Vast fortunes have been made in coin investments, but vast sums have been lost as well. Generally, the greatest gains have gone to those who have taken the time to learn about coins, investigate the subject carefully, and make purchases with patience. Those who have taken the losses generally have been those who have viewed coins as a get-rich-quick scheme and who have spent large sums of money without taking the time to learn even the first thing about grading (in particular), rarity, demand, and other considerations.

Buying Coins

Coins can be bought in several different ways. Many coin dealers issue price catalogues that describe and offer coins for sale. In addition, dealers will service want lists given by customers. Advertisements in *Coin World, Numismatic News*, and other periodicals also list coins for sale. Some firms offer special groups or packages to potential investors, and others have monthly or periodic investment plans.

Each year in the United States, there are several dozen rare-coin auctions. Many of these are unreserved and unrestricted, and offer the buyer the chance to bid competitively for desirable coins. However, to bid intelligently, requisite knowledge is necessary, so auctions usually are the realm of the advanced collector. Still, for the beginner, they furnish a good guide to comparative market values.

Selling Coins

Selling to a Dealer. Most dealers are eager to buy choice and rare coins and will make an offer for them. The amount of the offer will depend on the market conditions at the time, the size of the dealer's stock, economic conditions, the cost the dealer incurs when borrowing money from the bank, and the dealer's demand or desire for the coin. Not all dealers want all coins at all times. Yet, there are enough dealers to constitute a generally strong market. Most dealers will buy coins at 60 to 80 percent of the retail price, with certain high-demand pieces selling for even closer to the posted value. Generally, coins that are very inexpensive are bought for deeper discounts, simply because of the handling involved. A few examples follow.

A dealer may want to pay only fifty cents or one dollar for a coin that retails at two dollars, simply because a large part of that coin's value lies in dealer handling. In the 1989 edition of *A Guide Book of United States Coins*, a recent Lincoln cent, an Uncirculated 1980, listed for ten cents. This does not mean that 10,000 of these pieces, having a total face value of $100, could be sold for $1,000. Rather, the pieces would be worth just face value or slightly more. The listing of ten cents per coin, or ten times face value, reflects the dealer's handling cost.

A coin that sells for $10 may be bought for about $5 to $7 by a dealer, depending on the dealer's stock at the time. A $1,000 coin is apt to be more closely traded on a percentage basis and will wholesale for $700 to $800 in many instances.

Selling Through an Auction Catalogue. Auction cataloguers charge a commission for their services. The fee, generally expressed in terms of a percentage, is usually all-inclusive, covering expenses of insurance, photographing important pieces for the catalogue, advertising, printing, preparing and distributing the catalogue, and many other considerations. In recent years, it has been typical in the rare-coin field to have a split arrangement whereby the purchaser of the coins pays a 10 percent fee called a buyer's charge. This has been the rule in art and antique auctions as well. The seller also pays a commission, typically 10 percent, but there are exceptions. Often, extremely valuable coins can be sold for a lower commission rate, especially if they do not require extensive catalogue descriptions. On the other hand, tokens, medals, numismatic books, and items requiring lengthy descriptions in comparison to their value may be charged more than 10 percent.

When selling coins in an auction catalogue, it is important to investigate what services the seller can receive. If a dealer has a very small mailing list and distributes only one or two thousand copies of a catalogue, the dealer can charge a seller a lower commission and possibly make more profit than another dealer who charges 10 percent but who distributes several thousand catalogues. However, it is obvious that it is more beneficial to reach many thousands of potential buyers, so in this instance, the higher commission rate might well be the better deal.

In view of the spread between buying and selling prices, it is wise to consider coin investment on a long-term basis. Investors who buy coins today and sell them a month or even a year from now may make a lot of money for the dealers involved, but not necessarily for themselves. On the other hand, if the investor holds coins for a long time, the dealer markups become less important. For example, a 1932-D Uncirculated quarter listed at $33 in 1950, $90 in 1960, $250 in 1970, $3,000 in 1980, and $4,000 in 1988. (See Table 4.) Assume, for exmple, that pieces sell for precisely their catalogue value (in practice, some sell for more and some for less). An investor who paid $250 for a piece in 1970 and sold it for $4,000 in 1988, paying a 20 percent commission on doing so, would net $2,950, or about twelve times the purchase price. Few would begrudge the dealer's profit in such a situation. On the other hand, an investor who purchased the coin in March 1988 for $4,000 and attempted to sell it in December of the same year might find that the price did move a bit and that he had taken an $800 loss, certainly not a pleasant situation.

Deciding When to Sell. How long should one hold coins? There is no hard-and-fast rule for this, although a minimum of three to five years is advisable, and ten years or longer is even better. As the *Price Performance Tables* in this article vividly demonstrate, those who have held coins for a decade or more generally have done well. The longer the coins are held, assuming the market is trending upward, the greater the profits will be, and the buying and selling fee will have less impact.

ACQUIRING A COIN COLLECTION

Future Considerations

The future for rare-coin investment is unknown, as is the future for investment in the stock market, real estate, and the money market. The best thing to do is consider the factors and come to a reasonable decision.

The future of coin prices will depend on demand. While investors who buy coins help to create a market, the ultimate consumer is the collector. If the number of true collectors increases, then the price of coins will generally increase. If the number of collectors declines, then coin prices will decline.

From all indications, coin collecting is on the increase. As of late 1988, membership in the ANA stood at nearly 40,000, an all-time record. (The organization was formed in 1891.) The current trend in our society is for more leisure time to conduct pursuits such as coin collecting, which is a favorable indication. Personal earnings are on the increase, permitting more disposable income for hobbies.

In recent years, coins have become established as an investment medium. Financial institutions have added coins to their portfolios. Many investors, particularly individuals, begin by buying coins strictly as a hedge against inflation. After they have been involved for some time, they learn how fascinating coins can be from a historical, artistic, and romantic viewpoint, and then they become collectors. Once this happens, another true collector or consumer is established, and the market is strengthened.

Market Volatility

The coin market is subject to cycles. In 1979 to 1980, certain coins, rare and bullion-type alike, rose sharply in value, doubling and tripling in many instances. This was due to a worldwide fever for precious metals. Fortunes were made with the rising price of these metals, and, as a result, dealers who made large sums of money often reinvested it in the rare-coin market, driving prices up. After the high point in the market, which came early in 1981, prices for many pieces subsided sharply; this cycle was one of several since 1953. In 1957, there was a market break, another in 1966, and another in 1975. Undoubtedly, there will be many more in the future, as coin prices do move in cycles. In fact, the market began trending upward again in late 1982 and has risen steadily until today. However, by and large, the cycles trend upward, like a saw blade rotating on an angle. Several things can be done to avoid the effects of cycles. First, when the price of a coin rises sharply, beware. It may indicate that the coin is under speculative pressure. The time to buy is when the market is rather quiet. However, during the quiet periods, there is very little done in the way of promotional advertising, so it takes a measure of individual determination and fortitude to buy. Working against the trend is best—the greatest profits have gone to those who have bought during dips in the cycle, not during rising periods.

Diversification also will help counter the effects of cycles. An investor should buy some gold coins, some silver coins, some copper coins, and some nickel coins, or buy some coins from the early 1800s, and some minted 150 years later. It is a good idea to buy some very scarce coins and, at the same time, some that are not so scarce; it would also be helpful to study numismatic reference books and build a diversified collection or portfolio.

An investor who studies the field before investing and buys carefully will be in a position to get the most value from investment dollars. It is important to buy with a long-term commitment in mind; as the market trends upward, as it has done in the past, an investor will be in an ideal position to take advantage of the profits.

Ways to Collect Coins

By Date, Mintmark, and Variety. For example, Franklin half-dollars were minted from 1948 to 1963. There were several varieties minted each year, each one distinguished by a mintmark on the reverse. Thus, a complete collection of Franklin half-dollars would include such issues as 1948 (without mintmark—struck at Philadelphia), 1948-D, 1949, 1949-D, 1949-S, 1950, 1950-D, 1951, 1951-D, 1951-S, and so on through 1963 (thirty-five varieties in all).

Collections of Indian cents from the first year of issue, 1859, to the last, 1909, Liberty nickels from 1883 to 1912, Buffalo nickels from 1913 to 1938. Mercury dimes from 1916 to 1945, and other series have attracted the attention of collectors.

Certain early coins (e.g., one-cent pieces from 1793 to 1857) can be collected by die varieties. During the early years, individual dies used to strike coins were hand-cut, resulting in many interesting variations. Sometimes, letters were punched backward in the die, words were misspelled, numbers were incorrectly put into the die, and so on. Each die had its own characteristic. Such studies form a fascinating area for the specialist.

The date and mintmark collector aspires to own one of each of the different dates, mintmarks, and major varieties with a series. Completing a set by finally acquiring a major scarcity or rarity in the series is akin to the feeling of putting the last word in a crossword puzzle.

By Design Type. With the demand for coins very strong and the supply of older coins necessarily limited, no one can seriously aspire to collect one of each and every date and mintmark variety of U.S. coins from 1793 (the year the Philadelphia Mint first made coins in quantity for circulation) to the present. Even if one had the necessary financing—which would run to many millions of dollars—certain pieces simply are not available. A practical alternative is to collect by design type. Such a collector wants to obtain one of every major design. Thus, to illustrate the Franklin half-dollar in his collection, the type collector does not want thirty-five different dates and mintmarks from 1948 to 1963; rather, any Franklin half-dollar from 1948 to 1963 (a single example) will suffice. Likewise, any dime, quarter, or half-dollar from the 1892 to 1915 years will illustrate the Liberty head or Barber (named after the designer) style. A set of major types of U.S. coins offers a fascinating panorama of many different styles, artistic concepts, metals, and ideas.

Recommendation: It is wise to collect a type set at first. In this way, a collector will become familiar with the different types of coin designs available and, at the same time, will diversify his holdings, as he will not acquire more than one of any given type or issue.

Colonial Coins. U.S. coins cover a wide collecting area. Before the establishment of the Philadelphia Mint in 1792 and its first commercial coinage production in 1793, coins were issued by many private authorities. The field of early American coins or colonials, as they are called, is rich and varied and furnishes an interesting area for study. The Massachusetts Bay Colony issued threepence, sixpence, and shilling issues in silver, including the famous Pine Tree shilling, from 1652 until 1682. The denominations were patterned after the British monetary system, for the American system of dollars and cents did not come into use until the establishment of the Philadelphia Mint.

The Rosa Americana issues in copper composition, dated 1722 to 1724, were made in England for circulation in America and are popular with collectors today.

Different states issued their own coinage. Vermont issued copper coins from 1785 to 1788, as did Connecticut. New Jersey produced copper coins from 1786 to 1788, and Massachusetts issued cents and half-cents in 1787 and 1788.

The 1776 so-called Continental dollar bears the name of the thirteen original colonies on the reverse and has a design authorized by the Continental Congress. Many tokens and coins honoring President George Washington were circulated during the late eighteenth century and form an interesting part of the colonial series today.

When the Philadelphia Mint opened for business in 1793, it produced coins of only two denominations: the cent and half-cent. Thus was set the stage for American coinage. As of 1988, there are five denominations of coins being produced: the cent, nickel, dime, quarter, and half-dollar. Only the first four circulate with any regularity. Half-dollars, once plentiful in circulation, are now seldom used, despite the fact that there is no shortage of them. The Susan B. Anthony dollar, introduced with much fanfare in 1979, has been a flop as far as the public is concerned, and examples are rarely seen in everyday commercial transactions. Their mintage was discontinued in 1981.

Many different U.S. denominations have been produced over the years. These include:

- Half-cents: 1793 to 1857
- Large-size cents: 1793 to 1857
- Small-size cents: 1856 to the present time
- Two-cent pieces: 1864 to 1873
- Silver three-cent pieces: 1851 to 1873

- Nickel three-cent pieces: 1865 to 1889
- Nickel five-cent pieces: 1866 to the present time
- Half-dimes (silver five-cent pieces): 1795 to 1873
- Dimes: 1796 to the present time
- Twenty-cent pieces: 1875 to 1878
- Quarter-dollars: 1796 to the present time
- Half-dollars: 1794 to the present time
- Silver dollars: 1794 to 1981 (struck in metals other than silver in later years)
- Trade dollars: 1873 to 1885
- Gold dollars: 1849 to 1889
- Gold $2.50 (quarter eagles): 1796 to 1929
- Gold $3: 1854 to 1889
- Gold $4 (patterns only): 1879 to 1880
- Gold $5 (half eagles): 1795 to 1929
- Gold $10 (eagles): 1795 to 1933
- Gold $20 (double eagles): 1849 to 1933
- Gold $50 (1915-S Panama-Pacific Commemorative issue)

Within the various denominations are many different designs. For example, the collector of half-dollars encounters the following: 1794–1795 type with flowing hair of Miss Liberty on the obverse (collectors' term for the front of a coin) and small eagle reverse; 1796–1797 great bust obverse and small eagle reverse; 1801–1807 great bust obverse and heraldic eagle reverse; 1807–1836 capped-bust-type with lettered edge; 1836–1837 capped-bust-type with reeded edge, reverse reading 50 CENTS; 1838–1839 capped-bust-type, reeded edge, reverse reading HALF DOL.; Liberty-seated-type 1839–1891, including the following subtypes: 1853 (arrows at date and rays on the reverse); 1854–1855 (arrows at date), 1873–1874 (arrows at date), all issues 1866–1891 (IN GOD WE TRUST and all caps on the reverse); 1892–1915 (Barber design); 1916–1947 (Liberty-walking design); 1948–1963 (Franklin type); 1964 to date (Kennedy type); 1776–1976 (Kennedy Bicentennial type).

In addition to the regular U.S. issues, special commemorative coins have been produced from time to time. From 1892 to 1954, forty-eight different designs of commemorative silver half-dollars were produced. These were struck at several different mints, and some were produced with minor design varieties, giving a total of 142 date, mintmark, and design varieties. Commemorated events were varied and included the 1892 Columbian Exposition, the Bicentennial of Norfolk, Virginia, the 1915 Panama-Pacific International Exposition, the Centennial of Maine, and many others. The 1893 Isabella commemorative quarter and the 1900 Lafayette commemorative silver dollar were the only commemoratives of their type ever made.

Thirteen varieties of commemorative gold dollars and quarter eagles were produced, with the most impressive of all commemorative coins being the $50 issues made in octagonal (eight-sided) and round shapes for the 1915 Panama-Pacific International Exposition.

These items are exceedingly rare today. Only 483 round pieces were issued, and only 645 octagonal pieces were distributed to collectors.

In addition to coinage produced at the various mints, collectors desire tokens, medals, various types of U.S. paper money, and other issues that serve as currency from time to time. Tokens, in particular, are collected avidly. While such diverse areas are not recommended for the beginning investor (as they require a certain degree of expertise to study), they are highly recommended for the advanced numismatist who seeks a challenge. As is true of many fields, the more one learns about coins, the more one finds there is to know.

CUSTODIAL CARE

Expenses such as insurance and upkeep are very low. The cost of safe-deposit box rentals is trivial compared to the value of coins stored within them, and insurance rates for coins stored in banks are likewise low. Therefore, the holding cost of coins is minimal.

Care must be taken, however, to handle coins properly. Fingerprints, bruises, scratches, or careless handling can damage a coin. For this reason, most collectors and investors prefer to keep their coins in either special transparent envelopes provided for the purpose, or lucite holders. It is also important to keep pieces away from dampness and harmful industrial fumes.

TABLE 1. Price Performance of Ten Colonial Coins, 1950–1988

	Grade	1950	1960	1970	1980	1988
Fugio cent, 1787, pointed rays	Unc	$10	$ 43	$125	$ 500	$ 950
Talbot, Allum and Lee cent, 1795	Unc	6	20	75	350	800
Kentucky, 1792 plain edge	Unc	8	33	125	375	700
Vermont, 1787, bust right	Fine	4	12	65	175	250
New Jersey, 1788, horse head left	Fine	6	23	90	300	400
Connecticut, 1787 draped bust left	Fine	2	7	20	45	85
Massachusetts, 1787, half-cent	Fine	5	11	30	70	125
Constellatio, Nova, 1795, pointed rays	Fine	3	9	25	65	110
Virginia, 1773, half-penny, period	Unc	4	15	70	425	725
Washington cent, 1791, large eagle	Unc	15	40	175	775	1,350
Total		$63	$213	$800	$3,080	$5,495

Note: This group contains selected examples of early American coins that circulated prior to the year 1800 and are generally known as "colonials" by collectors today.

Source: R. S. Yeoman, *A Guide Book of United States Coins*. Fourth through forty-second editions, 1951–1989. Racine: Western Publishing Co., with permission.

PRICE PERFORMANCE TABLES

Tables 1–8 indicate the price performance of selected U.S. coins in approximate ten-year intervals from 1950 to 1988. Several types of coins were selected for these charts, including colonial coins, rare coins, classic coins, and modern coins.

TABLE 2. Price Performance of Ten Rare Coins, 1950—1988

	Grade	1950	1960	1970	1980	1988
1802 Half-dime	Fine	$ 500	$ 675	$ 3,000	$ 10,000	$ 14,000
1894-S Dime	Unc	2,250	3,625*	12,250	97,000	77,000*
1823 Twenty-five cents	Fine	500	725	1,250	5,500	9,000
1838-0 Fifty cents	Proof	2,000	4,500	14,000	62,000	50,000
1804 $1 Type 2	EEF	3,125	8,000	29,000	400,000	308,000
1848 CAL $2.50	Unc	250	750	6,000	30,000	30,000
1875 $3	Proof	2,750	5,000	25,000	91,000	121,000
1815 $5	Unc	2,250	3,250	6,500	150,000	150,000
1858 $10	Unc	2,500	4,000	6,200	30,000	22,000
1927-D $20	Unc	750	900	32,000	225,000	242,000
Total		$16,875	$31,425	$135,200	$1,100,500	$1,023,000

* Prices not provided in source. These are estimates based on averages from auctions.

Note: This chart includes selected major U.S. coin rarities and gives a vivid indication of price performance over the years.

Source: R. S. Yeoman, *A Guide Book of United States Coins*. Fourth through forty-second editions, 1951–1989. Racine: Western Publishing Co., with permission.

TABLE 3. Price Performance of Fifteen Classic Coins, 1950–1988

	Grade	1950	1960	1970	1980	1988
1793 Half-cent	Fine	$ 50	$ 140	$ 650	$ 1,500	$ 2,500
1793 Chain one-cent	Fine	100	215	800	2,500	3,750
1793 Wreath one-cent	Fine	60	130	600	1,150	1,500
1795 Half-dime	Unc	45	200	950	6,000	6,750
1829 Half-dime	Unc	3	12	93	600	400
1827 Dime	Unc	9	28	180	2,100	1,250
1796 Quarter	Unc	175	1,450	5,750	23,000	25,000
1834 Quarter	Unc	5	23	300	1,900	1,100
1807 Bust right fifty cents	Unc	23	85	425	8,000	4,750
1815 Fifty cents	Unc	65	240	875	3,000	5,250
1795 Flowing $1	Unc	150	400	1,600	16,000	16,000
1807 $2.50	Unc	100	400	1,500	8,500	16,000
1800 $5	Unc	75	160	850	6,000	9,500
1812 $5	Unc	50	145	650	4,500	9,500
1801 $10	Unc	100	290	1,200	8,000	15,000
Total		$1,010	$3,918	$16,423	$92,750	$118,250

Note: Shown here are moderately scarce classic U.S. coins of the eighteenth and nineteenth centuries, with emphasis on high-conditioned pieces.

Source: R. S. Yeoman, *A Guide Book of United States Coins.* Fourth through forty-second editions, 1951–1989. Racine: Western Publishing Co., with permission.

TABLE 4. Price Performance of Twenty Modern Coins, 1950–1988

	Grade	1950	1960	1970	1980	1988
1878 One cent	Unc	$ 7	$ 29	$ 88	$ 135	$ 135
1909 SVDB one cent	Unc	13	98	200	400	475
1914-D One cent	Unc	20	275	560	750	1,000
1883 NC Five cents	Unc	1	4	11	50	40
1926-S Five cents	Unc	70	175	440	625	1,300
1910 Dime	Proof	4	44	100	600	800
1911-D Dime	Unc	4	15	23	275	150
1916-D Dime	Unc	10	360	675	2,500	3,200
1942 Dime	Proof	1	5	20	425	750
1895 Quarter	Proof	7	43	100	600	1,100
1897-O Quarter	Unc	16	100	125	1,500	825
1917 Type I quarter	Unc	3	10	48	275	550
1930 Quarter	Unc	3	8	33	150	300
1932-D Quarter	Unc	33	90	250	3,000	4,000
1936-D Quarter	Unc	9	25	245	900	2,000
1892 Fifty cents	Unc	4	20	100	800	525
1915 Fifty cents	Proof	30	500	550	1,200	1,900
1916 Fifty cents	Unc	6	25	110	400	450
1936 Fifty cents	Proof	16	118	265	2,400	3,500
1949-S Fifty cents	Unc	1	5	24	250	300
Total		$258	$1,949	$3,967	$17,235	$23,300

Note: This chart shows a variety of modern coins, most of which were minted within the past hundred years, and many of which are from the past fifty years.

Source: R. S. Yeoman, *A Guide Book of United States Coins.* Fourth through forty-second editions, 1951–1989. Racine: Western Publishing Co., with permission.

TABLE 5. Price Performance of Ten Silver Dollars, 1950–1988

	Grade	1950	1960	1970	1980	1988
1881-S	Unc	$ 3	$ 4	$ 4	$ 60	$ 475
1884-S	Unc	15	16	65	13,500	27,500
1885	Unc	4	3	4	55	475
1889-CC	Unc	13	150	950	23,500	27,500
1892-S	Unc	25	125	1,800	18,500	35,000
1902	Unc	5	4	9	450	1,500
1921 Peace	Unc	4	13	40	2,800	3,850
1924	Unc	3	3	5	75	550
1925	Unc	7	3	4	65	550
1934-S	Unc	15	60	275	10,000	7,000
Total		$94	$381	$3,156	$69,005	$104,400

Note: Silver dollars have always been a popular collecting field. This chart shows representative price changes of a mixture of scarce as well as common issues.

Source: R. S. Yeoman, *A Guide Book of United States Coins.* Fourth through forty-second editions, 1951–1989. Racine: Western Publishing Co., with permission.

TABLE 6. Price Performance of Eight Bullion-Related Gold Coins, 1950–1988

	Grade	1950	1960	1970	1980	1988
1904 $2.50	Unc	$ 14	$ 35	$ 65	$ 525	$ 900
1925-D $2.50	Unc	8	24	50	500	425
1901 $5	Unc	15	21	55	425	400
1909-D $5	Unc	14	20	80	800	1,000
1901-S $10	Unc	35	34	70	500	450
1932 $10	Unc	40	35	90	1,000	900
1904 $20	Unc	75	60	85	775	700
1927 $20	Unc	85	58	85	850	750
Total		$286	$287	$580	$5,375	$5,525

Note: The coins shown here are made of gold and respond more in relation to the price movement of precious metals than to the considerations of collecting. This is particularly true of the $5 to $20 denominations.

Source: R. S. Yeoman, *A Guide Book of United States Coins.* Fourth through forty-second editions, 1951–1989. Racine: Western Publishing Co., with permission.

TABLE 7. Price Performance of Ten Commemorative Coins, 1950–1988

	Grade	1950	1960	1970	1980	1988
Isabella quarter	Unc	$10	$ 39	$ 85	$ 1,200	$ 4,000
Lafayette $1	Unc	15	50	180	7,000	12,000
Albany fifty cents	Unc	6	28	50	625	950
Bridgeport fifty cents	Unc	4	12	28	400	1,100
California fifty cents	Unc	7	13	25	750	1,250
Cleveland fifty cents	Unc	3	6	18	160	875
Columbian fifty cents	Unc	2	5	9	120	1,500
Hawaii fifty cents	Unc	33	165	465	3,400	6,000
Norfolk fifty cents	Unc	8	33	58	900	900
Vermont fifty cents	Unc	7	28	38	1,000	1,900
Total		$95	$379	$956	$15,555	$30,475

Note: Price performances of selected silver commemorative coins over the years.

Source: R. S. Yeoman, *A Guide Book of United States Coins.* Fourth through forty-second editions, 1951–1989. Racine: Western Publishing Co., with permission.

TABLE 8. Price Performance of Five Territorial Gold Coins, 1950–1988

	Grade	1950	1960	1970	1980	1988
1849 Norris, Gregg and Norris, P. E. $5	Unc	$ 225	$ 385	$1,000	$ 8,000	$15,000
1849 Moffat $5	Unc	65	115	575	4,500	7,000
1849 Miners' Bank $10	Unc	575	1,500	3,500	25,000	27,500
1852 Wass Molitor $5	Unc	900	1,900	2,500	10,000	16,000
1860 Clark, Gruber $10	Unc	275	600	2,000	10,000	16,000
Total		$2,040	$4,500	$9,575	$57,500	$81,500

Note: During the developmental years of the American West, many private firms issued gold coins. This served as a convenience to the miners, who were distant from regular U.S. mints, and also served to furnish coins for use in circulation. Today, these privately issued gold coins, known as territorial issues, are avidly desired.

Source: R. S. Yeoman, *A Guide Book of United States Coins.* Fourth through forty-second editions, 1951–1989. Racine: Western Publishing Co., with permission.

GLOSSARY

Almost Uncirculated—Showing the slightest trace of wear.

authentication—Authoritative determination of the genuineness of a numismatic item.

bag marks—Minor abrasions on an otherwise Uncirculated coin caused by handling in mint bags.

Choice—A desirable, superior, or better-than-average numismatic item.

coin—Usually a piece of metal, marked with a device, issued by a governing authority and intended to be used as money.

condition—The state of preservation of a numismatic item; same as *grade*.

counterfeit—An object made to imitate a genuine numismatic piece with the intent to deceive or defraud.

Extremely Fine—Degree of physical condition, inferior to Almost Uncirculated.

Fine—Degree of physical condition, inferior to Very Fine.

gem—A relatively flawless numismatic item of superlative quality.

Good—Degree of physical condition, inferior to Very Good.

grade—The state of preservation of a numismatic item, expressed either descriptively (such as Very Good) or numerically (such as MS-60).

intrinsic—As applied to value, the net metallic value as distinguished from face value.

luster—The sheen or bloom on the surface of an Uncirculated numismatic object resulting from the centrifugal flow of metal caused by striking with dies.

mint—(1) A location where coins are struck, usually under the auspices of the government; (2) term for uncirculated, a condition or grade.

mintmark—A letter or other symbol indicating the mint of origin, for example, S, for San Francisco.

mint set—Grading term referring to a coin in condition as it left the mint; Uncirculated.

numismatics—The science, study, or collecting of coins, tokens, medals, paper money, and similar objects.

numismatist—One who studies rare coins or who collects them while at the same time learning their history.

obverse—The side of a numismatic item that bears the principal design or device.

patterns—A proposed coin prepared officially by the mint or prepared unofficially by an outside entrepreneur usually for submission to a coin-issuing authority.

Proof—A piece produced by a technique involving specially prepared dies and planchets and usually special striking resulting in sharpness of detail and flawless surfaces.

prooflike—Having a surface as flawless and brilliant, or nearly so, as a Proof but struck from working dies and sold to collectors as above-average specimens.

proof set—A set of one Proof coin for each denomination issued by a recognized mint for a specific year.

restrike—A numismatic item produced from original dies at a later date.

reverse—The side opposite to that on which the head or principal figure is impressed.

type set—A collection composed of one of each coin of a given series.

Uncirculated—A numismatic item in new condition, as issued by the mint.

Very Fine—Degree of physical condition, inferior to Extremely Fine.

Very Good—Degree of physical condition, inferior to Fine.

TRADE ORGANIZATIONS

American Numismatic Association, Colorado Springs, Colo.

American Numismatic Society, New York, N.Y.

International Association of Professional Numismatists, London, England

Professional Numismatists Guild, Van Nuys, Cal.

DIRECTORY OF DEALERS

David W. Akers, Inc., Miami Shores, Fla.

Bowers and Merena Galleries, Inc., Wolfeboro, N.H.

Christie's, New York, N.Y.

Cohen, Jerry, Beverly Hills, Cal.

Rarcoa, Chicago, Ill.

Sotheby Parke Bernet, New York, N.Y.

Stack's, New York, N.Y.

Superior Coin and Stamp, Beverly Hills, Cal.

J.J. Teaparty, Boston, Mass.

GRADING SERVICES

American Numismatic Association Certification Service, Colorado Springs, Colo.

Numismatic Guaranty Corporation of America, Parsippany, N.J.

Professional Coin Grading Service, Newport Beach, Cal.

SUGGESTED READING

PERIODICALS

Coin Dealer Newsletter. Published in Torrance, Cal. Weekly.

Coin World. Published in Sidney, Ohio. Weekly.

Numismatic News. Published in Iola, Wis. Weekly.

The Numismatist. Published in Colorado Springs, Colo. Monthly.

PRICE GUIDES

Krause Publications. *Auction Prices Realized.* Iola, Wis., 1982–1988. Annually.

Yeoman, R. S. *A Guide Book of United States Coins*, 42nd ed. Racine, Wis.: Western Publishing, 1989. Annually.

REFERENCE BOOKS

General/Historical

Bowers, Q. David. *Adventures With Rare Coins.* Los Angeles: Bowers and Ruddy Galleries, Inc., 1979.

______. *United States Gold Coins: An Illustrated History.* Wolfeboro, N.H.: Bowers and Marena Galleries, Inc., 1982.

______. *The History of United States Coins as Illustrated by the Garrett Collection.* Wolfeboro, N.H.: Bowers and Ruddy Galleries, Inc., 1979.

Breen, Walter. *Encyclopedia of U.S. and Colonial Coins.* New York: Doubleday, 1988.

Coin World Almanac, 5th ed. Sidney, Ohio: Amos Press, 1987.

Taxay, Don. *The U.S. Mint and Coinage.* New York: Arco Publishing, 1966.

______. *The Comprehensive Catalogue and Encyclopedia of United States Coins.* New York: Scott Publishing, 1976.

Grading Coins

Bagg, Richard A., and Jelinski, J.J., eds. *Grading Coins: A Collection of Readings.* Portsmouth: Essex Publications, 1977.

Bressett, Ken, and Kosoff, Abe, eds. *The Official American Numismatic Association Grading Standards for United States Coins*, 3rd ed. With an Introduction by Q. David Bowers. Colorado Springs: American Numismatic Association, and Racine, Wis.: Western Publishing, 1987.

Ruddy, James F. *Photograde: A Photographic Grading Encyclopedia for United States Coins.* Wolfeboro, N.H.: Bowers and Merena Galleries, 1988.

Investing in Rare Coins

Bowers, Q. David. *High Profits from Rare Coin Investment.* Wolfeboro, N.H.: Bowers and Merena Galleries, 1988.

______. *Collecting Rare Coins for Profit.* New York: Harper & Row, 1975.

Berman, Neil S. *The Investor's Guide to United States Coins.* New York: Coin and Currency Institute, 1986.

Forman, Harry J. *How You Can Make Big Profits Investing in Coins.* New York: Nummus Press, 1972.

Hoppe, Donald J. *How to Invest in Gold Coins.* New York: Arco Publishing, 1973.

Specific Areas of Interest

Akers, David W. *United States Gold Coins: An Analysis of Auction Records*, 6 vols. Englewood, Ohio: Paramount Publications, 1975–1982.

Breen, Walter. *U.S. Gold Coins*. Chicago: Hewitt, 1964–1966.

Crosby, Sylvesters. *The Early Coins of America*. Reprinted. Lawrence, Mass.: Quarterman Publications, 1974.

Judd, J. Hewitt. *United States Patterns, Experimental and Trial Pieces*, 7th ed. Racine, Wis.: Western Publishing, 1982.

Kagin, Donald H. *Private Gold Coins and Patterns of the United States*. New York: Arco Publishing, 1981.

Miller, Wayne. *The Morgan and Peace Dollar Textbook*. Helena, Mont.: Adam Smith Publishing, n.d.

Sheldon, William H. *Penny Whimsy*. Reprinted. Lawrence, Mass.: Quarterman Publications, 1976.

COLLECTIBLES

Charles E. Wooley
Gary Darrow

BASIC CHARACTERISTICS

Collectibles represent the synthesis of technology and the human urge for entertainment. Whether they take the form of baseball cards, movie posters, or antique toys, they are the modern equivalent of the primitive amusements found in all nonindustrial societies. In addition to providing enjoyment, collectibles help preserve and transmit information about American culture that would otherwise be lost, and they almost always either retain or gain value. If you're tired of the same old investments, and you're not looking for a quick return on your money, collectibles are an enjoyable alternative.

Several things influence the decision to purchase collectibles, including their scarcity, significance, and condition. The number one factor that influences a buyer to make a purchase, however, is the personal reason. If the collectible is related to the buyer's childhood or has some other personal significance, chances are it will be bought, even if it is not in the best condition. Of course, a collector buys carefully whenever making a purchase, but an item in mediocre condition can always be upgraded.

Major Categories

Thousands of categories fall under the vague term "collectible," including autographs, beer cans, bottle openers, cameras, cigarette lighters, circus memorabilia, combs, fishing tackle, medals, menus, old fountain pens, photographs, pipes, political souvenirs,

---

Charles E. Wooley is an author and consultant in the collectible investment field; he prepared this article in its original form for the first edition. Gary Darrow is the owner of Darrow's Fun Antiques, New York, New York; he revised and updated this article.

postcards, radio premiums, punchboards, scrimshaw, sheet music, telephones, comic watches, and World's Fair souvenirs. All these things are fun to collect, but the most important factor in starting a collection is finding the category or subject that is meaningful to you personally. It is best to collect items that mean something to you—or to your past, your family, or your profession. (If you use your collection to decorate your place of business, it becomes a tax write off.)

Few collectibles possess serious investment potential, although the nine collectible categories described in the following paragraphs have established themselves as legitimate investment media during the last twenty years. Active markets, in which investment-grade merchandise is regularly traded, exist for all of them.

Advertisements. Color printing techniques became widespread in the 1850s, and popular advertising collectibles date from that decade onward. Older advertising pieces do exist, mostly in the form of three-dimensional object signs, but these are extremely scarce, and most collections of advertisements commence with the introduction of color printing.

Advertising collectibles are often divided into three technological time frames. First, there are the early pieces produced from 1850 to 1890. The great majority of these are simply colorful, postcard-type scenes printed on small sheets of paper. These pictures may or may not be related to the item being advertised. Second, there are the advertising messages printed between 1890 and 1920. Stone lithography was perfected during the 1890s, and the brilliantly rich colors that are found on advertising pieces of that era are unequaled. As technology blossomed, printers learned to print color onto metal, and the most desirable metal advertising pieces also date from that period. Produce labels and Coca-Cola trays are examples of highly desirable items produced during the same era.

Finally, collectors seek advertising objects produced from 1920 through World War II. The color printing process known as photolithography was widely used by 1920. The colors produced by this process are not as rich as those that were previously made with stone lithography. However, the fascinating themes that occur during this period tend to compensate for the muted colors. Further, neon and other gaseous signs were introduced in this country from France in about 1924; choice examples are scarce and in great demand.

Recently produced neon is also collectible. Signs and clocks made from the 1930s through the 1960s can be found for less than $1,000; neon beer signs can be bought for less than $200. These later signs have a place in history, not to mention the fact that they look great in the game or recreation room.

Baseball Cards. First issued during the 1860s and still marketed in quantity today, baseball cards have always been a popular collectible. Now more than ever, people are buying mint sets of cards and never touching them. There are rookie cards from the 1980s bringing close to $100 (book value). There seems to be no end in sight, because today's kids collect the cards of today. Today's rookies are tomorrow's superstars. I don't know how many collectors are willing to spend $10,000 for a 1952 Mickey Mantle rookie card, but I'm sure there are a few. With baseball cards, it is important to collect cards that are in top condition.

Comic Books. Comic books were originally marketed as collections of comic strip reprints. They quickly became the most popular entertainment for kids too old to play with toys (all this, of course, before television). Comic books have traditionally featured superheroes who could single-handedly defeat the Nazis, spies from unfriendly countries, or any evil empire trying to take over the United States or some colorful character, such as Donald Duck, who gets into trouble, learns a lesson, and makes amends.

The comic book format was standardized in 1933, when Max Gaines produced *Funnies on Parade,* the first modern comic book. Five years later, the most successful character ever, Superman, made his debut in the June 1938 issue of *Action Comics #1,* now worth about $20,000. The wonderful superheroes from Marvel Comics were born in the early 1960s. The first issues of *The Amazing Spiderman, X-MEN, The Fantastic Four,* and *Daredevil* are much sought after and, if found in really clean, like-new condition, can bring around $100 from a dealer. The first ten issues of a comic book are usually the most desired, but there are exceptions, such as the first appearance of a newly introduced villain or hero.

Fantasy Art. Fantasy artwork includes pictorial elements, such as elves and dragons, that are not found in real life. This type of art became widespread in the United States during the 1890s, when major artists, such as Aubrey Beardsley, began experimenting with the genre at the same time that color printing techniques were perfected. In response, such illustrators as Parrish, Pyle, Mucha, and Wyeth created fantasy artwork for various markets, including the mainstream magazines of the day. America's fascination with the pictorially fantastic reached a peak during the 1930s with the sensuous magazine covers of Margaret Brundage and the animation art of Disney, Fleischer, and Iwerks.

Animation Art. The hottest new collectible is animation art. A cel (short for celluloid) is a painting (for example, of Mickey Mouse or other cartoon characters) on a clear sheet of acetate, usually 10″ × 12″ or larger. Cels are the basic building blocks of animation. There are two kinds of cel paintings—production cels and limited edition cels. Production cels are strictly one of a kind and actually appear in an animated cartoon, filmed in sequence to create the illusion of motion. Limited edition cels are created expressly as fine art and have not appeared in a film. The artist, not limited by the constraints of a particular film, presents the characters in classic poses, just the way he wants them to be remembered. Limited editions are small in number, and the cels are often numbered and hand-signed by the animator.

Popeye, Superman, Porky Pig, Betty Boop, all the Disney characters, and more can be found. Look for the characters you loved as a child, and you can build a collection of animation art that will not only appreciate in value but bring back fond memories. Cels can range in price from $60,000 down to $25 for animation art from television commercials. Any animation art is a good investment as long as you get a receipt that assures it is genuine.

Movie Memorabilia. First produced about 1896, movie-related items have been collectible for many decades. Many different types of items qualify as movie memorabilia. Aside from the films themselves, the studios issued a variety of posters, cards, and glossy stills, as well as an assortment of press kits. They also granted licenses to numerous publishers and novelty promoters who issued items that either were outright movie adaptations or featured major studio stars.

Further, the studios have sold many of their own props at public auction. Around 1970, a pair of Dorothy's ruby slippers (worn by Judy Garland in the 1939 MGM production of

The Wizard of Oz) sold at the MGM auction for about $10,000. More recently, old Disney cartoon posters, which regularly sold for $4 or $5 in the 1960s, have begun selling at public auction for as much as $2,000.

When Ronald Reagan became president elect in 1980, many items from his movie career increased in value by a multiple of 10 to 100 almost overnight. During his presidency, Reagan material was in great demand and appreciated in value. Now that Reagan is no longer president, his movie career items are not as sought after.

Posters. Poster art, accessible to more people than fine art, is becoming increasingly desirable. Prices realized at gallery auctions, as well as at quality antique and collectible shows, have dramatically increased during the past decade.

Certain posters, such as those produced for advertising purposes and by movie studios, are mentioned above. Others, however, such as the magnificent propoganda posters created during both world wars, fit into their own categories.

Most collectors feel that a poster's value lies in both its graphic design and its historical context. Largely because of this, many posters from the turn of the century have commanded prices in the $3,000 to $6,000 range. A world record was set when an incomplete version of Toulouse-Lautrec's first poster, *Moulin Rouge*, sold at auction for $52,000.

Games. The ancient Sumerians produced the oldest extant games thousands of years before Christ's birth, and nontechnological peoples throughout the world still produce games of their own, independent of modern influences. Most collectors, however, only purchase games that contain colorful boards or boxes. The first such game produced in the United States, the Mansion of Happiness, was initially offered for sale in the mid-1840s. Of great historical significance, it is credited with the creation of the basic linear progression format, in which players follow a prearranged course, which has come to be characteristic of modern games.

American games have always reflected contemporary life in a clear and dramatic manner. Just a few years after baseball was officially created, a version of our national pastime was marketed as a boxed game. As bicycling became a national fad in 1890s, board games captured on pulp paper the characteristics of high-wheeling. The international sport of ping pong was created as a boxed game in about 1901. During the Depression, many games were issued that enabled the players to become wealthy, if only on paper; the original Monopoly game, first issued in 1935, is a classic and valuable example. In the past decade, games about space exploration have proliferated and become collectible. Currently, the most desirable games are those issued by Parker and McLoughlin Brothers during the era of perfected stone lithography (1890 to 1920).

Toys. Antique toys are fun to collect. They also represent simpler times, of horse-drawn carts, the Industrial Revolution, the radio as the center of entertainment in the home, or the golden age of television.

Cast-iron cars, trucks, and banks all have a wonderful charm. For very good examples, expect to pay a fair amount of money, $500 or more. Some of the major manufacturers were Arcade, Dent, Wilkins, Williams, Stevens, Kenton, Hubley, Ives, Harris, Carpenter, and Kilgore. Unfortunately, most of these manufacturers did not mark their toys with their names or trademarks; they simply stamped an inventory or a mold number somewhere on the bottom. Because of the increase in value of these toys in recent years, there are more reproductions than ever before. The only way to avoid them is to follow a few simple guidelines.

1. Check the quality of the casting. The iron toys made today generally have a rough instead of a smooth surface. In addition, the castings on most of the reproductions do not fit together as well as they do on originals. Sharp edges and grind marks are common on reproductions.
2. Examine the paint. The patina on old iron toys is hard to capture with the paints of today; the aging process naturally darkens and the paints fade slightly with time, unless well preserved and kept away from sunlight. In looking for signs of a reproduction, note burn marks, obvious scratches, and other unnatural aging.
3. Always ask the dealer for a receipt with an approximate date of when the toy was made, just for your own information. This document gives you recourse if you later find you've been taken. Be wary of dealers unwilling to provide such a receipt—and this advice goes for all collectibles.

Character toys are in demand now more than ever. America's fascination with the comics dates back to 1896 when Richard Outcault's *Yellow Kid* comic first appeared in the *New York Journal.* Since then, the comic strip has reflected society in a way no other medium could have.

Buster Brown and his dog Tige first appeared around 1902. Other popular comic characters that debuted around the turn of the century were the Katzenjammer Kids (1896) and Mutt and Jeff (1907). In the 1920s and 1930s, we had the cartoon strips of Skeezix (who was left on the doorstep of Uncle Walt, in *Gasoline Alley*), Barney Google and Spark Plug, Moon Mullins, Felix the Cat, Mickey Mouse, Blondie and Dagwood, Henry, Alley Oop, Li'l Abner, and Happy Hooligan. These characters were all immortalized in the form of toys.

Comic character toys dating from the 1920s and 1930s are sought after by collectors and dealers from all over the world. The toy manufacturers used everything from paper to cast iron to make toys of every description. The one thing the investor should consider more than anything else when buying a toy from any period is its condition. For investment purposes, a comic toy should have its original box; there should be no fading in the color, and no cracks or chips.

Toys from the 1940s and 1950s are very collectible. There are markets for items from the 1960s and 1970s, as well.

Special Attributes

Perishability. Most collectibles are extremely fragile and are created for limited use. Many comic books are offered at newsstand sale for a period of only two days. Fantasy artwork that appeared in magazines such as the original *Life* was intended to survive only until the next week's issue came out. Advertisements are rarely continued for more than a month. Movie memorabilia generally endure only until the motion picture concludes its original run. And many toys do not survive beyond Christmas morning.

Even collectibles with better survival prospects, such as games and baseball cards, are not created to last for more than a few years. Approximately 500,000 copies of *Action Comics #1*, in which Superman first appeared, were originally printed; about forty-five still exist. Before they were perceived as legitimate investment media, collectibles survived only in curious ways, and then primarily by chance. Very few have survived in fine condition.

Timeliness. The best collectibles are very timely. Baseball cards traditionally feature current players, not those who have retired. Comic book superheroes fight menaces of immediate danger to the nation: Nazis in World War II and environmental pollution and nuclear destruction today. Just as few games issued during the 1930s dealt with space exploration, so there are few new games that concern earning a fortune from a minimal investment. A good collectible directly reflects the contemporary culture that produced it.

Mass-Market Appeal. Collectibles are intended to possess widespread appeal. For the most part, they originally retail for a nominal amount, and thus the producers must rely on a large volume of sales to earn a profit. In order to accomplish this, most issuers of collectibles package their products in a dramatic, even gaudy, fashion. An investment-grade collectible, therefore, not only will have mass appeal when issued, but will similarly appeal to a wide variety of collectors in later years. The best collectibles make impressive display pieces, either framed or in a case.

Continuing Production. The collectibles with the best investment potential mark either the beginnings or the high points of specific collectible genres that are still being produced. The reason for this phenomenon seems to be that some people who enjoy the contemporary products decide that they would like to see and own significant earlier examples. In all the collectible fields discussed here, new merchandise is being created today, helping sustain and increase the value of top-grade collectible investments by generating new collectors year after year. For example, Roger Rabbit collectibles are in demand, and the new Batman movie, released in 1989, may spark a refurbished interest in related collectibles.

How Collectibles Differ From Traditional Investments

Collectibles Are Tangible Objects. The value of collectibles lies in their physical being. They do not represent something in the way that a Treasury bill represents an obligation of the U.S. government. Rather, the collectible itself is an object of value. If one needs cash quickly, a tangible investment that can be picked up and carried to a broker may be preferable to a bond, which promises to pay a certain amount at a given time in the future. On the other hand, if one loses a Treasury bill receipt or a stock certificate, the paper can be replaced. If one loses a prized collectible, it is unlikely that it will ever return. Further, if one accidentally creases the corner of a stock certificate, the stock retains its full value. If the corner of the only known near-mint copy of *Marvel Comics #1* were creased, it would instantly be worth about $4,000 less.

Market Is Not Standardized. In the stock market, anyone with sufficient cash can quickly and easily find a broker. Further, such investors realize that specific stocks are virtually always available and can be purchased within a narrow price range; market value seldom varies more than two points in a single day.

The purchase of investment-grade collectibles is a very different matter. Prices are not standardized, and very rare items may be traded only once or twice each decade. Further, few dealers clearly understand the history of their field or its market dynamics, because of scarcity of rare collectibles and the rapid rise of the market.

Importance of Expertise. The acquisition of investment-grade collectibles is best accomplished in one of two ways. The lowest acquisition prices are realized by the investor who is willing to become an expert in a given field. Such a person will read the available literature and initiate contact with major dealers who are willing to impart the information they possess to the serious investor. By becoming friendly with a variety of such dealers, the investor finds that most are occasionally willing to sell rare collectibles at substantially below market value.

The investor who lacks the time or desire to become so intimately involved with the field should instead find a reputable dealer who is willing to sell investment-grade material at current market value. Since market value is often difficult for the nonprofessional to determine, however, it is necessary that the dealer be honest and well informed. When a dealer of known integrity agrees with a purchaser on the price of a choice collectible, they actually create fair market value by virtue of completing the sale. Thus, it is particularly important to choose a dealer whose judgment one trusts.

ATTRACTIVE FEATURES

Growth Potential

Since many people still do not consider collectibles to be particularly desirable, many outstanding investment opportunities exist. Most major museums are devoting increasing display space to collectibles; it is only a matter of time before collectibles are widely perceived as being as legitimate an investment as other tangibles. As their role in our culture becomes more widely understood, the demand for choice collectibles is growing. Further, as investors increasingly perceive collectibles as legitimate investments, new collectors enter the marketplace.

Coin and stamp collectors point with pride to the strength of their market, which they often relate to the existence of millions of numismatists and philatelists worldwide. Many investors fail to realize, however, that there are millions of comic book and toy collectors too. As with coins and stamps, such broad interest is the hallmark of a healthy market.

Because of this worldwide demand, investment-grade collectibles are selling for ever-increasing prices. Almost every week some specific collectible sets a new price record. Beyond question, the best collectibles are being recognized worldwide as legitimate investment media. This realization in itself is certain to infuse new money into the marketplace, and that new money will compete for, and increase the value of, the best investment-grade collectibles.

Given this apparent inevitability, based on past market performance and steadily increasing interest among various types of investors, it would seem that this is an excellent time to invest in fine collectibles. In a time when more traditional investment media, such as fine art and household furnishings, climb in value, collectibles may do even better than the more established tangible investment media because many more people can afford them.

Few Sophisticated Buyers

Persons who invest in widely accepted media, such as stocks, bonds, and Treasury bills, are in constant competition with other well-trained investors. At present, however, there are few sophisticated, investment-oriented buyers in the collectibles market. Given the allure of substantial values that are increasing with dramatic speed, this situation is bound to change. Those experienced investors who enter the marketplace early, however, will find little real competition.

Enjoyment

There is much fun to be had in the purchase, ownership, and sale of collectibles. Compared to that of the floor of the Chicago Board of Trade, the general level of competition is minimal, and this relatively relaxed atmosphere helps to make working conditions pleasant. Then, too, looking for an investment in a good transportation toy can be an experience that is much more enjoyable (not to mention rewarding) than looking for a good transportation stock. Similarly, inspecting a comic book for defects can be infinitely more pleasing than inspecting a New York City bond for defects. Collectibles are created to be entertaining, and investing in them usually is entertaining also.

Relative Market Stability

Many institutional investors still perceive collectibles as a faddish investment with values liable to crash at any moment. However, at least 98 percent of all collectibles are controlled not by dealers who must trade continually to survive, but by individuals who normally resist selling under any circumstances. The market is, in that sense, very stable. Further, most collectors have been motivated to assemble their collections out of love for their chosen fields and the desire to possess specific pieces. Many are aware of the investment potential present in their collectibles, but that is usually secondary to them. Their primary goal is simply to own and enjoy, on a long-term or permanent basis, the objects that comprise their collections.

Because of this, the collectibles marketplace has never experienced a dramatic general sell-off, such as what happened to the stock market on October 19, 1987 or when gold reached $900 per ounce. Unlike investors who own stocks and bonds because they wish to profit from their ownership, collectors own collectibles because they wish to own the objects collected. This situation would seem to preclude the possibility of significant panic selling in the collectibles market during the foreseeable future.

The collectibles market, then, seems as unlikely to crash as does the quality antiques market, and for much the same reasons. Naturally, it is possible that certain values might slide, but the possibility that a typical investment-grade collectible will lose its value during the foreseeable future is small.

POTENTIAL RISKS

Although there are tremendous profits to be made by wisely investing in collectibles, there are distinct risks.

Misrepresentation

Investors must be certain that the investment-grade collectibles they are buying are actually in the condition in which they believe them to be. One of the greatest risks faced by the novice is winding up with items of lower quality.

Volatility

Investors also must consider the relationship between popular taste and collectible values. Collectibles that decline in popularity do not appreciate as quickly as those that must be divided among ever-growing numbers of collectors. Even if the number of collectors increases steadily, the sale of a collectible still should be timed to take advantange of the various market cycles. Poor judgment can be costly.

Government Regulation

Government intrusion into the marketplace also may affect values adversely. Coins and stamps, the tangibles of choice for many trust and Keogh plans, suddenly became subject to millions of dollars being withdrawn annually from their marketplace by government fiat. Other market disruptions are certainly possible.

Reproductions and Forgeries

Most investment-grade collectibles are printed in a variety of colors, and this makes them difficult to forge convincingly. Unscrupulous persons do attempt forgeries on occasion, but in the past these have apparently been successfully distributed only when the forged item was a black-and-white piece. We don't know of any attempt to forge a complete four-color comic book. However, one convict (in jail for counterfeiting) made some four-color 1952 Mickey Mantle baseball cards, several of which may still be in circulation.

There have been attempts to forge cast-iron toys in the past, but in such instances the forgers, lacking access to the original master molds, were forced to make their forgeries from actual toys. This method always results in loss of detail, and the forgeries, although they have fooled casual collectors, should be obvious to professional dealers.

Most collectibles cannot be forged convincingly enough to fool an expert. Novice investors must rely on either the professional dealers or their own common sense. People do try to forge black-and-white items and easily copied metal pieces, although these pieces must be of distinct value to make the illegal enterprise worthwhile. Some color baseball cards have been forged. However, color and metal forgeries probably will not withstand careful scrutiny when professionals compare them with original items.

At any rate, even though a certain risk does exist, there is generally a much smaller risk of encountering forgeries in the collectibles marketplace than in most of the other tangibles marketplaces. A reputable dealer should be willing to guarantee authenticity if asked to do so.

Effect of Warehouse Finds

A warehouse find involves the discovery of a large quantity of a specific type of collectible. Usually, such finds occur when someone searches a printer's personal files or gains access to stores that have been closed, complete with contents, for a very long time. A quantity of a given collectible, heretofore unknown, might thereby emerge onto the marketplace.

If such a find is handled properly, the hoard will quietly find its way into the hands of private collectors who are happy to pay market value for the items. More often than not, this delicate situation is handled tactfully, and the market emerges stronger than ever. Occasionally, however, an inexperienced dealer runs across a warehouse find and virtually destroys all confidence in the value of a specific collectible.

Luckily, this happens only very rarely. During the 1970s, several warehouse finds made their way into the hands of comic book dealers. All but one of these finds were handled properly, however, and the market was strengthened in most cases. The risk of a warehouse find adversely affecting the value of a particular piece does exist, but the odds of it affecting any given investment are minimal.

Physical Risks

Most items that have become collectibles are extremely fragile. Because the items were intended to be used quickly and discarded, manufacturers gave little thought to making them capable of withstanding the rigors of aging; in fact, an overwhelming majority of paper items utilize the cheapest pulp paper available. Such paper normally contains a high sulfur content that will destroy the cellular bonds that hold paper fibers together unless that process is prevented; temperatures of more than 60 degrees greatly accelerate the process. If left in a normal environment, pulp paper will crumble into dust in 50 to 100 years.

Most collectibles that are not made of paper are made, at least in part, of metal. As with paper items, metal collectibles are not intended to endure for long periods. They are not rust-proofed, and many fine old metal toys that are stored in a normal household eventually will begin to rust.

In addition to their intrinsic fragility or obsolescence, collectibles are subject to a variety of environmental hazards. If they are purchased in excellent condition, however, they are relatively easy to keep that way. (See *Custodial Care*, later in this article.)

TAX CONSEQUENCES

Capital Gains

A collectible purchased as an investment is a capital asset for federal income tax purposes. Profit from the sale of such a collectible is taxed as long-term capital gain, to an individual who has owned it for more than a year. Since the very best short-range profits are made by investing in collectibles just as the demand for them is about to rise and selling them just as demand peaks (a process that usually takes one to two years), this type of investment can take full advantage of the long-term capital gains tax, if lower rates for capital gains exist. Presently the rates are the same for long-term as for short-term capital gains or ordinary income.

Controlling the Year of Taxation

Another advantage of investing in collectibles is that one can control when one is taxed. Many investors buy collectibles when their income is high and sell them when their income is low.

Furthermore, those who invest in collectibles can increase their net profit by controlling how frequently their profits are taxed. Until the taxable sale or exchange of a collectible occurs, one need not pay any tax on its increased value. In comparison, one usually must pay taxes on the earnings from the bank account every year, and earnings from the bank account are necessarily smaller because of the tax owed on it. Since the government does not tax the increased value of collectibles until they are actually sold, however, the collectibles investor is able to realize compounded appreciation in value each year without taxation until a sale.

As compared with many investments, then, collectibles are taxed at favorable rates and give the investor some control as to when and how frequently he is taxed.

For a more detailed discussion of tax factors, including deductions for contributions of tangibles to qualified organizations, see article "Tax Considerations for Collector-Investors," elsewhere in this volume. For complete guidance in these matters, a professional tax advisor should be consulted.

REPRESENTATIVE TYPES OF INVESTORS

Private Individuals

Most investors in the collectibles field are private individuals. They range from the impoverished to the wealthy, and they live in all parts of the United States, Western Europe, and Japan. These investors are divided into three groups: those who buy collectibles primarily for fun and nostalgia (keeping a reasonable eye open for value and investment potential); those who believe that collectibles are valuable as an intrinsic part and reflection of our culture; and those who buy collectibles strictly for profit. Some, of course, collect for all these reasons; but for most, one or another motive is primary.

Universities

As universities come to realize that the popular culture of technological societies is equivalent to the myth and folklore of primitive societies, they become increasingly interested in collectibles. As such items become better appreciated as a valuable—and very accessible—subject for research, more and more papers are being written at the university level about movies, comic books, and other collectibles. Bowling Green, Syracuse, and Berkeley are currently the academic leaders in the development of popular culture resources.

Museums

Many major museums now display collectibles. The Metropolitan Museum of Art in New York hung a striking paper ephemeron collection in May 1976. Since this show, an ever-increasing number of museums are devoting attention to the cultural and aesthetic value of collectibles.

Corporations

Although there are currently few corporate investors active in the collectibles marketplace, many seem likely to enter into it. Certain corporations already are assembling significant collections of toys and advertisements.

IMPORTANT FACTORS IN BUYING AND SELLING

Dual Markets

All collectibles markets operate simultaneously on retail and wholesale levels. To realize full retail price at any given moment, the seller must take a variety of factors into account. However, collectibles can always be sold immediately on the wholesale market. In that sense, collectibles are as liquid as stocks. Prices thus realized average about one half of retail for investment-grade items, but it is possible to liquidate a major collection on wholesale terms in just one day. The fear that collectibles can be very difficult to sell is simply not true.

Grading

Most beginning collectors find it difficult to describe accurately the physical condition of collectibles. The purpose of this descriptive process, called grading, is to define how near an item is to being in perfect condition. A collectible's age has no relationship to its grade. Since its value is based predominantly on its grade, it is important for the investor to either learn to grade collectibles or find a reputable dealer to do it.

Typically, collectibles are graded on a scale of approximately twenty points, ranging from poor to fair, good, very good, fine, very fine, near mint, mint, and pristine mint. Each of these has its own refinements. For example, the difference between fine-minus and fine-plus currently can amount to several thousand dollars on a key collectible.

How does someone become an accurate grader? Trial and error is the best method. The new collector should read whatever literature is available and then attempt to grade a number of items. Most price guides and specialty publications contain guidelines for grading. Once an understanding of the grading system has been developed, the collector should approach as many dealers as possible, perhaps at a specialty convention, and quiz them about the condition of various items. A certain amount of disagreement is to be found even among professionals, but each field also has a hard-core group of dealers who grade very strictly. Since grading is very important, it is advisable to locate these dealers and buy from them.

Market Cycles

Collectibles markets develop in related cycles, and it is critical that the investor understand the nature of these cycles. Investors whose timing is inaccurate will tie up their capital needlessly.

Collectors tend to make as many discriminations of collectibles types as they can. Thus, comic book collectors divide their field into about seventy types of comics, such as superhero, war, love, adventure, western, and horror. Baseball card collectors regularly discriminate among manufacturers, individual teams, and different styles of cards. All nine of the basic collectibles fields discussed above have numerous subcategories.

The key to understanding market cycles is to realize that collectors tend to focus their energies on one type of item at a time. When these items become hot, dealers cannot hold onto them. When superhero comics are hot, dealers with fair prices find that their superhero comics sell as soon as they reach the market. All of this consumer interest, and the subsequent depletion of dealers' stocks, results in a typical supply and demand situation that forces up the market value of hot items. Meanwhile, most of the other types of comics sell less quickly, each following its own market cycle.

In a major marketplace like that governing comic books, about seventy separate cycles operate at once. Naturally, the best time to purchase any given type of item is when the demand for that type is at its lowest ebb, as most dealers are anxious to move slow sellers. In fact, investors can often buy items at the lowest point on the demand cycle at a very favorable price.

Similarly, the best time to sell is when the demand is just about to peak. These cycles take an average of three to eight years to progress through a full turn, and full retail is realized quickly when the demand is peaking. Investors should take careful note of this and plan to purchase and sell accordingly. The cycles are particularly important because most collectors are unaware that they exist. Consequently, many tend to buy while the demand is rising and sell when the demand has fallen.

Investors should also note that these ostensibly separate cycles are, in fact, related to one another in an orchestrated fashion. Over the long term, relative market values seldom fluctuate widely. Investors who understand this can make dramatic short-term gains.

For example, one type of comic begins a sharp upward journey in demand. This type of collectible (e.g., superhero comics) thus becomes hot. Meanwhile, other types of comics (e.g., Donald Duck comics) are apparently following their own independent market cycles. Within a period of about a year, the hot superhero comics have nearly doubled in value while the cool Donald Duck comics have maintained the same basic price level.

At about this point, two market phenomena occur simultaneously. First, the demand for superhero comics begins to cool. Collectors, realizing that the same superhero comics cost twice as much today as they did a year ago, decide that they are unwilling to pay the ever-increasing prices that dealers are forced to ask. Thus, the demand for (though not the value of) superhero comics begins to decline.

Meanwhile, the dealers are not overly concerned, as they realize that this merely means that some other type of comic will now become hot. For example, the collectors of Donald Duck comics, which were at a low point on their own demand scale when the superhero comics were peaking, now stop to consider the current market. They realize that their favorite comic, which in the past usually was valued at half the worth of superheroes, is now valued at only one quarter. As this realization spreads among collectors, the demand for Donald Duck comics will increase dramatically as collectors rush to purchase those comics before the market again balances. The pent-up demand of these collectors then bursts forth, and the Donald Duck comics themselves become hot as the demand for them shoots sharply upward.

Since all seventy types of comics follow their own demand curves at all times, these curves will be in varying positions relative to each other at any given moment. Over the long term, however, relative values have remained remarkably consistent, regardless of the collectibles genre, and short-term fluctuations in value have tended to eventually regain the relative market values that were established in the middle 1960s. For those who understand market cycles, knowing the best time to buy and sell becomes simple.

Price Guides

An accurate price guide is a boon to investors in any collectibles marketplace. Unfortunately, few, if any, price guides are totally accurate. It is critical for the sophisticated investor to understand the limitations under which most price guides operate. Inaccuracies occasionally occur even in generally accurate guides, such as Overstreet's *Comic Book Price Guide*, and for arguably legitimate reasons. For example, let us examine the history of the Overstreet *Price Guide* values of a very rare, anti-Communist comic book known as *Blood Is the Harvest*, which was published by the Catholic Church in 1950. First listed in the Overstreet *Price Guide* in 1973 (presumably Overstreet was unaware of its existence previously), a mint copy was valued at $2. By 1977, its value was officially $9, and in 1978, mint copies were listed at $45.

During this period, various collectors discussed with Overstreet the fact that because there were only two known copies of this historically important comic, a fairer value for it would be between $500 and $1,000. However, Overstreet refused to raise his valuation significantly because his *Price Guide* is a report of prices asked and sales made. Overstreet was worried that if he increased the valuation of *Blood Is the Harvest* without the justification of an actual sale, he might be blamed for attempting to manipulate the market.

During 1979, a Catholic priest surfaced at a Philadelphia comic convention with approximately nine copies of *Blood,* as well as various other comics that the Church had published during the 1950s; he sold these comics to several dealers for a total of about $10,000. These dealers, aware of the true importance of *Blood,* proceeded to ask and receive an average of about $1,200 per copy. Overstreet then raised his valuation of *Blood* from $45 in 1978 to $1,200 in 1979.

In retrospect, it is clear the *Blood Is the Harvest* was worth far more than the $45 listed in Overstreet's guide in 1978. After all, even with an official *Price Guide* value of $45, dealers still managed to sell all the copies they could acquire for about $1,200 each. On the other hand, one may respect Overstreet's determination to avoid influencing the market in advance of actual sales.

To sum up, price guides are very useful tools, but they have their limits. Investors should note carefully that the greatest profits in the collectibles field are made by those who possess the courage and foresight to predict future values, not by those who merely rely on last year's market reports.

CUSTODIAL CARE

Preservation of Materials

Most collectibles from the popular culture were not made to last. In particular, paper is liable to disintegrate over a long period, and metal is liable to rust. However, professional restoration experts (on staff at many major museums) can neutralize the acid content in pulp paper, thus preventing the cellular breakdown that would otherwise occur. As for metal collectibles, they tend to rust only if their environment is humid.

Collectibles can be kept in excellent condition by maintaining the humidity level at about 40 percent and the temperature at 50 to 60 degrees. Collectibles can be stored in such a fashion for many years without requiring further care.

Collectibles that are stored or displayed under adverse conditions constitute a different matter, however. For example, a curator who decides to display a grouping of World War II posters in a bank lobby should have the acid content of the paper neutralized before the acid is energized by the adverse effects of sunlight, heat, and air pollution.

Environmental Hazards

Collectibles are occasionally subjected to more dramatic dangers than inappropriate temperature and humidity. For example, many fine collectibles have been destroyed when basements have flooded; others have been damaged by earthquake and tornado. Vermin, particularly mice and silverfish, but also cockroaches, rats, and bats, have destroyed innumerable fine pieces. Further, air pollution is as dangerous to collectibles as it is to asthmatics. Perhaps the most bizarre environmental hazard of all is that constituted by other collectibles, as acids and molds can migrate from one paper to another. Thus, choice paper items must not be stored with pieces in poorer condition.

All the commonly used transport companies (including the post office, air freight, boats, trains, and trucks) have damaged fine collectibles. Unfortunately, theft is also an ever-present danger. Therefore, valuable items are often stored in safe-deposit boxes.

Insurance

As with other tangible investments, valuable collectibles should be insured. Further, with prices increasing dramatically, it is advisable to have them reappraised every few years.

MARKETS FOR COLLECTIBLES

There are eight basic types of collectibles marketplace and seven types of dealer engaged in them. A brief examination of these types will enable the investor to choose the best market situation and type of dealer.

Periodicals

Three basic types of periodicals serve as marketplaces for the investor. They are the general interest newspapers or magazines that carry advertisements for collectibles among many other kinds of merchandise, such as *The New York Times;* the collector's magazines, which carry advertisements directed at collectors generally, such as *The Antique Trader;* and the specialty publications, which are directed at a very narrow audience, such as *Antique Toy World.*

Most of the collectibles transactions that result from a public notice in a periodical are conducted through the mail. Because of the frequency of mail fraud, it is necessary to take greater precautions with these transactions than are normally required in face-to-face transactions. Buyers should be certain that any item not in the condition described can be returned for a complete refund; it is also wise to put in writing that the shipper is responsible for insuring the parcel and to try to telephone the seller before sending a check or money order. If it is impossible to contact the seller by telephone, it may be just as difficult to collect the merchandise.

Flea Markets

These sales, conducted all over the country on a weekly basis, are advertised in both general circulation and trade publications. They normally feature between 20 and 400 dealers, and the larger gatherings often have a tremendous display of prized collectibles. What makes flea markets so attractive to collectors is that key pieces are often available at bargain prices, because flea market dealers handle a vast array of material for which they pay very little and which they prefer to turn over quickly. Further, these dealers, like many other collectibles dealers, are often willing to haggle over prices.

When shopping at flea markets, it is best to arrive as early as the first dealers do. Although the best bargains do not always sell before the public arrives, it is true that the exceptional values normally sell to the first person who recognizes them as such. It should also be noted that more reproductions are turning up at flea markets than ever before. Know what you're buying, or at least get written assurance as to the age of an item, as well as the dealer's home address.

Antique Shops

The typical antique shop is a mom and pop operation, run by an independent individual who has a broad knowledge of many fields and an in-depth expertise in one or two. Most antique shops feature a wide assortment of merchandise, some of which is fairly priced and a small percentage of which is underpriced. Investors seeking to make acquisitions through the antique shop circuit should obtain antique shop directories and then map out an efficient shopping tour in advance. These directories are available through antique trade papers, flea markets, antique shops, better business bureaus, and local chambers of commerce.

On entering each shop, it is advisable to quietly scout for one's chosen specialty, buying any desired items that are fairly priced or underpriced, and then to ask if the shop owner has any other interesting items. Often the owner will have desirable items in storage or will recommend other shops that the buyer might visit. Most shop owners will haggle over prices; don't be afraid to ask, "Can you do any better?"

General Auctions

These events occur throughout the country on a daily basis. Public announcements of the auction and its contents are made prior to the sale date. On the day of the auction, the items are sold, on a nonreturnable basis, to the highest bidder.

Auctions frequently are held in order to settle an estate or a bankruptcy, or because someone who is moving does not wish to transport possessions to a new locale. Because these sales generally feature something for every taste, they can draw a large crowd.

Auctions usually last three to ten hours. Even though most items sell at bargain prices, persons interested in just a few pieces often feel that when the cost of their time is computed, the overall cost of acquisition is unreasonable.

Estate Sales

Often many items in an estate have value but are unwanted by the heirs. Notices of an estate sale are placed in a local newspaper, detailing many of the items to be sold. At the appropriate time, the public lines up outside the deceased's home, waiting for admission. By pricing items very cheaply, the managers of the sale normally sell everything in the house within three days. As a result, there is keen competition for the choice items, and minor melees are not uncommon. For the hardy who appreciate a bargain, however, estate sales can be an excellent source of collectibles.

Conventions, Quality Shows, and Specialty Auctions

These gatherings, which are advertised in general, trade, and specialty publications, feature hundreds, and occasionally thousands, of fine collectibles. Since they require a minimum of the investor's time, they are favored by many. The average sale price often will be higher than at the marketplaces discussed above, but the abundance of merchandise is considered by most collectors to be more than adequate compensation for the higher prices. It should also be kept in mind that many of the specialty auction houses accept mail bids. All auction houses have the same policy: They make no claims as to the age or origin of anything they sell. Caution should be used when buying at auction. It is sometimes least effective to pay a dealer to attend an auction on your behalf.

Specialty Shops

As collectibles gain ground as legitimate investment media, specialty shops around the country that deal primarily in collectibles have opened their doors. Although some shops are run in only a semiprofessional manner, most are excellent. The owners of the top-quality shops usually are knowledgeable individuals who feature a wide selection of fine collectibles. These owners pay fairly high prices to acquire their merchandise and usually maintain a high overhead. Although this means that investors who purchase through these quality shops will pay top dollar, it is often reasonable to do so. Knowledgeable specialty shop owners often discover the best investment-grade material and, because of their intimate contact with their chosen marketplace, can sometimes locate unique or hard-to-obtain collectibles. Such shops are usually listed in the Yellow Pages.

Fellow Collectors

As an investor becomes active in the collectibles market, he invariably meets fellow collectors. Most collectors, however attached to the items they own, occasionally have material to sell; often they prefer selling to a fellow collector. Although the average dealer pays about half of retail value for investment-grade collectibles, collectors sell to each other items at three quarters of retail. The seller thus receives 50 percent more than he would from a dealer, and the buyer saves 25 percent.

TYPES OF DEALERS

The various types of dealers active in the marketplaces described above are listed, in order of increasing sophistication, below. Dealing with each has its advantages and disadvantages.

Junkmen

Junkmen seldom exhibit any genuine appreciation for the material they are handling; rather, they concentrate on converting unwanted objects into cash. Most junkmen tend to undervalue quality collectibles.

Naïve Experts

Such individuals believe that they are experts in their fields; unfortunately, they are not. At first encounter they can be somewhat convincing, however, and it is worthwhile to keep in mind that there are more alleged experts in the collectibles field than there are true authorities. Like junkmen, such individuals occasionally underprice what they have for sale.

Minor Collectors

The minor collector often has a well-defined collection that, although small, brings its owner great pleasure. Such people are generally accurate in their statements and tend to sell items at low prices.

Medium Collectors or Minor Dealers

This type of dealer is usually transitory. As collections grow, people generally discard their less desirable objects and acquire others that they find more interesting. Existing market dynamics make it difficult to be a small-time dealer, however, and most people in this position are somewhat surprised by the business realities that they encounter. As a result, they either return to the relatively carefree status of a minor collector or progress into the market in a significant way.

Major Collectors and Medium Dealers

Such individuals spend a fair percentage of their conscious thought on market consideration. They deal in valuable or large quantities of material, much of it investment grade. As collectors, they are important customers for major dealers; as dealers, they often introduce new collectors to the field. Their selling prices vary as their understanding of market dynamics develops.

Major Dealers

Although few in number, major dealers control the bulk of the investment-grade collectibles that are offered at public sale. They have access to large amounts of cash as well as to major collections, and their behind-the-scenes maneuverings affect many collectors. Serious investors should meet and come to know as many major dealers as possible.

Market Masters

Within their limited field, these individuals have significant power. They often control large quantities of investment-grade collectibles and are constantly engaged in original research within their chosen field. Although they are welcome contributors to price guides, the market masters do not generally use such guides in business dealings. Rather, they create their own price levels based on their interpretation of current fair market value. They are few and far between.

GLOSSARY

auction—A public sale where the purchaser is the highest recognized bidder.

bid—The amount offered for an item being sold at auction.

book value—The suggested listed price for a particular item.

dealer—One who stands willing to buy or sell a collectible of a certain kind; prices are often negotiable.

grading scale—A 20-point scale ranging from poor to pristine mint, used in evaluating investment-grade collectibles.

lot—An item or a group of items sold together at an auction.

market master—A specialist who trades large quantities of investment-grade collectibles.

LEADING DEALERS AND OTHER SOURCES

Collector's Bookstore, Hollywood, Cal. Comic books, fantasy art, movie memorabilia, and posters.

The Collectors Gallery, New York, N.Y. Museum-quality toys, trains, and art.

Comic Investments, Philadelphia, Pa. Baseball cards and comic books.

Darrow's Fun Antiques, New York, N.Y. Toys and collectibles, arcade machines, and animation art.

Empire State Collectibles, Long Island, N.Y. Baseball cards.

Forbidden Planet, New York, N.Y. Books and comics.

Gallery Lainzberg, Cedar Rapids, Iowa. Animation and fantasy art.

Hake's Americana and Collectibles, York, Pa. Advertisements (emphasizing political souvenirs) and other collectibles.

International Comic Book Co., Manitoba, Canada. Comics.

Johnsons, San Francisco, Cal. Toys, folk art, and advertisements.

M. Kenyon & Co., New York, N.Y. Largest selection of comic watches.

John Knight, Rockville, Md. Comics.

Redbeard's Book Den, Crystal Bay, Nev. Comics.

Robert W. Skinner Inc., Boston, Mass. Auctioneers and appraisers.

Waves, New York, N.Y. Old radios, phonographs, advertisements, and television sets.

SUGGESTED READING

PERIODICALS

Antique Toy World. Published by Dale Kelly, Chicago, Ill. Monthly; articles and toy advertisements.

Antique Trader. Published by Babka Publishing Co., Dubuque, Iowa. Weekly; features many advertisements.

Comics Buyer's Guide. Published by Krause Publications, Iola, Wis. Biweekly; articles, comics, and toy advertisements.

Collector's Showcase. Published by Keith and Donna Kaonis, San Diego, Cal. Bimonthly; toys, early advertisements, folk art, dolls, and lots of advertisements for these items.

Film Collector's World. Published by Alan L. Light, Rapid City, Il. Biweekly; movie memorabilia.

Toy Shop. Published by Krause Publications, Iola, Wis. Biweekly.

BOOKS

Enes, Bill. *Silent Salesmen* (an encyclopedia of collectible gum, candy, and nut machines). Lenexa, Kan.: Enes Publishing, 1987.

Fey, Marshall. *Slot Machines*. Las Vegas: Stanley Paher, 1983.

Fried, Frederick. *Pictorial History of the Carousel*. New York: Vestal Press, 1964.

Garratt, John G. *The World Encyclopedia of Model Soldiers*. Great Britain: Frederick Muller Ltd., 1981.

Hake, Ted, and King, Russ. *Collectible Pin-Back Buttons*. York, Pa.: Hake's Americana & Collectible Press, 1986.

Murphy, Katherine. *Antiques & Collectibles Price Guide*. Dubuque: Babka Publishing Co., 1986.

COMMERCIAL PAPER

Patricia D. Segall

BASIC CHARACTERISTICS

Brief Description

Commercial paper is a short-term promissory note issued by a corporation to raise large amounts of money. If the paper is issued for less than 270 days and used to finance current transactions, the paper is exempt from the Securities Exchange Commission (SEC) registration requirements. This minimizes the time and cost of preparing a commercial paper issue. The average maturity is about thirty days.

ATTRACTIVE FEATURES

Ratings

Typically, commercial paper was issued only by blue-chip corporations. The few defaults that did take place were mainly smaller companies, so the effect was to limit the market to bigger, better known firms. However, in 1970, Penn Central went bankrupt with $82 million in commercial paper outstanding. Name recognition was no longer good enough. The credit rating of a company was now very important. In 1977, the SEC ruled that commercial paper bought by institutional investors would have to be backed by additional capital held by the dealers if the paper was not rated by at least two rating firms. Since the dealers did not want to bear the cost of raising additional capital, virtually all commercial paper is now rated. Clearly, this feature heightens its attractiveness to investors. Three

Patricia D. Segall is a Senior Analyst with IDD Information Services, Inc.

popular services that rate commercial paper are Standard & Poor's Corporation, Moody's Investors Service, Inc., and Fitch Investors Service.

Placement

Commercial paper can be placed either directly by the issuing company or through dealers. Direct placement eliminates dealer commissions but is cost-effective only for those firms that issue paper on a regular basis and thus maintain a regular sales force. Alternatively, an issuer can sell the paper through dealers, which are the large investment banks. Small companies typically do not have the resources to maintain their own sales force and, therefore, make use of dealers. Thus, the increase in paper placed through dealers is a good way to note the entrance of smaller companies into the market.

REPRESENTATIVE TYPES OF ISSUERS AND INVESTORS

Issuers

As previously stated, issuers of commercial paper are typically big firms. These can be broken down into financial and nonfinancial companies. Financial companies, which do the bulk of the issuing, are entities such as bank holding companies, insurance companies, and leasing companies. Nonfinancial companies are transportation companies, public utilities, manufacturers, and so forth.

Investors

Although available data on investors in commercial paper is quite limited, one thing is clear: institutional investors are the largest buyers. It is used as a safe short-term investment. Other investors include insurance companies, pension funds, local governments, and bank trust departments.

TAX CONSEQUENCES

Commercial paper interest is fully taxable as interest income. The exception is commercial paper issued by tax-exempt authorities.

POTENTIAL RISKS

Commercial paper is a relatively short-term investment. It is issued by financially sound companies or companies that at least have some kind of backup line of credit in place. In addition, a very small percentage of commercial paper is redeemed prior to maturity. Clearly a potential risk would be an investment in paper of lesser quality (lower rating) to obtain a higher yield, which could possibly lead to loss.

SOME RECENT DEVELOPMENTS

Bank Lines of Credit

A semirecent development is the introduction of bank lines of credit to accompany new issues of nonfinancial paper. In 1966, interest rates rose above legal ceilings on bank CDs. This made it difficult for banks to raise funds for corporate loans. Consequently, banks encouraged their strongest customers to issue commercial paper and provided backup lines of credit to be used in the event of liquidity problems or inability in rolling over expiring paper. While bank fees for these lines are less profitable than direct bank loans, they do not tie up capital. Instead, these arrangements establish a contingent liability which ensures payment if the issuer cannot repay. This commitment provides safety for the investors and since issuers do not always use their bank lines, it has little effect on the bank's capital. In addition, banks earn a fee for supplying lines of credit to commercial paper issuers. The issuer pays the bank a fee in exchange for the right to borrow money should liquidity problems arise.

Entrance of Small Companies

Seeing that commercial paper was an efficient way to obtain cheap short-term funds, small companies became interested. By using bank lines of credit, insurance company guarantees, letters of credit, and the like, these companies entered the market. In essence, these devices enhance the credit standing of the issuer by borrowing the name of a larger financial institution. A slight variation of this theme is the use of collateral to back an issuer's paper. Government-backed securities, credit card receivables, and mortgage obligations all serve as collateral. This allows companies that otherwise would have been denied access to the market, or which would have received very low ratings, to become well rated participants in the market.

Unrated Commercial Paper

Another feature to take hold is the emergence of unrated commercial paper. Although this market is still quite small, $7 billion versus $360 billion in rated commercial paper, many expect it to grow rapidly.[1] Investors looking for higher rates of return than that offered by a Treasury bill or rated commercial paper began to selectively buy this unrated paper. Companies can obtain funds at between 50 and 125 basis points below the prime rate.[2] Owing to a corporate restructuring (either a leveraged buyout or acquisition), a company may not be able to obtain a decent rating, or they may just wish to avoid the time and cost of obtaining a rating, as was the case with Avis. They found the price of their unrated paper was reasonably close to the price of its rated paper. The biggest problem with this new market is on the demand side. Only sophisticated investors, those who are capable of performing their own credit analysis of a company, will invest in unrated paper.

Universal Commercial Paper

In October 1986, Goldman Sachs released a new twist in the commercial paper market. Universal commercial paper is paper that is issued in the United States by U.S. companies and sold to U.S. investors. However, it is denominated in a foreign currency. It works like this: the bank finds a U.S. investor who would like to buy commercial paper in a foreign currency. A U.S. company agrees to borrow the U.S. dollar equivalent at a predetermined rate. Two business days later, the investor pays the foreign currency to the issuer via the bank. The bank does a currency swap with the issuer, selling the foreign exchange spot, buying it forward, and offering U.S. dollars to the issuer. On maturity of the paper, the issuer pays back principal and interest to the bank in dollars. The investors are paid in the

---

[1] David Neustadt, "Market Grows for Unrated Paper," *American Banker*, May 27, 1988, p. 30.

[2] Theodore Justin Gage, "Unrated CP Offers High Yields, Modest Short-Term Risk," *Cash Flow Magazine*, Dec. 1987, p. 11.

foreign currency. This universal commercial paper is subject to the same rules and regulations as U.S. commercial paper, yet it offers investors a foreign currency play without leaving their familiar U.S. credit risks and accounting principles.[3]

BUYING AND SELLING

When a company issues paper through a dealer, the company tells the dealer the quantity and maturity of the paper it wants to sell. The dealer, in turn, determines the rate at which he can place the paper by contacting prospective customers. Based on this, the dealer determines the rate at which he will buy the paper from the issuer. A transaction of this sort is usually settled in one day. Only about 5 percent of paper bought through dealers is held for their own inventory. The majority of it is sold to investors.[4] For those companies that issue paper directly, the issuer decides daily how much he wants to borrow and of what maturity. The issuer then releases offering rates based on his forecast of investor demand at each maturity. The money flow is watched throughout the day, and rates are adjusted accordingly.

THE EUROPEAN MARKET

The European counterpart to the U.S. commercial paper market developed from the Euronote market. Euronotes are defined as short-term promissory notes arranged with a form of medium-term bank backup, that is, a source that the issuer can draw on if his note cannot be placed at an attractive rate.

Attractive Foreign Regulations

From the Euronote market, today's European commercial paper (ECP) has evolved. ECP is defined as a Euronote without a committed backup facility. In the 1970s, the European commercial paper market's main participants were big American multinationals. They used the market to obtain funds for the operations of their foreign subsidiaries, due to the Interest Equalization Tax Act (IETA) and the Office of Foreign Direct Investment (OFDI) regulations.

The IETA was a tax on foreign securities in the domestic market. The controls set by the OFDI were restrictions on the outflow of capital from parent companies to their foreign affiliates. The IETA raised the cost for foreign subsidiaries of U.S. companies to issue securities in the U.S. market, while the OFDI made it disadvantageous for parent companies to export funds abroad. Both sets of regulations drove multinational companies to the European market for their financing needs. Once these restrictions were dropped, the European market, which was not offering great cost advantages, disappeared.

That has all changed. The ECP market is back and beginning to boom. The volume (as of December 1987) of ECP outstanding was approximately $50 billion.[5] Considering the fact that ECP did not make its comeback until late 1984, this growth is impressive.

---

[3] Cathy A. Lazare, "Another Way of Hedging," *Institutional Investor*, May 1987, p. 233.

[4] Timothy Rowe, "Commercial Paper," *Instruments of the Money Market*, 1986, p. 111.

[5] Fiammetta Rocco, "The New Eurocommercial Paper Game," *Institutional Investor*, Dec. 1987, p. 52.

Factors Contributing to ECP's Growth

Several factors have contributed to ECP's recent growth. One is the decreased attractiveness of syndicated loans to borrowers. Other forms of debt financing appeared that offered more appealing rates. Many issuers became dissatisfied with the Euronote market; setting up a note facility, arranging the backup, and so forth became costly and time-consuming. Another reason for growth was that many investors felt uneasy about parking all their money in banks. They wanted to diversify out of bank risk and wanted attractive alternatives to bank deposits. ECP provided one.

Recent developments in the ECP market suggest that it is developing along the lines of the U.S. market. Average maturity in the United States is about thirty days. A three- or six-month maturity for ECP is the norm, although the market is experiencing more and more odd-dated maturities, akin to the domestic market. This feature allows borrowers to tailor the paper to fit specific short-term financing requirements.

LIBOR (the London interbank offer rate on Eurodollar deposits traded between banks) is still used as a "proxy" for the rate on ECP, since most ECP is tied to LIBOR. This, too, is changing as the market shifts away from bank investors. Although approximately two thirds of the participants in the market are still banks, a growing proportion of them are nonbank investors. The market has recently witnessed several issues where the pricing was done on an absolute rate basis.

Until recently, ECP could be issued only in Eurodollars and European Currency Units. Absence of denomination in other currencies was perhaps due mainly to regulatory prohibitions by the home country of the issuer regarding short-term securities. Recently, there have been programs denominated in Euro Dutch guilders and sterling, due to the lifting of these regulations. However, two things should be noted. First, most of the big Euro Commercial Paper houses are institutions that have had good experience with U.S. dollar investors, and as such, the U.S. money center and investment banks lead the market. Second, the demand for ECP may only be for that which is denominated in "strong" currencies.

Increased Competition Between European and U.S. Markets

The issuance costs of the European and U.S. markets have become increasingly competitive. Previously, the "classic arbitrage" was to issue commercial paper in the United States and then reinvest the funds in either Euro CDs or LIBOR deposits. Increased arbitrage helped narrow the spread between U.S. and European rates, which in turn increased participation in the European market. The most important decline is that of the LIBOR/U.S. commercial paper rate spread. As spreads between the two markets narrow, borrowers may find it hard to resist another source of short-term funds.

GLOSSARY

collateralized commercial paper—Commercial paper which has some form of asset or collateral backing up the issue; this feature enhances the credit worthiness of the issuer and thus lowers the borrowing cost.

commercial paper—A short-term promissory note usually issued by corporations.

ECP (European commercial paper)—Commercial paper that is offered in Europe and developed as an outgrowth of the Euronote.

financial companies—The largest issuers of commercial paper; these are entities such as bank holding companies and insurance companies.

LIBOR (London interbank offer rate)—An interbank money market rate on Eurodollar deposits traded between banks.

nonfinancial company—Issuers of commercial paper, which include such entities as transporation companies and public utilities.

unrated commercial paper—Commercial paper that does not have a rating assigned to it by one of the rating agencies.

SUGGESTED READINGS

Brealey, R. *Principles of Corporate Finance*, 2nd ed. New York: McGraw-Hill, 1984, p. 685.

Evans, Nick. "Where Can Euro-CP Go Now?" *Euroweek* 22, Jan. 1989.

Rocco, Fiammetta. "The New Eurocommercial Paper Game," *Institutional Investor* 51, Dec. 1987.

Rowe, Timothy. "Commercial Paper," *Instruments of the Money Market* 111, 1986.

COMMON STOCKS

David J. Skinner

BASIC CHARACTERISTICS

The many characteristics of common stocks are discussed under the three main headings of definitions, purposes, and classification.

Definitions

Common stock is an equity security granting certain rights to stockholders. This section also discusses the shareholder's limited liability, the continuous existence of corporations, and the financial nature of common stocks.

Equity. Capital stock represents ownership in a corporation, and holders of capital stock are subject to the success or failure of the business. Some corporations choose to raise capital only through stock; others use additional securities, such as bonds and convertible bonds.

There are two types of capital stock: common and preferred. Preferred stock is covered in another article, "Preferred Stocks," elsewhere in this volume, but three aspects of it are relevant here. First, preferred stock dividends are fixed and must be fully paid before dividends may be paid on common stock. Second, preferred shares take precedence over common shares in the event of liquidation of the corporation. Third, preferred shareholders have a limited voice in the management of the company, unlike common-share holders, who have full voting rights.

David J. Skinner is a stock and bond broker with Edward D. Jones & Co., College Station, Texas. He holds an MBA and is a Certified Financial Planner.

As an equity security, common stock offers no guarantees; dividend payments are not required. Because there is no maturity of a common share, return of principal is not provided for. By contrast, a bond is a debt security that requires timely payment of interest according to a set schedule, as well as a return of the face amount, on a given maturity date. In common stock investments, the uncertainty of both the income stream and the market value of the shares is a significant risk factor. A result of this increased risk is that the total return on common stock investments has far exceeded the total return on bond investments over the long run (total return includes dividend or interest payments and gain or loss on sale over a given holding period). Historical rates of return from common stocks, bonds, and other investments are compared in another article, "Historical Returns on Principal Investments," elsewhere in this volume. In short, bondholders settle for a fixed return and have the right to sue if the corporation fails to make the required interest and principal payments; stockholders have no such right.

When a corporation is formed, a maximum number of authorized shares is stated in the charter and may not be changed unless the charter is amended. Otherwise, it would be possible for a corporation to issue an ever-increasing number of shares, thereby diluting the voting power and value of previously issued shares. The board of directors decides how many of the authorized shares they wish to issue to investors; the remaining authorized shares are known as unissued shares. Some or all of the issued shares will be held by investors, and these are known as outstanding shares. Issued and outstanding shares that have been bought back by the corporation are known as treasury stock (see Figure 1).

Treasury stock is treated as unissued for accounting purposes; that is, no dividends are paid, and no voting rights are available. Treasury stock can (1) be traded to other corporations in the course of a merger or acquisition; (2) be distributed to or held for the benefit of employees for stock option plans, deferred compensation arrangements, or other employee-related benefit plans; and (3) be sold (again) to the public in order to raise capital in a secondary offering.

FIGURE 1. Distribution of Common Stock

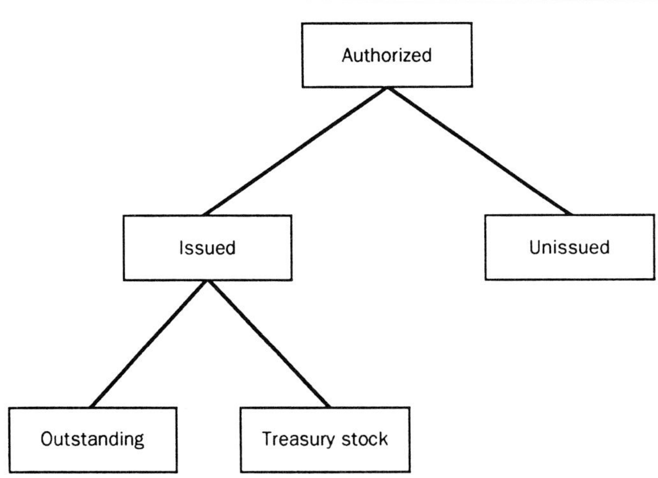

The original shares of a corporation are given an arbitrary value for accounting reasons; this is the par value. Par value is of little concern to investors.

The market value of a common stock is the price at which a buyer and seller agree to exchange shares for money. During each business day, numerous trades occur, and the execution prices are reported almost instantly by wire services. The most recent trade determines the current market value. If the most recent trade occurred at a higher market price than the previous trade, an uptick is said to have happened. A downtick is the opposite situation.

Rights of Common Shareholders. Ownership of common stock entails rights that are listed in the corporate charter. These rights usually include dividends, voting, order of liquidation, transfer of ownership, inspection of corporate documents, and subscription rights.

Dividends. A dividend may be either a cash payment or a distribution of additional shares to existing shareholders. Earnings per share (EPS) describes the amount of net income remaining after the preferred dividend is paid, divided by the number of outstanding common shares. If the board of directors votes to pay part of these earnings to common stockholders, they will declare a dividend. The dividend payout ratio is the percentage of EPS that is paid out as dividends. Earnings that are not paid out are known as retained earnings. Dividends are usually paid quarterly.

Once a company begins paying a sizeable dividend, it often becomes a matter of great importance to maintain or increase the dividend. The Bank of New York, for example, has paid a dividend annually since 1785 and is one of forty-eight companies that have paid dividends for at least forty-five years.[1]

In analyzing a stock's dividend, it is important to note the relationship between EPS and dividends per share. For example, EPS of $2 with a dividend of $1 might be quite reasonable (a 50 percent payout ratio). If, however, a company pays a $1 dividend and inspection of the annual report reveals earnings of only fifty cents, it would be wise to inquire why more was being paid out than taken in. Companies with outstanding dividend payment records might be tempted to do so in an unprofitable or marginally profitable year in order to avoid omitting or reducing the dividend. If the dividends were to be reduced or cut out completely, the price of the stock could drop precipitously as income-oriented investors sold out and sought alternative investments. There is no immediate cause for concern if a corporation pays out more than it earns, but the fact that the company will be depleting capital in the process is relevant to evaluation of the company's future prospects; in other words, it is not a good sign.

Dividends may take the form of either cash or additional shares or fractions of a share; in the latter case, the dividend is known as a stock dividend. Stock dividends do not represent an increase in the dollar value of the shareholder's position; rather, they are merely a distribution of additional shares that dilute the value of previously outstanding shares. In the case of both cash and stock dividends, the market price of the shares is reduced by an amount equal to the dividend on the day it trades ex-dividend (that is, the purchaser does not receive the current dividend). A stock split is a type of stock dividend: it is only a recapitalization and is not an increase in wealth. However, a 2–1 split, for example, reduces the

---

[1] See *Standard & Poor's Stock Guide.*

price of the stock to half its previous price, which some think will make the shares more attractive. Splits may have various ratios, such as 2–1 (two new shares for each old share) or 3–2. A reverse split is the opposite process. For example, a person holding 100 shares of a $50 stock would, following a reverse split, receive fifty new shares worth $100 each.

Voting. Each common share carries one vote, which may be cast at the stockholder's discretion in whatever matters come to the ballot. Whether statutory or cumulative voting is in effect for common share votes depends on the company. Under statutory voting, each share is entitled to one vote. Cumulative voting allows the shareholder to multiply the number of shares held by the number of candidates for the board of directors and then divide this total number of cumulative votes among any or all of the candidates. This allows minority shareholders to gain representation on the board if their votes are properly concentrated.

Order of Liquidation. Common-share holders receive the remainder of a corporation's assets in a complete dissolution, after other obligations have been satisfied, in the following order:

- Taxes
- Wages
- Senior lienholders
- Bank loans, accounts payable, debentures
- Subordinated debentures
- Preferred stock
- Common stock

The last-in-line position of common-share holders is the most risky, but it also has the greatest potential for return.

Transfer of Ownership. Shares of stock may be sold or transferred to another owner very easily. (See *Important Factors in Buying and Selling,* later in this article.)

Inspection of Corporate Documents. Common-stock holders must be provided certain financial statements and may request other documents, if they wish. As owners, they have the right to an extensive amount of corporate information.

Annual and quarterly reports are usually mailed to stockholders of record without stockholder request. These reports contain the balance sheet and income statement for the period covered, along with other information, such as sources and uses of funds and management's analysis of the results. Other documents concerning a corporation are available to the stockholder, such as Form 10-K, which is on file with the Securities and Exchange Commission (SEC).

Subscription Rights. If a corporation wishes to raise more capital by selling stock, it may (or must, depending on the circumstances) grant existing shareholders the right to buy some of the new shares at a certain price before the general public is allowed to buy. This is called a rights offering and is designed to allow existing shareholders to maintain their proportionate share of the company's assets. These rights usually have a value and may be sold or exercised within a relatively short specified time (approximately thirty to ninety days). A warrant is a long-term right to purchase additional shares at a given price, five to ten years is a typical period, although some warrants have no time limit. (See "Warrants and Rights," elsewhere in this volume.)

Rights offerings have taken on a new role in the 1970s and 1980s—that of the poison pill defense against a hostile takeover. A hostile takeover occurs when a raider acquires a significant block of voting shares of a corporation and threatens to vote out the existing board of directors and subsequently replace the existing management. The raider might then break up the company and sell off the pieces; conversely, the raider might implement new programs to improve the company's prospects. In either event, if the existing management fears that a hostile takeover might occur, a rights offering designed to alter the voting power of the common stock could thwart such a move. Whenever a shareholder acquires more than 5 percent of the outstanding shares of a company, a Form 13-D must be filed by the shareholder with the SEC. The shareholder's position therefore becomes a matter of public record, and is usually accompanied by a flurry of media exposure.

A poison pill defense can work in two ways. First, subscription rights may be granted to existing shareholders that would allow them to purchase additional shares at a given price if certain events occur. These events are spelled out in the agreement and usually include the acquisition by a new shareholder of more than 5 percent of the outstanding stock. The old shareholders would then be able to purchase additional shares at a dramatically reduced price (sometimes $0.01 per share). Because these rights are not transferable, the raider cannot get them. The second poison pill strategy is to grant subscription rights to the board of directors, which are again nontransferable and are offered at a deeply discounted price. Usually, the shares purchased under this arrangement would come out of unissued shares, whereas the shares sold under the first method would come out of treasury stock.

A poison pill defense may be invalidated by a court of law, depending on the circumstances. It is interesting that a seemingly obscure characteristic of common stock, subscription rights, has become pivotal in the financial markets.

Limited Liability. Owners of common stock are liable only for the amount of money they have invested.

Continuous Existence. Once a corporation is formed, it exists until it is dissolved and is not contingent on the lives of the owners or employees, as is the case with proprietorships and partnerships.

Financial Nature. A common stock is a financial asset (e.g., bonds, warrants, rights, and options) as opposed to nonfinancial tangible, or hard, assets (e.g., coins, gold, ceramics, and real estate). Financial assets usually perform well in times of low interest rates and low inflation, whereas hard assets generally do well during times of high inflation.

Purposes of Common Stock

The concept of selling shares of equity in an enterprise is an old one, and the motivations for such an arrangement are many. Three main purposes of common stock are (1) as a means of raising capital, (2) as a way to allow unrelated parties to share in the benefits of the business; and (3) as a way for entrepreneurs to sell out.

Raising Capital. When a business is first formed, money is needed to purchase the inventory and supplies necessary to produce the product or service that is to be sold. The person starting the business may or may not have sufficient funds to accomplish this. The entrepreneur has the option of borrowing the money or selling shares of ownership; these shares will presumably generate a fair return for investors. The first time a corporation sells shares to the public is called a primary stock offering, also known as an initial public offering (IPO). The market for a firm's shares that is expected to spring up after the IPO is known as the secondary market. After the IPO, sometimes years later, additional capital may be needed to finance further expansion. If there are unissued shares or treasury stock available, the corporation may sell all or part of these to the public in a secondary market offering.

In a primary offering, the issuing corporation sells shares to the public (usually through a brokerage firm). In the secondary market, investors trade these shares among themselves without the issuing corporation's involvement. There are also third and fourth markets. When a company's stock is listed on a major exchange but for some reason also trades in the over-the-counter market between non-exchange-member broker-dealers and institutional investors, it is said to be trading in the third market. The fourth market is the name given to trades between major institutional investors without the use of brokerage firms. For example, if a mutual fund wishes to purchase a large block of Exxon stock directly from an insurance company's portfolio to save money on brokerage commissions, the transaction is referred to as a trade in the fourth market.

Reasons for going public (selling shares in a corporation include:

- Access to additional capital
- Access to additional capital markets
- Increased visibility for the company, which may enhance its ability to sell its products

Two characteristics distinguish the IPO market from other markets. First, stocks that have recently gone public tend to be more volatile than stocks from more established companies. Second, IPO stock may be harder to sell back into the secondary market, should the investor so desire. Because of these potential problems, a diversified portfolio should have limited exposure to new issues. On the positive side, the potential returns from new issues have been markedly higher than those from more conservative issues. If the investor is willing to endure high volatility and limited liquidity, IPO stocks may be appropriate.

Many companies have gone public, only to go bankrupt later. Others, such as Xerox and Polaroid, have risen to success in recent years. In 1945, a retail store business was founded by Sam Walton. It was incorporated in 1969, and shares were sold to the public for the first time in 1970 for $16.50 per share. From 1971 through 1987, the shares traded as high as 42⅞ and as low as ⅛ per share, adjusted for splits. Once a penny stock (one that sells for less than $1 per share), the Wal-Mart Stores Corporation can be counted on the plus side of the IPO success/failure ledger; by the 1980s, Wal-Mart commanded a major part of the retail market.

Unrelated Parties. A second purpose of common stock is to allow investors to participate in the potentially dramatic returns available from equities without having any detailed knowledge about the business. History has shown that, in the long term, ownership of assets (business, real estate, tangibles) has proven to be a superior method of wealth accumulation when compared to the lending of money for interest (bonds). But not all investors have the expertise necessary to operate a business nor the capital with which to start one. Common stock allows these investors to take a position they would otherwise be unable to take. This aspect of common stocks is the answer to the question of who owns the means of production in a capitalistic society: stockholders.

Freedom for the Entrepreneur. Certain individuals are highly motivated to discover new methods of producing goods and providing services and also to structure systems for the efficient delivery of these goods and services. It is not uncommon, however, to find an entrepreneur who, after starting a business from nothing, has absolutely no interest in operating the now successful, established corporation with hundreds or thousands of employees. This task is then best left to professional management. Another factor is that the entrepreneur may wish to withdraw capital from the established business and tackle a new, larger, or more interesting task. Selling the ownership of the company to the new management and to other investors frees both capital and entrepreneur, while providing management with the motivating force of ownership and investors with a means of participating in a business that they otherwise would not have.

Classification of Common Stocks

Investors have a wide range of investment objectives, and common stocks may be divided into several classes corresponding to these objectives. The classes are not precise, but they do serve to help both seasoned investors and neophytes to simplify the process of evaluating investment prospects. It is interesting to note that an entire industry, as well as an individual issue, may fall into one or more of the following categories.

Income. An income stock typically pays a generous dividend and has a history of maintaining or increasing this dividend. Prospects for growth in share price exist but are not great. Strong balance sheets and conservative management are also found with income stocks. Utility stocks are good examples of income stocks, and oil stocks have also been known to pay fairly attractive dividends, though not on a level with utilities. Another name for this class of stock is widows' and orphans' stock. A classic example is American Telephone & Telegraph (AT&T), known as Ma Bell. Since the breakup of the telephone company, the new regional companies, collectively referred to as Baby Bells, also promise to be good income stocks.

Blue Chip. Blue Chip stocks are generally the highest quality on the market. The dividend may not be as large as that of an income stock, but it will have been paid for many years, and the chances of its being reduced or omitted will be minute. The balance sheet of a blue chip company will exude strength by being low in debt and high in cash and current assets. The company's products will be well known, and the possibility of bankruptcy or major mishap will be small. It is ironic that the term "blue chip" probably came from the field of gambling, where the player in a casino or friendly poker game exchanges cash for chips of various colors, with blue chips representing the greatest value. Blue chip stocks would be sold only in a drastic emergency, or if the stockholder's investment objective became more aggressive, in which case blue chip stocks would probably no longer be suitable. International Business Machines (IBM) is the most prominent of today's blue chips.

Others are Exxon, Coca-Cola, and Anheuser-Busch. Because classifications of stocks may overlap, a blue chip could also be an income stock, and both could be suitable for widows and orphans.

Growth. Dramatic potential for growth in share price with little possibility for dividends in the short term makes for a growth stock. A famous example is Xerox in the 1960s. Growth stocks would be suitable for investors with distant horizons, perhaps a minimum of three years and as long as thirty. An investor should be willing to leave capital invested during both good and bad times because both may occur before a growth stock begins to realize its potential.

Cyclical. A cyclical stock is one that is noticeably affected by the swings of the business cycle, which is a gauge of business activity. About twenty indicators are considered in determining the current phase of the cycle. Some of the indicators are the consumer price index (CPI), the producer price index (PPI), the stock market, housing starts, consumer demand, machine tool orders, plant capacity utilization, and consumer sentiment. Cyclical stocks include automobile makers and manufacturers of big-ticket items, such as appliances and houses.

Defensive. A defensive stock is one that shows little volatility in the face of business cycle changes. Regardless of the times, people must buy food, drugs, and other essentials. McDonald's, Albertson's, and Johnson & Johnson are examples.

One might wonder why an investor would buy a defensive stock at all. If the feeling was that the stock market was poised for a decline, why not just sell out of stocks completely? There are two reasons for maintaining at least a minimal stock position, even in the face of a down market. First, predicting down markets is not easy, and one could be wrong. Moreover, because dividends are usually unaffected by market value swings, why should an income-oriented investor give up a generous dividend to escape from an event that would probably not affect the dividend? Second, defensive stocks have performed quite favorably in down markets when compared to other types of stocks. For example, one mutual fund, established in the 1950s, must at all times invest at least 95 percent of its assets in common stocks and securities convertible into common stock. On October 19, 1987, the Dow Jones industrial average (DJIA) fell by 23 percent, and the Standard & Poor's (S&P) Index fell by 20 percent, but this mutual fund fell by only 18 percent. The reason it outperformed both indexes was probably that the fund was positioned primarily in defensive stocks.

ATTRACTIVE FEATURES

The attractive features of common stocks are discussed in three general categories: limited liability, continuous existence, and rate of return. The reader interested in theories about buying and selling stock will find them covered in the third category. The mechanics of how to place orders with brokers to buy and sell stocks are found in the section entitled *Important Factors in Buying and Selling*, later in this article.

Limited Liability

Limited liability is a primary feature of common stock. Regardless of the possible crimes of a corporation and its management or employees, stockholders are liable only for the amount of money they have invested in the corporation's shares. In privately held corporations, however, it is possible that this limited liability feature might not offer total protection against court sanctions.

Another aspect of the limited liability feature is that the common stockholder has no role in management other than to elect the board of directors and vote on other issues that are presented to shareholders. This means that (1) a shareholder need not know anything about the business in order to participate in the benefits and (2) the shareholder may reap the benefits of the business without any of the problems of day-to-day management. For example, sewage treatment, garbage disposal, and the disposal of toxic wastes are essential activities and can be profitable businesses. Still, an investor might be reluctant to gain hands-on experience in these activities, but would rather participate in the profits, liabilities, and management in a limited way. This is an attractive feature of common stock.

Continuous Existence

Once a corporation is chartered, it remains in existence until it is dissolved. The Ford Motor Company, for example, has long outlived its founder. This feature is attractive to investors for many reasons, two examples of which follow.

A wealthy individual might desire to provide for the future welfare of his heirs or to sustain the programs of a particular school or charity. A bequest or gift of common stock or common stock mutual funds would accomplish this goal and would be a source of great comfort to the donor. Other equity assets, such as real estate, gold, and antiques, also fall into this category, but none have the liquidity and rate of return expectations of common stocks.

The continuity of common stock is also attractive to an institutional investor, such as a pension plan or a mutual fund. The time horizons of these investors are much more distant than an individual's; in fact, an infinite horizon exists for many institutions. Accordingly, assets that are perpetual in nature would be suitable for such an investor.

Rate of Return

The information in this section is divided into six parts, which in the aggregate provide a sound framework within which stock investment decisions can be evaluated.

Total Return. The total return on a common stock is the dividend paid plus or minus the capital gain or loss over a given period. The S&P Index of 500 common stocks has averaged about a 9 percent compounded annual rate of return since the mid-1920s. Bonds have averaged in the range of 4 to 6 percent, and short-term Treasury securities and inflation have both averaged about 3 percent. From this cursory view, it is clear that holding common stocks over the long run has generated a compounded rate of return that exceeds fixed-rate investments and inflation by a factor of at least two. (See the article on "Historical Returns on Principal Investments," elsewhere in this volume, for a more detailed review of these rates of return.) Although it has been correctly argued that many common stock mutual funds have not been able to equal the past rate of return of the S&P 500, several mutual funds have consistently outperformed both the S&P 500 and the Dow Jones industrial average over multiple ten-year periods. For further discussion of mutual fund results, see article on "Mutual Funds," elsewhere in this volume.

Income Return. This term refers strictly to the dividends paid by a company. The dividend yield, or current yield, for a stock is found by dividing the annual dividend by the market price. This percentage is conveniently displayed in the stock market pages of most newspapers. Throughout the past sixty years, the dividends on common stocks have generally kept pace with inflation and provided investors with rising income. Services such as the *Standard & Poor's Stock Guide* and the *Value Line Investment Survey* are excellent sources of information on dividend payments.

It is interesting to note the effect of interest rate changes on dividend-paying stocks. As interest rates rise, the market values of dividend stocks tend to decline as do those of bonds. If an investor can receive 7 percent in an insured bank account or a short-term Treasury security with little or no market risk, why should a dividend-paying stock that fluctuates in value even be considered as an alternative? The reason is that, although rates on short-term securities change from day to day, stock dividends on income and blue chip stocks tend to be dependable and to rise slowly over the years. For example, Exxon common stock closed at 48⅞ on September 3, 1987, and at the time was paying an annual dividend of $1.90, resulting in a dividend yield of 3.9 percent, which compared unfavorably with the 7 percent then available on short-term securities. However, at the end of the dramatic market decline on October 19, 1987, Exxon closed at 33½, which resulted in a dividend yield of 5.6 percent. This yield was nearly what one might have earned on a short-term account, but with the key difference that the income from a stock such as Exxon is more likely to be consistent and rise over the years to come (Exxon increased the dividend in 1988 to $2.20), whereas the income from a short-term security changes each time it is renewed, which is often—perhaps annually, semiannually, or even quarterly. Of course, the financial position of Exxon Corporation could change, which would affect this analysis. The important consideration for investors is that when the stock market enters a panic-stricken slide, a search for financially strong, dividend-paying companies might yield some real values.

Various Markets. Common stocks may be traded between buyers and sellers who have located each other. Nothing else need be done beyond execution of the transfer form on the back of the stock certificate. The task of finding a buyer and seller for a given stock at a given price is not easy, however, and it is in this process that the public markets have become dominant.

A listed security is one that trades on an organized exchange. Exchanges include the New York Stock Exchange (NYSE) and the American Stock Exchange (AMEX), as well as regional exchanges, such as the Pacific, Midwest, and Canadian exchanges. Stocks that are not listed on a major or regional exchange trade in the over-the-counter (OTC) market. Each stock in the OTC market has one or more market makers, which are brokerages willing to buy or sell 100 shares of the stock at a quoted price. Stocks that are actively traded in the OTC market are quoted on the National Association of Securities Dealers Automated Quotation (NASDAQ) network. If an investor wishes to know the current market value of a stock trading on an exchange or OTC, a phone call to a broker with access to a listed securities quotation service and to the NASDAQ will yield this information. Quotes may also be obtained directly from quotation services, such as Quotron and S&P, by subscribing.

Some OTC stocks do not qualify for quotation on the NASDAQ and are listed only in a publication known as the National Daily Quotation Service pink sheets. Stocks that do not have an active enough market to warrant a listing in the pink sheets may be traded by contacting brokers in the local area of the company in question.

With the advent of computers has come more rapid exchange of information, and stock markets in London, Hong Kong, Tokyo, and many other cities throughout the world are becoming increasingly important as a means of trading various securities.

The primary market refers to the mechanism by which corporations sell newly issued shares to the public for the first time. The secondary market is the name given to the trading that arises between investors through the major and regional exchanges, the OTC, the pink sheets, and the international markets; brokerage houses are the conduit for these transactions. The third market arises when a listed security is traded in the OTC markets, again with brokers as the conduit. The fourth market operates without brokers, directly between institutional investors.

A final note about the various financial markets: Although some discrepancies exist, the price of a given security in one market is usually close to the quoted price in a different market at a given time. This is a major advantage to the investor in stocks, since the forces of the marketplace and the rapid exchange of information tend to protect the investor from inequities in pricing. Other such investments as coins, art, and diamonds are more subject to such variations. Still, it is possible to find a stock selling, for example, on the NYSE at one price and at a different price elsewhere. By buying the lower-priced shares and simultaneously selling the higher-priced shares, an arbitrageur need only wait until the prices come together, after which both transactions may be profitably reversed.

Valuation of a Corporation's Assets. Before deciding to buy into a business (whether directly or through common stock), the prospective buyer must place some value on the company's assets and also on the income that those assets may be expected to some during the buyer's investment term. This value can then be compared to the price that the seller is asking. For example, if, through analysis of its assets and income, it is estimated that the Exxon Corporation stock is presently worth $80 per share, then $80 per share would seem to be a fair price. If the stock market is in a state of euphoria, however, Exxon might be selling for $100 per share, in which case a purchase should not be made. Conversely, if the market has just crashed and Exxon can be bought for $50 per share, the value-oriented investor would probably begin to acquire shares.

The following discussion of the intrinsic worth of a company comprises six elements: the economy, industry analysis, book value, net current asset value, future dividends, and ratio analysis.

The Economy. The economy as a whole has an effect on the value of a common stock. The nature of that effect is a matter of intense scrutiny by the media, the government, investors, newsletters, and advisory services. The level of economic activity in the United States is measured by twenty or so indicators, which are reported in the financial press. A thorough explanation of these indicators is offered in *The Dow Jones-Irwin Guide to Using the Wall Street Journal*, by Michael B. Lehmann. Many experts feel that the investor who is well informed about these indicators will profit more than those less well informed.

Although initially it may seem that a firm command of economic data would be essential to investment success, a case can be made for a neutral position, perhaps even for a healthy skepticism about such data. Economists Steven Strongin and Paula S. Binkley have questioned the usefulness of economic data and forecasts:

> Forecast revisions, during the year being forecast, are as likely to worsen as to improve the accuracy of the forecast with as much as six months' additional economic information. These results make a strong case for policy makers or any other users of economic forecasts to be extremely cautious when responding to current economic statistics. We found that forecasts were often revised significantly in the *wrong* direction in response to supposedly clear economic signals. Early forecasts were often more accurate than their mid-term forecast revisions. In such an environment, it is important for policy makers to wait for full verification of economic trends before acting. Early signals simply are not reliable.[2]

The article examines forecasts of gross national product and of inflation and measures the accuracy of the initial forecast each January as well as of the forecasts for the rest of the year, for several different years.

Forecasts of stock market activity have been as difficult to make as those of economic activity. Benjamin Graham eloquently stated this position in *The Intelligent Investor*:

> We are equally sure that if [the intelligent investor] places his emphasis on [stock market] timing, in the sense of forecasting, he will end up as a speculator and with a speculator's financial results. . . . As a matter of business practice, or perhaps of thoroughgoing conviction, the stockbrokers and the investment services seem wedded to the principle that both investors and speculators in common stocks should devote careful attention to market forecasts.
>
> The farther one gets from Wall Street, the more skepticism one will find, we believe, as to the pretensions of stock-market forecasting or timing. The investor can scarcely take seriously the innumerable predictions which appear almost daily and are his for the asking. Yet in many cases he pays attention to them and even acts upon them. Why? Because he has been persuaded that it is important for him to form some opinion of the future of the stock market, and because he feels that the brokerage or service forecast is at least more dependable than his own.
>
> We lack space here to discuss in detail the pros and cons of marketing forecasting. A great deal of brain power goes into this field, and undoubtedly some people can make money by being good stock market analysts. But it is absurd to think that the general public can ever make money out of market forecasts. For who will buy when the general public, at a given signal, rushes to sell out at a profit? If you, the reader, expect to get rich over the years by following some system of leadership in market forecasting, you must be expecting to try to do what countless others are aiming at, and to be able to do it better than your numerous competitors in the market. There is no basis either in logic or in experience for assuming that any typical or average investor can anticipate market movements more successfully than the general public, of which he himself is a part.[3]

The preceding passage appeared in the 1973 edition of Graham's book, years before the advent of programmed trading, financial futures, options trading, and other events that have caused upheaval in the financial markets. If stock market forecasting could gain no praise from Graham in 1973, it could scarcely do better now.

Economic data, including stock market data, are worthy of awareness and review, but have not proven to be an investment panacea.

---

[2] Steven Strongin and Paula S. Binkley, "A Policy Maker's Guide to Economic Forecasts," *Economic Perspectives*, Federal Reserve Bank of Chicago, May/June 1988.

[3] Benjamin Graham, *The Intelligent Investor*, 4th ed., New York: Harper & Row, 1973, p. 95.

Industry Analysis. Studies have shown that being in the right industry at the right time would have generated investment results superior to being in and out of the stock market as a whole at the right time. The *Value Line Investment Survey* has identified about fifty different industry groups into which corporations may fall. In selecting equities, a diversity of industries should be represented.

Book Value. This is perhaps the most basic measure of a company's worth, but it is misleading. To find book value, list all a firm's assets and subtract all the firm's liabilities. Divide the remainder by the number of common shares outstanding, and the result is the book value per share. In other words, if the company was terminated and all the stockholders received a check for their residual interest in the firm, they would supposedly receive book value.

An example of a problem with the book value measure will serve to illustrate that book value must be viewed from more than one perspective. Real estate is typically shown on a company's books at the value for which it was purchased; subsequent appreciation therefore does not show up on the balance sheet. If the company purchased its headquarters location for $1 million in 1964, and the appraised market value of that land in 1988 is $4 million, the book value of the asset would still be $1 million, even though, if the firm was liquidated, the residual interest to the stockholders would be four times book (assuming no debt remained on that property). For reasons such as this, the stock market (as measured by the Dow Jones Industrial Average) has historically traded at about 2.2 times book value.

Net Current Asset Value. A stricter view of a firm's worth is given by net assets. Start with current assets (all assets that will become cash within a year) and subtract current liabilities (debts due within a year) and long-term debt. The remaining figure does not include property, plant, or equipment and represents the working capital of a company. If the market value of a firm's shares falls below the net current asset value, a bargain situation could result. If an investor paid $20 per share for a company whose net current assets represented $30 per share, the investor would be buying a dollar for sixty-six cents and getting the property, plant, and equipment to boot. The investor then need only wait until the firm's true value is recognized by the market. The *Standard & Poor's Stock Guide* is an invaluable tool for searching for stocks selling for less than net current asset value. Also available are computer data disks with the balance sheet information for a wide range of companies. These disks may be screened with special computer programs. The ready availability of such information has possibly made these value situations even more transient and difficult to capitalize on.

Future Dividends. The prospect of future dividend increases is a primary consideration in evaluating a company's stock. Constructing accurate models of dividend growth is extremely difficult, however, because of the number of assumptions that must be made concerning interest rates, price levels, and other parameters. In general, a history of consistent and increasing dividends would be one favorable indicator, as well as management's stated intention to continue such payments.

Ratio Anaylsis. The final tool that is offered for the valuation of a company's stock is analysis of several ratios derived from the firm's financial statements. The following six factors can help the investor to estimate the underlying value of a company. Once this value is reached, it may be compared with the price at which the stock is currently trading, known as market value.

1. *Price/earnings ratio* (PE). PE market price divided by earnings per share. A PE of less than 9 could indicate a good value, and a PE in excess of 18 might indicate an expensive stock, while the middle range would be neutral. *The New Contrarian Investment Strategy*, by David Dreman, is an excellent source for those interested in the low PE investment theory.

2. *Price/sales ratio* (PSR). Kenneth Fisher, author of *Super Stocks*, is perhaps the main proponent of this measure of a firm's value. To find the PSR, divide the total market capitalization (outstanding shares multiplied by market price) by annual sales. Generally, companies should be bought if the PSR is less than 0.75 and sold when the PSR exceeds 3. Other factors augment this rule, however, and a review of the entire theory is recommended prior to use.

3. *Current ratio*. This measure is equal to current assets divided by current liabilities. A ratio of 1.5 or higher is favorable for many companies, representing a strong balance sheet.

4. *Dividend yield*. Dividing the annual dividend by the current market price gives the dividend yield. This figure is found in the stock section of most newspapers on the same line as the daily price quotation for a given stock. Dividends are usually fixed for a period of a year or more, and a company that intends to raise the dividend will typically do so once a year. For example, Exxon Corporation has paid these annual dividends: 1984, $1.68; 1985, $1.72; 1986, $1.80; 1987, $1.90; 1988, $2.15. Since the price of a stock can fluctuate widely, the dividend yield can be an indicator of the relative value of the stock at a given time. For example, if Exxon stock fell to a price of $20 during 1988, its dividend yield would be nearly 11 percent. It is doubtful that investors would let Exxon fall that far, however, because they would notice that dividend yield rising and begin buying when that yield began to exceed the current yield on alternative investments. Buying Exxon at a yield of 11 percent would be extremely attractive, though, because the total return on stocks are general has averaged only 9 percent over the long run. A dividend yield of 11 percent, plus whatever growth in share price occurs in the future, could be a promising situation.

5. *Market price to book value*. Market price divided by book value, or the market to book ratio, is a general tool for valuation. The stock market as a whole has traded for about 2.2 times book value over the long term. If a stock can be purchased for less than half its book value, it might be a real bargain. A stock trading at more than three times its book value could be expensive.

Measures of Market Value. The market value of a given stock can easily be found by calling a broker or checking a newspaper. Whether the market value is high or low depends on its relationship to the intrinsic value of the company as estimated by the investor. The DJIA is frequently used as a proxy for all stocks, and there are several rules of thumb that might help the investor surmise whether the market as a whole is high or low.

The DJIA, one of four stock averages compiled by Dow Jones, contains thirty stocks. The other three averages are the transportation index, with twenty issues; the utility index, with fifteen issues; and a composite average of all sixty-five companies combined. Now calculated in seconds by a computer, the Dow Jones averages are transmitted around the world every half hour of the trading day by the Dow Jones News Service. Another popular average is the S&P 500, an average of 500 companies likely to be in an investor's portfolio. Other measures include the NYSE Composite Index and the Value Line Composite Index.

The following four rules of thumb concerning the DJIA have proved useful to many common stock investors.

The Rule of 20. The number 20, minus the current inflation rate, should equal the PE of the DJIA. If, for example, the inflation rate is 5 percent, then the DJIA PE should be near 15. If the actual Dow PE at the time is 9, the market might be poised to rise over the next few years; perhaps a high percentage of a portfolio might be allocated to stocks, and the selection of industries might lean toward cyclical industries such as steel, automotive, paper, and chemical. If the market PE in this case is instead in the area of 22, as it was before the October 19, 1987 crash, then perhaps stocks should be limited in a portfolio, both in percentage allocation and in industry position. Defensive industries such as electric utilities and telephone, financial, energy, and beverage industries might be emphasized. The use of ratios in this manner is not meant to be a timing tool; rather, it is meant to be a tool for gauging the general market climate.

The Dow PE Ratio. In addition to the rule of 20, some general parameters of the DJIA PE have been useful. The Dow PE ratio since 1926 has averaged about 13.6. As with individual stocks, a PE of less than about 9 would be favorable, but a PE above 18 could indicate an unfavorable time for new stock purchases.

The Dow Dividend Yield. The dividend yield of the DJIA has also been a good indicator of market levels. When the DJIA rises, its dividends yield falls. The further the DJIA rises, the lower the dividend yield and the more risk to the market. When the DJIA dividend yield has been below 3 percent, a down market has usually followed. The market has been more favorably priced when the dividend yield was above 5.5 percent.

The Dow Market/Book Ratio. Since 1926, the DJIA has traded at about 2.2 times book value. At 1.5 times book, the DJIA would appear inexpensively priced; above 3.0 times book, the opposite could be true.

These ratios are not meant to be tools for short-term timing of the markets. They are merely statistics and should be regarded as such. If all four of them are giving the same signal, however, the investor should take notice.

With this background, the safest prediction that can be made about common stock prices in the short run is that they will fluctuate widely without any logical or explicable basis. In the long run, common stock prices can be expected to correlate substantially with corporate earnings, but the investor's patience will often be tired sorely before this relationship becomes apparent.

Two Strategies for Investing in Common Stocks. Why should a given stock be bought or sold, or why should an investor buy stock at all? There are at least two approaches to these questions: conservative and aggressive.

The Conservative Approach. The most conservative standard that one could impose on the investment decision would perhaps be one with legal implications. Trustees and others with fiduciary responsibility for assets with which they have been entrusted are required to observe the prudent man rule, as enunciated by the Supreme Court of Massachusetts in 1830:

> All that can be required of a trustee to invest is that he shall conduct himself faithfully and exercise a sound discretion. He is to observe how men of prudence, discretion, and intelligence manage their own affairs, not in regard to speculation, but in regard to the permanent disposition of their funds, considering the probable income, as well as the probable safety of the capital to be invested.

In 1934, Benjamin Graham also drew a precise line between these two strategies: "An investment operation is one which, upon thorough analysis, promises safety of principal and an adequate return. Operations not meeting these requirements are speculative."[4]

With a clear idea of the distinction between investment and speculation, the following three steps are offered as a strategy for conservative investment in common stocks:

Identification of Financial Limits. The investor should identify clearly the level of fluctuation of principal value that can be withstood from both a financial and an emotional standpoint. These limits should not be exceeded.

Projection of Investment Time. The time horizon, or projected length of the investment, should be determined. For individual investors, two scenarios are possible. The independently wealthy person may consider investment, from the institutional point of view discussed below. The modest individual investor, after emergency cash needs are met with an adequate cash reserve fund and any life insurance requirements are fulfilled, may commit funds to common stocks through the allocation model in step 3.

Generally, a person's financial life has four phases: early years, working years, saving years, and retirement years. The investment time horizon shortens with each phase, and the percentage of the investor's portfolio allocated to common stocks and other equities should accordingly decrease. Under normal circumstances, in the early years (ages 25 to 35), up to 75 percent of a securities portfolio might be allocated to equities; in the working years (ages 35 to 55), equities might make up 60 percent of a portfolio; during the savings years (ages 55 to 65), a portfolio might have 40 percent in equities; and during retirement (age 65+), a minimum of 25 percent should be allocated to stock. These percentages should be tempered by the investor's risk tolerance.

Institutional investors are somewhat disadvantaged in that it is frequently difficult to determine exactly what time frame should be used for their investments. Banks, for example, exist both in the short term and the long term. Loans being made and maturing, deposits swelling and depleting—these dynamic factors wreak havoc with the efforts of the careful bank portfolio manager. Mutual funds have a similar problem, especially those funds that allow shareholders to switch easily between funds in the same fund family. A mutual fund portfolio manager might be operating under the objective of growth and income, which would require certain positions in income stocks and others in growth-oriented stocks. If a major market downturn started, some of the shareholders might switch to

---

[4] Id., p. 1.

the money market fund in the same family to escape the downturn. If enough shareholders switch, the conservative portfolio manager might have to liquidate high-quality stocks, perhaps at a loss, in a falling market, in order to generate cash to redeem shares for the departing shareholders.

During the process of allocating a portfolio's assets, the question of time frame should be addressed and some parameters set. For conservative investors, both individual and institutional, it is suggested that a two- to five-year time frame be allowed for a stock to meet its objective.

Allocation of Stocks. In *The Intelligent Investor*, Benjamin Graham offers information concerning the allocation of common stocks in a conservative portfolio. A 50–50 ratio of stocks to bonds would be a conservative allocation. The ratio may be changed in either direction, but in no case should there be less than 25 percent in either category. For individuals, a minimum of ten issues and a maximum of thirty issues should be purchased, from several different industries. Buying at prices below net current asset value is recommended. In the long run, stocks should average about 7.5 percent in total return. Whenever bonds can be purchased with a yield that exceeds 7.5 percent, the bond component of the portfolio should be expanded. (The 7.5 percent figure for stock performance was offered by Benjamin Graham in 1973. As of the late 1980s, stocks have performed at a higher rate, in the range of 9 percent, since the 1920s. Accordingly, the rule about buying bonds might be adjusted to reflect this higher performance of stocks to, say, 9 percent instead of 7.5 percent.)

The Aggressive Approach. With respect to investments, speculation may be defined as buying or selling stocks, commodities, land, or the like in the hope of taking advantage of an expected rise or fall in price, or as taking part in any risky business venture or enterprise on the chance of making huge profits. Four aggressive strategies are as follows:

Technical Analysis. One of the most common aggressive approaches to market timing is technical analysis. An incredible amount of literature exists on the subject of technical analysis of the stock market. The debate between fundamental analysts and technicians has raged for years and will no doubt continue. Technicians are chided sometimes for spending tedious hours poring over their charts and tables, even earning the nickname elves on a popular weekly financial television program. Most brokerage firms have technicians on staff, and among investors there is a strong interest in this type of thought.

Briefly, a technician believes that the past price moves of a stock provide insight into future moves. By plotting these moves on a chart, the technician hopes to discern a pattern, to grasp an opportunity. A stock might make the following price moves during the course of several weeks: 15 to 20, then back to 15, up to 25, back to 15, up to 20, then back to 15. A sketch of this pattern resembles the front silhouette of a human head and shoulders (see Figure 2). The theory is that a support level of 15 would exist in this case, and that after this level had been tested and then broken through on the downside after a completed head and shoulders pattern, several weeks of price decline might be expected. An inverted head and shoulders pattern would signal the opposite.

Another favorite measure used by technicians is the thirty-nine week moving average. The DJIA closing prices for the past thirty-nine weeks are averaged every day, with the oldest close dropped and the most recent added. If the DJIA breaks through its thirty-nine week average, it theoretically signals a trend in the direction of the break.

These technical trading tools are designed to help the investor to buy low and sell high.

FIGURE 2. Head and Shoulders Pattern

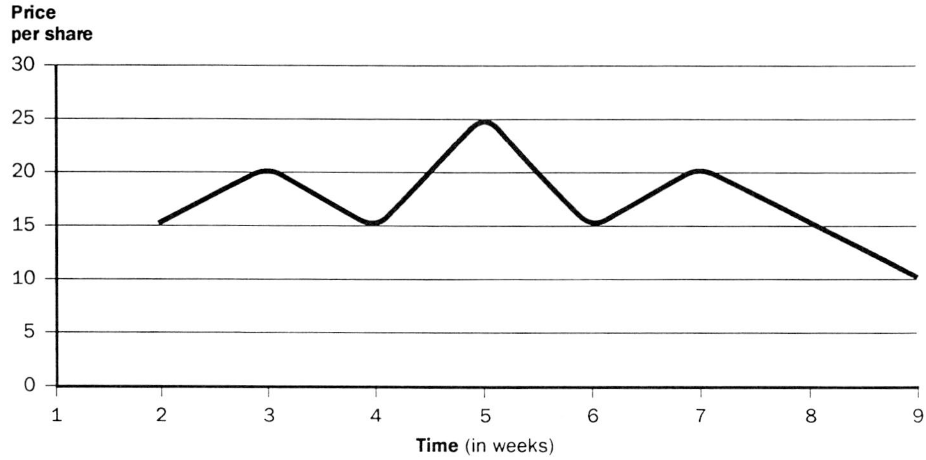

Speculation. A second aggressive strategy would be to speculate in growth stocks. Many of these companies sell for less than a dollar per share and are referred to as penny stocks. Other growth stocks sell for higher prices but have at least one thing in common with low-price stocks: extreme price volatility. Through research, the investor might discover a company that has a unique product or a new, untested drug. Selective investments in this area are risky but have the potential for high return.

Bargain Shopping. Taking advantage of a bargain situation is a third aggressive technique. The Chrysler Corporation required assistance from the federal government in the late 1970s, and its stock traded as low as 1⅜ during that period. Union Carbide Corporation stock tumbled when many deaths occurred in a 1984 plant accident in Bhopal, India. During a lawsuit between Texaco and Pennzoil Corporation in the mid-1980s, Texaco common shares traded at below book value for an extended period. The Three Mile Island nuclear disaster put General Public Utilities common stock under extreme pressure. Whether these situations are bargain speculations or conservative value purchases is hard to determine. If the key criterion for making this distinction is the expectation of a short-run price increase, then the speculative label would apply.

Arbitrage. Finally, two types of arbitrage are noteworthy: price arbitrage and risk arbitrage. Price arbitrage occurs when similar securities are purchased and sold in different markets in an effort to profit from price discrepancies. Risk arbitrage is the accumulation of shares of a company that is expected to undergo an imminent event that would drastically change the price. Tender offers are the most newsworthy of risk arbitrage operations. If a speculator can identify a buyout prospect and buy the shares before the tender offer starts to command media attention, profit could result. The main risk in this situation has nothing to do with the financial soundness of the company; rather, the main risk is whether the expected event will occur.

Other Strategies. Two additional topics of importance with regard to stock market strategy are averaging and diversification.

The concept of averaging is a way to reduce risk and potentially improve returns. For the conservative investor, dollar cost averaging involves the periodic purchase of a dollar amount of stock, regardless of the price. This method ensures that the investor buys during both up markets and down markets, and the average cost per share acquired will be neither the highest nor the lowest. The strategy can also reduce anxiety regarding timing of purchases: A basis is chosen, such as monthly or quarterly, and observed regardless of market conditions.

For aggressive investors, the averaging down strategy would be more suitable. Suppose an investor identified a stock that was believed to be a bargain. Shares are purchased at $20. Immediately the shares fall to $15. If the investor buys an equal number of shares for $15, the average cost for the entire position is $17.50. If the expected share price increase occurs, the overall profit will be higher because the cost of the shares has been averaged down.

Diversification is an important part of both conservative and aggressive strategies. The highest return on an investment might be achieved with no diversification at all: Buy a growth stock for $3 and sell it seven years later for $400. However, an extremely high degree of risk accompanies that strategy. A number of different stocks (ten to thirty) is suggested for conservative portfolios, chosen from a number of different industries. Industry diversification is the subject of a most interesting article, which shows that from 1940 to 1974, perfect industry timing would have generated investment returns far exceeding those generated by perfect stock market timing.[5] Diversification by security type, that is, stocks, bonds, convertible bonds, and others, will provide additional stability. Cyclical stocks and industries can complement growth stocks and industries, enabling the investor to tailor a portfolio to the specific objective and risk tolerance desired.

The most important aspect of diversification is time diversification. Figure 3 shows the performance of a particular common stock mutual fund since its inception in 1933. This fund is one of the several that have outperformed both the DJIA and the S&P 500 in every ten-year period ending December 31 from 1947 to 1987. A mutual fund was chosen for this illustration for two reasons. First, it represents a diversified portfolio of selected stocks, which is what a conservative investor should attempt to obtain. Second, unmanaged indexes such as the DJIA and S&P are typically used as a baseline but are inappropriate because the typical investor could not have bought the entire DJIA or S&P 500 (at least not until the advent of index mutual funds). Use of an unmanaged index also conveniently allows some writers to claim that the market can't be beaten. In the short run, this statement is difficult to disprove. In the long run, however, time diversification and conservative selection of stocks can generate quite satisfactory results.

Of the eighty-two common stock funds that are at least thirty years old, seven have outperformed both the DJIA and the S&P 500 on a ten-year basis as of 1987. Figure 3 shows the performance of one of these funds. A most interesting insight to be gained from this graph is that for periods ten years and longer, there are absolutely no negative rates of return. In other words, the patient investor with a ten-year investment horizon was consistently rewarded, regardless of market fluctuations. Time heals all wounds. The seven mutual funds, if viewed as a proxy for conservatively managed stock portfolios in general, serve to illustrate that common stocks are an excellent asset to include in portfolios with long-time horizons.

A concluding thought on how much stock an investor should own follows:

---

[5] "Common Stocks and the New Investor," *Wiesenberger Investment Companies*, Boston: Warren, Gorham & Lamont, 1975, p.66.

FIGURE 3. Rates of Return, 1934—1987, of a Particular Growth-and Income Common Stock Mutual Fund

Note: There are several mutual funds with similar performance data. The Investment Company of America was chosen for this example simply as a case in point; no recommendation or endorsement of this investment plan is implied.

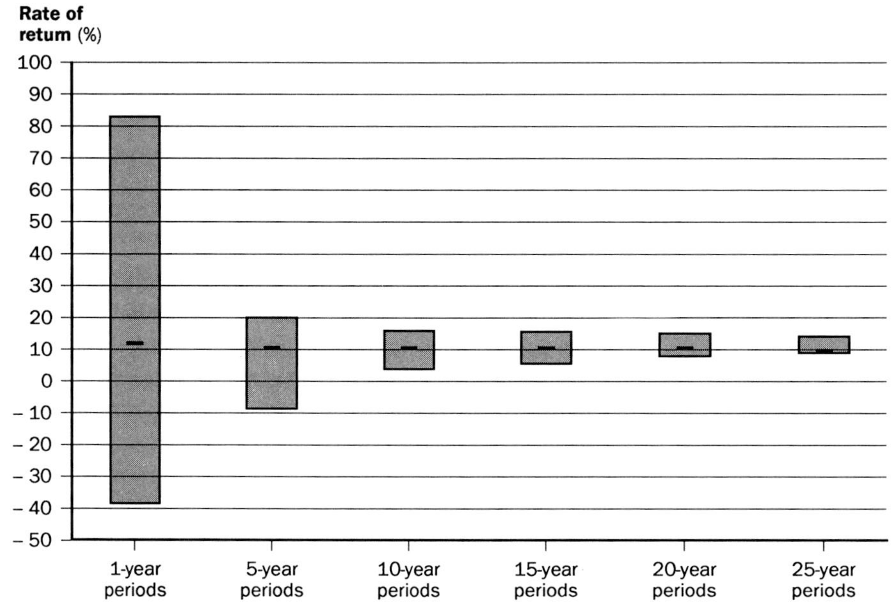

	1-year periods	5-year periods	10-year periods	15-year periods	20-year periods	25-year periods
High	83.2	20.1	16.5	15.7	15.1	14.5
Average (▬)	12.9	10.4	11.6	11.6	11.8	11.4
Low	- 38.4	- 8.2	4.3	6.0	8.2	9.6

Recognizing that higher returns are the incentive and reward for investors taking—and sustaining—an above-average market risk and the highest returns therefore come from equity investments, clients should set their portfolio's asset mix at the highest ratio of equities that their economic and emotional limitations can afford and sustain.[6]

POTENTIAL RISKS

The risks of owning any investment may be grouped into five categories: business risk, financial risk, interest rate risk, purchasing power risk, and market risk. In each category, the nature of the risk is defined, the effect of the risk on common stock is described, and a method for reducing the risk is identified.

Business Risk

Definition. Business risk is the risk associated with the business venture. Business risk manifests itself in many ways. General liability is a risk: Should a customer or employee be

[6] Charles D. Ellis, *Investment Policy: How to Win the Loser's Game*, Homewood, Ill.: Dow Jones-Irwin, 1985, p. 78.

injured on the premises of a business, the company runs the risk of a suit for damages. Product liability is one of the more celebrated types of business risk, perhaps the most notable example being that of the Ford Pinto automobile that exploded because of a faulty fuel tank design, resulting in a multimillion-dollar judgment against Ford Motor Company. The obsolescence of a product can also cost a corporation dearly; the classic example is the decline of buggy whip companies at the advent of the automobile, while more recently tobacco companies have been aggressively seeking alternative ways to market cigarettes and otherwise diversify their product lines. Fraud, weather, arson, acts of God, changing demographics, and changes in public opinion are all risks to which businesses may be subject.

Effect. Business risk can have a dramatic effect on the common stock of a corporation, the most damaging being outright bankruptcy. Since common stockholders receive only the residual assets after other claims are satisfied in a liquidation, business risk is of the utmost concern. Business risk has a similar effect on bonds, but in the event of liquidation the bondholders are in a superior position.

Reduction. Business risk may be diluted by an investor to the point where it is inconsequential. A useful rule of thumb is never to invest more than 10 percent of a portfolio in a given industry, nor more than 5 percent of a portfolio in a given stock. Stocks with conservative managements should balance stocks with more aggressive managements. The key to reducing business risk is trite but true: Don't put all the eggs in one basket; diversify your investments.

Financial Risk

Definition. Financial risk increases with the extent to which an enterprise is financed by debt. For example, if an enterpreneur with $10,000 approached a banker with a proposal to purchase an attractive tract of land and wanted a loan for $90,000, the banker, on reflecting that the enterprise would be 90 percent financed by debt, might be concerned about the financial risk involved and therefore decline. Conversely, if an entrepreneur with $90,000 approached the same banker for a $10,000 loan to buy the land, the banker would probably invite the customer to lunch and ultimately accept.

An investor may determine the amount of debt in a corporation by reviewing the balance sheet in the annual report. Additionally, services such as the *Standard & Poor's Stock Guide* and the *Value Line Investment Survey* display this information in a quite accessible format.

Effect. Common stocks of companies high in debt are at substantial financial risk. Should the business fail, there will be many claims to pay before the stockholders receive what, if anything, is left. Bonds are affected similarly, again with priority over stocks.

Reduction. Financial risk may be virtually eliminated by diversification. In a balanced portfolio, stocks without debt and risky stocks with increasing levels of debt would complement each other. It is worth noting that heavy debt leverages the assets of a company and will therefore magnify profits, possibly resulting in a much higher total return for the common stockholders. This situation is not without increased financial risk, however.

Interest Rate Risk

Definition. Historically, interest rates have fluctuated widely and without consistent pattern; thus the safest guess about interest rates is that this unpredictability will continue. Rising interest rates affect stock prices in a generally adverse way, driving the prices down. Falling interest rates usually have the opposite effect.

Effect. Rising interest rates portend higher costs for carrying inventory and borrowing money, which in turn means that the cost of supplying products will rise, squeezing profits and driving stock prices down. Another effect interest rates have is to drive down the prices of stocks in interest-sensitive industries more than those of stocks in general. For example, utility stock prices tend to fall as rates rise because, as the rates on short-term bank accounts and Treasury securities rise above the yields available on these stocks, investors have a strong incentive to sell the stocks and invest in the short-term investments. The reverse is also true. Bond prices vary almost inversely with interest rates for the same reason that utility stocks do.

Reduction. For the stock investor, two strategies might help. First, a portfolio should not be overconcentrated in stocks. Second, a stock portfolio should not be inundated with interest-rate-sensitive stocks.

Purchasing Power Risk

Definition. Purchasing power risk is the loss of buying power that results from inflation of the dollar.

Effect. Common stock dividends have historically outstripped the pace of inflation. However, there have been times when the total return of stocks did not outstrip inflation, usually in short time frames, such as five years or less. Over the long run, bonds can be devastated by inflation. As inflation fears arise, investors in the past have sought out hard assets for protection of buying power; as a result, gold usually fares well in times of rising interest rates.

Reduction. A portfolio should include assets that fare well in times of inflation as well as assets that have other strengths. (See article on "Historical Returns on Principal Investments," elsewhere in this volume.) Asset allocation is the name given to the process of selecting the percentage of money in a portfolio that is to be invested in a given asset class. Examples of asset classes include cash, stocks, bonds, real estate, precious metals, and collectibles. By evaluating the return, risk, and sensitivity to inflation of a class, an investor may reduce purchasing power risk to an appropriate level. Emphasis on dividend-paying stocks, real estate, and precious metals decrease purchasing power risk in a portfolio.

Market Risk

Definition. Market risk is the constant fluctuation of the market value of a given investment. It is measured by beta, a value that is reported in the *Standard & Poor's Stock Guide*. A beta of 1 means that the volatility of the stock is equal to the volatility of the market as a whole. Lower betas indicate lower volatility, and higher betas indicate greater volatility.

Effect. The specter of market risk can be a double-edged sword: Speculators love it and conservative investors wince. For the investor whose time horizon is matched to the assets held in the investor's portfolio, market risk is not a major factor.

Reduction. Because speculators seek fluctuation, they should avoid stocks with limited market risk, as indicated by the S&P beta value. Conservative investors should gain a thorough understanding of the time it takes for a serious common stock investment to succeed. Figure 3 is relevant, showing that common stock investments lend themselves to longer time frames.

TAX CONSEQUENCES

In investing, tax considerations should be secondary to economic considerations. That is, investments should be made because they are financially sound, not because they have tax advantages. Two types of taxable income generated by stocks are reviewed. Three tax-saving ideas are presented in the second part of this section.

Types of Taxable Income from Stocks

Dividend Income. For individual taxpayers, dividend income from common stocks is generally taxed as ordinary income. Corporations are allowed to exclude 70 percent of dividend income received from domestic corporation stock. Some corporations, in order to maintain a consistent dividend, may add cash from a source other than earnings to make the dividend payment. This may result in the part of the dividend not attributable to earnings being deemed a return of principal and therefore not subject to taxation. Although this treatment might be favorable to the investor in terms of taxes, the investor should determine whether paying out more money than was earned will have a deleterious effect on the future prospects of the company. A final note about dividends is that they are doubly taxed, that is, a corporation pays taxes on profits; from after-tax profit comes the cash to pay stockholders a dividend, which is included in the taxpayer's income and taxed again. This is a disadvantage of the corporate form of organization.

Capital Gains or Losses. A profit or loss on the disposition of a position in common stock is treated as a capital gain or loss. In 1988, capital gains are taxed at the same rate as ordinary income. It is noteworthy that Congress did not remove the distinctions of capital gains or losses from the tax code, even though the favorable treatment was eliminated (before the Tax Reform Act of 1986, only 40 percent of capital gains was taxable). Capital losses may offset capital gains, but there is a limit of $3,000 a year on such offsets for individual taxpayers. Losses beyond that may be carried over to future years.

Deferral of Capital Gains. Because capital gains and losses are taxable only when they are realized, an investor can defer taxation on a profit indefinitely by buying stock that is expected to grow in share price without a dividend payment.

A note about the taxation of mutual funds that invest in common stock is relevant. Capital gains that are realized within a mutual fund must be distributed annually to the fund's shareholders and are taxed to the shareholder in the year of receipt. This prevents efforts to defer taxes through share growth. An investor may control when a gain is realized with an individual stock, but not with a mutual fund.

Qualified Plans. Both dividend income and realized capital gains on stocks held within qualified retirement plans are not taxed until funds are distributed from the plan. Examples of qualified plans include individual retirement accounts (IRAs), defined contribution plans (both money purchase and profit sharing), defined benefit plans, 403(b) plans, and others.

Wash Sales. A wash sale occurs when a stock is sold at a loss and the same stock is purchased within thirty days either before or after the sale. An investor might do this in an attempt to establish a tax loss near the end of the calendar year without giving up the position in the stock, but the tax law prevents the loss from being recognized for tax purposes when the stock is purchased within thirty days.

REPRESENTATIVE TYPES OF INVESTORS

Investors in common stock may be grouped according to who they are, what their objective is, and the nature of their tax situation.

Individual or Institution

Individual investors are persons who have elected to buy or sell stock, usually in small amounts ranging from several hundred to thousands of dollars. These people own roughly two thirds of the stock that is on the various markets. Institutional investors may be individuals with huge sums of money to invest (usually $100,000 or more) or pension funds, trust funds, mutual funds, insurance companies, or any other entity that trades in stock in large blocks (multimillion-dollar trades). Institutional investors own about one third of the value of common stocks in the marketplace. On the other hand, individuals account for only about one third of the volume of trading in stocks, while institutions are responsible for two thirds.

Investment Objective

Preservation of Capital. The investor who wants to preserve capital will be most interested in blue chip, income, and defensive issues that can be expected to keep up with inflation and pay reasonable dividends.

Income. An income-oriented investor will be interested in maximum dividend payments and less concerned about principal fluctuations. Utility stocks or other high-dividend-paying stocks will be the most suitable.

Growth. The growth-oriented investor will be concerned with total return over the long run. Growing industries will interest this investor more than basic or cyclical industries.

Growth and Income. This type of investor will find that a diversified list of stocks, including high and low dividend payers, will be most suitable.

Speculative. The speculator is most likely interested in making the most money in the least time, and risk is a secondary consideration. Lower-priced stocks, growth stocks, bargain situations, arbitrage, and the seemingly never-ending stream of new ideas and concepts offered by Wall Street will be the speculator's primary concern.

Tax Situation

Low Tax Bracket. An investor with low income taxes will be able to purchase stocks without regard to tax consequences; that is, current dividends will not be a problem, nor will multiple transactions in the same tax year (unless great success causes a capital gains tax problem).

High Tax Bracket. The highly taxed investor will be interested in the tax-deferred nature of investing through qualified plans or in stocks that pay little or no dividends. Corporations in high tax brackets will find the 70 percent dividend exclusion quite favorable.

IMPORTANT FACTORS IN BUYING AND SELLING

The investor may either assume the responsibility for execution or delegate it. The investor may also delegate the selection and management process.

Self-Management

The decision whether to manage one's own money or to delegate hinges on these factors: Does the investor wish the investment decisions to be based on his or her research or that of a professional money manager? Does the investor wish to be involved in registering the securities in the appropriate name, collecting dividends, and tendering certificates for splits, mergers, and other details? Self-management is appropriate for those to whom these activities have appeal. Others should delegate these tasks. Following are several decision areas in the management of common stock purchase and ownership.

Type of Broker. Stock and bond brokers may be classified as either full-service or discount. The range of services offered by brokerage firms varies substantially from one organization to another. Some firms offer the complete gamut of investments: money market funds with checkwriting, Treasury bills, notes, and bonds, corporate bonds, municipal bonds, stocks, mutual funds, options, commodity contracts, limited partnerships, precious metals, international currency, and other programs. Other firms specialize in just a few of these activities. Discount brokers typically offer no advice and no research, but their commission rates for trade execution can be up to 70 percent lower than full-service firms. Full-service firms usually discount, however, in order to maintain the business of substantial customers.

Since brokers are usually compensated by commissions, it is possible that some brokers may not be completely objective about a client's buy/sell decision. Caution should prevail if a broker seems more interested in the immediate execution of the trade in question rather than the interests of the client. Brokers who are serious about being in the business for the long term will always put their clients' interests ahead of their own. It is extremely easy for a client to fire a broker and seek the services of another; this is perhaps the most effective policing mechanism offered by the marketplace, and clients should be willing to use it, if necessary. Brokers at discount firms might be compensated on a salary and as a result not have to deal with this conflict of interest, but, on the other hand, providing advice is not usually in their job description. Some of the leading brokerage firms are identified at the end of this article.

The actual transfer of stock is quite simple: The back of the stock certificate must be filled out, the seller's signature must be guaranteed by a commercial bank or a member of NYSE, and the executed certificate must be sent to the transfer agent named on the front of the certificate. A stock power may be signed when the certificate is in the broker's name. The stock power is attached to the certificate.

Types of Accounts. Brokers maintain both cash and margin accounts for their customers.

Cash. A cash account is one in which securities are purchased and paid for by cash or check within five business days. To open a cash account, the client must provide name, date of birth, address, and Social Security or taxpayer identification number and perhaps answer other questions.

Margin. A margin account operates on credit. When securities are purchased, the brokerage firm lends the customer some of the money to cover the transaction. The maximum amount of money that can be borrowed initially and to maintain the account is a percentage set by the Federal Reserve System; each brokerage firm can set minimum maintenance requirements above the regulation. The customer must sign a margin agreement, that gives the brokerage firm the authority to pledge the customer's securities against loans.

Buying stock on margin increases the risk involved in the transaction; it is possible to lose more than the amount of cash initially placed in the account. In the same way that increased debt increases the financial risk of a business enterprise, margin debt increases the financial risk of a given stock transaction. The potential return is magnified, but not without a commensurate increase in risk. Margin trading is of most interest to speculators. Conservative investors and those with fiduciary responsibilities should carefully evaluate and probably avoid margin accounts.

Types of Orders. There are several types of orders for common stocks and several variations of these orders. For a comprehensive discussion of these, the reader should refer to Allan H. Pessin's *Fundamentals of the Securities Industry.*[7]

Market Orders. A market order is intended to be executed at or near the current trading price and as soon as possible. Investors wishing an immediate disposition of their order regardless of price should place a market order.

Limit Orders. Limit orders are to be executed at a given price, or at a better price. For example, a limit order to buy a stock at 30 would fill at 30, or 29⅞, or any lower price. A limit order to sell at 30 would fill at 30, 30⅛, or higher, provided there is a buyer at that price.

Stop Orders. An execution price is specified on a stop order; when this price is reached, a stop order becomes a market order. A stop order to sell might be placed under

[7] Allan H. Pessin, *Fundamentals of the Securities Industry*, New York: Institute of Finance, 1985.

the current market price of a stock, by 2 points, for example. This would be a sell stop order. If the market price fell to the sell stop price, the order would become a market order and be executed next, regardless of the price. Sometimes, these orders are referred to as stop-loss orders, but this is a misnomer. It is true that if a stop order is placed below the current market price and the market price falls to the stop price, the stop order will become a market order, but if the market price is dropping rapidly, the order may fill at a price far below the stop price.

The following types of orders may be qualified in certain ways.

Short Sales. A stock may be sold in a short margin account, even though the seller has no shares of that stock in the account at the time. The brokerage firm borrows shares from another account to deliver to the buyer. For example, Mr. Speculator believes that the price of ABC Inc. stock will fall as a result of bad publicity on one of ABC's products. Speculator sells short 100 shares of ABC common at $50. The price falls to $40, and he buys the shares back at the lower price, making a profit of ten points.

A short sale must be made on an uptick or a zero plus tick. An uptick is a transaction that took place at a higher price than the previous transaction and is also higher than the last transaction that was at a different price. For example, if a stock trades at 49⅞ and then at 50, 50 is an uptick. If the same stock trades again at 50, the second trade at 50 would be a zero plus tick. When selling short, the investor must put up part of the cost of the stock sold and is liable for all dividends paid on the stock.

Day Orders. A day order must be executed the day it is placed, or it is canceled. All orders are assumed to be day orders unless otherwise specified.

Good-till-Canceled (GTC) Orders. These are valid indefinitely until canceled. Usually, brokerage firms will evaluate GTC orders periodically to ensure that the customer still desires that they remain in effect and that the relationship of the market price to the limit price is not far out of line. For example, one brokerage firm automatically cancels GTC orders that are more than thirty days old and more than 25 percent away from the market price.

All or None. For transactions exceeding 100 shares, the customer may specify that the entire order be executive at the same time and price or not at all.

Fill or Kill Orders. A fill or kill order must be executed immediately or it is canceled. A price limit is specified.

There are a few more combinations of orders and qualifications, but the foregoing should give the reader an idea of the flexibility of the trading system and provide a basis for discussion with brokers.

Types of Settlement. The two main types of settlement are cash and regular way. Cash settlements are made within a day or two of the trade day; that is, the actual stock certificates will be exchanged for payment within that time. By far the more common type is the regular way settlement, whereby the exchange takes place on the seventh calendar day after the trade date, excluding holidays. The seventh calendar day would normally be the fifth business day.

In a delivery against payment transaction, payment is given only on the actual delivery of the certificates. Banks and institutional investors frequently wish to use the delivery against payment form of settlement. In some circumstances, settlements may be extended past the seventh day. The National Association of Securities Dealers manual explains in detail circumstances that allow delayed delivery settlement.

Types of Ownership. Legal ownership of an account is extremely important. Only persons whose names appear on an account's registration may place orders in or remove money from the account. They may authorize a third party to place trades or remove money by executing a limited or full trading authorization, which the broker provides. Since securities are assets that could be included in an estate, the ownership of these assets is critical.

Single. The customer's own name and Social Security or taxpayer identification number are used.

Joint. A joint account has more than one name on it. Any person so named may operate the account. The owners may be tenants in common or joint tenants with the right of survivorship. Some states have laws that draw further legal distinctions. It is most important that the customers seek legal counsel to determine the desired form of ownership. Otherwise, an undesired distribution of the property may result at the death of one of the joint tenants.

Uniform Gift to Minors Act (UGMA). Because a minor may not have a brokerage account, a custodian may set up an account on the minor's behalf. If the value of the account belongs to the minor, it is intended that the assets in the account be distributed to the minor on achieving majority, a UGMA account would be appropriate.

Partnership. A partnership may operate a brokerage account. The broker should provide the forms required—usually a copy of the partnership agreement and written instructions concerning who may operate the account.

Corporation. Corporations may also set up accounts. Stocks purchased in a corporate account would qualify for the 70 percent dividend exclusion previously mentioned.

Estate Accounts. An executor may set up an estate account for the purpose of liquidating securities or transferring them into another name.

Custodial Care. The best criteria in deciding whether to hold securities in customer name or in some kind of custodial agreement would be (1) involvement—the more involved with the details the customer wants to be, the more attractive a customer name looks and (2) activity—the more active the account will be, the more convenient a street name account will be.

Once an account is set up, the customer must decide where the assets are to be stored. There are four choices.

Customer Name. The term "customer name" refers to the process of printing the name of the customer on the face of the stock certificate and then delivering the actual certificate to the customer's address, which usually takes four to six weeks. The advantages of holding securities in customer name are that (1) some customers feel more secure if they are in possession of the certificates; (2) the customer can sell the security at any brokerage; and (3) dividend checks and other communications come directly to the customer and are not delayed in a brokerage firm's back office. Disadvantages of holding one's own certificates are that (1) it may be inconvenient for the customer to get a safe deposit box; (2) on execution of an order, the customer must mail or deliver the certificates to the broker within seven days; and (3) if a dividend check gets lost, the customer must pursue the matter alone unless a broker is willing to help.

Street Name. Leaving securities in a broker's street name causes no security problems: Brokerages are usually covered by the Securities Investors Protection Corporation (SIPC), which protects customers from the failure of the brokerage firm up to certain limits. When selling stock that is held in a street name account, a phone call is all that is required, since the broker is already in possession of the item to be sold. Lost dividend checks should be tracked down by the brokerage firm. One other note about street name accounts is that if a customer signs a margin agreement, the brokerage may pledge the customer's securities as collateral for loans to the brokerage and may also lend the shares to other customers for short sales.

Banks. Bank trust departments will handle all the preceding matters for a fee. If desired, they will also provide money management services.

Qualified Plans. IRAs and other types of qualified plans must be held by trustees, which attend to the details of holding securities.

Initial Public Offerings. Some research and planning is necessary if the customer wishes to be active in the IPO or new issues market. First, since this is a speculative activity, the investor should take care to become educated in the fine points of the business. Second, the investor might seek out a brokerage firm that specializes in IPOs. Usually brokers allot shares of fast-selling IPOs to established and substantial clients. A red herring prospectus, covering the details of the offering but without key items such as selling price and underwriting concessions, is issued prior to the offering. The final prospectus will contain all the material facts.

During an offering (initial or secondary), a broker might mention to the customer that there is no commission added onto the price. This means that the stock is sold on a net basis and that, technically, the customer pays no commission. However, the amount of the commissions received by the underwriting brokerages is spelled out in the prospectus, and the public can review this document and realize that less than 100 percent of the offering proceeds will go to the issuing company. As a result, it is not unusual for the price of a new issue to drop by the amount of the underwriting discount almost immediately after the offering, unless some other market factor is at work. The point here is that the old saw "There's no such thing as a free lunch" applies to securities offerings with no commission.

Delegated Management

If an investor does not wish to become involved with the selection and management of a stock portfolio, this task may be delegated.

Investment Counselors. There are many firms that, for an annual fee ranging from 0.5 percent to 2 percent or more, will manage a portfolio and tend to the details of owning stock. A small account for an investment manager might be between $100,000 and $500,000. Most professionally managed private accounts exceed $1 million. There is a growing trend in the brokerage community for a broker to introduce a client to a money manager; if the client agrees, the money manager will make the investment decisions and instruct the broker to execute them, while the broker retains custody of the assets. This arrangement removes the conflict of interest that brokers must deal with, that is, receiving commissions and giving advice on which commissions are contingent. The investor in this case pays a fee to the manager and commissions to the broker. It should be mentioned that, although a conflict exists in broker compensation, many brokers manage this conflict to the complete satisfaction of their clients; if this were not the case, the brokers would have no clients.

Bank Trust Departments. A bank trust department will perform the services mentioned above, for a fee.

Mutual Funds. Investors may own stocks by purchasing common stock mutual funds. The annual expense of owning shares of an established, efficient fund is about 0.5 percent of total assets annually. The track records of mutual funds are a matter of public record. Excellent services that provide fund performance information include *Wiesenberger's Investment Companies*, *Standard & Poor's Stock Guide*, and *Johnson's Charts*. Mutual funds are covered in "Mutual Funds," elsewhere in this volume.

GLOSSARY

capital stock—Units of ownership of a corporation; common stock and preferred stock are the two types.

common stock—One type of capital stock; represents equity ownership in a corporation.

Dow Jones industrial average (DJIA)—An average of the share prices of thirty industrial companies, reported at half-hour intervals every business day; used as an indicator of market volatility.

fourth market—Name given to the trading of stock between institutional investors without the use of brokers.

fundamental analysis—Scrutiny of all available information about a company, including, but not limited to, earnings, capital structure, history, financial statements, and management. Compare to *technical analysis*.

par value—An arbitrary value assigned to shares for accounting purposes.

preferred stock—A type of capital stock, equity ownership in a corporation. Called preferred because dividends must be paid on it before any dividends on common stock may be paid. Preferred stock can be nonvoting and can also be convertible to common stock.

price/earnings ratio (P&E)—Market price divided by earnings per share.

primary market— The selling of shares of a corporation to the public for the first time; also referred to as initial public offering (IPO).

prospectus—A document that spells out material facts about a new offering.

secondary market—Trading in a company's stock that arises after the primary offering.

short selling—Selling a security that one does not own, by borrowing the stock, in the hope of a price decline.

third market—Trading in the over-the-counter (OTC) market of stocks listed on an organized exchange (such as the New York Stock Exchange or the American Stock Exchange).

technical analysis—Study of historical price and volume data of stocks in search of patterns that might help predict future price trends. Compare to *fundamental analysis*.

total return—A measure of investment performance found by considering the dividends received plus or minus the capital gain or loss over a given time period.

value approach—An approach to investing in common stocks that stresses that the underlying value of a company's assets should be determined and then compared to the current market price in order to make a buy or sell decision.

yield—The amount of money received per year divided by the amount of money invested. With respect to stocks, the *dividend yield* is the annual dividend divided by the market price (or price paid). The *earnings yield* is earnings per share divided by market price.

BROKERAGE FIRMS

FULL-SERVICE BROKERAGE FIRMS

A.G. Edwards & Sons, Inc.

Dain Bosworth, Inc.

Dean Witter Reynolds, Inc.

Donaldson Lufkin & Jenrette Securities Corp.

Edward D. Jones & Co.

First Boston Corp.

Goldman Sachs & Co.

Gruntal & Company

Kidder Peabody & Company, Inc.

Merrill Lynch, Pierce, Fenner & Smith, Inc.

Morgan Stanley & Company, Inc.

Newhard Cook

Paine Webber, Inc.

Piper, Jafray & Hopwood, Inc.

Prudential Bache

Shearson Lehman Hutton

Smith Barney, Harris Upham & Company, Inc.

Thomson McKinnon Securities, Inc.

DISCOUNT BROKERAGES

Charles Schwab & Company, Inc.

Olde Discount Corporation

Rose & Company Investment Brokers, Inc.

SUGGESTED READING

Cottle, Sydney, Murray, Roger, and Block, Frank. *Security Analysis*, 5th ed. New York: McGraw-Hill, 1988.

Dreman, David. *The New Contrarian Investment Strategy*. New York: Random House, 1982.

Ellis, Charles D. *Investment Policy: How To Win the Loser's Game*. Homewood, Ill.: Dow Jones-Irwin, 1985.

Fisher, Kenneth. *Super Stocks*. Homewood, Ill.: Dow Jones-Irwin, 1984.

Graham, Benjamin. *The Intelligent Investor*, 5th ed. New York: Harper & Row, 1973.

Hallman, G., and Rosenbloom, J. *Personal Financial Planning*, 3rd rev. ed. New York: McGraw-Hill, 1985.

Lehman, Michael B. *The Dow Jones-Irwin Guide to Using the Wall Street Journal*. Homewood, Ill.: Dow Jones-Irwin, 1984.

Loll, L., and Buckley, J. *The Over the Counter Securities Markets*, 4th ed. Englewood Cliffs, N.J.: Prentice-Hall, 1981.

Mayo, H. *Investments: An Introduction*. Chicago: Dryden Press, 1984.

National Association of Securities Dealers, Inc. *Reprint of the Manual*. Chicago: Commerce Clearing House, 1988.

Pessin, Allan H. *Fundamentals of the Securities Industry*. New York: New York Institute of Finance, 1985.

Pike, W. *Why Stocks Go Up (and Down): A Guide to Sound Investing*. Homewood, Ill.: Dow Jones-Irwin, 1983.

CONVERTIBLE SECURITIES

Thomas H. Dinsmore

BASIC CHARACTERISTICS

Convertible securities are senior investment instruments (bonds or preferred stock) that can be converted by the holder into a predetermined number of shares of common stock, usually the common stock of the issuing corporation. Convertibles have all the fundamental characteristics of bonds or preferred stocks, such as the scheduled payment of interest or dividends and, in the case of bonds, the repayment of principal (if they should mature unconverted). They are also senior to common stock in claims on corporate assets.

The purchase of a convertible provides the investor with two separate investments in one instrument: (1) a corporate bond or preferred stock, the value of which is affected by current interest rates and (2) a right or warrant to exchange for common stock, the value of which is directly affected by the price of the common stock. The investor pays one price for the combination of these features.

As a bond or preferred stock, the convertible will be more expensive than similar nonconvertible issues. As a right or warrant, the price will be at a premium over the value of the stock. The convertible market is generally efficient at recognizing the value of these features when pricing an issue, but there are often good buys available. It is the combination and the way that combination works that makes convertibles attractive.

Convertible securities provide an excellent investment alternative when the investment objectives are both capital appreciation and income. Capital appreciation comes from the conversion feature. As the underlying common stock moves up, the convertible

---

Thomas H. Dinsmore, C.F.A., is President of the Davis/Dinsmore Management Company, New York.

participates (to the extent that the premium over conversion value, or parity, is not reduced). In the end, if the stock moves up very strongly, then the convertible would reflect most of that rise. Conversely, if the stock falls sharply, the convertible should fall only to the level where the dividends or interest payments would support it as if it were a nonconvertible (straight) issue.

Basic Analysis of Convertible Securities

Buying a convertible security is not difficult. There are many major brokerage firms that have specialists devoted to the brokering of convertibles. This market has grown to approximately 5 to 10 percent of the entire equity market. Including private placement issues, the convertible market value is probably more than $100 billion today. However, determining whether buying a particular issue is right is another matter, and ignorance can be painful.

The basic analysis of a convertible security is mostly an objective process, but one that should start with the company and its common stock. Convertibles are really equity investments, and the investor must decide if the common stock would be worth owning.

After analyzing the common stock, there are specific tools that can be used to judge an issue. These factors include the yield, conversion premium, break-even (or payback) time, and investment value. For the purposes of our discussion here of a basic analysis, we will use the sample analysis of the IBM 7.875 percent convertible debentures maturing in 2004 as shown in Table 1. In the following discussion, all numbers shown in parentheses will come from the sample analysis.

Common Stock and Debt Analysis. The investor should first determine, by using the appropriate equity analysis methods, if the stock underlying the convertible is attractive and one that would be satisfactory to own. The company's balance sheet and earning prospects should then be examined to determine the safety of principal and interest. If the balance sheet is weak, then the convertible may be as risky as the common stock.

Conversion Premium. The premium to conversion value is the percentage (or dollar) difference between the current market price of the convertible and the value of the common stock the issue is convertible into. A lower premium is more attractive than a higher one, but the most appropriate premium is a function of a number of factors.

Conversion premium is not difficult to figure out. First, find the conversion value (or parity) by multiplying the conversion rate by the current stock price (6.508 shares multiplied by the $126.375 price equals $822.449). This is the dollar value of the stock that the bond could be exchanged into if converted at these levels.

Next, to get the dollar premium, subtract the conversion value from the current market price of the bond ($1,047.50 − $822.449 = $225.051).

Finally, to get the percentage conversion premium, divide the dollar premium by the conversion value ($225.051/$822.449 = 27.36%). The premium on the IBM 7.875 percent bonds is 27.36 percent. All other things being equal for a convertible bond selling near par ($1,000), an appropriate premium would be in the 20 to 30 percent range. A higher premium may be acceptable if the current yield is high. Larger premiums may also be appropriate where the conversion rate is very high because the leverage of a high rate can mean large swings in parity on very small moves in the common stock; for example, on a bond with a conversion rate of 200 shares per bond, a 50 cent price change in the common stock would move parity by 10 points, or $100 per bond. Premiums should be lower if the common dividend yield is high or if the common stock is at or near record high levels.

TABLE 1. Sample Analysis of Convertible Bonds

IBM 7.875% due 11/21/2004 Convertible Subordinated Debentures

Conversion rate:	6.508 shares
Conversion price:	$153.66
Call protection:	Not callable until 11/21/1988
First call price	104.725 ($1047.25)
Bond price:	104.75 ($1047.50)
Common stock price:	$126.375
Common stock dividend (annual):	$4.40 per share

Determining Conversion Premium

	Common price	$126.375
Times:	Conversion rate	× 6.508
Equals:	Conversion value	$822.449
	Bond price	$1,047.500
Minus:	Conversion value	−822.449
Equals:	Dollar premium	$225.051
	Dollar premium	$225.051
Divided by:	Conversion value	÷ 822.449
Equals:	Conversion premium	27.36%

Determining Current Yield and the Yield Advantage

Annual bond coupon (7.875% × $1000)		$78.75
Divided by:	Bond price	/1,047.50
Equals:	Current yield	7.52%
	Common dividend	$4.84
Divided by:	Common price	/126.375
Equals:	Common yield	3.83%
	Convertible yield	7.52%
Less:	Common yield	−3.83%
Equals:	Yield advantage	3.69% or 369 basis points

Determining Break-Even Time

(1) Premium method (a "quick and dirty" method)

Conversion premium		27.36%
Divided by:	Yield advantage	/3.69%
Equals:	Break-even time	7.41 years

(2) Dollar method (the most exact method)

A. Calculate stock equivalent income

	Bond price	$1,047.50
Times:	Common yield	× 3.83%
Equals:	Stock equivalent income	$40.12

(continued)

TABLE 1. *(continued)*

Determining Break-Even Time

B. Calculate dollar income advantage

Annual bond income		$78.75
Less:	Stock equivalent income	− 40.12
Equals:	Income advantage	$38.63

C. Calculate the break-even time

	Dollar premium	$225.051
Divided by:	Income advantage	/38.63
Equals:	Break-even time	5.83 years

Shortcut: The dollar break-even is equal to the premium break-even divided by one plus the percent premium:

(Dollar break-even = 7.41/1.2736 = 5.82 years)

This shortcut is convenient for spreadsheet analysis, as it is easy to program.

(3) Income method

A. Determine income advantage of bond over common stock

Annual bond income		$78.75
Minus:	Stock income (6.508 × $4.84)	−31.50
Equals:	Income advantage	$47.25

B. Divide dollar premium by income advantage

Dollar premium		$225.051
Divided by:	Income advantage	/47.25
Equals:	Break-even time	4.76 years

Determining Investment Value and Premium to Investment Value

Determine the yield* of a similar nonconvertible instrument, issued either by the same company or by an equally rated company in the same industry:

Compare IBM 7.875% convertible subordinated debentures of 2004 to the IBM 9.375% debentures of 2004 priced at 99:

Coupon of convertible		7.875%
Divided by:	Current yield of straight	/9.47
Equals:	Investment value	83.16 or $831.60
Dollar difference (1047.50 − 828.93)		$218.57
Divided by:	Investment value	/828.93
Equals:	Premium to investment value	26.37%

* For this analysis, using the current yield is acceptable. If either of the bonds were selling at a large discount or if the maturities were short, then yield to maturity should be used.

Yield and Yield Advantage. It is a yield on a convertible security that makes it possible for it to outperform a declining or flat common stock. The market pays a premium over the conversion value because of the yield advantage the convertible has over the common stock.

On new issues or issues near par, a rule of thumb is that the yield should be near or above current short-term interest rates. There should also be a yield advantage to the issue over the common stock. In the IBM example, the bond yields 7.52 percent and the common stock yields 3.83 percent, so the yield advantage is 7.52 percent minus 3.83 percent, or 3.69 percent. The yield advantage should vary with the premium: A high yield advantage is worth a higher premium than a low yield advantage. How much the yield advantage will vary from issue to issue is indicated, in part, by analyzing a statistic known as break-even time.

Break-Even Time (Payback Period). This statistic is used to measure the time that it takes the yield advantage of the convertible security to pay back the premium paid over conversion parity. Thus, the break-even time equals the premium/yield advantage. Break-even time provides the investor with an objective measure of how long the holding period might be for that investor to find the convertible and the common stock equally attractive.

There are three methods for figuring break-even time. All three are shown in the sample analysis. The dollar method is the most accurate, and the income method gives the shortest period. The premium method is a "quick and dirty" method that slightly overestimates break-even time. Simply take the premium and divide it by the yield advantage (27.36%/ 3.69% = 7.41 years). This method is useful because it is simple and, as will be shown later, can be used in a shortcut process for determining a more accurate number.

The dollar method is more complex, but it is the most accurate of the three methods. The premium used for this method is the dollar difference between the bond price and conversion parity ($1,047.50 − 822.449 = $225.051).

The yield advantage is the difference between the bond's annual coupon and the dividend income that would be generated by an equal dollar amount of common stock. The dollar yield of the common stock can be figured by taking the bond price and multiplying it by the current yield of the common stock ($1,047.50 × (4.84/126.375) = $40.12). The dollar yield advantage is $78.75 − 40.12 = $38.63. Break-even would be $225.051/ 38.63, or 5.83 years.

There is a shortcut that can be used to determine the dollar break-even. Take the premium method break-even (percent premium/percent yield advantage) and divide it by one plus the conversion premium. In the sample analysis, it is shown to be (27.36%/3.69%/ 1.2736 = 5.82 years. This is simple to program for spreadsheet analysis.

The income method is popular among some brokers, even though it often understates break-even time. It is similar to the dollar method, except that the yield advantage is figured differently. In this case, the income from the common stock is based on the shares the issue is convertible into. The IBM sample analysis shows that the dollar premium is divided by the income advantage to obtain a break-even time of 4.76 years. Note that this method compares the income from a $1,047.50 investment (the price of the bond) with the income from an $822.45 investment (6.508 shares of stock).

Important Factors in Break-Even Analysis. There are several criticisms of break-even analysis, and they should be understood. Three main criticisms are as follows:

1. The analysis ignores the net present value of the cash flows involved.

2. It implies that a convertible would be more attractive if the company were to cut its dividend.

3. The statistic becomes less meaningful for an issue where the underlying common stock has a very large dividend, especially when the income method is used.

Break-even analysis is useful when the investor has a specific time horizon in mind, or if the convertible is subject to maturity, redemption, or a put. In such cases, the investor can determine what the likely holding period of the investment might be. If the break-even time is much longer than this, the common stock may be a better investment.

Investment Value. Investment value is the price level that a convertible issue would sell for in the market if it was not convertible. To determine investment value, examine similar nonconvertible issues with equal seniority and maturity from the same company (or industry, if necessary). If such an issue is available, compare the yields, and determine the price that the convertible would have to sell at to provide the same yield.

In the IBM sample analysis a direct comparison between the IBM 7.875 percent convertible subordinated debentures maturing in 2004 can be made with the IBM 9.375 percent subordinated debentures of 2004. The 9.375 percent bonds recently sold at 99 for a current yield of 9.47 percent. For an issue with a 7.875 percent coupon to provide the same yield, it would have to sell around $832 (7.875/9.47 = 83.2%; 83.2% × $1,000 = $832).

For bonds with short maturities or large discounts to par, yields to maturity should be compared instead of current yields. Current yields are fine for preferred stocks.

Other Important Features. There are other important features that should be investigated before using convertibles in a portfolio. Some of these are unique to just a few issues, and the only complete source of information is the indenture or prospectus.

Call Provisions. An investor should understand the call protection included with any convertible selling with a premium at or above the call price. For example, Ben and Jerry's Homemade Ice Cream has a 9.5 percent convertible bond outstanding, it is selling at 118, parity is just under 102, and its call price in 1989 is 107.60. If they were to call the bond, it would immediately lose 9.45 points. Fortunately, it has provisional call protection that is in place until December 1989. Provisional call protection is essentially the same as standard call protection except that if the stock trades above a certain level (in this case $21.70 per share) for a set period (20 of 30 trading days), then the bonds are callable. Here, the stock is trading around $15.75, so the provisional call is not of immediate importance; however, if the stock did get to $21.70, then parity would be $1,400, and it would have been a good investment. The purpose of the call feature, especially the provisional call feature, is to allow the company to force conversion of the bonds or preferred stock into common stock; this is usually beneficial to the company's balance sheet and income statement. The purpose of call protection is to allow the investor time to take advantage of owning the convertible rather than the common stock.

Conversion Features. All convertibles have conversion features, but some are slightly different from others. Most are straightforward and include the following:

- Convert by submitting issue to conversion agent.
- Conversion rate is adjusted for stock splits, stock dividends and, sometimes, spinoffs of assets.
- Take-overs or mergers require issues to either remain convertible into the surviving company or to receive the same offer of cash or stock per share (assuming conversion).
- Interest accrued but not paid will be lost on conversion.
- No fractional shares will be issued; cash will be paid instead.
- Conversion feature usually expires just before or on the maturity date or redemption date.

Significant differences used to be common, often to the detriment of the holder; however, the above has become standard and few recent issues are different.

Sinking Fund Provisions. Most convertible bonds and some convertible preferred stocks have provisions that obligate the issuer to buy back a portion of the issue (often 5 percent) every year after a set date, usually ten years after issue. This helps increase buying interest in an issue that has been around for a while and is selling below call price.

Puts, Take-over Provisions, and Resets. A put feature is an extremely attractive feature that few convertibles have. This feature gives the holder the right to sell the bond or preferred back to the company at a set time in the future at a set price. The Helen of Troy 7.25 percent of '07 has a put feature that allows the holder to sell the bonds back to the company at a price of 117 in May, 1992. Those who bought the new issue for $1000 would get a $170 profit in addition to the yield generated by the coupon (provided, of course, the company remains solvent).

Takeover provisions (TOPs) involve a variety of situations. If a convertible is selling with a big premium and the company is taken over, it is possible that the issue would go down in value. Recently, some new issues have included provisions that help prevent this. The provisions vary from puts to mandatory calls to voting rights. The convertible market has not yet settled on a standard TOP.

Resets currently take two forms. The first resets the conversion rate on a set date in the future so that conversion parity is no less than a specified amount. International Game Technology 7 3/4 percent of '02 has this form of reset. The bonds were issued in May 1987. On May 14, 1988, the bond's conversion price would be reset to the lower of (1) the current conversion price or (2) 120 percent of an average of recent closing prices of the stock. This provision provided strong support for the price of the convertible during October 1987. The stock did well thereafter, so the conversion price did not need to be reset in May 1988. The second is a take-over provision that resets the conversion price (and hence the conversion rate) if the take-over price is below the current conversion price. This form is still being discussed by the industry.

Market Factors

Liquidity. The convertible market is very liquid, but there are many issues that are not. The IBM 7.875 percent bond is easily bought and sold in almost any quantity at prices that can be obtained from almost any quotation service. The Ben and Jerry's 9.5 percent bond is not as liquid because only $6 million worth were issued. Buying ten such bonds should be simple, but buying 250 of them would be difficult without paying a high price for them.

Broker Capability. Most major brokerage firms have special convertible traders. Large sales through these brokers are done on a net basis for bonds—the buyer and seller do not pay a commission, the broker profits from the difference between the purchase and sale prices—and on a commission basis on listed preferred stocks. Small buyers usually have to pay a commission on bonds and preferred stocks, and some small brokers have great difficulty in providing a good market of any size in small issues of bonds and unlisted preferred stocks.

Yield Disadvantage. If the issuer boosts its dividend high enough, the common yield will eventually be above the convertible yield. When this occurs, the investor should consider swapping out of the convertible and into the common market or converting the issue into common stock.

TYPES OF CONVERTIBLE SECURITIES

Convertible bonds and preferred stock are by far the most common forms used for the issuance of convertible securities. Other types of convertible issues in the market include the following:

- *Convertible bonds*. These are usually issued as subordinated debentures—a low level of general obligation debt but still ahead of preferred and common stock. This is the most common form of convertible and is exchangeable for the issuer's common stock company at the holder's option.
- *Convertible exchangeable debentures*. These issues are bonds that are convertible into the common stock of a company other than the issuer. Unlike the case with most convertibles, the holder of these bonds often gets the right to vote the shares their bonds represent. A tax liability may be incurred if the bonds are converted (see following discussion).
- *Euro-converts*. Some American companies issue convertible bonds in foreign markets through foreign subsidiaries. These bonds are convertible into the parent company's common stock and usually pay coupons and principal in dollars. Since these issues are not registered with the SEC, they cannot be bought by Americans until they have traded for a time (usually ninety days) on foreign markets. There are tax, liquidity, and deliverability problems that will be discussed later in this article (see *Tax Consequences* and *Important Factors in Buying and Selling*).
- *Adjustable convertible bonds (and preferred stock)*. These are issues where the coupon rate (or dividend) is adjusted at some time in the future to meet some specific requirement, such as keeping the yield above that of the common stock.
- *Convertible preferred stock*. This preferred stock has a fixed dividend rate that is convertible into the common stock of the issuing company at the option of the

holder. The dividend qualifies for the dividends received deduction when owned by a corporation.

- *Convertible exchangeable preferred stock.* This convertible preferred stock can be exchanged, at the issuer's request, into convertible bonds with the same yield and conversion price.

- *Zero coupon convertible bonds.* These convertible bonds pay no coupon, are issued at a deep discount to par (e.g., $200), and mature at par ($1,000) on a specified date. The return on these issues comes from either the gradual accretion to par over time (yield to maturity) or by the rise in the common stock. In taxable accounts, taxes must be paid on the annual accretion (the imputed interest).

- *Original Issue Discount (OID) convertible bonds.* These bonds are like zero coupon bonds except they do pay a modest coupon. They are issued at a modest discount to par and mature at par so that the yield to maturity is higher than the coupon rate. Taxable accounts must pay taxes on the annual accretion (the imputed interest).

- *Units.* Units are corporate bonds that are issued with warrants attached. The warrants can be separated from the bond so that the holder can sell either the bond or the warrants. When kept together, units act like convertible bonds and can be evaluated as such. In most cases, the holder can use the bond instead of cash to exercise the warrants.

- *Synthetic convertibles.* This term is used to describe the strategy of combining a warrant with a bond in a portfolio to have both income and the potential for capital gains.

- *Warrants.* Warrants are essentially long-term call options. They can be converted into common stock for a set price during a specific period. If they are not exercised during this time, they expire as worthless. They do not pay any coupon or dividend.

ATTRACTIVE FEATURES

It is the ability of convertible securities to provide the combination of potential for capital gains, a higher yield, and reduced risk and volatility characteristics relative to common stocks that makes them attractive to many investors. Proper use of convertibles within a portfolio can simplify the management of that portfolio.

Potential for Capital Appreciation. Because of the conversion right, convertibles can participate in an upward move in the price of the underlying stock. When the conversion premium moves toward zero, the convertible will appreciate at a rate virtually equal to that of the common stock. A good convertible can give returns very similar to those of a strong common stock.

Yield Advantage. Convertibles provide a predictable cash income stream that is usually higher than the common stock. Further, it is this yield advantage that makes it possible for the convertible to outperform a flat or weakly rising common stock. Finally, it helps the convertible hold more of its value when the price of the common stock is declining. When this happens, the premium grows, but the issue's price declines less rapidly as it approaches investment value.

Reduced Risk and Volatility. Investment value and conversion value provide a double floor to the downside risk of the issue. If the underlying stock falls sharply while the balance sheet of the company remains satisfactory, then the convertible will not decline below investment value. If interest rates rise while the common stock holds steady or even rises, as happened to many natural resource issues in the 1970s, then the convertible will not decline past conversion value and may rise in price. Only the conversion premium would be reduced.

A Hedged Instrument. The convertible is a hedged instrument. It sacrifices some of the appreciation potential of the common stock for some extra income and an expected reduction in risk and volatility. In the case of convertible bonds, a dramatic reduction in the risk to principal can often be gained.

Seniority of the Issues. Bonds and preferred stocks rank ahead of common stocks with regard to claims on assets of the corporation if a liquidation, bankruptcy, or reorganization of the company occurs. There are a few issues that have covenants in their indenture or prospectus that give the convertible holders substantial rights over those of common shareholders with respect to a number of other financial events that might occur (even without the threat of bankruptcy). These may include provisions governing the condition of the balance sheet or a right to vote on a leveraged buyout, or the spinning off or selling of significant assets. These types of covenants are not common. However, there appears to be a movement toward including them in new issues, so they may become common in the near future.

Other Areas of Opportunity. Many sophisticated investors go beyond purchasing domestic convertible securities for capital gains and income. Some alternative techniques are noted here.

- *Euro-convertibles.* The Euro-convertible market is different from the U.S. market. Foreign buyers look to the safety of the interest and principal rather than conversion value. This can make the price of these bonds differ from what the U.S. market would make them. For sophisticated investors with brokers with good foreign contacts, these bonds can be very attractive.
- *Hedging.* Convertible bonds and preferred stocks can be hedged by shorting the appropriate number of shares of common stock against a position in the convertible. If the conversion premium is very low and the yield advantage high, a nearly risk-free return can be made. There are three forms of the hedge: (1) bull hedge, which gains from price rises; (2) bear hedge, which gains from price declines; and (3) dollar for dollar, which should neither gain nor lose from common stock price changes; profits come strictly from the yield advantage.
- *Selling covered calls.* Income, in the form of short-term capital gains, can be generated by selling covered calls against the underlying common stock.

- *Swapping.* There are times when the common stock is more attractive for short-term reasons than the convertible. There are also occasions when the company has more than one convertible outstanding. In 1985, American General Corporation had four different convertible issues outstanding: two convertible debentures, a convertible preferred, and a convertible adjustable preferred. By monitoring all four issues and swapping when one of the issues became significantly more attractive, returns were improved by over 5 percent after commission costs by some sharp investors. This may not appear to be much, but the swaps appear to have reduced overall risk as well.

- *Convertible funds.* A number of funds specializing in convertible securities are available to investors. These funds provide professional management and institutional size; thus, small investors can participate in a diversified convertible portfolio.

POTENTIAL RISKS

Convertible securities are not risk free. They have almost all the risks associated with bonds or preferred stock issued by the same company. If the business fails, only the remaining assets or the reorganized company will be available to pay off the issue.

Other risks that the investor needs to monitor to receive the full performance of the convertible include the following:

- *Missing a call.* When parity is greater than the call price, value can be lost if the conversion right expires. When a convertible is called, this right ends on or before the call date. If the bonds are not put in for conversion before then, the company only owes the call price.

- *Missing a coupon due to a call.* If a convertible is called and its conversion value is greater than the call price, the investor should be aware that the timing of conversion can affect payment of interest or dividends.

- *Changes in the conversion ratio.* Convertibles change their conversion ratios for stock splits, stock dividends, resets, and other events. The changes are often small, but they should be monitored by checking one of the convertible statistical services, such as Value Line or RHM. (See *Suggested Reading* at the end of this article.)

- *Buying at excessive premium over call.* If the call protection has or nearly has run out and the issue is trading over the call price, the conversion premium paid should be modest because it may be lost if the issue is called.

- *Take-overs.* Convertibles selling with premiums of 40 to 50 percent or more are at risk of losing value in the event of a take-over if the bid is not high enough to cover the premium. This is why some new issues have puts and take-over provisions.

- *Lack of dilution privilege.* Most issues have a specific dilution privilege, making it mandatory for the company to adjust the conversion ratio in the case of a stock split, stock dividend, sale of significant assets, or an extraordinary dividend. Not all issues are fully covered for these, however. In the late 1980s, to fight off a take-over, Harcourt, Brace and Jovanovich paid a cash dividend of roughly 80 percent of the price of the stock. The convertible holders were not protected against the drop in the price of the stock when it went ex-dividend. To protect what value they had, convertible holders were forced to convert into the common stock to get the dividend.

TAX CONSEQUENCES

Convertible preferred stocks and bonds are treated exactly like preferred stocks and bonds by the Internal Revenue Service (IRS) when they are bought and sold by the investor. Interest received is taxed at ordinary rates. Dividends are taxed at ordinary rates, and corporations can take advantage of the dividends-received deduction.

If a convertible bond is purchased at a discount, gains resulting from its sale may be broken into two parts: accreted income and capital gain. Since these are currently taxed at the same rate, the distinction is only important if there are losses to offset. Otherwise, gains from the sale of convertible bonds and preferred stocks are treated as capital gains, which can be offset by capital losses but can only be deducted against ordinary income in amounts of up to $3,000 per year (with any carry-over to be used in the future). With the tax laws changing, the investor should check with a professional tax advisor on these matters.

Conversions. Converting most issues into common stock generally does not cause any "taxable event" to occur. However, on Euro-convertibles and on convertible exchangeable issues, if the issue is converted into the common stock of a company other than the issuer of the convertible, even if the issuer is a subsidiary corporation, a taxable event has occurred. It is as if the convertible had been sold at the current conversion value and the common stock bought at the current price.

Zero Coupon and OID Issues. The IRS assumes that the holder of zero coupon and OID issues is receiving income from them as they move toward maturity equal to the yield they provide (on OIDs plus what they call the imputed interest rate). Taxable holders may have to pay taxes on income that will not be received for years. It may be better for these to be kept in untaxed accounts, such as individual retirement accounts and pension funds.

Convertible Mutual Funds. The tax consequences of purchases, sales and income derived from investment activities in most convertible funds flow through directly to the investor. Investors should receive capital gains and income breakdowns from the fund so that they can pay the proper tax. The dividends-received deduction also flows through to corporate holders for the equity portion of the dividends received from equities.

Mergers and Restructuring. Securities or cash received for convertibles from mergers, take-overs, or other restructurings may or may not be taxable. There should be proxy material sent to all holders spelling out the exact tax consequences.

Covered Calls. Profits from writing unexercised covered calls are short-term capital gains. Exercised covered calls force a calculation of profit based on the exercise price minus the cost of the common stock: (convertible issue cost minus the call premium) divided by the conversion rate.

REPRESENTATIVE TYPES OF INVESTORS

All institutions and individual investors that use corporate debt and equity should understand convertible securities. At any given time, there may be a convertible alternative to a current holding. Further, since convertibles make up 5 to 10 percent of the equity market, they should not be ignored.

The types of investors that use convertibles include the following:

- *Tax-exempt institutions.* Most pension funds and many endowment funds set aside a specific percentage of their funds to be invested in convertibles.
- *Banks and insurance companies.* These investors have used convertibles for many years. Because of regulations, some financial institutions cannot invest in non-dividend-paying common stocks. Since many growth stocks do not pay dividends, convertibles are the only way these companies can invest in them. They also use them for the attractive features listed earlier.
- *Mutual funds.* There are at least thirty-two mutual funds representing billions of dollars that specialize in convertible securities. Many other funds also use convertibles. Individuals looking for convertible investments should probably look for a good fund.
- *Individual investors.* Few individuals invest in convertibles. This may be due to ignorance on the part of either the individual or the broker. Also, convertible markets are institutional markets; most sales are in lots worth $100,000 or more, and small individuals are not well served by them.

How to Determine a Convertible Strategy

The graph in Figure 1 depicts how a convertible's price will move with changes in the price of the underlying common stock (given stable interest rates). If the price of the common stock goes up, the price of the convertible moves up at a slower (but increasing) rate. If the price of the stock falls, the convertible also falls, but at a decreasing rate, until it nears its investment value floor. Historically, convertibles do not fall below investment value unless there is a serious question about the viability of the company. The area between the line depicting the convertible price and the line depicting conversion parity represents the conversion premium. The area between investment value and the line depicting convertible price represents the premium over investment value.

There are essentially three possible strategies within a portfolio that uses convertibles. These are portrayed on the graph in Figure 1 and consist of the following:

1. *Bond equivalent strategy.* Convertible bonds and preferred stocks that have fallen to discounts because the common stock has dropped while the company remains sound have yields close to or equal to straight issues. If one or two stocks return to their former levels, even over a long period, then the total portfolio can outperform a similar portfolio of straight issues.

FIGURE 1. Convertible Price Versus Common Stock Price

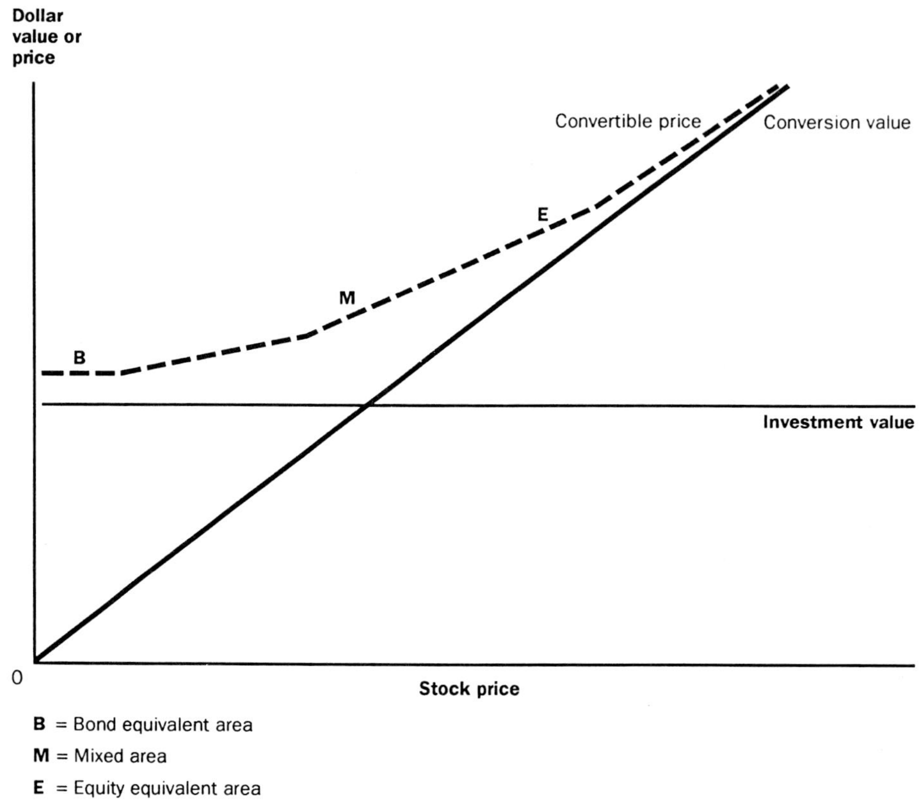

2. *Mixed or balanced convertible strategy*. This is the most common approach to investing in convertibles. The issues in the portfolio have moderate conversion premiums (usually 15 to 30 percent) and significant yield advantages (perhaps 5 percent) over the common stock.

3. *Equity equivalent strategy*. Some convertible issues reach a stage where they have little or no premium (0 to 5 percent) while still retaining serious advantages over the common stock (perhaps a small yield advantage). If there is no serious disadvantage to the issue (e.g., threat of call, lack of voting privilege), then the convertible would be bought to replace the common stock, even in a strictly equity account.

Table 2 presents issues that might be attractive to each strategy.

IMPORTANT FACTORS IN BUYING AND SELLING

It is easier to buy and sell convertibles today than it was just a few years ago. This is especially true of preferred stock, but it is also true of bonds.

TABLE 2. Convertible Strategies and Related Issues

Bond Equivalent Issues

Issue	Price*	Yield	Premium
Transco $4.75 preferred	46.75	10.16%	69%
Comsat 7.75% of 1998 (Euro)	91.25	8.49	54
Seagate 6.75% of 2012	69.75	9.68	66

Mixed Issues

Issue	Price*	Yield	Premium	Dollar Break-Even
Compaq 6.5% of 2013	114.50	5.68%	19%	2.8 years
Freeport McMoRan 8.75% of 2013	110.25	7.94	24	4.0 years
Holly Farm 6% of 2017	82.50	7.27	23	4.3 years

Equity Equivalent Issues

Issue	Price*	Yield	Premium	Dollar Break-Even
Helen of Troy	122	5.94%	− 1%	—
RPM 5.75 of 2001 (Euro)	100	5.75	5	2.2 years
Unisys $3.75 preferred	62.75	5.98	5	1.5 years

*Priced as of 7/7/88.

Convertible Preferred Stock. Most convertible preferred stocks are listed on an exchange or on the NASDAQ and trade like common stocks. The liquidity of any one preferred issue is, like common stock, a function of the size of the issue. Any broker should be able to efficiently buy, sell, or quote convertible preferred stock.

Convertible Bonds. Many convertible bonds are listed on an exchange or on NASDAQ, but few are actually traded there. Quotes and markets can be obtained from some quotation services, but they are often only close approximations of the actual markets. For very small buyers (ten bonds or less), these quotes may be accurate. For large buyers, the best markets are made over the counter on convertible trading desks. Among the major brokerage firms that have active convertible desks are Drexel, Kidder Peabody, Merrill Lynch, Morgan Stanley, First Boston, Thomson McKinnon, and Goldman Sachs.

Less Active Issues. For unlisted or less active convertible bonds and preferred stocks, there are specialty firms such as Wechsler, Krumholz & Co. and Murphy & Duriea.

Euro-convertible Bonds. Euro-convertible bonds are difficult to buy or sell through any broker that does not have Eurobond expertise. The best markets are made through firms with either an office in Europe (usually London) or strong foreign contacts. Some of the major firms that have such expertise include Merrill Lynch, Morgan Stanley, and First Boston. Smaller firms such as Cresvale International and Jesup and Lamont can also be helpful.

Once a trade has been made, delivery and payment can be difficult. It is expensive and probably unnecessary to take a Eurobond in certificate form. Letting it remain with the broker (in "street name") often reduces transaction costs, as the bonds will most likely remain in Europe or in book entry form on a computer. This may also ease future sale or conversion.

Commissions. Convertible bonds bought or sold in large lots are usually traded over the counter on a "net" basis. The broker makes money on the spread between the cost of the bonds and the price the buyer pays. Smaller lots trade with a commission. The commission used to be $2.50 per bond, but most firms have a minimum charge per transaction. Preferred stocks trade like common stocks, and commissions are similar.

GLOSSARY

bear hedge—A hedging strategy of owning a convertible position and being short a greater dollar amount of the common stock. The convertible position partially offsets the common position and generates extra income through the yield advantage.

break-even time—The time it takes for the yield advantage to pay back the conversion premium.

bull hedge—A hedging strategy of owning a convertible position and being short a lesser dollar amount of the common stock. The common position partially offsets the convertible position, which generates extra income through the yield advantage.

call—The right of the issuer to buy back bonds or preferred stock at a set price (call price).

conversion price—The exercise price of the conversion right.

conversion rate—The number of common shares into which a bond or preferred stock is convertible.

conversion value—The market price of the common stock multiplied by the conversion rate.

convertible—A bond or preferred stock convertible into common stock.

current yield—The rate of return on a fixed income issue based on the current price and assuming no future change in price.

dollar for dollar hedge—A hedging strategy of owning a convertible position and being short an equal dollar amount of the common stock. This is sometimes referred to as a riskless arbitrage, since losses in one position should be offset by gains in the other. The profit in this strategy comes from the yield advantage.

Euro-convertible—Convertible bonds payable in dollars but issued on a foreign market; not available to U.S. investors on the original underwriting.

investment value—The value of the bond or preferred stock without the conversion feature.

parity—Conversion value.

payback period—Break-even time.

premium—The amount, stated in dollars or percent, by which the market price of the convertible exceeds parity.

put—A provision that allows the holder to force the issuer to buy back the bond or preferred stock.

reset—A provision that forces the issuer to change the conversion rate to the benefit of the holder.

SEC—The Securities and Exchange Commission.

synthetic convertible—A bond and a warrant combination.

yield advantage—The difference in income of the convertible over the common stock.

yield to maturity—A measure of the total rate of return on a bond that will mature on a fixed date. It includes both the income from the coupon and an annualized measure of the change in price as the bond moves toward maturity.

SUGGESTED READING

The *Value Line Convertible Survey* and the *RHM Convertible Survey* are among the most useful publications available. In addition, the major brokerage firms that have convertible specialists often publish material on convertible securities.

PUBLICATIONS AVAILABLE TO THE PUBLIC

RHM Convertible Survey, 172 Forest Avenue, Glen Gove, N.Y. 11542

Value Line Convertible Survey, 711 Third Avenue, New York, N.Y. 10017

BROKERS THAT PUBLISH CONVERTIBLE REPORTS

Merrill Lynch, Pierce, Fenner & Smith, Inc.

Morgan Stanley & Co., Inc.

The First Boston Corporation

Kidder, Peabody & Co., Inc.

Thomson McKinnon, Inc.

Cresvale International, Inc. (Euro-convertibles)

Shearson Lehman Hutton, Inc.

Salomon Brothers, Inc.

CORPORATE BONDS

Irving D. Friedman

BASIC CHARACTERISTICS

Corporate bonds are the contractual obligations of a corporation to pay a fixed amount of money at a specified date, called the maturity date, with interest, usually paid at semiannual intervals until the bonds are paid. A bondholder's rights, and the corporation's obligations, are found in the bond and in a related contract called an indenture.

A corporate bond is often considered a corporate note. The two terms are synonymous. However, the term "note" describes a short-term obligation, usually one that matures in ten years or less from the date it is issued, while the word "bond" more correctly describes a long-term obligation. Sometimes, the corporate obligation is called a debenture, which is a special type of note or bond that is unsecured. It is usually guaranteed by the general creditworthiness of the issuer.

A corporation may also borrow money by issuing and selling bonds convertible into its own stock. (For a discussion of convertible bonds, see article on "Convertible Securities," elsewhere in this volume.)

A secured bond or note is one that is backed by collateral of real or personal property. If the collateral is real estate, the bond is called a mortgage bond. If it is personal property, the obligation is called a secured note or a secured bond. An equipment trust bond or certificate is one that is secured by a pledge of specific property, such as one or more locomotives, box cars, or trucks.

Irving D. Friedman, Esq., is a private investor, retired attorney, and stockbroker in New York City. He holds an L.L.B. degree from Fordham University.

The secured bonds of a corporation are ranked according to seniority. For example, there may be first mortgage bonds, second mortgage bonds, and subordinated bonds. The seniority of a secured bond becomes important when the company's business fortunes become so bad that default and insolvency occur. Obligations of greater seniority receive better treatment in insolvency proceedings than obligations of lesser seniority.

Although corporations issue bonds of millions of dollars, the bonds are sold to the public in denominations of as little as $1,000. On the New York Stock Exchange, the unit of trading is one bond of $1,000 denomination. The expression "fifty bonds" thus refers to fifty $1,000 bonds. However, the usual minimum denomination in which bonds are now issued and sold is $5,000.

Interest on Bonds

Bonds usually pay interest at a fixed rate, set when they are issued, on fixed dates until the bond matures unless the bond is paid before maturity. For example, a 12 percent bond (of $1,000 denomination) pays interest of $120 a year, in semiannual installments of $60 on January 15 and July 15 of each year. Normally, bond interest is paid semiannually; however, some bonds pay the interest quarterly and some annually.

Income Bonds. Income bonds are a type of bond on which the issuing corporation is not required to pay bond interest if it does not have sufficient income to pay it. The omitted interest is either lost to the bondholder for that interest period or becomes cumulative, depending on the bond. If the interest is cumulative, the issuing corporation is obligated to pay it in the future if its income available for the payment of interest justifies or requires it. The formula for computing the corporation's income available for the payment of income bond interest, and whether or not such interest is cumulative, is found in the bond indenture.

Floating-Interest-Rate Bonds. In certain bonds, interest is computed on the basis of a floating interest rate. The bond contract in such cases provides that the interest rate be adjusted, usually every six months, to the prevailing interest rate in the marketplace. Many floating-interest-rate bonds provide that the interest rate for the following six months be adjusted by adding either one-half or one percentage point to the rate the U.S. Treasury then pays on its three-month bills. The basis for the rate fixing is stated in the bond indenture.

Zero Coupon Bonds. An innovation in the issuance of corporate bonds is the zero coupon or zero interest bond. Zero coupon bonds do not pay any annual interest. Instead, the return to the investor is the difference between the low original purchase price and the redemption value of 100 at maturity. (See article on "Zero Coupon Bonds," elsewhere in this volume.)

Junk Bonds. Bonds of relatively low credit ratings have been referred to as junk bonds for many years, perhaps since the early 1900s when bond rating systems were established. Junk bonds offer a potentially high yield with a commensurate level of risk. In fact, they are also called high-yield bonds, especially by those who are opposed to the stigma of the term "junk." Generally, the result from a turn for the worse of companies whose business has soured.

In the 1980s, junk bonds became closely associated with Drexel Burnham Lambert's former employee, Michael A. Milken, a financial expert in corporate take-overs who sold junk bonds to facilitate the take-over. Some previously strong companies became so laden with debt that their issues were called junk bonds. With good business conditions in the 1980s, most junk bonds have performed admirably. However, in late 1988, Southmark, a Dallas-based real estate company suffering from the downturn in the oil patch, experienced difficulty with its junk bond plan. In mid-1989, Integrated Resources experienced severe trouble. Some analysts fear that a general recession will cause default on many issues of junk bonds, as the corporate debtors might not be able to withstand a business setback.

With leveraged buyouts being used by increasingly larger companies, there is a threat that the increased debt in a buyout will turn a high grade bond into a junk bond. This is a new wrinkle in bond risk factors, demonstrated in 1989 by the RJR Nabisco buyout.

Prepayment of Bonds

Virtually all bonds have a fixed maturity date (although a few are perpetual). However, the corporate borrower may want to pay its bonds before maturity to get out of debt, to borrow money at a lower interest rate, or to get rid of restrictions that the bond contract puts on its operations. Some bonds are noncallable and thus cannot be prepaid. Many bond contracts, however, include a prepayment provision.

Call Price. The call price of a bond is the amount required for prepayment of a bond, often at a premium above face value. The corporation may, for example, be required to pay a premium of 10 percent, that is, 110 percent or $1,100 for each $1,000 bond. Some bonds provide for prepayment without a premium, in which case the call price is equal to the face value of the bond.

Other bonds are noncallable for a certain period after they are issued, such as five or ten years; thereafter, they are callable at premiums that decline according to a fixed schedule.

Sinking Fund Requirements. In addition to the prepayment provisions, the bond may contain a sinking fund requirement. This means that the company must redeem a specified number of its bonds each year before maturity to reduce its debt. This provision has advantages and corresponding disadvantages for the bondholder. The chief advantage is that the bondholders may get their principal paid back earlier than the maturity date. The main disadvantage is that if the bond is a good one with a good interest rate, they may not want to be prepaid.

When bonds are to be prepaid, either by call for payment or by sinking fund requirements, the bondholders are notified by the corporation by mail or newspaper advertisements, or both. After a call for payment is effective and complete, the bondholder must take the money, because interest on such bonds ceases on the specified prepayment date.

Value of Bonds

The value of a bond depends on two factors. One is the financial strength of the issuer: bonds of a strong, rich, and successful corporation are a better investment than bonds of a weak company. The other is the interest rate. For example, if a bond carries a fixed interest rate of 9 percent, and interest rates rise to 12 percent, the 9 percent bond will decline in value until its price returns a competitive rate near 12 percent.

Another example is the highly rated American Telephone & Telegraph 7 percent bonds, due in 2001. This rate is less than the 1989 interest rate on comparable bonds, which is about 9 percent. On July 6, 1989, these bonds were selling at about $870 each, or 87 cents on the dollar for each $1,000 bond. Thus, an investor who bought these bonds at their original price of $1,000 for a $1,000 debenture suffered a 13 percent loss of market value. When interest rates were higher, as in the early 1980s, the potential loss on these bonds was as much as 50 percent.

The investor or speculator who purchases bonds at a discount and holds them to maturity will receive a yield at maturity that is higher than the fixed interest rate. The difference between cost and the matured value of the bond is a capital gain. It is not necessary to wait until maturity of the bond to realize a capital gain from a bond purchased at a discount. The bond can be sold at the price prevailing in the marketplace at any time.

Reduction of Risk

The only way to avoid the risk of major losses of principal on bonds because of an increase in interest rates is not to buy them. No one can forecast the future of interest rates with certainty. However, if the investor buys a bond at the current price of $870 for a $1,000 debenture, and interest rates decline sharply, the investor will enjoy an appreciation in the value of the bond. It should be noted, however, that a decline in interest rates makes it likely that the corporate obligor will prepay the bond with money it can borrow at a lower rate, if the provisions of the bond contract so provide. One investor solution to violent fluctuations in the value of bonds due to interest rate changes is the purchase of floating-rate bonds. In these bonds, the interest rate changes annually or semiannually in accordance with a well-known interest rate index.

The other risk in corporate bond investments is the loss of financial strength of the corporation. There is no sure way to prevent such a loss, because a successful corporation can turn into a failure. A case in point is First Republic Bank, Dallas, which suffered through bankruptcy. Another example is LTV Corporation, a formerly prosperous corporation whose bonds are now selling as low as 20, or $200 for a $1,000 bond. The serious financial problems of this corporation, plus the general increase in interest rates since the bonds were issued, have caused the bondholders to suffer an 80 percent market value loss.

One way to reduce the risk of such losses is to favor the bonds of financially strong electric companies, telephone companies, and banks, which are generally among the most stable types of corporations. (However, some investors will avoid utility company bonds when the company produces nuclear energy.) Another way to reduce risk is by diversifying. The investor can do this by investing in a bond fund. The advantage of investing in such a fund is that the investor gets expert management as well as diversification. (See article on "Mutual Funds," elsewhere in this volume.) The disadvantage of owning stock in a bond investment company rather than the actual bonds is that management expenses reduce the income received by the investor.

Variety of Corporate Bonds

Bonds are issued by corporations doing business in all areas of human activity. The basic categories of bonds are industrials, public utilities, transportation, and finance. There are shipping company bonds, railroad bonds, airplane bonds (both manufacturing and transportation), entertainment company bonds, insurance company bonds, oil company bonds, paper company bonds, and even gambling company bonds.

ATTRACTIVE FEATURES

Current Return

One advantage of a corporate bond investment is that the bond pays a fixed amount of interest; for example, a 12 percent bond will pay $120 a year on each $1,000 bond. The issuing corporation cannot reduce the interest rate unless it files a petition under the Bankruptcy Code. Thus, the bondholder is entitled to the payment of interest even in bad times.

Seniority

Interest on a corporate bond must be paid before any dividends can be paid or distributed on the common or preferred stocks of a corporation. Furthermore, interest on a corporate bond is payable ahead of federal, state, and city corporation income taxes. These are important priorities. Short of bankruptcy, a bondholder cannot be deprived of the principal and interest on the bond without giving written consent. The Trust Indenture Act of 1939 provides that no bond indenture issued under that law shall restrict an individiual bondholder's right to the prompt payment of the principal and interest.

The relative safety and seniority of bonds was demonstrated on October 19, 1987. Although the stock market plunged, with stock indexes down more than 22 percent in one day, the Dow Jones Bond Average fell that day to 81.26 from 82.28, a drop of only 1.25 percent. The Bond Index closed that week at 84.56, a gain of 2.28. Prices of high grade bonds were strong—some rose more than a point on October 19—and ended the week with large gains, reflecting the investor's flight to quality.

Capital Gains Potential

If a bondholder buys a bond at a discount from the face amount of $1,000, and sells it or redeems it at maturity for a profit, the profit is taxed at capital gains rates, subject to the required holding period. Tax law has changed capital gains tax rates many times. The effective capital gains tax rate has varied in recent years from under 20 percent to 33 percent. The bondholder who buys corporate bonds at a discount knows that a $1,000 bond will not be worth more than $1,000 unless interest rates decline. Therefore, a bond bought for $500, $600, or $800 should be sold at a profit when the price approaches its $1,000 face value.

Safety of Principal

The principal value of the bond will fluctuate with interest rate changes, and safety of the principal depends on the financial strength of the corporation. To protect against loss of principal caused by interest rate fluctuations, the investor should buy short-term bonds or floating-rate bonds. To protect against loss of principal caused by a possible bankruptcy of the corporate obligor, the investor should favor the highest-rated bonds of utilities and banks and should also diversify.

Also, to reduce the risk of fluctuations in the prices and values of bonds due to market forces, it is recommended that the bond investor maintain a presence in all maturity sectors of the market. Maturities should be spaced out among short-term, medium-term, and long-term. This diversification in maturity dates is as valuable as diversification of issuing corporations.

Liquidity

In buying and selling bonds on the New York and American Stock Exchanges, the unit of trading is one bond of $1,000 denomination. This is a very big advantage to the small investor, whose one- or two-bond order will get the same treatment on the floor of the exchange as a big order for 500 bonds.

POTENTIAL RISKS

Market Volatility

As mentioned earlier, the risk of loss from fluctuating interest rates is a very great one. Although the income and principal on a bond may be safe because the obligor is a credit-worthy corporation, the market value of the bond can be diminished by a general increase in interest rates. In 1981, for example, a 4 percent bond went down from $1,000 to as little as $300 because interest rates went up to about 18 percent; this was an extreme example, which was corrected as interest rates declined in the mid-1980s, and as the bonds advanced toward maturity.

Risk of loss due to increases in interest rates can be minimized by buying short-term bonds; no matter how low the interest rate is, the bondholder will get the full principal back at an early maturity. The bondholder can then reinvest the money at the then-prevailing rate. Bonds maturing in less than two years are recommended to reduce this type of loss.

Not a Hedge Against Inflation. Since they provide for the payment of the interest and principal at future dates, fixed-interest corporate bonds are not a hedge against inflation. In a period of inflation, the money from the interest and matured principal will buy less.

Corporate Reverses. Changes in the affairs of the corporate borrower are another source of market volatility. For example, the bonds of Financial Corporation of America and First Republic Bank, Dallas, were hurt by losses in their operations. To reduce the risk of loss because of an adverse turn in the corporation's business affairs, the bond investor should buy highly rated bonds. Standard & Poor's rates bonds from AAA for the highest down to D for the lowest. This is an excellent guide, although the investor should keep in mind that corporations and their ratings constantly change. Successful corporations can suffer a drop in profits, lose money, and go bankrupt just as poor corporations can become rich.

To reduce losses, it is recommended that bonds of major utilities and banks be favored. New York Telephone Company bonds and bonds of J.P. Morgan & Company are outstanding examples of financial strength. The prudent investor will favor bonds of corporations that have enough net working capital and profits to pay the interest and principal on their bonds even if business becomes bad; it is also wise to diversify by buying bonds in many companies or a bond mutual fund.

Fixed Current Return

The fixed return on a fixed-interest bond can also be a disadvantage. A stockholder has the possibility of a dividend increase, whereas the bondholder cannot get an interest increase. Exceptions are floating-rate bonds and the rare cases where an indenture is renegotiated by the company. There have been recent situations in which a corporation has aked its bondholders to release it from rigid indenture requirements, such as the maintenance of high collateral or working capital. In exchange, the corporate debtors are willing to compensate the bondholders by increasing the interest rate on the bonds.

Imperfect Liquidity

Although bonds are readily marketable, they are not as marketable as active stocks. Bonds enjoy a good market on the New York Stock Exchange, on the American Stock Exchange, and in the unlisted market. However, it is not unusual for a bond to sell at 70 ($700) with the bond quoted in the postsale market at 65 bid ($650) and offered at 75 ($750).

Inactive bonds, of course, are more difficult to buy and sell than active ones. It is better to buy an active, marketable, high-grade bond, unless the inactive one gives a much higher yield or a price advantage, or both.

Buyouts

The latest wrinkle in bond risk is the leveraged buyout. If a great amount of debt is added to a corporation's burden, as is typical in a leveraged buyout, the new bonds are often described as junk bonds. However, the credit rating on pre-buyout debt may be adversely affected. Courts may have to decide whether holders of pre-buyout debt will have priority.

TAX CONSEQUENCES

There are no special tax advantages attached to the ownership of corporate bonds. The profits and losses on the purchase and sale of bonds are taxed at capital gains rates, depending on how long they are held. Bonds held for more than six months are taxed as long-term capital gains.

There are limits on the offset of capital losses against ordinary income. Individuals and corporations may carry forward unused capital losses; corporations must first carry them back. Investors who repurchase bonds on which they realized losses should be mindful of wash sale rules.

While the individual or corporate investor pays regular income taxes on bond interest received, nonprofit institutions (e.g., labor unions and universities), which are exempt from income taxes in general, do not pay income taxes on bond interest.

As a possible tax-saving inducement, some corporate bonds were originally issued well below face value. For example, the deeply discounted 5.5 percent debentures of General Electric Credit Corporation were originally sold at $379.24 for each $1,000 bond, a discount of 62 percent. They yield 15.8 percent to maturity in 2001. These debentures are rated AA by Moody's. Another example is the deep-discount debenture offered by General Motors Acceptance Corporation in 1981. Its 6 percent debentures were sold at 44.51 percent of par value. This issue is rated AA− by Standard & Poor's.

The purchase of such bonds gives the bondholder a potental capital gain play if interest rates should decline. However, since the interest on deep-discount bonds must be amortized, they are especially suitable for purchase by tax-exempt organizations and funds.

REPRESENTATIVE TYPES OF INVESTORS

There is no single type of investor who buys corporate bonds. Some investors buy them to get higher interest than is available from banks or from U.S. government bonds. Other investors buy bonds that sell at a discount to get the high return plus a capital gain potential. Many investors buy corporate bonds simply to get a return on their money.

Some investors like the idea of a fixed rate of return and a fixed maturity date. Investors also buy bonds because of the superior rights bondholders have over stockholders, and because interest is tax deductible by the paying corporation.

IMPORTANT FACTORS IN BUYING AND SELLING

Selecting a Broker or a Dealer

All members of the New York Stock Exchange, American Stock Exchange, or National Association of Securities Dealers offer the services required to buy and sell bonds. The major difference among them is what they will charge for their services.

Substantial investors in corporate bonds should go to the big houses, which do a wholesale bond business. Such establishments are Asiel & Company; Bear Stearns & Company; Dillon Read & Company, Inc.; First Boston Corporation; Goldman Sachs; Merrill Lynch Capital Markets; Morgan Stanley & Company; Prudential-Bache; Salomon Brothers; and Shearson Lehman Hutton. Although these firms are headquartered in New York, most of them have networks of regional branch offices in the major cities of the United States.

A complete list of security dealers can be found in a Standard & Poor's publication called *Security Dealers of North America*. This book is available in almost every brokerage office. The *New York Stock Exchange Directory*, published annually, lists its members.

The big city banks, such as Bank of New York, Chase Manhattan, Manufacturers Hanover Trust Company, and Morgan Guaranty Trust Company also have corporate bond departments that will service the bond investor.

Commissions

The commission to buy and sell bonds is subject to mutual agreement and negotiation between the customer and the broker. Some brokers charge $2.50 a bond; others charge $5.00, $7.50, $10.00, or $20.00, and many have a minimum charge of $30.00. The bond purchaser should shop around to get the lowest commission charge available.

The most economical time to buy bonds is when they are originally issued. On a new issue, the customer pays nothing in commissions. The selling expense is absorbed by the corporation selling the bonds, or the underwriter, or both.

Markets

The market for listed bonds is the exchange on which they are listed. Big blocks of bonds, including the listed bonds, are also traded in the over-the-counter bond market. The over-the-counter market consists of brokers and dealers who buy and sell securities among themselves without using the facilities of an exchange.

Judging Quality

The easiest way to judge the quality of a bond is to use Standard & Poor's rating, which is contained in their *Bond Guide:*

AAA—Highest rating
AA—Next to highest rating

A—Below AA
BBB—Adequate
BB, B, CCC, CC—Speculative
CI—Income bonds not paying interest
D—Bonds in default

Plus or minus signs are used in ratings AA through CC to indicate relative standing within the category.

Moody's Investors Service has a similar rating system. If no rating is available, the bond investor should examine the corporation's balance sheet and income statements. The higher the coverage of interest and other fixed charges, the better the bond is; the higher the net working capital, the better the bond is.

For example, if a corporation's interest and fixed charges amount to $1 million a year, and the corporation has earned in each of the ten previous years $5 million to cover this charge, it has a record of earning its interest five times over, which is very good coverage. If the corporation has a total debt of $1 million, and its net working capital has been $5 million or more for the previous ten years, then its net working capital is five times its debt, which is very good.

Using Professional Advisors and Appraisers

The use of professional advisors and appraisers is not necessary. One can get excellent professional advice at a cost of $155 a year by subscribing to Standard & Poor's *Bond Guide*. Their ratings are as good an appraisal as one can get from any other professional. Some brokers even give these *Bond Guides* free to their customers.

Appraisers are not needed because bond prices are adequately quoted in *The New York Times* and the *Wall Street Journal*. The bond market prices are the best appraisals of all, and they can be obtained for the price of a newspaper or a telephone call to a bond broker or dealer.

The Dow Jones Bond Index comprises prices of bonds of ten public utilities and ten industrials. It is the bond counterpart of the widely tracked Dow Jones Industrial Average. The bond index is reported daily in the *Wall Street Journal* and weekly in *Barron's*. The following issuers are included:

Public utilities	Industrials
Alabama Power	Bank America
American T&T	Bethlehem Steel
Commonwealth Edison	Eastman Kodak
Consolidated Edison	Exxon
Consolidated Power	Ford Motor
Detroit Edison	General Electric
Michigan Bell	GM Acceptance
Pacific Gas and Electric	IBM
Philadelphia Electric	Socony
Public Service Indiana	Weyerhaeuser

CUSTODIAL CARE

Physical Safety Precautions

Most bonds issued now come in registered form. They are issued in the name and address of the owner. Checks for the interest are mailed by the corporation directly to the bondholder.

It is recommended that, when bonds are bought and paid for, the broker be instructed to transfer and ship the bonds to the bondholder. The bonds should then be placed in the bondholder's safe-deposit box.

Some bondholders prefer to leave their bonds with their broker for convenience. When bonds are left with the broker, the bondholder assumes the risk of the broker's insolvency. Although brokers' customer accounts are insured by the Securities Investors Protection Corporation and private insurance companies for up to $2.5 million (and more in some cases), insolvency of a broker creates problems of confusion and delay, which may cause losses to the bondholder.

Aside from the possibility of bankruptcy of a broker, when bonds are left with a broker, they are usually registered in the broker's name or in the name of a nominee. In such a case, the interest payments are mailed by the corporation to the broker or the broker's nominee. The broker, in turn, credits the interest to the customer's account and then remits the interest check to the bondholder. All this requires processing and causes delay, so an interest payment due on the first of the month may not reach the bondholder until the tenth. In addition, brokerage house bookkeeping volume may delay payment of interest and principal to the bondholder.

If the account is inactive, the broker may impose a service charge for taking care of the bonds. The broker may also have a lien on bonds in its possession for any money the customer owes on other business transactions.

Some bonds are issued in bearer form, with coupons attached for payment of interest. Such bearer bonds should also be sent by the broker to the customer as soon as they are paid for.

Ownership of such bonds can pass by delivery, in the same way that currency does. Therefore, they should be put in the bondholder's safe-deposit box, and a record should be made of the interest payment dates. When the interest is payable, the interest coupons for that date should be detached from the bond and deposited in the bondholder's bank account.

Income Collection Procedures

Income collection on registered bonds is easy. The bondholder gets a check in the mail for the interest. With bearer bonds, the interest coupons should be detached on the due date and deposited in the bondholder's bank account.

Professional Custodial Care

A bank will open a custodial account for a bondholder if the account is large enough to interest the bank. It may be worthwhile for a bondholder with substantial holdings to hire a bank to take care of the bonds, collect the interest, remit it, and send a monthly and annual report for tax and record-keeping purposes. The custodial bank will also monitor for redemption notices, tender offers, exchange offers, extension plans, and reorganization plans affecting the bonds. It will notify the bondholder when action is required. The ordinary registered bondholder does not need all this service because all important notices will be mailed. Such notices are also published in the financial pages of leading newspapers in major cities.

A holder of bearer bonds should watch published financial notices for a possible call for payment of the bonds, since nothing will be mailed because the corporation has no record of the bondholder's name and address. Many holders of bearer bonds learn for the first time that their bonds have been called for payment when they deposit an interest coupon for payment and have it returned because the bond has been previously called and paid. This results in a delay in payment and a loss of interest.

GLOSSARY

bond—A paper or document that sets forth the provisions for the payment of interest and principal. The term "a bond" refers to a bond of $1,000 denomination.

call price—The price the corporation is required to pay if it wants to pay the bond before maturity. If the call price is above $1,000, the excess is called a premium.

debenture—An unsecured note or bond. The difference between a debenture and an unsecured bond is just a matter of nomenclature, like a dollar and a buck.

deep-discount bond—A bond originally issued by the corporate obligor at a price much lower than its face value because the interest rate it pays is below prevailing interest rates. A corporation will sell a $1,000 bond for $500 or $600 because it agrees to pay only 6 or 7 percent when normal interest rates are much higher, say 10 to 13 percent. A deep-discount bond can also be created by market forces. A $1,000 bond, originally issued and marketed for $1,000, can become deeply discounted in the market if interest rates soar after it is issued.

floating-rate bond—A bond on which the interest rate is adjusted usually every six months, with the interest rate effective for the subsequent six months, according to a formula based on the then-prevailing interest rates. The prime rate, federal funds rates, commercial paper rate, and Treasury bill rates are the standards usually used.

income bond—A bond on which interest is payable only if the obligor corporation earns enough income to pay it.

indenture—A contract between the corporate obligor and a trustee, called the indenture trustee, that itemizes in detail all the obligations of the debtor corporation under the terms of the bond issue. This includes the remedies the indenture trustee and the bondholders have to enforce their rights in the event the debtor defaults.

interest—The money the borrowing corporation contracts to pay to the bondholder.

point—$10 for each $1,000 bond. If a bond's market price fluctuates 3 points, it has gone up or down $30. If it fluctuates half a point, it has gone up or down $5 for each $1,000 bond.

redemption—The act of the obligor to pay all the interest and principal due on its bonds on or before the maturity date.

secured bond—A bond that is secured by the pledge of personal property as collateral security for the payment of the bond. Where real estate is the collateral security for a bond, it is called a mortgage bond.

sinking fund requirement—A stipulation in the bond that obliges the corporation owing the money to pay a certain number of bonds, at specified dates, before the maturity date.

spread—The difference between the bid and asked prices when the bond is quoted. If a bond is quoted at 93 bid, 94 offered, the spread is the difference between 93 and 94, which is a point, or $10 on a $1,000 bond.

yield—The percentage return the bond pays. Current yield is the interest rate divided by price; yield-to-maturity reflects current income and the effect of the value change from its current price to value at maturity.

zero coupon bond—A bond that pays no interest during the life of the bond. The principal of the bond, when it is paid at maturity, includes the payment of interest.

LEADING DEALERS

The leading bond underwriters, from Standard & Poor's *Bond Guide*, are as follows:

Advest Inc., Hartford

Allen & Co., Inc., New York

Asiel & Co., New York

Baird (Robert W.), Milwaukee

Bankers Trust Co., New York

Bateman Eichler Hill Richards, Los Angeles

Bear, Stearns & Co., New York

Blair (D.H.) & Co., New York

Blunt, Ellis & Loewi, Milwaukee

Bradford (J.C.), Nashville

Brown (Alex.) & Sons, Baltimore

Brown Bros. Harriman & Co. New York

Burns, Fry, Ltd, Toronto

Burns Pauli & Co., St. Louis

Butcher & Singer, Philadelphia

Chase Manhattan Bank, New York

Chicago Corp., Chicago

Citicorp Investment Bank, New York

Cutter & Dixon, New York

Dain Bosworth, Minneapolis

Daiwa Securities America, New York

Dean Witter Capital Markets, New York

Dickinson (R.G.) & Co., Des Moines

Dillon, Read & Co., Inc. New York

Dominick & Dominick, Inc., New York

Dominion Securities, Toronto

Donaldson, Lufkin & Jenrette, New York

Drexel, Burnham, Lambert, New York

Eberstadt, Fleming Inc., New York

Edwards (A.G.) & Sons, St. Louis

Eppler, Guerin & Turner, Dallas

Equitable Securites, Nashville

Ernst & Co., New York

Fahnestock & Co., New York

First Boston Corp., New York

First Southwest Co., Dallas

Freeman Securities, Jersey City

Furman Selz Mager D&B, New York

Goldman Sachs, Inc., New York

Herzig (P.R.) & Co., New York

Hill Samuel Securities Corp., New York

Illinois Co., Inc., Chicago

Interstate/Johnson Lane, Charlotte

Investment Corporation of Virginia, Norfolk

Johnston, Lemon, Washington, D.C.

Jones (Edward D.) & Co., St. Louis

Kidder, Peabody & Co., New York

Kuhns Bros. & Laidlaw, Inc., New York

Ladenburg, Thalmann & Co., New York

Laidlaw, Adams & Peck, Inc., New York

Lazard Freres & Co., New York

McDonald & Co., Securities, Cleveland

McLeod, Young, Weir, Toronto

Merrill Lynch Capital Markets, New York

Milwaukee Co., Milwaukee

Morgan (J.P.) Securities, Inc., New York

Morgan Stanley & Co., Inc., New York

Moseley Securities Corp., New York

Nesbitt, Thomson Securities, New York

Nomura Securities International, New York

Offerman & Co., Minneapolis

Ohio Co., Columbus

Oppenheimer & Co., New York

PaineWebber, Inc., New York

Piper, Jaffray & Hopwood, Inc., Minneapolis

Prescott, Ball & Turben, New York

Prudential-Bache Capital Funding, New York

Rauscher Pierce Refsnes, Dallas

Raymond, James & Associates, St. Petersburg

Robinson-Humphrey, Atlanta

Rotan Mosle, Houston

Rothschild (L.F.) & Co., Inc., New York

Salomon Bros., Inc., New York

Seligman Securities, Inc., New York

Shearson Lehman Hutton, New York

Smith Barney, Harris Upham, New York

Sterling, Grace & Co., New York

Stern Bros. & Co., Kansas City

Stifel, Nicolaus & Co., St. Louis

Thomson McKinnon Securities, New York

Troster Singer, Jersey City

UBS Securities, Inc., New York

Underwood, Neuhaus, Houston

Wedbush Securities, Los Angeles

Wertheim-Schroder, New York

Wheat, First Securities, Richmond

Wood, Gundy & Co., New York

Ziegler (B.C.), West Bend

To buy or sell bonds, it is not necessary to go to these leading underwriters. Any broker who is a member of the New York Stock Exchange can put a bond order for one bond or more on the floor of the Exchange. American Stock Exchange brokers can do the same on their Exchange. Nonmember brokers can execute orders in unlisted bonds and give their listed bond orders to a member firm to be executed on the Exchange.

SUGGESTED READING

The *Wall Street Journal* and *The New York Times* have excellent news sections about bonds. The *Wall Street Journal* features news of credit markets, financing business, money rates, and corporate debt offerings. Both papers list bond quotations for the New York Stock Exchange, the American Stock Exchange, the Pacific Stock Exchange, and the Philadelphia Stock Exchange.

For unlisted corporate prices, the Bond Section of the National Daily Quotation Service is available; however, for most bonds, this service lists only the names and telephone numbers of the brokers, not the prices. Since most bond dealers will not give a quotation on the telephone to an unknown individual caller, a better way to obtain a quotation on an unlisted bond is to ask one's own broker to get it.

Standard & Poor's *Bond Guide* is an excellent reference work, which gives summary bond information for individual companies. For more complete bond information, consult Standard & Poor's *Corporation Records*, a reference service that is readily available in most brokerage offices.

A classic textbook on bond values is *Security Analysis* by Benjamin Graham, David Dodd, Sidney Cottle, Roger F. Murray, and Frank Block, 5th ed. (New York: McGraw-Hill, 1988). Other suggested references are as follows:

Bond Market Roundup. New York: Salomon Brothers, weekly.

Fischer, Donald E., and Jordon, Ronald J. *Security Analysis and Portfolio Management*, 4th ed. Englewood Cliffs: Prentice-Hall, 1987.

Hirt, Geoffrey, and Block, Stanley B. *Fundamentals of Investment Management*, 2d ed. Homewood: Richard D. Irwin, 1983.

Levy, Haim, and Sarnet, Marshall. *Portfolio and Investment Selection: Theory and Practice*. Englewood Cliffs: Prentice-Hall, 1984.

Standard & Poor's Ratings Guide. New York: McGraw-Hill, 1989.

Tinic, Seha, and West, Richard W. *Investing in Securities*. Reading, Mass.: Addison-Wesley, 1979.

EQUIPMENT LEASING

Joseph J. Dini

BASIC CHARACTERISTICS

Equipment leasing was originally seen as a source of financing for marginal credit companies or companies with special needs, such as utilities. As the customer base broadened, some leasing companies found it difficult to define market segments. Many leasing customers initially avoided leasing because they found little help in applying this new source to their needs. Industry focus and customer understanding have improved to the point that, in 1988, more than $95 billion in equipment was placed under lease. According to the American Association of Equipment Lessors, leasing was used to acquire equipment more than any other form of third-party financing by American companies in that year.

With each change in tax laws and accounting rules, investors have watched the leasing industry face new challenges. Each challenge has added direction and definition to this emerging method of equipment financing.

The Participants

There are two main participants in a leasing transaction: the lessee and the lessor. This terminology is used to differentiate these groups from their counterparts in a real estate leasing transaction, the tenant and the landlord.

Many articles have been written detailing tiers of subparticipants, including trustees and financing sources. Only large corporate investors continue to use these intricate structures.

Joseph J. Dini is Vice-President of DPF Group, Ltd., an equipment leasing company in Burlington, Mass., and Woodcliff Lake, N.J.

The Lessee. The lessee is the user of the equipment that is leased, for which the lessee pays an agreed-on rent. Some leases require the lessee to maintain and insure the equipment, while others provide these benefits as part of the contract.

Lessees lease for a number of reasons, the most important being economic. Financial analysts convert real and implied benefits of a lease transaction to measurable monetary units. The monetary costs and benefits of the transaction must justify the choice of leasing versus another form of acquiring the equipment. The measurable benefits are cash flow, preservation of working capital, transfer of risk of obsolescence, and operating flexibility.

Users of equipment acquired on their behalf by income funds or corporate lessors range from major U.S. airlines to small printing companies, government agencies, and Fortune 100 companies. To limit this discussion to any one type of lessee or equipment would limit the imagination as to the potential of this market.

Income Funds. Publicly offered funds are able to tap into a very large segment of investors by registering with the Securities and Exchange Commission (SEC), providing extensive disclosure, and setting strict investment guidelines.

Because income funds are designed to provide investors with high cash flow, rents need to be sufficient to satisfy projected distributions. Lessees are only willing to pay rents that are commensurate with term or credit. Therefore, income funds must take the risk of residual value.

Lessees with good credit tend to lease equipment with short-term leases. These lessees are willing to pay for the flexibility, which offers them a hedge against obsolescence. Terms as short as six months are written by some funds, and almost none offer terms longer than ten years. Equipment as diverse as aircraft and computers satisfy these terms and requirements.

For example, if an airline finds that it expects to have use for a particular aircraft for the next twenty to thirty years, it can find a financial institution or a corporate lessor willing to enter into a twenty-five-year leveraged lease at a rent of $7,500 per month per million. For an aircraft that the airline can use for only three years, it may be willing to pay an income fund or other lessor a rent of $15,000 per month per million. A company that finds itself quickly moving through computer generations may be willing to lease peripheral equipment for eighteen months for $25,000 per month per million.

The lessee with marginal credit may look to some income funds as a source for last chance financing. Not many income funds seek this type of lessee for equipment leased for the first time. However, as an income fund begins to remarket off-lease equipment, it may seek out these types of users. Such lessees can continue to provide high rent and, if the terms are short enough, the fund can limit its exposure. This lessee group can get its equipment needs fulfilled reasonably by obtaining off-lease equipment from income funds. This market is just beginning to emerge.

Either the good-credit initial lessee or the marginal-credit second user can fall into the situation in which an expected short-term use becomes long term. Most funds are not willing to give purchase options, and some are reluctant to give rental renewal options. After paying a sizable rental for flexibility or marginal credit, lessees may find that they have to continue to pay a rent in excess of that of originally longer-term leases—a shortcoming that lessees may be able to avoid by better planning. Additionally, second users should set up contingency plans to avoid possible problems of improperly operating equipment. Such plans could include a continuation of a manufacturer's service plan, where available.

The biggest threat to the continued success of income funds comes from unrestrained growth. As more funds are introduced and existing ones increase in size, lessees will begin to benefit from the lower rentals resulting from the competition, and investors will suffer from lower cash flow and yields. Growth that is too rapid could also force the syndication group to reduce its fee structure while its exposure increases. There is some elasticity in the market, in that some lessees may lease equipment that they would have otherwise purchased, thereby adding equipment to the pool of equipment available for lease, when and if rents become low enough. However, the amount of new equipment manufactured each year is finite. The severest blow resulting from an overactive market would come from the vast amount of used off-lease equipment vying for the same users and simultaneously competing against new equipment deliveries.

The Lessor. The lessor is the owner of the equipment. Some lessors buy (invest in) equipment that they feel they can readily rent. Others buy equipment specified by a lessee who is under contract to place the equipment in use and pay rent. Lessors are entitled to all the benefits and bear all the risks derived from ownership.

Classification of Lease Transactions

Equipment lease transactions fall into two classifications for accounting purposes: operating leases and finance leases. The Internal Revenue Service (IRS) has issued both regulations and guidelines defining ownership and expensed rentals, thereby defining a true lease.

Within these three classes, a further breakdown exists. Leases that have total rentals equal to or greater than the cost of the equipment are called full payout leases. Those with total rent obligations that are less than the cost of the equipment are called nonpayout leases. Lessor investors that borrow part of the cost to purchase leased assets structure leveraged leases. No financing is used in what is called a single investor transaction.

Accounting Classification. Since 1974, the Financial Accounting Standards Board has defined and redefined leases from the standpoint of the lessee and lessor. Board Statement Number 13, which details the definitions, is available to the public. The Statement defines an operating lease as one in which the lessor has significant risks as to residual value. This requirement is satisfied by adjusting the lease term or rentals. A finance lease is a lease that provides minimal risk (except for credit) of the lessor recovering its investment. This minimal level of risk is accomplished by charging a high enough rent or providing a long enough term so that little reliance is placed on residual value.

A lessee expenses rentals under an operating lease and footnotes future obligations. Under a finance lease, the lessee capitalizes its obligation on its financial statements. The obligation is amortized over the lease term. So long as a lessee does not share in ownership or economic benefits resulting from ownership, the IRS will treat an operating lease as a true lease. Finance leases look like and are treated like a method of financing, whereas short-term operating leases resemble rental contracts.

ATTRACTIVE FEATURES

As an investment, equipment leasing provides many benefits to the lessor. Lessors can be corporations, partnerships, trusts, or individuals. The basic economic nontax benefits of ownership are equal for all lessors. However, current tax law limits and restricts tax benefits to all noncorporate lessors or owners. Noncorporate lessors generally are limited partnerships called income funds. These funds are structured to provide cash income to investors.

Expected annual cash distributions for most income funds range from 10 to 15 percent of gross investment. The overall expected after-tax yield ranges from 8 to 10 percent. Those familiar with basic lease analysis know that yield can be enhanced with leverage. Therefore, some funds employ leverage up to 50 percent of acquisition costs. Too much leverage, however, can limit cash distributions. Some funds employ no leverage. A third option is to retain some of the cash flow generated from rents and sales and use it to purchase additional new equipment. To achieve a positive yield, a fund must return the full investment and provide a return on that investment. If the rents cannot provide a full return of investment and a return on investment, the fund manager must achieve sufficient residual values to satisfy investors' expectations.

POTENTIAL RISKS

The investor in any lease has to pay attention to cash distributions to determine what portion is return on investment and what portion is return of investment. Some analysts have argued that too much emphasis is placed on receiving above-average residuals to make a sufficient yield. They state that it would be less risky to invest in residual-sharing debt programs. Planning adequate expected distributions based on wise equipment purchases can satisfy most investors' needs for yield and cash flow. The corporate investor also has to monitor residuals on a periodic basis. Accounting rules do not allow a lessor to increase the book value of residuals if they are higher than planned, but they require a write down if residuals are expected to be lower.

The IRS also limits the amount of tax deferral for corporate investors, through the alternative minimum tax (AMT). A corporation must take into account all its tax preference items, including accelerated depreciation, in determining its AMT. This requirement may limit the amount of benefits from tax deferral to a corporation.

Credit problems can cause a corporate lessor or income fund a loss of revenue. Such a situation can be temporary, as in a loss of rent through a bankruptcy, or it can take on more dramatic aspects, as in the loss of an uninsured asset or a loss in the residual value of improperly maintained equipment.

A review of the benefits and shortcomings associated with each participant's involvement in income funds and those of corporate investors reveals an equitable balance. If each gets what they set out to achieve, then it is a good deal for all. If there is a major imbalance as to risk and reward, the open free-market system will cause investment capital to flow to the opportunity with the highest expected yield.

Although most corporate and individual investors in equipment leasing are passive, the industry is not. To protect yield and return of investment, professional lease managers should be employed. Income funds provide such management. Corporate investors are beginning to employ managers in increasing numbers.

TAX CONSEQUENCES

Corporate Investors and Financial Institutions

A widely held regular corporation that is a lessor or owner of leased equipment can take all the deductions allowed by the IRS in true leases. These deductions include accelerated depreciation, interest expense on any loans (recourse or nonrecourse), and amortized expenses. The deductions can be used to offset the rental income from the lease. If the deductions exceed rental income (which they do in the first one to five years), they can be used to offset other corporate income.

The tax payments deferred from a lease transaction generate cash to the corporate investor. The return on investment from the cash flow plus the after-tax cash from residuals at the end of the lease term are measured against the investment to determine yield. Yield methods vary. The simplest method is to use an internal rate of return (IRR) analysis. Alternately, the corporation can use a multiple investing sinking fund (MISF). This method uses a dual discounting stream, eliminating the possibility of multiple answers found in some IRR analysis. Typical desired MISF yields range between 1.25 to 3 percent above similar credit risk after-tax yields available from bond investments.

The Individual Investor

Since the 1986 change in U.S. tax law, individuals with dollars available for equipment leasing investment have been directing them into publicly offered equipment leasing income funds. Having evolved from the early publicly offered blind-pool real estate leasing funds, the current crop of equipment leasing income funds finds the basis for their structure in the early blind pools offered by Integrated Resources and Phoenix. The early public equipment funds offered tax deferral, tax shelter (when investment tax credit was available), and cash flow. Private partnerships offered higher apparent write off benefits because of staged-in equity. However, because of suitability requirements, many investors were closed out of private offerings. Consistent with the new tax law, current income funds offer investors sheltered cash flow with little or no excess losses. (Excess losses can no longer be used to offset ordinary income, only to offset income of a like kind.) Up-front and continued cash flow exclusive of tax benefits is what sets these investments apart from their older cousins.

REPRESENTATIVE TYPES OF INVESTORS

Institutions

Corporate Investors. Corporations that have elected to participate in equipment leasing participate as a lessor in the form of an equity owner. In many situations, this investment is made as part of a trust arrangement with the investor as the beneficial owner. These corporate investors represent companies that generate high pretax income and produce little depreciation expense from capital expenditures. These investors borrow as much of the cost of the lease as possible without incurring recourse. This debt provides leverage that generates the losses that create tax deferral.

Some corporations elect to invest in the debt instruments used in leasing. These corporations benefit from the security of the asset, the down payment of the lessor, the predictable cash flow, and the liquidity.

Financial Institutions. Banks, savings and loans, insurance companies, and credit companies make up the largest dollar volume segment of investors in equipment leasing. They are typical high-pretax-income low-capital-expenditure institutions. Each has a clear understanding of how leasing fits into a lessee's capital acquisition plans and growth. These institutions participate as equity owners in leveraged leases, 100 percent investor-owners in single investor leases and/or as debt providers in leveraged leases. Independent leasing companies also use this pool of institutions as a source of borrowing.

Financial institutions that have had the experience of obtaining higher than expected returns from the sale of equipment at lease-end are investing in leasing companies by lending up to 100 percent of the value of a pool of on-lease equipment at current rates in consideration for a share in the residual value of the equipment. This is a good investment for an institution during periods when it has little need of tax deferral.

Not-for-profit institutions, such as pension funds, also participate in equipment leasing. They invest a portion of their funds in high quality debt instruments that support leverage leases to investment grade lessees.

In the past several years, investment bankers have structured public debt offerings for large leveraged leases. This product has been used to support the billions of dollars in new commercial airline aircraft leveraged leases. This pooled debt offers the investor liquidity and security. The purchasers of this investment are almost exclusively institutions.

Individuals

Individuals are attracted to investing in publicly offered equipment leasing income funds because of the high cash flow expectations, upside potential in times of high inflation, return of capital, and, in some cases, partial sheltered early cash flow. Sophisticated and knowledgeable individuals or investors who employ financial planners can make good use of an income fund's cash flow as part of an overall investment strategy.

Less sophisticated but knowledgeable individuals purchase shares in income funds as part of their portfolio for an inflation hedge. They recognize that equipment residual values are proportional to the cost of new replacement equipment. This investment strategy works well in a retirement account. However, using a non-real estate or other qualified investment in a retirement account or pension portfolio may cause an unrelated business tax. Each situation must be evaluated by a tax expert to determine if and to what extent this tax is applicable.

A large number of individuals who own income funds are retired people living on fixed-interest investments, such as certificates of deposit (CDs). An income fund's cash flow of 10 to 15 percent per year in the early years of an investment is partially or fully sheltered from income tax. Investors benefit substantially in the first three to five years on an after-tax basis as compared to a CD. However, the risks of a CD and an income fund are not comparable, and an evaluation has to be made on a risk/reward basis.

Some individual investors use the cash flow generated from income funds for universal life purchases, using the sheltered cash flow to purchase another sheltered income generator.

IMPORTANT FACTORS IN BUYING AND SELLING

The Broker Dealer Network

Because income funds are registered (but not approved) by the SEC, they can be and are sold by broker dealers ranging in size from local one-man shops to the major wire houses, such as Shearson Lehman Hutton. This type of product, usually sold in minimum dollar units of $2,500 ($2,000 for individual retirement accounts, or IRAs), provides gross selling allowances of anywhere between 7 to 9 percent of the amount sold. Besides the fee income, the selling of income funds provides other benefits.

In times of a lackluster or a cautious stockmarket, income funds provide an alternative product with immediate cash returns for investors. Income funds, because they are different from real estate and other nonstock investments, add diversification to investor portfolios. Since the quarterly cash distributions are sheltered in the first few years, they can be offered as an alternative to municipals. Along with real estate partnerships, they are offered as an inflation hedge.

Some short-sighted brokers see these partnerships competing for their customers' finite investment dollars. Imaginative brokers use income funds in several ways. One is to compete against banks for IRA funds. Another is to convert CDs held by retired people who are concerned about current income to partnership shares offering sheltered high cash flow. Other brokers have set up automatic reinvestment of distributions into another broker-controlled investment.

All but a few older funds have no formal secondary market. Lack of liquidity can be one of the toughest selling negatives for a broker. The 1986 tax law provides that any limited partnership that has developed a formal secondary market for the trading of units must be taxed as a corporation. To help create liquidity, many of the funds provide informal lists of those willing to buy or sell outstanding units of their funds.

The General Partner, Manager, and Syndicator

In many of the funds, these three are part of the same family of companies which was formed to sponsor a limited partnership. This group spends the money to structure the partnership, receive SEC approval, hire the accounting and law firms, print offering memorandums and related sales material, provide the seller with due diligence information, and set up a wholesaling and equipment acquisition network. The group takes these economic risks in hope of recovering its expenses out of reimbursements from the partnership proceeds.

After the minimum stated sales of partnership units have been accomplished (breaking escrow), the manager begins to acquire equipment and receives its contracted acquisition fee. This fee ranges from 1.5 percent of acquisition cost to more than 4 percent of acquisition cost. If the partnership uses leverage to acquire equipment, the acquisition fee as a percentage of the funds raised increases in proportion to the leverage.

This syndication group can receive overall present valued gross fees equal to more than 14 percent of gross investment. However, there is a statutory limit to up-front syndication costs and fees equal to 10.5 percent of gross investment, including fees paid to the broker dealer. A generalized fee structure is shown in Table 1.

If the syndication group is not successful in raising the minimum investment, substantial losses can be incurred. A poor performing initial partnership, although it may cover initial expenses, will guarantee poor sales of subsequent partnerships. Therefore, all the fiduciary responsibilities have to be taken seriously. Because of the public nature of the product, any hint of failure can be disastrous.

The Investor

Without the investor—the individual who provides all the fuel for the machine—there would be no income funds. Generally, investors purchase units in income funds for all the reasons that brokers sell them. The limited partners are entitled to all net proceeds generated by the activities of the fund.

Summary

Opponents of income funds often point to the fees in a fund as being excessive. They point out that only 80 to 85 percent of the amount raised is spent on revenue-producing assets. They state that continuing management fees and the general partner's share leave as little as 85 percent of income for the investor. For paying all these fees, it is argued, the limited partner's risk is too high.

All income funds issued to date have commenced the paying of cash distributions the quarter after closing. Income funds have little liquidity and are designed to terminate ten to twelve years after commencement, necessitating long-term plans by investors for reinvestment. Some current income funds are shown in Table 2.

Managing the Investment

The manager receives a percentage of actual rents received. This fee can range from 2 to 10 percent. In most cases, the management fee derived from rentals is subordinated to the investors' right to receive a pre-agreed-on quarterly cash distribution percentage. For example, if the prospectus calls for a quarterly payout equal to one fourth of 8 percent of

TABLE 1. Income Fund Fee Distribution

	Percentage of Equity	Percentage of Equipment Cost
Sales commission	8.0%	
Organizational & offering expenses	2.5	
Acquisition fees		3.5%
Continuing management fees		7.2[1]
Remarketing fees		1.0[2]
General partner's share		9.0[3]

[1] Based on 5 percent of an average rental of 1.5 percent of cost over eight years.
[2] Based on an average residual of 33 percent of cost at a 3 percent fee.
[3] Based on an average 5 percent of all cash flow.

TABLE 2. Some Current Income Funds

Name	Type of equipment	Dealer manager
American Income Partners	Diversified and transportation	American Finance Group, Boston
CSA Income Fund	IBM peripherals	CSA, Inc., Boston
National Lease Income Fund	Information and transportation	Integrated Resources, New York
Polaris Aircraft Fund	Used commercial jet aircraft	Polaris, Inc., San Francisco

gross investment prior to any management fees being paid, then for every $1,000 raised, a quarterly distribution of $20 must be made before the manager receives any fees. However, the management fee is cumulative and can be paid at a later date. Finally, there is usually a subordinated incentive fee due the manager on sale of the assets. Any amount due the manager is subject to the partner's receiving payout, that is, a return of gross investment plus a minimum return on the average outstanding investment. This fee is usually 3 to 5 percent of the proceeds from sale of the used equipment.

For taking all the risks of a general partner (full liability and responsibility of all actions or lack thereof of the partnership), the general partner receives a percentage of all profits and losses, usually in the range of one percent. However, after payout or some other measure, some partnerships allow for the general partner share to increase to as much as 10 percent of distributions.

GLOSSARY

capital lease—A lease in which all the benefits and risks of ownership are substantially transferred to the lessee; usually, lease term is for at least 75 percent of the useful economic life of the property; often includes an option to purchase; accounting and tax treatment differ from those for an operating lease; also called full payout lease.

full-payout lease—See *capital lease.*

lessee—An individual, corporation, or other entity that leases equipment or other property from another in order to obtain its use.

lessor—An individual, corporation, or other entity that owns equipment or other property and leases it to another.

leveraged lease—A lease for a substantial part of the useful life of the property, in which a portion of the property's acquisition cost is raised from borrowed funds.

money-over-money transaction—A straight (nonleveraged) leasing transaction.

net lease—A lease in which the lessee is responsible for maintenance and other costs of ownership of the equipment, including taxes, while the lessor is entitled to the tax benefits of ownership.

operating lease—A lease in which the expenses of ownership may be the responsibility of the lessor; usually, lease term is for only a portion of the useful economic life of the property; accounting and tax treatment differ from those for a capital lease.

residual value—Value of the equipment at the end of the lease term.

sale/leaseback—A leasing transaction in which one party buys the equipment from another and then leases it back to the second party (the lessee).

sinking fund—A fund set up and accumulated, usually by regular payments or by interest-earning deposits, for paying off the principal of a debt when it falls due.

SUGGESTED READING

A careful reading of current periodicals in the accounting, business, and tax areas is essential to keep abreast of the latest developments in equipment leasing.

Barron's. Published by Dow Jones & Company, New York, N.Y. Weekly.

Business Week. Published by McGraw-Hill, Inc., New York, N.Y. Weekly.

Financial Executive. Published by Financial Executives Institute, New York, N.Y. Monthly.

Forbes. Published by Forbes, Inc., New York, N.Y. Biweekly.

Fortune. Published by Time, Inc., New York, N.Y. Biweekly.

Harvard Business Review. Published by Harvard University, Graduate School of Business Administration, Boston, Mass. Bimonthly.

The Stanger Register. Published by Robert A. Stanger & Co., Shrewsbury, N.J. Monthly.

FOREIGN EQUITIES

Nancy J. Kyle

BASIC CHARACTERISTICS

In recent years, individuals have been attracted by both the generous financial returns on foreign equities and the excitement of owning shares of exotic companies in faraway places. Foreign equities for the U.S. investor consist of the shares of companies incorporated and listed on overseas stock exchanges that generally are not subsidiaries of U.S. corporations.

Foreign equity markets are capitalized at about $6 trillion, compared with a capitalization of $2.7 trillion for the U.S. and Canadian markets. European equity markets are currently capitalized at about $1.9 trillion, with the United Kingdom having the largest by far, despite its smaller gross national product than France or Germany. In the Far East, Japan has the largest equity market, with a capitalization of above $3.8 trillion; smaller markets thrive in Australia, Hong Kong, and Singapore. In the past several years, many very tiny and less well-known markets in Latin America, Southern Europe, and the Far East have been attracting attention. Known as emerging markets, these countries—Brazil, Mexico, Thailand, Philippines, Turkey, Greece, Portugal, Chile, and Argentina—are opening to foreigners, while Taiwan, India, and Korea allow U.S. investors to buy special mutual funds. All together, the market capitalization is only $350 billion.

These overseas stock markets have taken on greater importance than ever because of the lessening dominance of U.S. business and finance in worldwide economic affairs. In many instances, particularly over the last decade, the growth of foreign economies has far outstripped that of the United States. Other nations' equity markets naturally have grown

Nancy J. Kyle is a Vice-President of Morgan Guaranty Trust Company, New York.

at a pace commensurate with their general economic expansion. For example, yearly growth of Japan's gross national product (GNP) has averaged 3.6 percent since 1977 while the U.S. GNP growth rate has been just 2.6 percent over the same time span. This difference is reflected in the changing positions of the U.S. and Japanese equity markets: Their respective shares of total worldwide equity market value shifted from 56 percent (U.S.) and 15 percent (Japan) in 1977 to 29 percent (U.S.) and 44 percent (Japan) in 1988.

ATTRACTIVE FEATURES

Higher Potential Rewards

An investment in foreign equities creates the opportunity for an American investor to diversify his portfolio on an international basis—over an increasingly interdependent world economic spectrum. This means taking advantage of different growth rates in various national economies, and limiting risk exposure through insulation of the portfolio

FIGURE 1. Total Rate of Return on Foreign Equities, 1978–1987

Source: Morgan Stanley Capital International S.A., Geneva

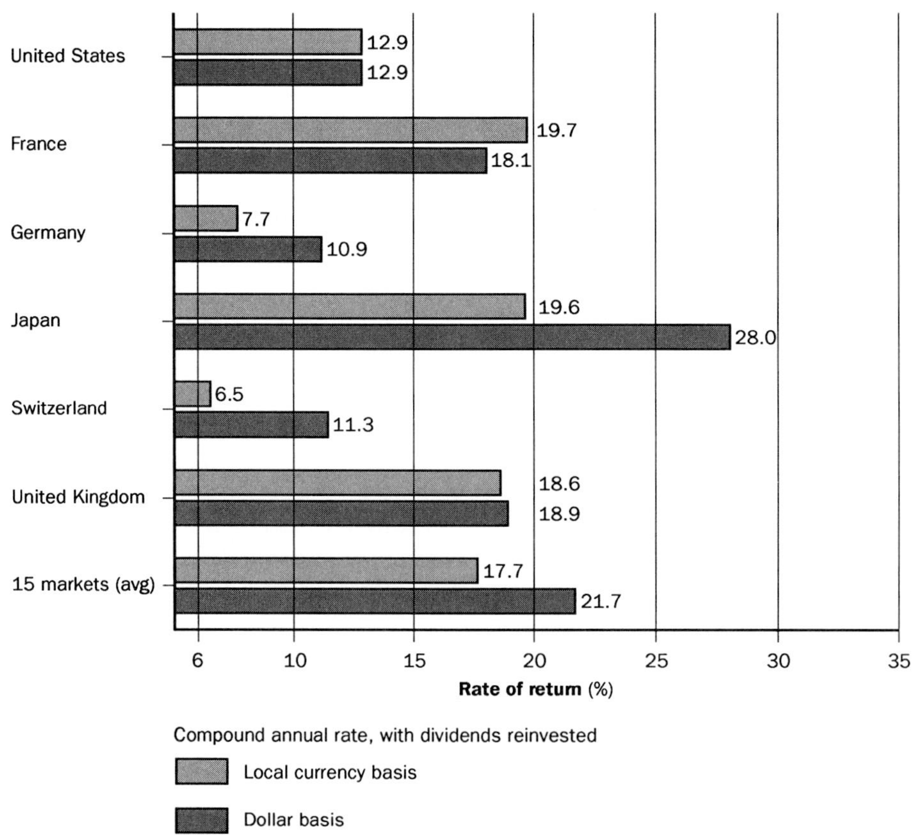

TABLE 1. Correlation of Equity Rates of Returns by Country and Industry, 1978–1987*

Country	Coefficient of Correlation with U.S.
Canada	.72
France	.43
Germany	.35
Japan	.21
Spain	.29
Switzerland	.48
United Kingdom	.57
15 markets (avg)	.46

Coefficient of Correlation U.S. Industry Group	With S&P Stock Index
Chemical	.75
Drug	.73
Gold	.36
Oil	.66
Retail stores	.70

* Return, excluding dividends, dollar basis

Source: Morgan Stanley Capital International S.A., Geneva

from localized economic problems in any one country—including the investor's. The result, in many instances, has been a higher rate of return than might have been possible with a portfolio limited to U.S. equities. As shown in Figure 1, most foreign equity markets outperformed the United States in total rate of return in both local currency and U.S. dollars during 1978–1987.

Less Variable Returns

It also appears likely that an investor's portfolio is less vulnerable to variability in returns if it is diversified among foreign equities and industry groups. A study by J.P. Morgan Investment Management, Inc. shows that the Morgan Stanley Capital International world index, as compiled by Morgan Stanley Capital International S.A. of Geneva, has been 10 percent less variable than Morgan Stanley Capital International's U.S. index over the last twenty years. These phenomena, taken together, indicate that the potential exists to create international portfolios with both higher rates of return and lower variability of return. (See Tables 1 and 2.)

Currency Exchange Impact

Moreover, the higher the degree of economic integration between any two countries, the more the rates of return on their stock markets are apt to move together. Skeptics will argue

TABLE 2. Correlation Coefficients: Foreign Equity Markets With United States

	Monthly Data					
	1960–79	1960–64	1965–69	1970–74	1975–79	1980–87
LOCAL CURRENCIES						
Australia	.40	.00	.30	.57	.36	.59
Austria	.13	.38	(.17)	.06	.13	.22
Belgium	.50	.46	.55	.44	.55	.46
Canada	.75	.79	.31	.79	.63	.77
Denmark	.16	.03	(.04)	.21	.32	.37
France	.36	.44	.13	.40	.41	.52
Germany	.31	.48	.16	.30	.27	.48
Italy	.22	.30	.13	.15	.28	.25
Japan	.22	.05	.13	.27	.48	.37
Netherlands	.58	.69	.69	.41	.58	.66
Norway	.29	.36	.05	.34	.34	.59
Spain	.14	.08	(.11)	.28	.21	.35
Sweden	.34	.34	.33	.40	.30	.45
Switzerland	.50	.53	.45	.53	.49	.68
United Kingdom	.42	.35	.27	.50	.47	.69
Average of 15	.35	.35	.25	.38	.39	.48
U.S. DOLLARS						
Australia	.41	.00	.30	.59	.36	.54
Austria	.15	.38	(.17)	.12	.14	.20
Belgium	.45	.45	.57	.41	.48	.42
Canada	.74	.80	.82	.78	.63	.74
Denmark	.19	.02	(.03)	.26	.34	.36
France	.35	.44	.09	.37	.43	.45
Germany	.33	.49	.21	.33	.27	.42
Italy	.21	.29	.13	.18	.21	.25
Japan	.22	.05	.13	.31	.32	.25
Netherlands	.57	.69	.69	.44	.57	.65
Norway	.30	.36	.05	.34	.39	.57
Spain	.12	.08	(.10)	.26	.18	.30
Sweden	.35	.33	.34	.39	.34	.43
Switzerland	.48	.53	.45	.49	.43	.56
United Kingdom	.40	.35	.25	.49	.44	.59
Average of 15	.35	.35	.25	.38	.37	.51

Source: Morgan Stanley Capital International S.A., Geneva

TABLE 3. Correlation: Stock Prices and Currency Exchange Rates in Foreign Countries

	Coefficient of Correlation Between Equity Price Index and Price of Local Currency in Terms of U.S. Dollars			
	1960–79	1970–79	1975–79	1980–87
Canada	.16	.16	.27	.48
France	.09	.14	.19	.07
Germany	.00	.01	−.01	−.06
Japan	.00	−.01	.07	.15
Spain	.18	.22	.29	.01
Switzerland	−.12	−.15	−.12	.14
United Kingdom	.09	.12	.13	.01
15 markets (avg)	.03	.04	.05	−.06

Source: Morgan Stanley Capital International S.A., Geneva

that foreign investment returns are mainly a result of currency gains, as the dollar declined against most other foreign currencies in the late 1980s. Other studies show, however, that changes in each of the world's equity markets are almost entirely uncorrelated with changes in their dollar exchange rates, as illustrated in Table 3.

Thus, market valuations and currency valuations should be regarded as separate considerations when international equity-investment decisions are made. Indeed, analysis of the total dollar returns of Morgan Guaranty Trust Company's international equities fund shows that its relatively better performance, against the Capital International index for non-U.S. stock markets (EAFE Index), results less from currency factors than from the direction and magnitude of stock market movements.

Still, foreign exchange rate movements can provide opportunities for higher returns, particularly for the institution or money manager with a good track record in currency forecasting. Conversely, it remains possible through poor stock selection for an internationally diversified portfolio to realize either a lower rate of return or a higher variability of return, or both. Here, as elsewhere, there can be no guarantees affecting the performance of freely traded equities.

Inflation Hedge

Owning foreign stocks gives the U.S. investor an opportunity to hedge against domestic inflation by participating in rapidly growing economies abroad—not only through diversification in a larger universe of assets but also through concentration among industries with growth prospects currently much brighter than may be the case with their American counterparts. The mining industry provides an outstanding example: While American investment opportunities diminish as a merger/takeover wave sweeps through the industry here, they literally abound in other countries, particularly Australia, where publicly traded mining companies continue to offer some of the few remaining vehicles for investor participation in commodity cycles anywhere in the world.

Other examples involve gold, shipping, real estate, cement, steel, and consumer electronics. There are any number of additional special situations, such as the Japanese advertising and computer software sectors, considerably less mature than their aging U.S. counterparts, with attractive growth potential that the American companies already have left behind.

Since the three sources of return from foreign shares are (1) capital gains in local currency; (2) dividends in local currency; and (3) currency gains or losses, they may, of course, provide that hedge against inflation only when the dollar is declining in relation to the currency in which they are denominated. This was precisely the case in the mid-1980s, when the dollar declined relatively while U.S. inflation declined more slowly in relation to elsewhere. Securities denominated in other currencies at that time provided a way to protect the purchasing power of dollar-denominated assets.

POTENTIAL RISKS

Currency Losses

Just as a U.S. investor in foreign shares may gain from a weakening dollar, he may sustain a loss when selling foreign shares and reconverting to dollars—if the dollar has appreciated relative to the currency in which that stock is denominated. The risk can be reduced by hedging in the forward markets. This allows the currency risk to be separated from the inherent market risk.

For example, an investor might purchase shares of a British exporting company, whose sales would benefit from a declining exchange rate of sterling against the dollar. At the same time, to minimize the potential loss in equity value (since the shares are denominated in sterling), the U.K. currency would be sold at the one-year forward rate, thereby locking in a specific exchange rate of sterling against the dollar. At the end of the year, the actual sale proceeds of the shares may differ from the amount of sterling sold forward, so some of the foreign-exchange transaction may have to be done at spot prices. Continued holding of a fully hedged position has its own cost. (See article on "Futures," elsewhere in this volume.)

Transactional Losses

Each foreign stock market has, to some extent, its own way of doing business; thus, at the very least, an American needs on-the-scene expertise to steer clear of pitfalls peculiar to a given territory. On the whole, the larger exchanges attracting most U.S. capital abroad have greatly improved their technical and mechanical procedures in recent years, to the point that many compare favorably with Wall Street and, on occasion, can be even more efficient than the U.S. model, although foreign trading and custodial costs are generally higher.

Trading in foreign securities is hardly without risk, as the 1974 collapse of Germany's Herstatt Bank made abundantly clear. Herstatt Bank was an active trader in foreign exchange markets and had entered into a number of deutsche mark-U.S. dollar transactions with U.K. and U.S. institutions. On that particular day in 1974, Herstatt Bank had entered into a transaction to deliver U.S. dollars in the United States against the deutsche marks that were delivered, in Germany, by U.S. and U.K. institutions (banks). The deutsche marks were delivered in Germany but, because of the time lag between the United States and Germany, the Herstatt never delivered the dollars in the United States.

Instead, it was closed down by the Bundesbank (the central bank of Germany) owing to overextension of the Herstatt. Therefore, before Herstatt had the opportunity to meet its obligation in New York during New York banking hours, it had been forced to close its doors. Many of these losses to other banks were never recovered. The moral of the story is that anything short of a simultaneous transaction, where both parties are meeting their obligations at the same time, is subject to risk.

A reputable institution or broker reduces the risk of a fraudulent transaction by dealing with only a limited list of well-run and well-capitalized foreign banks and brokers. (The Herstatt, for example, was not well capitalized.) Moreover, all the major stock markets have legal provisions similar to those in the United States, which allow a transaction to be dissolved if either party fails to deliver a security or make payment. Temporary delays in settlement, however, on both the cash side and the securities side, are not unusual.

Political Factors

Adding to the discomfort level of investors in foreign stocks is the political risk inherent in doing business abroad. The spectrum ranges from how effectively a government promotes private enterprise all the way to the extreme of sudden expropriation of assets. The attitudes of government and workers toward productivity, wage levels, medical and insurance benefits, and each other all have an impact on equity values. For example, in Japan, the close cooperation among government, business, and labor has been a factor helping to build a strong automobile industry whose products have achieved a dominant position in world markets, and whose equities, as a result, are highly prized.

Possible tax changes and the treatment of profits are equally important. For example, Hong Kong provides an attractive environment for locally registered companies by taxing profits at 16½ percent and by not taxing investors at all. The aforementioned Australian experience very clearly shows the impact of government policies on shareholders' wealth. Although endowed with rich resources of oil, gas, and other raw materials, the share prices of Australian mining companies were not participating in the 1973 to 1976 commodity price boom because the Labour government then in power discouraged foreign investment by severely taxing corporate profits. After the election of a Conservative party administration in 1976, which immediately reduced taxes, the country has seen record inflows of capital from abroad and a sharply rising stock market. More recently, the Labour party has treated corporations more kindly and has instituted pro-business policies.

Confiscation Threats

Of greatest concern to international investors is a situation where locally owned assets are left untouched while those held by foreigners are confiscated or devalued. The 1980 change in Ottawa's petroleum industry policy forced many U.S. oil companies to divest themselves of Canadian holdings at distress prices. (At the other extreme is a scenario in which foreign investors are prohibited from selling their shares or, if sold, the proceeds are denied convertibility into foreign currency.)

Most countries whose stock markets are attracting U.S. investors are, as it happens, politically stable Western-style democracies. Most also have citizens and companies with substantial investments in U.S. markets—subject, at least implicitly, to the restraints imposed by reciprocity. However, anything can happen in an era that features both multinationalism in business and fired-up nationalism in public affairs. To minimize the risk of unexpected losses that shifts in the political winds can suddenly create, careful and continuous monitoring of foreign governmental policies is essential to the management of an international equities portfolio.

Liquidity Limitations

Illiquidity is yet another common risk in international trading, but this is often more a function of the small size of a stock market or a negative market sentiment. With the exception of the Japanese, German, and British stock markets, turnover on foreign exchanges is not substantial relative to the United States, but turnover on all stock markets has increased dramatically between 1983 and 1989. Furthermore, the turnover of a particular stock is no more related to its share capitalization than the turnover of a particular stock market is to that market's capitalization. For example, British Telecom is Europe's largest telephone utility and is comparable in size to AT&T, but it trades at less than one-fourth the turnover of AT&T owing to large government ownership.

The low turnover in foreign stocks does not necessarily indicate a low level of sophistication or maturity in those markets. Germany provides a case in point. The number of listed companies on the five German stock exchanges is around 500. Moreover, trading volume of $150 billion a year (compared with $2 trillion on the New York Stock Exchange alone) is almost minuscule in relation to the size of Germany's huge and highly developed economy. The reason is not naiveté but ingrained national tradition. Historically, German industry draws its capital from retained profits and bank loans rather than through equity financing. Moreover, something over 40 percent of all German equities are held as virtually permanent investments by companies, banks, and government agencies. Whatever the reasons, the result is that many key German corporations have stock that is not only unlisted but also unquoted and, hence, not readily marketable. However, since markets are dynamic, proposed capital gain changes in Germany could usher in a period of rapid expansion of listed shares.

A long-standing relationship with reputable local brokers may help to protect against possible illiquidity, and the individual investor new to foreign markets is well-advised to search out an established institutional entree before plunging in. Being a prime institutional customer to major foreign brokers does not guarantee the best prices in a thin market, but it does demand attention from them and allows the institution to select the right broker for each transaction.

TAX CONSEQUENCES

Withholding Taxes on Dividends

No U.S. government restraints on foreign equity investments have existed since the expiration, in 1974, of the interest equalization tax and related controls. However, foreign governments (except Hong Kong and Singapore) withhold a tax on the dividends received by nonresident shareholders. In most countries, some of this tax can be reclaimed through the application of U.S. treaties. A U.S. taxpayer can offset this withholding tax to some extent by filing IRS Form 1116 with the 1040. The effective withholding tax currently applicable to a stock portfolio owned by a U.S. investor, and invested in most of the major stock markets, runs to about 15 percent on average.

A qualified U.S. pension trust benefits not only from the general provisions of double taxation agreements with foreign countries but also, in a few instances, by means of exemptions from foreign taxes that have been granted to pension and charitable trusts. Where withholding taxes are levied, there is a wide range of procedures for claiming refunds or for applying to have payments made under the concessionary rates of tax specified in the relevant double taxation agreement. Handling of these reclaims and applications is usually done by the custodian.

Capital Gains Tax

Generally, there is no capital gains tax imposed by any foreign government on securities sold by a U.S. investor. However, a U.S. citizen must, of course, include foreign capital gains when filing a federal income tax return; the same rate applies as for domestic capital gains.

REPRESENTATIVE TYPES OF INVESTORS

The serious long-term investor, whether individual or institutional, will find foreign equities an interesting alternative to many domestic securities. While limited liquidity and changing conversion rates present problems, these investments demonstrably have the potential to decrease the portfolio's variability of return and increase its overall rate of return.

IMPORTANT FACTORS IN BUYING AND SELLING

Transaction Costs

Trading expenses include brokerage commissions and, in some foreign markets, turnover or local stock-transfer taxes. While Table 4 does not reflect precise extracts from regular commission scales, it shows best estimates of the cost likely to be incurred when dealing on

TABLE 4. Transaction and Custody Costs: $10 Million International Portfolio

	Approximate Cost in Basis Points	
Country	Transactional	Custodial
Japan	120	12
Germany	100	10
United Kingdom	80	10
France	100	10
Australia	140	10
Netherlands	100	10
Switzerland	100	10
Weighted foreign average	100	10
Comparable U.S.	40	0

Source: Morgan Guaranty Trust Company of New York

stock exchanges for a reasonably substantial portfolio. The figures shown include fiscal charges such as stock transfer taxes.

It is often possible to reduce quite substantially the effective transaction expense by purchasing American Depositary Receipts (ADRs), discussed next, or by trading directly with off-floor net market makers. In the latter case, trades are not normally subject to brokerage commissions as such, and approximately 0.5 percent (e.g., $100 bid, $100.50 asked) is a fair indication of the spread between bid and asked prices. Because most, if not all, of the securities in an international portfolio will be non-U.S.-dollar-denominated, there are added costs of foreign exchange dealing.

The overall rate of transaction expense will depend on both the portfolio mix and its activity rate. As a very broad indication, the one-way expense in a characteristically diversified portfolio might be one percent for stocks on either the buy or sell side. Comparable numbers for a wholly U.S.-invested portfolio might be 0.40 percent. Overseas expenses, therefore, run about 60 basis points higher than those in the United States. (Note: Double commissions may be charged by a U.K. or continental bank to buy equity securities outside its national market. Additionally, stamp, duty, or government transfer taxes may be incurred.)

American Depositary Receipts

In addition to the direct purchase of shares overseas or from among the small number of foreign shares listed on the New York and American Stock Exchanges, investors can buy ADRs. ADRs remove many of the more formidable custodial and trading inconveniences that go with owning foreign equities. An ADR is a negotiable receipt issued by an American depositary in lieu of the underlying shares it holds in custody overseas. (Morgan Guaranty Trust Company and Citibank are two of the principal issuers of ADRs.) Normally, they are issued only for shares that are traded on recognized foreign securities exchanges, and an ADR may represent one share or, as is often the case with Japanese ADRs, many shares.

ADRs are traded and transferred in exactly the same way as U.S. stock certificates. If the holder of an ADR wishes, the underlying shares can be obtained in the United States by surrendering the ADR for cancellation and requesting shipment of the stock. A 0.5 percent fee is charged by the depositary for this cancellation. ADRs are traded on the New York and American Stock Exchanges and on the over-the-counter market.

Dividends on ADRs. An ADR holder automatically receives a dividend in U.S. dollars at no additional charge. Under the tax conventions between the United States and other countries, an ADR holder may claim, for federal income tax purposes, certain credits for foreign withholding taxes on dividends. Rights offerings, stock splits, and stock dividends are monitored by the U.S. depositary, which then notifies the ADR holder of such corporate actions.

ADR Subscription Rights. A rights issue by a foreign company that has complied with the requirements of the U.S. Securities Act of 1933 can be taken up by the ADR holder. If a foreign company has not so complied, which is more often the case, the rights are sold, and the dollar proceeds are forwarded by check to the ADR holder. A list of companies for which ADRs are issued is available from any U.S. stock exchange, the National Association of Securities Dealers, or any ADR custodian bank.

Use of Investment Professionals

Brokerage Firms with Foreign Expertise. Many American brokers have expanded their in-house capability to research as well as trade in foreign equities. In some cases, the U.S. broker trades directly as an associate or full member of an overseas stock exchange. More often, the orders are placed with a local foreign broker on a particular stock exchange. Some brokers prefer to deal only for institutional clients. (See *Brokerage Firms in the United States With Foreign Expertise* at the end of this article for a directory of leading U.S. and foreign brokers with at least one office in the United States. Many foreign banks located in the United States also distribute information about foreign securities.)

International Investment Managers. U.S. investors' growing interest in foreign equities has led to a sharp increase in the number of international portfolio managers vying for American clientele. Although London remains the base for most leading managers specializing in this area, other cities around the world—New York, Boston, Chicago, San Francisco, Geneva, Paris, Zurich, Hong Kong, and Tokyo—also are being chosen as headquarters for international management operations. Their services vary in terms of investment style, performance results, risk levels, active/passive management, research-capability depth, and cost. (See *International Investment Managers* at the end of this article.)

CUSTODIAL CARE

Administration

The time lag between a trade and settlement can be so short that it would be impossible to meet settlement deadlines if foreign securities were held in the United States, even in New York. For example, the settlement period for Hong Kong shares is twenty-four hours, although negotiable. Income collection from a distance can also be complicated; coupons on bearer securities must be clipped and mailed to local paying agents. Accordingly, while an unsophisticated investor might believe that the risks inherent in owning foreign stocks can be reduced by keeping the certificates at home, the disadvantages outweigh any apparent gains. Indeed, the cost of insuring and then physically moving the securities back to their base market for sale is usually a sufficient deterrent. Foreign stocks should be kept in the country in which they are purchased.

Loss Protection

The major markets in Europe—Germany, France, Switzerland, Belgium, and the Netherlands—all have computerized central clearing systems. These stock markets also operate under laws that ensure that trade settlements will not expose one party to a loss if the other fails during the settlement process. Even where centralized clearing has not yet been introduced, notably in Britain and the Far East, that protection is fairly well organized. Also, while many foreign banks do not carry custodial insurance—unlike American banks, which regard it as a routine precaution—investors will find that their U.S. custodian's insurance policy, in fact, covers its overseas agencies where the custody should be maintained.

Custody Costs

Many institutions do not quote separate custodial fees. Instead, the charge may be lumped in with investment-management transaction commissions, underwriting concessions, or even the spreads on other banking business. The aggregate cost of these foreign custodial services, which average around 10 basis points for a large institutional client, are shown in Table 4. Individual investors, it should be noted, often pay more. Custody costs are also a function of activity in the portfolio, just as they are in U.S. equity investing.

GLOSSARY

ADR subscription rights—Stock purchase rights issued by a foreign company. Such rights may or may not be exercisable by the U.S. investor; if not, the rights are sold with dollar proceeds payable to the investor.

American depositary receipt—A negotiable receipt issued by an American depositary institution in lieu of underlying shares of a foreign company held in custody overseas.

basis point—Commission pricing broken down into one hundredths. One hundred basis points equal one percent.

capital gain—The excess of selling over purchase price realized upon sale of a security.

coefficient of correlation—The correlation of performance between two investments, measured as a percentage of 1.0.

hedging—Trading in the forward markets in opposite directions with similar or related securities.

par value—The dollar value assigned to a share of stock by the issuer at time of issue.

price/earnings ratio—Market price per share divided by net earnings per share in the preceding year.

stock index—A composite historical record of market prices of a selected group of stocks.

variable return—The suboptimal earnings from a portfolio over time because of limited breadth of holdings.

yield—The total of dividend and interest payments.

BROKERAGE FIRMS IN THE UNITED STATES WITH FOREIGN EXPERTISE

Bear Stearns & Co., New York, N.Y.; San Francisco, Cal.

Arnhold S. Bleichroeder Inc., New York, N.Y.

Cazenove Inc., New York, N.Y.; San Francisco, Cal.

Daiwa Securities America Inc., New York, N.Y.

Drexel Burnham Lambert Inc., New York, N.Y.

Eberstadt Fleming Inc., New York, N.Y.

Goldman, Sachs, New York, N.Y.

James Capel, New York, N.Y.

J.B. Were & Co., Inc., New York, N.Y.

Merrill Lynch, Pierce, Fenner & Smith, New York, N.Y.

J.P. Morgan Investment Management, Inc., New York, N.Y.

Nikko Securities Co., Ltd., New York, N.Y.

Nomura Securities Co. Ltd., New York, N.Y.

Oppenheimer & Co., Inc., New York, N.Y.

Paine Webber, New York, N.Y.

Prudential-Bache Securities, New York. N.Y.

Salomon Brothers, New York, N.Y.

Shearson Lehman Hutton, New York, N.Y.

Warburg Securities, New York, N.Y.

INTERNATIONAL INVESTMENT MANAGERS

ABD International Management Corp.

Aetna Multinational Asset Management

AIG Global Investors

Bankers Trust Investment Management

Baring International Investment, Ltd.

Batterymarch Financial Management

Beutel, Goodman International, Inc.

Boston International Advisors, Inc.

Brown Brothers Harriman & Company
Capital Guardian Trust Company
Capital Management International
Chase Investors Management Corp.
CITICORP Investment Management, Inc.
County NatWest Investment Management, Ltd.
Credit Suisse Asset Management
Daiwa Int'l Capital Management Corp.
Fidelity Int'l Investment Advisors
First Chicago Investment Advisors
Grantham, Mayo, Van Otterloo & Co.
HD International Limited
Henderson International, Inc.
Hill Samuel Investment Advisors, Ltd.
IDS International, Inc.
INVESCO Capital Management
J. P. Morgan Investment Management, Inc.
Julius Baer Investment Management
Kemper-Murray Johnstone International, Inc.
Matuschka Moser Partners
Mercator Asset Management, Inc.
Morgan Grenfell Investment Services
Oechsle International Advisors
PCM International
Posthorn Global Asset Management
Putnam International Advisors
Rothschild, Inc.
Schroder Capital Management International
Scudder, Stevens & Clark, Inc.
State Street Bank & Trust Company
UBS Phillips & Drew International Investment, Inc.
Warburg Investment Management
Wardley Investment Services International, Ltd.
Wertheim-Philippe International
WorldInvest Limited

SUGGESTED READING

PERIODICALS

Euromoney. Published by Euromoney Publications, Ltd., London, England. Monthly.

Financial Times. Published by Bracken House, London, England. Weekly.

International Investor (international edition). Published by Institutional Investor Systems, Inc., New York, N.Y. Monthly.

South East Asian Review. Published by South East Asian Studies, Gaya, India, Semiannually.

The Economist. Published by Pearson, London, England. Weekly.

REFERENCE BOOKS

Euromoney Publications PLC, *Guide to World Equity Markets*. Published by First Boston Corporation with Euromoney Publications PLC and GT Management PLC, Boston, 1987.

FURNITURE

John A. Hays

Once upon a time in America, a man lived and died, leaving one highboy and two sons. The highboy was rare, the sons needed money, and eventually a buyer was found, making everybody happy.

From this simple beginning has flowered the multimillion dollar business of buying and selling American furniture. It is an industry dependent on two passions: aesthetics, or the desire to live with beautiful objects, and scholarship, or the act of learning about America in an earlier time through the furniture that has survived to the present day. The two motives may and often do overlap, depending on the investor.

Buying American furniture demands careful subjective and objective considerations on the part of investors, who may have to live with their selections for long periods before having the opportunity to sell to the best advantage. The staggering rise in prices for American furniture during the 1980s was largely owing to the increase in the number of collectors and a continued supply of good to excellent pieces. Five years ago, many market watchers wondered audibly when the market would peak. Despite dips in the stock market and other economic indicators, the prices of American furniture have continued to rise. This suggests that buying American furniture remains a good investment, one that is less vulnerable to vicissitudes in the national and international economy than are many others.

John A. Hays is Assistant Vice-President, American Decorative Arts, at Christie's in New York.

BASIC CHARACTERISTICS

American furniture is classified according to styles and periods, which run from the seventeenth to the early twentieth century. Most collecting has concentrated on high-style country and urban furniture from these centuries. Certain basic characteristics shared by the furniture from each period help identify and authenticate individual pieces.

Seventeenth Century

Examples of American furniture from the seventeenth century, or the pilgrim period, are rare. Part of the problem is their advanced age; another major difficulty is that such pieces bear so much similarity to their English prototypes that they are often misclassified as English furniture. In addition, the woods used in crafting American furniture during this period were frequently the same types found in Europe and can be distinguished only by using microanalysis. Recent scholarship has only begun to differentiate American from European characteristics, let alone one American group from another. In spite of these drawbacks, the interest and excitement for great and even good examples of seventeenth-century furniture have never been stronger. The most frequently encountered furniture forms from this period are carved and joined armchairs known as great chairs, blanket chests, Bible boxes, benches, and stools.

Between 1981 and 1988, prices have surged in this relatively low-priced field to the point where a rare seventeenth-century example will bring as much as one from the eighteenth or nineteenth century. For example, in October 1987, a Connecticut chest made of oak and poplar sometime between 1690 and 1710 sold at auction for $209,000. The price was four times the estimate set by the auction house that sold it. A great chair, made in Essex County, Massachusetts, circa 1675, sold for $400,000—this amount was ten times the price estimated by the auction house that sold it.

Eighteenth Century

Furniture design in eighteenth-century America was directly influenced by the most popular English pattern books, such as Chippendale's Director, available in the colonies. This desire to be in step with current taste in England, combined with the fact that many cabinetmakers were trained in Europe and the Continent before they immigrated to the young nation, gave American furniture an English bias. Nevertheless, American furniture is far more linear and unembellished than its English counterparts, reflecting the taste of the American merchants in contrast to the opulent taste of the English aristocrats. As cabinetmakers influenced by various tastes and training settled in America's port cities, specific regional styles developed, allowing us today to identify a desk made in Boston or Newport and a chair made in Philadelphia or New York. The basic connoisseurship of furniture made in each of these port cities has been call regionalism, and the value of furniture can fluctuate dramatically as one region becomes more popular than another among today's collectors. The four major port cities are Boston, Newport, New York, and Philadelphia. Other important regional styles centered around the ports of Baltimore and Charleston. There are many other smaller centers with their own distinct styles, including Salem, Massachusetts; Portsmouth, New Hampshire; and the Connecticut River Valley.

Philadelphia. The most sophisticated and high-style eighteenth-century American furniture was made in Philadelphia. Philadelphia was the political and cultural center of the colonies and for decades was the largest city in America, looking up only to London. The high-style design preferences of the clientele, combined with the sturdy construction techniques inherited from the German immigrants who settled in this area, created the very distinctive Philadelphia Queen Anne and Chippendale styles. Such techniques as mortise-and-tenon construction of chairs, tables, and cabinets, often using lemon-shaped pegs, are unique aspects of this distinct regional style. The secondary woods most frequently used in drawer linings and backboards are yellow pine, oak, and poplar. Walnut was frequently interchanged with imported mahogany as a primary wood, used in both solid carved cases and veneer.

Philadelphia furniture has surrendered little or none of its popularity over the centuries. In fact, in the last decade, its intrinsic value has been augmented by fierce competition among collectors who desire its academic purity and somewhat austere form.

The prices paid for Philadelphia furniture in the 1980s were the highest for any region and, in fact, set world records for individual forms. Four of the five top prices for American furniture were set by Philadelphia examples and all exceeded $1 million:

1. A wing chair that sold in January 1987 fetched $2.75 million, then a world record for any piece of furniture. The chair, with carved knees and hairy-paw feet, was made for General John Cadwalader, a prosperous Philadelphia merchant and patriot. (See Figure 1.)
2. A suite of furniture, comprising a mahogany highboy and matching lowboy and a pair of side chairs, was sold for $1.76 million in May 1987. The furniture was made in Philadelphia by Thomas Tufft and Thomas Affleck for Richard Edwards, a prosperous lumber merchant who later settled in New Jersey.
3. A wing chair with carved knees and claw-and-ball feet, made in Philadelphia circa 1770 by an unknown craftsman, sold in October 1986 for $1.1 million.
4. A tea table with a carved base and piecrust top, made in Philadelphia between 1760 and 1780, was sold for $1.04 million in January 1986. (See Figure 2.)

Newport. Newport's religious pluralism, strategic location, and successful marine economy made this island a cosmopolitan center in eighteenth-century New England. Among the many trades that flourished in this busy port was cabinetmaking, the demand for which was fueled by an ever-growing merchant class that made its money in shipping and onshore trade. Two families are considered preeminent cabinetmakers in this region: the Goddards and the Townsends. From a small workshop on Newport's waterfront, these families developed a furniture style that is highly sought after by collectors today. The most distinctive features of this regional style are plain, curvilinear desks and chairs and chests of drawers embellished with very distinctive lobed, stylized scallop shells. Newport craftsmen often used very dense, figured mahogany as a primary wood along with chestnut as a secondary wood, although because of their proximity to the brisk sea trade, these craftsmen are said to have always had first pick of the woods imported to America.

The scarcity of Newport masterpieces surfacing in the market in recent years may be responsible for the relative sluggishness of prices for this type of furniture, compared to Philadelphia furniture. Between 1983 and early 1989, no major piece of Newport furniture had been publicly sold. However, interest was very high among buyers when a kneehole bureau from the Goddard-Townsend workshop was sold in January 1983 for $687,000.

FIGURE 1. The General John Cadwalader Chippendale Wing Chair, Philadelphia, 1770

Note: This wing chair set a record price for American furniture on January 31, 1987, selling for $2.75 million at Sotheby's.

Source: Photo is courtesy of Sotheby's, Inc., New York. Copyright ©1988 Sotheby's, Inc.

FIGURE 2. A Chippendale Carved Mahogany Tea Table, Philadelphia, 1760 to 1780

Note: This tea table is the first piece of American furniture to sell for more than $1 million dollars ($1,045,000, at Christie's, January 25, 1986.)

Source: Photo is courtesy of Christie's, New York.

A masterpiece of Newport cabinetmaking—the magnificent Nicholas Brown desk and bookcase—sold at Christie's on June 3, 1989 for $12.1 million (Figure 3). This desk and bookcase, one of nine made in Newport with carved shells on the exterior lid and upper blocked panel doors, was probably made by John Goddard for Nicholas Brown of Providence, Rhode Island in the 1770s. This extraordinary price is four times the previous record for any piece of furniture sold.

New York. Created in a port whose heritage is English and Dutch, New York furniture exhibits an integration of styles from both. Broad Dutch and four-square New York

FIGURE 3: The Nicholas Brown Desk and Bookcase

Note: This masterpiece of Newport cabinetmaking set a new record high price for American furniture when sold at Christie's on June 3, 1989 for $12.1 million.

Source: Photo is courtesy of Christie's, New York.

furniture proportions tend to be wider and broader than other American regional styles. Examples are rare, largely because of two major fires that broke out during the eighteenth century and destroyed much of the furniture that was made and kept in New York City. The surviving examples give a fairly complete picture of the styles preferred in this region. Chairs were made in a robust, thicker style, suggesting a Dutch approach but obviously meant to copy English patterns established by such cabinetmakers as Thomas Chippendale. Carving, when it appears, is more stringy, and chairs and chests often include a heavy gadrooned molding.

Because they are so rare, masterpieces of New York furniture bring very high prices when they are publicly sold. In October 1983, two important Queen Anne side chairs, made for the New York merchant Charles Apthorp (1698 to 1758), sold for $473,000.

The value of New York furniture has not achieved parity with Philadelphia, Boston, or Newport. This is largely because fewer collectors have focused on New York, in part because the examples so seldom appear for sale, thus reducing the competition. However, many experts feel that New York furniture is significantly undervalued and predict stronger prices will follow as more collectors turn their attention toward it.

Boston. The extremely successful maritime trade between Boston and London in the eighteenth century created a wealthy mercantile class on both sides of the Atlantic. The most up-to-date furniture designs and fashions in London were easily imported to Boston, which were then copied by American craftsmen. Many of these designs, such as the highboy, blockfront and bombé chests, were embraced by American cabinetmakers and were favored long after the fashion for them changed in London. The intolerable tax acts, which led to the Boston Tea Party, severed the economic and cultural bonds between these two cities. Numerous examples of furniture from this region survive today, and outstanding pieces fetch record prices. For example, a Chippendale bombé chest of drawers sold publicly in 1986 for $600,000. A blockfront desk and bookcase, by John Chipman of Salem, sold in January 1987 for $352,000. White pine, maple, and birch are the principal secondary woods used in this region.

Nineteenth Century

Classical or late Federal American furniture from the first half of the nineteenth century was inspired by designs from the English and French pattern books printed in the early nineteenth century, which were influenced by the archaeological discoveries made during the eighteenth century, especially those at Pompeii and Herculaneum. For example, the klismos chair and récamier sofa was taken directly from Roman designs, as were many of the classical motifs such as saber legs, columnar supports, Greek keys, and other patterns. Americans were also inspired by the urge to inject Roman republican ideals into their own fledgling nation. The nineteenth century saw a dominance of important furniture by New York cabinetmakers, including Duncan Phyfe, Charles-Honoré Lannuier, and Michael Allison. Other cities also produced important furniture during this period, and examples include pieces by Anthony Quervelle and Joseph Barry in Philadelphia and Isaac Vose in Boston. Baltimore favored its furniture from this period fancy painted, work which was dominated by the shop of Hugh and John Finlay.

In 1987, an inlaid brass-mounted secretaire à abattant, made in Philadelphia circa 1815, sold at auction for $302,500. In 1988, a painted and stenciled brass-mounted slate-top center table, attributed to John Finlay, circa 1825, sold at auction for $75,000. In 1985, a carved mahogany sofa, attributed to Duncan Phyfe, circa 1810, sold at auction for $82,500.

Twentieth Century[1]

The furniture of the American arts and crafts period, spanning roughly from 1895 to 1915, is characterized by a reaction against the increased mechanization and mass production of the Victorian era and a return to the purity of form of earlier handmade objects. This medievalizing aesthetic, first promoted in the nineteenth century, greatly influenced America's premier designer and builder of arts and crafts furnishings, Gustav Stickley. Working mainly in native oak, and less frequently in imported mahogany, Stickley and his complement of craftsmen fashioned, by hand, tables, chairs, bureaus, beds, sideboards, bookcases, and china closets in a style virtually devoid of any unnecessary decorative embellishment. The partnership of Harvey Ellis and Gustav Stickley, for a brief period from 1903 until Ellis's untimely death in 1904, provides the one exception to this rule. Ellis, who created some of the most prized designs for the firm, did embellish his designs with certain stylized copper and mica inlays. Although there were many other shops producing this type of furniture—the firm of L. & J.G. Stickley, the Roycroft Shops, and Charles Limbert, to name a few—the work of Gustav Stickley and Harvey Ellis for Stickley command the highest prices in today's market. In June of 1988, a high-back settle made for the vestibule of Gustav Stickley's house was sold for $93,500. In the same auction, an Ellis-designed rocker sold for $19,800, and an oak and copper work cabinet fetched $18,700.

In addition to the work of the arts and crafts movement, the designs of several prairie school architects, notably Frank Lloyd Wright, George Washington Maher, and Charles Sumner and Henry Mather Greene (Greene and Greene), command substantial sums at auction. Like the furniture of Gustav Stickley, these designers generally executed their pieces in native oak. However, while Stickley furniture was made for use in any house, these architect's pieces were designed for specific commissions as part of the total design concept. Therefore, one should be able to identify the works of these architects through stylistic similarities to other known pieces, or by locating the actual piece in question (or one similar to it) in period photographs, which, for the more major commissions of this period, are widely published.

In June of 1988, an oak spindle armchair designed by Wright for his Ward W. Willits house, circa 1901, sold at auction for $93,500. In June 1985, an inlaid Honduras mahogany desk designed by Greene and Greene for the Charles M. Pratt house, circa 1909, sold at auction for $242,000.

ATTRACTIVE FEATURES

American furniture has proven to be a safe, long-term, exciting investment with very active participation on the part of the investor. In most cases, the investment potential is strictly a secondary consideration to the scholarly and aesthetic goals of the collector. Nevertheless, careful selections, the opportunity for bargains, and the increasing number of

---

[1] The author wishes to acknowledge the assistance of Patrick J. Meehan, Specialist in Twentieth-Century Decorative Arts at Christie's, New York, in the preparation of this discussion.

collectors have proven that American furniture has enormous investment potential, sometimes outpacing aggressive growth financial investments. Collecting American furniture also fulfills the desire to contribute to one's community through historic preservation, provides the opportunity to live with beautiful objects, has a potential tax benefit if investments are donated to museums, institutions, or historical societies, and can become either a scholarly avocation or even a profession for an investor.

A comparison of record American furniture prices according to form demonstrates examples of growth potential at the very top of the American furniture market during the 1980s. Selected comparisons of comparable forms in the middle range of the market show many of the same percentage gains. Although not every area of the market has increased so dramatically, generally investments did not lose ground in the worst cases and increased 20 to 30 percent between 1984 and 1988.

IMPORTANT FACTORS IN BUYING AND SELLING

The eight standard criteria used in determining the value of American furniture are rarity, aesthetics, condition, documentation, provenance, freshness to the market, previous prices, and fashion. Although there is always the potential for aberrations, the application of these basic criteria are the standard way to gauge the potential value of furniture.

Rarity

American furniture to begin with is rare, especially those examples from the seventeenth and eighteenth centuries. Nevertheless, some forms are rarer than others, and thus, the competition for them is greater. For example, in 1985 a Queen Anne dressing table sold at auction for $99,000, which was then a record for this form. The buyer had a clear objective—he owned the matching high chest and wanted to put the two together again. The underbidder came to the sale to bid on a painting, which had been exhibited over the dressing table. Liking the arrangement of the painting over the table, this bidder hoped to put the two together. The contrasting reasons of the two bidders for acquiring the same piece led to this extraordinary price. One important caveat: Unique or unusual forms do not always translate into high prices. Collectors prefer to be able to compare a particular form to others in order to understand its merits or to have some precedent for the existence of the object itself during the period.

Aesthetics

The success of the design and proportion of a piece of furniture, along with comparison to similar forms, is the standard way to judge its value. This good, better, best, masterpiece approach analyzes the height, width, depth, color, finish, embellishments, quality of wood selection, and other visual criteria. These factors are not all subjective, but are judged by the standards of the period in which the piece of furniture was made. In other words, the successful design of an eighteenth-century chair must be seen by eighteenth-century standards as well as twentieth-century ones. This requires an understanding of the aesthetics of the period from which a piece of furniture was made.

Condition

The condition of a piece of American furniture factors greatly in determining its value. The intense scrutiny a piece of American furniture goes through is a phenomenon unique to the American field and probably has to do with the number of forgeries and clever restorations that pervade the market. Honest repairs made on a piece of furniture, such as patches to drawer fronts or feet, replaced hardware, or minor inlay restoration, will have less of an effect on the price than the entire replacement of feet or legs. Case pieces that are married, or were not made to be together, or embellishments made or added at a later date, such as the addition of an inlaid eagle to a Federal piece, are significant condition problems.

If such alterations are determined to exist, the value of the piece may be only a fraction of what it would have been before the alteration. Some of the biggest disagreements among twentieth-century furniture experts have centered on which standards to apply—the period or contemporary aesthetics. The decision to refinish or reupholster an antique chair is often the result of the desire to bring the chair up-to-date. But in the view of some collectors, that action reduces the value of the chair because it strips it of some of its original aesthetics.

Documentation

Documentation essentially is any written piece of information that circumscribes a piece of furniture's place in history. It may take the form of a cabinet maker's label or signature, an entry in an account book, a written bill of sale, or an entry in a household inventory. If a document can illuminate the relationship between a patron and a craftsman, identify other pieces of furniture made by that cabinetmaker through stylistic comparisons to the documented example, or further help to understand that period of America, collectors are often willing to dramatically increase what they are willing to spend for that object. An example of this kind of documentation is a Federal tall case clock, made by Simon Willard in Boston in 1806, which sold at auction in 1985 for $104,000. The dial of this clock was signed by the clockmaker and warranted for the owner, Edward Killeran, a prominent state senator from Cushing, Massachusetts. The clock was accompanied by its printed instructions label, engraved by the silversmith and patriot Paul Revere, and the original bill of sale from William Fiske, maker of the case, who sold the clock on May 21, 1806, to Edward Killeran and received an amount of lumber as payment. This clock links a clockmaker, a cabinetmaker, a state senator, and a silversmith in the America of 1806.

Provenance

The history of ownership of a piece of American furniture can affect its price if one can document each time it changed hands. In particular, if furniture has been owned by a famous or illustrious collector, especially if it was owned by such a collector during the period, there will be greater competition for it today. For example, in 1984 a Queen Anne high chest of drawers, which had descended in the family of President John Adams, sold at auction for $165,000, which was four times its estimate and a record for this form. As a general rule, the provenance of a piece of American furniture must be accompanied by written documentation or other proof of its ownership.

Freshness to the Market

Nothing can beat the thrill of selling or buying a piece of furniture that has been tucked away and forgotten about for a few generations. This is especially true if a particular piece has never been on the market, giving it a certain amount of purity to potential buyers. On the other hand, if a piece of furniture, even a major piece, appears on the market several times in a short period, the value is diminished and can lead to very disappointing results. This may be due to several reasons: First, the challenge of collecting involves seeing and learning new things, which a fresh piece to the market can provide. Second, a piece that constantly reappears on the market may develop a stigma—however unfair—about either its authenticity or its success in design. Third, the availability of the piece reduces the urgency to buy it on the part of collectors.

Previous Prices

Previous prices are generally used by collectors, dealers, auction houses, and most important, the Internal Revenue Service (IRS) to establish the parameters of furniture values. The majority of buyers are aware of the recent prices paid for American furniture, and generally use these prices as a guide for the limits of what they are willing to spend. There is an awareness of the fact that the market is not stationary, and collectors often have to adjust their expectations from sale to sale to anticipate what they will have to spend. In the end, it is the price the buyers are willing to pay that establishes the market value of American furniture.

Fashion

Swings in taste and fashion do change among furniture collectors. The goals and aspirations of several collectors can create and destroy sections of the market. A case in point are the rococo revival pieces made by John Henry Belter, which surged in value during the late 1970s and early 1980s. The exit of two collectors from this field has almost completely evaporated this market. In general, however, there is a great deal of depth in the number of collectors of American furniture, especially for furniture made between 1725 and 1825. (See Figure 4).

POTENTIAL RISKS

Forgeries

The most common risk in collecting American furniture is the premeditated or uneducated misrepresentations made to collectors, known in the business as fakes. This can range from overlooking certain condition problems that affect the value to intentionally selling a fake to an unaware buyer. The most difficult forgeries to detect are period pieces that have been enhanced with embellishments, such as pictorial or figured inlay, applied carving where there was none, or pieces that are made to complete sets, such as groups of chairs.

The investor has a number of options to reduce the risks in this area: First, learn as much as possible about the field of collection by reading the pertinent bibliography; seeking advice from dealers, auction house specialists, and museum curators; and visiting as many auctions, exhibits, and shows as possible. Second, pay an independent specialist to render an opinion before purchasing a piece, and request a written warranty of the age and authorship of a piece with the clear understanding that there will be a full refund if the warranty is not met.

Illiquidity

If a collector desires to sell a piece of furniture at auction, a period of one to six months may be required in order for it to be placed into an appropriate sale, sold, and paid for. If furniture must be sold promptly, it is usually not done to the best advantage. Direct sales

FIGURE 4. A Chippendale Carved Mahogany Blockfront Chest-On-Chest, Boston, 1750 to 1785

Note: This chest-on-chest exhibits all the characteristics of an outstanding investment: excellent proportions, completely original including the water-gilt carved eagle, and a history of ownership in the Bliss family of Boston, Massachusetts.
This piece was sold May 31, 1986, at Christie's, for $297,000.

Source: Photo is courtesy of Christie's, New York.

can be made to dealers, and cash advances are made by auction houses as a percentage of the value of the collection being sold. The lack of competition for the former and the finance charges for the latter should be considered.

Insurance and Custodial Care

The potential damage from fire, water, or neglect is always a factor when collecting fine art. Although the cost of insurance increases with the value of the collection, it is possible to obtain reasonable policies from insurance companies. Collectors should research several companies, some of whom specialize in fine art coverage, before choosing a policy.

TAX CONSEQUENCES[2]

The tax consequences of a sale of antique American furniture by an individual are determined by the facts of each situation. Therefore, individuals should consult their own tax advisors as to the particular consequences of a specific sale.

As a general rule, however, an individual's sale of furniture is treated as the sale of a capital asset. As of 1989, gains on the sale of capital assets are taxed in full at the same rates as ordinary income, rather than under the more favorable treatment that used to be afforded to capital assets. Gains generally are calculated as the difference between the sale price and the individual's basis in the furniture. (Basis is generally the price the individual paid to acquire the furniture.) Where furniture was inherited from a decedent's estate, however, the basis has probably stepped up to the furniture's fair market value at the time the decedent died. Because of this step up, individuals who inherit antique furniture may be able to sell it tax-free or at little taxable gain, even though the value of the antique furniture may have increased tremendously during the time it was owned by the decedent.

Finally, antique furniture enjoys a tax advantage over certain other investment options because it does not give rise to any current income taxation, As just noted, no appreciation in value is taxed until the furniture is sold, exchanged, or otherwise disposed of. At that time, the seller can use at least part of the sales proceeds to pay the tax. This is far more favorable tax treatment than, for instance, the treatment of appreciation on original issue discount bonds or zero coupon bonds: Any appreciation on those bonds is taxed annually regardless of whether the bond pays any income or is held rather than sold. Although bonds are often touted as a way to finance a future expense, such as a child's college education, current tax laws may make a prudent investment in antique American furniture a more attractive alternative from a tax perspective.

REPRESENTATIVE TYPES OF INVESTORS

Basically, investors can be divided into three groups: dealers, private collectors, and institutions, including museums, historical societies, and foundations. Dealers generally specialize in broad or specific areas of the market, such as eighteenth-century furniture or Frank Lloyd Wright furniture. They buy for resale purposes and for inventory, or on commission bids on behalf of their clients, usually taking a percentage of the selling price or a prearranged fee. The purchase of a piece of furniture by a respected, well-established dealer can increase its value, because the dealer's name becomes part of the provenance.

---

2 The author would like to acknowledge the assistance of Victoria B. Bjorklund of Simpson, Thacher & Bartlett, in New York, in the preparation of this discussion.

On the other hand, these dealers are well aware of the influence they can have in the marketplace, and as a result, pieces sold by them are often marked up at least 100 percent. Private collectors, often beginning out of curiosity or sentiment, frequently focus on specific regional examples and styles. Small investors have stricter limits on how much they can spend, generally $10,000 to $100,000, and try to buy a few pieces of furniture a year, with a long-term collecting strategy in mind. Many important collections were formed, and continue to be formed, in this way.

In the past ten years, a new type of collector has become an important player at the top of the American furniture market. These extremely wealthy collectors have paid staggering prices for major pieces and have assembled major collections in a relatively short period of time. Although the average collector may have to deaccession several pieces in order to acquire an important piece, these major collectors have had the luxury of choosing from the top of the market from the moment they began to collect American furniture. The direct result of this type of buying has been an escalation of prices, which in turn has encouraged sellers to consign important pieces that otherwise might not have come to the market. Although smaller collectors have felt sidelined by the rising prices, they have also welcomed the increase in value of their own investments.

Institutions represent the third major group of buyers. Recent deaccessioning policies have allowed institutions to sell examples that are duplicates or not appropriate for the collection. This has increased the supply of fine pieces to the market, increased their acquisition funds, and allowed museums to be competitive at the top of the market. Museums in particular are the best places to start learning about American furniture because of the outstanding quality of the examples they own and their special exhibits, which are designed to teach as well as to display.

TABLE 1. Selected Examples of Appreciation in American Furniture, Auction Records for 1984 and 1988

Furniture Forms	1984 Record	1988 Record	Percentage
Tea table	$253,000 (Sotheby's) 12-8-84	$1,045,000 (Christie's) 1-25-86	+313
Sofa	$264,000 (Christie's) 1-22-83	$605,000 (Christie's) 10-18-86	+129
Dressing table	$69,000 (Sotheby's) 6-7-80	$264,000 (Christie's) 5-28-87	+282
Side chair	$275,000 (Sotheby's) 10-23-82	$341,000 (Christie's) 1-24-87	+ 24
Chest-on-chest	$242,000 (Christie's) 1-22-83	$308,000 (Sotheby's) 2-2-85	+ 27
Tall case clock	$82,500 (Sotheby's) 2-2-80	$440,000 (Oliver's) 6-25-88	+433

FIGURE 5. A Chippendale Mahogany Serpentine-Back Sofa, Philadelphia, 1765 to 1785

Note: Sold January 22, 1983, at Christie's for $264,000.

Source: Photo is courtesy of Christie's, New York.

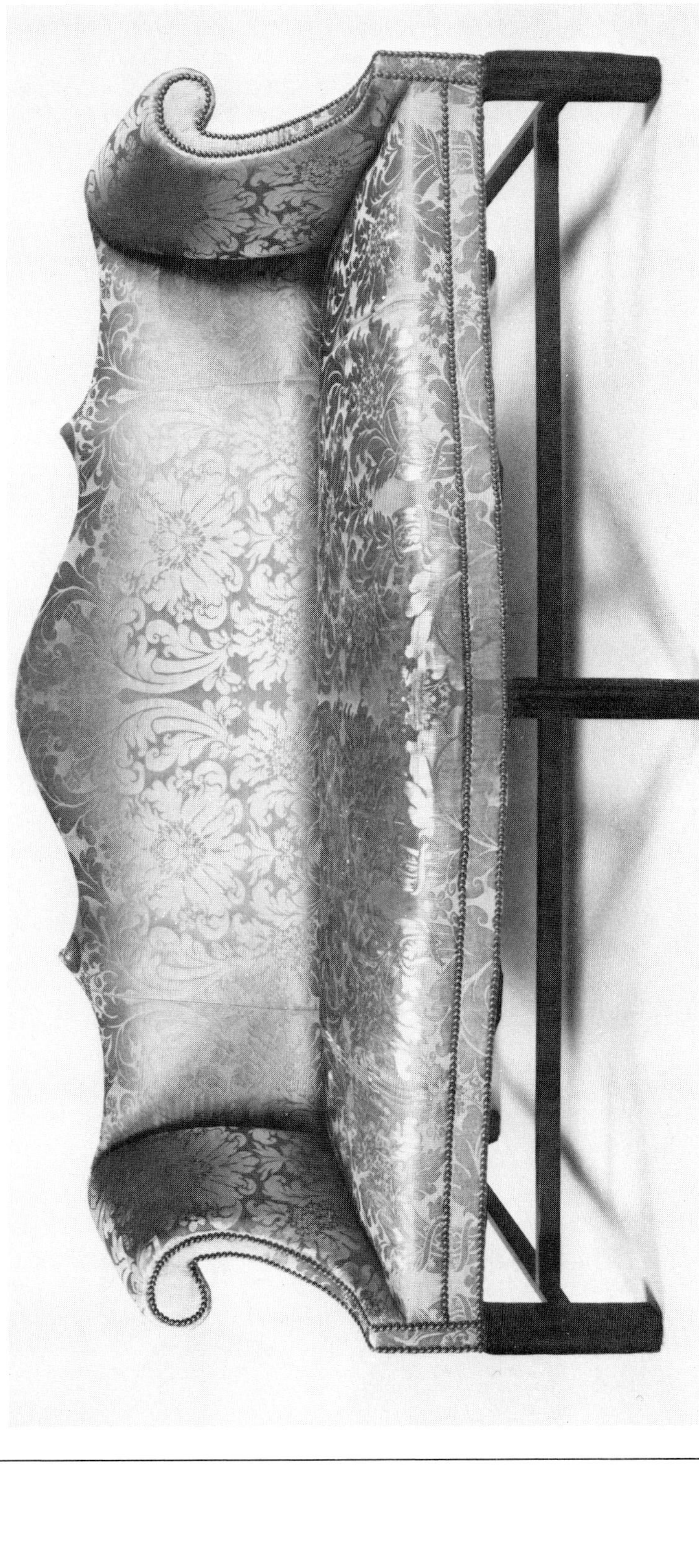

FIGURE 6. A Chippendale Carved Mahogany Serpentine-Back Sofa, Philadelphia, 1765 to 1785

Note: Sold October 18, 1986, at Christie's for $605,000.

Source: Photo is courtesy of Christie's, New York.

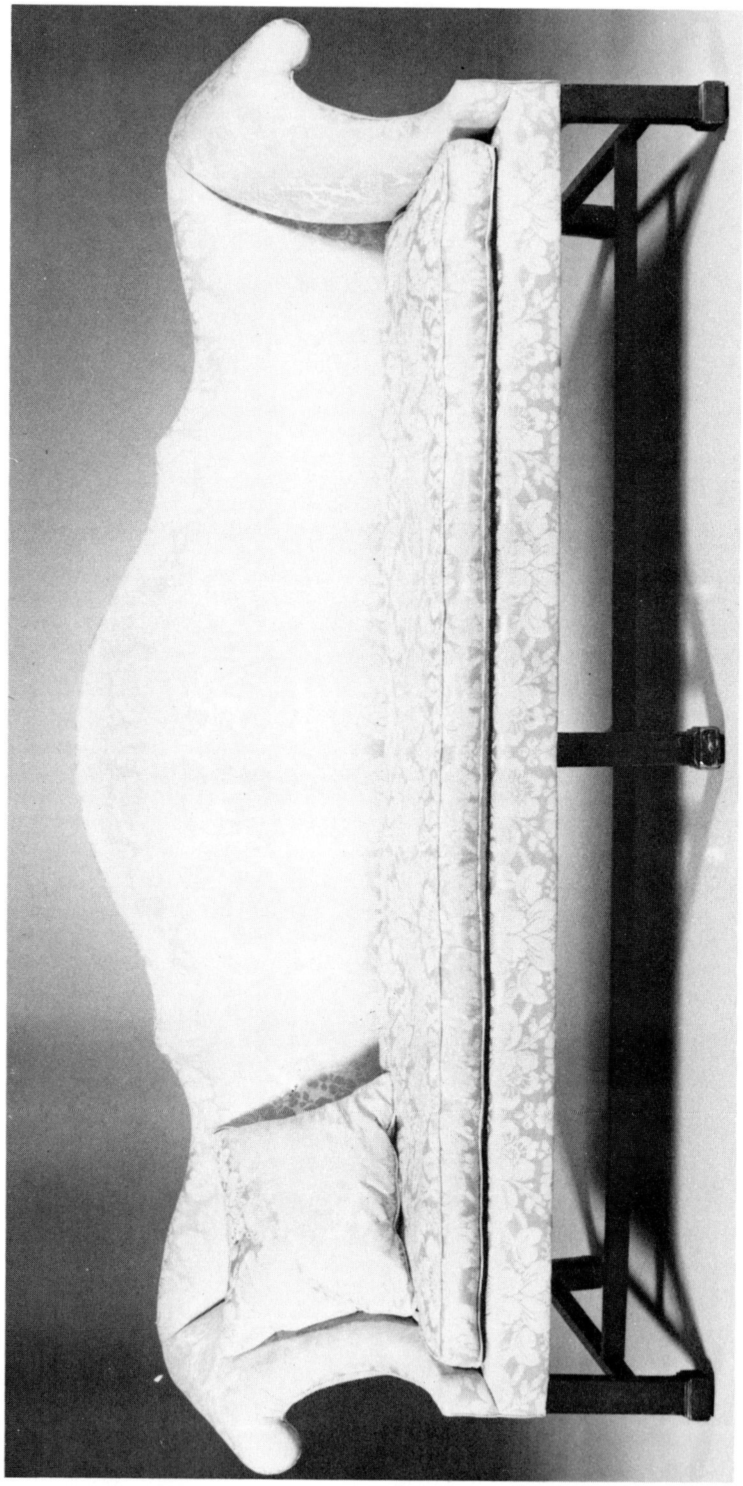

GLOSSARY

auction house—An establishment where pieces are sold to the highest bidder, usually for a commission charged to both buyer and seller. The auction catalog is a useful indicator of the range of prices associated with various pieces.

broker—An agent who specializes in buying and selling pieces for a commission, for the account of a collector.

cabriole—The style of forming an S shape in leg of a chair, table, or other piece of furniture, beginning with an outward curve and descending in a reverse curve to the foot.

dealer—A buyer and seller of antiques who maintains an inventory and stands ready to offer advice to clients.

marquetry—A mosaic created through the use of small pieces of wood or other material to form a pattern in wood veneer. Geometrical patterns in marquetry are usually called parquetry.

ormolu—Base metal (usually bronze) finished to resemble gold.

pier piece—A piece of furniture designed to be put between two doors or windows; hence the terms "pier mirror," "pier table," and so forth.

pilaster—A vertical projection on the face of a piece, simulating a classical column, often carved or fluted.

AMERICAN FURNITURE DEALERS

Philip H. Bradley, Downington, Pa.

G.K.S. Bush, Inc., Washington, D.C.

Chalfant & Chalfant, West Chester, Pa.

Colwill/McGehee, Baltimore, Md.

Elizabeth R. Daniel, Chapel Hill, N.C.

John M. Delaney, West Townsend, Mass.

Valdemar F. Jacobsen, Cold Spring Harbor, N.Y.

Leigh Keno, New York, N.Y.

Bernard & S. Dean Levy, New York, N.Y.

Deanne Levison, Atlanta, Ga.

Nathan Liverant & Son, Colchester, Conn.

C.L. Prickett, Yardly, Pa.

Priddy & Beckerdite, Richmond, Va.

Donald R. Sack, Inc., Buck Hill Falls, Pa.

Israel Sack, Inc., New York, N.Y.

Peter Sawyer, Exeter, N.H.

David Stockwell, Inc., Wilmington, De.

Robert O. Stuart, Limington, Me.

Tom Schwenke, Inc., New York, N.Y.

John Walton, Inc., Jewett City, Conn.

SUGGESTED READING

Carpenter, Ralph E. Jr. *The Arts and Crafts of Newport, R.I. 1640–1820*. Newport: The Preservation Society of Newport County, 1954.

Cooke, Edward S. Jr., ed. *Upholstery in America and Europe From the Seventeenth Century to World War II*. New York: Norton & Co., 1987.

Cooper, Wendy A. *In Praise of America*. New York: Alfred A. Knopf, Inc., 1980.

Downs, Joseph. *American Furniture, Queen Anne and Chippendale Periods*. New York: Bonanza Books, 1952.

Failey, Dean F. *Long Island Is My Nation*. New York: Society for the Preservation of Long Island Antiquities, 1976.

Flanigan, J. Michael. *American Furniture From the Kaufman Collection*. Washington, D.C.: National Gallery of Art, 1986.

Forman, Benno M. *American Seating Furniture 1630–1730*. New York: W.W. Norton & Co., Inc., 1988.

Garvan, Beatrice B. *Federal Philadelphia, 1785–1825*. Philadelphia: The Philadelphia Museum of Art, 1987.

Heckscher, Morrison H. *American Furniture in The Metropolitan Museum of Art*. New York: Random House, 1985.

Hornor, William MacPherson. *Blue Book of Philadelphia Furniture*, rev. ed. Washington, D.C.: Highland House, 1977.

Jobe, Brock, and Kaye, Myrna. *New England Furniture, The Colonial Era*. Boston: Hougton Mifflin Company, 1984.

Kane, Patricia E. *300 Years of American Seating Furniture*. Boston: Little Brown and Company, 1976.

Monkhouse, Christopher P., and Michie, Thomas S. *American Furniture in Pendleton House*. Rhode Island: Rhode Island School of Design, 1986.

Montgomery, Charles F. *American Furniture, The Federal Period*. New York: The Henry Francis du Pont Winterthur Museum, 1978.

Roque, Oswaldo Rodriquez. *American Furniture at Chipstone*. The University of Wisconsin Press, 1984.

Sack, Albert. *Fine Points of Furniture*. New York: Crown Publishers, Inc., 1950.

Santore, Charles. *The Windsor Style in America, Vol. II*. Philadelphia: Running Press Book Publishers, 1987.

Ward, G.W.R., and Hosley, W.N., Jr., eds. *The Great River, Art & Society of the Connecticut Valley, 1635–1820*. Hartford: The Wadsworth Atheneum, 1985.

Weidman, Gregory R. *Furniture in Maryland, 1740–1940*. Baltimore: Schneidereith and Sons, 1984.

FUTURES

FINANCIAL, AGRICULTURAL, CURRENCY

Thomas C. Coleman
Jay L. Gottlieb

This article focuses on the U.S. commodity futures and options business. The U.S. is the dominant force in worldwide commodity futures and options trading. As of June 1989, 69 percent of all commodity futures and options contracts were traded on U.S. exchanges. However, from 1984 to 1988, trading on foreign exchanges grew from 19.4 to 30 percent of the worldwide market. This growth in foreign trading has been primarily spurred by the success of U.S. financial futures. Foreign exchanges have developed their own U.S. Treasury bond futures as a hedging medium for foreign citizens and institutions that hold U.S. debt. Furthermore, they have developed futures contracts for the national government debt instruments of their respective countries.

BASIC CHARACTERISTICS

Futures were originally developed in the middle 1800s for grains as a means to find protection from the risk of price changes. Price volatility is characteristic of many basic commodities, both physical and financial. Through the years, futures have been developed for many nonagricultural commodities, including energy, metals, equity indices, currencies, and financial instruments. Futures markets have been evolving to meet the needs of a growing international business economy. An example is the night session of the Chicago Board of Trade (CBOT) for selected financial and metals products.

Thomas C. Coleman is Vice-President and Director and Jay L. Gottlieb is an Advisory Economist in the Department of Economic Analysis and Planning at the Chicago Board of Trade.

A commodity futures contract is a firm commitment to make or accept delivery of a certain quantity and quality of a commodity during a designated month in the future, at the price determined through open bidding in a central exchange. An individual can buy or sell a contract for any of the designated delivery months currently being traded on an exchange. Using soybean futures as an example, a person buying a January soybean contract at $9 per bushel is obligated to accept delivery of 5,000 bushels of soybeans during the month of January at a price of $9 per bushel. Buying a contract is referred to as taking a long position and selling a contract is known as taking a short position.

Futures Contracts

Futures markets are different from other markets. Unlike transactions in cash markets, where contracts are designed to meet the individual needs of the contracting parties, futures contracts are based on standardized terms. The contract size, quality, and delivery requirements are fixed and explicitly stated. The only thing that is not stated in the contract is price, which is determined in the marketplace.

All transactions, including orders from the public, are executed in a central location via an open outcry competitive auction. This arrangement provides an information advantage. Every bid by a buyer is known to every seller, and every offer by a seller is known to every buyer. Everyone knows the price at that moment. Since the market participants are in the same location (the trading pit), this competition should result in a better price—a narrower bid-ask spread—than may occur in a decentralized market in which many prices can be in effect at any given moment.

Delivery terms directly affect futures prices. Although very few contracts are settled by delivery of the commodity on which the contract is based, it is always a possibility. Anytime before the month the contract matures, the buyer or seller may close out his obligation through an equal but offsetting trade in the same delivery month. The difference between the price at which the trade is initiated and the price at which it is offset, less transaction costs, is either profit or loss. For example, the purchase of a January futures contract resulting in a long position may be liquidated by selling a January contract (for the same year) anytime before the calendar month of January. This situation is different from a cash forward contract in which delivery is intended. Although the vast majority of futures contracts are settled by offset, the fact that sellers and buyers have the option of offsetting or taking delivery of the commodity is an important and, indeed, essential facet of futures trading. The possibility that delivery can take place assures that future prices will reflect the commodity's cash value.

Since a futures price is just that—a price for future delivery—buyers and sellers must take into account the cost of storage and other expenses such as financing costs and insurance. These expenses are usually lumped together and called carrying charges. In consideration of carrying charges, grain prices for future delivery are normally higher than prices for immediate delivery. There is an exception in times of shortage when buyers in urgent need of a product may be willing to pay a higher price. This is an inverted market, in which the nearby price is higher than the distant price.

Futures contracts are standardized. Unlike transactions in the cash market, in which commodity specifications, delivery location, payment terms, and time of delivery (spot or forward) must be explicitly stated, buying or selling a futures contract is limited to one variable: price. Thus, futures contracts allow ease of quotation and trading. The contract terms themselves are subject to constant review by the exchanges and are revised as necessary to reflect changes in the marketplace.

Options

Options on futures have greatly expanded the range of trading strategies for both hedgers and speculators. A call (put) option on futures gives the buyer the right, but not the obligation, to purchase (sell) the underlying futures contract at a specified price, called the strike price, at any time up to the option's expiration date. The cost of the option is called the premium. Since the option buyer is not obligated to buy the underlying futures contract, the option buyer's maximum loss is the premium paid. However, the option buyer has the potential for unlimited gains. In the hedge example discussed later in this article (see Financial Markets) the fund manager could have bought put options on Treasury bond futures instead of selling Treasury bond futures. If interest rates rose (as they did), the put options would have increased in value, offsetting the loss in the cash bond position. If, instead, interest rates fell, the put options would have declined in value, with a maximum loss limited to the premium paid. However, as rates fell, the value of the cash bond position would continue to increase without limitation. By using put options, the fund manager limits possible losses while allowing the possibility for unlimited gains. The cost of this flexibility is the premium paid for the options. It should be noted that hedging using futures, which have no premiums cost, insulates the fund manager from potential profits (if interest rates unexpectedly fall) as well as from potential losses (if rates rise, as expected.) For a detailed explanation of options, see the separate article in this encyclopedia.

As with futures contracts, options on futures are standardized contracts that are traded through the "open auction outcry" system on an exchange floor. Financial instrument options accounted for 49.5 percent of all U.S. commodity options trading in the first half of 1989, while agricultural futures options accounted for 14.6 percent.

Hedging and Speculating

Those who buy and sell on commodities futures markets can be classified as either hedgers, who want to minimize risk, or speculators, who are willing to assume risk.

Hedgers. The basic principle underlying hedging is that cash market prices and futures prices tend to move in a predictable relation to each other and generally tend to move higher or lower in an approximately parallel fashion.

A firm that would be hurt by declining price, perhaps because it owns a large inventory of a commodity, takes a position in the futures market that enables it to benefit from declining prices, by selling a futures contract that can be bought back later at a lower price. If prices decline, the gain in the futures market roughly equals the decline in the market value of the inventory. Cash prices and futures prices tend to move up and down together in response to varying market conditions, although they do not fluctuate by precisely equal amounts.

Speculators. Attitude toward risk separates the hedger from the speculator. The hedger uses the futures market as a means of protection against unpredictable and potentially damaging price changes. The speculator uses the futures market to assume price risk in pursuit of profit opportunity.

Speculators either buy or sell futures contracts, depending on their opinion about future price movement. A speculator will buy a contract when his forecast suggests an increase in price (decrease in interest rates), expecting later to make an offsetting sale at a higher price, and at a profit. A speculator will sell a contract when his forecast suggests a decrease in price (increase in interest rates), expecting later to make an offsetting purchase at a lower price, and at a profit. Also, speculators can participate in these markets through commodity mutual funds, or discretionary accounts.

FINANCIAL MARKETS

Description and Definition

The terms "financial futures" and "interest rate futures" describe futures contracts based on financial instruments, the price of which fluctuates with changes in interest rates. As with all futures contracts, financial futures represent a firm commitment to buy or sell a specific commodity or financial instrument during a specified month at a price established through open outcry in a centrally regulated marketplace. During the first half of 1989, more than 42.8 percent of all futures traded were financial contracts.

Importance of Delivery Terms. Some financial futures contracts (for example, eurodollar and municipal bond index futures) are settled in cash at the expiration of the futures contract. Cash settlement means that the actual gain (or loss) on the futures position is received by (or paid by) the holder of the position in cash, based on cash market prices. Actual physical delivery of the underlying security (e.g., a eurodollar deposit) is not permitted. Many other financial futures contracts (e.g., Treasury bond futures), however, require physical delivery for contracts held until expiration.

The delivery process has a significant effect on the price at which these futures contracts trade. The market trades with the knowledge that delivery can occur at contract maturity. However, few financial futures contracts—fewer than 3 percent of contracts traded, are settled by the buyer receiving and the seller making delivery of the actual instrument on which the contract is based. Depending on the delivery specifications for a particular contract, the price may move differently from that of another contract that, on the surface, looks very similar. Although financial futures contracts that allow physical delivery have a range of deliverable issues, the choice of which issue is actually delivered remains with the seller. The market tends to trade the issue that is best for the seller to deliver. Thus, anyone participating in the financial futures market should have an understanding of the delivery procedure and its ramifications even though he may never take delivery.

For example, the CBOT Treasury bond futures contract allows delivery of all Treasury bonds with fifteen or more years to maturity, or the right to call if callable. Currently, there are thirty-one different Treasury bonds with fifteen or more years to maturity or call. In a typical delivery month, five or six different bonds have been delivered.

Interest Rate Protection—A Useful New Commodity. Financial futures are based on the principle that interest rates—the cost of credit—can be viewed in the same way as the price of other commodities, and that certain kinds of institutions need a means of protecting themselves from volatile interest rates. Just as futures in soybeans or silver do, financial futures such as Treasury bond or eurodollar futures represent a viable market for transferring the risk of price volatility.

Hedging in Financial Instruments

Portfolio managers, bond dealers, and others who hold fixed-income securities, such as bonds and notes, can protect their holdings from rising interest rates (i.e., falling prices) by hedging through the sale of futures. Since cash and futures markets tend to move in parallel, any loss caused by a declining cash market price will be offset by the gain received when futures contracts previously sold at high prices are offset at lower prices. See the example of a short hedge with Treasury bonds futures in Figure 1.

FIGURE 1. Hedging With Financial Futures

Background. On June 1, a pension fund manager is holding $1 million of 11.75 percent Treasury bonds due 2005-10. He plans to sell the bonds in September and is concerned that their value will decline if interest rates rise. The current market price for an 11.75 percent bond is 117–23 with a yield of 9.89 percent.

Objective: To protect his portfolio against a possible interest rate increase, he hedges his position in the financial futures market. Since he is long in the cash market, he hedges by going short, or selling, in the futures market. But how many futures contracts should the fund manager sell? The variety of deliverable Treasury bond coupons and maturities is related by means of a conversion factor to the nominal 8 percent CBOT coupon. Therefore, use of the appropriate conversion factor is the shorthand method for adjusting hedge amounts. (For more detailed hedging methods, see Figlewski (1986).) For this particular period, a ratio of 1.4 bond futures contracts (corresponding to the 11.75 percent bond's CBOT conversion factor of 1.3957) will produce a more effective hedge. Therefore, the fund manager sells fourteen September bond futures contracts ($100,000 per contract) at their current price of 83–06. By selling futures contracts, the fund manager has transformed his long-term high-risk investment into a short-term low-risk investment.

Outcome: By September 1, rising interest rates have reduced the price of 11.75 percent bonds to 104–12 (yielding 11.24 percent) and the price of September bond futures to 74–09.

Cash Market		Futures Market	
June 1: Holds $1 million 11.75 percent bonds priced at 117–23. Market value:	$1,177,187.50	June 1: Sells fourteen September bond futures contracts at 83–06. Market value:	$1,164,625.00
September 1: Sells $1 million 11.75 percent bonds priced at 104–12. Market value:	$1,043,750.00	September 1: Buys fourteen September bond futures contracts at 74–09. Market value:	$1,039,937.50
Plus accrued interest earned:	$ 29,375.00		
Loss	$ 104,062.50	Gain:	$ 124,687.50

Result: The manager's weighted futures position offset the cash market loss in the fund's 11.75 percent bonds. The excess of the futures gain over the cash market loss corresponds to the return on a short-term low-risk investment.

Types of Financial Futures Contracts

Few financial innovations have attracted as much attention in as short a time as financial futures. The first interest rate futures contract, Government National Mortgage Association (GNMA) Collateralized Depositary Receipt (CDR) futures, was introduced in 1975 at the CBOT. In their first full year of trading, GNMA futures contracts equivalent to $15 billion were traded at the CBOT.

As of early 1989, many financial futures contracts are trading (on U.S. exchanges), including Treasury bonds (CBOT and Midam), ninety-day Treasury bills (Chicago Mercantile Exchange) (CME), eurodollars (CME), five-year and ten-year Treasury notes CBOT and Mid-America Commodity Exchange (MACE), and municipal bonds (CBOT). Contracts pending government approval by the Commodity Futures Trading Commission (CFTC) include Japanese government bonds.

The most successful financial futures contracts have been the Treasury bond contract offered by the CBOT and the eurodollar contract offered by the CME. The CBOT's Treasury bond contract ranks in 1989 as the most actively traded futures contract in the world; eurodollars rank second. Table 1 presents a history of the volume and open interest of these contracts.

Trading in options on financial futures began in 1982 and has experienced tremendous growth in volume. Options on Treasury bond futures in 1989 is the third most active contract of all futures and futures options contracts (see Table 1).

AGRICULTURAL MARKETS

Background

Active futures and options markets exist for virtually all major domestically produced agricultural commodities, several agricultural products, and selected imported commodities. The domestic commodities include corn, wheat, oats, soybean, cotton, live cattle, and live hogs. The agricultural products include soybean oil, soybean meal, frozen pork bellies, and frozen concentrated orange juice. Imported commodities include coffee, sugar, and cocoa. Although not strictly agricultural, one forest product, lumber, also has an active futures market. The agricultural futures markets accounted for just under 23.6% of all U.S. futures activity in the first half of 1989.

Price Determination

For most of these commodities, futures markets are the primary points for price determination. Actual cash as well as forward transactions are priced in relation to futures prices. The fundamental determinants of futures prices are the supplies available and the demand for the specific commodities. Thus, factors important in determining prices (and expected price changes) include domestic production, imports and/or exports, domestic use, and stockholdings. Estimates of these numbers are regularly provided by the U.S. Department of Agriculture. These estimates provide a baseline for commodity brokerage firms' analyses and are typically included in commodity newsletters. Much additional analysis by commodity firms examines the assumptions lying behind the projections and analyzes supplementary data.

Nature of Futures Contracts

Agricultural commodity futures markets are among the oldest commodity futures markets. In fact, the institution of futures trading originated in agricultural markets—a logical

TABLE 1. Historical Volume and Open Interest for Selected Financial Futures and Futures Option Contracts 1977–1988

	Treasury Bond Futures (CBOT)[1]		Treasury Bond Futures Options (CBOT)[2]		Eurodollar Futures (CME)[3]	
Year	Volume	Open Interest	Volume	Open Interest	Volume	Open Interest
1977	32,101	2,864	NA	NA	NA	NA
1978	555,350	41,246	NA	NA	NA	NA
1979	2,059,594	90,676	NA	NA	NA	NA
1980	6,489,555	243,614	NA	NA	NA	NA
1981	13,907,988	221,680	NA	NA	15,171	1,461
1982	16,739,695	182,772	118,772	12,879	323,619	18,012
1983	19,550,535	183,664	1,664,921	82,863	891,066	45,602
1984	29,963,280	202,488	6,636,209	214,518	4,192,952	85,128
1985	40,448,357	300,571	11,901,116	407,947	8,900,528	121,537
1986	52,598,811	229,286	17,314,349	356,829	10,824,914	214,401
1987	66,841,474	262,326	21,720,402	402,344	20,416,216	292,326
1988	70,307,872	361,658	19,509,425	506,296	21,705,223	528,913

NA = Not available.

[1] Treasury bond futures began trading on the CBOT on August 22, 1977.
[2] Treasury bond futures options began trading on the CBOT on October 1, 1982.
[3] Eurodollar futures began trading on the CME on December 9, 1981.

Source: Futures Industry Association

outgrowth of the extensive forward trading that accompanied the marketing of products that were produced only once during the year (harvest), were storable, and were used continuously during the year. Futures contracts are standardized forward contracts. The standards or contract specifications are fixed by the exchange on which the particular future trades. Specifications include quantity (e.g., 5,000 bushels of corn), quality (No. 2 yellow corn), form of delivery (in approved elevator storage), and location (Chicago). Often, contract specifications also include provisions for differences from these standards in the actual delivery of the commodity, normally with fixed premiums or discounts for the difference. In addition, futures contracts are traded only for specified delivery months during the year (for example, December, March, May, July, and September, in the corn market).

Futures contracts may be bought and sold only on regulated commodity exchanges. All orders are executed by open auction outcry, buyers and sellers meeting to determine price. Once an order is executed, a buyer has found a seller, and price has been agreed on, the exchange (technically the clearinghouse of the exchange) becomes a third party of the transaction. Rather than having an obligation to each other, both the buyer and seller now have separate obligations to the exchange. For example, the buyer of a March soybean futures contract has an obligation to the exchange to accept delivery of soybeans in March, according to the predetermined contract specifications, and the seller has an obligation to the exchange to deliver soybeans in March. Since the obligations of both buyer and seller are with the exchange, neither has to find the person with whom the original transaction was made. Rather, someone who has futures must simply sell a like amount (a transaction called offset) to become even in the records of the clearinghouse and out of the market. The clearinghouse's third-party role in all futures contracts thus facilitates market entry and exit and increases market liquidity.

Types of Agricultural Markets

Table 2 provides a comparative view of the size of the major agricultural futures markets. It presents information commonly reported with the summary of a day's trading activity in such sources as the *Wall Street Journal*. First, for each commodity, the principal exchange is designated. For each agricultural commodity, there is normally one principal exchange where the majority of futures trading in that commodity takes place. There are two exceptions: The more obvious exception in the table is wheat, which is more or less actively traded on three exchanges, although the CBOT market clearly dominates. In fact, each wheat market is different in that a different variety of wheat is being traded on each exchange. All three markets have survived because they provide a pricing vehicle for specific groups of users. The less obvious exception is those commodities traded on the MACE in smaller-sized contracts. For example, the standard CBOT contract for corn is 5,000 bushels; the MACE contract is 1,000 bushels.

The second column in Table 2 indicates the amount of the commodity represented in a single futures contract. The grains and soybeans are uniform contracts of 5,000 bushels; otherwise, contract size tends to reflect an amount commonly used in commercial trade for that commodity. The next column shows the units in which prices are quoted. Next are the two most often used indicators of market size, open interest and volume of trading, both in thousands of contracts. The open interest is the number of buy or sell contracts outstanding on a specific date (here, the last trading day in 1988). Since every buyer must have found a seller to have entered the market, positions on only one side of the market are counted in these measures of activity. Volume of trading is the number of contracts that have been traded (again, on only one side of the market), either on a specific day or during a specific period. The latter is used here and the volume numbers are totals for the year. Total volume for each market for which options are traded is also shown.

Participants in Agricultural Futures and Options

Hedgers who actively participate in these markets include country elevator operators, terminal elevator operators, grain merchandisers (including exporters and importers), feed manufacturers, food processors, and food product companies.

OTHER MARKETS

The breakdown of U.S. futures trading volume among other markets in 1988 includes equity indices, 5.8, energy, 11.0; foreign currencies, 9.0%; and metals, 7.6%.

Equity Indices

A major innovation in the application of futures trading took place in February 1982 when the Kansas City Board of Trade introduced the first futures market based on a stock index,

TABLE 2. Agricultural Commodity Futures and Options Markets

	Principal Exchange(s)[1]	Contract Size	Price Quote/Unit	Futures Activity: Volume of Trading in 1988	Futures Activity: Open Interest on Dec. 31, 1988	Options Volume
Grains and Oil seeds						
Corn	CBT	5,000 bushels	¢/bu.	11,105,516	224,670	1,591,223
Wheat[2]	CBT	5,000 bushels	¢/bu.	3,377,738	64,378	445,575
	KCBT	5,000 bushels	¢/bu.	1,338,711	31,554	30,178
	MGE	5,000 bushels	¢/bu.	423,542	6,938	1,847
Oats	CBT	5,000 bushels	¢/bu.	354,578	9,751	
Soybeans[2]	CBT	5,000 bushels	¢/bu.	12,497,096	120,877	3,245,134
Soybean oil	CBT	60,000 pounds	¢/lb.	4,896,194	72,108	124,131
Soybean meal	CBT	100 tons	$/ton	5,313,081	71,884	172,428
Livestock Products						
Live cattle[2]	CME	40,000 pounds	¢/lb.	5,477,205	75,383	1,067,593
Feeder cattle	CME	42,000 pounds	¢/lb.	702,438	13,383	163,433
Live hogs[2]	CME	38,000 pounds	¢/lb.	2,008,750	33,064	130,206
Pork bellies	CME	38,000 bushels	¢/lb.	1,186,599	19,362	12,143
Foods and Fibers						
Coffee	CSCE	37,500 pounds	¢/lb.	1,149,710	23,156	65,204
Sugar	CSCE	112,000 pounds	¢/lb.	5,819,121	143,241	1,536,345
Cocoa	CSCE	10 metric tons	$/ton	1,268,050	36,762	95,509
Orange juice	NYCE	15,000 pounds	¢/lb.	358,039	7,905	5,873
Cotton	NYCE	50,000 pounds	¢/lb.	1,370,249	30,573	124,260
Wood Products						
Lumber	CME	130,000 board feet	$/1,000 bd. ft.	371,489	6,872	22,171

[1] The exchanges are the Chicago Board of Trade (CBT), Kansas City Board of Trade (KCBT), Minneapolis Grain Exchange (MGE), Chicago Mercantile Exchange (CME), New York Mercantile Exchange (NYME), Coffee Sugar and Cocoa Exchange (CSCE), New York Cotton Exchange (NYCE), and the Citrus Associates of the New York Cotton Exchange (Citrus).

[2] Also traded on the Mid-American Commodity Exchange (MACE) in smaller contracts.

Source: Futures Industry Association

Value Line Average Stock Index futures. Since then, new futures markets have been introduced based on the Standard & Poor's 500 and 100 stock indices, on the New York Stock Exchange (NYSE) Composite Index, and on the American Stock Exchange (AMEX) Major Market Index.

Stock indices are used primarily to evaluate the price performance of individual stocks and groups of stocks compared with the movement of the total stock market. Among the stock indices currently followed, the primary differences are in methods of sampling, weighting, and averaging. A stock index can be based on all traded stocks or on a smaller sample of stocks. Two examples of these kinds of indices are the NYSE Composite Index of all stocks traded on that exchange and, on the other hand, the AMEX's Major Market Index of 20 stocks.

When selecting a sample of stocks for an index, the problem is one of choosing stocks whose aggregate price movement reflects as closely as possible the movement of all stocks. An examination of the performances of stock indices through the years reveals that a relatively small number of stocks, carefully chosen, will experience price movements that are nearly identical to the price movement of the entire stock market.

The second challenge in constructing a stock index is that of weighting individual stocks used in the sample so that the index reflects the relative importance of each stock in a manner consistent with the purpose of the index. Some indices weight stocks according to their individual market values; this method is thought to be most appropriate in indicating the combined movement of all stocks the index represents. Other indices assign equal weights to all stocks in the sample for relatively equal price changes; this method is regarded as most appropriate for reflecting the price movements of typical or average stocks.

In constructing a stock index, one must choose a method of combining the prices or price movements of the several or many stocks into an index number. Most stock indices widely followed today are computed using the arithmetic mean of the stock prices in the sample.

Various studies have shown that there is relatively little difference among the movements of the various stock indices over longer periods of time. However, in the short term, there can be very marked movement differences. In some uses of stock indices, these differences are of little importance; in others, they are critical.

Futures and options on equity indices currently being traded include Standard & Poor's 500 Index at the CME, the AMEX Major Market Index at the CBOT, the Value Line Index at the Kansas City Board of Trade, and the NYSE composite index at the New York Futures Exchange. Options are traded on these futures: Standard & Poor's 500 and the NYSE composite.

Energy

The New York Mercantile Exchange introduced petroleum futures with heating oil in November 1978. Since then, these markets have been very successful—more than 32 million futures and options traded in 1988—with the addition of gasoline and crude oil. Options are traded on both heating oil and crude petroleum.

Foreign Currencies

In May 1972, the CME introduced the trading of foreign currencies with the trading of seven different currencies. Their array of futures contracts today includes British pound, deutsche mark, Swiss franc, Japanese yen, Canadian dollar, and Australian dollar.

Options on futures are traded for each of these currencies, except the Australian dollar. The MACE trades futures on the same contracts in smaller contract units. In addition, the New York Cotton Exchange, through its Financial Instruments Exchange (FINEX) subsidiary, trades a trade-weighted U.S. Dollar Index. Total currency volume in 1988 exceeded 32 million futures and options contracts.

Metals

Metals trading began in the United States in 1933 when trading in silver futures began on the Commodity Exchange Inc. (COMEX). Trading was suspended in 1934 because of the Silver Purchase Act, which authorized the Treasury to purchase silver until the price rose to $1.2929 or until the value of the U.S. silver stock equaled one third of the value of U.S. gold stock. The Treasury's price for newly mined silver was much higher than the prevailing market price, and users were forced to purchase silver abroad. Silver futures trading resumed in 1963 and now takes place on three U.S. exchanges: the CBOT, the COMEX, and the MACE.

The New York Mercantile Exchange began trading platinum on 1956 and palladium in 1968. Gold futures began trading in the United States on December 31, 1974, when it became legal for Americans to own gold. It is traded at the COMEX of New York, the CBOT, and the MACE. Abroad, gold futures and options are traded on more exchanges than any other commodity, including ones in Amsterdam, Hong Kong, Montreal, Rotterdam, Sydney, Tokyo, Vancouver, and Winnipeg. Copper and aluminum are also traded on the COMEX. U.S. trading volume for metal futures and options exceeded 21 million contracts for 1988.

ATTRACTIVE FEATURES

The basic economic functions of futures contracts are hedging and price discovery. Investors can use these markets for risk transfer or for profit opportunity. Attractive characteristics of these markets include leverage, contract integrity, and liquidity.

Leverage

Because margin requirements are relatively low for commodities, a trader can benefit from the price movement of a contract for a fraction of its full value. This feature, called leverage, offers speculators the opportunity for returns that are relatively large compared with the amount of margin money they have committed. The speculator can benefit substantially from a small change in the value of a contract. Under adverse conditions, however, such leverage can lead to losses in excess of the margin committed. Low margins also make it economical and practical for hedgers to use futures markets to transfer risk. For example, as of March 1989, the initial speculative margin on the CBOT $100,000 Treasury bond futures contract is $2,500.

While stock markets and futures both have margin requirements, there is a significant difference in the nature and purpose of these payments in the two markets. In the stock market, margin is a down payment on a loan to purchase securities, and an actual transfer of property rights occurs. The balance on the sale is financed with the borrowed funds.

In contrast, margins in futures markets act as a performance bond. Margin is placed on deposit by both parties to the transaction; it provides the funds that ensure contract performance and financial integrity.

Contract Integrity

In futures markets, unlike in forward markets where parties to a transaction deal only with each other, all transactions are ultimately between clearing members and the clearinghouse. A member of an exchange who is also a member of the clearinghouse is a clearing member. In this manner, the clearinghouse becomes a party to every trade; in effect, it becomes the buyer to every seller and the seller to every buyer. For those who trade futures, this arrangement enhances market performance in several critical ways. It eliminates concern over the credit rating of the party on the other side of the transaction; it frees the original trading partners from delivery or offset from each other; and it provides maximum flexibility in deciding when and how to close out a position.

Clearinghouse Responsibilities. Between the close of one day's business and the next day's market opening, the clearinghouse matches that day's trades, settles gains and losses on all transactions, monitors margin calls on all open positions, and matches those buyers and sellers who intend to make or take delivery.

Unlike the responsibility of the clearinghouse of a stock exchange or a bank, the responsibility of the clearinghouse of a futures exchange does not end with reconciling and clearing the traders' transactions. By interposing itself as a party to every trade, the clearinghouse also guarantees financial performance from clearing member to clearing member. However, it does not explicitly guarantee that every entity possessing a license to handle customer money will properly and fully safeguard customer funds. Any transaction of a futures exchange must be made through a member of that exchange. Any member who trades futures and is not a member of the clearinghouse must clear and settle trades through a clearing member.

Source of Guarantee. The guarantee of contract integrity comes primarily from the daily margins on deposit as well as from the clearing members. The members of the clearinghouse, that is, individuals and firms that are also members of the exchange, provide the financial integrity that guarantees performance on every contract traded at the exchange.

Liquidity

Several factors make for a successful futures market. The liquidity of a market describes how easy it is for participants to enter and exit from their positions. This is primarily a direct function of the volume; the higher the volume, the easier it is to enter and exit from a position. The strong interaction between the cash and the futures markets, based on sound contract design, contributes to high levels of liquidity. As Tables 1 and 2 have shown, exchange-traded commodity futures and options exhibit a great deal of liquidity. Liquidity in a specific contract can be evaluated by examining its current volume and open interest.

Market Regulation

Regulation of commodity futures markets is founded on self-regulation combined with federal oversight. The markets are regulated both by the exchanges on which they trade and by an independent regulatory agency, the CFTC. The markets are monitored quite closely for signs of unusual behavior and potential manipulations. All traders with large positions (currently defined as half a million bushels in the grains, for example) must report their trading directly to the CFTC. All individuals dealing in or advising about commodity futures positions are required to be registered with the CFTC. Brokerage firms are subject to an audit of their customers' funds (margin money must be kept in a segregated account) and of the financial condition of the firms (firms must meet minimum exchange and/or CFTC designated financial requirements.)

In addition, the CFTC has adopted industrywide customer protection rules, including the requirement that brokers provide customers with risk disclosure statements, monthly profit and loss statements, and margin statements. Brokers cannot trade for an individual's account unless specific permission has been given. Finally, the CFTC has established reparations procedures by which customer complaints against a commodity broker may be heard and adjudicated in an orderly manner.

TAX CONSEQUENCES

Taxation of speculative gains and losses from commodity futures positions changed fundamentally with the Economic Recovery Tax Act of 1981, which established the current procedures for taxing gains and losses from both commodity future and option transactions.

POTENTIAL RISKS

Like other financial markets, commodity futures and options markets entail market or price risk—the risk of the absolute change in price. For a hedger, this price risk can be reduced to basis risk, where basis is the difference between the cash price and the futures price. Unlike most other financial markets, futures market gains and losses are settled on a daily basis. Investors must meet any daily margin calls or their futures positions will be liquidated.

Market or Price Risk

Price volatility has become a major factor in our economic life. For the performance-minded trader, speculating in the commodity futures and options market offers the possibility of attractive returns. Before entering into any speculative trades in such futures or options, however, traders should carefully assess their financial capacity to withstand risk. Experienced speculators recommend that only a small proportion of an individual's capital be risked on a single trade. Also, traders should limit their open positions to as many as they can adequately follow, while keeping some capital in reserve for additional opportunities or margin requirements. Because market conditions can and do change rapidly, it is essential that traders maintain flexibility.

Basis Risk

Cash and futures prices tend to move in the same direction, in a roughly parallel pattern. The arithmetic difference between them (the cash price minus the futures price) is called the basis. Changes in the basis tend to be more stable than either cash or futures price movements. Understanding basis relationships is the key to placing and lifting effective hedges.

Cash and futures prices also move together because, at expiration, the cash commodity can be delivered against the futures contract, or, for cash-settled futures, the futures cash settlement price equals the cash price. Many market participants engage in cash-futures arbitrage, seeking to profit from any misalignment of the cash and future prices.

Positive and Negative Basis. Basis can be positive or negative, depending on whether the cash price is higher or lower than the future price. In financial instruments, contract prices for delivery in distant futures months usually have been priced lower than those for nearby futures months, and prices for financial futures normally have been lower than cash prices, reflecting a positive cost of carry. For financial instruments, the term "cost of carry" refers to the net financial costs (coupon income minus financing costs, i.e., short-term interest rates). For physical commodities, prices for distant futures months are normally higher than nearby months, reflecting the cost of carry (composed of interest expense for owning the commodity) and the costs for storing and insuring the commodity over that period. Cost of carry can be represented by a positive or negative number.

Effect of Changes in Basis. Changes in the basis can influence the final result of a hedging transaction. Whether the basis strengthens or weakens has an influence on the hedge's overall profit or loss. The basis strengthens, or becomes more positive, when futures prices decline faster than cash prices, or when cash prices rise faster than futures prices. (A short hedge always benefits from a strengthening basis). Conversely, the basis weakens, or becomes more negative, when futures prices increase faster than cash prices, or when cash prices fall faster than futures prices. (A long hedge always benefits from a weakening basis.)

Margin Calls

Because either buyer or seller could lose money on a subsequent offsetting trade, both sides post margin. As the price changes, each side's account is marked to the market, debited or credited to reflect the most recent settlement price. When the account falls below a prescribed maintenance level, additional margin must be deposited to maintain the position. Additional margin can also be called for when the price volatility of a commodity warrants it.

Margin calls that are not met will result in an investor's futures position being liquidated. Therefore, sufficient funds should be available to meet margin calls if investors want to maintain their futures positions. The closing of futures positions will result in a hedger moving from a hedged position to an unhedged position. If prices then move in the opposite direction, losses for hedgers could result from both their futures positions and their cash positions.

REPRESENTATIVE TYPES OF INVESTORS

Participants in commodity futures and options markets are generally categorized as either hedgers or speculators. The distinction reflects a fundamental difference in the initial position of the participant. Hedgers are those whose business involves them in the underlying commodity. Many types of institutions use financial futures to reduce their exposure to interest rate risks. They include banks, bond dealers, pension funds, investment bankers, money managers, savings and loan associations, portfolio managers, financial executives, trust funds, insurance companies, mortgage bankers, corporate treasurers, and state and local governments. In agricultural commodities, the commercial firms include producers, merchants, processors, storers, and exporters. Speculators have no such commercial interests in the underlying commodity. Both types of participants are necessary for functioning markets.

Commercial Firms

Commercial firms use commodity futures to earn a return on their primary cash market activity, to provide a substitute transaction for an intended cash market transaction, and to reduce the risk of commodity price fluctuations. A particular hedging decision may have elements of all three motives. A hedging example for financial institutions is shown in Figure 1. A common example of hedging in agricultural markets uses an elevator operator who is storing grain. In the absence of futures markets, the operator's return from grain storage is simply the difference between the purchase price and the price at which the grain is later sold. The returns are fundamentally speculative, since time must elapse between the two transactions. With futures markets, the elevator operator can, on the same day as he purchases cash grain, sell an equivalent amount of futures contracts and know with reasonable certainty what the return to storage will be. When the cash grain is sold, the futures positions are bought back in and the actual profits calculated. This action will depend on the relationship between the cash and the futures price when the hedge is lifted. This basis relationship is generally much more predictable than are price changes over time. Thus, in this simple hedge, the futures transaction enabled the elevator operator to earn a predictable return to storage. The initial futures transaction could be viewed as a substitute for an intended later cash transaction, and the risks of commodity storage have been significantly reduced.

Speculators

Speculators in commodity futures markets are classified as one of three distinct kinds of traders: (1) floor traders; (2) spread traders; and (3) position traders. As speculators, these traders have no other commercial interest in the commodity. Their profits come solely from their futures trading. Although outside investors will most likely be position traders, the functions and the type of trading characteristic of each are described below.

Floor Traders. Floor traders are members of the exchanges, trading on the floor of the exchange. They trade in large volume during the trading session but rarely carry a position overnight. Floor traders, also called scalpers, are the market makers. They have been described as always ready to buy or sell at a tick below or above the price of the last transaction. Unlike stock market specialists, they are independent traders and are not assigned specific commodities to trade, nor do they hold a deck of outside orders to be executed at various prices. Income from their trading depends entirely on how skillfully they make a market, that is, how skillfully they accommodate the flow of orders into the market during the day.

Spread Traders. Unlike scalpers, spread traders hold open positions at the end of day, endeavoring to profit from somewhat longer-term changes in price relationships. Basically, a spread trader will maintain offsetting positions in different maturities of the same commodity or in similar maturities of related commodities. An intramarket spread involves two different delivery months of the same futures contract. An example of this would be a trade long December corn and short March corn on the expectation that the long December option will gain in relation to the short March option. An intermarket spread involves the sale of a given delivery month of a futures contract on one exchange and the purchase of the same delivery month of the same commodity on another exchange. A well-known intermarket spread includes positions in Chicago versus Kansas City or Minneapolis wheat.

Position Traders. Position traders take long-term positions in the market, based on their forecast of price changes. Position traders are sometimes distinguished according to the kinds of analysis they use to anticipate price changes. Fundamental analysis examines the determinants of supply and demand. Technical analysis, on the other hand, focuses on discerning patterns in past price changes and ignores fundamental factors. Both methods are used extensively, most often together rather than exclusively.

IMPORTANT FACTORS IN BUYING AND SELLING

Futures trading is regulated by the CFTC, the National Futures Association (the industry's self-regulatory arm), and the exchanges themselves. All new futures contracts must receive prior approval from the CFTC, as must certain changes in rules and regulations. Only members of the exchanges who are subject to the rules and regulations of the exchanges and of the CFTC may execute trades on the floor of the exchange. Members can either be commission brokers, who execute trades for nonmember customers and other members, or locals, who trade for themselves.

Futures commission merchants (FCMs), or brokerage firms, are the link between the broker and the customer. Such firms range in size from international investment firms, which are active in both commodities and securities markets, to one-person operations. These firms employ registered commodity representatives (RCRs), also known as account executives, to handle customer accounts. Both the commission firm and the RCR must be registered with the National Futures Association. RCRs serve their customers by placing orders, handling margin money, providing basic accounting records, and counseling customers on their trading programs.

GLOSSARY

basis—The difference between a cash price and the price of a particular futures contract. If the cash price of a commodity exceeds its futures price, the basis is said to be positive; a negative basis is the converse.

cash market—A market in which transactions for the immediate sale and purchase of the physical commodity or financial instruments are made under terms agreeable to both buyer and seller.

clearinghouse—An agency connected with a commodity exchange through which all futures contracts are reconciled, settled, guaranteed, and, later, either offset or fulfilled by delivery of the commodity, and through which financial settlement is made. It may be a fully chartered separate corporation rather than a division of the exchange itself.

Commodity Futures Trading Commission (CFTC)—A federal regulatory agency charged and empowered under the Commodity Futures Trading Commission Act of 1974 with regulation of futures trading in all commodities. The CFTC is comprised of five commissioners, one of whom is designated as chairman. All commissioners are appointed by the

President subject to Senate confirmation, and the commission is independent of all Cabinet departments.

contract month—The month in which a futures contract may be fulfilled by making or taking delivery. Most interest rate futures contracts are liquidated prior to the contract month.

cover—To offset a previous futures transaction with an equal and opposite transaction. Short covering is a purchase of futures contracts to cover an earlier sale of an equal number of the same delivery month; liquidation is the sale of futures contracts to offset the obligation to take delivery of an equal number of futures contracts of the same delivery month purchased earlier.

cross hedge—Hedging a cash market risk in one commodity by initiating a position in a futures contract for a different but related commodity. A cross hedge is based on the premise that while the two commodities are not the same, their price movements correlate.

daily price limit—The maximum advance or decline from the previous day's settlement permitted for a contract in one trading session. This limit is set by the exchange.

discretionary account—An arrangement by which the holder of the account gives written power of attorney to another, often his broker, to make buying and selling decisions without notification to the holder; often referred to as a managed account or controlled account.

forward contract—A cash market transaction in which two parties agree to the purchase and sale of a commodity at some future time under conditions on which the two agree. In contrast to futures contracts, the terms of forward contracts are not standardized; a forward contract is not transferable and usually can be canceled only with the consent of the other party, which must often be obtained for consideration and under penalty. Forward contracts are not traded in federally designated contract markets.

fundamental analysis—An approach to market behavior that stresses the study of underlying factors of supply and demand in the commodity, in the belief that such analysis will enable one to profit from being able to anticipate price trends. Compare with technical analysis.

futures contract—A firm commitment to make or take delivery of a standardized quantity and quality of a commodity or financial instrument during a specified month in the future, under terms designated at the exchange where the contract is traded.

hedging—The initiation of a position in a futures market that is intended as a temporary substitute for the sale or purchase of the actual commodity; the sale of futures contracts in anticipation of future sales of cash commodities as a protection against the possibility of price declines, or the purchase of contracts in anticipation of future purchases of cash commodities as a protection against the possibility of increasing costs.

long—As a noun, one who has bought futures contracts and has not yet offset that position. As a verb (going long), the action of taking a position in which one has bought futures contracts (or the cash commodity) without taking the offsetting action. For example, if an investor had no position and bought five contracts, he would be a long. However, if his previous position was one of having sold five contracts (i.e., being short five), and he then bought five contracts to offset that position, the second action would not be referred to as going long because his position when the second action was concluded would be zero.

long hedge—The purchase of a futures contract or contracts in anticipation of actual purchases in the cash market; often used to lock in a cost (favorable yield).

margin—Money deposited by both buyers and sellers of futures contracts to ensure performance of the terms of the contract (making or taking delivery). Margin in the futures market is not a down payment on equity; it is a performance bond or security deposit for an executory contract.

margin call—A call from a clearinghouse to a clearing member, or from a brokerage firm to a customer, to bring margin deposits up to a required minimum level. A member of an exchange who is also a member of the clearinghouse is a clearing member.

mark to market—The debits and credits assigned to each account after the close of every trading session. Each day, all market losses are collected and all gains disbursed.

offset—The liquidation of a purchase of futures, or the covering of a short sale of futures contracts, through the purchase of an equal number of contracts of the same delivery month. Either action transfers the obligation to make or take delivery of the actual commodity to another principal.

open interest—The contracts that have not yet been offset by opposite transactions in the futures market or fulfilled by delivery. Although each transaction has a buyer and a seller, the calculation of open interest reflects only one side of every trade.

original margin—Term applied to the initial deposit of margin money required of clearing members by clearinghouse rules, or to the initial margin deposit required of customers by exchange regulations.

physical—The underlying physical commodity in a futures transaction.

price limits—(See daily price limit).

short—As a noun, one who has sold futures contracts and has not yet offset that position. As a verb, the action of taking a position in which one has sold futures contracts (or made a forward contract for sale of the cash commodity) without taking the offsetting action. For example, if an investor had no position and sold five contracts, the action would be shorting the futures, and he would then be a short. However, if his previous position was one of having bought five contracts (i.e., being long five), and he then sold five contracts to offset that position, the second action would not be referred to as shorting because his position when the second action was concluded would be zero.

short hedge—The sale of a futures contract or contracts to eliminate or reduce the possible decline in the value of an asset.

speculator—In an economic sense, one who attempts to anticipate commodity price changes and to profit through the sale and purchase, or purchase and sale, of commodity futures contracts or of the physical commodity.

spreading—Taking opposite positions in two futures contracts with the objective of profiting through changes in relative price relationships.

technical analysis—An approach to analysis of futures markets and future trends of commodity prices that examines the technical factors of market activity. Technical analysts normally examine patterns of price change, rates of change, and changes in volume of trading and open interest, often by charting, in the hope of being able to predict and profit from future trends. (Compare with fundamental analysis).

Volume—The number of contracts traded on any given day.

TRADE ORGANIZATIONS

Futures Industry Association Inc., Washington, D.C.

National Futures Association, Chicago, Ill.

SUGGESTED READING

PERIODICALS

American Banker. Published by American Banker, Inc., New York, N.Y. Daily.

American Metal Market. Published by Fairchild Publications, New York, N.Y. Daily.

Commodity Futures Professional. Published by Education and Marketing Dept., Chicago Board of Trade, Chicago, Ill. Monthly.

Futures: The Magazine of Commodities and Options. Published by Futures Magazine Inc., Cedar Falls, Iowa. Monthly.

Financial Analyst Journal. Published by Financial Analyst Federation, New York, N.Y. Monthly.

Financial Exchange. Published by Chicago Board of Trade, Chicago, Ill. Bimonthly.

Institutional Investor. Published by Institutional Investor Inc., New York, N.Y., Monthly.

Intermarket. Chicago, Ill. Monthly.

Journal of the Futures Markets. Published by John Wiley & Sons, New York, N.Y. Quarterly.

Pensions and Investment Age. Published by Crain Communications, Inc., Chicago, Ill. Biweekly.

Pro Farmer. Professional Farmers of America, Cedar Falls, Iowa. Weekly.

REFERENCE BOOKS

Chicago Board of Trade. *Interest Rate Futures for Institutional Investors*. Chicago, 1985.

______. *Financial Instruments Markets: An Advanced Study of Cash-Futures Relationships*. Chicago, 1986.

______. *Using Interest Rate Futures in Portfolio Management*. Chicago, 1988.

Fabozzi, Frank, and Pollack, Irving (eds). *The Handbook of Fixed Income Securities*, 2nd ed. Homewood: Dow Jones-Irwin, 1987.

Figlewski, Stephen. *Hedging with Financial Futures for Institutional Investors: From Theory to Practice*. Cambridge: Ballinger Publishing, 1986.

Hieronymous, Thomas. *Economics of Futures Trading*. New York: Commodities Research Bureau, 1977.

Kolb, Robert W. *Understanding Futures Markets*. Glenview: Scott, Foresman and Company, 1985.

Labuszewski, John, and Nyhoff, John. *Trading Options on Futures: Markets, Methods, Strategies, and Tactics*. New York: John Wiley & Sons, 1988.

McMillan, Lawrence G. *Options as a Strategic Investment*. New York: New York Institute of Finance, 1986.

Powers, Mark J., and Vogel, David J. *Inside the Financial Futures Markets*. New York: John Wiley & Sons, 1984.

Schwarz, Edward, Hill, Joanne, and Schneeweis, Thomas. *Financial Futures: Fundamentals, Strategies and Applications*. Homewood: Dow Jones-Irwin, 1986.

Stigum, Marcia, and Mann, John. *Money Market Calculations: Yields. Break-Evens, and Arbitrage*. Homewood, Dow Jones-Irwin, 1988.

Teweles, Richard J., Harlow, Charles V. and Stone, Herbert L. *The Commodity Futures Game: Who Wins? Who Loses? Why?* McGraw-Hill, 1987.

GEMSTONES

Antoinette Leonard Matlins

BASIC CHARACTERISTICS

In A.D. 77, the Roman historian Pliny the Elder wrote, "Some precious stones are valued beyond all price, or at least at a higher price than any other of the world's goods." Throughout history, the fascination with precious gems and the desire to possess them have remained constant. Kings, noblemen, and political refugees have all found gems to be a source of real wealth and a hedge against political and economic uncertainty.

As investments in the Wall Street sense, however, gems are relative newcomers. Very few people understand what gems are, the factors that determine their value, and how the gemstone market works.

To be considered a gem, a stone must possess the following characteristics: rarity, beauty, desirability, and portability. Diamonds, rubies, sapphires, and emeralds have always been considered gems. Because these stones have proven track records, they make the best choices for investment. Other stones that might be considered for investment include natural (not cultured) pearls, jadeite, black opals, and alexandrite; there is an increasing Asian market for the latter three.

Four factors (sometimes known as the four C's) determine the overall quality of a gemstone, and any of the four can have a significant effect on a stone's value. For colored

---

Antoinette Matlins advises investors and collectors around the world on buying and selling gems. She is also the author of several books on gems and frequently lectures on the topic.

Portions of this article are based on information in Jewelry and Gems: The Buying Guide, *by Antoinette Matlins and Antonio C. Bonanno, and in* How to Buy and Sell Gems, *by Benjamin Zucker.*

gems, purity of color is the most important determinant of value. For diamonds, it is the whiteness of the stone (or intensity of color, if one is considering a natural colored diamond) and the purity of crystallization (clarity). The price of a gem can vary enormously with only a subtle difference in color or clarity, often referred to as the flaw grade. *Cut* (not shape, but the symmetry, proportioning, and precision that goes into the cutting) and *carat* (that is, weight, not size) can also significantly affect the value of a gem.

Several certification systems can aid the investor, but certificates cannot be relied on solely. The most widely recognized ones are issued by the Gemological Institute of America (GIA), in New York City and Santa Monica, California; the American Gemological Laboratory (AGL), in New York City; and the Gemmological Laboratory Gubelin (GL), in Lucerne, Switzerland.

Investing in gems does not yield quick and easy profits, nor is it for the unsophisticated investor. It is an area that requires knowledge, a major financial outlay, and normally a long-term commitment on the order of ten years or more. Gemstone investment should be regarded as a means of preservation of wealth or as a holding that may provide a hedge against the decline of paper assets and unfavorable political conditions.

Investors must exercise extreme caution. Gemstone investment can be profitable, but only for those who thoroughly understand the pros and cons. It is a complex area that should not be entered casually.

ATTRACTIVE FEATURES

Gems have always provided psychic and aesthetic pleasure. In literature, gems and treasure have been synonymous. Since the Middle Ages, some people have believed that gems aid health and spiritual well-being. Good stones are not trendy; they do not go in and out of fashion. And there is no reason to think that the demand for gems will diminish.

Beauty and Wearability. One of the most attractive features of gems as investments is their natural beauty. Unlike many other beautiful purchases, gems can be used and enjoyed without adversely affecting their value.

Portability. Gems are portable. Easily moved and stored, they can be made readily available to the owner and are easy to show when the need arises.

Stability. During inflationary times and periods in which the stock market has been volatile and unpredictable, the demand for gems has been good and market prices strong. On the day following the stock market crash of October 19, 1987, gems set all-time records at Sotheby's and Christie's auction houses in New York City. A 64.83-carat pear-shaped D/Flawless diamond sold at Christie's for $6.4 million, the highest price ever paid for a gem at auction. During the three days from October 19 to October 21, 1987, Christie's jewelry auction brought in $23.6 million, and Sotheby's, a record $26.7 million.

Strength as Tangible Assets. Following a study of compound annual rates of return for a twenty-year period ending June 1, 1989, Salomon Brothers, Inc., revealed that by comparison to other tangible assets, diamonds and precious stones have a good track record. The Salomon study, which compared diamonds to twelve other alternatives (U.S. coins, oil, gold, silver, U.S. Treasury bills, Old Master paintings, stocks, bonds, Chinese ceramics, housing, U.S. farmland, and foreign exchange), ranked diamonds number 5, ahead of the consumer price index (CPI), foreign exchange, oil, U.S. farmland, gold, and silver. Jewelry industry figures show diamond prices are the strongest since 1981, and auction indicators continue to show investor interest, with major jewelry sales setting world records.

POTENTIAL RISKS

Gemstones offer no current income. In addition, investors should consider the following risks.

Market Volatility

Although gemstones historically have provided a sound means to long-term preservation of wealth, and current indicators reflect an upward movement in the gemstone market, demand for gems over time is unpredictable and subject to many influences, such as the volatility of the stock market, political conditions in gem-rich lands, fashion trends, and the discovery of new mines.

The discovery of a new ruby or emerald mine, for example, can result in declining prices. The DeBeers cartel reduces this risk for diamonds, but it is an ever-present risk with colored gems.

The most dramatic recent example of price volatility occurred in the late 1970s, when gem prices rapidly escalated to unprecedented levels. By December 1980 to January 1981, the wholesale price of a 1-carat, D/Flawless diamond was $60,000. By the end of 1981, the price for the same stone had plummeted to less than $15,000 per carat, and, eight years later, the wholesale cost was still less than one third the price paid in November 1980. Following the plummet in diamond prices, prices for colored gems also declined. Investor losses were significant. Many gem investment companies went out of business. Many investors, unable to recoup even their initial investment, are still holding gems purchased then.

Since 1987, the gem market has shown signs of stabilizing and strengthening. Most investment reports appearing in 1988 show gemstones as long-term investments (more than ten years) outperforming many other investment vehicles. The figures look very attractive, the rewards are often exaggerated and over simplified, but the risks are understated.

Illiquidity

Gemstones are not liquid assets, and selling gems purchased for investment can be difficult; the selling process can take months, even years. Normally, one disposes of gems by selling them to a jewelry retailer or through a broker or auction house. Each of these avenues has its pros and cons, and the particular circumstances under which one must sell usually determine which way will be most appropriate. Whichever way is chosen, it is critical to know the quality and current value of the holding to ensure getting a reasonable price. For many people, assessing the holdings may pose a problem in and of itself. (See *Disposing of Your Gem Investment,* later in this article.)

TAX CONSEQUENCES

Under current tax law, profit from the sale of gemstones held for more than one year is taxed as a capital gain. Gemstones can be exchanged for others of equal or greater value in a tax-free transaction under certain conditions. (See article on "Tax Considerations for Collector-Investors," elsewhere in this volume.) For specific guidance in these matters, investors are urged to consult a professional tax advisor.

REPRESENTATIVE TYPES OF INVESTORS

Wealthy people have been buying gems for thousands of years, and persons of substantial means who buy stones as a hedge against economic or political instability most likely will continue to be the principal investors. During recent years, many rising female executives have begun to purchase fine, gem-quality jewelry; they may become an important factor in the gem investment field.

IMPORTANT FACTORS IN BUYING AND SELLING

Diamonds, rubies, sapphires, and emeralds have always been the stones of primary interest to the investor. Stones of sufficiently fine quality to be considered for investment can easily cost more than $15,000 per carat. With so much invested in a single stone, the investor who is seriously considering gems as an investment must make every effort to understand fully the elements that influence decisions about buying and selling.

Most buyers lack the expertise to evaluate the item in which they are investing. Verifying genuineness and being able to judge the four quality factors requires extensive training. Investors who fail to seek the advice of an expert risk buying a gem that is not what it is represented to be.

For counsel and aid in verifying the facts, the investor should seek a gemologist who holds one of the following titles: Fellow of the Gemmological Association of Great Britain (FGA); Graduate Gemologist (GG), awarded by the Gemological Institute of America (GIA); Master Gemologist Appraiser (MGA), awarded by the American Society of Appraisers; or Certified Gemologist (CG) or Certified Gemologist Appraiser (CGA), the latter two awarded by the American Gem Society (AGS). The names of local gemologists can be obtained from the Accredited Gemologists Association (AGA), (801) 581-9900; the American Society of Appraisers, (ASA), (703) 478-2228; or AGS, (213) 387-7375.

Is the Gemstone What It Appears to Be?

Just one color or flaw-grade difference or the presence of natural or enhanced color can significantly alter the value of a fine gem. Theoretically, any serious investor can learn the four C's, but most lack the knowledge and expertise to know for certain that the stone is genuine or that the quality is as represented. This situation can be particularly dangerous because today's technology has provided the means to alter or conceal any of the four quality factors—especially color and clarity. Although most jewelers are reliable professionals with high standards of integrity, sometimes a treated stone escapes their detection.

Certificates are not enough, and should not be relied on exclusively. Few laypeople understand the importance of particular details in terms of quality and value. For colored gems, many certificates have limited value because they verify only genuineness and possibly country of origin; few evaluate color, clarity, and cut, and many colored gem certificates, such as those issued by the GL, omit critical information about color enhancement.

Is It a Genuine Stone? There are many synthetic stones currently on the market, some so sophisticated that even a professional may have difficulty distinguishing them from the natural. In addition to the synthetics, there has been an increase in the number of stones that are made from parts of stones or that look like a more valuable stone; attempts are made to sell both types of stones as something they are not.

On recent trips to Thailand, professional buyers have had to deal with an increasingly serious problem of synthetic sapphires and rubies that are represented as natural. Imitation stones called doublets or triplets (made by cementing together two or three parts of some material—sometimes poor-quality genuine stone—with colored cement) have also been sold as genuine.

Many stones look like other, more valuable, stones. Although sometimes honest mistakes are made, often substitution is deliberate. Among the British Crown Jewels, mounted in the center of the State Imperial Crown, is a magnificent red stone, the Black Prince's Ruby. In relatively recent gemological studies, it was discovered that this ruby is not a ruby, but a red spinel. Red spinels are beautiful stones, and some are, in fact, gems; but a red spinel is not a ruby.

What Is Its Quality? Not all diamonds, rubies, emeralds, and sapphires are gems. Only stones of fine, rare quality can be called gems; of these, only stones of the very finest, rarest quality should be considered for investment. Although many advertisements seem to offer gems at attractive prices, one gets what one pays for. Rubies, sapphires, and emeralds offered at $500 or $1,000 per carat are not gems of investment quality. Learning to recognize quality differences and their effect on value and cost is a critical aspect of gemstone investment.

Unfortunately, misrepresentation of quality is not uncommon. Recently a large diamond was purchased for investment from a Boston jeweler, who represented it to be very fine, even including a full description of the stone in writing on the bill of sale. At the urging of a friend who questioned the stone's quality (given the stated quality, the price seemed too low), the purchaser obtained an independent appraisal from a registered gemologist and learned that the stone was four color grades and two clarity grades lower than represented.

Many factors must be evaluated to determine the overall quality of a gem, and accurate evaluation requires years of skill and training. Value can be affected by very subtle differences, which cannot be seen by the nonprofessional, even when stones are compared side by side.

Several internationally accepted standardized grading systems have been developed to assist in grading and describing gem quality. Some of the most widely used systems include those developed by the GIA, the AGS, the International Confederation of Jewelry, Silverware, Diamonds, Pearls, and Stones (CIBJO), a European system, the Scandinavian Diamond Nomenclature (Scan DN), and the Belgian Diamond High Council (HRD). The GIA system, the most widely used in the United States, also has wide acceptance internationally.

Is the Price Right? Few buyers have access to pricing information that enables them to evaluate the investment merit of a purchase. Most gemstones bought by the average consumer are purchased at retail prices but are sold at wholesale prices or below, and it usually takes many years for the current wholesale price to exceed the previous retail price.

Information on current prices at which stones are being traded, that is, their wholesale cost, is usually not available to the public. Without knowledge of this base line, it is very difficult to determine the soundness of any purchase as an investment. As an example, a Florida-based gem investment company offered stones at wholesale prices, fully certificated. When a buyer took his purchase to an appraiser to learn its retail value, he found that the price he paid was almost four times the wholesale price, higher than he would have paid in any jewelry store. Because he didn't know the current wholesale price of comparable stones, the buyer had made a very poor investment.

For a list of publications that report wholesale prices, see *Are You Buying at a Good Price?* later in this article.

If one does know wholesale prices, the next problem to be faced is where to go to obtain gems at or close to those prices. Without expert advice, finding a reliable source with prices close to wholesale can be very risky; the same problem occurs in disposing of a gem.

Judging the Quality of Diamonds

Several systems provide very precise, easy-to-understand, and highly reliable grading information about diamonds. Their color and flaw-grading scales make comparison of quality and pricing quite reliable. Judging color and clarity (flaws) alone, however, is insufficient; cut and carat (weight) are equally important in terms of beauty and desirability, and price is also a factor.

Diamond Certificates. Diamonds bought for investment should be accompanied by a grading report, or certificate, issued by a recognized laboratory, such as the GIA. The GIA report gives important, precise information fully describing the stone; verification of genuineness, weight, shape, measurements, information about the proportions of the cutting, culet size, polish, symmetry, clarity and color grades, and a plot showing the location and type of inclusions and blemishes.

Investors should verify the genuineness of the certificate. There have been cases in which counterfeit reports or certificates have accompanied a stone. Because each is dated and numbered, it is easy to verify a report. One simply contacts the lab and gives them the date and number; the lab confirms whether they issued the report.

One must be sure that the diamond matches the stone described on the certificate. Normally this is easily done by comparing the weight and millimeter dimensions of the stone with the description on the report; it is highly unlikely that more than one diamond will exist with the same weight and exactly the same millimeter dimensions. However, to avoid any doubt, the type and location of flaws shown on the plot can be checked by an expert.

Colored (fancy) diamonds should always be accompanied by a report verifying the genuineness and origin of the color (to ensure it is natural), as well as such other factors as weight, shape, and millimeter dimensions. The clarity grade is not so critical in colored diamonds (certain colors, such as red, always have flaws visible to the naked eye), but there are acceptable standards for a particular color. Color is normally described by hue (for example, yellow) and vividness (from light through intense). Stones described as fancy light should be avoided for investment.

A new grading system for fancy diamonds has been developed by Colored Diamond Laboratory Services, Inc., in New York City. It is superior to other certificates for colored diamonds because it provides a more precise description of color. Because color is the principal determinant of value in colored diamonds, precision is critical. This system has been praised by the U.S. jewelry trade and is also gaining acceptance internationally.

The Importance of Cut and Proportion. The cut of a diamond and the proportioning of the cut (the make) are of extraordinary importance, because they have the greatest influence on the fire and brilliance of the stone.

The round brilliant-cut stone is the most popular cut. It usually displays the stone's qualities to their greatest potential and is, therefore, the best investment cut.

Figure 1 illustrates, in simple terms, the effect of cut and proportion on fire and brilliance in a round brilliant-cut stone. As a general rule, if the crown (see Glossary) appears to be roughly one-third of the pavilion depth, the proportioning is probably acceptable (see Figure 2).

Types of Diamond Proportioning. Various combinations of width and depth create differences in a diamond's fire and brilliance (see Glossary). The degree of brilliance and

FIGURE 1. The Importance of Cut to Brilliance

Source: A. Matlins and A.C. Bonanno: *Jewelry and Gems: The Buying Guide*. South Woodstock, Vermont: GemStone Press, 1987, p. 23.

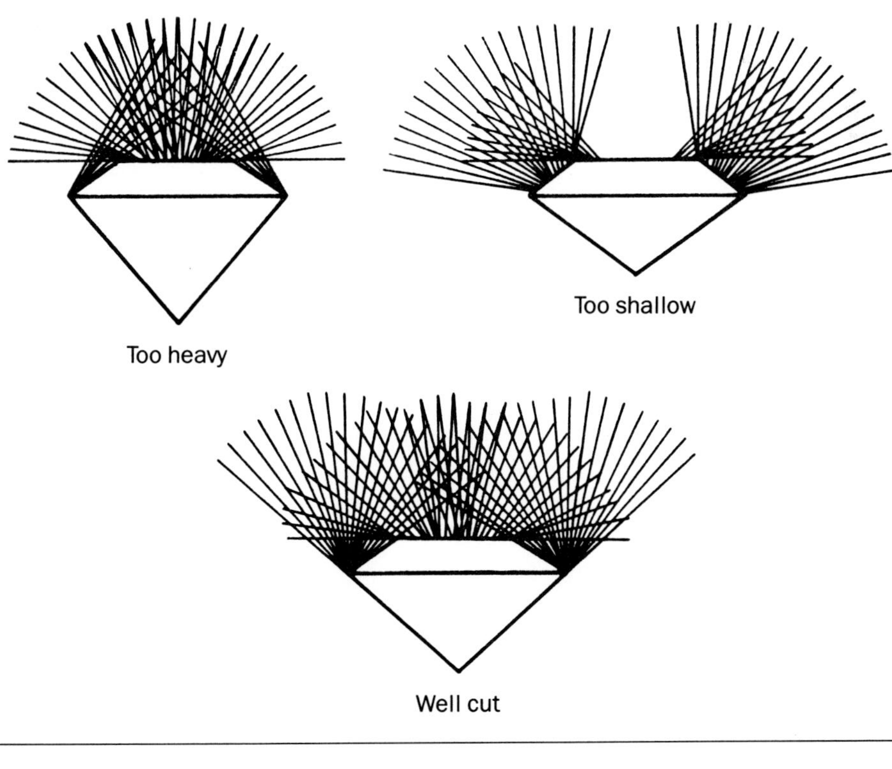

FIGURE 2. A Well-Proportioned Stone

Source: A. Matlins and A.C. Bonanno: *Jewelry and Gems: The Buying Guide*. South Woodstock, Vermont: GemStone Press, 1987, p.24.

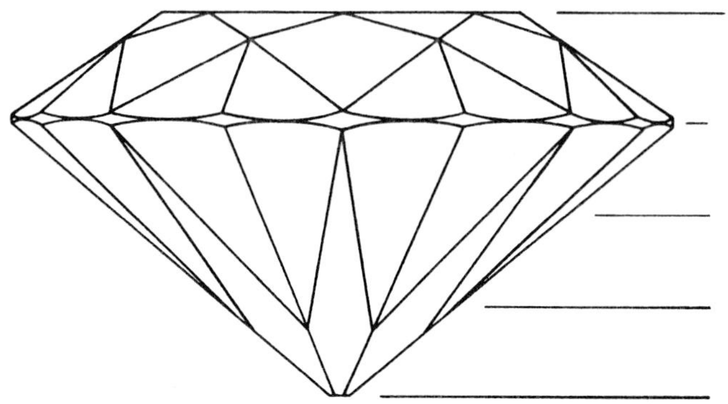

fire depends primarily on the table spread and the crown and pavilion angles. A large table area can create greater brilliance but will cause some reduction in fire, and a small table can increase fire but may reduce brilliance; the former seems to be more in fashion today. The ideal would be a compromise that would allow the greatest brilliance and fire simultaneously. There is a lack of agreement, however, on what the percentages should be. Some people prefer fire to brilliance, and vice versa. Thus, several accepted types of proportioning are found, and choice is a matter of personal preference.

Faulty Cuts. Many errors can occur in the cutting that affect the appearance and value of a stone. Figure 3 shows a few faults to watch for.

Fancy Cuts and Standard Deviations. Other popular cuts include the pear shape, emerald cut, marquise, and oval. These are referred to as fancy cuts (Figure 4). Within the popular fancy shapes, certain deviations have been established as standard. Moderate deviations will not affect the beauty or value of a stone; however, deviations that exceed acceptable tolerances can seriously reduce a stone's beauty and value.

One of the most obvious deviations in proportion in fancy shapes is the bow tie, or butterfly, effect, a darkened area across the center of widest part of the stone, depending on the cut. The bow tie is most commonly seen in the pear shape or marquise but may exist in any fancy shape. The degree of misproportion is directly related to the degree to which the bow tie is pronounced (Figure 5).

As with the brilliant-cut diamond, fancy shapes can also be cut too broad or too narrow, and the pavilion can be too deep or too shallow (Figure 6).

The Effect on Value. Excellently cut and proportioned stones (ideal cut) cost significantly more per carat than those that are not cut well. The following list gives a basic idea of the monetary effect of some of the most frequent defects in cut and proportion.

FIGURE 3. Faulty Cuts

Source: A. Matlins and A.C. Bonanno: *Jewelry and Gems: The Buying Guide*. South Woodstock, Vermont: GemStone Press, 1987, p. 27.

Off-center culet

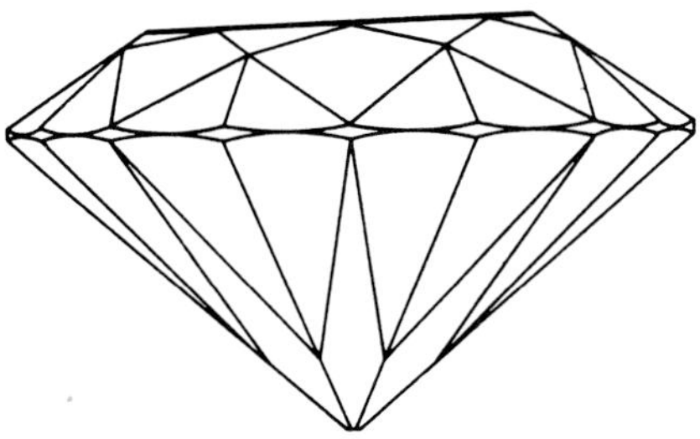

A brilliant-cut stone with a sloping table

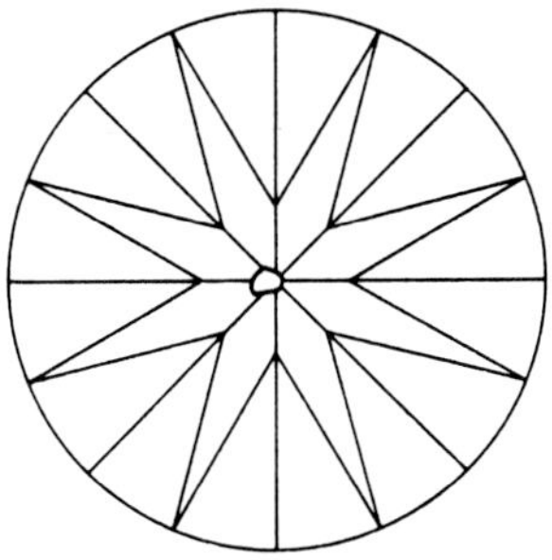

Open culet (viewed from the bottom)

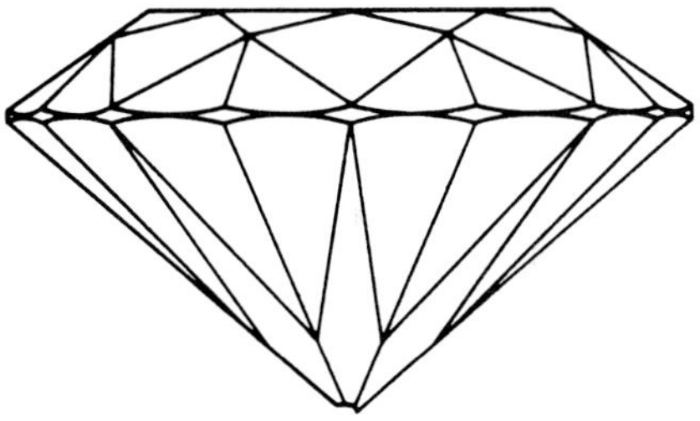

Broken or chipped culet

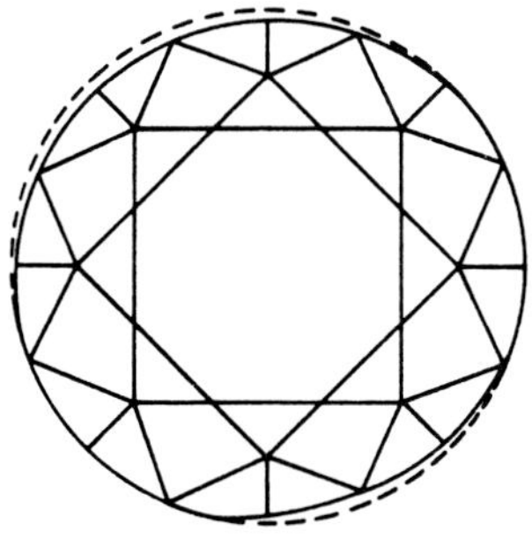

Poor symmetry

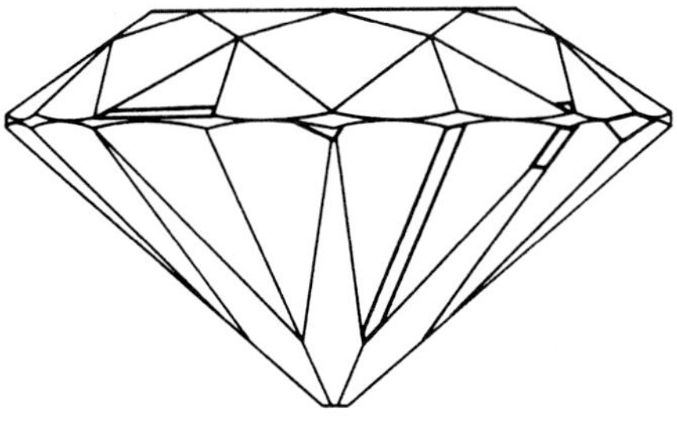

Stone with extra facets

FIGURE 4. Fancy Cuts

Source: A. Matlins and A.C. Bonanno: *Jewelry and Gems: The Buying Guide*. South Woodstock, Vermont: GemStone Press, 1987, p. 11.

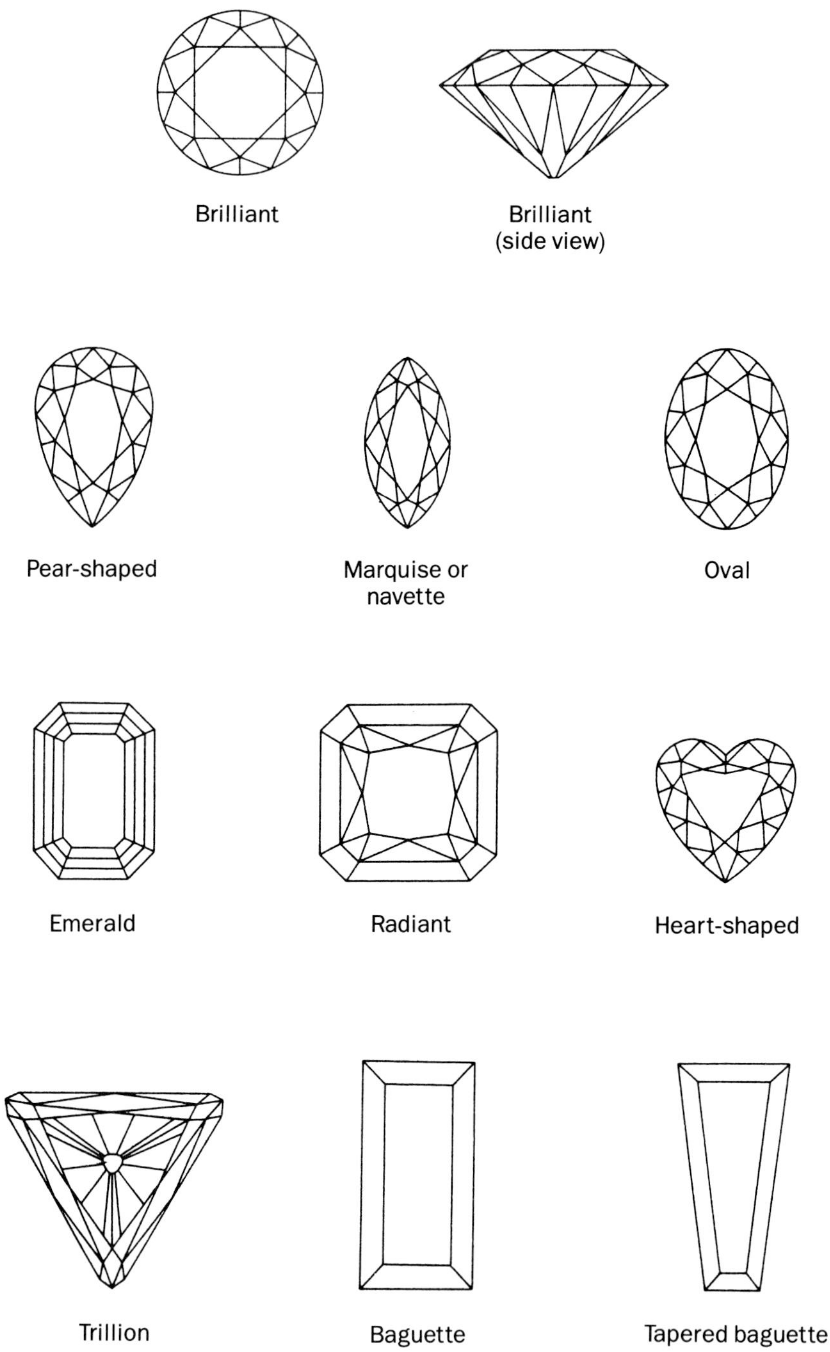

FIGURE 5. Marquise With a Pronounced Bow Tie, or Butterfly

Source: A. Matlins and A.C. Bonanno: *Jewelry and Gems: The Buying Guide*. South Woodstock, Vermont: GemStone Press, 1987, p.31.

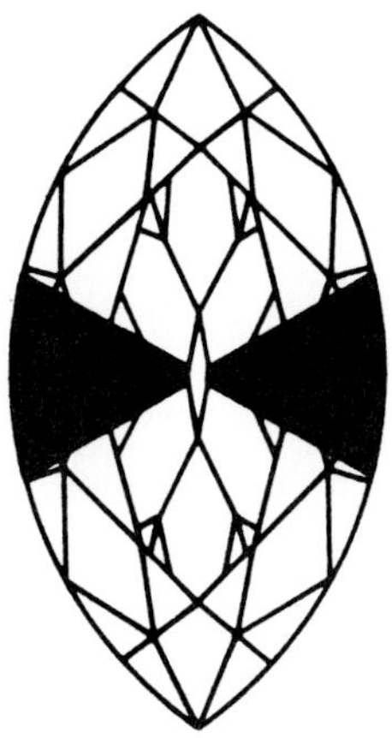

- Table not a reasonably accurate octagon: 2 to 15 percent off
- Girdle too thick: 5 to 20 percent off
- Symmetry of crown facets off: 5 to 15 percent on round, less on fancy cuts (defect is not so easily seen)
- Asymmetrical culet: 2 to 5 percent off
- Misaligned culet: 5 to 25 percent off
- Stone too shallow: 15 to 50 percent off
- Stone too thick: 10 to 30 percent off
- Slightly thin crown: 5 to 20 percent off
- Slightly thick crown: 5 to 15 percent off

Only an experienced professional can determine the extent to which the value of a given stone may be lessened. But a stone that suffers from several errors could certainly have its price per carat significantly reduced.

Body Color. Body color refers to how much yellow or brown tint is observable in a colorless diamond. It does not refer to the shades of colors found in the rare natural colored diamonds designated in the trade as fancies.

The color designation frequently used to grade an absolutely water-clear colorless diamond is the letter D. This letter designation is part of a color-grading system introduced by the GIA and used extensively in the diamond trade. The GIA classification progresses from D, the finest classification on this scale (colorless), through the alphabet to Z, getting progressively more yellow, brown, or gray. The grades D, E, and F can be grouped as very

FIGURE 6. Faulty Cuts of Fancy Shapes

Source: A. Matlins and A.C. Bonanno: *Jewelry and Gems: The Buying Guide.* South Woodstock, Vermont: GemStone Press, 1987, p. 31.

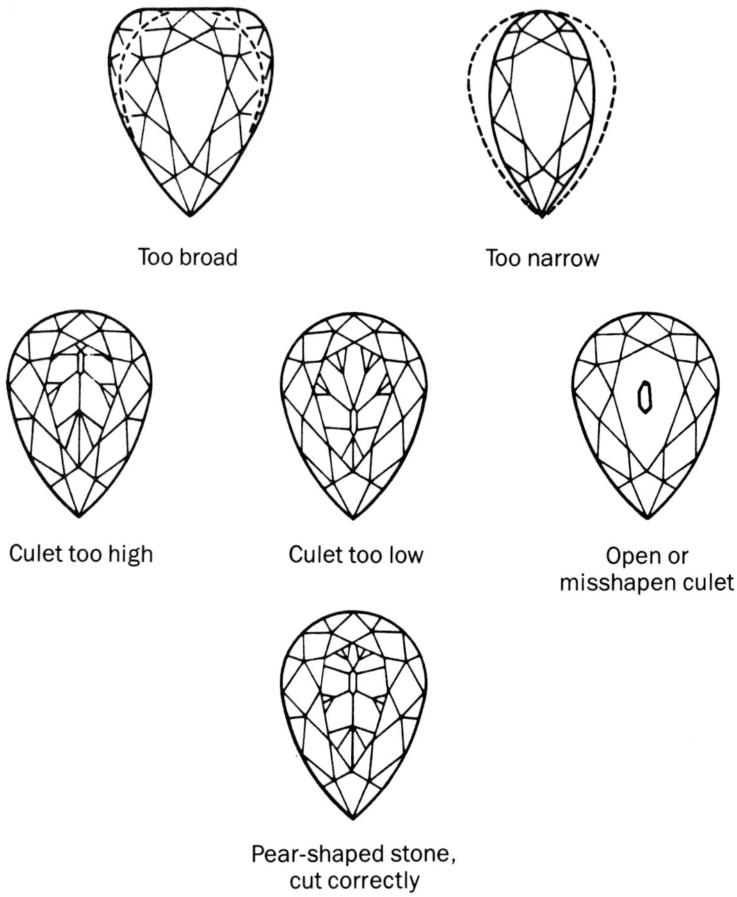

fine and may be referred to as colorless, gem, or gem-white. G and H may be referred to as fine white. These grades are all considered to be very good, and good for investment.

Evaluating Color. It is impossible to determine accurately color grade in a mounted stone, but even an amateur can learn to see color differences in an unmounted stone if the stone is viewed properly. It is best to observe color by examining the stone through the pavilion with the table down, against a flat white surface, such as a white business card, or in a plastic grading trough (available from a jewelry supply house for a few dollars). Next, view the stone with the pavilion side down and the culet pointing up.

Fancies. Diamonds have been found to occur naturally in almost every color and shade—blue, red, green, yellow, lavender, pink, gunmetal blue, coffee brown, and black. The color can be intense or very pale. Colored diamonds are called fancies.

Fancies are very expensive because they are rare—and some more than others. The most common fancy colors are shades of yellow (very intense, bright yellow, or canary), orange, and brown. Among the most rare and most valuable are the reds, greens, and blues. The least valuable, yet still expensive, are the blacks. At Christie's auction in New York City in April 1987, a purplish red diamond weighing 0.95 carat brought almost $1 million per carat, the highest price in history for a red diamond. At Sotheby's auction in New York in April 1988, a 20-carat pink diamond brought $236,500 per carat, yielding a price of over $4.75 million. Then, in May 1989 Christie's in Geneva set a new record, selling a 21.06-carat fancy pink diamond for $287,428 per carat, for a total amount over $6 million.

Buyers must be aware, however, that it is possible to use sophisticated radiation technology to alter poor-quality brownish and yellowish diamonds so that they become beautiful fancy-colored stones. These should sell for much less than their naturally occurring counterparts. There are tests—spectroscopic examination, electroconductivity, and ultraviolet response—that differentiate the natural from the treated colored diamond.

Flaw Classification. Flaw classification is one of the most important criteria for determining the value of a diamond. The four systems commonly used for grading flaws are:

- CIBJO (International Confederation of Jewelry, Silverware, Diamonds, Pearls, and Stones); participating nations who use this scale include Austria, Belgium, Canada, Denmark, Finland, France, Great Britain, Italy, Japan, the Netherlands, Norway, Spain, Sweden, Switzerland, the United States, and West Germany.
- Scan DN (Scandinavian Diamond Nomenclature)
- GIA (Gemological Institute of America)
- AGS (American Gem Society)

The major grading system in the United States is the GIA system. Most of the other systems are being revised to conform to the GIA scale.

These systems grade the stone for its imperfections, both internal (inclusions) and external (blemishes). Flaws can be white, black, colorless, or even red or green in rare cases. The flaw grade is more commonly referred to as the clarity grade today. Clarity and flaw, however, may be used interchangeably.

FL is the grade given to a stone that has no visible flaws, internal or external, when examined under 10× magnification. Only a highly qualified person is able to determine this grade. Also, it is difficult for inexperienced people to see flaws that are readily observed by the experienced jeweler, dealer, or gemologist. A flawless, colorless, correctly proportioned stone, particularly of 1 carat and more, is extremely rare and is priced proportionately much higher than any other grade. Some jewelers insist that there is no such thing in existence today.

IF is the grade given to a stone which, under 10× magnification, exhibits no internal flaws and only minor external blemishes (nicks, pits, or girdle roughness not on the table) that can be removed with polishing. These stones, in colorless, well-proportioned makes, are also rare and are priced proportionately much higher than other grades.

VVS_1 and VVS_2 are grades given to stones with internal flaws that are very difficult for a qualified observer to see, under 10×. These grades are also difficult to obtain and are priced at a premium.

VS_1 and VS_2 are grades given to stones with very small inclusions difficult for a qualified observer to see under 10×. These stones are more readily available in good color and cut, and their flaws will not be visible except under magnification. These are excellent stones to purchase.

SI_1 and SI_2 grades are given to stones with flaws that a qualified observer will see fairly easily under 10× magnification. They are more prevalent and so command a lower price, and their flaws may sometimes be visible without magnification when examined from the back side or laterally. They are highly desirable for good jewelry, but are not recommended for investment. Exceptions are made for rare fancy colors. Red and green diamonds, for example, have set record prices even with inclusions visible to the naked eye.

The imperfect grades are given to stones in which the flaws may be seen by a qualified observer without magnification; they are readily available and much less expensive, except in rare, intense fancy colors. They are graded I_1, I_2, and I_3—called first pique, second pique, and third pique in some classification systems. Imperfect grades should not be considered for investment because they will be difficult to resell.

Weight. Diamonds are sold by the carat (ct), not to be confused with karat (kt), which in the United States refers to gold content.

The carat is a unit of weight, not size. Since 1913, most countries have agreed that a carat weighs 200 milligrams, or one-fifth gram. Most people think that a 1-carat stone is a particular size. They expect a 1-carat diamond and a 1-carat emerald to look the same size or to have the same apparent dimensions. This is not the case. Because emerald weighs less than diamond and ruby weighs more than diamond, a 1-carat emerald will look larger than a 1-carat diamond, and a 1-carat ruby will look smaller than a 1-carat diamond.

Diamond weight is also described in points—100 points to a carat. A stone that is 0.9 carat might be described as weighing 90 points or as a 90-pointer.

Diamonds are sold on a price-per-carat basis. Diamonds of fine quality sell for a higher price per carat than lower-quality stones. For example, the finest-quality diamond in a certain size might sell for $30,000 per carat; a stone of the same weight, in a less fine quality, might sell for only $10,000 per carat.

As a rule, because large stones are increasingly limited in supply, there is an increase in the price per carat as one goes from smaller to larger stones. That is, stones of the same quality weighing 1 carat will sell for more per carat than stones weighing 0.5 carat; stones weighing 2 carats will sell for more per carat than stones of the same quality weighing 1 carat.

The price of a diamond does not increase proportionately with its weight; there are disproportionate jumps. All else being equal in terms of overall quality, the larger the stone, the more disproportionate may be the increase in cost per carat. A 2-carat stone will not cost twice as much as a 1-carat stone; it could easily be four times as much. A 5-carat stone would not cost five times more than a 1-carat stone; it could easily cost ten times more.

Types of Misrepresentation. There are four areas in which diamond fraud or misrepresentation usually occurs. Investors should be cautious with regard to:

- Weight misrepresentation
- Color alteration and misgrading
- Flaw concealment and misgrading
- Counterfeit production or alteration of certificates

Judging the Quality of Colored Gemstones

Systems for evaluating colored stones are relatively new and not yet as widely used within the trade as the systems for evaluating diamonds. One can find certificates accompanying colored gems that confirm genuineness and, in some cases, verify the country of origin; some provide ratings for color, clarity, and brilliance. The most widely used reports for colored gems are issued by the GIA Gem Trade Laboratory, the AGL, and the GL.

Whereas almost all diamonds today of more than 1-carat size have been precisely graded for each of the four C's, very few colored gems have. We are just beginning to see the evolution of standardized systems that could be considered comparable to those used for diamonds. Several sytems gaining acceptance for grading colored gems are GIA's ColorMaster, the AGL's ColorScan, and Howard Rubin's GemDialogue. However, there is still very limited use of these systems.

It is particularly difficult to evaluate the comparative quality and value of colored stones. Furthermore, colored stones do not have the organized strength of a central selling organization standing behind their price, as is the case with the DeBeers organization and diamonds. However, the rarity of colored gems is much greater than that of diamonds.

Color. The principal determinant of value in colored gems, color is affected by many variables that make it difficult to evaluate truly. Color is affected primarily by light—the type of light and its intensity. In addition, color can be very subjective in terms of what is considered pleasing and desirable. As a general rule, the closer a stone comes to being the pure spectral hue of that color, with no strong undertone of any other color, the rarer and more valuable is the stone.

Key Elements. The spectral colors go from pure red to pure violet, not including brown, white, black, and gray. These latter colors, in combination with the spectral colors, affect the tone of the color seen and make the classification of color difficult. For example, if there is white present with red, the tone of red is lighter; if there is black, it is a darker shade of red. In describing color, one refers to these factors:

- *Hue:* The precise spectral color
- *Intensity:* The brightness or vividness (or dullness or drabness) of the color
- *Tone:* The depth of the color (light or dark)
- *Distribution:* The even (or uneven) distribution of the color

Both intensity and tone of color can be significantly affected by the proportioning of the cut. A good gem cutter, working with a fine stone, will be able to bring out its inherent, potential beauty to the fullest, making it very desirable. A poor cutter may take the same rough material and create a stone that is not really desirable; a poor cut reduces the vividness and alters the depth of color, usually producing a stone that is too dark to be attractive.

In general, stones that are either very light (pale) or very dark sell for less per carat. There is a common belief that the darker the stone, the better, but this is true only to a point. A rich, deep color is desirable, but not a depth of color that approaches black, or looks black in certain types of light. It is important to differentiate between a nice depth of color and a stone that is too dark.

To develop an eye for colored gems, one must become attuned to the four elements of color. Some stones exhibit a more intense, vivid color than others, but only by extensive visual comparison can one recognize the differences.

The finest rubies are Burmese, the most highly prized and the most expensive because of their color and scarcity. Although not a pure red, they come the closest to it, with the tone varying from very light to very dark. As with most stones, the very light and the very dark stones sell for less per carat.

Thai rubies vary tremendously in hue and tone, from light to dark red, with varying degrees of blue undertone giving them a purplish cast and making them look like the much cheaper reddish-purple gemstone, the garnet. Some shades of Thai ruby are very expensive, but most are much less so than the Burmese.

Tanzanian rubies have a tint or undertone of brown or orange, making them much cheaper than the Burmese reds but more valuable than Thai rubies, depending on the color of the latter.

Ceylon rubies are usually classified as pink sapphires and not as rubies, since the tone is consistently pale. (Ceylon is now called Sri Lanka, but its rubies and sapphires are still referred to as Ceylon.) Ruby must be deep red, not pink. Sapphire and ruby are physically and chemically the same stone, corundum. Only red corundum is called ruby, while the equally popular blue is called sapphire, as are varieties that are green, yellow, pink, and colorless.

Blue sapphires, intensely colored gems, come in numerous tones of blue—from light to very dark, some so dark that they look black in artificial light. Many contain some degree of green—the more green, the lower the price. Some exhibit a color change, turning purple or lavender in incandescent light, while blue in fluorescent light. The lighter blues are generally referred to as Ceylon-colored sapphires although they may not come from Ceylon. Also, stones that do come from Ceylon (Sri Lanka) may also exhibit a rich, deep blue. The finest and most expensive blue sapphires are Burmese, which exhibit a rich, true blue in all kinds of light. Some people prefer the more subdued, soft, velvety looking blue exhibited by the rare Kashmir sapphires, which are also very expensive.

Today, some of the finest emeralds come from Colombia. The Colombian emerald is the color of fresh, young green grass—a pure spectral green with a faint tint of either yellow or blue. The drop-of-oil emerald from Colombia is considered absolutely the finest; it is a deep green (do not confuse with dark green, which has black in it) with a very slight blue undertone. This most valuable color is unique to Colombian varieties.

The African emerald is also a nice shade of green, but it has a blue undertone that sometimes can have a slight darkening effect (probably owing to traces of iron), which make the stone less valuable than the Colombian. However, it usually has fewer flaws than the Colombian, so, when cut, the stone can appear more brilliant. Therefore, some of the African stones, depending on depth of color, compare aesthetically very favorably with the Colombian, while costing less per carat.

The Importance of Environment. A stone's color can be drastically affected by the kind of light and the environment in which it is examined; for example, the color of the wallpaper or the color of a shirt can have a significant effect. If examined under a fluorescent light, a ruby may not show its fullest red, because most fluorescent lights are weak in red rays, causing the red in the ruby to be diminished and to appear more purple-red. The same ruby examined in daylight or under incandescent light, which is not weak in red rays, will appear a truer, fuller red. The same ruby would look even redder if examined against a piece of orange-yellow paper.

Color Distribution, or Zoning. In some stones, color is not evenly distributed but exists in zones, adding color to colorless areas around the zone. This phenomenon is frequently observed in ruby and sapphire. These zones may be seen by looking through the side of the stone, while tilting and rotating it slowly (Figure 7). If the zoning is easily seen from the top, beauty and value can be significantly reduced.

Sometimes in the rough a stone is colorless, or nearly so, but has a spot or layer of color. If cut so that the culet is in the color spot, the entire stone will appear to be that color. If there is a layer and the cutter cuts the stone so that the layer lies in a plane nearly parallel to the table, the stone will look completely colored. Evenness and complete saturation of color are very important in determining the value of colored gems.

Clarity. With colored gemstones, as with diamonds, clarity refers to the absence of internal flaws (inclusions). Flawlessness in colored stones is perhaps even rarer than in diamonds. However, although clarity is important, and the clearer the stone the better, clarity in colored stones does not usually carry the premium that it does with diamonds. Light, pastel-colored stones will require better clarity because the flaws are more readily visible in lighter colors. In darker toned stones, the flaws may not be as important a variable because they are masked by the depth of color.

The type and placement of flaws is a more important consideration than the presence of

FIGURE 7. Zones of Color in a Stone

Source: A. Matlins and A.C. Bonanno: *Jewelry and Gems: The Buying Guide*. South Woodstock, Vermont: GemStone Press, 1987, p. 97.

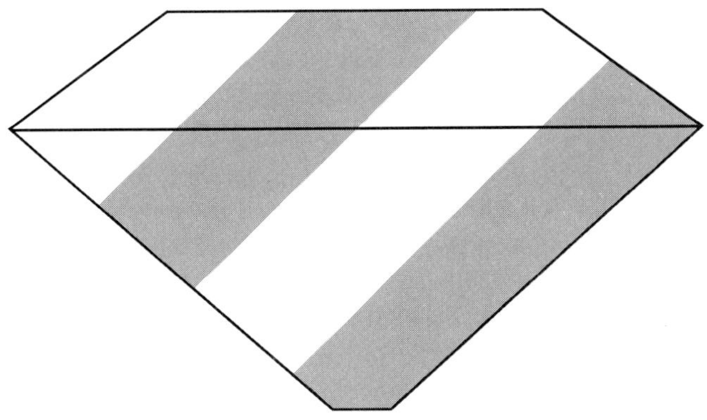

flaws in and of themselves. For example, a crack (called a feather) that breaks the surface of a stone can be dangerous because it weakens the stone's durability and breaks the light continuity; also, it may cause an iridescent effect that detracts from the stone's beauty and value.

If flaws weaken a colored stone's durability, affect color, or are easily noticeable, or are too numerous, they will significantly reduce the value. Yet, if a flaw is small and positioned unobtrusively, it will have minimal effect on its durability, beauty, and value. Certain types of flaws that are characteristic of specific gems and localities may detract very little from the value; in some cases, a particular flaw may provide positive identification of a stone's exact variety or origin and cause an increase in the per-carat value. A very fine colored gem that is flawless will bring a disproportionately high price per carat because it is so rare.

The Importance of Cut. The cut and proportion of colored stones are important for two reasons: They affect the depth of color of the stone and the liveliness projected by the stone.

Cut is an important criterion in determining value in colored stones. If a colored stone is of good-quality material, a good cut enhances its natural beauty to the fullest and allows it to exhibit its finest color and liveliness. If the same material is cut poorly, its natural beauty is lessened, causing it to look too dark, too light, or even "dead."

Obtaining Gems for Investment

What To Buy. If history goes on repeating itself, there will continue to be a good market for diamonds, rubies, sapphires, and emeralds. Natural (not cultured) pearls, jadeite, black opal, and alexandrite also offer good investment opportunities and should continue to do so as long as the Asian market remains strong.

Regardless of the type of gem being considered, investors should adhere to the following guidance:

Buy Only Gems That Are Natural and Unenhanced. Avoid gems that have been treated to conceal flaws or heated, dyed, or irradiated to enhance color.

Buy Only the Finest Gem Material. Top quality gems have always been in demand, even in economically difficult times. For diamonds, buy well-cut and well-proportioned stones of D/E/F color, FL/IF/VVS clarity, and more than 4 carats. For fancy colored diamonds, consider only natural colored stones accompanied by certificates verifying that the color is natural. Red diamonds are the rarest and most collectible, in any size from 0.5 carat up. Even if they have inclusions, if the color is truly red they are acceptable. Green diamonds are next to red in rarity, but the color must be very good for them to do well as an investment. Blue diamonds have an excellent track record, but those designated fancy blue, as opposed to fancy light blue, do best. The stronger the color—fancy intense blue—the less critical is the clarity; the lighter the color, the more critical a high clarity rating becomes. Fancy intense yellow diamonds, especially in FL/VVS clarity and more than 5 carats, have an excellent track record. Light yellows, browns, and blacks should be avoided.

For sapphire, the best track record has been with stones of Burma or Kashmir origin, which possess unusually fine color, clarity, brilliance, and size (ideally, more than 5 carats). Fine Ceylon sapphires, especially in sizes of more than 10 carats, make good investments as long as they are of exceptionally fine quality and show no indication of heating to enhance color.

For ruby, stones of more than 4 carats, of Burma origin, with unusually fine color, clarity, and brilliance are in greatest demand. However, exceptionally fine, unheated rubies from other locations, with fine Burma-like color, may also make good investments.

For emerald, the stones in greatest demand are those of Colombian origin, which possess unusually fine color, clarity, brilliance, and size (ideally, more than 5 carats). Exceptionally fine stones from other locations, with a Colombia-like color, may also make good investments.

Natural pearls, jadeite, alexandrite, and black opal require specialized skills to evaluate. When considering these gems, one must be sure to work with a specialist.

Buy Only Gems Accompanied by an Internationally Recognized Certificate. For diamonds, certificates from the GIA Gem Trade Laboratory are the most widely recognized. For colored gems, certificates from the AGL or from the GL are the most widely acknowledged. For investment purposes, the certificate should indicate the genuineness of the stone, the country of origin, and whether the color or clarity have been altered. If this information is not included, seek additional verification or obtain certification from a laboratory that will provide this information.

Where To Buy. Once a buyer has knowledge of what he or she wants to buy, the next problem is finding the best source from which to obtain the gem—a source through which one can buy at a price as close as possible to wholesale, or below. (See *Are You Buying at a Good Price?* later in this article.)

The Retail Jeweler. One source may be a retail jeweler who handles fine gems and jewelry. Some jewelers will work with a customer to obtain fine gems at a price significantly below retail. Because the cost of a very fine gem with investment potential is usually significantly above the cost of gems used in commercial jewelry, the jeweler may still be able to enjoy an attractive profit, even on a lower mark-up percentage. Of course, only by having knowledge of the wholesale price can one judge the price offered by the jeweler. Also, when buying from a jeweler be sure that the stone is accompanied by the proper certification from a recognized laboratory.

The Broker. Some brokerage firms are reliable; some are questionable. Usually brokers will charge a fee from both the seller and the buyer. Typically fees range from 15 to 30 percent. A broker does not own merchandise, make any promise about return on investment, or offer a buy-back guarantee.

The Auction House. Many fine diamonds, rubies, sapphires, and emeralds go up for auction from important estates and, with the exception of rare or unique pieces, frequently sell at less than current wholesale prices. The auction house also functions as a source for rare gems that may be difficult, if not impossible, to obtain today in the normal wholesale jewelry trade, for example, fine Burmese rubies, unusually large, very fine diamonds, or Kashmir sapphires.

At Christie's auction in New York City on October 10, 1988, a magnificent, rare bracelet containing seven Kashmir sapphires (weighing a total of more than 45 carats) and eight natural yellow diamonds sold for almost $1 million. Because such gems are no longer being mined, locating such stones is exceedingly difficult and time consuming.

On October 18, 1988, Sotheby's in New York City offered one of the finest, largest Burmese rubies (15.97 carats) known to exist. It brought more than $3.5 million. There was nothing comparable to such a stone in the wholesale market. At the same auction, a magnificent cabochon emerald and diamond bracelet of exceptionally rare quality was offered, bringing almost $2.5 million. Such gems are no longer being mined, and finding so many fine, matched Colombian emeralds through wholesale channels would be extremely difficult. If they could have been found, based on the cost of comparable single stones, the wholesale cost to produce the bracelet would have been close to $3 million.

Anyone can buy at auction. An interested buyer registers with the auction house and obtains a bidding paddle—a numbered paddle that is raised to place a bid. In addition to the bid at which one succeeds in obtaining an item, a 10 percent buyer's premium is paid to the house. Thus, the total price for a piece bought at auction is the highest bid plus 10 percent.

The major deterrent to bidding on gems at auction is, for most people, their lack of knowledge and their inability to ascertain genuineness and quality. The key to being successful is to work with someone not affiliated with the auction house to verify the genuineness and quality of the stones being offered and to determine current availability of similar stones and current wholesale and retail value for comparison.

One must be on guard against relying on certificates accompanying stones at auction, because such reports often omit information pertaining to quality or neglect to indicate whether the stone has been treated to conceal flaws or enhance color.

A Private Party. One can learn of items available from private sources through local jewelry appraisers. Having provided an appraisal, they are frequently contacted when a client decides to sell any of the appraised pieces. The appraiser may also arrange for the parties to meet and safely view pieces that are offered for sale.

Buying from a private party can be profitable, but it can also involve serious risk. Dealing with a private party requires the utmost caution on the part of both buyer and seller. No matter what the source, the investor should be sure to have any gem under consideration fully examined by a qualified gemologist or gemologist-appraiser. No purchase should be made based on trust. Erroneous descriptions and documentation often accompany family heirlooms.

Are You Buying at a Good Price? Several fairly reliable monthly publications make wholesale price information available to the trade. These price indexes are listed at the end of this article. Serious gem investors should try to obtain access to at least one of these publications, by contacting the publisher directly or through a jeweler, consultant, or dealer.

A Gem-Buying Consultant. Increasingly, investors are seeking skilled gem experts to consult with them and assist them with their gem searches. Ideally, consultants should not be gem dealers or traders themselves, or be affiliated in any way with the company or auction house from which the purchase might be made. The consultant should be a highly trained professional who knows and understands gems, and who also understands current market value, demand, and availability of the gem under consideration. See the opening paragraphs under *Important Factors in Buying and Selling,* earlier in this article, for advice on locating a gem consultant.

Resale Considerations

The better the price at which one acquires a gem for investment, the easier it will be to sell. Nonetheless, the selling process can take months, even years. Depending on the price paid and the rate of appreciation, the sources suggested for buying may offer a means through which to dispose of your gems at a profit.

If you made a purchase at auction, at a price substantially less than wholesale, you may find an interested buyer in your jeweler. In tracking auction prices for comparables, you may find that the auction house is a viable means for disposing of your investment. If you made your purchase through a broker, you may be able to sell through the broker. And, if you exercise caution, you may be able to sell to a private collector; a gem consultant or gemologist-appraiser may be of assistance in locating an interested party.

Pricing Gemstones

Colored Gemstones. It is difficult to define prices for colored gems because a slight difference in hue or clarity, often not discernable without side-by-side comparison, can dramatically affect the price. Although experience can help develop the eye to spot fine color, clarity, and brilliance, where possible try to compare stones side by side, in the same light, before making a final decision.

Another important factor that makes pricing difficult is size. A gem of rare quality and unusually large size can often dictate its own price, namely, whatever the market will bear at the time.

Nonetheless, the rise in overall prices for fine colored stones over the past ten years has been dramatic, despite the decline in the early 1980s. However, past increases in price do not guarantee future increases. To yield profit as an investment, stones usually need to be held for at least five years.

Rubies. On November 10, 1977, a superb, lively, gem-quality 7+-carat ruby, accompanied by a Gubelin report stating it was Burmese, sold for $40,000 per carat. In April 1986, at Sotheby's in New York City, a 15+-carat ruby, accompanied by a Gubelin report stating it was Burmese, sold for $110,000 per carat. In October 1988, a 15.97-carat ruby, possibly the finest of its size anywhere in the world, also accompanied by a report stating it was Burmese, sold for almost $220,000 per carat.

Sapphires. In April 1978, a superb Kashmir cabochon sapphire, cut in the old-fashioned, pointed sugarloaf style, sold for $15,000 per carat. In April 1981, a 9.5-carat gem Kashmir sapphire brought $30,000 per carat at Sotheby Parke Bernet in New York City. In April 1987, a very fine 41+-carat sapphire, accompanied by a Gubelin report stating that it was Burmese, brought only $23,600 per carat at a Sotheby's auction in New York City; in October 1988, a very fine 32.77-carat Kashmir sapphire brought only $18,500 per carat at a Sotheby's auction in New York. Although prices for other gems were skyrocketing in 1985 to 1988, sapphires seemed to be less popular. This situation may well change as prohibitive prices for other gems force attention onto sapphires.

Emeralds. In 1968 in New York City, a beautiful 34-carat emerald sold for $6,000 per carat. In 1972, the same stone sold for $10,000 per carat. In 1987, at a Christie's sale in New York, a 5+-carat stone of exceptionally rare quality sold for $80,000 per carat. In October 1988, at Sotheby's in New York, an 11+-carat stone of exceptionally fine quality sold for more than $48,500 per carat.

Diamonds. Diamond prices are much easier to evaluate because of the standardization in grading that is now almost universally applied. On the establishment of precise diamond-grading systems, fairly precise pricing guidelines followed.

Table 1 gives a history of wholesale prices for round brilliant-cut D/Flawless diamonds.

However, it is important to understand the relationship of the four C's to price. Tables 2 and 3, showing retail diamond prices, demonstrate the effect of differences in color, clarity, and size on price.

Methods of Sale

As a general rule, if you offer gems to a jeweler, he will offer a price somewhere between one half to one third of the current wholesale price, depending on quality and availability of comparable merchandise through the trade. A jeweler can usually obtain anything he needs on memo without tying up any cash, so the incentive to buy for cash is usually a price that is substantially below the wholesale cost.

By selling through a broker, one can usually do better than by selling directly to a jeweler. Although often an unpredictable amount of waiting time is involved, one can expect eventually to obtain a price 10 to 20 percent less than wholesale.

TABLE 1. History of Wholesale Prices for Diamond

Year	Weight in Carats	Value per Carat	Total for Diamond
1970	3	$ 4,000	$ 12,000
1974	3	11,000	33,000
1978	3	18,000	54,000
1981	3	55,000	165,000
1982	3	21,000	63,000
1988	3	40,000	120,000
1970	1	1,500	1,500
1974	1	5,000	5,000
1978	1	10,000	10,000
1981	1	35,000	35,000
1982	1	18,000	18,000
1988	1	20,000	20,000

Note: These prices are for internally and externally flawless diamonds of D color, in a round brilliant cut diamond.

Source: Author's data

TABLE 2. Effect of Color and Flaw Grade on Retail Diamond Pricing: 1-Carat Round Brilliant (1.00+)*

	Flaw (Clarity) Grade†							
Grade Color	IF	VVS_1	VVS_2	VS_1	VS_2	SI_1	SI_2	I_1
D	$32,000	$20,000	$16,000	$11,600	$10,400	$8,400	$7,500	$5,300
E	20,000	16,000	13,000	10,400	9,400	7,600	7,000	4,900
F	16,000	13,000	11,000	9,400	8,400	7,500	6,600	4,600
G	13,600	11,000	9,400	8,400	7,400	7,000	6,200	4,400
H	11,600	9,400	8,400	7,400	7,000	6,700	5,900	4,300
I	8,400	8,000	7,700	7,000	6,600	6,200	5,500	4,200
J	7,700	7,200	6,800	6,200	5,900	5,700	5,100	4,000
K	6,400	6,000	5,700	5,500	5,300	5,100	4,900	3,800

*Dollar prices quoted are per carat (using GIA scale for comparison).
†These grade designations are defined earlier in this article under Flaw Classification.

Note: Observe both the tremendous price fluctuation among stones of the same size owing to differences in the flaw grades and color grades and the disproportionate jumps in cost per carat, depending on size.

Source: Author's data, 1989

Through selling privately—a process that can take months or even years—a price close to wholesale may be obtained, or even 15 to 30 percent more than wholesale. Unfortunately, most private sales involve very expensive, rare, unusual pieces, which might take an investor a very long time to sell.

At auction, prices tend to be about half of wholesale, except for very unusual or rare items. In addition, the seller must pay a 10 percent seller's fee to the auction house. Thus, selling at auction is usually profitable only for very unusual or rare items. When considering selling at auction, the investor should try to identify comparables sold at recent auctions and track prices brought. Also, auction houses will usually estimate what the gem will bring. Auctions may also provide one of the fastest means of disposal, and, by stipulating a reserve below which the item cannot be sold, some measure of safety against a major loss.

One Last Word

For insurance purposes, as well as for deriving the greatest pleasure from gem investment, it is recommended that investment stones be set in jewelry. The mounting should not account for more than 10 percent of the value of the entire piece, including the price of the gems. Many insurance companies will insure only jewelry, not unmounted gemstones. Jewelry can be insured under a floater policy. Additional coverage, attached to your normal insurance coverage, insures each jewelry item separately. Each piece requires an appraisal.

TABLE 2. Effect of Color and Flaw Grade on Retail Diamond Pricing: 1-Carat Round Brilliant (1.00+)*

	Flaw (Clarity) Grade†							
Grade Color	IF	VVS_1	VVS_2	VS_1	VS_2	SI_1	SI_2	I_1
D	$39,000	$26,000	$22,400	$16,800	$14,000	$11,800	$9,400	$6,800
E	27,000	22,000	19,400	15,800	13,400	11,400	9,000	6,400
F	23,000	19,000	16,400	14,400	12,800	10,800	8,600	6,000
G	20,000	16,400	14,400	13,400	11,400	9,600	8,200	5,600
H	17,000	14,400	13,400	11,400	10,400	8,800	7,600	5,400
I	12,000	10,400	10,000	9,400	8,400	7,600	6,800	5,200
J	10,000	9,400	9,000	8,200	7,600	6,800	6,200	4,800
K	9,000	8,000	7,600	7,200	6,800	6,000	5,600	4,400

*Dollar prices quoted are per carat (using GIA scale for comparison).
†These grade designations are defined earlier in this article under Flaw Classification.

Note: Observe both the tremendous price fluctuation among stones of the same size owing to differences in the flaw grades and color grades and the disproportionate jumps in cost per carat, depending on size.

Source: Author's data, 1989

Gemstones can make a sensible investment choice, but gem investment should be undertaken only by people who are determined to learn about the gem market, who can make a substantial, long-term financial commitment, and who will find a qualified gem expert with whom to work.

GLOSSARY

AGL—American Gemological Laboratory, a New York-based laboratory specializing in colored gemstone testing, detection of treatments, and providing internationally recognized grading reports, which frequently accompany pieces offered at auction by such houses as Christie's and Sotheby's.

brilliance—The reflection of light back to the eye; the liveliness or sparkle of a stone.

cabochon—A cutting style that produces a stone with a smooth surface rather than a faceted surface.

carat—A unit of weight (one fifth of a gram) for gemstones.

CG or CGA—Certified Gemologist or Certified Gemologist Appraiser, a prestigious title awarded to gemologists in the United States by the American Gem Society.

clarity—A stone's freedom from inclusions; sometimes called the flaw picture.

comparable—Term used to indicate that a gem or piece of jewelry compares well to another in its overall quality—color, clarity, make and size.

corundum—The mineral aluminum oxide, also known as ruby and sapphire; red corundum is ruby; all other shades (blue, green, yellow, pink and colorless) are called sapphire.

crown—The top portion of any faceted stone; the part above the girdle.

culet—A tiny flat facet that runs parallel to the girdle and is located at the very tip of the pavilion of a faceted stone; it is so small that to most people it looks like a point.

DeBeers syndicate—The so-called diamond syndicate; the organization that controls diamond prices.

diamond—Carbon arranged with a particular atomic structure; the hardest natural substance.

dispersion—The splitting of white light into various colors; the fire, or flashes of color, observed while turning certain stones in the light; diamond is known for its high dispersion.

doublet—An assembled stone, created by man by fusing or cementing two pieces of material together (doublet); when three pieces are used, it is called a triplet.

emerald—The green and most highly valued variety of the mineral beryl; the blue variety of beryl is known as aquamarine and the golden yellow variety is called golden beryl.

faceted—A cutting style that places small faces around a transparent stone at precise angles, to affect the way light travels through the stone.

fancy—A colored diamond or unusual cut or cutting style.

feather—A crack or fracture.

FGA—Prestigious gemological title meaning Fellow of the Gemmological Association of Great Britain (gemmological, in this case, uses the British spelling, with a double "m").

fire—The variety and intensity of rainbow colors seen in a gem; another word for dispersion.

fluorescence—A property found in some diamonds and colored gems that enables them, when viewed under ultraviolet light, to produce a color not seen by the naked eye in normal light.

GG—Graduate Gemologist, the highest gemological title given by the GIA.

GIA—Gemological Institute of America; operates the Gem Trade Laboratory (New York and Santa Monica), which issues reports on diamonds, colored gems, and pearls, often accompanying pieces auctioned at Christie's and Sotheby's.

girdle—The edge of the stone that forms its perimeter; the point (border) at which the top portion of the stone meets the bottom portion; its dividing line, the portion usually grasped by the setting.

ideal-cut—A term applied to round, brilliant-cut diamonds that conform to one of several strict standards of proportioning.

inclusion—Something included inside the gemstone, such as an irregularity in the crystal structure, a break or crack, a little cavity filled with liquid or gas, or crystals of other minerals.

iridescense—A rainbow-like effect that occurs when light hits a fracture (crack) in a stone, especially noticeable when the crack breaks through the surface.

lasered diamond—A diamond that has been bombarded with laser beams to remove visible flaws, making the stone more aesthetically desirable; lasered diamonds should sell for much less than other diamonds.

luster—The reflection of light from the surface of a stone; poor luster reduces beauty and value.

make—A term applied in the trade to the cutting and proportioning of a stone; a stone with a poor make is not a well-cut and proportioned stone; a stone with an ideal make has been cut to ideal proportions.

melee—A term used in the trade when referring to small stones, usually less than one-quarter carat.

Master Gemologist Appraiser (MGA)—The highest title awarded to gemologist-appraisers of the American Society of Appraisers and Accredited Gemologists Association.

pavilion—The bottom portion of a stone, that below the girdle.

rough—Uncut gem material.

ruby—Corundum that is red.

sapphire—Corundum that is blue or any color other than red.

silk—Inclusions of the mineral rutile, interwoven so as to resemble silk; trade term used for rutile arranged in a crisscross pattern, as seen in ruby.

spinel—A gem, often red or blue, that can resemble ruby and sapphire.

synthetic stone—Manmade stone that, unlike a cheap imitation, has essentially the same physical, chemical and optical properties of the genuine stone it is trying to imitate. New synthetic materials can easily be mistaken for genuine stones.

table—The horizontal flat surface at the center of the top of a facet stone.

translucent—Transmitting light imperfectly so that one cannot see through the material clearly; although translucent material is normally not of investment quality, exceptions may include the fine star ruby, star sapphire, and fine, precious cat's-eye.

treated stone—A stone that has been dyed, stained, heated or irradiated to enhance color as with heated sapphire or irradiated fancy-color diamonds.

zoned—A term that refers to *uneven* distribution of color, usually occurring in parallel planes; often present in sapphire and ruby; can significantly reduce beauty and value.

GEM LABORATORIES

These laboratories provide internationally recognized reports on genuineness and quality, often accompanying gem/jewelry pieces.

American Gemological Laboratory, 580 Fifth Ave., 12th floor,, New York, N.Y. 10036 (Services available to the jewelry trade and to the public)

Colored Diamond Laboratory Services, Inc., 15 West 47th St., New York, N.Y. 10036 (Issuing reports on colored diamonds only)

Gemmological Laboratory Gubelin, Denkmalstrasse, 2, Ch-6006 Lucerne, Switzerland (Only to the jewelry trade)

GIA Gem Trade Laboratory, Gemological Institute of America, 580 Fifth Ave., New York, N.Y. 10036 (Only to the jewelry trade)

GIA Gem Trade Laboratory, Gemological Institute of America, 1660 Stewart St., Santa Monica, Cal. 90404 (Only to the jewelry trade)

These accredited labs and gemologist appraisers are listed with the U.S. Accredited Gemologists Association. An asterisk indicates that an MGA is on staff.

*American Gemological Laboratory, 580 Fifth Ave., New York, N.Y. 10036
(212) 704-0727
C. R. Beesley, MGA

Antique Appraisal Service, P.O. Box 27903, Houston, Tex. 77227,
(713) 665-8245

*Balzans Gemological Laboratory, 915 Lootens Place, San Rafael, Cal. 94901
(415) 454-8553
Courtney Balzan, MGA

*B.J. Caldwell Appraisers, 7225 North Oracle Rd., Tucson, Ariz. 85704
(602) 742-3687
B. J. Caldwell, MGA

Brewsters, 6052 Magnolia Ave., Riverside, Cal. 92506
(714) 686-1979

*Colonial Jewelers, 9 West Patrick St., Frederick, Md. 21701
(301) 663-9252
Jeffrey Hurwitz, MGA

*D. Atlas & Co., Inc., 732 Sansom St., Philadelphia, Pa. 19106
(800) 441-1312
David Atlas, MGA

*Dick Bennion Jewelers, 59 South Main St., Salt Lake City, Utah 84111
(801) 364-3667
Robert Rosenblatt, MGA

*European Gemological Laboratory, 608 S. Hill St., Suite 1013, Los Angeles, Cal. 90014
(213) 623-8092
Thomas Tashey, MGA

*Fauquier Gemological Laboratory, P.O. Box 525, Main St., Marshall, Va. 22115
(703) 364-1959

Frank Gooden Co., Inc. Gemlab, 1110 Grand Ave., Kansas City, Mo. 64106
(816) 421-0281

Gem Profiles, 416 West Santa Ana, Fresno, Cal. 93705
(209) 229-7361

*Gemological Appraisal Assocs., Inc., 666 Washington Rd., Pittsburgh, Pa. 15228
(412) 344-5500
Donald Palmieri, MGA

Jaylyn Gemologists Goldsmiths, 30 S.E. 4th St., Boca Raton, Fl. 33432
(305) 391-0013

Joseph W. Tenhagen Gemstones, Inc., 36 NE First St., Suite 419, Miami, Fl. 33132
(305) 374-2411
Joseph Tenhagen, MGA

International Gem Trade Lab, 650 S. Hill St., No. 229, Los Angeles, Cal. 90014
(213) 688-7837

*Lourdes Gemological Laboratory, Rt. 6 & Hill Blvd., Jefferson Valley, N.Y. 10535
(914) 245-4676
Howard Biffer, MGA

*Mackley & Co., Inc., 8906 Kingston Pike, Suite 214, Knoxville, Tenn. 37923
(615) 693-3097
Joseph Mackley, MGA

*National Gem Appraising Laboratory, 8600 Fenton St., Silver Spring, Md. 20910
(301) 588-7770
Antonio Bonanno, MGA; Karen Ford, MGA

*NC Gem Lab, 107 Hunter's Ridge Rd., Chapel Hill, N.C. 27514
(919) 966-2227
William Benedict, MGA

*Neil Cohen, Gemologist, 99 Pratt St., Hartford, Conn. 06103
(203) 247-1319
Neil Cohen, MGA

*San Diego Gemological Laboratory, 3957 Goldfinch St., San Diego, Cal. 92103
(619) 291-8852
Thomas Underwood, MGA

*Spectrum Gems, 1615 South Foothill Drive, Salt Lake City, Utah 84108
(801) 581-9900
Dana Richardson, MGA

Suncoast Accredited Gemological Laboratory, Bayshore Office Bldg., 6221 14th St. West, Suite 105, Bradenton, Fla. 34207
(813) 756-8787

The Gem Lab, 20776 St. George Court, Bend, Or. 97702
(503) 389-6790

United States Gemological Services, 14801 Yorba St. No. 237, Tustin, Cal. 92680
(714) 838-8747

SUGGESTED READING

POPULAR MAGAZINES AND GEMOLOGICAL STUDIES

Gems & Gemology. Published by the Gemological Institute of America, Santa Monica, Cal.

Jewelers' Circular-Keystone. Published by Chilton, Radnor, Pa.

Journal of Gemmology. Published by the Gemmological Association of Great Britain, London.

Lapidary Journal. Published by Lapidary Journal, Inc., San Diego, Cal.

Modern Jeweler. Published by Vance Publishing, Lincolnshire, Ill.

National Jeweler. Published by Gralla, N.Y.

PRICE INDEXES

The Diamond Registry, 30 West 47th Street, New York, N.Y. 10036;
(212) 575-0444

Gemstone Price Reports, UBIGE SPRL, 26/08 Avenue General de Gaulle, B-1050 Brussels, Belgium

The Guide. Gemworld International, Inc., 5 South Wabash Avenue, Chicago, Ill. 60602
(312) 263-3342

Michelson Gemstone Index, 1401 South Dixie Highway East, Pompano Beach, Fla. 33060
(305) 785-9018

Precious Stones Market Monitor, 666 Washington Road, Pittsburgh, Pa. 15228
(412) 344-5500

Rapaport's Diamond Report, 15 West 47th Street, New York, N.Y.:
(212) 354-0575

REFERENCE BOOKS

Anderson, B.W., *Gem Testing*. London: Butterworth, Ltd., 1971.

Arem, Joel E. *Color Encyclopedia of Gemstones*. New York: Van Nostrand, Reinhold, 1977.

Bank, Hermann. *Precious Stones and Minerals*. New York: F. Warne, 1970.

Bauer, M. *Precious Stones*. Trans. by L.J. Spencer. Rutland, Vt.: C.E. Tuttle Co., 1971.

Bruton, E. *Diamonds*, 2nd ed. London: Northwood, 1977.

Geological Museum. *A Guide to the Collection of Gemstones*. London: Her Majesty's Stationery Office, 1950.

Gubelin, E.J. *The Internal World of Gemstones*. Zurich: ABC Edition, 1974.

______, and Koivula, J.I. *Photoatlas of Inclusions in Gemstones*. Zurich: ABC Edition, 1986.

Liddicoat, R.T., Jr. *Handbook of Gem Identification*. Los Angeles: Gemological Institute of America, 1986.

Matlins, A., and Bonanno, A. *Gem Identification Made Easy*. S. Woodstock, Vt.: Gemstone Press, 1989.

______, *Jewelry & Gems: The Buying Guide*, S. Woodstock, Vt.: Gemstone Press, 1988.

Moyersoen, J.S. *Investing in Diamonds*. New York: Wolf Publications, 1980.

Pough, F. *The Story of Gems and Semiprecious Stones*. New York: Harvey House, 1969.

Shipley, R.M. *Dictionary of Gems and Gemology*. Los Angeles: Gemological Institute of America, 1951.

Sinkankas, J. *Emeralds & Other Beryls*. Philadelphia: Chilton & Co., 1982.

Webster, R. *Gem Identification*. New York: Sterling Publishing, 1975.

______. *Gems*. London: Butterworth & Co., 1970.

______. *Practical Gemology*, 6th Ed. London: Northwood, 1976.

Zucker, B. *Gems and Jewels: A Connoisseur's Guide*. New York: Thames and Hudson, Inc., 1984.

______. *How to Buy and Sell Gems: Everyone's Guide to Rubies, Sapphires, Emeralds and Diamonds*. New York: Times Books, 1979.

MUSEUM COLLECTION STUDIES

Desautels, P. *Gems in the Smithsonian Museum*. Washington, D.C.: Smithsonian Institution Press, 1972.

Holmes, M. *The Crown Jewels*. London: Her Majesty's Stationery Office, 1955.

Meen, V.B., and Tushingham, A.D. *The Crown Jewels of Iran*. Toronto: University of Toronto, 1968.

HORSES

James M. D. Maloney

BASIC CHARACTERISTICS

Horses are big business. According to a 1987 report by the American Horse Council, there are 5.25 million registered horses in the United States, and the horse industry accounts for $15.2 billion per year.[1]

Forms of Ownership

Investment in horses can take many forms. Sole ownership, general partnerships, limited partnerships, public and private stock companies, and stallion syndications are now common, as horse investments become more popular.

Breeds

Other than unregistered riding horses and workhorses, horses fall into two categories, race breeds and show breeds (see Figure 1). Racehorses include quarter horses, thoroughbreds, and standardbreds (trotters and racers). Show breeds include Arabians, Morgans, saddlebreds, quarter horses, and a number of less well-known breeds.

---

[1] The Economic Impact of the U.S. Horse Industry, American Horse Council 1987 by the policy economics group of Peat, Marwick, Mitchell & Co.

James M.D. Maloney is Executive Vice-President of Arabians Ltd., Inc., China Spring, Texas. He is a well-known consultant and lecturer on successful equine investing.

FIGURE 1. Categories of Horses

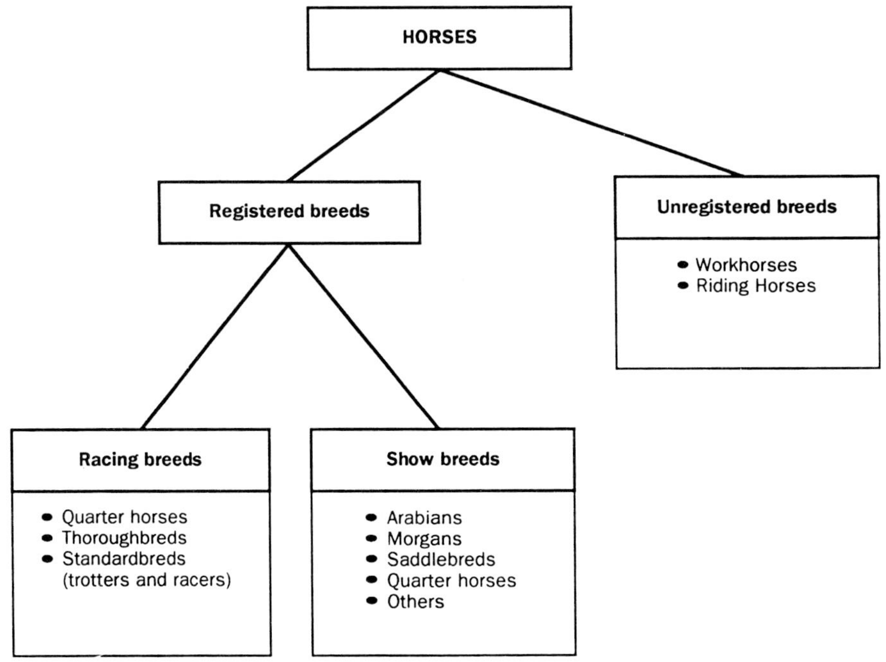

Roles With Horses

Regardless of the horse's breed, a person is involved with horses in one of two roles: as a user or as a producer (breeder). Most horse owners are users involved in riding, racing, or showing.

Users are involved primarily for sport and recreation. Most horse users do not make a profit. Production (breeding) has traditionally been the most profitable part of the horse business.

Users. Approaching horse investments as a user involves high risk. In spite of highly publicized purses for races, each year fewer than 10 percent of thoroughbred race horses pay their way on the track. In 1987, the average thoroughbred yearling cost $35,441; in the same year, the average earnings per horse was $7,871.[2] Show breeds also earn low purses in relation to the capital costs of horses and training expenses.

Yet, many horse operations are highly profitable. With few exceptions, the profitable horse investor is the producer (breeder), not the user.

Producers. The producer is the breeder or manufacturer, supplying products (horses) to users. Cash flow is more predictable for the breeder than for the user; it is not dependent on a highly competitive race or show. Breeders supply horses to users involved in many

---

[2] *The Blood-Horse*, Feb. 27, 1988.

different aspects of the horse industry. Therefore, the breeding business is more stable and less dependent on conditions in one isolated segment of the business. "The chief advantage of an equine investment . . . is that new aspects of value are created . . . the real money is made in the breeding shed."[3]

Male or Female

Stallions (mature males) provide the glamour and glitter for an emotional horse community. Males are certainly necessary for a breeding program. However, with staggering promotional costs and the use of artificial insemination, very few stallions are needed. Only colts (young males) of impeccable quality have high value. Most other colts end up gelded and are used as riding horses. Because of their popularity, the top stallions pass both market demand and high prices on to their foals (offspring of either sex).

Mares (mature females), however, are the true economic backbone of the breeding business. They are the "factories," making their owners the "manufacturers" of the horse business. From three years of age until well into their twenties, mares produce a foal every eleven months.

Top females bred to top stallions produce foals that are sold for profit or retained to build equity. Ownership of females is the most conservative and consistently profitable approach to horses as a business.

Age

Investors planning to become breeders often purchase fillies (young female horses) as yearlings. Fillies appreciate significantly between birth and age 3, when they are ready to produce cash flow. By purchasing at yearling age, the investor can purchase top quality stock at reasonable prices and become the recipient of this appreciation. Often, broodmares (mature females used for breeding) of exceptional quality are either not offered for sale or are extremely expensive.

Quality

Of all the principles offered to the horse investor, the most lasting and important one continues to be: Start with top quality. Throughout history, the highest quality horses have always been the most profitable. Top quality can be defined as the top 5 to 10 percent of any breed at any time. See *Important Factors in Buying and Selling*, later in this article, for a discussion of how to determine quality.

Breeding only top quality will result in higher prices when foals are sold. An age-old adage in the horse business is that it costs the same to feed low-quality and high-quality horses. The difference becomes apparent when offspring are sent to market, and the price levels of offspring ultimately determine success or failure.

Breeding Racehorses

Thoroughbreds are the elite among racing breeds. Each year, the highest quality thoroughbred yearlings are sold at the Keeneland Summer Sale in Lexington, Kentucky. In 1988, yearlings at Keeneland averaged almost $360,000, with fillies averaging more than $310,000.

---

[3] *National Law Journal*, Dec. 22, 1987.

Costs for breeding to the top thoroughbred stallions fall in the $100,000 to $250,000 range. Thoroughbred fillies typically sell for two-and-a-half to three times the stud fee. This ratio, coupled with the high cost of females, has historically made most racing breeds less profitable than certain show breeds.

Breeding Show Horses

Breeding high quality show horses has been profitable for three reasons:

1. *Lower capital costs:* Investors can start at the highest quality levels for a fraction of the cost of top-quality racehorses.
2. *Higher Return:* Yearling show fillies often sell for 8 to 10 times their stud fees, as opposed to 2.5 to 3 times in racing.
3. *Less risk:* Racehorses are single-purpose horses. Show horses are more versatile, multipurpose horses. Thus, there are multiple markets for top-quality show breeds.

Not all show breeds, however, can be considered profitable investment horses. Some are simply hobby or pleasure horses. It is important to understand the difference.

- Investment horses: Yearlings consistently sell for more than their production costs.
- Hobby/pleasure horses: Yearlings usually sell for less than their production costs.

Which Breed of Show Horse. Of all major show breeds, Arabians have had the greatest investment potential since the early 1970s. There are three reasons:

1. Arabians have the highest value of any major show breed; they sell for the highest prices.
2. Since the early 1970s, Arabians have been the fastest growing of any major breed.
3. Arabians are the most versatile breed; as such, they appeal to more markets.

Over the past ten years, a small, elite group called Egyptian Arabians have been the best investment among Arabian horses, for four reasons:

1. Highest value among all strains of Arabians
2. Consistency of value
3. Scarcity
4. A market supported by a well-funded breeder's organization (the Pyramid Society)

"Arabians because of their scarcity are the 'blue chip stocks' of the horse market. Of all the Arabians the handful of Egyptian Arabians offers the greatest profit potential."[4]

Compared to breeding racehorses, breeding Arabian show horses is more affordable. Each year in Lexington, Kentucky the Pyramid Society hosts the highest quality sale of

---

[4] *Texas Business*, Nov. 1984.

Egyptian yearlings. At this sale, in 1988, yearling fillies averaged $61,000. The price of the average Egyptian yearling filly in 1987 was more than four times the average price of a yearling filly of all Arabian strains.[5] With stud fees to the top Egyptian stallions in the $5,000 to $8,000 range, yearling fillies sell for 8 to 10 times the stud fee as opposed to racing fillies that may sell for only 2.5 to 3 times the stud fee.

Polish Arabian horses also command high prices in relation to other Arabians, although not as high as Egyptians. One reason is that Polish horses are not as scarce as Egyptian yearlings. The prices of Polish Arabians are less stable and have lately fluctuated widely, based on market and economic conditions.

History of Arabian Horses. All Arabian horses have pedigrees that can be traced back hundreds of years to the Arabian Peninsula. These desert war-horses were exported to Russia, Spain, Poland, England, and, in the late nineteenth century, the United States. However, prior to any of these early exportations, the very best Arabian horses (a group of 1100) were exported to Egypt by Mohammed Ali the Great, who conquered the entire Arabian Peninsula in 1840.

Arabian horses that can be directly traced to this original group of 1100 are termed "straight," or "pure," Egyptian Arabians. Today, there are about 300,000 purebred Arabian horses of all bloodlines in North America. Of these, only about 4,000 (1.3 percent) are straight Egyptians.

Superior show records, highly refined pedigrees, and extreme scarcity cause Egyptian Arabians to be sought after worldwide to upgrade the quality of other, less refined Arabians. Since the turn of the century, Egyptians have demanded a premium in the marketplace.

Showing and Competing. The biggest advantage of the breeding business is that top-quality females do not have to compete in any way to establish their value, which is determined by the quality of their pedigrees. Although they are sometimes shown as fillies, their entire mature life can be devoted to foal production and cash flow.

Stallions, on the other hand, must be winners of major events in order to pass on market demand and enhance the price of their offspring.

A Success Formula

To be a successful horse investor, focus on these elements:

- Consider only top quality, the top 5 to 10 percent of the highest quality strains.
- Concentrate on specialized bloodlines, such as pure Egyptian Arabians.
- Stay in the breeding business and out of the performance, racing, or showing part of the horse world, where a high-risk contest determines your future.
- Invest in females only; leave the high risk and high cost of breeding and promoting those few superstar stallions to full-time professionals.
- Breed only to the best stallions; choose one of the handful of prominent winners that best compliments your mare.

---

[5] *The Arabian Horse Digest*, Santa Monica, Cal.

ATTRACTIVE FEATURES

The increasing popularity of horse breeding as an investment results from three of its attractive features:

1. Profit potential
2. Favorable tax treatment
3. Enjoyment/involvement

Profit Potential

Historically, breeding and selling high-quality horses has been a highly profitable business. Breeders produce foals to keep or sell. Foals that are retained become additional "factories" and build herd equity. Regardless of quality, overhead is relatively constant. Therefore, high-quality offspring that command high prices generate the profits in the breeding business.

Tax Treatment

Horse breeding remains one of the few tax shelters that survived the 1986 Tax Reform Act. Horse breeders continue to use depreciation and expense deductions to offset taxes on active income. The most attractive features are short depreciation schedules (three and seven years) and write-offs of all associated expenses (see *Tax Consequences*, later in this article).

Enjoyment and Involvement

Enjoyment and involvement are also compelling reasons for the popularity of horse investments. With pedigrees tracing to the 1700s, Arabian horses are often described as "living works of art." For those with an affinity for horses, they provide tremendous pride of ownership.

For centuries, Arabian horses were bred for intelligence and people-oriented dispositions. As a result, they are more adaptable to the neophyte. In a short time, a newcomer can become relatively expert at handling and training Arabians, as compared to other breeds.

Broodmares (mature females used for breeding) are often ridden as family horses. Even though many are in foal (pregnant) eleven months of the year, they can be ridden during most of their pregnancy.

The International Arabian Horse Association conducts local and regional shows throughout the United States. Louisville, Kentucky and Albuquerque, New Mexico host the National Championships on alternating years. Many amateur shows are also held where nonprofessional owners show their own horses in a variety of classes.

Most investors do not own farms. Mare care farms in every part of the country provide excellent care of broodmares at reasonable rates.

POTENTIAL RISKS

Downside risks of horse breeding include death of the animal(s), low quality foals, health problems, infertility, and adverse market conditions.

Horse breeders commonly insure against death by natural causes, humane destruction, and even theft. Many reputable insurance carriers provide complete coverage for 3 to 4 percent per year of insured value.

Low-quality foals are a potential risk. Successful horse breeders reduce that risk by starting with high-quality females and breeding them to the top stallions. It is a common mistake among newcomers to purchase a marginal mare and breed her to a top stallion with the thought of producing a highly marketable foal.

Health problems pose risks and can be expensive. Horses are hardy animals. Most health problems can be reduced, and many can be avoided, by proper veterinary care of the mare and her foals. Choose a mare care facility that has an outstanding health record. Be sure it has an adequate staff and a good feeding and care program. If you keep your own horses, educate yourself and enlist the continuing services of a veterinarian who specializes in horses.

Most fertility problems can be avoided before a purchase is made. This is accomplished in three ways: (1) arrange a careful examination of health records and physical examination of the mare; (2) purchase a female whose pedigree clearly demonstrates a family of females void of fertility problems; and (3) buy from a reputable, financially stable farm or agency.

Two principles help breeders to weather market fluctuations:

1. *Stay with only the highest quality*. Breeders who produce the best usually find a buyer willing to pay a good price, even when those down the quality ladder may be suffering.

2. *Be patient*. Horses should be considered long-term investments. Those unable, or unwilling, to be patient until a down market recovers should not consider equine holdings.

TAX CONSEQUENCES[6]

Horse farming received favorable treatment under the 1986 Tax Reform Act. *Newsweek* calls horse breeding "one of the ten hottest tax shelters/direct investments."[7]

With proper structure and documentation, horse investments can be treated as a business, not a hobby; associated expenses and depreciation can be written off against active income from other sources. For many breeders, one-to-one tax write-offs are not uncommon.

Hobby or Business

The Internal Revenue Service (IRS) states that losses generated by an activity cannot be deducted unless that activity is "engaged in for a profit."

If horse activities generate a profit in two of seven specific years, then the IRS presumes the activity to be a business. Note that with other businesses, the IRS applies a two-of-five-year rule. However, a lack of profit does not necessarily create a hobby presumption with horses.

Disguising a hobby as a business is risky. However, a profit-motivated horse-breeding

[6] The author wishes to thank Gay Calabro of Calabro & Assoc., CPA firm, Dallas, Tex., for their assistance with this section.

[7] *Newsweek*, "Looking for Shelter?" Aug. 25, 1986.

business with good documentation should be deemed a business, not a hobby, even if scrutinized by the IRS.

Active or Passive Participation

Owning horses is one of the few remaining ways to reduce taxes on active income from your job or business. To use deductions actively, participation on a regular, continuous, and substantial basis is necessary.

To satisfy this definition, the IRS says a person must satisfy at least one of the following tests:

- Participate more than 500 hours per year.
- Spend 100 hours per year as long as your participation is not less than any other individual involved.
- Devote 500 or more total hours to several activities but not less than 100 hours to any one activity.
- Participate on a regular, continuous, and substantial basis during the year, and spend at least 100 hours on the activity.

Eight hours and twenty minutes per month (100 hours per year) is a reasonable amount of time to devote to an investment with the potential of substantial return. The IRS even allows time spent by a spouse, whether or not the spouse is an owner and whether or not you file a joint return.

Depreciation

Horses may be depreciated over a short term (three or seven years). Investors use accelerated depreciation (150 percent declining balance), guided by the Modified Accelerated Cost Recovery System (MACRS) drafted by the IRS.

A three-year schedule is used for racehorses over two years old and all horses over the age of twelve. All other horses are depreciated on a seven-year schedule. On a seven-year schedule, approximately 70 percent of the purchase price can be written off in the first sixty months of ownership.

Expenses

All ordinary and necessary business expenses with horses are fully deductible in the year paid. In addition, up to 50 percent of annual expenses for the next year can be prepaid and deducted.

Deductible expenses include boarding fees, medical expenses, transportation, mortality and other insurance, interest on associated loans, stud fees, training fees, feed, and supplies. Other horse-related business expenses, including most travel and 80 percent of entertainment, are also deductible.

Tax Risk

One of the advantages of using horses as a tax shelter is that the IRS has specific, distinct guidelines for horses. Following these guidelines should greatly reduce the risk of losing tax benefits.

Assistance

This brief overview of horse taxation is by no means a complete explanation. Potential investors should consult an equine tax expert. A number of certified public accountants specialize in horse taxation and accounting.

REPRESENTATIVE TYPES OF INVESTORS

Horse investors come from all walks of life. Some could be considered pure investors who discover the benefits of horse investments. Others have a natural affinity for horses. They range from those who have only dreamed of owning a horse to experienced riders.

Horse investors are motivated by three aspects of ownership: (1) profit potential; (2) tax benefits; and (3) enjoyment, family involvement, and lifestyle. Horse ownership is certainly not exclusively for the very wealthy. Purchasers of top-quality horses often have annual incomes of $75,000 to $100,000. They start small, usually with one horse, and build from there. "It's hard to fall in love with a stock or bond," says Tom Aronson of the American Horse Council, "but it's easy to fall in love with a horse."

IMPORTANT FACTORS IN BUYING AND SELLING

The quality of the horse you buy and the price you pay will probably determine the success or failure of your investment.

Buy only absolute top quality. Don't be blinded by low prices. It costs the same to breed and maintain a top-quality mare as a low-quality mare. Dropping below top quality, however, will lower the value of foals by 50 percent or more.

How do you determine top quality? Enlist the services of a qualified appraiser to help you make that determination. The Pyramid Society (see Organizations) can help you find an appraiser for a straight Egyptian.

Appraisers consider three factors in determining quality and, ultimately, the price of a filly or mare:

1. Conformation (the way the horse looks)
2. Pedigree (ancestry)
3. The show record of her male ancestors

Good conformation ensures a top-quality individual. Pedigree determines the predictability with which the female can duplicate, or improve, her own quality in her foals. The show records of the sire (father) and grandsire (grandfather) determine the demand for offspring in the marketplace. All three of these factors, considered together, determine quality and value.

Financing can be considered in making a horse purchase. There are financial institutions that finance horses, even though most traditional banks reject the idea. These willing institutions deal with the most reputable farms and agents. The seller should have knowledge of financing avenues that can be explored.

Trusted advisors are particularly helpful to the newcomer. In considering advisors and appraisers, be sure they exhibit longevity, integrity, and success. Ask and verify how long they have been in business. Ask for and check a list of clients and references.

GLOSSARY

Arabian—Breeding can be traced back to the Arabian Peninsula.

bloodstock agent—Agent in the business of horse selection.

board fee—Fee charged to care for a horse.

breeding stock—Males or females used to produce offspring.

broodmare—Mature female used for breeding.

colt—Young male.

Crabbit Arabian—Arabians bred in or traced to England.

dam—Mother.

domestic Arabian—Arabians bred in or traced to the United States.

filly—Young female.

foal—Baby, male or female.

gelding—Castrated male.

granddam—Grandmother.

grandsire—Grandfather.

in foal—Pregnant.

mare—Mature female.

pedigree—Genealogy of a horse.

performance stock—Horses raced or ridden in competitive shows.

Polish Arabians—Arabians bred in or traced to Poland.

pure, or straight, Egyptian Arabian—Bloodlines traced to an original group of 1100 exported from Arabia to Egypt in the 1800s. About 4,000 in North America, about 6,000 worldwide today.

purebred Arabian—Arabians of all bloodlines, approximately 300,000 in North America today.

quarter horse—A registered breed combining native American stock horses and thoroughbreds.

sire—Father.

Spanish Arabian—Arabians bred in or traced to Spain.

stallion—Mature male.

stud fee—Fee charged by a stallion owner to breed a mare.

thoroughbred—Horses originating from English and Arabian breeding and used primarily for racing.

TRADE ORGANIZATIONS

Arabian Horse Registry of America, Inc., Westminster, Colo.

Arabian Horse Trust, Westminister, Colo.

International Arabian Horse Association, Denver, Colo.

The Pyramid Society, Lexington, Ky.

SUGGESTED READING

PERIODICALS

Arabian Horse Digest. Published in Santa Monica, Cal.

Arabian Horse Express. Published in Coffeyville, Ky.

Arabian Horse Times. Published in Waseca, Minn.

Arabian Horse World. Published in Palo Alto, Cal.

Inside International. Published in Denver, Colo.

REFERENCE BOOKS

Brown, Gladys. *The Arabian War Horse to Show Horse.* Westminster, Colo.: Arabian Horse Trust, 1980.

Byford, Sharon. *The Arabian—The Guide for Owners.* Westminster, Colo.: Arabian Horse Trust, 1987.

Forbis, Judy. *The Classic Arabian Horse.* Lexington, Ky.: The Pyramid Society, 1976.

The Pyramid Society, *Reference Handbook of Straight Egyptian Horses.* Lexington, Ky.: 1987.

Schimanski, Walter, and Forbis, Judy. *The Royal Arabians of Egypt & The Stud of Henry Babson.* Lexington, Ky: The Pyramid Society, 1976.

INDIVIDUAL RETIREMENT PLANS

Donald S. Grubbs, Jr.

BASIC CHARACTERISTICS

An individual retirement plan is a plan to which an individual can make tax-deductible contributions for personal savings. The amount of contribution is generally limited to $2,000 or to $2,250 for certain married persons, but not more than 100 percent of compensation. The plans are for four different types: individual retirement accounts (IRAs), individual retirement annuities, accounts established by employers or employee associations, and retirement bonds. The term "IRA" is popularly used for all four types of plans. Simplified employee pensions (SEPs) are IRAs established by employers under rules that allow deductions as large as $15,000.

IRAs may be established by employees or self-employed individuals or may be established for such individuals by employers, unions or employee associations.

Prior to 1982, an individual could not contribute to an IRA if he were covered under an employer's pension plan. This made about half of all workers ineligible. Use of IRAs is substantially greater by upper-income individuals, reflecting their greater ability to save and their greater interest in tax deductions. A 1988 report of the Internal Revenue Service showed the percentage of tax return filers, by income class, who had IRAs in 1986:

Donald S. Grubbs, Jr., is an actuary and is President of Grubbs and Company, Inc., Silver Spring, Md.

Family adjusted gross income	Percent of filers making IRA contributions
$ 0– 10,000	1.9%
10,000– 20,000	7.1
20,000– 50,000	22.7
50,000–100,000	51.4
Over 100,000	70.2

Beginning in 1982, all individuals who received compensation or self-employment income were allowed to contribute to an IRA. However, since January 1987, individuals with incomes above a stipulated level may not claim a tax deduction for their IRA contributions. (See *Deduction of Contributions*, later in this article).

IRAs — Legal Requirements

An individual retirement account is a trust created or organized in the United States for the exclusive benefit of an individual, for which the trust agreement meets the following requirements:

- Except for rollover contributions, the trust will accept contributions only if they are in cash and do not exceed $2,000 on behalf of any individual for the taxable year.
- The trustee must be a bank or individual allowed under regulations.
- No trust assets may be invested in life insurance contracts.
- An individual's interest in his account must be nonforfeitable.
- Trust assets may not be commingled with non-IRA property, except in a common trust fund or common investment fund.
- Benefit distributions must be made within certain periods.

Timing of benefit distributions. Benefit distributions must begin no later than April 1 following the calendar year the individual attains age 70½. The amount of distribution in that year and each year thereafter must be at least equal to the account balance at the beginning of the year divided by the individual's life expectancy or the life expectancy of the individual and his spouse. Based on regulations, these life expectancies are 16.0 years for a person age 70. The combined life expectancy of a husband and wife depends on their particular ages; for example, if both husband and wife are age 70, the combined life expectancy is 20.6 years. Alternatively, benefits can be paid as a life annuity payable during the lifetime of the individual or during the combined lifetimes of the individual and his beneficiary.

If the individual dies after distribution has begun but before his entire interest has been distributed to him, the remaining interest must be paid at least as rapidly as under the period that was applicable just prior to his death.

If the individual dies before the distribution has begun, his interest generally must be paid within five years of his death. An exception applies if payments begin within one year of death and are paid over the lifetime of the beneficiary or over a period not exceeding the life expectancy of the beneficiary; but if the beneficiary is the spouse of the deceased, payments need not begin before the spouse attains age $70^1/_2$.

The penalty for failure to satisfy these minimum distribution requirements is a 50 percent tax on any amount that was required to be distributed but was not distributed.

Custodial accounts. A custodial account may be used in lieu of a trust if the account is held by a bank or individual allowed under regulations, provided the custodial account otherwise satisfies the requirements for trusts. For tax purposes, such custodial accounts are treated as trusts.

Investments. Most kinds of investments may be used for IRA funds. The only legal restriction under federal law on the type of assets an IRA may invest in is a prohibition on life insurance contracts. However, in effect, there is a restriction against investing in collectibles such as art and stamps, since such investments are treated as distributions and included in the individual's gross income. If an IRA is established by an employer under an employee pension plan, it is governed by the fiduciary requirements of the Employee Retirement Income Security Act of 1974 (ERISA). (See article on "Pension Plan Investments," elsewhere in this volume.) The trust laws of the various states may also affect investments, although use of a custodial account may avoid such requirements. (See *Prohibited Transactions*, later in this article.)

Individual Retirement Annuities

An individual retirement annuity is an annuity contract in which

- The contract is not transferable by the owner.
- The contract provides for flexible premiums.
- The annual premium on behalf of an individual may not exceed $2,000.
- Dividends must be applied to increase benefits or pay premiums, and may not be distributed in cash.
- The entire interest of the owner is nonforfeitable.
- Benefit distributions must be made within the same periods as required for individual retirement accounts.

It is allowable for contracts to provide for waiver of premium on disability. A group annuity contract with individual accounts can be used. Certain endowment life insurance policies are also allowed.

Accounts Established by Employers and Employee Associations

Employers, labor unions, and other employee associations may establish a trust to provide IRAs. Such trusts must satisfy all the requirements for IRAs. The assets of the trust may be held in a common fund, but there must be separate accounting for the interest of each employee or member. Few, if any, such trusts have been established. Employers have preferred to avoid the additional responsibility and expense, particularly since many alternative forms of IRAs are already available for employees.

TAX CONSEQUENCES

Deduction of Contributions

Individuals are allowed a deduction from gross income for their IRA contributions, regardless of whether or not they itemize deductions. The basic maximum deduction equals the lesser of $2,000 or 100 percent of the individual's compensation. Compensation includes earned income of self-employed individuals. IRA contributions for a year can be made by the due date (including extensions) for the individual's tax return. It is not necessary to establish the IRA before the end of the year.

Contributions for spouses. A married person is allowed a deduction for contributions to an IRA for his spouse, provided they file a joint tax return and the spouse does not work for pay. The maximum deduction equals the lesser of $2,250 or 100 percent of the working spouse's compensation, reduced by the deduction taken for the working spouse's own IRA. The $2,250 can be split between the two IRAs in any manner, except that not more than $2,000 can be contributed to either one.

The two IRAs must be separately owned. A joint trust can hold the accounts of both, but their interests must be separately accounted for. This does not prevent each from naming the other as beneficiary with a right of survivorship.

Restricted Deduction for Pension Plan Participants. As of January 1987, if an individual is an active participant in a qualified pension plan, profit-sharing plan, stock bonus plan, tax-sheltered annuity plan, or SEP, the amount of IRA deduction allowed is limited or eliminated. This restriction applies only if the adjusted gross income of the individual (determined before subtracting any IRA deduction) exceeds the "applicable dollar amount." In the case of married persons filing jointly, the restrictions apply to both if either one is an active participant in a plan and if the adjusted gross income for their joint return exceeds the applicable dollar amount. This amount is as follows:

Married filing jointly	$40,000
Not married	25,000
Married filing separately	0

If the adjusted gross income exceeds the applicable dollar amount by $10,000, no deduction is allowable. If the excess is less than $10,000, the deduction is proportionately reduced. For example, if a single person has adjustable gross income of $26,000, his maximum deduction is $1,800 because the $2,000 maximum deduction is reduced 10 percent for each $1,000 his adjusted gross income exceeds $25,000.

Restrictions. No deduction is allowed if the individual has attained age 70½ before the close of the taxable year.

Contribution by employers. If an employer contributes to an IRA for an employee, the entire contribution is included in the employee's gross income, but the employee is allowed to take the appropriate deduction. (See *Simplified Employee Pensions* for deductions for SEPs, later in this article.)

Rollover Contributions

Distributions from qualified pension and profit-sharing plans are ordinarily taxable when received. But if an individual contributes part or all of a qualifying rollover distribution to an IRA within sixty days of receipt, he is not taxed currently on the amount of the rollover. A qualifying rollover distribution is a lump-sum distribution or a distribution made on termination or discontinuance of a qualified plan. The maximum amount that may be rolled over may not exceed the fair market value of the cash and property received in the distribution, reduced by the sum of any employee contributions included in the distributions. If the employee receives property other than cash, the property received may either be transferred to an IRA or sold and the proceeds transferred to an IRA. If a participant rolls over only part of a distribution received from a qualified plan, the remainder is taxable as ordinary income.

Rollover contributions are not subject to the $2,000 limitation or the limitation for pension plan participants. Of course, there is no deduction on the rollover, which is a tax-free transfer. Similar rollover rules apply to distributions from tax-deferred annuities. In addition to rollovers from qualified plans, IRA-to-IRA rollovers are allowed tax-free if the entire amount received from an IRA is rolled over into another IRA within sixty days. Only one such tax-free rollover is allowed in any 365-day period.

Excess Contributions

If an individual makes a contribution to an IRA (other than a rollover contribution) that is larger than can be deducted, a 6 percent excise tax is imposed on the excess contribution. But if an excess contribution, together with the net income it has earned, is returned to the individual before his tax filing date (including extensions) for the year the excess contribution was paid, there is no excise tax and only the net income paid is taxable income.

The excise tax on excess contributions is assessed not only for the year in which the excess contribution is made, but for each year that it remains in the IRA. To avoid continuing excise taxes, an individual may either withdraw the excess contribution or offset it against IRA contributions that could have been made in future years.

Excess contribution—Illustration. For example, assume that John Doe contributes $2,000 to an IRA in 1989, but because of business difficulties his total earned income for 1989 is only $800. Since he is allowed to deduct only $800, he has made an excess contribution of $1,200 for 1989. Unless he withdraws this $1,200 together with the net income it earns by his tax filing date (April 15, 1990, unless extended), he must pay an excise tax of $72 (6 percent of $1,200). Assume John Doe fails to withdraw the $1,200 by his tax filing date; and assume that in 1990 he has only $1,000 of earned income, makes no IRA contribution, and again fails to withdraw his 1989 excess contribution of $1,200. Because John Doe makes no contribution in 1990 while he is entitled to contribute and deduct $1,000, $1,000 of his excess contribution will be treated as contributed in 1990 and John Doe will be entitled to a $1,000 deduction in 1990. However, he will have to pay a 6 percent excise tax in 1990 on the remaining $200 of the excess contribution, unless he withdraws it.

Investment Earnings

An individual retirement account or individual retirement annuity is exempt from taxation. Thus, there is no current tax on investment income received or on realized and unrealized appreciation of assets, so long as the investment return is retained within the IRA.

Distributions

Except as noted below, all distributions from IRAs are taxable as ordinary income when received by an individual. Except for any nondeductible contributions, the individual's tax basis is zero. Therefore, the total amount of any distribution, excluding any nondeductible contributions, is included in gross income.

There is no tax on distribution from an IRA if the entire distribution is rolled over into another IRA within sixty days. However, only one such tax-free rollover is allowed in any 365-day period. In the case of an IRA under which all of the contributions were rollover contributions from a qualified plan, there is no tax on distribution from the IRA if the entire distribution is rolled over into another qualified plan within sixty days. A similar rule applies to rollovers from and to tax-deferred annuities.

Distributions of Excess Contributions. There is no tax on the distribution of any excess contribution if the distribution is received by the individual's tax filing date (including extensions) for the year the excess contribution was made, and if the distribution of the excess contribution includes any net income attributable to the excess contribution.

If a distribution of an excess contribution is made from an IRA after the tax filing date for the year of the contribution, the distribution will still be recovered tax-free (to the extent no deduction was previously claimed) if the aggregate contributions did not exceed $2,250 in the year in which the excess contribution was made. If an individual has erroneously made a rollover contribution larger than allowed because he or she received incorrect information from the plan administrator, the excess can be recovered tax-free even if it is larger than $2,250.

Transfer of Account Upon Divorce. A transfer of an individual's ownership interest in an IRA to his spouse, incident to a divorce, is not a taxable transfer. The spouse will pay no tax until distributions are made from the IRA.

Penalty for Premature Distributions. If a distribution is made from an IRA before the individual for whom the IRA was established attains age 59½, it is a premature distribution, unless the individual is disabled (as defined in the Internal Revenue Code). Any premature distribution included in gross income is subject to an additional 10 percent tax.

Penalty for Insufficient Distributions. IRAs are required to make distributions beginning April 1 following the year the individual attains age 70½. In any year in which the minimum distribution required exceeds the amount actually distributed, a 50 percent tax is assessed on the excess. The IRS may waive this severe penalty if the shortfall was due to reasonable error and reasonable steps are being taken to remedy it.

"Worst Case" Illustration. Fred Brown, whose salary puts him in the 28 percent tax bracket, changes employers at age 45. He participates in his new employer's pension plan and is not eligible for IRA deductions before or after the job change. He receives a $300,000 distribution from the old employer's profit-sharing plan on June 1, 1989 and rolls it over into an IRA on August 1, 1989. He excludes the distribution from his 1989 gross income as a tax-free rollover. Upon auditing Fred's 1989 return in 1991, the IRS notices that it was sixty-one days between June 1 and August 1, and therefore Fred was not eligible for a tax-free rollover. The IRS recomputes Fred's 1989 tax, including additional income for 1989 of $300,000. This increases Fred's 1989 tax by $84,000 for the year. But the $300,000 contribution (less $2,000 treated as an allowable but nondeductible contribution) was also an excess contribution in 1989 subjecting Fred to an additional $17,880 excise tax (6 percent of $298,000). In addition, because he failed to withdraw the excess in 1990, there was $296,000 remaining excess contribution ($298,000 less a $2,000 allow able contribution for 1990) for which the 1990 excise tax of 6 percent is $17,760.

Fred needs to withdraw the $296,000 to prevent the continuing annual excise taxes; he also needs the money to pay his back taxes. But he cannot obtain a tax-free withdrawal of the excess contribution because his tax-filing date for 1989 has passed, the 1989 excess exceeds $2,250, and it was not caused by a reporting error of the plan administrator. If he withdraws the $296,000 in 1991 to avoid the annual 6 percent excise taxes, the distribution will be taxed as ordinary income, increasing his 1991 income tax by $82,880. In spite of the fact that Fred has already paid tax on the money once and received no deduction, his case is still subject to the rule that withdrawals from an IRA are generally taxed as ordinary income and have zero basis. In addition, since Fred is under 59½, distribution of the $296,000 excess contribution in 1991 will be a premature distribution, resulting in an additional 10 percent tax of $29,600.

In addition, his IRA distribution would be subject to state income tax. Based on the state's tax laws, his estimated state income tax would be $22,500 in 1989 and $22,200 in 1991, a total of $44,700.

The total tax liability incurred by Fred's $300,000 profit-sharing distribution is as follows:

1989 income tax on distribution	$ 84,000
1989 excise tax	17,880
1990 excise tax	17,760
1991 income tax on distribution	82,880
1991 tax on premature distribution	29,600
Total federal tax	$232,120
Total estimated state taxes	44,700
Total tax on distributions	$276,820

Fred could have avoided this disastrous result initially by making his rollover contribution within sixty days, or by withdrawing his excess contribution by his tax filing date for 1989.

Summary of Tax Advantages and Disadvantages of IRAs

The principal tax advantages of IRAs are the deduction of contributions and the tax deferral of investment income. The principal disadvantages of IRAs are the low limits on contributions and restrictions on when money can be withdrawn.

For individuals not eligible for a deduction, the only tax advantage is the tax deferral for investment income. For such an individual, additional disadvantages include the requirement to complete IRS Form 8606 for the year of deduction and the need to maintain records that will enable the individual to prove, many years later, that a portion of his distribution is not subject to tax.

SIMPLIFIED EMPLOYEE PENSIONS

SEP Objectives

Congress established simplified employee pensions (SEPs) in order to encourage small employers to establish pensions for their employees. Some small employers have been discouraged from maintaining qualified plans for employees because of the complexity of ERISA and the burdensome nature of its reporting and disclosure requirements. With simpler requirements, Congress felt more small employers would adopt plans, particularly employers who, as owners, could thus set aside more for themselves than allowed under regular IRAs. But to assure that rank and file employees would also receive equitable treatment, it was necessary to require that the SEPs be nondiscriminatory.

Limits on Contributions and Deductions

A SEP must prohibit contributions greater than $30,000 per year on behalf of an individual. Employer contributions to a SEP are included in the employee's gross income, but are deductible by the employee. The largest employer contribution that an employee may deduct in a year is the lesser of $30,000 or 15 percent of compensation. Unlike regular IRAs, SEPs provide no special allowance for employer contributions on behalf of a spouse.

In addition to any employer contributions, an employee may also make his own contributions and deduct them under the usual IRA rules and limits. Such employee IRA contributions may be made to the same SEP as employer contributions are, or may be made to a separate regular IRA. (See *Restricted Deduction for Pension Plan Participants*, later in this article.)

Participation Requirement

If an employer contributes to a SEP in a given year, contributions must be made for each employee who has attained age 21 and has worked for the employer in at least three of the preceding five years. Exceptions are allowed for employees covered under a collective bargaining agreement that includes an agreement on pensions, and also for certain nonresident aliens.

Nondiscriminatory Contributions

Employer contributions must be a uniform percentage of total compensation up to a stated limit. The limit may not exceed $200,000, and may exceed $100,000 only if employer contributions are at least 7.5 percent of compensation.

Integration With Social Security. In determining whether employer contributions meet these requirements, Social Security taxes paid by the employer may be taken into account. It is permitted to have two levels of contributions: (1) a uniform percentage of total compensation and (2) a uniform percentage of compensation in excess of the Social Security taxable wage ($48,000 in 1989). The percentage that applies to such excess compensation may not exceed the lesser of 5.7 percent or the percentage that applies to total compensation.

Two examples of contribution formulas that would be acceptable in 1989 are as follows:

1. 4 percent of total compensation, plus 4 percent of any excess of total compensation over $48,000

2. 9 percent of total compensation, plus 5.7 percent of any excess of total compensation over $48,000

Elective Salary Deferrals. An exception to the general rule concerning nondiscriminatory contributions allows individual employees to elect to have their employer reduce their compensation and contribute it to the SEP on their behalf. Such elective deferrals are allowable only if the employer has twenty-five or fewer employees and if at least 50 percent of all employees of the employer elect to make deferrals. The elective deferral percentage for each "highly compensated employee" (as defined in Section 414(q) of the Internal Revenue Code) may not exceed 125 percent of the average of the elective deferral percentages of all other employees.

Other Rules

A SEP allows the employer complete flexibility to determine whether or how much to contribute during any given year, so long as the maximum limits are not exceeded. But it must include a written allocation formula specifying how each contribution is to be allocated.

All contributions must be 100 percent vested in the individual participant's account. The employer cannot restrict an employee's right to withdraw any portion of his account. However, the employee is subject to the tax on premature withdrawals and the funding media can impose penalties for early withdrawal.

SEPs may be funded through individual retirement accounts or individual retirement annuities, but not through retirement bonds.

IRS Form 5305—SEP

The IRS has published Form 5305-SEP, "Simplified Employee Pension—Individual Retirement Accounts Contribution Agreement." A similar Form 5305A-SEP is available for plans that include elective salary deferral. An employer completing this model agreement form has assurance that his plan complies with IRS requirements. The form should not be submitted to IRS. No advance determination from IRS is needed or possible.

The IRS model SEP will not meet the needs of all employers. For example, an employer using the form cannot integrate contributions with Social Security taxes. Therefore, some employers will prefer to use an individually designed SEP or an approved prototype SEP of an insurance company, bank, or other institution.

Reporting Requirements

For employers using model forms, reporting requirements are very simple. The employer must provide each employee with a copy of the form at the time the employer becomes eligible to participate. At the end of each calendar year, the employer must give a written statement of the amount of any employer contribution. If the employer selects, recommends, or otherwise influences the choice of the particular IRA or of the type of IRA, and if the particular IRA restricts withdrawals (e.g., by a penalty for early withdrawal), the employer must provide a clear explanation of the restrictions, including a statement that other IRAs may not have such restrictions.

Reporting requirements for employers that do not use model forms are much more rigorous. Department of Labor regulations fail to reflect congressional intent that such plans have simplified reporting.

INVESTMENT MEDIA FOR IRAs

At the end of 1987, IRA assets totaled $297 billion. In 1984, about 15 million tax returns claimed deductions for $35 billion of IRA contributions. Beginning in 1987, the new contributions were reduced because of the restriction on IRA deductions by pension plan participants.

There is almost no limit to the kinds of investments that may be used for IRAs, except for collectibles and insurance contracts. However, the small amount of each IRA, except for rollover IRAs, places a practical restriction on some types of investments. The investment alternatives differ in their rates of investment return, in the existence and nature of guarantees on principal or interest, in liquidity, and in expense charges.

Variety of Investment Objectives

Individuals have differing needs and objectives, and therefore the same form of investment is not suitable for all. For everyone, the goals during the period after withdrawals begin are usually different from the goals during the earlier accumulation period.

For all investors, the objective is to maximize the total investment return within acceptable limits of risk. But individuals differ greatly in the extent they desire or can afford to take the risk of greater market value fluctuation in the pursuit of greater investment return. During a long accumulation period, the individual may be little concerned with year-to-year fluctuation if the long-term prospect of appreciation is good. But many retired persons cannot afford the risk of fluctuation.

For most, the greatest risk is not that the dollar amount of their IRA will fluctuate but that its purchasing power will decline with inflation. Selecting investments to counter inflation over both short periods and long periods is difficult.

During the payout period, an individual who needs to use both capital and income but must avoid outliving his capital should consider some form of annuity. For example, a person may have an individual retirement account invested in mutual funds during the accumulation period, but roll it over into an individual retirement annuity during the payout period.

Savings and Loan and Mutual Savings Bank Media

About one quarter of all IRA assets are held by savings and loan associations and mutual savings banks. The funding arrangements of federally chartered institutions differ slightly from those of state-chartered ones, and differ from state to state. The three principal investment alternatives offered are money market accounts, certificates of deposit (CDs), and passbook savings accounts.

The Federal Savings and Loan Insurance Corporation (FSLIC) or Federal Deposit Insurance Corporation (FDIC) guarantee both passbook savings and CDs in federally chartered savings and loans and mutual savings banks up to $100,000. State agencies usually provide similar guarantees for state-chartered institutions.

Money Market Accounts. Many savings institutions have established money market funds, which they invest in short-term debt instruments, such as three-month Treasury bills and commercial paper. Individual accounts are credited with the average rate of return of the fund less a margin for expense and profit. A minimum deposit, such as $2,000, may be required.

Certificates of Deposit. Often, a single institution will offer two or more alternative forms of CDs, differing in duration, interest rates, and other features. CDs have a substantial penalty for early withdrawal, but a minimum return such as 5.5 percent may be guaranteed in any event. Minimum deposits, such as $250 or $500 or more, are required for CDs. Some CDs allow additional deposits to be added after the initial purchase, while others do not. If an additional deposit is made, some banks treat the entire CD, including prior deposits, as a new CD for purposes of determining the period when early withdrawal penalties apply.

Passbook Savings Accounts. Passbook savings accounts guarantee the right to withdraw the entire principal and interest at any time. Interest rates on such accounts are generally unattractive, usually 5.5 percent in 1989. A passbook savings account may be used for an IRA when the amount is less than the minimum required for a CD or money market account.

Commercial Bank Media

Commercial banks are used to fund IRAs in two ways: as the investment medium and as the trustee or custodian for other investments.

Acting as the investment medium, commercial banks fund individual retirement accounts in much the same way as savings and loan associations and mutual savings banks do. CDs and savings accounts are the principal vehicles used. Commercial banks hold about one quarter of all IRA assets.

A bank may serve as a trustee through an individual trust arrangement. The small amount involved in most IRAs, however, usually makes this uneconomical. Some banks serve as trustees for all of the IRAs funded through a particular mutual fund or a particular broker-dealer.

Mutual Funds

Almost the whole range of types of mutual funds, including growth stock funds, income stock funds, balanced funds, and money market funds, are used to fund IRAs. Tax-exempt bond funds are not used for IRAs, since there would be no tax advantage for an IRA, already tax-exempt, to invest in such funds, which have relatively low yields. Mutual funds hold approximate one quarter of all IRA assets.

Broker-Dealer Plans

Stock brokerage firms arrange for IRA funding, some passively accepting the business and others actively seeking it. Brokers actively seeking the business often have their own approved prototype plans. These plans generally fall into two categories: mutual fund IRAs and self-directed IRAs.

Mutual funds whose investment manager and distributor are affiliated with the broker sometimes may be used. If self-directed investment is chosen, a custodial account is established; the individual directs the investment of his own account. Prototype plans of brokers may limit investments to marketable securities. One major brokerage firm will not allow investments in commodity futures or in precious metals.

Insurance Company Investments

Insurance companies usually fund IRAs with individual flexible premium annuities. A flexible premium annuity allows the policyholder to vary the time and amount of premiums, or to pay no premium at all. If a flexible premium annuity is used as an individual retirement annuity, it must prohibit premiums in excess of $2,000 per year except for rollover contributions.

An expense charge is subtracted from the premium received and the balance is accumulated at an interest rate that is guaranteed for the life of the contract. Interest guarantees vary greatly from company to company. Often, there is a high first-year guarantee, with successively lower guaranteed rates applying to more distant years. Most companies actually credit interest higher than the guaranteed rates when their investment earnings substantially exceed the guaranteed rates.

The policyholder may receive his account balance in a lump sum or have it applied to provide a monthly income for life under one of several forms of annuity. Annuity purchase rates are guaranteed in the contract, but more attractive current rates are used when they provide a larger income.

Previously, endowment contracts and level premium annuity contracts were issued for IRAs; some of these are still in force, but amendments to the Internal Revenue Code no longer allow such contracts to be issued for IRAs.

Expense Charges

Expense charges take a variety of forms. There may be a charge deducted from deposits, as in the case of an annuity contract or a load mutual fund. There may be a direct deduction from investment income, or an indirect deduction because the funding medium credits less than it earns on its investments. There may be brokerage fees for buying and selling investments. There may be a charge on distributions, particularly a penalty for early withdrawal if the deposit is not held for a minimum period. If annuities are purchased at retirement, the purchase price includes an expense charge. There may be a flat dollar fee to establish the IRA and a flat annual fee to administer it.

Utilization of Various Investment Media

The American Council of Life Insurance reports that the amount of assets of IRAs invested with selected financial institutions as of the end of 1986 were as follows:

Institution	Amount ($ billions)
Life insurance companies	$22.7
Savings and loan associations	Not available
Mutual savings banks	13.1
Commercial banks	Not available
Mutual funds	53.7
Credit unions	19.4

SUITABILITY OF IRAs FOR INDIVIDUAL INVESTORS

Every employee who receives compensation and every person who has self-employment income is eligible to invest in an IRA. Any such person who can afford to defer current income until age 59½ or beyond should consider the tax advantages and disadvantages. The current deduction of contributions and deferral of tax on investment income are most favorable. But all distributions will be taxable when received. This is unfavorable for a person who expects to receive a distribution from an IRA during a period when his tax rate is substantially higher than his current tax rate. Thus, IRAs are generally most suitable for a person who expects to withdraw the money in installments during retirement years and who expects to be subject to a lower tax rate during the years of withdrawal than during the years of deferral. Even for the individual who expects to be taxed at the same rate during the years of withdrawal as during the years of deferral, there is an advantage in deferring the payment of the tax. For individuals who are not eligible to deduct IRA contributions, the relatively small advantage of tax deferral on the investment income may be outweighed by the burden of record keeping and filing IRS forms.

PROHIBITED TRANSACTIONS

An IRA may not engage in a prohibited transaction with a disqualified person. The general effect is to prevent self-dealing by persons who exercise control over the IRA.

Disqualified Persons

The term "disqualified persons" includes fiduciaries, persons providing services to the IRA, employers, unions, and certain persons related to any of the above by blood, employment, ownership, or otherwise. A fiduciary is any person who exercises authority or control over the plan or its assets or renders investment advice for a fee or other compensation. The individual for whom the IRA is established is ordinarily a fiduciary, since he ordinarily has authority to roll over the IRA into a different funding medium.

Prohibited Transactions Defined

All transactions between the IRA and a disqualified person are prohibited transactions, unless an exemption is granted. This includes the sale, exchange, or leasing of any property, lending money, extending credit, furnishing goods or services, and similar transactions. The prohibition on loans precludes such practices as buying securities on margin or making policy loans on annuity contracts. Such transactions are prohibited even if they are at arm's length for full consideration. For example, an individual could not even sell a listed security to his own IRA for its current market value.

Penalties

If an individual engages in a prohibited transaction with his IRA, the IRA loses its tax-exempt status and the entire assets of the IRA become current taxable income to the individual.

If some other disqualified person, such as the trustee, engages in a prohibited transaction, that disqualified person must pay an excise tax equal to 5 percent of the amount involved. If the 5 percent tax is assessed and the transaction is not corrected within the correction period (generally ninety days after IRS sends a notice), an additional 100 percent tax may be imposed.

GLOSSARY

custodial account—An account held for the benefit of an individual by a bank or individual in lieu of a trust, but meeting the requirements for trusts.

individual retirement account (IRA)—A trust set up for the exclusive benefit of an individual in conformance with federal income tax law.

individual retirement annuity—A retirement plan based on an annuity contract providing for a flexible premium, and nontransferable by the owner.

rollover contribution—That portion of a lump-sum distribution of a qualified plan, or distribution on termination of a qualified plan, that is contributed to an IRA within sixty days of receipt of the distribution.

simplified employee pension (SEP)—An employee pension plan that relieves employers of the burden of meeting ERISA reporting and disclosure requirements.

SUGGESTED READING

Allen, Everett T., Jr., Melone, Joseph J., and Rosenbloom, Jerry S. *Pension Planning*, 6th ed. (see Chapter 21, "Individual Retirement Arrangements and Simplified Employee Pensions"). Homewood: Richard D. Irwin, 1988.

Commerce Clearing House. *Planning for Your Retirement: IRAs and Keoughs*. Chicago, 1987.

Internal Revenue Service. *Individual Retirement Arrangements* (Publication 590). Washington, D.C., 1987.

______. *1987 Required Distributions From Individual Retirement Arrangements (IRAs)*. Washington, D.C., 1987.

McGill, Dan M., and Grubbs, Donald S., Jr. *Fundamentals of Private Pensions*, 6th ed. (see Chapter 28, "Individual Retirement Plans and Voluntary Employee Contributions"). Homewood: Richard D. Irwin, 1989.

Rabel, William H., and Martin, Ernest L. *Individual Retirement Arrangements (IRAs) and Simplified Employee Pension (SEP) Plans*, Handbook of Employee Benefits. Homewood: Dow Jones-Irwin, 1988.

LIFE INSURANCE

GUARANTEED INTEREST CONTRACTS

Gordon J. Munro
Jonathan L. Wooley

BASIC CHARACTERISTICS

Guaranteed interest contracts (GICs) are custom-designed, fixed-dollar funding arrangements offered by many life insurance companies to large, tax-qualified corporate pension and profit-sharing plans and to tax-exempt foundations and government plans. Although a GIC is similar in many ways to an unmarketable bond, the contract that evidences the arrangement is not considered a security. It is a group annuity contract, subject to regulation by the various state insurance departments, and as such is currently exempted from regulation by the SEC. Because it is a group annuity contract, it will contain ancillary features that are not generally available with any of the traditional investment vehicles. Among these are the options to (1) accept future deposits within an "open window" period of up to twelve months; (2) allow withdrawals to provide participant-directed benefit payments; and (3) purchase, at predetermined rates, pension benefits guaranteed for life. Furthermore, the insurance company can often make available a variety of administrative services, such as participant record keeping or payment of retired life benefits, if these services are required. These services, however, are increasingly being provided by third-party administrators instead of insurance companies.

The essential function of a GIC is to provide guarantees of principal, interest, and expense charges on funds deposited with the insurance company for as long as those funds remain with the company, up to a maximum specified period. Such fund deposits may be

Gordon J. Munro is retired. He was formerly a Vice-President in the Pension Department of New York Life Insurance Company. Jonathan L. Wooley is a Corporate Vice-President and Actuary of New York Life Insurance Company.

made in a single sum or on a recurring schedule during the open window period. Interest is usually at a fixed rate but sometimes is offered on a minimum-floor basis with higher rates credited if earned by the insurance company. Interest may also be at a "floating" rate that is related to an outside, widely recognized index. Expenses may be billed separately or withdrawn directly from the net accumulation of deposits less withdrawals. At the end of the period of guaranteed accumulation, the remaining funds held by the insurance company will be paid out, without any market-value adjustment, either in a single sum or in installments over a period of years with interest credited at the guaranteed rate on the declining balance. This general statement should not obscure the fact that these arrangements are custom-designed; hence, the variations that may be built in are virtually endless.

Types of GICs

The design of a GIC is dictated by the needs of the plan it will serve. Some features may present a problem or risk of loss to the insurance company and thus may be difficult to obtain without some hedging or special device established for the protection of the insurance company. What a prospective GIC purchaser will look for in a contract varies greatly, depending on whether the plan being funded is a defined benefit plan or a defined contribution plan.

GICs for Defined Benefit Plans. A defined benefit pension plan is one in which the plan document specifies a formula by which the amount of pension payable to a participant on retirement is determined. The employer's objective is to provide the promised benefit as economically as possible, subject to the fiduciary and other constraints of the Employee Retirement Income Security Act of 1974 (ERISA). A superior investment result reduces the employer's cost; it does not increase the benefit payable to participants. The decision to purchase a GIC, to deposit or withdraw funds under it, or to terminate the contract is made by a single entity. This may be the plan's investment manager, a board of trustees, or the employer, acting perhaps on the guidance of a third-party consultant.

For defined benefit plans, therefore, the key factors in the design of a GIC are its ability to accommodate the projected cash flow requirements of the plan and the level (and duration) of the interest guarantee net of all expenses.

GICs for Defined Contribution Plans. A defined contribution plan is one in which the plan document stipulates a formula that determines the amount of contribution to be made by the employer each year for the benefit of each participant. The amount actually collected by a participant is the accumulated value of his vested account. A superior investment result increases the benefits payable to participants but, for all practical purposes, has no effect on the employer's cost. Usually, all decisions to deposit funds in or withdraw them from a GIC issued to such a plan are decisions made by the participants themselves, not by the employer, the trustees, or the investment manager. Such decisions are, of course, subject to whatever restrictions may be contained in the plan.

The usual structure of these plans is to provide the participants with a certain range of investment options, typically a fixed-dollar investment option, one or more equity funds, and other funds with specialized investment objectives, such as market value bond funds, a convertible securities fund, or a short-term money market fund. A participant may always change an election with regard to future contributions and, typically, may opt once a year to transfer existing funds from one form of repository to another. Often, however, there are restrictions on which funds may be transferred where. Finally, some plans permit participants (or their beneficiaries) to withdraw vested accumulations in whole or in part on retirement, death, disability, or termination of employment; for hardship or after a fixed period of years; and certain plans permit participants to borrow against their accounts.

For defined contribution plans, therefore, a GIC that is to serve as the repository for fixed-dollar funds must be designed to provide participants with (1) an easily understood, fully guaranteed account and (2) maximum flexibility to move funds in and out without penalty or market value adjustment. The precise level of interest guaranteed is secondary. One or more insurance companies will normally be designated, after competitive bidding, to receive the funds placed under the plan's fixed-dollar election in one plan year, with renewed competitive bidding for each succeeding year's fixed-dollar contributions. In this situation, participants with balances under the plan's fixed-dollar election will often have interest credited to these balances at the average rate of return on all the in-force GICs, not at the rate being earned by the individual GICs in which the participants' contributions are actually deposited. However, under a more recent form of crediting interest to these balances, the class-year method, interest is credited at the rate being earned by the individual GICs in which the participants' contributions are actually deposited.

Comparison With Alternative Investment Options. The principal alternative investment options for the funds to which GICs are sold are the following:

Certificates of Deposit (CDs). CDs give an interest yield that may be higher than that for GICs, for example, when an inverted yield curve exists. Like GICs, they have a fixed maturity date with substantial penalties for early withdrawal. CDs are short- to medium-term and may pay out interest periodically. They also have a limited Federal Deposit Insurance Corporation (FDIC) protection.

Money Market Funds. These funds reflect current short-term market yields, but there are no guarantees of principal or interest. They have the advantage, compared to GICs, of substantial liquidity.

Deep-Discount Bonds. These bonds offer yields to maturity for a tax-exempt purchaser comparable in level to those available from GICs, and for at least as long a period. They are effectively free from the risk of premature call; and the zero coupon variety, under which no interest is payable prior to maturity, eliminates all reinvestment risk prior to maturity. However, they lack the custom-designed flexibility of GICs, particularly in setting the term to maturity and the payout option at maturity. They are not adaptable to the participant withdrawal options of defined contribution plans, and, of course, they are subject to the same risk of default as any other bond portfolio.

Immunized Bond Portfolios. These investments provide a measure of protection against fluctuating interest returns and can be arranged to give yields similar to those for GICs. The effective period of immunization, however, is limited to only a few years, and the portfolio requires constant managing.

Common Stocks. Common stock investments are the antitheses of GICs. They offer a low current yield, give no guarantees of any kind, and have to be sold at market value to realize cash. However, they offer the possibility of capital growth.

ATTRACTIVE FEATURES

GICs can be responsive to many investment problems faced by the trustees of pension or profit-sharing plans. They lock in current interest levels not only on the principal but also, depending on the option selected, on the reinvestment of interest. This, coupled with the fact that the entire accumulating amount may be carried at book value according to current Internal Revenue Service (IRS) regulations, provides a very desirable measure of stability and predictability in the operation of the fund. GICs can thus be used to maintain fixed-income return in a falling interest market, to hedge aggregate market portfolio performance, to accumulate cash for specific future needs, and to control future cash flow.

Matching Cash Flow

For defined benefit plans, in the optimum arrangement, projected positive inflow of funds would be channeled into a GIC contract constructed to release these funds back to the plan at a time and in a manner designed to match a projected outflow of funds. Such projections of cash flow are, of course, subject to a good deal of uncertainty. However, within reasonable limits of practicability, a GIC contract can be designed to accommodate projected cash flow, a flexibility that is not available under conventional investment vehicles and that greatly facilitates financial planning. A word of caution, however: If the projected need for cash in future years is underestimated (as might happen, for example, if the impact of inflation is not given adequate recognition), the amount paid out by the GIC under its terms will not meet actual cash flow requirements, and supplementary funding will be necessary.

Shedding the Investment Risk

In defined benefit plans that are large enough to absorb the mortality risk inherent in providing pensions to their participants, many of the trustees are adopting a variation of GIC that retains the mortality risk with the fund while transferring the investment risk to the insurance company. The plan's own enrolled actuary develops a schedule of anticipated monthly payments to participants over the next thirty-five or forty years. A GIC contract that undertakes to make those scheduled payments to the plan trustee is then purchased for a single premium.

This can lead to a significant freeing-up of funds, since the single sum currently called for under a GIC normally would be less than the amount that would be set aside by the enrolled actuary in his valuation of plan benefits. This, in turn, can make it possible to improve plan benefits without additional outlay or, alternatively, to reduce the outlay needed to provide the present level of plan benefits.

Note again, however, that the GIC will pay out only what it promises. If the schedule of payments proves to be underestimated for any reason, the amounts received from the GIC will be correspondingly inadequate.

Flexibility in Duration of Guarantees

The duration of GICs ranges generally from a minimum of one year to a maximum of ten for single-sum payout, but may be up to forty years for a regular schedule of disbursements. Over the past few years, funds have been seeking shorter rather than longer periods, since investment managers have not wanted to commit monies long-term in an increasingly volatile interest rate environment.

Flexibility in Payout Terms

The most recent trend has been for funds to seek more flexible payout terms to accommodate participant-directed withdrawals or loans under defined contribution plans, especially the newer 401(k) plans, since investment managers have learned that projections of cash flow requirements can be very unreliable.

Guaranteed Interest on Recurring Contributions

A single-sum deposit under a GIC is less common now than it used to be. Funds that project a recurring excess of cash inflow over outflow, such as under a 401(k) plan, may very well wish to enter into a contract that will accept regular, periodic contributions, locking in minimum levels of interest rates on future deposits during an open window period that can be as long as twelve months from contract issue.

Known Return in Employee Elections

When a GIC is issued to handle the fixed-dollar elections under a defined contribution plan, the rate that will apply for the guaranteed period to all such elections made in the ensuing plan year will usually be declared in advance. This greatly facilitates the participants' choice of elections and the plan administrator's task in explaining them.

Diversification of Investments

ERISA requires plan fiduciaries to diversify the investments of a plan to minimize the risk of large losses unless there are circumstances in which it is clearly prudent not to do so. It is now well settled that a plan may be invested wholly in an annuity contract, such as a GIC, without violating the diversification rules, since the insurance company's assets are invested in a diversified manner.

Option to Receive Single-Sum Payment

GICs issued to fund the fixed-dollar elections under defined contribution plans can provide that at the end of the guaranteed accumulation period, the remaining funds will be paid out at book value in equal, annual installments over a period (usually three to five years). This is designed to minimize any reinvestment problem for the plan administrator or trustee. However, the GIC sometimes provides that if, at the end of the accumulation period, the insurance company that issued the GIC is offering a guarantee of interest on new contracts of this type lower than the rate at which the accumulation has actually been made, the trustee may have the option of receiving payment of the accumulated amount in a single sum without market value adjustment.

Relieving Past Mistakes Through Contract Innovation

Several years ago, many GICs were issued for long terms (sometimes up to twenty years) at guaranteed rates of interest that were low in relation to market rates in the years shortly after contract issue. These contracts could have been terminated in those later years, but the funds recovered would have been reduced by a substantial market value adjustment.

If the GIC in question was issued to handle the fixed-dollar elections under a defined contribution plan, any market value adjustment resulting from termination of the contract would, of course, be reflected as a pro rata capital loss in all the participants' fixed-dollar accounts. Participants would be understandably dissatisfied with their returns.

A modified GIC was developed to relieve this situation. This form of GIC would accept the reduced amount of cash transferable, after market value adjustment, from a terminated GIC contract, but would credit the fund with the full book value amount that had accumulated under the prior contract before the market value adjustment. Participants in a defined contribution plan would continue to exercise their withdrawal and transfer rights without market value adjustment, and hence the individual account balances did not need to be reduced. The difference between cash received by the insurer and the amount credited under the GIC was made up, over a period of years, by crediting a rate of interest to the book value funds that was lower than that being earned on cash funds. At the end of this period, the market value of the transferred funds would have been restored to book value and they could then be reinvested at the rates available at that time. If this type of GIC was discontinued before the difference between cash received and book value credited was fully recovered, any outstanding balance and any other termination charges that may apply at that time would be debited by the insurer.

This was an ingenious solution to a difficult problem that existed in the early 1980s but is currently not as popular, since new money interest rates are currently back down from the lofty heights in those years. Whenever interest rates are on the rise, however, this arrangement could become actively used once again. If it is, it should be approached with caution and subject to expert analysis. Depending on the rates of interest involved, the extent of the market value adjustment applied, and the future course of interest rates, it is quite possible for a fund to be worse off under this arrangement than it would have been had it either continued under the original contract or had bitten the bullet by accepting the market value adjustment and then negotiating a new, straightforward GIC on current terms.

Capital Gain GICs

The typical GIC provides guarantees of principal and interest at the cost of forgoing the chance of any capital gains that might have been enjoyed had the purchaser bought marketable bonds. However, a version of GIC has been available under which interest is guaranteed for only one year with the proviso that if the interest credited after that year is at a lower rate, the purchaser has the option of cashing out the GIC at the higher of book or market value. Strictly speaking, there is no market value for a GIC, but an approximation is developed by accumulating the deposit(s) under the GIC to maturity date at the guaranteed rate and discounting that amount back at the yield given by a specified bond index. This appears to restore the possibility of participating in capital gains if interest rates should fall. However, this result may be more apparent than real, since the insurance company controls the interest rate that triggers the option.

POTENTIAL RISKS

Recurring Contributions Under an Open Window GIC

A GIC that will accept recurring contributions within an "open window" period of up to twelve months is generally available from most life insurance companies. Typically, there are maximum and minimum limits on the amount of future contributions that will be accepted under the contractual interest guarantee, since the insurance company will insist on having predictable cash flow on which to base pricing decisions.

Withdrawal Options Under Defined Contribution Plans

Withdrawals from a GIC without market value adjustment are allowed only during the accumulation period when they are a result of the exercise of the withdrawal, transfer, and loan options of the participants in a defined contribution plan. During the same period, employer-originated withdrawals usually are not permitted at all, but may be allowed under limited circumstances with a market value adjustment. Once the payout phase has started, however, no withdrawals are permitted other than the contractual repayments of the accumulated funds.

Withdrawals of vested benefits without market value adjustment by participants (or their beneficiaries) on retirement, death, disability, or termination of employment, under normal circumstances, are reasonably predictable and will be allowed for automatically in the pricing of the GIC. However, withdrawals of vested benefits on termination of employment due to unusual business conditions, such as sales, mergers, spin-offs and closings of all or part of an employer's operations, are not predictable in any quantitative way and are not often permitted without a market value adjustment.

The terms that an insurance company is willing to offer are significantly affected by the anticipated degree of permanence of the deposits under a GIC. In this regard, it is interesting to note that the Tax Reform Act of 1986 made all withdrawals of vested benefits prior to age $59\frac{1}{2}$ (other than on account of death or disability) subject to a 10 percent penalty tax. This would appear to encourage terminated employees to leave their balances in the plan. In fact, however, there has been no significant reduction in withdrawals of vested benefits on termination of employment. In such instances, if the participant has not already reached the earliest retirement age under the plan, he or she often exercises an option (permitted by the IRS) to rollover the withdrawal into an Individual Retirement Account (IRA) within a specified period without incurring the 10 percent penalty.

The option that causes a prospective issuer of a GIC the greatest concern, and that will affect the terms it will offer, or even its willingness to bid at all, is the option allowing participants in a defined contribution plan to transfer funds between the GIC contract and other investment options. The insurance company will look closely at the nature of the other investment options to judge whether or not any of them may create a significant risk of a concerted withdrawal of GIC funds by the participants. A competing fund that is invested exclusively in equities normally would not be a matter of concern, since the considerations that would induce a participant to invest in equities on the one hand or in a GIC on the other hand are totally diverse. If, however, one of the competing investment outlets were, say, a money market fund, rising short-term rates could lead to the wholesale withdrawal of GIC funds.

The insurance company may simply refuse to issue a GIC to a plan that has an unacceptable competing fund. However, if it does agree to issue a GIC, it will undoubtedly insist on certain safeguards, of which the following are typical:

1. Both the plan document and the GIC may prohibit transfers from the GIC to such of the other funding outlets as would create unacceptable investment selection. In this case, the insurer will also closely examine the plan transfer

provisions to ensure that the prohibited transfer cannot be achieved by an indirect route.

2. The GIC may provide that if a competing fund is added to the plan later, transfers from the GIC to that new fund may be prohibited, or the GIC itself may be terminated.

3. In the typical situation, where more than one insurance company GIC has been or will be issued covering contributions of different years, each issuer of a GIC will require:

- A prohibition against transfers between the GICs and
- A contractual provision requiring fixed-dollar withdrawals to be made pro rata from all such GICs.

4. The insurance company may require that the transfer option in the plan be exercisable by a participant only once in each plan year, perhaps on the anniversary of the individual's participation, rather than optionally or on a single, fixed date within the year.

These kinds of plan and contractual provisions emphasize the negotiated nature of a GIC. The prospective issuer always has the right to bid as requested, to offer an alternative, or to decline to quote.

Recapture Provisions

If the risk involved in issuing a proposed GIC appears to the insurance company to be too great to accept in its entirety, it may offer a contract with the right to recapture losses through future guarantees. These provisions are most often found in connection with GICs issued to defined contribution plans where a new interest crediting rate is declared each year.

Premature Termination of a GIC

An insurance company is able to offer guaranteed interest rates and payments at book value because it writes a volume of such business large enough to arrange its own portfolio of investments with repayments scheduled so that sufficient liquid funds will be available when a GIC contract calls for a disbursement. Predictability of cash flow is very important in this context. If a GIC contract holder should wish to terminate a contract and receive payment prior to the date established in that contract, a cash flow problem for the insurer can result. For this reason, insurance companies take particular care in writing the discontinuance provisions of their contracts, protecting themselves from the possibly adverse effect of a premature withdrawal. In evaluating such contracts, therefore, special attention needs to be paid to the discontinuance terms.

The usual termination calculation, which is designed to approximate a market value, accrues the GIC funds at the guaranteed rate of interest to the end of the guaranteed accumulation period and then discounts this sum back to the date of payment at some (higher) rate of interest, representing currently available interest levels. A published bond yield, such as Salomon Brothers' BBB (long-term) industrials, often is used to define the current interest rate for this purpose. If the current interest rate used in this calculation should be less than the guaranteed rate, payment will normally be made at book value, not at the higher theoretical market value.

It is most desirable that the termination provisions spell out in detail how any discontinuance calculation will be made and the specific bond index or other measure that will be used to compute the market value adjustment.

TAX CONSEQUENCES

Since GICs are generally available only to tax-exempt funds, federal income tax is not a consideration for the buyer. In a few states, if the option to purchase paid-up annuities is exercised, a state premium tax would be incurred on the amount applied to purchase the annuity. This tax (if any) would be added to the guaranteed purchase rates.

IMPORTANT FACTORS IN BUYING

The leading life insurance companies compete vigorously in the GIC market, and it is most important for a fund to obtain competitive bids, quite apart from the requirement to do so that seems implicit in ERISA. However, the complexity and inherent difficulty of matching the needs of a fund to the product available generally require that the fund receive expert, professional guidance in developing specifications, analyzing and evaluating the various responses, and negotiating the best available offer. A partial list of consultants in this field is given at the end of this article.

The offers that will be made on a given set of specifications vary significantly not only from insurance company to insurance company but also from one time to another for any one insurance company, because each company must respond to changing financial conditions, both current and anticipated, and to its own internal requirements. It is quite normal for an insurance company to be extremely active and competitive in this market one month and totally uninterested the following month. The risks and financial strains incurred by life insurance companies in writing this type of business can be significant; therefore, most will place internal limits on how much will be accepted during any period.

It would seem a logical corollary for the purchaser to be satisfied about the surplus strength of the insurer chosen to write GIC business. Information regarding the amount of surplus carried and its relationship to total company liabilities can be readily obtained from the insurance company's most recent annual statement. Furthermore, claims paying ratings are currently available for many insurance companies. The ratings of Moody's Investors Service, Standard and Poor's Corporation, and Duff and Phelps, Inc., among others, can be reviewed to give the purchaser an independent appraisal of the financial stability of the company.

Under conditions of financial volatility, a purchaser will often have to accept a bid and pay over funds within not more than fifteen days of the bid being made, and periods as short as one to three days are not unknown. It is essential, therefore, for a GIC purchaser to be ready to move before soliciting bids. This particularly includes having the necessary assets in readily available funds.

In conclusion, there is currently intense competition for pension fund monies among banks, investment managers, and insurance companies. This battle is being waged with, among others, CDs, money market funds, original issue deep-discount zero coupon bonds, immunized bond portfolios, and GICs. This last is the result of some very creative thinking on the part of the major life insurance companies, a creative process that is still unfolding. The best advice to a prospective purchaser of a GIC is expressed in the old shopping adage, "If you don't see it, ask for it."

GLOSSARY

book value—The arithmetic sum of deposits made and interest added, less any amounts withdrawn, all without regard to the market value of the underlying assets.

enrolled actuary—An individual who, having satisfied certain educational and experience requirements, has been enrolled by the Joint Board for the Enrollment of Actuaries, established by ERISA, as qualified to perform the actuarial valuations for defined benefit pension plans and authorized to sign Schedule B of Form 5500 regarding the solvency of such plans.

ERISA—The Employee Retirement Income Security Act of 1974. This Act established minimum funding standards for defined benefit pension plans, set tough fiduciary standards for those having responsibility for the running of such plans, prohibited particular transactions, and required a large number of plan provisions designed to protect the pension rights of plan participants. It also established the Pension Benefit Guaranty Corporation (PBGC) to insure accrued pension rights in the event of plan termination.

fixed dollar—A term indicating that fluctuations in market value will not be reflected in the value of a fund or benefit. However, the fixed-dollar account of a GIC will reflect any reduction in market value in the event of premature withdrawal of the funds.

401(k) plan—Any arrangement that is part of a qualified plan having a salary reduction provision, under which a participant may elect to have the employer make payments as contributions to a trust under the plan on behalf of the participant. These payments, i.e., salary reductions, are not currently taxable to the participant and are strictly limited under IRS regulations.

funding arrangement—Any contractual arrangement entered into by a life insurance company to accept and accumulate monies contributed in connection with a pension or profit-sharing plan.

inverted yield curve—In so-called normal conditions, the longer the period to maturity of a bond or other debt instrument, the higher the yield, reflecting increased reward to the lender for increased risk. When unusual financial conditions result in short-term rates exceeding long-term rates, the resulting pattern of interest rates is referred to as an inverted yield curve.

individual retirement account (IRA)—A trust created or organized in the United States for the exclusive benefit of an individual or beneficiaries meeting the requirements of pertinent IRS regulations. Certain individuals not presently covered by a corporate pension plan or with income earnings below a specified level may contribute up to $2,000 annually to the trust, with the benefit of tax deferral on both principal and interest earnings. Other individuals may also contribute up to $2,000 but without the benefit of tax deferral on the principal amount.

market value adjustment—When funds are withdrawn from a GIC fixed-dollar account before the contractual maturity date, the amount payable may be reduced to reflect any drop in the value of the underlying assets. Such reduction, which may be calculated in a variety of ways, is referred to as a market value adjustment.

mortality risk—In calculating the amount of money to set aside to provide pensions to retired lives, the actuary will discount for mortality; that is, he will assume that the mortality of participants in the plan follows some appropriate mortality table, and, as each participant is assumed to die, the funds set aside for him become available to provide pensions to the survivors. If participants live longer, on the average, than was assumed, additional funds (which may be substantial) will be needed. The greater the number of lives, the more likely that mortality will follow closely the assumptions made by the actuary; hence, the smaller the risk of having to find additional funds. The smaller the number of lives, the greater the risk, and the more need to have this risk underwritten by a life insurance company.

open window period—A period, often up to twelve months, measured from the effective date of certain GIC contracts during which additional contributions will be accepted by the insurance company under the contract at the specified interest rate guarantee.

tax-qualified plan—A pension or profit-sharing plan that meets the requirements of Section 401 of the Internal Revenue Code. Contributions made by the employer are tax deductible to it and are not taxable to the employee during the accumulation period. Investment returns on the fund are also exempt from income tax during the accumulation period.

vested benefit—A benefit that has become nonforfeitable to the individual under the provisions of a pension or profit-sharing plan.

CONSULTANTS

The following is only a partial list of consultants. Locations are given for the main U.S. office of each consultant. However, many of these firms maintain offices in other locations across the country.

Alexander & Alexander Consulting Group Inc., Lyndhurst, N.J.

Buck Consultants Inc., New York, N.Y.

Hewitt Associates, Lincolnshire, Ill.

Fred S. James & Co., New York, N.Y.

Kwasha Lipton, Fort Lee, N.J.

William M. Mercer-Meidinger-Hansen Inc., New York, N.Y.

Milliman & Robertson Inc., Seattle, Wash.

Martin E. Segal Co., New York, N.Y.

The Wyatt Co., Washington, D.C.

SUGGESTED READING

Burroughs, Eugene. "Perspective on Investments: Acquiring and Managing Guaranteed Investment Contracts Today." *Pension World* 47, Apr. 1988.

Feinberg, Phyllis. "Defined-Contribution Plans Give Boost to GICs." *Pension World* 26, July 1988.

Perry, David M. "GIC Service Firms: Brokers, Consultants, Managers." *Pension World* 42, Nov. 1987.

Vosti, Curtis. "GIC Still Tops With 401(k)s." *Pensions & Investment Age* 14, July 11, 1988.

Williams, Fred. "Banks Aiming at GIC Market." *Pensions & Investment Age* 8, Aug. 8, 1988.

LIFE INSURANCE
SEPARATE ACCOUNTS

David L. Renz

BASIC CHARACTERISTICS

Separate accounts are investment vehicles made available under contracts offered by insurance companies, primarily to institutional investors. Although the types of purchasers have broadened over the years, pension plans have always been the primary market for these products.

In the United States, qualified pension plans are required to be advance funded. The sponsoring organization must contribute amounts to the plan over the working career of the covered employees such that sufficient assets will be available at retirement to provide for the employees' benefits. Hence, a plan will begin to accumulate funds that it may not need to pay out for another thirty years or more.

Under defined benefit pension plans, contributions are determined by actuaries using an assumed rate of investment return on plan assets. If the plan earns a higher return, it can increase benefits or reduce future employer contributions. Conversely, shortfalls will typically increase the employer's cost.

Pension plans use a wide array of insurance contracts. The products can be differentiated by the nature of the insurer's contractual liabilities into general or separate account products.

An insurance company's primary portfolio is called the general account. This account stands behind the company's promises to pay benefits under many different types of policies and contracts, such as traditional life insurance, group insurance, and health insurance.

David L. Renz, FSA, is Vice-President and Director of Financial Services for The Prudential Asset Management Co., Inc., in Florham Park, N.J.

The benefits guaranteed in these products are not contingent on the investment results of the general account. The insurer bears the investment risk. The purchaser may participate in excess performance through the crediting of dividends, but these are not guaranteed. The fixed or predictable nature of the company's outflows coupled with stringent limitations from state regulatory authorities lead the general account to be invested primarily in fixed income securities, such as bonds and mortgages.

Prior to 1962, the general account was the only portfolio available to insurance companies. It was used to back all lines of business. The general account was appropriate for many types of pension contracts, particularly those assuring annuity benefits or containing a guarantee of principal and interest. However, most pension plans were in the accumulation phase wherein current contributions plus income exceeded disbursements, resulting in large funds that needed to be invested with a long-term horizon. In such cases, there was growing interest in equities, which were expected, to provide superior returns over time. Consequently, pension plans were turning more and more to independent advisors and bank trust companies. The wider range of investments available from these sources allowed a plan to tailor its portfolio to its individual needs for current income, long-term return, and risk tolerance. Insurance companies, hampered by state and federal regulations, were at a disadvantage. This led insurance companies to seek and obtain enabling legislation to permit operation of separate accounts.

A separate account is a portfolio of investments that is legally segregated from all other investments of the insurance company. The insurance company is the nominal owner of the underlying assets, but the beneficial owners are the customers of the separate account. Under a separate account, all income, including unrealized gains and losses, is credited to the account. The insurer's liability to customers is defined in terms of the account's investment results.

Separate accounts have shown rapid growth since their introduction. As shown in Table 1, assets exceeded $112 billion at the end of 1987. (This does not include assets managed under investment advisory agreements.) Although the initial development of separate accounts was concentrated in common stocks, other categories now comprise over half of separate account assets.

Insurance Contracts

Separate accounts are issued under an insurance company contract, such as a group pension contract or variable life insurance policy. The contract may provide for investment services only. In such a case, the contractual obligation is limited to the investment results of the account. Alternatively, the contract may contain guarantees of certain retirement or other benefits, such as under an immediate participation guarantee (IPG) arrangement.

Administration

One or more investment professionals will be designated the portfolio manager and will have responsibility for investment decisions relating to the account. The portfolio manager may be a member of the company's investment department or may be located in a subsidiary that specializes in institutional investments. The increasing use of subsidiaries and special units is designed to increase focus on the special needs of institutional investors and to encourage an entrepreneurial approach to asset selection.

The accounting area will track deposits, withdrawals, receipt of investment income, and

TABLE 1. Separate Account Assets (in millions of dollars)

Year	Bonds & Cash	Stocks	Mortgages	Real Estate	Other	Total
1967	127	1,064	14	0	2	1,207
1968	281	1,946	20	1	21	2,269
1969	690	2,793	36	1	99	3,619
1970	947	4,041	37	2	34	5,061
1971	851	6,499	87	24	62	7,523
1972	1,016	8,744	120	96	82	10,058
1973	1,645	7,953	171	186	75	10,030
1974	2,383	6,192	202	372	127	9,276
1975	2,608	9,323	200	563	279	12,973
1976	2,791	12,219	214	653	346	16,223
1977	4,612	10,997	268	803	678	17,358
1978	6,649	11,528	311	1,146	792	20,426
1979	9,237	12,902	410	2,097	998	25,644
1980	12,699	17,705	687	3,341	1,340	35,772
1981	18,603	16,957	1,401	5,030	2,103	44,094
1982	25,034	20,641	2,556	5,686	3,364	57,281
1983	27,826	25,118	4,372	6,437	4,103	67,856
1984	29,180	24,316	3,341	7,816	5,027	69,680
1985	34,763	34,158	4,402	8,561	6,217	88,101
1986	40,057	42,486	5,897	9,084	11,052	108,576
1987	37,576	47,872	4,095	9,291	13,295	112,129

Source: American Council of Life Insurance

any other flows and will keep the portfolio manager apprised of the availability of investable funds. Any cash position will be managed to produce additional investment income.

A customer service area or representative is normally assigned to provide assistance and give the customer a central contact with the company. Periodic reports will be produced showing the value of the client's contract and the assets held in the account.

Pooling

Separate accounts, whether commingled or pooled, operate much like mutual funds. Multiple clients invest in a single account. A customer's equitable interest is expressed in terms of units. Unit values are redetermined periodically to reflect interest, dividends, and changes in market value. The effect of this approach is to provide automatic reinvestment of income. Deposits or withdrawals can only be made on a day a current unit value has been calculated. Frequency of calculation will vary, depending on the type of underlying investment (for example, common stock may be daily, while real estate might be quarterly).

If a client is willing to deposit sufficient funds (e.g., $10 million or more, depending on the type of investment), an insurance company may develop a single-customer separate account. This allows investments to be tailored to the client's specific needs. However, there may be less diversification and liquidity than in a similar, but larger, commingled account.

Regulation

Certain states require separate account contracts to be filed with their various state insurance departments. In New Jersey, for example, the filing will include an essentials of operation summary, which will specify the type of contract, type of clients to which it will be sold, any applicable guarantees, limitations on investments, method of asset valuation, and method of determining the liability to customers. Prior approval of the insurer's board of directors or finance committee will normally be obtained before the contract is filed with the state.

Separate account investments are reported in their own financial statements of the insurance company and are carried at market value.

Pension plans come under the jurisdiction of the Employee Retirement Income Security Act of 1974 (ERISA), which is jointly administered by the Internal Revenue Service (IRS), Department of Labor (DOL), and the Pension Benefit Guarantee Corporation (PBGC). Plan assets, including separate accounts, must be administered solely for the benefit of participants and beneficiaries and thus fall subject to federal regulation. A series of prohibited transaction exemptions have been issued by the DOL to facilitate the efficient operation of separate accounts.

Registration

Separate accounts are legally considered to be investment companies by the Securities and Exchange Commission (SEC) and, as such, would normally be subject to the requirements of the Securities Act of 1933, the Securities and Exchange Act of 1934, and the Investment Company Act of 1940. However, the Investment Company Amendments Act of 1970 exempted separate accounts issued to qualified plans from the most burdensome provisions of these laws. Administrative exemptions are also available for large sophisticated investors, such as foundations. These exemptions do not apply to separate accounts used to fund variable life insurance, variable annuities (except under Section 401(a) plans), and Section 403(b) annuities. Such accounts are required to register with the SEC, must provide a prospectus, and can be marketed only by registered representatives.

Investment Management Fees

Investment management fees (IMFs) are typically expressed as a percentage of assets managed. It is common to have fees downscale as a client's assets increase. For example, an account might charge 0.65 percent on the first $10 million, 0.50 percent from $10 million to 25 million, 0.40 percent on the next $75 million, and 0.30 percent on amounts over $100 million. There is usually either a minimum deposit requirement or a minimum total fee. IMFs may be deducted from the unit value, or they may be paid separately by the client.

IMFs are designed to cover the insurer's investment expense. Transaction costs such as trading commissions or bid-asked spreads are reflected in the account's investment performance. The IMF may include a charge for standard administrative services or such costs may be paid in addition to the IMF. Special services, such as benefit payments, are not covered.

There has been increasing exploration of the use of performance fees wherein the level of investment management fee is determined by reference to the account's performance in relation to a predetermined index or target. Proposals from the SEC and DOL are expected to ease existing restrictions and open the doors to this type of arrangement. Interest among plan sponsors remains to be determined.

Separate accounts compete not only with each other but with banks, brokerage houses, and other investment advisors. Thus, there is substantial pressure on IMFs, and fee schedules tend to be quite competitive.

The most important factor influencing fees is the investment strategy and type of underlying investment. Fees for a stock index account may be 0.125 percent or lower, while real estate or foreign investments may be 1.00 percent or higher.

Guarantees

Separate accounts may be issued with certain guarantees. The most common is guaranteed minimum annuity purchase rates. These rates tend to be conservative, and actual purchases will be charged at the prevailing rates, if more favorable. Bond accounts are occasionally issued with guarantees of principal or interest.

In 1986, regulatory approval was received for a new form of contract under which the insurance company may guarantee fixed annuity benefits backed by separate accounts. Under this participating annuity arrangement, the contract holder retains significant control over investment decisions, and excess investment performance (positive or negative) is retained by the plan rather than the insurance company, as it would under a guaranteed general account contract. Separate accounts now guarantee that the total return will be at least equal to those under some external index, such as the Salomon Brothers bond index or the S&P 500.

Types of Separate Accounts

Large insurance companies will offer dozens of separate accounts. The accounts are differentiated by the types of underlying securities and the investment management style. Although most accounts invest primarily in one class of assets, there will always be a need for some short-term cash management. If permitted, an account may also employ derivative instruments, such as futures and options, to increase return or decrease risk.

Index Accounts. In recent years, interest increasingly has centered on passive management. Index accounts are designed to track closely the performance of an external index, such as the S&P 500 or the Wilshire 5000. Fees for index management are quite low and, historically, results have outperformed the majority of equity money managers. In addition to domestic stock accounts, index funds are available to track various bond indices and the Europe-Australia-Far East index.

Equity Accounts. Considering the nature of their obligations, most pension plans have a long investment horizon. Their tax-exempt status allows them to concentrate on total return without artificial distinctions between income and appreciation. They are well suited to invest in common stocks; in practice, the most prevalent investment strategies have historically allocated over half of the plan's assets to equities. As a result, institutional investors have become a dominant force in the daily trading activity on the major stock exchanges.

Most insurance companies will offer a number of different actively managed stock funds, each of which attempts to add value by using a specific investment style. Possible approaches include value oriented, quantitative, earnings momentum strategies, low or midsize capitalization, contrarian, segment specific, and income oriented.

Preferred stocks are not a major factor in separate accounts, amounting to only $220 million in 1987. While they may be viewed as a form of fixed income security, their pricing reflects a tax advantage (i.e., the intracorporate dividend exclusion) that has no value to pension plans. One exception is convertible preferred stock, which has certain hybrid characteristics that may make it attractive.

Bond Accounts. Insurance companies are most widely recognized for their investment expertise in the fixed-income marketplace. The experience gained from running their extensive general account holdings has been readily transferable to the operation of separate accounts.

Companies operate multiple bond accounts. Some may target specific maturities (e.g., intermediate and long) or may use a spaced (laddered) maturity approach. They may be passively (e.g., buy and hold) or actively managed. Active management will attempt to add value through swaps or interest rate anticipation strategies.

Accounts may be defined in terms of quality. A commonly offered type of separate account is invested in high yield or junk bonds (which are below investment grade quality). Variable life insurance products often have an account restricted to U.S. government debt securities, which are viewed as having no default risk. Of course, such accounts are still subject to market value loss if interest rates rise.

The tax advantaged position of separate account purchasers makes investment in tax-free municipal bonds rare.

Immunized Bond Accounts. Institutional investors may need to have a given sum of money available at a specific later date. For example, a hospital or college endowment fund may have amassed contributions for future construction that will not be spent for some time. One approach to meeting the investor's goal is to purchase zero coupon bonds of the appropriate maturity. If coupon bonds are used, the entity faces reinvestment risk—the uncertainty of the rates at which interim cash flows may be invested. Also, if the maturities of the bonds do not coincide with the target date, there is uncertainty as to the future market value of the securities. A solution is the use of immunized bond accounts, which employ duration matching to produce the desired maturity value regardless of the intervening level of general interest rates. While the insurance company does not normally guarantee the maturity value, rebalancing should add value versus the results that could be obtained from the purchase of a portfolio of zero coupon bonds. Because of the need for a specific maturity value and date, such accounts are normally run on a single-customer basis.

Dedicated Bond Accounts. Pension plans have liabilities coming due at different times. Rather than using a series of immunized bonds accounts, they may employ dedication, which aims to assure that assets will be sufficient to support a specified cash flow in the future. The fund may be managed via cash flow matching or duration matching. In either approach, frequent rebalancing is required.

Dedicated bonds have occasionally been employed to justify the use of a higher assumed actuarial rate of interest. If this is the primary purpose, such use is questionable. Acquisition of dedicated bond accounts should be pursued based on their merits as an investment (e.g., for risk reduction).

Mortgage Accounts. An alternative in the fixed-income arena is the use of mortgages, which tend to have higher coupons than bonds. However, they also incur additional servicing costs and have more reinvestment risk due to the uncertainty of the level and timing of prepayment. The ongoing receipt of principal produces a shorter duration than bonds with similar maturities. Some companies offer accounts that deal only in mortgages on properties built with unionized labor. Such accounts have special appeal to Taft-Hartley Plans.

Separate accounts need to invest very large sums. Thus, the mortgages tend to be commercial rather than residential. If desired, residential mortgages can be acquired via mortgage pass-through securities, such as the Government National Mortgage Association (Ginnie Maes) or collateralized mortgage obligations (CMOs), which are available in large denominations.

Private Placement Accounts. Private placements are debt instruments negotiated directly between the borrower and lender. The borrower avoids the time, cost, and public disclosure of registration and underwriting. In return, such securities will provide a higher rate of return than public offerings. Insurance companies are a primary purchaser of private placements.

Since private placements have no public market value, unit values are determined by the insurance company using its own valuation methods. The limited marketability of private placements may impact the liquidity of such separate accounts.

Real Estate Accounts. Historically, real estate has proved to be an excellent inflation hedge. This can be particularly attractive to defined benefit pension plans where payments may be linked, through salary increases, to inflation. Also, since real estate performance is weakly correlated with the stock and bond markets, its inclusion can reduce the volatility of the total portfolio returns.

Real estate accounts invest in direct ownership of real property, primarily commercial. Day-to-day management may be provided by the insurance company or contracted out to a professional realty management firm. Such accounts may be open or closed ended. In a closed-end account, units may be acquired only during a limited period. The account is then invested in properties and distributes both investment income and principal as received.

Determination of market value is based on periodic appraisals. It is important that real estate accounts be diversified both geographically and by exposure to specific industries and other economic factors.

Cash Accounts. Most insurance companies offer a separate account investing in short-maturity obligations. This is similar to a money market fund. Many plans include an allocation to short-term instruments in their investment strategy. Cash accounts may also be used either to pay current annuity benefits or as a holding vehicle while awaiting movement to other separate accounts.

International. There is rising interest in investing abroad. Foreign markets do not correlate perfectly with those in the United States. Hence, a mixture of domestic and foreign securities should lower risk as measured by the standard deviation of returns. Also, it may be possible to achieve superior returns by investing in equities of countries whose economies are growing faster than that of the United States.

The research and analysis required to manage foreign securities successfully is more complex and less accessible than for domestic investments. Since most plans allocate only a small portion of their funds to the international sphere, only the largest institutions are in a position to operate directly in this field. Separate accounts provide a convenient means to incorporate these instruments into a portfolio.

Separate accounts have been established to invest in foreign stocks, bonds, or both. Accounts may be invested internationally or globally. Global accounts will invest in both foreign and U.S. securities.

A major source of variance in the total return on foreign investments is the volatility of currency exchange rates. An account may hedge this risk by use of forward contracts. It is important that the purchaser determine the account's intentions in this regard to make an informed decision.

Balanced Accounts. Separate accounts may invest in differing classes of assets under a balanced approach. Thus, the account may contain equities, bonds, mortgages, and real estate. In such cases, the insurance company typically will determine the weighing of one type of security versus another, based on its judgment as to the relative expected returns and risk from each class.

Alternatively, a company may offer a service providing asset allocation among its existing separate accounts. In either case, the objective is to add value versus the results that would be produced under a passive or static asset allocation.

Other Vehicles. Separate accounts can invest in a wide range of other vehicles. Examples might include venture capital, leveraged buyouts (LBOs), or oil and gas exploration. At times, an insurance company may offer to its institutional clientele investment products that have a legal structure other than that of a separate account. For example, a company may create a limited partnership to invest in specific real property.

ATTRACTIVE FEATURES

Diversification

Commingled separate accounts can acquire a wider range of instruments than the individual investor could reasonably assemble in a portfolio. This added diversification reduces unsystematic risk. By spreading its funds among a number of separate accounts, a plan may further increase diversification by asset type.

Liquidity

Separate accounts normally keep a small holding of cash or short-term investments to facilitate transactions.

In commingled accounts, cash flows from interest, dividends, and client deposits provide liquidity. Also, since any given withdrawal tends to be small in relation to the total account, sales of securities can usually be made in a rapid and orderly fashion to accommodate payouts.

Movements of funds from one separate account to another usually can be arranged quite easily, facilitating changes in investment strategy. Large deposits and withdrawals are commonly processed by bank wire, thus eliminating any "float."

Professional Money Management

The investment departments of insurance companies are responsible collectively for investing hundreds of billions of dollars. This enables them to acquire and develop a highly qualified team of professional money managers. They can afford to have specialists focused on subsegments of the various markets. This size enables them to provide continuity of portfolio management. They are likely to engage in more research than the typical pension plan might do on its own. For example, large companies often have full-time economists and supporting staff.

Economies of scale may produce savings in investment expenses. Their trading volume allows them to negotiate minimal commissions. Large insurance companies have inhouse traders and computerized trading rooms and are usually in a position to get the best price on purchase or sales.

Wider Availability of Investments

The diversification inherent in commingled accounts may enable clients to purchase investments that they would be unable to acquire on their own. For example, a plan wishing to invest $2 million in commercial real estate would find limited opportunities and most likely would be limited to a single property (with the attendant unsystematic risk). However, the same deposit into a pooled real estate account would be quite practical. Large commingled accounts may be able to purchase sizable pieces of property or other deals that might be beyond the capacity of an individual plan.

Insurance companies also have access to investments such as private placements or LBOs, which are not typically available in the open market.

Benefit Payment Services

Insurance companies are quite efficient in making payments to retirees. They also have the required expertise to comply with the often complex governmental reporting requirements. Benefit payments may be processed directly from separate accounts. Alternatively, separate accounts may be used to accumulate funds during an employee's working career, and such funds may be applied to purchase guaranteed benefits under an IPG or guaranteed investment contract (GIC).

Regulation

In addition to the ongoing review by internal and external auditors, insurance companies are subject to examination by the insurance departments of the states in which they are licensed. Separate account contracts will also be filed with the states. Although such reviews will not address investment selection, they are an important independent verification of the financial integrity of insurance companies.

POTENTIAL RISKS

Separate accounts present risks to the investor. Of course, these same risks are present under other methods of direct investment.

Systematic Risk. Since separate accounts typically invest in a specific type of asset, results are subject to significant systematic risk. Thus, equity accounts may be expected to rise or fall with the overall stock market. Similarly, bond accounts will respond to the general level of interest rates.

Performance. As with any money manager, separate accounts may over- or underperform the market. An account's investment approach may be effective over an economic cycle but nevertheless can underperform during shorter periods.

Liquidity. Primarily with respect to real estate or private placements, an insurance company may not be able, at all times, to accommodate all withdrawal requests. This risk should not apply to accounts invested in stocks or publicly traded bonds.

TAX CONSEQUENCES

Federal Income Tax

Separate accounts must meet the requirement of Section 817(d) of the Internal Revenue Code (the Code), which specifies that the investment return and market value of the segregated asset account be reflected in the annuity account value or, for life insurance contracts, in the amount of the death benefit or period of coverage. If all requirements are met, the insurance company may take a deduction for the change in its reserves (liabilities to customers) annually. This will offset the income from such sources as realized and unrealized gains, interest, and dividends, leaving the company in a position of paying tax on its economic income (i.e., revenues received less expense).

The tax treatment to the purchaser is dependent on the tax status on that entity. Employee benefit plans are covered by Sections 401–420 of the Code. If qualified under the Code, the plan itself is not subject to taxation. Taxation to individual participants is deferred until such time as payments are received.

Separate accounts may also be used to fund individual retirement accounts (IRAs) and Section 403(b) annuities. Again, if the requirements of the Code and regulations are met, the growth in assets is tax deferred until distributed. Purchasers of variable annuities or variable life insurance normally receive tax deferment until distribution and, in the case of life insurance contracts, death benefits may be received tax-free.

A number of events or actions can give rise to penalty taxes to plan sponsors or individuals. These taxes are in addition to any regular tax that may be due. For example, a plan distribution before age 59½ may result in a 10 percent excise tax if it is not rolled over into another qualifying plan. Underpayment of required plan contributions can lead to an excise tax of up to 100 percent of the amount of the deficiency.

Taxation of employee benefits is quite complex and constantly changing. A competent tax advisor should be consulted to help manage plans and assist individuals.

State Taxes

Currently, only California, Kentucky, Alabama, and the District of Columbia charge premium tax on amounts used to purchase annuities under tax qualified plans. Variable life insurance is subject to premium tax in most states.

Insurance companies may be subject to state corporate income taxes but usually receive a credit for premium taxes paid. Tax-qualified plans are not subject to state taxation. Taxation of distributions to participants varies, but many states provide tax advantages on receipt of retirement income.

REPRESENTATIVE TYPES OF INVESTORS

Defined Benefit Plans

Defined benefit plans make promises to pay retirement benefits to employees, usually based on length of service or compensation. Such plans may be viewed in two pieces: (1) benefits to current retirees and (2) benefits to employees who have not yet retired. Benefits to retirees represent a reasonably predictable stream of outflows. These payments may be funded through a GIC, an IPG, a similar annuity contract, or a dedicated bond fund; or they may be funded out of current cash flow. An accumulation amount will be needed to pay benefits to employees who have not yet retired. The emphasis on the latter funds is on maximizing total return within the predetermined risk limitations of the plan's investment strategy. Separate accounts can be well suited to this purpose.

Defined Contribution Plans

Defined contribution plans include money purchase, profit sharing, and 401(k) salary reduction arrangements. Here, the employer's obligation is to contribute a predetermined amount of money (or percentage of profit) each year. The amounts ultimately payable to participants will reflect the actual investment performance of the underlying accounts. Often, each individual employee selects the investment vehicle for his own account and may periodically move money among accounts. In such cases, the majority of participants tend to elect an option providing a guarantee of principal and interest. The primary funding vehicle for such allocations is a GIC. Separate accounts are often offered as additional options.

Public Employee Retirement Systems

These systems operate in much the same manner as defined benefit or defined contribution plans but typically are not qualified under the Code. Political subdivisions may also offer deferred compensation arrangements under Section 457. Large state plans may use single-customer accounts. Public plans often have investment limitations (e.g., maximum percentages that can be invested in equities or the requirement that portfolios be South Africa-free).

Other Employee Benefits

Benefits such as medical expense reimbursement or disability coverage may be administered on a "self-insured" basis by health and welfare plans. In this case, the plan or union will receive contributions and pay benefits either directly or via an outside administrator. While large sums may accumulate, payments are constantly being made. Liquidity is a prime consideration. The short investment horizon makes the use of cash accounts appropriate for the majority of assets.

Corporations may use separate accounts to prefund the cost of life insurance for current and future retirees. Most of the tax advantages of qualified pension plans are not available for prefunded life insurance.

Currently, there is a major controversy over prefunding the cost of providing medical and long-term care insurance for retirees. While the potential employer liabilities have been estimated by the General Accounting Office to be at least hundreds of billions of dollars, a lack of tax incentives has impeded the creation of any significant pool of assets to provide for such benefits. (Section 401(h) permits some funding within a qualified pension plan, but it is quite limited and restrictive.) The proposal by the Financial Accounting Standards Board (FASB 97) and any possible legislative action on the tax questions could open up this market. If so, separate accounts are likely to have a significant role as a funding vehicle.

Other Institutional Investors

Foundations, endowments, and institutions (e.g., colleges, hospitals) often have large funds that require professional management. Corporations may require short-term management of amounts to be used in acquisitions or liability settlements.

Individual Arrangements

IRAs may be offered on a group basis through a separate account contract issued to an employer. Similarly, tax deferred annuity plans (such as Section 403(b) annuities) are often funded using separate accounts.

Variable Life Insurance

Variable life insurance is a form of life insurance in which cash values and the amount or duration of insurance coverage are related to the performance of the underlying sep-arate accounts. In essence, the insurance company retains the mortality and expense risk while the policyholder assumes most of the investment risk (receiving the reward in return). Variable life insurance may allow an insured to increase coverage over time in response to inflation (assuming that the underlying investments prove to be an inflation hedge). Typically, policyholders may move their cash values among a number of separate accounts.

Variable Annuities

Immediate variable annuities provide a periodic payment to the recipient, usually for life. The amount of each payment varies according to the performance of the underlying separate account. These products were originally designed for use by pension plans. The concept was that the excess performance of common stocks should provide some protection against inflation. However, the uncertainty as to the amount of payment proved unpopular, especially to those relying on their pension as a major source of income. Today, this market is relatively small.

Nonqualified deferred variable annuities operate in a manner similar to mutual funds. Deposits purchase units of a separate account with the unit values reflecting current investment results. A difference is that the income under deferred annuities purchased by natural persons is tax deferred until received. Under the Tax Reform Act of 1986, there is a 10 percent penalty tax that applies to annuity withdrawals prior to age 59½, which is waived in the case of death or disability or for payment in the form of life annuity.

IMPORTANT FACTORS IN BUYING AND SELLING

Underlying Investments

The single most important decision facing the purchaser is the type of investment used. Over long periods, the difference in returns among equities, bonds, and real estate will be more significant than the value added by any individual investment manager. The decision as to the types of investments used will depend, for example, on the client's needs for appreciation, liquidity, and safety. An important factor will be whether the plan is in an accumulation phase or the payout phase. The nature of the plan's promises will also be important. Plans with benefits related to inflation such as those with final salary benefit formula may be more inclined to invest in real estate and equities than plans with benefits based on career average earnings.

Purchases should be consistent with the plan's predetermined investment strategy in terms of both the class of asset and the investment philosophy of the separate account.

Impact on Financial Statements

Under FASB 87, investment results from pension plans can, in certain situations, flow through to the sponsoring organization's balance sheet. Since separate accounts reflect market value, they are more volatile than a GIC, for example. A company's tolerance for such fluctuations should be considered.

The level of funding versus accrued or projected liabilities may influence the risk a plan is willing to assume and thus the type of investment used.

Past Performance and Reputation

Once the type of investment has been selected, separate accounts should be examined as to the company's experience with these assets and the particular investment style, the level of professionalism of the staff, and past performance. If a contract or insurance policy contains guarantees, the financial condition of the company should be considered. Many of the larger carriers are rated by Moody's and Standard & Poor's as to claims-paying ability (i.e., the financial wherewithal to make good on guarantees). The highest S&P classification is AAA. The A.M. Best company rates most insurance companies annually. The highest rating in their system is A+.

Fees

The investor should assess fees in terms of value added and services provided. The relevant factor in this phase of the decision-making process should be the net expected total returns after fees and any other expenses.

CUSTODIAL CARE

In commingled accounts, the insurance company retains custody of securities. This includes responsibility for physical receipt and safekeeping, collection of income, responding to tender offers, and, in some cases, proxy voting. The cost of this service is included in the IMF.

Custody of foreign securities is extremely complex. The insurance company will normally subcontract parts of this function to one of the small number of organizations with the international network required for this specialized activity.

Single-customer accounts may be nominally owned by the insurance company, which is then responsible for custody, or they may be externally held. If they are externally held, the arrangement is actually an investment advisory contract, not a separate account.

GLOSSARY

actively managed account—A separate account in which securities are continually traded to add value to the account's performance.

duration—The time-weighted present value of future cash flows divided by the unweighted present value of future cash flows.

duration matching—A process for minimizing reinvestment risk based on the fact that if two portfolios have the same modified Macauley duration, changes in their respective market values due to changes in overall interest rates will be highly correlated.

forward contract—An agreement to exchange a set amount of two currencies at a predetermined exchange rate at a specified date in the future.

institutional investors—Entities with large sums of money that need to be managed. This includes pension and welfare plans, foundations, endowments, institutions such as hospitals and colleges, and corporations.

passively managed account—A separate account managed by application of a formula or set of rules governing the composition of the portfolio.

rebalancing—Purchase and sale of securities to realign a portfolio's holdings with its stated goals.

separate account—A legally segregated portfolio of assets beneficially owned by the account purchasers under which realized and unrealized appreciation as well as investment income are credited to the account.

systematic risk—The risk inherent in a class of securities as a whole. In the case of equities, this is often approximated by the use of a broad-based stock index.

unsystematic risk—The risk unique to a specific security as opposed to the total market. This risk can be reduced or eliminated in a portfolio through diversification.

TRADE ORGANIZATIONS

The American Council of Life Insurance, Washington, D.C.

The Life Insurance Marketing and Research Association, Farmington, Conn.

SUGGESTED READING

PERIODICALS

Life Insurance Fact Book. Published by the American Council of Life Insurance, Washington, D.C. Annually.

Pension and Investment Age. Published by Crain Communications, Inc., Chicago, Ill. Biweekly.

Pension Facts. Published by the American Council of Life Insurance, Washington, D.C. Annually.

REFERENCE BOOKS

Cummins, J.D., ed. Investment Activities of Life Insurance Companies. Homewood: Richard D. Irwin, Inc., 1977.

Maginn, J. and Tuttle, D.L., eds. Managing Investment Portfolios. Boston: Warren, Gorham & Lamont, 1983.

______. Managing Investment Portfolios: 1985–1986 Update. Boston: Warren, Gorham & Lamont, 1985.

McGill, D.M., and Grubbs, D.S. Fundamentals of Private Pensions, 6th ed. Homewood: Richard D. Irwin, Inc., 1988.

Note: Life insurance companies publish annual and quarterly reports on their pooled separate accounts.

METALS

GOLD, SILVER, PLATINUM, PALLADIUM

Alvaro Meneses-Diaz
Luis Vigdor

BASIC CHARACTERISTICS AND HISTORICAL PERSPECTIVE

Although each precious metal has qualities that make it unique, all share certain characteristics: relative rarity, durability, malleability, irreplaceability, and versatility. Precious metals are symbols of wealth and highly tangible and liquid assets. Precious metals today are part of everyday life: as industrial components, jewelry, household objects, the stuff of many people's dreams, and investments.

Precious metals concentrate a great deal of value in small weight and volume. All are bought and sold as industrial materials, used in the manufacture of sensitive components of the strategic industry in the space era and in the manufacture of jewelry. They are held in bullion form for investment and in futures and options contracts for hedging and speculation. Gold and silver traditionally have been part of the world's monetary systems; even platinum was part of the official coinage during more than twenty years in czarist Russia.

Because the price of precious metals tends to rise when nontangible assets (stocks and bonds) are shaky and cash is an eroding asset, metal-related investments are a stabilizing element in a diversified portfolio.

The characters of all the precious metals markets underwent major changes in the 1970s, the result, in part, of an oil-fired inflation that rocked the economies of the world and deteriorated the currencies of oil-importing countries to the benefit of the producers. The changes also resulted from the appearance of a major market force, the American

---

Alvaro Meneses-Diaz and Luis Vigdor are Vice-President and Executive Vice-President, respectively, of MTB Banking Corporation.

investor, who for forty years had been legally forbidden to buy gold for investment or speculation and who rarely thought of silver and platinum.

Unlike the people of Europe, Asia, and the Middle East, during most of their history Americans were not particularly enamored by gold. The European settlers who populated the continent in the seventeenth century came not for gold but for land, freedom, and stability. Gold was for ornaments and coinage, and the Californian and Alaskan gold rushes did not touch significantly the lives of the great mass of American farmers, factory workers, and ordinary citizens.

The federal government hoarded gold to support its currency and to settle foreign obligations, but, for the average saver, gold held little attraction as an investment. When the dollar was a symbol of solidity and retained most of its purchasing power from one decade to the next, gold, which does not yield an income, was a less attractive holding than land, a business, or interest-bearing securities.

But in 1934, when the solidity of the dollar was at stake, the economy stagnant, and unemployment rampant, President Franklin D. Roosevelt devalued the dollar against gold, increasing its official price from $20.67 to $35 an ounce. To discourage profiteering, he put a legal ban on the private ownership of gold for investment or speculation. The United States, which had minted more than 70 million Saint Gaudens double eagles between 1907 and 1933, melted most of them. The records of the Philadelphia mint alone show that, during 1934, about 22.5 million double eagles were melted.

During the years that followed the ban on gold ownership, a potential buyer of physical gold in the United States had only two alternatives: purchasing jewelry or declaring himself a numismatic collector in order to be able to acquire semibullion coins minted prior to 1933.

The watchdog for the U.S. Treasury Department was a unit in Washington, D.C., called the Office for Gold and Silver Operations. This office was directly responsible for setting the guidelines for the industry. All gold bullion dealers and manufacturers needed a license issued by this office, which was very difficult to obtain. The law was strict, and Treasury agents were prompt in responding whenever they received reports of noncompliance.

Coin dealers selling coins minted before 1933 to collectors did not need this license and could therefore take full advantage of the American public's developing gold fever. Americans bought any coin available in quantity as long as it passed the 1933 dating test. Little by little, French napoleons, English sovereigns, Swiss vrenelies, Italian twenty-lires, and Colombian five-pesos coins found their way into the United States. Millions of coins were imported.

By 1974, the world had changed profoundly, and the U.S. government had ceased to guarantee its currency in terms of gold. The official price of gold had risen to $42.22 an ounce, a legal fiction in a world in which the free market price was no longer controlled by the U.S. Treasury. The actual price had soared in anticipation of a gold boom following the opening of the gold window by the United States on January 1, 1975, when all restrictions on the purchase of gold by U.S. citizens were to be lifted.

On December 30, 1974, gold reached $197.50 an ounce, yet American investors were supremely indifferent. The gold boom market fizzled, and bullion fell to $101.50 an ounce once again in 1976. Soon, however, world investors began to realize that precious metals offered an alternative to unstable stocks and tumbling bonds affected by the soaring price of crude oil and the increase of inflation rates.

In a world in which instant communications can spread alarm with the speed of light, several factors came together to create a textbook condition for a bull market in gold. American buyers entered the market with strength, operating through the new futures markets in New York and Chicago and purchasing gold coins. Buying increased by the newly affluent oil-producing countries of the Middle East, and demand grew in Europe, especially for gold jewelry.

Late in 1979, the Iranian hostage crisis and the Soviet invasion of Afghanistan raised the threat of a major confrontation in the Middle East. At the same time, a decline in oil production in Iran put new upward pressure on oil prices. The seizure of the Grand Mosque in Mecca endangered the stability of Saudi Arabia, the world's largest crude oil exporter. These events, coming together, set off new waves of anxiety worldwide and triggered widespread panic-buying of gold as a hedge against disasters that seemed imminent.

In January 1980, the price of gold peaked at $887.50 an ounce, and the price of platinum reached $1,085 an ounce. The final assault on silver by the Hunt brothers, combined with other events to put silver at its maximum price ever, $52 an ounce. These prices were anything but realistic, and the world saw the unpredictable: People decided to melt down all their precious metal holdings, such as flatware, candelabra, and jewelry, to sell it at market price. The price of all three metals tumbled.

In spite of these events, during the 1980s investors came to recognize the value of precious metals. Gold hoarding outside the United States and Europe went from 73.2 tons in 1983 to 274.6 tons in 1987. The futures and options contracts in the exchanges of the United States have been expanding since 1985 and continue to experience substantial growth. Total investment in platinum has been constantly rising since 1983, from 155,000 ounces to 490,000 ounces in 1987.

Palladium also has experienced a growing interest on the part of the industry. Demand in the western hemisphere grew 12 percent in 1987 over the previous year, and in Japan it grew 15 percent. The palladium futures contract in the New York Mercantile Exchange (NYMEX) celebrated its twentieth anniversary in January 1988 with 168,532 contracts traded during 1987, 16 percent more than the year before.

The industrial demand for silver also rose for the fourth consecutive year in 1987. Total consumption in the non-Socialist world increased to an estimated 340 million ounces, 14 percent higher than in 1981, but still well below the all-time peak of 16,065 tons (516 million ounces) achieved in 1973.

The range of possible investment in precious metals is remarkably varied, from the very conservative to the highly speculative. Ownership of metals offers an equity in a commodity of intrinsic value rather than in an arbitrary number of units of currency. In a world in which inflation has become an alarming fact of life, the ownership of a tangible commodity that has been historically in demand offers not only a hedge against inflation but also some prospect of real capital growth if purchases are timed well.

TYPES OF PRECIOUS METAL INVESTMENTS

Gold

Gold is a heavy, yellow, inert, metallic chemical element with a high degree of ductility and malleability; it is a precious metal and is used in the manufacture of coins, jewelry, alloys, and the like: symbol, Au (from Latin aurum); atomic weight, 197; atomic number, 79; specific gravity, 19.4; melting point, 1063° C; boiling point, 2600° C.

These coolly enumerated characteristics have made gold an object of human desire and greed throughout recorded history. The Egyptians were the first to mine gold extensively. For them, gold was not only for jewelry and ornamentation. It proclaimed wealth and power, and its ownership was the prerogative of kings, who were buried with gold artifacts. Gold was the royal treasure for Old Testament kings and was the doom of Midas. Zeus transformed himself into a shower of gold to possess Danae. Gold led adventurers to the discovery of new worlds, was the ransom of kings, and is part of the mythology, folklore, and literature of all the peoples of the world.

Although market prices of all precious metals have fluctuated wildly since 1974, a longer perspective suggests that ownership of metallic gold has been a surprisingly safe and stable form of investment. One ounce of gold purchased a well-made man's suit in the eighteenth and nineteenth centuries, and so it does today. Two hundred ounces of gold would buy a family home at almost any time during the last 200 years except during the period when gold was artificially priced at $35 an ounce. Twenty-five ounces of gold would pay for a Model T Ford in 1927 or any of a variety of domestic and imported cars in 1989. Gold prices during the last twelve years are compared in Figure 1.

Gold has never lost its appeal. Inflation, the oil crisis, political upheaval in the Third World, war in the Arabian Gulf, unending political tension in the Middle East, uncertainties in the future of the South African supply, terrorism, social and economic depression in developing countries—all have done much to establish gold, silver, and platinum as worthy components of well-planned portfolios.

Moreover, historically, gold has outperformed alternative investments. For instance, an investor who held Treasury bills during the fifteen-year period 1972 to 1987 would have had a yield of about 240 percent, while the consumer price index rose 181 percent. In the same period, gold achieved 990 percent.

For gold, the normal market factors of basic producer supply and consumer demand are an intricate chain of relationships, in which political and psychological forces play major roles. The price of gold is a sensitive barometer of world anxiety, rising in times of tension and fear and declining in times of relative tranquility.

Gold is traded all over the world, around the clock, with the price always swinging back and forth in London, Zurich, Hong Kong, Sydney, Winnipeg, New York City, and other major gold-trading centers. However, prices published in local media are usually based on either prices issued at noon and at the close of trading by the New York Commodity Exchange (COMEX), or in the famous twice-daily London fixing by major bullion dealers there.

In a ritual carried out since 1919, each member of the London gold market is represented at the fixing. The representatives are in direct communication with their own trading rooms. A representative of one of the major bullion houses acts as chairman. After considering the price at which gold has been trading so far each day, the chairman suggests a price, which the gold market members communicate to their own traders. The traders indicate whether they wish to buy, wish to sell, or have no interest. Then the chairman suggests other prices until all buyers and sellers agree on both price and quantity. At that point, worldwide supply and demand comes into balance, and the chairman declares the price fixed. Thus, for a moment twice a day, London gold is as close to an authentic price as the market can offer. Immediately thereafter, traders begin to change the price according to the realities of supply and demand in their own trading areas.

London's role as the world's leading bullion market was underlined in 1987 with the

FIGURE 1. The Average Price of Gold From 1977 to June 30, 1988

Source: Based on data provided to the authors by Platinum Guild International, Inc.

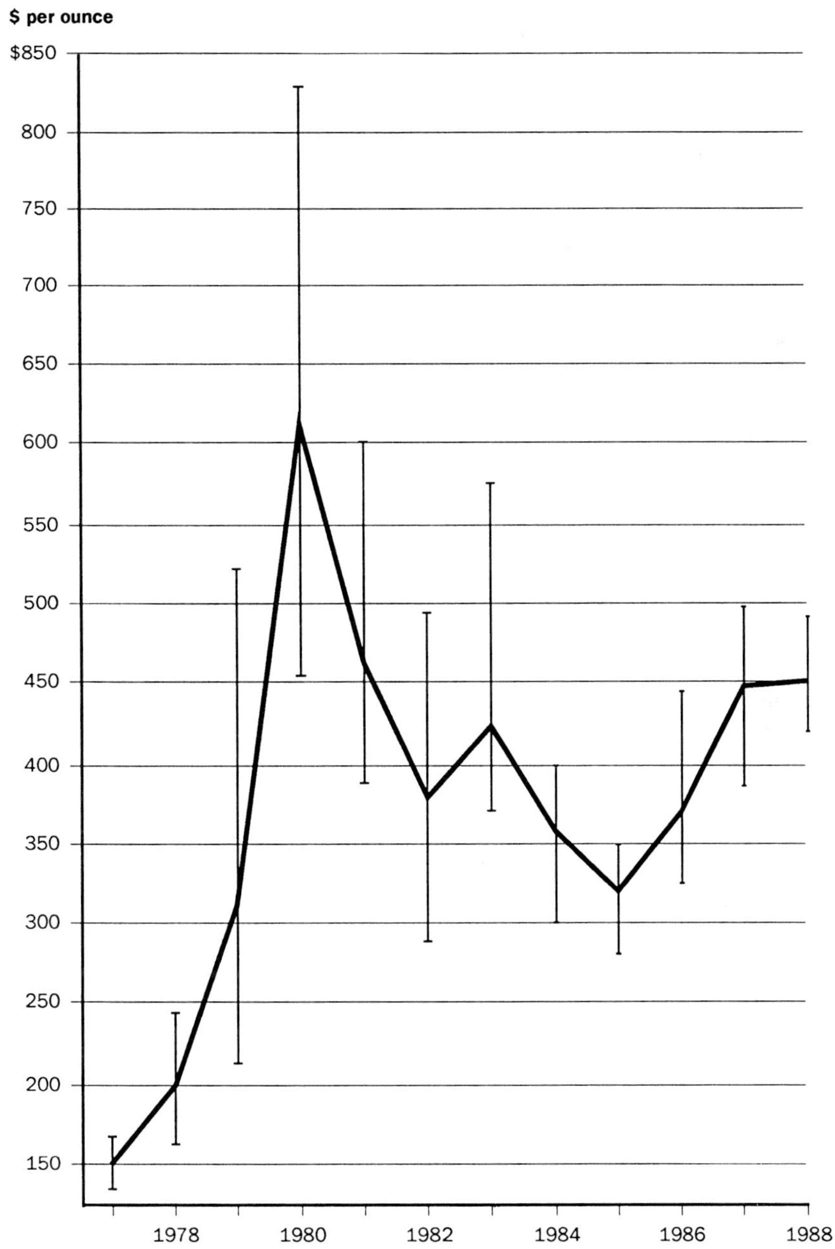

formation of the London Bullion Market Association (LBMA), which resulted from the flourishing growth of participants in the London gold and silver markets. The LBMA has become the official body with which the Bank of England is in regular contact as supervisor of the London markets.

The formation of the LBMA sprang from within the London gold market to bring together all major bullion dealers. The five members of the London fix have been joined as market makers during the past five years by six more houses as associate members, plus at least fifty recognized associate members who deal actively but do not make markets. The market members are designated as market-making members or ordinary members, and the association sets tests and rules for membership. Among its responsibilities is approving the "good delivery" list of acceptable members and assayers.

Bullion Bars. The most common form of gold bullion investment is the purchase of bullion cast in bars or ingots. Bullion bars can be held in a depository in the United States; in a foreign banking center, such as Zurich, London, or Luxemburg; or in the designated storage facilities of the investor, such as a safe deposit box in any bank or a safe in his own home.

The standard unit of gold in international trading is the 400-troy-ounce bar (12.5 kilograms) with a fineness of .995, known as the London good delivery bar (LGDB), but gold bullion bars are available in several sizes and weights. The most typical investment bars range from the one-kilo bar to the 400-ounce LGDB. This variety offers a wide spread in gold bar prices. The vast majority of the bars in the market, excluding the London good delivery, are of a .9999 fineness, which is what today's market demands most. In the Middle East and in the Far East, other measures than the troy ounce and kilos (grams) are used; the tola and the tael are common trading units for purchasing physical gold.

Bullion Coins. According to Herodotus and Xenophon, Croesus, king of Lydia (561 to 546 B.C.) struck the first gold coin. Since then, gold coins have fascinated the world's collectors and investors.

Bullion coins are favored by many investors who wish to have physical possession of their gold; coins may be purchased in smaller units than the regular bars; they are legal tender in the country that issues the coin; and the fine content is guaranteed by the issuing nations. Although the face value of a bullion coin does not represent its real value, which depends on its gold content, it does represent a bottom redeemable value in case of a gold price catastrophe.

In recent years, bullion coins have achieved great importance and popularity, especially since the introduction in 1967 of the Krugerrand, which had an easy-to-understand weight of exactly one troy ounce of fine gold, a very low premium, and legal tender status. Today, the investor has the choice of a variety of bullion coins; the maple leaf from Canada, the American eagle, the panda from China, the Australian nugget, and the Manx cat and the Britannia from the United Kingdom are the most popular. All have a pure content of one troy ounce of gold. Although the assay is not exactly the same, they all are legal tender and have a low premium.

An additional advantage of modern bullion coins is that all are available in fractionals, from the one-half ounce to one-twenty-fifth ounce, opening the doors to gold investment for small savers. (See Table 1.)

TABLE 1. Bullion Coins

Coin	Country of Origin	Fineness	Weight in Ounces	Comments
American eagle	United States	0.9167	1,½,¼,⅒	Launched October 1986. Face value $50
maple leaf	Canada	0.9999	1,½,¼,⅒	Launched in 1979. Face value C$50
panda	China	0.999	1,½,¼, ⅒,1/20	Launched in 1982; early issues have appreciated greatly. Face value 100 yuan
golden nugget	Australia	0.9999	1,½,¼,⅒	Launched April 1987. Face value Au$100
Britannia	United Kingdom	0.9167	1,½,¼,⅒	Launched October 1987. Face value £100 (the highest value of any bullion coin)
Manx cat	Isle of Man	0.9999	1,½,⅕, ⅒,1/25	Officially launched December 1988; was in the market since September. Face value 1 crown
gold ecu	Belgium	0.90	½	Successful since its launching; no continuation plans known. Face value 50 ecu
sovereign	United Kingdom	0.9167	0.2354	Produced intermittently; millions trade in the secondary market. Face value £1.00
Krugerrand	South Africa	0.9167	1,½,¼,⅒	Available only in the secondary market; trades at low premiums; importation forbidden

During 1987, Belgium successfully launched the ecu, but plans to continue it are not known. The Isle of Man, which has the angel, introduced the Manx cat in 1988 with some variations in the denomination of the fractional coins. In addition, other bullion coins are still available in the market: the Krugerrand, banned from importation to the United States in 1985 but still minted in limited quantities; the English sovereign (a touch less than one-quarter ounce); the Mexican fifty-peso coin (which is no longer legal tender but continues to be struck by the Banco de Mexico); and a variety of other coins that have enjoyed popularity in the past.

Bullion coins are traded by the major international traders, who make markets by publishing bid-and-ask prices on the best-known data carriers, such as Reuters and Telerate, thus ensuring their great liquidity. Bids for most of the bullion one-ounce coins fluctuate from 2 to 3 percent over melt value, and ask prices are from 4 to 7 percent over melt value. Bullion coins can be stored in depositories or kept in private safes.

Small Bars and Medallions. Also on the market are a large variety of small bars that range from the tiny 1-gram bar to 10-ounce and 500-gram ingots. These bars are popular among small savers who wish to accumulate gold little by little. The smaller bars are also popular in the jewelry industry, where they are used for pendants and rings.

Some assayers and private mints also produce coin-like medallions in round form and normally in only four sizes. These medallions are generally minted with attractive designs. Because they are not coins and have no legal tender status, their premium over gold is comparable to the cost of normal bars. The most popular sizes range from one-tenth ounce to one ounce.

Gold Certificates. The certificate is a relatively new type of gold investment designed to allow the small investor to trade gold in smaller quantities than the standard exchange contracts. Issued by many Canadian and U.S. Bank groups, certificates obligate the issuer to deliver a given quantity and fineness to the buyer.

The gold certificate gives the investor the same exposure to gold as does bullion, with the added advantage that he does not pay manufacturing charges and is provided with convenient storage as long as he does not take actual delivery.

Because the certificate is an obligation of the issuing institution to deliver gold, it can be exchanged for the underlying gold at any time. In that case, the investor is charged the fabrication costs plus a commission. Alternatively, the certificates can be sold through the issuing institution.

In the United States, there is now a certificate that is traded in lots of five or more ounces, which is considerably below good delivery weight and exchange contracts, and can be freely traded in any of the group member banks. Many financial institutions issue certificates in fractional amounts and provide the opportunity to invest in relatively low dollar amounts; some even accept credit card orders.

Forwards, Futures, and Options. Forwards, futures, and options contracts may be entered into either for hedging purposes or as speculative investments. See articles on "Futures: Financial, Agricultural, Currency" and "Options: Puts and Calls," elsewhere in this volume.

Gold forwards and futures are in essence the same thing: firm commitments to take or make delivery of a specified quantity of gold at a specific future date at a specific agreed-on price. The difference between forward and futures contracts is that forwards are custom made. They are traded on a principal-to-principal basis, that is, by a bullion dealer who makes a market to a client (normally a producer) out of a centrally cleared system. Such a contract requires a credit risk evaluation (line of credit). Settlement of a forward contract can be at any date agreed on by the parties. Forward positions are not easily offset or transferred to other participants.

Futures trading is conducted in a competitive arena of an exchange, known as the pit, by open outcry of bids, offers, and amounts. Sizes of contracts are uniform,[1] and delivery

---

[1] Contracts are of various sizes in the several exchanges of the world: the most common is 100 ounces, but Winnipeg also has a contract of 400 ounces, while on the Tokyo Commodities Exchange (TOCOM) the standard is one kilo and in the Sydney Futures Exchange it is fifty ounces.

is on a specific day of specific months. Margins are required of all participants. Market participants are usually unknown to one another. All positions, short or long, are very liquid and can be liquidated easily prior to delivery, thereby requiring only paper transactions. Very few futures contracts end in actual delivery.

The use of the forward and futures markets for hedging purposes is made by an operator who is already in the (cash) market as producer, consumer, or merchant. The hedge is the establishment of a position in the futures market that is opposite to the position held in the actual commodity. The hedge provides a means to lock in the price to be received or paid for gold at a given point in the future. By selling futures, producers can ensure the price of the future production and free themselves from market fluctuations. The consumer buying a futures contract locks in the price of his future needs, thereby eliminating the risk of rising prices.

The principle behind establishing equal and opposite positions in the cash and future markets is that the loss in one market will be offset by a gain in the other market. In short, the hedger fixes a future price for his metal in today's market.

At the other side of the hedger is a speculator, an investor who puts his capital at risk in the hope that the market will move in his favor. The existence of the speculator is essential to the futures market, as he is the willing taker of the risk that the hedger wishes to avoid. Investors in the futures market constantly study the markets and normally provide valuable assessments of market trends.

Speculators use a number of trading techniques to limit their risk. The most common is the purchase of options on futures, but many also employ arbitrage, the simultaneous purchase and sale of a future in different markets to take advantage of price differentials that may prevail for a very short time. With today's instant communications, such differentials are minimal, but the existence of more than one market always provides the possibility of an arbitrage.

The major gold futures markets cover the world around the clock. The first exchange that provided a gold futures contract was the Winnipeg Commodity Exchange, in 1972, but the dominant market is the COMEX, which inaugurated its gold contract on December 31, 1974; its volume has reached almost 100 times the combined volume of the rest of the exchanges of the world.

Options markets are becoming very important for both speculative and hedging purposes. An option gives the purchaser the right, but not the obligation, to buy or sell a futures contract at a given price within a specific time period. The underlying transaction in the options contract is the futures contract, while in the futures contract the underlying transaction is a cash position.

The option contract is a right that the operator or speculator purchases at a fixed price or premium, which is his only risk. Options can be exercised at any moment during the life of the option or can be allowed to lapse. In that case, the holder of the option loses the premium paid. Thus, the option can be compared with an insurance policy for which the insured pays a premium, or a *fond perdu*, if the insured risk does not occur.

The option that gives the right to buy a futures contract is a call option; the one to sell a futures contract is a put option.

Options are an efficient tool for hedgers, especially producers who can protect themselves from market fluctuations at a fixed cost, which is the price of the option, without entering into a futures position that involves margin calls. For the speculator, the purchase of an option contract gives an unlimited potential for a gain with a fixed limited potential loss. Options can be liquidated at any time, and part of the premium paid may be recoverable.

The options markets have generated enormous flexibility when used alone or in conjunction with other instruments, both as speculative investment or for hedging. Many highly sophisticated techniques have been developed to increase or decrease leverage, or minimize risk.

Gold options were introduced in 1982 by COMEX, which has become a dominant market in this field, with more than 2 million options contracts traded in 1987. Also active are the European Options Exchange in Amsterdam, which started in 1981 with a ten-ounce option, and the Montreal Options Exchange, where nearly a half million options were traded in 1987.

Gold-Mining Shares. There are three main markets for trading mining shares: North America (United States and Canada), Australia, and South Africa. Each has different characteristics, quite independent of the intrinsic merits of the companies involved. Gold-mining shares offer an attractive and highly leveraged way to go into gold-related investment, and they have the advantage of earning dividends. The availability of stocks is vast.

The North American mining stocks are vehicles more for capital growth than for yield, because most of the companies' profits are reinvested instead of being paid out as dividends. The major stocks are highly capitalized, with multiples (price/earnings ratios) ranging between ten and thirty. But there is also a plethora of new companies offering a wide scope for capital growth.

South African gold shares pay dividends out of all profits and set no reserves, because the South African gold-mining companies treat their mines as depleting assets. Moreover, owing to the discount between the financial rand, through which the shares are bought and sold internationally, and the commercial rand, through which the dividends are paid, the yield on these securities can be high. On the other hand, the perceived instability of South Africa requires these shares to be of a low risk/reward ratio.

Production cost is a variable that normally is closely followed by the investor. In the recent past, local costs in South Africa have been rising, thus making the purchase of anything but shares of gold companies with the lowest production costs less attractive. In general, the profitability of South African shares is declining with time, but because the South African stocks are usually highly capitalized, the trade of these shares is very liquid.

The Australian market is becoming increasingly liquid as a consequence of a series of takeovers, mainly during 1987, which has increased the number of gold-mining companies with large market capitalization. Also, the growing production of Australian gold is enhancing the appeal of Australian gold shares. In Australia, there is an increasing number of large, medium-sized, and young but growing gold-mining companies.

Shearson Lehman Hutton Securities in London publishes *Mining Weekly*. The section called "The Gold Page" lists the gold-mining companies of Australia, Canada, the United States, and South Africa whose shares are traded internationally, with updated information on the price of shares, the estimated production for the year, market capitalization, and other news. An important point of information is the rating for the short- and long-range period. The rating goes from one to five (with one the best and five the worst), thus giving the investor a clue as to when to buy or sell a position in a given mine company.

The investor or potential investor in this sector has to look at not only the multiple or price/earnings ratio, but other international economic considerations, including the exchange rates.

Bonds. The structure of gold bonds is quite sophisticated and offers a number of trading alternatives.

In 1973, the French government issued the famous Rente Giscard: 6.5 million bonds with a par value of Fr 1000 backed by gold and carrying a 7 percent coupon with maturity in January 1988. The French government guaranteed that, should the existing relationship between the French franc and gold be severed before maturity, the redemption value of the bond and the coupon would be based on the then-prevailing price of gold. This severence took place five years later when the international monetary system severed all links with gold.

As the par value of the bonds at issue was 1,000 francs, the bond holder was entitled to receive at redemption of each bond the franc equivalent of 3.07 ounces of gold as well as the equivalent to 0.215 ounces for the final coupon or 7 percent of the principal. The price of the redemption was based on the Paris fix for one kilobar over the thirty final trading days of 1987.

Although this instrument was useful for the French government in raising capital and was very attractive for the buyers, it ultimately proved to be expensive for the government. The market also proved to be sophisticated, as the bond was to a large extent hedged in the international gold markets.

With the exception of the above precedent, this type of gold-related investment is relatively new. Essentially there are two types of bonds: those that actually can be converted into bullion, and those with warrants attached, which give the holder the right to convert the warrants into gold within a certain period. (*Warrants* are discussed later in this article.)

Bonds that can be fully converted to bullion are mainly issued by mining companies. A well-known bond of this type is the eight-year Eurobond issued in 1986 by Brunswick N.L., which is listed on the Luxemburg Stock Exchange. The principal of each bond is equivalent to three ounces of gold and carries an annual coupon of 4.5 percent. After a minimum investment period, the bonds are fully convertible at any time to the cash equivalent of three ounces of gold plus 4.5 percent annual interest.

Bonds with detachable warrants seem to be more common, as they are issued not only by mining companies, but also by a variety of others, such as American Telephone and Telegraph (AT&T), General Motors, and Standard Oil.

These bonds generally can be traded either combined or without the warrant; the warrant can usually be traded separately. On this basis, the warrants are geared to the gold price just as the share warrants are geared to the price of the shares. A combined bond is also geared to the price of gold, but much less so, as the bond has its own intrinsic value based on the coupon payment.

Unit Trust and Mutual Funds. Unit trusts and mutual funds are pools of funds managed on behalf of investors. A number of these are based on gold and gold shares. By purchasing shares in these trusts or funds, the retail investor eliminates the burden of managing his portfolio on a day-to-day basis. Unit trusts and mutual funds usually require a minimum initial investment; purchases thereafter can be as low as $50. These funds normally have a diversified portfolio and take positions in gold and other precious metals to take advantage of the changes in the supply and demand in each of the precious metals markets.

Warrants. A share warrant is basically an option that grants the holder the right to purchase common stocks on the tender of further payment.[2] A warrant can be exercised at any time before the due date but generally is not exercised sooner. As the warrants give the right to the shares at a future date, they have a time value or, at worst, drop to zero if the underlying shares fall heavily. See article on "Warrants and Rights," elsewhere in this volume.

A separable gold warrant is a unit that, on payment of a specific sum on a due date, converts into gold metal. A warrant of this type operates as an option on physical gold, with a much longer period to run than the traditional options traded in the gold markets.

Both types of warrant are basically issued by mining companies for the purpose of raising capital.

Silver

Silver is a white metallic chemical element that is extremely ductile and malleable; it is capable of high polish and is the best metal conductor of heat and electricity. It is a precious metal and is used in the manufacture of coins, jewelry, alloys, and the like: symbol, Ag; atomic weight, 107.868; atomic number, 47; specific gravity, 10.5; melting point 960.8°C; boiling point, 1950°C.

Silver is second only to gold as an object of human desire. Thirty silver coins were the price paid for the betrayal of Christ; two rooms full of silver were part of the ransom paid for the last Peruvian king, Inca Atahualpa. Traditionally, silver is also the second prize for Olympic athletes. Man has been extracting large quantities of silver probably since 4000 B.C., but evidence suggests that by 2000 B.C. Mesopotamian merchants were the first to disburse silver as money. Silver is inextricably bound to India's history, a country where as much as 150,000 tons of silver are said to be in private hands.

Since it is considered a strategic metal, governments maintain stocks of silver in unknown quantities. By the end of 1987, the United States reportedly had a stockpile of 3,524 tons held by the General Services Administration, 75 tons held by the Defense Department, and 1,253 tons in the hands of the Treasury. U.S. Treasury coinage programs currently under way through the U.S. Mint will reduce these holdings.

The relationship between gold and silver has often been discussed. Before 1980, silver and gold tended to move symmetrically with each other, responding to economic, financial, and political changes. After 1980, gold continued to be regarded as a hedge against inflation because of its position as official reserve; silver lost favor for many reasons, but maintained its appeal for individuals mainly in the Middle East, India, and the United States. (See Figure 2.)

Silver is also the subject of an unending debate: Should it be considered a precious metal or a mere industrial metal, as the industrial demand for silver is the largest. The industrial aspects of silver are clearly important, but as long as silver is used for jewelry, coinage, and as an investment vehicle for the individual who wants to hoard it, silver is without doubt a precious metal.

Contrary to gold, whose production in the Western Hemisphere extends from South Africa to Brazil and from Australia to North America, silver production is largely concentrated in the Americas. Sixty-three percent of the estimated world production for 1988 is in

---

[2] In this it is similar to the so-called partly paid shares. Partly paid shares are those for which the balance of the full price of the share is payable at a specified date in the future.

FIGURE 2. The Price of Silver From 1973 to 1987

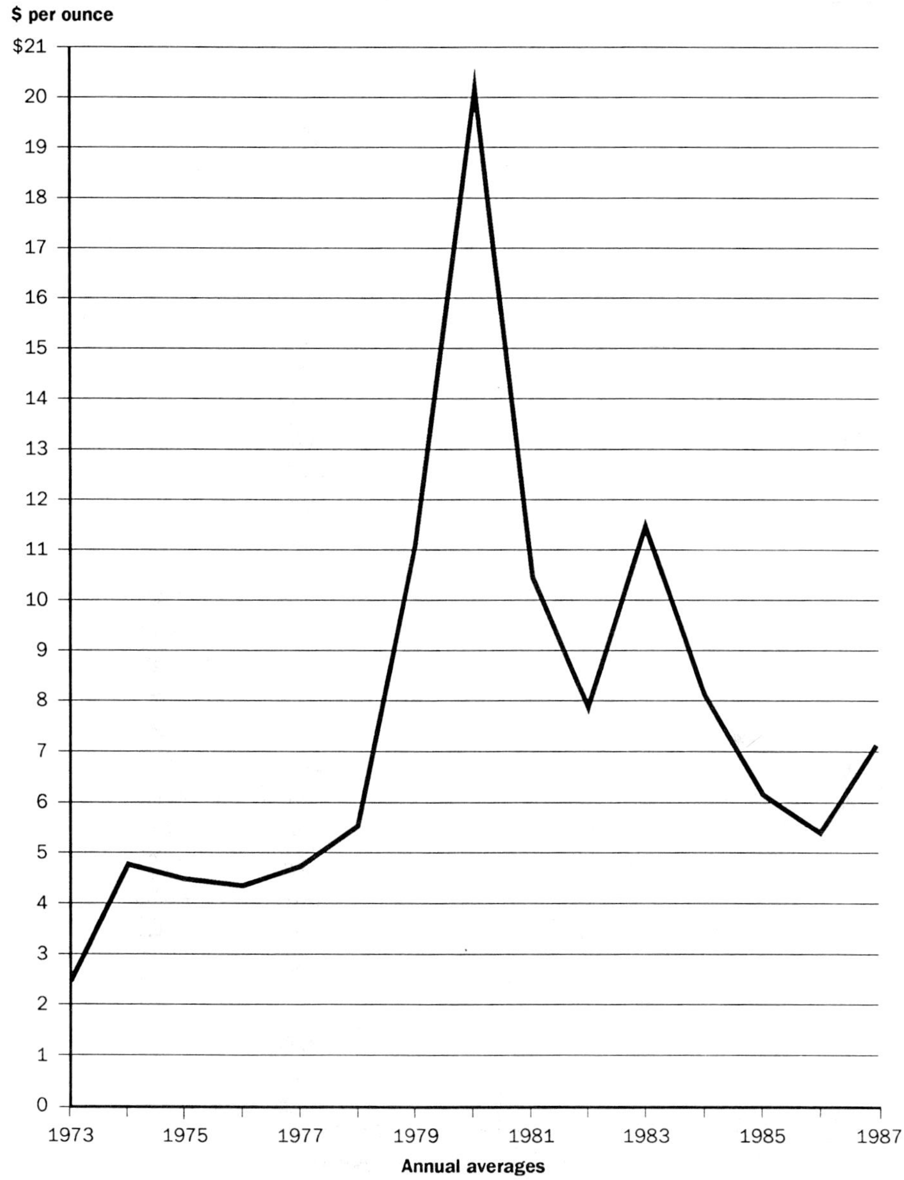

the hands of Mexico, Peru, the United States, and Canada. Ten percent comes from Australia and 27 percent from the rest of the Western Hemisphere.

For generations, the annual production of newly mined silver has been at least one-fifth lower than demand. The deficit is traditionally covered by Indian sales of privately owned silver (which, however, is not a regular but cyclical source); the melting of coins, bars, and decorative objects; the use of government stockpiles; and secondary recovery or industrial recycling, which becomes more and more profitable with advances in technology.

Bullion. London is the most important center for trading in physical silver bullion. The system for silver operates basically in the same way as for gold, with a number of trading houses making markets on a principal-to-principal basis and dealing on behalf of clients. The price, like that of gold, is fixed every day by three of the London houses.

The fixing member have orders from the market to sell and buy; the fix is produced when selling and buying orders are balanced. The fix is quoted in U.S. dollars per ounce and immediately converted into pounds sterling in such a way that the two prices are practically simultaneously established.

The trading unit in the London market is 100 ounces and is commonly referred to as *lakh* (Hindu for 100), but the market is flexible, and, as is normal in a principal's market, an order of any size may be executed.

At the COMEX and the Chicago Board of Trade (CBT), the standard delivery bar is of 1,000 ounces of 0.999 silver, plus or minus small tolerances. Other than these bars, which are cumbersome, the market offers a variety of small bars and coin-like, round medallions to the investor. Today, the investor has a choice of bars from one ounce to 100 ounces, including one-kilogram bars, which are quite liquid, because they are manufactured by reputable smelters and assayers, who guarantee their fineness. Small denomination bars are also used by the jewelry industry and small industries that cannot afford to carry standard-contract-size positions.

The purchase of bars carries a premium reflecting basically the manufacturing cost of the bar, which is totally lost when the bar is resold. Retail traders normally repurchase bars at a few cents below the market.

Silver Coins. The first silver coin was probably an irregularly cast planchet of silver introduced by Mesopotamian merchants some 4,000 years ago. Weight determined value, and silver was sliced or shaved to separate the exact amount for payment. As expanding trade intensified the need for equivalent monies, coins of specific weight and purity appeared.

When the Holy Roman Empire was at its prime, silver was less scarce than gold and thus less valuable; therefore, silver served as money for the merchant class, while gold was the currency only of kings and the very wealthy. This silver came from the Spanish lead-silver mines, which Rome had gained as spoils of the Punic Wars and which supplied most of the world's silver until the eighth century, when the Moors occupied Spain and closed the mines.

No new significant silver production was to occur for another eight centuries. After the ransom was paid by Atahualpa, the Spanish realized the large extent of silver availability and developed the mines of Mexico, Perú, and Bolivia. After that time, the Spanish colonies provided most of the world's silver until the colonies gained independence in the first part of the last century. Silver coins minted in American Spanish colonies circulated all over the world and were the preferred currency. The Spanish "Real de 8" minted by the Mexico mint (founded in 1535), the first silver "dollar," was the basis for the U.S. silver dollar.

In 1792,[3] the United States tied the price of silver to the price of gold under a bimetallic

[3] The U.S. Mint was established in 1792, but the first coin was minted in 1793.

monetary system. As the then-circulating dollar contained .77 ounces of silver, the monetary value of the metal was set at $1.29 per ounce. Bimetallism lasted in the United States until 1900, when the gold standard was adopted. However, silver dollars continue to circulate, and some U.S. paper money (silver certificates) was fully redeemable in silver until the early 1960s.

Until 1965, more than 50 percent of silver production in the Western world was used in mintage of coins, most of them for U.S. coin issues, in line with the American tradition for silver investments. When U.S. silver coinage declined in the late 1960s, silver consumption decreased accordingly. The price surges of the 1970s took their toll, and silver coinage declined in 1981 to less than 3 percent of total production.

In the last few years, particularly during 1986 and 1987, silver coins have experienced a renaissance. In fact, coin issues have gone back to 9.2 and 9.3 percent of silver production in 1986 and 1987, up from the low levels of the first half of the 1980s. North American silver coins account for more than half the resurgence, mainly because of the Statue of Liberty and U.S. Constitution commemorative programs, as well as the silver eagle program, which enjoy excellent sales. They practically have eliminated the Mexican onza from the market, which had been the only legal tender silver bullion on the market during most of the 1980s.

New programs have been launched in 1988, increasing the silver coinage available to the investor. In addition to the Olympic programs of Canada and Korea and the U.S. programs, Canada has put the silver maple leaf on the market as a logical companion to the gold maple leaf. An important feature of the silver maple leaf is its legal tender face value of C$5, considerably higher than that of the silver eagle (US$1) and consequently much closer to the intrinsic value of the silver. If one bears in mind that in 1973 the average price of silver was only $2.56 an ounce and that as late as 1977 it was only cents above four dollars per ounce, the silver maple leaf actually guarantees a long-term floor price for silver. The silver maple leaf has gained popularity very rapidly.

Bags of Silver Coins. These are bags containing U.S. standard silver coins of 90 percent fineness minted from 1896 to 1964 with a total face value of $1,000. Silver bags are traded in the market as any other form of bullion, that is, exclusively according to their fine silver content. This is a popular form of non-interest-yielding investment; U.S. silver bags are widely quoted on the market, are quite liquid and are a relatively inexpensive investment. Each bag contains 720 ounces of silver.

As with any other bullion investment, silver bags need storage facilities that are normally available in all trading houses. Storage is needed for U.S. silver bags, which weigh around sixty-five pounds and are, therefore, somewhat cumbersome.

Forwards, Futures, and Options. These forms of the silver trade have exactly the same fundamental characteristics as those of gold and, as a matter of fact, of most of the commodities traded in open markets. The specific terms differ, but the basic use for hedging purposes and speculative investment remains the same.

Silver contracts for forward delivery are predominantly traded in London. Although delivery can be set for any business day, there are two common contracts. One contract is the spot, which is for delivery two business days after sale, and the other is three months forward. Delivery is made through a warehouse receipt. The basic difference with the futures contract is that normally actual delivery of the metal terminates this transaction.

Future silver contracts are traded in the United States at the COMEX; at the CBT and its affiliate, the Mid-America Commodity Exchange; at the London Metal Exchange, which has two contracts, both quoted in U.S. dollars; and at the Tokyo Commodities Exchange (TOCOM), which has one contract denominated in yen per gram.

As with gold, the dominant market for silver futures is the COMEX. Out of 25,175 million ounces traded during 1987 in London and New York, COMEX accounted for 25,039 million ounces, leaving no doubt as to its preeminence, in spite of the problems in the spring.

In 1987, the CBT obtained approval from the Commodity Futures Trading Commission to trade during the night trading session gold and silver contracts identical to those traded during the day. Night trading commenced in September 1987 and most probably will mirror the TOCOM precious metals trading, where silver is in third place after gold and platinum, reflecting the preferences of the Far Eastern markets.

The main characteristics of the international silver futures contracts are shown in Table 2.

Options on silver futures contracts continue to expand, owing to the intrinsic merits of the option contract in general, and will probably continue to grow, as options prove to be a viable way to hedge and to speculate within a well-defined risk.

COMEX also is the leading market for silver options contracts. In 1987, COMEX traded almost a million contracts. As of 1988, other than COMEX, only the agreement between the exchanges of Montreal, Vancouver, and Sydney has had a silver options contract. In 1987, the London Metal Exchange inaugurated its silver options contract, which, however, has had little activity because of the low level of its futures contract in silver. During the first part of 1988, the CBT obtained authorization to trade a silver options contract, indicating that this market will continue to expand in the future.

Certificates. The only available silver certificates are Latin American certificates, though they carry some restrictions. The Mexican and Peruvian governments, aware of

TABLE 2. International Silver Future Contracts

Exchange	Contract	Trading Dates	Quotations
London Metal Exchange	10,000 ounces 2,000 ounces	Three months forward plus all other dates by adjustment	U.S. cents per ounce
COMEX	5,000 ounces	January, March, May, July, September, December, and two months following spot	U.S. cents per ounce
CBT	1,000 ounces	February, April, June, August, October, December, and two months following spot; same for night session	U.S. cents per ounce
Mid-America Commodity Exchange	1,000 ounces	All months	U.S. cents per ounce
TOCOM	10 kilograms	Spot plus six months forward, up to one year forward	Yen per gram

the importance of silver to their economies and of the fact that they are the two largest producers of silver in the world (the two countries account for 40 percent of the western world production) have been trying to stimulate both domestic production and local investment.

The Peruvian government has traditionally had a strategic stockpile of silver in the hands of its Central bank; in 1988, it monopolized the purchase and export of silver in order to better control the foreign-exchange revenues of the metal (half of which leaves the country anyway as part of polymetallic lead and zinc concentrates). The Peruvian government has a program of silver certificates available only to residents who can purchase them in local currency up to 3,000 ounces per person. (Companies are allowed to purchase up to the equivalent of $50,000.) These certificates are fully redeemable in physical silver. All that is known about the mechanism of the certificates is that a total of 3 million ounces of metal has been earmarked by the Central Bank. It is known, however, that Peruvian investors bought about 200,000 ounces in the first few days and that the authorities stopped the program. Some investors have actually taken delivery and later exported the physical silver, thus making, in effect, a foreign exchange profit.

Mexico has a more clearly defined silver certificate mechanism. *Ceplatas*, or silver certificates, are issued and guaranteed by a group of trustees led by the Banco de Mexico, Banca Cremi, and two mining houses, Industrial Minera Mexico and Peñoles. The metal backing the certificates is stored at Banca Cremi. Each certificate is for the value of 100 ounces of 0.999 fineness and has been issued to the general public with some tax advantages. These certificates are available to any purchaser regardless of nationality and have been very successful. During 1987, two issues were sold for a total amount of 7 million ounces.

Silver-Mine Shares. Unlike gold mine shares, which are plentiful, silver-mine shares are rather scarce, for several reasons. First, actual silver mines account for only about 35 percent of production; the rest of the silver comes in polymetallic geological formations, mainly associated with lead, zinc, and copper. Second, the vast majority of pure silver mines are in Peru and Mexico, and large multinational companies—mainly American, Canadian, and British—already have interests in Mexican and Peruvian silver-mining concerns. In Mexico, for instance, Asarco, Amax, Lacana, Placer Dome, and BP, among others, have substantial participation. In Peru, the following are major shareholders in silver production: The Hochschild Group, Peñaroya, Asarco (through Southern Peru Copper Corporation), Geomin, and others.

In the United States and Canada, several registered mine companies produce silver as a primary product, and their shares are available to the investor. The criteria for investing in this type of equity are similar to those for gold shares; they must be carefully researched, with appropriate information and expert guidance.

Rare Coins. Rare coins in gold and silver have all the merits of the precious metals, combined with an aesthetic appeal. A famous chart created by Salomon Brothers, reproduced by several coin dealers, shows how rare coins have appreciated in comparison with other investments. Independently of the values given in that chart, the truth is simple: Rare coins do appreciate with time, are a long-term investment, and, in many cases, can also be considered as authentic objects of art rather than merely tangible assets.

Rare coins have to be purchased carefully. Grading of coins has become much more sophisticated than in the recent past, and, as a consequence, price variations are very significant from one grade to the other. Anyone wishing to invest in rare coins has to do careful homework before going into the market, and should rely only on coin dealers with the highest integrity. See article on "Coins," elsewhere in this volume.

Platinum

Platinum is a steel-gray, malleable, ductile metallic chemical element, highly resistant to corrosion and electrochemical attack; used as a chemical catalyst, for acid-proof containers, ignition fuses, jewelry, dental alloys, and the like: symbol, Pt; atomic weight, 195.09; atomic number, 78; specific gravity, 21.45; melting point, 1773.5°C; boiling point, 4300°C.

The dictionary does not define platinum as a precious metal, but it is, and the rarest of the traditionally accepted ones. It is what we call the *primus inter pares* of the precious metals. Moreover, platinum is foremost among the rare strategic precious metals called the platinum group metals (PGM), or the platinum related metals (PRM). In addition to platinum, these are palladium, iridium, rhodium, osmium, and ruthenium, all of great rarity. Out of this group, only platinum and palladium exist in sufficient quantity to support a commodity market structure. Nonetheless, compared with gold and silver, platinum supply is almost 19 times lower than gold and more than 120 times lower than silver. In fact, in 1987, 3.1 million ounces of platinum entered the market, as opposed to more than 56 million ounces of gold (without considering recycling of scrap and official sales) and the more than 362 million ounces of newly mined silver that were produced in the western world.

Most of the current demand for platinum and platinum-related metals is met by newly mined material. Very little is held in inventories above ground, as is the case with gold and silver; therefore the price of platinum group metals is more sensitive to perceptions of instability in the economic and political scenarios of the producing countries.

Platinum supply depends basically on the production of South Africa and the Soviet Union. South African mines produce between 80 and 85 percent of the total world output. Soviet platinum is basically dependent on its palladium production. Canada also produces platinum as a by-product of nickel and copper; therefore, Canadian platinum production depends on that of these basic metals. Since the times of the Spanish colonies in South America, Colombia has been a producer of platinum from alluvial deposits, but its production is very small. The United States has an insignificant production as a by-product of palladium.

The United States and Japan are dominant in the demand for platinum. During 1987, Japan consumed 50 percent of the world's output, the United States 27 percent, and western Europe, 17 percent. The balance (6 percent) was shared by the rest of the world. Preliminary data for 1988 shows that Japan has absorbed 53 percent of the total demand, while the U.S. consumption remains below 28 percent; total supply increased by 7 percent. Investment demographics parallel consumption (See Table 3).

Only recently has platinum begun to attract widespread attention. Until the 1950s, the world market was less than 10 percent of what it is now. The demand has grown rapidly with the introduction of platinum catalysts and the advance of technology. Today, platinum is used in the petrochemical industry, in fertilizers, electronics, medicine, and fuel cells, but the primary consumer of platinum is the autocatalyst industry; the jewelry industry is in second place; and investment is third.

TABLE 3. Platinum Investment

	North America	Japan	Rest of Western World
1980	N.A.	160	N.A.
1981	N.A.	195	N.A.
1982	40	115	5
1983	40	70	45
1984	30	165	125
1985	130	205	95
1986	300	(90)*	115
1987	85	335	70
1988	70	430	130

N.A. = Not available.

* Japanese investors are divided into small and large. During 1986, large investors disinvested 125,000 ounces; small investors invested 35,000 ounces.

Note: All measurements shown are in thousands of ounces.

Source: Based on the statistics of platinum consumption provided by F.J. Smith and G.G. Robson, *Platinum 1988*, London: Johnson Matthey, 1988, p. 25.

This distribution of the uses is representative of global consumption, but priorities differ according to region. In 1987, 54 percent of the total Japanese consumption was in the form of jewelry; second in preference was direct investment, which accounted for 20 percent of Japan's consumption, while the autocatalyst industry was third, with 17.8 percent.

The consumption structure is North America is quite different. Sixty-five percent of 1987 consumption was absorbed by the autocatalyst industry, while investment was less than 10 percent and jewelry a mere 1.6 percent.[4]

In any case, the growing demand for platinum, whatever its final use, has contributed to the creation of awareness about its investment potential, but much has yet to be done in the western hemisphere to make platinum a long-term investment, as the Japanese seem already to have done.

The pricing of platinum was for a long period dominated by the South African producers who still stick to their practice of establishing their price for their clients on the basis of long-term contracts. Until the 1950s, one of the producers, Inco, sold only through Engelhard, and another, Rustenburg, sold through Johnson Matthey. Thus, these two houses controlled most of the platinum pricing worldwide. This price system still exists and is known as the producers' price. During the 1950s, South African production tripled, creating an active and substantial dealers market in London and Zurich. In 1956, NYMEX introduced its platinum futures contract, thus giving a hedging mechanism to consumers. At the end of the 1960s, Impala became the second largest South African producer and sold only through Ayrton, but by then the free market had consolidated and was

[4] Figures calculated based on the statistical data provided by F.J. Smith and G.G. Robson, *Platinum 1988*, London: Johnson Matthey, 1988.

FIGURE 3. The Platinum-Gold Price Ratio From 1977 to June 30, 1988

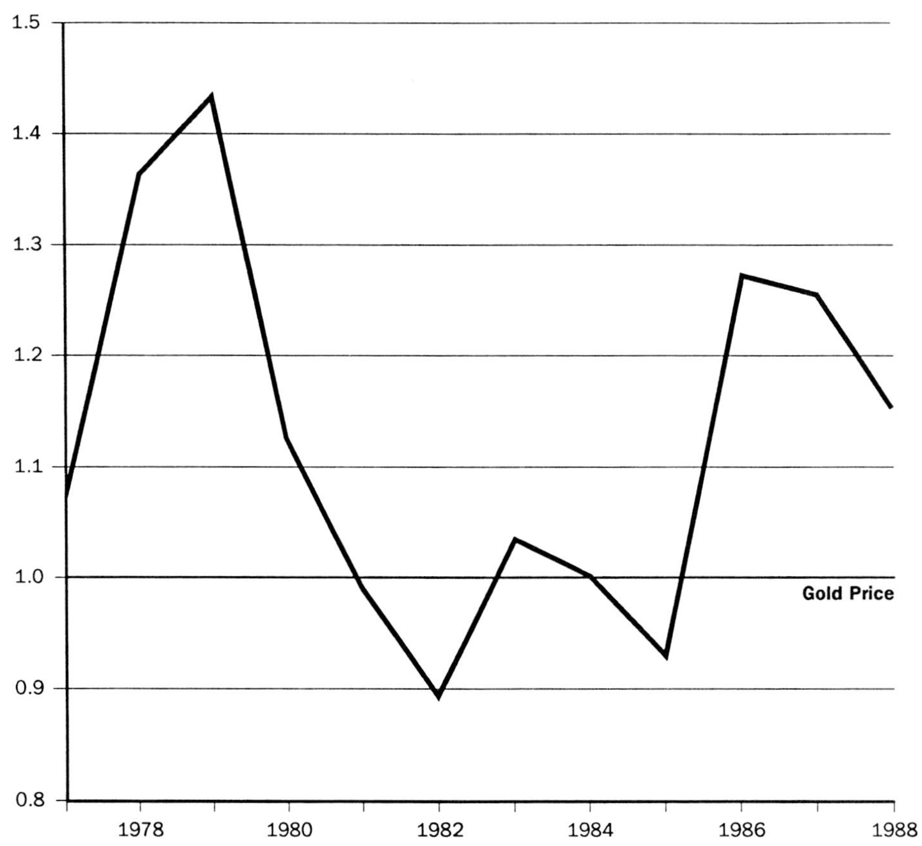

very liquid, and the volatility of the precious metals prices during the 1970s did not permit the sole use of the producers' price.

Platinum's price has always been measured in comparison to the price of gold. Figure 3 was prepared with data provided to the authors by Platinum Guild International (U.S.) Inc.; it clearly shows that in the past eleven years the average price of platinum was higher than the average price of gold, by a comfortable margin—with the exception of 1981 (0.971), 1982 (0.869), 1984 (in which it was at par), and 1985 (0.921). The implication is that if gold, as an alternative investment and/or hedge against inflation, has performed very well, platinum has done at least as well.

Bullion. Platinum bars are of a standard 0.9995 fineness. Bars exist in a variety of sizes and weights, although these are not as diversified as gold and silver bars. The largest platinum bar is the fifty-kilogram bar; more common are the kilo bar, the half-kilo, the ten ounce, and the ounce and half-ounce bars. These bars are produced by the most active platinum refiners: Johnson Matthey, Engelhard, Tanaka, and Degussa.

A number of coin-shaped round bars, or medallions, have entered the market in the last few years. Among them are the swan, produced in Japan; the Swiss shooting thaler; the American prospector; the liberty trade platinum, which is produced in one ounce, one-half ounce, and one-quarter ounce; and a variety of other pieces produced in limited quantities, and destined probably more for the collector than the investor. The latter include two different dragons produced in the fall of 1987 and 1988 (for the Year of the Dragon), one in Hong Kong and the other in Singapore; a rabbit and a tiger, also produced in Singapore; and a Mexican peso.

Platinum bars are quoted by the major precious metals dealers. The most serious of them publish bid and ask prices, through the traditional Reuters and Telerate systems, which the prospective buyer can take as reference prices. The price of a bullion piece depends on the size of the bar, which is linked to the current spot market quotations. A premium per ounce is charged to cover manufacturing and trading costs.

The Japanese market has already realized that platinum is as good a long-term investment as gold. In America and in the Western world in general, platinum bullion is not yet considered a long-term investment, but more a short-term, speculative one. This attitude is erroneous; platinum should be explored and considered by precious metals investors as a suitable complement to other precious metals-related investments.

A careful attitude about where and when to invest is always advised, especially regarding a proper differentiation between the coin-shaped medallions and actual coins. A reliable dealer is always the best hedge against risks for the novice.

Bullion Coins. In August 1988, there was only one platinum bullion coin on the market: the noble, from the Isle of Man. Two more entered the market during the last part of 1988: one from Australia, the koala, and one from Canada, the platinum maple leaf. A few other modern platinum issues exist, but they are seminumismatic, not bullion, coins.

The first real circulating platinum bullion coin was the Russian three-ruble introduced in 1828. It was issued until 1849 and circulated for many more years, at least until it was replaced by the gold three-ruble coin in 1869. During the same period (1829 to 1849), the Russians also minted a six-ruble and a twelve-ruble coin in platinum, but the reported issues are so small that they cannot be considered bullion coins.

In 1983, the Isle of Man introduced the first contemporary bullion platinum coin: the noble, consisting of one ounce of legal tender platinum with 0.9995 fineness. This coin is distributed by precious metals dealers and banks around the world.[5] The noble is very liquid and now is also available in one-half-ounce, one-quarter-ounce, and one-tenth-ounce sizes. The small denominations are very popular among small investors and the jewelry industry, where they are used for pendants, rings, and cuff links. A proof version is produced in limited quantities for the collector's market.

Since 1987, two official distributors in the United States have maintained the secondary market and created the liquidity for the coins; the prime world distributor does not make the secondary market. Before 1987, the distribution was in the hands of German banks who sold to dealers in the United States and elsewhere in the world, but rarely, if ever, repurchased coins sold to other markets. The noble retails at around 5 to 6 percent over metal and is repurchased at slightly over 2 percent.

The introduction of the two new platinum bullion coins has had a very positive stimu-

[5] In the United States, banks are an exception because they are not allowed to trade in platinum.

lating effect on platinum investments around the world. Competition and the importance of the issuing countries has provided new excitement in the market. Furthermore, the massive advertising campaigns of both countries are producing a major and healthy awareness of platinum investments.

The Australian platinum coin is struck by the Perth Mint and distributed by GoldCorp Australia. The coin, which depicts a koala bear, is produced in four denominations: one ounce, one-half ounce, one-quarter ounce, and one-tenth ounce. Contrary to the nugget, which is produced exclusively of gold mined locally, the koala uses imported platinum, as Australia is not yet a platinum-producing country. Tanaka of Japan is the purchasing agent and manufacturer of the blanks. Reportedly, the platinum used is from the USSR.

The Canadian coin, a platinum maple leaf, complements the successful gold maple leaf and the silver maple leaf. This coin has the same characteristics of the noble and the koala in terms in size and fineness, but it is minted only with platinum produced in Canada; therefore, it is a wholly Canadian product. The Royal Canadian Mint is the minter and the prime distributor. Both coins have distributors in the United States.

The investor interested in platinum legal tender coins, other than bullion coins, has a number of modern platinum coin issues with seminumismatic characteristics from which to make a choice. Besides the nineteenth-century three-ruble coin, which can be found at numismatic dealers, there are five commemorative coins issued by the USSR from 1977 to 1980, for the Moscow olympic games. These coins, in uncirculated and proof quality with a half-ounce fine content and having a face value of 150 rubles, can be found in the secondary market.

The French 100 franc coin, issued in 1986, commemorates the Statue of Liberty. With a fine content of 0.6430 ounce of platinum, it is available on the secondary market. In 1987, France commemorated General Lafayette with four 100-franc coins in gold, silver, palladium, and platinum. The platinum coin is of the same fineness and weight as the one of the Statue of Liberty and is also available on the secondary market. Minted by the Royal British Mint in 1987, a one-ounce platinum coin commemorating the 165th anniversary of Napoleon's death on Saint Helena can be obtained on the secondary market.

China produced its first platinum coin in 1987: the platinum panda, in proof quality and in a limited issue only. The coin, also produced in 1988 and programmed as a permanent issue, contains one ounce of 0.9995 fineness. The 1987 coin has already appreciated over the issue price. Commemorating the Year of the Dragon, China also produced a one-ounce platinum coin, mainly for the Far Eastern market, but more than half of the issue was sold in the United States. This coin is also beginning to show signs of appreciation over the issue price. At the end of 1988, another platinum coin was produced commemorating the Year of the Snake.

At the end of 1988, the first of a ten-year series of USSR gold, silver, palladium, and platinum commemorative coins were launched. Because gold coins from the USSR are banned from the U.S. market, the U.S. investor may only buy the "white" coins. The platinum coin is one-half ounce of pure platinum and has a face value of 150 rubles.

Futures and Options. The concepts of futures and options described in the previous parts of this chapter cover platinum in exactly the same way. A futures or an options contract serves both for investment purposes and for hedging a cash position.

The leading futures contract, launched in 1956, is the fifty-ounce contract at the NYMEX. Because the platinum price was dominated by producers for many years, one of the most important features of the platinum futures contract is price discovery. As the NYMEX conducts continuous auctions in the trading pits in which offers and bids are given by open outcry, the price transparency is enhanced. A sign of recognition of the free market's importance is that Rustenburg, the world's largest producer, has used the NYMEX since 1983 for most of its production; Impala, the second largest producer, continues to publish the producer's price.

The specifications of the standard platinum contract at the NYMEX are as follows:

Unit: 50 troy ounces

Price: U.S. $ per ounce

Delivery: Warehouse receipt on NYMEX approved depository

Contract months: Spot month and January, April, July, and October

Par grade (good delivery): Ingot or plate of 0.999 fineness

Although the industry standards are of 0.9995 fineness, the good delivery ingot is of lower purity; this fact does not pose any problem to the hedger, as a price differential will be part of the hedge calculation. Upgrading of the good delivery purity is a goal that cannot be achieved in the near future, as good delivery status for existing warehouse stocks is effective until fifteen years after the date of the assay.

Another futures contract is available in Japan. In 1984, TOCOM began to trade a platinum 500-gram futures contract. Although the dominant platinum market in Japan is still the physical trade loco Zurich, London, or Amsterdam, the volume of platinum contracts traded in 1987 at the TOCOM was already larger than the silver and gold contracts traded on the same exchange.

The investor willing to use futures contracts has more alternatives than taking long or short positions. One is, for instance, arbitrage between the different markets, buying or selling on one and making the opposite transaction on the other. Because the platinum price is constantly referenced to the gold price, the investor can also build so-called spreads, which consist of taking opposite positions in the gold and platinum futures contracts, depending on the investor's assessment of whether platinum is underpriced or overpriced in relation to gold.

In May 1987, the London Platinum and Palladium Market (LPPM) opened its operations. Although the LPPM is not recognized as an exchange by British authorities, its pricing mechanism is widely used as a reference price, although by users and traders more than by investors, and seems to be growing in acceptance. The founding members, Samuel Montagu, Ayrton Metals, Sharps Pixley, Mase Westpac, Johnson Matthey, and Engelhard have been joined by Inco Europe, Mitsui, and Alexander Relf.

The creation of LPPM in London was followed by the first platinum options contract introduced by the International Options Clearing Corporation (IOCC). It is traded on the European Options Exchange in Amsterdam and on the exchanges of Vancouver, Montreal, and Sydney, which are IOCC members. This options contract is for ten ounces and is priced in U.S. dollars. The NYMEX has submitted to the Commodity Futures Trading Commission a proposal for a platinum options contract likely to be approved in the near future. Meanwhile the IOCC option contract is the only one available.

Platinum Shares. South African platinum shares are dominant in this form of platinum-related investment. Rustenburg, Impala, Gold Fields of South Africa, West

platinum-related investment. Rustenburg, Impala, Gold Fields of South Africa, West Plats, Western Platinum, and Lefko are the most important mine companies that directly extract platinum and whose shares are quoted on the Johannesburg Stock Exchange, and, in some cases, on other exchanges, mainly London. As is the case with gold-mining shares, South African platinum shares are available to nonresidents through depository receipts rather than actual voting stock. As South African companies normally distribute all profits, their platinum shares, like their gold shares, tend to yield high dividends.

In the United States and Canada, platinum is extracted as a byproduct of base metal mines; therefore there are no companies mining only platinum. However, Madeleine in Canada and Stillwater in the United States have platinum projects under exploration.

In Australia, a number of mining companies are exploring platinum deposits. Among them are Reynolds of Australia, Helix Resources, and Hunter Resources. Ashton Mining, one of the leading mining companies of Australia, is reported to be exploring for platinum in Alaska where placer deposits formerly yielded a few thousand ounces per year.

In South America, some mining companies are also exploring for platinum. British Petroleum Mineração is exploring in Brazil, and Overseas Platinum of Canada in Ecuador.

The trend shows that, aside from the South African production and the USSR sales, a number of organizations in the western hemisphere are enriching platinum-related investment potential. Anyone interested in this type of investment must remember that, although the share investment may yield dividends or provide capital accumulation, it is subject to the risks of high production costs and poor management, among others. Hence it is imperative to do thorough research and to seek expert advice before investing.

Palladium

Palladium is a rare, silver-white, ductile, malleable, metallic chemical element of the platinum group; it is used as a catalyst, especially in hydrogenation processes, or in alloys with gold, silver and other metals: symbol, Pd; atomic weight, 106.4; atomic number, 46; specific gravity, 11.97; melting point, 1549.4° C; boiling point, 2200° C.

Palladium was the material of the legendary statue of the Greek goddess Pallas Athena, on which the safety of Troy depended. It is symbolic of anything that ensures safety; it is synonymous with safeguard.

Palladium, one of the platinum group metals, has many important industrial applications, mainly in the electrical, dental, and petrochemical industries. The first autocatalysts were made of palladium. It is largely used in dentistry as a substitute for gold. An alloy of gold and a small quantity of palladium produces the white gold that is very popular in the jewelry industry. Rarer than platinum, correctly priced between silver and gold, it offers an interesting investment potential. (See Figure 4.)

The USSR is the largest producer of palladium, as a byproduct of nickel; it produces palladium in much larger quantities than it does platinum. South Africa is the second largest producer of palladium, as a byproduct of platinum. Canada is the third largest producer of palladium, as a byproduct of nickel.

The Soviet Union's sales of palladium to the western world averaged 56.5 percent of the total supply between 1983 to 1987. South Africa's share of the market in the same period averaged 34.7 percent. In short, these two countries account for practically nine tenths of the total supply of the western world.

Japan is the leading consumer in the western world of palladium as well as platinum. During the period 1983 to 1987, Japanese consumption averaged about 40 percent of the

FIGURE 4. The Palladium Price Ratio Versus Platinum, Gold, and Silver Prices, 1985 to June 30, 1988

Note: Gold, Silver, and Platinum Prices are the Annual Average. Palladium price is the annual average of the last day of trading for the nearest delivery month at NYMEX.

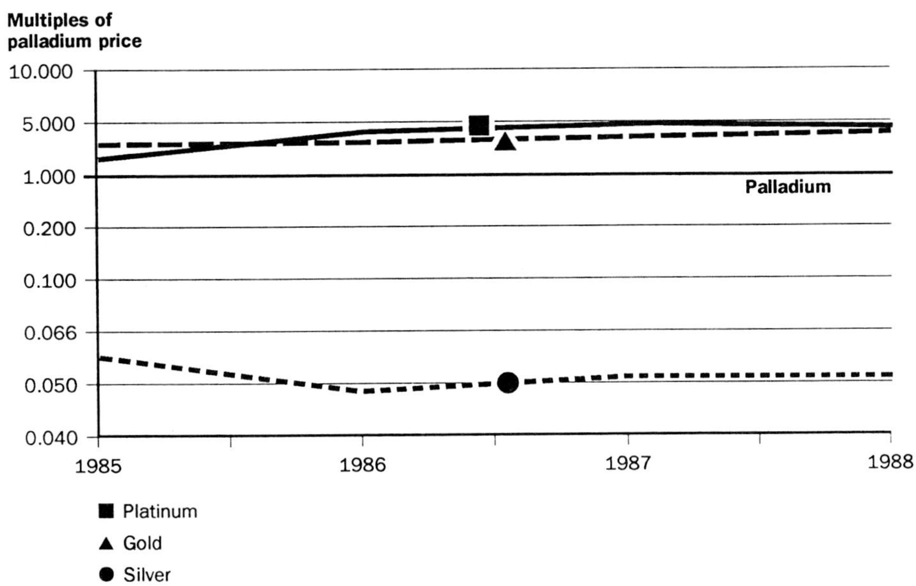

total demand (45 percent in 1988), while North America accounted for about one third. The electrical industry is the largest consumer of palladium in the western world, with a share that has gone from 40 percent in 1983 to 49 percent in 1987. Dentistry is the second, jewelry the third, and the autocatalyst industry the fourth. There are no segregated figures for investment in palladium, which falls statistically within the "other" category of consumption; this category, in the last few years, has been quite constant in absolute terms, but has lost in relative terms.

The structure of demand in North America is different from that in Japan. Japanese consumption follows exactly the pattern of the rest of the western world; in North America dental application is the leading consumer, and electrical industry follows in second place.

As in the case of platinum, the price of palladium has been largely dominated by producers and dealers. Producers have sold the greater part of their production to consumers through long-term contracts. The prices were set or negotiated at a level that producers thought would stimulate consumption.

The London dealers who make the fix for platinum also make the twice-a-day fixings for palladium, in exactly the same way as described in the previous section; they control a very important share of the market.

In spite of the attractive features of palladium as an investment, investors have shown a relative lack of interest in this precious metal. Several explanations are given by different analysts, but all seem to concentrate on the view that each one has on the motivations of the Soviet Union. As one example:

> Investors believe that the Soviet practice of offering non-contract material within the spot market range, albeit at the high end, limits opportunities for profit. Market analysts emphasize different characteristics of Soviet policy. Most see the USSR interested in making steady supplies available to the West at relative stable prices in order to discourage a search for substitutes. Others see the Soviets as watching carefully for profitable opportunities for themselves and using their contract offerings for that purpose. These analysts fear that a sharp price increase would result in a large amount of palladium from Soviet inventory being dumped on the West.[6]

According to statistics, supply in the last few years has been lower than demand. In three out of five recent years (see Figure 5), the gap has been covered by inventories and scrap recycling, which contradicts some of the views of the market analysts. On the other hand, the USSR does not publish production figures, and its inventories are totally unknown. Thus anything that may be said about Soviet intentions is pure speculation. Moreover, as development and modernization progresses, the Soviet Union has to be facing an increase both in the domestic demand and demand from the Eastern Bloc. Projected increases in platinum production in South Africa and North America will yield larger quantities of palladium, thereby reducing the proportion of Soviet share in the market.

Bullion Bars. A number of bullion bars are available to the investor. Ingots from one ounce to 100 ounces are easily obtained at the major precious metals dealers. These bars, as any other bullion bar, are produced by the platinum refiners: Johnson Matthey, Engelhard, Degussa, Tanaka, and others. Of a standard 0.999 fineness, the 100 and the ten ounce bars are good for delivery at the NYMEX. Another ingot, the Soviet three-kilogram bar of .9995 fineness, better known in Europe and in Japan, is also available for the investor. This bar is the one most used for physical deliveries in Japan.

Palladium bars are widely quoted by the major precious metals dealers, whose prices are disseminated together with those of gold, silver, and platinum by the various data carrier systems, such as Reuters and Telerate. These dealers make a dual market and provide liquidity for the bars.

Palladium Coins. As yet, there is no palladium bullion coin on the market, but no doubt in the near future we will see one. The U.S. Congress already has a proposal for a palladium coin. Such a project would have an enormous impact on the precarious equilibrium in the supply and demand of the palladium market. This may be considered an exaggerated assertion, but if the U.S. Treasury mints palladium coins for only one tenth of the gold ounces consumed the first year of the American eagle, it would need about 150,000 ounces of palladium. Those 150,000 ounces would represent a reduction of almost 5 percent of the already short supply.

The Kingdom of Tonga produced the world's first palladium coinage in 1967. The issue, consisting of three denominations, can be acquired as a numismatic item. During 1987, two palladium coins entered the market: the 100-franc Lafayette, issued together with a gold silver and platinum coin commemorating *égalité*, and a twenty-five dollar Bermuda coin, the sea venture, commemorating the adventurous arrival of that ship in Bermuda in the early seventeenth century.

---

[6] From *Metals in the News—Nymex Palladium Futures: 1968–1988,*" New York Mercantile Exchange, Winter 1988, New York.

FIGURE 5. Palladium Supply and Demand Ratio, 1983 to 1987

Source: Based on statistical data of F. J. Smith and G. G. Robson, *Platinum* 1988, London: Johnson Matthey, 1988.

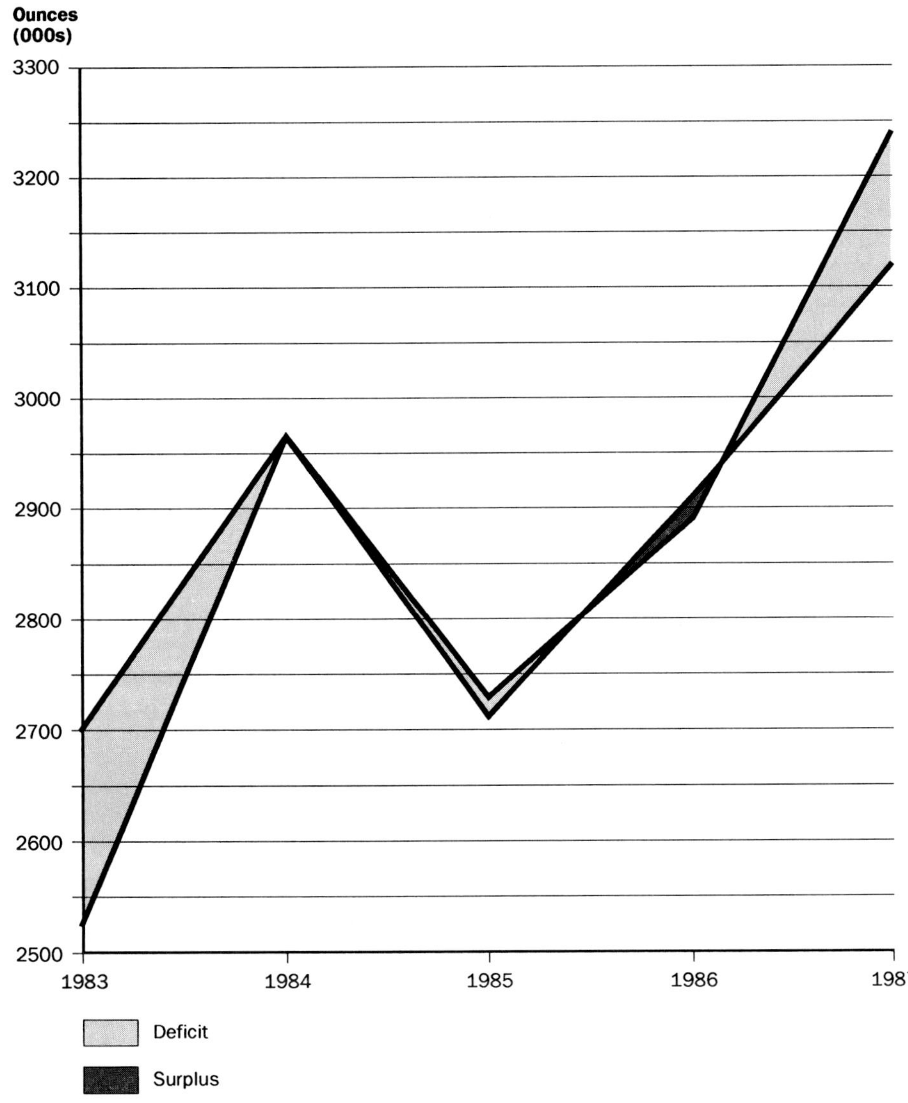

In December 1988, the first of ten series of palladium, gold, silver, and platinum coins from the USSR were launched. These series commemorate a number of events in Russian and Soviet history. The first one commemorates the millennium of Christianity in Russia. The issues are of limited quantity.

On December 1988, China introduced a very small issue of a palladium medal as a forerunner of the first palladium coin to be launched during 1989, a panda.

Palladium Futures. The mechanics of the future contracts at the exchanges have been explained earlier in this chapter. There is little to add, except for the particulars of the only palladium future contract.

On January 22, 1968, the NYMEX introduced its palladium futures contract. With the strong role played by producers in the palladium market—mainly the Soviet Union, which sells only through a state company—the importance of the NYMEX futures contract has to be underlined, as NYMEX is the only market where price discovery is conducted by a continuous auction in the trading rings.

It would be incorrect to say that the NYMEX contract is the only outlet that the operator has for hedging a cash position, as this also can be achieved through forward contracts in the dealers market. However the NYMEX is the only market where both operator and investor can participate in palladium trading with advantages unique to the future contracts—anonymity, liquidation of the contract at any time, no need to take delivery, and guarantee of contract performance.

The specifications of the palladium future contract are as follows:

Unit: 100 troy ounces

Price: U.S. $ per ounce

Delivery: Warehouse receipt on NYMEX approved depository

Contract months: Spot month and March, June, September, and December

Good delivery: Ingot or plate of 0.999 fineness
100-ounce bars or ten 10-ounce bars

Until March 1985, ingots of 0.998 fineness were certified for delivery at the exchange. As ingots or plates of such grade still exist, they may be delivered at a discount.

Since palladium is a byproduct and its market, as compared to the gold and silver markets, is still small, the investor does not have the variety of investment alternatives that those other markets offer: there is no options contract for palladium, neither are there palladium mining shares or certificates or warrants. Therefore, the person who wishes to invest in palladium has fewer alternatives: the physical purchase of bars or ingots, spot or forward contracts in the dealers market, or futures contracts at the NYMEX.

> Expanding South African production and new sources of supply in Canada, Australia and New Zeland will necessitate greater dependence on the spot market, which will alter traditional contract-market relationships. This last factor will have the most striking effect on the future of the palladium market.
>
> As new production increases, users will have more choices among suppliers. New producers can be expected to seek long-term contracts with major users to assure a steady demand for a portion of their output.
>
> At the same time, given the structure and size of the contract market, the remainder of new production can be expected to move through spot-market channels as suppliers seek new markets and create market niches.
>
> The importance of the spot market as a legitimate supply balancing mechanism will therefore grow. It should provide more transparency and market efficiency than in the past.[7]

[7] Elizabeth L. Saxe (manager of metals marketing at NYMEX), "NYMEX Ready for 20 Year Palladium Party," *American Metal Market: Platinum Group Metals*, special issue, Dec. 1987.

ATTRACTIVE FEATURES

Hedge Against Inflation

The primary attraction of precious metals investment is the protection it provides against inflation. Gold, in particular, tends to retain purchasing power over very long periods of time. This is true to a lesser degree for silver. Because platinum has been recognized as a medium for investment for only a few decades, its record as a shield against inflation is not as clear. Nonetheless, an extremely useful metal—such as platinum, with a constantly increasing demand, produced in small quantities by a costly extractive process principally in two countries (South Africa and the Soviet Union)—should sustain value over a long period.

Liquidity

Most of the investment forms in precious metal described in this article are highly liquid and therefore instantly convertible into cash. Precious metal bars and bullion coins are internationally negotiable, and their prices are widely quoted.

The liquidity of precious metals in physical form has made them a valid means for capital flight, mainly in regions where political tensions, wars, and persecutions have forced people to protect their assets or even leave their homelands.

In recent history, when Jews in Nazi Germany and Vietnamese of Chinese extraction found themselves persecuted, many were able to use their accumulated savings in gold to obtain documents, bribe officials, make an escape, and reestablish themselves in other countries. In the Middle East, the Iranian revolution of 1979, followed by the rise of Islamic revolutionary movements in conservative Arab states around the Arab Gulf, created an unrest to which many wealthy and influential leaders of the region responded by converting their assets to gold and placing it in banks in Zurich and London.

Premium and Handling

Most forms of physical precious metal investment carry a low premium over metal and are easy to transport. Security types, such as certificates, unit trusts, and mutual funds have the additional advantage of being easy to store and keep safe. Open-market investments, such as futures and options, have speculative appeal and tie up relatively small amounts of capital.

Long-Term Appreciation and Aesthetic Appeal

Some forms of physical precious metal have great beauty and may be considered as works of art. Those who are attracted by the aesthetics of lovely objects and wish the security of precious metals may find in the market a variety of old and modern gold and silver coins that are both collectors items for their beauty and investments for their fine content.

POTENTIAL RISKS

Lack of Current Return

There are few disadvantages in owning physical metals. One is that they tie up substantial amount of capital; another, that they provide no current return in the form of dividends, interest, or rent.

Market Volatility

Another disadvantange is that precious metal investments are subject to price fluctuations that, depending on the form of investment, may represent a higher or lower potential loss should the investor be forced to liquidate.

Physical precious metal holdings have appreciated in the long term, but the potential for a loss in the short term is very real. Likewise, other types of investments tied to the current price of gold, such as certificates and shares, are subject to the same price fluctuation as gold.

Storage

A third disadvantage of physical precious metal investment is that it needs secure storage facilities. Although most banks offer safekeeping services to their clients, storage poses a risk when the investor prefers to keep physical holdings at home. (See *Custodial Care*, later in this article.)

Limited Liquidity

Some precious metal types of investment are less liquid. Forwards are less liquid than futures. Platinum in general is less liquid than gold and silver because the investor's market, other than in Japan, is very thin and the industry has its own sources for supply. Certain forms of partnerships are also less liquid than traditional forms of investment. In many instances, the investor needs the assistance of expert advice and sophisticated trading ability.

TAX CONSEQUENCES

Precious metals are capital assets, and profits are taxed as long-term or short-term gains under the prevailing rules of the Internal Revenue Service (IRS) and state taxing authorities. Many states impose sales tax on bullion and coins purchases if delivery is taken. There is active lobbying by representatives of the precious metals industry to eliminate sales tax in all the states of the union. Thirteen states charge no tax, the others have a large variety of systems.

IMPORTANT FACTORS IN BUYING AND SELLING

Some banks and bullion and currency dealers, and a number of brokerage firms, offer facilities for the purchase of small amounts of gold or silver bullion or coins by customers who wish to build accounts, averaging costs over a period of time.

An investor contemplating the purchase of bullion or coins should check a number of institutions and deal only with the most reputable houses. Brokerage fees and service charges are generally competitive but do vary. The Industry Council for Tangible Assets, based in Washington, D.C., has produced a pamphlet geared to guide and protect the prospective investor.

For an investor dealing in the futures market, it is important to do business with a broker who has access to all the active markets, such as Zurich, London, Sydney, and Hong Kong. Participation in these markets extends the trading day to nearly twenty-four hours.

In the case of numismatic coins, a viable and growing branch of the larger precious metals market, the services of only a well-qualified dealer should be considered. In the case of traditional numismatics (coins that are no longer produced), the value of the coin depends not only on its rarity but on its physical condition, which requires a very expert grading capability. In the case of modern numismatics, accurate information about mintages, quality, and secondary market is necessary.

CUSTODIAL CARE

Coins, small ingots, and large bars need to be safely stored. A personal safe-deposit box may be enough for relatively small quantities. For substantial amounts or large bars, special arrangements are required. In any case, the investor should check carefully into the rules of bailment that regulate the liability of the institution owning the storage facility, in case of fire or theft. Sometimes the institution's legal liability is minimal; in this case, the owner should take out special insurance to guard against risk of loss.

Owing to the variety of state sales taxes, many bullion dealers and banks have storage and delivery arrangements in the state of Delaware, where precious metals transactions are tax-free.

Investors who wish to take delivery and keep their precious metals in their homes should have adequate safekeeping facilities. A small amount of coins or small bars will fit comfortably in almost any safe, but a 400-ounce gold bar or a 1,000-ounce silver bar, which will not fit in most household safes, requires special facilities and insurance.

GLOSSARY

ask price—Price at which precious metal is offered for sale.

assay—A test to determine the quantity of pure metal; a test to determine the fineness of a precious metal.

bid—Price at which an operator is prepared to buy precious metal.

bullion—Precious metal in ingots, bars, or plates, of at least 0.995 fineness.

bullion coins—Contemporary precious metal coins minted in large numbers and marketed at a premium of no more than 5 to 7 percent above the value of the precious metal content.

carat—Unit of fineness for gold jewelry.

commodities—Goods traded on specialized markets in the form of standardized contracts.

contract unit—Prescribed unit of trading on a futures exchange.

depository—An authorized safekeeper who issues certificates for the bullion held in deposit.

double eagle—U.S. gold coin with a face value of $20, minted until 1933.

face value—The monetary value given by the issuing state to a coin.

fineness—Proportion of pure precious metal in an alloy, expressed as parts per thousand by weight.

fixing—Setting of the price for the spot metal.

forward contract—Contract of sale or purchase of a commodity or financial instrument under which delivery and payment take place at a later date; usually made between principals.

futures contract—A contract covering the purchase or sale of a commodity or a financial instrument for future delivery on a commodity exchange.

futures market—Market or exchange on which commodity future or financial futures contracts are traded.

good delivery—Conditions of delivery in terms of weight and fineness established by the exchanges.

good delivery bar—Bars that meet the recognized conditions of delivery established by the exchanges or by the London market.

good delivery weight—Unit weights accepted as good delivery by the exchanges; for example, COMEX accepts 100-ounce and 400-ounce bars, and Brazilian exchanges accept 250 gram and one-kilogram bars.

hedge—The purchase or sale of a futures contract as a temporary substitute for a transaction to be made at a later date; usually it involves opposite positions in the cash market and in the futures market at the same time.

hoarding—Accumulation of assets in the form of precious metals and/or cash.

legal tender—The coin or currency that the monetary authority of a country declares to be universally acceptable as a medium of exchange.

loco—A quotation "loco" means that the metal will be delivered at that place free of any further charge.

long position—A purchase position in the futures market or a holding of metal in the cash or spot market.

margin—A cash amount that must be deposited for each futures contract as a guarantee of fulfillment of the contract; also called security deposit.

melt value—The value of the fine content less the refining costs.

option contract—A right to buy or sell a futures contract at a future date at a specified price.

position—An interest in the market, either long or short.

Saint Gauden—American sculptor, designer of the double eagle coin in 1907.

share warrants—Option issued by a company granting the holder the right to buy common stock at a specified price, usually for a limited time.

short position—A sale position in the futures market; a sale for future delivery of a metal that the seller does not own at the moment of the sale.

spot—Transaction in which payment and delivery take place immediately.

tael—Any of various units of weight of eastern Asia; formerly a Chinese unit of money.

tola—Traditional unit of weight for gold in the Middle East and Indian subcontinent; equal to 11.6638 grams.

troy ounce—Traditional unit of weight for gold and other precious metals; equal to 31.10348079 grams.

white gold—Alloy of 75 percent gold and either 25 percent palladium or 15 percent nickel and 10 percent copper.

SUGGESTED READING

PERIODICALS

Futures and Option World. Published by Metal Bulletin Journals, Ltd., Surery, Eng. Monthly.

Metals in the News. Published by the New York Mercantile Exchange, New York. Monthly.

Mining Weekly. Published by Shearson Lehman Hutton, London. Weekly.

The Precious Metals Outlook. Published by Philipp Brothers. New York. Monthly.

ARTICLES

Meneses-Diaz, A. "Variable que determinan el precio del oro," *Latin American Finance*, Mar.–Apr. 1986.

BOOKS

Annual Review of the World Gold Industry, 1988. London: Shearson Lehman Hutton, 1988.

Annual Review of the World Silver Industry, 1988. London: Shearson Lehman Hutton, 1988.

The Educated Investor's Guide to Precious Metals. Washington, D.C.: Industry Council on Tangible Assets, 1988.

Gold. New York: MTB Banking Corporation, 1987.

Gold. London: Consolidated Gold Fields, 1988. Annual.

Gold Handbook. Zurich: Credit Suisse, 1983.

Gold Myth and Reality, 2nd ed. Zurich: Swiss Bank Corporation 1985.

An Illustrated History of Modern Coinage, New York: MTB Banking Corporation, 1988.

Introduction to Investing in Gold. New York: The Gold Institute, 1986.

Micklus, Stephen G. *Palladium Plating*. New York: AT&T Nassau Metal, 1986.

Palladium—Completing Your Precious Metals Portfolio. New York: MTB Banking Corporation, 1987.

Smith, F. J., and Robson, G. G. *Platinum 1988*. London: Johnson Matthey, 1988.

Trading in Tomorrows. Chicago: Chicago Mercantile Exchange, 1984.

MORTGAGE-BACKED SECURITIES

Thomas G. Gillis

BASIC CHARACTERISTICS

A mortgage-backed security (MBS) is a fully amortizing instrument that makes monthly payments of principal and interest with a variable and unknown maturity. These securities fall into two categories: fixed rate and adjustable rate. The important elements of any MBS are the characteristics of the loans backing it. What is the weighted average interest rate, the weighted average maturity? Are the loans credit enhanced? Who is the originator and servicer? This article details each of these elements and describes and analyzes the various MBS products available to investors.

MBSs are backed by mortgage loans made to individuals. Banks, savings and loans, and mortgage bankers make the loans and then package them for sale in the secondary market. When loans are packaged for sale in the secondary market, the MBS is created. The ability of these insititutions to sell MBSs provides them with a constant stream of funds for making more mortgages. How these loans are made or originated affects how the security will perform.

A pool of mortgages is usually credit enhanced before it is sold in the secondary market. Although credit enhancement can be obtained through the government and its instrumentalities or in the private market, most mortgage pools are credit enhanced by the government and its instrumentalities. The government entered the mortgage credit business by creating the Federal Housing Administration (FHA) in 1934 to insure mortgages

Thomas G. Gillis is a Senior Vice-President of Financial Institutions/Structured Finance, Debt Rating Services Division, Standard & Poor's Corporation, New York, New York.

against loss. The FHA was the catalyst for changing the single-family mortgage to a long-term instrument that was fully amortizing.

During the Great Depression, many lenders lost large sums of money on mortgage lending. The government, wanting lenders to return to the mortgage market, created entities to facilitate this. The FHA was created to provide credit protection, and the Federal National Mortgage Association (FNMA), to provide liquidity. Since that time, the role of the government in the mortgage market has changed often and has expanded. Today, the government's presence is as great as at any time in history.

The largest and most uniform mortgage pools are those sponsored by the government and government-sponsored enterprises: the Government National Mortgage Association (GNMA), the Federal Home Loan Mortgage Corporation (FHLMC), and the FNMA. FNMA and later FHLMC and GNMA were created to provide liquidity for lenders throughout the country in regions where home mortgage funds were not readily available. These three entities are dominant forces in the secondary mortgage market. All three facilitate the packaging of mortgage pools and indemnify investors against loss.

GNMA guarantees pools of mortgage loans insured by the FHA and the Veterans Administration (VA) against timely and ultimate loss. This guarantee is backed by the full faith and credit of the United States of America. GNMA offers approved originators two major programs: the GNMA I and GNMA II.

Both programs typically are pools of like mortgages; however, GNMA I pools tend to be issued in minimums of $1 million and to have mortgages of the same interest rate. GNMA II pools can be packaged in principal amounts of as little as $250,000, and the interest rates on the mortgages can vary within 1 percentage point of the certificate rate. GNMA I certificates are originated, packaged, and issued by the originator of the FHA/VA loans. The originator is responsible for payment on the certificates. Payments on GNMA I certificates are made monthly, on the fifteenth, with a fifteen- to forty-five-day delay. Chemical Bank is the payment agent for GNMA II certificates. Payments on GNMA IIs are made to investors monthly, with a twenty- to fifty-day delay.

FHLMC purchases conventional mortgages, packages them, and issues participations in these pools through documents known as participation certificates (PCs). Participation certificates carry FHLMC's guarantee of timely payment of interest and ultimate repayment of principal. FHLMC is not backed by the full faith and credit of the United States. Standard & Poor's (S&P) has evaluated FHMC PCs as eligible for AAA-rated transactions. FHLMC PCs are paid monthly, with a forty-five- to seventy-five-day delay.

FNMA is a federally chartered, privately owned stockholder corporation. FNMA, like FHLMC, purchases conventional mortgage loans, and packages and issues ownership interest in these pools. Commonly referred to as FNMA MBSs, these securities are guaranteed by FNMA to pay timely principal and interest and to hold investors free from loss. FNMA, like FHLMC, is evaluated by S&P as eligible for AAA-rated transactions.

Table 1 lists the key factors in comparing the different instruments that are available. Payment delays are an important consideration in the purchase decision. The longer a certificate takes to pass through payments, the less time remains to reinvest. GNMA and FNMA payment delays are within days of each other. An FHLMC can take up to a month longer in passing through its payments. The maximum spread of underlying mortgages to certificate rate is the difference in the interest rate of the MBS and the mortgages backing it. This factor is important in assessing prepayment speeds. An example is an investor who

TABLE 1. Agency Mortgage-Backed Securities Fact Sheet

Characteristics	GNMA I	GNMA II	FHLMC	FNMA
Payment frequency	Monthly	Monthly	Monthly	Monthly
Payment delay	15 days on schedule; P&I up to 45 days on prepayments	20 days on schedule; P&I up to 50 days on prepayments	45 days on schedule; P&I up to 75 days on prepayments	25 days on schedule; P&I up to 55 days on prepayments
Maximum spread of underlying mortgages to certificate reat	50 bp	100 bp	25–250 bp	25–250 bp
Credit	Full faith & credit of the United States	Full faith & credit of the United States	Evaluation of AAA by S&P	Evaluation of AAA by S&P
Liquidity	Excellent	Excellent	Excellent	Excellent

P&I = Principal and interest.
bp = Basis points.

owns one each of the four certificates, all with the same 10 percent interest rate. The mortgages backing the certificates could have rates of 10.5 percent on the GNMA Is, 11 percent on the GNMA IIs, and 12.5 percent on the FNMA and FHLMC certificates. As will be seen later, a mortgage's interest rate helps determine assumptions about its prepayment.

Mortgage pools that are credit enhanced in the private market are generally made up of loans that were not eligible for purchase by FHLMC and FNMA. There are a number of questions to be asked on privately credit-enhanced mortgage pools. Who originated the loans and how were they underwritten? Origination and underwriting constitute the process in which the decision whether to lend is made. The more thoroughly loans are underwritten, the better the pool will perform in terms of mortgage delinquencies. Who is the servicer? The loan servicer is the entity that collects the mortgage payments from homeowners and passes them on to investors. The servicer is also responsible for collecting late payments and foreclosing on delinquent properties, if necessary.

How much credit enhancement is provided and who provides it? Different mortgage loans behave differently. Mortgages with low down payments tend to default more often than those with high down payments. Where are the properties located? The more concentrated the pool, the greater the risk; a pool's performance is generally tied to the economy in which it is located. Is the credit protection in the form of mortgage insurance, letter of credit, or subordination?

Private issues require a good deal of analysis. Most investors look for a private security to be rated by S&P. S&P rates practically all privately issued MBSs, and its rating methodology is publicly available. Most privately issued MBSs, known as pass-throughs, are rated AA.

Adjustable Rate Mortgages

The increasingly popular adjustable rate mortgage (ARM) has many variables, including the teaser, index, margin, servicing spread, payment and interest rate caps, and frequency of adjustments. Whether an ARM negatively amortizes is an important consideration. Teasers are the initial rates at which mortgages are offered, often initial discounts of 1 or 2 percent to entice people into ARMs; they determine the first year's cash flow. On privately issued mortgage pass-throughs, the teaser also has credit implications. The larger the teaser or discount, the easier it is to qualify for the mortgage.

The index is also very important. Two main indexes are employed: the one-year Treasury and the Federal Home Loan Bank's eleventh district cost of funds (COF) index. The COF is the average cost of deposits of the members of the Federal Home Loan Bank's eleventh district, made up mostly of California savings and loan associations. The COF index, the more stable of the two, is a lagging index, because it trails U.S. Treasury rates both up and down. The one-year Treasury index is highly volatile.

The contract rate on an ARM is the index plus the margin less the servicing fee and any other expenses. The margin is the spread added to the index. The margin is a fixed percentage that remains constant for the life of the mortgage. Margins can vary in amount. If the contract specifies a 2 percent margin, the lender checks the index and adds 2 percent. If the index is 10 percent, the mortgagor is charged 12 percent. The servicing fee (including any other expenses) must be subtracted to calculate the net interest rate to the investor. If the servicing fee (plus any other expenses) equals 25 basis points, the net interest rate is 11.45 percent (10 percent index + 2 percent margin − 0.25 percent servicing).

Payment and interest rate caps, as well as how often they occur, are key variables. Two items, how much and how often, must be looked at in conjunction with each other. For example, a 2 percent payment cap provides immense flexibility if payments are adjusted monthly. At the other extreme, a 2 percent payment cap does not provide much interest rate protection if it is adjusted every ten years. ARMs with annual adjustments generally have both annual caps and lifetime caps. Negative amortization (in which interest earned exceeds interest paid) occurs when interest rate caps exceed payment caps.

Two ARM programs have dominated the ARM market. Both programs are referred to by their index, the one-year Treasury ARM and the COF ARM. The one-year Treasury ARM has an annual interest rate cap of 2 percent and no payment cap. Interest rates are capped over the life to 5 or 7 percent of the initial rate. This instrument has no negative amortization. The COF ARM has monthly interest rate adjustments and an annual payment cap of 7.5 percent. Over the life of the mortgage, the interest is capped at 5 to 7 percent above that of the initial rate. This instrument can negatively amortize. At the fifth year, no payment cap is applied, so that the loan payment can be adjusted to amortize fully by maturity.

ARMs are not supposed to eliminate a mortgage investor's interest rate risk but are designed to share this risk. This aspect is important in two ways. First, the holder of an ARM security is still exposed to interest rate risk. Second, as interest rate risk shifts to the mortgagor, credit risk increases. ARMs are packaged and issued by FNMA and FHLMC. The nongovernment, public pass-through market is also very active in ARM transactions.

Credit quality is a key component that should be addressed in discussing MBSs. There are many elements that an investor must consider before investing in mortgages. Credit is not one of them. Investors should look for government backing or a AAA or AA rating from S&P. With credit quality taken care of, investors can focus on the other aspects of an MBS.

Prepayments

The variable and unknown maturity of the investor's security is the most challenging aspect of MBSs. Mortgages have an unknown maturity because homeowners are allowed to prepay their mortgage at any time. This prepayment risk is one that should be understood fully prior to investing in MBSs. What causes prepayments? Interest rates and social and economic factors contribute to how a pool of mortgages may prepay.

Interest rates have the single largest impact on prepayment rates, as was clearly seen in 1985 and 1986. Those years were affected by the largest decline in interest rates ever to occur. During that period, more people refinanced their mortgages than ever before. Interest rates and prepayment rates have a direct relationship to one another. A homeowner paying $1,028.61 a month on a 12 percent $100,000 mortgage is likely to refinance the mortgage if 10 percent mortgage money is available, because a 10 percent mortgage will cost only $877.57 a month, a saving of $151.04. This saving will pay for points of 2.5 percent over a seventeen-month period. On the other hand, when interest rates rise, prepayments slow down. In addition, as rates rise, an increasingly smaller percentage of the population can qualify for new mortgages. In a rising environment, the financial incentive for the homeowner to prepay is no longer present.

When the economy is expanding, prepayments are likely to increase, because of the job creation that usually occurs during economic expansion. Job creation causes people to move to locations of new employment, and thus entails the sale of homes and the prepayment of mortgages. Also, companies have a tendency to transfer employees more in expansion periods.

Social factors, such as divorce, play a role in prepayments. In a divorce, the home is often sold in order to settle the terms of the estate. Other factors are important as well. "Due on sale" clauses require the prepayment of the mortgage on the sale of the home. The seasoning of a mortgage, or how long it has been outstanding, indicates the likelihood of prepayment. Prepayments are low in the early years when homeowners are just settling into their new homes. As time goes on, prepayments increase to a point and then level off. Knowledge of the factors that affect mortgage prepayments is important in understanding how mortgage securities will perform.

For the most informed judgment on prepayments, the following questions should be answered. What is the weighted average interest rate and the range of interest rates on the mortgage pool backing the MBS? The relationship of these rates to current rates will show if there are incentives present for prepayments. What is the weighted average maturity of mortgages? The more seasoned the pool, the more likely that mortgages will prepay. Do the mortgages contain "due on sale" provisions? Where are the mortgages located? Certain areas of the country, such as California, are more mobile than others.

The Public Securities Association's (PSA's) standard prepayment model provides a standard measure of prepayments. With this standard measure, pools of mortgages can be compared and contrasted. The PSA has established an expected norm of how prepayments will occur over the life of a pool. Pools are compared against an expected norm, called 100 percent PSA. A pool paying down at twice the normal rate will have a PSA of 200 percent. Likewise, a pool paying down at half the normal rate will have a PSA of 50 percent. Figure 1 shows these various PSA speeds. PSA speeds account for the increasing number of

FIGURE 1. The Public Securities Association's Prepayment Speeds

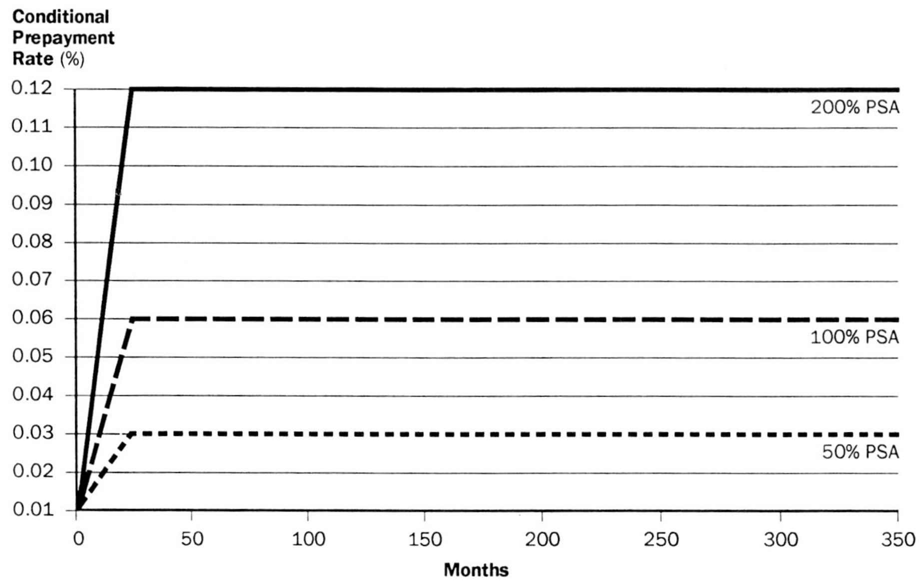

prepayments that occur in the early years of a mortgage pool's life. Table 2 highlights the exact percentage breakdown of PSA and how it compares to other methods of measuring mortgage payments.

Just as the method of measuring prepayments is important, so is the application of that method. Unfortunately, certain areas of common misunderstanding exist. One is that actual prepayments will follow the PSA curve. Actual prepayments on any pool go through cycles of accelerating rates of prepayments, as well as slowdowns. A pool may average 100 percent PSA while never actually prepaying at 100 percent. Because prepayments do speed up and slow down, looking at their average experience since origination can be very misleading. Recent historical speeds for the most recent three- and six-month periods should be considered. Also, the origination of the mortgages should not be confused with the origination of the certificates. Because mortgages prepay based on how long the mortgage has been outstanding, when looking at MBS look to the underlying mortgages.

Prepayment measures are key to understanding how MBSs are priced. PSA and the cashflows it represents provide a tool that investors can use in measuring investment maturity. Investment decisions cannot always be in absolute terms. How an investment performs relative to other investment alternatives is an important consideration. Maturity is a key factor in choosing alternative investments, and prepayments and prepayment measures provide a tool for measuring maturity.

The fact that mortgages have a maturity schedule of thirty years is useless in the investment decision process. Prepayments, causing a substantial return of an investment prior to its scheduled maturity, must be factored in. The mortgage market employs two popular

TABLE 2. PSA Standard Prepayment Experience

Month	PSA Standard	CPR Equivalent	SMM Equivalent	Month	PSA Standard	CPR Equivalent	SMM Equivalent
0	0.00%	0.00%	0.00%	16	3.20%	3.20%	0.27%
1	0.20	0.20	0.02	17	3.40	3.40	0.29
2	0.40	0.40	0.03	18	3.60	3.60	0.31
3	0.60	0.60	0.05	19	3.80	3.80	0.32
4	0.80	0.80	0.07	20	4.00	4.00	0.34
5	1.00	1.00	0.08	21	4.20	4.20	0.36
6	1.20	1.20	0.10	22	4.40	4.40	0.37
7	1.40	1.40	0.12	23	4.60	4.60	0.39
8	1.60	1.60	0.13	24	4.80	4.80	0.41
9	1.80	1.80	0.15	25	5.00	5.00	0.43
10	2.00	2.00	0.17	26	5.20	5.20	0.44
11	2.20	2.20	0.19	27	5.40	5.40	0.46
12	2.40	2.40	0.20	28	5.60	5.60	0.48
13	2.60	2.60	0.22	29	5.80	5.80	0.50
14	2.80	2.80	0.24	30	6.00	6.00	0.51
15	3.00	3.00	0.25	360*	6.00	6.00	0.51

CPR = Conditional prepayment rate.
SMM = Single monthly mortality.
*For months 30 through 360, the values remain the same.

methods in determining maturity: average life and duration. Average life, the method most often used in the mortgage market, is calculated by taking the sum of principal received (Pr) times the months outstanding (Mo), divided by total principal (Pt):

$$\frac{\text{Pr} \times \text{Mo}}{\text{Pt}}$$

For example, consider a $400 loan at 10 percent for five years with annual payments:

Year	Principal Received	Year × Principal
1	$ 65.52	$ 65.52
2	72.07	144.14
3	79.28	237.84
4	87.21	348.84
5	95.93	479.65
Totals	$400.00	$1275.99

$$\text{Average life } \frac{12.75}{400} = 3.19 \text{ years}$$

Average life and duration both address the same problem. The returns on investments are received in the form of cash flows spread over time. To compare investments, investors need a way of judging the timing of the expected cash flows.

Average life allows investors to ask, "How long will it take to repay the average dollar of principal in the cash flow?" Its formula is a weighted average of the number of payments, using principal dollars received as the weights.

Duration asks a slightly different question. It is concerned about total dollars received, including both principal and interest. To measure the time value of money, it uses present values. It then computes a weighted average of the present values. Duration allows investors to ask, "What is the average present value of the payments in the cash flow?"

$$\frac{\sum P \times \frac{1}{(1 + R)^t} \times Mo}{\sum P \times \frac{1}{(1 + R)^t}}$$

For example:

Year	Principal and Interest Received	Present Value at 12% Discount	Weighted Present Values
1	$105.52	$ 94.21	94.21
2	105.52	84.12	168.24
3	105.52	75.11	225.32
4	105.52	67.06	268.24
5	105.52	59.87	299.37
Totals		$380.37	1055.38

$$\text{Duration} = \frac{1055.38}{308.37} = 2.77$$

Once a prepayment speed is picked and a maturity is calculated, an investment decision can be made. Now the yield on the security can be compared to U.S. Treasury security yields. The spread between an MBS with comparable maturity and a Treasury security will be a major factor in the decision to sell or buy an MBS. MBSs generally trade between 125 basis points and 200 basis points over the seven-year Treasury rate. Depending on the certainty and outlook for prepayments, the amount of yield pickup can be judged. In a situation where prepayments are highly volatile or decreasing, a higher spread to U.S. Treasuries should be sought. Conversely, when prepayments are stable or increasing, a lower spread to Treasuries is appropriate. The spread over Treasuries is meant to compensate investors for the uncertain maturity, or prepayment, risk.

ATTRACTIVE FEATURES

MBSs are among the safest investments available. Agency securities are assessed AAA by S&P, the highest credit rating possible. Private pools are usually AA rated. Mortgages are such safe investments because they are secured by real property. Home mortgage payments are the last payment to be missed by a homeowner. When evaluated alongside other investments, such as corporate or municipal debt, mortgages compare well on a credit basis. If a corporation or municipality stops paying principal and interest on debt, investors lose more than half the face value of their investments. Mortgage securities are not likely to lose more than 10 percent of their value, even in a depression. During the Great Depression of the 1930s, losses for fully amortizing mortgages are estimated to have been less than 10 percent.

Yields on MBSs provide high returns for investors. The yields of MBSs trade at a spread over comparable maturity U.S. Treasury securities. This additional yield is mostly provided to compensate the investor for the risk of the unknown maturity. Investors who are not sensitive to maturity will find these securities very attractive. By carefully analyzing the prepayment risk, other investors can eliminate much of the uncertainty associated with prepayments.

MBSs are highly liquid. Investors can buy and sell MBSs as easily as corporate bonds. New issuances of MBSs generally equal or exceed new issuances of corporate bonds. Trades occur daily. All major investment banks, as well as more and more regional investment banks, have trading desks. Derivative products cause demand for these securities. The constant turnover of homes and newly constructed homes creates the supply.

POTENTIAL RISKS

The single biggest risk is mortgage prepayments. Prepayments and their effect on maturity can mean the difference between a good investment and a poor one. Assume that an investor receives a spread of 100 basis points over the seven-year Treasury rate for an MBS with an expected life of seven years. Prepayments are slower than expected, and the average life of the mortgages stretches out to ten years. The 10-year Treasury rate was 100 basis points over the seven-year Treasury rate. The investment for ten years ended up earning 10 basis points less than a Treasury. The Treasury bond provides the ultimate credit and call protection because it is noncallable and backed by the full faith and credit of the United States.

To further complicate matters, mortgages tend to prepay at the worst time. They also remain outstanding when the investor would rather that they prepay, a situation called negative convexity. When rates are dropping, prepayments increase, returning the principal from a higher rate investment to a lower one at a time when only lower-yielding investment alternatives exist. Assume that an investor holds a 12 percent GNMA. Rates drop to 8 percent. The GNMA prepays heavily, with the investor receiving the money in an 8 percent interest rate environment.

On the other hand, treasuries and corporate debt have convexity. When rates drop, the investor is left with a high-return instrument. To use the previous example, assume the investor owns an 11 percent Treasury and interest rates drop to 7 percent. In this scenario, the investor receives 4 percent more than market.

In a rising-rate environment, both MBS and Treasury investors lose. The MBS holder, however, will probably lose more. When rates rise, investors in either security are left with below-market-rate instruments. This situation is also the result of prepayments. During a rising-rate environment, prepayments will slow down, lengthening average lives; this lengthening of maturity causes greater price declines.

TYPES OF MORTGAGE-BACKED SECURITIES

MBSs have been sliced up and reconstructed to accentuate some of the attractive features as well as some of the risks. They range from instruments very similar to traditional corporate and Treasury obligations to high-risk investments similar to equity-type instruments. This section describes each of these investments, pointing out the individual risks and the features that are attractive in these securities.

Stripped Mortgage Securities

These securities are manufactured from MBSs. The most popular "strips" are interest only securities (IOs) and principal only securities (POs). "Stripping" is accomplished by splitting an MBS payment into an interest stream and a principal stream or a combination of the two. The possibilities of the proportions of the strips are infinite. Who does the stripping? FNMA and FHLMC issue strips. Instead of purchasing mortgages and issuing an MBS, the agencies issue an IO and a PO. Investment banking firms purchase securities on the open market and strip them. Securities are stripped because the value of the parts—IOs and POs—exceeds the value of the whole MBS. For example, assume a 10 percent GNMA is priced at $99. By stripping these securities, the IO sells for $20 and the PO, for $81. The sum of the parts (20 + 81 = 101) exceeds the value of the whole.

IOs are the interest portion of an MBS. If $1 million 10 percent GNMA MBS is stripped, the IO consists of the interest payments that are made on the GNMA. This stream of income is a declining annuity, subject to prepayment risk. IOs are considered bearish securities, in that the purchaser is betting that interest rates will rise. IOs are priced by discounting this income stream at current rates by some prepayment assumption. The prepayment assumption is critical in that it determines the length of the income stream. If prepayments slow down, the stream lasts longer, increasing the holder's return. If prepayments increase, this stream of interest is terminated early, causing a lower yield and possibly a loss of the investment. IOs are most beneficial as part of a hedge by sophisticated investors.

POs are the opposite of IOs. The principal portion of an MBS is stripped and sold at a deep discount. Pricing relies heavily on prepayment assumptions. Unlike IOs, POs will always return the investment if held to maturity. PO buyers are bullish and expect rates to drop and prepayments to increase. This scenario enhances the investor's return because the PO is purchased at a discount and paid back at par.

Mortgage-Backed Bonds

The mortgage-backed bond (MBB) is similar to corporate debt. Unlike most mortgage securities, MBBs do not depend for their repayment on the cashflow payments of a mortgage pool. This debt is a general obligation of a bank or savings and loan. The issue pays like any corporate obligation, with semiannual interest payments and a bullet principal payment. It is called an MBB because it is secured by the market value of a pool of mortgages. The market value is the price the pool could be sold for in the marketplace. The bank or savings and loan pledges the bondholders a pool of MBSs. If the institution fails to make a bond payment, the trustee is instructed to liquidate the pool of MBSs and redeem the bonds. So, through the use of mortgage collateral, banks and savings and loans can provide bondholders with greater security, which often leads to a AAA rating on these bonds.

MBBs are straight corporate debt. There is no uncertainty to prepayments. Bond repayments are fixed and made by the institution issuing the bonds. The elimination of prepayment risk makes these bonds much easier to price and sell.

However, MBBs do not provide call protection to investors. Most institutions that issue these types of securities are not of strong credit quality. If an institution becomes insolvent during the life of the bonds, the receiver (FDIC or FSLIC) may accelerate the bonds and pay them off. The AAA rating assessed on these bonds is a comment that bondholders will receive principal and interest in full. The rating makes no comment on call protection. To judge call protection, an assessment of the unsecured credit strength of the issuing institution must be made.

Collateralized Mortgage Obligations

The collateralized mortgage obligation (CMO) is a debt security backed by cashflow generated from a pool of mortgages. Its payment characteristics have been modified to provide investors with some call protection. The CMO does this by splitting up the issue into several classes, or tranches. The cashflows from the mortgages are directed to repaying the principal of one tranche at a time, mitigating to a large extent the prepayment risk from any holder. Table 3 provides an example of a traditional CMO issue.

The data in Table 3 clearly show how the CMO takes advantage of the yield curve. Notice that the largest class is the first. This positioning is done by design. The first class has the lowest interest cost because of its short average life; therefore, the issuer places as many bonds as he can in this class, helping to reduce the overall cost of the issue. The stated maturity shown in the table is not the date investors rely on. The stated maturity is how long it would take the investor to receive his full investment if no prepayments were to occur. The stated maturity is all but ignored in CMO issues, which are sold on an average life basis, assuming some prepayment rate. Table 4 details these assumptions for the strategic mortgage trust issue.

Table 4 demonstrates the amount of call protection provided by the CMO structure. Class A bonds differ by 2.2 years in weighted average life, given some fairly large changes in the prepayment assumptions. The example provides prepayments ranging from 75 percent PSA to 225 percent PSA. Class B bonds differ in weighted average life by 4.8 years. The Class B bonds have a 5.4-year difference, with 8.1 years being the change in a Class

TABLE 3. A Traditional CMO Issue

	Stated Principal Amount	Interest Rate	Stated Maturity	Price to Public
Class A	$50,000,000	7.85%	September 1, 2003	$99.78125
Class B	20,000,000	8.95	March 1, 2006	99.00000
Class C	20,000,000	9.30	March 1, 2008	98.71875
Class D	10,000,000	9.50	December 1, 2017	85.96875

Note: $100,000,000 Strategic Mortgage Trust 1986 I, date of issuance, October 29, 1987; Collateralized Mortgage Obligations, Series 1986 I, date of issuance, December 3, 1986.

TABLE 4. Percentage of Initial Principal Balance Outstanding on Various Bonds

	Class A Bonds				Class B Bonds			
Date	0%	75%	150%	225%	0%	75%	150%	225%
December 16, 1986	100.0	100.0	100.0	100.0	100.0	100.0	100.0	100.0
December 1, 1987	96.9	94.4	91.8	89.2	100.0	100.0	100.0	100.0
December 1, 1988	93.5	85.0	76.5	68.3	100.0	100.0	100.0	100.0
December 1, 1989	89.8	72.7	56.6	41.2	100.0	100.0	100.0	100.0
December 1, 1990	85.7	60.3	37.3	16.4	100.0	100.0	100.0	100.0
December 1, 1991	81.2	48.0	19.2	0.0	100.0	100.0	100.0	85.9
December 1, 1992	76.2	35.8	2.3	0.0	100.0	100.0	100.0	36.7
December 1, 1993	70.7	23.5	0.0	0.0	100.0	100.0	65.5	0.0
December 1, 1994	64.6	11.3	0.0	0.0	100.0	100.0	27.4	0.0
December 1, 1995	57.9	0.0	0.0	0.0	100.0	97.3	0.0	0.0
December 1, 1996	50.5	0.0	0.0	0.0	100.0	66.0	0.0	0.0
December 1, 1997	42.4	0.0	0.0	0.0	100.0	34.2	0.0	0.0
December 1, 1998	33.5	0.0	0.0	0.0	100.0	1.8	0.0	0.0
December 1, 1999	23.6	0.0	0.0	0.0	100.0	0.0	0.0	0.0
December 1, 2000	12.7	0.0	0.0	0.0	100.0	0.0	0.0	0.0
December 1, 2001	0.7	0.0	0.0	0.0	100.0	0.0	0.0	0.0
December 1, 2002	0.0	0.0	0.0	0.0	68.7	0.0	0.0	0.0
December 1, 2003	0.0	0.0	0.0	0.0	32.2	0.0	0.0	0.0
December 1, 2004	0.0	0.0	0.0	0.0	0.0	0.0	0.0	0.0
December 1, 2005	0.0	0.0	0.0	0.0	0.0	0.0	0.0	0.0
December 1, 2006	0.0	0.0	0.0	0.0	0.0	0.0	0.0	0.0
December 1, 2007	0.0	0.0	0.0	0.0	0.0	0.0	0.0	0.0
December 1, 2008	0.0	0.0	0.0	0.0	0.0	0.0	0.0	0.0
December 1, 2009	0.0	0.0	0.0	0.0	0.0	0.0	0.0	0.0
December 1, 2010	0.0	0.0	0.0	0.0	0.0	0.0	0.0	0.0
December 1, 2011	0.0	0.0	0.0	0.0	0.0	0.0	0.0	0.0
December 1, 2012	0.0	0.0	0.0	0.0	0.0	0.0	0.0	0.0
December 1, 2013	0.0	0.0	0.0	0.0	0.0	0.0	0.0	0.0
December 1, 2014	0.0	0.0	0.0	0.0	0.0	0.0	0.0	0.0
December 1, 2015	0.0	0.0	0.0	0.0	0.0	0.0	0.0	0.0
December 1, 2016	0.0	0.0	0.0	0.0	0.0	0.0	0.0	0.0
Weighted Average Life (Years)*	9.4	4.9	3.4	2.7	16.6	10.6	7.5	5.8

Date	Class C Bonds 0%	75%	150%	225%	Class D Bonds 0%	75%	150%	225%
December 16, 1986	100.0	100.0	100.0	100.0	100.0	100.0	100.0	100.0
December 1, 1987	100.0	100.0	100.0	100.0	109.8	109.8	109.8	109.8
December 1, 1988	100.0	100.0	100.0	100.0	120.7	120.7	120.7	120.7
December 1, 1989	100.0	100.0	100.0	100.0	132.5	132.5	132.5	132.5
December 1, 1990	100.0	100.0	100.0	100.0	145.6	145.6	145.6	145.6
December 1, 1991	100.0	100.0	100.0	100.0	159.9	159.9	159.9	159.9
December 1, 1992	100.0	100.0	100.0	100.0	175.7	175.7	175.7	175.7
December 1, 1993	100.0	100.0	100.0	92.4	192.9	192.9	192.9	192.9
December 1, 1994	100.0	100.0	100.0	52.1	211.9	211.9	211.9	211.9
December 1, 1995	100.0	100.0	90.8	15.1	232.8	232.8	232.8	232.8
December 1, 1996	100.0	100.0	55.6	0.0	255.7	255.7	255.7	217.3
December 1, 1997	100.0	100.0	21.3	0.0	280.9	280.9	280.9	177.9
December 1, 1998	100.0	100.0	0.0	0.0	308.5	308.5	284.0	144.0
December 1, 1999	100.0	68.5	0.0	0.0	338.9	338.9	248.0	114.8
December 1, 2000	100.0	34.3	0.0	0.0	372.3	372.3	215.2	89.6
December 1, 2001	100.0	0.0	0.0	0.0	408.9	406.5	185.3	68.0
December 1, 2002	100.0	0.0	0.0	0.0	449.2	373.1	158.0	49.5
December 1, 2003	100.0	0.0	0.0	0.0	493.4	340.4	133.1	33.6
December 1, 2004	92.0	0.0	0.0	0.0	542.0	308.3	110.4	19.9
December 1, 2005	47.7	0.0	0.0	0.0	595.3	276.8	89.7	8.2
December 1, 2006	0.0	0.0	0.0	0.0	651.6	245.9	70.8	0.0
December 1, 2007	0.0	0.0	0.0	0.0	608.3	215.3	53.5	0.0
December 1, 2008	0.0	0.0	0.0	0.0	560.2	185.2	37.7	0.0
December 1, 2009	0.0	0.0	0.0	0.0	506.9	155.2	23.3	0.0
December 1, 2010	0.0	0.0	0.0	0.0	447.8	125.5	10.1	0.0
December 1, 2011	0.0	0.0	0.0	0.0	382.2	96.0	0.0	0.0
December 1, 2012	0.0	0.0	0.0	0.0	310.2	66.6	0.0	0.0
December 1, 2013	0.0	0.0	0.0	0.0	230.5	37.3	0.0	0.0
December 1, 2014	0.0	0.0	0.0	0.0	143.0	8.1	0.0	0.0
December 1, 2015	0.0	0.0	0.0	0.0	48.7	0.0	0.0	0.0
December 1, 2016	0.0	0.0	0.0	0.0	0.0	0.0	0.0	0.0
Weighted Average Life (Years)*	19.0	13.6	10.3	8.2	25.5	21.5	17.0	13.4

*The weighted average life of a bond is determined by (1) multiplying the amount of each principal payment by the number of years from the date of bond issuance to the related principal payment date; (2) adding the results; and (3) dividing the sum by the total principal paid on the bond.

Note: Percentages are according to the prepayment model.

D's weighted average life. It is important to note that these swings in average life are at the initial issuance dates. As the issue pays down, larger prepayment moves are necessary to cause these differences.

This bond pays interest quarterly. The mortgages backing the bond had a weighted average coupon of 10.37 percent. The interest rates on the collateral ranged between 9.50 percent and 11.99 percent. The weighted average term to maturity was 354 months. These factors help in forming a judgment about prepayments. If the weighted average coupon approximates current mortgage rates, prepayment expectations will likely be in line with general expectations. Prepayments can be expected to be faster than usual if rates are falling or are below 10 percent. Likewise, if rates are above 11 percent, slower than average prepayments can be expected. The weighted average maturity of 354 is only six months off the maximum 360, meaning that the pool is recently originated. As the PSA assumptions suggest, prepayments should be slow for the first few years.

The payment flow of the Strategic Mortgage Trust 1986 I CMO pays interest to the A, B, and C bonds. All principal is applied to the Class A bond until it is paid in full. Principal is then applied to Class B and Class C sequentially. Class D bonds react differently from the other classes. This is a Z bond. The Z bond accrues but is not paid interest, which is why its bond balance grows. Each period the interest earned is added to the principal balance of the bond. Once all the prior classes are paid in full, the Z bond begins to fully amortize. The fact that it negatively amortizes at first helps the Z bond remain outstanding longer, providing the holder with some additional call protection.

The Z bond's price sensitivity changes over time, as does its payment stream. In the early years, when the Z bond behaves more like a zero coupon security, the bond price is highly sensitive to interest rate moves. The price will be highly volatile in a changing rate environment. Once the Z bond begins amortizing, however, the price becomes stable. At this point, owning it is similar to owning the first tranche.

Planned amortization class (PAC) bonds attempt to provide call protection to investors. This protection is accomplished by redirecting the deal's cashflow. A PAC promises holders a set amortization schedule within a range of prepayment rates. The prepayment range will change from deal to deal. Assume the range to be between 50 and 300 percent PSA and the PAC class to be the second class of the CMO. If the CMO is experiencing 100 percent PSA in prepayments, Class A, the PAC, and Class C are paid down sequentially. If prepayments are only 50 percent of PSA, payments are redirected from the first class to the PAC. If prepayments are 200 percent PSA, Class A is paid down. The PAC is paid only as planned, with the excess cashflow used to paydown Class C. This action has the effect of providing considerable certainty to the PAC holder. If prepayments fall outside the range established, the PAC holder is exposed to maturity uncertainty. This example demonstrates that the stability of cashflows given to the PAC class is accomplished by increasing the instability of payments to any other class.

Targeted amortization class (TAC) bonds also attempt to provide greater certainty of bond payments to investors, but not as much as PAC bonds. PACs try to protect investors against prepayment moves in either direction, whereas the TAC's aim is to protect holders from being called early. TACs promise to pay principal at the pricing speed. Assume that the pricing speed is 100 percent PSA. If prepayments exceed 100 percent and rise to 200 percent PSA, the excess prepayments over the 100 percent PSA pricing speed are redirected to other classes. Unlike PAC bonds, TACs extend in average life if the prepayment rate is less than expected.

CMOs commonly offer one class as a "floater." This floating rate class promises to pay investors an interest rate that is based on an index and that is capped. The indices that have been used to date are the London Interbank Offering Rate (LIBOR), the Federal Home Loan Bank's eleventh district COF index, the consumer price index, the one-year Treasury bill, and the one-month certificate of deposit composite rate. The bonds promise to pay a rate that floats with the designated index. These bonds do have an interest rate cap, which places a limit on the maximum amount of interest that the bond will pay. Investors should be aware of the index and the interest rate cap before making an investment decision.

Residuals (R bonds) are generally the class of CMO with the lowest principal amount and the highest interest rate. The R bond is, in fact, the residual of the CMO. R bonds represent excess cashflows generated from mortgage collateral over the amount required for the CMO issue's debt service and ongoing administrative expenses. Any mortgage security has a certain inherent risk level. Because the objective of the CMO structure is to isolate the bondholder from many of the risks associated with holding an MBS, the risks are shifted to the residual holder.

The residual holder is compensated for these risks through higher yields. To predict his ultimate rate of return, the residual owner must consider how prepayments, interest rates, and ongoing expenses will effect the CMO structure and, therefore, his payment stream. The R bond has many characteristics of an IO security, but with greater risk; it is closer to an equity type investment than a bond investment. R bonds generally have short average lives of approximately four years.

The difficulty in analyzing residual cashflows can be seen in Table 5, which illustrates how more and more CMOs are issued. As structures of CMO become more complicated, the analysis of the R bond becomes more complicated.

TAX CONSEQUENCES

Taxes for MBSs are very complex. Like all taxation, the complexity increases as one becomes more specific. This section highlights the issues and describes the various tax concepts that apply. Tax law in the mortgage securities area has been evolving. The tax reform acts of 1984 and 1986 have further defined the tax treatment of these securities. Investors can anticipate that the IRS will define further the tax treatment of these securities.

Tax treatment of a security depends on the type of security it is and on whether the security was purchased at par, at a discount, or at a premium. The tax treatment discussed here is for all currently issued mortgage securities. Seasoned issues may or may not have to comply, depending on when they were issued. To maximize the tax treatment of seasoned issues, investors should consult with a tax lawyer or tax accountant.

For tax purposes, GNMA certificates, FNMA, MBS, FHLMC, PCs, and pass-through certificates are all treated the same. Holders of pass-throughs must report income as received by the trust and not when received as payments under the certificates. This income should be reported as gross income for the amount of interest earned on the underlying mortgages. Deductions are allowed for servicing fees and other expenses.

Original issue discount usually does not apply to pass-throughs because mortgages are originated at par. However, any pass-through that has provision for increasing interest payments other than because of change in index, as for adjustable rate mortgages, must be accounted for as original issue discount. This would apply to teaser rates on ARMs and

TABLE 5. American Southwest Financial Corporation $250,250,000 Mortgage-Collateralized Bonds, Series 67

	Principal Amount	Type of Class	Interest Rate	Stated Maturity
Class 67 A	$14,190,000	PAC	8.65	March 1, 1999
Class 67 B	33,750,000	PAC	9.00	August 1, 2008
Class 67 C	13,150,000	PAC	9.30	October 1, 2010
Class 67 D	37,680,000	PAC	9.45	March 1, 2015
Class 67 E	45,000,000	Floater	Floater	December 1, 2015
Class 67 F	15,700,000	PAC	9.45	July 1, 2016
Class 67 G	23,160,000	Standard	9.75	January 1, 2017
Class 67 H	28,400,000	PAC	9.45	August 1, 2018
Class 67 I	39,220,000	Standard	5.95	August 1, 2018

graduated payment mortgages. The amortization of the discount should be done under the constant yield method for each period the security is held. Market discounts can also be amortized under the constant yield method, although other treatments are possible. Premiums must be amortized under the constant yield method. IOs and POs must both be treated as original issue discounts. These discounts should be amortized into income using the constant yield method.

The Real Estate Mortgage Investment Conduit (REMIC) established the tax treatment for CMOs. Commonly misunderstood as a structure or an issuer, REMIC is a provision of the tax code. REMIC provides treatment for investors of CMOs and pass-throughs that make a REMIC election. REMIC provides that all interest must be either regular interest or residual interest. Regular interest holders are taxed like all debt holders. Discounts and premiums must be amortized into income by the constant yield method. Residual interest of a REMIC is responsible for taxes on the issuing entity net of all expenses.

MBBs are taxed like all corporate debt. Discounts and premiums should be amortized into income using the constant yield method.

REPRESENTATIVE TYPES OF INVESTORS

MBSs have a broad investor base. Banks and savings and loan institutions are the largest investors in mortgage securities. GNMA, FHLMC, and FNMA securities are all purchased by financial institutions. Early tranches of CMOs are also purchased by these institutions. IOs and POs are purchased by savings and loan institutions.

Insurance companies and pension funds purchase the agency pass-throughs, MBBs, and longer classes of CMO. Pension funds also purchase private pass-through securities. Certain classes of CMO are sold in Europe. European as well as Japanese investors purchase LIBOR-based floating-rate classes of CMOs.

Retail investors have purchased CMOs and MBBs. Before tax reform, many CMO Z classes were sold to IRA accounts. Residual bonds of CMOs are purchased by real estate investment trusts and certain money market funds.

IMPORTANT FACTORS IN BUYING AND SELLING

Investors can easily purchase MBSs. Most firms actively trade these instruments. There are two components of an MBS, the minimum unit size and the dollar amount outstanding. The unit size is the minimum face amount in which a security is issued. For GNMAs, this is $25,000. This minimum does not mean an investor necessarily must invest $25,000 to purchase GNMAs. Like all mortgage securiities, GNMAs are constantly paying down their principal balance. An investor, therefore, may invest $12,500 for a GNMA that has a face of $25,000 but has paid down in half. FHLMC and FNMA offer units as low as $1,000. Nongovernment-issued pass-throughs and CMOs are generally issued in units of $10,000.

The key aspect of buying and selling is knowing the product. An investor who buys an agency security or pass-through certificates should know the characteristics of the loan pool backing the security. Weighted average coupon and maturity are key to the description. All major investment banking houses publish their expectations of prepayment speeds.

With CMOs, investors should know what tranche they are buying, as well as the other classes of the CMO and how they work. If another class is a PAC, a class under consideration may be more volatile than expected. Loans backing the CMO are also important. What is the prepayment assumption? How sensitive is the security to changes in interest rates and prepayments?

MBSs are complicated to understand and complicated to put together. Investors should look for either highly rated securities or issues of GNMA, FNMA, and FHLMC. Many factors may affect the investment, but credit should not be one of them.

GLOSSARY

AA—Second-highest rating category assigned by S&P.

AAA—Highest rating category assigned by S&P.

ARM—Adjustable rate mortgage; a residential mortgage loan with an interest rate that may change over time.

amortize—To pay down the principal balance.

annual cap—For ARMs, the largest possible interest rate change allowed in one year under the mortgage.

basis points—1/100 of a percent.

call protection—Provides protection against being redeemed.

CMO—Collateralized mortgage obligation.

conventional mortgage—Any mortgage loan that is not insured by the Federal Housing Administration.

COF—Cost of funds index.

credit enhance—To increase the credit quality.

Due on sale—A provision of mortgage loans that requires the full repayment of the mortgage on the sale of the home.

FDIC—Federal Deposit Insurance Corporation.

FHLMC—Federal Home Loan Mortgage Corporation.

FHA—Federal Housing Administration.

FNMA—Federal National Mortgage Association.

FSLIC—Federal Savings and Loan Insurance Corporation.

floater—Term referring to the class of a CMO whose interest rate is adjustable.

GNMA—Government National Mortgage Association.

IO—Interest Only portion of a mortgage certificate or loan.

lifetime cap—Maximum interest rate that can be charged on an adjustable rate mortgage.

LIBOR—London Interbank offering rate.

margin—The spread or the difference between an index and a rate charged on the mortgage loan.

MBB—Mortgage-backed bond.

MBS—Mortgage-backed security.

mortgage pool—A group of mortgage loans segregated in some fashion.

PC—Participation certificate.

pass-through—A privately issued mortgage-backed security.

payment cap—Maximum permitted increase in a mortgagor's payment under the mortgage contract for ARMs.

PAC—Planned amortization class.

P&I—Principal and interest, the two components that usually make up a monthly payment on a mortgage loan.

PO—Principal only portion of a mortgage certificate.

PSA—Public Securities Association.

REMIC—Real Estate Mortgage Investment Conduit.

R bonds—Residual bonds; a class of a CMO that generally sells at a high premium.

seasoned—Has aged or been in existence for a number of years.

secondary market—The sale of mortgage loans after they are originated.

servicer—The organization that collects the monthly mortgage payment from the consumer.

servicing spread—The difference between the gross interest rate on a mortgage loan and the net interest rate paid to investors.

stripping—The slicing up of mortgage payments into different components from the scheduled principal and interest.

TAC—Targeted amortization class; a class of a CMO that stabilizes principal payments.

teaser—The initial rate offered on an ARM that is at an initial discount to its contract rate.

tranches—A term for the different classes of a CMO.

underwriting—The process a lender goes through in making mortgage loans; the checking and approving of applications for mortgage loans.

Z bond—The class of a CMO that initially accrues interest until previous classes are paid.

MAJOR RETAIL FIRMS TRADING MORTGAGE-BACKED SECURITIES

Dean Witter Reynolds, Inc.

Merrill Lynch Pierce Fenner and Smith, Inc.

PaineWebber Group, Inc.

Prudential-Bache Securities, Inc.

Shearson Lehman Hutton, Inc.

SUGGESTED READING

Fabozzi, Frank J., ed., *The Handbook of Mortgage-Backed Securities.* Chicago: Probus Publishing Co., 1988. A comprehensive look at mortgage-backed securities.

Goldman Sachs & Co., New York, publishes and regularly updates the following:

CMOs Revisited: The Impact of Structure on Value

Mortgage-Backed Bonds: Structures and Value

Stripped Mortgage-Backed Securities

ARM Securities: A Product Review

Mortgage Residuals

An Introduction to the Mortgage Market and Mortgage Analysis

Floating Rate CMO's: A Primer for First Time Buyers

S&P's Structured Finance Criteria. New York: S&P, 1988. An in-depth look at the structures and credit risk associated with mortgage securities.

MOTION PICTURES

David Nochimson

BASIC CHARACTERISTICS

Historical Background

From its rudimentary beginnings at the turn of the century, the motion picture industry has grown at an extraordinary rate. By 1946, in the United States alone, 3 billion tickets were sold annually, producing gross box-office receipts of $1.6 billion. Without any real competition for the leisure dollar, Hollywood was turning out an average of 400 pictures per year for the world market. The film industry during these years was dominated by nine companies (MGM, Columbia, Paramount, Twentieth Century Fox, United Artists, Universal, Warner, Walt Disney, and RKO), which were integrated production-distribution-exhibition companies known as the studios or the majors. The studios were dominated by a handful of autocratic and, in some cases, charismatic studio heads whose members included Louis B. Mayer, Jack Warner, and Harry Cohn; their combined judgments determined the motion picture fare for the entire world.

The stranglehold of the majors on the production, marketing, and exhibition of feature films led to the Department of Justice-imposed consent decree in 1950, pursuant to which the majors were required to divest themselves of their American theater holdings. To compound the impact of the consent decree, the studios were losing large portions of the public to the new, free visual entertainment medium—television. The results were nearly fatal. As a direct consequence of the huge drop in audience and income, Hollywood production operations went through a drastic shake-up. Several companies retired from the scene,

David Nochimson is a member of the Los Angeles law firm of Ziffren, Brittenham & Branca.

studio executive staffs were cut to the bone, production departments were mothballed, and large areas of studio real estate were sold off.

As a consequence of this restructuring, the studio heads, whose numbers were severely depleted by death and retirement during this period, lost control of the industry. The important actors, directors, writers, and producers, freed from long-term studio employment agreements, formed their own production companies, created and developed their own material, assembled the casts and directors, and sought from the studio only its funds for financing and its marketing organization for distribution. This shift from studio production to independent production became, and remains today, the basic way in which feature films are financed, produced, and distributed.

Current Industry Trends

New Growth. As the novelty of free television entertainment began to wear off in the early 1960s, audiences that had forsaken the theaters began to return, and U.S. box-office receipts grew slowly but steadily until 1975, when they reached $2.1 billion. Aided by a series of blockbuster films, box-office receipts rose to above $3.0 billion in the early 1980s and to $4.2 billion in 1987. (See Table 1 for 1966–1987 theater industry statistics.)

This growth and income also reflected impressive changes and the fundamental economics of the marketplace for feature films, including the following:

- Box-office prices from 1973 to 1987 generally rose faster than the rate of inflation.
- New theater construction, accelerating a trend that began in the late 1960s, contributed to a total number of theaters in 1987 of 23,555 (compared to 17,590 in 1980, 14,055 in 1971, and 11,000 in 1963). One factor in this growth was the increasing use of multiplexing (using several motion picture screens in a single building or complex), which in turn was aided by a change in union rules that permitted a single projectionist to handle the projection of more than one picture in the same building.
- While the number of English-language films released continued to drop during the period 1972 to 1979 (from 279 in 1972 to 248 in 1979), revenue earning potentials of pictures released increased during the 1970s. The number of films released has dramatically increased in the 1980s to 478 in 1987.
- The decrease in supply and increase in demand for films has resulted, for the most part, in the higher percentage of gross box-office dollars being paid by exhibitors to distributors. Exhibitors were being forced to compete more aggressively in bidding for an increasingly scarce product, resulting in higher film rental terms. Although the distributor share of box-office receipts declined from 1982–1985, it has again increased over the past three years.
- The attempt to develop meaningful centers for the production and international distribution of indigenous theatrical motion pictures in England, Italy, France, Germany, and Mexico collapsed, leaving the worldwide theatrical motion picture industry almost totally dependent on American films.

Ultimately, however, two factors have played and are continuing to play the major role in the resurgent economic strength of the industry. The first is the growth and

TABLE 1. U.S. Motion Picture Theater Industry Statistics, 1966–1987

	Number of Films Released	Box Office Gross		Average Price Per Ticket		Number of Admissions	
		Amount (in millions)	Percent Change	Amount	Percent Change	Number (in millions)	Percent Change
Average (1966–1987)			7.0%		6.7%		0.3%
1987	478	$4,252.9	12.6	$3.907	5.2	1,088.5	7.0
1986	398	3,778	0.8	3.714	4.6	1,017.2	(3.7)
1985	371	3,749.4	(7.0)	3.550	5.6	1,056.1	(11.9)
1984	398	4,030.6	7.0	3.361	6.8	1,199.1	0.2
1983	395	3,766.0	9.1	3.146	7.1	1,196.9	1.8
1982	365	3,452.7	16.4	2.937	5.7	1,175.4	10.2
1981	N.A.	2,965.6	7.9	2.779	3.3	1,060	4.5
1980	N.A.	2,748.5	(2.6)	2.691	6.9	1,021.5	(8.9)
1979	248	2,821.3	6.3	2.517	7.4	1,120.9	(0.6)
1978	203	2,653	11.8	2.343	5.1	1,128.2	6.1
1977	226	2,372	16.5	2.23	4.7	1,063	11.1
1976	174	2,036	(3.7)	2.13	3.9	957	(7.4)
1975	176	2,115	10.8	2.05	8.5	1,033	2.2
1974	238	1,909	25.3	1.89	7.4	1,011	16.9
1973	219	1,524	(3.7)	1.76	3.5	865	(7.4)
1972	296	1,583	17.3	1.70	3.0	934	13.9
1971	256	1,350	(5.5)	1.65	6.5	820	(11.0)
1970	236	1,429	10.4	1.55	9.2	921	1.0
1969	235	1,294	0.9	1.42	8.4	912	(6.8)
1968	235	1,282	15.5	1.31	9.2	979	5.6
1967	N.A.	1,110	4.0	1.20	10.1	927	(4.9)
1966	N.A.	1,067	N.A.	1.09	N.A.	975	N.A.

N.A. = Not available.

Source: Motion Picture Association of America

entrenchment of the practice among the majors of requiring guarantees as a condition to renting their films to exhibitors. Second, sequential markets for films after their theatrical release are major sources of income today, a fact that has dramatically reduced the downside risk historically accompanied by investing in motion picture production. However, the performance of the ancillary markets has begun to flatten and prospects are for a downward cycle in the industry.

New Markets. New markets for motion pictures include the following:

- U.S. prime-time network television
- Local nonnetwork television and all foreign television, referred to generically as television syndication
- The pay-television market, including pay per view
- The nontheatrical market, such as airlines, ships at sea, offshore oil rigs, colleges, hospitals, libraries, construction camps, and defense installations
- Video cassettes and video discs

The motion picture industry accounted for total worldwide revenues (at the distributor-studio level) of $3.1 billion in 1980, and revenues exceeded $6.2 billion in 1988.

Pay Television. Pay television, in particular, has experienced extraordinary growth since its introduction in the early 1970s. In a report published in 1976, Arthur D. Little, Incorporated, developed certain projections for the pay-cable industry. It estimated that the number of pay subscribers would be 3.4 million in 1980 and 5.7 million in 1985. These projections were vastly understated. In fact, the number of subscribers grew to 24.2 million in 1985 and, in 1987, reached 24.6 million. However, the market has undergone its most rapid growth and is starting to plateau. The number of subscribers declined by 2.1 percent from 1985 to 1986 (after increasing by 19.8 percent in 1985) but increased more modestly (by 3.8 percent) from 1986 to 1987.

The potential profitability of pay television is far greater than that of commercial television because, instead of underwriting programs by advertising revenues (at pennies per viewer), revenues from pay television are based on a per-subscriber charge.

Although the pay-television industry is still experiencing growth and increased earnings, the revenues derived by the motion picture companies from that segment of the marketplace has recently flattened out and is expected to decline in the short term.

Pay Per View. The new technologies of the 1980s—pay television and home video—have had an explosive effect on the motion picture business, and now that these industries have matured, there has been a debate about what impact pay per view will have on the future of the motion picture industry. Until now, the pay-per-view market has been limited because of two factors. First, there is a small number of addressable homes (i.e., homes to which pay-per-view programming is available). Although this number has increased dramatically from 1.5 million in 1982 to 15 million in 1987, it is still insufficient to generate the kind of revenues that will have a substantial impact on overall profits. Second, pay per view is still an "event driven" business—major sports or musical events—and the revenues from a continuing stream of feature films is yet to occur. The real impact of pay per view will not be realized for three to five years when the pay-per-view population will reach a critical mass. Estimates are that by 1990, the pay-per-view universe will reach 20 million addressable homes. Paul Kagan Associates estimates that the percentage of motion picture revenues from pay per view will reach six percent by 1997,[1] a point at which this segment of the market will be significant.

Home Video. The 1980s witnessed a dramatic growth in the home video market, and motion picture companies have been one of its biggest beneficiaries. VCR households

---

[1] Paul Kagan Associates, *The Pay TV Newsletter*, March 31, 1988.

grew from 1,850,000 in 1980 to 45,800,000 in 1987 and sales of prerecorded cassettes to U.S. dealers grew from 3 million in 1980 to 110 million in 1987. The video cassette market accounted for 3 percent of revenues from feature motion pictures in 1980, while in 1987, it represented 33 percent (see Table 2). Although this growth has been dramatic, as the video cassette industry matured, there has been an accompanying leveling off and even decline in the revenues from this area of the marketplace. The reasons for this are as follows:

1. The video business is now largely a hit driven or "A-title" business, and secondary offerings are no longer generating the revenues they initially could achieve.
2. The video business is substantially a rental business and the small retail market (in stores and through mail order), combined with the inability of the major producers to participate in rental revenues, has deprived the production companies of additional revenues.
3. The novelty of the business has worn off.
4. The move to an $89 retail price has lessened unit and dollar volume.
5. With the depletion of "library" titles (old movies), the business has become dependent on current releases.
6. There has been a reduction and consolidation of retail outlets.

Subsidiary Rights. In addition to the income from pay television, television syndication, and home video, the subsidiary rights to the literary materials on which a picture is based are of growing importance. Subsidiary rights include theatrical sequels and remakes, television series rights, publishing rights, merchandising exploitation of characters, the marketing of phonograph records and tapes using the soundtrack of a film, and music publishing income.

Until 1970, the amount of income derived from the exploitation of a theatrical motion picture in these sequential markets and the subsidiary rights was relatively insubstantial, rarely amounting in the aggregate to more than 20 percent of the production cost of a picture. In the last decade, the rate of growth in these areas has been even more dramatic than the growth in theatrical exhibition income. Indeed, it has been generally accepted that the extraordinary interest expressed by outside investors and lenders in the motion picture industry has been prompted by the substantially reduced downside risk in theatrical film investment resulting from the high income potential from these sources. This attitude is undergoing a significant change.

Current Status of the Industry and Short-Term Trends. The motion picture industry is presently undergoing a shake-out that will result in a leveling out and perhaps decline in earnings, accompanied by a consolidation (due to a combination of acquisitions and failing companies), which will be preparatory to another upward cycle (see Table 3). For the short term, however, there is caution about the profitability for the industry as a whole. The easy access to equity markets from 1980 to 1986 has evaporated due to some major failures of companies that were taken public. In 1986, Wall Street raised $1.6 billion for the entertainment industry in the public market; in 1989, estimates are that this number will barely reach $400 million. As a result, there will be a culling out among the

TABLE 2. Total Revenues by Source for Feature Films

By Percentage of Total Revenues

	1978	1979	1980	1981	1982	1983	1984	1985	1986	1987
Domestic theatrical	46	45	38	34	35	32	30	25	21	20
Foreign theatrical	29	33	29	25	19	20	15	14	15	15
Domestic pay television	2	3	5	8	9	9	11	13	10	8
Foreign pay television	0	0	0	0	0	0	0	0	1	1
Network television	11	6	8	5	7	6	4	3	3	3
Domestic syndication	5	3	5	5	5	6	7	8	8	8
Foreign syndication	5	3	5	5	5	6	7	8	8	8
Domestic home video	0	1	4	10	9	9	12	18	19	18
Foreign home video	0	0	0	2	5	7	8	8	12	15
Other	1	1	1	1	1	1	1	1	1	1
Total revenues	100	100	100	100	100	100	100	100	100	100

By Amount of Total Revenues
(in millions of dollars)

	1978	1979	1980	1981	1982	1983	1984	1985	1986	1987
Domestic theatrical	1186	1142	1178	1160	1337	1302	1323	1131	1134	1243
Foreign theatrical	747	837	899	853	726	814	662	633	814	932
Domestic pay television	51	76	155	270	344	367	485	588	543	497
Foreign pay television	0	0	0	0	0	0	0	0	55	62
Network television	283	152	248	170	267	244	176	136	165	186
Domestic syndication	128	76	155	170	191	244	309	362	434	497
Foreign syndication	155	203	310	341	382	407	529	452	543	684
Domestic home video	0	26	125	341	344	367	529	814	1031	1119
Foreign home video	0	0	0	68	191	284	353	362	651	933
Other	26	25	31	34	38	41	44	45	55	62
Total revenues	2576	2537	3101	3413	3820	4070	4410	4523	5427	6215

Source: Wertheim Schroder & Co.

TABLE 3. Operating Income Before Taxes (Film and TV Divisions Only) (in millions of dollars)

Studio	1977	1978	1979	1980	1981	1982	1983	1984	1985	1986	1987
Columbia	$ 31	$ 80	$ 59	$ 60	$ 78	$ 47	$ 91	$121	$161	$205	$(120)[1]
Disney	46	54	40	49	31	20	(33)	2	34	59	131
MGM[2]	27	39	48	23	35	28	50	35	(84)	29	(81)
Orion						11	10	9	(38)	13	15
Paramount	15	40	82	72	71	66	68	111	78	115	297
Tri-Star								(15)	2	17	(23)[3]
20th Century Fox	70	91	67	55	15	3	52	(58)	(70)	36	88
United Artists	53	58	48	20	(39)						
Universal (MCA)	107	160	174	134	72	212	164	62	146	89	162
Warner Bros.	58	80	118	61	25	102	109	150 (112)[4]	160	172	176
Totals	$407	$602	$636	$474	$288	$489	$511	$305	$389	$735	$708

[1] Through February 29, 1988.
[2] MGM/UA since 1982.
[3] Estimated.
[4] Disney special write-off.

Source: Wertheim Schroder & Co.

mid-level independent production companies, most likely resulting in a greater concentration among the majors (which will continue to control distribution), with a few substantial independents and a variety of small players left to compete. The ultimate beneficiaries of this shake-out will be the small number of major studios. A recent Oppenheimer & Co., Inc., report concluded as follows:

> Despite record box office grosses in 1987, the movie industry's 1988 outlook is not encouraging, particularly for the smaller independent producers. The majors have stepped up their production rate, and because of their generally higher movie budgets, are fighting each other for wider coverage to hopefully increase their grosses. They are also expanding their release schedule beyond the normal large attendance periods of the Christmas and summer seasons. As a result, we believe the independents will have difficulty obtaining broad exposure for their films. This should force some of the weaker suppliers out of the business and/or to combine forces.[2]

A significant cause for this development has been the maturing of the new technologies—pay television and home video. In the early 1980s, the industry's growth was stimulated by pay-television revenues. With a slackening in pay-television revenues, dramatic video cassette revenues fueled continued growth. As a Goldman Sachs' report stated:

[2] "Movie Industry Review," Oppenheimer & Co., Inc., Report Number 88–126, January 28, 1988.

Almost 85% of the total revenue growth between 1980 and 1986 came from paying cassette. The growth of these markets altered the structure of the industry and deferred the shakeout that is now taking place. For the first time in almost ten years, there is no significant stimulative replacement technology on the horizon.[3]

Film Distribution and Exploitation

Typically, a film is produced either by an independent production company or by a major. In the case of a film financed by a major, the studio distributor retains worldwide control over all rights and will take a distribution fee depending on the media and territory, thereafter recouping all its distribution expenses and finally recovering its production costs plus overhead plus interest. The balance is referred to as net profits and is shared with certain creative elements (e.g., stars, directors, and individual producers). In the case of an independent production company, funds for the production of the film are, in whole or in part, raised independently of the studio; as a result, the independent has a greater opportunity to drive a harder bargain with the distributor and, in addition, to withhold certain rights from the theatrical distributor. For example, an independent may give U.S. and Canadian theatrical rights to a major, reserving the right to make the network and pay-television sale itself, turning over foreign theatrical sales to a sales agent on a territory-by-territory basis, and giving television syndication rights to an independent syndication company.

The independent producer also has a better opportunity to obtain a gross or adjusted gross deal, as opposed to a net profit deal, from a distributor. Instead of the distributor recouping a full distribution fee and all expenses before remitting any money to the independent producer, at negotiated levels of revenues, the producer will get a varying percentage of the revenues received by the distributor. If the independent producer is able to furnish the cost of prints and advertising to the distributor, the distribution terms will become even more favorable.

Break-Even Rule. As a rule of thumb (which seems to be more an exception than a rule), a film must generate gross film rentals (as opposed to box-office receipts) of approximately three times its production cost to break even. Depending on the cost of the film, its advertising budget, and whether there are so-called gross participants (superstars who participate from the first dollar of film rental), the breakeven point can even be at a higher multiple. It is more common now to see a picture break even at a factor of 4 to 5.

Distributor-Exhibitor-Producer Exploitation. There are three levels in the U.S. theatrical exploitation of motion pictures: the distributor, the exhibitor, and the producer. As noted previously, with studio-financed pictures, the producer is also the distributor. Typically, a film is first distributed to motion picture theaters, and the exhibitor (or theater owner) collects box-office receipts. The theater owner receives a share of box-office receipts as negotiated with the distributor, which typically ranges from 10 to 75 percent but averages 45 percent. When the theater owner retains a lower percentage of box-office receipts, he usually recovers the negotiated charge to cover overhead and, in addition, is able to deduct the cost of advertising he is advanced. The balance is remitted to the distributor and is called film rental, from which the distributor must cover its distribution

---

[3] "The Movie Industry—1988" by Richard Simm, Goldman Sachs Investment Research Report, December 4, 1987.

expenses, such as advertising and prints. From film rentals, the distributor will typically deduct a distribution fee (ranging from 30 to 35 percent) and thereafter recoups distribution expenses. If the distributor has not financed the picture, it will remit the balance to the independent producer, but if the distributor is also the financier, it will recoup its production costs plus interest and overhead plus a share of the profits.

Foreign theatrical distribution takes two forms. Films may be licensed by the producer on a territory-by-territory basis with foreign distributors, in which case the producer will receive an advance against a percentage of receipts (after recoupment by the distributors of their fees and expenses); alternatively, the film can be licensed on a fixed fee or outright sale basis where the producer receives a fixed license fee but not participation of revenues of the film. If the studio or U.S. theatrical distribution controls foreign theatrical rights, it will customarily charge 40 to 50 percent of the film rentals as its distribution fee for foreign theatrical distribution. If the film is licensed on a territory-by-territory basis by a foreign sales agent, the fee charged by the sales agent will be typically 20 percent, which is based on amounts remitted by the territorial distributors (who themselves will take a distribution fee).

In the television markets, films are licensed by producers to pay television and free television (network and syndication) directly or through a distributor (often by the distributor who has the theatrical distribution rights). If licensed through a third-party distributor, the distribution fee charged by the distributor will range from 25 to 40 percent of the license fee.

Production and Marketing of Television Films

Although the focus of this article is on theatrical motion pictures, some attention should be given to an alternative pattern of motion picture production, namely, film production for initial exhibition on television. While the network license fees for theatrical motion pictures escalated until the early 1980s, the prices paid by advertisers were not elastic enough for the networks to pass on all of their costs, and the earlier exposure of the films in the home video and pay-television markets virtually eliminated the possibilities for networks licensing feature films (except for major blockbusters). As a result, the networks are relying more on film made directly for television. The lower cost, the ability to control the time of release, and the general popularity point to a further emphasis on "Movies of the Week."

A two-hour motion picture for television, as opposed to a television series or miniseries, requires little risk (although the rewards, too, are commensurately limited). Little money will be committed without first submitting the proposed project to the network, and, if the network approves the material, it will underwrite the cost of the script and perhaps defer some of the producer's overhead cost. When the teleplay is completed, it will be budgeted and submitted to the network, and, if the network approves the project, it will negotiate a license fee with the production company, typically covering two network runs of the film. Current network license fees range from $2 million to $2.4 million (plus so-called cast breakage to cover the additional cost for major television stars). Following the network telecast, the producer, who owns the film, will be able to license the film for television syndication, pay television, and the ancillary markets. If the film has special attributes (such as an actor well known in the foreign theatrical market), the film can be sold to and exploited by local foreign theatrical distributors before being sold to television stations in the market (and concurrently with the U.S. network run).

The production of a "Movie of the Week" can be done by either the television arm of a major studio, a major independent production company, or an individual producer. Because the network will require producers who are not well established to furnish evidence of financial responsibility (since the producer is responsible for costs in excess of the network license fee), those producers must make arrangements in the form of a co-venture with an umbrella company (a studio or major independent). It should be noted that the network license fee often may not cover the entire production cost, so it is important to arrange for deficit financing, which can be done through an umbrella company or by preselling syndication rights. The attractive characteristics of producing "Movies of the Week" include the following:

- The essentially limited nature of the front-end risk, since, except for general overhead, the only investment is in the acquisition of rights in the underlying material, which may be passed along to the network.
- On occasion, the network license fee may exceed the production costs of the film.
- After deducting distribution fees and residuals, there may be an opportunity for foreign theatrical income.
- Worldwide syndication income has grown at an attractive rate (although since early 1982, this market has softened), and it is possible for a supplier to gross from \$500,000 to \$600,000. The weak dollar and the privatization of foreign television (resulting in increased competition) has fostered higher foreign revenues over the past three years.

Types of Motion Picture Investments

Investments in motion pictures take a variety of forms and may involve a single picture or multiple pictures.

Development or Seed Capital Investments. The active production of a motion picture is preceded by a development process in which literary material is acquired or developed by a producer, a director is assigned to the project, proposed casting is determined, and a budget is formulated. Development costs are relatively modest compared to the production itself but nevertheless can be substantial, depending on the nature of the project. For example, an option on underlying literary material, such as a novel, may cost from \$10,000 to \$50,000 (although the option for a blockbuster novel may cost from \$100,000 to \$250,000); the preparation of a screenplay may cost from \$100,000 to \$250,000; and the supervisory services of a director or producer may range from \$10,000 to \$50,000, plus miscellaneous costs for budgeting, travel, and other expenses.

Investments in Production. After the project has been developed, the screenplay finalized, and the budget approved, actual production occurs. The average cost of a studio feature motion picture today is \$17 million, although low-budget pictures can cost from \$2 million to \$5 million.

Investments in Completed Films. Investments in completed films take one or both of the following forms: copyright acquisition, which is the acquisition of the copyright on the completed motion picture after it has been produced; or a distribution expense fund, wherein, instead of or in addition to the copyright acquisition, an investor may advance funds to underwrite the distribution or marketing costs of a motion picture, such as prints and media advertising.

Investments in a Publicly Traded Motion Picture Company. An investor also has the opportunity to make an equity or debt investment in an existing public company that produces or distributes motion pictures. Some of the companies are exclusively involved in the motion picture production business and distribution (e.g., MGM-UA, Orion), while others are diversified entertainment entities (e.g., Warner Communications, Inc., Columbia Pictures, MCA, and Walt Disney). In addition, Gulf & Western, which owns Paramount Pictures, is a major diversified conglomerate. The performance of these publicly traded companies is set forth in Table 3.

Structure of Investments

The investment in a development, production, or completed film deal can take several forms, depending on the number and nature of the investors and the securities and tax aspects.

General Partnership. The investor may elect to form a partnership with the producer.

Limited Partnership. In a limited partnership, which is the most common form of motion picture investment, the investor is a limited partner who does not participate in the management and control of the project. (See article on "Real Estate: Limited Partnerships," elsewhere in this volume, for a discussion of the legal and financial aspects of this method of investment and participation.)

Corporation. Except in the public company context, an investment in capital stock of a motion picture company is rarely used. In certain situations, the Subchapter S corporation may be employed, but this may pose special tax problems.

Types of Deals

In the prototypical motion picture investment (which is not unique to this industry), the money recoups first, after which money and talent each receive 50 percent of the profits. Therefore, the investor would recoup his investment, pro rata with the other investors, out of the first receipts[4] of the film; thereafter, the investor would receive 50 percent of the profits, and the talent (e.g., producer, director, and cast) would receive the remaining 50 percent. There are many variations on this theme, each with its own special characteristics.

---

[4] It should be noted that first receipts are not box-office receipts or even film rental. It customarily means the first receipts received by the production entity from a third-party distributor, after deduction by the distributor of distribution fees and expenses.

ATTRACTIVE FEATURES

Disproportionate Return on Successful Projects

One of the major benefits of a motion picture investment is directly related to its greatest risk, namely, the highly speculative nature of the investment. The reward for a successful motion picture investment can be quite disproportionate to the investment. A motion picture, unlike a manufactured item, does not have a fixed production markup for each item sold; therefore, once its cost has been recouped, all income after marketing expenses is pure profit. It must be noted, of course, that the blockbuster picture is not commonplace, but an investor who chooses the right project (which may be more accidental than planned) will reap the reward of making back many times his investment. The blockbuster mentality that permeates the industry can be dangerous and misleading; one cannot predict which film will be the next *Star Wars*.

Intangible Benefits

There is a certain psychological benefit associated with motion picture investment. The glamour of being associated with a film production certainly has intangible rewards irrespective of its economic benefits.

Modest Fixed Costs

Unlike other investments, the motion picture industry requires no significant investment in plant or equipment. It is basically a service business. Personnel can be hired on a project basis, and a film can be marketed through existing distribution organizations.

Sequential Marketing

A motion picture has the potential of generating significant revenues long after its initial release by way of reissues, remakes, sequels, and exploitation in new markets.

Contra-Cyclical Nature of the Business

There are many indications that the motion picture industry is contra-cyclical and may even prosper during periods of economic recession. For example, in 1974 and 1975, the poorest years for the economy since the 1940s owing to the Arab oil embargo, movie attendance rose 17 percent. In contrast, in 1976, a boom year for the economy, box-office receipts declined nearly 4 percent. However, the decline in attendance (by 9 percent) in 1980 runs counter to this theory.

Rapid Return on Investment

The theatrical release of a film takes a small amount of time (three to nine months); thereafter, if the film is successful, the return on capital can be accomplished quite quickly. This is especially likely in a completed film acquisition; development and production deals involve a period when the investment funds are not producing revenues.

POTENTIAL RISKS

The film business, perceived by the public as glamorous, exciting, and lucrative, must be viewed by the investor as a business and, as such, must be considered highly speculative. The chances are greater for substantial losses than for meteoric profits.

TABLE 4. Advertising Costs for 1980 to 1987

	Combined Advertising and Print Costs			Advertising Costs		
Year	Average Cost ($ millions)	Yearly Percentage Change	1987 Versus Given Year	Average Cost ($ millions)	Yearly Percentage Change	1987 Versus Given Year
1987	$8.840	+ 32.5%	—	$6.564	+ 20.8%	—
1986	6.673	− 7.4	+ 32.5%	5.435	+ 4.6	+ 20.8%
1985	7.210	+ 8.4	+ 22.6	5.194	− 3.2	+ 26.4
1984	6.651	+ 27.8	+ 32.9	5.363	+ 28.2	+ 22.4
1983	5.205	+ 5.4	+ 69.8	4.182	+ 3.0	+ 57.0
1982	4.936	+ 12.0	+ 79.1	4.182	+ 3.0	+ 57.0
1981	4.407	+ 1.8	100.6	3.541	+ 0.1	+ 85.4
1980	4.329	—	+ 104.2	3.544	—	+ 85.2

Source: Motion Picture Association of America

High Production and Marketing Costs

The cost of producing a motion picture has increased substantially owing to such factors as inflation, high union payments, higher talent payments, and higher media costs. Accordingly, the revenues that must be generated to break even become even greater. The average cost of a studio film was $5.5 million in 1978 and jumped to $9.4 million in 1980. The average cost of a studio film in 1987 was $17 million ($20 million if overhead and capitalized interest were included). Advertising costs are on the rise as well, increasing 20 percent a year in recent years. In 1980, the average studio film required nearly $3.5 million of advertising for its domestic release; this increased to $6.6 million in 1987 (see Table 4).

Over-Budget Costs. There is the general risk of the production cost of a motion picture going over budget. One way of dealing with this risk is to ensure that there is a reputable completion bond (or guarantee) on the picture pursuant to which a third-party guarantor will cover over-budget costs. However, completion guarantors charge a premium equal to 6 percent (50 percent of which may be rebated if the guarantee is not called upon) of the budget, which can add significantly to the cost of the film.

Project Inadequacy

Producers can miscalculate the ability of any particular motion picture to attract audiences due to a lack of interest in the subject matter or a creative failure in execution. It is the nature of the motion picture business that with any film, even starting with an excellent screenplay and major talent, there is no assurance of the quality or commercial profitability of the end product. Furthermore, there is no assurance that the film will sufficiently meet public taste so that, at the time of release, it will be able to compete with rival films.

Maldistribution

Theatrical performance of motion pictures is dependent on the time at which they are released. If a film does not enjoy a good distribution window, it may fail at the box office despite its quality. The best times to release a film are in the summer, at Christmas, and at Easter; the best months, in descending order, are June, April, July, August, December, and May. Release is often timed to coincide with the school vacation periods, since 80 percent of the theatrical box office is represented by the age group twelve to twenty-five.

Lack of Salvage Value

As opposed to tangible assets, motion pictures are worth nothing if they are not shown. If the market does not respond to the product, there is no residual or salvage value.

No Public Market

With the exception of the investment of public motion picture companies, there is seldom any public market for the investment in motion pictures.

Lack of Tax Benefits

Until the recent changes in the tax laws, such tax benefits as the investment tax credit and depreciation deductions were available. These and other deductions resulted in leveraged write-offs and considerable tax shelter benefits. Due to the disallowance of passive losses, these benefits are no longer available.

Risk Reduction Strategy

The risks previously referred to can be reduced in a number of ways: investing in more than a single film; making sure that distribution is guaranteed, preferably by a major distribution company; and investing in a completed motion picture rather than in a preproduction (development) deal or a production deal. Acquisition of films in preproduction stages involves significantly greater risks because production can be delayed or abandoned due to labor disputes, death or disability of a cast member, or budget overruns.

TAX CONSEQUENCES

Before 1986, motion picture investments enjoyed certain tax shelter benefits and the investment tax credit. With the passage of the 1986 Tax Reform Act, however, the investment tax credit has been repealed and, as a result of Section 469 of the Internal Revenue Code, no passive activity losses are permitted, and the new limitations on the ability to deduct passive losses have all but eliminated any meaningful tax benefits from motion picture investments.

REPRESENTATIVE TYPES OF INVESTORS

Representative investors in the motion picture industry are customarily film industry laymen who have been successful in their own businesses. Some investors choose to bear the entire financial obligation, while others choose to group together, spreading the risk in limited partnerships.

IMPORTANT FACTORS IN BUYING

At one time, motion picture limited partnership offerings fell into two distinct categories—those that were predominantly structured to maximize tax shelter benefits and those that were basically equity deals emphasizing the return on investment with the tax benefits having secondary, if any, impact. With the elimination of tax benefits, investors should carefully review the investment to make sure it is structured to meet their particular investment objectives, since such investments are no longer "tax driven." Over the past several years, another type of offering has achieved a level of popularity—the Delphi offerings (managed by Merrill Lynch) and Silver Screen offerings (managed by Shearson/Lehman/Hutton) have raised substantial amounts of money to help underwrite the production slate of major studios, such as Columbia/Tri-Star in the case of Delphi, and Walt Disney in the case of Silver Screen. Investing in motion pictures is not for the faint of heart, and most motion picture investment opportunities are not penny stock situations. They require substantial minimal investments (usually in excess of $25,000 and often in minimum units of $150,000), and, as previously noted, the risks are substantial. The minimum investment in the Delphi and Silver Screen offerings has been $5,000.

In the case of limited partnership investments, it is important to analyze the prospectus or private placement memorandum carefully and to have the advice of a good accountant and attorney, as well as an industry consultant if possible. The motion picture industry is closely knit and is centered largely in one city, Los Angeles. It is therefore possible to determine quickly the reliability and qualifications of the promoters and the filmmakers. Specific areas of concern should include the following:

Up-Front Commissions and Fees

Broker-dealers usually charge from 8 to 10 percent of the sales price as a commission. Promoters' fees and organizational fees should be scrutinized carefully, along with the percentage of the sales price that is allocated to the actual acquisition or production of the film and distribution and marketing expenses.

Specific Issues to Consider

Distribution Guarantee. Is distribution guaranteed and, if so, is it by a major distributor? One of the greatest disappointments, and one that occurs all too frequently, is for a film to be completed but go begging for a distributor.

Completion Guarantee. If it is a production deal, how has the producer provided for the completion of the film, and is there a reputable completion guarantor? In addition, is there any overcall right, whereby the general partner can require that the limited partners put up additional funds in the case of cost overruns? If there is no overcall right, how will cost overruns be satisfied, and is the general partner willing to step into the breach?

Investor Recoupment Position. Is the investor in first position with respect to the recoupment of his investment and what, if any, fees and other compensation are payable to the promoter-producer prior to recoupment?

Investor Profit Position. What share of the profits go to the investors? As noted earlier, investors customarily receive 50 percent of the profits of a motion picture.

Tax Opinions. Is there tax opinion from reputable counsel as to the tax effects of the transaction, and how heavily is the opinion qualified?

Projections. Are there financial projections? If so, who prepared them (the promoters or an outside accounting firm)? They should be carefully reviewed to make sure the assumptions underlying the projections are reliable.

Judging Film Quality

This is a most difficult factor in deciding on a motion picture investment. Filmmaking is both an art and a business. Artistic achievement may not always result in economic reward; conversely, a mediocre film (from a critical point of view) can reap a veritable harvest at the box office. Decisions as to what film to make and how to make it are highly subjective, involving a collective process among various creative elements. It is difficult enough to determine, after a film has been made, whether the marketplace will give it a good reception. It is significantly more difficult to predict its success when it is still on the drawing board. Filmmaking has certain similarities to wildcatting in the oil business, and professional advisors are useful in trying to cope with the decision as to whether or not a project makes sense. As with any investment, a key factor is the proven track record of the producer and his creative team.

Selecting a Broker or Dealer

Several of the motion picture private placements are marketed through major investment houses. Merrill Lynch; Kidder Peabody; Paine Webber; A.G. Becker; Drexel Burnham Lambert; and Shearson/Lehman/Hutton, to name a few, have been involved in recent offerings. Other investments are marketed without the use of broker-dealers by the producer alone.

MANAGING THE INVESTMENT

Motion picture investors seldom manage their own investments; therefore, careful evaluation of the film professionals involved is essential. The fees paid to the producer and promoter should be evaluated to make sure they are consistent with these individuals' prior deals as well as competitive within the industry. Again, a professional consultant is advisable in such matters. In a production deal, investors will rely exclusively on the producer to ensure that the picture is made within the budget and in accordance with the screenplay, and to see that it is properly exploited and marketed. Those entrusted with the management of the investment should be experienced, and an investor should carefully check out the producer's track record as well as the past performance of the promoters.

GLOSSARY

break-even rule—The rule of thumb that a film must generate gross film rentals equivalent to three to four times its production costs.

completed film investment—The outlay required for acquiring copyright to a produced film and distribution and marketing expenses.

development investments—The funds required to cover literary acquisition and other preproduction costs up to the beginning of production.

film rental—The share of box-office receipts paid by the theater owner to the distributor.

general partnership—Form of organization in which the investor forms a partnership with the producer.

independent production company—A company that raises funds independently of the studio. Typically, it negotiates distribution terms on a more favorable basis than if the studio financed the picture.

limited partnership—The arrangement whereby the investor (limited partner) participates in profits but not in management or control of the project.

negative cost—All costs incurred in producing a motion picture project up to the point of distribution.

production investment—An investment in the cost of producing a motion picture as it is being made.

studio—The integrated production-distribution-exhibition company dominated the film industry until the 1950s; today, it distributes the motion pictures it finances or those financed by independent producers.

subsidiary rights—Ancillary film rights, such as theatrical sequels, television series rights, publishing rights, recording rights, and merchandising rights.

television syndication—The market of local nonnetwork television stations and all foreign stations.

SUGGESTED READING

PERIODICALS

Boxoffice. Published by Associated Publications, Inc., Kansas City, Mo. Weekly.

Electronic Media. Published by Crain Communications, Inc., Chicago, Ill. Weekly.

The Hollywood Reporter. Published by H.R. Industries, Los Angeles, Cal. Daily.

The Independent Film Journal. Published by Robert Sunshine, New York, N.Y. Monthly.

The Motion Picture Investor. Published by Paul Kagan Associates, Inc., Carmel, Cal. Monthly.

The Pay TV Newsletter. Published by Paul Kagan Associates, Inc., Carmel, Cal. Monthly.

Variety. Published by Syd Silverman, Los Angeles, Cal. Daily.

Variety. Published by Syd Silverman, New York, N.Y. Weekly.

The VCR Newsletter. Published by Paul Kagan Associates, Inc., Carmel, Cal. Monthly.

REFERENCE BOOKS

Baumgarten, Paul A., and Farber, Donald C. *Producing, Financing and Distributing Film*. New York: Drama Book Specialists, 1973.

Blivan, William A., and Squire, Jason E., eds. *The Movie Business: American Film Industry Practice*. New York: Hastings House, 1972.

Kopple, Robert C., and Stiglitz, Bruce M. *Taxation of the Motion Picture Industry*. Washington, D.C.: Tax Management, 1978.

Litwak, Mark. *Reel Power: The Struggle for Influence and Success in the New Hollywood*. New York: William Morrow & Company, Inc., 1986.

Motion Picture Almanac. New York: Quigley Publishing Co. Annual.

Squire, J.E., ed. *The Movie-Business Book*. Englewood Cliffs, New Jersey: Prentice-Hall, 1983.

Television Almanac. New York: Quigley Publishing Co. Annual.

Vogel, Harold L. *Entertainment Industry Economics*. Cambridge: Cambridge University Press, 1986.

MUNICIPAL SECURITIES

Mark Rosen

BASIC CHARACTERISTICS

Not all bonds are created equal. The debt obligations of corporate entities and the federal government are different from those of state and local governments in one very important way: Interest income earned on corporate and federal bonds is taxable, while interest on municipal securities is exempt from all federal income taxes and, frequently, from state and local taxes levied within the state of issuance. The judicial precedent that granted federal income tax-exemption dates back to 1803 and the U.S. Supreme Court case of *Marbury v. Madison*. Subsequent court rulings reinforced the legitimacy of tax-exemption in a series of cases that upheld the principle of reciprocal immunity. The extent to which the federal government is prevented from interfering in the affairs of state governments has been tested in the courts and found to include the areas of taxation.

The allure of tax-free income is clear from the perspective of the investor, but this feature also conveys enormous benefits to the issuer. When they turn to the capital markets to raise funds, municipal governments have a distinct advantage over corporate debt issuers: Tax-exemption enables municipal borrowers to issue securities at interest rates substantially lower than those on comparable taxable bonds. Tax-exemption, therefore, serves as a type of subsidy to state and local governments. In providing an increasing amount of goods and services to an expanding population, the municipal securities market has experienced

---

Mark Rosen is an Institutional Bond Trader at Ehrlich Bober & Co., Inc., New York. This article is based on earlier work, which appeared in the first edition, by Burtt R. Ehrlich and Douglas R. Albert, President and Associate Municipal Note Trader, respectively, at Ehrlich Bober & Co., Inc., New York.

dramatic growth since the imposition of the federal income tax in 1913. In that year, state and local borrowings were only $5.5 billion. By 1986, the value of municipal government bonds outstanding was in excess of $725 billion.

Municipal securities provide funding for over 82,000 state and local governments and the diverse financial needs of their citizens. These governments increase the quality of life for their population through the construction, expansion, and maintenance of a broad range of public and private facilities, such as roadways, hospitals, airports, courthouses, and other public buildings. Resource purification and recovery, public utilities, and transportation facilities are also common recipients of the billions of dollars in municipal securities that are brought to market each year. In fact, there is scarcely any area of infrastructure development that has not benefited over the years from the issuance of municipal securities. These securities, possessing varied rates of interest and maturities, are fixed-income obligations of their issuers.

Description and Composition of Municipal Borrowings

Municipal notes, which may have maturities ranging from one month to three years but generally mature in one year, are used for construction lending and cash-flow purposes. Municipal bonds, in contrast, have maturities ranging from one to thirty years, and serve to finance long-term capital projects. Similar to long-term corporate obligations, municipal bonds return to the investor a stream of semiannual interest payments (coupons) and a repayment of principal in the full face amount of the issue on maturity. Municipal notes, however, are generally redeemed in one of two ways: Interest-bearing notes return the principal plus an interest payment at maturity, while discount notes carry an implicit interest payment, since they sell below par and are redeemed at face value. The use of discount notes has declined substantially in recent years. Municipal notes with maturities beyond one year usually provide coupon payments similar to those associated with municipal bonds.

Types of Municipal Securities

In addition to being classified with respect to their maturities, municipal securities may be further characterized by the purpose for which they have been issued and by the sources of income that provide for their repayment.

General Obligation Securities. These securities are backed by the full faith, credit, and taxing powers of the municipal borrower. In a sense, they may be considered senior municipal debentures because they place a lien on municipal revenues. That is, general obligation securities attach a legal claim to the unencumbered revenues received by a municipal government. These typically include tax receipts plus federal and state aid. General obligation notes fulfill short-term borrowing needs of state and local governments, while general obligation bonds raise funds for municipal capital improvements. Facilities built with these long-term issues serve the entire community and include schools, municipal buildings, streets, and highways.

Municipal revenues raised through tax levies differ, between state and local governments, as to sources. State governments generally call on sales and income taxes for the repayment of borrowed funds. Local governments rely primarily on property tax receipts to meet interest and principal payments. General obligations of local governments, therefore, tend to assume price and risk characteristics that reflect the value of property and the municipalities' ability to levy property taxes. Securities issued by communities that experience rising property values, for instance, are deemed less risky than are those issued by communities in which property values remain constant or are declining. Similarly, securities issued by municipalities with limited taxing powers are perceived by investors to be less marketable than are issues of a municipality that possesses greater taxing flexibility.

Importance of Taxing Powers. How a municipality's taxing powers may affect the security of its issues is best exemplified by the recent taxpayer revolts in both California and Massachusetts. One of the effects of the 1978 passage of Proposition 13 in California, which put a ceiling of one percent of fully assessed property values on property taxes, was a significant reduction in the general obligation borrowings of local governments in that state. In November 1980, the voters of Massachusetts supported a measure to limit their property taxes by passing Proposition 2½. This limits the property tax that local governments may impose to 2.5 percent of fully assessed values.

The ramifications experienced in the market for the general obligations of cities and towns in Massachusetts were more serious than those for California municipalities after passage of Proposition 13. When the latter was approved, California enjoyed a budget surplus. The presence of these funds and their potential transferability to faltering municipalities placated investors who feared a loss of liquidity and marketability. Actually, Proposition 13 provided special measures that assured the repayment of outstanding issues. In Massachusetts, however, no such provisions were associated with Proposition 2½. As a result, no municipality in Massachusetts issued a general obligation bond in the last two months of 1980, and the yield levels on outstanding issues rose substantially, relative to the market, as their prices plunged.

As electorates throughout the nation confront the issue of limiting government's power in levying the property tax, it will become increasingly important to evaluate both the way local units finance their operations and the nature of the financial relationship that exists between a state and its local governments.

Revenue Bonds. In contrast to general obligations, revenue bonds provide funding for the construction of specific municipal projects. Toll roads, bridges, and water and sewer projects are among the facilities that municipal governments finance through revenue bonds. These projects attempt to tax only the component of the populace that makes use of the facility. Revenue bond borrowings are repaid from the income (user fees) generated by these facilities. Because revenue bonds are not included in the general indebtedness of a municipality, they provide state and local governments with a powerful instrument with which to raise funds.

Through revenue bonds, municipalities have been able to expand their use of tax-exempt borrowing without burdening taxpayers. This makes the issuance of revenue bonds a practical and desirable form of funding.

In the 1950s, revenue bonds were issued primarily for highways, turnpikes, and public utilities. During the 1970s and 1980s, tax-exempt revenue bonds were issued to provide financing for housing, hospitals, industrial pollution control equipment, public power plants, sports stadiums, and convention centers. It is essential to note that changes in the 1986 tax laws require that many industrial development bonds (IDBs) be subject to the alternative minimum tax (AMT).

The fact that revenue bonds may be issued without having to pass a voter referendum also accounts for their frequent issuance. If traditional sources of tax revenues become uncertain, the use of revenue bonds may reasonably be expected to play an even larger role in municipal financing. Revenue bond issues include several distinct types of borrowings. The form of a given borrowing is determined, necessarily, by the intended use of the funds to be raised. Figure 1 shows the major uses of revenue bonds in 1986.

Housing Revenue Bonds. These bonds are generally issued by a housing agency created by a state or local government to finance the construction of single-family or multifamily residential units. The proceeds raised by the bond issue may be loaned to a developer or directly to a home buyer. It is not uncommon for the housing agency to turn over the funds to a lending institution for administration of the project.

Public Utility Bonds. These bonds serve to finance the building of sewer and water projects as well as public power facilities. How these services are delivered to the public varies by how much the public utility participates in the ownership of its facility. Hence, different systems assume different risk characteristics, and each issue must be analyzed carefully. In general, the bond proceeds are repaid from the fees charged to users of the system.

FIGURE 1. Major Uses of Revenue Bonds in 1986

Source: IDD Information Services/PSA Municipal Securities Database

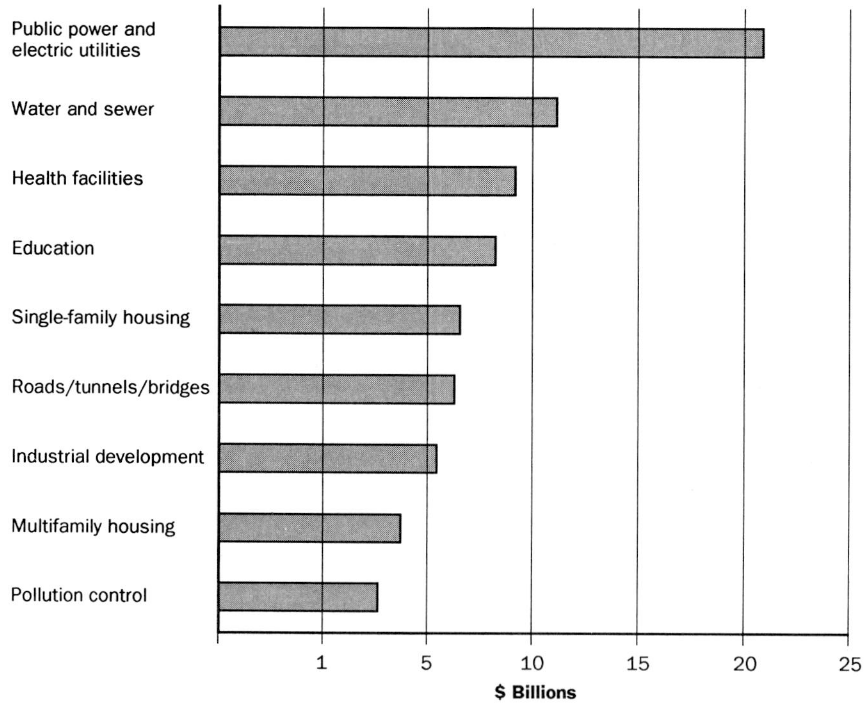

Hospital Revenue Bonds. Hospital revenue bonds fund construction of new hospitals and renovations in existing ones. They are sometimes used to purchase expensive hospital equipment. In general, they are repaid from hospital revenues.

Industrial Development Bonds. IDBs are a class of revenue bonds issued to finance construction of such projects as factories, sports stadiums, and industrial parks. Once construction is completed on behalf of the government unit, the facility is leased to a private corporation whose lease payments provide the revenue to repay the borrowed funds. Generally, the tax-exempt status of interest on municipal securities benefits the investor and the issuing state or local government. Here, the benefit that normally accrues to the issuer, in effect, is transferred to a private corporation. Pollution control revenue bonds, for example, are a type of IDB through which environmental equipment is purchased by the government unit and leased to a corporation. Since the lease payments provide the security on these bonds, the corporate entity represents the underlying credit risk. It is important to note that changes in the 1986 tax laws make a great deal of new IDBs subject to the AMT.

Hybrid Bonds. Hybrid bonds combine characteristics of both general obligation bonds and revenue bonds. For instance, a revenue bond may be issued to finance the construction of a new state highway. The primary revenue source that secures the issue is the income earned through the collection of user tolls. The bond may be further secured, however, by the proceeds raised through a fuel tax. These hybrid issues are also referred to as double-barreled bonds. The purposes for which state and local governments issued bonds of all types through 1986 are shown, relative to one another, in Figure 2.

Municipal Notes. Essentially short-term financing, these notes are issued for cash-flow and construction-loan purposes. Frequently, state and local governments find themselves with a temporary cash shortage or deficit caused by timing differences in the expenditure and receipt of funds. For example, a city may need to purchase new fire-fighting equipment, but finds the money not readily available; officials may then decide to borrow the necessary funds through an issue of short-term municipal notes. The equipment is then purchased and the debt repaid from tax revenues received later in the year. Similarly, a local government may wish to begin the construction of a parking facility at a heavily congested railroad station. The project may be started by issuing a note to raise construction funds. The local government anticipates repayment of the note with proceeds from a later bond sale that ultimately will provide long-term funding for the project.

Although these short-term issues are usually redeemed at maturity, it is not uncommon for them to be rolled over in a manner similar to that used by the U.S. Treasury in refinancing its outstanding debt. However, while the Treasury may refinance its debt continuously, there are mandatory redemption periods for municipal issues. The number of times a municipal government may roll over its debt varies from state to state; usually the limit is a period of, at most, seven years.

There are four basic types of municipal notes, with many common features.

Bond Anticipation Notes (BANs). These notes provide interim financing for projects that ultimately are to be funded with a long-term bond. Because the notes are paid down

FIGURE 2. Major Uses of Municipal Debt, 1967–1986, as a Percentage of Total Long-Term Borrowing

Note: Changes in the major uses of debt financing over the years reflect both the evolution of new financing techniques and the demand for government-provided services. Only new capital issues are included for use of proceeds purposes; all issues are included for total long-term figures.

Source: Public Securities Association Municipal Securities Database, 1967–1985; IDD Information Services/PSA Municipal Securities Database, 1986

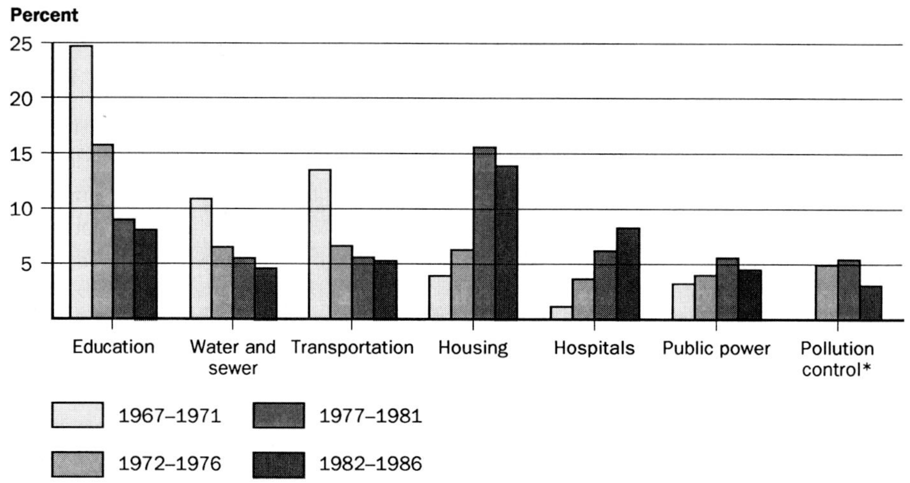

*Pollution control figures for 1966–1971 are not available

from proceeds of the bond issue, they may often be secured only by the municipality's long-term borrowing capability. In many communities, therefore, BANs are also a general obligation, secured on a parity with outstanding general obligation bonds.

Tax Anticipation Notes (TANs). These notes are general obligations of the community, used to fulfill interim financing needs, and are secured by projected tax receipts plus any other unencumbered revenue of the community.

Revenue Anticipation Notes (RANs). These, too, are general obligation notes to fund current operations. They are paid down from municipal revenues other than taxes, especially federal and state aid.

Project Notes. Housing authorities use these notes to provide construction funds for urban-renewal and redevelopment projects. They are secured by the full faith and credit of the federal government, and in fact are sold at bimonthly auctions conducted by the U.S. Department of Housing and Urban Development on behalf of local authorities. Because of their backing, these issues are equal in security to U.S. government notes, although they may not be as readily marketable.

ATTRACTIVE FEATURES

In general, investors are attracted to municipal securities for two basic reasons: tax-free interest income and relative safety of both principal and income. As with any fixed-income obligation, a decline in interest rates will increase the price of outstanding issues, and any capital gain that may be realized thereby is not exempt from federal and state capital gains taxes. An investor even may choose to hold municipals for potential capital gain; but if the intent is to defer earnings beyond the investor's peak income years, it probably would be wiser to purchase a long-dated maturity bond for its higher ultimate yield.

Tax-Free Income

The willingness of investors to supply funds to municipal governments is directly related to their respective income tax rates. The benefits of tax-exemption increase for taxpayers in progressively higher tax brackets. Households and institutions that earn substantial taxable income, therefore, are the more prominent investors in municipal securities. Yields are proportionately less than pretax yields on comparable corporate securities, but this difference is almost entirely due to the tax-exempt feature of municipal securities. Table 1 provides a comparison between yields on municipal securities and their equivalent taxable yields for various federal income tax brackets.

The yield that an investor in municipal securities can expect to earn over the life of the bond may be calculated in a number of ways, most commonly by the current yield and the yield to maturity.

Current Yield. This approach offers a rough approximation of the more precise yield-to-maturity calculations. The current yield is simply the interest payment divided by the purchase price. For example, a bond bought at 80 ($800 per $1,000 face value) with a 7 percent annual coupon ($70 per year) would have a current yield of 8.75 percent; that is:

$$\frac{\$70}{\$800} = 8.75\%$$

Yield to Maturity. A more sophisticated approach, the yield to maturity, adjusts the coupon payments for the timing of their receipt. That is, it allows for the fact that interest payments received earlier in the life of the bond are worth relatively more than identical payments received later. In the preceding example, if the issue were a ten-year bond, the investor would adjust the $70 annual interest payments according to when they will be received. The general formula is as follows:

$$P = \sum_{n=1}^{t} \left(\frac{C}{(1 \times k)^1} + \frac{C}{(1+k)^2} + \frac{C}{(1+k)^3} + \cdots + \frac{C}{(1+k)^n} + \frac{R}{(1+k)^t} \right)$$

where P = the price of the bond
C = the annual coupon payment
k = the yield to maturity
R = the principal repayment amount
n = the number of periods to maturity
t = the number of periods to repayment

TABLE 1. Tax-Exempt/Taxable Yield Equivalents for 1988

TAXABLE INCOME Single Return	\$0 to \$17,850	\$17,851 to \$43,150 or over \$100,480	\$43,151 to \$100,480
Joint Return	\$0 to \$29,750	\$29,751 to \$71,900 or over \$171,090	\$71,901 to \$171,090
TAX BRACKET	15%	28%	33%*
TAXABLE YIELD EQUIVALENTS For a tax-exempt yield of...	The taxable yield equivalent is...		
4.0%	4.71%	5.56%	5.97%
5.0	5.88	6.94	7.46
6.0	7.06	8.33	8.96
7.0	8.24	9.72	10.45
8.0	9.41	11.11	11.94
9.0	10.59	12.50	13.43
10.0	11.76	13.89	14.93
11.0	12.94	15.28	16.42
12.0	14.12	16.67	17.91

*This 33 percent bracket is based on a 5 percent surtax and a phase-out of the personal exemption amount for certain income ranges. The income ranges listed above assume (1) a single person with no dependents and (2) a married couple filing jointly with no dependents. If there are dependents, the upper end of the 33 percent bracket will increase by \$10,920 per dependent. Note that once a taxpayer's income exceeds the upper end of the 33 percent bracket, any income in excess of that amount is taxed at a marginal rate of 28 percent.

$$800 = \left(\frac{70}{(1 \times k)^1} + \frac{70}{(1 + k)^2} + \frac{70}{(1 + k)^3} + \cdots + \frac{70}{(1 + k)^9} + \frac{1000}{(1 + k)^{10}} \right)$$

Therefore, k = 10.3 percent. Embodied within this yield-to-maturity formulation, however, is the implicit assumption that coupon payments can be reinvested at the coupon rate.

Relative Safety

Municipal security offerings are being protected essentially by the viability of a taxpayer-supported public body. To bolster this relative safety, each new issue is accompanied by documentation that attests to the validity of the liability of the issuing entity, explains the specific features of the issue and the intended use of the borrowed funds, provides financial information relating to the economic health of the issuer and, most important, sets forth the terms of the loan and the schedule of repayments. This information is offered in detail within the Official Statement. Representative samples of the title pages of two different official statements are shown in Figures 3 and 4.

Most of the pertinent information regarding a security may be found on the title page of the official statement. At the top of the title page, the prospective investor will find verification from bond counsel that the issue is exempt from federal (and/or state and local) income taxes. In the case of the City of New York general obligation bonds, all three exemptions apply. The Coldwater Bond anticipation notes are exempt from federal and state income taxes. As general obligations, both issues are backed by the full faith and credit of the borrowers. All unencumbered revenues plus the full measure of the taxing power of the borrowers can and must be applied to pay the bonds.

Beneath the legal opinion and the issuer's name, the prospective investor will find a short description of the security (here G.O.'s and G.O. Bans). At the bottom of the title page are the underwriters' names (syndicate). The New York City general obligations list the names of the dealers and banks which conducted the underwriting.

The Coldwater notes were underwritten in "single-handed" fashion (without a syndicate). With issues as large as the $400 million New York City issue, not all syndicate members will appear on the title page. Appearance on the title page is usually limited to the managers and co-managers. The proportionate amount of bonds allocated to each syndicate member may be determined by the position of the bank or firm name in descending order. In the case of the New York City bonds, Merrill Lynch and Goldman Sachs will have the lion's share of the bonds. Interested parties might contact any of these firms to buy bonds.

Repayment Schedule. Both securities accrue interest from the given date; January 19, 1988 for the Coldwater notes, and date of delivery for the New York City bonds. The amounts due on specific dates (maturities) were to be paid at stipulated rates of interest, and each issue was priced to the investor to provide the yields prescribed. All this information is presented in the repayment schedule. Beneath the repayment schedule is further information pertaining to the law firm that served as bond counsel and confirmation that the loans are legal liabilities of the issuing entities.

There are two types of repayment schedules, conforming to the length of municipal financing involved. In one, the note issue, the debt obligation is retired at a single stated maturity term. In the other and more common form, the serial issue, a portion of the outstanding issue is repaid annually or semiannually prior to final maturity.

Term Issues. Term issues are usually associated with the retirement of revenue bond borrowings. Because the flow of income generated by revenue-producing facilities is subject to uncertainty, it is difficult to project the amount of borrowings that can be paid down from these revenues in future years. Consequently, revenue bonds typically provide a sinking fund into which revenues are placed for the ultimate repayment of the entire issue on a single maturity.

Serial Issues. Serial issues, on the other hand, usually connote general obligation bonds. This form of repayment was originally tailored to suit the needs of commercial banks, which prefer to receive step-wise repayments of their loans to municipal borrowers. The banks' reasons are to maintain liquidity and the flexibility to move into the commercial loan market and to match more easily the maturities of their assets and liabilities.

FIGURE 3. Sample Title Page From Official Statement—Municipal

NEW ISSUE

In the opinion of Bond Counsel, assuming continuing compliance with the provisions of the Internal Revenue Code of 1986, as amended, as described herein, interest on the Bonds will not be includable in the gross income of the owners thereof for Federal income tax purposes. See "Tax Exemption" herein for certain provisions of the Code that may affect the tax treatment of interest on the Bonds for certain Bondholders. Interest on the Bonds will be exempt from personal income taxes imposed by the State of New York or any political subdivision thereof, including the City.

$400,000,000

The City of New York

General Obligation Bonds

Fiscal 1989 Series B

Dated: Date of Delivery — Due: December 1, as shown below

The Bonds will be issued as registered bonds and, when issued, will be registered in the name of Cede & Co., as nominee of The Depository Trust Company, New York, New York, which will act as securities depository for the Bonds. Purchasers will not receive certificates representing their ownership interest in the Bonds purchased. Interest will be payable semi-annually, beginning June 1, 1989 and on each December 1 and June 1 thereafter. See "The Bonds—Book-Entry Only System". The Bonds will be subject to redemption prior to maturity as described herein.

Maturity	Amount	Interest Rate	Price or Yield	Maturity	Amount	Interest Rate	Price or Yield
1989	$20,800,000	6.10%	100%	2004	$6,290,000	7½%	7.60%**
1990	20,800,000	6⅜	100	2005	6,290,000	7⅞	99
1991	20,800,000	6.60	100	2006	9,430,000	7⅞	99
1992	20,800,000	6.80	100	2007	9,435,000	7⅞	99
1993	25,125,000	7	100	2008	9,435,000	8	100
1994	26,845,000	7.20	100	2009	4,935,000	8	100
1995	31,200,000	7⅜	100	2010	4,935,000	8	100
1996	31,200,000	7½	100	2011	4,935,000	8	100
1997	31,200,000	7.60	100	2012	4,935,000	8	100
1998	31,200,000	7⅛	7.20*	2013	4,935,000	8	100
1999	6,290,000	7¾	7.80	2014	7,400,000	6¾	86½
2000	6,290,000	7¾	7.85	2015	7,400,000	6¾	86½
2001	6,290,000	7.40	100**	2016	7,400,000	6¾	86½
2002	9,170,000	7½	100**	2017	7,400,000	6¾	86½
2003	9,435,000	7½	7.55**	2018	7,400,000	6¾	86½

(Accrued interest, if any, to be added)

* Insured by Municipal Bond Investors Assurance Corporation
** Insured by Financial Guaranty Insurance Company

The Bonds are offered subject to prior sale, when, as and if issued by the City and accepted by the Underwriters, subject to the approval of the legality of the Bonds by Brown & Wood, New York, New York, Bond Counsel to the City, and subject to certain other conditions. Certain legal matters in connection with the preparation of this Official Statement will be passed upon for the City by Lord Day & Lord, Barrett Smith, New York, New York. Certain legal matters will be passed upon for the Underwriters by Rogers & Wells, New York, New York. It is expected that the Bonds will be available for delivery in New York, New York, on or about December 15, 1988.

Merrill Lynch Capital Markets — **Goldman, Sachs & Co.**

Bear, Stearns & Co. Inc. — **Morgan Stanley & Co. Incorporated** — **PaineWebber Incorporated**

Prudential-Bache Capital Funding — **Shearson Lehman Hutton Inc.**

Dillon, Read & Co. Inc. — **Drexel Burnham Lambert Incorporated** — **Ehrlich Bober & Co., Inc.**

WR Lazard & Laidlaw Incorporated — **Manufacturers Hanover Securities Corporation**

J.P. Morgan Securities Inc. — **Pryor, Govan, Counts & Co., Inc.**

Smith Barney, Harris Upham & Co. Incorporated — **Dean Witter Capital Markets**

December 8, 1988

FIGURE 4. Sample Title Page From Official Statement—State

OFFICIAL STATEMENT

NEW ISSUE

In the opinion of Bond Counsel, under existing law and assuming compliance with certain covenants, interest on the Bonds is excluded from gross income for federal income tax purposes, is not treated as an item of tax preference for purposes of the alternative minimum income tax imposed on individuals and corporations under the Internal Revenue Code of 1986, as amended (the "Code"), and is exempt from certain taxes imposed by the State of Ohio. The Bonds are not "private activity bonds" within the meaning of the Code. Interest on the Bonds may be subject to certain federal income taxes imposed on certain corporations, and certain taxpayers may have certain other adverse federal income tax consequences as a result of owning the Bonds. See "Tax Exemption" herein.

$4,980,000

COLDWATER EXEMPTED VILLAGE
SCHOOL DISTRICT

MERCER COUNTY, OHIO

GENERAL OBLIGATION BOND ANTICIPATION NOTES

(Unlimited Tax)

FOR SCHOOL BUILDING CONSTRUCTION AND IMPROVEMENT

Voted November 3, 1987

Dated: January 19, 1988 Due: September 19, 1988

Interest and principal will be payable upon maturity in federal funds at the principal office of Security Pacific National Trust Co., New York, New York. The Notes will not be subject to prior redemption and will be issued in bearer form in the denomination of $25,000 each or such other denominations as shall be selected by the original purchasers. The interest rate will be as set forth in the note legislation to be adopted on January 13, 1988.

Certain legal matters relating to the issuance of the Notes are subject to the approving opinion of Bricker & Eckler, Bond Counsel, Columbus, Ohio, (see "Legal Matters" and "Tax Exemption" herein).

This Official Statement has been prepared by the School District in connection with the original offering for sale by it of the Notes. It is expected that delivery of the Notes in definitive form will be made on or about January 19, 1988. The date of this Official Statement is January 1, 1988, and the information herein speaks only as of that date.

EHRLICH BOBER & CO., INC.

Columbus, Ohio

POTENTIAL RISKS

Given its constitutional rights to print and coin money, there is no fear that the federal government will default on its borrowings; U.S. Treasury securities therefore are accepted by investors as risk-free assets. The bonds and notes of state and local governments, with regard to their ability to meet interest payments and principal repayments, are generally considered to rank second only to Treasury obligations. What this means, of course, is that municipals cannot be regarded as absolutely risk-free. The risk factors fall, essentially, into three categories: (1) erosion of principal value: (2) potential for default; and (3) regulatory pitfalls. (It should also be noted that there may be market limitations for a particular issue, as described in *Important Factors in Buying and Selling*, later in this article.)

Erosion of Principal Value

The risk of erosion in principal value is not unique to municipal securities. Rather, it is common to all fixed-income debt obligations. Although municipalities are extremely unlikely to suffer the debacle of bankruptcy, to which any corporate security is exposed, they are not inflation-proof. They cannot protect against the potential depreciation of principal value caused by unanticipated increases in interest rates.

Risk of Default

Municipal securities that either fail to make interest and principal payments or delay these payments are considered to be in default. This situation might arise for a number of reasons. Actual collection of tax receipts may be significantly lower than had been anticipated, or underlying income-generating facilities might not produce the projected revenues. Although both extensive and relatively safe, the income sources of municipal governments are associated with some degree of risk and uncertainty.

It follows that the ability to meet debt-repayment schedules without undue strain varies widely among municipal borrowers. However, for an individual investor to become familiar with the financial, demographic, and managerial strengths of all issuing entities would present an impossible task. Consequently, rating agencies such as Moody's and Standard & Poor's (S&P) are engaged by the state or municipality or by the public borrowing authority to grade their creditworthiness. (Fitch's Investor Service is a smaller rating agency specializing in the area of hospital issues.) By carefully evaluating a community's strength according to a number of different factors, the rating agencies convey to investors a sense of the municipality's ability to meet interest and principal payments (i.e., how much risk is present) and, in so doing, markedly affect the rate of interest that community must offer investors in order to market its debt.

Rating General Obligations. The rating agency begins its analysis by examining the sources of funds from which debt issues can be repaid. Thus, with regard to general obligation securities, a thorough understanding of the strength of the issuer's tax base is developed and a forecast made of how it may change over time. The agency further evaluates the community and its economic assets. A highly diversified economy is preferable to one in which local employment is concentrated in a single major corporation or industry or in relatively few businesses. The community in which population is stable or growing steadily is stronger than one in which population is declining. The proportion of working-age residents to those under age 18 and over 65 is another vital determinant. The current debt and potential debt capacity of the community are important considerations in judging the ability both to service outstanding debt and to take on additional obligations. Finally, the rating agency interviews municipal leaders personally and reviews their track record to evaluate managerial effectiveness and their general competence as financial controllers.

Rating Revenue Bonds. Analysis of the quality of revenue bonds is similar to that for general obligations; of course, the income sources that underlie revenue bonds require specific cash-flow evaluation. Both major rating agencies employ analysts with expertise in particular project-financing areas, to facilitate evaluation and maintain continuity from one issue to the next. As with general obligations, credit risk is graded according to historical economic performance, the ability to control finances and collect revenues, and the borrowing entity's managerial competence. Table 2 provides a description of the ratings assigned to municipal bonds by S&P and Moody's. Table 3 describes the ratings assigned to municipal notes by Moody's.

Insurance Protection. A recent market innovation is the insurance-backed municipal bond. The Municipal Bond Insurance Association and the American Municipal Bond

TABLE 2. Municipal Bond Ratings

Description of Ratings	S&P[1]	Moody's[2]
Capacity to pay interest and repay principal is extremely strong.	AAA	Aaa
Very strong capacity to pay interest and repay principal and differ from highest-rated issue only to a small degree.	AA	Aa
Strong capacity to pay interest and repay principal, although they are somewhat more susceptible to the adverse effects of changes in circumstances and economic conditions than bonds in higher-rated categories.	A	A
Adequate capacity to pay interest and repay principal; while they normally exhibit adequate protection parameters, adverse economic conditions or changing circumstances are more likely to lead a weakened capacity to pay interest and repay principal for bonds in this category than for bonds in higher-rated categories	BBB	Baa
Ability to pay interest and repay principal deemed speculative.	BB	Ba
Speculative in nature—low grade.	B	B
More speculative than higher-rated bonds—poor grade.	CCC	Caa
Highest speculative grade.	CC	Ca
Lowest-rated class of bonds. May be paying no interest or extremely poor prospect of reaching investment status	C	C

[1] Standard and Poor's may add a plus (+) or minus (−) on grades AA through BB to indicate relative strength within these categories.
[2] Moody's adds the number one (1) to the grades A and Baa to indicate greater strength within these categories.

Source: Moody's Investor Service and Standard & Poor's Corporation

TABLE 3. Municipal Note Ratings

Description of Rating	Moody's Grade
Loans bearing this designation are of the best quality, enjoying strong protection from established cash flows of funds for their servicing or from established and broad-based access to the market for refinancing, or both.	MIG 1
Loans bearing this designation are of high quality with margins of protection ample though not as large as in the preceding group.	MIG 2
Loans bearing this designation are of favorable quality, with all security elements accounted for but lacking the undeniable strength of the preceding grades. Market access for refinancing, in particular, is likely to be less well established.	MIG 3
Loans bearing this designation are of adequate quality, carrying specific risk but having protection commonly regarded as required of an investment security and not distinctly or predominantly speculative.	MIG 4

Source: Moody's Investor Service

Assurance Company will insure the interest and principal payments on tax-exempt issues. Although Moody's continues to rate variously the credit risk of the issuing entity, S&P gives bonds that carry this insurance feature an automatic AAA, presuming that the issue would have achieved at least a BBB on its own standing. From the perspective of the municipal borrower, the decision regarding insurance comes down to whether the reduction in interest costs, arising from the enhanced credit rating, will exceed the cost premiums on the insurance itself.

Legal Recourse. To assure that a municipal security represents a legal and binding liability of the issuer, all new issues must be verified with regard to the legality of the debt obligations and the tax-exempt status affecting interest payments. This practice grew out of the general panic of the 1870s and the number of municipal issues that did default during that period. Investors found that they had no legal recourse. To restore investor faith in these obligations, municipalities thereafter engaged legal counsel to attest to the validity of the claim on municipal revenues. As municipal securities proliferated through the 1960s and 1970s, the responsibilities of legal counsel expanded. Today, the legal opinion is rendered by an outside bond counsel—usually a legal firm specializing in this area—and must accompany all issues when delivered to investors.

Pitfalls of Regulation

Historically, the federal government has been reluctant to assume regulatory authority over the municipal securities industry. In adhering to the concept of reciprocal immunity, the separation of state and federal powers had, until 1975, provided the industry with virtual freedom from the Securities and Exchange Commission (SEC). The Securities Act of 1933 and the Securities Exchange Act of 1934 were primarily concerned with bringing order and integrity to the markets in which flagrant abuses appeared to be rampant. Although a number of municipal securities did go into default during the Depression, the

SEC considered the borrowings of state and local governments to be rather small and, in general, relatively free from default risk.

Self-regulatory Limits. In the early 1970s, however, the sale of municipal securities in both Florida and Tennessee were marred by accusations of unethical behavior on the part of certain broker-dealer firms. Then in 1975, New York City's temporary default on some maturing notes prompted an evaluation of the regulatory environment surrounding the entire municipal securities industry. Following congressional review, in 1975 the SEC set up the Municipal Securities Rulemaking Board (MSRB). Acting as a self-regulating authority composed of representatives from broker-dealer firms, banks, and the public, the MSRB was charged with setting forth administrative, definitional, and general procedural rules for the industry.

The MSRB remains an independent body, requiring only SEC approval of its membership, and specifies areas of mandatory rulemaking. The areas to which its regulatory authority extend include monitoring underwriter and dealer registration fees, defining market participants, and promulgating rules for such procedures as record keeping and clearing. However, whereas underwriters and broker-dealer firms must register corporate new-issue securities with the SEC before bringing them to market, municipal securities do not have to be registered. The issuance of municipals, accordingly, is far less regulated than the marketing of corporates.

Accounting Practices. With regard to state and local government financial reporting, neither the SEC nor the MSRB may authorize or enforce supervisory review, disclosure procedures, or standard accounting practices. However, without uniform reporting requirements, the users of municipal financial information have not been well-served. To accommodate them, private organizations (e.g., the American Institute of Certified Public Accountants and the National Committee on Government Accounting) are working with municipal governments, broker-dealer firms, and investor groups to develop a uniform accounting system for state and municipal reports.

TAX CONSEQUENCES

Income Tax Exemption

The most important characteristic of municipal securities to the investor is their special tax feature, specifically, exemption of interest payments from federal income taxes. That benefit increases with higher tax brackets. For instance, a 9 percent tax-exempt yield to the investor in a 28 percent marginal tax bracket is equivalent to a 12.50 percent yield on a taxable issue.

The Internal Revenue Service (IRS), however, disallows interest deductions on money that is borrowed by individual investors expressly for purchasing tax-exempts. If this were not the case, a double tax benefit would result. The taxpayer could deduct from the federal income taxes the interest expense on indebtedness while earning tax-free income. Similarly, the potential for corporations to use borrowings to purchase tax-exempts motivated the IRS to restrict to 2 percent the total value of assets invested in municipals for those corporations with debt on their balance sheet.

State and Local Taxes. Municipal securities are usually exempt from state and local taxes within the issuing state as well. However, they are often subject to state taxes outside the state of issuance. The significance of the federal tax-exempt feature is greatest to the investor whose income from municipals is also exempt from all state and local taxes. (When determining the equivalent taxable yield for any municipal security, however, it must be borne in mind that state and local taxes constitute federal income tax deductions.)

Equivalent Taxable Yields. The mechanism most widely used to determine a municipal security's equivalent taxable yield is the following:

$$\frac{\text{Tax-exempt yield}}{1 - \text{Marginal tax bracket}} = \text{Equivalent taxable yield}$$

For example, to calculate the equivalent taxable yield on an 8 percent tax-exempt for the investor in a 28 percent marginal tax bracket:

$$\frac{8\%}{1 - .28} = \frac{8\%}{.72} = 11.11$$

Thus, an 8 percent tax-free yield is equivalent to a 11.11 percent taxable yield.

Capital Gains Treatment

Any capital gain that accrues on municipal securities is not exempt from federal income taxes, with one exception. The gain realized on securities purchased in the secondary market at a discount, and held to maturity or sold at a profit before final redemption, is subject to all capital gains taxes. However, the capital gains tax does not apply to securities originally issued at a discount; that discount is considered an implicit interest payment.

Similarly, a deductible capital loss is incurred if securities are sold below their purchase price. The rule does not apply to issues purchased at a premium and held to maturity. Instead, the premium is amortized on a straight-line basis over the life of the bond, and at final maturity the amortized basis is equivalent to the principal repayment. For issues purchased at a premium and sold before maturity, a capital loss may be incurred if the sale price is less than the amortized basis. For example, a bond purchased at $1,100 with a twenty-year maturity would normally be amortized at $5 per year. At maturity, the basis would equal the principal repayment of $1,000. After ten years, the adjusted basis would be $1,050. If the issue is sold at $1,020 after ten years, a taxable loss of $30 would be sustained.

REPRESENTATIVE TYPES OF INVESTORS

Municipal securities hold the strongest attraction for individuals in relatively high income tax brackets, as well as for certain taxpaying institutions. Since pension funds pay no income taxes, they are not investors in the municipals market. Neither (because they are subject to low tax rates) are savings (thrift) institutions and life insurance companies among the substantial buyers of tax-exempts. The primary suppliers of funds to state and local government borrowers are the commercial banks, fire and casualty insurance companies, corporate treasuries, and high-bracket individual investors. Because these investment groups require significant and secure after-tax interest income, tax-exempt bonds and notes are usually favored for their portfolios.

Cyclical Patterns

Historically, the aggressiveness with which these groups have pursued municipal securities has been cyclical.

Commercial Banks. Traditionally, commercial banks were large holders of municipal securities. When credit demand was strong, commercial banks would sell off parts of their municipal portfolios and use those funds to provide commercial loans. When loan demand was weak, these institutions were heavily involved in municipals. For example, in the early 1970s commercial banks realized greater after tax yields in real estate and leasing. By 1977, banks built up holdings of municipals. As Figure 5 shows, however, pursuant to changes in the 1985 and 1986 tax laws, banks had all but disappeared as holders of municipal bonds.

Fire and Casualty Insurers. When underwriting business is strong at the fire and casualty insurance companies, they are extremely active buyers in the municipal area. When business is slack and underwriting losses are anticipated, however, the expectation of narrow profits encourages these firms to enter the higher-yielding corporate market.

Growth of Individual Investors

Individuals assumed an increasingly active role in the municipal securities market throughout the 1970s. With nominal incomes rising rapidly throughout the decade, households sought to reduce their overall taxable incomes by investing heavily in municipals. By 1981, they held 24 percent of outstanding municipal securities. In that year, commercial banks held 42 percent of all outstanding issues and fire and casualty insurance companies held 26 percent. The remaining 8 percent of outstanding issues was held by other financial intermediaries and nonfinancial corporate businesses. In 1983, 1984, and 1985, municipal holdings of individuals soared as households sought to acquire municipals that would be "grandfathered" in and circumvent new tax laws. In 1986, in the midst of confusion over new tax ramifications, households bought significantly fewer municipal securities.

IMPORTANT FACTORS IN BUYING AND SELLING

Primary Market

When a state or local government or agency must borrow funds, it turns to the capital markets. However, rather than selling new issues directly to the ultimate holders of municipal securities, municipal borrowers typically engage the services of one or more financial institutions that act as a conduit through which private funds are made available to the borrowing entity. The process that includes the functions of pricing and structuring the loan, and of selling the issue to the public, is referred to as underwriting. The source of funds for such new offerings is known as the primary market. Issues come into this market through either negotiated or competitive underwritings. Negotiated underwritings are usually more expensive than their competitively bid counterparts, but they require more work for the underwriter. In many states, municipal borrowers are instructed by law to conduct competitive underwritings for general obligation issues. Revenue bond issues, on the other hand, are usually sold on a negotiated basis.

FIGURE 5. Net Changes in the Holdings of State and Local Government Securities by Major Investing Groups, 1975–1986

Source: Federal Reserve Flow of Funds Accounts

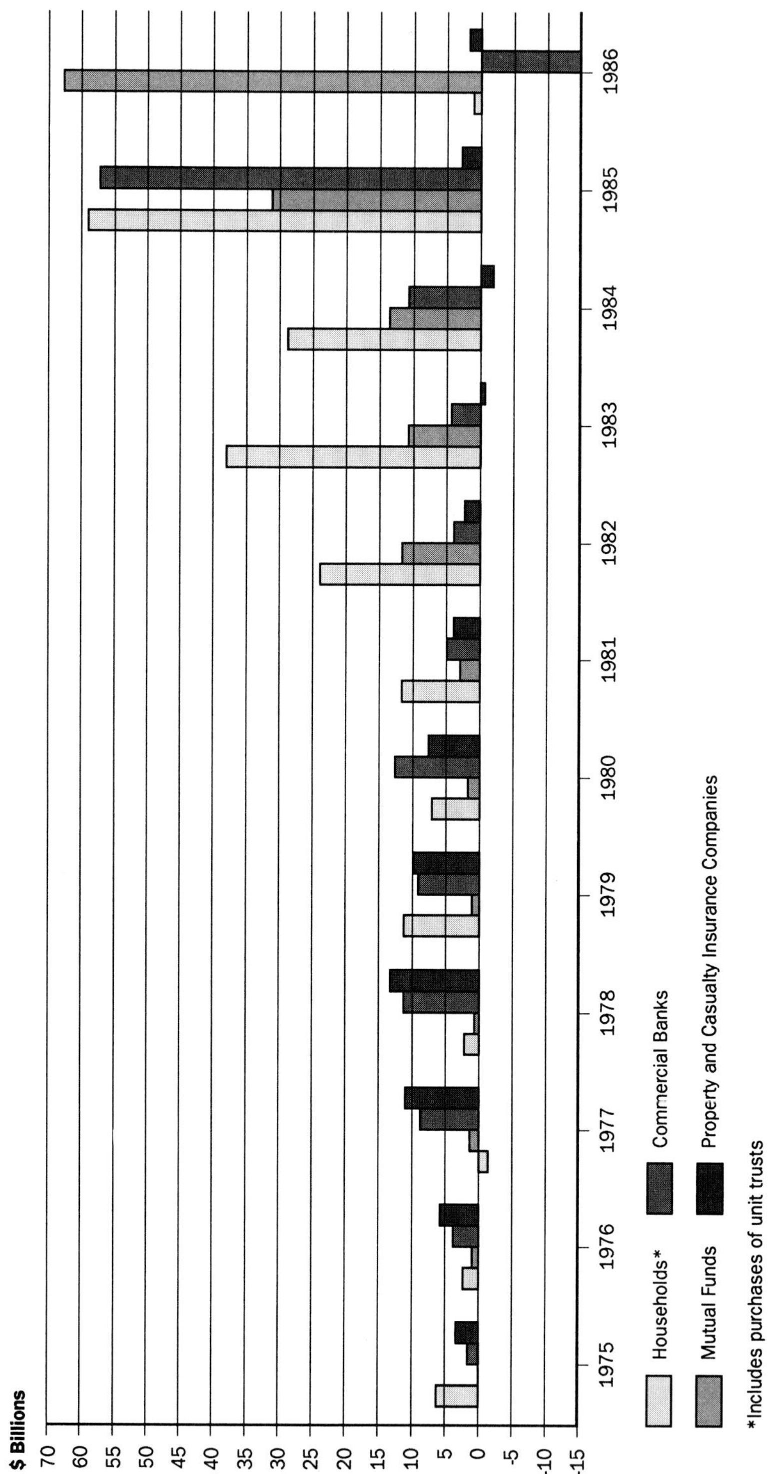

*Includes purchases of unit trusts

Negotiated Underwritings. These involve the selection of an underwriter or syndicate by the municipal borrower, and are common when the size of the issue is large and distribution capabilities important, or when a new type of security must be carefully explained to potential investors. Usually, the government unit will ask certain prospective underwriters to submit proposals. From an evaluation of both the cost of their plans and the managerial and distributive strength of the participating firms, a single underwriter or syndicate is chosen.

Competitive Underwritings. Competitively bid offerings require prospective underwriters or syndicates to submit their proposals to the municipal borrower in a sealed envelope. Once the sealed bids are reviewed by the issuing entity, the bond is sold to the group that offers the lowest interest costs to the government unit.

General Underwriting Procedures. While the mechanics that precede the final bid proposal by an underwriting syndicate are often complicated, the procedure itself has become largely routine. Underwriters are made aware of municipal borrowing needs through solicitations for bid proposals that appear in a variety of trade publications, most notably the *Daily Bond Buyer.* Frequently, the municipality extends invitations to bid on an issue directly to municipal dealers. The larger municipal-dealer firms usually assume the responsibility of managing the syndicate and earn managing fees for their efforts. Depending on the size of the issue, some deals may be co-managed by two or more dealers.

Generally, a manager tries to reassemble the same syndicate with which it has participated on previous issues. This patronage is extremely important, since a strong allegiance between the firms facilitates development of final bid proposals. Through a series of meetings conducted by the manager, the syndicate participants discuss the rate they intend to submit. Once the bid is in, the syndicate participants are bound by contract (the legal syndicate letter) to the provisions relating to the reoffering price and the percentage of the issue to be sold by each participant. Competing syndicates are ethically bound to develop their bids in the strictest privacy—with the reputation of each firm's name at stake.

Secondary Market

The buying and selling of older or seasoned issues, after completion of the underwriting and up until final maturity, is known as the secondary market. In this nationwide over-the-counter market, broker and dealer firms maintain close relationships with each other through telephone communication. Although most individual investors purchase and hold municipal notes until maturity, institutional portfolio managers tend to trade their longer maturities actively to capitalize on changes in interest rates and to time the realization of taxable gains and losses. As a result of this active trading—particularly in the larger and better-known municipals—the securities provide liquidity and marketability to a significant degree for their investors. *The Blue List,* a daily bulletin published by Standard & Poor's, lists those securities that dealer firms are willing to sell each day. On any given day, *The Blue List* will contain municipal bond offerings having a total par value of perhaps $1 billion, as well as industrial development bonds, obligations of some federal agencies, and municipal notes with a total par value exceeding $750 million.

Market Limitations. Although the trading of municipals in the secondary market may be extensive, the activity in any particular issue may be quite small. As a result, unlike the price listings for corporate stocks and bonds, which appear in a variety of daily and weekly business publications, there are no comparable postings of municipal security prices. Investors in municipals will find that they must engage the services of a municipal securities dealer to obtain such ongoing price and yield information. However, the great number of banks and dealer firms that underwrite and sell municipal securities demands investor caution. A dealer's strength in a number of areas should first be evaluated.

Choosing a Dealer. To begin, the dealer should be capable of making a market in any security in which the investor is interested. This ability derives from a broad client base and a reputation position vis-à-vis the industry. The maintenance of a competitive market is an important consideration to any municipal securities buyer. Making competitive bids and maintaining spreads suggest that the dealer is extremely market-sensitive. In this way, the investor can be assured that liquidity and marketability are available for most municipal securities.

In addition, the investor should have confidence in a dealer's ability to understand thoroughly the credit risk represented by the issuing entity. (See *Potential Risks*, earlier in this article.) A municipality's rating from Moody's or Standard & Poor's should be augmented with independent analysis conducted by the dealer. Prior to New York City's default on a note issue of 1975, to illustrate, both rating agencies had given the city an A rating. If a dealer has reservations about the creditworthiness of a particular community, despite widespread feelings to the contrary, the dealer should convey that information to the customer. The dealer must also understand each customer's needs in order to judge the amount of risk to which each is willing to be exposed. Dealers that underwrite bad credit risks in hopes of earning wider spreads are firms of which newcomers to the municipals market should beware. When a dealer meets all the positive criteria, an investor can reasonably anticipate a satisfying relationship.

CUSTODIAL CARE

Repayment procedures differ, depending on whether the issue is a coupon bond or a registered bond, and this difference is significant. Registered bonds require the bearer's name to be recorded on the books of the municipality. It is difficult to effect interparty transfers of these bonds, since title exchange requires the bearer to endorse the issue. Although registered bonds provide safety to the owner, they are unwieldy and not easily pledged in collateralized transactions. Since the security thus loses much of its marketability, registration should be discouraged. Coupon bonds, in contrast, are physically delivered to the bearer, and although more susceptible to theft, they are much more marketable and easily pledged.

The registered-bond owner receives semiannual or annual interest payments via check on prescribed dates over the life of the bond. Coupon bonds may be registered with respect to interest or principal or both. If, for example, the interest is registered, payments are sent directly to the registered owner in the form of a check. The payment procedure usually entails the separation and retention of the coupons by the borrower. On interest payment dates, the borrower mails a check to the registered owner. If the bond is sold prior to its maturity, the new owner must be registered with the municipal borrower.

If interest and principal are not registered, the bonds are considered in bearer form and ownership extends to whoever is in possession of the security. Payment of interest on bearer bonds requires the holder to clip coupons from the bond on payment dates, and redeem them at particular paying agent banks specified by the borrower. (Paying agency banks typically include a regional bank in the area of the municipal borrower and a co-paying agency bank in New York City.)

Municipal note owners generally take physical possession of the security and redeem the note at designated banks upon maturity, receiving both interest payment and principal repayment.

RECENT DEVELOPMENTS IN MUNICIPAL FINANCING

The long period of increasingly high interest rates has directly affected the market for municipals in a number of ways. With short-term rates at historically high levels, investors appear averse to holding long-term bonds, preferring instead to purchase securities at the shorter end of the maturity scale. While the requirement that any general obligation issue be approved by a voter referendum effectively limits municipal borrowers' innovations to the revenue-bond-type of financing, several new methods have developed with which to raise funds in the capital markets.

Tax-Exempt Commercial Paper

In the early 1970s, tax-exempt commercial paper was introduced to the market. This consists of short-term unsecured promissory notes of a state or local government or its agencies, usually backed by a bank line or letter of credit. Issued in bearer form, tax-exempt paper is sold at a discount from par and redeemed at full face value. From the perspective of the issuer, it allows the raising of funds more quickly and at lower cost than do municipal note issues. Furthermore, it provides the borrower with the flexibility to roll over the issue continuously. From the investor's standpoint, commercial paper offers greater liquidity, since most issues mature in fifteen to ninety days. Although not all states permit this method of raising funds, if high interest rates persist it can be expected to account for an ever-increasing share of the market for new municipal securities.

Put Options

To attract investors back to the bond market, some municipal borrowers have experimented with attaching a put option feature to their bond offerings. Thereby, the borrower pays the underwriter (typically a bank), a flat fee against the eventuality that investors may sell the bond at par before its maturity. For instance, a twenty-year bond may provide a put option to be exercised after five years. That is, at the end of five years, the investor may choose to sell the issue back to the bank at par value, presumably because interest rates have moved up and the principal can be reinvested in higher-rate offerings. Moreover, after five years, the issue is regarded as a series of successive one-year notes. The investor is willing to accept a lower yield for the privilege of redeeming the bond before final maturity. The bank usually charges a fee equal to 2 percent of the total issue. For a bond with a five-year put option, the market would compare its return to other five-year offerings. In essence, then, the put option is a mechanism to enhance long-term financings in an otherwise sagging bond market.

Variable Rate Issues

The advent of variable rate issues is another device to enhance the attractiveness of long-term bonds. Variable rates depart from typical long-term issues to the extent that the interest rate is not fixed but tied—for example, to the ninety-day Treasury-bill rate or the prime lending rate. That is, the bond's interest rate is tied to, say, the average prime rate over a designated period as charged by a preselected money-center bank. An investor does not purchase a variable rate bond for speculative reasons since they generally trade at or around par.

Enhanced Security Issues

In an effort to reduce their financing cost, tax-exempt borrowers often attempt to gain higher credit ratings on their issues. For example, dormitory authorities that need to borrow construction funds may pledge part of the university's endowment fund to enhance the security of the bond issue. Similarly, a municipal borrower may obtain a bank letter of credit to provide further collateral on a bond offering. The bank would usually charge a flat fee for the potential use of these funds. In both of these circumstances, the greater security enhances the quality of the issue and reduces the overall financing costs to the borrower.

Open- and Closed-End Municipal Bond Funds

Over the last two decades, legislative changes in many states have cleared the way for the creation of tax-exempt municipal bond funds, both closed- and open-ended. These changes have been enacted primarily to make the market for municipal securities more accessible to individuals. As a result, a variety of funds have emerged to meet a wide array of investor needs.

Fixed-Unit Investment Trusts. Instituted in 1961, fixed-unit investment trusts have come to play an increasingly dominant role in the demand for municipal securities. The trust is simply an investment company that assembles a fixed portfolio of municipals, shares that are then sold to the general public. Because these shares are typically denominated in $1,000 to $5,000 blocks, they have become a viable investment alternative that may be likened to a closed-end fund for municipal bonds. Once the fund is created, only under very special circumstances may the shares in it be traded or sold. (Sales and trading are generally allowed if the trust's ability to meet interest payments or principal repayment becomes seriously impaired.) Because active trading is restricted, most shareholders incur only a sales charge upon initial investment; there are no yearly management fees. In addition, for some unit investment trusts whose shareholders are solicited by direct mail, there may be no sales charge to buy into the fund.

Fixed-unit trusts are usually organized by an investment firm (the sponsor), which selects the securities that are to be held in the fund's portfolio. Frequently, a fixed-unit investment trust may be tailored for a particular class of investors. Thus, a specialized fund may be set up to hold only municipal securities issued by the same state, making interest income exempt not only from federal taxes but also from state and local taxes. Administration of the fund is usually assigned to a bank (the trustee), whose responsibilities include safeguarding the securities, collecting interest payments and executing any income distributions. Such a trust provides the shareholder with safety, diversification, and liquidity:

- Safety is derived from the investment quality of the bonds held in the portfolio (Standard & Poor's AAA to BBB and Moody's Aaa to Baa).
- Diversification is achieved through the holding of a large number of municipals, typically ten to fifty different securities.
- Liquidity is gained through the assurances given to investors that their shares may be redeemed at any time. If the sponsor chooses not to repurchase the shares, the trustee usually is obligated to do so.

The value of both the outstanding shares and the underlying portfolio will fluctuate with general market conditions. Shares that are sold before their final expiration are retired and not resold to other investors. If all outstanding shares should be retired—or when all securities in the portfolio reach final maturity—the entire principal is distributed to the shareholders of the trust, and it loses its character as a legal investment entity.

Municipal Bond Mutual Funds. In 1976, Congress enacted legislation to facilitate the establishment of open-ended tax-exempt municipal bond funds. Unlike the fixed-unit trusts, open-end or mutual funds may be actively managed and, when they are, a management fee is usually charged. Some open-end funds are passively managed, however, and simply held until the portfolio reaches final maturity. Open-end funds that are managed actively may be less susceptible than unit trusts to erosion of principal value caused by inflation. In 1976, when these funds first became legal, sales of the shares in them totaled $475.5 million. By year-end 1988, total net assets of short-term municipal bond funds had soared to more than $65 billion.

GLOSSARY

amortization—Periodic charges to premium bonds that gradually reduce the book value of the debt.

bearer security—A security that extends ownership privileges to the holder. Bearer securities do not require that the owner be registered with the borrower.

bond—An interest-bearing debt obligation that promises to pay the principal on a specified date.

bond anticipation note (BAN)—Short-term borrowings of states and municipalities to obtain interim financing for projects that will be funded long-term through the sale of a bond.

broker—An agent who brings together a buyer and a seller in the exchange of a security in the secondary market. The broker does not assume a position in the security but earns a commission on the trade.

callable bond—A bond that the issuer has the option of repaying prior to its stated maturity date. Repayment is usually made at a specified price above par.

competitive underwritings—A bond sale conducted by prospective underwriters submitting sealed bids.

coupon—The annual rate of interest on the bond's face value or interest payment to be made by the issuer. It also refers to the physical certificate that is often detached from the bond and presented for collection of interest payments.

dealer—An agent who assumes a position in a security. The dealer is involved in underwritings and in the buying and selling of securities.

debt service—The amount of income required for annual interest on and principal repayment of borrowed funds.

discount bond—A bond that sells below the face amount or par value.

discount notes—Non-interest-bearing securities that, when issued, sell below par, but are redeemable at full face value upon maturity.

double-barreled bond—A bond that has at least two potential sources of funds for repayment.

equivalent taxable yield—The pretax yield on a taxable security that would provide an investor with the same return after taxes as a given tax-exempt security yields.

general obligation bond—A municipal debt issue backed by the full faith, credit, and taxing powers of the borrowing state or locality.

industrial revenue bond—A bond issued by a municipality or public authority to finance the construction of a facility to be leased to a private corporation. They are secured by the private corporation's credit.

municipal securities rulemaking board—An independent, self-regulatory authority established by the SEC in 1975 to promulgate rules for the conduct of brokers, dealers, and banks that participate in the municipal securities market.

negotiated underwritings—A bond sale performed by the municipal issuer, preselecting an underwriter or group of underwriters to price and distribute the new issue.

new issue market—The market for original issues or newly issued securities. Also referred to as the primary market.

notes—Debt obligations with maturities of one month to three years, although generally recognized as one-year issues.

over-the-counter market—A securities market created by dealer negotiations rather than the auction system typical of organized exchanges.

par value—The principal amount of a security that is to be repaid at maturity, generally $1,000.

premium bond—A bond that sells above the principal amount or par value.

project notes—Short-term debt obligations issued on behalf of public housing authorities by the U.S. Department of Housing and Urban Development for the purpose of financing housing and urban development projects.

refunding—The process by which a new bond issue is sold to redeem an outstanding issue.

registered bond—A bond whose owner is registered on the books of the borrower.

revenue anticipation note (RAN)—Short-term borrowings of state and local governments in anticipation of future receipt of revenues.

seasoned issue—An issue that has been sold and trades actively in the secondary market.

serial bond—A bond issue in which a portion of the debt obligation matures annually or semiannually until final maturity.

spread—1. Difference between bid and asked prices on a security. 2. Difference between yields on or prices of two securities of differing maturities. 3. In underwriting, difference between price realized by the issuer and price paid by the investor.

tax anticipation note (TAN)—Short-term borrowing of states and municipalities to finance current operations. TANs are repaid out of anticipated tax revenues.

term bonds—A bond issue in which the debt obligation is repaid on a single date.

trading market—The market for buying and selling issued bonds.

yield—The annual rate of return on an investment.

DEALERS

Like corporate securities, municipals are widely available in securities brokerage firms where qualified personnel are prepared to discuss specific issues in light of individual requirements.

SUGGESTED READING

PERIODICALS

Municipal Finance Journal. Published by Panel Publishers, Greenvale, N.Y. Quarterly.

Municipal Registered Bond Index. Published by Standard & Poor's Corporation, New York, N.Y. Weekly.

Government Finance Review. Published by Government Finance Officers Association, Chicago, Ill. Bimonthly.

Public Finance Quarterly. Published by Sage Publications, Newbury Park, Cal. Quarterly.

REFERENCE BOOKS

Cooper, James J. *Investing in Municipal Bonds: Balancing Risks and Rewards*. New York: John Wiley, 1987.

Fabozzi, Frank J., and Feldstein, Sylvan G. *The Municipal Bond Handbook*. Homewood: Dow Jones-Irwin, 1983.

Feldstein, Sylvan G. and Fabozzi, Frank J. *The Dow Jones-Irwin Guide to Municipal Bonds*. Homewood: Dow Jones-Irwin, 1986.

Fundamentals of Municipal Bonds. New York: The Public Securities Association, 1987.

Lamb, Robert, and Rappaport, Stephen P. *Municipal Bonds*. New York: McGraw-Hill, 1980.

Stigum, Marcia. *The Money Market: Myth, Reality and Practice*. Homewood: Dow Jones-Irwin, 1983.

MUTUAL FUNDS

John C. Bogle
Jeremy G. Duffield

Investment companies, both open-end and closed-end, have enjoyed a remarkable resurgence in asset growth in the past decade. Total assets of investment companies, which had risen from $19 billion at year-end 1960 to $67 billion at year-end 1972, were just $62 billion at year-end 1978. Assets quadrupled to $248 billion at year-end 1981 and more than trebled to $844 billion at mid-year 1988.

This chapter discusses the two basic types of investment companies:

- Open-end funds, commonly referred to as mutual funds, which issue and redeem shares daily at a price representing the underlying net asset value of the shares;
- Closed-end funds, which have a fixed number of shares outstanding. Shares may be traded at an auction market price that may be more or less than their underlying value.

There are many similarities, but also some profound differences, between these two popular types of investment company. Section I discusses the open-end variety, and Section II, closed-end funds.

John C. Bogle and Jeremy G. Duffield are Chairman and Senior Vice President, respectively, of The Vanguard Group of investment companies in Valley Forge, Pennsylvania.

OPEN-END (MUTUAL) FUNDS

BASIC CHARACTERISTICS

The past decade has been an extraordinary period of growth and evolution for mutual funds, witnessing the transformation of what was once a small component of the financial services industry into one of the industry's most important and fastest-growing sectors. From year-end 1978 to June 1988, mutual fund assets grew from $56 billion to $811 billion, and the number of shareholder accounts increased from 9 million to 55 million.

Mutual funds, first formed in the United States in the 1920s have enjoyed intermittent periods of substantial growth. These growth spurts have usually coincided with strong equity markets, reflecting the almost complete concentration by mutual funds on equity investments through the mid-1970s. From 1945 to 1972, the Dow Jones industrial average (DJIA) rose from a level of 150 to more than 1,000, and mutual funds, which provided competitive absolute rates of return, grew from $1 billion to $60 billion in net assets. However, the period 1973 to 1974 saw a substantial drop in stock prices, and with it a severe slowdown in investor purchases of mutual fund shares.

A number of factors explain the renaissance of mutual funds that began in the late 1970s and accelerated in the 1980s:

The Money Market Fund Innovation

The money market mutual fund must rank as one of the great financial services innovations of all times. First conceived in 1971, the money market fund attracted some attention in the high interest rate period of 1973 to 1974 as a safe, although uninsured, way for investors to avoid the interest rate ceilings then imposed on bank and savings and loan deposits. But it was the even higher interest rate period of 1978 to 1982, when short-term interest rates averaged 11 percent and soared to as high as 18 percent, that kicked off the astounding growth of this new type of mutual fund. Assets grew from $3 billion at the end of 1977 to $207 billion in 1982.

Expanding Types of Funds

The money market fund phenomenon made it clear to mutual fund executives that the industry was no longer a one-product supplier of broadly diversified common stock funds. Indeed, mutual funds could be used to provide convenient, cost-effective, and diversified access to many types of securities, and soon corporate and U.S. government bond funds, municipal bond funds, and funds focusing on particular segments of the stock market were formed by the hundreds. Although in the past, mutual fund companies had offered one or just a handful of mutual funds, fund families (a group of funds under common sponsorship) moved toward offering a panoply of investments—a mutual fund for seemingly every investor need.

No-Load Distribution

An additional innovation spurring mutual fund growth was the development of no-load fund families. Until the early 1970s, the vast majority of mutual funds were distributed by sales people who were compensated by sales commissions. These sales commissions were often referred to as front-end loads, and, for the typical stock fund, they amounted to 8.5 percent of the investor's initial purchase. However, with the rise of money market funds and the difficulty of raising money through brokers in the wake of the 1973 to 1974 stock market decline, a growing number of fund companies began distributing funds directly to customers, without sales charges, that is, on a no-load basis. These firms appealed to self-reliant investors willing to make their own investment decisions. By 1982, no-load firms had captured a market share of 34 percent.

The no-load trend was really just the start of a trend toward divergent pricing schemes. It has been said that the mutual fund industry in the 1980s engaged in a massive price war. But, unlike traditional price wars, it has been a war to raise prices, not to lower them. The trend has been to develop pricing systems that appear more attractive than the traditional 8.5 percent front-end load system. Some approaches have indeed cut costs to investors, as in the case of true no-load funds; others, ingenious though they may be, have increased costs to investors by spreading charges out over a number of years. Today, mutual fund pricing comes in many forms. (See *Sales Charges and Operating Costs*, in this chapter.)

The Great Bull Market: Stocks and Bonds

On August 12, 1982, the stock and bond markets exploded out of their doldrums. Long-term interest rates began to decline from their highs of more than 15 percent, causing a remarkable rally in the bond markets. The rally in the stock market continued for five years, taking the DJIA from a low of 777 in August 1982 to 2,700 in August 1987 before it began a dramatic tumble culminating in the October 1987 stock market crash. In this five-year period, common stocks (as measured by the Standard & Poor's (S&P) 500 stock index) provided an historically exceptional return, averaging 32 percent on an annualized basis. During the same period, the supposedly staid bond market also provided exceptional returns, averaging 17 percent annually.

In this period, as Figure 1 shows, investors poured money into stock and bond mutual funds as the most efficient way to participate in the great bull market. Although stocks provided the higher returns, bond funds touting high yields captured the lion's share of mutual fund sales. As a result, by 1988 bond fund assets had risen to 23 percent of industry assets, up from 8 percent in 1978.

Types of Mutual Funds

Mutual funds come in an extraordinary variety, with a diversity of objectives and policies that enable most investors to find mutual funds that meet their needs. Although it is not possible to catalog funds into a series of precise categories, the principal groups are listed below.

Stock (Equity) Funds. Stock funds invest primarily in common stocks. Within this category are (1) growth and income funds, placing relatively equal weight on capital growth and dividend income; (2) growth funds, primarily seeking capital growth, with income incidental; (3) aggressive growth funds, investing in smaller or riskier stocks, seeking maximum capital gains; and (4) equity income funds, selecting high-yielding common stocks for maximum income, with capital growth a secondary goal.

Bond Funds. Bond funds emphasize fixed income investments, such as bonds and mortgages. Reflecting the diversity of types of fixed-income securities available, there are a variety of bond funds. Among the major types are (1) U.S. government bond funds, owning only issues with federal government guarantees; (2) mortgage funds—most

FIGURE 1. Mutual Fund Industry Assets by Objective Category

Source: Investment Company Institute

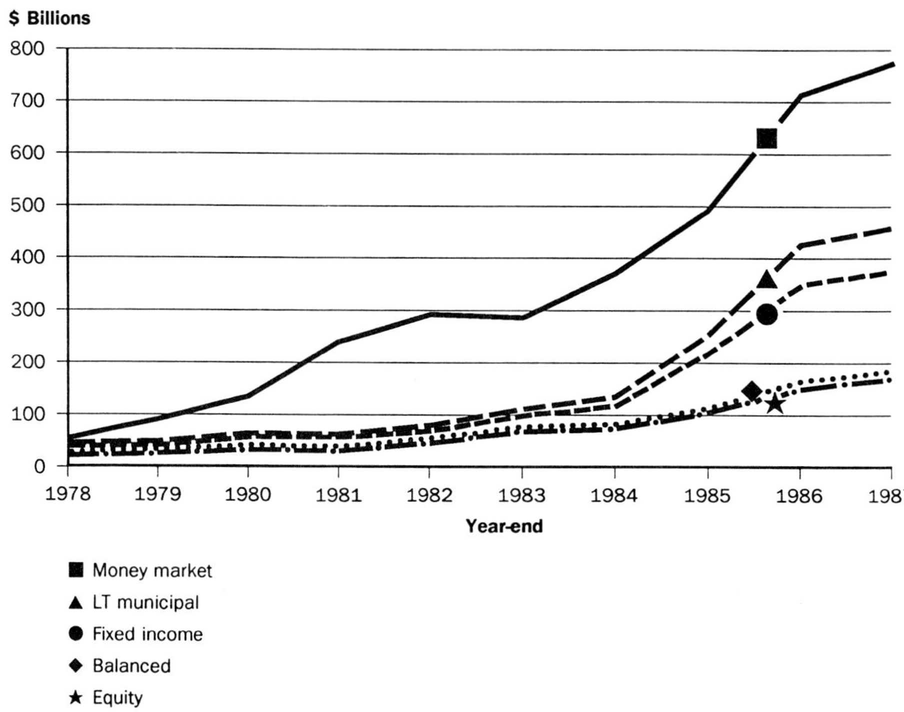

popularly, Government National Mortgage Association (GNMA) funds, which invest in securities backed by residential mortgages, pay attractive yields, and, in the case of GNMAs' are backed by the U.S. government as to payment of interest and principal; (3) investment-grade corporate bond funds, emphasizing top-rated corporate bonds in order to offer higher yields with limited credit risk; and (4) high-yield bond funds that own lower-quality corporate bonds, with greater credit risk, in order to maximize income. In addition to differing by security type, bond funds also vary importantly in terms of the average maturity of their investments. Most funds maintain long maturities; others shorten maturity length to reduce principal risk.

Balanced Funds. Balanced funds combine bonds and stocks in a complete investment program to conserve capital, pay reasonable income, and provide some capital appreciation. Balanced funds include (1) traditional balanced funds, which are typically composed of about one-third bonds and two-thirds stocks, and (2) income-balanced funds, which aim to pay generous income by emphasizing bonds when interest rates are high relative to dividend yields and then reversing the emphasis when this relationship is reversed.

Municipal Bond Funds. Municipal bond funds are a completely separate category of bond fund, providing tax-free income to investors. The principal types are (1) short-term or limited-term bond funds with average maturities of one to four years, offering a reasonable degree of principal stability and higher yields than tax-free money market funds; (2) long-term bond funds, which take greater price risk, by owning high-grade bonds with long maturities, and seek higher income; (3) intermediate-term bond funds, which fall between the first two types; and (4) high-yield bond funds, which own lower-grade long-term bonds for maximum income. In addition, there are now municipal bond funds tailored to residents of particular states, providing income exempt from federal and state, and sometimes local, taxes.

Money Market Funds. Money market funds invest in short-term money market instruments. By maintaining a short average maturity, usually less than sixty days, and investing in high-quality instruments, money market funds are able to maintain a stable $1 net asset value. As money market funds usually offer yields higher than insured bank money market deposit accounts, they are a very attractive haven for savings or temporary investment dollars. Like bond funds, money market funds come in both taxable and tax-free municipal versions. Reflecting their tax-free status, municipal money market funds pay consistently lower before-tax yields than taxable money market funds.

International Funds. International funds (which invest in foreign securities) and global funds (which combine foreign and U.S. securities) have proliferated rapidly, aided in large part by the substantial fall of the U.S. dollar from 1985 to 1987. As the dollar fell, other currencies rose commensurately, giving foreign securities markets a relative return advantage. (Of course, the reverse would be true when the dollar rises.)

Specialized Funds. Specialized funds that concentrate on a particular sector of the stock market also come in a wide variety. Some of the more popular areas are gold mining stocks, energy funds, technology funds, health care funds, and utility funds.

Diversity of Objectives

Table 1 illustrates the diversity of mutual fund objectives by providing summary data for each fund category, including performance records for the one-, five-, and ten-year periods ending June 30, 1988. Performance is defined in terms of total return, which takes into account the change in a fund's net asset value, adjusted for income dividends and capital gains distributions.

The table shows that the year ending June 30, 1988 was difficult for equity and balanced funds, encompassing as it did the crash of October 1987. However, the five- and ten-year periods ending on that date were quite exceptional for stock funds, balanced funds, and bond funds (taxable and tax-free).

Table 1 also indicates the average yield for funds in each category on June 30, 1988. Income yields offered by the fund categories differ, and the various types of funds provide different levels of income stability. Bond funds typically provide a high and stable level of income. Money market funds usually offer a lower level of income (although sometimes, as in the early 1980s, money market fund yields may exceed bond fund yields), which may be expected to fluctuate substantially with the level of short-term interest rates. Equity

TABLE 1. Major Categories of Investment Companies

	Number of Funds	Assets (Billions)	Total Return Period 1 Year	5 Years	10 Years	Current Yield
Stock funds						
Capital appreciation	163	$19.8	−6%	+35%	+357%	1.5%
Growth	249	55.5	−6	+54	+335	1.7
Small company growth	64	8.4	−5	+33	+337	0.6
Growth & income	180	62.7	−4	+80	+323	3.3
Equity income	53	18.1	−4	+84	+344	6.1
Total	709	$164.5				
Bond funds						
U.S. government	148	$61.8	+6%	+61%	+160%	8.5%
GNMA	43	48.4	+8	+71	+131	9.2
Investment grade*	47	9.8	+7	+69	+166	8.9
High yield	89	31.6	+6	+70	+190	12.0
Total	327	$151.6				
International funds						
Equity	92	$18.0	−3%	+157%	+416%	1.0%
Bond	27	3.0	+10	+113	N.A.	7.4
Total	119	$20.9				
Balanced funds						
Traditional	45	$12.1	−1%	+84%	+289%	4.3%
Income	19	3.1	+4	+67	+231	7.8
Convertible	27	3.8	−3	+62	+296	6.2
Total	91	$19.0				
Specialized funds						
Gold	27	$3.7	−14%	−2%	+414%	2.2%
Science & technology	25	2.2	−9	+22	+283	0.6
Natural resources	14	2.4	−10	+49	+371	2.2
Other	71	6.1	−6	+81	+216	2.1
Total	137	$14.4				
Municipal bond funds						
Intermediate-term	40	$7.0	+6%	+44%	+87%	6.0%
Long-term	129	36.9	+7	+68	+105	7.1
High yield	29	13.3	+7	+67	+105	8.0
Single-state	256	31.1	+7	+63	+80	6.9
Total	454	$88.3				
Money market funds						
Taxable	401	$261.7	+6%	+44%	+158%	6.2%
Tax-free	170	63.9	+4	+26	+44	4.2
Total	571	$325.6				
Totals	2,408	$784.3				

N.A. = Not applicable.
*Lipper Category = corporate bond funds, A rated.

Note: Data as of June 30, 1988.

Source: Prepared by Vanguard Statistical Services Department using data provided by Lipper Analytical Services, Inc.

TABLE 2. Cumulative Performance of Equity Funds

	Aggressive Growth		Growth		Growth and Income	
	Total Return	Annual Return	Total Return	Annual Return	Total Return	Annual Return
Total period	+ 1,243%	+ 10.9%	+ 974%	+ 10.0%	+ 972%	+ 10.0%
Market rise 1963–1968	+ 263	+ 24.0	+ 153	+ 16.7	+ 120	+ 14.0
Market decline 1969–1974	– 50	– 11.0	– 36	– 7.1	– 24	– 4.5
Market rise 1975–1987	+ 638	+ 16.6	+ 559	+ 15.6	+ 543	+ 15.4

Note: For period 1963 to 1987.

Source: Prepared by Vanguard Statistical Services Department, using data from Wiesenberger Investment Companies Services, *Investment Companies*, 1963 to 1974, and Lipper Analytical Services, Inc., 1975 to 1987.

funds, generally offering the lowest of income, may be expected to provide a growing level of dividends over time.

Table 2 shows the performance of equity mutual funds over a longer period, divided among three sets of market conditions: (1) the great bull market of 1963 to 1968, (2) the generally bearish market of 1969 to 1974, and (3) the ensuing recovery of 1975 to 1987. The first and last of these periods provide some idea of the rewards available through three types of equity mutual funds (few other types have as extended a history): (1) aggressive growth funds (the riskiest of the three types); (2) growth funds (generally riskier than average); and (3) growth and income funds (carrying a marked level of risk).

Table 2 makes it clear that mutual funds—and even equity funds—may be sharply differentiated under various market conditions. In the first bull market, the riskier the fund, the larger the gain; in the bear market, the riskier the fund, the larger the loss; and, in the later bull market, aggressive growth funds again led the way by a modest margin, with growth funds and growth and income funds providing similar returns. Although conventional wisdom tells us that high risk is usually associated with high return, these comparative figures suggest that this principle should be viewed with healthy skepticism.

It should be emphasized that equity funds should not be picked at random, for there are significant differences not only in past performance, but in risk, quality, cost, and management competence. In particular, investors should choose carefully the broad objective group that best matches their own investment goals, picking from the aggressive growth, growth or growth-and-income categories. Funds with greater emphasis on growth have usually exhibited higher rates of return, but the aggressive fund should be selected only by those investors who have the heart and stomach to ride out not only the inevitable swings in the stock market, but the sharp magnification of these swings by the aggressive funds.

Organization of Mutual Funds

Most mutual funds are organized, sponsored, distributed, managed, and administered by an external management compamy. (The Vanguard Group funds are believed to be the

TABLE 3. Expense Ratios for Categories of Mutual Funds

Fund Objective	Average Expense Ratio Highest 10%	Lowest 10%	All Funds
Stock funds	2.51%	0.53%	1.35%
Bond funds	1.91	0.36	1.01
Long-term municipal bond funds	1.51	0.29	0.79
Money market funds—taxable	1.36	0.26	0.74
Money market funds—tax-free	1.06	0.23	0.63

Note: Sample excludes funds with expense ratios that are less than or equal to 0.10 percent and greater than or equal to 3.00 percent.

Source: Prepared by Vanguard Statistical Services Department, using data from Lipper Analytical Services, Inc.

only major exception to this rule.) Although a fund normally has a board of directors, a majority of whom are independent of the management company, the company generally exercises de facto control of the fund. The management company manages and markets the fund, creates new funds, and assumes responsibility for providing a family of funds with a diversity of objectives. Under these circumstances, the fund may be viewed as the product of the company. If investors are dissatisfied with the performance or management of the fund, they may "vote with their feet" by cashing in their investments. This will be an expensive decision for an investment of short duration when a sales charge has been paid (or if a back-end sales charge is due), but essentially is a cost-free decision if a no-load fund is involved.

A typical mutual fund organization sponsors a family of funds with a variety of objectives. For example, a fund family may offer a number of stock funds with varying levels of aggressiveness, a number of bond and municipal bond funds with varying maturities and degrees of credit risk, a balanced fund, an international fund, and a money market fund. Each fund within the family is normally a separate corporation or business trust, although there is increasing use of the series fund, a single corporation with a series of completely independent portfolios (e.g., a municipal bond fund with a long term portfolio and a short-term portfolio).

Sales Charges and Operating Costs.

Mutual funds levy widely disparate sales charges and operating fees. Therefore, the investor should remember that, as with most goods, the expression caveat emptor holds. The first category of costs is sales charges, which reflect the three principal ways mutual funds are sold:

1. Historically, mutual funds were sold by brokers with a front-end sales charge of 8.5 percent. More recently, front-end sales charges on many new funds have been lowered to the 4 to 5.5 percent range. Low-load funds, often sold directly to investors by the fund company, charge front-end sales loads of 3 percent or less.

2. A more recent, but now very common development, has been to substitute a more complex arrangement for compensating the broker. The investor pays no up-front sales commission, but the fund, and therefore the investor, is charged a distribution, or so-called 12(b)1, fee that usually ranges from 0.25 to 1.00 percent per year in addition to investment advisory fees and fund operating expenses. If the investor decides to redeem during the first year, he is charged a back-end sales charge of, say, 6 percent; that charge may be reduced to 5 percent if he redeems after the first year, 4 percent after the second, 3 percent after the third, and so on. This method of charging sales commissions can be just as expensive to the investor as the traditional front-end load.

3. True no-load funds are sold without sales commissions. In this seemingly vanishing category, the fund's sponsor typically pays the costs of marketing and recaptures those expenses through advisory fees, although in recent years even some no-load funds have added 12(b)1 fees, principally to provide resources for direct advertising.

The second category of costs that investors should consider in selecting among mutual funds is ongoing expenses, consisting of the advisory fees, shareholder servicing, and other costs that all funds incur. Once again, these costs can vary widely. As illustrated by Table 3, ongoing costs for mutual funds are summarized in a fund's expense ratio, which expresses total costs as a percentage of assets. Because this expense ratio directly reduces the amount of investment income paid out to investors, the higher the expense ratio, the lower the income yield, other things being equal.

In 1988, new rules promulgated by the Securities and Exchange Commission (SEC) required tabular disclosure in fund prospectuses of all sales charges and fees. The new table greatly simplifies the investor's task in comparing the cost of investing from fund to fund. Lower costs can significantly increase investor returns over time, and so investors should include costs among their criteria for selecting mutual fund.

Industry Regulation. All mutual funds are organized and operate under the Investment Company Act of 1940. Administered by the SEC, the act requires disclosure in a variety of areas, including advisory contracts, sales charges, composition of the board of directors, capital structure, and insider transactions. The stringent regulation of the industry by the SEC over a period of more than forty-five years has been an important contribution to the facts that few marginal operators have entered the industry and that major scandal has been virtually unknown. Nonetheless, investors should be aware that the SEC's regulatory purview does not extend to fund investment objectives and portfolio management.

ATTRACTIVE FEATURES

The concept of mutual funds is really quite simple: Investors seeking similar goals combine their resources so as to diversify over a large number of securities (thus reducing risk) and to obtain professional investment management that they could not employ individually (thus enhancing the possibility of reward). This concept is hardly of recent vintage. The first known ancestor of today's mutual fund was the Société de Belgique, formed in 1822. More than a century ago, in 1875, an English barrister named Arthur Scratchley gave a particularly good description (albeit in somewhat turgid prose) of the purposes of a mutual fund:

> Whether a man has a large sum or a small sum to invest. . .if he subscribes to a general fund, which (assisted by the advise of persons of experience in such matters) would divide its purchases carefully among a selected variety of investments—each member would derive greater benefit with much security from loss by the distribution of the risk over a large average.[1]

Performance

One reason for the spreading acceptance of mutual funds by investors, individuals and institutions alike is the growing perception that mutual funds provide access to some of the best investment management talent available. Although there is an enormously wide variety of performance results among funds, available evidence suggests that common stock mutual funds, as a whole, have provided investment results comparable, and perhaps superior, to those of other types of equity managers, such as managers of bank and insurance company pooled funds.[2]

Mutual fund managers may have a number of advantages relative to other types of investment managers in approaching their task. First, they work with well-defined objectives. Mutual funds usually seek specific objectives (e.g., growth or a combination of growth and income) and adhere closely to them. Investment managers who have more open charters may be whipsawed by shifting their objectives and polices at inopportune times. Second, mutual fund managers deal with a spectrum of investments. Mutual funds are typically well diversified. Common stock mutual funds are more likely than banks and insurance company equity funds to have a wide spectrum of investments beyond giant blue chip companies. Third, mutual funds benefit from their size. Generally, mutual funds are large enough to warrant the full-time attention of a dedicated portfolio management group, rather than being just one of a large number of relatively smaller accounts under the supervision of a single portfolio manager.

Risk Spreading

Diversification is almost universally acclaimed by investment advisors and academic researchers, who have found there is virtually no value added in holding only a limited number of stocks. Investors who do not (or cannot) hold a broadly diversified portfolio are taking a risk that is not offset by a higher reward potential. Fund diversification usually means owning a relatively large number of stocks (50 to 100 or more) issued by a wide range of industries or by companies with different investment characteristics (e.g., a growth fund may own seasoned growth stocks, cyclical growth stocks, and emerging growth stocks), or even owning stocks of corporations in different nations. The table below

Number of Stocks	Risk Ratio
1	6.56
2	3.77
4	2.38
10	1.55
50	1.10
100	1.04
500	1.00

[1] Arthur Scratchley, *On Average Investment Trusts*. London: Shaw & Sons, 1875.

[2] John C. Bogle and Jan M. Twardowski; "Institutional Investment Performance Compared," *Financial Analysts Journal*, Jan.–Feb. 1980.

Table 4. Ten-Year Total Return on Types of Equity Funds

	Number of Funds	Average	Highest 10%	Lowest 10%	Range
Aggressive growth funds	56	+ 352%	+ 617%	+ 20%	597%
Growth funds	118	+ 335	+ 676	+ 123	553
Growth and income funds	80	+ 323	+ 486	+ 182	304

Note: Period ended June 30, 1988.

Source: Prepared by Vanguard Statistical Services Department, using data from Lipper Analytical Services, Inc., *Mutual Fund Performance Analysis*, June 30, 1988.

shows the relationship between diversification and investment risk, defined as the relative variability of annual return of a stock portfolio.

Note that the variability of return, or risk, associated with holding just one stock is more than six times as great as the risk of a 100-stock portfolio typical of a mutual fund. Yet, a study of 1971 tax returns showed that 51 percent of households listing dividends owned just one or two dividend-pay stocks and that 89 percent held nine or fewer stocks.[3] Given the fact that the typical American investor is diversified among only a few stocks, mutual funds obviously fill a critical need.

Diversification is also important in bond portfolios. A corporate bond fund will own the debt securities of many different companies in a variety of industries; a municipal bond fund will own the debt securities of many different governmental bodies, such as cities, states, and school districts, in different parts of the country. In either case, there is a significant reduction of the risk in holding any one bond, with no sacrifice in yield. The same principle holds with respect to portfolios of short-term securities held by money market funds.

Skilled Management

Professional management is a primary characteristic of mutual funds. The idea that a trained, skillful, professional management organization can successfully select a stock portfolio and adjust it as conditions change is hardly counterintuitive. Nonetheless, despite the high degree of professionalism exhibited by mutual fund investment advisors as a group, the ability to outpace the performance of stock or bond market averages is remarkably difficult to come by. The records of hundreds of mutual funds support this conclusion. A few are outstanding, many are more or less average, and some are distinctly poor. The performance range is large, even among funds sharing similar investment policies and characteristics. Table 4 shows the differences among equity funds in various categories over the past decade.

The chief reasons for this range of results are as follows:

---

[3] Marshall E. Blume and Irwin Friend, *The Changing Role of the Individual Investor*. New York: John Wiley & Sons, 1976.

1. Despite comparable investment objectives within each of the three categories, investment policies may differ, and often substantially so. Thus, in various types of markets, some funds will certainly surpass others. For instance, some long-term growth funds emphasize seasoned growth stocks, while others tend to own stock of smaller, less well-known companies. Similarly, some growth and income funds hold cyclical stocks (General Motors, USX) or income stocks (e.g., electric utilities or telephone companies), while others take a different tack altogether, perhaps choosing out-of-favor stocks with low price-to-earnings ratios.

2. Some markets favor stocks in one industry versus another; technology stocks prospered from 1975 to mid-1983, only to slide into a long period of underperformance through 1987.

3. Management competence does vary; when all explanations have come and gone, some fund advisors simply do better than others. It may be luck, or it may be skill. The challenge to the mutual fund investor is to evaluate the past by giving appropriate weight to the fund's relative return numbers (e.g., what rate of total return has been earned by the fund, compared to similar funds and to the stock market averages in general), but not getting carried way with picking the best in retrospect, a recipe for possible investment disaster.

Given the dispersion in results of managed portfolios, many investors in recent years have opted for an unmanaged alternative, index funds, which provide competitive performance and, to a degree, enhanced predictability of return (see *Indexing: An Alternative to Active Management*, later in this article).

Investor Convenience

Simplicity is an important, if often overlooked, characteristic of mutual funds. Although a shareholder often owns 50 to 100 or more individual securities through a mutual fund investment, the investment program is pooled, and the shareholder need not be concerned with the bookkeeping, tax records, and sheer flow of paper associated with owning a diversified portfolio of many individual issues. Instead, he owns a single investment—admittedly one whose success or failure depends on the net accomplishment of its stock or bond portfolio—making it easy for the investor to judge the performance of his investment program. The mutual fund represents a conveniently packaged investment program, offering the advantages of diversification and professional investment counseling, with management, custodial, and administrative services provided, often at remarkably low cost relative to alternative investment programs.

Service

A key element in the success of the funds is service. It is simple to purchase shares, either directly from no-load funds, through sales representatives from brokerage firms, or from direct sales forces of mutual fund distributors. Examples of no-load fund groups are Scudder, T. Rowe Price, and Vanguard; brokerage firms include Merrill Lynch, Paine Webber, and Shearson Lehman Hutton, among many others, who sell their own funds as well as funds offered by third parties, such as the American Funds and Putnam, and direct sales firms, such as Investors Diversified Services, which often sell insurance as well as their own mutual funds. In each case, the investor's purchase of fund shares, with or without a sales charge, buys a diversified, professionally managed investment program. Further, the fund handles all the income collection and bookkeeping and distributes the net income (after fund expenses) to shareholders, who may receive these dividends either in cash or in additional shares of the fund through a dividend reinvestment program.

Mutual fund shares are easy to purchase. They are also easy to redeem on demand, by contacting the fund directly, or through a broker or salesperson. Plans for adding regular monthly investments to the fund are available, along with plans for receiving regular monthly withdrawal checks, the former for investors accumulating assets in their earning years, the latter for investors who require income in their retirement years. An annual statement showing the tax treatment of fund distributions is provided. Tax-deferred retirement plans established under self-employed retirement plan programs or under the Individual Retirement Act have been an important part of the industry's growth.

In recent years, the exchange privilege has found increasing favor in the eyes of investors, as the single funds of yesterday have blossomed into the fund families of today with a variety of funds, usually ten or thirty or even more. Investors may exchange their shares for shares in another fund in the family usually without commissions and often by a simple telephone call. For example, an investor might purchase shares in a stock fund during his accumulation years and exchange them with shares in an income fund in the same fund family on retirement. Or an investor might exchange shares in a growth fund with those in money market fund to protect his assets when he expects stock market declines and reverse the process in anticipation of stock market rises. The exchange privilege, then, offers a new dimension of investment flexibility to the fund investor.

POTENTIAL RISKS

Mutual fund investments involve the risks associated with the types of underlying securities purchased. Investors in common stock funds should have an understanding of the volatility of the equity markets. Bond fund investors need to be aware of principal risk associated with rising interest rates and credit risk incurred by investing in lower-quality instruments. And even money market fund investors should think about risk, not so much in terms of safety of principal, but in terms of inflation risk (i.e., the likelihood that their investment will be a poor hedge against inflation over time).

Investors should focus on the risk associated with an entire investment program rather than with its various components. Just as risk can be reduced by forming a portfolio of stocks that move to some degree independently of one another, creating a portfolio of mutual funds—with either differing investment objectives or differing investment policies—reduces the volatility or risk of the overall investment portfolio. Thus, even extremely conservative investors may reasonably hold a small commitment in an aggressive fund, given judicious holdings in more conservative stock funds, as well as bond and money market funds.

INDEXING: AN ALTERNATIVE TO ACTIVE MANAGEMENT

Although skilled management may significantly enhance mutual fund portfolio returns, it is also true that investment managers, as a whole, have a difficult time trying to outpace broad market averages, whether in the stock or bond markets. This result should not be surprising when one considers that, all investors in the aggregate, can only earn the market return. And with brokerage costs, advisory fees, and ongoing fund operating expenses, mutual fund investment advisors have an additional hurdle to surmount in attempting to beat the market indices.

In fact, results show that only 14 percent of equity mutual funds have managed to beat the S&P 500 Index in the five years ending June 30, 1988. The same phenomenon has been observed among managers of pension funds; 66 percent of such managers have underperformed the index in the past decade, even before considering the effects of investment management fees.

In recognition of the efficiency of our securities markets and the difficulty of outperforming unmanaged indexes, passively managed indexed funds have grown in popularity, especially among institutional investors. Index funds attempt to match the investment performance of a target index by holding all, or a representative sample, of the securities in the index. Instead of selecting securities to outperform the index, index fund managers emphasize broad diversification, low portfolio turnover, and low transaction costs. At midyear 1988, it was estimated that more than $200 billion were invested in index funds.

Indexing is available in mutual fund format, as well. The first indexed mutual fund was formed in 1976, and there are now seventeen indexed mutual funds with assets of $2.4 billion.

In addition to their performance appeal, indexed funds are also popular because of the broad diversification they provide—typical S&P 500 Index funds own all 500 securities in the index. The funds also provide a reassuring measure of predicatiblity of relative return; they eliminate the risk of substantially underperforming the market in any year.

Investors should pay careful attention to costs in selecting among index funds. Given the same index as a benchmark, the difference in return from investment in two index funds is mostly dependent on the relative costs incurred in each.

TAX CONSEQUENCES

The tax impact of mutual funds should always be considered. Mutual fund dividends are normally taxed to individuals at rates from 0 to 33 percent, depending on the investor's tax bracket, and are generally considered to be dividend income even though their source (in a bond fund) may be interest. The income from municipal bond funds, however, is in a special category under federal tax law, and investors pay no federal tax, although the income may be subject to state and local taxes.

Investors also pay taxes on capital gains realized on their fund investments. When a fund realizes net capital gains during a year, it is required to distribute them to shareholders in the form of a capital gains distribution, which may be either short term or long term in nature. Short-term capital gains distributions are included with dividend income. Long-term capital gains distributions must be reported separately on the tax forms. Investors also are required to report net capital gains or losses realized on the redemption of mutual fund shares. Under present tax law, capital gains are taxed at the same rate as dividends and other income.

Because of the variety of funds available, their low cost, and investor convenience, as well as the ability to exchange between funds with different objectives within one fund family, mutual funds are ideal vehicles for investors eligible to take advantage of the tax and retirement planning benefits of individual retirement accounts (IRAs), plans for the self-employed (Keoghs), and company-sponsored savings and retirement plans, such as 401(k)s and profit-sharing plans. These plans provide the dual benefits of tax-deferred building up of investment return—which can be an enormous advantage over time—and a means of regular investing that represents a sensible way to build a long-term investment program.

Representative Types of Investors

Originally considered as an investment principally for the average individual, today mutual funds are owned by an extraordinarily wide range of investors—large as well as small, institutional as well as individual. Table 5 shows the broad range of mutual fund ownership at year-end 1987. The profile of mutual fund shareholders is hardly a static one. For example, in recent years the mutual fund industry has attracted growing investments from institutional investors formerly not considered to be prime prospects for mutual fund investment, as shown in Table 6.

The recent increases in institutional use of mutual funds are impressive. Although mutual funds are used in many ways by institutional investors, two uses predominate. First, money market funds have become a very important institutional cash management tool, especially for bank trust departments and corporations. Second, mutual funds have captured an increasing share of defined contribution plan assets, such as 401(k)s; the combination of a diversity of fund choice, daily valuation, participant communications, and record-keeping services have made mutual funds a popular choice for corporations of all sizes. By contrast, mutual funds have made less headway in the field of pension investments. Despite the fine long-term performance record of many mutual funds, pension plan assets in mutual funds at the end of 1987 amounted to only about 2 percent of the total $1.6 trillion pension fund assets.

IMPORTANT FACTORS IN BUYING AND SELLING

Purchasing Shares

Fund shares may be purchased from a stockbroker, insurance agent, fund salesperson, or directly from the fund. In each case, the purchase price is directly related to the fund's current net asset value per share (the market value of its assets, less liabilities, divided by the number of shares outstanding). However, there may or may not be a sales charge associated with the purchase. Funds sold through commissioned brokers and insurance agents typically assess front-end sales charges of up of 8.5 percent, although increasingly the trend has been to lower or eliminate the unsightly front-end fee and instead recapture the commission through 12(b)1 fees and contingent deferred sales charges (back-end loads). Fund shares bought directly from the fund are usually sold without sales commissions (i.e., no load), but some may charge sales commissions of 2 to 3 percent (low load). Whether purchased from brokers, insurance agents, or directly from the fund, money market fund purchases should involve no sales commissions, although 12(b)1 fees are often incurred.

Redeeming Shares

Just as the baseball manager is described as hired to be fired, so a mutual fund share is bought to be sold, sooner or later, as the investor's objectives are reached. For example,

TABLE 5. Types of Mutual Fund Shareholders

	No. of Accounts (Thousands)	Value of Accounts (Billions)
INDIVIDUALS		
Regular	31,240	$425.5
Retirement	15,000	72.3
Total individual	46,240	487.7
INSTITUTIONAL		
Pension & profit-sharing plans	2,138	40.8
Trust accounts	4,196	156.3
Business corporations	442	30.3
Financial institutions	114	22.0
Self-employed retirement plans	15,853	10.1
Other institutional	663	22.7
Total institutional	8,406	282.2
TOTAL INDUSTRY	54,646	$770.0

Note: Data as of December 31, 1987.

Source: Investment Company Institute, *Mutual Fund Fact Book, 1988*

TABLE 6. Institutional Accounts

Year	Assets (Millions)	Total
1966	$3,984	11.4%
1970	6,174	13.0
1976	10,720	22.5
1980	17,665	29.3
1987	282,200	36.6

Source: Investment Company Institute, *Mutual Fund Fact Book*, 1988

the accumulation of fund shares for a child's college education must be sold in order to pay tuition bills and room and board. Fund shares are normally sold by tendering them back to the fund for redemption at the current net asset value. This liquidation is normally handled simply and expeditiously; the liquidity of mutual funds is one of their important advantages.

Of course, other reasons exist for fund redemptions. The need for cash (e.g., to build a house or purchase other investments) is one. Dissatisfaction with the fund's management policies or performance is another. Until recent years, two other reasons were significant: a change in the investor's investment objective (e.g., seeking retirement income after the accumulation phase), and an investor's preference for liquidity versus risk (e.g., redeeming a stock fund and putting the proceeds in a savings account, perhaps to lock in profits or to act on a perception that stocks are overpriced). However, the growth of families of funds with a broad range of objectives is gradually converting redemptions to exchanges, wherein the first shareholder in the examples above might switch from a growth fund to an income fund, and the second, from a stock fund to a money market fund. In neither case would there normally be any additional commission cost.

Mutual Fund Distributions

There are two common types of mutual fund distributions: income dividends and capital gains distributions. Both types of distribution may be taken in cash or reinvested in additional shares of the fund at no cost (although some funds charge an additional sales commission on these purchases).

Income Dividends. Income dividends represent the interest and/or dividends earned by the fund's portfolio less the fund's expenses. The level of such dividends depends on the types of securities held by the fund; dividends are typically high for bond funds, moderate for money market funds, and low for equity funds.

Capital Gains Distributions. Capital gains distributions arise during years in which the fund realizes profits in excess of losses on the sale of portfolio securities and may be either short-term or long-term, depending on the fund's holding period. Capital gains distributions are usually erratic and, for most investors, should be reinvested to keep 100 percent of principal at work.

Performance Measurement

Mutual fund performance should be measured on a total return basis, taking into account not only the change in asset value, but also all dividends and distributions as if they were reinvested in additional shares. Using a total return approach puts all types of investments on a common measurement standard, expressed as a compound annualized rate of return. Thus,

Initial purchase price	\$10,000
Sale price ten years later (including reinvested dividends)	\$25,000
Total gain	\$15,000
Compound annual rate of return	+ 9.6%

It requires only a moment's reflection to see the soundness of this concept of compound annual rate of return. Compare, for example, a bond fund paying dividends of 12 percent per year (assuming the principal value to be unchanged) with a growth fund paying 2 percent of the initial capital invested per year, but with its asset value growing at the annual rate of 10 percent over ten years (see Table 7).

Note that, on a compound interest basis (assuming dividends are reinvested), both investments have the same rate of return, namely 12 percent. However, the simple-

TABLE 7. Comparison of Bond and Equity Fund

	Bond Fund		Stock Fund	
	Simple Interest	Compound Interest	Simple Interest	Compound Interest
Initial investment	$10,000	$10,000	$10,000	$10,000
Final value (ten years later)	10,000	10,000	25,937	27,549
Dividends paid	12,000	21,059	2,000	3,510
Final value (including dividends)	22,000	31,059	27,937	31,059
Annualized rate of return	8.2%	12.0%	10.8%	12.0%

interest computations (assuming dividends are not reinvested) result in misleadingly lower annual returns, because they ignore the time value of the dividends paid during the holding period.

Selecting a Fund—Individuals

A number of considerations should enter into the selection of a mutual fund by an individual investor. Among the more important factors are the following:

Personal Objectives. As mutual funds usually seek specific investment objectives, a prerequisite for successful fund selection is that the investor's objectives be compatible with those of the fund chosen. Thus, an individual seeking current income without risk to principal will likely select a money market fund; a bond fund would be chosen by an individual seeking stable income; and a growth equity fund would likely be selected for the purpose of obtaining capital appreciation. However, a single fund will not necessarily fulfill all an investor's objectives. A retired investor with a lump sum to invest will likely want a combination of funds, perhaps including a stock fund for inflation hedging, a bond fund for durable income, and a money market fund for safety of principal. The relative balance among these three asset classes depends on such factors as financial objectives, other income, age, risk tolerance, and number of dependents.

Fund Size and Investment Policies. Normally, it is best to avoid very small and new funds and fund families unless the investor is satisfied with the resources available and the probity and skill of the fund's management. Huge size, on the other hand, may limit an equity fund's ability to differentiate itself from the stock market in general.

The fund's prospectus should be examined carefully to see what its objectives are and the policies through which it proposes to achieve them. Its policies should appear reasonable and sound. Also, it is wise to examine the fund's latest shareholder report to learn about the advisor's investment approach and to find out about the specific portfolio under consideration. What type of stock portfolio is being purchased—a collection of blue chips or stocks of small, emerging companies? What is the average quality of the bond fund—is the portfolio's high yield explained by an emphasis on lower-quality bonds? In other words, investors must know what they are buying.

FIGURE 2. Combined Effect of Loads and Expenses, Cumulative Investment Values

Note: The chart shows the ending value of a $10,000 investment in three mutual funds, each earning a 10 percent gross annual return over one-, five- and ten-year periods. The no-load, low-expense fund has no sales commission and a 0.50 percent expense ratio. The deferred load, 12(b)1, fund has no initial sales charge, but a contingent back-end sales charge of 5 percent on redemptions during the first year, 4 percent during the second year, 3 percent during the third year, 2 percent during the fourth year and 1 percent during the fifth year, and an expense ratio of 1.5 percent (of which 0.75 percent represents a 12(b)1 fee). The front-end load fund has an 8.5 percent sales charge and an expense ratio of 1.5 percent.

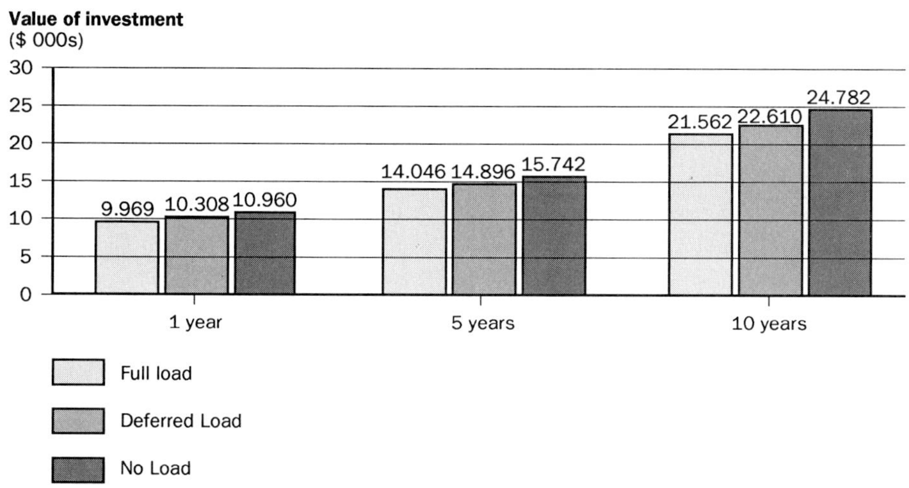

Costs. The investor should determine what it will cost to own the fund, including the initial sales charge (if any), the operating expenses (annual operating expenses as a percentage of average net assets are referred to as the expense ratio), and any back-end sales charges or redemption fees. Differential sales charges and operating expenses can make a big difference over time in the investor's accumulation of capital (see Figure 2). The effect of the sales charges is obvious. But even what may seem like small differences in annual expense ratios can add up over time. These differences are perhaps most obvious in money market funds, where lower expense ratio funds can and do have higher yields without any sacrifice in investment quality. In equity funds for which returns are more volatile, however, a lower expense ratio is equally beneficial, but this effect may be swamped by differences in performance.

Fund Performance Record. Although the fund's record of past investment returns is a very important factor in the fund selection process, it is listed last in this criteria for several reasons. First, the investor should consider personal goals, the fund's objectives and policies, the cost of investing, and the amount of risk he is willing to assume before getting down to the brass tacks of evaluating the performance of comparable funds. Second, there is no conclusive evidence that the past record of relative performance provides a reliable criterion for judging future performance. Third, investors often make their worst mistakes by "investing in a rear view mirror," namely, by focusing on what has happened in the recent past, for example, buying aggressive growth funds after they have achieved their best results and, often, just before they go into a decline.

Consider that the five top-performing equity mutual funds in the five-year period 1978 through 1982 provided an average total return of 43 percent compared to 14 percent for the S&P 500 Index. In the next five years, 1983 through 1987, these same funds provided an average return of 9 percent, compared to 16 percent for the index. Clearly then, selecting funds on their superior past records provides no guarantee of excellent results in the future.

Timing. Once the investor has selected a fund or group of funds, the next decision is when to invest. If the investor is going to invest regularly, the time to begin is now. Individuals investing a large lump sum, however, should not be in a hurry to invest, but should consider spreading the purchase over a year or more on a quarterly basis, perhaps by starting with the entire investment in a money market fund and periodically exchanging into an equity fund within the same family. Such a program of dollar averaging is an effective way to reduce the risk of investing.

What about using mutual funds for market-timing? Why not switch from money market funds to stock funds at market lows, and reverse the process at market highs? Why not emphasize aggressive funds in ebullient markets, and conservative funds in trading markets? Unfortunately, what sounds utopian on paper is essentially just that. Given the volatility and the efficiency of securities markets, it is extremely difficult for investors to add value to their portfolio in this manner. It is also very hard to avoid being influenced by the emotions and the sway of the crowd. For these reasons, investors may find it more rewarding to let their objectives and risk tolerances set their asset mixes among various types of funds, changing this mix not as markets fluctuate, but only as their objectives change. However, if an investor wishes to take a more active approach to rebalancing his portfolio, he may either utilize an asset allocation mutual fund as a portion of his portfolio or make allocation decisions himself to modestly alter the proportions in different asset classes.

Selecting a Fund—Institutions

Mutual funds serve a variety of needs for institutions, some of the most important of which are:

Cash Management. Money market mutual funds can be an ideal temporary investment for institutional cash managers. By pooling investors' assets, money funds are available to provide a level of diversification, liquidity, and, often, yield that many institutions cannot achieve on their own. Money market funds with low expense ratios (there is little justification for paying more than 0.5 percent) and services (such as wiring and check-writing privileges) tailored to an institution's needs can be a much more efficient means of maintaining temporary investments than directly purchasing money market instruments.

Defined Contribution Plans. The recent trend in employee benefits away from emphasizing defined benefit plans and in favor of defined contribution plans has been accompanied by a shift toward giving employees more control over their defined contribution investments. Accordingly, plans today offer participants more investment choices and the flexibility to make periodic changes in their investment choices. Not surprisingly, then, more and more defined contribution plans have been turning to mutual fund companies to fulfill these needs. A number of mutual fund companies have developed a full range of fiduciary and record-keeping services designed for defined contribution plans, such as 401(k)s, profit-sharing plans, and 403(b) plans (for non-profit institutions). In selecting among fund families, sponsors usually seek out a fund family offering good and consistent long-term investment performance, excellent administrative services, and reasonable costs.

Pension Plans. Defined benefit pension plans also use mutual funds. Funds can be an extremely effective way for smaller plans (those up to $25 million or even somewhat larger) to build a complete investment program. Many larger plans use mutual funds to incorporate a specialty style of investment management into their mix of investments or to gain access to a fund manager with particular skills. In selecting among mutual funds, pension sponsors should use basically the same criteria employed when selecting separate account managers.

CLOSED-END FUNDS

Closed-end investment companies, like mutual funds, have enjoyed dramatic growth in recent years. As recently as 1984, closed-end funds seemed to be a moribund second cousin to mutual funds; in that year, assets of only $6.5 billion were held by just fifty funds. Since 1985, closed-end funds have made a substantial comeback. By mid-1988, there were 133 funds with $34.3 billion in assets. This growth has been matched by a proliferation of types of closed-end funds that makes the closed-end universe an interesting and diverse mosaic.

BASIC CHARACTERISTICS

A Comparison With Mutual Funds

Closed-end funds, like mutual funds, serve the primary function of pooling shareholders' monies for investment purposes. As such, they offer many of the same benefits: diversification, professional management, stated investment objectives, and cost-efficiency.

The basic difference between open- and closed-end funds is in the form of capital structure. Closed-end funds generally raise money from shareholders only once, in underwritings sponsored by brokerage firms. They are typically structured with an infinite life, although closed-end funds may liquidate or become open-end on a specified date in the future. Unlike mutual funds, closed-end funds do not stand ready to redeem their shares at net asset value. Instead, shareholders wishing to sell their shares must do so by trading them on a national exchange or in the over-the-counter market, at a price determined by the market. The market price may be higher or lower than the fund's net asset value (at a premium or discount, in the jargon of the industry).

Thus, mutual funds and closed-end funds differ in terms of liquidity. Although the stock exchange where the closed-end funds may be liquid enough to assure that shares can be traded, the market mechanism does not assure that investors receive a sales price equal to or even approximating the fund's underlying net asset value per share. Discounts, and indeed premiums, from net asset value may be wide and add an extra degree of uncertainty to the investment equation.

TABLE 8. Closed-End Funds

	No. of Funds	Net Assets ($ Billions)
Bond funds	70	$22.1
Diversified equity funds	17	5.5
Specialized equity funds*	41	5.6
Dual-purpose funds	5	1.1
	133	$34.3

*Includes convertible funds.

Source: Lipper Analytical Securities, Inc.

Types of Closed-End Funds

There is now a wide diversity of closed-end funds, as shown in Table 8. The funds may be categorized into the following broad groups:

Stock Funds. Diversified stock funds, the first type of closed-end fund to be developed, today represent a minority of the industry. There are just a few broadly diversified U.S. equity funds, among them Tri-Continental Corporation and Adams Express Company. Additionally, there are a number that focus on a particular equity management style, such as growth stocks or small company stocks.

International and Single-Country Funds. After the U.S. dollar peaked in early 1985, a rash of funds emphasizing foreign stock markets were developed. Some of these were global (including U.S. stocks), and some were diversified across a variety of foreign markets only. But the largest group represented funds that invested in only one foreign market. Today, single-country funds exist that invest in Australia, Brazil, Canada, France, Germany, India, Italy, Korea, Malaysia, Mexico, Spain, Switzerland, Taiwan, Thailand, and the United Kingdom.

Bond Funds. Most important in terms of dollars raised in recent years have been the closed-end bond funds. In the first six months of 1988 alone, more than $13.8 billion was invested in this type. These funds emphasize high income, whether obtained simply by purchasing bonds or by using strategies to enhance income as options programs or the use of leverage. An array of taxable bond and municipal bond funds has been created.

Specialty Funds. A number of funds specialize in equities of particular industries, emphasizing, for example, precious metals mining companies, utilities, financial institutions, or energy and resources companies. In addition, several funds invest principally in convertible securities.

Dual-Purpose Funds. One unusual type of closed-end fund is the dual-purpose fund. Its name derives from the fact that there are two classes of shares: income shares and capital shares. At the underwriting, each class of shareholders puts up capital—usually, but not always, 50 percent each. The income shares are essentially a preferred stock in the closed end fund and are entitled to all net investment income earned by the fund. By contrast, the capital shares represent common stock entitled to all capital appreciation earned by the fund. The two classes of shares appeal to differing investor groups, one seeking a high, steady, and possibly growing level of income, and the other favoring a leveraged investment in pursuit of capital gains over the long term.

ATTRACTIVE FEATURES

Proponents of closed-end funds offer two justifications for accepting the closed-end fund's added element of risk, resulting from discounts and premiums, as compared with that of open-end funds. The first is that the closed-end manager, free of the need to worry about mutual fund shareholder cash flows, can invest with a longer-term horizon and incur less portfolio turnover (and lower portfolio transactions costs). Arguably, too, the closed-end fund manager may maintain a fully invested portfolio, while a mutual fund manager usually maintains a small buffer of cash reserves to handle shareholder redemptions. These arguments make most sense for funds investing in illiquid securities, such as stocks of companies in foreign countries where securities markets are not yet well developed.

A second argument for investing in closed-end funds refers to buying shares in the secondary market, at some point after the initial underwriting. It may be to an investor's advantage to buy closed-end funds at a discount, because by doing so he acquires assets at less than their true value, while purchasing them in an initial offering involves paying a premium (i.e., the initial sales commission). At some point in the future, the investor may be able to sell the shares at their net asset value or at least a smaller discount and conceivably even at a premium, thus making a gain in excess of that realized by the fund itself. However, in doing so the investor takes the risk that the discount will widen and the return will be reduced. In addition, the effective dividend yield on the investment may be higher than it would be otherwise. For example, a mutual fund bought at a net asset value of $10 per share with a fifty cent annual dividend per share provides a dividend yield of 5 percent. If the same portfolio could be purchased at $9, or at a discount of 10 percent, the yield would now be fifty cents on a $9 investment, or 5.56 percent.

Potential Risks

The chief disadvantages of closed-end funds relate to their lack of liquidity. They can only be sold through a broker in a national market, resulting in brokerage commissions and the uncertainty of how the price will relate to the fund's net asset value per share. In addition, shareholders purchasing closed-end fund shares in the initial public offering of the fund usually incur substantial sales charges, typically 5 to 7 percent of the amount invested. Meanwhile, advisory and operating expenses of closed-end funds can be quite high, as illustrated in Table 9, often reflecting the smaller size of the closed-end funds. A further disadvantage relative to mutual funds relates to the issues of convenience and service. Closed-end funds do not offer many of the services provided by mutual funds, such as the exchange service, simplified additional purchase plans, and redemption plans; although some offer dividend reinvestment plans, most do not.

The closed-end fund investor assumes an element of risk in addition to the portfolio risk taken by participating in a managed investment pool, that is, the market risk associated

TABLE 9. Closed-End Fund Expense Ratios

	Lowest 10%	Highest 10%	All
Total closed-end funds	0.42%	2.32%	1.16%
Closed-end bond funds	0.67	1.82	1.01
Closed-end equity funds	0.33	2.45	1.32

Note: Data excludes ratios less than or equal to 0.10 percent and greater than or equal to 3.00 percent. The expense ratio represents total annual expenses of the fund divided by average net assets.

Source: Lipper Analytical Services, Inc.

with varying discounts and premiums. Therefore, investors considering closed-end funds, whether in an initial underwriting or in a secondary market purchase, should understand this risk.

Investors considering purchasing shares in a new closed-end fund should recognize that, in most cases, they would be purchasing shares at a substantial premium to their net asset value. In a typical offering, shares priced at $10 typically will have a net asset value of just $9.30. This difference of $0.70 goes to pay the underwriter as sales compensation, which is a 7 percent load on the amount invested, or 7.5 percent on net asset value. Equivalently, an investor can think of paying a 7.5 percent premium for the shares.

After the underwriting is completed, closed-end fund shares begin trading at values determined by the marketplace (although the underwriters may try to support the price temporarily). If the fund were immediately liquidated, proceeds would approximate net asset value. But assuming there are no plans for liquidation, the shares will trade at a price at which investors are willing to exchange them. Usually this price is tied to net asset value but may vary dramatically above or below net asset value—usually the latter for stock funds—with smaller variations for bond funds, given the price support provided by their higher dividend yields.

Although there are prolonged periods in which closed-end funds, either particular funds or a category of funds, may trade at a premium, more often closed-end funds are traded at a discount to their net asset value. One reason for the discount is the lack of sponsorship. After the initial underwriting, brokers have little self-interest in promoting the purchase of closed-end fund shares; higher fees can be garnered by selling a new fund or an open-end fund. And the management company advising the closed-end fund has little incentive to promote the fund; a promotional campaign will not result in additional assets under management. A second reason is that the discount is necessary compensation to the secondary market buyer for the lack of liquidity and for the risk that the discount will actually widen after the time of his purchase.

Arguably, a fund purchased at a steep discount to net asset value entails a reduced level of risk as compared to an identical open-end fund purchased at net asset value. By contrast, a fund bought at a sizable premium incurs substantially increased risk. For example, the investor buying at a premium takes the risk that the fund's assets will decline in value, as well as the risk that the premium will decline.

TAX CONSEQUENCES

Generally, investors of a closed-end fund think of the investment as shares of common stock of a corporation and report dividends and capital gains or losses realized on sale in the same manner as for other stock holdings. Similar to open-end mutual funds, closed-end funds may pass through all dividends and realized capital gains to investors without paying tax at the fund level. However, some closed-end funds elect to pay out all dividends but not to distribute realized gains to shareholders; instead, in order to keep capital at work in the fund, the fund pays taxes on the realized capital gains. Shareholders, in such circumstances, should report the gains realized by the fund and also claim a credit on their tax return for the taxes paid by the fund; the cost basis of their shareholdings should also be increased by the amount of the undistributed long-term capital gains (less the amount of capital gains tax paid by the fund).

REPRESENTATIVE TYPES OF INVESTORS

Typically, closed-end fund shares are sold by brokers in a public offering to individual investors. Institutional investors may also buy closed-end fund shares; many do so through the secondary market as they are reluctant to pay the sales charges associated with initial public offerings.

IMPORTANT FACTORS IN BUYING AND SELLING

Investors considering closed-end funds should evaluate the factors discussed in the section on selection of open-end funds: objectives, investment policies, costs, performance record. Given the unique risks associated with varying premiums and discounts, investors should also pay close attention to the market price relative to net asset value.

In doing so, smart investors will wish to ask especially hard questions before buying a fund selling at a substantial, or indeed any, premium. Perhaps a premium is justified as a unique means of investing in a particular category of assets (e.g., a fund that represents the only available means for investing in a foreign equity market) or with an investment manager of particular skill. Or perhaps the premium is justified in terms of an unusually high level of dividend income, as is sometimes the case with the income shares of dual-purpose funds. But, as the premium may at some point decline or even be replaced by a discount, the investor should be especially reluctant to invest on a belief that the premium will increase.

Purchasing closed-end funds at a substantial discount can be much more attractive. Investors should rarely, however, invest in a fund simply because it is trading at a large discount. The investor, as distinct from the speculator, should invest only if the investment objectives of the fund coincide with his own.

When deciding to buy, the investor may find it helpful to analyze trends in the general level of discounts and premiums on closed-end funds and trends in particular funds of interest. Discounts and premiums narrow and widen based on market forces and are more or less attractive at some times than at others. Figure 3 shows the varying trends in discounts and premiums of closed-end funds over the past several years.

Another factor to consider when purchasing funds at a discount is the possibility of the future elimination of the discount through reorganization of the fund. Occasionally, a

FIGURE 3. Closed-End Funds, Showing Average Premiums and Discounts

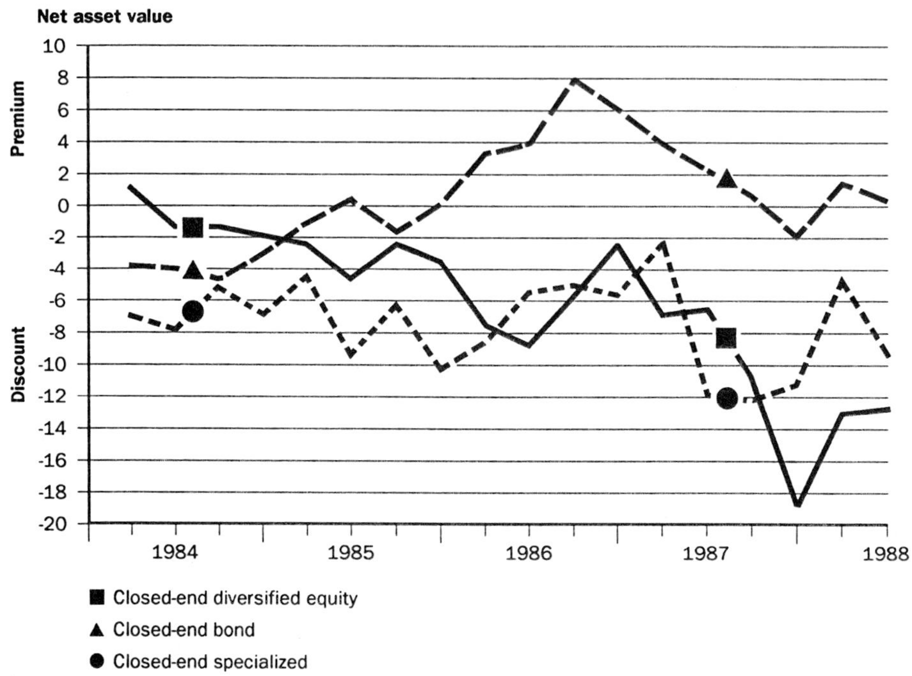

shareholder group will campaign to reorganize the fund, typically to convert it to an open-end company, in order to eliminate the discount. Generally, such reorganizations are not viewed favorably by the fund's management and so the funds often employ a host of antitakeover defenses. Investors selecting closed-end funds at a discount with the thought of benefiting from a possible reorganization may then wish to understand what antitakeover provisions a fund has in place.

Like a mutual fund, a closed-end fund is originally offered with a prospectus. However, it may be more difficult to obtain information about a fund after its initial underwriting is completed and it is trading in the secondary market. Investors should contact the closed-end fund for a copy of the latest shareholder report. Additional information may be gathered from brokers with research staffs following the funds or from stock guides, such as those issued by the S&P Corporation. Information on daily prices is contained in the stock price listings of most major newspapers, and a comparison of market price versus net asset value is published once weekly in certain newspapers, including *Barron's*, the *Wall Street Journal*, and *The New York Times*.

GLOSSARY

capital gains distribution—A distribution representing a fund's net realized capital gains, either short- or long-term. The shareholder is taxed for capital gains distributions based on the fund's holding period, not the shareholder's.

closed-end fund—An investment company characterized by having a fixed number of shares outstanding. Unlike a mutual fund, the closed-end fund does not redeem or buy back its shares at net asset value; rather, shares are bought and sold at market-determined prices.

diversified investment company—An investment company that meets certain standards of diversification under the Investment Company Act of 1940, primarily that in regard to 75 percent of its assets, it has not invested more than 5 percent of its total assets in any one company and owns no more than 10 percent of the voting securities of any single company.

dividend—A distribution of the fund's net investment income (i.e., income net of expenses). Dividends may be paid daily, monthly, quarterly, semiannually, or annually, depending primarily on the role of income in the fund's investment objectives.

dollar averaging—Purchasing mutual fund shares regularly in constant dollar amounts. It results in an average cost per share lower than the average price at which purchases are made, because fewer shares are purchased when prices are high and more are purchased when prices are low.

exchange privilege—An option offered by most mutual fund complexes allowing the sale of shares in one fund and the use of the proceeds for purchase of shares in another fund within the same fund family, usually for a nominal charge.

expense ratio—Total annual expenses of the fund divided by average net assets.

hedge fund—A specialized and speculative mutual fund seeking maximum capital appreciation. Such a fund may generally borrow money to purchase stocks and may also sell securities short in pursuit of its objectives.

individual retirement account (IRA)—A retirement plan originally for individuals who were neither self-employed nor covered by a qualified pension plan, offering special benefits (tax-deferred status and deductibility of contribution). Under the Economic Recovery Tax Act of 1981, IRAs were made available to any individual with earned income, beginning January 1, 1982. However, beginning in 1987, only individuals in certain income brackets may make tax-deductible contributions. An individual may rollover the assets tax-free into an IRA on ending participation in a qualified pension plan. An individual qualified to establish an IRA may use a mutual fund as the chosen investment vehicle.

investment advisor—The organization employed by a mutual fund to invest the fund's assets. Usually the investment advisor also sponsors the fund, distributes its shares, and provides many of the necessary administrative services.

Keogh account—Offers self-employed individuals and their employees benefits similar to those of an IRA.

mutual fund—An open-end investment company, which is distinguished from a closed-end investment company by the fact that shares may be redeemed at net asset value, rather than at a market-determined value, as is the case with closed-end funds.

net asset value per share—The per-share value of the assets—(securities, cash, and accrued earnings) in an investment company's portfolio, net of such liabilities as accrued expenses, represents the share price at which shares of open-end companies are redeemed.

non-diversified investment company—An investment company with fewer investment restrictions than a diversified investment company, permitting, for example, investments in a single industry or in a group of related industries.

transfer agent—The organization that maintains shareholder records and processes shareholder transactions. The fund's transfer agent may be a bank or part of the mutual fund organization itself.

unit investment trust—A type of investment company that holds a fixed portfolio of securities (most commonly consisting of long-term municipal bonds) usually sold through brokerage houses with a sales commission.

MAJOR MUTUAL FUND COMPANIES

Fidelity, 133 funds, $73,678 in assets

Merrill Lynch, 39 funds, $67,816 in assets

Federated, 45 funds, $38,949 in assets

Dreyfus, 75 funds, $35,593 in assets

Dean Witter, 23 funds, $34,561 in assets

Franklin, 49 funds, $33,542 in assets

Kemper, 29 funds, $32,853 in assets

The Vanguard Group, 52 funds, $31,181 in assets

Putnam, 40 funds, $31,055 in assets

Prudential-Bache, 45 funds, $22,943 in assets

SUGGESTED READING

PERIODICALS

Annuity & Closed-End Survey. Published by Lipper Analytical Distributors, New York, N.Y. Monthly.

Management Results. Published by Wiesenberger Investment Companies Services, New York, N.Y. Quarterly.

Mutual Fund Performance Analysis. Published by Lipper Analytical Distributors, New York, N.Y. Weekly.

Portfolio Analysis Report on Fixed Income Funds. Published by Lipper Analytical Distributors, New York, N.Y. Quarterly.

Risk-Adjusted Mutual Fund Performance Review. Published by Computer Directions Advisors, Silver Springs, Md. Monthly.

REFERENCE BOOKS

American Association of Institutional Investors. *The Individual Investor's Guide to No-Load Mutual Funds*. Chicago, 1988.

Herzfeld, Thomas J. *The Investors Guide to Closed-End Funds*. New York: McGraw-Hill, 1988.

Ibbotson Associates, Inc. *Stocks, Bonds, Bills and Inflation 1988 Yearbook*. Chicago, 1988.

Investment Company Institute. *Mutual Fund Fact Book*. Washington, D.C., various years.

Wiesenberger Investment Companies Services. *Investment Companies*. New York, various years.

OIL AND GAS

Fred Williams
Richard Mark

BASIC CHARACTERISTICS

Petroleum is the world's most valuable commodity. As such, investors of all types have been seeking opportunities in the oil patch for decades and will continue to do so because the world economy will remain tied to oil for much of the next century.

The enthusiasm for oil has been spurred in part by the eighteen-fold jump in the price of crude oil from around $2 per barrel in 1973 to a post-Arab embargo price of about $35 per barrel in 1981. As of 1989, oil prices have settled back to the $18 to $20 range, but energy economists continue to look to the depleting nature of petroleum and forecast increasing prices over the next several decades.

Investor interest has followed the cyclical nature of oil prices and exploration activity. Public involvement in oil and gas programs has remained high, hitting a record high of $2.9 billion in 1983 and dropping to a ten-year low of $594 million in 1988.[1]

Investors should recognize that investments in oil and gas exploration made today often will not be selling the major share of their production at today's market prices, but in future years when higher prices may be expected. This is why major oil industry exploration and development expenditure budgets have remained at relatively high levels. Total

---

[1] Robert A. Stanger & Co., Shrewsbury, N.J.

Fred Williams is a Staff Reporter for Pensions and Investment Age, The Newspaper of Corporate and Institutional Investing, *Dallas, Texas. Richard Mark is Associate Professor of Accounting at the University of Texas at Arlington.*

company capital and exploration expenditures for twenty-one of the industry's major companies totaled $51.8 billion in 1987.[2]

Energy Stocks

The simplest way to participate in the oil and gas industry is through the purchase of energy stocks, which make up about 18 percent of the Standard & Poor's 500 Composite Stock Index. The major advantage of this investment strategy is its liquidity. Energy stocks are easily traded in exchanges throughout the country. Any amount can be purchased, and the timing of both purchases and sales is at the discretion of the investor. The risks involved are not much different from those of any other stock. Unfortunately, energy stocks do not directly reflect the jump in oil and gas prices and are subject to the pricing vagaries of the stock market as a whole. Consequently, they do not rate high as long-term hedges against inflation.

Oil and Gas Programs

A more direct participation can be accomplished through what is known as oil and gas programs or drilling funds. These are not the same as mutual funds, although the two share some common characteristics. Both are investment pools run by professional managers. In both there is a pass-through of profits and losses to investors, and both are diversified in their holdings. Mutual funds, however, buy and sell the securities of businesses over which they have little control and provide a certain liquidity for their members.

The purpose of oil and gas programs, on the other hand, is to explore or drill for oil, or purchase producing oil wells. This is not a passive investment but a principal interest in a closed-end business. These programs are normally joint ventures or limited partnerships offered for a given number of months and then closed off from further trade. Therefore, each program is a distinct operating business. Their size can vary from $1 million up to $300 million, and minimal investments for individuals are usually $5,000 to $10,000.

The public offerings of oil and gas programs are regulated by the Securities and Exchange Commission (SEC) as well as by the individual states in which the offerings are sold. Private placements involve much larger amounts of money, are unregulated by the SEC, and are normally purchased by wealthy individuals, insurance companies, and institutional investors, such as pension funds.

Institutional investors have become a major source of capital for the oil and gas industry. Although precise figures are not available, it is not difficult to show that such institutions as insurance companies, public and private pension funds, endowments, and foundations may have surpassed individual investors as a major funding source for the energy industry. Compared with public oil and gas programs at the $594 million level in 1988, a group of pension funds and endowments committed $325 million to two direct private placement deals in 1987 and 1988.[3] This figure does not include the ongoing commitments being made by major insurance companies to direct oil and gas deals. Since 1985, CIGNA has nearly doubled its energy portfolio from $800 million to about $1.3 billion in 1989.[4]

---

[2] Arthur Andersen, *World Oil Trends*, Cambridge, Mass.: Cambridge Energy Research Associates, 1988–1989.

[3] *Pensions and Investment Age*, May 20, 1987, and Aug. 22, 1988.

[4] *Oil and Gas Investor*, May 1989.

As members of a limited partnership, each participant in the program receives a pro rata share of the profits, losses, and assets of the enterprise. Unlike a corporation, a partnership pays no income tax of its own. If the undertaking is successful and substantial oil reserves are discovered, developed, or acquired, the investors should benefit substantially and are taxed accordingly.

Increasingly, investors in oil and gas limited partnerships are looking for superior cash flow from the investment rather than tax shelter aspects. The major tax shelter benefits in these limited partnerships were removed in the Tax Reform Act of 1986. Any tax benefits arising out of passive activity associated with involvement in a limited partnership are limited to offsetting income from other passive activities but not to shelter income from wages or income from a trade or business or investment portfolio income, as was the case prior to 1986. (See *Tax Consequences*, later in this article.)

Organizers of Oil and Gas Programs. Oil and gas programs are put together and offered to investors either by independent oil companies or by oil investment managers.

Oil Companies. The oil companies have their own staffs of supervisory engineers, geologists, and technicians, although they may hire outside contractors to do the actual drilling. Some people feel that oil company management provides a higher level of industry expertise, better supervision over wells, and reduced overhead and fees. If the company has been successful in its drilling of wells, it can also show investors an impressive track record of past experience. However, if the company has only had experience in one geographic location, and little exposure to other prospects, its chances for success may be limited.

Oil Investment Managers. Oil investment managers normally do not maintain their own geologists, landsmen, or engineers. Rather, they acquire prospects and enter partnerships with operators of various geographical areas and rely on the operators' technical staffs. Some investors feel that oil investment managers, who choose prospects from a broad range of geographical areas, can provide greater diversification and improved chances of success. The ability to enter into contracts with local exploration offices also provides oil investment managers with a flexibility that may not be available to oil companies with their own staffs. Oil investment managers are also less likely to run into conflicts of interest since they are merely managers of funds and do not directly participate in the oil business as oil companies do.

Types of Programs. Both management approaches play major roles in oil and gas investing and both can offer the five types of oil programs available today. They are exploratory, development, balanced, income-producing, and royalty programs.

Exploratory Programs. An exploratory program is one whose goal is to discover new petroleum reserves. Exploration normally takes place in untested areas not part of known commercial reservoirs or deposits. Consequently, the success rate for exploratory drilling is not high. One or two prospects may result from ten drillings. And only one in forty may be an economic success. Obviously, then, the more test wells the program puts into the ground, the higher the chances of success.

Since an exploratory or wildcat well must be developed after discovery, additional capital and time are necessary before any cash flow is seen. This is not an investment for someone interested in an immediate return on capital. A purely exploratory program is a high risk/high reward venture. Consequently, it is recommended for only the upper-bracket taxpayer who is comfortable with risk. An investor in a 33 percent tax bracket, for example, could save $3,300 on a $10,000 oil and gas program. An investor in the 15 percent bracket would only save $1,500. If the program were a complete loss, the higher bracket investor would lose only $6,700 while the fellow investor in the 15 percent bracket would lose $8,500.

Development Programs. These programs set up wells near existing oil reserves in areas where production is already under way. Naturally, the chances of success in development programs are higher than they are in exploratory ones. On average, about 70 percent of developed programs end up with productive wells. Since the drilling takes place in a proven area, these programs must pay higher prices for their leases and usually drill on a smaller prospect or block of acreage than exploratory programs will. Since the chances of finding oil are greater with these programs than with exploratory programs, investors can expect a quicker return on their investment. They will probably hit a greater percentage of productive wells, and the wells will be located in developed areas where pipelines for transporting the oil are in place, thus reducing the costs and perhaps eliminating the need for additional money from investors.

In short, development programs have a higher success ratio but their return on capital is often proportionately less than exploratory programs. Consequently, they are good investments for people who want less risk than wildcat drilling involves. Investors in development programs can usually get an earlier and more favorable cash surrender on their interest than owners of exploratory programs, whose involvement is longer term.

Balanced Programs. These investments include both exploratory and development wells in similar proportions in one program. They try to combine the advantages of higher yields produced by successful exploratory wells with the early cash flow and lower risk of development wells. It should be kept in mind, however, that few programs can be classified either all exploratory or all development. Even programs that title themselves as development might follow a drilling policy in which 80 percent of their capital goes into development prospects and the balance goes toward drilling exploratory wells.

The difference between one kind of program and the next is a matter of degree. Each oil and gas program will set out in its prospectus, under the title "Proposed Activities," exactly what its drilling policy is and the mix of wells it expects to drill.

Income Programs. These investments are unlike either exploratory or development programs in that they purchase producing properties rather than develop drilling sites themselves. The risks inherent in income programs are considerably less than in the other kinds of oil and gas investments. The benefits include participation in established production capabilities with little reserve risk. An additional upside is the potential to participate in higher oil prices. The principal advantage of these programs is their income stream over the life of the oil well, which is normally ten to fifteen years, or the gas well, which may last fifteen years or more. As the oil or gas is removed from the well, the income to investors decreases until the well is abandoned as nonproductive. Because these programs produce income with less risk, they appeal to a broader market of investors and not just to higher-income investors.

The bulk of the capital raised in public oil and gas partnerships from 1982 through 1988 was for income-producing programs.[5] During this period $6.7 billion was raised in income-producing programs while only $3.3 billion was raised in drilling deals.

Royalty Programs. The first royalty fund designed to invest in landowner royalties was introduced in 1979. The popularity of royalty programs has resulted in rapid growth in this type of investment. Royalty funds are attractive to both the institutional and the individual investor. Some royalty funds can be assembled to offer wide diversification and lower risks than drilling funds with potential returns that equal or exceed the more aggressive programs.

A royalty interest is a percentage of future production retained by the landowner when his land is leased for oil and gas production. The royalty interest bears no part of the cost, risk, or expense of drilling or producing the wells. It is a gross interest in oil and gas revenues.

Master Limited Partnership. The master limited partnership is also a relatively new way to participate in the drilling and production of oil and natural gas wells. It is not a direct participation in the business, but is closer to an equity deal. Many master limited partnership units are publicly traded on major exchanges. In a master limited partnership, specific properties or producing wells are packaged into a partnership unit and spun off as a single entity. Stock or limited partnership units are exchanged for direct interests in the property. The units provide a stream of income and offer greater liquidity and diversification than traditional partnership units. Proceeds from the sale of the tradable units are normally subject to capital gains taxation and recapture.

ATTRACTIVE FEATURES

Oil and gas programs offer a number of attractive characteristics to both the taxable and tax-exempt investor. For the taxable investor, the benefit may be divided between the potential large return on investment a successful well or wells can generate together with some immediate tax benefit through the partnership's special allocation of certain deductions to the investor. This latter feature enhances the investor's return by lowering the after-tax risk.

A large institutional investor can also benefit from oil and gas investments. The attraction may center on the potential cash flow, the relatively small amount of money required for a minimum investment (generally $2,500 to $10,000), or the fact that the investment represents a diversification in the institution's portfolio.

Tax-exempt entities may typically view an oil and gas investment as a less conservative but reasonable means to generate a future income flow. This future regular income flow benefits the tax-exempt investor in the valuation of his portfolio as well as insuring cash when other illiquid investments in the portfolio may not be generating the cash necessary to fund its programs.

[5] Robert A. Stanger & Co., Shrewsbury, N.J.

Overview of Typical Investment Arrangements

Investments Through a Program. Typically, investors in any of the types of programs described earlier will receive a limited partnership interest expressed in terms of unit or interest. The unit or interest represents the investor's percentage share of total contributions to the partnership by all investors. In many circumstances, the general partner makes little or no contribution to the partnership.

Many investors expect that their partnership interest will reflect the amount of each item of income, gain, loss or deduction generated by the partnership. Instead, however, the tax rules allow the partnership to specially allocate certain beneficial deductions, such as intangible development costs (IDC) or depletion, to the investors to reflect the fact that it was the investor's money that allowed the partnership to generate the deduction.

In an exploratory partnership, the partnership will incur both geological and geophysical (discussed below) as well as development costs (including IDC) if the prospect proves to have potential reserves. Although both types of costs are incurred, the investor normally will be allocated only the IDC.

In either case, an investor who contributes $10,000 may be allocated $10,000 of IDC in the first year of the partnership's operation. This $10,000 deduction, at regular tax rates, could result in a $2,800 tax savings. However, this calculation presumes that the investor's deductions are not limited in any way by passive losses, at-risk rules, or his basis in the partnership.

Similarly, if the oil and gas venture were a complete loss, the investor would be able to take the investment as a loss, which would generate as much as $2,800 in tax savings. Consequently, the investor would end up losing $7,200 in actual investment net of tax benefit. This analysis does not consider the potential offset that such a loss might have against the investors' other taxable gains or income for the same period, nor does it consider the character of the loss as capital or ordinary.

The substantial changes to the federal tax rules brought about through the numerous acts of Congress passed between 1984 and present have placed greater emphasis on the economic rather than tax consequences of an oil and gas investment. This is particularly true because the federal tax rules have been strengthened to limit or deny deductions to both passive participants in ventures and participants in ventures that attempted to generate tax deductions through nonrecourse borrowing (the at-risk rules).

Direct Investment in an Oil or Gas Well. An investor may be offered the opportunity to share directly in the costs of drilling and developing a well. In this case, the owner of the working interest in a well will not have the funds to complete the development. To acquire the funds, the working-interest owner will approach a number of investors and offer each a fractional interest in the working interest from the well in exchange for a cash contribution. The investors' cash contributions will then be used to fund the development drilling. The amount of cash contributed is not equal to the working-interest share obtained. One frequently used phrase to describe the arrangement is a "third for a quarter."

What the phrase means is that each investor is being asked to contribute, say, one third (33⅓ percent) of the cash necessary to fund the drilling and development but will only receive one quarter (25 percent) of the working interest in the well. In this instance, all costs will have been covered by the three investors, yet those same three investors will only share in 75 percent of the working interest. The remaining 25 percent of the working interest stays with the original owner.

POTENTIAL RISKS

Oil and gas exploration investments are highly speculative and involve a large number of risks that investors should consider before investing. These are not just limited to drilling risks, but could include problems relating to liquidity and assessment calls as well as management, regulatory, and legal considerations.

Oil and Gas Drilling Risks

The most publicized risks among oil and gas programs are those associated with dry holes and low-production wells. This can mean a substantial investment loss—up to 100 percent, in fact—in a drilling program.

The prospectuses for all types of direct-investment partnership programs—exploration and development and production purchases—have detailed explanations concerning associated risks to investors. Most say essentially the same things. The specific wording may vary but generally the prospectus in a drilling program will warn that completion of a well does not assure investors that the well will produce any oil or gas for commercial sale or that it will produce for any meaningful period of time. The prospectus usually specifically warns that investors have no assurance that they will recover any part of their investment.

Further risks in drilling include unusual or unexpected formations, pressures, downhole fires, blowouts, or other conditions that, although infrequent, may either delay or prevent completion of a well. Most operators further warn that these conditions may result in substantial losses and possible liability to third parties. These risks may not be covered by insurance, because it is either unavailable or considered impractical owing to high premium costs. If these costs are incurred in most partnerships, the funds available for exploration and development are reduced accordingly.

Income Program Risks

Income programs have few of these risks. They do, however, have some risks associated with oil and gas production. Producing oil and gas properties are purchased for the programs on the basis of geologic and engineering data. In addition, the operators make certain assumptions when they purchase properties regarding the future price of the oil and gas and the future development and production costs of the well. To the extent that these estimates and assumptions are incorrect, returns will be lower.

The 1987 prospectus for Swift Energy Income Partners III program provides a representative example of how risks are specified. It states:

> Generally the managing general partner would prefer to acquire properties for the partnerships which are in the early stages of their development, in an attempt to acquire properties with oil and gas reserve potential in relation to the price of acquisition. Properties of this nature usually have a limited production history and in many instances will require further developmental activity. Consequently, the acquisition of such properties is more speculative than the acquisition of other producing properties with longer production histories and less required development, and involves a higher risk of loss. There is no assurance that properties can be acquired which possess any of the characteristics discussed, or which would permit the partnerships to earn any predictable return on their investment, or permit the recovery of limited partners' capital contributions.

Royalty Program Risks

In royalty programs, the partnership does not bear any costs associated with drilling or production, but an investment in a royalty will be affected if the drilling does not result in a commercial oil or gas reserve. The royalty may also be affected if natural hazards (such as blowouts) occur, to the extent that oil and gas reserves are diminished and income is delayed.

Return Risk

The riskier oil and gas programs—the exploratory and development programs—have widely varying success rates. Some will produce returns many times the original investment while others may lose almost the entire investment. Typically, the industry handles return risk by diversification across a sufficiently large number of prospects to average into the high returns available. Clearly, large institutions are more able to commit the investment funds required for a variety of programs than individuals are, yet both should commit sufficient investment dollars to diversify as widely as is practical.

Liquidity Risk

Investments in all types of oil and gas programs are essentially illiquid. The typical oil well generally produces for about ten years and profits to investors, if any, are received only as the well pays out. A problem could arise if an investor needed cash quickly. There is only a small market for the sale of limited partnership units.

Cash Redemptions. Most programs try in some way to reduce this liquidity risk. Many do this by providing cash redemptions. Essentially, the operator agrees to buy back investment units for an amount based on the company's valuation of that unit. Cash redemptions generally are not available, however, until several years into the program. In addition, the manager could run into a problem if there are too many redemptions. Unlike a mutual fund, redemptions cannot be paid by selling off assets.

Conversion Into Stocks. A conversion of the investment units to common stock is another method some programs use to increase liquidity. This alleviates the manager's problem of coming up with needed cash for redemptions. However, this too occurs only after several years into the program. The market for the common stock of a former partnership will likely be very thin.

Management and Performance Risk

Management risk is one of the more serious problems in oil and gas investments. The people responsible for managing a program and overseeing its prospects are the key to its success or complete failure. Conflict of interest and self-dealing can and do arise in these programs. These situations are not necessarily illegal or detrimental to the program, but the SEC requires that these problems be detailed in program prospectuses and that investors be aware of them. Despite detailed disclosures of possible conflict of interest and self-dealing in program prospectuses, it is still difficult to determine if these possibilities pose real dangers to a program.

Conflict of Interest. The type of program that is most susceptible to a conflict of interest is one that is managed by an oil company. The company is acting as an agent for the investor in the program, but at the same time it may be selling services to the program.

In addition, the company's geological staff will be evaluating properties in an attempt to generate oil and gas prospects. The staff may be doing this for both the company and the program. The conflict lies in determining into which portfolio the prospect will be placed—the oil company's or the program's.

Self-Dealing. Self-dealing can occur if the operating company has an affiliate or is itself providing services to the program. The operator then is acting as both buyer and seller. Operators that supervise a series of different programs will encounter conflict when they must decide which properties are going to go into the various programs.

Managerial Performance. Accurately measuring the past performance of managers is another investor problem, in spite of the reporting requirements of the SEC and the various states. Most programs will provide statistics regarding previous performance, but comparing these is difficult because not enough information is provided regarding the underlying values of the program.

For example, in exploratory programs, operators can drill wells on properties having a wide range of risk. A step-out well, or a well drilled near a proven well but in an unproven area, is still an exploratory well but is far less risky than one drilled far away from any proven areas. An exploratory program drilling a large number of step-out wells will have a higher success ratio—and a lower risk—than one drilling in unproven properties located away from proven areas. The two programs are both exploratory and both are drilling in the same geological area, but may have unreported differences in the risks involved, which accounts for their different success ratios.

Assessments Risk

Although assessments are generally a good sign, most investors do not like them, and therefore they are classed as risks. An assessment is made to provide funds to develop discoveries that are made using the funds from the original investment. If the drilling has been very successful, the operator will need a sizable amount of cash up front to develop the wells. This cannot be financed through the cash flow of the well.

These new costs are not predictable, so some programs will provide for assessments in which each investor must put more money into the program. The amount callable can be either limited or unlimited, according to the program's prospectus.

Regulatory Risks

The oil and gas industry is subject to extensive federal and state regulation governing both the conduct of operations and the marketing of petroleum products once production is established. New regulatory legislation affecting this area is being enacted continuously. Most of the regulatory risk involves the pricing of oil and gas and could affect oil and gas investments.

President Reagan decontrolled the price of crude oil and refined petroleum products in early 1981. These had been subject to the allocation and price controls adopted in the Emergency Petroleum Allocation Act of 1973.

Natural gas prices were deregulated more slowly under the Natural Gas Policy Act of 1978. By 1985, this Act deregulated newly discovered natural gas. High-cost natural gas was decontrolled effective November 1, 1979. In addition, federal controls were imposed on intrastate gas marketing for the first time.

Natural gas production is regulated by the Federal Energy Regulatory Commission (FERC), which is part of the Department of Energy. The FERC has control over the transportation and marketing of natural gas and can change the selling price of gas.

The U.S. government has the power to increase or decrease the amount of imported oil, which directly affects oil and gas prices in the United States. It can also pass laws and regulations regarding pollution controls and the conservation of oil and gas that would affect the prices of these commodities.

ERISA Considerations

The nature of oil and gas investment opportunities offered to pension fund investors is restricted by the tax and Employee Retirement Income Security Act of 1974 (ERISA) considerations applicable to pension funds. Some programs would make tax-exempt institutions liable for unrelated business income tax. The Internal Revenue Code (the Code) defines unrelated business taxable income to mean the gross income derived by an organization from any unrelated trade or business regularly carried on by it, less the deductions allowed by the Code, which are directly connected with the carrying on of such trade or business. Most problems with unrelated business income arise from tax-exempt institutions taking a working interest in an oil or gas program. The owner of the working interest in an oil and gas lease generally is regarded as being engaged in a trade or business for tax purposes. Consistent with this approach, the Code and the Internal Revenue Service (IRS) rulings provide that income from working interests in oil and gas leases constitutes unrelated business income unless the exempt organization is relieved of its liabilities for development costs and operating costs by the terms of an agreement with the operator. Income to tax-exempt institutions that are partners in a partnership that is carrying on a trade or business through the ownership of working interests would most likely be treated as unrelated business income.

Passive income realized by an exempt organization is generally not subject to the tax imposed on unrelated business income. Income from royalty or net profits interest is generally considered passive since the owner of such an interest has no right to participate in the development and operation of the property.

An acquisition of working interests, directly or as a limited partner, is usually not suitable for qualified plan trusts and other tax-exempt institutions since such investors would be subject to federal income tax on income from such investments. In addition, investments in oil and gas by fiduciaries of ERISA-covered institutions must be consistent with the general requirement of the law that the fiduciary discharge its duties "with the care, skill, prudence and diligence under circumstances then prevailing that a prudent man in a like capacity and familiar with such matters would use. . . ."

TAX CONSEQUENCES

In recent years, the changes in the federal income tax rules have altered the way investors view oil and gas investments. For the most part, although there are tax advantages to oil and gas investments, the current limits on deductions make the economics, rather than tax, the primary evaluator for an investment.

Some of the more significant deductions attributable to an oil and gas program are reviewed here. The discussion also briefly covers the current rules that may deny, limit, or defer one or more of those deductions. When reviewing this portion, it should be kept in mind that the written material is just a thumbnail sketch of the many tax ramifications. Any investor seriously considering an oil and gas investment whose tax ramifications will affect his choice should consult with a knowledgeable tax advisor.

Intangible Drilling Costs

A significant tax advantage to an oil and gas program is the ability to currently deduct IDC. Only working interests can deduct IDC. Consequently, the deduction is not available to royalty or income programs since neither program shares in the costs of developing the well. An election to deduct IDC on successful wells must be made on the program's first tax return. If the election is not made properly, all IDC must be capitalized. Separately, the program can elect to deduct IDC on dry holes.

Also, the IDC can be deducted only to the extent of the working interest share. The result of this rule is most often seen in situations in which the investor is a direct participant in the well rather than being involved in a drilling program. If the investor is a direct participant, he may, as previously indicated, agree to contribute more funds to the drilling program than his working interest share would require. If the investor agrees to contribute funds sufficient to cover one third of the costs yet gets only a one quarter working interest share, only those costs equal to one quarter of the total costs can be deducted. For example, if the investor agrees to fund one third of the total $300,000 drilling costs, he must fund $100,000. Yet, the same investor receiving a 25 percent working interest would be liable for only 25 percent of the $300,000 costs ($75,000). Consequently, the investor can deduct only $75,000 of the $100,000 contribution. The remaining $25,000 is treated as leasehold and equipment cost.

As the name implies, IDC are costs paid or incurred during the development stage of a well that do not constitute the direct costs of depreciable assets. Such costs can include fuel, labor, hauling, surface preparation, and costs of the drilling. The program can pay the IDC directly or, as often happens, will pay third-party contractors for the development work on the well. The development stage during which IDC is incurred can be thought of as beginning when drilling on the well is begun and ending at the time the "Christmas tree" is installed on the well.

The IDC are usually incurred in the first twelve to twenty-four months of a program. Often, up to 99 percent of the IDC are allocated to the limited partner investors to reflect the fact that it was their money that allowed the development work to continue.

This type of investment can make an excellent gift. After taking the IDC deduction, the investor, when the well has begun production and will generate revenue, can gift the investment to a family member in a lower income tax bracket. After the development stage of a program, its liquidation value is still relatively low, and the value of such an investment as a gift can be below the annual gift limitation of $10,000 per donee per year. As with other tax areas, there is significant risk that the IRS will restructure the transaction to negate the perceived tax benefits.

Timing of IDC Deduction. Congress has, in recent years, tightened the timing of the IDC deduction. Many early programs had attempted to accelerate the IDC deduction by entering into a drilling contract with a drilling contractor. In many of these contracts, although drilling would not begin until some months into the future, there would be a prepayment clause requiring or allowing the program to currently pay for IDC. Thus, a program may pay millions of dollars (often through borrowing) to the driller in 1986, although drilling would not begin until 1987 or 1988. The programs would then allocate the prepayment to the investors as an IDC deduction in this instance, in 1986.

To eliminate this type of arrangement, Congress has placed most programs on the accrual basis of accounting and now requires that the IDC deduction match the time at which the drilling occurs, no matter when the funds are paid. In the preceding situation, the program would be unable to deduct any of the IDC in 1986 and would pro rate the deduction over the period in 1987 or 1988 during which the actual drilling occurs. The types of arrangement affected by these rules are accrual basis taxpayers as well as cash basis tax shelters. Although complicated, the general concept of a tax shelter is any program that has a tax avoidance motive (as determined by the IRS).

There is one exception to these rules. If prepayment is made in one year and drilling is begun within two and one-half months after the end of the year of prepayment, the deduction can be claimed in the year of prepayment. Thus, if the program pays all drilling costs in October 1989 and drilling begins before March 15, 1990, the investors could be allocated their share of the IDC deduction for their 1989 tax returns.

Depletion

If a program is successful in developing oil properties, the production from the properties will offer the owners the right to deduct the greater of cost or percentage depletion on the property.

Cost Depletion. Cost depletion, like depreciation, allows the investor to recover the costs in a productive oil property as barrels of oil are produced. As might be expected, the calculation compares the remaining basis in the property (adjusted for prior year's depletion) to a fraction whose numerator is the property's production for the year and whose denominator is the property's remaining reserves.

Although it does not happen often, it is possible for an investor to be admitted to the program at a time when investors receive no allocable share of the program's oil property's basis. In that case, no cost depletion can be taken because the investor does not have a basis in the oil property.

Percentage Depletion. Unlike cost depletion, percentage depletion does not depend on the property's cost basis. Instead, it is a deduction currently based on 15 percent of the investor's gross income from the oil property. Percentage depletion is available only to particular types of investors, and is limited to a given amount of production on certain types of oil properties. The investor should review his tax status as well as each program's written material to see if any of these limits may apply.

If percentage depletion is available, it is calculated initially at 15 percent of the property's gross income from production. The amount calculated above is denied (i.e., may be neither deducted nor carried forward) to the extent it exceeds 50 percent of the property's net income. This limited amount of percentage depletion is deferred further (i.e., it cannot be used in the current tax year but can be carried forward indefinitely) to the extent it exceeds 65 percent of the taxpayer's taxable income, to be calculated with some adjustments.

An example of the depletion calculation can be shown for an investor in a program who is allocated $100 of gross income from oil production. This $100 represents one percent of the investor's reserves from the property. The investor has a $600 cost basis in the property.

The investor has no IDC deduction for the year attributable to the property, and operating costs are $20. In this event, he can deduct the greater of

1. Cost depletion equal to one percent of $600, or $6; or
2. Percentage depletion equal to 15 percent of $100, or $15 (the 50 percent limit would not affect this particular set of facts).

If the investor were to be allocated $60 of IDC on the oil property in addition to the $20 of operating costs, the depletion calculation would change. Instead of the above calculations, the depletion deduction would be the greater of

1. Cost depletion equal to one percent of $600, or $6; or
2. Percentage depletion equal to 15 percent of $100, or $15. However, the $15 is limited by 50 percent of the property's net income of $20 or $10; so percentage depletion for the year would be $10.

In the second situation, the investor would still be able to deduct percentage depletion on his tax return but the amount would be only $10. The $5 difference between the originally calculated percentage depletion and the amount determined by the net income limitation is lost forever as a deduction to the investor.

Alternative Minimum Tax

All the deductions and tax benefits described above have a dark side. All IDC deducted as well as any depletion deducted that exceeds the lessee's basis (excess depletion) are treated as preference items for alternative minimum tax (AMT) calculations. Although the term preference sounds favorable, it is just the opposite. Any portion of a deduction that is treated as a preference, such as IDC and excess depletion, must be ignored in computing AMT. In other words, the deduction is treated as though it were not allowed during the year and cannot be used to reduce the AMT. Consequently, a taxpayer may end up paying a higher rate of tax under the AMT than he would have paid had there been no IDC or depletion to deduct. Although there are other preferences and adjustments to the AMT calculation, only those preferences particular to oil and gas are reviewed here.

IDC as a Preference Item. Not all IDC are considered a preference. To determine which portion of the IDC is a preference, the total IDC deducted must be adjusted by comparing the deduction to the amount that would have been deducted had the IDC been capitalized and amortized over either 120 months or cost depleted. This adjusted IDC is a preference to the extent it exceeds 65 percent of the taxpayer's net income from oil and gas operations. The taxpayer's net income from oil and gas operations is calculated by excluding from the deductions the adjusted IDC.

For example, $12,000 of IDC deduction on a lease acquired on January 1 of the year and having produced 5 percent of reserves would be adjusted as above for the greater of $^{12}\!/_{120}$ of $12,000 ($1,200) or 5 percent of $12,000 ($600).

If the lease had produced 15 percent of reserves during the year, the IDC deduction would be adjusted for the greater of $^{12}\!/_{120}$ of $12,000 ($1,200) or 15 percent of $12,000 ($1,800).

The taxpayer having preference IDC may eliminate the preference by electing to amortize all or any portion of the IDC ratably over a ten-year period. The calculations necessary to consider this secondary ten-year amortization are complicated and should be left to a tax professional.

Depletion as a Preference. Like a portion of the IDC, depletion in excess of the property's basis constitutes a preference item for AMT calculations. Thus, any percentage depletion available to the investor for the year that is in excess of the allocable share of the property's basis will not be allowed as a deduction in calculating AMT.

Tax Benefits and Caveats for Exploration-Development Investors

The tax benefits involved in exploratory and development oil programs are a significant characteristic. Oil and gas drilling offers taxpayers the benefit of immediate deduction of IDC, the percentage depletion allowance (if applicable), and the depreciation and amortization of capital assets. In addition, certain ordinary and necessary expenses of the program may be currently deductible, such as management fees and operating and overhead costs. These benefits are tempered, however, by the AMT as well as future ramifications to the deductions.

For example, a taxpayer must be careful of depreciation and amortization deductions. Although these deductions effectively will lower an investor's current tax liability, they could return to haunt him in the form of higher taxes if capital gains rates are ever reduced. If a program sells tangible property that has been depreciated, any gain on the sale must be treated as ordinary income to the extent of all depreciation previously claimed by the program on that asset irrespective of whether the gain would receive any special classification otherwise.

Similarly, IDC as well as depletion in excess of basis, like depreciation, are recaptured on the sale of the oil property. Just like depreciation, to the extent of the previously deducted IDC and depletion in excess of basis, all gain on sale must be treated as ordinary income.

Passive Loss Limitation

Congress felt that many investors were able to offset various types of income, such as salary, dividends, and royalties, with losses from their investments. The result, it felt, was that the investor was being able to reduce substantially taxable income through losses generated from investments. To eliminate this perceived abuse, Congress set up rules that require certain of an investor's activities to stand on their own. That is, losses from these types of activity could only be used to offset income from the same types of activity. Any excess losses could not be used to reduce the investor's tax liability from salary, royalties, dividends, or capital gains.

To accomplish its purpose, Congress divided activities into types. Activities could, by definition, be income-generating and were called portfolio income. Most other activities could be considered a passive investment or could be a trade or business activity, depending on whether the investor materially participated. Any activities in which the investor did not materially participate were called passive losses and were subject to the loss limitation rules described above. In addition, Congress felt that certain activities were inherently passive. Included in this last group are all rental activities as well as most limited partnership interests and publicly traded partnerships. Only those matters particular to oil and gas investments are reviewed here.

Except for certain transition rules, that phase out in 1990, an investor must keep track of all passive activity deductions and income separately from all other activities and deductions. To the extent of passive activity income, those deductions are currently deductible. Passive activity deductions in excess of passive activity income are deferred and carried forward to future years to be applied against those future years' passive activity incomes.

There is a special rule applicable to publicly traded partnerships. A publicly traded partnership is treated and taxed as a corporation unless 90 percent or more of its income is from oil and gas activities. Partnerships operating before December 17, 1987, are not subject to these rules until 1997. A partnership is publicly traded if its interests are sold on an established securities exchange or on a secondary market. Also, losses from a publicly traded partnership can only be used to offset against income from that same partnership and cannot be added to other activities in calculating income or deductions.

In the oil and gas area, working interests not held through an entity that limits the taxpayer's liability (as would limited partnership interests and most S corporation interests) are excluded from the passive activity rules. In other words, any deductions from working interests held directly by the investor may be used to offset any other type of income. The IRS has placed some restrictions on this working-interest exception if the investor converts a directly owned working interest into an interest in an entity that limits liability.

Royalty interests held directly by an investor may or may not be passive, depending on whether the investor materially participates and holds the royalties in a trade or business. As with almost all other activities, if the royalty is owned through an entity that limits the investor's liability, income and deductions from the royalty are considered passive.

At-Risk Limitations

Separate from the passive loss rules, an investor's deductions from an activity may only be deducted currently to the extent of the activity's income during the year. If the investors' deductions exceed income from an activity, the excess may be deducted only to the extent the investor is considered to be at risk in the activity. Generally, to the extent an investor has contributed cash or unmortgaged property or has signed recourse borrowing, he is considered to be at risk. Any nonrecourse financing (except for limited circumstances in real estate transactions) will not be considered to be part of the investor's at-risk basis.

Consider two investors. Investor A contributes $50,000 cash to an investment. Investor *B* contributes $10,000 cash and signs a nonrecourse note for $40,000. If the investment generates $110,000 of deductions (and no income) that are shared equally between the investors, A may deduct $50,000 of the $55,000 deductions allocated to him. *B*, however, may deduct only $10,000 of the $55,000 because *B* is considered to be at risk only to the extent of the cash contribution. Both may carry the unused deductions forward to future years.

Sale of a Partnership Interest

Investors in an upper tax bracket may be attracted to an oil or gas program's deductions rather than its income. As such, they may wish to dispose of their oil and gas program after exhausting most of its deductions during the first two years or so of the program. Of course, the taxpayer can gift the interest to a lower-income member of the family, as was discussed earlier. However, if this is not possible or practical and the program is sold back to the general partners, the investor probably may be entitled to treat some of the resale proceeds as long-term capital gains if he has held the interest for more than twelve months.

In most oil and gas programs, investors must offer to sell their interest to the general partners or to the program itself, through the general partners. The program, if it is a partnership, will be careful to limit the number of transfers since frequent transfers may result in the partnership being reclassified as a corporation and taxed accordingly. Usually, a general partner will limit the number of transfers per year to 10 to 20 percent of the outstanding interests.

Investors must remember to take into account the adjusted basis in their asset when considering gain or loss on a sale. If an investor originally contributed $10,000 cash to a program but has been able to take $8,000 of deductions during the first two years, that investor's tax basis in the program is now $2,000. If the investor then sells the interest for $7,000, the investor realizes a gain of $5,000, not a loss of $3,000. Rather, an investor will have a $5,000 capital gain to be reported on his tax return. If part of this sales price is attributed to appreciated inventory or from recapture of the depreciation, IDC, or depletion discussed above, that portion of the sale price must be treated as ordinary rather than capital gain.

Other Taxes

In addition to federal income taxes, partnership interests also may be subject to state income, gift, inheritance, and estate taxes.

Certain kinds of oil and gas investment may subject tax-exempt institutions to taxation. Tax-exempt organizations that participate directly in business ventures through limited partnerships may be generating unrelated business income as defined in the Code. In such cases, these organizations will have to pay unrelated business income taxes on revenues received from the investment. The partnership itself may be obligated to withhold tax on the unrelated business income before distributing any proceeds to the tax-exempt entity.

REPRESENTATIVE TYPES OF INVESTORS

In the public oil and gas programs, the high net worth individual traditionally has been the most significant investor. But the industry has developed various programs that have made oil and gas investments more available to a broader base of investors, thus including investors with more modest means.

High-Income Individuals

Investors in drilling programs are generally well to do. Most oil and gas programs have minimum investment requirements of at least $5,000, and many investment counselors recommend investing in two or three programs to diversify and minimize risk. In addition, many programs have high net worth requirements. For example, the Stone Oil Corporation 1981-II Ltd. drilling program has a minimum subscription of $25,750. It is also limited to persons with a net worth of not less than $225,000 (excluding home, furnishings, and automobiles) or to persons with a net worth of not less than $60,000 (excluding home, furnishings, and automobiles) and taxable income for the previous year of $60,000 or more.

These investments can be used by taxpayers in a variety of different ways. They can also be purchased by a high-income investor just prior to retirement. Income generated from the investment, if any, would be received several years later, when the individual is in a lower tax bracket. Obviously, someone who is about to retire would not invest in such a speculative area without having a significant amount of other, more conservative, investments. These investments also are used by high tax bracket individuals who wish to gift their assets.

Lower-Income Individuals

Investors in the less risky income programs are looking for consistent cash flow from their programs. Lower tax bracket individuals invest in these programs, which include individual retirement accounts (IRAs) and pension plans. Income programs also have reinvestment provisions allowing investors to build their asset bases for future retirement income. And the fairly consistent rate of return enables pension plans to do benefit-cost projections.

Corporations

Although their number is still small, corporations also are starting to enter the oil and gas arena through private placements. The investment is used as a hedge against future energy costs that the company may be forced to incur as energy prices escalate.

Insurance Companies

Insurance companies also are investing in oil and gas exploration, largely through private placements. Insurance companies have the available capital to invest in such placements for relatively long periods and, in addition, can take advantage of some of the tax-shelter aspects. The attraction is the inflation-hedged return. Firms active in this area include Prudential, Aetna, Equitable, Allstate, and Northwestern Mutual Life.

Tax-Exempt Institutions

Tax-exempt institutions are starting to invest in oil and gas for similar reasons. These investments also have been largely through private placements and, most recently, have been in the form of natural gas exploration and development and royalty programs. Traditionally very conservative, pension funds appear to favor this relatively passive approach to oil and gas investing; in addition, the royalty interests appear to provide the best legal arrangements in light of ERISA requirements. Another indirect participation enjoyed by pension funds has been debt offerings with equity kicker features.

An advantage of the private placement is that the deals can be structured specifically for the pension funds involved in the deal because of the large amounts of capital the funds are able to put up. Pension funds also have invested smaller amounts in some public offerings, a few of which have been set up primarily for institutions.

A representative sampling of major pension funds that have invested in oil and gas deals includes the pension funds of Hughes Aircraft, General Electric, DuPont, Beatrice Foods, AT&T, IBM, and Atlantic Richfield, and the Harvard University endowment. Investment amounts are as great as $20 million, and many have been for less than $1 million.

IMPORTANT FACTORS IN BUYING

Not all oil and gas programs are successful. The bewildering number of oil and gas drilling programs may look much the same to the inexperienced investor. Nothing is further from the truth. Even the good programs can have a bad year and, without doubt, there are poor programs. It is always advisable to make this kind of investment through a reputable financial intermediary. In addition, the following broadly applicable guidelines may be useful. Note that some of the information needed may only be available verbally pursuant to current securities regulations.

Past Performance

The most important information the potential investor can get is how the drilling company has done in the past. Past performance is measured in terms of net future revenues from proven oil and gas reserves in relation to limited partner capital contribution. Net future revenues are the estimated sale value of oil and gas discovered less estimated operating costs and borrowings. The limited partner's capital contribution is the original investment plus any assessments. Essentially, a desirable return is an average of twice the limited partner investment in net future revenues (undiscounted) as an average over the preceding three to five years. Even more desirable is about 1.4 times the investment in net future revenues discounted at a rate of about 10 percent.

In making comparisons, the investor should use only proven reserves, not probable or possible reserves, and notice what price escalation formulas are used; the most reliable figures are those provided by an independent reserve engineering firm.

The past performance information provided in a prospectus, such as the so-called success ratios and the cash distribution tables, can be meaningless or very hard to interpret. A better success ratio does not necessarily mean a better economic result. The success ratio is the percentage of all wells drilled that are completed as producers. Drilling should be successful 90 percent of the time in the Appalachian Basin (Ohio, West Virginia), but perhaps only 30 to 40 percent of the time in Louisiana. Why, then, drill in Louisiana? The answer is more prolific reserves, potentially more dollars back per dollar spent.

The cash distribution tables show the cash actually paid out to the investor. This too can be deceptive. Some types of wells pay out (or produce) over 50 percent of all that they will ever pay out in the first two years of their productive lives and do not produce any significant revenues after the first four or five years. Other types of wells produce a lower percentage of the total early on, but produce over a twelve- or fifteen-year life.

Front-End Costs

Another factor to consider is how much of the investor's capital contribution goes into the ground. The rule of thumb is 87.5 percent. This applies to oil and gas drilling or leasing costs, as opposed to management fees, general and administrative overhead, brokerage commissions, and offering costs. An investor who is asked to pay more front-end bills can seriously dilute the chance for a good investment.

Importance of Expert Advice

The most important step that a potential investor should make is to seek the help of an expert in determining whether an investment in oil and gas is prudent, based on the investor's particular financial condition.

An outside advisor can provide both taxable investors and tax-exempt institutions with the expertise needed to determine the appropriateness of such an investment and to evaluate the different kinds of programs available. For the taxable investor, it is advisable to have an accountant or tax advisor review the investor's tax situation and the effect the potential investment will have on it.

For further advice on the different kinds of programs, a reputable stockbroker can provide a wealth of research information. For tax-exempt institutions, a number of firms provide advice on oil and gas investing. (See *Companies Offering Programs and Institutional Placement Advisors*, at the end of this article.)

A good advisor should provide an investor with the following:

- Help in determining the risk tolerances the investor can live with
- Help in determining if the investment will assist the investor in achieving particular financial objectives and needs
- Help in evaluating alternative investments and setting up a suitable asset mix for the investor's portfolio
- Help in determining which of the numerous oil and gas programs available would be best for the particular investor
- Research on many of the programs to help eliminate the questionable ones
- Help in evaluating the tax implications of a chosen investment for the taxable investor
- Assistance in structuring a private placement suited to the needs of the large institutional investor

Judging the Particular Program

There are numerous oil and gas programs on the market at any given time. Evaluating them properly is difficult and time-consuming.

Management Record. One of the most important features in an oil and gas investment is management, and this is one of the most difficult areas on which to find information. Brokers and investment advisors can provide some help in this area. Familiarity with management—either through previous investments or through the experience of others—is also a plus in judging programs. Some background information on the general partners is also provided in program prospectuses.

Financial Structure. Investment consultants strongly recommend that investors study the financial structure of the program. The general partner should share in some of the program costs. How those costs are divided among the general and limited partners is also important, particularly in drilling programs. Limited partners should pay the intangible costs so as to benefit from the tax write-offs. At the same time, revenues should provide the general partner with some incentive fee. This probably will mean that the general partner will receive a proportionally larger percentage of the revenues than that to which the general partner's capital contribution would entitle him. A typical agreement would give the general partners a 40 percent share of the revenues based on a 15 percent contribution of capital.

It is also important to see if the managing general partner or investment company that structured the deal is investing any of its own funds along with the limited partners or investors in a joint venture. If the managing general partner is not investing along with the limited partners, it may be advisable to find out why or find another program.

Obviously, it is better for the investor if the general partner's profit is based on the success of the program and not simply on the successful selling of the program. Also, management fees and sales commissions among the various programs should be compared.

Other Considerations. Investors should check to see if the program will incur any indebtedness. If so, there should be limitations on the amount.

The size of the oil and gas program should be substantial to provide enough capital for proper diversification. Programs probably should be investing in a fair number of wells (at least twenty-five) in a number of different locations.

Investors also should be aware of the conflict-of-interest potential in the different programs, and the possibility of future assessments. If the program will be making such changes, they should be limited in size. In addition, the consequences of not paying the assessment should be examined.

Redemptions are important because they provide the investment with at least a small amount of liquidity. Some programs may provide for redemptions earlier than others. Transferability of the units is also important, since programs often have limitations on this.

For investors interested in a program for its cash flow, a prospectus should indicate when revenues can be expected.

MANAGING THE INVESTMENT

Investments in oil and gas programs should be treated with the same kind of care given to any security. The investor should make sure that the program's general partner provides detailed, audited annual reports on the financial status of the partnership, including fees and commissions paid to the general partner. Generally, unaudited reports on the partnership activities are provided quarterly.

General partners also provide the limited partners with necessary tax reporting information on the program. At the end of the calendar year the general partner files tax information on the partnership with the IRS and sends each limited partner a schedule indicating his share of the deductions and tax credits, if any.

GLOSSARY

assessments—Additional capital contributions that may become required of the limited partners during the course of the partnership's existence, after capital formation of a limited partnership.

blind pool—An oil and gas partnership that has not committed to specific prospects or properties at the time of capital formation.

carried interest—A fractional working interest in an oil and gas lease that comes about through an arrangement between co-owners of a working interest. The owner of a carried interest is not liable for certain development and operating costs.

carved out interest—a fractional interest that has been transferred to another party by the original owner of the entire interest.

completion costs—The costs associated with completing a well.

depletion allowance—The income tax deduction allowed for the exhaustion of a natural resource.

economic interest—An interest in oil and gas in the ground.

engineering appraisal—An appraisal of the proven and probable reserves in a region; it includes a future net income estimate and is conducted by an independent petroleum engineer.

farm out—An agreement by which the responsibility for exploration and development is shifted from the working-interest owner to another party who wants to drill a well on the property.

front end costs—Costs paid out of initial investment in a venture before the venture actually gets under way.

intangible drilling costs—Expenditures incurred in drilling a well on items that do not have salvage value, such as labor, fuel, repairs, and hauling, which are allowed as tax deductions.

net profits interest—An agreement providing that the holder shall receive a stated percentage of the net profts from the operation of the property.

operating costs—Costs incurred from completed wells in the producing and marketing of oil and gas.

overriding royalty—A royalty interest carved out of the working interest.

royalty interest—A fractional interest in the gross production of oil or gas or other minerals under a lease.

production payment—A specified share of the production from oil or gas in place or the proceeds from the sale of such production.

working interest—The interest that bears the costs of drilling and operating a property in the production of oil and gas properties.

TRADE ORGANIZATIONS

American Association of Petroleum Landmen, Fort Worth, Tex.

American Petroleum Institute, Washington, D.C.

Gas Research Institute, Chicago, Ill.

Independent Petroleum Association of America, Washington, D.C.

International Association of Drilling Contractors, Houston, Tex.

International Association of Oil Well Drilling Contractors, Houston, Tex.

International Oil Scouts Association, Austin, Tex.

Mid-Continent Oil and Gas Association, Tulsa, Okla.

National Petroleum Council, Washington, D.C.

National Petroleum Refiners Association, Washington, D.C.

Petroleum Equipment Institute, Tulsa, Okla.

Petroleum Marketing Education Foundation, Columbia, S.C.

Society of Exploration Geophysicists, Tulsa, Okla.

Texas Independent Producers and Royalty Owners Association, Austin, Tex.

COMPANIES OFFERING PROGRAMS AND INSTITUTIONAL PLACEMENT ADVISORS

Below is a sampling of the companies offering oil and gas investment programs.

Apache Corp., Denver, Colo.

Callon Petroleum Co., Natchez, Miss.

Coastal Corp., Houston, Tex.

Geodyne Resources Inc., Tulsa, Okla.

Merrico Resources Inc., Ardmore, Okla.

New York Life Oil & Gas Producing Properties II, New York, N.Y.

Prudential-Bache, New York, N.Y.

Red Eagle Exploration Co., Oklahoma City, Okla.

Shearson Lehman Hutton, New York, N.Y.

Swift Energy Co., Houston, Tex.

Torch Energy Corp., Houston, Tex.

INVESTMENT BANKERS

Dean Witter Reynolds, New York, N.Y.

Lawrence Energy Associates, Boston, Mass.

Merrill Lynch, New York, N.Y.

Shearson Lehman Hutton, New York, N.Y.

INVESTMENT ADVISORS

Chase Investors Management Corp., New York, N.Y.

First Reserve Corp., Greenwich, Conn.

Investment Advisers Inc., Minneapolis, Minn.

Petroleum & Resources Corp., Baltimore, Md.

Trust Company of the West, Los Angeles, Cal.

SUGGESTED READING

PERIODICALS

Institutional Investor. Published by Institutional Investor Systems, Inc., New York, N.Y. Monthly financial magazine covering institutional investments.

Oil and Gas Investor. Published by Hart Publications, Inc., Denver, Colo. Monthly magazine for oil and gas investors.

Oil and Gas Journal. Published by Petroleum Publishing Co., Tulsa, Okla. Weekly newspaper covering news of the American oil producers.

Pensions & Investment Age. Published by Crain Communications, Inc., Chicago, Ill. Biweekly newspaper for the tax-exempt investor.

Platt's Oilgram News Service. Published by McGraw-Hill Inc., New York, N.Y. Daily newsletter giving all oil news and the prices of main petroleum products.

REFERENCE BOOKS

Adelman, M.A. *The World Petroleum Market.* Chicago: Johns Hopkins Press, 1977.

American Petroleum Institute. *Basic Petroleum Data Book.* Tulsa, 1978.

Dam, Kenneth W. *Oil Reserves: Who Gets What How?* Chicago: University of Chicago Press, 1976.

Griffin, James M., et al. *Energy Economics & Policy.* New York: Academic Press, 1979.

Johnson, William A., et al. *Competition in the Oil Industry.* Washington, D.C.: Energy Policy Research Project, 1976.

Lattes, Robert, ed. *Energy: The Countdown.* London: Pergamon Press 1979.

O'Connor, Harvey. *The Empire of Oil.* New York: Monthly Review Press, 1963.

Orban, John. *Money in the Ground: Oil and Gas Investments Explained,* 2nd ed. Oklahoma City: Meridian Press, 1987.

OPTIONS

PUTS AND CALLS

Gary L. Trennepohl

BASIC CHARACTERISTICS

Definitions

Options are of two types: calls and puts. A call option is a contract giving the option buyer the right, but not the obligation, to buy an asset (for example, 100 shares of common stock) for a fixed price—exercise or strike price—on or before a specified future date—the expiration date. The buyer of a put option has the right to sell the underlying asset to the seller of the put. The seller of an option is called the option writer, and the price paid the option seller by the buyer is called the premium. An option that can be exercised at any time before its expiration date is known as an American option; options that can be exercised only on the expiration date are called European options. With few exceptions, noted later, options traded on exchanges in the United States are American options.

Options are exercised on or before expiration if it is in the economic interest of the buyer to do so. The call buyer chooses to exercise the option if the asset price is above the option exercise price (S>E), or in the money. However, for investors who cannot trade personally on the floor of the exchange at minimum transaction costs, the return from the position usually is greater if the option is sold rather than if the actual security is sold. If the security price is below the call's exercise price at expiration, or out of the money, the call will be allowed to expire worthless. The put buyer will exercise only if the asset price is below the

---

Gary L. Trennepohl, Ph.D., is Chairman of the Department of Finance at Texas A&M University, College Station, Texas. He is also a member of the faculty of the Options Institute, Chicago Board Options Exchange.

put strike price (S<E) and, just as with calls, will sell the option on the exchange, rather than delivering the asset.

The Marketplace for Options

Exchanges for Options. Options on individual stocks have been traded for many years in the over-the-counter (T) market. However, numerous trading disadvantages—such as high transaction costs, illiquidity, and individualized contract specifications—severely limited investor participation. In 1973, the Chicago Board Options Exchange (CBOE) began trading standardized call options (listed options) on sixteen stocks. Investor interest in these contracts grew dramatically. Today, listed options are available on more than 200 stocks, several stock indices, U.S. Treasury bonds and bills, financial and commodity futures contracts (options on futures), and foreign currencies.

Options contracts are traded on many security exchanges. Options on individual stocks, stock indices, and bonds are traded on the CBOE, and options on stocks and indices are traded on the American Stock Exchange (AMEX), the Pacific Stock Exchange (PSE), the Philadelphia Stock Exchange (PHLX), and the New York Stock Exchange (NYSE). Options on currency futures are available on the International Monetary Market (IMM); options on foreign currency are traded on the PHLX. Options on commodity futures are traded on the Chicago Board of Trade (CBT) and most other commodity futures exchanges, and options on financial futures are traded on the CBT. Many overseas markets also offer trading in listed options on individual securities, indices, and foreign currencies.

Standardized Contracts. For a secondary market in options to exist, it is necessary to standardize the option contract in terms of exercise price, expiration date, characteristics of the underlying security, and exercise procedures.

Exercise Price. The exercise prices of individual stock options on stocks selling for more than $25 per share are set at $5 increments (e.g., $25, $30, $35). Stocks selling for less than $25 have exercise prices at $2.50 intervals (e.g., $10, $12.50, $15, $17.50). New strike prices usually are offered for trading when the security closes above the midpoint of the strike price interval for at least two days running. For example, if a stock now at 21 closes above $22.50 for two days in a row, the $25's would be offered for trading. The exercise price is adjusted for stock splits and stock dividends, so from time to time listed contracts are traded that do not appear to fit the rules described above.

The exercise prices for index options typically are in 5-point intervals in the index value. Exercise prices of foreign currency options are in terms of the dollar exchange rate for the currency, and options on debt securities are in terms of percentage of par value.

Expiration Date. Significant changes have occurred since 1979 in the assignment of expiration months for options on individual stocks. On the CBOE in 1973, expiration months for options on the thirty-two underlying stocks were January, April, July, and October. Trading took place in options having nine months or less to expiration. For example, in February trading was allowed in the April, July, and October options. When the Aprils expired, the January series was added. As more underlying stocks were added, two additional cycles were developed: the February cycle with expiration in February,

May, August, and November; and the March cycle with expiration in March, June, September, and December.

As the market developed, investor demand for near-term options grew, and the exchanges introduced trading in options with shorter maturities. Today, options on individual stocks are offered with expiration in the nearest two months in addition to the intermediate and long-term months from the cycle to which the stock previously was assigned. For example, in late September International Business Machines (IBM) which is on the January cycle, will have options traded that expire in October, November, January, and April.

The specific expiration time for individual stock options is 11:59 P.M. Eastern time on Saturday after the third Friday of the expiration month. However, trading in the option stops on the business day prior to expiration (usually a Friday) at 4:10 P.M. Most brokerage firms require clients to provide notice of exercise before 3:00 P.M. on this day.

The expiration date for stock index options and U.S. Treasury bond options is the same as that of individual stock options. However, foreign currency options expire on the Saturday preceding the third Wednesday of the expiration month, and U.S. Treasury bill options expire on the second business day preceding the earliest day of the expiration month on which a one-year Treasury bill has thirteen weeks remaining to maturity. Treasury bill options are European options, as are the options on the Institutional Investors Index (XII) and the Standard & Poor's 500 Index (SPX).

If the option is in the money, most investors will close their option position by selling the option, to avoid paying commissions on buying and selling the underlying asset. The option premium just prior to expiration will closely reflect the difference between stock price and exercise price (S-E), called intrinsic value. Market makers on the exchange who can trade options and the underlying asset with low transactions costs will buy these options at a slight discount from intrinsic value and exercise them against the seller, thus capturing an arbitrage profit. Only by neglect will an in the money option not be exercised.

Contract Size. All individual stock option contracts call for delivery of 100 shares of the underlying stock. Stock index option contracts are denominated in dollars and based on a specific multiplier of the index (e.g., $100 times the option exercise value). Foreign currency options are traded in a specific amount of the foreign currency, and U.S. Treasury bond options are traded in units of $100,000 principal value per contract. Contracts on Treasury bills are against $1 million of principal value.

The Option Clearing Corporation (OCC). The OCC is an indispensable participant in all listed option trading because it provides liquidity and guarantee of performance for all options. It is the intermediary between the buyer and seller of every option contract, becoming the buyer for every option seller and the seller for every option buyer. If an option buyer chooses to sell the option before expiration, the position is closed by selling the contract to a buyer on the floor of the exchange. The original buyer's name is replaced on OCC records by the person who bought the option. The original option seller still holds the position and is not involved with the second transaction, because the contract is with the OCC rather than an individual. More importantly, an equal number of buyers and sellers for each contract still exists. The number of existing contracts, called open interest, is reported daily in many financial publications.

If the option is exercised, the buyer's brokerage firm delivers the exercise notice to the OCC through a clearing member. The OCC notifes a randomly selected option seller of exercise. In the rare instance when the seller does not comply, the OCC steps in to honor the contract to the buyer, in effect guaranteeing performance of the contract. Two problems of the OTC options market are thus avoided: illiquidity and uncertainty about the seller complying with an exercise notice.

Underlying Assets

Individual Stocks. Option contracts on more than 200 individual stocks currently are traded on four different options exchanges. Each contract calls for delivery of 100 shares of the individual stock if the option is exercised. Individual stock options are traded by investors who desire to speculate or hedge positions in an individual security.

Stock Indices. In 1983, options on various stock indices were made available for trading, and several new ones have been added since that time. Popular index options include those on the S&P 100 Index (OEX) and the SPX, traded on the CBOE, and the Major Market Index (MMI) and XII, traded on the AMEX. OEX contains 100 of the 500 stocks in the SPX; the MMI is composed of twenty blue chip securities, seventeen of which are in the Dow Jones industrial average (DJIA). The XII is composed of seventy-five stocks that are widely held by institutional investors.

Index options are designed for portfolio managers who desire to hedge equity positions using options and for investors wishing to speculate or hedge the direction of the market. Two distinctions between individual and index options should be recognized. First, index options are settled in cash rather than by delivery of the underlying asset. Assume you exercise a call on the OEX having a striking price of 260. If you exercise your option on the last trading day before Saturday expiration and the index closes at 267, you will receive in cash the difference between the index value at the close and the option exercise price (267 − 260), times the index multiplier (7 × 100 = 700). Second, some index options are European rather than American (e.g., the SPX and the XII). These options can be exercised only at maturity; however, they can be traded on the exchange at any time before expiration.

U.S. Treasury Bonds and Bills. The market for interest rate options is developing rapidly, and changes in the characteristics and nature of these instruments undoubtedly will occur. Currently, the only Treasury bond options traded call for delivery of a specific bond issue (e.g., the 9⅛ percent of 2018). These are called price-based options, and their exercise price is as a percent of par. A Treasury bond call with an exercise price of 98 would allow the buyer to purchase 100,000 par value of the underlying bond for 98,000 plus accrued interest. Proposals are under consideration to make available cash settled Treasury bond options called yield based options. Cash settlement procedures similar to those used for stock index options would be used. Treasury bond options are designed for investors, such as bond portfolio managers, who wish to speculate or hedge against changes in long-term interest rates.

Treasury bill options are European options that call for delivery of thirteen-week Treasury bills having a principal value of 1 million. Treasury bill options allow investors to hedge or speculate in short-term interest rates.

Foreign Currency. Standardized options contracts against major foreign currencies are available in the United States on the PHLX. These options specify delivery of a fixed amount of foreign currency on exercise (e.g., £31,250), and contracts include both European and American options. The exercise price is in terms of the exchange rate between the U.S. dollar and the foreign currency (e.g., $1.70/£). It is expected that trading of currency options will become common on most major world exchanges in the future. Major traders of foreign currency options are banks and multinational corporations who hedge foreign currency cash positions or expected foreign currency cash flows.

Options on Futures. Options are available in which the underlying asset is a futures contract rather than the asset itself. (For a description of financial futures, see the article "Futures: Financial, Agricultural, Currency," elsewhere in this volume.) Most popular are options on foreign currency futures, stock index futures, and U.S. Treasury bond futures. On exercise of a call option on a futures contract, the buyer receives a futures contract expiring in a specified month at a price equal to the exercise price of the option.

Assume that on October 1 you buy a call option on the January British pound futures with a strike of $1.70. On December 2, the exchange rate rises to $1.75/£ and you exercise the option, obtaining a futures contract against £62,500 at a cost of $1.70/£, which expires in January. The futures contract is immediately marked to market value, producing a gain in your account because the spot exchange rate is above $1.70. Thereafter, as the exchange rate fluctuates, you will gain or lose on the futures position, which is marked to market value daily. (Differences between futures and options are described below.) Options on futures are used by banks, institutional investors, and money managers to create hedged or arbitrage positions incorporating the option, future, and underlying asset.

Comparison to Other Securities

Options and Futures. Options frequently are confused with futures contracts, although they are very different instruments. Options give the holder the right but not the obligation to buy (call) or sell (put) an underlying asset. The buyer of a call option pays the premium for the privilege it offers. He profits if the asset appreciates; but if the asset's price falls, the buyer will never lose more than the premium paid for the option.

A futures contract is a contract for delivery of the underlying asset at a future date. There is no premium paid on a futures contract: margin, amounting to 5 percent to 10 percent of the contract's value, is deposited by both the buyer and seller when the contract is created to provide assurance that they will honor the contract. The buyer of a futures contract is obligated to purchase the underlying asset at a future date, and the seller is obligated to deliver the asset. The buyer (seller) profits dollar for dollar if the asset appreciates (falls) in price and loses (profits) dollar for dollar if the price declines.

Futures contracts are marked to market value at the close of each day, and if the asset falls far enough in price (5 to 10 percent in value), the buyer of a futures contract is required to deposit additional funds to his account. Theoretically, the maximum possible loss on a futures contract is unlimited; the maximum loss on an option is the cost paid.

Options and futures are similar in that both provide highly leveraged means of participating in the market. The option premium represents a small amount of the underlying asset's value. Percentage changes in the prices of an option are greater than the percentage changes in the prices of the underlying asset. Similarly, the margin required on a futures contract represents a small portion (5 to 10 percent) of the contract's value. Percentage changes in the margin account of a futures contract are greater than the percentage changes in the price of the underlying commodity. Both instruments are ways to buy leverage in the market.

Another point of comparison is open interest. In the futures and options market, the number of outstanding contracts is called open interest. However, the net (buyers minus sellers) number of contracts in either market is always zero. Clearing corporations exist for both markets to provide contract liquidity and guarantee performance.

Since buyers match sellers and no new money is raised by corporations, options and futures contracts have been compared to side bets and to gambling, contracts without an economic purpose. Options and futures both have economic purposes; they enable investors to fashion patterns of returns that suit their particular objectives, thereby facilitating the functioning of the primary and secondary markets in the underlying assets.

Options and Warrants. Warrants are essentially long-term European call options issued by a corporation rather than created by investors. Most warrants originate as part of a corporate debt issue. Basic terms and characteristics are identical to options on individual stocks except that the expiration date usually is five to twenty years after issue, and each warrant covers one share of underlying stock. When the option is exercised, the holder submits the warrant plus cash amounting to the exercise price to the issuing corporation in exchange for the company's stock. (For further detail, see the article "Warrants and Rights" elsewhere in this volume.)

Options and Other Securities. Options and option-like securities are imbedded in numerous financial assets. Executive stock options are similar to listed call options except that they are originated by a corporation and usually are given rather than sold to employees or management; they have no developed secondary market. Convertible bonds are part bond and part option. Homeowners insurance contracts are put options that give you the right to sell your house to the insurance company at its market value in case of total calamity. Even the common stock of a corporation with bonds in its capital structure can be viewed as an option. Shareholders have the right to buy back the assets of the firm from the bondholders by paying off the face amount of the debt at the bond's maturity. If the firm is not worth the value of the debt, shareholders will default (i.e., allow their options to expire worthless). A knowledge of put and call options will be helpful in understanding many other financial assets.

Primary Determinants of Value

Value at Maturity. At option expiration, the value of the contract will be zero if the option is out of the money; if the option is in the money, it will be worth the difference between the exercise price and asset price. Consider a call with an exercise price of \$85; if the stock is at \$93, the call's value at expiration will be \$8; if the stock is below \$85, the call will be worthless. A put having a strike of \$95 on the same stock would have a value of \$2 (i.e., \$95 – \$93), whereas a put with a strike of \$90 would have no value.

Value Before Maturity. In 1973, Fischer Black and Myron Scholes published an article describing a model for pricing options and warrants on stocks. A pivotal theoretical breakthrough, the Black-Scholes option pricing model has formed the basis for significant research in option pricing during the past fifteen years. In 1979, a mathematically less complex formula, the binomial option pricing model, was derived. Today, option valuation programs developed from these pricing models are available for personal computers and hand-held calculators. They are widely used by market makers on the floor of the options exchanges and by other professional option traders.

The Black-Scholes insight regarding stock option pricing was that payoffs identical to an option could be replicated by continuously rebalancing a position in the underlying stock and a riskless asset. Consequently, if a listed option's value deviates too far from the price specified by the model, an arbitrager will sell (buy) the listed option and buy (sell) a synthetic option constructed with the underlying stock and Treasury bills, thus locking in a riskless profit. Listed option prices will be driven toward the price indicated by the option pricing model. The following six factors are incorporated into the Black-Scholes option valuation model to determine the value of an option before maturity.

Current Price of the Underlying Asset. The value of an option depends strongly on the current price of the underlying security. The greater the current price of the underlying asset, the greater the value of a call and the less the value of a put. At the extremes, a call will never be worth more than the underlying asset nor less than its exercise value.

Prior to maturity, an American put or call must sell for at least its exercise value. If the striking price of a call is $50 and the stock is at $55, the call must sell for at least $5; otherwise, a sure profit can be made by buying the option and exercising it. The same relationship does not hold for European puts. Since they cannot be exercised until maturity, the in-the-money European put will sell for at least its discounted intrinsic value. It sometimes appears in prices reported in the financial press that boundary values are violated in actual trading. The usual cause for these discrepancies is that the reported prices are those of the last trade of each asset. If the last option trade occurred at a different time than the last trade of the stock, mispricing will seem to occur, when in reality investors would not be able to trade at the reported prices the next morning.

Interest Rates. Percentage premiums on call options increase with increases in short-term interest rates. All else being constant, the higher the rate of interest on riskless bonds with the same maturity as the option, the lower is the present value of the striking price that would be paid for the underlying asset. The striking price, however, is paid only if the option is exercised. As a result, the effects of changes in the rate of interest on the value of an option depend on the probability of exercise; the greater the probability of exercise, the greater the effect of a change in the rate of interest. Increasing the rate of interest is the same as reducing the striking price: Both increase the price of the call. Since a put option is more valuable if the striking price is high relative to the price of the underlying asset, higher interest rates reduce the value of a put option.

Volatility of Returns of the Underlying Asset. The volatility of the return on the underlying security influences the value of an option proportionally more than any of the factors. The more volatile an underlying security, the greater the price movements of the security either up or down. The buyer of a call gains on the upside and has limited loss on the downside (the reverse is true for a put); therefore, the more volatile an underlying stock, the more valuable an option on that stock. When using option pricing models, the expected security volatility is the only pricing model variable not directly observable; it must be estimated using past data or other information. Differences in option prices calculated from the same option pricing model will occur because the option traders using them have differing expectations of security price volatility.

Time to Maturity. In general, the longer the time to maturity of a call option, the greater the value of the contract. Time works to increase volatility by allowing more time for the underlying security to experience wider price fluctuations. Time also works to reduce the present value of the exercise price; increasing the time period is similar to increasing the interest rate. For a put option, the effect of time on value is ambiguous. When the put is out of the money (S>E), a longer maturity option generally will have greater value than a shorter maturity one. However, if a European put is deep in the money, its value may increase as time to maturity declines.

Exercise Price. The higher the exercise price of a call option, all else being constant, the lower the value of the call. A greater appreciation in the price of the underlying asset is required to produce a profit from the call. For a put, the effect is reversed; higher exercise prices move the put deeper in the money and increase its value.

Anticipated Dividends or Interest Payments. Dividends or interest payments expected to be paid on the underlying asset prior to the maturity of the option are another important determinant of value. The holders of listed stock options do not receive the rights to any cash dividends. On the ex-dividend date, the price of the underlying security will fall by approximately the amount of the cash dividend. A call option on a high-dividend-paying security such as American Telephone & Telegraph (AT&T) is not as valuable as a call option on an underlying security with exactly the same terms and market characteristics except for the payment of dividends. Losing dividends has approximately the same effect on the value of a call as does reducing the price of the underlying security by an amount equal to the present value of the lost dividends. Reducing the stock price relative to the striking price reduces the value of a call option by making it less likely that the option will be exercised. By the same reasoning, dividends increase the value of put options. Interest payments on debt options produce the same effects on their premiums as dividends on stocks, increasing the value of their puts and reducing the value of their calls.

The timing and amount of dividends on individual stocks can be estimated fairly accurately from company records and incorporated into the valuation of options on dividend-paying stocks. However, the effect of dividends on the premiums of index options is more complicated to measure because the timing and amount of each dividend on every stock in the index must be estimated. Cash payments on debt securities can be estimated with great certainty because they are specified contractual obligations. Because foreign currency and futures contracts do not pay dividends or interest, the values of their options are not affected by cash distributions.

To summarize: (1) The greater the asset price to striking price ratio, the greater the percentage call premium and lower the percentage put premium. (2) Call options on longer-term options almost always sell at a higher price than near-term options with the same characteristics. For puts, the effect of time to maturity is ambiguous, depending to a great extent on the relationship of the stock price and exercise price. (3) Puts and calls on more volatile assets will have greater percentage premiums than options on less volatile assets.

The estimate of security volatility is a key factor in determining an option's value. (4) Given the other factors, the higher the level of interest rates, the greater the percentage call premiums, and the lower the percentage put premiums. (5) Dividends or interest payments act to reduce the prices of call options and increase the prices of put options.

Other Factors Influencing Value. Although the factors described above are the primary determinants of the value of options, other factors—some basic and some institutional—have been suggested, and may influence the price of an option. The expected rate of return on the underlying security, for instance, does not directly affect the value of an option; however, higher expected rates of return on the underlying security influence the price of the underlying security, and this price, in turn, is used to value an option. In addition, higher (or lower) expected returns may suggest an increase in the security's volatility, thus increasing an option's price.

Institutional rules, such as tax laws, margin requirements, and transaction costs, may also be factors in the pricing of options. Even with these rules, investors do price options and other assets, however difficult it is to quantify their effects on market pricing. Prices in the market may be set as if no one individual were subject to these institutional restrictions. The investors, who set prices in the market, may profit by buying or selling options until prices are the same as those that would have been set without these institutional rules.

For example, investors using options to obtain leverage may find that the prices of options are the same with margin rules and borrowing costs as they were without them. Transaction costs may be significant in managing an option portfolio. With transaction costs, however, option prices may still be efficient. Even when differential transaction costs between options and other equivalent investments may affect values, competing market makers and brokerage houses—buying and selling options at close to zero marginal transaction costs—bring the prices of option contracts extremely close to the prices of the option contracts that would prevail in the absence of transaction costs.

Prices of American Versus European Options

American options offer something that European options do not: the ability to exercise before option expiration. Consequently, it may be expected that an American option always will sell for a higher price than an identical European option. It general, this is true, but some important exceptions exist. An American call on a non-dividend-paying stock, or a stock that will not pay a dividend before option expiration, should sell for the same price as a European call. The American call premium always includes time value in addition to any intrinsic value (S-E) that would be realized if the option was exercised. The time value would be lost if the option is exercised early; consequently, the holder of an American option should sell rather than exercise to unwind the position. In this case, the early exercise feature is of no added value to the American option.

Calls on dividend-paying stocks are a different matter. The holder of an American call option always should evaluate exercising the option immediately prior to the ex-dividend date to capture the dividend. The opportunity for early exercise in this situation makes an American call option on a dividend-paying security worth more than a European call.

For an American put, the ability to exercise early has value regardless of whether the stock pays dividends. At some stock price, the holder of an in-the-money put (i.e., $E > S$) will gain by exercising the put and placing the proceeds in Treasury bills rather than holding the put to expiration. As noted above, the effect of time on put value is ambiguous, and a deep-in-the-money American put may have zero time value, in which case early exercise is appropriate. Dividends have the opposite effect on put prices, as compared to calls. An American put should be exercised early, if at all, immediately after a dividend payment, since the stock price should fall by the amount of the dividend. The payment of dividends reduces the likelihood that an American put will be exercised early.

Relationship Between Put and Call Prices

For European puts and calls with identical characteristics on the same underlying security, a relationship called put-call parity exists between their prices. Consider having available a put and call with ninety days to maturity, both having an exercise price of $50, for a stock selling for $50 and a riskless bond (e.g., Treasury bill) whose present value equals the exercise price of the options. The put-call parity relationship is given by:

$$\text{Put} + \text{stock} = \text{call} + \text{bond}/(1 + r)^t$$

where r = the daily interest rate of the bond and t = days to maturity

Two implications of this relationship are important. First, if the value of the call is known, the proper value of the put can be determined, and vice versa. Second, the payoffs from alternative strategies can be developed by rearranging the put-call parity equation.

For example, the relationship shown above illustrates that the strategy of buying a put and a share of stock (put + stock) provides the same payoff as the strategy of buying a call and a discounted riskless bond (call + bond/$(1 + r)^t$). Rearranging the equation

$$\text{Put} + \text{stock} - \text{call} = \text{bond}/(1 + r)^t$$

shows that a portfolio containing a long put, long stock position, and short call should give the same return as the riskless bond. Unfortunately, put-call parity doesn't hold exactly for American options because of the effects of dividends and early exercise, but it does provide a good working approximation of their values. The put-call parity formula is used below to explain some of the attractive features about options in risk management of portfolios.

ATTRACTIVE FEATURES

Using Options To Modify Patterns of Returns

The attractive characteristics of options become evident when options are combined with other securities. Combining options with other assets transforms the returns and risks of an option into the returns and risks of an investment strategy: Options combine with other investments to produce patterns of returns for a portfolio of investments. In short, options can alter the return and risk in portfolios.

There are several ways to limit the risk of investing in securities. Diversification is one of the primary ones. The larger the number of assets held in a portfolio, the smaller will be an investor's exposure to the risks of any one security in the portfolio, and the risk of the portfolio will approach the risk of a widely diversified market portfolio. Another approach to limit risk is to invest less than 100 percent of available cash in stocks and allocate the remainder to bonds or money market funds. The larger the fraction of the portfolio in bonds or money market funds, the less risk. (See article on "Modern Portfolio Theory," elsewhere in this volume.)

Puts and calls also enable investors to modify the risk in their portfolios. Using options, investors can reduce risk by insuring against adverse changes in the prices of their holdings of securities or against adverse changes in the value of a portfolio of assets. Options provide patterns of returns that cannot be duplicated at reasonable cost by traditional ways of combining stocks and bonds in portfolios. The economic justification for options is that they enable investors to mold the payoffs of their investment strategies to fit their investment objectives.

Options as Investment Insurance

Put Options as Insurance. One strategy for reducing the risk of a stock portfolio is to buy puts against stock held by the investor. This is one form of portfolio insurance, a technique that limits losses in a down market yet allows the investor to participate in market increases. A put option is like a term insurance policy in which the term or maturity is the length of time between the purchase of the put and its expiration date; the item being insured is the value of the underlying asset. For an option on an individual stock, the face value of the policy, or maximum claim that is paid in the event that the underlying stock becomes worthless, is equal to the number of shares specified in the contract times the exercise price. For partial losses, the amount received is equal to the number of shares times the difference between the exercise price and the market price of the underlying security at the time the put is exercised.

Depending on the relation between the striking price and the price of the underlying asset when the put is purchased, the put option will have features quite similar to an insurance policy with a deductible amount. Assume that an investor owns 100 shares of a stock that has a value of $100 per share. The purchase of a put with an exercise price of $100 totally insures the investor against any decline in the stock's price during the life of the option. The cost for this protection is the put premium, which can be compared to a premium on an insurance policy.

If, however, the investor buys a put with a $90 exercise price, the first $10 decline in the price of the stock is not insured; in insurance terms, the position has a $10 deductible. Just as with an insurance contract, the cost of the insurance will be reduced because the premium on the put with a $90 exercise price is less than the put with a $100 exercise price. Even a negative deductible can be obtained by buying a put that is in the money. If the investor purchases a put with an exercise price of $110, he is insured against not only price declines, but against the stock appreciating $10 in value. Unlike traditional insurance, the investor can buy this insurance without owning the asset.

The same principles of portfolio insurance apply to other options and their underlying assets. The purchase of stock index puts can be used to insure a stock portfolio against declines in value. A similar result could be achieved by buying puts against each stock held in the portfolio, but this would overinsure the portfolio and be more costly than the use of index puts. When using index puts to insure a portfolio, options should be selected on the index that most closely tracks the portfolio being insured. Managers of bond portfolios can purchase puts on debt securities to insure against declines in value due to interest rate fluctuations, and companies or financial institutions exposed to foreign currency risk can insure against declines in a currency's value by purchasing the appropriate foreign currency puts.

Call Options as Insurance. A call option by itself is a highly leveraged means of investing in the underlying asset. Rearrangement of the put-call parity equation shows that call options are equivalent to a long position in the underlying asset levered by a term loan with a face value of the exercise price, plus a put that provides insurance against declines in the stock price below the exercise price:

$$\text{Call} = \text{stock} - \text{bond}/(1 + r)^t + \text{put}$$

Although the leverage component of a call option is its most commonly known characteristic, the insurance characteristic distinguishes call option strategies from simple stock strategies, such as buying stock on margin.

For two calls with the same maturity, the one with the higher striking price will have more leverage; also, it will have a larger insurance component. A call option on a volatile stock is more valuable than a call on one that is less volatile; the source of this greater value is the insurance component.

Further analysis of the put-call parity relationship reveals that the payoffs from a protective put strategy (stock + put) can be replicated by allocating a portion of investable funds to the purchase of calls (say 10 percent) and investing the remainder (90 percent) in Treasury bills:

$$\text{Stock} + \text{put} = \text{call} + \text{bond}/(1 + r)^t$$

Although the purchase of calls by themselves is highly risky, combining calls with investment in Treasury bills is a conservative strategy. The greater the percentage invested in Treasury bills, the lower the risk of the call-buying strategy.

Using Options To Generate Current Income. Covered call writing is the strategy of selling calls against an asset held in a portfolio. Consider buying XYZ stock at $110 and selling a 110 call for $5. Because current income is increased from the premiums received, this strategy is used by some conservative portfolio managers to meet payout objectives. In a flat market, the portfolio return should be increased because of receipt of the option premiums; however, in a rising market, this strategy will underperform the stock only portfolio, because when the calls are exercised the stock is sold at a price below its market value. If XYZ rises to $130 by option expiration, the call will be exercised, and the covered writer will receive only $110 for the stock. The sale of puts also can be used to increase current income, but it exposes the put writer to a potential future cash outflow if the stock price falls and the put is exercised.

Rearrangement of the put-call parity equation shows that covered call writing is equivalent to investing the discounted exercise price of the option in U.S. Treasury bills and selling a put:

$$\text{Stock} - \text{call} = \text{bond}/(1 + r)^t - \text{put}$$

The covered-call-writing strategy is more conservative than buying only calls or allocating 100 percent of investable funds to a stock portfolio. However, investors should be aware of what they are doing when using covered-call-writing; it is the equivalent of selling a put and escrowing the exercise payment in Treasury bills. If the stock goes down, the investor will have the put premium and interest to offset part of the loss on the stock; if the stock goes up, the investor will have the put premium plus interest only. By using fully covered writing strategies, investors are selling insurance on securities and lending money.

Speculation on Asset Price Changes. The purchase of a call option is identical to a levered investment in the underlying asset. An investor who believes a stock will rise in value can either purchase the stock or a call on the stock to speculate on this belief. Conversely, an investor who believes a stock will decline in price can speculate by shorting the stock or buying a put. Buying a put may be more attractive than shorting the stock because (1) the short sale rules of exchanges are avoided and (2) losses are avoided if the stock appreciates in value. Exchange rules require that investors wait for an increase in the price of the stock before making a short sale of stock (the up-tick rule). However, a put can be purchased at any time; just like a short sale, it produces profits if the asset declines in price. Puts and calls on stock indices, Treasury securities, foreign exchange, and futures enable investors to speculate on the price behavior of these securities as well.

Trading on Market Volatility. Unlike other investments, puts and calls enable an investor to trade on the volatility expected in the market. An increase in volatility makes calls and puts more valuable; a decrease in volatility reduces their price. For example, an investor who believes the market will become more volatile but is uncertain of the direction of the market can purchase a straddle, a put and call on the same underlying asset, with identical characteristics.

Consider XYZ stock at $110. A ninety-day call sells for $4, and a ninety-day put sells for $3, both options having a strike of 110. The investory buys a straddle by purchasing both the put and call. If XYZ appreciates to $125, the call will be worth $15 and the put worthless. A profit of $8 ($15 – $7) will be earned from the straddle. If XYZ stock falls to $95, the put will be worth $15 and the call worthless. The straddle again will provide a profit of $8. Only if the stock stays at $110 will the investor lose the entire premium of $7 spent on the options.

Conversely, an investor who believes the market will become less volatile should sell the straddle by selling both the put and call. A profit will be realized if the stock closes between $103 and $117 at option expiration.

POTENTIAL RISKS

Exaggerated Effect of Market Swings

To understand the risks of buying and selling options, it helps to consider why an option differs from the underlying asset. An investor acquires leverage by buying an option. Although the change in price of the option always will be less than the change in the price of the underlying security, the percentage change in the option's price always will be greater than the percentage change in the price of the underlying security. If the exercise price of a call is $100 and the stock is $125, the option could not sell for less than $25; for example, it might sell for $26. If the stock price declines by 10 percent to $112.50 at option expiration, the option would fall more than 50 percent in value, from $26 to $12.50. Holding one option was five times riskier than holding the common stock.

The differences between the risk of the option and the risk of the underlying asset change dramatically with changes in the ratio of the price of the underlying asset to the exercise price of the option. If the price of the underlying security was below the exercise price of the call (i.e., out of the money), investors would view the probability of exercise as low; small changes in the price of the underlying security would cause small changes in the price of the option. If the price of the underlying security, however, was above the striking price, the probability of an exercise would be greater; a change in the price of the underlying security would cause a larger change in the price of the option—less than the change in the price of the underlying security but greater than the change in the price of the option when there was less probability of an exercise. When the price of the underlying security was \$125, a \$1 change in its price would cause about a \$1 change in the option's price, or a change of about 3.8 percent. However, when the stock is at \$80, the call option with the \$100 strike price is worth about \$1; a \$1 change in the price of the underlying security might cause a \$0.05 change in the price of the option, a 5 percent price change. The dollar change in the price of the option always will be less than the dollar change in the price of the underlying security. The percentage change in the price of the option always will be greater than the percentage change in the price of the underlying security.

The prices of options are very sensitive to changes in market prices of the underlying asset. If the market is a boom, the prices of call options explode. If the market is a bust, the prices of call options fizzle. Since options are a leveraged instrument, their prices are sensitive to any changes in the prices of underlying securities.

Risk of Total Loss

Options have the reputation of being highly risky because, when purchased alone, they frequently produce total loss of the investment. Consequently, it is best to consider options in a portfolio context, as a means to shape the pattern of returns of a portfolio to best meet investment objectives. Option buyers never hold only call or put options as their entire portfolios; option sellers never sell only put or call options alone. Although the buyers of options expect a positive return, the risk of holding only a portfolio of options is so great that an investor could go bankrupt; all the options could expire worthless.

Consequently, buyers of call options unlever their position and reduce their risk by allocating a large percentage of investable funds to the purchase of Treasury bills. The purchase of put options by themselves is riskier than holding the underlying asset, but buying individual or index put options against assets held in a portfolio is a risk-reducing activity.

Cash Versus Asset Settlement

The writer of an American call option on an individual asset such as a common stock stands ready to deliver the security any time the buyer elects to exercise the option. If the call writer owns the underlying asset, it is called a covered call; if the writer does not, it is known as a naked call position. As shown above, unless the stock pays a large dividend, it is unlikely that the option will be exercised until maturity. Just prior to expiration the writer of an option that is in the money can close the position by purchasing the option, or hold the position and deliver the underlying asset. A covered call writer has a choice, and thus less risk than the naked call writer, because he possesses the underlying asset at a known cost.

The seller of a stock index call that is settled in cash does not have the opportunity to provide in advance the potential cost of settlement and thus is in a position similar to the naked call writer. Even if the index call writer holds a diversified portfolio that approximates the underlying index, it is unlikely that (1) he will sell the entire portfolio at the time the call expires or (2) the portfolio's change in value will exactly match the change in value of the underlying index. Strategies involving cash settled options thus contain a greater degree of risk than asset-settled options.

TAX CONSEQUENCES

The Tax Reform Act of 1988 made a significant change in the tax treatment of investment income by taxing capital gains and ordinary income at the same rate. Options are considered capital assets, and net gains from long option positions that are closed will be combined, along with stock and bond gains, to the investor's income and taxed at the ordinary income rate. However, tax treatment differs if the option is exercised. Also, options on individual stocks are treated differently than options on indices, debt instruments, and foreign currencies.

Call and Put Options on Individual Stocks

If an investor buys a call or put and later sells it for a profit, the gain is taxed as ordinary income. If a loss results from the sale, it can be deducted from ordinary income, up to a maximum of $3,000. However, if the investor exercises the call, the call premium is added to the price of the stock to determine the basis in the stock, and no tax liability occurs until the stock is sold. If the investor exercises the put, the amount received for the stock, less the put premium previously paid, is considered the sale price of the stock. Taxable gain or loss is determined by subtracting the stock's basis from this sale price. For the call or put writer who buys back the option at a profit, or profts by allowing it to expire worthless, the gain from the premium is included as ordinary income. If the option is bought back before expiration at a loss, the loss can be deducted from ordinary income up to the $3,000 limit.

For the option writer, if a call is exercised, the call premium is added to the price received from the sale of the stock and stock basis is subtracted to determine the gain or loss in the position. If the put is exercised, the put seller subtracts the put premium from the exercise price of the option to determine the basis in the stock. No tax liability occurs until the stock is sold.

Options on Other Assets

The tax treatment of options on stock indices, debt instruments, and foreign currencies differs from that of individual stock options in the following way. At the end of each calendar year, the investor must include all net realized and unrealized gains as ordinary income and can subtract losses from taxable income up to the $3,000 limit. Thus it is assumed for tax purposes that all open positions on these options are closed on the last trading day of the year.

Options and the Wash Sale Rule

The wash sale rule prevents investors from creating losses for tax purposes while retaining a position in the taxable asset. An investor cannot take a loss on the sale of a security if he acquires an identical security during the thirty days prior to or thirty days after the date of sale. For tax purposes, options are considered identical assets to their underlying security; thus investors cannot take a tax loss on a stock if they purchase a call option of the stock during the thirty days before or after the sale of the stock.

Taxation of Options Compared to Underlying Assets

Taxable investors incur potential extra tax costs by trading in options compared to buying and holding the underlying asset. For example, if stocks are bought and held, only the dividends they generate during the year are taxable; unrealized gains are not taxed. Tax liability is not incurred until the asset is sold. However, options on individual stocks, because of their short life, will generate frequent taxable transactions, and the options on other assets can create tax liabilities from unrealized gains at year end.

Options in Tax-Deferred Retirement Accounts

If investors want to use options to insure investments against price declines, it may be more efficient to insure stocks within a tax-deferred account, such as a pension fund, Keogh plan, or individual retirement account (IRA). Within these accounts, all income earned by the assets is taxed as earned income, but only when withdrawn from the accounts; consequently, the potential tax disadvantages of options noted above are avoided. Following a strategy such as buying calls and Treasury bills or buying puts against stocks held in the accounts can benefit investors. They automatically maintain a balanced program, buying insurance on stocks just as they buy insurance on automobiles. This prevents a common error in many investment programs, that of switching between bonds and stocks in anticipation of market moves or when the market has moved already.

Timing the market by switching between bonds and stocks increases risk for little, if any, extra return. In contrast, the strategy of using calls and bonds or puts and stocks is a perfect timer of movements in the market. Investors participate in up movements in the market and protect against the down movements. A major advantage of these strategies is that they change the patterns of returns on investments; the new patterns discipline investors to stay in the market and to maintain a constant level of risk for their holdings of assets. For long-term investments, such as pension accounts, keeping risk constant is the best strategy; for a given level of expected return, it has the minimum risk.

REPRESENTATIVE TYPES OF INVESTORS

Individuals

The examples above illustrate that puts and calls can be used in a variety of risk-modifying strategies that mold return patterns to fit the needs of any investor. Conservative individuals may increase current income by selling insurance-writing call options against stock that they hold or selling puts and escrowing the exercise price in riskless securities. Alternately, they may buy insurance by purchasing puts against their assets or by buying calls with a portion of their wealth and allocating the remainder to money market securities. Investors who believe they have superior information may purchase options to obtain leverage; others may buy options merely to gamble. The tremendous growth in participation by individuals in the options markets since 1973 indicates that options fulfill the investment objectives of a variety of investors.

Institutional Investors

Fixed-Income Portfolio Managers. Mutual funds, mortgage companies, pension funds, and financial institutions exposed to interest rate risk by positions in bonds, loans, and other debt instruments can modify their risk exposure using options on debt securities and options on debt futures. For example, the purchase of puts on Treasury bonds will insure the fixed-income portfolio against price declines caused by rising interest rates. Insurance also is obtained by the purchase of Treasury bond calls that can be combined with money market securities, thereby shortening the maturity of the debt portfolio. Current income can be increased by the sale of debt options. Attention must be given to state statutes and fund charters regarding permissible strategies of regulated investment companies and financial institutions. Because debt options have been available only since 1982, the use of these securities by professional fund managers is a recent phenomenon.

Equity Investment Managers. Equity investment managers in charge of pension funds, college endowment funds, mutual funds, and insurance company investments are recognizing the benefits of using options to manage risk in their stock portfolios. Strategies followed generally are of two types: the purchase of options to create insured portfolios and the sale of options to reduce portfolio variability and increase current income.

Pension and endowment funds have generally defined payment and earnings requirements. Fund managers are concerned with meeting earnings objectives and avoiding large losses, rather than merely maximizing return. Consequently, the implementation of a portfolio insurance strategy can assist them in meeting their investment objectives. To insure equity portfolios, fund managers buy stock index puts at a strike price that defines the maximum loss they are willing to incur. If the market declines, the fund loses a defined amount; if the market appreciates, the fund's stocks appreciate, but the return is reduced by the cost of the puts. The protective puts thus reduce risk while allowing the fund to participate in market advances.

Other fund managers purchase portfolio insurance by buying call options with a small percentage of investable funds and balancing the risk by investing the remainder in short-term Treasury bills. The strategy can be implemented with individual or index calls, but the return patterns differ.

Other institutional investors follow programs that involve the sale of insurance: the covered-call-writing strategy of selling individual or index call options against stock held in their portfolios, or selling puts and escrowing the exercise price in short-term Treasury bills. The writing of index puts or calls generates a different pattern of returns compared to options on the individual securities, and the risk is different because of the cash settlement procedures followed for index options.

The covered-call-writing strategy is popular not because it is thought of as the writing of insurance on common stock, but because it appears to produce extra income, the premium, and to reduce the risk of holding common stock. The worst application of this strategy is to assume that the underlying stock will never be sold; therefore, the premium is extra income, or the premium income cushions declines in the price of the stock, or the premium income covers small advances in the price of the stock. As with writing insurance generally, the equity fund participates in down markets and gives up the gains in up markets.

Big up-market movements are lost under the fully covered strategy when stock that was never to be sold is called away at the exercise price; in reality, the in-the-money call option is repurchased at a loss. The fully covered strategy and its variations produce patterns of returns resulting in more current income, usually balanced with an occasional big loss when compared to holding the underlying stock outright. For this reason, managers of funds following a covered-writing strategy during the bull market from 1982 to 1987 typically underperformed stock-only funds.

Multinational Companies and Financial Institutions

Foreign currency options and options on foreign currency futures can be used to hedge foreign currency exposure of multinational companies and financial institutions. For example, the sale of computers by an American company to a French firm, in which the contract price is stated in French francs, exposes the American firm to foreign exchange risk until the francs are received and converted into dollars. Assume the exchange rate is $0.20 per French franc today and the payment in francs will be made in ninety days. The American company can hedge the exchange rate risk by purchasing three-month puts on the French franc with a striking price of 0.20 $/Fr. Depreciation in the franc will cause the put to increase in value, thus offsetting the loss incurred when the francs are received and converted to dollars.

Institutional Investors, Options, and Program Trading

The term "program trading" received publicity in the early 1980s in reference to mechanistic trading routines designed to arbitrage mispricing between stock index futures and the underlying stocks of the index. These trading strategies were used by institutional investors for their own accounts or were sold as a service to their clients. In general, the price of a stock index futures contract should bear a relationship to the current value of the index defined by the cost-of-carry model

$$\text{Futures price} = \text{spot price} \times [1 + (\text{interest rate} - \text{dividend yield})]^t$$

where t indicates the time to expiration of the futures contract. For example, if the value of the SPX is 300, short-term interest rates 8 percent (annualized), and the annual dividend yield on the S&P 500 stocks is 3.5 percent, the three-month futures contract should sell for 303.32.

This model reflects the idea that is possible to take a position in the index with no capital investment using futures, whereas direct investment in the stocks themselves requires an outlay of capital (i.e., a cost of carry). Since Treasury bills can be used to satisfy the 5 to 10 percent margin required for an index futures contract, virtually no capital commitment is required for a futures position. Because short-term interest rates have exceeded the 2.5 to 4.0 percent yield on the stocks in the index since index futures were introduced, the cost-of-carry model generally has indicated that the futures prices should be greater than the spot price of the index.

Using computer programs that continuously compare the theoretical value of the futures contract to the spot value of the index, program traders can identify when the futures are mispriced relative to the underlying basket of stocks composing the index. Continuing the example from above, if the futures price is 307.50, it is overvalued compared to the cost of carry price of 303.32. Program traders will create a hedge by selling the overpriced futures and buying the underlying stocks in the index, using the automated computer trading system on the NYSE. (If the futures value is underpriced, program traders will buy the futures contracts and short the underlying stocks.)

The value of the index three months hence is unknown, but the program traders are perfectly hedged; at futures contract expiration, the value of the futures must equal the value of the index. At futures expiration, they reverse their hedge, buying back the futures at a gain or loss and selling their stock positions for an approximately offsetting loss or gain.

A profit will be earned on this position, which is greater than the short-term interest rate on a riskless investment.

Although traditional program trading involves futures contracts, the prices of stock-index options, options on futures, and the futures contracts themselves are inexorably linked. A synthetic long position in a futures contract can be created by buying an option on a futures call and selling the identical put. Put-call parity for options on futures must hold or arbitrageurs will create a hedged position from selling the overpriced security and buying the underpriced one. Sophisticated program trading strategies can be implemented using options on the futures and options on the indexes in addition to trading index futures contracts.

Market critics have blamed program trading for accentuating volatility in the market and magnifying the market's decline on October 19, 1987. While this controversy has not been resolved, use of the computerized trading system on the NYSE has been curtailed when a daily market move is greater than fifty points on the DJIA, effectively suspending program trading because orders must be delivered by runner to the various posts on the floor.

Institutional Investors and Portfolio Insurance

Prior to the market break of October 1987, more than $100 billion in institutional equity portfolios was managed under strategies called dynamic asset allocation, a form of portfolio insurance. An insured portfolio is one in which losses are limited to a known value, including zero, if the market declines; but if the market rises, the portfolio will appreciate in value by a proportional amount. As explained above, insured portfolios can be created using put or call options.

Another means to insure a portfolio is to create synthetic options using dynamic asset allocation. Synthetic options are created by institutional investors because (1) the listed options markets may not be large enough to absorb the funds involved or (2) requirements may exist for options with a particular expiration date and striking price that are not traded on an exchange (e.g., a three-year European put with a striking price equal to the current value of the equity portfolio).

A synthetic put can be created by shorting a fractional share of stock and lending money at the riskless rate, the proportions of stock and riskless asset being determined from an option pricing model. The allocation between the short stock position and the riskless asset must be rebalanced frequently (e.g., daily) as the stock price changes. A fall in the stock price requires an increase in the short stock position, which provides more funds to lend; an increase in the stock price means that lending will be reduced and stock purchased to reduce the short position. These synthetic option strategies will lead to increased buying activity in a rising market and increased selling activity in a falling market. For reasons of trading efficiency, most dynamic asset allocation strategies use stock index futures (see article on "Futures: Financial, Agricultural, Currency," elsewhere in this volume, for an explanation of these instruments) instead of individual stocks to create the short position required for synthetic puts.

The continuous trading required by dynamic portfolio insurance strategies led many critics to assert that these strategies along with program trading increased market volatility and accentuated the market decline during October 1987. As the market fell during October 15, 16, and 19, portfolio insurers were selling stock index futures in an attempt to maintain required short equity positions. Selling pressure on the index futures contracts should lead to buying of the underlying stocks as arbitragers attempt to profit from the mispriced futures. However, on October 19 the stock and futures markets became delinked when stock price quotations trailed actual trading activity by more than sixty minutes. At one point on October 19, stock index futures were selling at a 20 percent discount from what appeared to be their theoretical value, causing many dynamic allocation investment advisors to suspend trading of stock index futures. The equity portfolios then became uninsured. Since the difficulties of implementing dynamic allocation strategies were experienced in October 1987, the amount of equity funds insured by this strategy has declined dramatically.

A major difference between dynamic portfolio allocation insurance and the insurance provided by individual or index options is that the dynamic strategies are dependent on the path followed by security prices. Higher than expected volatility in stock prices reduces the effectiveness of dynamic strategies and increases their costs. Extreme stock price volatility can cause the strategy to become inoperable. Conversely, the cost and effectiveness of the insurance provided by put and call options is known when the options are purchased. The insurance protection will remain in place until the option expires or is exercised.

IMPORTANT FACTORS IN BUYING AND SELLING

Trading Options Through Brokers

Almost all major retail brokerage firms and discount brokers will trade options for clients who can meet minimum net worth requirements (e.g., $10,000) and open a margin account. A few brokerage firms will not open option accounts for their clients because their management believes that options do not serve the needs of their customers.

A buyer acquires an option by making an opening purchase transaction and cancels an option by making a closing purchase transaction. Writers are willing to be on the other side of an opening purchase transaction. In either case, brokers send their order to their firm's booth on the floor of the exchange; then a floor broker trades it at a designated location either with another floor broker, a market maker, or, on the AMEX, a specialist. Although the other floor brokers represent other writers or buyers, the market makers trade for their own accounts, thus providing significant liquidity to the market. Exchange rules prohibit market makers from trading ahead of public orders.

Position and Exercise Limits

The OCC and option exchanges limit the number of options that can be held by a single investor on the same side of the market (i.e., calls purchased and puts sold, or puts purchased and calls sold). These position limits vary across the different types of underlying assets and should be ascertained by the investor before trading large positions. Exercise limits specify the total number of puts or calls on the same underlying asset that an individual may exercise during any five consecutive business days.

Types of Orders

As with trading in common stock, investors may place various kinds of orders to execute option trades. A market order instructs the floor broker to buy or sell the options at the best price possible when the order reaches the exchange floor. A limit order specifies execution at or better than a particular price. Orders for multiple contracts may be specified all or none, which instructs the broker to hold the trade until all the contracts can be placed on the same ticket. When trading spread positions (e.g, two or more different contracts on the same underlying security), instructions may be given to trade the entire order at a set spread or better.

Exercising Options

Option buyers should understand their broker's rules for exercising options and the procedures used by the OCC to assign exercise notices. American options can be exercised at any time before the expiration date, but European options can be exercised only on that date. Most brokerage firms require that instructions to exercise be given before 3:00 P.M. on the business day preceding expiration. The firm then notifies the OCC of the order to exercise, and the OCC randomly selects a writer of the option to deliver the asset. Investors should assume that any option in the money near the hours of option expiration will be exercised.

Transaction Costs

Trading costs include bid-asked spreads and brokerage fees. The liquidity of the market is such that competition keeps the spreads and brokerage fees relatively low when compared to stocks; however, options are traded more frequently relative to stocks because of their set expiration dates. Investors should expect to incur higher relative transaction costs trading in options than in common stocks.

GLOSSARY

American option—An option that can be exercised at any time before the expiration date.

arbitrage—Buying an asset and selling an identical asset to make a riskless profit.

at the money—An option whose strike price equals the current price of the underlying asset.

binomial option pricing model—A mathematical model used to find the value of American and European puts and calls.

Black-Scholes Option Pricing Model—A mathematical model used to find the value of European puts and calls.

call option—The right to buy the underlying asset at a specified price.

cash settled options—Options in which exercise means that the writer pays the buyer the difference between the asset price and the exercise price in cash, instead of delivering the underlying asset.

CBOE—Chicago Board Options Exchange, founded in 1973.

commodity option—An option whose underlying asset is a commodity.

covered call—A position in which the call option writer owns the underlying asset.

debt option—An option whose underlying asset is a debt security (e.g., a U.S. Treasury bill).

dynamic asset allocation—A strategy that allocates investment between the underlying asset and the riskless security to create a synthetic option. The option is constructed to insure the portfolio against loss.

European option—An option that can be exercised only on the expiration date.

exercise notice—Indication that an option is being exercised against the writer.

exercise value—Value of an option if it is exercised; also called intrinsic value.

expiration date—Last date an option can be exercised.

foreign currency option—An option whose underlying asset is foreign currency.

futures contract—Buying or selling an asset for future delivery.

futures option—An option whose underlying asset is a futures contract.

hedging—Reducing risk by creating an opposite position in an identical asset.

index option—An option whose underlying asset is a stock or bond index rather than an individual asset. Index options are cash settled.

in the money—An option that has immediate exercise value. A call is in the money if the asset price is above the strike price. A put is in the money if the asset price is below the strike price.

intrinsic value—Value of an option if it is exercised immediately; also called exercise value.

naked call option—The call writer does not own the underlying asset; called an uncovered option.

Option Clearing Corporation (OCC)—A regulated agency that is the buyer for the seller of every option and the seller to every buyer.

open interest—The total number of options or futures contracts outstanding.

option buyer—Holds a long position in the option and has the right to exercise.

option seller—Holds a short position in the option and must deliver the asset if requested by the option buyer. The option seller also is referred to as the option writer.

out of the money—A call whose strike price is below the market price of the asset or a put whose strike price is above the market price of the asset.

portfolio insurance—A strategy that limits losses in a portfolio while allowing for proportional gains relative to a benchmark index.

premium—Price paid the option buyer to the option seller.

put-call parity—A mathematical relationship between the fair value of a European put and call option with identical terms on the same underlying asset.

put option—Right to sell an asset at a specified price.

riskless asset—A financial asset that has no risk; for practical purposes, represented by U.S. Treasury bills.

straddle—Buying (selling) a put and call on the same asset with the same strike price.

strike price—Price of the underlying asset that will be paid if the option is exercised; also called the exercise price.

synthetic option—A position that provides the same payoffs as an option, created by investing in the underlying asset and the riskless security.

time value—The part of the option premium that does not reflect exercise value. The premium of an out-of-the-money option is entirely time value.

underlying asset—The asset that must be delivered if the option is exercised.

volatility—A measure of dispersion of the price changes in a financial asset.

SUGGESTED READING

The CBOE, AMEX, and other option exchanges make available many information booklets describing trading procedures and the uses of options.

Black, Fischer. "Fact and Fantasy in the Use of Options," *Financial Analysts Journal*, July–August 1975, pp. 36–41, 61–72.

______, and Scholes, M. "The Pricing of Options and Corporate Liabilities," *Journal of Political Economy*, May–June 1973, pp. 399–417.

Bookstaber, Richard M. *Option Pricing & Investment Strategies*, rev. ed. Chicago: Probus Publishers, 1987.

Chance, D.M. *An Introduction to Options and Futures*. Chicago: Dryden Press, 1989.

Cox, J.C., and Rubenstein, M. *Options Markets*. Englewood Cliffs: Prentice-Hall, 1985.

Leland, H.E. "Portfolio Insurance and Ocober 19th," *California Management Review*, Summer 1988, pp. 80–114.

McMillan, L.G. *Options as a Strategic Investment*, 2nd ed. New York: New York Institute of Finance, 1986.

Merton, R.C., Scholes, M., and Gladstein, M. "The Returns and Risk of Alternative Put Option Portfolio Investment Strategies," *Journal of Business*, Apr. 1982, pp. 1–55.

______. "The Returns and Risk of Alternative Call Option Strategies," *Journal of Business*, Apr. 1978, pp. 183–242.

The Options Clearing Corporation. *Characteristics and Risks of Standardized Options*. Chicago, *Sept. 1987*.

Ritchken, P. *Options: Theory, Strategy, and Applications*: Glenview: Scott, Foresman, 1987.

Rubenstein, M. "Alternative Paths to Portfolio Insurance," *Financial Analysts Journal*, July–Aug. 1985, pp. 42–52.

Trennepohl, G.L., Booth, J., and Tehranian, H. "An Empirical Analysis of Insured Portfolio Strategies Using Listed Options," *Journal of Financial Research*, Spring 1988, pp. 1–12.

U.S. Government Printing Office. *Report of the Presidential Task Force on Market Mechanisms*. Washington, D.C., 1988.

PAINTINGS

J. Patrick Cooney

BASIC CHARACTERISTICS

The purchase and sale of paintings dominate the overall art market in terms of both dollar values and publicity. No other category of art attracts the international interest or the multimillion-dollar prices achieved by paintings. In fact, for many investors, paintings are synonymous with art. The market for paintings covers a broad range of periods as well as nationalities, ranging from twelfth-century Greek icons painted on wood panels to contemporary acrylic stained canvases. In the discussion that follows, paintings are presented in six major categories: Old Masters, nineteenth century, Impressionist and Postimpressionist, modern, contemporary, and American.

The value of a work of art is in large part subjective. Unlike many other investment instruments, art does not provide cash dividends; it is certainly not a substitute for money. Rather, the value of a painting is established by what buyers and sellers think that value is. Unlike paper money, shares, or coins, art is not related to a means of production, to the ability of a government to honor its obligations, or to skills organized to deliver a service. Works of art are created for a number of purposes. In some cases, they are embued with mystical qualities, as in religious pictures or artifacts. In other cases, they are commemorative, such as portraits and paintings of historic scenes. In still other cases, works of art are designed to be useful, as with furniture, silver, or many of the decorative arts. Ironically, the value of a work of art increases when it is no longer being used for the purpose for which it was created. For example, collectors during the early twentieth century paid

J. Patrick Cooney is Assistant Vice-President, Fine Arts Management Service, Citibank, New York.

enormous prices to coax portraits of English noblemen from their ancestral halls. Similarly, Meissen teacups that once were in daily use became priceless when sitting in a museum showcase. It could be argued that objects become more highly valued when they cease to be what their creators made and become something special—a work of art.

Determinants of Value

Various factors, some of them elusive, contribute to the market value of paintings. The following, although difficult to measure in dollar terms, are the principal determinants.

Quality. A number of characteristics affect the price of any work. Quality is undoubtedly the most important of these; it is also the most difficult to define, as it is based on connoisseurship, a consensus of scholarly opinions, and taste. Certainly no one today would question that Rembrandt's *Self Portrait* at the Frick Collection in New York is a work of supreme quality. However, this opinion has not always been held. During the eighteenth century, works by Rembrandt were not as highly prized as those of some of his contemporaries.

Authorship. Works by established, respected artists command higher prices than those by unknown artists. A signed work by Gauguin will sell for more than even a high-quality work by one of his unknown contemporaries.

Authenticity. It is essential that the work being purchased is by the artist to whom it is attributed. With works by modern artists, this can usually be checked with galleries, scholars or the artist himself. However, with Old Master paintings, questions often arise, and debates between scholars are frequent. Questions of attribution and authenticity can also change as scholars continue to research and study the history of art. If there is any doubt, the investor should check with several authorities.

Provenance. Provenance is the history of ownership of a painting, a listing of the collections through which a picture has passed. This history can be important in establishing the authenticity or identity of a specific painting. It can also affect price. A painting that has been in a royal collection or that of a distinguished collector frequently commands a higher price than a similar work without such a history.

Market Demand. The existence of a number of collectors willing to pay high prices for what they want is essential to establish and stimulate an active market. The investor who buys a work with the intent of selling it should be sure there will be a broad market. For example, Impressionist paintings are prized internationally and are avidly collected by Europeans, Americans, Latin Americans, and Asians. On the other hand, the market for Brazilian contemporary art is for the most part a localized national market.

Rarity. Prices continue to rise as high-quality works become less frequently available. However, in certain areas, rarity does not necessarily indicate value. A sufficient supply of work is necessary to stimulate interest in the market and make collectors competitive. A unique work may appeal only to a limited group of collectors and therefore may not command the highest price. Premium prices can be expected when supply is just below the market demand.

Condition. Collectors, investors, and institutions continue to seek works of art in pristine condition. Even slight damage may severely affect the value of a painting, particularly when similar works are available on the market.

Price Guides and Indexes

Price Lists. A number of aids are available to help the investor track the price of works of art. In almost all categories of art objects, it is usually accepted that the prices achieved at public auctions are the best general indicator of overall market trends. In June 1960, *Fortune* magazine stated, "It is a safe generalization that public auctions set basic price trends, and a dealer, while listening to hearsay of private transactions, takes prices reached through open bidding as the main basis for evaluating his own stock." A growing number of price guides are published on an annual basis. Following each public sale at the major auction houses, price lists are made available. Of the many lists of prices achieved at auction, *The Year's Art*, started in 1880, is probably the oldest and *The Annual Art Sales Index* by Richard Hislop is the best known. E. Mayer's *International Auction Records* covers a broader range of sales and includes prints, drawings, watercolors, and sculpture. However, these publications present merely the raw facts of the prices fetched by works of art. They do not provide reliable analysis of the changes in prices or trends.

Indexes. Since November 1980, Sotheby's has published a weekly art index presented in *Barron's*. This index is a highly sophisticated attempt to quantify the art and antiques market. It offers a statistical look at what has happened in twelve important areas in the overall market and provides a single aggregate figure to show how the market as a whole has performed. In each category, the index is based on a generic sampling that is representative of the types of objects that come on the market fairly frequently. Sampling specifically avoids the kind of blockbuster that come up only rarely and makes its way onto the front pages of *The New York Times* by virture of having reached an eight-figure price. The sampling of items is reevaluated following each major sale, approximately ten to fifteen times a year. Although Sotheby's index is constructed as accurately as possible, it cannot pretend to be as accurate as a stock market index. However, it is a good general guide to the movements of the art market.

ATTRACTIVE FEATURES

Art is not always a good investment, any more than any other vehicle is. However, art certainly can be regarded as a durable asset.

Independence of Money Economy

As Gerald Reitlinger has pointed out in *The Economics of Taste*, Vol. III, "The slump of 1968–69 produced a paradox which threatened to become an orthodoxy. It is that works of art go up in proportion as capital values, profits, and dividends decline, that as substitutes for money, works of art are not liable to the same erosions as money itself." Internationally collected art also has the advantage of generally selling in the strongest currency. Collectors and investors with strong currencies tend to be the most active at any given moment. Art goes where money flows. If a painting is purchased by a collector bidding with strong German marks, the seller has the advantage of realizing an increased return vis-à-vis his local currency.

Long-Term Appreciation

In case after case, particular pieces of art have provided investors with substantial increases in value. However, art must be looked at as a long-term investment, with a normal holding period of five to ten years. Works of art usually cannot be resold quickly with sizable appreciation. The costs of moving an item in and out of the market are considerable. Not only are high fees incurred in transactions, but works of art are adversely affected by appearing too frequently on the market. When a work of art is sold more than once within a short period, it is often considered burned.

Psychic Income

For most, the unrivaled benefit of investing in works of art is an intangible one: the pleasure of ownership. The profound psychological and aesthetic enjoyment provided by works of art has stimulated many of the best financial investments.

POTENTIAL RISKS

Limited Appreciation for Overall Market

The art market overall has moved in steady, consistent trends. Contrary to the impression one receives from newspaper headlines, the art market as a whole has shown only a gradual increase in prices over the past twenty years. Although there are specific examples of individual works returning 30 and 40 percent a year, for the past ten years the average painting has performed in a steady and much less dramatic fashion.

Low Liquidity

The art market is not as liquid as many other investment media. Liquidity to a large extent depends on market conditions. To sell a work of art at auction takes a minimum of several months for cataloging and publication of information. Following the sale, thirty days must be allowed for payment to be made. Private sales often can be arranged more quickly, depending on the desirability of the material being offered.

Risk of Fraud

As paintings become increasingly expensive, the proliferation of forgeries becomes a greater consideration. The best protection against fakes is to know the market and to seek expert advice. Certain dealers and auction houses will guarantee items they sell, but these guarantees are limited and vary widely. The terms of the guarantee are published in the front of the auction catalog.

Import and Export Regulations

Before investing in any work of art, the investor should make sure that the item being purchased has free and clear title and can be exported from the country in which it is purchased. It is not uncommon for a foreign government to prohibit the exportation of national treasures (i.e., works of art that it seeks to maintain as part of its national heritage). In many cases, export licenses are required before a painting can leave a country.

Changes in Fashions

The value of works of art to a certain extent depends on taste. In contemporary art, in particular, there is a great risk that today's master will be tomorrow's forgotten painter.

OLD MASTER PAINTINGS

Definition

Old Master Paintings are European paintings created up to, but not including, the nineteenth century.

Marketplace

Auction Houses. London traditionally has been the largest center for the sale of Old Master pictures. During April, July, and December, Sotheby's and Christie's, the two largest auction houses, hold major sales. In recent years, New York City has become an increasingly important center where auctions are held in January and June. Auctions are also arranged by the auction houses on a regular basis in Monte Carlo, Rome, Paris, and Amsterdam.

Dealers. Dealers play a very strong role in the Old Master market. Although the largest number of paintings may pass through the hands of the auction houses, dealers have traditionally handled many of the most important Old Masters. A dealer will often guarantee a selling price, either through outright purchase or by contract. It is not unusual for a dealer to guarantee anonymity to a seller or buyer. Anonymity can be of great importance in delicate situations and is not as easily achieved in the auction world.

Private Sector. The private sector of the market traditionally has been thought to be dominated by European buyers, but North and South Americans also provide a strong market. Foreign exchange fluctuations tend to discourage buying by holders of devalued currencies, and vice versa. For example, during the 1988 season European buying, especially by Germans and Italians, was particularly strong owing to the strength of foreign currencies against the dollar.

Important Factors in the Old Master Market

Stability. Old Master pictures are traditionally known for their stability. One reason is that museums have been the major purchasers of high-quality, important Old Masters. Established collections will pay high prices to enhance or round out their holdings. New museums, such as the Kimbell Art Museum and the J. Paul Getty Museum, reportedly push up the price of Old Masters in building new collections. However, the private collectors still dominate the market.

Quality and Reputation. Quality is a vital factor in the Old Master market as well as most other painting markets. High-quality works sell under all conditions, while lesser quality pieces are not sold. The inclusion of a painting in a show, catalog, or scholarly work strengthens its reputation and acceptance.

Attribution. Attribution is very important: a painting by the hand of the master is much more valuable than a school picture. A portrait believed to have been painted by Peter Paul Rubens was bought for $100,000 in 1901 by J.P. Morgan. In 1935, it was sold to the Metropolitan Museum of Art for more than twice that sum. Scholarship, however, has now shown the picture to be by the school of Rubens, and the picture was recently sold at auction for only $22,000.

Subject Matter. Subject matter often affects the salability of a picture. Portraits, popular earlier in this century, are not collected as enthusiastically today except by institutions. Landscapes, genre scenes, and flower pictures appeal to a broad international market. During recent seasons, there has been a doubling and tripling of prices for seventeenth- and eighteenth-century still lifes, which collectors find attractive and easy to live with.

Supply. The supply of first-quality Old Master pictures is very small. It is a rare occurrence for a masterpiece to appear on the market. When a major picture does appear on the auction market, it creates headlines in the press with its spectacular price. Rembrandt's *Aristotle Contemplating the Bust of Homer* sold to the Metropolitan Museum of Art, in New York City, for $2,300,000 in November 1961. Velasquez's *Portrait of Juan de Pareja* sold to the same institution for $5,544,000 in November 1970. During the 1978 to 79 season, two major works sold at auction in London: Dirk Bout's *Resurrection* for $3,740,000 to the Norton Simon Museum in California, and *Samson and Delilah*, by Peter Paul Rubens, for $5,400,000 to the National Gallery in London.

More recently, the market for Old Master paintings has become increasingly attractive. In 1985, Mantegna's *The Adoration of the Magi* sold to the Getty Museum for a world record price of $10,449,000. In 1986, a private collector purchased Rembrandt's *Portrait of a Girl* in London for $10,871,400, while another Rembrandt, *St. Peter in Prison*, sold privately for $8,000,000.

The price of Old Master paintings has increased dramatically. As the prices of Impressionist and modern pictures have risen above the reach of most collectors and investors, many have turned to Old Masters, which by comparison appear to be undervalued. This influx of new interest is reflected in new price levels. For example, David Teniers the Younger's *An Alchemist at Work* sold in 1984 for $291,384 and resold in 1988 for $572,000.

The market for Dutch still life paintings has also been very strong in recent years. In 1987, a Cornelius van Spaendonck *Still Life* sold for a record price of $105,000. One year later, Jan van Huysum's *Still Life of Flowers in a Vase* sold for $396,000 and Gerard van Spaendonck's *Still Life With Flowers in a Stone Vase* sold for $797,500. In January 1988, Jan Davidsz. de Heem's *Still Life* sold for $2,530,000, and on the next day this masterpiece brought $6,600,000.

The price performance of Old Master paintings from 1975 to 1988 is shown in Figure 1, which plots Sotheby's Art Index for Old Masters for those years. The graph shows that the index has risen 350 points, from 100 to 450, over the period, for an increase of 350 percent. For the period 1986 to 1988, the index rose from 350 to 450, an increase of 28 percent.

NINETEENTH-CENTURY PAINTINGS

Definition

This category includes all nineteenth-century paintings, exclusive of Impressionist and American paintings.

FIGURE 1. Price Performance of Old Master Paintings, 1975 to 1988

Note: Figures 1 through 5 in this article are based on data taken from Sotheby's Art Index. Sotheby's Art Index reflects subjective analyses and opinions of Sotheby's art experts, based on auction sales and other information deemed relevant. Nothing in Sotheby's Art Index is intended or should be relied upon as investment advice or as a prediction or guarantee of future performance or otherwise.

Source: Sotheby's Art Index, © 1989 Sotheby's Holding, Inc.

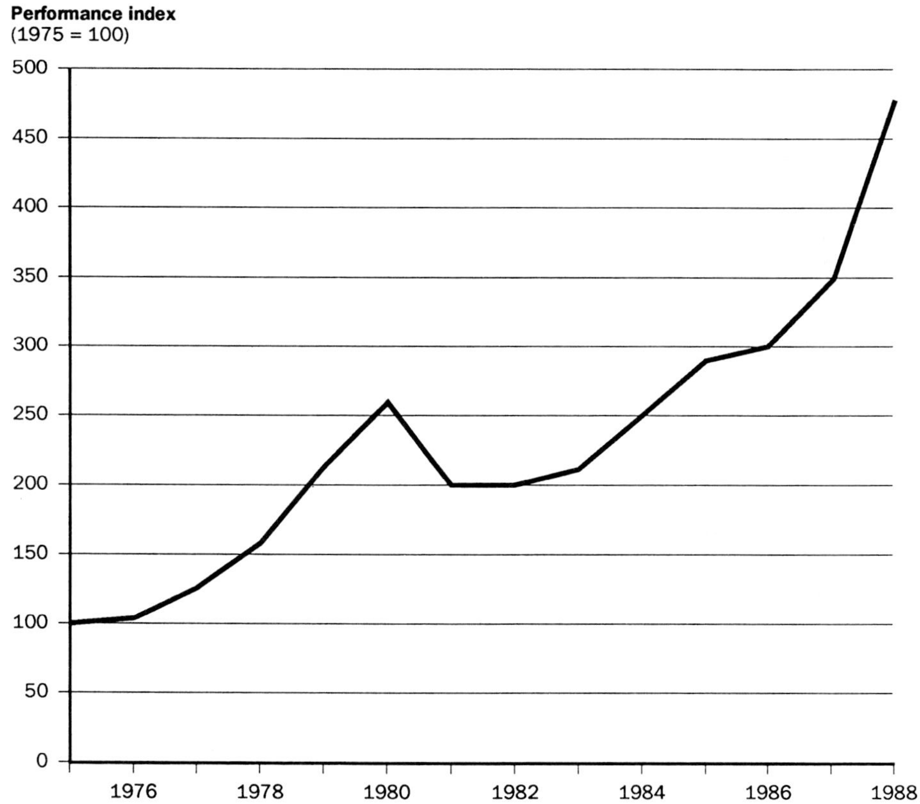

Marketplace

Nineteenth-century paintings are widely sold in Europe and in the United States. In the nineteenth century, American millionaires went to Europe and bought paintings right off the walls of the salons to hang in their homes. Therefore, large numbers of nineteenth-century European paintings are now in the United States. The demand for these paintings took a decided downward turn about the time of World War I. Many paintings came off the walls and went into storage, and are only now being rediscovered. The major buyers of nineteenth-century paintings today are Europeans themselves; national pride helps motivate the purchase of many of these paintings. German, Dutch, and Belgian collectors dominate the world market, while the English and French find paintings within their own borders. Sentimental subjects are very popular, and recognizable scenes bring heavy competition in the country involved.

A current subgroup consists of rich buyers from the Middle East who are looking for Middle Eastern, or "Orientalist," subjects, a popular theme during the nineteenth century. Collectors are so anxious to get works that they often fly to sales in American cities—New York, Boston, Philadelphia, San Francisco, and New Orleans—to buy particular paintings. Seventy percent of buyers at recent auction have been European.

In addition, many dealers have set up businesses just to handle nineteenth-century European paintings and to cater to the European market coming to the United States to buy. Small but growing interest is seen in U.S. museums, some of which are anxious to build collections while prices are still affordable. Dealers often show interest in artists whose work is given a major show in the United States, because the reputation and, therefore, the prices of an artist's work are often rehabilitated by a major show in a museum or reputable gallery.

Value of Nineteenth-Century Paintings

The average price range for high-quality nineteenth-century paintings is between $50,000 and $500,000. Recognized painters bring the highest prices. As with Old Master paintings, few major masterpieces reach the market. However, when they do, they obtain high prices. In 1987, Jacques Louis David's *The Farewell of Telemachus and Eucharis* sold to the Getty Museum for $4,070,000. Prices for works by such artists as Delacroix, Courbet, and Millet continue to demand high prices. During the past few years, the market has begun to appreciate the value of many of the lesser-known nineteenth-century artists. In 1979, John Frederick Lewis's *An Intercepted Correspondence* sold for $450,000; nine years later, it was auctioned for $1,265,000.

Even works by such Victorian artists as James-Jacques-Joseph Tisot have escalated in price; his *A Fête Day at Brighton* sold in 1988 for a record price of $962,500. The artist Albert Joseph Moore is also becoming more appreciated by the market; in 1986, his painting *Musk* sold for $243,320, while in 1988, a similar picture, *Topaz*, brought $715,000; a record for this artist. As the more popular artists' work becomes more expensive and less available, experts feel that the work of lesser nineteenth-century artists will enjoy a substantial escalation in price. The price performance of nineteenth-century European paintings from 1975 to 1988, according to Sotheby's Art Index, is shown in Figure 2.

IMPRESSIONIST AND POSTIMPRESSIONIST PAINTINGS

Definitions

The works of the French artists known as Impressionists attracted wide attention during the 1874 to 1886 period, when they were shown together at various exhibits in Paris. The Postimpressionists, whose work began about the same time and continued to the end of the century, repudiated the Impressionists through emphasis on form and structure.

Marketplace and Value

Impressionism has long been out of the most prestigious areas of art collecting. Works by the great Impressionist and Postimpressionist painters are prized by collectors all over the world. Europeans, North and South Americans, and Japanese are all actively bidding

FIGURE 2. Price Performance of Nineteenth-Century European Paintings, 1975 to 1988

Source: Sotheby's Art Index, © 1989 Sotheby's Holding, Inc.

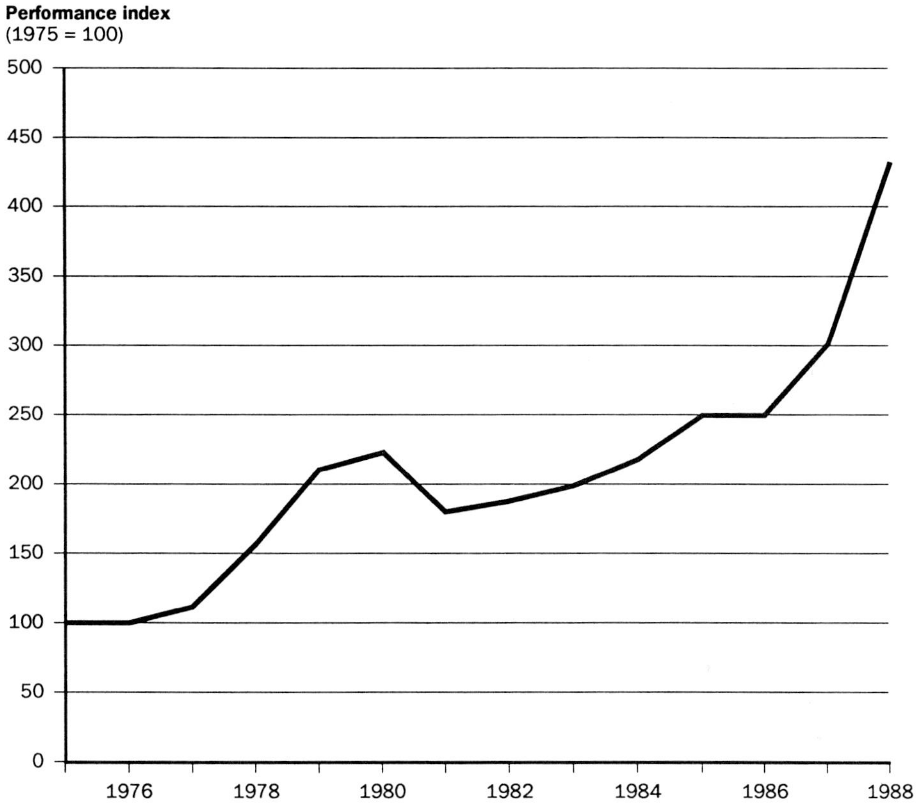

for these paintings. Ever since the London Goldschmidt auction sale in 1958, when Impressionist works first brought auction prices that rivaled the amounts paid for the most important Old Masters, French Impressionist and Postimpressionist paintings have been the money center of the art market. Fine Impressionist pictures are today the blue chips of the art world.

Although many of the Impressionist and Postimpressionist painters were unknown in their own lifetimes (Van Gogh sold only one painting during his entire life), by the turn of the century there was already a thriving market for these artists' work. In 1912, Dégas's *Danseurs à la barre* sold to the Louvre for $102,270. Renoir's *Les Cantoniers* sold to Duncan Phillips for $200,000 in 1923. During the early part of this century, great European and American private collections of Impressionist and Postimpressionist paintings were formed. Most of these collections were subsequently given to museums, providing the foundations of the great public collections now to be seen in Europe and America.

The major market for Impressionist pictures is now among private individuals. Only rarely do institutions buy, and usually it is to fill a gap in a collection. One notable exception in the United States was the Kimbell Art Museum of Fort Worth's purchase of Cézanne's *Peasant in a Blue Blouse* for $3,900,000 at the Henry Ford II sale in 1980. Japanese museums are also actively building collections. In 1987, a Japanese museum purchased Van Gogh's *Sunflowers* for the highest price as of that date ever paid for a work of art—$39,921,750.

During the 1979 to 1980 season at Sotheby's New York, 312 Impressionist paintings sold for $34,451,000, at an average price of $110,000.

During the 1988 season alone, Sotheby's Impressionist department sold more than $181,434,440. One picture alone, Van Gogh's *Irises*, sold for $53,900,000 at Sotheby's, more than the total sales of Impressionist paintings for the entire year of 1980.

Important Factors in the Market

Unlike the Old Master market in which attributions change frequently, new discoveries are made, and restoration and condition problems are numerous, the Impressionist and Postimpressionist market is relatively uncomplicated. Most attributions to an artist are firm, although a large number of convincing fakes plague this market as well as the modern market. Discoveries are rare, because most artists have been well cataloged and investigated. For each major artist, comprehensive catalogs, (catalogues raisonnés) have been published. It is unlikely that large numbers of important pictures have disappeared in old family homes and are waiting to be discovered. Condition problems, ever-present with Old Masters, are not as frequent, since Impressionist and Postimpressionist paintings are so much newer. This market is particularly attractive to a wide range of buyers, thanks to easy recognition of a painter's work (a Renoir always looks like a Renoir) and pleasant subject matter—landscapes and cityscapes, still lifes, and nudes.

The Impressionist and Postimpressionist market was extremely strong during the 1980s. In 1988, even lesser works by secondary Impressionist painters obtained record price levels. The market has been fueled by an influx of new investors and Japanese and European buying. Prices continue to rise at an unprecedented rate. In 1984, Renoir's *Le Jardin ou Dans La Parc* sold for $1,250,000. Four years later, it brought $6,600,000. In 1985, Renoir's *Baigneuse* sold for $1,650,000, only to resell in 1988 for $8,525,000.

When works of art sell for high prices at auction, the prices for similar works rise equally at private galleries. Although high prices have existed for Impressionist and Postimpressionist works sold privately, public sales of major collections increase values in the private sector. The price performance of Impressionist art from 1975 to 1988 is shown in Figure 3, which is based on Sotheby's Art Index.

MODERN PAINTINGS

Definition

Modern paintings have been defined as pictures created between 1900 and 1945. The modern market, comprising a relatively few years of artistic production when compared to the Old Master or the American painting markets, is nevertheless complex.

Marketplace

The modern market did not gain million-dollar status until 1979, when Matisse's *Le Jeune Marin I* brought $1,500,000 at auction. Until the 1960s, modern pictures could be

FIGURE 3. Price Performance of Impressionist Art, 1975 to 1988

Source: Sotheby's Art Index, © 1989 Sotheby's Holding, Inc.

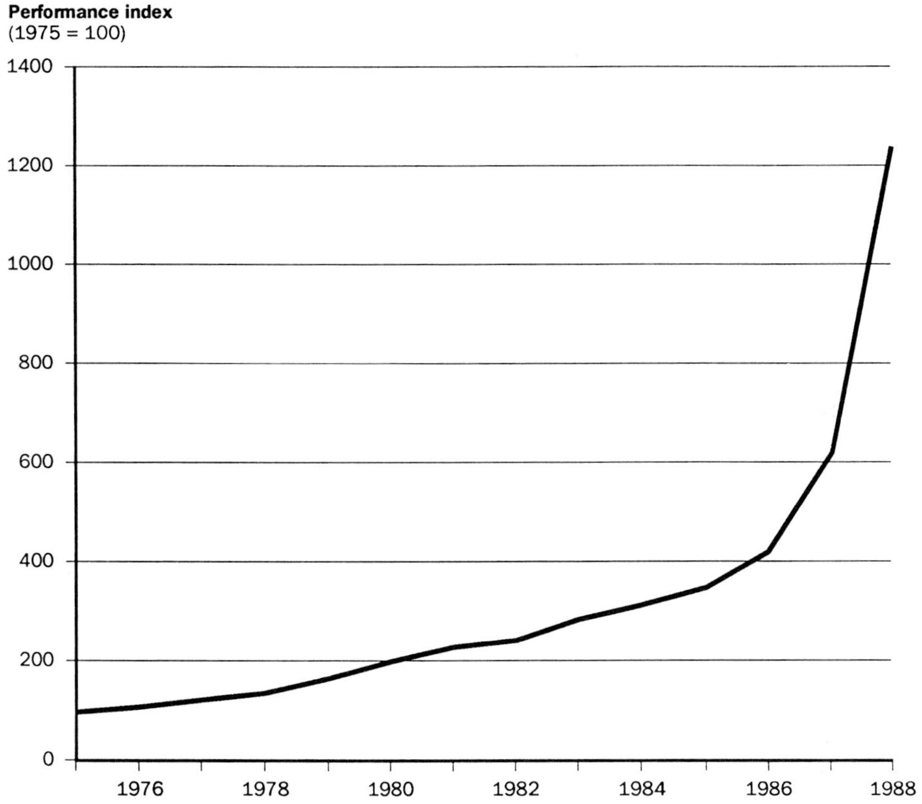

bought relatively inexpensively although the Impressionist and Postimpressionist market had already skyrocketed.

Investment interest in some modern artists is international. Picasso, Matisse, Chagall, Dali, and Leger are actively sought throughout the world. German expressionist paintings, works by Wassily Kandinsky, Emil Nolde, Franz Marc, and Ernst Ludwig Kirchner, rose in price in 1980, but the market remains mostly European, although recent shows in U.S. museums have sparked interest in the U.S. market. Works by Modigliani reflect the increase in prices of modern paintings. In 1984, Modigliani's *Giovanotto dai Capelli Rossi* sold for $1,925,000. In 1986, his *Jeane Hebuterne* sold for $3,013,200, while in 1988, the artist's *Portrait of Mario* sold for $8,886,240.

The surrealist market has remained relatively undervalued by comparison to other areas of the modern market. Although the sale of several single-owner collections, such as the William N. Copley collection in 1979 (in which Man Ray's A *l'heure de l'observatoire: les amoureux* brought $750,000) and the Julien Levy collection in 1981, excited public attention, major works by the surrealists continue to bring substantially less than those by their contemporaries. However, as the demand for modern works continues to grow and the supply of important twentieth-century paintings diminishes, the price of surrealist pictures has begun to climb.

The most famous and also the most prolific artist in the modern period was Pablo Picasso. The Picasso market is complex. The artist lived an unusually long life and produced tirelessly during his entire career. Following the death of the artist, there was speculation that prices might decline because of the vast holdings of the estate. This decline has not taken place, and major works by the master continue to be the most sought after on the market. Prices have continued to rise. In May 1980, *Saltimbanque Seated With Arms Crossed* sold by Sotheby's for $3,000,000. One year later, his *Self-Portrait: Yo Picasso* set a record, selling for $5,300,000; yet, on May 9, 1989, it was sold at Sotheby's at auction for $47,900,000!

The price performance for modern paintings from 1975 to 1988, according to Sotheby's Art Index, is shown in Figure 4.

FIGURE 4. Price Performance of Modern Paintings, 1975 to 1988

Source: Sotheby's Art Index, © 1989 Sotheby's Holding, Inc.

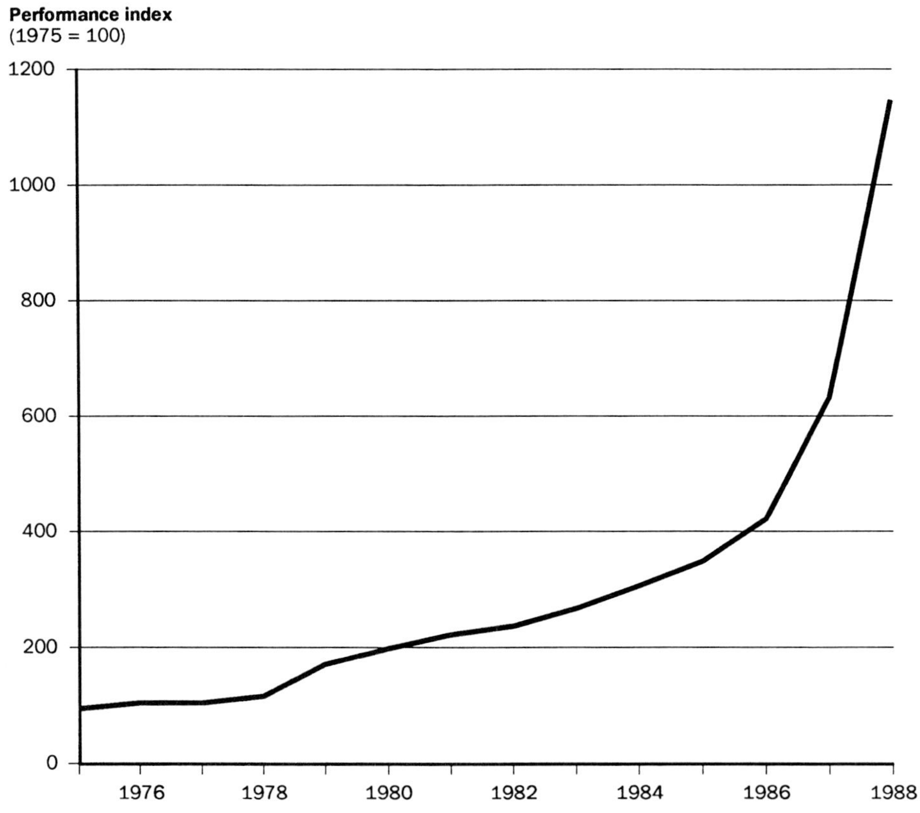

Fakes

Like the Impressionist and Postimpressionist market, the modern artist is hampered with the specter of fakes. Modigliani, Leger, and Rodin have all suffered from the existence of a large number of fakes, causing buyers to look elsewhere when not absolutely sure of authenticity. Experts among dealers, auction houses, and museums are generally highly cooperative and should be consulted in any case of doubtful authenticity.

CONTEMPORARY PAINTINGS

Contemporary art is usually understood to mean art produced after World War II. Although regional interest in local artists both in the United States and Europe exists to a certain extent, New York is indisputably the center of the contemporary art scene. The major activity in sales have traditionally taken place in galleries. During the 1980s, however, auction houses have made a strong play to capture the resale market for this "hot" area. The major buyers of contemporary art are Americans, with the Swiss, Italians, and Germans providing the major impetus from Europe.

The contemporary market got its start in the late 1950s with the work of Jackson Pollock and other abstract expressionists capturing the imagination of buyers. Although Pollock's work could be bought in the early 1950s for only hundreds of dollars, by the end of the decade his *Autumn Rhythm* had sold for $30,000; his *Blue Poles* sold in 1980 to the Australian National Gallery for a reported $2,000,000, while his *Lavender Mist* sold to the National Gallery in Washington, D.C., for a reported price in excess of $2,000,000. In 1988 Pollock's *Search* sold at auction for $4,840,000.

Contemporary pictures reached the $1,000,000 mark in 1981 when Jasper Johns's *Three Flags* was sold privately for that figure to New York's Whitney Museum of American Art; it was the highest price ever paid for a work of art by a living artist. By 1988, Johns's prices reached $17,000,000 with the sale of *False Start*. Works of other contemporary artists have also seen dramatic price rises. Andy Warhol's *Marilyn Monroe (Twenty Times)* sold in 1988 for $3,960,000, and Robert Rauschenberg's *Rebus*, which had been purchased in the 1950s for less than $10,000, brought $6,325,000 at auction.

AMERICAN PAINTINGS

Definition

This category includes all paintings produced in the United States up to World War II. Post–World War II works are considered contemporary. The most important schools are colonial portraiture, early American folk art, the Hudson River school, luminism, American barbizon, American nineteenth-century academic paintings (including genre painting and history painting), Western art, American Impressionism, the ashcan school, the Stieglitz group, the American modernists, regionalism, the American scene, WTA, and American abstract artists. Some, such as Western art, are thriving markets in themselves.

Marketplace

The overwhelming majority of buyers of American art, as expected, are Americans, both museums and private individuals. In the past few years, a number of Europeans have become interested in American art. New York City must be considered the center of the

American art market, with a large number of galleries and two large auction houses, Sotheby's and Christie's. However, thriving galleries exist in most cities on both coasts as well as in the Midwest and South, where regional schools are of particular importance.

The biggest monetary gains, rediscovery, and critical acclaim have been in nineteenth- and early twentieth-century American paintings. Long neglected and forgotten, and often stored in attics and basements, these paintings have come under scrutiny from art historians and dealers, and have found enormous acceptance and enthusiasm from an ever-growing number of museum-goers and private collectors. Although large prices, perhaps in excess of $1,000,000, may have been realized by dealers in recent years, the million-dollar mark was not reached in public auction until the 1980 sale of Frederic Edwin Church's *Icebergs*, found in an English home for boys and sold at Sotheby Parke Bernet for $2,500,000. The high price of Church's masterpiece has pushed prices higher in all categories of fine-quality American paintings. By 1989, the million dollar price was common.

As recently as 1978, the highest price ever paid at auction for an American painting was $320,000 for James Peale's *Washington and His Generals at Yorktown*. The June 1978 sale of George Caleb Bingham's 1848 *The Jolly Flatboat Men* at Sotheby's, Los Angeles, marks the beginning of the auction boom in American art. The piece was sold for $980,000 to New York's Hirschl and Adler Gallery and was later sold to the New Terra Museum of American Art in Evanston, Illinois for more than $1 million. In 1988, Georgia O'Keeffe's *Black Hollyhock with Blue Larkspur* sold for $1,980,000. Mary Cassatt's *The Conversation*, which sold in 1984 for a record price of $495,500, resold in 1988 for $4,510,000.

The price performance of American paintings from 1975 to 1988 is given in Figure 5, which plots Sotheby's Art Index.

TAX CONSEQUENCES

Under federal tax law, profit from the sale of a painting held by an individual for more than one year is taxed as a capital gain. Under certain conditions, paintings can be exchanged for others of equal or greater value in a tax-free transaction. As with other types of investments, it is also possible to realize a tax deduction on donating to a qualified organization a painting whose market value has appreciated. Separate rules apply to those who are recognized as investors by the Internal Revenue Service. (See article on "Tax Considerations for Collector-Investor," elsewhere in this volume.) For complete guidance in these matters, readers are urged to consult a professional tax advisor.

REPRESENTATIVE TYPE OF INVESTORS

Dealers

To a large extent, the market for paintings is dominated by dealers, the professional art market investors. As astute businesspeople, they must watch the market closely and buy with an eye to marketability.

Private Collectors

The second major force in the market consists of private collectors, those with a passion for acquisition who reach for the best and acquire the most desirable. It is the individual collector in most cases who is willing to pay the highest price for an object. There remains

FIGURE 5. Price Performance of American Paintings From 1975 to 1988

Source: Sotheby's Art Index, © 1989 Sotheby's Holding, Inc.

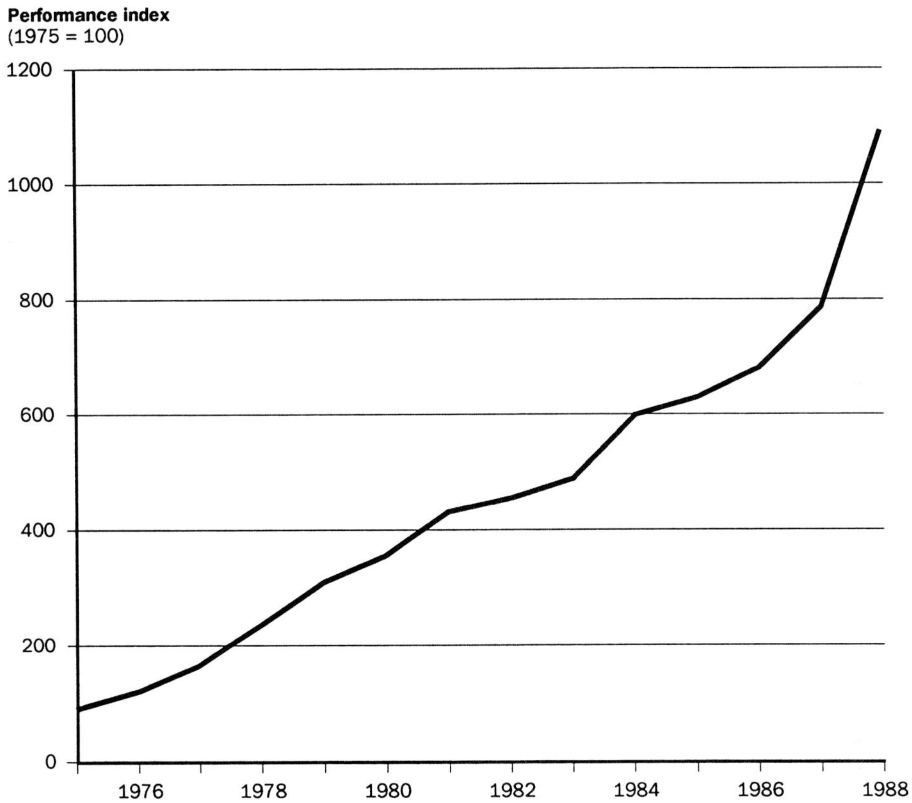

only a small number of individuals who approach the market solely with an investment motive.

Institutions

Museums and universities continue to play a role in the market. However, they are increasingly dependent on the generosity of private collectors and corporations. Only a small number of well-endowed institutions can afford to be active in today's market.

IMPORTANT FACTORS IN BUYING AND SELLING

Acquiring Information

The uninitiated buyer should find out what he really likes and then become educated in that area. As in every investment area, knowledge is the key to success. There is no substitute for one's own expertise. Information on art is readily available from museums, art libraries, auction houses, and major dealers.

Books on collecting, auctions, and art history give the investor an essential introduction to the market. For practical information on how the market functions, dealers and specialists at local auction houses can be consulted. Auction houses regularly have exhibitions of items a week before they are sold. The in-house specialists are happy to show prospective buyers these items and explain, for example, why one item is expected to bring a higher price than similar items in the sale. Similarly, dealers will talk readily about the items in their galleries. When beginning to buy, an investor should buy one or two objects of personal interest and live with them to see how he enjoys them after a few months. Perhaps it would be wise to start with smaller, less expensive items. An investor should start making acquisitions slowly while becoming familiar with the business.

Combining Taste and Investment Value

If personal inclination attracts an investor to well-known artists and art movements that command top prices, he may have to look for other less expensive collecting areas with greater potential for price appreciation. For example, someone whose favorites are the French Impressionists might look for the works of some lesser-known American Impressionists that are still considered underpriced by many experts. Another alternative is to look to the drawings and sketches by the artists he admires most.

Specializing Within the Field

By specializing, even within the general area of interest, an investor's knowledge increases dramatically. After having focused his attention, an investor will be able to spot good buys. When dealers know of an investor's specific interest, they will call him when they have exceptional pieces.

Moreover, specializing can make a collection more valuable. The total value of the items in a unified collection is greater than the sum of the prices of the individual paintings. The fact that a piece has come from a well-known collection may increase its price.

Selecting Quality

An investor should buy the very best affordable and always look for quality. Selection is vital. It is the quality pieces that will show the most appreciation in value. Even during recessions, higher-quality works usually maintain their value because they attract the wealthier, more recession-proof buyers. Auction experts, in fact, have recently noted the existence of a two-tiered art market: Museum-quality work continues to be in demand regardless of fluctuations in the economy, while the market for lesser-quality work attracts little interest in times of low prosperity.

Inspecting the Work

Before buying, an investor should be sure to get full information about the condition and history of the specific work. Knowing the broad price levels for similar works is not enough. Close inspection is especially important for works of art being sold at auction. Descriptions of condition in the catalog are not detailed. Certain damages, even tears and improper restoration, may not be immediately apparent, but they can make a big difference in the price.

Appearance is not everything. It is not unusual for a painting actually to have lost value because it has been restored. The quality of the restoration is extremely important. At the same time, slight damage can give the investor an opportunity to buy a painting by a major master at a lower price. If the condition problems are minor and do not affect important areas of the painting, a buyer may actually be able to purchase advantageously. Sophisticated buyers often prefer to purchase a painting uncleaned to be sure any restoration is done properly.

Working with Experts

It is a good idea for an investor to get involved personally with museum curators, art experts, dealers, and scholars who specialize in the area in which he is interested. These experts will give information and advice if the investor is serious about collecting. Even the most modest catalog that has a text by a respected scholar can bring a collection to the attention of other experts in the field. It can have a real impact, especially if the catalog is one of the few documents on the artist or school.

Buying and Selling Costs

Auction House Commissions. All works of art bought and sold at auction bear a commission payable to the auctioneer. In the case of major auction houses in London, Paris, and New York, this includes commission by both the buyer and the seller. These commissions change from time to time. In the 1930s, auctioneers in London charged a commission of only 7.5 percent to vendors of pictures. There was no buyers' commission. In New York, commissions are currently 10 percent for both the buyer and the seller. In London, commissions vary from house to house.

Value-Added Tax and Sales Tax. In London, there is also a value-added tax (VAT) of 15 percent on the auction commission; thus a buyer bidding £100,000 at a Sotheby's London auction would pay the following:

Hammer price (bid price)	£100,000
Buyer's premium	10,000
VAT (15%)	1,500
Total purchase price	£111,500

Therefore, immediately on purchasing a work of art, the buyer must pay 11.5 percent in addition to the hammer price.

In New York, although there is no VAT, a sales tax is levied on all works of art delivered to the purchaser in New York City. An example of this would be as follows:

Hammer price (bid price)	$100,000
Buyers' premium	10,000
New York City sales tax	9,075
Total purchase price	$119,075

Thus, a buyer receiving delivery of a work of art in New York pays an additional premium of 19.1 percent on the bid price.

Insurance. The expense of insuring a work of art is relatively low compared to the value of the items. Cost varies according to location and security. A reliable, objective appraisal is necessary in setting the value for insurance. Appraisal costs generally are set by most reputable appraisers at an hourly rate or flat fee rather than on a percentage basis.

CUSTODIAL CARE

A collection must be maintained properly. This costs money, but condition is an important part of the value. Paintings or water colors that are damaged by direct sunlight decrease in value. Room humidity and temperature should be maintained at an even level. A work of art must be handled carefully. A collection should be regularly appraised by an expert to ascertain its value for insurance purposes.

If restoration is necessary, the collector should consult a nearby museum for recommendations. Many museums have professional conservators on staff. The American Institute of Conservation, in Washington, D.C., can also recommend conservators. Museums should also be consulted about framers.

GLOSSARY

attribution—An educated assignment by an authority of the authorship of a work of art.

auction—Public sale where highest recognized bidder is purchaser.

bid—The amount offered for a painting being sold at auction before comissions are added.

buyer's commission—Fee charged to purchaser on top of the hammer price. At Sotheby's and Christie's in New York, a standard 10 percent is charged.

buy-in—Item at auction that does not reach the preestablished reserved price.

consignment—Item given to an auction house or dealer for sale. Auction houses usually charge a 10 percent sales commission, plus fees for insurance, storage, and catalog illustration. Dealers usually negotiate fees between 10 and 20 percent.

contemporary painting—American art produced after World War II.

hammer price—The accepted bid price for a lot. The buyers' commission is added on to this price.

Impressionist painting—A school of painting that started in France during the 1860s, of which the best known artists are Monet, Renoir, Manet, Pissaro, and Dégas. The Postimpressionists Cezanne, Van Gogh, and Gauguin are often included in sales with the Impressionists.

lot—An item, or group of items sold together, at an auction.

modern painting—Painting from the Postimpressionist period to 1945.

nineteenth-century painting—European and painting from 1800 to 1900.

Old Master painting—European painting to the nineteenth century.

order bid—A bid placed in writing before an auction. The bid is executed on a client's behalf by the auction house.

presale estimate—Range of prices set as an expert's best guess as to what a lot will bring at auction. These ranges are published by the auction house prior to the sale.

provenance—A record of the previous private collections, museums, artists, and dealers who have owned an object.

reserve—An amount set by the seller below which he will not sell the consigned material. The auction house will bid on the owner's behalf up to the reserve price.

seller's premium—Fee charged consigner by the auction house for arranging the sale. Usually this is a 10 percent charge; however, on major items the percentage can be negotiated.

SOME LEADING U.S. GALLERIES

A.A.A. (Associated American Artists), New York, N.Y.

Didier Aaron, Inc., New York, N.Y.

ACA Galleries/ACA Contemporary, New York, N.Y.

Acquavella Galleries, Inc., New York, N.Y.

Rachel Adler Gallery, New York, N.Y.

Brooke Alexander, New York, N.Y.

Babcock Galleries, New York, N.Y.

William Beadleston, Inc., New York, N.Y.

John Berggruen Gallery, San Francisco, Cal.

Berry-Hill Galleries, Inc., New York, N.Y.

Blum Helman Gallery, New York, N.Y.

Mary Boone, New York, N.Y.

Grace Borgenicht Gallery, New York, N.Y.

Leo Castelli, New York, N.Y.

Colnaghi USA Ltd., New York, N.Y.

The James Corcoran Gallery, Santa Monica, Cal.

Charles Cowles Gallery, Inc., New York, N.Y.

Terry Dintenfass, Inc., New York, N.Y.

Richard L. Feigen & Co., New York, N.Y.

Ronald Feldman Fine Arts, Inc., New York, N.Y.

Marian Goodman Gallery/Multiples, Inc., New York, N.Y.

Graham Gallery/Graham Modern, New York, N.Y.

Stephen Hahn, New York, N.Y.

Hirschl & Adler, New York, N.Y.

Sidney Janis Gallery, New York, N.Y.

Kennedy Galleries, Inc., New York, N.Y.

Coe Kerr Gallery, New York, N.Y.

M. Knoedler & Company, Inc., New York, N.Y.

R.M. Light & Co., Inc., Santa Barbara, Cal.

James Maroney, Inc., New York, N.Y.

Mary-Anne Martin/Fine Art, New York, N.Y.

Barbara Mathes Gallery, New York, N.Y.

Pierre Matisse Gallery, New York, N.Y.

Stephen Mazoh & Co., Inc., New York, N.Y.

Jason McCoy, Inc., New York, N.Y.

Robert Miller Gallery, New York, N.Y.

Newhouse Galleries, Inc., New York, N.Y.

The Pace Gallery, New York, N.Y.

Perls Galleries, New York, N.Y.

Rosenberg & Stiebel, Inc., New York, N.Y.

Salander-O'Reilly Galleries, Inc., New York, N.Y.

Holly Solomon Gallery, New York, N.Y.

Sonnabend Gallery, New York, N.Y.

Sperone Westwater, New York, N.Y.

Stair Sainty Matthiesen, New York, N.Y.

E. V. Thaw & Co., Inc., New York, N.Y.

David Tunick, Inc., New York, N.Y.

Washburn Gallery, New York, N.Y.

John Weber Gallery, New York, N.Y.

Richard York Gallery, New York, N.Y.

Zabriskie Gallery, New York, N.Y.

SUGGESTED READING

MAGAZINES

Apollo. Published by Bracken House, London, England. Monthly.

Art and Auction. Published by Auction Guild, New York, N.Y., Monthly.

Art in America. Published by Whitney Communications Corp., New York, N.Y. Monthly.

Artnews. Published by Artnews, New York, N.Y. Monthly.

Connoisseur. Published by The Hearst Corporation, New York, N.Y. Monthly.

The Magazine Antiques. Published by Straight Enterprises, New York, N.Y. Monthly.

Portfolio. Published by Grosvenor Publications, Inc., New York, N.Y. Bimonthly.

NEWSLETTERS

The Art/Antiques Investment Report. Published by Wall Street Reports Publishing Corp., New York, N.Y. Biweekly.

The Art Newsletter. Published by Artnews, New York, N.Y. Biweekly.

The International Art Market. Published by Art in America, Inc., New York, N.Y. Monthly.

REFERENCE BOOKS

Butler, John. *Art As Investment*. (Special Report No. 74, The Economist Intelligence Unit Ltd.) London: Spencer House, 1979.

Gordon, Martin. *Gordon's Print Price Annual*. New York: Martin Gordon, Inc., annual.

Hislop, Richard. *The Annual Art Sales Index*. Surrey (England): Art Sales Index Ltd., annual.

Mayer, E. *International Auction Records*. New York: Editions Publisol, annual.

Reitlinger, Gerald. *The Economics of Taste*. Volumes I to III. London: Barrie & Jenkins, 1970.

PENSION PLAN INVESTMENTS

Donald S. Grubbs, Jr.

BASIC CHARACTERISTICS

A pension plan is not an investment. Rather, it is a program that uses investments to accomplish its goals. There are many definitions of the phrase "pension plan." The Employee Retirement Income Security Act of 1974 (ERISA) defines pension plans extremely broadly as:

> [A]ny plan, fund, or program . . . established or maintained by an employer or by an employee organization, or by both. . .[that]
>
> (A) provides retirement income to employees, or
>
> (B) results in a deferral of income by employees for periods extending to the termination of covered employment or beyond,
>
> regardless of the method of calculating the contributions made to the plan, the method of calculating the benefits under the plan or the method of distributing benefits from the plan.

The ERISA definition applies both to plans that accumulate assets and to unfunded plans that are merely an employer's promise to make future payments. It applies to written plans and unwritten plans, to plans that are qualified under the Internal Revenue Code (the Code), and to plans that are not qualified.

Donald S. Grubbs, Jr. is an actuary and is President of Grubbs and Company, Inc., Silver Spring, Md.

Qualified Plans

Plans that meet certain requirements of the Code in order to receive favorable tax treatment are called qualified plans. All qualified plans must be in writing and must be funded. (See *Requirements for Qualification* in this article for a summary of the requirements for qualified plans.) The overwhelming majority of private employers' plans are qualified plans. This article generally discusses only qualified plans, although some statements apply equally to nonqualified plans. Many smaller employers establish a "simplified employee plan" (SEP) rather than a qualified plan. (See article on "Individual Retirement Plans," elsewhere in this volume.)

The Code describes several types of qualified plans: pension plans, profit-sharing plans, stock bonus plans, and annuity plans. Under the Code, "pension plan" refers to one particular type of qualified plan. Under ERISA, all qualified plans are called pension plans. This discussion follows ERISA in using the term "pension plan" to refer to all types of plans, including profit-sharing, stock bonus, and annuity plans.

Extent of Pension Plans

Approximately 900,000 qualified plans cover 48 million active workers in private employment. About 6,000 plans of state and local governments cover another 12 million workers. Within the federal government, sixty-eight plans cover about 3 million federal civilian employees. In 1988 pension plan assets of private employer plans totaled about $1,500 billion, and government employee plans held an additional $500 billion. The number of employees covered by a single private employer plan ranges from one employee to hundreds of thousands.

TYPES OF PLANS

All pension plans are either defined benefit plans, defined contribution plans, or a combination of the two. Each of these categories can be divided into subcategories, and many variations exist for each type. Investment objectives and legal requirements vary considerably according to the type of plan. The distinction between defined benefit plans and defined contribution plans is particularly important.

The design of pension plans is a very broad topic, and is subject to complex legal requirements. This article endeavors to summarize only those characteristics of plan types that bear on investment objectives.

Defined Benefit Plans

Definition. A defined benefit plan specifies the amount of benefit that will be paid. For example, a defined benefit plan may provide a pension on retirement at age 65 equal to one percent of the employee's average pay for his last five years of service, multiplied by total years of service. A monthly pension payable for life is the usual form of benefit, but many defined benefit plans also allow lump-sum distributions.

Funding and Costs. The amount of contributions needed to provide the benefits under the plan is not defined. Ultimately, the cost of a defined benefit plan is the sum of the benefits paid plus expenses of administering the plan, reduced by any investment earnings on the plan assets. An actuary determines the estimated amount needed to be set aside currently to provide for the ultimate cost of the plan. Some plans require employee contributions. The employer contributes whatever is needed, in addition to any employee contributions, to finance the plan.

Contributions for all employees usually are combined for investment purposes in a single fund. The fund generally is not allocated among employees. An individual employee has no claim to any part of the plan assets; his only right is to receive the benefits promised by the plan. Individual benefits generally are unaffected by increases or decreases in investment earnings.

The employer's cost is affected by investment experience. If the plan's investment return increases by one dollar, ultimately the employer's cost is reduced by one dollar. Because plan assets are invested over long periods of time, the effect of compound interest is great. In a typical plan, increasing the long-term investment return by one percent will decrease plan costs by about 20 percent. Thus, employers have a strong incentive to maximize the investment return in a defined benefit plan in order to reduce plan costs, and a corresponding incentive to minimize losses.

Most plans have a positive cash flow in almost all years. Usually, it is not necessary to liquidate investments in order to pay benefits. For this reason, defined benefit plans generally are more concerned with long-term investment returns than with short-term fluctuation.

Multiemployer plans. A multiemployer plan is a plan established under a collective bargaining agreement between one or more unions and two or more employers. Most multiemployer plans are defined benefit plans. The collective bargaining agreement specifies the amount of employer contributions to the plan (e.g., eighty cents per hour worked) but usually does not specify the level of benefits to be provided by the plan.

When a multiemployer plan is set up, a joint board of trustees is established, with an equal number of labor and management trustees. Both labor and management trustees must act in the sole interest of participants and beneficiaries. An actuary engaged by the board advises it of the estimated level of benefits that can be supported by the estimated future contributions. Based on the actuary's advice, the board establishes the plan and determines the level of benefits to be provided.

The actuary's estimate of the level of benefits that can be supported is based upon various actuarial assumptions, including the rate of future investment return. If the fund earns more than assumed, the excess can be used to increase the level of benefits. If it earns less than assumed, it may be necessary to reduce the promised level of benefits. Thus, participants and plan trustees acting in their behalf have an interest in maximizing the investment return. The investment return ordinarily has no direct effect upon employer costs, which are fixed by the collective bargaining agreement. However, poor investment performance may create greater union demands for employers to increase their level of contributions during the next bargaining period in order to maintain the promised benefit level.

The Multiemployer Pension Plan Amendments Act of 1980 created new liabilities for employers contributing to multiemployer plans. Employers who withdraw from a multiemployer plan are now liable for their share of the excess of the value of vested benefits over the value of plan assets. This gives employers a new interest in maximizing the investment return of such plans and in minimizing negative fluctuations in asset values in order to minimize the potential withdrawal liability.

Other Jointly Trusteed Plans. Sometimes, a jointly trusteed plan is established by an agreement between a single employer and a union. Such a plan may have all of the characteristics of a multiemployer plan except that there is only one employer. This type of plan generally has the same investment considerations as a multiemployer plan; however, it is not subject to the Multiemployer Pension Plan Amendments Act.

Mandatory Employee Contributions. At one time, a large proportion of defined benefit plans required participating employees to contribute. Mandatory employee contributions are not tax-deductible. Because of tax and other considerations, most plans have eliminated these contributions.

In a defined benefit plan with mandatory employee contributions, a withdrawing employee may be entitled to his own contributions with accumulated interest. Because of certain provisions of ERISA, interest is usually credited at 5 percent regardless of the rate of investment earnings of the plan's assets. Thus, the existence of mandatory employee contributions does not introduce any investment considerations.

Voluntary Employee Contributions. Some defined benefit plans allow employees to make voluntary contributions to increase their benefits under the plan. A separate account must be maintained for each employee's voluntary contributions. This account must be credited with its share of the plan's investment income and with realized and unrealized appreciation and depreciation. Voluntary employee contributions introduce investment considerations that are entirely different from those for funding the defined benefits. These considerations are similar to those for defined contribution plans.

Defined Contribution Plans

A defined contribution plan (also called an individual account plan) is a plan in which each participant has an individual account to which an amount defined by the plan is allocated each year. The sum of all of the individual account balances ordinarily equals the total assets of the plan. Each participant's account shares in the investment income and in the realized and unrealized appreciation and depreciation of the plan.

When an individual is eligible to receive benefits from the plan, his benefit is whatever his account balance can provide. The account balance may be paid in a lump sum or in installments, or may be applied to purchase an annuity payable throughout the participant's life. Some plans allow a choice between a fixed annuity, with unchanging monthly payments, and a variable annuity, under which monthly payments fluctuate with investment performance.

Effect of Investment Experience on Benefits and Costs. The amount of future benefits under a defined contribution plan, unlike those in a defined benefit plan, depends on the plan's investment return. Because of the effect of compound interest over the long period of an employee's career, the effect of the rate of investment return can be very substantial. An investment of $1,000 at the end of every year over a forty-year career will accumulate to $154,762 at 6 percent interest, or $199,635 at 7 percent — about 29 percent more for a one percent change in the annual return. Thus, there is a strong incentive to maximize the long-term investment return.

Fluctuation in market values can have an important effect on the amount of benefits. If a participant becomes eligible to receive a benefit at a time when the plan's market value is low, this benefit will be lower than it might have been at a different time. This may cause some defined contribution plans to avoid investments with substantial market value fluctuation, in part or all together.

Under a defined contribution plan, the investment performance usually has little or no effect on the employer's costs.

Money Purchase Pension Plans. A money purchase plan is one type of pension plan under the Code. Because it is classified as a pension plan under the Code, there must be a definite formula for determining employer contributions to the plan (e.g., 5 percent of pay). Contributions cannot be contingent on employer profits. All qualified pension plans are required to make benefits available in the form of an annuity, although a pension plan may allow participants to elect a lump sum as an alternative. Some money purchase plans allow the payment of lump sums, while others require every employee to apply his account balance to provide an annuity.

Some money purchase plans have invested all plan assets in annuity contracts and other fixed-dollar investments in an effort to protect the benefits from market value fluctuations. Other money purchase plans have endeavored to maximize the long-term investment return, with less attention to the problems of market value fluctuation.

The largest money purchase plan is the plan of the Teachers Insurance Annuity Association and College Retirement Equities Fund (TIAA-CREF). Most participants are college and university employees. TIAA-CREF allows each participant to elect what portion of his contribution is to be deposited in a fixed investment fund to provide a fixed life annuity, and what portion is to be deposited in an equity fund to provide a variable life annuity.

Target Benefit Plans. A target benefit plan is a money purchase pension plan that has some of the characteristics of a defined benefit plan. Like a defined benefit plan, a target benefit plan has a formula (e.g., one percent of pay multiplied by years of service). The employer is required to contribute to each employee's individual account a level annual amount that, together with interest at a total assumed rate of between 5 and 6 percent, is expected to be sufficient to provide the target benefit. Thus, the target benefit plan has defined contributions and individual accounts, like all other defined contribution plans. The amount of benefits is the amount that can be provided by the account balance. Unlike a defined benefit plan, a target benefit plan may miss the target. It may provide more or less than the target benefit, depending on whether the actual investment return is more or less than the 5 to 6 percent assumed.

A target benefit plan is often established in lieu of a defined benefit plan. It has a stated pension objective, a target. To avoid the possibility of missing the target on the low side, some target benefit plans invest in annuity contracts or other fixed-dollar investments that assure that the target at least will be met. Other target benefit plans are more willing to accept investment risk in the attempt to maximize benefits.

Deferred Profit-Sharing Plans. A deferred profit-sharing plan under the Code is another type of defined contribution plan. Some profit-sharing plans specify that the amount of contributions to the plan will be based directly on the amount of profits (e.g., 25 percent of profits in excess of $1 million). Other profit-sharing plans leave the amount of contribution completely at the employer's discretion each year.

Some profit-sharing plans are established primarily to provide retirement income.

Others are established for varying purposes, particularly when the employer also has a defined benefit pension plan to meet retirement income needs. They are often established to give employees incentive to make the business profitable. Almost all profit-sharing plans provide for lump-sum distributions. Some plans also allow the participant to elect to receive his account balance in installments or to have it applied to purchase a life annuity. Where provision of retirement income is not a primary purpose of the plan, the plan sponsor's concern about market value fluctuation may be less than it would be under a money purchase plan.

Particularly when employee profit incentive is the key purpose of the plan, the employer may decide to invest part or all of the profit-sharing plan assets in the employer's own common stock. Then the employees' benefits have a further dependency on employer profits, perhaps increasing the profit incentive.

Thrift or Savings Plans. A thrift plan (also called a savings plan) is a defined contribution plan under which employer contributions are made to match a stated percentage of employee contributions. Most thrift plans are qualified profit-sharing plans under the Code, but some are established as money purchase pension plans.

Under a typical thrift plan, employees may elect to contribute any amount up to 6 percent of pay. The employer agrees to contribute a stated percentage of whatever the individual employee contributes. Usually the matching percentage is 50 or 100 percent, although some plans have matching contributions as low as 25 percent or as high as 200 percent.

Thrift plans are often established, in part at least, to encourage employees to save. Employers usually want to encourage employees to participate in order to meet this objective. In addition, if participation falls too low, the plan's tax-qualified status may be in jeopardy. Therefore, employers may want the plan's investments to be attractive in order to encourage participation.

401(k) Plans. Section 401(k) of the Code provides for "cash or deferred arrangements." It allows employees to elect to direct their employer to pay part of their compensation (within prescribed limits) into a profit-sharing plan rather than paying the amount in cash. Elective contributions to the profit-sharing plan are excluded from current taxable income. The earliest of these cash or deferred arrangements, commonly called 401(k) plans, allowed employees to choose between having a profit-sharing bonus paid in cash or contributed to a deferred profit-sharing plan. Most modern 401(k) plans instead are for deferral of regular salary and include matching employer contributions like a thrift plan.

Investment Alternatives. Some employees want to be able to invest in common stocks in the hope that market values will appreciate. Others are more concerned about preservation of principal, preferring guarantees that their investment will not decline in market value. Therefore, many defined contribution plans maintain two accounts, one for equity investments and one for fixed-dollar investments. This allows each employee to determine what proportion of his contribution is to be deposited in each account. Some plans offer more than two investment alternatives. Most defined contribution plans allow the election of investments to apply to both employee and employer contributions, although some restrict the election to the employee's own contributions.

Some plans allow each individual employee the right to direct the investment of his own individual account, with little or no restriction on the investment choices. Under such an arrangement, each employee can, for example, establish an account with his own investment broker, investing in stocks, bonds, mutual funds, annuity contracts, and other investments. This approach substantially increases the work and expense of administering the plan.

Providing employees partial or complete control over the investment of their accounts gives them a sense of ownership and control and is popular with employees. Some employees invest their funds well, achieving superior results. However, there is substantial evidence that most employees achieve worse results than those of the typical pension fund managed entirely by professional investment managers.

Employee Contributions. Some defined contribution plans include employee contributions and others do not. In certain plans, all employees are required to participate and to make contributions to the plan. Some employers require employee contributions only if an employee elects to participate. Thrift plans and 401(k) plans, as noted previously, allow employees to elect whether and how much to contribute.

Some plans, unlike thrift plans, allow voluntary employee contributions that are not matched by employer contributions.

Regardless of whether employee contributions to a defined contribution plan are mandatory or voluntary, employees must share directly in the plan's investment return. In defined benefit plans, on the other hand, mandatory employee contributions generally are credited with 5 percent interest regardless of the rate of earnings of the plan's assets.

In defined contribution plans, some employers believe that principal preservation is more important for employee contributions than for employer contributions. Therefore, employee contributions may be invested in fixed-dollar investments with guaranteed principal, while employer contributions are invested in common stocks. Some employers believe that the employee should be entitled to direct the investment of his own contributions, at least among several alternatives. Others have taken the opposite approach, requiring employee contributions to be invested in fixed-dollar investments for safety, but allowing employee choice in the investment of employer contributions.

Stock Bonus Plans. A stock bonus plan is similar to a profit-sharing plan, except that the employer contributions are not necessarily dependent on profits, and the benefits are distributable in stock of the employer. Such plans are generally subject to the same requirements as profit-sharing plans.

The employer may contribute stock to the plan or the plan may purchase employer stock in the market. Although distributions from a stock bonus plan must generally be in stock of the employer, there is no general requirement that all assets of all stock bonus plans must be held in employer stock. Stock bonus plans are usually fully invested in employer stock, except for cash that is temporarily uninvested.

Employee Stock Ownership Plans. An employee stock ownership plan (ESOP) is a defined contribution plan that is designed primarily to invest in qualifying employer securities and that meets other Internal Revenue Service (IRS) requirements. It may be a qualified stock bonus plan or a combination of a stock bonus plan and a money purchase pension plan. A qualifying employer security is stock or a marketable obligation, but an S corporation may not establish an ESOP, since the stock of an S corporation may not be held by a trust.

The laws concerning ESOPs have changed annually in recent years, changing the plans themselves and the terminology applied to them. A leveraged ESOP is designed to meet financial objectives of the employer corporation or its key stockholders. Usually, the plan borrows money to purchase employer securities, either directly from the employer or from stockholders. Employer contributions to the plan are used to repay the loan. At times, ESOPs have been used to acquire the stock of a principal owner who dies or retires. They have also been used by corporations to spin off a subsidiary and sell it to their employees.

Combination of Defined Benefit and Defined Contribution Plans

Many employers have both a defined benefit plan and a defined contribution plan. In such cases, the defined contribution plan usually is a thrift plan or a traditional profit-sharing plan. The defined benefit plan usually is intended to meet retirement income needs, while the defined contribution plan primarily serves other purposes. Ordinarily, the investment objectives of each plan are not affected by the existence of the other plan.

Floor plans. A floor plan is a defined benefit plan under which the amount of monthly pension is determined first under a benefit formula, then reduced or offset by the amount of monthly pension that can be provided by a profit-sharing or other defined contribution plan. Floor plans provide a floor of protection, assuring that the combined benefit will never be less than the amount of pension determined under the benefit formula. When a new profit-sharing plan is adopted, it is often expected that this plan by itself will provide adequate pensions for younger employees. For older employees, there may not be enough time to build up adequate benefits. A floor plan can assure that minimum benefit requirements are met for older workers who will not have time to build up large profit-sharing accounts.

Sometimes, the floor plan is expected to benefit most of the members of the profit-sharing plan. In other cases, it is expected that the profit-sharing account will more than offset the entire calculated benefit under the floor plan, leaving no benefit to be paid from the floor plan. Unless the profit-sharing account balance is sufficient to provide more than the benefit under the floor plan, the effect of greater or lesser investment earnings of the profit-sharing plan is to decrease or increase both the benefit and the employer's cost under the floor plan. To the extent that this occurs, the employer, and not the employee, really is bearing the investment risk under the profit-sharing plan. This may change the investment objectives of the profit-sharing plan.

Combined Target Benefit — Floor Plan. Target benefit plans and floor plans can be combined, and the same benefit formula can be used for both. If the target benefit plan exactly meets its assumed investment objective of 5 ot 6 percent, it will exactly hit the target benefit and no benefit will be payable under the floor plan. If the target benefit plan earns more than the assumed rate, the excess increases the amount of benefit provided. If the target benefit plan earns less than the assumed rate, the floor plan picks up the difference. Thus, employees benefit from favorable investment experience, while the employer bears the risk of unfavorable experience. This feature makes the combination undesirable to many employers, but attractive to some. The employer, for example, may want to invest the target benefit plan assets in more speculative investments, expecting this to increase the investment return, but may establish the floor plan to assure employees that they will be protected if results are poor. This combination may also alleviate the problem of the target benefit plan's restriction on employer contributions, which occurs because of contribution limits under the Code.

Tax Advantages of Combinations. In the case of small close corporations, including professional corporations, the primary objective of establishing a pension plan may be to defer taxable income for the owner rather than actually to provide pensions. Section 415 of the Code limits the amount of benefits that can be provided under defined benefit plans and the amount of contributions that can be provided under defined contribution plans. The combination of a defined benefit plan and a defined contribution plan can often provide more tax deferral than either plan can alone. If the owners of the business are generally older than their employees and want to maximize their own tax deferral while minimizing costs for employees, a combination of a target benefit plan and a defined benefit plan (not a floor plan) may be the best way to accomplish those objectives. Projections of benefits and costs under assumed rates of investment return are needed to determine the most effective combination.

Annuity Plans

The Code defines an annuity plan as a plan, funded with annuities, that would meet the requirements to be a qualified trust except that there is no trust. Annuity plans can be either defined benefit plans or defined contribution plans, and can take almost all of the forms of benefit design previously discussed. The only exception is that an annuity plan cannot, of course, be a stock bonus or employee stock ownership plan, since an annuity plan is invested entirely in annuities. An annuity plan may be invested in any of a number of group or individual annuity contracts. (See *Insured Funding Media*, later in this article.)

Tax-Deferred Annuities. A separate type of plan is a tax-deferred annuity (sometimes called tax-sheltered annuity), established under Section 403(b) of the Code to provide tax-deferred savings for teachers and employees of certain nonprofit organizations.

Keogh (HR-10) Plans for Self-Employed Individuals

Plans established to cover partners or sole proprietors of unincorporated businesses are known as Keogh, or HR-10, plans. Partners and sole proprietors generally are treated as though they were employees, and their earned income is treated as compensation, provided their personal services are a material, income-producing factor in the business. Keogh plans generally are subject to the same requirements as other qualified plans.

TAX CONSEQUENCES

Tax Effects of Qualification

If a plan is qualified under Section 401(a) of the Code, it enjoys several tax advantages. Employer contributions to a qualified plan are deductible by the employer, up to certain limits, for the year in which they are paid to the plan; but they are not taxable to the employee at the time contributed, even if the employee has a nonforfeitable interest in the contributions. Investment earnings of the trust are not currently taxable to the trust, the employer, or the employee.

The employee generally is taxed on payments received only in the year in which they are received, even if he has an unrestricted right to receive them earlier. An employee who receives benefits in the form of a lump-sum distribution gets favorable tax treatment under a five-year averaging rule. If employer stock is distributed to the employee, the employee is not taxed on the unrealized appreciation at the time of distribution. "Excess distributions" in any year (generally lump-sum distributions exceeding $750,000 or other distributions exceeding $150,000) are subject to an additional 15 percent tax. Distributions paid before age $59\frac{1}{2}$ (age 55 in the case of termination of employment) are subject to an additional 10 percent tax, but distributions rolled over into another qualified plan or into an IRA are not currently taxable.

Investment Implications of Qualification

As an investment for the employee, participation in a qualified plan is quite favorable in terms of tax treatment. If the employee received the employer contribution in cash, he would pay current income tax on it. The employee could then invest the difference, paying tax currently on investment income. It can be shown that the usual effect of the tax-deferred buildup of a qualified plan ultimately is to produce a more favorable after-tax accumulation than individual investment of after-tax income will produce, if the rate of investment return is the same.

Employees who are considering investing their own contributions, even if they do not receive a current deduction for the contributions, will benefit most from the tax deferral on investment income. Thus, the qualified plan is generally a good investment for employees from the tax viewpoint. It is possible, however, that contributions may be made in years when employees are in tax brackets lower than when benefits are received.

From an employer's viewpoint, a pension plan is an expense, just as salaries are an expense. But the employer may be able to prepay its pension expense for future years. In effect, the employer may be investing money currently in a tax-exempt fund to pay for future years' expenses.

The tax-exempt status of the trust affects its investment considerations. It would be foolish to acquire tax-exempt bonds with their lower yields, for example, since tax-exempt income has no special value to a trust that already is tax-exempt.

Similarly, a qualified trust has no tax preference among investment income received, realized gains and losses, and unrealized appreciation. The decision as to whether to invest in low-income growth stocks or higher income securities with little growth potential need not be influenced by tax considerations as it is for individual investors. Similarly, the decision to buy or sell a security with unrealized appreciation or depreciation can be made strictly from investment considerations, since there is no tax effect on realizing the gain or loss.

Requirements for Qualification

The requirements for obtaining qualification of pension plans are numerous, detailed, and complex. The principal requirements are as follows:

1. The plan must be funded with a trust, a custodial account, or annuities.
2. It must be in writing.
3. It must be for the exclusive benefit of employees and beneficiaries.

4. It must not discriminate in favor of highly compensated employees.

5. Eligibility for participation must satisfy certain age and service rules.

6. It must meet minimum vesting requirements.

7. It must meet certain requirements for limiting plan mergers and transfers of assets and liabilities.

8. Benefits may not be assigned or alienated.

9. Benefits must commence within stated periods.

10. The plan must include certain limits on contributions and benefits.

11. Separate additional rules apply to qualified pension plans, profit-sharing plans, stock bonus plans, ESOPs, annuity plans, and other specific types of plans.

A plan sponsor may obtain an advance IRS determination of a plan's qualified status. Even if an advance determination letter is received, the IRS may determine on audit that the plan is not qualified in practice. Such determinations can be both prospective and retrospective.

INVESTMENT OBJECTIVES

Pension plans have the same general objectives as other investors do. However, the relative priorities given to liquidity, preservation of principal, investment income, and market value appreciation tend to be different for pension plans than they are for most investors. The need for these elements varies substantially according to the type of plan, and from one plan to another. There is extensive literature on investment objectives. This discussion deals only with the ways that pension plan investment objectives may differ from general investment objectives.

Liquidity

The liquidity requirement is related to the plan's cash flow. Apart from the purchase and sale of assets, the plan receives contributions and investment income and pays benefits. In the large majority of plans, projections will show that the plan's cash flow is positive for many years into the future. In such cases, there is little need for liquidity.

A minor need for liquidity may occur because of the timing of cash flow within a year. Many employers pay their entire annual plan contribution in a single payment, while benefits may be paid throughout the year. The plan may need to retain sufficient liquid assets to pay benefits between the annual contributions.

In a small plan, the termination of a participant entitled to a large benefit may necessitate liquidation of investments. If such events can be predicted, asset liquidity can be planned around the event. To the extent that a plan faces such events that cannot be predicted, liquidity may become an important investment objective for a portion of the plan assets.

Security of Principal

Security of principal is a consideration of every investor. Since most defined benefit plans expect a positive cash flow for many years into the future, they can take a long-term view of security. Short-term market value fluctuations usually are of little importance for defined benefit plans.

In defined contribution plans, the benefits paid to withdrawing participants will depend on the market value of assets at the date of withdrawal. Some defined contribution plans are concerned with preventing loss of principal, which could decrease benefits; others feel comfortable having the benefits vary with market value fluctuations, for better or for worse. Some employers are particularly concerned with preventing loss of principal with respect to the employee's own contributions. Individual employees differ in their desire for security of principal. To accommodate this, some plans allow employees to choose from alternative investments for their funds; others allow employees to make transfers between funds, particularly where retirement is only a few years away.

Investment Return

Maximizing the total investment return, within acceptable limits of risk, is an objective of every pension plan. Increased investment return will either increase employee benefits or decrease employer costs, depending on the type of plan.

The investment return that matters generally is not the investment income received, but the total investment return, including investment income and realized and unrealized appreciation and depreciation. As stated earlier, there are no tax reasons for a pension plan to prefer investment income, realized gains, or unrealized appreciation as a form of investment return. The form of investment return does affect the plan's cash flow, but the positive cash flow of most plans usually makes this a very minor consideration.

Plans differ as to the relative importance placed on short-term versus long-term investment return. A defined benefit pension plan is concerned primarily with the long-term investment return; a defined contribution plan, particularly a thrift plan or 401(k) plan, may be concerned with the short-term return.

For the purpose of funding defined benefit plans, assets are valued at their actuarial value, such as average market value over a period of years. Such methods tend to gradually recognize appreciation and depreciation of market values, while dampening the short-term fluctuations. This reduces the adverse effect of market value fluctuation, enabling the assets of a defined benefit plan to focus more on long-term investment return than on short-term fluctuations.

Risk

Like other investors, pension plans are concerned with investment risk. Some commonly used measurements of risk actually measure fluctuations, both positive and negative. Of course, pension plans only want to limit negative fluctuations. For example, a convertible bond for which the conversion price does not currently affect the market value may have the potential for substantial upward fluctuation but little downward fluctuation from its present value.

For a pension plan, it is the risk of the entire portfolio that matters. The risk associated with individual investments is important only as it relates to the risk of the whole plan. A highly diversified portfolio of fairly high-risk investments may represent less of a risk than does a less diversified portfolio of low-risk securities.

Another question as to how much risk is acceptable is the question of who bears the risk. Employers generally bear the risk in defined benefit plans, and are able to spread any investment losses over long periods. Employees bear the risk in defined contribution plans. In some defined contribution plans, employees select the amount of risk they bear by choosing between a guaranteed principal fund and a common stock fund. In such a situation, the two funds will be invested with entirely different risk objectives.

Compliance With ERISA Fiduciary Requirements

General Requirements. ERISA has imposed a number of requirements on those who control plan assets, called fiduciaries. A fiduciary must discharge his duties to the plan solely in the interests of participants and beneficiaries

- For the exclusive purpose of providing benefits to participants and beneficiaries and defraying reasonable administrative expenses.
- With the care, skill, prudence and diligence of a prudent man.
- By diversifying investments to minimize the risk of large losses.
- In accordance with plan documents.

Profit-sharing, stock bonus, thrift, ESOP, and certain money purchase plans are exempt from the diversification requirement to the extent that they invest in qualifying employer real property or qualifying employer securities. The definition of qualifying employer real property was designed to apply to the retail stores of one particular employer, and applies to few, if any, other situations. A qualifying employer security is a security of the employer that is either a stock or a marketable obligation satisfying certain ERISA criteria.

Exemption of qualifying employer securities from the diversification requirement does not exempt them from other fiduciary requirements. In one case, pending as of 1988, participants alleged that investing profit-sharing-plan assets in the employer's stock was imprudent and caused extensive damages.

No plan may acquire or hold any employer security that is not a qualifying employer security, or any employer real property that is not a qualifying employer real property. Defined benefit plans and certain money purchase plans may not acquire or hold qualifying employer securities or qualifying employer real property if they constitute over 10 percent of plan assets. This 10 percent rule also applies to any defined contribution plan that is used to offset benefits under a floor plan.

If a defined contribution plan allows individual participants to exercise control over their own assets, the fiduciary is not liable for losses resulting from the participants' decisions. Fiduciaries are liable for losses resulting from their own breaches of fiduciary duty, and, to a large extent, are liable for breaches by cofiduciaries. Trustees are not liable for breaches by an investment manager. Fiduciaries may obtain fiduciary liability insurance, and they must be bonded.

Prohibited Transactions. ERISA contains very broad prohibitions against transactions between pension plans and parties in interest. Parties in interest include all fiduciaries, persons providing services to the plan, the employer, any union involved, officers, directors, and 10 percent shareholders of any of the above, certain relatives, and others. Prohibited transactions include the sale, exchange, or leasing of property; lending or extending credit; furnishing goods, services, or facilities; and transfer of assets. There are statutory exemptions from the broad prohibited transaction rules, as well as a procedure for obtaining class or individual exemptions. Hundreds of individual and class exemptions have been issued by the Department of Labor. Prohibited transactions are the subject of an automatic excise tax equal to 5 percent of the amount of the transaction; if the transaction is not corrected, an additional 100 percent tax can be assessed.

Investment Objectives and Fiduciary Responsibilities. A major objective of all fiduciaries is to avoid prohibited transactions or fiduciary liability. It is argued that the prohibited transaction rules have prevented plans from taking advantage of good investment opportunities, and that fear of fiduciary liability has caused some trustees to become too cautious to be good investors. But the rules undoubtedly have deterred some improper investments.

Investment Expense

Minimizing unnecessary investment expense has the same effect as increasing the investment return. This affects decisions concerning which investments to acquire and how to acquire and manage them. The objective is to maximize the net investment return after expenses. Some types of investments, such as mortgages, have higher investment expenses than other types do. The real question is whether or not higher investment return offsets higher investment expense.

The fees of trustees, investment managers, and consultants are reviewed by plan sponsors who select them. If a particular trustee, investment manager, or consultant can increase the investment return by even a small amount, the increased return usually will more than pay for the fee. If an equal return can be obtained with less expense, any additional expense would be a waste of plan assets.

Social Investment

Some forces in organized labor, as well as some endeavoring to support broad public interests, argue that the investment of pension plan assets should serve social purposes as well as the usual investment goals.

Organized labor often sees a connection between jobs for union members and the investment of pension plan assets. For example, it is argued that the union-organized textile industry of the Northeast is losing out to new, lower-cost, nonunion textile factories in the South, and that the new factories are financed in part by the investments of pension assets of plans for Northeastern union workers. Unions would prefer that the assets instead be invested in the development of businesses that produce jobs for their members.

Another example is the investment of the pension assets for New York City employees in loans to the city in 1975. The city needed the loans to prevent a bankruptcy that, among other things, would have cost many of the covered workers their jobs. It was argued that the loans were imprudent investments for the pension funds, since the nation's leading banks had refused to extend comparable credit because they perceived the risk as too great.

Some want particular plans to make investments that will directly benefit participants in those plans, such as new housing or a children's day-care center in the area where the particular workers live. Others want pension funds invested in areas they believe serve broad social purposes, such as low-cost housing. Another aspect of social investing is the blacklisting of investments that are considered socially undesirable. These may include companies doing business in South Africa, or companies with an anti-union reputation.

Effects of Social Investment. Most employers and banks have argued that plan assets should be invested solely in the interests of plan participants and beneficiaries, and that social investment objectives may either increase investment risk or decrease investment return. Blacklisting certain investments has little effect on the investor or on the business being blacklisted. From the viewpoint of the pension fund, many good alternatives for investment are available, so eliminating one alternative does not matter. If the business being blacklisted is actually a good investment, it will have no trouble finding other investors at comparable terms. Positive investments for social purposes, however, may adversely affect a plan if it causes the plan to accept higher risks or lower investment returns than are otherwise available.

Funding Policy

Every employee benefit plan must, as ERISA states, "provide a procedure for establishing and carrying out a funding policy and method consistent with the objectives of the plan." Some have mistakenly assumed that "funding policy" means "investment policy." Legislative history makes it clear that a funding policy is not an investment policy; however, a funding policy is needed to establish an investment policy.

The funding policy is the employer's policy regarding how much to contribute to the plan and when to contribute it. Knowledge of the funding policy assists the trustee to project the plan's cash flow, which helps in planning the investment policy, particularly to meet any liquidity needs. In some plans, the employer has no flexibility to vary contributions. In others, there may be substantial flexibility to vary contributions from one year to another. In making the decision as to how much to contribute, the employer may compare the rate of investment return being earned by the pension plan with the amount that can be earned by investing more in the business, or with the rate the employer is paying on its indebtedness.

Investment Policy

Investment policy may be established by the plan sponsor, trustee, or investment manager. It may be written or unwritten. Many sponsors, particularly larger plan sponsors, adopt a written investment policy, primarily to describe in what types of assets the plan will invest and how assets will be allocated among the various types. The investment policy provides a framework for selecting insurance companies, trustees, and investment managers, as well as providing guidance when making investments and reviewing investment results.

Statements of investment policy vary from those that state broad, general goals to those that are quite detailed and specific. Investment policies usually are reviewed from time to time and revised as appropriate. Some employers believe that they can reduce their potential fiduciary liability by adopting a suitable investment policy. Others seek to reduce fiduciary liability by delegating investment policy decisions to the insurance company, trustee, or investment manager. If the latter approach is used, it is important that the investment manager be familiar with the investment needs of the particular plan.

TRUSTS AND TRUST INVESTMENTS

Trusts

In most cases, all assets of an employee benefit plan must be held in trust by one or more of the trustees. The principal exception is for plans invested in insurance and annuity contracts and certain other assets held by insurance companies. Government and church plans also are exempt from the trust requirement. The establishment and operation of trusts are controlled by state laws and vary somewhat from state to state.

A plan may use a custodial account in lieu of a trust if the custodian is a bank or a person satisfying IRS requirements. A custodian is responsible for the safekeeping and accounting of plan assets, but not for investments. The principal use of custodians has been for plans fully invested in mutual funds. Sometimes they are used to hold insurance and annuity contracts, although this is not required by law.

Trustees

A bank or trust company usually is named as trustee. Some plans designate an individual or a group of individuals as trustee. Multiemployer plans always have a joint board of trustees consisting of an equal number of union and employer representatives. Where there are individual trustees, they frequently enter a second trust agreement with a bank or trust company to hold and invest the plan assets.

The duties of the trustee are set forth in the trust agreement. These duties generally include responsibility for holding, investing, and accounting for plan assets. The trustee usually is authorized to pay benefits and expenses from the trust on direction of the plan administrator. In the case of trustees who are individuals, the trust agreement may give the trustees part or all of the responsibility of plan administration.

The trustee is given extremely broad discretion in the investment of plan assets in some trust agreements. In others, the investment is restricted in various manners, including the requirement that the trustee follow instructions of the employer or a designated outside investment manager. Even when it is not required by the trust agreement, the corporate trustee normally consults with the employer and gives serious consideration to any of the employer's investment preferences that do not breach the trustee's fiduciary responsibility. However, the trustee or trustees have exclusive authority and discretion under ERISA to manage and control the assets of the plan, unless the plan expressly provides that the trustee is subject to direction from a named fiduciary, or some authority is delegated to one or more investment managers.

Trust Investments

Trust assets may include almost any type of investment. These various types (e.g., bonds, common stocks, mutual funds) are all discussed in detail elsewhere in this volume.

Commingled Funds. Most banks that serve as pension plan trustees maintain one or more commingled trusts, which combine the assets of many qualified plans. These pooled funds operate very much like mutual funds. Most banks maintain a fund for bonds, a fund for common stocks and, often, a balanced fund. Some banks maintain many specialized pooled funds for income-producing stocks, growth stocks, money market instruments, mortgages, and other types of investments. These pooled funds are used as the investment intermediary for most small plans and for some quite large ones. The pooled funds may provide greater diversity of investment, better investment management, and lower investment expenses than are possible for small plans investing their assets separately. Since the pooled fund as a whole almost always has a positive cash flow, even when some of its individual plans have a negative cash flow, liquidity problems are minimized.

The investment considerations for each pooled trust are similar to those for the investment of a separate pension plan, except that each pooled trust may be restricted to specific classes of investments or to specific investment goals (growth or income). The assets of the individual plan can be invested in the combination of pooled trusts that are expected to accomplish the plan's investment objectives. Individual employers may designate the proportion of plan assets to be invested in each pooled fund, or that decision may be left to the corporate trustee. (See article on "Bank-Managed Investment Accounts," elsewhere in this volume.)

Marketable Securities. Most trusts limit their investments to securities that are publicly traded in established markets to reduce the problems of valuation, investment, and administration. But increasingly, trusts are investing in real estate and other assets that present valuation difficulties.

Distribution of Assets by Type. The market value of trust assets of private noninsured employer pension plans in 1986 was documented by the American Council of Life Insurance, as shown in Table 1.

INSURED FUNDING MEDIA

More than one-third of all private pension plan assets are invested with life insurance companies. Insurance companies fund plans under a wide variety of contracts. These contracts may be classified broadly as either group contracts covering a group of employees, or individual contracts for each employee. Contracts also may be classified as either annuity contracts or insurance contracts. Both types may provide annuities after retirement. The distinction is that on death before retirement, annuity contracts never pay death benefits exceeding the reserve, cash value, or premiums paid, whichever is greatest, while insurance contracts guarantee larger death benefits. Contracts also differ in the extent to which the insurance company guarantees the payment of benefits or the costs to the employer.

TABLE 1. 1986 Assets of Noninsured Private Pension Funds

	Market Value (billions)	Percent of Total
Cash and deposits	$ 41	5.0%
U.S. government securities	112	13.5
Corporate and foreign bonds	122	14.8
Corporate equities	437	52.8
Open market paper	32	3.9
Mortgages	5	0.6
Other assets	78	9.4
Total	$827	100.0%

Source: *Pension Facts, 1988 Update*, American Council of Life Insurance

Group Annuity Contracts

Deposit Administration Group Annuity Contract. Under deposit administration (DA) contracts, contributions to the plan for active participants are placed in a deposit fund. The insurance company does not allocate the fund among participants. The fund is credited with interest and charged with expenses. When a participant becomes eligible for a pension, the plan administrator notifies the insurance company, which makes a withdrawal from the deposit fund to purchase an annuity for the participant. If the participant is eligible for a lump-sum distribution, it is paid directly from the deposit fund.

The insurance company guarantees a minimum rate of interest to be credited to the deposit fund and guarantees the level of expense to be charged against the deposit fund. The insurer also guarantees the annuity purchase rates that will be used to purchase annuities and, after annuities have been purchased, payment of the promised pensions. It does not guarantee that the deposit fund will be sufficient to purchase the annuities.

The guarantees are conservative in nature. Experience more favorable than that assumed by the guarantees may be reflected in dividends or experience credits, which are added to the deposit fund. The insurance company may provide a full package of consulting, administrative, and actuarial services in connection with the plan, or the functions may be provided by the employer and consultants.

If the contract is discontinued, the employer may have the option of applying the deposit fund account balance to purchase annuities or withdrawing it for transfer to a trust or another insurance company. In case of withdrawal, the insurance company may subtract a surrender charge or a market value adjustment, and may require that the transfer be paid out over several years.

Separate Accounts. Insurance companies offering DA contracts generally make available one or more separate accounts for common stock investments to be used in connection with such contracts. The separate account is very similar to a mutual fund. The employer may direct that part or all of the contributions to the plan be invested in the separate account. Transfers can be made from the deposit account into the separate account. Any transfers out of the separate account are based upon the current market value.

In addition to separate accounts for common stock, many insurers maintain separate accounts for bonds, mortgages, real estate, and other classes of investment. Some insurers will establish a special separate account for a large individual plan, investing the account to meet its particular investment objectives. (See article on "Life Insurance: Separate Accounts," elsewhere in this volume.)

Immediate Participation Guarantee Contract. Also known as pension administration or investment-only contracts, immediate participation guarantee (IPG) contracts are similar to DA contracts. However, the insurer guarantees to credit its actual rate of investment earnings on its general portfolio rather than on a rate stipulated in the contract. The insurer charges the pension fund for an allocation of expenses for the particular contract based on accounting records, rather than using a stipulated expense charge. Although annuity purchase rates are guaranteed under the contract, usually there are no annuities actually purchased so long as the account balance is more than sufficient to purchase annuities for all those already retired, unless the contract is discontinued. Instead, pension payments are withdrawn from the account monthly as they are paid, just as in a trusteed plan. Some companies use an accounting device that has the appearance of purchasing annuities, but they actually operate the contract as though no annuities had been purchased. In addition, separate accounts are often made a part of IPG contracts in the same way as they are with DA contracts.

Guaranteed Investment Contract. Some employers desire contracts that guarantee the rate of interest to be credited to the deposit account and also guarantee that the full principal can be withdrawn with no surrender charge or adjustment. A guaranteed investment contract (GIC) offers just such guarantees. The interest guarantee may extend for five to ten years. It is contemplated that the account balance will be paid out at the end of the guarantee period, although the balance may be left on deposit and a new guarantee period established. The GIC may include annuity purchase options, but usually no annuities are purchased. GICs are widely used to fund defined contribution plans whenever the guarantee of principal is an objective.(For a more complete discussion, see article on "Life Insurance: Guaranteed Interest Contracts," elsewhere in this volume.)

Group Deferred Annuity Contracts. A deferred annuity contract is one in which the insurance company promises to pay a monthly annuity beginning at a specified future date. Under a group deferred annuity contract, the employer pays a premium to the insurer for each participant each year to purchase the amount of pension earned in that year.

Group deferred annuities once were the most common form of group annuity contract, but few new contracts have been issued in recent years, except to purchase annuities under terminated plans. Many plans that have changed to other methods of funding still have deferred annuities in force, reflecting the benefits funded before the date of change.

Individual Contracts

Many small plans fund each participant's benefit with the purchase of one or more individual annuity or insurance contracts. The premiums for such contracts contain substantially higher margins for expense than do the group contracts, previously discussed, in order to meet the higher commissions and higher administrative expense associated with such contracts. If higher expenses result in a low net return compared to other investments, this may be deemed a breach of fiduciary liability.

Level Premium Annuities. As the name implies, the individual level premium annuity contract has level annual premiums. An expense charge is deducted from each premium and the balance is accumulated at interest to obtain the policy's cash value. At retirement, the cash value is converted into a monthly annuity income. If the participant dies before retirement, a death benefit is paid equal to the greater of the cash value or the sum of the premiums paid.

Individual level premium annuities are sometimes used under defined benefit plans, but their use has declined in recent years. When an employee first becomes a participant, his projected pension at retirement age is calculated assuming that employment continues at the employee's current salary until that age. A level premium annuity contract is purchased for the level premium amount expected to provide the projected pensions. The premium is paid each year until retirement age. If the participant receives a salary increase the next year, resulting in an increase in the projected pension (above some minimum), a second annuity contract is issued to fund the increase in the projected pension. By retirement age, a large number of individual contracts may be in force for each participant.

Retirement Income Insurance. Retirement income insurance policies are similar to level premium annuities, except that the death benefit generally equals the greater of the cash value or 100 times the projected monthly pension. The death benefit usually exceeds the cash value for two-thirds or more of the policy's duration. Retirement income policies, like level premium annuities, were once commonly used for defined benefit pension plans but are no longer common.

Flexible Premium Annuity. A flexible premium annuity contract is similar to a level premium annuity contract, except that the premium may be changed each year. The flexible premium annuity contract may be used to fund defined benefit plans, just like a level premium annuity. If the participant receives a salary increase that increases his projected pension, the additional projected pension can be funded by increasing the future premiums rather than by issuing another contract. The flexible premium annuity also is used to fund profit-sharing plans and money purchase pension plans.

Split Funded Plans With Ordinary Life Insurance

Many plans, particularly small plans, are funded by a combination of individual ordinary life (whole life) policies and an auxiliary fund. The auxiliary fund, often called a side fund, may be a trust or an unallocated fund held by the insurance company and credited with interest. Many such funding programs were established to replace individual retirement income policies. The ordinary life policy is usually issued for 100 times the projected pension. At retirement, the policy cash value can be converted into an annuity to provide a monthly pension. Unlike the retirement income policy, the ordinary life policy does not have a cash value large enough to purchase an annuity for the entire pension. Therefore, a transfer is made from the auxiliary fund so that the transfer plus the cash value can purchase the needed annuity. Each year, the employer pays the premiums for the insurance and makes deposits to build up the auxiliary fund.

Trusteed profit-sharing plans often allow active participants to direct the trust to purchase an ordinary life insurance policy to provide a death benefit larger than the participant's account balance. Premiums for the policy are deducted from the employer's current contribution for the participant or from the participant's individual account balance.

Term Life Insurance

Some plans fund death benefits through the purchase of individual term life insurance policies. Term insurance is temporary insurance, often for a period of one year or five years. At the end of the term, the policy can generally be renewed for another term of the same length. In the past, some plans used policies that could not be renewed beyond age 70, but this is now generally prohibited by the Age Discrimination in Employment Act.

Premiums for term insurance are initially lower than those for whole life insurance, but they increase with age. Most term insurance policies have no cash value.

Universal Life Insurance

Some pension plans purchase universal life insurance contracts. A universal life policy is similar to a savings account plus term life insurance. Premiums paid are added to the account, which is credited with interest. The account is decreased by an expense charge and by the cost to purchase term insurance. The account balance is usually called the gross cash value or cash value. If the contract is surrendered, the policy holder will receive the "cash surrender value," which usually equals the gross cash value less a surrender charge.

The initial face amount of insurance generally doesn't change, but the policyholder can reduce the amount of insurance at any time. The policyholder may increase the amount of insurance if evidence of insurability (i.e., good health) is provided.

Two alternative patterns of death benefits are usually offered under universal life insurance. These are called level death benefit and increasing death benefit. Under the level death benefit alternative, the death benefit generally equals the face amount of insurance. This level death benefit consists of the policy's cash value plus a pure term insurance element. Each month, term insurance is purchased equal to the face amount of insurance less the cash value. The cost to purchase this amount of term insurance is deducted from the account.

Under the increasing death benefits alternative, the death benefit equals the face amount of insurance *plus* the cash value. Each month, term insurance is purchased equal to the full face amount of insurance. Because more term insurance is purchased under this alternative, less of the premiums are available for investment. The death benefit increases or decreases with any increase or decrease in the cash value.

The amount of each premium under a universal life policy is flexible. After the first premium, the policyholder may pay any amount desired, as long as the amount paid plus the surrender value is sufficient to pay the monthly expense charge plus the cost of insurance.

MANAGING THE INVESTMENT

Investment Management Decisions

After the type of pension plan has been decided on, certain important decisions must be made regarding pension plan investments. The plan sponsor, or a party delegated by the sponsor, must

- Determine investment policy.
- Select the party or parties to perform custodial functions.
- Select the party or parties to provide investment management.
- Make individual investment decisions.

It is generally desirable that the plan sponsor decide at least the broad direction of investment policy before selecting the parties to perform custodial functions and make investment management decisions, since investment policy is likely to influence the other choices.

Custodial Function

For an insured plan, the insurance company performs the custodial function of holding plan assets. For most trusteed plans, a bank or trust company almost always provides the custodial function. Although it is possible for an individual trustee to provide custodial functions, ERISA's requirements as to fiduciary responsibilities discourage that approach.

Investment Management of Insured Plans

If the plan sponsor chooses an insured approach without the use of separate accounts, the plan's assets are represented by the insurance company's contractual obligation. The insurance company combines the amounts it receives with all of its other assets, to be invested as part of its overall portfolio.

The insurance company also determines the investment of each of its separate accounts. The decision as to which of the insurer's separate accounts a plan should participate in, and the proportion of plan assets to be invested in each separate account, are investment management decisions that may be either made by the plan sponsor or delegated to the insurance company. Independent investment managers can be used for this function, but they rarely are.

Investment Management of Trusteed Plans

Commingled Funds. The investment management of commingled funds is entirely a function of the bank. The choice of which funds to participate in, and the proportion to be invested in each, is an investment policy decision that can be made by the plan sponsor or delegated to the bank. Independent investment managers are rarely used for this purpose.

Mutual Funds. Investment in mutual funds is comparable to investment in the commingled funds of banks. The employer or a party delegated by the employer can make the investment management decision as to the funds in which to invest and the extent to invest in each.

Other Trusts. The investment management function for trusts that do not use commingled or mutual funds may be performed by the trustee or by one or more independent investment managers.

Selecting Investment Management

The careful determination of investment policy is central to the choice of investment management and should take precedence over all other factors. For example, a decision to invest most plan assets in long-term bonds probably will lead to a different selection of investment management than will a decision to invest entirely in common stocks.

Judging Past Performance. The past investment performance of managers for funds will usually be compared by the sponsor with similar investment objectives. Past performance is not always a good indicator of future performance, but it may be helpful in evaluating the manager's style.

In studying the past performance of an investment manager, there is no consensus on how long a time should be examined. A period that is too short may give a misleading picture or show the manager's ability to invest only under certain circumstances, such as a falling market. A period that is too long may not reflect the manager's current personnel and practices. A five-year period is often used.

Obtaining appropriate information may be difficult. For a manager investing many trusts, complete information may not be available. Any manager investing hundreds of trusts can produce a few with outstanding results, but these may not be representative.

When in doubt, the funds of public record can be used. For insurance companies, the investment performance of the various separate accounts and the rates of interest credited to group annuity contracts can be examined. For a bank, the records of commingled funds can be examined, even if the sponsor contemplates separate management rather than commingled funds. Some investment managers also manage mutual funds, which provide a public record for comparison.

All comparisons must be made with considerable care to assure that assets with similar investment objectives are being compared. The same period should be used for all managers being compared. If this is not possible, each manager can be compared with an appropriate index for the period about which information is available. Care must also be taken to adjust for differences in accounting methods. Some banks, for example, apply investment income received in a commingled fund to increase the unit value; other banks use it to increase the number of units.

Management Personnel. The specific personnel of the manager may be considered. Their experience and qualification for investment under the sponsor's investment policy is important. Recent changes in personnel can be vital. An outstanding performance record can be meaningless if the individuals responsible for it are no longer with the manager.

Investment Philosophy and Methods. The manager's investment philosophies, strategies, and decision-making processes can be studied to determine if they are consistent with the plan's investment policy.

Fees. Investment management fees are an important part of any evaluation. For a small pension plan, the expense of separate investment management may dictate use of an insured approach, commingled funds, or mutual funds.

Pooled Funds or Separate Management. For a particular manager selected, there may be a choice between separate investment management and use of a pooled fund managed by the same manager. If he manages a commingled fund or a mutual fund with investment objectives similar to those of the pension plan, is there any reason to believe that the manager will produce better results with a separately managed fund? Unless the pension fund is quite large, it may receive less of the manager's attention and talent than will the mutual or commingled fund. For small plans, diversification is another reason for the pooled approach.

One Manager or More Than One. Some plans use a single investment manager and others use more than one. Different managers may be selected for different types of investments, since the same managers are not the best for all types. On the other hand, use of more than one manager increases the total management fees, which is a disadvantage, particularly for smaller funds. Some plans divide investments of the same type among two or more managers, perhaps in the hope that competition will spur them to greater effort. The only result of this strategy may be increased management fees.

If more than one manager is selected, the plan sponsor or a party delegated by the sponsor needs to develop guidelines for each, determine the amounts each should invest, and coordinate their work.

Use of Consultants. The plan sponsor may engage the services of an independent consultant to assist in establishing its investment policy and in selecting investment management. Consultants work with clients at each stage of the manager selection and coordination process. This includes helping plan sponsors determine what types of managers are appropriate for their situations and investment goals, examining a selection of suitable managers, presenting the leading candidates to the sponsor, participating in the interviewing process leading to the final selection of money managers, and assisting sponsors in developing instructions for each manager to assure implementation of overall investment policy, define expectations for each individual money manager, and make it easier to monitor results.

REVIEWING INVESTMENT RESULTS

Plan sponsors and their consultants may review all aspects of investment results to determine whether investment policy is being followed, whether performance is satisfactory, and whether any changes are advisable in investment policy and management.

Measuring Performance

Measurement of investment return and risk has become a highly sophisticated procedure. Dollar-weighted rates of return are calculated to determine the overall investment results; time-weighted rates of return are used to measure percentage return independent of the volume of assets available for investment during different periods. Some consulting firms provide extensive comparisons with other pension funds that have comparable investment objectives. Risk measurement is an important adjunct to performance measurement to ascertain whether investment policy is being followed and whether the return is appropriate for the risk.

Evaluating Investment Management

Reviewing investment results can be helpful in eliminating misunderstandings between the plan sponsor and investment managers, and in clarifying investment policy. This process can correct management problems. Review also assists the sponsor in deciding whether to retain existing managers or to seek a change. Results should be reviewed over a period of several years. Except for serious errors or unusual circumstances, the sponsor generally will not replace a manager for poor performance over a short period.

GLOSSARY

annuity plan—A plan funded with annuities, which meets the requirements of a qualified trust, but without a trust.

deferred profit-sharing plan—A type of defined contribution plan generally subject to fewer restrictions than a money purchase plan.

defined benefit plan—A pension plan that specifies the amount of the retirement benefit.

defined contribution plan—A pension plan in which a specified amount is allocated to each employee's individual account each year.

employee stock ownership plan (ESOP)—A defined contribution plan designed primarily to invest in qualifying employer securities.

Keogh plan—A plan for partners or sole proprietors of unincorporated businesses who generally are treated as though they were employees.

money purchase plan—A pension plan with employer contributions determined by a definite formula, independent of profits.

multiemployer plan—A pension plan established under a collective bargaining agreement between one or more unions and two or more employers, usually a defined benefit plan.

pension plan—A defined benefit plan or defined contribution plan, or combination plan, providing for employee retirement income.

qualified plan—A pension plan that meets the requirements of the Internal Revenue Code in receiving favorable tax treatment.

stock bonus plan—A pension plan in which benefits are distributable in the shares of the employer-company.

S corporation—A corporation that elects to be taxed as a partnership under Subchapter S of Chapter 1 of the Internal Revenue Code.

thrift plan—Also known as a savings plan—a defined contribution plan in which employer contributions match a stated percentage of employer contributions.

SUGGESTED READING

Allen, Everett T., Jr.; Melone, Joseph J.; and Rosenbloom, Jerry S. *Pension Planning*, 6th ed. Homewood: Richard D. Irwin, 1988.

Blodgett, Richard. *Conflicts of Interest: Union Pension Fund Asset Management*. New York: Twentieth Century Fund, 1977.

Brooks, John. *Conflicts of Interest: Corporate Pension Fund Asset Management*. New York: Twentieth Century Fund, 1975.

Dietz, Peter O. *Pension Funds: Measuring Investment Performance*. Columbia University, Graduate School of Business Dissertation Series, New York: The Free Press, 1966.

Ellis, Charles D. *Investment Policy*. Homewood: Dow Jones-Irwin, 1985.

Financial Analysts Research Foundation. *Evolving Concepts of Prudence: The Changing Responsibilities of the Investment Fiduciary in the Age of ERISA*. New York, 1976.

Grubbs, Donald S., Jr. *Target Benefit Plans*. Philadelphia: American Law Institute-American Bar Association, 1980.

Hannah, Leslie, ed. *Pension Asset Management: An International Perspective*. Homewood: Richard D. Irwin, 1988.

International Foundation of Employee Benefit Plans. *Investment Policy Guidebook for Trustees, rev. ed.* Brookfield, Wis., 1981.

———. *Investment Performance of Multiemployer Pension Funds: Measurement and Reporting, Comparison and Evaluation, Implications for Future Policy*. Brookfield, Wis., 1976.

Johnson, George E., and Grubbs, Donald S., Jr. *The Variable Annuity*, 2nd ed. Indianapolis: Research & Review Service, 1969.

Levin, Noel A., and Brossman, Mark E. *Social Investing for Pension Funds: For Love or Money*. Brookfield: International Foundation of Employee Benefit Plans, 1982.

Livingston, David T. *Investment Practices of Jointly Trusteed Pension Plans*. Research Survey Report No. 2. Brookfield: International Foundation of Employee Benefit Plans, 1975.

Mamorsky, Jeffrey D., ed. *Employee Benefits Handbook*, rev. ed. Boston: Warren, Gorham & Lamont, 1987.

Marcus, Bruce W. *The Prudent Man: Making Decisions Under* ERISA. Belleville: ESP Corporation Pensions and Investments, 1978.

McGill, Dan M., ed. *Social Investing*. Homewood: Richard D. Irwin, 1984.

———, and Grubbs, Donald S., Jr. *Fundamentals of Private Pensions*, 6th ed. Homewood: Richard D. Irwin, 1989.

President's Commission on Pension Policy. *Coming of Age: Toward National Retirement Income Policy*. Washington, D.C., 1981.

PORCELAIN

Michele Beiny
Rotraut Beiny
Paul Vandekar

BASIC CHARACTERISTICS

Porcelain collecting is a pursuit with a long history; for more than 1,000 years, porcelain has been esteemed in China, where it was first made, and for 500 years, it has been cherished and collected in the West.

Kinds of Porcelain

Hard-Paste (True) Porcelain. For true porcelain, two special ingredients are required: kaolin, or china clay, which produces a hard white material when fired at a high temperature; and petuntse, or china stone, which supplies the unique translucency. The mixture forms the paste, and the shaped ware is fired in a kiln at a very high temperature, between 1,300 and 1,400 degrees Celsius to produce a white, vitrified, translucent material. Many things can go wrong during the firing; forms can shrink, crack, sag, or collapse, or a series of fine cracks, called crazing, can develop.

Porcelain that has been fired but not glazed is known as biscuit, or bisque. It resembles white marble and has often been used to imitate sculpture. Usually, porcelain is glazed. Glaze is a thin coating of a glassy compound that fuses with the porcelain on firing to form

---

Michele Beiny and Rotraut Beiny are Vice-President and President, respectively, of The Antique Porcelain Company of New York, Inc.; they prepared this article in its original form for the first edition. Paul Vandekar is President of Earle D. Vandekar of Knightsbridge, Inc., a member of the National Antique and Art Dealers Association, New York; he revised and updated this article for this second edition.

an extremely hard surface. Various colored glazes are produced by the oxides of different metals. Glaze that is crackled has a pattern of small cracks that originate in the firing, either accidentally or intentionally, for effect, the latter being peculiarly Chinese.

Painted decoration can be applied before glazing; this is called underglaze decoration. Only colors that can withstand the high firing temperatures, such as cobalt blue and copper red, can be used for this purpose. A wide palette of enamel colors can be applied over the glaze. Such colors are fired on at a lower temperature, so signs of wear sometimes become evident.

Early Porcelain. This category includes not only "true porcelain" as defined in Europe, which must be white and translucent when fired, but also fine, hard, dusky, and gray materials fired to such a vitrified state that they emit a musical note when struck, as made in China in the T'ang and Sung Dynasties (618–1279). This resonance was the principal test of early Chinese porcelain.

Soft-Paste (Artificial) Porcelain. This is not readily distinguishable by eye from hard paste, but it shows a granular surface when chipped. Also, the glaze does not appear to be one with the body as in true porcelain. The recipe varies. One of several glassy substances, called frit, is mixed with white clay and water to form a paste. This is fired at about 1,000 degrees Celsius to produce a biscuit. A lead oxide glaze is sprayed over the piece and overglaze decoration applied. Kiln losses are heavy. Soft paste is a less useful ware than true porcelain; it is inclined to craze, and it chips, stains, and scratches more easily than hard paste does. But the beauty and softness of the material as well as the ability of the painted decoration to sink into the glaze have made soft paste irresistibly alluring to the collector. Soft-paste porcelain was used by the early French factories and by most eighteenth-century English ones, but it has rarely been used since the early nineteenth century.

Bone China. This has been the standard English porcelain since the early nineteenth century, the formula being credited to Josiah Spode II. Burned animal bones are added to the basic hard paste, making it more durable than most porcelain.

HISTORY

The history of porcelain manufacture in the Far East is distinct from that of Europe; however, they have had considerable reciprocal influence. The following brief summary deals with the most salient features of each and the most collectible ware from the main factories.

Early Porcelain of the Far East

Chinese porcelain is categorized first by dynastic periods, then by type of ware. The dynasties of greatest interest to the porcelain collector are as follows.

T'ang	618–906 A.D.	Yuan	1280–1368
Sung	960–1279	Ming	1368–1644
Northern Sung	960–1127	Ch'ing	1644–1912
Southern Sung	1127–1279		

It is generally believed that the first true porcelain was made under the T'ang dynasty, which is better known for its earthenware.

Under the Sung dynasty, extremely fine porcelains with outstanding monochrome glazes ware produced by hundreds of kilns in northern and southern China. *Kuan yao*, the imperial ware made specially for the emperor's court, is today considered one of the high points of Chinese art. Decoration, incised or moulded, is subtle and understated; motifs include floral designs, fish, ducks, and human figures. Among the best known Sung wares is *ying ch'ing*, which has a glaze tinged with a very pale, shadowy blue. The haunting color celadon, varying from delicate green to gray-blue, gave its name to objects glazed in that color. White porcelain is covered with an ivory glaze, imparting an orange translucency to the body; the decoration is carved or incised. Sung wares have always fetched very high prices.

Contemporary with the Sung dynasty, the Koryo period in Korea (918–1400) saw the production of superb celadons. Korean ceramics of this period, typically decorated under the glaze with cranes, waterfowl, and willow trees, have long been collected in the West.

During the Yuan period, hard-paste (true) porcelain was produced. A noteworthy development was the use of underglaze painting, especially in cobalt blue; this was to evolve into China's famous blue-and-white decoration. It was during the reign of Kublai Khan (1216–1294), founder of the dynasty, that Marco Polo visited China, which was to be an event of enormous cultural importance to Europe.

Ming wares were the first Chinese porcelains introduced into Europe in quantity, and are therefore the most widely familiar. They are noted for the rich palette of polychrome enamels on glazed porcelain; blue-and-white decoration also flourished. The painting has echoes of the noble Chinese art of calligraphy. Many pieces were monumental in size, four feet or more. Porcelain with a fine-grained body covered with a thick white glaze, called blanc de chine, was first made at Tehua in the Fukien province in the late Ming period.

Oriental Porcelain in Europe

By the fifteenth century, several European monarchs had some Chinese porcelain in their treasuries. The Chinese did not want European interlopers to learn much about China; in particular, they jealously guarded the lucrative secret of porcelain-making until the mid-nineteenth century. They were, however, willing to trade in porcelain with the Portuguese and later with the Dutch East India Company. Huge amounts of porcelain were imported into an insatiable Europe from the sixteenth through the eighteenth centuries.

Japanese Porcelain. The Dutch, who sought new sources of porcelain for importation into Europe, were responsible for the production of porcelain in Japan, already known for its pottery. The Japanese were eager to trade, and soon began to turn out porcelains based on Chinese and Korean models to satisfy European tastes. Kaolin was discovered at Arita in 1616; the earliest decoration in polychrome enamels is associated with a celebrated family of Japanese potters, of whom the most famous is Sakaida Kakiemon. He gave his name to an elegantly asymmetrical style of decoration that had the greatest influence on many eighteenth-century European factories. European Kakiemon-style wares are among the most collectible today. Imari ware has also been much admired and imitated in the West to the present day. It is prized for its colorful and amusing decorations. In the late seventeenth century, striking porcelain was manufactured at Kutani, with a nineteenth-century revival: the most sought-after wares are those decorated in gold on a coral red ground. Other Japanese porcelains collected today are Nabeshima (made after 1675), decorated in underglaze blue and enamels, and Hirado (made from 1712), with underglaze blue or relief decoration.

Chinese Export Porcelain. The porcelain that was manufactured in China for export to Europe is known today as Chinese export or in Europe as chine de commande. This porcelain was produced to Occidental specifications as to shape and decoration.

The trade between China and Europe began with the Portuguese and continued with the Dutch. By the 1750s, when most of the European maritime nations had East India companies, the British dominated. The Chinese authorities specified certain locations where this trade could take place, and Canton became the principal trade port.

A wide variety of products, including spices, silks, and gold, as well as porcelain were traded in Canton. The trade was carefully regulated by the Chinese authorities, who considered the Europeans barbarians. They wished for little contact between the European traders and the Chinese people and kept the Europeans to a small enclosed area of the city.

By the second decade of the eighteenth century, the production of porcelain had begun in Europe, but the European factories could not produce the quantity nor could they match the lower price of the porcelain being produced in China. By the end of the century, competition from technological innovators such as Wedgwood had brought the trade in porcelain in Europe almost to an end, although America, looking for new trading partners, considerably expanded its trade with China at that time.

A wonderful variety of items had been brought to Europe and America to adorn the furniture and decorate the rooms of the nobility and merchants. Large numbers of pieces were made for special order — from commercial objects of everyday use for the East India companies, to unique objects made for special orders placed from Europe by wealthy individuals. Sometimes, the design provided was drawn on paper; at other times, an actual silver or faience original was itself dispatched. Whole dinner services, including some with armorial decoration, were ordered, as were huge vases and jardinieres and fanciful, fantastic animals to be used for interior design. The decoration of these porcelains changed with fashion, and provide for us today a wonderful picture of the interests of the people at that time. Exotic "chinoiseries" reflected a newfound fascination with the East. The huge variety of botanical subject matter was the result of the growing interest in the exploration of the Pacific, while religious and political subjects mirrored the more personal outlooks of the European buyers.

Early European Porcelain

Throughout the eighteenth century, Oriental porcelains continued to be imported into Europe in vast quantities. This "Chinamania" was beginning to ruin whole families and, in some cases, countries, because of the enormous expenditures devoted to this luxury. Indeed, China was called the bleeding bowl of Saxony by one dismayed minister. Efforts to make porcelain in Europe were redoubled. Europe was well aware that domestic porcelain manufacture would be an excellent source of revenue.

German Porcelain. The greatest collector of porcelain in European history was Augustus II, Elector of Saxony and King of Poland (1670–1733). He bought Oriental porcelain in massive quantities, and even traded an entire regiment of dragoons to the

King of Prussia for a collection of 117 pieces of Chinese porcelain. He was determined to have his own factory producing porcelain as good as the Chinese wares. On January 15, 1708, the combined efforts of the physicist and philosopher, von Tschirnhaus, and a young alchemist, Johann Friedrich Boettger, produced the first piece of true hard-paste porcelain made in Europe. In January 1710, Augustus opened the Meissen factory by official decree.

The body of Meissen porcelain was equal in quality to the Chinese, and very soon the decoration and modeling were to surpass it. A series of master decorators, including Herold Loewenfick, Hauer, and Heintze, and of master modelers, especially Kirchner and Kaendler, with his assistants Reinicke and Eberlein, managed to create a new, totally European style of decorative art. Their artistic accomplishment in the first half of the eighteenth century made porcelain one of the clearest expressions of the baroque and then the rococo art in Europe.

Kaendler was a modeler of genius who worked at the Meissen factory from 1731 to 1775. He probably created over 1,000 different figures and groups. His animals and birds are worthy of particular mention. So, too, were his vivacious figures, which often formed sets that were very much to the eighteenth century taste: the Four Seasons, the Four Continents, the Italian comedy figures, peasants, street vendors, nationals, and crinoline groups depicting court life. Religious subjects were the topic of some of his greatest works.

Count von Bruhl became director of the factory in 1733 on the death of Augustus, and from then until the beginning of the Seven-Year War in 1756, Meissen enjoyed its greatest period. Magnificent tablewares and huge dinner services, such as the famous Swan Service, were in fashion.

The European courts were a ready market, with their taste for grandiose table decoration—large porcelain centerpieces, every imaginable type of tableware and vessel, and porcelain figures to replace those decorations which had previously been made of sugar and wax. Special importance was attached to the utensils used in the aristocratic pursuits of drinking tea, coffee, and chocolate. The Meissen collector can also choose from a whole range of small, highly decorative objects, such as needle cases, snuff boxes, scent bottles, cane handles, patch boxes, and pipe bowls.

Meissen at its height produced a wealth of enamel colors and an enormous variety of original painted decoration, all of excellent quality. The earliest decorations from 1715–1719 were usually straightforward copies of the Chinese; later, this developed into chinoiserie, the Europeans' naïve and charming idea of what Chinese life ought to be. Harbor scenes were a great favorite, as were the European landscapes. Kakiemon designs took on a European interpretation, especially the *indianische Blumen* (Oriental flowers), followed later by *deutsche Blumen* (naturalistic flowers). Pieces were often painted with an overall background color. As the rococo set in, a taste for pastoral and Watteau scenes emerged.

By 1756, the great days of Meissen has passed. The jealously guarded secret of the manufacture of hard paste managed to leak out by various devious means; defectors from Meissen were bribed, kidnapped, and coerced into revealing what they knew. Rulers in central Europe were intent on having their own factories; it was almost a necessity of the princely state. The end of Meissen's monopoly of the European market paved the way, during the second half of the eighteenth century, for the emergence of many factories in the German-speaking world. Their products are for the most part of very high quality, although, in some cases, they are primarily of interest to the more specialized collectors. At first, they were influenced mainly by Meissen; their artists worked in the rococo and later in the neoclassical style. Each factory produced both tablewares and figures in its own distinctive forms, colors, and decorative subject matter, although there was some overlap. Continuity was increased by the curious phenomenon of the eighteenth-century wandering workman: artists and modelers were in the habit of moving around Europe from one factory to another during their working life.

Half a dozen of these factories are the most important from the collector's point of view. Vienna (1719–1864), especially the early du Paquier period (1719–1744), was among the most noteworthy. This was the only German factory besides Meissen to use chinoiserie decoration frequently. Furstenberg (1747–today); Hoechst (1750–1798); Nymphenburg (1753–today) boasted a modeler, Bustelli, who rivalled Kaendler in the excellence of his figures; Frankenthal (1755–1800) specialized in a great variety of figures and groups; Ludwigsburg (1758–1824); and Berlin (1761–today) were all of great importance. There were many other factories, such as Fulda and Kelsterbach, that produced wares of extremely high quality and originality, although examples are now rare.

Other factories of note in Northern Europe were St. Petersburg, Zurich, and Copenhagen.

Italian Porcelain

In Italy, several factories started up in the eighteenth century, of which the most important in today's market are Cozzi, Vezzi, Doccia, and especially Capodimonte (1743–1759). The soft-paste porcelain made at Capodimonte, in the Kingdom of Naples, is today considered the finest Italian production, especially the figures modeled by Giuseppe Gricci. When King Charles IV of Naples became King Charles III of Spain in 1759 and moved to Madrid, his beloved factory followed him. Known as Buen Retiro, it remained in production until 1808. There are no longer many examples of Capodimonte on the market today.

French Porcelain

Soft-paste porcelain is a true reflection of eighteenth-century French taste, as epitomized in the production of the well-known Sèvres factory. Before this factory opened, there were a few others producing wares of great charm and delicacy, in a style totally distinct from that of the German factories. Soft-paste wares have a creamy, warm texture, and the softer coloring is most appealing to the eye.

St. Cloud (1677–1766) was the first French factory with any significant output and success. It specialized in making figures and many small objects for domestic use such as covered jars, potpourri vases, pastille burners, and snuff boxes. Its wares were often undecorated, relying on moulded decoration. Chinoiserie was very popular. Chantilly (1725–1800) was established by Louis-Henri de Bourbon, Prince of Condé. The style of the wares was very restrained; strong colors were seldom used, and by far the most popular decorations were Kakiemon designs, still the most sought-after by collectors. Figures of Orientals were popular. Mennecy (1734–1785) is especially known for its distinctive, delicate pink and blue enamel colors, which were used to decorate a wide variety of tablewares, vases, and figures. Their style of decoration was more European than Oriental, and the paste was a beautiful creamy white. Tournai (1751–1891) was one of the few major European factories of the eighteenth century to supply utilitarian wares destined for use in middle-class households. The factory was successful and the production large.

Sèvres is considered by many to be the queen of porcelain factories. Originally called

Vincennes, it first produced porcelain in 1745. The production of extremely realistic porcelain flowers accounted for about 80 percent of its sales. The flowers were either mounted on wire stems in vases or used as ornaments on other objects, often from other factories. In 1753, Louis XV took charge of the factory, thanks to the encouragement of his mistress, Madame de Pompadour, a great patroness of the arts. After 1756, the factory was known as Sèvres. Restrictions were placed on the production of porcelain at the other French factories, and these soon went out of business. Louis XV obliged his courtiers to purchase heavily. Production was very ornate, elegant, and refined to suit the highly sophisticated taste of a frivolous aristocracy whose life centered around the palace of Versailles. Many dinner and tea services were made, as well as flowerpots, large potpourri vases, covered bowls on stands, and elaborate clocks, often mounted on ormolu. Sèvres is celebrated for its ground colors, such as bleu céleste, dark royal blue, rose pompadour, and apple green. Gilding was richly tooled and applied. Favorite decorations included birds and flowers, putti, paintings inspired by Watteau and Boucher, marine scenes, and emblems. From the second half of the eighteenth century onward, Sèvres took over Meissen's position as the leading porcelain factory in Europe and greatly influenced the production of other European competitors from then on. It became the major supplier of dinner services and decorative vases to all the royalty and nobility in Europe.

English Porcelain

No princely sponsorship was bestowed on the English factories, which operated as private enterprises. Precise historical data and records are not readily available in many cases. All but three factories produced soft paste in the eighteenth century. English porcelain, like French, has a very distinct style and flavor.

Chelsea (circa 1745–1770) is classified by its marks, the Raised Anchor (1749–1752) and Red Anchor (1752–1758) periods being generally considered the finest. Silver shapes greatly influenced the form of the wares. The factory was very fond of Kakiemon designs, as well as botanical decoration, which attained a peak unrivaled by any other factory. Freshness and charm characterized the early English factories. Tureens and dishes in the form of vegetables and animals were popular. Chelsea's excellent modeling also produced some very fine figures and birds. During the final Gold Anchor period (1758–1770), Chelsea adopted the more formal Sèvres style with rich decoration, striking ground color, and much gilding. The factory excelled at toys, and is particularly famous for its many delightful scent bottles.

Bow (circa 1744–1776) was the busiest factory in eighteenth-century England, noted for its primitive charm. The most valued products include brightly painted and somewhat crudely modeled figures and animals, as well as tablewares decorated with Oriental designs or botanical motifs.

Derby (circa 1750–today) concentrated on figures in its early days, often copying Meissen originals; tablewares were decorated with flowers, birds, insects, and butterflies. In 1770 it acquired the Chelsea factory, and in 1776, Bow. Called Chelsea-Derby from then on, it increased its production of tablewares.

Worcester (1751–today) was successful from the start, its most important period from the collector's point of view being from 1751–1783, called Dr. Wall or First Period. It made many useful wares, especially sauceboats, jugs, baskets, leaf dishes, and mugs. Hardly any figures were produced. Worcester is noted for its decoration; its chinoiseries, transfer printing, extraordinary ground colors and scale ground colors that were overlaid to look like fish scales, and flamboyantly exotic birds and foliage.

Another factory of note was Longton Hall (1750–1760), producing charming botanical wares in a distinctive yellowish green, crudely modeled but colorful figures, and decorations by an unidentified artist called the Castle Painter. Caughley, Liverpool, Lowestoft, Plymouth, Bristol, and New Hall are also noteworthy.

Nineteenth-Century Porcelain

From approximately 1775 to 1850, porcelain styles were strongly affected by neoclassicism, showing Greek, Roman, and Etruscan influences. Vienna, Nymphenburg, and Berlin excelled in this style. The well-known factories of Hutschenreuther and Rosenthal, still operating today, were founded during this period. Royal Copenhagen flourished. Sèvres, which had now adopted hard paste, was very active, producing many large pieces with florid decoration. The Paris and Limoges factories were founded.

In England, porcelain factories flourished, especially those producing large dinner services that are still sought after today. The colorful Japanese Imari designs and the formal elegance of Sèvres were a great inspiration. Spode, Derby, Worcester, Coalport, New Hall, Minton, and Rockingham are all known for their tablewares. Wedgwood became one of the most successful business enterprises in England.

Some porcelain manufacturers existed in America during this period, but their wares are collected for patriotic rather than aesthetic reasons. Examples are Bonnin and Morris of Philadelphia, Tucker and Hulme, and the United States Pottery Company. Lenox, perhaps the best known, is still commissioned to make state dinner services for the White House.

Twentieth-Century Porcelain

Fresh techniques of manufacture and decoration, such as *pâte-sur-pâte,* were developed from the 1880s on. Art Nouveau influenced porcelain designs, especially at Sèvres. The Scandinavian factories of Rörstand, Royal Copenhagen, and Bing and Gröndahl were great innovators. In the 1920s, Sèvres produced elegant dinner wares in the Art Deco style, which also inspired Meissen and Nymphenburg. Dorothy Doughty and Edward Marshall Boehm are noted for their limited editions of bird sculptures. Royal Copenhagen's Flora Danica service is famous. At Sèvres today, the factory's director, Jean Mathieu, is encouraging contemporary artists and sculptors to express themselves in porcelain, with notable success.

ATTRACTIVE FEATURES

Few kinds of collecting have a grander pedigree than porcelain; today's collector begins against an impressive background. From the start, fine porcelain was enthusiastically sought after in the Far East and eagerly received by the Europeans, who found it equally irresistible. Their reverence for it often found expression in the custom of complementing objects with silver, gold, gilt, and ormolu mounts. The image of porcelain collecting is both elegant and aristocratic and carries with it a certain refinement of taste and an aura of sophistication.

Aesthetic Appeal

Initially, porcelain and other ceramics can be somewhat intimidating, considering the large number of factories, different materials, and different styles involved. However, once this confusion is overcome, porcelain can be one of the most rewarding areas of collecting. Porcelain is the only antique material that looks exactly the same today as the day it was made. Whatever one's interest — sailing, animals, new technology, the production of a particular factory — the wide range of subject matter can be the basis for a fascinating collection that is both personally satisfying and financially rewarding.

Investment Value

Although porcelain should never be purchased for investment purposes alone, those who have purchased good porcelain have seen the value of their collections rise significantly. Ceramics are affected by fashion, and thus, certain areas have increased in value more significantly than others.

Early Chinese porcelain has become one of the highest priced types of porcelain, with individual pieces now frequently making over $1 million. A Ming copper red vase in pristine condition sold in Hong Kong for a price of $2,183,099, which is a record for any ceramic object ever sold at auction to date.

Chinese export has also risen in value. Unlike much European porcelain, its appeal is international and its value is less linked to any fluctuation in a particular currency or economy. A Chinese export "tobacco leaf" dinner service recently made over $800,000, while a single dish decorated with the coat of arms of Leake Okeover made $132,000 at auction in New York.

English porcelain has also risen significantly in the last two years, having remained stagnant for a time. In July 1986, a Chelsea porcelain model of Hogarth's dog "Trump" made $136,800 at the Rous Lench sale. Meissen has also remained a porcelain factory that has brought high prices for important pieces.

It is still possible to purchase pieces of antique ceramics that represent the finest objects made by a particular factory and still pay less than $10,000. The prices previously mentioned were achieved for top objects in their field; yet, they are still significantly less than the prices achieved for top pieces in other collecting specialties, such as the fine arts or French furniture.

With an eye on the best, astute collectors can enjoy wonderful antiques and see their collections appreciate significantly in value. The help of an advisor, specifically a member of one of the top trade organizations, is highly recommended.

POTENTIAL RISKS

The art market as a whole is always affected by the current general economic situation. When money is scarce in times of recession, the art market suffers. On the other hand, when confidence in money and intangibles is shaken, investment in art becomes more favored. Overall, porcelain has proved to be a good hedge against inflation.

However, the porcelain market may tend to be more chauvinistic than most art markets; the prices fetched by various factories will often be closely related to the economic situation of the countries involved. This may be an advantage as well as a risk for a potential investor. While the Deutschmark and Japanese yen are strong, German and Oriental porcelains will continue to do best. The Americans with their strong dollar, the Australians, and the South Africans are now boosting the prices of English porcelains.

Value can also be affected by a variety of intangible factors: current vogue, the object's provenance, a successful show in a leading museum, publicity, and media coverage in popular magazines. The whims of fashion, an elusive factor, may be difficult to predict. For instance, at present, eighteenth-century French soft-paste porcelain, once very strong, is less popular and does not fetch such high prices as it had in the past. On the other hand, for the investor who also wishes to enjoy the beauty of his possessions, this is the time to acquire some good bargains in that area.

The market may be more volatile in highly specialized areas, rising suddenly if two or more collectors appear on the market competing for the same limited supply of objects. This happened recently in the field of Vienna-du-Paquier-period porcelain (1719–1744), where prices suddenly soared.

Many people worry about liquidity as regards investment in works of art. Of course, an investor cannot expect to liquidate a portfolio of tangibles overnight. However, an auction house or dealer will take the piece off a collector's hands and turn that asset into money quite quickly. If a forced sale takes place, the price realized will be by no means the best.

Whatever economic fluctuations occur, the golden rule is to always buy the best and the rarest in a chosen field of interest. Then, as experience has proved, the objects will retain their value and appreciate over time.

TAX CONSEQUENCES

Under federal tax law, profit from the sale of porcelain held by an individual for more than one year is taxed as a capital gain. Under certain conditions, objects of porcelain can be exchanged for others of equal or greater value in a tax-free transaction. As with other types of investments, it is also possible to realize a tax deduction on donating a porcelain piece whose market value has appreciated to a qualified organization. Separate rules apply to those who are recognized as investors by the Internal Revenue Service. (See article on "Tax Considerations for Collector-Investors," elsewhere in this volume.) For complete guidance in these matters, readers are urged to consult a professional tax advisor.

IMPORTANT FACTORS IN BUYING AND SELLING

Dealers and Auction Houses

A collector has a choice of operating through a dealer or an auction house. The latter is an important marketplace, and following auction results is one of the essential means of gauging current market prices and trends. However, there are disadvantages for a private collector working through the auction houses. In their conditions of sale, auction houses refuse to accept responsibility for the statements in their catalogs that are merely statements of opinion. They will not guarantee the genuineness, date, attribution, provenance, or condition of any piece they sell. Proven deliberate forgeries can only be returned within seven days of their sale.

In addition, many people, both buyers and sellers, dislike the publicity of an auction. In the art world, privacy and anonymity are highly valued; this element is lost at auction, where the identity of purchasers and sellers, as well as the prices paid, become public knowledge. If unsold, for whatever reason, an object becomes tainted in some way. Newspapers report the record prices fetched at auction, but tend to ignore those lots that do not reach their estimates. It is always considered more prestigious to acquire a piece that has not been offered to the world at large; therefore, on the whole, the best prices are obtained privately. The exception will be in the case of the occasional highly publicized and important object, especially as private individuals are more prone to get carried away, driving prices sky high; a dealer, who is far more aware of market value, will know when to stop bidding. Alternatively, it is possible for a seller to be unlucky; his piece may be included in a poorly attended or a nonspecialized sale where the price will be unnaturally low. An object invariably suffers if, unsold the first time, it is subsequently reoffered for sale. Again, it is possible for an object to be wrongly catalogued for auction, as the auction house has to deal with the thousands of pieces that pass through its hands. Attention to any particular object or person may be lacking. Finally, both buyer and seller must bear in mind the 10 percent minimum commission that an auction house will charge each of them on every transaction.

For several reasons, a reputable dealer is an invaluable advisor to the collector. Obviously, a knowledgeable collector can seek bargains in antique stores or take some risks by following the auction market. On the other hand, a reputable dealer has the advantage of many years' experience. He will guarantee the genuineness and condition of the pieces he sells. Also, a collector can be sure that a dealer will be willing to spend time with him, since the dealer is interested in establishing an ongoing relationship. He will often take great pride in the collection he is helping to form. A dealer's expertise is an invaluable barometer for many crucial factors: authenticity, quality, condition, price, the importance of the piece, historically or as it relates to other works of the same period.

Authenticity, Quality, and Condition

The eye and hand have to be trained to recognize the various indicators of authenticity, quality, and condition. This comes only with time and experience. Various scientific aids are being developed today to analyze the composition of the paste. Ultraviolet lights are most useful in exposing forgeries, marks that have been tampered with, and repairs that are undetectable to the naked eye, as well as differentiating hard from soft paste. Many collectors own hand-held lights that can be purchased at a relatively low cost.

The feel of the paste, its color as well as the colors used in the decoration, and the resonance of the porcelain when struck will tell an experienced person a great deal about the date, origin, quality, and condition of an object: whether it was decorated later or outside the factory, whether it is soft or hard paste, whether it is a forgery. For instance, a certain stickiness to the touch may indicate to the expert that the object he is handling has been restored.

Pastes vary a great deal in translucency and color. Each factory has its own distinctive traits. For example, a characteristic of Chelsea porcelain is the formation of transparent glassy spots in the paste, clearly visible when a piece is held to the light; early Worcester, which includes soapstone in its body, has a slightly greenish tone and its thin glaze tends to shrink away from the foot.

Marks

Marks on porcelain are a very useful guide to origin and identification. Many porcelains were marked, and comprehensive publications on the subject are available. There is, however, one great caveat: By no means are all originals marked, but almost all forgeries are.

Many factories forged the marks of other factories, or forged marks used in earlier periods at their own factory. As a result, most experts emphasize that, in establishing the origin and value of a piece of porcelain, marks are secondary to style and quality. The extreme irregularity of marks should also be noted; lack of uniformity in drawing and spelling is commonplace. In addition, marks of various kinds were added by modelers, gilders, decorators, and dealers. The absence or irregularity of a mark does not, therefore, necessarily detract from the value of a piece.

Forgeries

The problem of forgeries must be considered. As porcelains have always been highly prized, forgers have found their occupation a lucrative one; as early as the sixteenth century, there were potters renowned for their imitations of Sung wares. It was common for factories to sell off stocks of white porcelain that were decorated by the enterprising buyers and often passed off as genuine factory-decorated products. In the nineteenth century, for instance, some lightly decorated Sèvres pieces had their decoration removed with acid and a heavier decoration substituted to bring a higher price. Sèvres imitations were made by Martin Randall at Madeley, England, in the 1820s, as well as at Coalport. In this connection, special mention must be made of the nineteenth-century firm of Edmé Samson et Cie. of Paris, whose fame rests entirely on its excellent imitations. It was founded with the express purpose of making reproductions of ancient works emanating from museums and private collections, specializing in Chinese export, Meissen, and Sèvres. The products of this manufacturer have now become collector's items in their own right.

Finding the Right Market

A dealer's advice is helpful in deciding what to buy and when to buy it, whether to follow an existing fashion or to go against it. The collector who always seeks quality first and foremost cannot go wrong in the long run. The best pieces will always retain their value; in times of economic uncertainty, when money is short, it is the value of the mediocre that will suffer. With that in mind, many collectors choose to collect with a purpose or theme in mind. For instance, they may choose armorial porcelain bearing coats of arms, botanical motifs, wild animals and birds, or ground colors.

CUSTODIAL CARE

Condition

The condition of an item of porcelain is an important consideration. A porcelain object should not be ruled out automatically merely because it has some flaw, such as a chip to a leaf on an elaborate figurine. Some damage or repair is often to be expected in the case of a delicate object that is over 200 years old.

The question of how much the value of an object is affected by a flaw depends on several factors: (1) the type of piece, as a chip out of a plate will affect its value more than damage to a foot or finger in a figure; (2) the rarity or importance of an object; if a piece is very rare or important it will not lose its value simply because it has been broken and repaired; (3) the type of damage involved; there is a world of difference, for instance, between a firing crack that occurred while an object was being made and a crack that happened yesterday, when it was dropped. A broken arm on a figurine is regarded as relatively minor, while a head break is far more serious. If the broken arm has been completely reconstructed out of plaster, however, the value of the piece is seriously affected. There are a variety of possible flaws, such as discoloration, rubbing, crazing, and fritting, whose seriousness can be evaluated only with experience and good advice.

Restoration

The question of how extensive or invisible a repair should be is a controversial issue. On the one hand, some maintain that ceramics are decorative objects and should be restored as completely as possible if any damage is visible to the eye. On the other hand, many insist that, ethically, and for the sake of historical integrity, repairs should be clearly visible, only minimally affecting the work of the original craftsman. If a piece is tampered with too much, it may end up looking fake, especially if some inauthentic addition or reconstruction is undertaken. Very often, the extent of a repair must be an emotional and aesthetic personal decision on the part of the owner.

The quality and cost of repair can vary tremendously. With the techniques available today, it is possible to make totally invisible repairs that cannot be detected, even under ultraviolet light. An object intended for use can be repaired with strong epoxies, reinforcing pegs, and clamps. The cost can vary from under $50 to several thousand dollars. Dealers or museums can generally recommend a reputable and suitable restorer.

Day-to-Day Care

The care and preservation of porcelain is a relatively simple matter. There is no need for special humidity or temperature control devices, as in the case of many other collectibles. Porcelain is a strong and durable material, which needs little attention if it is housed in a safe place. It can be dusted with a camel's hair brush or washed in diluted dishwashing liquid with a soft paintbrush. It is best to let the object drip dry, especially if it has many projections and crevices.

GLOSSARY

arcanist—A craftsman who knew the secret of the formula for making true porcelain.

biscuit or bisque—Porcelain that has been fired once but not glazed.

blanc de chine—European name for fine Chinese porcelain with a milky white glaze, popular in Europe from the seventeenth century on, and much imitated by European factories.

bone china—A translucent ware, neither soft- nor hard-paste porcelain, that contains kaolin, petuntse, and bone ash.

celadon—European name given to Oriental stoneware and porcelain glazed in a color that varies from delicate green to gray-blue.

chinoiserie—A European interpretation and idea of what was characteristic of China and the Chinese taste. During the eighteenth century, chinoiserie was fashionable in all the decorative arts.

crazing—The formation of a web or mesh of fine cracks over the surface of a glaze.

enamels—Pigments made from metallic oxides and mixed with ground glass to produce a wide variety of colors for overglaze decoration on porcelain. Enamels fuse onto the surface of the glass when fired at relatively low temperatures.

famille—Rose, verte, jaune, and noire porcelain; a classification of Chinese enameled porcelain according to the predominant background color.

glaze—A glassy coating, produced in many colors, and applied to porcelain by immersion or spraying.

hard-paste porcelain—Porcelain made from china clay (kaolin) and china stone (petuntse), fired at a high temperature.

imari—Originally the name of a Japanese porcelain made at Arita and exported through the port of Imari; later indicating heavy decoration in polychrome enamels on European porcelain in the style of the Japanese product.

Italian comedy figures—A series of comic figures derived from the Italian theater, which was produced at many Continental and English factories in the eighteenth century. Among the most famous of these figures are Harlequin, Columbine, and Pantaloon.

kakiemon—Style of porcelain decoration; simple, delicate, and asymmetrical, with large spaces left white.

pâte-sur-pâte—Decoration in low relief and painted using liquid clay, called slip; a technique developed in Sèvres circa 1859 and later used in England and Germany.

repairer—A worker in a porcelain factory who assembles pieces made from several molds.

soft paste—Porcelain made by mixing clay and water with a glassy compound called frit. It is fired at a lower temperature than hard paste is.

TRADE ORGANIZATIONS

Collectors may rely on any national trade organization belonging to the Confederation internationale des Negociants en Oeuvres d'Art. This group includes the following:

The British Antique Dealers Association, London, England.

The National Antique and Art Dealers Association of America, Inc. New York, N.Y.

ANTIQUE SHOWS

January: The Winter Antiques Show, New York, N.Y.

June: The Grosvenor House Antiques Show, London, England.

June: The International Ceramics Fair and Seminar, London, England.

LEADING DEALERS

Armin B. Allen, Inc., New York, N.Y.

Bernheimer Fine Arts, Limited, London, England

Bluett & Sons, Ltd., London, England

Ralph M. Chait Galleries, Inc., New York, N.Y.

Eskenazi Ltd., London, England

Kate Foster Limited, London, England

Graham & Oxley (Antiques), Limited, London, England

Brian Haughton Antiques, London, England

Lefebvre et Fils, Paris, France

D.M.&P. Manheim Antiques Corp., New York, N.Y.

Rosenberg & Steibel, New York, N.Y.

Spink & Son Ltd., London, England

Jacob Stodel Antiques, Amsterdam, Holland

The Antique Porcelain Company, London, England

Earle D. Vandekar of Knightsbridge, Ltd., New York, N.Y. & London, England

Ets M. Vandermeersch, Paris, France

SUGGESTED READING

PERIODICALS

Antique Collector. Published by The Antique Collector, London, England. Monthly.

Apollo. Published by Apollo Magazine, London, England. Monthly.

Connaissance des Arts. Published by Societe Francaise de Promotion artistique, Paris, France. Monthly.

The Magazine Antiques. Published by Brant Publications, New York, N.Y. Monthly.

Die Weltkunst. Published by Kunst und Technik Verlagsgesell, Munich, West Germany. Semimonthly.

REFERENCE BOOKS

General

Boger, Louise Ade. *The Dictionary of World Pottery and Porcelain.* New York: Charles Scribner's Sons, 1977.

Charleston, Robert J., ed. *World Ceramics.* New Jersey: Chartwell Books, 1977.

Hillier, Bevis. *Pottery and Porcelain, 1700–1914: England, Europe and North America.* New York: Meredith Press, 1968.

Savage, George. *Porcelain Through the Ages,* 2nd ed. Baltimore: Penguin Books, 1963.

British

Books on British porcelain generally are specific to individual factories. Mr. Geoffrey Godden has written a number of excellent books covering different English factories, and he provides separate bibliographies for the major factories in his general works.

Godden, Geoffrey A. *British Porcelain: An Illustrated Guide.* New York: Clarkson N. Potter, 1975.

Godden, Geoffrey A. *English China.* London: Barrie & Jenkins Ltd., 1985.

Savage, George, *Eighteenth-Century English Porcelain.* London: Spring Books, 1964.

Continental

Ducret, S. *German Porcelain and Faience.* New York: Universe Books, 1962.

Paul-Eisenbeiss, Erika. *German Porcelain of the Eighteenth Century.* Fribourg: Office du Livre, 1972.

Eriksen, Svend and Bellaigue, Geoffrey de. *Sèvres Porcelain.* London: Faber & Faber, 1987.

Savage, George. *Eighteenth-Century German Porcelain.* New York: Macmillan Company, 1958.

Syz, Hans. *Catalogue of the Hans Syz Collection: Meissen Porcelain and Hausmalerei.* Washington D.C.: Smithsonian Institution Press, 1979.

Oriental

Beurdeley, Michel. *Chinese Trade Porcelain,* trans. Diana Imber. Rutland: Charles E. Tuttle, 1963.

Godden, Geoffrey A. *Oriential Export Market Porcelain.* London: Granada, 1979.

Howard, David, and Ayers, John. *China for the West,* 2 vols. London: Sotheby Parke Bernet, 1978.

Jenyns, Soame. *Japanese Porcelain.* New York: Frederick A. Praeger, 1965.

Williamson, George C. *The Book of Famille Rose,* reprint. Tokyo: Charles E. Tuttle Company, Inc., 1985.

Marks

Chaffers, William. *Marks and Monograms on European and Oriental Pottery and Porcelain,* 15th ed. New York: Dover Publications, 1966.

Godden, Geoffrey A. *Encyclopedia of British Pottery and Porcelain Marks.* New York: Crown Publishers, Inc., 1964.

PREFERRED STOCKS

Charles W. Lard
Joseph A. Schrank

BASIC CHARACTERISTICS

Preferred stock, like common stock, legally represents a portion of ownership in a corporation. It is classified on the balance sheet along with the common stock in making up the capital of the company.

Preferred stock has certain advantages over common stock in terms of receiving dividends and obtaining assets at liquidation. A specific dividend must be paid to holders of preferred stock before any dividends can be paid on the common stock. Also, preferred stock almost always takes precedence over common stock in the distribution of assets on dissolution of a corporation.

Usually, the dividend paid on preferred stock is set at a fixed rate, such as a percentage of the par value of a company's stock. In contrast, the dividend rate on common stock may be changed by the board of directors. Holders of preferred stock normally do not have voting power, as do common stock shareholders.

Under certain conditions, convertible preferred stock can be converted into a certain number of common shares. Nonconvertible preferred stock, however, does not offer this opportunity. Since the value of convertible preferred stock is affected by fluctuations in the value of the common stock, nonconvertible preferred is more stable in value. (For further discussion of convertible preferred stock, see article on "Convertible Securities," elsewhere in this volume.)

Value of preferred stock is also determined by the ratio of the dividend to the market

Charles W. Lard is President and Joseph A. Shrank is Vice-President of Alternative Investment Management Company, Hartford, Conn.

price and by the quality rating. Also important are the industry sector, the size of the issue, and the call price. The existence of a sinking fund is also important to the value and to increased liquidity. This is because the issuing company is required to repurchase a predetermined amount of the preferred at a certain price at a fixed maturity date.

A Hybrid Security

Nonconvertible or straight, preferred stock is a hybrid security. It has some of the features of a debt instrument and some of the characteristics of an equity investment. For instance, preferred stock is like a debt instrument in that it has a fixed rate dividend similar to the fixed-interest rate of a bond. But, as with common stock, the holder of preferred stock cannot claim a dividend unless it is earned and declared. The bond holder, on the other hand, has a legal claim to both the interest and the principal on maturity. Preferred stock is like an equity issue in that it has a prior claim on earnings up to the fixed amount of the dividend. However, rarely does it participate in the earnings available to stockholders after the dividend has been paid. The preferred stock shareholder stands between the bondholder and the common stock shareholder in legal status in that preferred stock stands after bonds but before common stock in terms of claims on the assets of a company at liquidation.

Contractual Features

A wide variety of contractual features is offered by the preferred stock of various companies, as stipulated in corporate charters, bylaws, stock certificates, and state statutes. These features include participation in profits, redemption clauses, and cumulative dividends. A current development is the adjustable rate preferred dividends. These issues feature a coupon rate that is tied to a percentage of or a fixed spread over or under the base rate (i.e., Treasury yields). An interesting development is the auction preferred dividend, which is determined by bids from current holders and potential buyers and is payable every seven weeks. In those rare instances where nonconvertible preferred stock is participating, the shareholders receive a stipulated dividend and then share in the earnings or dividends along with the common stock shareholders.

Some types of preferred stock have redemption clauses, which provide that the stock may be called in by the company and redeemed at a certain price. An example of a nonparticipating issue is a seasoned cumulative preferred with a dividend of $6. The issue is noncallable before May 1, 1990, at which time the call price is $100 on shares the company may decide to redeem at that time. On May 1, 1990, a $30 million sinking fund is established for 300,000 shares, which must be redeemed at $100 per share. The current price of $75 is lower than the sinking fund price or the call price, adding to the attractiveness of the investment if called in the near term.

Most preferred stock is cumulative in that any arrears in dividends from prior years must be paid to preferred stock shareholders before any dividends can be paid on the common stock.

Kinds of Issues

Nonconvertible preferred stock is issued by corporations in most kinds of industries. It can be publicly offered or privately placed. Utility companies, including electric, gas, telephone, and water, represent over 80 percent of the issues and 67 percent of the par value of the preferred stock outstanding. Industrial, financial, and insurance companies also offer

TABLE 1. New Preferred Stock Offerings (millions of dollars)

Year	Total Preferred Stock	Year	Total Preferred Stock
1987	7,099	1981	1,220
1986	8,540	1980	1,961
1985	5,626	1979	1,318
1984	3,191	1978	1,395
1983	5,649	1977	1,921
1982	4,859		

Source: Merrill Lynch Capital Markets

preferred stocks, with each industry category offering the investor a wide range of quality and risk from which to choose.

A total of $7.1 billion of nonconvertible preferred stock was offered in 1987, according to a statistical study by Merrill Lynch Capital Markets. The total value of all public and private nonconvertible preferred stock outstanding at the end of 1987 was estimated at $30.1 billion by Merrill Lynch. The average size of a nonconvertible preferred public issue was $30 million. Table 1 shows the market value of new preferred stock issues offered for the years 1977 to 1987.

ATTRACTIVE FEATURES

High Current Yield

The most attractive characteristic of a preferred stock for corporate investors is its high after-tax current yield. In the summer of 1988, the yield on A (third highest rating) utility preferred stocks was in excess of 10 percent. A corporation need report only 30 percent of these dividends as income. Thus, a corporation that pays taxes at a rate of 34 percent would realize an after-tax return of somewhat more than 8.98 percent. This yield is higher than that of tax-exempt bonds that yield 8 percent. The lower an investor's tax bracket, the more attractive the after-tax return.

The high-yield preferred stock is an ideal instrument to own when the inflation rate is low. However, in a highly unstable and inflationary period, the fixed coupon (dividend) and high sensitivity to interest rate changes make this investment a poor hedge against inflation.

The present yield on "A" quality preferred issues compared with tax-free municipal bonds for the last six and a half years is shown in Table 2.

Added Liquidity

The existence of mandatory sinking funds in certain preferred issues reduces the average life. This sinker provides a calculable return higher than the current yield. This return would include some guaranteed capital appreciation provided the preferred stock is selling at a price below the sinking fund repurchase price. Additionally, many preferred issues

TABLE 2. Yields on Preferred Stocks, Municipal Securities, and Corporate Bonds

	New "A" Electrical Utilities Preferred Perpetual Stocks		30-Year A Municipal General Obligation		Corporate "A" Long-Term Electrical Utilities	
	High	Low	High	Low	High	Low
1988 (6 months)	10.05%	9.10%	8.40%	7.50%	10.75%	9.65%
1987	10.75	7.75	8.60	6.75	11.00	8.85
1986	9.90	7.80	8.10	6.80	10.85	9.15
1985	12.90	10.10	9.85	8.50	13.20	10.80
1984	14.25	12.60	11.00	9.75	15.13	12.75
1983	12.95	11.60	10.00	8.85	13.38	11.63
1982	16.00	12.25	13.75	9.70	17.40	13.75

Source: Merrill Lynch Capital Markets, Fixed Income Research.

have call prices above the current market price that may be used by the issuing company. The sinking fund and call price provisions offer added liquidity relative to common stocks, which do not have these two provisions.

Protection of Income and Principal

The preferred stock features with regard to dividend and distribution of assets on liquidation are attractive in relation to common stocks. An investor would purchase preferred rather than common stock for the protection of capital, although no upside appreciation would be received if the common stock moves higher.

The higher after-tax yield for many corporate holders makes preferred stocks more attractive than bonds, although the preferred holder has inferior protection against liquidation of the issuer.

POTENTIAL RISKS

Possible Risk to Income

While the holder of preferred stock has preference over the common stock shareholder in the payment of a declared dividend, the company does have the discretionary right to spend the cash available for preferred dividends on other items (excluding common stock dividends) if the board of directors feels it is prudent to do so. If a company forgoes a preferred dividend, it is a sign of financial weakness, and the company is viewed negatively by the financial markets.

Risk to Principal

Risk to the principal is a function of the liquidation rights of the holder, although the preferred stock shareholder has liquidation preferences on the claim of assets over the common stock shareholder. The rights are generally stipulated in the case of involuntary or voluntary liquidation. In addition, some preferred stocks have sinking funds to further protect the safety of the principal.

Market Volatility

The market volatility of preferred stock is a function of interest rate changes. This means that the preferred stock acts as a yield instrument. Since the preferred stock does not have a stated maturity, the market value fluctuates inversely with the percentage change in the yield. Nonconvertible preferred stock has characteristics comparable to a perpetual bond, except when it has a sinking fund or purchase fund. Thus, if required yield increases from 8 to 10 percent (a 25 percent increase), the price of the preferred stock would fall by 20 percent.

Different industry sectors have yield-spread relationships that change as investors perceive greater risk. For example, utility preferred stocks today have higher yields than industrial preferred stocks.

Possible Illiquidity

Liquidity is mainly a function of the size and the quality of the issue. Larger issues have more market makers, and this increases the liquidity. However, large purchases of preferred stocks by insurance companies, for example, can later produce an imbalance in the market as these companies respond to policyholder redemptions and policy loans during credit crunches with block sales. An individual holder of a small issue may be forced to rely on a thin market.

TAX CONSEQUENCES

An important difference between preferred stocks and bonds is the 70 percent tax exclusion of dividends received on stocks by corporate owners. Since preferred stocks do not carry an income tax savings to the paying company, the receiving corporations generally can exclude 70 percent of dividend income from their federal taxes. (This exclusion also applies to dividend income from common stocks.) However, individuals do not receive this exclusion. Most states tax dividend income, which would reduce the net yield.

At present, comparable nonconvertible preferred stocks yield less than bond counterparts. This abnormality of getting less return for greater risk reflects the 70 percent dividend exclusion. Today, there is a shortage of preferred stocks for income-oriented corporate portfolios because of the demand created by the tax treatment of the dividend. Meanwhile, the preferred stock is vulnerable to any changes in tax legislation that might reduce this exclusion provision.

Of course, nonprofit institutions such as universities and qualified pension funds do not pay taxes and, consequently, do not benefit from the tax shelter now available to corporations. Table 3 shows how the corporate rate affects the net return on preferred stocks.

REPRESENTATIVE TYPES OF INVESTORS

The biggest holders of preferred stocks are institutions that can qualify under the 70 percent dividend income exclusion. This category includes corporations and insurance companies. Ideally, institutions that have a low income tax rate and a need for high income invest in preferred stocks, whereas investors in high brackets might use tax-exempt municipal bonds.

TABLE 3. Investor After-Tax Yield

Investor	Preferred Gross Yield	Dividend Exclusion	Tax Rate	Net Yield
Individual	10%	0%	28%	7.20%
Corporation	10	70	34	8.98
Insurance Company	10	70	25	9.25
Pension fund	10	0	0	10.00

Note: Tax rate is established for hypothetical investor. Dividend exclusion is established for corporations by the IRS. Effective tax rate for mutual insurance companies differ from that for the general insurance industry.

Life and property-casualty insurance companies are big purchasers of preferred stock because of the high after-tax return and favorable accounting treatment allowed by the National Association of Insurance Commissioners (NAIC). The NAIC has ruled that all preferred stocks that have a sinking fund of 2.5 percent per year or that amortize the issue over forty years, starting within ten years of the date of issue, can be carried at cost. The accounting entry at cost allows the insurance company to avoid write-downs in the market value if the interest rates increase, which would cause the yield on new offerings of preferred stock to increase and the market value of existing preferred stock to drop. In addition, life insurance companies can carry nonsinking fund preferred stocks at cost.

Pension funds and universities could use preferred stocks, but they can obtain higher yields with bonds and, at the same time, get higher safety in terms of claims on the issuing company's assets.

IMPORTANT FACTORS IN BUYING AND SELLING

Selecting a Broker

In selecting a broker, it is important to consider several factors. The integrity of the organization and its employees is of utmost importance. The more quantifiable factors that should be considered include the number of issues in which the organization is willing to make a market, the amount of capital it is willing to commit, and the number of professional analysts and preferred traders it employs.

Markets

Preferred stocks are traded in two markets. It is estimated that more than 40 percent of preferred stock outstanding can be traded on the major exchanges. The over-the-counter market handles the remaining trading.

Dealer Spread

Historically, the dealer spread is wider in preferred stocks than in common stocks, since it is not a continuous market. In some over-the-counter issues, there may be only one market (broker or dealer). The institutional trades are negotiated on an individual basis. The spread ultimately is determined by the individual issue's characteristics, not by the location of the listing.

Quality

The investor can use any of the standard reference books to judge quality of issues. Moody's and Standard & Poor's have proprietary grading systems. Both systems rate the highest quality AAA and the lowest CC. Several major brokerage firms, including Salomon Brothers and Merrill Lynch, Pierce, Fenner & Smith, publish tabulations that may also be useful.

CUSTODIAL CARE

The physical safety precautions for preferred stocks are the same as for any equity security. Almost all nonconvertible preferred stocks are registered; thus, dividends are mailed automatically to the holder of record.

LEADING DEALERS

Like common stocks, preferred stocks may be purchased from brokerage firms and dealers throughout the country, as listed in classified directories.

GLOSSARY

adjustable rate preferred dividends—Dividends adjusted at a fixed spread or percentage to a base rate, i.e., treasury yield curve.

auction preferred dividends—Dividends based on current credit standing, perceptions of the issuer, and conditions in the marketplace.

convertible preferred stock—Preferred stock that may be converted into a stipulated number of common shares.

cumulative preferred stock—Feature of preferred stock whereby the dividends not paid in any year will accumulate and must be paid berfore dividends can be paid on the common stock of the corporation.

liquidation rights—In a preferred contract, provision for preference above common stock in claims on assets in case of involuntary or voluntary dissolution of the issuing corporation.

participating dividends—Dividends paid in excess of the stipulated amount of the preferred stock.

redemption provision—Provision according to which the issuer can call and retire all or a portion of the issue, generally at a premium.

sinking fund—A fund established through periodic payments for meeting specific obligation, such as redemption of stock shares.

straight preferred stock—Term used to describe nonconvertible preferred stock.

voting rights—Right to vote stock, which may range from full voting to contingent voting, based on specific conditions. For example, holders of preferred stock may have the right to vote as long as accumulated dividends remain unpaid.

SUGGESTED READING

PERIODICALS

Commerce Clearing House. New York, N.Y. Daily; card system; notification of changes in capital structure of corporations.

Moody's Bond Record. New York, N.Y. Daily; details on features of preferred issues.

Moody's Bond Survey. New York, N.Y. Weekly; highlights on credit analysis.

Moody's Dividend Record. New York, N.Y. Daily; reporting preferred dividend record, payment date, ex-dividend date, and amount of dividend.

Standard & Poor's Daily Dividend Record. New York, N.Y. Reporting preferred dividend record date, payment date, ex-dividend date, and amount of dividend.

Standard & Poor's Fixed Income Investor. New York, N.Y. Weekly: highlights of credit analysis.

Standard & Poor's Monthly Stock Guide/Bond Guide. New York, N.Y. Key financial characteristics of preferred issues.

ARTICLES

Fischer, D.E., and Wilt, G.A., Jr. "Non-convertible Preferred Stock as a Financing Instrument — 1950–1965." *Journal of Finance* 23:611–624, Sept. 1968.

Gardner, D.R. "Sinking Fund Preferred Stocks: An Attractive Alternative." *Best's Review* (Property Edition) 80:22, Oct. 1979.

REFERENCE BOOKS

Wilson, Richard S. *Corporate Senior Securities*. Chicago: Probus Publishing Co., 1987.

REAL ESTATE

COMMERCIAL AND INDUSTRIAL

Ted R. Whitmer

BASIC CHARACTERISTICS

The broad categories of commercial and industrial real estate include office buildings, shopping centers, warehouses, factories, service centers, and other commercial and industrial properties.

Office buildings can be freestanding, single-tenant buildings; smaller multi-tenant mid-rise structures; and high-rise central business district buildings. Additionally, office buildings are often classed by construction type, from class A through D, with the premium buildings being classified as class A.

Retail properties include speciality, freestanding retail, strip centers (generally with relatively few tenants); neighborhood centers (up to approximately 100,000 square feet); community centers (up to approximately 250,000 square feet), with one to two major anchor tenants; and regional malls (up to 2 million square feet), with up to six or more major anchor tenants.

Industrial buildings include warehouses, service center buildings, high tech buildings, office-showroom facilities, and manufacturing facilities. In addition, industrial buildings are classified by construction type and as being with or without dock-height loading and as being rail or non-rail served.

Ted R. Whitmer, MAI, owns and operates his own commercial appraisal firm. The Ted Whitmer Company. He holds an MBA in finance and is a Member of the Bar in Texas.

Principal Characteristics of Value

When commercial or industrial real estate is purchased for its income potential, most investors base their purchase decisions on the future income benefits that would be generated from the properties. Generally, the income analyzed is net operating income, which is the income that flows from the investment after accounting for vacancy and collection losses and expenses of operation, that is, the amount of money available after all expenses are deducted from collected rentals and ancillary income. However, net operating income is income before depreciation or interest deductions from a mortgage are accounted for. Income taxes and expenses associated with corporations or other ownership entities are not considered operating expenses. Net operating income is analogous to a bond coupon or cash dividend on a stock.

Real estate appraisal considers generally the income, cost, and sales comparison approaches to value. The income approach values investment real estate by capitalizing future income benefits that flow from the ownership of real estate into present value. The cost approach is a measure of property value derived by adding the contributory value of improvements to the value of the site, as though vacant. The contributory value of the improvements is generally the replacement cost minus accrued depreciation (loss in value from any source). The sales comparison approach requires comparing the property to comparable properties that have sold, and adjusting the sales price for differences.

Although brokers, appraisers, and financial institutions generally consider all three approaches to value, an individual investor is typically more concerned with achieving a particular rate of return on an investment. Therefore, the income approach is most useful as a valuation tool to the investor.

TABLE 1. Traditional Income Approach: Direct Capitalization

Gross Potential Rental Income							
Units		Rental/Month		Months		Annual Rental Income
5	×	$ 600	×	12	=	$ 36,000
6	×	$ 875	×	12	=	63,000
10	×	$1,000	×	12	=	120,000
Total gross potential rental income						$219,000
Plus: Other income (vending, etc.)						20,000
Potential gross income (PGI)						$239,000
Less: Vacancy & collection loss (8%)						(19,120)
Effective gross income (EGI)						$219,880
Less: Operating expenses (40% of EGI)						(87,952)
Net operating income (NOI)						$131,928

Note: This example is an apartment property. Net operating income ÷ capitalization rate = value, that is, $131,928 ÷ 10% = $1,319,280.

Traditional Income Approach. The traditional income approach, or direct capitalization, indicates value by capitalizing a single year's net operating income by a capitalization rate. The net operating income used is either the next year's projected net operating income, from the date of valuation, or is an average or stabilized net operating income. The capitalization rate used is the market- or investor-required return on the net operating income. Table 1 illustrates valuation by way of the traditional income approach method.

In Table 1, an investor pays $1,319,280 for the apartment property and receives a 10 percent rate of return on the net operating income. Although easily understood, the traditional income approach has some limitations. For example, it is often difficult to estimate net operating income, even for the next year or a stabilized year. In addition, a reasonable capitalization rate is difficult to determine. A capitalization rate is usually derived by dividing the net operating income of a sale by the comparable's sale price. However, there are numerous ways to derive capitalization rates. An appropriate capitalization rate will reflect the available financing on the property, the risk of the investment, changes over time of net operating income and value, and other specific property characteristics.

Discounted Cash Flow Analysis. The increased use of computers has resulted in more sophisticated measurements of value for investment real estate properties. Because of the computer, discounted cash flow (DCF) techniques have become increasingly important. The discounted cash flow method allows for more flexibility in income patterns as well as property value changes. Table 2 reflects a DCF model used for an office building property.

A DCF, if generated on a computer, is useful for analyzing complex income relationships. In Table 2, vacancy, rentals, expenses, and value all varied over the five-year holding period. Although the investor will receive a total of $1,545,795 over the five-year holding period, the investor would pay only $914,650 for the investment. The investment would return the total capital outlay of $914,650 plus a 13 percent return on the capital invested. It should be noted that the DCF analysis in Table 2 does not consider after-tax income, but was a before-tax cash flow analysis. The primary strength of the DCF analysis is that the emphasis is on the overall yield to the investor. The yield on the real estate investment may be compared to overall yields on bonds, stocks, and other investments.

Cost Approach. The formula for the cost approach is to estimate a reproduction or replacement cost (new) of improvements, subtract accrued depreciation (which is loss in value from all causes), and add the site value. In other words, the contributory value of the improvements is added to the value of the site, as if vacant and in its highest and best use.

The cost approach is relevant as an indication of value because a prudent investor would not pay more for an existing building than the cost to construct a brand new building. This approach assumes that the cost to lease-up a new building to market occupancy would also be considered.

The limitation to the cost approach is that it is often difficult to estimate accrued depreciation. However, it is useful as a starting point for analyzing value before estimates of accrued depreciation are made. The cost to construct a new building and lease it to market occupancy should set an upper limit of value for a particular investment property.

TABLE 2. Discounted Cash Flow Yield Capitalization

Assumptions
Discount rate: 13%

Holding period: 5 years

Growth in rental rate & expenses: 5% per year

Value in 5 years: $1,000,000 (after expenses of sale)

	Year 1	Year 2	Year 3	Year 4	Year 5
PGI	$200,000	$210,000	$220,500	$231,525	$243,101
−Vacancy	(20%)	(15%)	(10%)	(5%)	(5%)
EGI	$160,000	$178,500	$198,450	$219,949	$230,946
Expenses	(80,000)	(84,000)	(88,200)	(92,610)	(97,240)
NOI	$ 80,000	$ 94,500	$110,250	$127,339	$133,706
×PV Factor*	× .8850	× .7831	× .6931	× .6133	× .5428
PV of NOI	$ 70,800	$ 74,003	$ 76,414	$ 78,097	$ 72,576

Note: This example is an office building. PV of income + PV of reversion = value; that is, $371,890† + $542,760‡ = $914,650.

* Present value (PV) factor @ 13%.
† The sum of the present value of NOIs.
‡ $1 million future value discounted to present value at 13 percent, five years.

Sales Comparison Approach. The sales comparison approach formula is to adjust a comparable sale, plus or minus the value of different features compared with the subject property. This is the most direct approach for achieving value and, when adequate sales are available, the most accurate indication of market value. However, the sales comparison approach does not necessarily explain the motivations or desires of particular investors in commercial or industrial properties. Additionally, few properties have identical lease structures.

A potential investor in commercial or industrial property should consult brokers or appraisers for sales of similar properties within the specific market location. Furthermore, sales are useful to abstract market-derived rates of return for particular property types.

Market Characteristics

All real estate markets, including industrial and commercial ones, are characterized by a lack of central trading, non-uniform pricing, and often a lack of information concerning the various property types. Because of the nature of the commercial and industrial real estate markets, there is added risk in purchasing real estate versus other investment vehicles that offer more accessible information. However, there is also a potential for below-market purchases of real estate, which make real estate a particularly attractive mode of investment for those willing to spend the effort to capture this market inefficiency.

TABLE 3. Effect of Positive Leverage

Assumptions	All Cash	Leveraged Investment
Purchase	$1,000,000	$1,000,000
Loan	0	$800,000
Terms	N.A.	10% interest only
Debt service	N.A.	$80,000 per year
Resale price*	$1,150,000	$1,150,000
Return to equity	15%†	54%‡

* Resale after a one-year holding period.
† $150,000 (profit) ÷ $1,000,000 (initial investment).
‡ $150,000 (profit) ÷ $280,000 (initial equity investment + interest).
N.A. = Not applicable.

ATTRACTIVE FEATURES

Leverage

Financial Leverage. Leverage occurs when a portion of the sales price of an investment is financed. The positive effect of leveraging real estate is to enhance return to the equity investor. This benefit is not available from other forms of investments that must be purchased with all cash or little financing. In particular, some investments are restricted by legal margin requirements (such as stocks), and it is difficult for an investor to finance most tangible personal property. The effect of positive leverage is illustrated in Table 3.

Table 3 is simplified to illustrate the effect of positive leverage. Given the ability to obtain 80 percent financing, the investor could control $5 million worth of real estate and would have returned 54 percent, given no transaction costs and assuming a mortgage interest rate of 10 percent. The table illustrates financial leverage that enhances return. Leverage is positive, before tax considerations, as long as the value of the property increases at a higher rate than the mortgage interest rate.

Operating Leverage. Operating leverage can occur when an investor lowers expenses, increases rental rates, or decreases vacancies by either pooling resources between properties, or by bringing better than average management expertise into one or more commercial or industrial properties. For example, assume two industrial warehouses that generate $100,000 in net operating income. Given a market rate of return of 10 percent; the properties would sell for $1 million each. If an investor could purchase both and, because of managing two properties instead of one, create economies that result in the two properties producing $10,000 more in net operating income each, then the value of each property would increase $100,000 ($10,000 net income divided by 10 percent). Operating leverage may also be affected by increasing rental rates, decreasing vacancies, or pooling marketing efforts that may be feasible for two properties but not for one. In the latter case, operating expenses may actually be higher for each property, but the increase in the rental or occupancy structures more than offset the expense increase.

Cash Flow. Cash flow from real estate is usually identified as being net operating income (NOI), before-tax cash flow (BTCF), or after-tax cash flow (ATCF). Given no mortgage, the NOI is equal to BTCF. BTCF is income after expenses and debt service are paid from Effective Gross Income (EGI). ATCF is income after expenses, debt service, and income taxes are paid from EGI.

Because of the tax benefits associated with real estate, it is possible to show a positive BTCF but a tax loss. This situation is advantageous because the investor can generate cash flow and use the tax loss to offset other income (but see *Tax Consequences*, later in this article, for limitations).

ATCF is computed by subtracting taxes from BTCF. Taxes are derived by deducting depreciation and interest from NOI, and then multiplying the taxable income by the applicable tax rate. Table 4 depicts the unique cash flow characteristics that apply to real estate.

In Table 4, the investor has a positive cash flow of $18,778 after paying debt service, does not pay taxes on the cash flow, and enjoys a tax savings of $1,504. Therefore, BTCF return to equity (equity capitalization or cash-on-cash rate) was $18,778 divided by $220,000 or 8.5 percent. The ATCF return to equity was $20,282 divided by $220,000, or 9.2 percent. Depreciation write-offs and interest deductibility are benefits to commercial and industrial investment properties that accrue through tax savings. A taxable bond would have to yield 12.8 percent to achieve a 9.2 percent after-tax yield, assuming the interest is taxed at 28 percent. This illustrates that a bond yield rate and a yield rate that applies to real estate are not the same. Comparing the two would require adjustments for the tax benefits.

TABLE 4. Before and After Tax Cash Flows

Gross income			$200,000
Vacancy and collection loss			(20,000)
Effective gross income (EGI)			$180,000
Operating expenses			(60,000)
NOI			$120,000
Debt service*			(101,222)
Before-tax cash flow (BTCF)			$ 18,778
Plus: Tax savings, calculated as follows:			
NOI		$120,000	
Less:	Interest†	(96,800)	
	Depreciation	(28,571)	
	Taxable income	(5,371)	
	× Tax rate (28%)	×0.28‡	
Tax Savings			$ 1,504
After-tax cash flow (ATCF)			$ 20,282

* Assume a value of $1 million with an 80 percent loan at 11 percent, and annual debtd service payments.

† Note that only the interest portion is deductible for tax purposes. Additionally, see *Tax Consequences*, later in this article, for discussion of limitations on the deductibility of investment interest.

‡ The maximum tax rate is assumed to be 28 percent.

Tax Advantages

The major tax advantage that commercial and industrial real estate have is the annual deduction allowed for depreciation. Depreciation is allowed even if the property value actually increases over the taxable year. (See *Tax Consequences*, later in this article.)

Appreciation

The value of a property may increase because of either inflation (general price increases) or supply and demand factors (relative price increases). Investor perceptions of a rising rental market, in excess of rising expenses, will generally result in expectations of property appreciation, assuming that the rate of return required in the future does not increase enough to offset higher future net income. For example, a retail center may be purchased for $500,000 based on NOI of $50,000 and a capitalization rate of 10 percent. An increase in NOI to $60,000 results in a future value of $600,000, if capitalized at 10 percent. Even if the capitalization rate is higher in the future, say 10.5 percent, the value would nevertheless increase to $571,429 ($60,000 ÷ 10.5 percent).

Commercial/industrial properties purchased in areas of depressed rental and occupancy rates are purchased largely for their appreciation potential, because the cash flow alone would generally not show an adequate return, apart from appreciation. Additionally, industrial and commercial real estate subject to long-term leases with fixed and low rents is often purchased for the appreciation potential that can be realized once the lease term expires.

Preservation of Capital

An investor requires a return *of* capital and a return *on* the investment. The return of capital is also called capital recapture. Real estate, being a tangible as opposed to an intangible asset, is suitable for preservation of capital. Even if the value of the property declines, generally there would be at least some recapture upon the future sale of the real estate. Given a current return through cash flow, along with long-term and relatively secure tenants, the capital invested may be secure even if the property declines in value over time. For example, assume a property is purchased subject to long-term leases that return 8 percent per year in net operating income for ten years. The property could decline 80 percent over time, and the capital would all be returned. The investor would have made a 0 percent return on the capital, but the example shows that an investor with a strong motivation for preservation of capital can minimize risk of loss. Additionally, the preservation of capital may be analyzed by worst, most probable, and best case scenarios considering cash flow and future potential price. In the above example, with fixed and long-term leases, the primary consideration in a sensitivity analysis would be future resale price. Potential variations in cash flows because of indexed or short-term leases complicates the analysis.

One simple method that focuses on return of capital is to rank investments based on payback period. The payback period method ignores the time value of money but is calculated by adding the cash flows, cumulatively, until the investment is returned fully. The payback period is the year in which the entire capital is returned. Since this method ignores the time value of money, its usefulness is limited for ranking properties (see Table 5).

Investment 1 returns all of the capital in year 5; investment 2, in year 8. Therefore, the payback period method would rank investment 1 over investment 2. The Internal Rate of Return (IRR) for investment 1 is 11.7 percent; for investment 2, it is 16.3 percent. Using

TABLE 5. Investment Performance: Payback Period Method

	Investment 1		Investment 2	
Time	Cash Flow	Cumulative	Cash Flow	Cumulative
1	$10,000	$ 10,000	$ 10,000	$ 10,000
2	20,000	30,000	10,000	20,000
3	25,000	55,000	10,000	30,000
4	20,000	75,000	10,000	40,000
5	25,000	100,000	10,000	50,000
6	15,000	115,000	10,000	60,000
7	30,000	145,000	10,000	70,000
8	20,000	165,000	200,000	270,000

Note: Initial Investment = $100,000.

IRR as the criteria, investment 2 is a better investment. Ranking by IRR is generally more useful because the time value of money is accounted for. Additionally, if the IRR is positive, then all capital will be returned to the investor.

Inflation Hedge

Inflation is a general rise in the price levels in an economy. During inflationary periods, real estate and other hard assets tend to rise in value directly with a rise in overall value. In comparison, existing bond and other security prices may decline because of rising interest rates. For example, if a $1 million loan were originated at 10 percent for thirty years and interest rates rise to 12 percent because of inflation, the loan would be sold at a discount in the secondary market. The same loan would be sold for approximately $855,000 to yield 12 percent. Security values would decline in inflationary periods.

Real estate rental rates usually increase directly with inflation. Therefore income and prices would be expected to increase over time. However, the required rates of return would probably also increase. Therefore, commercial and industrial real estate is an inflation hedge only if the rise in income and future sales price offset any rise in the required rate of return for real estate. As may be seen from the late 1970s and early 1980s, most investors view real estate as a hedge against inflation, indicating that the market perceives that the change in income and price more than offset a higher required rate of return. This perception is consistent with the greater investment activity in tangible assets, as compared to securities, that occurs in inflationary times.

POTENTIAL RISKS

Management Burden

A major expense category for commercial/industrial properties is a provision for investment management. Management expense is an operating expense to compensate for physically maintaining and marketing a property. Management expense associated with operating a property should not be confused with managing the investment. The property management expense is a deduction that reduces NOI and is included as a variable expense in an operating statement. On the other hand, the management provision for the investment is usually accounted for by raising the desired rate of return for the additional burden of handling a real estate investment over and above an alternative investment. A yield rate used to discount cash flows to value is made up of a risk-free (or safe rate), a risk premium, a provision for illiquidity, and a provision for investment management. The provision for investment management is usually higher for real estate than for alternative investments such as stocks, bonds, and other securities. Investors often put a great amount of time into selecting management companies, buying the real estate, assisting in major decisions concerning the property, and, eventually, selling the property. Therefore, managing the real estate investment is often burdensome.

Negative Leverage

The effect of leverage was previously discussed as a potential enhancement to equity yield because of the potential positive effect of borrowing on an investment. However, if a property increases in value but at a lower rate than the interest rate on the debt, negative leverage occurs. In fact, if a property that was purchased for cash declines in value 20 percent, then the equity loss is 20 percent. If the property was purchased with 80 percent financing, or 20 percent down, then 100 percent or the entire equity investment is lost. If the value declines further and the debt is recourse (the investor is personally liable on the debt), the investor may have to contribute additional money. Consider Table 6, which illustrates negative leverage.

In Table 6, the three examples assume before-tax returns, interest-only loans, and no NOI. Investment 1 had no debt; therefore equity declined 20 percent. Investment 2 declined 20 percent and $40,000 was paid in debt ($500,000 × 80 percent × 10 percent; the decline to equity was 140 percent, which represents a loss of original investment plus an out of pocket payment for interest. Investment 3 illustrates negative leverage even with a value increase, because the value increase was below the interest rate on the loan. If the property in the example increased 10 percent, then the change in equity would be 10 percent. The value would have increased $50,000, and $40,000 would be paid toward debt service, leaving a net increase to equity of $10,000 or 10 percent ($10,000 loss divided by $100,000). In summary, negative leverage can enhance loss to the same degree that positive leverage can enhance gain, because of mortgaging property.

TABLE 6. The Effect of Negative Leverage

	Investment 1	Investment 2	Investment 3
Purchase	$500,000	$500,000	$500,000
Mortgage debt	0%	$400,000	$400,000
Interest rate on debt	N.A.	10%	10%
Property value change	−20%	−20%	+5%
Interest (10%)	0	$40,000	$40,000
Resulting equity change	−20%	−140%	−15%

Depreciation and Obsolescence

Real estate, unlike most other investments, has a natural decline owing to wear and tear, and often because of obsolescence. Obsolescence is a decline in value, other than from wear and tear; that is, it results from external sources (factors outside the boundaries of the property) or from functional sources, such as over-improvement or under-improvement and poor layout or design. In other words, buildings are wasting assets.

In the purchase of commercial or industrial real estate, the potential increase in value owing to inflation or relative price increases (supply and demand factors) is often offset by the decrease in value because of wear and tear or outside forces that affect value over time. The wear and tear of a structure may be estimated and forecasted over the life of the investment. However, there is considerable risk when purchasing commercial property because land is immobile and because there is little or no control over potentially detrimental forces that are outside of the property boundaries. Therefore, there is considerable risk involved in owning real estate because of its inherent characteristics.

Another potential loss in value that is particularly applicable to commercial and industrial real estate is from functional obsolescence. Commercial and industrial properties are generally built to satisfy the need of a particular tenant. The value of the building on the open market may not be the same as the value to the particular tenant. Therefore, an investor in commercial or industrial real estate would need to consider adaptability of the property to the market requirements, once the current tenant's lease expires. Often a substantial expenditure is required at the end of a lease to enable the investor to lease the building to another potential tenant. In general, the more specialized the property, the greater the expenditure rèquired to market the property once the lease expires.

In summary, because real estate is a wasting asset and because it is immobile, there is a potential offset to inflation from depreciation and obsolescence. If the useful life of a building is forty years and depreciation is expected to occur on a straight-line basis, the buildings will depreciate 2.5 percent per year (one year divided by the forty-year estimated life). Assuming a land-to-building ratio of 20 percent, the property would have to increase in value 2 percent per year (2.5 percent × 80 percent) from other causes (e.g., inflation) to offset normal wear and tear.

Environmental Contaminants

Numerous environmental laws and agency requirements have been instituted during the 1980s that affect the values of both commercial and industrial real estate. For example, hazardous waste sites are often associated with industrially developed areas. A purchaser of industrial property should check with the Environmental Protection Agency (EPA) to verify the existence of any known potential hazardous waste. Often the cost to clean up the waste is greater than the value of the property. In addition, there may be hazardous waste that has not yet been discovered. Therefore, because of the costs that may be associated with clean- up, studies should be conducted of soil and subsoil conditions prior to the purchase of a site.

Many commercial and industrial properties are negatively affected by asbestos materials that were used as insulation and in other components of structures. Asbestos has been found to cause cancer; recent agency, federal and state enactments have required that the asbestos used in buildings be measured and the problem rectified. As with hazardous waste, the steps necessary to achieve acceptable levels of asbestos may be cost-prohibitive. An asbestos study should be made prior to purchasing improved properties.

Other considerations include the removal of underground fuel storage tanks, compliance with clean air laws, and dealing with radon gas level. Additionally, if the property is near a waterway, both state and federal laws should be researched to determine applicable standards for construction or operation of properties near the waterways. Site assessment studies are costly but necessary to prevent potential liabilities. The current owner of a property is responsible for complying with all the standards, even if a purchaser is not the original cause of the presence of hazardous substances.

Illiquidity

Real estate is usually a relatively illiquid asset. Illiquidity, in this context, refers to the extended time and effort needed to sell property compared to other easily transferrable properties, such as listed stocks and bonds. The salability of real estate is affected by the availability of mortgage loans, the supply of existing properties for sale, and the demand for the particular use of the property. The length of time needed is also affected by the specialized or general adaptability of the property, the value of the property, and the current tax laws at the time the property is to be sold.

Transaction Costs

The expenses associated with selling real estate are higher than with most other investments. Typical expenses incurred to close a transaction may include broker's sales commissions (4 to 8 percent), title insurance policy, survey, legal fees, advertising, appraisal fee, environmental and other studies, and often unanticipated renovations and repairs needed to bring the property to a salable condition. The costs could, and often do, exceed 10 percent of the sales price.

The seller generally incurs most of the cost to sell a property. However, some costs may be passed on to the buyer. A property may substantially increase in value. However, the seller would realize no gain for profit if the transaction costs offset the gain in value.

Personal Liability on Borrowed Capital

When a property is purchased with borrowed funds, the debt is typically evidenced by a note that contains the written agreement between the borrower and lender. The lender will obtain a lien against the real estate, evidenced by a mortgage or deed of trust document, depending on the state. The note is a promise to pay by the borrower. If the borrower defaults and the lender forecloses and sells the property, the distinction between recourse and nonrecourse debt becomes important. If the debt is recourse, the lender can legally proceed against other assets of the borrower to satisfy the deficiency (the debt that the sale of the property would not cover). If the debt is nonrecourse, the lender can look only to the collateral for satisfaction of the debt. Therefore, the classification of debt is important when assessing risk of an investment in commercial or industrial real estate.

If a property is sold with existing financing, the purchaser can either assume the note or take the property subject to the existing note, assuming there is no due-on-sale clause in the note. With a due-on-sale clause, the note is assumable. If the note is assumed, absent another agreement, the purchaser is liable for the entire debt. If the property is sold subject to the existing financing, then the purchaser is generally not liable to the lender.

TAX CONSEQUENCES

The current tax laws that affect real estate are reflected in the Tax Reform Act of 1986. Prior to the current tax law, real estate was given more favorable tax treatment than is currently available. However, the current tax code still provides for favorable income tax treatment for investors in real estate as compared to other investments. The following is a brief discussion of some of the relevant tax provisions as applied to commercial and industrial real estate investments. It should be noted that some of the provisions discussed below are gradually being phased in. Additionally, all of the tax provisions are subject to change. Therefore, a tax attorney or accountant should be consulted concerning income tax considerations prior to the purchase of commercial or industrial real estate for investment.

Interest Deduction

Interest is not considered an operating expense in deriving net operating income. However, interest paid on a mortgage may be deductible as an expense for tax purposes. If the property is subject to a net lease whereby the tenant pays operating expenses, the amount of interest allowed as a deduction may not exceed the net investment income of the taxpayer plus $10,000 for the taxable year. Net investment income is the excess of investment income (gross income plus any net gain for disposition of investment property) over investment expenses (which is all deductions other than interest). For example, assuming the following cash flows and no other investment income, the allowable interest deduction would be as follows:

NOI	$110,000
Less: depreciation	(28,571)
NOI after depreciation	$ 81,429
Interest paid	96,800
Maximum deduction allowable	$ 91,429
Interest to carry over	5,371

Interest of $5,371 would not be deductible in the current year, but would carry over to the following year. The above example would not apply if the investor were responsible for most or all of the operating expenses.

Depreciation Deduction

One of the major benefits of investing in real estate is the ability to depreciate the asset, even though the value of the property is rising. The applicable provision for depreciation, as related to industrial and commercial real estate, is the accelerated cost recovery system, which is contained in the Internal Revenue Code. Depreciation is deducted after NOI, and is not considered an expense when deriving NOI. Therefore, when analyzing NOI as a cash flow, an investor should remember that there is an additional benefit past the NOI line. Specifically, commercial and industrial real estate may be depreciated on a straight-line basis over thirty-one and one-half years. Therefore, the depreciation per year is 3.17 percent per year of the improvement value.

Depreciation is claimed for tax purposes as a paper loss. The value of the asset may be increasing, yet the current tax laws allow a depreciation deduction in each accounting year. Assuming a building-to-value ratio of 80 percent, the additional benefit to real estate would be approximately 2.5 percent per year (3.17 percent × 80 percent).

Other depreciation provisions that are applicable to nonresidential real property are that the property is assumed to be placed in service during mid-month of the month in which it is purchased. Also, an investor can choose to depreciate over forty years for nonresidential real property, instead of thirty-one and one-half years.

Capital Gains Treatment

A long-term capital gain is a gain from the sale or exchange of a capital asset held for more than six months. Under the existing tax code, there is no tax rate differential or exclusions applicable to capital gains; currently capital gains income is taxed at the same rate as ordinary income. However, the distinction between short-term and long-term capital gains is preserved in the current tax code.

Passive Investments

A passive activity is one that generates rental income or one in which the taxpayer does not materially participate. Material participation relates to the extent of involvement in the business. Rental property automatically is considered passive. Passive losses may be used only to offset passive gains from other properties. Passive losses can always be used to offset passive income.

If the taxpayer is an individual and actively participates in the rental real estate activity, then up to $25,000 in passive loss may offset other income in the current year if a person's adjusted gross income is less than $100,000. Furthermore, the amount that may be used to offset other income, called either active or portfolio income, is reduced $0.50 on the dollar until the adjusted gross income is $150,000, where the deduction is not available at all. It should be noted that actively participating is not the same as materially participating. Material participation is a greater degree of involvement than active participation.

Passive losses accumulate and carry forward indefinitely to offset future income or gains from passive sources.

At-Risk Rule

The at-risk rule limits the amount of losses to the amount of money at risk in a venture. Therefore, if a note is nonrecourse, then the at-risk rule would limit losses to the amount of actual equity in a property. An important exception is allowed for third-party (not property sellers) nonrecourse loans.

Exchanges

If a property is exchanged for property of like kind, and is held either for productive use in a trade or business or for investment, then no gain or loss will be recognized on the exchange of such property. The definition of like kind has been narrowed in the current tax laws, as compared to previous tax codes. The basis of the property traded for carries over from that of the property surrendered. However, the basis is decreased by any money received by the taxpayer, and that money is taxable, despite the exchange.

REPRESENTATIVE TYPES OF INVESTORS

Investors in commercial and industrial real estate provide either equity or mortgage funds for the purchase of properties. From the post–World War II period to the early 1970s, the real estate capital market was characterized by expansion; mortgage capital was provided by large institutions and, primarily, individuals providing equity capital. During this time, investors typically focused on cash flow, as opposed to property value increases, because the market was relatively stable and inflation was at low levels.

From the early 1970s to approximately 1986, the real estate capital markets changed significantly. Inflation caused significant price increases in real estate; therefore, cash flow became of secondary importance to most investors in investment real estate. Additionally, during this time period, there was favorable tax treatment for developing and holding real estate—an additional monetary benefit. Investors were allowed to depreciate, or write off, real estate even though the actual value of the real estate was dramatically increasing; furthermore, it was possible for an investor to write off more than what had actually been invested in equity funds over the investor's holding period. This time period was also characterized by higher loan-to-value ratios, a result of perceptions of increasing property values. Lenders felt secure with a higher loan-to-value ratio because property values were increasing at substantial rates. For example, considering a 90 percent loan-to-value ratio at the time of purchase and a 10 percent increase in property value with fixed debt, the loan-to-value ratio in the subsequent year, after a one-year holding period, was 80 percent. The real estate market at this time was also characterized by securitization, with mortgage-backed securities, governmental programs through the Department of Housing and Urban Development (HUD), and real estate investment trusts (REITs) investing substantial money in real estate.

Since the implementation of the Tax Reform Act of 1986, the real estate markets have undergone another significant shift. Depreciation write-offs that were formerly fifteen years at an accelerated rate on commercial properties are now thirty-one and one-half years at the straight-line rate. Therefore, depreciation deductions are not as significant as under the previous tax code. Additionally, because of the deteriorating financial condition of many of the traditional financing institutions, loan-to-value ratios are lower than before 1986. In addition, property values have not risen, in most locations, at the same rate as from 1972 to 1986. Because of the decline in returns from favorable tax treatments and inflation, investors are once again focusing on cash flows as a primary source of yield to the investment. The following is a brief discussion of the major players in the real estate capital markets. Their current effect in the marketplace can be assumed by their level of involvement.

Financial Institutions. Commercial banks and savings and loans have been gradually deregulated since the early 1980s, and their investments in the real estate capital markets have risen substantially. For example, commercial banks provided approximately $20 billion in loans in 1981 and approximately $64.2 billion in 1986 (these figures are in real dollars, using 1983 as the base year). Savings and loans provided $8 billion in capital in 1981, but $39 billion in 1986. In addition, mutual savings banks also increased their mortgage holdings in real estate over this period.

Life Insurance Companies. Life insurance companies provide both equity and mortgage capital to the real estate markets. Insurance companies are one of the largest investors in the real estate investment marketplace. Mortgage investments in 1986 were just under $30 billion, while equity investments were in excess of $30 billion.

Pension Funds. Pension funds provide both mortgage and equity capital but have a larger amount of equity capital than do insurance companies, as a percentage of holdings.

However, from 1982 to 1986, pension funds have declined in percentage of investment in real estate. A very small percentage of the pension fund assets are invested in real estate; therefore, pension funds could be an important source of real estate capital in future years.

Foreign Investors. In recent years, foreign investors have invested increasing amounts of money in commercial and industrial real estate in the United States. Most of the foreign money is from Canada, Japan, the Middle East, and Europe. U.S. investments have become popular because of the level of the dollar, and because the market is perceived to be more stable than most other national real estate markets. In addition, some foreign investors saw higher yields in the United States than in their own countries, given the same level of risk. Foreign investment is expected to continue as a major source of capital in the near term.

Public Syndicators. Most of the public syndications were a direct result of the Tax Act of 1981. A large amount of equity capital was provided in the period of 1981 to 1986, through public syndication offerings. However, because of the current tax code, public syndications have declined in importance.

As might be expected, the five largest institutional investors in the period of 1982 to 1986 were life insurance companies, REITs, pension funds, syndicators, and foreign investors. During this time period, life insurance companies provided approximately 52 percent of equity for real estate purchases, REITs approximately 10.2 percent, pension funds 10.9 percent, syndicators 22.5 percent, and foreign investors 4.5 percent. However, with commercial and industrial real estate, investors also compete with private individuals who purchase for investment and as users. An investor should note that the user market will tend to pay a premium for real estate that meets particular needs.

IMPORTANT FACTORS IN BUYING AND SELLING

Selection of Form of Business

Investment properties may be held either in sole proprietorship, general partnership, limited partnership, or some form of corporation. As may be expected, there are advantages and disadvantages to each type of ownership.

Table 7 summarizes the characteristics of each form of ownership.

Corporation. A corporation is treated legally as a separate entity. One of the disadvantages of a corporate form of ownership of real estate is that the corporation is taxed as an entity, and any dividends that are distributed to a shareholder are also taxed. This double taxation is a particular disadvantage to the corporate form of ownership of real estate. However, this form would be suitable for those properties that are associated with high liability, since the individual stockholders may be afforded some protection from general liability.

Most commercial properties are not held in a corporate form of ownership. However, corporate forms of ownership are often associated with industrial properties that may have high liabilities associated with either the activity on the premise or with other potential problems such as hazardous waste.

TABLE 7. Comparison of Ownership Entities

Characteristic	Corporation	Limited Partnership	General Partnership	Sole Proprietorship
Expense	High	High	Medium to Low	Low
Regulation	High	High	Low	Low
Continuity	Perpetual	High for limited Low for general	Low	Low
Transferability	High	Medium Low for limited	Low	Low
Management	High	High for general	Medium	High
Liability	Low for stockholders	Low for limited High for general	High	High
Tax treatment	Corporate plus individual on dividends	Individual	Individual	Individual

Limited Partnership. During the 1970s and 1980s, limited partnerships have grown in importance as an ownership vehicle for real estate. The primary advantages of a limited partnership are the tax conduit characteristic and reduced liability to the limited partners. Limited partners are liable only for their original investment in the property. Disadvantages include the expenses associated with a limited partnership, a substantial amount of governmental regulation, and the expenses that often accrue to the general partners. (For further discussion, see the article "Real Estate: Limited Partnerships," elsewhere in this volume.)

General Partnership. General partnerships are relatively inexpensive to form and are often used for purchasing commercial or industrial real estate. General partnerships are useful when each of the partners has a particular expertise that would contribute to the ownership of the property. For example, an advantageous partnership might be formed by one partner who is adept at acquisition and financing and another who has particular expertise in managing properties.

One disadvantage of a general partnership is the liability of all the general partners for the acts of one of the partners. In addition, disagreements between partners can often lead to poorly managed investments. Any ownership of investment real estate in a general partnership should involve a written agreement.

Sole Proprietorship. In a sole proprietorship, an individual, without entering into a partnership or taking a corporate form, purchases real estate, an advantageous situation from the standpoint of management and expense. However, often the management of the investment becomes burdensome to an investor, particularly if he is not experienced in managing the particular type of real estate. Additionally, the risks are high, with the individual being solely responsible for any liability that arises from the ownership of the property.

Selecting a Property

Once the decision is made to invest in commercial or industrial property, the particular property must be selected. An investor needs to consider a predetermined set of investment objectives and should purchase property that meets the criteria. For example, if the investor's primary objective is to enhance cash flow, then only properties that offer cash flow should be considered. A property that is expected to decline in value over the holding period may be a reasonable investment if the return could come from current cash flows from the property. However, in most cases, the investor's main focus is the overall yield, or internal rate of return, generated from holding the property.

Another important consideration is the level of management needed to operate the property. Management is considered an expense to the ownership of real property. Therefore, an investor who also wishes to manage the property will save in expenses by managing the property in lieu of a management company. However, there is additional risk if the investor does not have the needed expertise to manage the investment, and often the loss in income resulting from poor management will offset any savings from self-management.

The investor needs to consider the market or submarket. Some investors prefer to purchase property only near their residence, whereas others prefer to look for the best deal available.

In summary, the investor should first list a set of objectives concerning property type, management, and location, and then find the property that bests meets the particular investor criteria.

Brokerage

A purchaser should contact a broker that specializes in a particular property type or area that is of interest. Although the broker may represent either the buyer or the seller, the broker's commission is typically paid by the seller of the property; therefore the investor can benefit from the expertise of a broker without direct costs. The broker should be one who will communicate with the investor; the broker should be able to be trusted to look out for the investor's best interest and to work to find a property that meets the investor's needs.

Other Considerations

The following is a checklist of items to be considered prior to purchasing a property. This list is not all-inclusive but is representative of potentially relevant information:

- Plans and specifications
- Title policy, including legal description
- Financing
- Zoning and deed restrictions
- Structural and engineering study
- Appraisal
- Copy of lease and operating statements
- Other (depends on property)

—EPA study for hazardous waste and other problems
—Asbestos study
—Soils study
—Fault study

- Market or feasibility study
- Past sales history of the property
- Recent major maintenance and capital improvements
- Road or other off-site improvements that could impact on value
- Governmental or legislative bills that could affect value
- Community attitudes toward property
- Plot of land
- Personal property that is not included in the purchase
- Current architectural standards for newer properties of the same size or use
- Any easements or licenses granted
- Tax consequences, including proposed tax legislation
- Legal risks

The above listing of relevant considerations implies the complexities and the expense of purchasing commercial/industrial real estate. The following is a brief discussion of some of the factors listed.

Financing. Real estate may be seller-financed or financed through a third party. If feasible, the financing should be arranged prior to selecting the property. An investor should shop for favorable rates and lender requirements. In addition, advanced financing arrangements are desirable because the institution can provide the investor with a checklist of items required by the lender in order to finance a project. The investor should consider the available terms, including points, interest rates, and length of loan, as well as lender attitudes and expertise concerning particular property types.

Studies. Numerous studies are listed within the checklist, including structural and engineering, EPA studies, asbestos, soils, faults, and market or feasibility studies. Often the studies have already been performed by the current owners of the property and would be at no additional cost to the investor. Therefore, a prudent investor should ask the seller for any studies that may have been conducted concerning the property. However, if one of the studies was not conducted and it appears that there may be a potential problem, an investor should seek professional assistance.

Appraisal. If the property is to be financed through an institution, an appraisal will be required. Generally, the appraisal is ordered after a particular property is selected. Often, the buyer and seller have agreed on a purchase price, yet the appraised value is determined to be lower than the agreed-on contract price. Therefore, the sale of the property should be contingent on the appraisal being at some predetermined level of value.

Although most financial institutions have a list of approved appraisers, the Member of the Appraisal Institute (MAI) designation is the most recognized for commercial and industrial properties. In addition, the Society of Real Estate Appraisers offers an SRPA (Senior Real Property Appraiser) and an SREA (Senior Real Estate Analyst).

Transaction Costs

The high transaction costs involved in purchasing and selling real estate were discussed in the *Potential Risks* section of this article. The investor should research customary transaction costs within a certain market area. For example, the brokerage fee is typically paid by the seller of property but may also be paid by the purchaser. In addition, various closing costs, including title policy, legal fees, appraisals, inspections, and other studies may be negotiated and are customarily paid by buyer or seller, depending on the area. It should be noted that these fees are generally negotiable but do affect the ultimate price that may be received for property.

Selection of Management

Because real estate is typically considered a management-intense endeavor, it is important to consider, in advance of a purchase, who will manage the property. Various alternatives include owner management, an independent management company, and management retained by the seller of the property. Property management companies with designated members (e.g., a Certified Property Manager) may be desirable over companies that do not offer such expertise.

Because of the unique characteristics of real estate, a prudent investor will research the market area and particular property before making an investment decision. Investment in commercial and industrial real estate can result in high yields to the investor. However, because of potential risks, the immobile nature of real estate, and high costs to both operate and dispose of real estate, the investor should base a purchase decision on all relevant information collected concerning the property.

GLOSSARY

after-tax cash flow—Actual spendable income from an investment after income taxes; net income increased by depreciation and reduced by mortgage principal amortization payments, less income tax payments.

anchor tenant—A major chain or department store that is strategically located in a shopping center so as to generate traffic for the smaller, satellite stores; sometimes called a magnet store or traffic generator.

balloon mortgage—A mortgage for which the stipulated periodic payments do not result in complete amortization of principal at maturity, thus necessitating a final payment much larger than the previous ones.

before-tax cash flow—Actual spendable income from an investment before income taxes; rental income less cash payments for operating expenses and debt service.

capitalization rate—The rate at which a future flow of income is converted into a present value figure, expressed as a percentage.

commercial property—Improved real estate held by its owner for the production of income through leases for commercial or business use; for example, office buildings, retail stores, shopping centers.

debt service coverage ratio—The ratio of annual net operating income from a property to the annual debt service on a mortgage loan on the property; also, debt coverage ratio.

depreciation—The gradual loss or shrinkage of value of property (except land) due to wear and tear and the action of the elements; a tax-deductible expense for investment or business property.

equity—In accounting and finance, net ownership, that is the extent of the owner's right in a property above all claims and liens against it expressed in money value.

equity dividend rate—Before-tax cash flow divided by the initial equity investment.

financial leverage—See *leverage*.

gross rent multiplier—A rule-of-thumb method of appraising the fair market value of real estate by multiplying gross rental income by a factor that varies with the type of property and its location; also, gross multiplier or gross income multiplier.

internal rate of return—The discount rate that will produce a present value of cash inflows equal to that of cash outflows.

leasehold—An estate in realty that arises by virtue of a lease; the right of a lessee to the use and occupancy of real estate.

leverage—A financial term meaning a result that is disproportionate to the amount of equity investment; in real estate, a situation created when the debt service on funds borrowed to acquire the real estate is lower than the free-and-clear return from the real estate (upside leverage) or higher than the free-and-clear return (downside or reverse leverage).

net lease—A lease under which the lessee assumes the responsibility of paying all of the operating expenses of the property so that the rental received by the lessor is entirely net to the lessor; see also *triple-net lease*.

net operating income—The balance remaining after the operating expenses of a property are deducted from the gross rental income or gross receipts received from the property; in contrast to cash flow, net operating income is determined without deduction for debt service on any mortgages.

occupancy rate—The ratio of rented units or space to total rentable units or space in a property, expressed as a percentage.

percentage lease—A lease of commercial property under which the total rental to be paid by the tenant varies according to the business done by the tenant; the rental is usually determined by the gross sales, gross revenues, or gross receipts.

pro forma statement—A financial statement for real estate, projecting gross income, operating expenses, and net operating income for a future period (usually one year) based on specified assumptions; literally, according to form.

reappraisal lease—A lease under which the rental is to be reappraised at periodic intervals during the life of the lease; normally used only for long-term leases.

replacement reserve—A fund set aside for making replacements of property; typically required by a lender of a borrower in cases where owners install on the premises property with a short life expectancy, such as furniture, carpeting, or appliances.

triple-net lease—A net lease under which the tenant is responsible for operating expenses, including real estate taxes and debt service on a mortgage taken out by the landlord, as well as rental paid to the landlord; also, net-net-net lease.

variable-rate mortgage—A mortgage that calls for installment payments of varying amounts during its term based on interest rates and that may or may not be fully amortized (liquidated) at maturity.

TRADE ORGANIZATIONS

Building Owners and Managers Association, Washington, D.C.

Institute of Real Estate Management, Chicago, Ill.

National Association of Corporate Real Estate Executives (NACORE), Miami, Fla.

Real Estate Securities and Syndication Institute, Chicago, Ill.

Society of Industrial Realtors, Chicago, Ill.

LEADING DEALERS

Ackerman & Co., Atlanta, Ga.

Arthur Rubloff, Chicago, Ill.

Cabot, Cabot & Forbes, Boston, Mass.

Coldwell Banker, Los Angeles, Cal.

Gerald Hines, Houston, Tex.

Helmsley Spear, New York, N.Y.

Henry S. Miller, Dallas, Tex.

Trammell Crow, Dallas, Tex.

Vantage, Columbus, Ohio

SUGGESTED READING

PERIODICALS

The Appraisal Journal. Published by the American Institute of Real Estate Appraisers, National Association of Realtors, Chicago, Ill. Quarterly.

Commercial Investment Journal. Published by Realtors National Marketing Institute, Chicago, Ill.

Journal of Property Management. Published by the Institute of Real Estate Management, National Association of Realtors, Chicago, Ill. Bimonthly.

Mortgage and Real Estate Executive's Report. Published by Warren, Gorham & Lamont, Boston, Mass. Biweekly.

National Real Estate Investor. Published by Communication Channels, Inc., Atlanta, Ga. Monthly.

Real Estate Review. Published by Warren, Gorham & Lamont, Boston, Mass. Quarterly.

Real Estate Today. Published by National Association of Realtors, Chicago, Ill. Monthly.

SIR Reports. Published by the Society of Industrial Realtors, Washington, D.C. Monthly.

Valuation. American Society of Appraisers, P.O. Box 17265, Washington, D.C. 20041.

REFERENCE BOOKS

Arnold, Alvin. *The Arnold Encyclopedia of Real Estate*. Boston: Warren, Gorham & Lamont, 1978.

______. *Real Estate Investor's Deskbook*, rev. ed. Boston: Warren, Gorham & Lamont, 1987.

Britton, James A., ed. *Financing Income-Producing Real Estate*. New York: McGraw-Hill, 1977.

Building Owners and Managers Association International. *Downtown and Suburban Office Building Experience Exchange Report*. Washington, D.C. Annual.

Collins, Webster A. *Real Estate: A Hidden Corporate Asset*. American Society of Real Estate Counselors, 1986.

Friedman, Jack P., and Ordway, Nicholas. *Income Property Appraisal and Analysis*, 2nd ed., Englewood Cliffs, N.J.: Prentice Hall, 1988.

Johnson, Irvin E. *The Instant Mortgage-Equity Technique*. Lexington, Mass.: D.C. Heath & Co., 1972.

Kinnard, William N., and Messner, Stephen D. *Industrial Real Estate*. Washington, D.C.: Society of Industrial Realtors, 1979.

Messner, Stephen, D., et al. *Marketing Investment Real Estate*. Chicago: Realtors National Marketing Institute, National Association of Realtors, 1982.

Pyhrr, Stephen A., et al. *Real Estate Investment: Strategy Analysis, Decisions*, 2nd ed. New York: John Wiley & Sons, 1989.

Urban Land Institute. *Dollars and Cents of Shopping Centers*. Washington, D.C. Annual.

REAL ESTATE

CONDOMINIUMS, COOPERATIVES, TIME-SHARES, FRACTIONALS

Keith B. Romney

BASIC CHARACTERISTICS

History and Background

The concept of multiple ownership of a piece of real estate, especially a building, has been known since Roman times. Modern usage of this ancient concept started in the United States with the cooperative in the 1920s and the condominium in the 1960s. Time-share followed in the 1960s in Europe and in the 1970s in the U.S. Fractional ownership, the latest refinement, is a product of the early 1980s.

Cooperatives and condominiums first came about in response to the increasing cost and lack of availability in urban locations of single-family residences. Condominiums quickly became a second-home product also. Time-share and fractional ownership resulted from increasing prices and limited usage patterns of recreational, second-home condominiums.

A condominium has many of the characteristics of a single-family residence as an investment, but it is distinguished primarily by the required membership in a homeowner's association, involvement with management, and the ownership of common elements that generally have restrictions on their usage. The owner of a single-family residence could probably tear up the lawn and plant a garden. Because the owner of a condominium is not the sole owner of the lawn, garden, or grounds, these areas cannot be changed without the permission of the homeowner's association.

Cooperatives offer many of the same features as condominiums, but there is a major difference in the ownership form. In a cooperative, a nonprofit corporation owns the land

Keith B. Romney is Founder of Keith Romney Associates, Condominium, Timesharing, and Fractional Ownership Consultants, Salt Lake City, Utah.

and buildings. The corporation blanket-mortgages the entire property. Shares of stock in the corporation are sold by the developer. The purchase of certain shares allows the stockholder to use a certain dwelling unit in the building. Stockholders are assessed each month for their pro rata share of mortgage payments, taxes, and maintenance.

The following chart summarizes some of the major differences between condominiums and cooperatives.

	Condominium	Cooperative
Finance unit individually	Yes	No
Finance entire property	No	Yes
Owners personally liable for mortgage	Yes	No
Make up unpaid taxes on others' units	No	Yes
Make up unpaid principal and interest on others' units	No	Yes
Tax deductions for interest and property taxes	Yes	Yes, if certain provisions are met

Resort time-sharing received its impetus in an economy plagued by recession, where developers trying to market whole-unit condominiums found the solution in selling time to individual purchasers. Resort time-sharing is a hybrid, combining attributes of being an owner with attributes of being a guest, with all the attendant hospitality and management functions of a hotel. Good property management becomes very important to maintain the continuity and quality of the project because owners, many of whom live a long distance from the resort and buy only a few weeks' time, do not have the voice or influence of whole-unit owners. Fee time-shares are bought and sold in the same manner as other real estate, but right-to-use time-shares (no fee interest is required) can only be used and dealt with as allowed in the documentation.

Fractional ownership is an ownership product that occupies the area between whole-unit condominiums and one-week ownership time-share. Some real estate professionals have chosen to call fractional ownership bulk time-share, seeing it as the bundling together of some number of one-week intervals, usually at least four or five weeks, to escape the time-share nomenclature. Others see fractional ownership as a whole-unit product, just divided once or twice for more efficient usage, seeing a quarter of a whole unit as the standard fractional product.

To put each of these types of ownership into perspective, visualize a large tract of land. (1) Divide the land into separate parcels that can be deeded to various individuals. This is fee-simple land ownership. (2) Assume that some or all of these individuals build structures upon their land. This connotes single-building ownership. (3) Suppose an individual or corporation builds a multiple-unit structure. If the builder keeps the ownership of the building but allows usage of a unit to an owner through a stock ownership arrangement, this is a cooperative. If the building is legally divided, separately deeded, and sold so that each unit owner owns his own units, this is a condominium. (4) Divide the units as to usage of the time. If the usage is a substantial portion of the time in one whole unit, say 25 percent or at least 12.5 percent (a quarter or eighth, respectively), the product is called fractional ownership. If the usage is at least a week ($1/52$) or as much as several weeks, the product is called time-share.

Results of the decision as to what the ownership product is judged to be may determine public acceptance, lender/financing arrangements, regulatory agency jurisdiction, and so forth.

Current Standing

Condominiums, cooperatives, time-shares, and fractional ownership in the past have been inflation-responsive, and their popularity has increased substantially since their respective introductions. Inasmuch as they are composed primarily of land and building construction materials, like single-family residences, they continue to increase in value in an inflationary economy. The fact that there are economies achieved in construction of condominiums as compared to single-family residences has, in many instances, brought multiple-ownership dwellings into a more attractive relative price range. Time-share and fractional ownership have also been inflation-responsive, and many people who have purchased them in resort areas do so to avoid the ever-increasing costs of hotel or resort accommodations. By purchasing a time-share or fractional ownership, they are able to secure tomorrow's vacations at today's cost.

Condominiums and cooperatives, like single-family residences, can be found in most price levels. There are entry-level economy cooperatives and condominiums at one end of the spectrum, and luxury high-rise cooperatives or condominiums and luxury resort condominiums at the other end. The same holds true for time-share and fractional ownership products. Condominiums are found in most major cities and all major resort areas across the United States and are now available in many smaller cities and suburbs. Cooperatives have been quite popular in New York City and its surrounding area but, in other regions, have not spread as rapidly as condominiums. Time-share and fractional ownership are found primarily in either destination resort areas or regional resort areas. Time-share and fractional ownership projects have also been offered in urban locations such as San Francisco, New Orleans, New York City, and Salt Lake City.

ATTRACTIVE FEATURES

Psychological Benefit of Ownership

The American dream usually includes the ownership of land and property. Condominiums and cooperatives, like single-family residences, fulfill this dream and give the psychological benefit of ownership. Most people are aware of the many great fortunes that have been founded on ownership and development of real estate. *Forbes Magazine*'s annual review of billionaires and millionaires showed that, in 1988, real estate was still te leading source of wealth creation in the United States and much of the world. Americans like to consider themselves a landed class of people; therefore, there is a deep desire to own and control property. Properties in fee-simple ownership fulfill this desire.

Inflation Hedge

Given the length of time needed to construct a project, high inflation has in times past produced a narrow but lucrative investment opportunity: the investment or, in some cases, the speculation, on presales. Investors placed deposits on cooperatives, condominiums, time-shares, and fractional ownership in projects to be constructed and then sold them at a profit before closing on the unit. That practice was particularly prevalent in the "hot" areas of the early 1980s, such as Hawaii, California, and Florida.

A somewhat similar method of investment based on the expectation of future inflation has been to purchase condominiums in overbuilt or low-demand markets and hold them for resale until demand improves or the excess inventory is reduced.

Time-share and fractional ownership investments have had significant price increases at various times in their relatively short history. One survey in the early 1980s indicated that time-share investments were increasing in value at a rate of 26 percent per year. Specific examples of this were the Imperial in Hawaii, and Laguna Shores in California. One-week ownership of the "Ohia" unit (a studio unit) in the Imperial increased from $2,900 to $6,300 in the first eighteen months of the project. Likewise, the "Captain" unit in the Laguna Shores project increased from $3,500 to $6,500 in eight months. Much of this appreciation is developer-forced price increases rather than market-driven real growth in property value or even inflation-driven increases.

Overbuilding and a depressed economy in many areas of the country for the past several years have reduced this price escalation for time-share and fractional ownership. However, sales are still being made at healthy prices in many resorts.

Investors are well-advised to make condominium, time-share, and fractional ownership investments in projects that are well located, well built, and well managed, and not to rely on inflation to help them bail out of a buying decision that is not properly researched. To be sure, times of inflationary price increases will come around again; there are business cycles and monetary cycles. It is better to buy a property that makes sense in any economy, and then enjoy the added benefits should inflation push prices higher.

Life-Style Issues

Some of the price differential between condominiums and single-family homes has been eliminated in recent years as luxury condominiums with square footages comparable to single-family homes have come into the marketplace. The tendency toward extensive on-site amenities, including spas, pools, tennis courts, game/club rooms, and even golf courses, has also pushed up the price of condominiums in relation to single-family homes. The investment issue, then, becomes a decision as to whether the traditional single-family residence or the amenity-rich condominium has greater appeal to the buying public. This is a function of population demographics, baby boom phenomena, the aging of the population, and geographical regional peculiarities. In other words, yuppies and "empty-nest" couples are much more likely to buy condominiums than are rural or ex-urban or suburban young families. Knowing the market becomes critical in the investment decision. Two-job marriages are less likely to opt for the yard work and upkeep associated with single-family residence ownership. Retired and semiretired couples with extensive travel plans or with summer or winter second homes are more likely to favor condominium lifestyles.

Safety of Principal

A primary incentive for owning real estate has always been the safety of such an investment. Assuming some level of care in the selection of the property, including analyzing comparable real estate and getting a good property appraisal, an investment in real estate is usually quite safe. Land is one commodity that, in Will Rogers' terms, "they ain't making any more of." Thus, despite occasional brief periods of stagnation or recession in the economy, the overall trend for real estate values is at worst constant, and at best substantially upward. Real estate, traditionally, has not been as volatile as some other investments, such as stocks, bonds, commercial paper, and other money investments, which are subject to severe swings up and down for a variety of reasons that are difficult to predict.

There are times when real estate sells slowly, and periods during which prices stabilize, but it is rare when, over a moderate holding period, prices of real estate don't rebound and eventually escalate. Thus, investments in cooperatives, whole-unit condominiums, time-shares, or fractional ownership, especially in well-located urban or resort areas, provide safety of principal while holding out the possibility of market-driven or inflation-driven investment enhancement.

Cash Return (Income)

The cash return on condominium or cooperative ownership generally is less than on other investment mediums. However, many investors feel that this is a small price to pay for the safety of principal and for the potential for appreciation. The return on most condominium investments does not flow in on a monthly basis as does the return on a bond or other similar investments.

There is, of course, some rental income to be derived from condominium ownership and investment, but this is often insufficient to provide an adequate return on the monies invested. However, many investors have found that they can provide a periodic income by refinancing their properties. Borrowing money normally is not a taxable event. Therefore, properties can be refinanced and cash withdrawn. Later, on sale of the condominiums, there will be less cash proceeds and the same amount of tax to be paid. For simplicity's sake, assume the purchase of a condominium for $50,000 and assume the refinancing of that condominium whereby the investor gets $15,000 of the appreciated value of the property. This will not have any tax consequence at the time the cash is received, but will be deferred to point of sale. This method of providing a periodic income is contingent on the escalating value of the property.

Although substantial returns are not expected, rental receipts often do cover a majority of operating costs and mortgage costs, thereby allowing an investor to purchase something for his own occasional use that he would not otherwise be able to justify economically.

Capital Gains Treatment

A major benefit of holding investments in condominiums, cooperatives, time-shares or fractional ownership in the past was the capital gains treatment (a lower tax rate than for ordinary income) afforded to properties held for at least six months and up to twelve months before being resold. The Tax Reform Act of 1986 eliminated the capital gains benefits. However, the substantial reduction in tax rates on all types of income, including investment income from sale of real estate, helps to soften the impact of the elimination of capital gains tax treatment.

POTENTIAL RISKS

Market Volatility

The possibility always exists that overbuilding will occur in a particular area, making it difficult to sell any property. Resort properties (condominiums, time-shares, and fractional ownership) are especially prone to boom and bust cycles, since resort investments are some of the first to be curtailed in tough economic times and since every window of opportunity in prosperous times is quickly filled up by numerous developers. In the past, most resort areas have not done a good job of controlling and guiding growth to take the ups and downs out of the system. This is slowly changing, but for too long and still in too many jurisdictions the result is a pattern of too few units followed by too many units, followed by too few units, and so forth, with price swings as great as 50 to 100 percent.

The cure for such volatility is always the same: to wait until the bad cycle ends and the good cycle begins. Unless investments are made with this possibility in mind, individuals may not have the wherewithal or might not have properly planned to be able to stay the course through the problem cycle.

Liquidity

In a normal market, condominium, cooperative, time-share, and fractional ownership units would be salable within a reasonable period. This period can usually be determined by the average length of time it takes to sell similar properties in a particular area. Very often, local real estate boards keep accurate information on this period and will make it available on request. However, it should be pointed out that in times of recession, economic stagnation, high interest rates, market uncertainty, tax reformation, or a general unavailability of financing, these ownership products may take a longer time to sell than would be expected under normal conditions. This is a special consideration for investors in this medium and should be considered in the timing of investment sales to prevent having to cut price, and therefore profit, to accomplish a sale. Real estate does not have the liquidity of some other investments, such as stocks, bonds, or gold. Many feel that the protection and stability of principal are worth the loss of liquidity, but the investor should be aware of the issue.

Source of Income

Traditionally, single-family residences have not been an economically viable investment relative to income. Condominiums, cooperatives, time-shares, and fractional ownership share this characteristic. Demand for these products is expected to continue to grow, but land costs, building costs, and financing costs are also expected to increase or remain high. This may prevent them from being an economical investment for owners. Although subsequent increases in land and building value do not affect coverage for rent, they do affect return on equity and must be compared with alternative investments in that respect. Long-term, fixed rate mortgages do not affect rent coverage, but variable rate mortgages do.

An investor who holds a piece of real estate encounters costs for debt service, taxes, and expenses. He also must consider what his equity could earn in an alternative investment, and he is entitled to a return on that equity. Generally, obtainable rent will not cover debt service, taxes, expenses, and return on equity. After a time, the rental income may cover these costs, but it usually fails to cover them if consideration is given to the return on equity as that equity is increased by inflation.

Many condominium owners have found that if the investment is held long enough, and if inflation increases the rents that can be obtained, there is usually a point at which the rental income can carry the debt service and expenses. However, if a true investment approach is used, and the owner's equity is computed based on the inflated value of the condominium, the rental income will not yield the rate of return that would be expected from income-based investments. However, those who invest in condominiums generally are seeking safety of principal and appreciation (most of which has come through inflation) rather than income.

Regulatory and Political Risks

The risk factors in purchasing an existing condominium, cooperative, timeshare, or fractional ownership are relatively few. There are now environmental considerations as well as zoning considerations in nearly all areas of the country. Certain localities oppose condominium, time-share, and fractional ownership projects routinely. There are other areas that, for political reasons, make it difficult for a multiple-unit project to get the necessary construction permits and approvals.

The trend to convert apartment projects to condominiums often is opposed by local government authorities, both regulatory and political, who feel that widespread conversions could substantially reduce the number of available apartments for rentals. Not everyone can afford to purchase a condominium, and government authorities assume responsibility for either providing adequate rentals or making certain that adequate rentals are provided. Partially as a result of rent ceilings and controls, many owners of apartment house rental property are very interested in converting to condominiums, because their projects have become uneconomical as apartments. Similar opposition exists to converting condominiums, hotels, or apartments to time-shares or fractional ownership.

Therefore, although the risk associated with investing in an individual existing condominium, cooperative, time-share, or fractional ownership is minimal, particularly if the investor goes through the normal steps of checking out the location, zoning, and property, and reviewing the property documents, the risk of investing in proposed projects or conversion projects is greater because of government attitudes and restrictions.

TAX CONSEQUENCES

Ownership of condominiums, qualified cooperatives, time-shares, and fractional ownerships offers all the tax benefits to the owner-occupant that owning a single-family residence does. The owner-occupant can deduct mortgage interest and property taxes. This is true for primary residences and one second home. The Tax Reform Act of 1986 limits other deductions for depreciation and operating losses to those investments in which the investor is a material participant. The rules and regulations defining material participation specify 500 hours of involvement per year in the operations/management of the project, a requirement that few if any investors can meet. Alternatively, if the investor can show 100 hours of such participation and the managing agent for the property cannot show any more than that number of hours as their contribution to the operation of the project, then the investor may qualify as a material participant. Even this lesser number of hours is a tough requirement that few investors can or would attempt to meet.

REPRESENTATIVE TYPES OF INVESTORS

Because of their broad availability as well as the wide selection of types, locations, price ranges, quality, and down payment, condominiums, cooperatives, time-shares, and fractional ownerships have become an attractive vehicle to almost all classes of investors. The majority of investors have been individual rather than institutional or corporate investors.

However, corporations, universities, and similar institutions have found investment and ownership to be an asset because of both the appreciation and the opportunity to use the condominium facility for their own purposes. Since the Tax Reform Act of 1986, investments in these products are more likely to be made for personal usage than for appreciation or tax shelter reasons, although each is still viable for different segments of the market.

IMPORTANT FACTORS IN BUYING AND SELLING

Selection of Broker, Salesperson, or Developer

The investor in condominiums, cooperatives, time-shares, or fractional ownerships should use the same principles in selecting a broker, salesperson, or developer that he would use in selecting a doctor, accountant, or lawyer. While the writers cannot recommend specific brokers, salespersons, or developers, they can recommend that careful attention be given to the reputation for honesty and fair dealing of these people. An investor should check with the Better Business Bureau, the local Board of Realtors or real estate brokers, the local builders' association, and, of course, anyone who is known to be active in the business. Sometimes, real estate editors or real estate departments of leading newspapers can provide information on various brokers, salespersons, or developers.

Most people find that the commission a broker charges to handle the sale is well worth the cost. While commissions vary from location to location, in general they are approximately 6 percent of the sales price on condominiums and cooperatives; commissions on time-shares and fractional ownerships are generally higher, averaging 10 to 12 percent of the sales price.

Finding the Market

In today's aggressive real estate market, the market is usually brought to the investor much in advance of his seeking it. Mail campaigns, phone solicitation, and personal contacting at resort locations make it difficult to avoid an awareness of most major developments of the products under discussion. Newspapers, homebuyer's guides, chambers of commerce, rental agencies, tourist bureaus, and hotel/motel associations are other good sources of information.

Quality of Investment and Professional Advice

The investor who understands real estate and can judge the quality of construction as well as quality of maintenance may not need the help of a professional appraiser. The Yellow Pages usually lists local appraisers who specialize in housing and are experienced in appraising condominiums or cooperatives. These appraisers also can offer valuable input as to quality of construction, level of maintenance, and other areas of concern to the investor. Fees vary greatly and depend on the appraiser's workload and willingness to take the assignment.

Sources of Financing

One very important factor in purchasing a condominium, cooperative, time-share, or fractional ownership is the availability of financing. Most often, investors are seeking leverage. Financing terms, rates, and availability are generally very similar to those for single-family residences, although down payment requirements may be more stringent for investors than for owner-occupants. The leading banks, savings and loan associations, and some credit unions or pension funds are all possible sources. Some developers also offer financing themselves when other sources are not available.

As with any other service, the investor should carefully shop the sources to determine the points, current interest rate, length of loan, and any other factors that may affect the investment.

CUSTODIAL CARE

Physical Maintenance

Exterior maintenance and much of the management of a condominium, cooperative, time-share, or fractional ownership are handled by the homeowner's association, thereby relieving the investor of the responsibility for mowing the lawn, painting the exterior, calling a plumber, and many other tasks that the owner of a single-family residence must perform. However, the investor is responsible for the interior of his individual unit and any plumbing, maintenance, or similar expenses incurred or caused by a tenant. Having much of the maintenance taken care of by the homeowner's association relieves the investor of some of the burdens of ownership. This can be a definite advantage when compared to a single-family residence.

Collecting the Income

As with any other real estate rental, the condominium, cooperative, time-share, or fractional ownership investor should have written leases with his tenants or renters to ensure the rights of the investor to collect rental income and to maintain the unit in a state of good repair. Many investors use the services of banks or savings and loan associations as collection agents, particularly if they live out of the area. This also allows the flexibility to move from an area without disturbing the flow of rental income from a tenant.

Insurance

Although the homeowner's association will have insurance coverage and protection for the common areas, it is up to the unit owner or occupant to provide insurance coverage for the interior and for any personal property within the unit. The investor should give consideration to this and have adequate fire insurance. He should also either provide contents coverage for the tenants or make sure the tenants obtain that coverage.

Property Management

In all major cities and communities across the United States, there are real estate firms or companies that specialize in property management. For a fee plus actual expenses incurred, they will undertake to management condominiums or cooperatives as well as other real estate. If the investment is located in an area some distance from the investor, it may provide greater peace of mind to have a property manager overseeing the investment. Naturally, the property manager will not provide any services without charge. Under the normal arrangement, the manager is paid 10 percent of the gross income and is reimbursed for any expenses or extraordinary costs incurred. This fee is for the basic management function of receiving the telephone calls relating to tenant relations and contacting qualified people to do the repair, maintenance, and other work or services required. The services rendered to the property or for the owner are usually billed to the owner in addition to the basic management fee. For example, if the plumbing stops up in a unit, the management company will receive the call from the tenant and call a plumber as part of the basic management fee. The plumber's services for repairing the problem will be billed to the owner as a separate item, in addition to the basic management fee. Very often, the costs of owning property some distance away are increased because of the need to make extra trips, telephone calls, and so forth. The investor should consider those things when purchasing. Most resort projects have property management organizations for the ownership interests they sell.

Status of Homeowner's Association

The homeowner's association prepares or causes the preparation of a budget of the operating expenses, which are then divided among the various owners and assessed to them as their share of those expenses. One of the things that should be determined by the investor is the status of the homeowner's association. Are its assessments current? Is it functioning? Is there dissension or harmony? Does the project look like it has been receiving periodic maintenance? Are the yards, lawns, and shrubbery in good condition? The performance of the homeowner's association should be evaluated and considered. In addition, the investor who wishes to become a force in the homeowner's association, in order to change attitudes through action and involvement, should realistically evaluate the extent to which this is possible.

GLOSSARY

amenity—A feature of real property that enhances its attractiveness and increases the satisfaction of its occupants or users.

common elements—In a condominium, those portions of the building, land, and amenities owned by the condominium association and used by all the unit owners, who share in the common expenses of their operation and maintenance.

condominium—Individual ownership of units combined with joint ownership of common elements of building, structure, or development.

condominium owners association—An association of condominium unit owners, empowered to operate the condominium and to maintain the common elements. Where the association is incorporated, it is organized as a not-for-profit corporation.

declaration of condominium—An instrument in the form of a deed, which must be filed in the proper office by the developer or owner(s) of the property. When duly executed it binds the present owner and all future owners of the property.

fee simple absolute—Ownership without time limitation (in perpetuity); the most inclusive type of real estate ownership.

fee simple condominium—A form of real property ownership in which the condominium unit owner is the exclusive owner of his own unit only, and is an owner in common with respect to the land and other common elements of the property.

fractional ownership—The exclusive right to occupy a condominium unit for a specified period each year, not less than 1⁄16 of the year.

maintenance costs—Costs assessed on unit owners to provide for the needs of the common elements of the building and development.

time-shared ownership—The exclusive right to occupy a condominium unit for a specified period each year, usually one week.

LEADING FRANCHISE BROKERS

Century 21 Real Estate

Coldwell Banker

Electronic Realty Associates (ERA)

Gallery of Homes

International Real Estate Network

Meredith Publishing (Better Homes & Gardens)

Realty World Corporation

Red Carpet Corporation

TRADE ORGANIZATIONS

American Hotel & Motel Association, New York, N.Y.

American Resort & Residential Development Association, Washington, D.C.

Community Associations Institute, Arlington, Va.

National Association of Homebuilders, Washington, D.C.

National Association of Realtors, Chicago, Ill.

Urban Land Institute, Washington, D.C.

SUGGESTED READING

PERIODICALS

Developments. Published by American Resort & Residential Development Association, Washington, D.C. Eleven issues per year.

Multi-Housing News. Published by Gralla Publications, New York, N.Y. Monthly.

NAHB Builder. Published by the National Association of Home Builders, Washington, D.C. Monthly.

Perspective. Published by Resort Condominiums International, Inc., Indianapolis, Ind. Monthly.

Resort Development. Published by CHB Company, Inc., Bellingham, Wash. Nine issues per year.

Resort Timesharing Law Reporter. Published by Land Development Institute Ltd., Washington, D.C. Monthly.

Resort Timesharing Today. Published by CHB Company, Inc., Bellingham, Wash. Monthly.

Vacation Industry Review. Published by Worldex Corporation, Miami, Fla. Monthly.

REFERENCE BOOKS

Bloch, Stuart M., and Ingersoll, William B., eds. *Timesharing*. Washington, D.C.: Urban Land Institute, 1977.

California Association of Realtors. *How to Manage Condominium Developments*. Los Angeles, 1976.

Dombal, Robert W. *Residential Condominiums: A Guide to Analysis and Appraisal*. (Chicago: American Institute of Real Estate Appraisers, 1976.

Institute of Real Estate Management. *The Condominium Community: A Guide for Owners, Boards, and Managers*. Chicago, 1978.

Richard L. Ragatz Associates, Inc. *The Resort Timesharing Industry: A Socio-Economic Impact Analysis of Timesharing*. Volumes I and II. Washington, D.C.: The Resort Timesharing Council of the American Land Development Association, 1980 and 1981.

Rohan, Patrick J., and Reskin, Melvin A. *Condominium Law and Practice*. New York: Matthew Bender Co., 1965 (revised periodically since 1969 by Patrick J. Rohan).

Romney, Keith B. *Condominium Development Guide: Procedures, Analysis, Forms*. Boston: Warren, Gorham & Lamont, 1988 (annual supplements).

Keith Romney Associates. *Timesharing Guide for Buyers and Developers*. Salt Lake City, 1982 (updated periodically).

Wolfe, David B. *Condominium and Homeowners Associations That Work*. Washington, D.C.: Urban Land Institute, 1978.

REAL ESTATE

FARMS AND RANCHES

James E. Hamer
John R. Schumann
Gene L. Dunbar
Kim Ford

BASIC CHARACTERISTICS

The 1987 market value of the 2.2 million[1] farms and ranches in the mainland United States (forty-eight states) is estimated to exceed $576 billion[2] (total value of land and buildings). Roughly 25 percent of the farm and ranch land sold in the year ending June 1, 1988 was purchased by either absentee investors (not residing in the county of purchase), nonfarming corporations, or nonresident aliens (foreign buyers).[3]

Agriculture is one of the nation's largest businesses, with nearly $170 billion in sales in 1987 (fifty states), according to the U.S. Department of Agriculture. This huge volume has attracted a highly sophisticated network of producers and investors. To be successful in farm- or ranchland, an investor must buy well, operate efficiently, and sell profitably. This scenario has become increasingly difficult to achieve because of the large percentage of poor farm and ranch investment alternatives appearing in the marketplace.

---

[1] U.S. Department of Agriculture. Agricultural Statistics Board Crop Production, Aug. 1988, p. A-32.

[2] U.S. Department of Agriculture, Economic Research Services, Agricultural Land Values and Markets, AR-10, June 1988, p. 5.

[3] Id. at 19.

James E. Hamer is a former Trust Officer with The Northern Trust Company, Chicago. John R. Schumann was formerly a Vice-President and attorney in the Trust Department of The Northern Trust Company. Gene L. Dunbar is Vice-President and Senior Trust Officer with NBC Bank-San Antonio, San Antonio, Texas. Kim Ford is a Certified Public Accountant with Gerald L. Hill and Company, P.C., San Antonio, Texas.

Primary Determinants of Value

Farm and Ranch Income. Historically, the average return on the fair market value of farms and ranches in the United States has ranged from 1 to 5 percent (net operating income before taxes divided by market value of the land asset). When land appreciates rapidly, as it did during the early 1970s, this capitalization rate has decreased to as low as one percent. For example, in late 1980 in Illinois, an average farm cost approximately $3,100 per acre. Farm rents in Illinois were averaging about $155 gross income per acre, so an average investment would yield roughly 5 percent (before tax). Farm and ranch investors have traditionally realized more from capital appreciation than from net farm or ranch income.

Inflationary Pressure. This has been a major factor in the strong performance of farm and ranch values. Since the early 1930s, agricultural land has been an ideal inflationary hedge. During the early 1980s, land values far exceeded the rate of inflation, as illustrated in Figure 1.

Land Supply Factors. Nearly 3 million acres of agricultural land are lost annually to urban development, highways, rights of way, and so on. Farm- and ranchland cannot be manufactured, so the supply side of the land value equation is steadily decreasing.

Land Demand Factors. An increasing world population is requiring more food products annually. This increased demand has contributed to higher production levels, higher agricultural commodity prices, and increased land values.

Less than 3 percent of the total number of farms and ranches in the United States are sold each year. The competition for this land is usually led by farmers and ranchers, who use existing acres as collateral to bid at an advantage against nonagrarian competition.

However, farmers, speculator-investors, corporations, investment groups, and foreign buyers are becoming increasingly more competitive for available farm- and ranchland.

Variety of Investments

Before investing in a farm or ranch, potential buyers must determine which type of agricultural enteprise will satisfy their objectives. In choosing from among hundreds of crop and livestock alternatives, geography, economics, or personal preference may emerge as the deciding factor. Irrigated or dry land cultivation, row crop or permanent crop farming, grazing livestock, concentrated livestock, or combinations of crop and livestock may be considered. The investor needs to clearly define objectives and compare them to the risk-reward ratio of the alternative enterprises.

Permanent Crops. Permanent crops include perennial fruit- and nut-bearing trees and bushes. With a high risk-reward ratio, these agricultural enterprises require both sophisticated management and large capital input. They are among the most intensive operations in agriculture and are not recommended for the passive investor. Recently, among the most attractive regions for permanent crop investments have been the following:

- Imperial, San Joaquin, Napa, and Salinas Valleys in California (citrus, grapes, kiwi, nectarines, peaches, pears, and plums)

FIGURE 1. U.S. Farmland Value Compared With Inflation Rate

Source: U.S. Department of Agriculture, Economic Research Services, and U.S. Department of Commerce

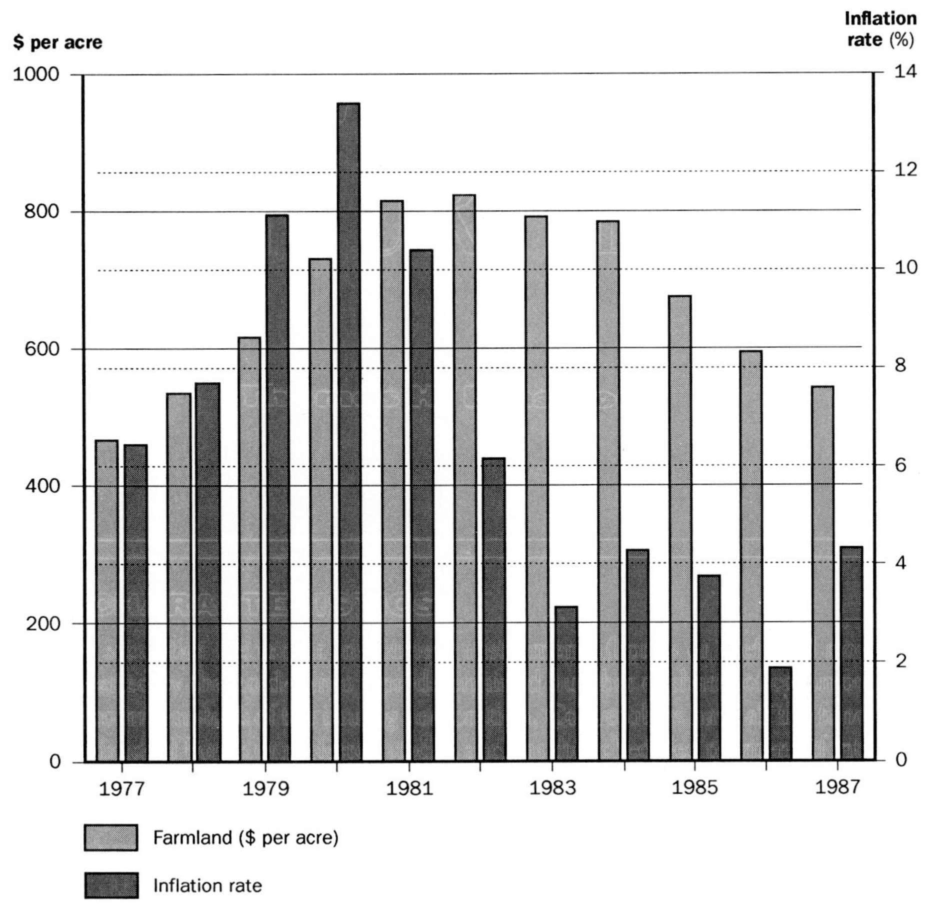

- Rio Grande Valley in Texas (citrus, avocados)
- Florida (citrus)
- Arizona (citrus, pecans, grapes)
- Texas and New Mexico (pecans, grapes)

Livestock or Dairy. Extremely large capital requirements make entry into livestock or dairy operations prohibitive. Land investors are best advised to enter livestock operations on a nonparticipating basis, that is, by renting land and facilities to a livestock operator. This, in effect, minimizes overall risk exposure and reduces or eliminates operating costs. There are, however, successful livestock share arrangements, which remain an alternative for the risk-tolerant investor who can sustain both heavy operating costs and volatile cash flow.

Vegetable Crops. These farms, selling to the fresh, canned, or packaged vegetable markets, are highly specialized in nature. Production costs are high, volume is relatively low, and intensive management is required. Although production and market risks are high, there is real potential for excellent operating returns. The San Joaquin and Imperial Valleys in California and the Rio Grande Valley and Winter Garden areas in Texas historically have attracted a large number of absentee investors in vegetable farms. These investors generally rent to a farm operator on a share basis or, if they wish to minimize risk, on a cash basis.

Field Crops. Feed grains, grasses, and cotton are typical of these farm or ranch operations. Extremely high in volume with liquid markets, these operations are typical of the Corn Belt, Plains states, and Cotton Belt. They require lower production costs and offer a more consistent return on invested capital than other types of farm and ranch operations. In the Corn Belt states, competition for land among tenant farmers has created a favorable climate for securing good cash-rent or share-crop operators.

The row crop alternative offers the lowest risk and is probably the most amenable to absentee investor ownership. The key factor is selection of a progressive and honest tenant-operator.

ATTRACTIVE FEATURES

Hedge Against Inflation

Throughout the world, land traditionally has served as an inflationary hedge. Inflationary pressure fueled tremendous gains in farm and ranch values during the mid-1970s and substantial increases in the early 1980s.

Safety of Principal

Given a stable political climate, continuing growth in world demand for food products, and continued inflationary pressure, farm- and ranchland will be an attractive investment for preservation of capital.

Current Cash Return

The absentee investor's potential for income is dictated largely by the type of lease arrangement that is negotiated with his tenant or resident-operator. The four major lease alternatives are the cash rental, the crop or livestock share, the custom arrangement, and the direct operation.

Cash-Rental Lease. Under the cash-rental lease, the landowner simply rents his property and facilities at some flat rate, usually on an annual per-acre fee. This type of lease eliminates most production risk and guarantees a steady cash flow. This lease also requires the least amount of management input by the absentee investor. Variations of this lease include rents payable in some predetermined crop or livestock quantity, regardless of production levels. Because of the limited management input required by the investor, there is a tendency to "under manage" and possibly allow the asset to deteriorate from a conservation standpoint especially if a marginal tenant is selected.

Crop or Livestock Share Agreement. Under this arrangement, the landowner accepts his share of income as a percentage of crop or livestock production. The landowner is also responsible for participating in a specified portion of production costs. A common crop-share lease in the Midwest is the 50-50 arrangement. Here, the landowner receives half of the crop production and pays for half of the seed, chemical, and fertilizer costs. Share agreements vary greatly according to crop, geographic locale, potential production levels, and community tradition. Under these leases, an owner participates in production risks, but can also benefit from increases in production or market prices. This arrangement requires considerable input from the landowner and may necessitate the retention of a professional farm manager if the owner lacks the necessary time or expertise.

Custom Arrangement. A variation of the direct operation, the custom farm contracts all its fieldwork individually with one or more custom operators. The landowner accepts all the production risk and receives all the farm or ranch receipts. Obviously, this type of arrangement requires that the owner have extensive farm management expertise or that a professional farm manager be retained.

Direct Operation. This is usually limited to a large-scale enterprise. The investor/owner owns all operating equipment and hires the labor necessary for production. Usually, a salaried resident-manager assumes operating responsibilities. As in the custom operation, the owner accepts all production risk and receives all farm or ranch income.

Intangible Benefits

The lifestyle associated with agriculture is attractive to many investors. For those with any agrarian spirit, pride of ownership has a very real impact on the value placed on a farm or ranch. Many investors also cite security as a motivating factor in pursuing an agricultural investment.

POTENTIAL RISKS

Despite impressive appreciation of farm- and ranchlands during the past quarter century, land values have at times yielded to economic pressures. During the great depression, for example, land values decreased by nearly 60 percent, and much land was sold as forced liquidations. Since 1985, land values in Texas, Oklahoma, and other parts of the Southwest have decreased by as much as 50 percent in specific areas, owing largely to the impact of lower oil prices that reduced the number of potential investors.

The investor must be aware of production risks, rapid fluctuations in commodity prices, and tenant or operator risks that exist in any agricultural enterprise. Political maneuvers, such as the Russian grain embargo of 1980, can also drastically affect farm income and, ultimately, land values.

Income Limitations

The low cash throw-off of 1 to 5 percent on farm and ranch investments is an immediate deterrent to many investors. However, farm- and ranchland has provided a safe,

FIGURE 2. Farmland Value Compared With Stocks (S & P 500 Index)

Source: U.S. Department of Agriculture, Economic Research Services

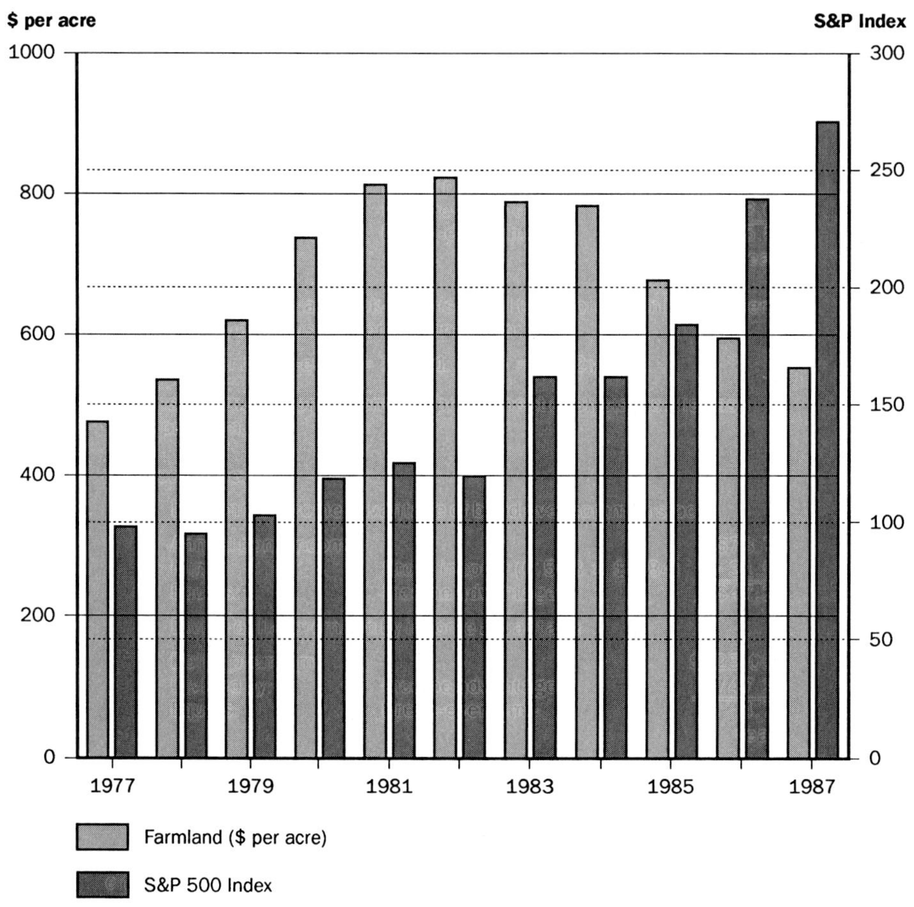

consistent, and attractive vehicle for preserving and increasing real dollar wealth. A comparison of stocks to farmland provides a good frame of reference (See Figure 2). Even though the positive trend for land over stocks was reversed in 1986 and 1987, the precipitous stock market drop in October 1987 would reestablish that trend.

Liquidity

Farm- and ranchland is not a highly liquid holding and should be considered only for long-term investment or speculation.

The propitious timing of a sale is dictated by the farm income situation, commodity prices, competing land prices, and available financing. To avoid an untimely offering, only those investors with staying power should consider including agricultural property in their portfolios. This is one of the most important factors to be considered when investing in agricultural land.

Special Risk Factors

The investor who is accustomed to the more traditional debt or equity vehicles will find several risk factors unique to agriculture. First, natural phenomena such as floods, drought, disease, and insect pests threaten agricultural production annually. Second, a pricing strategy is replaced by a marketing strategy in agriculture, and the market clearing price of commodities is determined largely by the buyer. Effective marketing of these commodities is an extremely sophisticated process, and usually determines the difference between profit and loss. Third, good management is absolutely essential. Locating the highly skilled, capable operator and farm manager is a critical factor for success in farm or ranch investments.

TAX CONSEQUENCES

Farm- and ranchland is, for the most part, very similar to other forms of real estate investments insofar as income taxes are concerned. As with an investment in an office building or an apartment complex, there are three distinct tax phases or stages in the full-cycle transaction:

1. Acquisition
2. Operation
3. Liquidation

With each phase of the cycle of farm and ranch ownership, there are, however, several tax-related aspects that are unique to involvement in agriculturally oriented enterprises. In this section, the basics of farm acquisition, operation, and liquidation are discussed briefly, and unusual tax treatments found only in agricutural land investments are presented in some detail.

Acquisition

Conflict between buyer and seller permeates the entire acquisition process. It is this conflict that comforts the Internal Revenue Service (IRS) when it reviews transactions between unrelated parties. The crux of the conflict between the buyer and seller is, of course, the allocation of value among assets involved in the transaction. The seller is interested in allocating as much of the total purchase price as possible to assets that will cause generation of neither recapture of investment tax credits nor depreciation. The farm investor is, however, interested in just the opposite. With the exception of some permanent crops (e.g., grapes, fruit, and nuts) and livestock properties, the normal ratio of depreciable assets to total investment is quite low.

Timing. As a result of the Tax Reform Act of 1986 (the 1986 Act), depreciation recapture to be included in ordinary income of the seller must be included in income in the year of sale, even though the total cash received may be less than the total amount to be recaptured. Therefore, the seller will normally want enough cash up front to at least pay the taxes due in the year of sale.

Even though the 1986 Act repealed the beneficial capital gains exclusion, the provisions that define capital assets are still intact and may be beneficial in the future. Unlike other forms of real estate investment, there are two areas in the acquisition of farm or ranch properties where, generally speaking, there is no inherent conflict between investor-buyer and seller. They are the purchase of raised production livestock and growing crops bought along with the land. Briefly stated, to the seller, the income is treated as capital gains, and the buyer receives basis in the assets purchased. Because of the lack of investor-seller conflict in these two areas, each is very closely scrutinized by the IRS.

Allocation Agreement. The preceding discussion on acquisition of farms assumes there will be an asset allocation agreement, in writing, between investor-buyer and seller noted in the sales contract. There are new sections of the Internal Revenue Code (the Code) that govern the consistency of allocations between the buyer and seller. One approach preferred by the IRS in determining allocations is to first value the land and then attribute the difference between land value and purchase price to the other assets. From an investor's point of view, however, it is usually better to first value the nonland assets and then allocate to the land the difference between other asset values and purchase price. In both cases, the allocation should be made on the basis of market values at the time of sale. In viewing the acquisition from an asset-by-asset perspective, most tangible items, other than land, traditionally associated with farms and ranches are depreciable. As with investment in other types of real estate, the depreciable lives of assets purchased depend on the class lives as determined by the Code.

OPERATION

There are basically four ways an investor can operate a farm or ranch: (1) cash-rental lease; (2) crop or livestock share agreement; (3) custom arrangement; and (4) direct operation.

Importance of material participation. From an investor's tax perspective, the key difference among all the operating alternatives listed is the classification of the activity as active or passive by the IRS. Briefly, an investor is considered a material participant in an activity if he spends over 500 hours per year involved on a regular continuous and substantial basis in the operation of the farm. If an investor is a material participant, he is considered active, and he can deduct any losses incurred against ordinary income. If an investor does not meet the material participation test, he is considered passive, and his losses may be limited.

If an investor cash-leases his farm, he is precluded from shifting income from one tax year to another. This shifting (growing a crop in one year and, if personal income tax exposure dictates, selling the crop in another year) is available to investors operating property by crop share, custom, or direct operation methods, subject to the material participation rules. Because cash rental of a farm is not the conduct of an active trade or business and is passive by definition, most of the tax advantages allowed to a farmer under the Code are not available.

Hobby Loss Rules. For tax years beginning after 1986, an activity is presumed not to be a hobby if it is profitable in three out of five consecutive tax years. In the case of breeding, training, showing, and racing of horses, this presumption arises if gross income exceeds deductions in two out of seven consecutive tax years. The IRS uses the following nine factors to determine whether a taxpayer can show that the intent has been to operate the farm or ranch at a profit:

1. Manner in which the taxpayer carries on the activity
2. Expertise of the taxpayer or his advisors
3. Time and effort expended by the taxpayer in carrying on the activity
4. Expectation that assets may appreciate in value
5. Success of the taxpayer in carrying on other similar or dissimilar activities
6. History of income or losses with respect to the activity
7. Amount of occasional profit
8. Financial status of the taxpayer
9. Elements of personal pleasure or recreation

LIQUIDATION

When selling a farm or ranch, an investor-owner bargains from the opposite side of the asset allocation table discussed earlier. Here, too, the rules of the game are very similar to the sale of other forms of real estate investment. Planning is the key to avoiding the pitfalls associated with recapture of investment tax credit and depreciation as well as land-clearing and soil- and water-conservation expenses.

The sale of land with unharvested crops involves no basic dispute between buyer and seller because their respective tax positions are not adverse, and it is therefore subject to IRS scrutiny. (See *Acquisition*, earlier in this article.) Interestingly enough, however, expenses to produce the crop must be recaptured. This is not true in the sale of other farm assets, such as breeding stock, where production expenses do not have to be recaptured. The recapture provision requires recapture in the year that crop production expenses are actually incurred and disallows deductions for items attributable to crop production.

To qualify for this special provision, the land on which the crops are grown must be held for more than one year and be used in a trade or business (precluded by cash rental). In addition,

- The seller can retain no direct or indirect right to reacquire the land on which the crop grows, except for a mortgage.
- The crop must be sold at the same time and to the same purchaser as the land.
- The unharvested crop cannot be on leased land.

Definition of "crop" includes all traditional crops, seasonal as well as permanent, and has been interpreted to include grass grown for sod. Crop is indeed broadly defined, but it is clear that something must be growing.

The sales contract must allocate portions of the sales price to land and crops in order to qualify. The allocation must be reasonable. The seller's position is that both land and crops receive capital gains treatment unless there have been land clearing or soil and water conservation expenses taken. The buyer, on the other hand, receives a basis in the crop equal to the amount allocated at the time of sale, and to minimize income taxation at the time of crop marketing seeks a high allocation of the total land transaction. Thus, the allocation of the sales price to unharvested crops is an important consideration for both buyer and seller. In light of this, the popular notion that farm sales should transpire only in dormant production cycles may not have credence.

It can be easy to let the tax benefits of a transaction cloud the decision to make an investment. There are some attractive tax reasons to invest in farmland, but the investor should not lose sight of the overall economic viability of a farm or ranch investment.

REPRESENTATIVE TYPES OF INVESTORS

The farmers' activity in the market will ultimately dictate the value of farms and ranches. In the year ending June 17, 1988, farm owners/operators accounted for roughly 64 percent of the land purchased.[4] Nonfarm investors, defined as those living outside the county in which land is purchased, account for 25 percent of land sales. Absentee investors fall into one of four general categories: the individual, the investment corporation, the limited partnership, and the foreign investor.

IMPORTANT FACTORS IN BUYING AND SELLING

A potential buyer should have professionals analyze the price, terms of agreement, and quality of a farm or ranch investment. Purchasing a quality farm or ranch is the first and most important of the three steps to a successful farm or ranch investment—buy well, operate efficiently, sell profitably. A good real estate broker, attorney, accountant, and farm consultant can prevent many unforeseen disasters. Most professional land traders use all four when buying or selling.

Selecting a Broker, Dealer or Salesperson

An agent who specializes exclusively in agricultural properties should be chosen. His credentials and reputation should be checked carefully. A good place to do this is with the Realtor's Land Institute in Chicago. This affiliate of the National Association of Realtors maintains accreditation standards and can refer members by geographic location. In addition, the American Society of Farm Managers and Rural Appraisers in Denver is an excellent place to seek professional consultation.

Commissions and Fees

Determining a sales commission is a major part of the negotiation process. The standard range is from 3 to 10 percent of the gross sales price. The seller is responsible for this fee.

An agent-consultant usually represents the buyer and typically requires 1 to 5 percent of the purchase price. He usually charges a minimum fee, which varies according to the complexity of the investment.

Judging Quality

This is the most difficult and critical factor in securing a good farm or ranch investment. Soil productivity, water quality, water and mineral rights, irrigation requirements,

---

[4] Id. at 19.

conservation factors, physical facilities, markets, transporation, and availablity of labor are but a few of the many considerations that must be thoroughly analyzed. There are many more poor farm and ranch investments than good ones. Quality should be judged by a professional consultant.

MANAGING THE INVESTMENT

The same management input that makes any type of business successful also makes a farm or ranch investment work. Planning, organizing, and controlling an agricultural operation in a professional manner is the key to a profitable farm or ranch business. The investor-owner may choose to manage the investment alone, may rely solely on the tenant or operator, or may hire a farm and ranch management firm to represent him.

Professional Management

The typical absentee investor does not have the time, interest, or expertise to manage the property efficiently. In addition, most tenant farmers are not accustomed to preparing the inspection reports, budgets, cash flow projections, year-end reports, insurance reviews, and other communications required by the absentee investor-owner. Most investors seek professional management services to represent their interests.

Quality farm and ranch management, whether by a qualified operator or an organization, should include at least the following services:

- Negotiation of leases and contracts
- Three- to five-year development plan
- Cash flow projections and production budgets
- Detailed inspection reports
- Monthly or quarterly reports
- Marketing services
- Budgeting management services
- Rent or income collection
- Ad valorem tax services
- Payment of bills
- Annual tax summary

Fees for these services vary from 6 to 12 percent of the owner's share of gross farm or ranch income.

GLOSSARY

acre—A measure of land area equivalent to 43,560 square feet.

cash-rental lease—An arrangement whereby the landowner leases property and facilities at a flat rate, usually a per-acre fee.

crop—All traditional plants grown and harvested for profit and/or subsistence, seasonal as well as permanent, including grass grown for sod.

crop or livestock share agreement—An arrangement whereby the landowner accepts a share of income as a percentage of crop or livestock production.

custom arrangement—A variation of the direct operation, whereby the custom farm contracts all its fieldwork individually with one or more custom operators.

direct operation—An arrangement whereby the investor-owner owns all operating equipment and hires labor necessary for production.

farmland—Land used for cultivation of crops or for the maintenance of livestock to produce food products; includes the land on which the farm buildings stand.

liquidity—The condition of an individual or business wherein a high percentage of the assets can be quickly converted into cash without involving a considerable loss by accepting sacrifice prices.

ranch—Grazing acreage used for the raising of livestock.

LEADING DEALERS IN AGRICULTURAL ACQUISITION SERVICES, BROKERAGE, AND MANAGEMENT

ACQUISITION CONSULTATION

Capital Agricultural Property Services, Oakbrook, Ill.

Doane's Farm Management Co., Bettendorf, Iowa

Farmers National Co., Omaha, Neb.

FARM AND RANCH BROKERAGE SERVICES

In addition, most national and regional real estate brokerage firms maintain farm and ranch specialists at local offices.

Doane/Western Company, Fresno, Cal.

Farmers National Company, Omaha, Neb.

Huber Farm Services, Memphis, Tenn.

FARM AND RANCH MANAGEMENT

There are many regional management firms in addition to these national operations. Check with the American Society of Farm Managers and Rural Appraisers in Denvers for referrals.

Agri Vest, Glastonbury, Conn.

Capital Agricultural Property Services, Inc., Oakbrook, Ill.

Doane/Western Company, Fresno, Cal.

Farmers National Co., Omaha, Neb.

First Interstate Bank of Oklahoma, Oklahoma City, Okla.

Texas American Bank, Ft. Worth, Tex.

Huber Farm Services, Memphis, Tenn.

NBC Bank-San Antonio, San Antonio, Tex.

Norwest Capital Management & Trust, Des Moines, Iowa

Plantation Services, Albany, Ga.

Wells Fargo, Sacramento, Cal.

SUGGESTED READING

PERIODICALS

Agricultural Financial Outlook. U.S. Department of Agriculture, Washington, D.C. Monthly; summarizes agricultual production and farm real estate values.

Agricultural Statistics. U.S. Department of Agriculture, Washington, D.C. Annual.

Agri Finance Magazine. Skokie, Ill. Monthly; deals with farm management problems and frequently publishes articles appropriate for farm and ranch investors.

Doane's Agricultural Report. Doane's Agricultural Services, St. Louis, Mo. Weekly; a concise newsletter with excellent reporting on farm price trends.

Farm and Land Realtor. Realtor's Land Institute, Chicago, Ill. Monthly; geared directly toward farm and ranch real estate brokers.

Farmline. U.S. Department of Agriculture, Washington, D.C. Monthly; tracks current government activities, price cost data, and farm and ranch values.

Farm Real Estate Market Developments. U.S. Department of Agriculture, Washington, D.C. Monthly; tracks farm and ranch transfers and land values.

Landowner. Professional Farmers of America, Cedar Rapids, Iowa. Biweekly; a series of short articles on farmland real estate. Geared mainly toward the Midwest, it is valuable both for buyers and sellers.

Progressive Farmer. Progressive Farmer, Inc., Birmingham, Ala. Monthly; published regionally, it offers many good tips on buying, managing, and selling agricultural land.

Successful Farming. Meredith Corporation, Des Moines, Iowa. Monthly; most appropriate for the owner/operator or farm manager, but frequently prints articles on farm and ranch acquisition and sales.

REFERENCE BOOKS

Realtor's Land Institute. *Realtor's Land Real Estate Manual*. Chicago, 1975.

Jurdt, Dwight W. *Buying or Selling Farms*. St. Louis: Doane's Agricultural Services.

U.S. Government Printing Office. *National Agricultural Lands Study*. Washington, D.C.

Warren, Gorham & Lamont. *Real Estate Review Portfolio No. 22. How to Evaluate an Investment in Agricultural Real Estate*. Boston, 1988 (updated annually).

REAL ESTATE INVESTMENT TRUSTS

John B. Nicholson

BASIC CHARACTERISTICS

Publicly held real estate investment trusts (REITs) were designed ostensibly to combine the best features of Wall Street's stock market with Main Street's realty markets by creating a liquid investment traded daily on the stock exchanges but with all the benefits of otherwise illiquid income-producing real estate.

Although REITs grew tremendously in the early 1970s and have experienced a resurgence of interest in the mid-1980s, several built-in conflicts indicate that their continued growth and development may be limited; REITs may become not much more than an interesting appurtenance to the stock market.

Passive Funnel of Funds

A REIT is designed for tax purposes to have many of the characteristics of a mutual fund that invests in stocks. Originally, it had to be a trust that was to be treated as a corporation for tax purposes, but changes now permit full use of the corporate form. Its trustees (or directors) must agree to invest passively in primarily real estate assets on behalf of the shareholders. The portfolio of realty investments—ownership in realty, in other REITs, or in mortgage loans secured directly by real estate—must conform to certain rules in order to be qualified for tax purposes as a conduit and thereby escape taxation at the trust/corporate level. (See *Qualifying Tax Rules*, later in this article.)

The portfolios of the publicly traded REITs tend to specialize. Some invest regionally, others nationally. Some own only strip shopping centers, while others deliberately seek a

John B. Nicholson is President of Berryhill Associates, a consulting firm in Washington, D.C.

mix of property types. Many specialize in creative finance, making loans that have equity kickers or other features that give the lender virtually the same position as an owner or joint venturer. Because REITs, unlike banks or savings and loans, are not subject to regulatory constraints (they do not solicit depository funds from the public), the REIT form has attracted mostly operators from real estate experience rather than from major financial institutions or other participants in the national stock markets.

Whatever the composition of the portfolio, all publicly held REITs have the following three characteristics:

1. The individual REIT investor owns a share of a real estate portfolio rather than an operating business. Although this distinction encourages investors to look to the REIT's assets and analyze them separately instead of looking on the REIT as an operating entity, in fact the management of realty has been shown to be more important than the realty itself. It also means that the operator of the REIT fund often has a reputation independent of the REIT management (such as a bank-sponsored REIT that trades on the reputation of the bank that runs it).

2. The REIT investor derives income almost exclusively from the passive ownership of realty. Capital gains (or losses) cannot be the primary source of dividends, so cashing in on inflation's effect on asset values must be done piecemeal, and the emphasis is on income generation by the various properties. Because income from trading is prohibited, a qualified REIT cannot, for example, develop a condo project and derive income by selling off the units, except in highly unusual circumstances. Thus, a REIT cannot speculatively own vacant land for the purpose of resale, but it can buy raw land on which to build income-producing improvements, and it can improve its own properties to make them more profitable.

3. Some REITs, spawned to facilitate highly creative finance, buy residuals or other kinds of mortgage-related loans. To remain qualified, they must seek only funds that are directly secured by realty, such as interest income derived by mortgage payments from a pool of home loans. (Because short-term partcipations in long-term pools often carry lower rates of interest, the REIT specializes in owning the residual difference between the higher coupon rate on the mortgages and the lower face rate to be paid on the short-term participation.) Similarly, subordinated land sale-leaseback transactions used to be REIT "meat" because of the direct relationship of the financial transaction to realty (even though the creditworthiness of the tenant is the major true security of the transaction).

REIT's Role in the Stock Market

Because REITs have existed on the stock market for nearly thirty years, they command a limited but faithful following. Real estate enjoys the reputation of being an asset mostly for antiinflationary purposes. Just as gold stocks' values fluctuate along with the price of gold, so REIT shares tend to reflect popular esteem for real estate values, even though realty owned by REITs is characterized (in terms of its ability to generate income) quite unlike home real estate values.

Wall Street tends to sell REITs to individual investors when real estate is a popular topic. Institutional investors (pension fund managers) tend to avoid REIT shares because few have enough shares outstanding to enable big blocks to be sold easily without affecting price. Although there are a few REITs of REITs, or mutual funds specializing in realty stocks (and limited partnership shares), in general the REIT sector holds down its corner of the marketplace but must await periodic investor fascination with real estate to augment its presence.

After the 1981 tax amendments changed the depreciation rules, income-producing property generated substantial paper losses that could be used to shelter earned income. REIT managers had difficulty competing with non-REIT syndicators for the better properties, because tax-shelter benefits were of marginal value to the REITs. During the mid-1980s, partnership syndicators used Wall Street salesmen to sell limited-liability partnership shares aggressively to the public, but further changes through the 1986 amendments reduced the syndicators' appeal. By drawing Wall Street back into the real estate world, the partnerships' attractiveness did revive interest tangentially in REITs. And now that publicly traded partnerships are on the wane, there is preliminary evidence that the increasing numbers of investors and Wall Street's educated realty sales force are turning their spotlights onto the REIT sector.

Types of Holdings

As a practical matter unrelated to tax qualification procedures, REITs have tended to buy or finance all forms of income-producing real estate, especially the more novel or unusual types in which unproven, or creative, finance is involved.

Bankers, insurance company investment officers, and others who evaluate standard large projects compete on price aggressively, so the REITs operators tend to see only the more challenging investment opportunities. One REIT, for example, eschews looking at the huge shopping centers but specializes in buying smaller strip shopping centers where the REIT as the new owner can have a turnaround appeal.

Apartments tend not to be favored by most REITs because of the inability to raise rents quickly enough to keep pace with rapid inflation. Also, the emotional reaction to rapidly rising rents for housing tends to concern operators of publicly traded financial vehicles. REITs cannot hold condo units for resale (that's not passive ownership) except when the condo is acquired through foreclosure, and then special rules apply.

For a while, miniwarehouses in industrial areas relied on REIT financing. In the late 1980s, health care facilities became a favorite of newly formed REITs. In general, new REITs are being sold more on the strength of their sponsor (or the REIT's role in the sponsor's business) than for just being a strong portfolio of realty holdings.

Occasionally, realty projects are so big that they can be financed by just one REIT, as was the case with Rockefeller Center. Generally speaking, major corporations can sell their real estate assets through investment banking sources at a better price than REITs are willing to pay, although one REIT got its start by owning Chrysler warehouses. The variations in REIT investment polices make REIT-to-REIT comparisons tricky except by dividend record, the workhorse of total return analysis.

Qualifying Tax Rules

REITs incur no tax liability while acting as a conduit to pass income through to their stockholders. To qualify for conduit treatment under sections 856 to 860 of the Internal Revenue Code, the REIT must declare its intention and then must fulfill several requirements concerning structure, sources of income, nature of assets, and dividend distribution. Among other obligations, the REIT must

- Pay out at least 95 percent of its taxable income to its shareholders.
- Invest more than 75 percent of its capital in real estate or real estate-related investments.
- Never have more than 30 percent of its income in any one year derived from the sale of real estate held less than four years.
- Always be a passive investor, that is, never derive gains from the sale of property held for sale. If so, the gains are taxed 100 percent. Up to seven sales can be made in any one year if the properties have been held four years or more. (There are some minor exceptions to this rule, aimed mostly at allowing the sale of assets acquired through foreclosure on property securing a mortgage loan.)
- Comply with certain organizational strictures designed to keep the REIT from being closely held; that is, there must be more than 100 shareholders, and no five or fewer of the 100 can be people owning 50 percent or more.

Origins and History

The trust form in which many REITs were created and exist today reflects the somewhat tortured history of the oldest survivors. In the late 1800s, New England legislators truncated the company-town movement by requiring that all operating (mill) corporations could own only the realty needed to do business. They were not allowed ownership of realty investments such as employees' houses. Thus, individual investors who sought to own income-producing property through professionally managed companies were forced to adopt the trust vehicle.

These trusts were deemed to be taxable like corporations, and thereby became subject to the federal corporate income tax during the 1930s. However, just before World War II, when the mutual fund lobby won its conduit-type exemption from taxation, the dozen or so REITs in business at that time set their legislative sights to gain similar tax treatment. Throughout the 1950s, the real estate lobby battled back, fearing takeover by the major companies once REITs had won their tax-favored status. Thus, in 1961, after an Eisenhower veto, the survivors won. The tax-favored treatment was limited to trusts—no corporations—and only passive investments were explicitly permitted.

Growth and Development. REITs grew slowly as instruments for owning income-producing properties. Some of the larger regional real estate brokerage houses found the sponsorship of a REIT a suitable device for unloading income-producing project listings that had not attracted the interest of more established institutional owners. However, any underwritten issue of a new REIT created substantial amounts of money to be invested all at once (not the usual way to buy deals), so managers from the realty world were reluctant to seek huge new offerings.

Two types of trust evolved that pursued radically different investment philosophies. One type invested in mortgages, the other owned real estate. The cash flow of a mortgage-lending operation provided stark contrast to the rather dowdy dividends of equity ownership, and the difference was not overlooked by Wall Street. That seven- or eight-year record difference was tailor-made for the Wall Street hot-stock specialists.

At the same time, federal rules were amended, and the regulatory agencies decided commercial bank holding companies could create advisors to REITs as a financially related activity. Thus, the stage was set for the bank-sponsored REITs to take off, sold on the reputation of the sponsor, with the history of mortgage-lending REITs to support the theory.

The investment banking community had just concluded a period of rapid growth of retail sales forces. Suddenly, with tight money, stocks were not quite attractive. New product was needed to keep active the massive sales force of account executives. The new issues of REITs graced by famous sponsors' names were launched and soon kept retail brokers busy.

An additional factor favoring the rise of REITs was that the real estate world was contracting because of tight money, and REIT money—equity dollars without a fixed rate of return required—could be committed on deals that others were shunning. Investors believed that REITs were countercyclical, although in retrospect they were really supercyclical, exacerbating the ups and downs.

Eventually, Wall Street's excessive enthusiasm resulted in equity leveraging. When new equity issues became treacherous because the numbers were catching up with the new REITs, Wall Street invented the dealer-placed commercial paper backed by bank lines of credit to the REITs. Because bankers did not have to provide reserves against standby lines of credit, the placement fees went directly to current earnings for the bankers.

By 1975, the industry had grown from \$2 billion to \$21 billion in five years. REIT managers had more money than they could invest wisely. Innovative lending techniques flowered. Incentives were based on leverage, so bankers were encouraged to lend more at virtually no cost through providing back-up lines of credit.

Decline and Stabilization. As part of the 1974 recession, the REIT bubble burst quickly when oil prices increased and fuel shortages exacerbated the short supply of asphalt. Developers were forced to terminate projects prior to completion and defaulted on their construction loans. Stock market prices plunged, making rich those clever enough to sell short extensively. REITs turned to the banks, which were urged to honor their standby lines of credit so that no investor in REIT commercial paper ever lost money by default. But the banks suddenly owned many REITs.

At least throughout the latter half of the 1970s, much of the industry's manpower was devoted to cleaning up the wiped-out REITs. Because all REIT share prices suffered, many of the smaller REITs were purchased for their hidden value in real estate owned. (See *Valuation of Assets*, later in this article.)

During the early 1980s, investors continued to be fascinated by real estate's potential value. Growth resumed, but at a much slower pace in three sectors of the REIT marketplace. First, the shake-out of the 1970s enabled some survivors to seek new financings, during a brief window of opportunity in 1985 to 1986. Second, a newer concept was heavily sold by smaller, regional investment salesmen: the deliberately finite lifetime of the REIT, with the promise to dissolve and return (presumably appreciated) asset values to the investors in seven or so years. Third, there were some conversions from limited-partnership shares to REITs. (See article on "Real Estate: Limited Partnerships," elsewhere in this volume.)

There also arose a new kind of investment that uses the REIT form as its base, but that is promoted and sold as an adjunct to mortgage banking operations. Known as collateralized mortgage obligation (CMO) REITs because they specialize in bonds, these investment vehicles were created by Wall Street as an adjunct to the mortgage banking practice of assembling a pool of home loans and then selling off participations backed by the pool. For Federal Housing Authority (FHA) insured and Veteran's Administration (VA) guaranteed home loans, the mortgage-backed security program applies the full faith and credit of the U.S. government on such securities by the Government National Mortgage Association (GNMA, or Ginnie Mae). CMOs are a form of privately backed Ginnie Maes. Some REITs were created to issue CMOs, backed by the mortgages rather than the REIT's own credit. Others were spawned to buy up the residuals of a CMO offering. The CMO bonds are usually tailored to maturity lengths sought by the large (often savings and loans) buyers, which can carry a lower rate of interest than the mortgages in the pool; thus there are often amounts of interest left over. These residuals are purchased by the CMO REIT, whose shares are then sold largely on the basis of computed yield almost as if it were a money-market instrument. Although the gross book value of these CMO REITs is substantial, because of their financing attributes they are not widely considered to be like other REITs.

A further revision of the tax laws appears likely to make more popular a new form of mortgage intermediary called the Real Estate Mortgage Investment Conduit (REMIC). REMICs are expected to take the place of CMO REITs, eventually becoming a major new weapon in Wall Street's arsenal of products tailored to satisfy the investors' desire for liquid secondary marketing of real estate, including pools of residental mortgages. (See article on "Mortgage-Backed Securities," elsewhere in this volume.)

Revised Tax Law. Partly as an outgrowth of the chaotic history of REITs, in 1976 Congress revised the REIT tax provisions to provide more flexibility and to avoid penalizing investors when standard work-out procedures were to be used. Again in 1986, further tinkerings with the REIT tax law were made by Congress, largely to ease the start-up process for new REITs.

At both times, the industry held its breath because some tax-policy reformers still question the valid purpose of tax avoidance just to give small investors access to major realty financings. And in both instances, the changes deliberately avoided opening more loopholes. The IRS and the government look over the shoulders of REIT managers not to protect investors but to try to maximize tax collection, whenever possible. Thus, to say a REIT is tax qualified is not to imply government supervision other than for revenue-generating purposes.

Types of REIT

Most REIT managers have learned to advance themselves with the few REIT analysts by selling a story about their investment objectives:

- Some REITs deliberately buy older projects and then upgrade them to create value, promoting their growth-inducing formula to Wall Street.
- Others own specialized facilities such as day care centers and then promote themselves as adjuncts to that growth sector of the economy, anticipating parallel stock price movement.
- Some specialize in fast-food structures, stressing location in case the affiliated franchise wanes.

- Some intentionally seek property in a variety of locations so as to spread out regional risks, while others specialize in only a few areas in order to obtain a regional following of stock owners.
- Some REITs are composed essentially of just one property. The former New England Patriot's stadium is one, and the Rockefeller Center property was recapitalized as a REIT by itself.

Recent changes in the REIT tax law, permitting a REIT to spread out its purchase of realty over the first two years of its existence, have induced a new set of sponsors to consider forming equity REITs. In the past, when a new REIT had to own property immediately to generate qualified income, realty-holding institutions sponsored REITs because they could then transfer assets to the REIT once it was formed. Otherwise, proposed deals to purchase properties had to be stacked up ready to close as soon as the REIT was formed, an awkward method undermining the trade practice of using the timing of the closing as one element in the deal making. Now a new REIT can be sold on the reputation of its manager without regard to specific properties, which is why most of the newer, larger REITs are being created by developers (such as Koger Properties) with a well-established reputation.

Another subset of REITs, the so-called finite life ones, have been sold to investors with the stated intent of dissolving in seven to ten years. The appeal, presumably, is that investors will capture appreciation through final distributions while obtaining income over seven to ten years. To date, however, the final chapters in the saga of the finite life REITs have not yet been written. Since most such REITs were sponsored and sold through smaller regional investment brokers, their history has been characterized by having been sold more than bought, a situation that has limited the pricing effect of the secondary markets. Once several have dissolved and final distributions have been made, the secondary market will have a track record by which to assess the current value of the newer ones.

Major foreign interests with significant funds have chosen to own American realty, and some have created their own REITs (managed by their Wall Street advisors) to do so since recent foreign-held taxation amendments do not apply to foreign holdings of REIT shares. Shares in these foreign-owned REITs are not publicly traded, however. Other privately distributed 100-shareholder REITs are also believed to exist, managed by Wall Street interests, but because of the secretive nature of their owners and managers, not much is known about them.

The recent decline in favor of publicly traded partnerships has caused several to convert to REIT status. Just how popular this conversion may become, however, is limited by the nature of the partnership agreements; many do not permit conversion without a vote of all limited-partner shareholders.

Especially in the wake of the 1974 crash, some investors have bought controlling interest in the weaker REITs and have used them as conduits to buy into other REITs. One such investor in Mississippi owns a major position in several REITs and keeps them, as he says, "on a string, like catfish, ready to [pull] up whenever a buyer happens by." REITs tend to merge together, apparently because it takes one real estate operator to successfully value another's portfolio. The most recent REIT tax law changes now permit REITs to own 100 percent subsidiaries, which is expected to facilitate inter-REIT mergers, too.

Because the complexities of sophisticated realty investment in income-producing properties are not well understood on Wall Street, REIT stocks remain potentially volatile. Every year or so, retail stockbrokers become excited about some REIT's hidden assets, and a flurry of orders takes place. More than once in the industry, the net outcome from such a flurry has been for the REIT either to liquidate or to merge out of the public securities market. Also because of the Street's lack of understanding, some REIT stock prices have languished unduly. As a result, most of the institutions that sponsored REITs in the 1970s have dumped their REIT association, and the few that are still managing REITs (Mutual of New York (MONY) Property Capital Trust, and Wells Fargo, among others) have announced plans to divest themselves of their REIT involvement.

For many years, the National Association of Real Estate Investment Trusts (NAREIT), the industry's trade voice, legitimized the distinction of three types of REIT: equity (or ownership) REITs, mortgage REITs, and hybrids. The distinction arose largely because the bank-sponsored REITs of the early 1970s mostly specialized in making construction and development (C & D) loans, and the so-called equity REITs sought to differentiate themselves from the lenders.

However, during the past two decades, the legal distinction between lending and owning has blurred substantially. Joint venturing has become the standard method of advancing funds for construction and development. Today only one or two REITs make straightforward C & D loans (without equity kicker features or other aspects that make the lender act like an owner). REIT loans are often convertible debt that, on rent-out, switch the REIT's holdings from interest-bearing to ownership.

Equity REITs. Traditionally, REITs managed by trustees intending solely to buy and own (or develop) income-producing properties were called equity REITs. They owned the equity of a project and then leveraged it with separate, nonrecourse realty-secured financing. Owning a realty project traditionally creates slow but steady income, however, so Wall Street (fascinated with quarterly earnings and upside potential) tended to overlook the equity REITs.

Many equity REITs are self-managed, sometimes through a set of complex arrangements designed to obviate the so-called independent contractor rule that used to require REITs to have a third party operate the project for the owner as a further step in the insistence on passive management. (Tax changes in 1986 alleviated that requirement.) Many of the equity REITs are regional in nature, such as Federal Realty and Washington REIT, which capitalized on the growth of the Washington, D.C., area.

Pricing equity trusts remains an enigmatic problem. Usually, stock analysts capitalize the dividend or, more precisely, the periodic distribution of the REITs. Some equity REITs choose to pay out their depreciation (characterizing a portion of their cash flow dividend as a return of equity). Later on, when mortgage repayments of capital exceed taxable income, these REITs anticipate that their ability to refinance will avoid cash flow crunches.

Mortgage REITs. Only two dozen or so REITs still make mortgage loans, reflecting widespread skepticism among investors about using the REIT to make short-term loans. The few that are still in the business generally make development loans that convert to a joint ownership at the time the project is rented up.

The REITs' unregulated capacity to make loans of unusual nature attracted traditionally highly regulated sponsors: banks and insurance companies, primarily. Today, few major lending institutions manage REITs. MONY has announced its intention to get out of the REIT business, and MassMutual still has a small REIT. But the days of a large institution, such as Equitable Life or Bank of America, sponsoring a REIT as a way to put its lending prowess on parade down Wall Street are gone, and not likely to return. The memory of Wall Street using investors' long-term equity to make short-term risky loans is not fading quickly.

Hybrid REITs. The classic formula from investment bankers who brought the public the institutionally sponsored REITs was to match the shareholders' equity with ownership of projects, to make long-term mortgage loans roughly comparable to subordinated debt, and to balance short-term C & D loans in proportion to commercial paper or other short-term REIT debt. Symmetry in the balance sheet was the goal, until the 1974 crash when short-term debt became long-term holdings almost overnight.

Today, most REITs are hybrid entities. So-called equity REITs often issue financing that culminates in ownership, and lending REITs now take kickers or other forms of quasi ownership. Thus, the distinction among the three types, while of historical interest, is more image than reality.

Valuation of Assets

Traditionally, real estate is valued by comparison (which does not work well for income-producing property since leases and their terms and conditions are the guts for knowing the true value of property use); by replacement cost (which means little in income-producing property management, except for insurance purposes); or by capitalization of income. Computing the value of a future stream of income, while logical, depends on significant assumptions: future cap rates; sales volumes, if there are percentage leases; and, not uncommonly, lease concessions that kick in only at later stages of development, a factor not often known to an outsider.

Consequently, valuation of a REIT's assets is not easily determined with specificity. Many REITs tried preparing a present-value estimate of their holdings, revealed publicly. However, the stock market valuation tended not to be influenced by the management's estimate. Security lawyers feared that valuations would encourage lawsuits if the marketplace began to see value that management allegedly was hiding from owners. Consequently, with no valid purpose served and with the threat of lawsuits pending, most REITs no longer provide present value estimates. (The process also opened up the proverbial can of worms in the appraisal process: assumptions that are dictated by management to the appraiser about future conditions not directly related to the property, such as whether an all-cash sale is to be anticipated.)

The ultimate value of a REIT's assets can be determined only if they are sold. Even then, selling assets from a company that has announced formal dissolution does not necessarily result in shareholders obtaining full value. (When the buyer knows the seller must sell for cash, the price reflects that knowledge.) The few REITs that have announced formal liquidation and sold off all assets have paid shareholders much beyond book value, but the prompt turnover by the buyers of the formerly REIT-held property at nearly double the price suggests shareholders may not have received full value. Probably for most income-producing property and especially for undeveloped land, the future intentions of the developer-owner are as much a part of the value as the real estate.

ATTRACTIVE FEATURES

The problems inherent in REITs do not negate some powerful benefits available only through the REIT investment vehicle. The REIT has demonstrated its staying power. People remain fascinated with realty investments, and the REIT is one instrument required (if tax purposes are to be met) to stick to real estate. There are several other advantages, especially when compared to other realty investments.

Liquidity

No other form of owning real estate provides the liquidity of a REIT. Direct ownership of real estate, even through other devices such as publicly traded limited-dividend partnership shares, requires specialized knowledge of the terra firma at stake. The negative side to this attribute is that Wall Street often prices REIT shares at a discount to the book value or other stated value of the realty, because investors do not know or trust the appraisals of the real estate. Most REIT shares are traded actively, but investors buy REITs for income and, hopefully, appreciation over the longer haul, so there is not much short-term movement in and out of a stock. Consequently, the REIT stocks' markets are generally thin, a potential problem for institutional portfolio managers.

Well-Defined Purpose and Yield

In contrast to publicly held real estate development companies (which can mix income from owning past projects with gains or losses from current active business transactions), REITs must only own real estate (not operate it in the sense of managing others' investments) to remain tax qualified. The total yield to investors does not depend on the investor's tax status; the benefits of owning REIT shares are its dividend and its share price/ potential. Because income-producing property is generally stable, historic trends are often a good indication of future yield, in contrast to the speculative promise of many realty offerings.

Daily Pricing

Many institutional funds require the ability to value their portfolios as of a certain day. REIT shares are the only form of concentrated realty investment that can be priced daily, without engaging the services of an appraiser. (See *Liquidity*, earlier in this article.) REIT shares are traded on the New York, American, and National Association of Security Dealers' Automated Quotation system (NASDAQ) markets.

Disclosure

The REITs are the most exposed segment of the income-producing real estate business, an industry characterized by secrecy, widely disparate notions of value, bluff and adept timing in negotiations, and confidence belied by widespread use of others' funds. Ownership of each project must be made known. To meet public disclosure requirements, lending and investment policies must become well defined and publicly stated (words that buyers or sellers can use for their own advantage in negotiating with a REIT manager). When a REIT loan goes sour and is of a magnitude to be material, it must be so declared publicly (limiting the lender's role in secretly attempting to maneuver a workout). Accounting procedures have been created solely because of the REIT experience. The role of the trustees/directors to shareholders has been clarified and expanded, through the consensus-making security commissioners' organizations, creating a somewhat higher level of requirements as compared to directors of general corporations.

POTENTIAL RISKS

Several built-in conflicts of policy have plagued REITs since their inception. Some of the following problems are characteristic of income-producing real estate in general; others arise as a result of the blending of stock market and real estate market attributes.

Valuation

Affixing a value to an income-producing project is an art; even immediately after a sale the value can change dramatically. (A project owned by weak owner unable to carry it through the next down cycle has a value different from the same project owned by a shrewd strong owner, in that it will probably be for sale sooner than later.) Book value, current value, liquidation value, and all-cash value can be different; appraisals are a function of the assumptions given. Stock market investors sometimes are understandably confused.

Quality

Top-graded income-producing real estate (and potential developments) go to personal investors or (insurance) institutions willing either to pay top dollar or to provide financial backing for the nation's biggest development companies. For many years, REITs were known in the income-producing brokerage community as the way to package and sell to the public those projects that could not be sold to institutional investors. Today, the industry has attracted leaders who relish their somewhat public role, managers who have become more established and better known in order to attract better-quality projects, operators who take pride in a reputation for turning around projects or using novel procedures to extract higher yields. Better management is resulting in better-quality projects in REIT portfolios.

Risky Loans

Lending short-term construction money is the riskiest business known to banking; the REIT industry grew in the early 1970s primarily by making C&D loans while selling shares to the public that were backed by real estate's reputation for solidity (often using the old adage that employees cannot steal the inventory of land). Today, few REITs lend for construction or development; those that do usually act as partners in a joint venture, so that the lender knows as much as the borrower.

Asset Play

The benefit of a REIT is a dividend untaxed at the corporate level, when 95 percent of all income is paid out to shareholders. Yet this income-generating vehicle is often sold on Wall Street to satisfy investors' desire for a real estate hedge against inflation, a so-called asset play.

Long-Term View

Investment in real estate is usually for the long haul; rents and returns are inched up as tenants become accustomed to their overhead costs. Wall Street lives quarter by quarter, seeking hot prospects for quick price movements. The conflict between long- and short-term views is always a source of tension between companies and customers' men on the Street; for followers of REIT stocks, that tension often turns into somnolence.

Goldfish Bowl

Striking a lucrative real estate deal is intensely private and personal, yet REITs must operate in the goldfish-bowl atmosphere of full disclosure of the securities laws.

Analysts

After the 1974 downturn, many security analysts stopped following REITs or decided to violate the wall between being analysts with no stake in the outcome of advice and becoming investment bankers or managing portfolios of money. Some analysts also sought ownership positions for control purposes, resulting in a scarcity of pure analysts advising the public. The moderate upswing during the mid-1980s restored some interest, but generally the number of analysts remains few, limiting the stock market following.

TAX CONSEQUENCES

There are no tax advantages to owning REIT shares. Only the REIT escapes taxation, if qualified, and no tax benefits (such as artificial losses) flow through to REIT shareowners. Presumably, because REITs must pay out 95 percent of income to qualify for special tax status, investors get a higher-than-usual dividend. This benefit is also widely regarded as attractive to tax-exempt investors such as pension funds.

Some REITs have chosen to characterize part of their dividend as a return of capital (when depreciation expense exceeds repayment of principal on mortgages). That portion of the dividend would be tax-free, of course, as well as reducing the basis of the stock's value in determining future gain on sale of the stock. However, because of recent changes in depreciation rules, few REITs are structured to maximize return-of-capital dividends.

Recent technical changes in the REIT taxation law have removed the potential for the REIT to lose its tax-qualified status and thereby be forced to recharacterize the dividends paid. For example, if gains from a property sold are subsequently determined to have been from property held for resale because the REIT acted as a dealer, the new law provides for a 100 percent tax on such gains rather than disqualifying all dividends paid by the REIT for that period.

Sometimes REITs pass along proceeds from sale of property to shareholders, thereby characterizing a portion of the dividend paid as a capital gain; if not, the REIT must pay capital gains tax on profits retained. Many REIT trustees believe the capital gains characterization only causes investor headaches (unless it is a significant amount). Since sales are usually unplanned or nonrecurring events, dividends partially treated as capital gains are also regarded as unusual.

REPRESENTATIVE TYPES OF INVESTORS

Having ridden out several shake-outs and enjoyed several renaissances, the REIT industry seems certain to remain a viable segment of the stock market, at least as long as the U.S.Treasury Department is willing to condone its tax-exempt status as a social benefit to the small stockholders who seek to share in the benefits of large, professionally managed real estate financings.

As the real estate businesses consolidate and grow larger, the ability to tap Wall Street for funds becomes increasingly important, and the REIT is the best vehicle to date, spawned by the imaginative salesmen in the financial centers. Among personal investors, the desire to own real estate is substantial, as proven by the explosive growth of limited partnership units in the 1980s. Salesmen still look to the REIT as one way to meet that investor desire.

Institutional ownership of REIT shares has been documented to be substantial (REITs must survey shareholders periodically, to be able to assess the REIT ownership tests), but most pension fund managers have expressed concerns about REIT holdings because the stock market tends not to value REIT holdings successfully, that is, as bullishly as realty operators believe, and most REITs do not have enough shares being actively traded to enable the large institutional holder to get out of a position without affecting price.

Instead of being used by financial intermediaries (such as banks, life insurance companies, and others) as a different kind of fund to be managed, increasingly the REIT is being positioned alongside other intermediaries as a source of funds for the developers and owners of major realty projects, one that is able to be managed by the users of the funds themselves. The new REIT law changes let REIT managers act more like developers, and therefore developers can act more like REIT managers.

Localized equity REITs run by real estate professionals who are captivated by managing a publicly held company, however, remain the backbone of the industry. Trained by the investment bankers who bring REITs public to think in terms of size large enough to enable a successful secondary market, the REIT managers recognize that too large an inventory of income-producing (management-intensive) projects invites trouble, so there is a natural tension between portfolios that are too big to manage and those that are too small to service investors' needs. Such tension can be expected to limit the size of growth of individual REITs, which means the industry's expansion can be expected reasonably to come mostly from new REITs entering the scene.

As long as the prime properties continue to be developed and sold to life insurance companies, or savings and commercial banks that specialize in real estate, only the second- and third-level properties will be available for REITs. Forced to be marginal (but not insignificant) players in the top-grade commercial real estate markets, REITs will continue to have their following but cannot be expected to reclaim Wall Street's attention as they did when they were so much in favor in the early 1970s.

IMPORTANT FACTORS IN BUYING AND SELLING

What to Look for in a REIT

NAREIT formerly published a brochure entitled *What to Look for in a REIT*, which was extremely circumspect in its text. (NAREIT is not a registered investment advisor and, like most trade associations, cannot be expected to favor one member over another.) Although it is no longer published, the NAREIT brochure described REITs with investment potential as having the following:

> *An intention to pass through earnings.* Trusts or corporations that intend to meet the REIT qualification standards established in the Internal Revenue Code generally state that intention in the annual report, prospectus and Securities and Exchange Commission (SEC) filings.

A term of existence. Some REITs are self-liquidating, or of a specified term; others are intended to exist indefinitely. Either case is generally specified in the annual report and prospectus.

Experienced real estate management. Most REIT financial reports, proxies, prospectuses, and SEC filings carry the names and credentials of executive and advisory officers and trustees.

An investment orientation. The real estate investment types in which a REIT will concentrate are generally specified in some form in the prospectus. Changes in investment orientation are usually described in the annual or other financial reports.

Actual real estate investments. The types and locations of a REIT's investment holdings are usually included in the annual report and SEC filings.

Using REIT Analysts

The REIT industry has not been of sufficient magnitude to attract much academic attention. Some studies have indicated that REIT share prices are less volatile than the market in general, but no one has yet tackled the issue of why REITs almost always trade at a discount to book, for example.

Partly reflecting the renaissance of interest in REITs during the mid-1980s, several individuals follow the industry closely:

Kenneth Campbell, of Audit Investments (Montvale, N.J.), has followed REITs ever since his days as editor of *House & Home* magazine in the 1960s. A personal advisor and money manager, as well as editor of his newsletter, Campbell and his advisory firm follow other realty-oriented securities.

Burl East and Robert Frank, at Alex, Brown & Sons, Baltimore, Maryland, are some of the closest followers of REITs, including several that the firm helped bring to market. Frank advocates the regional REIT because management can stay on top of its investments; he publicly asserts that no REIT should begin with less than $100 million capitalization if a secondary market is to be achieved.

Thomas J. Kearns, of Merrill-Lynch in New York City, has followed REITs since the heyday of the 1970s and is widely regarded as a dean of REIT specialists on Wall Street. Within the firm, he and Jim Donohue give corporate finance advice while Rita Dominguez handles retail advisories.

Bruce Garrison, name partner in the Houston, Texas, investment banking firm of Lovett Mitchell Webb & Garrison, began as a REIT analyst at Alex, Brown before going to Texas, first with Underwood, Neuhaus and now his own firm.

Michael Oliver, formerly of Alex, Brown, is the senior REIT expert for PRA Securities Advisors, San Francisco, managing funds for institutional investors in publicly traded real estate securities.

Jon A. Fosheim, Green Street Financial, Newport Beach, California, analyzes REITs on contract to institutional investors and eschews money management or corporate finance activities.

Anne Mengden, Cohen & Steers Capital Management, New York City, follows REITs for their mutual funds specializing in real estate.

NAREIT is especially anxious to maintain a critical mass of individuals who follow the industry closely, believing that only with numerous opinions focused on the various REITs can somewhat accurate pricing in the secondary market take place. Its research director maintains an up-to-date listing of the money managers, investment bankers, and analysts.

GLOSSARY

advisor—Pursuant to a one-year renewable contract, a person or company that provides investment analysis, management functions, and other services for a REIT. Until recently, the separate advisor was one way to help demonstrate that the REIT was a passive (rather than an active, self-managed entity) for tax purposes.

beneficial owner—Shareholder (not nominee); the person who ultimately benefits from ownership of shares or other securities; an important concept for REITs in determining ownership to meet tax law requirements.

collateralized mortgage obligation—(CMO) A bondlike offering backed by a pool of mortgages, with offerings usually of different maturity dates, stated interest rates, and prepayment clauses that allow returns of principal (when a mortgage is prepaid, for example) to flow through directly to the offering holder (investor).

declaration of trust—A document establishing the legal existence of a REIT organized as a business trust; analogous to the charter of a corporation.

equity—The difference between the current market value of a property and the liens or mortgages on it; also, the value of what shareholders own in a company, usually measured by paid-in-capital and undistributed income. When applied to REITs, the name connotes property ownership rather than making loans secured by real property.

fiscal year—For companies formed after 1976 that seek REIT tax treatment, the fiscal year must end on December 31.

indenture—Deed of trust, the legal document setting forth conditions of issuance of a bond offering; often a bank's trust department acts as indenture trustee to represent the interests of owners of a publicly offered issue.

land purchase-leaseback—Now a common transaction in which the land under improvement is simultaneously sold and leased back by the owner of the improvements. The owner thereby retains (taxable) control of all depreciable interests, usually having financed them by a first mortgage, to which the land lease is subordinated. Early REITs specialized in the transactions until they became sufficiently commonplace to become highly competitively priced.

passivity—The state of owning for the purpose of investment (not holding for resale, i.e., as a trader); passivity is implicit in several of the REIT tax requirements.

personal property—Any property not real estate, such as furniture, fixtures, and equipment. REITs investing in hotels or medical facilities must be especially careful to separate income from personalty as from realty; for example, dining rooms are not qualified for REIT tax purposes. The so-called candy machine problems frustrate realty operators while fascinating tax lawyers.

qualified assets—Realty, not personalty (see above). The REIT tax rules require that in any one year a REIT must have 75 percent of its assets invested in realty (except for certain start-up provisions). A partially qualifed asset is passive but not realty, so its income meets the tax rule that 90 percent of a REIT's income must come from passive investments.

secured debt—For REITs, senior mortgage debt secured by specific properties. In case of default on the nonrecourse mortgage, the lender may take property but not pursue other assets for satisfication.

shares of beneficial interest—Analogous to common stock of a corporation, shares of the REIT that is organized as a business trust can be publicly traded.

SUGGESTED READING

PERIODICALS

Real Estate Law Report (newsletter); Warren, Gorham & Lamont, Boston.

Real Estate Review (quarterly); Warren, Gorham & Lamont, Boston.

Realty Stock Digest (statistical), Audit Investments, Inc., Montvale, N.J.

Realty Stock Review (advisory), Audit Investments, Inc., Montvale, N.J.

REIT Line (statistical monthly); National Association of REITs, Washington, D.C.

REIT Report (quarterly newsletter); National Association of REITs, Washington, D.C.

RECENT ARTICLES

Bary, Andrew. "CMO Residuals: A New and Risky Breed of REIT," *Barron's*, Aug. 22, 1988.

Reid, Jeanne L., and Willis, Clint. "No Sweat Ways to Make Money in Property," *Money* (79–82), June 1988.

Sing, Bill. "REITs Offer Investors Entree to Real Estate," *Los Angeles Times*, May 7, 1988.

Thompson, Terri. "A Growing Trust in Real Estate," *U.S. News & World Report*, May 9, 1988, p. 83.

Vinocur, Barry. "REITs Aren't Likely to Keep Up Their Early Pace," *Barron's*, May 16, 1988, p. 102.

REFERENCE BOOKS

Campbell, Kenneth D. *Real Estate Trusts: America's Newest Billionaires*. New York: Audit Investments, 1971.

Derenthal, Paul J. *Real Estate Investment Trust, Formation and Initial Public Offerings*. New York: Sorg Printing Company, 1988.

Jarchow, Stephen P. *Real Estate Investment Trusts; Tax, Securities and Business Aspects*. New York: John Wiley & Sons, 1988.

National Association of Real Estate Investment Trusts, Inc. *REIT Fact Book*. Washington, D.C., 1988. Annual update.

Practicing Law Institute. *Real Estate Securities: Public and Private Course Handbook* (Real Estate Law and Practice Course Handbook Series). New York, 1986.

REAL ESTATE LIMITED PARTNERSHIPS

Stephen E. Roulac
Katherine A. Foulser

Over the past fifteen years, the limited partnership, or syndication, has widened the availability of real estate investment to a broad range of investors. Once exclusively the province of the wealthy and financially sophisticated, real estate has emerged as a viable alternative investment for anyone with a few thousand dollars to invest.

Prior to the 1970s, the real estate business lacked a sustained capital market, and investors lacked participation options comparable to those available in the corporate securities markets. Real estate syndication provides both.

BASIC CHARACTERISTICS

Syndication is essentially a pooling of resources, both financial and managerial. Typically organized as a limited partnership, the syndication combines the financial resources of many individual investors with the managerial expertise of a professional real estate organization. The individuals, known as limited partners, contribute capital; as with a common stock investment, they have little say in the management of the entity, and their liability for its actions is limited to the amount of the investment.

In contrast, the general partner, as the syndicator of the investment is known, makes only a nominal capital investment, but assumes responsibility for the operations of the

Stephen E. Roulac is Partner in Charge of the Roulac Real Estate Consulting Group of Deloitte Haskins & Sells, with offices in New York, Los Angeles, and San Francisco. The author of numerous books and articles, he is the editor of Roulac's Strategic Real Estate *newsletter and is a frequent lecturer on real estate topics. Katherine A. Foulser is a Manager with the New York office of the Roulac Real Estate Consulting Group of Deloitte Haskins & Sells.*

partnership, including investing the partnership funds, managing the real estate owned by the partnership, and finally selling the real estate and distributing the proceeds according to the terms of the partnership agreement. For such services, the general partner may receive certain fees and a share in the cash flow and capital proceeds of the investments.

One of the primary distinctions among real estate limited partnerships is that between public and private offerings. Private partnerships are exempt from registration with the Securities and Exchange Commission (SEC) by virtue of their being small in terms of either total capitalization or number of investors, excluding those accredited investors who are deemed sufficiently wealthy to be able to withstand total loss of the investment. Partnerships marketed exclusively intrastate are also exempt from SEC registration.

Because they are typically marketed to accredited investors, private partnerships tend to be somewhat more speculative in nature, and they may derive a higher proportion of their total returns from tax benefits than from current cash distributions. The real estate investments of private partnerships are typically specified in the offering documents. In contrast, the time-consuming registration process makes it difficult for public partnerships to control the real estate prior to the offering; hence, most public offerings are blind pool, acquiring real estate only after funds are raised.

The limited partnership concept is not new. In fact, more than $10 billion of mortgage bonds were sold in the 1920s, and a significant amount of real estate limited partnership activity took place in New York State in the 1950s. Its emergence, however, through the 1970s and 1980s represents the third wave of syndication activity, one that has become an integral part of real estate finance.

ATTRACTIVE FEATURES

Real estate limited partnership does provide investors with an attractive alternative investment. Among the reasons real estate securities are attractive are the following:

1. *Favorable real rates of return.* Real estate provides an effective inflation hedge and also has been shown to provide returns competitive to other forms of investment during periods of low inflation.

2. *Volatility of corporate securities values.* The stock market crash of October 1987, during which one third of the value of corporate securities was lost in a day, caused many investors to seek investments less subject to the whims of Wall Street.

3. *Lure of an inefficient market.* Unlike commodities for which the markets are homogeneous, real estate investments can vary substantially from one market to the next. Although increasingly sophisticated means are needed to evaluate them, there are always good real estate investments to be found, providing opportunities for those who can find and take advantage of them.

4. *Diversification.* The benefits of diversification in providing superior risk-adjusted returns are well recognized by the modern portfolio manager.

5. *Fundamental soundness of a usable asset.* Because of its uses by both households and businesses for space, location, and production, real estate always will offer investment opportunities. This usable quality distinguishes real estate from stocks, bonds, and other investments whose value depends to a large extent on such

financial indicators as interest rate fluctuations and general investor confidence in the stock market.

6. *Influence of foreign investors.* The strong value of American real estate is expected to be reinforced by foreign investors, for whom it represents a stable, high-yield investment that can be purchased at a bargain relative to similar quality real estate overseas.

7. *Favorable tax status.* Despite the recent tax reform, which eliminated some tax shelters, real estate still enjoys a favorable tax status compared to investment alternatives. Limited partnerships and investment trusts, the most common forms of real estate investment ownership, are still exempt from the double taxation of corporate securities.

During the early 1980s, when syndications attracted new sources of money (particularly tax-exempt Individual Retirement Account (IRA)/Keogh funds and pension dollars), new participants were encouraged to enter the market, making real estate investments available through most financial planning and securities firms. In response to the strong investor appeal of the real estate syndication concept, there has been a veritable explosion over the past decade in the diversity of available investment opportunities.

From the investor's standpoint, factors favoring investment in real estate syndication interests over direct ownership of real estate include the following:

- *Professional management.* Investment in a real estate security buys not only a share in the real estate but also the services of a professional real estate organization to provide property and portfolio management.
- *Superior investment selection.* The larger amount of capital available when individuals pool their investment resources through a syndication removes the barriers to entry caused by high price tags for investment-grade real estate.
- *Limited liability.* For passive investors, individual liability is limited to the amount of their investment.
- *Diversification.* Pooled resources create the opportunity for portfolio diversification even with a limited investment amount.
- *Prepackaged investment.* Investors are saved the substantial time required to put together all the elements of a successful real estate investment.
- *Flexible investment size.* Small investment unit sizes enable investors to have a high degree of control over their portfolio allocation decisions.
- *Staying power.* Pooled investments provide deeper pockets for investors to weather temporary downturns in investment performance.
- *Disclosure requirements.* Securities regulations require that substantial information be provided to potential investors. This reduces the risk of poor investment returns.
- *Due diligence.* Where initiated by the syndication sponsor or securities broker, due diligence provides the investor with additional security in the form of an independent opinion about the fairness of the investment structure and the likelihood that investment objectives will be met.

A compelling factor in the growth of the real estate limited partnership business has been its outstanding investment performance. Public partnerships that had sold their properties by 1984 returned an average 14.3 percent compounded annually to investors in the 50 percent tax bracket. The earliest of these programs was begun in December 1970, and the latest, in May 1980. Stocks, bonds, and U.S. Treasury bills averaged 9.0 percent, 9.9 percent, and 7.9 percent, respectively, from 1971 to 1984. With inflation averaging 7.3 percent, real estate provided a superior inflation hedge.

Although inflation is no longer as much a source of concern as it was a decade ago, real estate may continue to provide superior real (inflation-adjusted) rates of return. From 1960 to 1970, when inflation was relatively stable and averaged about 3 percent, real estate provided favorable rates of return in comparison with other asset categories.

POTENTIAL RISKS

As with any investment, real estate limited partnership carries certain risks. Generally, real estate investments are reasonably insulated from inflationary and interest rate risks, but are subject to risks involving declines in property values, lack of continuity in management, and illiquidity.

Real estate investment risk is the risk that properties purchased by the partnership will be worth less than their acquisition price. Most investment managers require appraisals prior to acquisition, although the quality of these may vary. The best indicator of real estate investment risk is the sponsor's track record in achieving appreciation on their prior real estate investments.

An often unconsidered element of real estate investment risk is the risk that the sponsor will be unable to invest in properties that meet the objectives of the partnership within a reasonable time frame, leaving investors with the returns from the money market or similar accounts in which funds are temporarily invested. Such risk is most prevalent in blind pool funds where capital is invested prior to identification of specific real estate investment opportunities. The risk increases with the size of the fund unless the sponsoring organization is large enough to handle the volume of investment capital.

Development and leasing risks for properties that are not yet built or fully leased may affect both cash flow and property value. The risk that these activities may not be completed in a timely manner, or at all, depends on the overall health of the market, the specific demand for the unique features of the property, and the capabilities and financial health of the sponsoring organization.

Cash flow risk is the risk that cash flow from real estate operations will decline or fail to achieve the levels anticipated by investors. Among the most prevalent causes for disappointing cash flow are overly optimistic assumptions regarding the leasing of currently vacant space, underestimation of expenses, especially capital expenses required to cure existing property deficiencies, and declines in market rental rates owing to overbuilding and/or economic declines in the market where the property is located. Despite recent trends in guarantees provided by the sponsors, most real estate investments, with the exception of mortgage partnerships, should not be counted on for stable cash flows. A portfolio diversified by property type and geographic area is less subject to such risks than one that is not diversified.

Inflationary risk is the risk that cash flow will decline because of inflationary increases in property expenses. With the ability to raise rents in response to expense increases, real estate generally provides a reasonable hedge against inflation risk and has historically provided reasonable real rates of return. Mortgage partnerships or partnerships that own properties with long-term fixed-rate leases may still be susceptible.

Interest rate risk is the risk that returns from the partnership, while meeting expectations in terms of a nominal rate of return, will seem inadequate because of an increase in current interest rates. The ability to raise rents makes real estate investments less susceptible to interest rate risk than most other forms of investment. Even partnerships that invest in mortgages typically structure their investments with either adjustable rate loans or some participation in property cash flow or appreciation to provide a hedge against rising interest rates.

Liquidity risk is the risk that investors may not be able to sell their investment at their own discretion to meet changing personal financial circumstances. Limited partnership investments are generally not to be considered liquid investments. Although certain sponsors will assist investors in selling partnership units on a limited basis, and many are traded on the secondary market, public partnerships often trade at a steep discount to value. REITs are better investments for those who prize liquidity or anticipate any change in financial circumstances.

Organizational risk is the risk that the sponsoring organization, because of financial or other difficulties, will no longer be able to manage the investments properly. When investing in a management-intensive asset, such as real estate, gauging the overall financial health of the general partner and the extent of and risk from its obligations to other partnerships or entities is critical.

In the face of soft markets and the resultant declining investment volumes, syndicators are using a variety of structural devices to try to mitigate the risks of real estate investment. Many recent public programs that have been successful in attracting investor capital provide guarantees of cash flow or minimum appreciation level. Obviously, the financial health of the guarantor is an important consideration in judging the value of any guarantee.

Preferred returns have long been used to ensure investors of the general partner's financial incentives to provide the limited partners with a reasonable rate of return. More recently, some syndicators have taken out insurance on the lease payments that provide cash flow. Investors may judge the cost of such insurance, typically 5 to 6 percent of funds raised, to be too high.

Clearly, risks should be commensurate with potential returns. Investors should be aware of the investment objectives of a fund before they invest, and evaluate the proposed investment policies in light of both the risks and potential returns of the investment.

Gauging the ongoing performance of real estate partnerships is difficult because a disproportionate share of total returns comes from appreciation in the latter years of the investment. Returns in early years may be low or even negative, as the partnership invests in property improvements and as organization and investment fees are paid. As fees are absorbed and if properties appreciate, returns improve. Thus, even partnerships with negative returns in early years may provide good returns over the life of the investment.

TAX CONSEQUENCES

Tax reform has been a major factor in a declining investor interest in real estate syndications. Syndication activity peaked in 1985, with nearly \$20 billion raised. In 1988, investors committed \$8.7 billion to real estate syndications, including public and private real estate limited partnerships and real estate investment trusts (REITs).

Private partnerships, which raised only $1.5 billion in 1988 versus an estimated $10 billion in 1984, have been particularly affected by the elimination of certain tax benefits. Public partnerships, which have raised an average of $6 billion, and REITs, raising $4 billion annually since 1985, have been less affected by changing tax law provisions, but have suffered volume declines because of soft real estate markets and investor wariness in the wake of the October 1987 stock market crash.

Although interest in real estate securities investment is unlikely to return soon to the levels seen during the pre-tax-reform days of the mid-1980s, there can be little doubt that it will continue. In a sense, the 1980s can be seen as an aberration, a time when liberal tax benefits and other investment incentives encouraged capital commitment to real estate without regard to the fundamental supply of and demand for office, hotel, residential, industrial, and retail space in the nation's real estate markets. Tax reform essentially reestablished the linkage between the developer's need for capital and the investor's willingness to commit capital.

Real estate remains a tax-advantaged investment, but most real estate investments rely on good property economics, drawing only a fraction of their returns from tax benefits. For real estate limited partnerships that had sold their properties by 1983, when tax benefits were relatively high, only 9 percent of the returns were due to tax savings. The majority were due to cash flow (24 percent) and property appreciation (67 percent).

In earlier, more liberal tax environments, losses from real estate investment could be used to offset taxable income from other sources. Thus, an investor who earned $100,000 from employment could deduct from this amount any investment losses (including, for example, a pro rata share of the excess of investment property expenses over property income) before calculating tax payments. In the days when accelerated depreciation artificially inflated expenses, tax losses were common in spite of good economic performance of the real estate assets.

The current tax law makes a distinction between passive and portfolio income. Losses from passive investments, primarily those unrelated to employment or direct business ownership, may be used only to offset income earned from other passive investments. Thus, the investor with $100,000 of employment-related income and passive real estate investments which generated $10,000 in tax losses and $2,500 in income can offset only the $2,500 in passive investment income.

For those with existing investments at the time the new tax laws went into effect, there is a phase in of the passive loss provisions such that in 1989, 20 percent of passive losses may be used to offset other income; in 1990, the percentage will decline to 10 percent, with none allowed in 1991 and thereafter.

Depreciation schedules have been lengthened and simplified under the most recent tax laws to 27.5 years for residential properties and 31.5 years for commercial properties, both straight line. The prior law allowed considerably faster depreciation (19 years), with the double declining balance method allowed for residential or commercial properties. The result is to decrease the depreciation expense allowed over, for example, the first five years of the investment by a factor of approximately 60 percent.

The elimination of installment plan provisions that had allowed individuals to defer paying some capital gains taxes discourages individuals from selling properties. Especially in states with high capital gains tax rates, such as New York and California, this has given new impetus to participating mortgage deals.

Tax credits for rehabilitation of historic properties are still available, but reduced from 25 percent to approximately 13 percent of qualified expenditures. The investment tax credit has been repealed.

REPRESENTATIVE TYPES OF INVESTORS

The variety of real estate investment programs available make it impossible to define the typical real estate investor. Investor suitability is the paramount consideration in choosing a real estate investment. Choices range from those suitable for relatively conservative IRAs to those designed more for wealthy individuals in need of tax deductions. Changes in the tax laws have eliminated the so-called deep shelter investments for high tax bracket individuals, narrowing the range somewhat; at the same time, syndicators continue to be creative in their design of new investment products to appeal to other market segments.

The return objectives of different investors depend primarily on the tradeoffs each investor is willing to make between risk and reward. Other considerations include liquidity needs, the ability to make use of tax benefits, and the typical time frame for investment returns. All these factors combine to determine the appropriateness of an investment for a particular investor.

The three primary elements of return from real estate investments are cash flow, appreciation, and tax benefits. Different types of investments provide some or each of these to varying degrees.

For example, a land development partnership, which invests in undeveloped land that it plans and rezones for future development without making any physical improvements, receives its benefits almost exclusively from appreciation. Although returns can be extraordinary and are typically achieved in a relatively short time, investors also face substantial risks that the property may not be developable to a higher economic use or that the planning and political processes required to improve its value may become protracted. Such an investment may appeal to young investors who primarily desire capital appreciation, have a long investment time horizon, can tolerate relatively high risk, have little need for cash distributions, and may not be in tax brackets that would make full use of tax benefits.

A partnership involved in the development or rehabilitation of real property receives its benefits from a combination of appreciation and tax advantages. The risk profile is high, and investors who cannot make use of the tax advantages may find the risk outweighs the benefits. Relatively well-off individuals in their prime income-producing years may be most attracted to such investments because they primarily desire capital appreciation, have a relatively long investment horizon, have sufficient income to tolerate some degree of risk and eliminate the need for cash distributions, and can make maximal use of tax benefits.

The more typical buy-and-hold partnership, which invests in existing, fully developed real estate, benefits from a combination of cash flow, appreciation, and tax advantages, which may vary in their importance and thus in their investor appeal, depending on the amount of leverage and numerous other factors.

Mortgage partnerships rely primarily on cash flow benefits, with some appreciation possible where equity kickers and participation structures are employed. IRA and Keogh funds—which focus on a combination of capital appreciation and control of downside risk, are not subject to income tax, and have low liquidity requirements—have become significant investors in such funds since their establishment in the mid-1980s.

Generally, publicly traded REITs are more suitable than partnership investments for investors requiring liquidity and desiring to meet a minimum return requirement, although such individuals may desire to invest in real estate partnerships as one element of their portfolio.

CHOOSING A REAL ESTATE SYNDICATION

One of the primary considerations in choosing a real estate syndication is the investor's preference for current versus future returns. Much like the choice between a high coupon and zero coupon bond, real estate partnerships may be structured to emphasize returns from current cash flow or from property appreciation, or a combination of the two. The investor's age and financial position will determine the appropriate emphasis.

The following should be considered in choosing real estate syndication programs.

Debt versus equity position. Partnerships may invest in mortgages or buy properties. Mortgage funds typically emphasize current cash flow, although they may also share in appreciation on the sale of underlying properties.

Property life cycle. Fully leased properties generally provide current cash flow and a relatively low degree of risk. Properties that are yet to be leased are close to providing cash flow, although there is risk that the leasing may not be completed on time and at the expected rates. Properties under development are the most risky, but have the potential to provide outstanding overall returns. In any case, the prospective gains to a partnership must be weighed carefully against development and leasing risks.

Specified versus unspecified properties. The majority of the public, SEC-registered programs first raise investor funds and then seek to buy properties, whereas the property for a privately placed deal is most often identified before the syndicator seeks investor capital for the acquisition.

Open- or closed-end fund. A closed-end fund provides that once the properties are sold, the proceeds of sale will be distributed to investors and the venture terminated, whereas the open-end fund provides that the proceeds from sale may be reinvested in additional properties.

Legal structure. Most real estate syndications are organized as limited partnerships, although the REIT is also utilized. A REIT may be publicly traded while still maintaining favorable tax status, although certain restrictions regarding distributions and property transactions impair its flexibility. REITs tend to be oriented more toward cash flow than appreciation because of the requirement that they distribute 95 percent of their income every year. Master limited partnerships, which combine the flexibility of a partnership with the liquidity of a REIT, were popular until tax law changes made them taxable as corporations.

Portfolio diversification. Funds may be invested in a single or multiple properties. In the case of a multiple property fund, the portfolio may be diversified in terms of property type, geographic area, and property size or it may be concentrated on a particular real estate attribute.

In addition to these general, structural differences, each real estate investment is unique because of its location and market. The unique nature of each property is both the beauty and the difficulty of real estate investment. On the one hand, it provides constant opportunity for those who are willing, and have the resources, to investigate potential investments. On the other hand, increasingly sophisticated means are needed to evaluate markets.

Choosing a real estate investment means choosing a syndicator, a professional who will provide the real estate expertise for the venture. The sponsor of a limited partnership syndication performs numerous entrepreneurial and management functions, bringing together the many elements necessary to create and manage a real estate investment program. The sponsor designs and structures the investment program, coordinating the tax and legal advisors and ensuring regulatory compliance; acquires, manages, and eventually sells the real estate; manages the investment portfolio and maintains investor relations; and ultimately disposes of the investment proceeds and dissolves the venture.

For these services, the sponsor typically receives compensation in a variety of forms. For each dollar invested in a real estate program, typically eight cents are paid for securities underwriting commissions and another two cents for expenses of organizing the partnership. Acquisitions fees and other expenses may be paid to the sponsor or to the seller, although the trend recently has been to defer the acquisitions fees pending establishment of cash flow to the investors, or even until sale of the properties.

Over the life of the investment, the sponsor may collect fees for managing the properties (perhaps 5 percent of gross rents) as well as administering the business of the partnership (typically a percentage of partnership revenues). It is not unusual for the sponsor to share in operating cash flow. On sale of the property, the sponsor is typically paid a fee for selling the property plus a share in the appreciated value.

Investors should investigate a syndicator's track record, particularly the track record of the individuals, not just of the corporate name, and judge the following:

- Ability to identify appropriate markets for property acquisitions, in line with established investment policy
- Effectiveness in analyzing and negotiating acquisitions
- Property management capabilities to preserve and create values
- Internal financial controls
- Sense of market timing for property dispositions
- Management capability to coordinate the syndication process and oversee the organization

The top ten sponsors of publicly registered real estate limited partnerships, listed in Table 1, have each raised at least $1 billion in partnership capital. With the exception of Johnstown/Consolidated Capital, which sold a controlling interest to the Southmark Corporation of Dallas in early 1988, all continue to actively raise money for real estate programs.

The top ten money raisers in identified private limited partnerships for 1988 are listed in Table 2. Other significant players include VMS Realty, Inc., of Chicago, Lepercq Capital Partners & Co., Inc., of New York, and First Equities Corporation of Atlanta.

Syndication makes it possible for all investors to participate in the real estate investment market. As the industry evolves, new products continue to be offered to meet the needs of every portfolio.

TABLE 1. Top 1988 Money Raisers in Public Real Estate Limited Partnerships

Rank	Firm/Headquarters	Capital Raised in 1988 (in millions)
1.	JMB Realty Corp., Chicago	$3,740.1
2.	The Balcor Co., Skokie, Ill.	3,272.8
3.	Integrated Resources, Inc., New York	1,950.9
4.	Merrill Lynch, Hubbard, Inc., New York	1,860.7
5.	The Krupp Co., Boston	1,605.1
6.	Metric Partners (Fox Group), Foster City, Cal.	1,526.5
7.	Public Storage, Inc., Glendale, Cal.	1,456.5
8.	Consolidated Capital, Dallas	1,298.5
9.	Franchise Finance Corp. of America, Phoenix	1,150.2
10.	Paine Webber Properties, Inc., Boston	1,053.7

Source: Roulac Real Estate Consulting Group of Deloitte Haskins & Sells.

TABLE 2. Top 1988 Money Raisers in Identified Private Real Estate Limited Partnerships

Rank	Firm/Headquarters	Capital Raised in 1988 (in millions)
1.	First Winthrop Corp., Boston	$76.3
2.	Public Storage, Inc., Glendale, Cal.	74.2
3.	Integrated Resources, Inc., New York	64.5
4.	CRI, Inc., Rockville, Md.	55.3
5.	Prudential-Bache Properties, Inc., New York	52.2
6.	Lepercq Capital Partners & Co., Inc., New York	37.5
7.	Bennett Consolidated, San Ramon, Cal.	37.0
8.	Fogelman Partners, Ltd., Memphis, Tenn.	35.4
9.	Boston Capital Services, Inc., Boston	33.7
10.	Cardinal Industries, Inc., Columbus, Ohio	28.9

Source: Roulac Real Estate Consulting Group of Deloitte Haskins & Sells.

Although real estate syndications historically have been regarded as tax shelters, most real estate returns come from the cash generated by property sales. Recent tax law changes may work to the long-term benefit of investors by reducing the amount of capital committed to new real estate development, thereby allowing the demand to catch up to supply in currently overbuilt markets.

The large proportion of returns from property sales makes it difficult to judge performance of ongoing partnerships. Because real estate partnerships are generally not liquid, they should be viewed as long-term investments. Fluctuations in current cash distributions do not necessarily indicate that overall investment performance will be less than expected.

Properly structured, real estate limited partnerships generate three sources of returns: cash distributions from ongoing operations, cash distributions from property sales, and tax savings. Investors should be careful to choose an investment that has been structured to provide the mix of benefits most appropriate to their own portfolio.

GLOSSARY

after-tax cash flow—Actual spendable income from an investment after income taxes; net operating income (or loss), reduced by mortgage principal and interest payments, less income tax payments.

equity capital—Funds invested in property or in an enterprise in consideration of receiving a share of future profits but which bear the first risk of any loss. These funds are distinguished from debt capital, which represents funds loaned to the enterprise or to acquire property in which specific interest is to be paid and which represents a claim on the assets that is superior to the claim of the equity capital.

general partnership—A partnership in which all the partners share in the profits and losses of the enterprise and in the management and operation of partnership affairs.

limited partnership—A partnership in which a general partner (or partners) manages the partnership affairs and can bind the partnership, and limited partners are passive investors in the enterprise. Limited partners cannot by their acts or conduct bind the partnership, and their liability is limited to the amount of their contribution to the partnership.

nonrecourse loan—A loan in which the lender waives any personal liability by the borrower; in case of default, the lender is limited to foreclosing on the mortgage and acquiring the real estate.

partnership—An association of two or more persons for the purpose of carrying on a business for profit and sharing both profits and losses.

securities broker—Any person or entity engaged in the business of effecting transactions in securities for the account of others (as defined by the Securities Exchange Act of 1934).

syndication—An organization through which a real estate professional, who is the syndicator or sponsor, obtains investors who provide the funds required to engage in a real estate enterprise.

SUGGESTED READING

Adelstein, S. Thomas. *How to Read and Select Private Real Estate Offerings.* Longman Financial Services Publishing, Inc., 1985.

Arnold, Alvin K. *Real Estate Syndication Manual.* Boston: Warren, Gorham & Lamont, 1985.

Bloomenthal, Harold S. *1985 Securities Law Handbook.* New York: Clark Boardman Company Ltd., 1985.

Ellsworth, John D. *Real Estate Securities Offerings Handbook*, 4th ed. San Francisco: Questor Associates, 1982.

Fass, Peter M., and Haft, Robert J. *Real Estate Syndication Handbook.* New York: Clark Boardman Company, Ltd., 1985.

Jarchow, Stephen P. Real Estate Syndication: Taxes, Securities and Business Aspects. New York: John Wiley & Sons, 1986.

Questor Real Estate Syndication Yearbook. San Francisco: Questor Associates, 1982–1985.

Roulac, Stephen E. "Real Estate Syndication Digest—Principles and Applications," *Real Estate Syndication Digest*, 1972.

———. *Syndication Landmarks*. Practicing Law Institute, 1974.

———. *Modern Real Estate Investment: An Institutional Approach*. Property Press, 1976.

———. "Syndication Emerges to Transform the Real Estate Capital Market," *Real Estate Finance*, Winter 1985.

———. "Games the Stock Market Didn't Teach You," *Real Estate Investing*, monograph published by The Institute of Chartered Financial Analysts and Dow Jones-Irwin, 1985.

———. "How to Value Real Estate Securities: Harder Than It Looks," *The Journal of Portfolio Management*, Spring 1988.

———. "Real Estate Securitization: Prologue and Prospects," REF Special Report, 5 *Real Estate Finance*, Spring 1988.

———. and Sobolik, Douglas E., "Real Estate Tax Reform: Historic Perspectives and Economic Implications," 2 *Real Estate Finance*, Summer 1985.

REAL ESTATE

MULTIFAMILY RENTAL

Harris Lawless

BASIC CHARACTERISTICS

General Description

A multifamily rental is usually described as a building or series of buildings that includes more than four living units that share certain common facilities. These common facilities may include hallways, entrances, heating and air-conditioning facilities, laundry room, and parking lots, as well as amenities, and certain common-area facilities provided for the tenants' recreation. Some typical amenities are swimming pools, saunas, club houses, tennis courts, wading pools, children's play areas, computer game rooms, and even computer modems. A profusion of amenities not only makes the units easier to rent but also justifies higher rents.

Groups of rental units consisting of fewer than four are generally referred to as duplexes, triplexes, or fourplexes and usually have separate entrances. The smaller complexes are usually managed and maintained by the owner who, most likely, will also occupy one of the units. Many people jokingly remark that purchasing a rental unit of four or fewer units is not an investment—the owner bought a job. That is not entirely true, as the units provide the owner with living space at a lower occupancy cost in addition to a certain amount of tax shelter. For the investor, the primary motive is long-term appreciation, as there will probably be little, if any, positive cash flow from the investment, except from some more expensive units.

Some people invest in single-family houses, condominiums, or cooperatives that they intend to rent to others rather than use for personal occupancy. Under current rental levels

Harris Lawless is President of Harris Lawless & Associates, Freedom, Cal.

and interest rates, in some cases, the owner will put out cash to carry the unit. The investment motive is a certain amount of tax shelter and an appreciation potential. These smaller investments are usually thought to be inflation hedges.

Common Rules of Thumb

Economy of Scale. Although every investment is different and must be dealt with individually, as a general rule of thumb, the more living units contained in a multifamily rental unit, the better the return to the investor. There are certain fixed or semivariable costs associated with any complex that, spread over a larger number of units, will result in a better return. Also, the greater the number of units, the more likely it will be that the complex can afford the professional management fees necessary to manage the complex efficiently. If the complex is too small, the owner-investor is going to have to invest sweat equity to operate the complex.

For economic efficiency, it is generally agreed that a multifamily complex should have a minimum of fifty units. Anything smaller usually cannot pay professional management fees, which means that the owner will have to be involved in the management. Even that rule of thumb is not completely reliable. In a very high-rent area where apartments rent for $1,000 a month or more, possibly as few as twenty units would be sufficient. In a low-rent area where rents are $300 or so a month, it might be necessary to have a minimum of seventy-five or more units.

Gross Multipliers. Economy of scale also affects another commonly used rule of thumb called the gross multiplier. A gross multiplier is a factor that is used to multiply the anticipated gross annual income from a multifamily complex to arrive at an approximate value. The gross multiplier for a reasonably large complex will usually be between six and ten. The factor will reflect the quality of the complex, the location, and the nature of the tenancy. Assume, for example, that the annual scheduled rentals are $200,000 and the gross multiplier is seven. The approximate value would be $1.4 million. This, of course, is only an approximate value. Every investment must be individually analyzed.

The fewer the number of units, the higher the factor will be. For example, a duplex may sell with a factor of twelve to fourteen. With rents of $600 per unit, the annual gross income from both units would be $14,400. Using a multiplier of thirteen, the approximate value would be $187,200. Since a smaller number of units will usually carry a higher multiplier, an investor pays more for the income stream from the smaller complex.

The reason for the variance in the factor is simply the effect of supply and demand. There are probably millions of people who can afford to invest in a fourplex. There are probably only a few hundred who can invest in a $4 million complex. As a result, the cost for the income stream from the smaller complexes is relatively higher than it is for the income stream from the larger complexes. There is a far larger market for the smaller complexes.

Another reason for the higher relative cost of the income stream from the smaller complex is that the people who buy the smaller units tend to invest on an emotional rather than a rational basis. The investor (and the seller) of the $4 million complex will not get emotionally involved in the purchase and will buy on the basis of a rational analysis of the potential returns. Pride of ownership is a valid emotion, but it should not interfere with investment.

The investor must keep in mind that the gross multiplier is only a rule of thumb and not a financial analysis. It is not even uniformly applied. Some investors will apply the multiplier to the total of the scheduled rents (i.e., the amount of rent charged for each apartment on an annual basis) without regard for existing or expected vacancies. Others will apply a 5 or 10 percent vacancy factor before using the multiplier. At best, it is only a very rough estimate of value. It is useful in screening out opportunities that probably would not be appropriate candidates for the detailed financial analysis that should be done.

There are no rules of thumb for valuation of a single-family or condominium rental unit, since the income stream does not establish the value. An appraiser would base his value judgment almost entirely on comparable sales of similar units in the same area and on some consideration of the replacement cost. In fact, under current conditions, the income stream probably would not be enough to carry the property financially, and hence, the equity would have a negative value.

Subsidized Housing Programs

The U.S. Department of Housing and Urban Development (HUD) offers forty-six programs to provide government subsidized housing. It would be impossible to discuss all of them here, but for an investor who is interested and wants to gain a general understanding of the programs, HUD publishes a booklet entitled *Departmental Programs*, which is frequently updated. It can be obtained by writing to the Office of Public Affairs, Department of Housing and Urban Development, Washington, D.C. The booklet also contains the addresses for all the regional and area HUD offices.

Tax Orientation. Generally, most investors in subsidized housing programs in the past were tax motivated. The once popular Section 8 programs are now available only on a limited basis. Programs offering the most tax benefits are rehabilitation projects, and these also are limited, largely because of local community opposition. The entire area of subsidized housing has no clear programs on a national basis. As a result, such programs are usually available on a local basis and often depend on local political and financial support. If such programs do become available, each must be considered individually in the same manner as a conventional investment.

ATTRACTIVE FEATURES

Potential Returns

Figure 1 represents the four benefits of investing in real estate in general and in multifamily units in particular, since all four returns usually will be available.

Cash Flow. Cash flow can be described as any cash remaining from operating income after payment of all operating expenses and interest and principal on any debt, and setting aside any funds needed for reserves. Cash flow can be increased over time by raising rents, controlling expenses, and arranging for loans that carry better terms for the borrower. Neglecting to set aside reserves for replacement of material, equipment, and contingencies, although it will increase cash flow, is usually a mistake.

Cash flow in the real estate industry can best be described as feast or famine. At the present time and probably for some time in the future, cash flow is a significant benefit

FIGURE 1. Four Investment Benefits From Real Estate

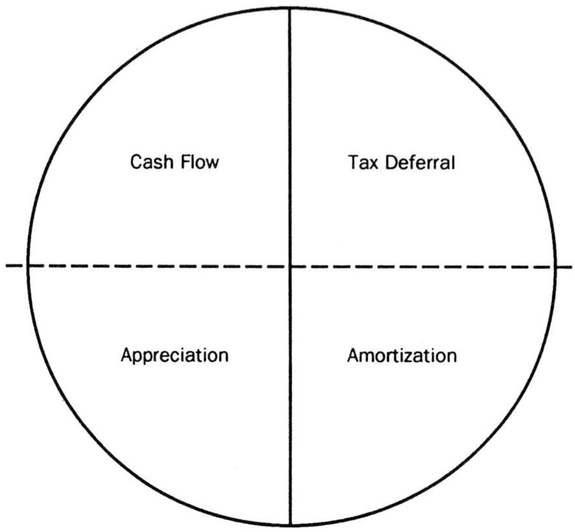

from ownership of multifamily developments. This is largely the result of a dearth of new apartment development in recent years and a growing number of family units exerting an upward pressure on rental rates. The relative stability of interest rates and lower inflation of operating expenses have all contributed to increased cash flow to the owner.

Rents from multifamily units tend to lag behind increases in operating expenses. Until recently, the lag between operating expenses, interest, and rental levels was so great that very few new multifamily units were being built except in some very rapid-growth areas that were not, as yet, sensitive to resistance to increasing rents. When interest and expenses do reach a parity with rental levels, it is financially feasible to develop new complexes. Since it takes up to three years to plan and build a multifamily unit, there will be a period when owners of such units enjoy a handsome cash flow. This will not last indefinitely, however, since the real estate industry periodically overbuilds. Overbuilding creates a high vacancy level that, in turn, results in lower rents or lower rent increases. These periods of underbuilding and overbuilding seem to occur in seven- to eight-year cycles.

Tax Shelter. Improved real estate can provide what is commonly described as tax shelter. That shelter is the result of the noncash expense of depreciation of the improved portion of the investment. The bulk of this so-called shelter is deferral of taxes to a future date.

In the past, it was possible to convert ordinary income to capital gains with real estate. With ordinary income and capital rates at the same level, this distinction is now academic. Investment tax credits are no longer available to real estate. The remaining tax benefit is the deferral of current taxes to a future date. However, that deferral is not as valuable as in the past, when accelerated depreciation was available and could also be applied to other regular income.

The Tax Reform Act of 1986 (the 1986 Act) limits depreciation (now referred to as asset cost recovery). In the case of residential income-producing property, the cost is recovered over a period of twenty-seven and one-half years and must be taken on a straight-line basis. (The owner may elect a forty-year cost recovery.)

The 1986 Act also divides income into three categories: (1) active or earned; (2) portfolio or income from dividends and interest; and (3) passive. All rentals are considered passive income, and from 1990 on, losses from passive sources can only be deducted from passive income or profits from other passive sources. Any excess of passive losses that cannot be taken in a given year can be carried forward to future years.

If a taxpayer satisfies an "active participation" test, he may be able to offset up to $25,000 of active income. Depending on the circumstances, it would usually be possible to defer taxes on the principal payments of a mortgage and possibly some cash flow. The limitation is caused by restrictions on the amount of interest that can be deducted.

The amount and the value of tax deferral will vary from individual to individual, depending on other investment income. Individuals are subject to the alternative minimum tax (AMT), which also affects the value of the deferral.

Current Versus Deferred Benefits

The pie chart of benefits shown in Figure 1 has a dotted line through the center of the pie. The two benefits above the dotted line are current benefits that can be measured on at least an annual basis. Some refer to the benefits of cash flow and tax shelter as the here-and-now benefits.

The two benefits below the dotted line, appreciation and amortization, are deferred benefits. Appreciation will not be realized until the property is sold, and there will only be appreciation if the property did in fact increase in value. Amortization benefits will be realized only when the property is sold for an amount at least equal to its cost or when it is refinanced at some point in the future. These two returns are sometimes called the if-and-when returns.

Current Returns

Cash flow is the cash left over after all expenses and the principal and interest payments have been made and cash is left for the investor. A certain amount of the excess cash may be held for reserves to pay future taxes and insurance or to upgrade and rehabilitate the property. Those reserves should always be held in an interest bearing account until needed.

Tax deferrals are the taxes that will eventually be paid. In the meantime, the owner has the use of that cash for investment or other purposes.

Deferred Returns

Appreciation. Currently, most investors in conventional multifamily housing (i.e., not government subsidized) are investing for appreciation. Appreciation is any increase in value that may occur as the result of inflation and increasing rents. Many other factors may affect appreciation. A complex located in an area that is improving in residential desirability will appreciate more than one located in a deteriorating area. Generally speaking, a quality complex is likely to appreciate. The general economy of the area in which the complex is located also will affect the appreciation rate. Upgrading the property and adding amenities have a direct effect on appreciation, often in excess of the cost to do so.

If equity represents 25 percent of the purchase cost and debt represents 75 percent, all the increase in value accrues to the equity. Therefore, a 1 percent increase in value will result in a 4 percent increase in equity to be realized on resale or refinancing.

Amortization. Amortization is the pay-down of the principal amount of the mortgage(s). In effect, it increases the owners' equity in the property. Had that principal not been paid, the owner would have had more cash flow.

Unless it is a long-term investment, amortization generally does not have a significant effect on return. For example, assuming a $1 million self-amortizing 12 percent loan for a term of thirty years, at the end of five years the balance of the loan would still be $977,000, and at the end of ten years $934,000. The higher the rate of interest, the slower the rate of amortization, and conversely, the lower the interest rate, the greater the rate of amortization.

Present Value and Internal Rate of Return. Most knowledgeable real estate investors agree that the only way to measure return on investment is by a present value computation on a completely after-tax basis. The fact that a substantial part of the return from a multi-family investment is represented by tax shelter makes this method of calculating the return even more useful. In present value analysis, each future period's cash flows are discounted to their present value.

The terms "internal rate of return" (IRR) and "present value" are used interchangeably and most of the time give equivalent answers. Very simply, the concept behind either is that a dollar in hand today is worth a dollar. The promise of a dollar to be delivered at some future date is worth less than a dollar. The difference is the amount that could have been earned with that dollar between now and the delivery date, if it had been invested at current interest rates.

Any investor in apartments should understand and use IRR. Not only is it the truest way to measure an after-tax return, it is also the best way to compare alternative investment opportunities, not just real estate. The investor should be certain, however, to compare all investments on an after-tax basis. A real estate investment that promises an 18 percent after-tax IRR is equivalent to an 18 percent municipal bond, or a 27 percent corporate bond for someone in the 33 percent tax bracket.

Computing Present Value. While the IRR calculations are rather complex, many accounting firms, real estate offices, banks, and savings and loans associations have access to computer programs that can calculate the returns very quickly. Investors who do not have access to a computer program can compute returns by using tables available for that purpose. A word of caution: The IRR calculations usually assume that the returns will continue to earn or be reinvested at the rate shown. In the case of a very high or low rate, this will tend to skew the result. Most computer programs will accommodate a fixed reinvestment rate. Such a program is usually called an adjusted internal rate of return. In fact, many CPA firms use a zero reinvestment rate based on the theory that the investor will receive the money and spend it.

The investor must be wary of sellers or brokers who represent the deferred returns as current. For example, they may claim that he will receive a 10 percent cash flow on the funds invested. This is then added to the value of the tax shelter of, say, 4 percent a year, that debt amortization will average 2 percent a year, and the annual appreciation will increase the equity by 5 percent. By adding those four percentages together, there is an annual return of 21 percent on the investment. Clearly that is not so. The investor must not be misled.

The investor also must be careful to distinguish between current and deferred benefits when negotiating special terms. The effects of special terms should be analyzed on a present value basis. For example, it might be worthwhile to give up all or part of the long-term appreciation to receive the short-term benefit of the here-and-now cash flow.

Structuring the Purchase for Deferred Benefits. It is possible to structure the purchase of multifamily units to increase one or more of the returns or to remove some of the risk of losing the return. The investor should keep in mind that structuring a purchase to achieve a greater amount or more certainty in one or more of the benefits may decrease the likelihood of receiving the other benefits. The investor who wants to secure a known amount of cash flow on a regular basis might get the seller to lease back the property or guarantee a certain cash flow. To assume that risk, the seller will want a higher price for the property. The higher price means that the investor has given up all or part of future appreciation. If the investor obtains an interest-only loan, he will not realize any amortization. If, on the other hand, the investor buys a property with a very high ratio of debt, he increases tax shelter at the expense of cash flow. However, if there is any appreciation, his portion will have increased through the use of leverage.

POTENTIAL RISKS

Return on Investment

Potential risk in this area is difficult to measure, since every property is different and every location is different. Rent control in some communities can have a profound effect on return on investment. The tax bracket of the investor and the purpose of the investment can make a difference. For example, most investors in subsidized housing programs usually invest for the tax deferral the investment will provide. The cash flow remaining after expenses, debt service, and reserves will usually be minimal, if any. Many investors in subsidized housing go into a project with the assumption that there will be a foreclosure after several years. Why would anyone invest in real estate who expected to lose through foreclosure? Investors do so because of the projected IRR on a completely after-tax basis.

Illiquidity

Another potential risk is the relative illiquidity of the investment. If the investor has a need for cash, it may take several weeks to several months to find a buyer and effect a sale. To obtain cash, the seller might even be forced to sell at a price less than full value. He may obtain junior mortgages on the property at inordinate terms and interest rates to obtain cash.

Overbuilding

There is also the possibility of overbuilding of apartment units. This will create vacancy rates that could lower the value of the property. In times of overbuilding, public acceptance of investment in apartment units wanes, thus lowering the value of the units.

Changes in the Market

The investing public is very fickle. There is a herd instinct in investing. In late 1989, the herd wanted to invest in so-called trophy properties. As a result, prices of trophy properties were bid up to unreasonable levels. Just as in the stock market, the key to success is to buy low and sell high. It is never advisable to buy at the peak of public interest.

Variations in Income and Operating Expenses

Income and operating expenses vary widely from project to project. A very broad rule of thumb is that the expenses will range from 40 to 60 percent of the gross operating income. The largest variable will usually be real estate taxes and insurance. Many investors fail to recognize that the sale of a property will usually trigger an increase in assessment for tax purposes based on the selling price. They blithely expect future real property tax bills to be the same as those the seller had been paying. A.knowledge of the policies of local tax assessors is helpful in making reasonable, accurate estimates of future annual taxes.

The same is true of insurance. The investor always gets a quote from his own agent. While the seller may have some type of discount due to a "master" policy or a very high deductible, the investor may not qualify for a master policy or may not want to live with a high deductible.

Income also will vary widely, depending on the location and quality of the multiple-housing units and the existence or lack of rent control. Rents will also vary in relationship to the vacancy level of competing units. There is sometimes a tendency for developers to overbuild when rentals reach a profitable level.

TAX CONSEQUENCES

As has been demonstrated, ownership of multifamily rental properties, as with many kinds of real estate, brings substantial tax benefits. (See *Tax Shelter*, earlier in this article.)

REPRESENTATIVE TYPES OF INVESTORS

Investors in multifamily housing represent a wide spectrum of individuals and entities. Generally speaking, individuals usually invest in the smaller properties, although a few individuals do invest in very large complexes. Most individual investors are involved in a pooled investment with one or more other investors. Some are formally organized as limited partnerships, others as informal general partnerships or as joint tenancies. Corporations are generally not used because of double taxation and lack of tax loss pass-through.

Many of the more active purchasers of larger complexes now are public and private syndications. Again, generally speaking, the average investment in a public syndication will be less than $10,000. In private syndications the individual investment may be well in excess of $50,000.

Many banks and insurance companies have commingled funds that acquire apartments. They usually do not get involved in projects that require less than $3 million or $4 million of equity money, since it does not take much more time to acquire a larger project than to acquire a smaller one.

A recent entry into the field of apartment investments consists of pension funds. They usually do so through credible real estate firms or advisors who can also manage the projects.

Some real estate investment trusts also invest in apartment projects, but they usually participate as owners of the land, which is then leased to the owners of the building and the other improvements.

In terms of total numbers, most smaller multiple-housing units are owned by individuals. How they make the investment is based on their attitude toward the degree of management responsibility they will undertake. Active investors are those who will manage the project in their own name. Passive investors will only do so if someone else is going to manage the day-to-day details. Managing an apartment project is an endless succession of small problems that may not be of interest to the high-capital investor.

IMPORTANT FACTORS IN BUYING AND SELLING

Selecting the Property

It is often said that the key to successful real estate investment is based on three things: location, location, and location. The average multifamily developer or investor does not have complete control over location. Local zoning laws in most areas dictate where a multifamily project can be built. Even so, location should be given careful consideration.

Location. It is important to know whether or not the local area is improving in quality, is static, or is deteriorating. The investor is usually well-advised to invest in a community where property is appreciating; the cost per square foot in a neighborhood that is declining will be lower, but the property will probably lose value rather than appreciate.

People who rent multifamily units usually do not have the same degree of mobility as those who own single-family homes. They are more likely to depend on public transportation than to own one or more personal cars. Therefore, the proximity to shopping facilities, schools, industry, and public transportation becomes more important. A multifamily project located near a major hospital can expect that most of the tenants will be employees of that hospital. If the hospital closes, there will be an exodus of tenants. The same would be true of a single-purpose industrial plant or office building area.

Physical Condition. Before an investment in an apartment project is decided on, a careful physical inspection should be made to ascertain the physical condition. It is important to know whether or not there is deferred maintenance, which will create future higher costs. If the investor does not have the expertise to do so, in most cities of any size, there are experts who specialize in making such inspections. The few hundred dollars of cost is a good investment. If deferred maintenance is found, it can often be used to negotiate a lower price.

In addition to the inspection of the soundness of the basic structure, all mechanical equipment, such as furnaces, air conditioning, kitchen appliances, and sprinkler systems, should be inspected. Every apartment should be visited to determine the condition of the rugs and drapes, the need for paint, and general cleanliness. Common areas such as hallways, parking lots, and entrances as well as lighting, landscaping, swimming pools, and saunas should be reviewed. If necessary, experts should be hired in each of these areas, and for environmental concerns, especially asbestos.

Appraisal. Unless the investor is able to conduct his own appraisal, an independent appraiser should be hired to make an appraisal. The investor should not rely on an appraisal prepared for the seller. Not only will the independent appraisal be a less biased view of the value, but the independent appraiser can also be helpful in establishing value. Appraisers often can call attention to items that might have been overlooked by a less sophisticated buyer. This might include neighborhood information, comparable rents in the area, physical faults, the condition of the industrial base, and potential competition.

Quality of Tenancy. An apartment investor should probably avoid a unit in which there is a high rate of tenant turnover because of dissatisfaction with the facilities or past management. Such dissatisfaction is very difficult to turn around.

The ideal tenants enjoy a relatively high income and are not transient workers. The physical inspection of the occupied units assist in judging the nature of the tenancy. If the parking lots contain a number of abandoned vehicles or vehicles with flat tires, there might be reason to suspect a low-income transient tenancy. A lot full of expensive cars would tell another story.

If possible, the investor should try to talk to some of the tenants, away from the seller, to determine their attitude toward the complex and what they do for a living. Their ages can be important. A group of newlyweds living in studio apartments can have a high turnover rate as babies are born.

Resale

The owner of a multifamily unit must not be so involved in its day-to-day operations as to lose the overall view. This overview should include the current market for multifamily units, availability of mortgage money, the current market for real estate, and the area in which the property is located.

In addition to these basic considerations, other factors must be taken into account, including the following:

- *Condominium conversions*—Owners should be constantly alert to the possibility of converting the units to condominiums, which generate the highest possible price. Conversion, however, requires some capital for improvements and may require paying taxes on the profits.
- *Cross-over point*—It is also necessary to watch for the cross-over point, that is, the point at which all tax deferral of other income and the cash flow are lost. Tax deferral is an important return from real estate, so this could be a vital consideration in determining the time to sell.
- *Improvements*—Once the investor decides to sell, he should make cosmetic improvements to the property, such as repainting, landscaping work, and parking lot striping.
- *Use of a broker*—The next decision is whether or not to use a third-party broker. Before making that decision, the property should be offered to adjoining owners. They often want to add to their holdings in a particular area for management efficiency.

If a third-party broker is engaged, he should not be given a long-term exclusive listing. Two months should be the limit. The seller should also ascertain if the property will be placed in a multiple-listing service if one is available in the area. Commissions are negotiable; there is no such thing as a fixed commission rate. The greater the value of the property, the lower the commission rate should be as a percentage of the sales price.

MANAGING THE INVESTMENT

Increasing Income

In the past several years, rents have lagged far behind the cost of building multifamily units. Simple economics dictate that, eventually, rent levels must increase to reflect costs, and that rentals charged for existing units eventually must reflect the higher rentals required to make new units profitable.

If a seller tells the investor (the potential buyer) that his multifamily unit is always 100 percent occupied, what he is really saying is that the rents are too low. To obtain the optimum rents, a constant upward pressure on the rent levels must be maintained. Every time a unit is vacated, it should be put back on the market at a higher rent level. If it does not rent in a reasonable time, the rental can always be put back to its original level. In the meantime, the investor has tested the market.

After a number of units have been rented at the higher level, the investor should consider raising the rents for all occupied units. If the units are renting at the current market rate, there is little danger of a massive evacuation by existing tenants.

Controlling Expenses

Some expenses, such as taxes, insurance, and utilities, are considered by many to be relatively fixed. That is only partially true. The property owner can appeal, or can engage a specialist to appeal, the tax assessment. The owner must be able to make a good case based on income or on assessments of comparable units. Real estate tax specialists usually receive a percentage of the tax savings over two or more years.

The owner should shop around for insurance among agents that specialize in his particular type of property, asking for competitive bids. There is no such thing as a fixed rate for fire and casualty insurance. One owner of about $60 million of real estate was able to decrease his annual premiums from $115,000 to $30,000. He obtained a master policy and increased the deductible from $1,000 to $10,000, feeling that the additional risk was well covered by the reduction in premium.

Services are available to review utility bills. Utility companies are not infallible and often will apply rates higher than those allowed. Again, the fee is usually a share of the savings.

For other operational expenses, budgeting is essential. Any deviation from the budget should be studied and fully justified. One of the budgeted expenses will be a vacancy factor. An on-site manager should be asked to make sure that careful records are kept of vacancies. In addition, it is important to make periodic audits of the units that are listed as vacant. This point is particularly critical if many of the tenants pay rent with cash rather than by check.

Reserves

The owner of a multifamily property should plan to keep a certain amount of cash in reserve for (1) necessary replacements and (2) contingencies. Unless the owner is willing to furnish funds from other sources, the reserve should be set up from operating income.

Replacement Reserve. Planning the replacement reserve is a mathematical exercise. The owner must calculate when the replacements will be necessary and accumulate the needed funds. For example, carpets normally last about five years, kitchen appliances seven years, and roofs fifteen years.

Contingency Reserve. This reserve is set up to cover any unexpected event that might occur. The owner of a multifamily property on the West Coast that was slipping downhill used his contingency reserve to shore up the slope to avoid losing his building. Although it would be impossible to provide reserves that cover complete destruction (e.g., damage done by an earthquake), most owners set aside some funds for unexpected expenses.

Reserves need not be unproductive if and when they are unused. They can be invested and earn interest. In the current market, reserves may earn more cash than the real estate itself.

Property Management

Poor management can turn a good property into an investment disaster, whereas good management can sometimes turn a marginal investment into a good one. Management of a multifamily property entails responsibility for the ongoing maintenance, renting, rerenting, and general supervision of all ongoing activity. Records must be maintained and goods and services ordered and paid for. Disputes between tenants must be resolved. Data must be provided, and access to the property assured when requested by government agencies. These functions can be accomplished by the owner or through an independent third-party management group. Smaller properties are usually owner-managed, while larger ones are frequently managed by a third-party management group.

Executive Management. Executive management sets the general policy of the operation, handles the money, and hires and supervises the on-site manager. Advertising and promoting the project will usually be accomplished at this level also.

On-Site Management. If the owner is not personally managing the property, there will usually be a resident on-site manager. Quite frequently, this will be a husband and wife combination, who share responsibility for cleaning and repainting apartments for new tenants. In addition, traditionally the wife has shown and rented apartments and kept the office records, while the husband has performed or supervised on-site work, such as landscape maintenance, plumbing, electrical, and other mechanical repair. If there is a swimming pool, it is common practice to hire a pool service.

The on-site managers should participate in the preparation of and agree to the annual budget. They should also be provided with a written policy covering their jobs so that they clearly understand their responsibilities, duties, and limitations. Usually, the on-site managers collect rents and deposit them into a rent depositary account, which is under the owner's control. The managers generally have a small petty cash fund and the right to order goods and services up to a limited amount without the owner's approval.

Usually, the compensation for on-site management consists of a living unit plus a monthly salary. Smaller projects may provide only the living unit. Some incentive arrangement may increase the on-site managers' income if certain occupancy or gross income goals are achieved. The managers' living unit also may serve as the on-site office, but most larger properties have a separate office.

The on-site managers should be reasonably personable and intelligent, as they are often the owner's only contact with tenants. In addition, in some states, anyone who rents out apartments must have some type of real estate license. There is usually a high rate of turnover among on-site managers. Often, the job is looked on as an interim occupation or as a stepping stone to a better one.

Third-Party Management. In some cases, the owner may not have the time to manage a property, even with the help of on-site managers, and must hire a third party. Arrangements for third-party management vary greatly from region to region. For example, in some of the southeastern states, the on-site manager is an employee and on the payroll of the third-party manager. In other areas, the on-site manager may have been hired by the third-party manager but the owner pays the salary directly. In some cases, the third party will handle the money and keep the books, while in others, the owner will perform these functions. It should be clearly understood what the third party's responsibilities include and they should be specified in a contract.

Third-party managers are usually paid a percentage of the gross income. Normally, for multifamily housing, if the owner is paying for the on-site management, the fee will be 4 to 6 percent of the gross income. If the management company is paying the cost of the on-site management, the percentage will be higher.

Leases

The region of the country and the relative value of the project usually determine the nature of the lease. The most common form of lease is the month-to-month lease. Under this arrangement, the tenant need give only thirty days' notice to vacate and the owner needs to give only thirty days' notice to have someone move or to raise rents. The disadvantage of the month-to-month rental is that it leads to higher turnover rates, since the tenant can move at any time. A high rate of turnover increases operating expenses because the units must be prepared for new tenants.

In some areas, particularly in larger cities, a longer lease period is used. Properties are often leased for periods of at least one year and as long as five years. Sometimes, the lease will provide for cost-of-living increases in the rent and for renewal options at a rental to be negotiated. The latter provision really is not of much value to the tenant and of no or negative value to the owner.

Owners who negotiate longer-term leases should try to avoid granting the tenant the right to sublease the unit. In so doing, the owner loses control over tenant quality and mix.

GLOSSARY

***after-tax cash flow**—Before-tax cash flow less the income tax effect of ownership.*

amenity value—The value of the pleasures of the property, such as good neighborhood, schools, parks, playgrounds, etc.

assessed value—Value placed on property for the purpose of computing real property taxes.

balloon payment—The large final payment on a debt.

before-tax cash flow—Net operating income minus debt service. The amount available to the equity owner after cash operating expenses and debt service are subtracted from the effective gross income.

cash flow—See before- and after-tax cash flow.

deferred maintenance—Negligent or "put off" care of a property. An excessive form of deterioration.

depreciation—Loss in value due to any cause. Also a tax deduction that allocates the cost of property over its useful life.

effective gross income—Actual cash receipts from income-producing property. Includes rental receipts, parking, and other miscellaneous income.

exclusive agency listing—An agreement giving a broker the right to a commission if the listed property is sold during the listing period by anyone except the owner.

exclusive right to sell listing—An agreement giving broker the right to a commission if the listed property is sold during the listing period, regardless of who obtains the buyer.

graduated lease—A lease that provides for a varying rental rate, often based on some future determination, such as a periodic appraisal of the property.

gross income—Total income before deduction of expenses.

lessee—Tenant; a person who receives the right to occupy property by a lease.

management fee—An operating expense paid for overseeing the operations of real estate.

mortgage—A document used to make property security for payment of a loan.

net operating income (NOI)—Property operating expenses subtracted from effective gross income.

occupancy rate—The ratio of the space rented to the total amount of space available for rent.

operating expense ratio—The relationship of operating expenses to potential gross income or effective gross income.

partnership—A method of persons joining together for operation of a business for a profit. Tax benefits flow through the partnership to the partners.

potential gross income—Gross receipts that would be collected if all available rental units were leased and all rents were paid by tenants.

rent—Consideration paid for the use and possession of a property.

sinking fund method of depreciation—Setting aside from the income of property an amount that, with accrued interest, will pay for the replacement of improvements when needed.

special assessment tax—Charge against real estate by a public authority to pay the cost of public improvements for the property, such as sewers and street lights.

straight-line depreciation—Depreciation spread evenly over the useful life of property.

sublease—A lease given by a lessee.

TRADE ORGANIZATIONS

National Apartment Owners Association, 1101 14th Street, NW, Washington, D.C. 20005

Institute of Real Estate Management (IREM), 430 North Michigan Ave., Chicago, Ill. 60611

Both of these organizations publish annual operating data gathered from their members. They also both have a variety of publications on the industry and bibliographies.

TAX INFORMATION

The "Big Eight" CPA firms offer publications on real estate taxation as well as frequent updated information. Contact one of their offices in your area to receive their publications and to be included in their mail list.

LEADING BROKERS

Ackerman & Co., Atlanta, Ga.

Arthur Rubloff, Chicago, Ill.

Cabot, Cabot & Forbes, Boston, Mass.

Coldwell Banker (various cities)

Gerald Hines, Houston, Tex.

Helmsley-Spear, New York, N.Y.

Henry S. Miller, Dallas, Tex.

Trammell Crow, Dallas, Tex.

Vantage, Columbus, Ohio

SUGGESTED READING

BOOKS

Downs, James C., Jr. *Principles of Real Estate Management*. Chicago: Institute of Real Estate Management, National Association of Realtors, 1980.

Freeman, Roland. *The Encyclopedia of Apartment Management*. Washington, D.C. National Apartment Association, 1976.

Friedman, Jack P., and Ordway, Nicholas. *Income Property Appraisal and Analysis*. Englewood Cliffs, New Jersey: Prentice-Hall, 1987.

Kelley, Edward N. *Practical Apartment Management*. Chicago: Institute of Real Estate Management, National Association of Realtors, 1981.

Messner, Stephen D., et al. *Marketing Investment Real Estate*. Chicago: Realtors National Marketing Institute, National Association of Realtors, 1982.

Pyhrr, Stephen A., et al. *Real Estate Investment: Strategy, Analysis & Decision*, 2nd ed. New York: John Wiley & Sons, 1989.

PERIODICALS

Apartment Management Newsletter. Mattco Equities, Inc., 48 West 21st Street, New York, N.Y. 10010-6976. Monthly.

Income/Expense Analysis: Apartments. Institute of Real Estate Management, 430 North Michigan Avenue, Chicago, Ill. 60611. Annual.

Journal of Property Management. Institute of Real Estate Management, 430 North Michigan Avenue, Chicago, Ill. 60611. Bimonthly.

Mortgage Banking. Mortgage Bankers Association of America, 1125 15th Street, NW, Washington, D.C. 20005. Monthly.

Multi-Housing News. Gralla Publications, 1515 Broadway, New York, N.Y., 10036. Monthly.

Novick's Income Property Finance Report. IPFR Publishing Corp., 111 John Street, Penthouse, New York, N.Y. 10038. Twenty-two issues per year.

Real Estate Finance. Federal Research Press, 210 Lincoln St., Suite 700, Boston, Mass. 02111. Quarterly.

Real Estate Finance Journal. Warren, Gorham & Lamont, 210 South Street, Boston, Mass. 02111-9902.

REAL ESTATE

SINGLE-FAMILY RENTAL

Glenn E. Crellin

BASIC CHARACTERISTICS

The single-family owner-occupied residence has long been referred to as the American Dream. It is considered part of the "good life" by 87 percent of Americans—renters and owners alike—a higher rating than that given to any other material or psychological attribute. While providing shelter and privacy, it has traditionally entitled the owner to important tax advantages (with favored status traceable to the financing of the Civil War). In addition, on sale, the home has often brought a price well in excess of the purchase price. The combination of tax benefits and appreciation has also made the single-family residence attractive to many investors, especially since a house as an investment is also entitled to additional tax advantages.

Industry statistics indicate that the typical selling price of a resale home in the United States has increased by 344 percent in the last twenty years, from $20,100 in 1968 to $89,300 in 1988, an annual increase of just over 7.7 percent. Overall and regional home prices for selected years are shown in Table 1. During the same twenty-year period, the overall consumer price index rose only 239 percent, an annual inflation rate of 6.3 percent. Clearly, ownership of single-family homes has been an effective storehouse of real wealth during the last twenty years.

While the potential for appreciation is clear, for some people, the negative aspect of residential rental investment is the need for most investors to assume the role of landlord, a position carefully avoided by those who wish to remain passive investors.

Glenn E. Crellin is Division Vice-President for Economics and Research at the National Association of Realtors.

TABLE 1. Selling Price of Existing Single-Family Homes

Year	United States Median	United States Average	Northeast Median	Midwest Median	South Median	West Median
1968	$20,100	$ 22,300	$ 21,400	$18,200	$19,000	$ 22,900
1973	28,900	32,900	32,800	25,300	29,000	31,000
1978	48,700	55,500	47,900	42,200	45,100	66,700
1983	70,300	83,100	72,200	56,600	69,200	94,900
1988	89,300	112,800	143,000	68,400	82,200	124,900

Note: Prices are not seasonally adjusted.

Source: Economics and Research Division, National Association of Realtors.

Developments in Housing Finance

Housing finance has undergone major changes in recent years. In the 1920s, home mortgage credit was available only on a short-term basis for a modest portion of the purchase price. Typical terms from a commercial bank were a five-year loan for 50 percent of the purchase price; the borrower expected, but was not promised, a renewal every five years—until the crash and Depression came. In the 1930s, the Federal Housing Administration (FHA) was created to insure lenders against loss and to encourage them to make long-term, fully amortizing loans for a high percentage of the purchase price. The Federal Home Loan Bank System was created to strengthen savings and loan associations, the specialized housing lenders. Through the joint efforts of governmental and private entities, housing mortgage credit grew more available and liberal.

By 1971 to 1972, loans were available for 95 percent of purchase price (with FHA or private mortgage insurance) for thirty years at fixed interest rates. These terms were better than those available to most high-quality corporations. Active secondary markets and pooling of mortgages for mortgage-backed securities offerings, standard mortgage instruments, and the use of passbook savings at 5 percent interest to fund mortgages at 7 to 8 percent made housing credit plentiful and cheap. However, this system was based on the use of short-term funds borrowed at low interest rates to provide the money for long-term mortgage lending at rates only some 2 to 3 percentage points (200 to 300 basis points) in yield over the savings rate.

Several credit crunches in the 1970s and early 1980s proved the fallacy of borrowing short and lending long. For example, in 1981 and early 1982, the thrift industry (savings and loan and mutual savings banks) portfolios were full of 7 to 9 percent mortgages with long maturities. Their only sources of funds were the popular certificates of deposit with interest rates tied to Treasury bill rates that floated between 12 and 15 percent. Current mortgages were offered at rates up to 17 percent, and home sales activity fell to less than 2 million units.

By the late 1980s, there was concern for the traditional financial institutions themselves. Problems in the agricultural and energy economies led to significant levels of default on all types of loans, including mortgage loans in those communities. The result has been the highest number of bank failures since the Depression. Many other thrift institutions have been the focus of forced mergers to keep the problem from spreading. The secondary market, created to add liquidity to the residential finance system, has made its purchase criteria more selective to better protect the purchasers of mortgages from default.

Alternative Mortgage Instruments. The untenable position of traditional mortgage lenders resulted in a major redesign of contracts between lender and purchaser. Many mortgage arrangements now feature variable interest rates, graduated or balloon payments, sharing of appreciation with lenders, wraparound mortgages, and renegotiation of rates every several years. Traditional, fixed rate mortgages are preferred by most borrowers; however, for investment purchases, lenders often require the adjustable rate instrument.

Lender Resistance. Of even more importance was the withdrawal from the home mortgage market of many lenders who preferred to invest their funds in short-term, high-yield paper. Those lenders who offered fixed term mortgages to home buyers offered them at rates that exceeded the market rates for other long-term investments. (A 16 to 17.5 percent mortgage rate in 1982, when the official prime was 15.5 percent, implied that the local savings institutions were protecting themselves against an inflation rate of 11 to 12 percent throughout the term of the mortgage.)

The 1980's have not been kind to homeownership. The homeownership rate has declined from 65.6 percent in 1980 to 64.2 percent in 1987, the first sustained decline since the Depression. While a modest increase may have taken place in 1988, affordability conditions imply that further declines in homeownership may be in the offing.

Housing is more affordable in most parts of the country now than it was in the early 1980s, primarily because mortgage interest rates are below the 15 to 17 percent levels of 1982. Nevertheless, housing affordability is significantly worse than it was in the early 1970s, when the typical American family had 50 percent more income than the bare minimum required to carry a mortgage on a mid-priced home with a 20 percent down payment. Now the cushion is closer to 15 percent.

More troublesome for home buyers, but perhaps encouraging to potential investors, is the growing gap in affordability for potential first-time buyers. Not only do they have to clear the hurdle of saving the significant down payment required, but it is becoming increasingly difficult for renter families to manage the monthly payments to carry a mortgage.

This affordability gap for owning the American Dream must be balanced against an apartment market that is experiencing the highest level of vacancies in a generation. Such high vacancy rates will tend to keep rental prices for apartments more competitive and may make it harder for the investor-owner of single-family homes to achieve the rental income that the property might otherwise produce. However, it is still possible to make a profit in the residential rental market for considerably less cash outlay than is required for other forms of real estate investment. Although many popular real estate investment manuals suggest the leveraged purchase of a two- to four-family unit as offering the greatest return, the first-time investor might well choose to start with a single-family dwelling. With a possible lesser return on investment, it also promises fewer headaches.

ATTRACTIVE FEATURES

Capital Appreciation

Although a rental residence produces low periodic cash flow in times of high mortgage rates, for two decades the single-family home has proved an effective insulator against the erosion of capital by inflation. However, the expectation of property appreciation can be justified only if property values are likely to rise in the general area and if the subject property is well located, well constructed, and well maintained.

Prices of one-family houses rose dramatically during the late 1970s, sometimes as much as one percent per month. While it is unlikely that in the 1990s overall appreciation will exceed inflation substantially, particular markets may continue to see higher appreciation because of local conditions. In regions of growing population, the prices of existing residences may well continue to rise at least as fast as the cost of building new houses.

Tax-Sheltering Benefits

The investor in residential real estate may deduct from his rental income all mortgage interest as well as depreciation on the property. He may further deduct operating costs—repairs, maintenance, heating, and utilities (if they are included in the lease)—and local property taxes. In the early years of an amortized mortgage, the investor is certain to enjoy the benefits of a considerable tax loss that may offset other income, particularly if the investment is active, that is, the investor is managing the rental of the property.

Leverage

The initial cash down payment for investor-owned single-family residences is often relatively low, with such payments generally running from 20 to 30 percent of purchase price. In times of easy money, buyers have put down as little as 5 percent. Some creative financing techniques (see *Important Factors in Buying and Selling*, later in this article) provide for the seller's offering a second mortgage that requires little initial cash investment. Be wary of quick money schemes that promote real estate investment with no money down. The adage "A deal that seems too good to be true probably is" applies.

Steady Demand

If the investment is wisely made in terms of community and neighborhood, there is usually a steady demand for desirable rental houses. The rental house is the first choice of many corporate transferees. It gives other newcomers who are prospective homeowners the opportunity to get acquainted with the community before assuming the burden and complications of outright ownership.

Investment Advantages Over Multifamily Units

Single-family houses are often a more attractive investment than multifamily structures, since there is less of a threat of rent control. Single residences are usually exempted in most of those municipalities that impose rent controls unless the investors own a great many units. Further, individual dwellings are easier to sell than large, multiunit buildings; management may be less onerous to the extent that fewer tenants are involved, and the chance for appreciation may be greater.

POTENTIAL RISKS

Uncertain Market Values

During economic slowdowns, prices may not keep up with inflation. In some areas of the country and in some neighborhoods, prices of residential real estate deteriorate as strong industries decline and towns have difficulty maintaining physical plants and services. The Oil Patch has given ample evidence in the last few years. The lesson to be learned is obvious: Location is all-important. (This point is discussed in *Important Factors in Buying and Selling*, later in this article.)

Limited Cash Flow

The investor in today's market must be sure to have sufficient cash reserves to offset negative cash flows and to make necessary repairs and replacements. He must also be prepared to meet increases in property taxes and energy costs.

Most important, it is always possible that the investor will find himself without tenants for a month or two, or even longer. Lenders offer no forgiveness of carrying charges because of nonoccupancy. Mortgage payments are due even when no rent is coming in.

Lack of Liquidity

An investor should not get involved in any kind of real estate investment if he is not in a position to tie up his money for some time—at least four years, in the case of residential property. Real estate is not a liquid investment, and if the house must be sold within a year or two, broker's commissions and other transaction costs may well eat up any appreciation in value. Transaction costs, unlike those of marketable securities, are high. Moreover, selling takes time; houses cannot be sold for cash with a telephone call.

Tenant Problems

Destructive or irresponsible tenants are always a risk. Although most leases provide for one month's rent as security, this amount may prove insufficient to cover damage caused by a destructive tenant. Moreover, the court process for collecting delinquent rent and evicting tenants who violate leases may be time-consuming. The investor must be certain he is emotionally suited to the landlord role; it is essential to maintain a reasonably harmonious but businesslike relationship with tenants.

Overall Investment

There is always the risk of making improvements that cannot be justified in terms of prospective resale price. Houses normally do not sell for a great deal more than surrounding properties that are comparable in major respects. The buyer, therefore, should think carefully before making changes that may not affect the selling price. Any necessary repairs, of course, should always be made promptly.

Managerial Requirements

Managing a rental residence may periodically require concentrated time and labor, particularly in making the property ready for a new tenant. In addition, the prudent owner visits the property frequently as part of routine surveillance. Street observation is usually sufficient for this purpose.

TAX CONSEQUENCES

An advantage to investment in single-family homes is the ability to claim depreciation for income tax purposes. Because land is considered not to wear out, depreciation cannot be claimed on it. Appliances and furniture may be expensed in the year acquired, or depreciated over a relatively short life; buildings may be depreciated over a longer period.

Depreciation allows a tax deduction that the owner does not pay for in cash, giving the owner a tax deduction without reducing cash flow, and possibly resulting in a tax saving that increases after-tax cash flow. For example, suppose an investor buys a single-family house for $110,000 of which $10,000 is land, leaving $100,000 to be depreciated. A 27.5-year depreciable life is allowed using the straight-line method. The owner may deduct $3,640 annually each year for 27.5 years. Table 2 offers the depreciation percentages for single-family rental property.

The tax depreciation deduction, created by a bookkeeping entry, can be claimed even when the property rises in value. Thus, the owner gains from property that provides cash flow and reduces taxable income. Not to be confused with an actual reduction or loss in value, tax depreciation does not measure the actual loss in value of property; it is an arbitrary deduction allowed by tax law.

Land is not depreciable for tax purposes. When an investor buys an existing house, an allocation must be made between its parts: land, buildings, and appliances. It is to an investor's advantage to allocate as much as possible to depreciable components rather than land. The relative fair market value of each component is required for this allocation by tax law, permitting appraisals, tax assessments, and replacement costs being introduced as guidelines to establish relative values. By contrast, a builder's basis in land and components are their actual cost.

TABLE 2. Depreciation Percentages for Single-Family Rental Property

Month Placed in Service	Recovery Year 1	2–27	28	29
1%	3.48%	3.64%	1.88%	0%
2	3.18	3.64	2.18	0
3	2.88	3.64	2.48	0
4	2.58	3.64	2.78	0
5	2.27	3.64	3.09	0
6	1.97	3.64	3.39	0
7	1.67	3.64	3.64	.05
8	1.36	3.64	3.64	.36
9	1.06	3.64	3.64	.66
10	.76	3.64	3.64	.96
11	.45	3.64	3.64	1.27
12	.15	3.64	3.64	1.57

TABLE 3. Single-Family Demonstration: Financial Profile

Holding period for property: 10 years	
Resale expense rate: 6%	
Annual gross income	$12,000
Gross income annual growth rate: 5%	
Vacancy rate: 0%	
Annual miscellaneous income	0
Miscellaneous income annual growth rate: 0%	
Annual operating expenses	$ 1,600
Operating expenses annual growth rate: 5%	
Investor's first year tax rate: 28%	
Investor's last year tax rate: 28%	
Depreciable assets	$100,000
Land cost	10,000
Total assets (purchase price)	$110,000
Annual growth rate for combined assets: 5%	
Total debt	$ 80,000
Initial equity (down payment)	$ 30,000

Tables 3 to 5 provide output from a computer program that projects results from income-producing real estate, based on data input and application of mathematics. In the example, the first-year depreciation was $3,480 rather than $3,640 because of the "mid-month convention" built into the depreciation tables by the Internal Revenue Service.

After the first year, it is assumed that rental rates, operating expenses, and the potential resale price increase by 5 percent annually, compounded. For simplicity, the loan is demonstrated as requiring no amortization payments, although the computer can accommodate virtually any amortization schedule. It should be noted from the demonstration that cash flow increases with time because of rising rents, while taxable income increases or tax losses diminish with time. If there were mortgage amortization or rapid/short life depreciation, any tax losses would diminish with time, or taxable income would rise more sharply.

The model includes a 6 percent resale expense rate and calculates an internal rate of return (a true rate of return) on equity invested to any holding period up to the ten-year projection.

Suppose an investor paid $100,000 for a rental house and mortgaged it for $80,000 at 10 percent interest. He received $12,000 annual rent, and paid out $1,600 for operating expenses and $8,000 interest. Before-tax cash flow is $2,400 ($12,000 rent minus $8,000 debt service and $1,600 operating expenses). The $2,400 cash flow represents an 8 percent return on the equity of $30,000 ($110,000 cost less $80,000 mortgage requires $30,000 equity). A depreciation deduction of $3,640 allows the investor to show a tax loss of $1,240 ($12,000 rent minus $8,000, $1,600, and $3,640 depreciation). The investor, although subject to limitations, may be able to use the tax loss to offset other income, thus reducing taxes on other income and saving tax money. If the losses cannot be used currently, they may carry over to future years.

TABLE 4. Single-Family Demonstration: Calculation of After-Tax Cash Flow

Year	Potential Gross Income	Vacancy Allowance	Miscellaneous Income	Operating Expenses
1	$12,000	$0	$0	$1,600
2	12,600	0	0	1,680
3	13,230	0	0	1,764
4	13,891	0	0	1,852
5	14,586	0	0	1,945
6	15,315	0	0	2,042
7	16,081	0	0	2,144
8	16,885	0	0	2,251
9	17,729	0	0	2,364
10	18,616	0	0	2,482

Year	Net Operating Income	Interest Expense	Principal Amortization	Before-Tax Cash Flow
1	$10,400	$8,000	$0	$2,400
2	10,920	8,000	0	2,920
3	11,466	8,000	0	3,466
4	12,039	8,000	0	4,039
5	12,641	8,000	0	4,641
6	13,273	8,000	0	5,273
7	13,937	8,000	0	5,937
8	14,634	8,000	0	6,634
9	15,366	8,000	0	7,366
10	16,134	8,000	0	8,134

Year	Depreciation Expense	Taxable Income	Passive Loss Used	Passive Loss Carryover	Tax Paid (-Savings)	After-Tax Cash Flow
1	$3,480	$−1,080	$1,080	$0	$ −302	$2,702
2	3,640	−720	720	0	−202	3,122
3	3,640	−174	174	0	−49	3,515
4	3,640	399	0	0	112	3,927
5	3,640	1,001	0	0	280	4,361
6	3,640	1,633	0	0	457	4,816
7	3,640	2,297	0	0	643	5,294
8	3,640	2,994	0	0	838	5,796
9	3,640	3,726	0	0	1,043	6,322
10	3,640	4,494	0	0	1,258	6,876

TABLE 5. Single-Family Demonstration: Decrease in Adjusted Tax Basis Over Time

Sale Year	Selling Price Before Expenses	Selling Expenses	Selling Price After Expenses	Mortgage Balance	Adjusted Tax Basis
1	$115,500	$ 6,930	$108,570	$80,000	$106,520
2	121,275	7,276	113,998	80,000	102,880
3	127,339	7,640	119,698	80,000	99,240
4	133,706	8,022	125,683	80,000	95,600
5	140,391	8,423	131,967	80,000	91,960
6	147,410	8,845	138,566	80,000	88,320
7	154,781	9,287	145,494	80,000	84,680
8	162,520	9,751	152,769	80,000	81,040
9	170,646	10,239	160,407	80,000	77,400
10	179,178	10,751	168,428	80,000	73,760

If losses are used to offset other income, the investor may have to return the benefits received from depreciation when the property is sold. Basis is the point from which gain or loss is measured. Depreciation reduces the basis of property, and that reduction increases the gain when property is sold. If the single-family house does not decline in value, all of the depreciation becomes taxable as a gain when sold.

Restrictions of the Tax Reform Act

The Tax Reform Act of 1986 (the 1986 Act) placed restrictions on tax losses potentially generated by real estate. It defined three categories of income: passive, portfolio, and active. Losses from a passive activity cannot be used to offset either portfolio income or active income, and a tax credit generated by a passive activity can offset only the tax attributable to passive income. The tax act limited depreciation allowances, increased capital gains rates, extended at-risk rules to real estate, and expanded the alternative minimum tax (AMT).

Passive activities are those that fall into either of two categories:

1. Any trade or business conducted for profit in which the taxpayer does not materially participate
2. Any rental activity

Thus, rental of a single-family house is passive. Rental activities also include long-term rentals of apartments, net leased property, office equipment, and automobiles. In contrast, the rental of hotel rooms or transient apartments and short-term car rentals are not passive because of the extent of the services provided.

Portfolio income consists of interest, dividends, and royalties. Portfolio income also includes gain or loss on the sale of investment property or property that generates portfolio income.

Active income includes salaries, fees, and income from businesses in which the taxpayer materially participates.

Because rental real estate is a passive activity, owners may not use losses to offset or shelter other types of income. There are two exceptions:

1. Property acquired before October 22, 1986, the enactment date of the 1986 Tax Act. Losses on property acquired before then are phased out over a four-year period, with only 10 percent of losses allowed in 1990 and none thereafter.
2. Active participants in rental real estate are allowed to shelter up to $25,000 per year of losses against other income, provided their adjusted gross income from sources other than real estate is less than $100,000. If income exceeds $100,000 but is less than $150,000, the $25,000 allowance is reduced. If other income exceeds $150,000, the $25,000 allowance cannot be used. It is this $25,000 allowance that gives a tax break to the "mom and pop" single-family home operator.

Indicators of active participation in real estate include the following:

- Approving new tenants
- Deciding on rental terms
- Approving capital or repair expenditures

The definition of active participation, however, excludes the following:

- Ownership of a 10 percent interest or less
- Limited partners

Residential real estate placed in service after December 31, 1986, is eligible for a 27.5-year depreciable life. To be classified as residential depreciable property, 80 percent of the income must come from dwelling units. Residential real estate includes manufactured homes when they are rented as residences but does not include hotels, motels, and other transient establishments.

Instead of the 27.5-year life, a taxpayer can depreciate property over a forty-year period. The advantage of this alternative is that depreciation deductions are not added back to income when figuring the AMT liability.

Each year, up to $10,000 of personal property acquired for business use can be expensed, up to the taxable income for the year. Qualifying property is depreciable personal property bought for use in an active trade or business, such as appliances and furniture in a rental apartment unit. However, each dollar over $200,000 spent on qualifying investments reduces the amount eligible for expensing. Thus, if more than $210,000 is spent on personal property in a year, none may be expensed.

The term "placed in service" has reference to the date when real estate was rented or available for rent by that taxpayer. Real estate placed in service after 1986 is depreciated using the modified accelerated cost recovery system (MACRS). Real estate placed in service during 1981 to 1986 is generally depreciated using the more rapid accelerated cost recovery system (ACRS). In 1981, ACRS permitted a fifteen-year life and an accelerated schedule that provided very generous tax depreciation deductions during the years immediately following acquisition.

Each property owner begins the depreciation cycle again for their property, with the price they pay as the starting point. They must use the depreciable life and method permitted by law when they place that property in service. During the 1981 to 1986 period of ACRS, tax law stimulated asset sales. Investors would sell their mostly depreciated property, report their capital gain at a low tax rate, and then buy another property that provides rapid depreciation that can be used to offset ordinary income earned from nonreal estate sources.

Capital Gains and Losses

Under the 1986 Act, there is no distinction in tax rates for capital gains. However, all of the differences in types of income remain in the tax law, paving the way for restoration of differences in tax rates. Furthermore, there are differences in the way capital losses are used to offset other gains or income, while nuances in the tax law introduce complications.

A single-family residence that is rented to tenants is considered used in a trade or business, causing it to be classified as a Section 1231 asset rather than as a capital asset. Under Section 1231, gain would be taxed as a capital gain; a loss can be used to offset ordinary income in contrast to the $3,000 limit on capital losses. Section 1231 of the Internal Revenue Code applies to real property used in a trade or business, including single-family rental units. The tax treatment of gains under Section 1231 is similar to capital assets, except for its treatment of depreciation claimed by the taxpayer during ownership. Accelerated depreciation claimed by the taxpayer is recaptured as ordinary income on the sale of real estate at a gain.

At-Risk Rules

At-risk rules were extended to real estate as part of the 1986 Act, and thus apply to property placed in service after 1986. This means that losses on real estate investments are deductible only to the extent of money the equity investor stands to lose. For example, if an investor has $10,000 at risk in a real estate investment that generates $3,333 per year in tax losses, the losses may be used for only three years. Thereafter, the losses may be used only if the investor contributes more money or property (net of withdrawals) or becomes liable to repay borrowed money. Amounts at risk include the following:

- Cash contributed to the activity
- Money borrowed for which the investor is personally liable for repayment
- Property pledged as security for the real estate activity, provided the property is not used in the activity

An exception is made for qualified third-party nonrecourse financing.

Alternative Minimum Tax

The alternative minimum tax applies a 21 percent rate to a broader base of income than the regular income tax. After subtracting the appropriate exemption, a taxpayer compares the tax due on the broader-based income at the 21 percent rate to the regular income tax and pays the greater amount.

AMT income begins with the regular taxable income, then adds in certain preference income. Preference income generated by real estate investments include the following:

- Depreciation of real estate acquired after December 31, 1986, in excess of a forty-year straight-line life
- Depreciation in excess of straight line on real estate and leased personal property acquired under ACRS or pre-ACRS
- Losses from passive activity investments allowed under a phase-in rule (but depreciation will not be counted twice)

The following exemptions are in effect: Married individuals filing joint returns have a $40,000 exemption, singles $30,000, and marrieds filing separately $20,000. These exemptions begin to be phased out when AMT income exceeds a certain level: $150,000 for married filing jointly; $112,500 for singles.

REPRESENTATIVE TYPES OF INVESTORS

A present or former homeowner who has had a satisfactory investment experience with his own house and who is interested in a moderate-risk, low-liquidity investment with better than average growth potential is a logical investor in residential real estate. The temperament to deal with sometimes demanding and inconsiderate tenants is probably one of the most important requirements, unless one is prepared to sacrifice income for the services of professional management. With professional management, any investor looking for long-term growth may want to consider residental real estate.

IMPORTANT FACTORS IN BUYING AND SELLING

Does the disappearance of 6 to 9 percent mortgages make housing an unattractive investment? Clearly, some spectacular rates of return, which were available in the late 1970s because of high inflation, low levels of housing production, and very attractive fixed-rate mortgage credit, made investment ownership of homes especially attractive. Again, recently, on a regional basis because of shifting demographics and limited new construction, rapid increases in prices reinforced with mortgage rates well below those of the early 1980s made investment very attractive. However, these situations are the exception rather than the rule. If moderate inflation persists and new housing starts continue to fall below basic demand for housing needed for new household formation, replacement, and relocation, prices of housing can be expected to continue to rise strongly in areas to which people want to migrate. The investor therefore will have to pay close attention to demographics and supply and demand, as well as to carrying costs.

Where to Buy

In selecting a single-family house, the investor should concentrate on one factor above all: location.

Geographic Guidelines. In general, communities with a moderate amount of transient population are preferable to towns with little population turnover. The suburbs of major metropolitan areas are attractive, since they are sought out by families transferred from other parts of the country. If one can sense major population shifts before they are too far underway, there are excellent rental prospects in and near the major cities at the center of these migrations, as long as the migration is inward.

Neighborhood Guidelines. The value of a property is largely determined by houses in the immediately surrounding area. Most neighborhoods are in a state of transition, and it is very important to determine whether a particular neighborhood is in a period of growth, stability, or decline. Judgments can be made on the basis of property maintenance and the types and quality of municipal services.

In lower-income neighborhoods, proximity to public transportation and shopping facilities is important. In upper-income neighborhoods, the availability of desirable schools is particularly important.

Price

The price paid by the investor must be reasonable and fair. It will probably be based on recent sales prices of comparable properties in the general area. There will also be additional factors to consider: costs of repairs and renovation and the prospects for appreciation. Above all, the investor should beware of being carried away by a property that appeals to his particular esthetic values. Location must still remain the primary factor. A beautifully maintained house is worth only a slight premium in price, since it will not remain in that condition after having been occupied by two or three tenants, despite the landlord's reasonable maintenance efforts. If it is in an undesirable neighborhood, the risks escalate.

Financing the Purchase

While the traditional approach to financing is to deal with commercial banks and thrift institutions, the investor should be aware that other avenues may be available, especially if mortgage rates rise above 14 percent. This usually means persuading an eager seller to take back a mortgage (either first or second), often at rates that are below the current market. There may be definite advantages to paying a seller's price if one can get a below-market mortgage. At a later date, it may be possible to refinance the property at a comparable rate, using a traditional source of mortgage credit.

Selling the Property

When it is his turn to sell, the investor may have to resort to the same devices that made the purchase of the property possible in the first place. The investor must be prepared for the possibility that some profits at the time of resale—and perhaps some down payment—may have to remain invested and that a portion of the equity may convert to a note.

It generally pays to develop a working arrangement with local brokers. A professional can easily keep abreast of the market—what is happening in the area and prevailing prices—and has access to serious buyer prospects.

Necessary repairs plus cosmetic renovation—painting, cleaning, and possibly landscaping—always should be done because the cost will be returned several times over by a higher selling price. However, the investor must think very carefully before making substantial improvements that will overimprove the house in terms of the market prices of other homes in the neighborhood.

A final but important tip: It is well worth the time, effort, and cost to put the interior of the house in immaculate condition, with special attention to the kitchen, bathrooms, and all appliances. This factor alone persuades many prospects to close the deal, possibly at a higher price than they were prepared to pay.

MANAGING THE INVESTMENT

It is very difficult to succeed by oneself as an absentee landlord. The only substitute for personal surveillance is to retain the services of a broker or other person who is willing to manage the property and possibly collect rents. Few brokerage firms specialize in rental management of individual houses. When the house is in good condition and the tenant has a long-term lease and pays rent promptly, the usual fee is too high; if there are problems with the property or the tenant, it may be too low.

The best course for the strictly passive investor probably is to seek out an individual who owns rental homes in the area and who manages them actively. The agreed-upon fee reflects the manager's expertise in knowing which plumber, electrician, or painter to hire, and how much to pay; it also may include deciding on appropriate rent and explaining it to the tenant, finding a new tenant, or dealing with or evicting a delinquent tenant.

GLOSSARY

alternative mortgage instrument—A mortgage instrument created by varying one or more of the four factors that are held fixed in the usual mortgage: amount of principal, interest rate, periodic or monthly payment of principal and interest, and repayment terms.

amenity value—The value of the pleasures of the property, such as good neighborhood, schools, parks, and playgrounds.

assessed value—Value placed on property for the purpose of computing real property taxes.

balloon payment—A large final payment on a debt.

basis points—One basis point is one hundredth of one percent in yield. The difference between a mortgage yielding 10.25 percent and one yielding 10.75 percent is 50 basis points.

closing—In the case of a sale of real estate, the final meeting of the parties at which title passes from the seller to the purchaser and the consideration for the purchase passes from the purchaser to the seller, the final documents are signed and delivered, expenses are prorated, and other final adjustments are made.

closing costs—The expenses incurred in the consummation of a real estate or mortgage transaction.

deposit receipt—Document by which a prospective purchaser makes an offer to buy and submits a deposit to accompany that offer; also known as agreement of sale and earnest money contract.

due-on-sale clause—A clause in a mortgage permitting the mortgagee to accelerate the mortgage debt (so that it becomes immediately payable) in the event of a sale of the real estate by the borrower.

equity buildup—The increase in value of a property owner's equity as a result of mortgage loan amortization or appreciation in the total value of the property, or both.

exclusive agency listing—An agreement giving a broker the right to a commission if the listed property is sold during the listing period by anyone except the owner.

exclusive right to sell listing—An agreement giving a broker the right to a commission if the listed property is sold during the listing period, regardless of who obtains the buyer.

gross lease—A lease in which the landlord pays operating expenses.

housing starts—The number of residential units for which construction has begun within a specified period. Used together with number of construction permits, issued as an indicator of real estate and construction and mortgage activity and trends.

imputed rent—The fair rental value of owner-occupied or otherwise unrented property.

loan-to-value ratio—The ratio (usually expressed as a percentage) of the mortgage loans to the value of the mortgaged property.

net lease—A lease in which the tenant pays operating expenses.

occupancy value—Fair imputed rent for the occupancy of a property.

private mortgage insurance—Protection to the lender for the riskiest 25 to 30 percent of a loan; if the borrower defaults and foreclosure becomes necessary, the private mortgage insurance company will pay the lender an amount equal to 25 to 30 percent of the mortgage balance.

Realtor—A registered mark that identifies a professional in real estate who subscribes to a strict Code of Ethics as a member of the National Association of Realtors.

renegotiable rate mortgage (RRM)—An automatically renewable three-to five-year loan note, secured by a mortgage of up to thirty years for residential dwellings, providing for renegotiation of the interest rate on each renewal (similar to rollover mortgage, except that the latter involves both short-term notes and short-term mortgages).

reverse annuity mortgage (RAM)—A form of mortgage that permits a homeowner to draw on the accumulated equity in the home (cash inflows and outflows are in reverse of those associated with a conventional mortgage loan).

shared appreciation mortgage (SAM)—A mortgage plan under which the lender offers the home buyer an interest rate that is, for example, one-third lower than the rate prevailing in the market. In return, the lender receives a third of the appreciation in the value of the property when the property is sold or the mortgage matures.

tax-free sale of residential property by taxpayer over age 55—A taxpayer who is age 55 or over at the time of the sale may exclude from gross income up to $125,000 of gain on the sale of a principal residence (Section 121 of the Internal Revenue Code).

wraparound mortgage—A second mortgage that, instead of being wholly independent of the first loan, wraps around it; that is, the borrower pays debt service on the entire wraparound loan to the second mortgage lender, who then pays the first lender its share.

LEADING FRANCHISE BROKERS

Century 21 Real Estate

Coldwell Banker Residential Affiliates

Electronic Realty Associates (ERA)

Gallery of Homes

Meredith Publishing (Better Homes & Gardens)

RE/MAX

Realty World Corporation

Red Carpet Corporation

SUGGESTED READING

American Institute of Real Estate Appraisers. *Appraising Residential Properties*. Chicago, 1988.

Arnold, Alvin L., and Kusnet, Jack. *The Arnold Encyclopedia of Real Estate*. Boston: Warren, Gorham & Lamont, Inc., 1978 (supplemented annually).

______, Wurtzebach, Charles H., and Miles, Mike E. *Modern Real Estate*. Chapters 3, 9, 14, 16, 19. Boston: Warren, Gorham & Lamont, Inc., 1980.

Boyce, Byrl, and Kinnard, William. *Appraising Real Property*. Chicago: Society of Real Estate Appraisers, 1984.

Brueggeman, William B., and Stone, Leo D. *Real Estate Finance*, 7th ed. Homewood: Richard D. Irwin, 1981.

Downs, James C., Jr. *Principles of Real Estate Management*, 12th ed. Chicago: Institute of Real Estate Management, 1980.

Federal Research Press. *Real Estate Finance.* Boston. Quarterly.

Friedman, Jack P.; Harris, Jack C.; and Lindeman, Bruce. *Dictionary of Real Estate Terms*, 2nd ed. Hauppage, N.Y.: Barron's Educational Series, 1987.

Friedman, Jack P., and Harris, Jack C. *Keys to Investing in Real Estate.* Hauppage, N.Y.: Barron's Educational Series, 1989.

Friedman, Jack P., and Ordway, Nicholas. *Income Property Appraisal and Analysis*, 2nd ed., Englewood Cliffs, N.J.: Prentice-Hall, 1988.

Harrison, Henry S. *Houses.* Chicago: National Association of Realtors, 1984.

Lyons, Paul. *Investing in Residential Real Estate: A Guide to Increasing Your Income and Profit.* Reston: Reston Publishing Co., 1981.

Marshall & Swift Publication Co. *Marshall Valuation Service.* Los Angeles, Cal. Updated regularly.

National Association of Realtors, Economics & Research Division, Washington, D.C. *Home Sales.* Monthly and annual reports.

Bureau of the Census, U.S. Department of Commerce. *New One-Family Houses Sold and for Sale.* Washington, D.C.

Phyrr, Steven A., et. al. *Real Estate Investment: Strategy, Analysis, Decisions*, 2nd ed. New York: John Wiley & Sons, 1989.

Seldin, Maury, ed. *The Real Estate Handbook.* Chapters 20, 21, 28. Homewood: Dow Jones-Irwin, 1980.

Unger, Maurice A. *How to Invest in Real Estate.* New York: McGraw-Hill Book Co., 1975.

Vidger, Leonard P. *Borrowing and Lending on Residential Property.* Lexington: Heath Lexington Books, 1981.

Warren, Gorham & Lamont. *Real Estate Finance Journal.* Quarterly.

Weidemer, John. *Real Estate Finance.* Englewood Cliffs, N.J.: Prentice-Hall, 1988.

Wright, Arthur L. *Investing in a Small Residential Rental Property.* College Station, Tex.: Real Estate Center, Texas A&M University, Dec. 1986.

REAL ESTATE

UNDEVELOPED LAND

Terrence L. Love, Sr.

BASIC CHARACTERISTICS

Undeveloped land is one of the most speculative types of investment, with potential for the highest returns as well as for the greatest risks. It requires expertise in political matters; creativity and judgment in terms of the issue of highest and best use and physical engineering and environmental matters; plus staying power to weather the economic cycles that occur during many holding periods. Undeveloped land is defined here as land having the potential of going under development or being redeveloped to a higher use within ten years. The land may be presently lying fallow or otherwise not put to its potential highest and best use. Thus, undeveloped and underdeveloped land, although perhaps currently in use as farmed, differs from farms and ranches because of its potential for development. Undeveloped land also differs from small recreational lots, suburban lots, and urban lots, which have already been provided with infrastructure and demographics (people), and site improvements (utilities). It is useful to think of undeveloped and underdeveloped land as currently undergoing a use transition period; development can be expected within the foreseeable future. The purchaser hopes to benefit financially during this transition period by buying at or just above raw land prices and selling at a predevelopment or user price.

City Forms

Among the several forms that cities take are multiple nuclei, linear, and concentric ring; most metropolitan areas have some of each. The quantity of land in the urban, suburban,

---

Terrence L. Love, Sr., is Chairman of L.D.A., Inc. (Land Development Analysts) in Atlanta, Georgia.

exurban, and rural rings increases exponentially (the square of the radius). The astute land investor realizes the increase in the quantity of undeveloped/underdeveloped land that occurs as he moves away from the city's center. It is imperative to recognize the volume of land that is brought into competition as one moves out.

The largest potential returns or losses obviously belong to the largest land assemblages. The greatest incentives for large assemblages are mixed-use development; attraction to large lenders, investors, and intermediate buyers; and ultimate site users. The predeveloper (packager) needs to differentiate his assemblage from all the others in his urban, suburban, or exurban ring.

Unique Characteristics

Every investment has certain characteristics that differentiate it and its special group of investors from all others. Undeveloped land has certain physical qualities from which unique economic and investment attributes flow. These characteristics include immobility, indestructibility, and nonhomogeneity (i.e., no two parcels are identical). Economic attributes include scarcity, modification potential, and location.

Undeveloped land is tangible and immobile, has the ability to satisfy certain human needs, and is scarce in many geographic areas. Therefore, it offers desirable investment characteristics. Value may be enhanced by real appreciation, zoning, and inflationary gains; by the possibility of receiving periodic income from rents; and by income tax deductions for business expenses, real estate taxes, and interest. Land also offers the opportunity to magnify gains through financial leverage, and the possible monopoly inherent in a specific location.

Cash Flows

Cash flows during ownership of undeveloped land are seldom significant. Some parking lots or farmable parcels are rented, but seldom does property bring an annual rent of more than 5 percent of its market value. Such rent may pay the taxes, but rarely is there cash flow. The sale of timber, mineral rights, hunting rights, easements, and other partial interests is often helpful in offsetting property tax payments and some of the interest expense. Income tax deductions for property taxes and interest reduce the net carrying costs of undeveloped land.

Four Primary Factors Affecting Values

Factors that affect the value of undeveloped land fall into four categories: (1) physical; (2) economic; (3) governmental; and (4) sociological.

Physical Attributes. The size of a parcel of land must be adequate for development to its highest and best use. Small or awkwardly shaped parcels may be difficult to develop; hence marketability is affected. Topography is important; not all land is suitable for construction. Some will be lost to flood-prone areas. Adequate drainage is important, because low areas may require costly filling.

Vegetation can be important for some parcels. Wooded residential lots and office sites are generally more valuable than open, farmed parcels. Soil and subsoil conditions affect the types of buildings that can be erected and the construction techniques used. Ground water, percolation, and drainage capabilities are important. Soil boring tests can be performed to assess these factors. Soil contamination from leaking underground storage tanks and pesticide applications are among major environmental problems.

Economic Factors. Since the rationale for buying undeveloped land is based on its growth potential, a trend toward growing employment in the local area is an important factor. The economic base consists of industrial activity; wholesale, retail, and service trade; productivity; and sensitivity to influence by outside forces. Strong growth areas with a diversified economic mix are preferred by investors.

Total area income growth and rising per capita or family income is desirable. Investing in land located in a declining income region is unwise unless the land can be acquired at an extremely depressed price and held for longer than the typical length of time.

High interest rates tend to depress the price of non-income-producing land; investors put their money elsewhere. If the high interest rates are a symptom of anticipated high inflation, land prices will rise along with other tangibles. Land buyers should be prepared to ride out the storms created by fluctuating interest rates.

Governmental Factors. Landowners will, of course, want the best services at the lowest cost, and the greatest possible freedom from hindrances to development. Prices for adjacent parcels can vary sharply when the parcels are separated by municipal or school district boundaries.

Utilities (water, sewer, gas/electric, telephone) are essential to development. A land investor should be certain that someday they will be available to the property. Municipal services include fire and police protection, education, refuse collection, and such controls as planning, zoning, and building codes. Transportation facilities are generally within the government's purview. Some governments will require the landowner to supply utilities at his cost or may assess the landowner for the cost.

Some local governments have adopted no-growth policies and rent controls. Although attitudes may change someday, a land investor must have great fortitude to buy undeveloped land in such an area or one where similar controls might be implemented. Some local governments will tax a property into development by basing the rates on zoning rather than existing use. Governments can tax lower income families and marginal businesses out of their jurisdiction.

Sociological Factors. Demographics includes the population of an area, natural increases and immigration trends, household and family size, age and sex composition, ethnic background, density, and geographical distribution. Growth in population combined with shrinking household size indicates a growing need for housing units and therefore a promising potential for development.

Local tastes and attitudes are also important. Preference for high or low density may be indicated by the composition of the population (permanent, transient, or mixed), the climate, and transportation facilities. The investor must understand his ultimate user thoroughly. Such preferences do not transfer easily from one section of the country to another. As a result, regional architecture, density, transportation mode, and the like will evolve in ways in which the land speculator must be well versed.

ATTRACTIVE FEATURES

Appreciation Gain on Resale

Appreciation gain realized on resale is the primary motivating force behind most undeveloped land investments. Two main avenues of gain are local growth and inflation.

Local Growth. Local growth may be in the form of geographical expansion or population and employment increases. As a city and its suburban areas grow, highways and other transportation arteries are planned and built to accommodate existing and future demand. Utility lines are extended; other public facilities, such as parks, schools, and libraries, are built in newly developed areas, as are shopping centers, office buildings, and factories. As this development ensues, land that was formerly fallow is put to a higher and better use. Development potential becomes more obvious for land that was once considered too distant from the city. Although appreciation gains generally occur gradually, some changes can cause rapid appreciation. These include the announcement of plans for or the actual completion of roads, utilities, reservoirs, annexation by a city or town, rezoning, speculative interest, and new employment opportunities.

Hedge Against Inflation. Because it is tangible, indestructible, and useful, undeveloped land is considered an excellent hedge against inflation. As the purchasing power of money shrinks, it takes more dollars to buy the same parcel of land. Some investors have paid more for land than it was worth and were disillusioned when they tried to sell but could not realize what they paid, as least not for many years.

Leverage

Leverage, the ability to borrow, can enhance capital gains from land. Some institutional lenders are willing to lend with raw land as collateral; however, in most situations, owners must finance the property that they sell. Down payments have typically ranged from 10 to 40 percent, the balance financed over five to twenty years. Interest rates are sometimes lower than what lending institutions are charging, and properties are frequently sold on an interest-only basis.

With a typical 25 percent down payment at 10 percent interest, a 33 percent property appreciation rate is magnified to a 100 percent rate of return on equity. Such returns can occur in raw land, but rarely with improved properties. However, leverage is a double-edged sword. Unless the property appreciates at a rate above the interest rate paid for borrowed money, the equity will be eroded. Such conditions, leaving little way to achieve a positive return, generally result in abandonment or foreclosure.

Financing from the seller can often be arranged on a nonrecourse basis, which means that the property is the sole collateral for the loan. A 60 to 80 percent loan-to-value ratio is sought. In the event of default, the mortgage holder has no recourse to the personal assets of the debtor. Release provisions, whereby portions of the property are deeded free and clear to the purchaser on payment of part of the principal owed, are commonly used. They are quite desirable to the buyer who employs leverage. Typically, the less attractive acreage will be released first, generally on a payment of 25 percent more than the average acreage price.

Security of Investment

In most cases, land cannot be wasted or stolen (exceptions include erosion of beachlands, adverse possession, and political upheavals). Although environmental restrictions occasionally may reduce or otherwise retard value, land is generally solid security. Except in rare instances following speculative binges and the troughs of economic depression, the value of most undeveloped land in the United States has steadily climbed upward.

Intangible Benefits

Land ownership provides intangible benefits for many. Notable among these groups are American farmers and their families, Europeans, and Japanese. For them, land provides safety, security, a feeling of well-being and pride for community involvement. Development of the land offers a sense of artistic and business accomplishment.

Interim Income

Drive-in theaters, low-density office areas or industrial parks, and dairy farms are among the last feasible users of large land assemblages appropriate for higher and better uses. Downtown parking lots may pay taxes while the uneconomical older buildings create large negative cash flow. Investors frequently underestimate land holding times, and interim expenses contribute greatly to the high carrying costs.

POTENTIAL RISKS

Variable Rates of Return

Rates of return from undeveloped land investments exhibit an extremely wide range of variability. Land investments are unlike U.S. Treasury bills, which offer a certain income. Landowners cannot tell their brokers to sell and expect to receive a check next week for market value. Land is subject to many other risks, including illiquidity; regulatory and political risk; and market volatility.

Illiquidity. Unlike many other investments, land cannot be sold at market value within a short marketing period. It is difficult to parcel out or subdivide land into undivided interests. The selling of the back forty to send a child to college is not always possible. Land may require several months or years on the market for the owner to realize its market value. Impatient or desperate sellers may be forced to sell at a loss, or may fail to sell at all. Investors should be cognizant of this significant drawback and not purchase land unless they have liquid assets sufficient to meet their needs.

Regulatory and Political Risk. A government agency enforcing environmental regulations can cause expensive development delays or even prevent full development of the land. The states of Florida and California require environmental impact statements (EISs) for many kinds of development. Regional and local planning councils have become increasingly concerned with the environmental impact of proposed projects. Powers beyond review and recommendation have been awarded some planning commissions within a specified area (e.g., river corridors of 2,000-foot width). When a Federal Housing Administration (FHA) mortgage-insurance project is to be requested on a development proposed for more than 500 homes, the Department of Housing and Urban Development (HUD) requires an EIS to be prepared and made available to specified public agencies, as well as to the public at large.

Rezoning applications, no matter how justified the owner feels they are, may be disapproved by political bodies. In recent times, courts have been hearing complaints from landowner-developers that zoning councils have acted capriciously and arbitrarily. At first, the courts declared some land free of zoning, then rezoned other land, and now appear to be remanding cases back to the original zoning body. In some cases, they are upholding the zoning boards. These cases, however, may be considered a step forward for the landowners in that for many years the courts refused to hear such cases at all, declaring zoning issues to be the exclusive domain of the zoning boards.

Private ownership is subject to the government's right of eminent domain. Landowners sometimes feel that condemnation awards are insufficient. They have always had the right to contest these awards and have frequently won in court. Juries can go either way, however, and litigation is expensive, with attorney and appraisal fees paid by the landowner. These risks often affect the maximum gain realized. However, they seldom cause substantial losses to careful buyers who compare actual resale prices to original costs. In fact, for some investors, having land condemned can be highly profitable.

Market Volatility. Markets for undeveloped land are generally local. They are subject to influence at all levels of government and the economy: national, state, and, particularly, local. Stability is the general rule, but wide swings can occur for specific property. Lack of activity often masks volatile prices. In periods of tight money, such as the mid-1970s and early 1980s, transactions may be infrequent and characterized by distress selling at depressed prices. Generally, after a year or two activity resumes and prices continue to ratchet upward, as they did in the late 1970s and late 1980s.

TAX CONSEQUENCES

Land Speculation Under Earlier Tax Laws

In the period between 1969 and 1973, several areas—particularly in the Sun Belt states, including the cities Atlanta, Dallas, Houston, Orlando, and Phoenix—experienced such strong speculator markets that the marketing techniques that were used then are still associated with investment in raw land. This is true despite the fact that they were oriented to tax advantages that no longer exist.

The syndications popular at that time were almost always limited partnerships composed of a broker-general partner and numerous limited partners who were not knowledgeable in land values or development but typically sought tax shelter for other income. The bulk of the shelter was achieved through prepaid interest paid to sellers as an inducement to offer attractive purchase-money notes. Prepaid interest is no longer allowed as a tax deduction. A second tax law that has subsequently been revised, affecting installment sales, tended to hold the down payment required by a landowner to less than 30 percent of the purchase price. Many aggressive general partners were able to get their limited partners to borrow cash for the down payment, resulting in purchase with no cash of their own (mortgage-out).

Deductions for interest were the only tax deductions available to these partnerships, but they were sufficient to create an artificial land boom. The mortgaging-out situation of paying "interest only" results in what brokers term one-to-one write-offs; that is, every dollar paid is deductible. Deduction for prepaid interest was disallowed in the Tax Reform Act of 1976. However, many partnerships had matured by that time into principal-paying periods and many land investments, perhaps most, were abandoned; this situation brought a whole new condition of tax setback in that some foreclosures/abandonments can be treated like sales by the Internal Revenue Service (IRS), with tax due on profits that never occurred.

With raw land speculators quickly pushing prices beyond levels that subdividers could feasibly pay, the only prospective purchasers were other syndicators. Although this market soon collapsed with losses to many participants, many people still associate the excitement of that period with raw land investing.

Phases in the Life Cycle of Land

The three phases of the life cycle of land as an investment are acquisition, holding, and resale.

Acquisition

Purchase. The acquisition cost for property purchased serves as the purchaser's initial tax basis in the property. This cost includes both the equity paid and any debt burdens taken on in the purchase. The cost of title insurance, survey costs, legal fees, appraisal, option payments, broker commissions, and most other items paid at closing are included in the initial tax basis. Prorated property taxes and unexpired insurance paid by the purchaser at closing are generally deductible as expenses in the period to which they relate.

Gift. The recipient of a gift takes the donor's basis as his own. In computation of a donee's gain or loss on resale, the basis is the lower of the donor's basis or fair market value at the time of the gift. In many situations, part or all of the federal gift taxes paid can be added to the donee's basis.

Inheritance. The basis of inherited property is generally its fair market value at the time of the decedent's death or an alternative valuation date, which is ordinarily six months after death. Tax law as to basis of inherited property changed in 1976, but implementation was delayed and the law essentially reversed in 1980. Consequently, unrealized appreciation at death generally skips income taxes.

The basis of property acquired in an exchange is carried over from the property surrendered. (Exchanges are described in *Tax-Deferred Exchange*, later in this article.)

Holding. During the period of ownership of land, deductions are permitted for expenses, including real estate taxes, insurance, and interest. Deductions for investment interest expenses on land are generally limited (except for corporations) to $10,000 plus the taxpayer's net investment income. Unused investment interest expenses can be carried over indefinitely.

Capital improvements, such as the cost of a new fence or costs to connect to utility lines, are generally added to the landowner's tax basis. Deductions for depletion and depreciation, for example, generally reduce the original tax basis. Raw land itself, however, is not depreciable.

The Tax Reform Act of 1986 (the 1986 Act) made major changes in loss computations. Losses can now be deducted from passive activities only to the extent of income from passive activities. However, the new law provides exceptions for certain activities, and it also contains phase-in rules for some losses. A passive activity generally is any activity involving the conduct of a trade or business in which the investor does not participate materially. The IRS considers an investor involved on a regular, continuous, and substantial basis in the operation of an activity as participating materially in that activity. The passive loss rules that apply limit the income to a level that excludes most persons who can invest in land.

The popular seller mortgage was frequently a nonrecourse loan; that is, since land was a nonwasting asset, it could be returned to the seller and would probably have the same or a higher value. Institutional lenders will sometimes make such loans, although on a shorter-term basis and to borrowers having a firm subdividing/disposition plan. Losses from any activity, including the holding of real property (other than mineral property) placed in service after December 31, 1986, fall under new at-risk rules that prevent deductions beyond the amount an investor stands to lose. Amounts protected against loss by a guarantee, stop-loss agreement, or similar arrangement also trigger these rules.

Resale. On the resale of land that had been held as an investment, capital gain or loss is recognized. The amount realized (sales price less expenses of sale) less the adjusted tax basis (original basis modified by improvements or subtractions) is the amount of capital gain or loss.

If the property has been held for more than six months, long-term capital gains status results. The 1986 Act repealed the capital gains deduction that had long been enjoyed by land investors. The holding periods varied in the prior tax acts from six months to a year, and investors have always been very careful that they did not involve themselves in the development of the land to the extent that profits would be tainted, that is, treated as ordinary income. There were limits on how many parcels (lots) could be subdivided from a large tract before the investor was classified as a dealer. The new law provides no rate differential for capital gains.

The interest required to carry the land investment is deductible against income from it or other income from passive activities, but the interest cannot be directly applied to reduce the investor's ordinary income. Land has been a poor tax shelter for the last decade or more and the 1986 Act made it more so.

Installment Sale

Land sellers who finance the land that they sell can use installment sale provisions. However, the 1986 Act changed the recognition of the portion deferred. The new rules make investors recognize current income to the extent of allocable installment indebtedness (AII). AII is determined by dividing the application installment obligation outstanding at year end by the investor's total assets (including the applicable installment obligations) and multiplying the results by the investor's average indebtedness. Amounts recognized in prior years reduce AII for the current year. Amounts collected are first used to offset amounts previously recognized under these new rules. The purpose of this rule is to prevent an investor from increasing his liquidity by direct or indirect borrowing against outstanding notes receivables. For some, the installment sale will now be dropped from the tax tool kit.

Tax-Deferred Exchange

Section 1031 of the Internal Revenue Code states that "no gain or loss shall be recognized if property held for productive use in trade or business or for investment is exchanged solely for property of a like kind to be held either for productive use in trade or business or for investment." A tax-deferred exchange occurs when property held for productive use or for investment is exchanged for property of a like kind to be held for productive use or for investment.

The provisions of Section 1031 apply to both gains and losses. Further, the section is mandatory if all requirements are met. Consequently, if property is traded and the transaction meets all the requirements, the taxpayer cannot elect to pay a tax on the gain or to recognize a loss. Alternatively, a taxpayer can sell property to recognize a gain or loss.

The three basic requirements for a tax-deferred exchange are as follows:

1. There must be an exchange. A sale and separate purchase can qualify if strict requirements are met (Starker's provision allows forty-five days to find/contract for new property).
2. Both the asset surrendered and the one received in the exchange must be held for productive use in trade or business or as an investment.
3. The exchange must involve property deemed to be of like kind. Generally, one form of real estate may be exchanged for another.

Other Provisions

The 1986 Act is a complex act, and such of its provisions as investment interest expense, at-risk rules, investment tax credits, and alternative minimum tax are beyond the scope of this article. None applies specifically to land. The 1976 and 1986 tax law changes combined have had a negative impact on land investing and have thus helped to remove some speculation from it. Land investing is now mostly based on ordinary income objectives.

REPRESENTATIVE TYPES OF INVESTORS

Land ownership appeals to a wide variety of investor types: individuals, pension plans, insurance companies, savings and loan associations, partnerships, corporations, developers, and others. The nature of land investments—their illiquidity, the uncertainty of returns, and the likelihood that returns will be deferred—makes the most suitable investors those who can wait for the time it takes for the property to reach desirable fruition and those who can pay carrying costs (interest, taxes, insurance) with money from sources outside the property. Because most carrying costs are tax-deductible, after-tax costs are least for those in the highest tax brackets.

Patient but persevering investors are being suited to investing in undeveloped land. Since returns are deferred, the rewards occur years after the investment. Moreover, an investor should be prepared to upgrade the land's value, an activity that often requires action and reaction to proposed utility lines, thoroughfare extensions, and zoning changes. It may be possible for an investor to purchase land near his own residence; if not, it is wise to establish a rapport with brokers and attorneys where the site is located. The investor benefits from rapidly learning of pending changes that affect the land's use and its value.

Individuals

A popular technique by which the small investor can participate in land value appreciation is to live on it—that is, to find a small home on acreage. Property taxes are limited by homestead exemptions in most states; the primary residence has always been favored by other tax advantages at the time of resale, and the owner-occupant is frequently in the best position to know when the most opportune time has come for subdividing.

However, this technique is fading along with the ownership dream. A recent article in *Mortgage Banking* points out that in the 1950s the typical house payment took 14 percent of a thirty-year-old's paycheck, while in 1985, it required 44 percent. Homeownership rates among twenty-five- to thirty-year-olds have dropped by more than 10 percent in the 1980s alone. Land investment, like many other investments, is left to more mature participants.

The farmette of three- to five-acre homesites may work for the owner of fifty-plus acre assemblages, but further subdividing of the property will probably be infeasible for many years. However, the home on a three- to five-acre site in close-in areas is adequate for the resubdividing of that lot into its own cul de sac or mini-neighborhood. In highly desired neighborhoods in Hawaii, a half million dollar home is frequently razed for the site for another more highly valued home. It is not unusual in Atlanta or Dallas for the developers of postage stamp lots in an in-fill project (five to ten lots) close to downtown to offer lots at the same or higher prices as larger lots in the market and at prices just under that of improved properties.

Syndications

Although small investors can purchase amounts of land that suit their own pocketbooks, such tracts are seldom among the most desirable. Syndicates (limited partnerships) often serve the best interests of the small investor. Reputable, experienced syndicators often arrange purchases of large tracts with good potential by a group of small investors. Twenty investors who each put up $10,000 cash for the down payment can frequently control a choice $1 million tract. However, syndicates may fail to accomplish their goal for many reasons, including market downturns, setbacks on other properties experienced by the syndicator, and the unwillingness or inability of investors to continue their annual financial commitment to the property. Consequently, investors must be careful in their selection of the syndicator and other investors, as well as of the property under consideration. Since most syndications are limited partnerships, the general partner has total control of decisions. (See article on "Real Estate: Limited Partnerships," elsewhere in this volume.)

Foreign Investors

For various reasons, raw land has become a favored investment of foreign investors. Tens of thousands of acres of farmland and raw land have been quietly acquired by non-American investors during the 1980s. These investors have frequently paid cash and have been able to outbid many local investors. Government agencies are monitoring this activity, although no quotas are known to be in the making nor are other federal restrictions being developed. In many areas, the new money has been most welcome.

Developers

Real estate developers may purchase land three to five years in advance of their needs. In some areas, it takes a minimum of one year to secure the necessary building approvals, but the motivating force is more often fixing the land cost and excluding competitors for a particular site.

Other Investors

Insurance companies and most pension plans are obligated to meet certain actuarially determined commitments. Because returns are uncertain, investing in raw land is virtually prohibitive except for a small portion of money. State or federal laws may prohibit large-scale raw land investments.

Some savings and loan associations are partners in real estate developments through their service corporations. They may hold some raw land as a small fraction of their assets, with an eye toward development. Few will invest in land unless it has obvious immediate development potential, although they may make acquisition and development, construction, and permanent home loans.

Industrial and retail corporations sometimes will acquire land prior to needing it for business expansion. The land cost is locked in at an early date, and the potentially best site is purchased. However, land purchase in advance of need is often perceived as an inefficient use of corporate capital.

IMPORTANT FACTORS IN BUYING AND SELLING

The critical concerns when buying and selling are (1) selecting a broker, (2) finding the right market, (3) determining highest and best use, (4) using professional advisors, (5) negotiating the purchase or sales price and the terms of sale as well as acceptable terms of financing.

Selecting a Broker

In 1988, there were more than 2.5 million licensed real estate salespersons or brokers in the United States. Of these licensees, about half were active in real estate on a full-time basis. Because most full-time agents concentrate on sales of single-family homes, selecting a real estate salesperson at random to help buy or sell a parcel of land suitable for investment can be a uncertain proposition.

It is important to find a local person who is knowledgeable about land: its physical, economic, governmental, and social environment. It is crucial that a land salesperson have a reputation for honesty and knowledge. Other professionals such as lawyers, accountants, and bankers are sometimes able to recommend good land salespeople. Real estate appraisers and developers are also potentially good sources.

Membership in the Realtors Land Institute and/or the Securities and Syndications Institute indicates some commitment to professionalism in the field. Both organizations are affiliates of the National Association of Realtors. Membership also denotes adherence to a code of ethics.

Finding the Right Market

The market for land is imperfect. In a given local area, there are generally few buyers and sellers. In contrast to securities or commodities markets, transactions are infrequent and private. Several speculator markets have experienced the phenomena of churning and pyramiding, in which land values have been artificially inflated. Some accounts of fraud have lead to the financial failure of some lending institutions.

The investor should approach land buying in a disciplined and systematic manner. One approach is to find the specific site wanted and to negotiate with the owner. The other is to select from what is offered on the market. In either case, it is prudent to plot known offerings and sales on a map. Consider what is known about each sale, including prices and terms, topography, utilities, flood-prone areas, nearby roads, and other special features. Try to ascertain why the sale of one site realized more (or less) per land unit (acre, foot) than that of a comparable site. A real estate appraiser can be of great help. When selling, the information will help an investor to price the land intelligently. When buying, the investor will be able to recognize obvious bargains (there could be desperate sellers or overpriced parcels). Whether buying or selling, investors are wise to be patient. Marketing land or making investment tastes known takes time.

Determining Highest and Best Use

Deciding how to use it is the most creative aspect of investing in undeveloped land; this judgment is an art built on the physical and economic sciences. The purpose of the analysis that any investor in vacant or underimproved land makes is to determine its highest and best use. The American Institute of Real Estate Appraisers offers three definitions of this concept, as follows:

1. The reasonable and probable use that supports the highest present value of vacant land or improved property, as defined, as of the date of the appraisal.
2. The reasonable, probable, and legal use of land or sites as though vacant, found to be physically possible, appropriately supported, financially feasible, and that results in the highest present land value.
3. The most profitable use.

Implied in these definitions is that the determination of highest and best use takes into account the contribution of a specific use to the community and community development goals as well as the benefits of that use to individual property owners. Hence, in certain situations the highest and best use may be for parks, greenbelts, preservation, conservation, wildlife habitats, and the like.

In situations of rapid land-use change and volatile business conditions, professional analysis may be required to determine the optimal mix of land uses. Three tables illustrate a case study in which three possible investments are analyzed over a development period of four years. The highest and best use mix is the one that produces the greatest present worth of the three combinations. Reference may be made to alternative investments in the selection of the discount rate used in the cash flow analysis. The rate may be built up, beginning with the interest rate on the land loan (say 12 percent) plus allowance for nonliquidity (1 percent), management (1 percent), and risk (1 percent), which produces the 15 percent discount rate used in examples herein.

In the scenario depicted in Table 1, a $1 million beachfront property is held for three years before being sold for redevelopment. The small house on it is rented during the holding period. What is the present value of these incomes, assuming a 15 percent discount rate? The pro forma statement shows it to be worth about $690,000.

The $1 million land sale projected to occur in the fourth year has a present value of $571,800; however, if there is a downturn in the market and the developer cannot realize

TABLE 1. Valuation of Condominium Land Investment

Land Uses	1 Year	2 Years	3 Years	4 Years	Totals
Beach house rentals	$ 80	$ 100	$ 120	$ 50	$ 350
Sales for condo development	—	—	—	1,000	1,000
Total revenue	$ 80	$ 100	$ 120	$ 1,050	$ 1,350
Expenses	− 45	− 50	− 55	− 40	− 190
Net income	$ 35	$ 50	$ 65	$ 1,010	$ 1,160
Discount factor @ 15%	× .8696	× .7561	× .6575	× .5718	NA
Present value	$ 30.436	$ 37.805	$ 42.738	$577.518	$688.497

NA = Not available.

Note: Amounts in thousands of dollars.

that price until the tenth year, the value today has been eroded to $247,185. This is an example of why it is necessary for a lender to foreclose on a property before the development is ever completed. Values can be determined to be lower than outstanding loan balances when sales do not occur as originally projected.

Table 2 reflects the subdividing of a 100-acre land parcel for multiple land uses; in both cases, ten acres are lost to streets. This table and Table 3 focus on the same parcel and mix of uses, but the absorption period varies. The first produces a present value of the assemblage at $32,120 per acre ($3,212,000 ÷ 100 acres), although the gross retail sales over the four-year period total $75,000 per acre ($7,500,000 ÷ 100 acres).

Table 3 depicts a more aggressive development scenario of the same land assemblage. The impact of time of development is reflected in the resulting present value. Expenses are lower, as are holding costs. This scenario produced a value for the raw development site of $3.2 million, whereas the cash flow projections in Table 3 support a $3.97 million investment.

There are as many values as there are combinations of parcel sales over time. It is imperative that a purchaser not pay the seller the gross retail sellout. Subtractions are for (1) necessary expenses, (2) hard costs, and (3) the time value of money (discounting). The gross retail sellout in the case study is $7.5 million, which would quickly result in catastrophe for the buyer were his negotiation to pay that amount.

Using Professional Advisors

Appraisers, attorneys, planning consultants, brokers, and accountants are the professionals commonly used by land buyers and sellers (Table 4). Depending on the complexity of the property and the transactions, others can be helpful. These include farm, ranch, and timber specialists, counselors, mortgage brokers, architects, and engineers.

Those dealing in land should select professionals with care. Some real estate appraisers concentrate in residential or commercial property, and so have little experience with land. Many attorneys are specialists in matters other than real estate, and the same is true for

TABLE 2. Valuation of a Mixed-Use Development Over a Four-Year Period (Scenario A)

Land Uses	1 Year	2 Years	3 Years	4 Years	Totals
Commercial	$ —	$ —	—	10 a × $ 200/a $ 2,000	$ 2,000
Office	—	—	30 a × $ 100/a $ 3,000		$ 3,000
Industrial	50 a × $50/a $ 2,500	—	—	—	$ 2,500
Total revenue	$ 2,500	0	$ 3,000	$ 2,000	$ 7,500
Expenses	− 1,500	− 200	− 600	− 400	− 2,700
Net income	$ 1,000	(200)	$ 2,400	$ 1,600	$ 4,800
Discount factor @ 15%	× .8696	× .7561	× .6575	× .5718	NA
Present value	$ 870	$ (151)	$ 1,578	$ 915	$ 3,212

a = acre; NA = Not available.

Note: Amounts in thousands of dollars.

TABLE 3. Valuation of a Mixed-Use Development Over a Two-Year Period (Scenario B)

Land Uses	1 Year	2 Years	Totals
Commercial	$ —	10 a × $ 200/a $ 2,000	$ 2,000
Office	—	30 a × $ 100/a $ 3,000	$ 3,000
Industrial	50 a × $ 50/a $ 2,500		$ 2,500
Total revenue	$ 2,500	$ 5,000	$ 7,500
Expenses	− 1,500	− 900	− 2,400
Net income	$ 1,000	$ 4,100	$ 5,100
Discount factor @ 15%	× .8696	× .7561	—
Present value	$ 870	$ 3,100	$ 3,970

a = acre.

Note: Amounts in thousands of dollars.

most accountants. Property buyers and sellers are advised to seek out professionals who have participated in and are knowledgeable about the type of transaction involved.

A farm or ranch acquired by an investor is not the same as idle land. It is a business, and experienced management is needed. Land with timber can be managed to maximize profits or reduce holding costs; planting, harvesting, and maintaining healthy trees is a science.

When land approaches the development stage, architects and engineers may be necessary to plot subdivisions and decide where utility lines and streets should be put. Counselors and marketing experts can be helpful in designing suitable improvements, targeting the market, and timing sales. As projects require mortgage financing, mortgage bankers or brokers may be called on for assistance.

Negotiating the Purchase and the Financing

Real estate owners who want to sell quote an offering price through their brokers. It is known that they will accept that price in cash, but negotiation is customary in real estate. Buyers, generally acting through their broker or the listing broker, will submit an offer at a lower amount and request generous financing terms. The offer also may stipulate certain conditions and subject the property to physical tests and title checks by experts. The owner may reject it with or without a counteroffer. Further negotiations ensue until an agreement is reached. Provided that all conditions to the contract have been met, closing takes place. Money and property change hands.

MANAGING THE INVESTMENT

Contrary to popular belief, land does require management, although it can be less intensive than that required for rented improved property.

Governmental Changes

Some zoning is reversionary; the predevelopment classification may expire and revert to an agricultural category if some form of construction is not initiated within a prescribed period. Condemnation of easements and rights of way require monitoring. Various public hearings may be carried out on road relocations, a reservoir development, or zoning of neighboring property.

Physical Inspection

Periodic physical inspections are recommended for landowners. Although the land itself cannot be destroyed, it is subject to forces of nature (e.g., erosion, drought, fires, pests, and flooding) and of people (e.g., waste dumping, encroachments, squatters, and theft of timber and minerals). Periodic inspections, at least annually, should uncover any problems.

Liability Insurance

Liability insurance is recommended to protect against unforeseeable events, such as an all-terrain vehicle accident, a fall, or a drowning on the property. Although such events are rare, liability insurance is particularly necessary when the land is used for recreational purposes.

TABLE 4. Professional Designations in Real Estate

Designation		Certifying Organization
REAL ESTATE SALES		
CRB	Certified Residential Broker	Realtors National Marketing Institute, Chicago
CRS	Certified Residential Specialist	Realtors National Marketing Institute, Chicago
GRI	Graduate, Realtors Institute	Graduate Realtors Institute, Chicago, and State Realtors Association
INDUSTRIAL, COMMERCIAL INVESTMENT		
CCIM	Certified Commercial Investment Member	Realtors National Marketing Institute, Chicago
CRSS	Certified Real Estates Securities Sponsor	Securities & Syndication Institute, Chicago
SIR	Society, Industrial Realtors	Society of Industrial Realtors, Chicago
MANAGEMENT		
AFLM	Accredited Farm and Land Managers	Realtors Land Institute, Chicago
AFM	Accredited Farm Manager	American Society Farm Managers & Rural Appraisers, Denver
CPM	Certified Property Manager	Institute of Real Estate Management Institute, Chicago
APPRAISAL		
ARA	Accredited Rural Appraiser	American Society Farm Managers & Rural Appraisers, Denver
ASA	Member, American Society of Appraisers	American Society of Appraisers, Washington, D.C.
IFA	Independent Fee Appraiser	Independent Fee Appraiser, St. Louis
MAI	Member Appraisal Institute	American Institute of Real Estate Appraisers, Chicago
RM	Residential Member	American Institute of Real Estate Appraisers, Chicago
SRA	Senior Residential Appraiser	Society of Real Estate Appraisers, Chicago
SREA	Senior Real Estate Analysts	Society of Real Estate Appraisers, Chicago
SRPA	Senior Real Property Appraisers	Society of Real Estate Appraisers, Chicago
SR/WA	Senior Right of Way Agent	American Right of Way Association, Chicago
ASSESSMENT		
AAE	Accredited Assessment Evaluator	International Association of Assessing Officers, Chicago
CAE	Certified Assessment Evaluator	International Association of Assessing Officers, Chicago
RES	Residential Evaluation Specialist	International Association of Assessing Officers, Chicago
COUNSELING		
CRE	Counselor, Real Estate	American Society of Real Estate Counselors, Chicago
FINANCIAL		
CMB	Certified Mortgage Banker	Mortgage Bankers Association, Washington, D.C.

Other Precautions

Tax payments are mandatory. Tax assessors should be notified of address changes, and the owner should be certain that taxes and other assessments are paid. Both may need to be contested if they are inequitable.

Foreign investors should be certain to maintain a relationship with a knowledgeable person in the United States to file necessary documents.

Predevelopment Work

Professional predevelopment work is generally called packaging, namely, getting raw land into a market-ready condition. Skilled buyers plan the ultimate sale of properties when they first acquire them. The minimization of risk requires aggressive management in the conversion of raw land into a valuable user asset.

The greatest increment of profit occurs with the repositioning of a land parcel's highest and best use—not necessarily its actual use. A land investor might commission a detailed survey, field-checked topographic study, hydrological analysis, subdivision lot layout, or other land-use plan; zoning approval; water-sewer layout approval; and perhaps soil borings and building permits.

GLOSSARY

acre—A measure of land containing 43,560 square feet.

discounted cash flow (DCF) analysis—A set of procedures in which an appraiser specifies the quantity, variability, timing, and duration of periodic income, as well as the quantity and timing of reversions; each is then discounted to its present value at a specified yield rate.

discount rate—A rate of return on capital used to convert future payments or receipts into present value.

eminent domain—The power to take (condemn) private property for public use on payment of a fair compensation.

forecasting—Predicting a future happening or condition based on past trends and the perceptions of market participants, tempered with analytical judgment concerning the continuation of these trends and the realization of these perceptions in the future.

highest and best use—The legally permitted and otherwise feasible use of the land that will bring the greatest income or value to the land.

internal rate of return—The discount rate that equates the present value of expected cash inflows with expected cash outflows.

land residual process—Method of appraising vacant land.

leverage—Use of others' money to complete an investment transaction.

listing—An agreement to engage a broker to sell or lease.

nonrecourse loan—The lender may claim only the property as collateral; the borrower is not personally liable.

option—A contract providing the right to buy, sell, or lease property within a stated period and under certain specified terms.

parcel—Any area of land contained within one description.

purchase-money mortgage—A loan from the seller to the buyer of property.

raw land—See unimproved land.

release provisions—A clause in a mortgage that allows some property to be freed as collateral.

reversion—A lump-sum benefit that an investor receives at the termination of an investment.

unimproved land—Land in its natural state, undeveloped, with no building or other improvements.

water table—Level of water in the ground.

yield rate—In appraising, a measure of investment return that is applied to a series of incomes, including reversion, to discount each to present value (e.g., interest rate, discount rate, internal rate of return, and equity yield rate).

zoning—Local government control of the use of land.

LEADING BROKERS

Adam-Cates Co., Atlanta

Coldwell Banker, Chicago

Cushman Wakefield, New York

Grubb & Ellis, San Francisco

Laguarta & Co., Houston

Landauer & Company, New York

Henry S. Miller Company, Dallas

Sonneblick-Goldman Realty, Miami

SUGGESTED READING

PERIODICALS

Appraisal Journal. Published by the American Institute of Real Estate Appraisers, an affiliate of the National Association of Realtors, Chicago. Quarterly.

Federal Home Loan Bank Board Journal. Published by the Federal Home Loan Bank Board, Washington, D.C. Monthly.

Journal of the American Real Estate and Urban Economics Association. Published by the American Real Estate and Urban Economics Association.

Journal of Real Estate Taxation. Published by Warren, Gorham & Lamont, Boston. Quarterly.

Land Economcs. Published by University of Wisconsin, Madison. Quarterly.

Mortgage and Real Estate Executives Report. Published by Warren, Gorham & Lamont, Boston. Monthly.

Real Estate Appraiser and Analyst. Published by the Society of Real Estate Appraisers, Chicago. Bimonthly.

Real Estate Review. Published by Warren, Gorham & Lamont, Boston. Quarterly.

Real Estate Today. Published by the National Association of Realtors, Chicago. Monthly.

REFERENCE BOOKS

Achoris, Dominique. *Real Estate, Analysis and Appraisal*. Scarborough, Ontario: Butterworths of Canada, Fischer Presses, 1987.

American Institute of Real Estate Appraisers. *The Appraisal of Real Estate*, 9th ed. Chicago: American Institute of Real Estate Appraisers, 1987.

Anderson, Jerry D. *Success Strategies for Investment in Real Estate*, 2nd ed. Englewood Cliffs, N.J.: Prentice-Hall, Inc., 1987.

Benke, William. *All About Land Investment*. New York: McGraw-Hill Book Co., 1976.

Coopers & Lybrand. *Tax Planning for Real Estate Transactions*. Chicago: Farm and Land Institute, 1978.

Friedman, Jack P., and Ordway, Nicholas. *Income Property Appraisal and Analysis*. Englewood Cliffs, N.J.: Prentice-Hall, 1987.

Hinds, Dudley,Carn, Neil, and Ordway, Nicholas. *Winning at Zoning*. New York: McGraw-Hill Book Co., 1979.

Hines, M.A. *Shopping Center: Development and Investment*, 2nd ed. New York: John Wiley and Sons, Inc., 1988.

Jaffe, Austin J., and Simmons, C.F. *The Fundamentals of Real Estate Investment*. Englewood Cliffs, N.J.: Prentice-Hall, Inc., 1986.

Kendy, Lane H., Conner, Susan, Byrd, Cranston, and Heyman, Judy. *Performance Zoning*, reprint. APA Planners Press, 1988.

Messner, Stephen D., Boyce, Byrl, Trimble, Harold G., and Ward, Robert L. *Analyzing Real Estate Opportunities: Market and Feasibility Studies*. Englewood Cliffs, N.J.: Prentice-Hall, 1987.

Real Estate Review Portfolio No. 3. *Investing in Raw Land*. Boston: Warren, Gorham & Lamont, Inc. 1974. Updated periodically.

Seldin, Maury. *Land Investment*. Homewood, Ill.: Dow Jones-Irwin, 1975.

Thomas, Ronald L., Means, Mary C., and Grieve, Margaret A. *Taking Charge: How Communities Are Planning Their Futures*. Washington, D.C.: International City Management Association, 1988.

Wendt, Paul F., and Cerf, Alan R. *Real Estate Investment Analysis and Taxation*, 2nd ed. New York: McGraw-Hill Book Co., 1979.

RUGS

Archie Cherkezian

BASIC CHARACTERISTICS

Historical Background

To the sophisticated collector-investor, Oriental rugs are imbued with a mystique that combines beauty and material value with historical traditions derived from some of the most ancient of the world's surviving cultures. They are produced today by virtually the same methods as those practiced by Eastern weavers 2,000 years ago. They are of infinite variety (no two are exactly alike) but always for essentially utilitarian purposes. Yet, whether new or centuries old, Oriental rugs have the potential to appreciate over the long term.

This materialistic trait—unlike that affecting most other collectible media in the universe of art—began to appear in the design of Oriental rugs only in relatively recent times. In the countries where they are woven, rugs originally were used not only to cover bare floors, but as curtains to shield windows or conceal open entrances to rooms, and as shroud-like personal wraps to protect against the desert chill. They were used variously as decorative tapestries, as blessings to feudal lords, and as pillows on which to rest a weary head. They served as saddlebags to carry a family's worldly goods on camel-borne treks across the sands, and as prayer rugs, church aprons, even as a kind of personal "companion" with which an owner chose finally to be buried. In more modern times, rugs gradually have become a symbol of personal wealth.

Archie Cherkezian is President of William Cherkezian & Son, Inc., New York, and editor of the quarterly trade magazine, Oriental Rug Magazine.

FIGURE 1. Turkish Knot and Persian Knot

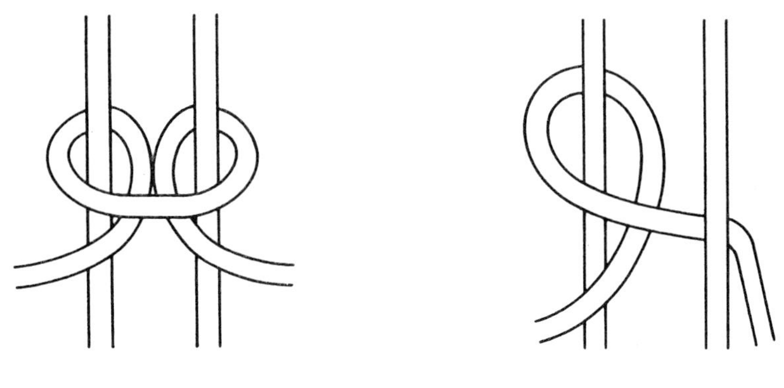

The pile of a handwoven rug is fashioned by tying knots to vertical threads called the "warp." After tying one line of knots the width of the loom, the weaver passes a weft thread horizontally over the row of knots and tamps it into place. The distance between warp threads determines the weave count or quality of the rug. Rugs are tied with either a Turkish or Persian knot, sometimes misnamed ghiordes and sehna knots, respectively. (See Figure 1.) The free ends of the knot form the pile. All Caucasian (essentially Eastern European) Oriental rugs are woven with the Turkish knot. A mixture of Persian and Turkish knots will be found in Ionian rugs (from Asia Minor) and those produced elsewhere in the Asian Orient.

A rug that is handwoven in Kansas or California is not, of course, considered an Oriental rug, no matter how well (or richly) it is fashioned. While a particular handwoven piece from a non-Oriental area may have value to some buyers — for example, because it commemorates a specific event — that carpet probably would not have a worldwide market value. Also, a machine-made rug from an Oriental-rug country is not an Oriental rug, even if it has an Oriental design.

Definitions

The Oriental Rug Importers Association of America (ORIA) defines the term "Oriental rug" as follows: "An *Oriental rug* is handmade of natural fibers, most commonly wool or silk, with a pile woven on a warp and weft, with individual character and design; it is produced only in the Near East, Middle East, Far East, the Balkans and the Caucasus." This definition conforms to standards used by the U.S. Department of Commerce and the U.S. Treasury Department.

The Near East is defined as including most countries of Southwest Asia—specifically Turkey, Lebanon, Egypt, Syria, Jordan, Saudi Arabia, and the smaller sheikdoms of Asia Minor on the Arabian Peninsula—as well as the Balkan States—Greece, Yugoslavia, Romania, Bulgaria, and Albania—which occupy the Balkan Peninsula in Europe. The Middle East is an extensive region consisting of Iraq, Iran, Afghanistan, Pakistan, India,

Burma, and the Caucasus (that region of European Russia situated between the Black Sea and the Caspian Sea). The Far East includes China, Tibet, Eastern Siberia, Japan, Korea, Cambodia, Laos, Vietnam, and the Malay Archipelago.

All of these nations and regions, at one time or another, have produced handwoven rugs for domestic use or export. The most prolific, traditionally, have been Turkey, Iran, Afghanistan, Pakistan, India, China, and the Caucasus. More recently, Yugoslavia, Romania, and Nepal also have become leading world-market suppliers of Oriental rugs.

Handmade rugs are pile textiles that serves as superb coverings for a floor or wall and, with proper selection, constitute a worthwhile investment vehicle as well. Handmade rugs are like fine paintings—they provide aesthetic benefits and simultaneously increase in value, even while being used. Not all handmade rugs are good investments, necessarily, nor is every rug woven by hand automatically an Oriental rug. Machine-made rugs (non-Oriental) are pile textiles used primarily as floor coverings. They are excellent as wall-to-wall broadloom carpeting or as area rugs, but have little, if any, investment value.

PRIMARY DETERMINANTS OF VALUE

Three factors are most important in determining both intrinsic value and appreciation potential for Oriental rugs. The first of these is age. The second factor is quality, relating to both construction materials (silk, wool, and cotton, in that order) and, more important, fineness (i.e., density) of weave. The third is place of origin, involving not merely the identity of village, region, or country where a rug was produced, but also the authenticity of that identification. A fourth factor that must also be considered in evaluating any rug is its size; in general, the larger it is, the more valuable it is. Showing the sharpest gains in investment value of late are the Oriental rugs of Iran, i.e., Persian rugs, whether classified as antique, semi-antique, or new; the Caucasus (antique and semi-antique); Turkey (antique only); China (antique, semi-antique); and India (all three varieties). Essentially, the balance of this discussion of investment-grade Oriental rugs will focus on these most valuable types.

Age

On world markets, Oriental rugs are classified by age according to relatively strict standards.

Classifications. An antique rug is one that is at least 100 years old; such a rug can be imported into the United States duty-free. Semi-antique rugs generally are twenty to fifty years old and of traditional design. A new rug usually means one recently woven, while a used rug is one that has been in use in a home for twenty years or more. While some degree of wear actually can enhance the worth of a fine rug provided it has been well maintained, the general experience has been that rugs literally worn to the warp-threads retain little more than sentimental value. Inevitably, the world supply of mint-condition antiques and semi-antiques has diminished; meanwhile, world demand continues to rise, forcing the prices up.

A certain unpredictability adds spice to such exotic markets. In a case still celebrated when American dealers convene socially, one of their number plucked an excellent, semi-antique, 3.6 × 5.2 foot Herez (Iranian) from a New Hope, Pennsylvania trash can in 1956; the rug, being of silk, had evidently been discarded by an unknown person because silk Orientals were out of vogue at the time. A goodly quantity of Caucasian, fine Persian, and old Turkish silks had been sold in the United States from 1895 to 1928. After that period, and up to 1956, Oriental rugs were not purchased in the United States; sales plummeted. This merchandise (1895–1928), much of which remained intact and in good condition in the estates or homes of the wealthy, became available for sale to Europeans after 1956.

Similarly, a prized antique may create headlines in the trade press just by coming to market. At the February 14, 1981 auction conducted by Sotheby Parke Bernet, New York, a fine *Lavar* Kirman (Iranian), 22.4 × 15.2 feet, woven in 1875, was offered for $7,000 to $10,000 and fetched $20,000. Questions of age have become all but academic with regard to the extremely rare antiques and semi-antiques of India and China; those from Iran and the Caucasus crop up more frequently, although a public sale usually remains something of an occasion.

Dating. Appearance of the actual date on a rug, generally woven into the design in such a way as to be more discernible on the back—will add glamour and investor interest (i.e., value). Dated rugs are in great demand around the world. A date is seldom found in Persian or Turkish rugs, but Caucasian rugs are frequently dated. The digits used would probably be Islamic and appear as follows:

۰	۱	۲	۳	۴	۵	۶	۷	۸	۹
0	1	2	3	4	5	6	7	8	9

To calculate the date that corresponds to the Gregorian calendar, divide the number of Islamic years by 33, round off the result, then deduct that figure from the number of Islamic years and add 622. However, word of caution: Many rugs have woven into their designs dates and signatures (the late Shah of Iran's, for example) that actually predate the year of manufacture. An expert should be consulted to authenticate the age of any antique. A newly developed technique of dye analysis is available, capable of throwing light on both the date and location of manufacture.

Quality

No single factor in the market's evaluation of a rug counts for more than quality, which involves both its major material of construction and the fineness of its weave.

Materials. The three major textiles used in Oriental rug-weaving are wool, silk, and cotton. Wool is by far the predominant fiber, accounting for the largest dollar volume of both current annual output and world-market annual sales. However, rugs of silk have enjoyed the greatest increase in value over recent decades. Thus, in 1959, a New York dealer sold six semi-antique silk rugs, each approximately 3 × 5 feet, to a dealer in Wiesbaden, West Germany, for $275 apiece. Five of the silks were sold during the ensuing ten years at prices ranging from $1,500 to $9,000 each. The last piece hangs in a place of honor in the dealer's shop. It's price tag: $16,000.

As of early 1982, short-term prices dropped on fine small wool and silk pieces because of smuggling from Iran, on some major pieces because of the collapse of the financial base in Iran, and on some new Iranian rugs because of liquidation of holdings by Iranian émigrés.

Fineness. Of all the elements that play a role in the long-term appreciation of Oriental rug values, fineness perhaps is the single most important one. This term describes how tightly the rug is woven, by means of a counting of the knots tied off by the weaver during its manufacture. Because quality affects both the look and feel of a finished rug, as well as its durability, fineness should be the paramount factor in selecting rugs for investment. Indeed, in the parlance of Oriental rug dealers, the term "quality" has come to mean specifically the knot-count measurement, which, as it happens, is determined and expressed differently (owing to tradition) when used to describe the fineness of rugs from different countries.

For Iranian (Persian) rugs, the number of knots in one inch of vertical count (direction of warp) is multiplied by the number of knots in one inch of horizontal count (direction of weft). The product is usually expressed as knots per square inch. Quality-counts for Persian rugs range from 36 to 1,300 knots per square inch. Those for Turkish, Afghan, and Caucasian rugs are determined in the same manner.

In Chinese rugs, quality is determined by the number of knots or threads to the linear foot. Counts range from 70 per line to 240 per line. Indian rug quality is measured by the knots in 36 linear inches. For Pakistani rugs, it is expressed as a ratio of the horizontal count to double the vertical count: Hence, 9/18 quality means 9 knots per horizontal inch and 18 knots per vertical inch. The range is from 7/14 to 20/20.

Regardless of origin, fine rugs have been a good hedge against inflation. Best of all have been the finest Persians from Iran, which have increased in value tremendously over the past thirty years. A fine, new 9 × 12 foot Kashan, sold in 1921 for $432, brought $1,296 in 1928, and will fetch about $12,000 today. The increase in price is logical: Fine, new Iranian rugs are in diminishing supply. As Iran marched toward industrialization, the best of its veteran hand weavers left their looms for better paying jobs in other, newer industries. Ever since then, mediocre rugs have been coming on the market.

Place of Origin

Historical Factors. The first known Persian carpet—predecessor of everything known today as Oriental rugs—was found in 1945 by Soviet archaeologists in the remote Altai Mountains of Outer Mongolia (i.e., the U.S.S.R. Mongolian People's Republic). It is the twenty-two-century-old Pazyryk Carpet, currently housed in the Hermitage Museum in Leningrad. From its unique, if primitive, techniques flowed rug-weaving developments, first in Persia (Iran), and then throughout the Oriental rug-making universe. Where a rug comes from, as has been noted, affects to greater or lesser degree its value.

Iran. Iran is credited with most of the artistically great creations, including the sixth-century Persian "Spring of Khosrov," usually cited as the most valuable carpet ever made. It is said to have measured 11,300 square feet in area; woven with silk, it was embroidered with gold and silver thread, and further studded with gems. The Persian rug has been the mainstay of the Oriental rug industry in the United States for the past half-century, so much so that the term "Persian rug" is still synonymous with "Oriental rug." From 1930 to

1978, Iranian rugs led both the artistic and investment parades, but very few Iranian rugs are currently being imported into the United States. This is because during the same period, most successful Iranian merchants lost faith in their banks. Savings and checking accounts were translated into piles of rugs in their living rooms. A fine *Nain* was their CD; an old silk Tabriz was even better than the common stock of IBM. Thus, even before the political strife of the 1980s, export trade to the United States and other world markets had diminished in Iran. Oriental rug stocks were hoarded at home rather than shipped abroad.

On October 29, 1987, President Reagan issued Executive Order No. 12613 prohibiting Iranian imports, with the exception permitted by specific license. These licenses may be issued authorizing the importation of nontangible goods of Iranian origin, such as carpets (Oriental) and artwork. This edict has not unduly influenced prices of Iranian goods. Prior to 1981, prices of Iranian new goods had touched remarkably new heights. For instance, double-wefted Bijars were retailing at $200 per square foot. For a period of about five years, Iranian exports were prohibited until 1986, then permitted until the recent ban. With the advent of the Iran-Iraq war, the presence of the U.S. fleet in Iranian waters, and other related events, the need for hard currency by the Iranian government and lack of consumer goods fostered an intense second market wherein the rial fell from 80 rials per dollar (official) to 600 to 1200 rials per dollar. Although the price of Bijar rugs climbed in Iran during this period, the increase was more than compensated by the exchange. New Bijars started selling at $80 per square foot in the short period prior to the October 29, 1987 ruling. Current market sentiment states that Iranian goods will be allowed to be imported, and their importation in the near future will be based on the present international situation. The Iranian exchange will strengthen, and the price of new goods will increase.

India. Indian rugs were produced from the eleventh century until the 1930s. Weaving then stopped until the 1950s. Today, Indian rugs and carpets are in full production and are sold throughout the world, in traditional and modern designs. They have been steadily increasing in wool quality and weave density; today they rival the finest of Persian rugs.

Turkey. Prior to the twentieth century, Turkish rugs were available and in great demand. However, when Kemal Ataturk assumed leadership in Turkey, he initiated a modernization program that did not including weaving. From then until recent years, Turkey produced only a few pieces for domestic consumption.

China. Chinese industry, led by the Nichols factories and others in Tiensin, supplied world markets, particularly an eager American public, until 1949. Then the United States banned trade with Communist China. From that date until the recent trade renewals, used Chinese carpets were bought by dealers at auctions. Today, Chinese carpets are again being imported by the United States in great quantities. China has also begun weaving Persian designs in 160, 200, 260, and 300 weave count. Although weaving was formerly controlled through centralization, autonomous factories are now in vogue, with each area producing designs and qualities independent of other areas, with competitive prices. China has assumed the lead, of all weaving countries of origin, with exports totaling 864,000 square feet valued at $69 million prime cost in 1987.

Afghanistan, Turkoman, Baluchistan. Semi-antique rugs from these areas have been in good demand for decades in the United States.

Pakistan. In Pakistan, rug weaving began in 1953, with the first carpets sold in Europe. As production increased and Pakistanis sought new markets, rugs were exported to this country, mainly in Bokhara and Gul designs.

Eastern Europe. Communist bloc production, notably in Yugoslavia, Romania, Albania, and Bulgaria, is primarily of Persian design.

Caucasus. Caucasian rugs of modern design are woven and sold in the Soviet Union, with export to Europe. It is the older (antique and semi-antique) rugs, however, that have captured the fancy of American buyers.

Identification Factors. The handwoven Oriental rugs from various countries are identified, and labeled, in different ways. A myriad of potentially confusing names confronts any investor-collector who is new to the market. (See Table 1 for names of Oriental rugs.) To properly assess the value of an Oriental rug, a professional dealer or collector must be able to identify it with confidence.

Iranian (Persian) rugs are usually named after the province, village, town, or hamlet where they are woven. For example, a Kirman rug is one woven in the city of Kirman. Generally, the rugs are knotted from readings by a master singer or woven from individual templates. Nomads weave from memory. Each region is noted for a traditional design that has been handed down from one generation to the next. The designs are often subtly and subconsciously modified by the weaver. A number of different types of rugs may be woven in a particular village; thus, twenty types of Tabriz rugs may be on display at the Tabriz bazaar.

It should be noted that rugs of India are named through an entirely different system than the others. Most Indian rugs are woven in the Varanasi area to specifications of U.S. importers. Importers who are astute entrepreneurs have submitted a weave count, designs, and colors to the supplier in India, and established a line. These lines have been named (e.g., *Super Darbar* and *Sovereign Anatole*); each name identifies the rug and represents a standard of value. Loom owners in India also will weave rugs based on traditional Iranian designs and sell them in the open market.

Chinese rugs are perhaps the easiest of all rugs to identify, with their unique designs, lustrous wool, and deep colors. They are usually sold by line count, such as 80-line or 90-line; thickness of pile, such as $3/8$ or $5/8$; and the designation open back or closed back. Open back signifies a loose tamping of the pile; closed back means that as each knot is tied, it is pressed into place over the previous row of knots, completely encasing the white weft thread. The entire designation of a Chinese rug might read: 90-line, $5/8$, closed back. (This rug would be more expensive than another in which any of those three elements were lower.)

Pakistani rugs are also identified by weave count and design name. A $9/18$ *Mori* design single would refer to 162 knots per square inch of a Bokhara design of single thickness. Caucasian rugs are identified by name in a manner similar to Persian rugs.

Tibetan carpets are made in Nepal by Tibetan refugees who fled from Tibet during the communist invasion. Such rugs are now capturing increased interest owing to their uniqueness of raw materials and design. An unusual look imparted to the nap surface through the unique method of loop weaving reveals an eye-appealing decorative surface, with arresting designs supplied by talented craftsmen for use with traditional and

TABLE 1. Selected Names of Oriental Rugs

Iranian rugs (usually woven in curvilinear designs)		
Birjand	Huseinabad	Khorrassan
Dergazine	Ingillas	Meshat
Genjtepe	Ispahan	Nain
Ghom	Kashan	Sarouk
Hamadan	Kirman	Tabriz
Iranian rugs (usually woven in geometric designs)		
Abadeh	Ferraghan	Serapi
Ahar	Herez	Shiraz
Bijar	Jooshaghan	Simsari
Gorovan	Karaja	Yallemeh
Caucasian rugs		
Baki	Genja	Shirivan
Capistan	Karabagh	Shousha
Chichi	Kazak	Tscherkess
Daghestan	Kupa	Tiflis
Derbend	Leshian	
Turkish rugs		
Anatolian	Konieh	Melez
Bergano	Korowan	Rhodian
Ghiordes	Kulah	Sivas
Kirshehr	Ladik	Yuruk
Indian rugs (trademarks)		
Agra	Panir	Super Darbar
Chindia	Rajagra Herez	Teremez
Shangrila	Sovereign Indian Rugs	Zeigler
Rugs from Nepal		
Two Grey Hills	Pinwheel	Divine
Kalsang	Nelson	Rose
Square Tilt	Kira	Allover Floral
Futura		

contemporary settings. The durability, resilience, and length of yarn combine for plushness, which has become the hallmark of Tibetan carpets and rugs.

ATTRACTIVE FEATURES

Appreciation of Investment

The 1960 to 1990 price increases in home furnishings have played havoc with household budgets. It is not pleasant to put $5,000 to $8,000 into floor coverings and, after a relatively short period, to find it is necessary to replace them with new floor coverings. One of the attractive features of the Oriental rug has been its remarkable price resiliency. When prices broke in Iran in 1929, dealers and collectors held on to their inventories and, by 1939, prices started to reaffirm themselves.

Similarly, the consumer who bought Oriental rugs at any time in the last fifty years not only received pleasure and joy from seeing works of art every time he walked into a room, but also had the pleasure of realizing an increase in capital when the rug was sold. In 1921, Macy's sold 9 × 12 foot Sarouks for $243. Those same rugs, if kept in decent (not mint) condition by the buyers and used for fifty-nine years, would have sold for $3,000 to $5,000 each to a New York dealer in 1980; in 1989, their value rose to $9,000 to $12,000 each.

Prices of Oriental rugs have held up extremely well since Black Monday of 1987. The following examples were reported by William Ruprecht, the expert in charge of rugs and carpets at Sotheby's in New York. A Polonaise carpet purchased at Christie's in London on June 10, 1976 was sold at Sotheby's in New York on July 4, 1988 for $264,000. A Shirvan rug from the East Caucasus was purchased at Sotheby's on October 30, 1982 for $30,000 and was sold on December 5, 1987 for $46,200.

Worldwide Marketability

Oriental rugs are now an art form that is valued in almost every country in the world. From the time of the Great Depression until 1956, the desire for, and consequently, the sales of, Oriental rugs in the United States were negligible compared with Europe. There were a number of reasons for this lack of appetite for Oriental rugs, among which must be the decorator's interest in other types of floor coverings and the public's complete unawareness of the attractiveness of Oriental rugs, old or new. The entire importation of new Oriental rugs from Iran to the United States in the period of 1950 to 1958 did not exceed $3 million per year. Iranian imports represented the bulk of handwoven rugs when Indian and Pakistani looms still were in infancy; imports from China were forbidden, and the Balkans had not yet begun to weave.

Postwar Reconstruction. As the European countries started to rebuild and prosper (particularly Italy, Germany, and Austria), European dealers surveyed the international art market for products to sell to millions of newly affluent consumers. Turning westward, these overseas dealers found a treasure-house of old Oriental rugs in the United States: *Khilas, Kazaks, Genjas, Capistans*, silks of all weaving areas, and a veritable bonanza of old Iranian and Chinese rugs with which neither the American public nor the American dealer knew what to do.

European dealers descended on the New York wholesale showrooms, invaded national auction houses, and visited every retail dealer in the country. Finally, they advertised in the local newspapers in forty-eight states to buy old rugs directly from homes. Prices climbed daily. It was no longer a matter of price or profit, only a matter of locating a piece.

Building Viable Markets. While overseas dealers were buying old U.S. treasures, they also were making our public rug-conscious—largely by word of mouth. The demand for new rugs grew to unprecedented heights and total importations into the United States from all weaving countries totaled $75 million. American demand for new goods was reflected in price rises in Iran. Contributing further to the spiral, the Iranian government initiated a program to locate and replace its national art treasures, in which rugs had priority. Another round of increases was inaugurated with agents around the world searching for old rugs of Iran.

Finally, the oil-producing countries, flush with tremendous incomes, demanded the finest new rugs Iran could produce. A world market was informally, but firmly, established. Today, an Oriental rug can be sold anywhere: in London, Geneva, Hamburg, Johannesburg, New York, Los Angeles, Milan, Vienna, or Tokyo. If the proper price is paid for the rug, the chances of a loss of capital are minimal, most notably when dealing in Iranian rugs (new or old), and in antique Caucasian or Chinese rugs.

Hedging

Small Oriental rugs have provided a means of moving capital from war zones and countries exiling their citizens. During the recent turmoil in Iran and Lebanon, individuals who were unable to unfreeze bank accounts and transfer their assets to safer havens purchased small, but expensive, Oriental rugs. These were shipped abroad or packed in suitcases to accompany the exiles when they left. Small silk rugs were particularly appropriate, for they were lightweight and readily marketable.

POTENTIAL RISKS

Lack of Income

Rugs, like gold, yield no investment income. The only source of potential profit in rugs bought as investments is through resale at appreciated value.

Potential Oversupply

It is very seldom that an internationally collected art form falls to extremely low prices. Hundreds of thousands of collectors and dealers throughout the world will continue to maintain proper price structures for old rugs, but there is a fear concerning new Iranian rugs. Because the prices of Iranian rugs have increased to a great extent, a large influx of new carpets into world markets may tend to deflate prices until such world markets settle to find their level. As of late 1988, price lists from Teheran did not indicate price reductions in any of the approximately 140 different Iranian weaves; rather, we are now seeing an increase in prices across the entire spectrum of qualities.

Misleading Advertising

It is possible, although unusual, to buy a machine-made Oriental-design rug, in the belief that it is an authentic hand made. These rugs are imported from Italy, Germany, and Belgium, among other areas, and some are even made in the United States. The designs are modified forms of traditional Iranian designs and the names of these rugs reflect the design. At present, most of the misleading advertising by department stores has been corrected; however, now and then one will read of a 9 × 12 foot Sarouk for $299 and, somewhere at the bottom of the page, find a statement in small letters that all rugs being advertised are machine-made. To verify that a rug is handmade, the nap of the rug along the weft thread should be broken, and the buyer should look for the knots. The appearance of design and color running through to the back of the rug should not be depended on.

Mislabeling

Occasionally, a dealer will misname a rug, usually due to a lack of knowledge. A *Sparta*—a handwoven Greek rug of little investment value—may be called a *Meshat*, which is a valuable Iranian rug. Unfortunately, many dealers with scant love for rugs have entered the market in recent years. Most of them are not unscrupulous, just uncaring. Caveat emptor.

TAX CONSEQUENCES

As with many intangibles, profit from the sale of a rug held by an individual for more than one year is taxed as a capital gain. Under certain conditions, rugs can be exchanged for others of equal or greater value in a tax-free transaction. It is also possible to realize a tax deduction on donating a rug whose market value has appreciated to a qualified organization. Separate rules apply to those who are recognized as investors by the Internal Revenue Service. (See article on Tax Considerations for Collector-Investors, elsewhere in this volume.) For complete guidance in these matters, readers are urged to consult a professional tax advisor.

REPRESENTATIVE TYPES OF INVESTORS

The great majority of Oriental-rug investments are made by individual collectors. In addition, many corporations have purchased Oriental rugs as floor coverings for board rooms and the offices of top executives, choosing them for aesthetic appeal but also with an eye toward prestige and potential appreciation. Moreover, numerous hotels and motels have purchased Oriental rugs in quantity, taking depreciation on the books but, in fact, often realizing a worthwhile appreciation in value. At least one bank in recent years accepted Chinese rugs as collateral on a loan.

IMPORTANT FACTORS IN BUYING AND SELLING

Studying the Market

Before spending any money, there are a number of steps that should be followed by the inexperienced investor:

1. *Read up on Oriental rugs.* Many books have been written and a few are really great (see *Suggested Reading* in this article). Read, not to absorb technical knowledge, but to get an idea of the industry's geography: the location of the weaving countries and the towns that have given the glamorous names to rugs. Start a mental classification system; get a "feel" for the weaving areas.

2. *Visit department stores and pre-auction exhibitions.* Look at the names of rugs and try to fit the rug into a mental classification. The more exposure, the more experience in seeing rugs, the surer will be the buyer's ultimate grasp of rugs as an investment medium. Rug viewing underscores the truth that a picture is worth a thousand words.

3. *Know the seller.* Once an idea has been formed about rugs, make friends with a dealer or a knowledgeable department store salesperson. Short of harassment, ask as many questions as necessary.

4. *Witness actual sales.* Attend auctions after looking over the gallery's exhibitions. Visit department stores on sale days. The buyer will soon start to recognize rugs.

5. *Specialize.* Whether as collector or investor, make a decision to concentrate on one area—perhaps 4 × 6 foot Capistans, or 3 × 5 foot Kashans, or 2 × 3 foot

rugs of all types. Studies and discussions will help to analyze that particular market for availability, dealer preference, price structure, and potential rewards.

Recommended Sources

Department stores. When buying Oriental rugs for a home, a major department store is a safe place to buy. Most major department stores have a "return" policy. However, a lot of grief can be saved by taking along both the measurements of the room and the desired color scheme.

Auctions. Seldom should rugs be bought at auction, whether itinerant auctions or standing auctions, without prior examination. The examination should be made with a dealer or broker who will charge a small fee for this service. He or she will put a price range on the rug. It is important that the dulcet tones of the auctioneer do not sway the buyer. Good buys for investors and for consumers can be had at auction when the rugs are truly of estate or home quality.

If ever there has been an itinerant auction whose stock consisted of rugs put up for sale by estates, this writer has yet to see it. The usual practice of the itinerant auctioneer is to obtain a large consignment selection of Oriental rugs from a wholesaler and peddle them from town to town. Obviously, this creates unnecessary risk for the unsophisticated investor. In sharp contrast, standing auctions can be relatively safe and rewarding sources of supply. The buyer should beware of gauging prices by what dealers may be bidding, however. They may be raising prices on their own merchandise. Standing auction houses such as Sotheby Parke Bernet and Christie's in New York are responsibly managed, and good purchases can be made there with confidence.

Specialty shops, wholesalers, agents. Most proprietors of specialty shops (new or old) will take the time and have the knowledge to locate the rug that a particular buyer wants. They will show samples of Indian continuity lines and procure the size needed. In addition, they will know who in the country (through the Oriental Rug Importers Association or the Oriental Rug Retailers of America) has the Iranian rug the buyer wants. Professional dealers buy their inventory from wholesalers, but this is not usually a satisfactory situation for consumers or other collector-investors. The wholesaler seldom has the time, facilities, or interest to sell one piece. Unfortunately for the collector, however, there is no middle market for old rugs. The collector, in the final analysis, must buy rugs where he finds them: wholesale, retail, or at auction.

The serious investor must seek a guide. This can be a broker, dealer, specialty agent, or another collector, but that person must know the world market in old and new rugs from all weaving countries.

CUSTODIAL CARE

Oriental rugs lose their value unless they are properly maintained. Periodic care by professionals is recommended, as it would be for any other valuable property or work of art subject to wear and exposure. Minor repairs, stain removals, and the like sometimes can be done by the owner with guidance from the reputable dealer or auction house at which the rug was purchased.

Wear

To prevent undue wearing in any one area, the carpet should be rotated once a year. This ensures even wear and even patination (softening of colors). As the carpet proceeds through the stages of new, used, and, in the fourth generation, antique, it will thus maintain an even pile.

Dry Rot. Dry rot (drying out and brittleness of warp threads) is highly destructive for rugs and carpets. It occurs when water or other liquid is allowed to remain on the rug, or the rug is alternately subjected to moisture and heat (such as in a screened area or patio), resulting in chemical decomposition of the wool or cotton warp and weft. To prevent dry rot caused by spillage, make sure water does not overflow or spill onto the carpet and remain for any length of time.

Cleaning

Weekly care, depending on the pollution in the area, consists of vacuuming, using a suction vacuum, but not one of sufficient strength to pull out the individual knots. The owner must be careful not to catch the fringe in the vacuum. If the fringe gets caught and rips off, fringe must be added to that area. A restorer should never be permitted to cut away the original fringe and then sew on domestic fringe. A $10,000 rug could be rendered valueless by such a measure. If fringe has been damaged, it is best to add new fringe over the old.

Rugs should be cleaned professionally once every five years. Of course, the time depends, again, on conditions in a particular area. Moths should be guarded against by frequent inspection of the rug in dark recesses, as under sofas. When calling a professional cleaner make sure he is not cleaning Oriental rugs along with machine-made rugs in the home. In-home cleaners are designed specifically for wall-to-wall carpeting and must not be used on hand-woven rugs. These machines are hot-water extractor units that build up hot water and jet it down onto the nap; such treatment could be injurious to the fine Oriental rug.

Grit. One element that can surely destroy your rug, and hence its value, is grit. Grit consists of tough, hard particles of dirt that we track into our homes. It sifts down into the roots of the wool nap and, as the rug is walked on, cuts against the strands of wool and saws off small pieces of pile. The grit must be removed by suction, rug beating, or a reliable cleaner.

Insurance and Safety

An Oriental rug is a thing of beauty that may readily be stolen. Take two or three photographs of the rug; note its measurements. If it is stolen, the pictures, which are much like fingerprints, can be circulated.

Pictures, a written description, and evaluations by two recognized appraisers are usually necessary for obtaining insurance. Rugs should be insured as individual pieces, not lumped together under one homeowner's policy.

Where there is a collection of small rugs that needs to be stored, some banks do have vaults large enough for that purpose. Note that the bank will allow only nominal insurance. The rugs must be insured with an outside source, for full value. They should be revalued for insurance every few years and, if stored, examined every six months for moth damage and mothproofing.

GLOSSARY

abraish —A streak of different shade, which might run the width of a rug.

all-over —A term for a pattern that is repeated all over the field of a carpet without any medallion or other central feature.

bote —Flower design.

dozar —A rug measuring 4 × 7 feet.

fereghan —A small, geometric medallion cornered on four sides by a fish-like pattern.

fringe —The end of the rug containing the warp threads. Many rugs have one end compacted into an apron.

Gul —The abstract form of a flower, usually woven as octagonal medallion.

kelleyi —A long and narrow carpet.

kurk —Top grade of wool.

Persian and Turkish knots —The method of tying the yarn to the warp, the upper parts of which form the pile. The knots sometimes have been misnamed "sehna" and "ghiordes" knots, respectively.

pile —The wool surface of the rug, forming the nap.

pushti —A mat measuring approximately 2 × 3 feet.

warp —The foundation threads running top to bottom on which knots are tied.

weft —The foundation threads running from side to side between rows of knots.

zar —Measurement of 36 inches (one yard).

zaronim —A rug measuring 5 × 3.6 feet.

TRADE ORGANIZATIONS

A number of trade and collectors' organizations exist in the United States. These organizations are very selective, accepting for membership only those firms or individuals with the highest credentials of reputation and integrity. They are as follows:

Oriental Rug Importers Association, Inc.— A nonprofit organization consisting of importers of Oriental rugs who have been in the wholesale business for a minimum of three years in the United States. The aim of the organization is to promote the best interests of the Oriental rug industry in the United States and abroad and to raise the standards of the trade.

The Oriental Rug Retailers Association—An association of some of the major retailers of new and old rugs in the United States.

Hadji Baba Club—An organization of Oriental rug collectors dedicated to pursuits of aesthetic and cultural life of the United States through Oriental rugs.

Pittsburgh Rug Society—Consists of individuals (about seventy members) in the Western Pennsylvania region who are interested in Oriental rugs.

Local rug societies have an extremely enthusiastic membership of collectors and frequently feature guest lecturers at their meetings. A few of these organizations are New York Rug Society, Chicago Rug Society, Oriental Rug & Textile Society of Great Britain, The Oriental Rug Society Inc. of Toronto, Canada, and The Rug Society of Paris.

LEADING DEALERS

Most specialty shops carry old and new rugs from various weaving areas. Department stores usually inventory only new rugs. The following is a list of well-known, established Oriental rug dealers.

Absolutely Rugs, Tamarac, Fla.

Aladdin Co., Greensboro, N.C.

B. Altman Oriental Rug Department, New York, N.Y.

Ara Seropian Oriental Rugs, Lancaster, Pa.

Azars, Birmingham, Mich.

Vojtech Blau, New York, N.Y.

Bedrosian, J.K. & Sons, Summit, N.J.

L. Boodakian & Co., Boston, Mass.

Brookline Oriental Rugs, Boston, Mass.

Carson Pirie Scott, Chicago, Ill.

Chuck Wells & Assocs., Denver, Colo.

D.S. Tiftickjian & Son, Buffalo, N.Y.

Lou Demanes Interiors, Peoria, Ill.

Dingilian, Inc., Cincinnati, Ohio

Donaldson's Oriental Rug Store, Minneapolis, Minn.

Einstein Moomjy, New York, N.Y.

Ellisons, Ft. Worth, Tex.

Fain's, Providence, R.I.

Hagopian, Oak Park, Mich.

Hofstatter, New York, N.Y.

Indich Collection, Honolulu, Haw.

John D. Sedlak Interiors, Cleveland, Ohio

Joske's Oriental Rug Department, San Antonio, Tex.

Landry and Arcari, Ipswich, Mass.

The Levant Oriental Rugs, Oakland, Cal.

Macy's Oriental Rug Department, New York; N.Y.

McKay's Interiors, Baton Rouge, La.

The Persian Rug Co., Springfield, Mo.

Richard R. Markarian, Inc., Cincinnati, Ohio

Scalamandre, New York, N.Y.

Sharian's, Atlanta, Ga.

Sharian, Inc. Decatur, Ga.

Stark Carpet Company, New York, N.Y.

Suniland Furniture, Houston, Tex.

Tinnin Carpets, Meridian, Miss.

W. Hirsh Orientals, Richmond, Va.

Wellesley Hills Rug Shop, Wellesley, Mass.

Zaven Kish, Memphis, Tenn.

SUGGESTED READING

PERIODICALS

Hali. Published by Hali Publications, London, England. A quarterly periodical, it has gained an international reputation for its scholarly articles and objective dissemination of information.

The Oriental Rug Review. Published by Ron O'Callaghan, Meredith, N.H. Monthly; features rugs sold at auction with descriptions and prices. Also has Oriental rug articles.

Oriental Rug Magazine. Published by the Oriental Rug Importers Association of America, New York, N.Y. Four issues a year; contains extensive editorial information pertinent to the trade. Sold only to dealers.

Rug News. Published by Trade Data Reports, New York, N.Y. Monthly; contains some news and statistics on Oriental rugs. Concentrates on auction sales.

Sotheby's Fine Oriental Rugs and Carpets Catalogs. Published by Sotheby's, New York, N.Y. Available at sale time, with superb color pictures and descriptions of original rugs.

JOURNAL ARTICLES

Amirian, Lemyel. "The Design of the Pazyryk Rug," *Ararat*, Spring 1979, page 2.

Cherkezian, Archie A. "Appreciating Persian Rugs," *Finance*, Jan. 1975, pages 52–53.

Dickinson, Ernest. "Rug Importers Thrive," *New York Times*, June 6, 1976, page 8.

Harb, Joseph H., "Oriental Rugs," *The Investing Professional*, vol. 1, no. 9, Oct. 1973, pages 12–16.

"Oriental Carpets: A Flying Start," *New York* April 19, 1972, pages 47–54.

"Oriental Rugs," *Changing Times*, May 1977, pages 45–47.

Powell, Jim. "Flying Carpets," *Barron's*, Aug. 16, 1976, page 9.

Whitney, Michelle. "Oriental Values for Occidental Floor," *Money*, vol. 3, no. 2, Feb. 1974, pages 52–56.

REFERENCE BOOKS

Bennet, Ian. *Oriental Carpet Identifier*. Secaucus, N.J.: Chartwell Books, 1985.

Black, David. *The Macmillan Atlas of Rugs and Carpets*. New York: Macmillan, 1985.

Cherkezian, A. *The Magic Carpet*, rev. ed. New York: Oriental Rug Importers Ass'n, 1980.

Collingwood, Peter. *The Techniques of Rug Weaving*, rev. ed. New York: Watson-Guptill Publications, 1983.

Dilley, Arthur Urbane. *Oriental Rugs & Carpets*. Philadelphia: J.B. Lippincott Co., 1959.

Edwards, Cecil A. *The Persian Carpet*, London: Duckworth & Co., 1975.

Eiland, Murray L. *Chinese & Exotic Rugs*. Boston: New York Graphic Society, 1979.

Haack, Herman. *Oriental Rugs*. London: Faber & Faber, Ltd., 1960.

Hackmack, Adolf. *Chinese Carpets & Rugs*. Translated by L. Arnold. Tientsin-Peking, China: Peiyang Press, 1973.

Hawley, Walter A. *Oriental Rugs—Antique & Modern*. New York: Tudor Publishing, 1970.

Hillman, M.C. *Persian Carpets*. Austin: University of Texas Press, 1984.

Izmidlian, Georges. *Oriental Rugs & Carpets Today*. New York: Hippocrene Books, Inc., 1978.

Jacobsen, C.W. *Oriental Rugs*. Rutland, Vermont: Charles E. Tuttle Co., 1962.

Jerrehian, Aram K. Jr., *Oriental Rug Primer*. Philadelphia: Running Press, 1980.

Nemati, Parvis. *Rugs as an Investment*. New York: Agate Press, 1981.

Schurmann, Ulrich. *Oriental Carpets*. London: George Allen & Unwin Ltd., 1979.

Stone, Peter F. *Rugs of the Caucasus Structure and Design*. Chicago: Greenleaf Co., 1984.

Tanavoli, Parviz. *Shahsevah Iranian Rugs & Textiles*. New York: Rizzoli, 1985.

SCULPTURE

Alice Levi Duncan

BASIC CHARACTERISTICS

Interest in medieval, Renaissance, and baroque sculpture is certainly not recent. The great investor-collectors of the early part of this century, Morgan, Frick, and Kress, to name a few, were avid buyers of bronzes at enormous prices. There are specialized sales of furniture and works of art (including sculpture) from these periods and there are many dealers who handle objects from this category exclusively.

Interest in nineteenth- and twentieth-century European and American sculpture for investment purposes, on the other hand, has evolved recently, along with the current fervor for collecting all fine and decorative arts. Sculpture of this period must be sought out by the investor; it is rarely the subject of specialized sales in the auction houses, and it is not handled exclusively by dealers in New York, London, or Paris. Investment in sculpture is dependent on the knowledge of the buyer and the choice of marketplace. Such an investment can be either a very exciting and beneficial choice or a very secure, but not necessarily profitable, one.

Major Categories of Sculpture for Investment

Three major categories of nineteenth- and twentieth-century sculpture for investment are animalier and academic bronzes, Art Nouveau and Art Deco, and American sculpture. To a lesser extent, medieval, Renaissance, and baroque works of art are still purchased for

Alice Levi Duncan is Director of Sculpture and Works of Art at Christie's, New York.

investment. However, quality sculptures from this early period rarely come on the market, and there are relatively few interested buyers.

Bronzes. Because they are of multiple mechanical facture, bronzes are generally classified as decorative arts. It cannot be assumed that two objects made by the same artist in the same medium and depicting the same subject will be priced similarly. Variables such as size, condition, quality and quantity of casting, and authenticity must be considered in determining the value of a bronze. Popular among collectors are animalier bronzes, which depict animals, and academic bronzes cast in a realistic or representational style.

Only within the past two years have new collectors and investors driven up the prices for animalier and academic bronzes. Once a stable market with a large supply of objects and a limited number of collectors, the prices were usually predictable. Now there is international interest in these animal bronzes by Barye, Meme, Bonheur, or the works by such salon artists as Gerome or Carpeaux. Record prices are set at each auction, and the dealers cannot keep up with the demand for quality casts.

Art Nouveau and Art Deco Sculpture. Art Nouveau and Art Deco sculpture has experienced dramatic price increases in the past several years. The Art Nouveau and Art Deco market has carried that period's sculpture into its recent sweep of public interest and resultant auction records. Works that would not have found their way into the salesroom—either because the artists were not known in this country (as the artistic endeavours were primarily European, particularly French) or because the offering prices did not justify selling them—are now comprising 25 percent of the number of lots offered in a typical Art Nouveau and Art Deco sale. Moreover, the galleries display their more important bronzes of that period, by such artists as Raoul Larche, Agathon Leonard, Gustav Gurschner, Emmanuel Villanis, and even Sarah Bernhardt, with furniture and lamps of the same period.

Art Nouveau and Art Deco sculpture is not collected or bought in a vacuum. The buyer usually has an interest in another aspect of the field (e.g., Tiffany lamps, Marjorelle furniture, Gallé glass) and has turned to sculpture as decoration. It is the least expensive part of a very strong and "pricey" market. The prices range from $1,000 for a bust by Villanis, to $75,000 for a vase with mounts by Louis Chalon.

American Sculpture. The American sculpture market is also very exciting, with enormous collector fervor, rising prices, and the resultant appearance of rare and interesting works of art. Although there are many collectors who buy American sculpture independent of paintings, it is still a field that is tangential to the more expensive and better-known world of paintings. Unlike those who live with Old Master oils or nineteenth-century paintings, the owners of American paintings are usually active and avid collectors of complementary works of art in bronze, marble, plaster, and wood. Even museum classifications and exhibitions accept American sculpture as an equal partner to painting. Because of recent museum exhibitions, monographs, and the influence of the art market, this plastic art is now studied, admired, and collected with a fervor that traditionally has been characteristic of painting connoisseurs.

Unlike the world of paintings, the sculpture market makes no distinction between monumental sculpture that is museum quality and that which is collectible—the only distinction is between what is monumental and what is small scale. Both institutions and individuals are possible purchasers of Hiram Powers marbles, Remington bronzes, or Frishmuth garden fountains. Museums may, however, be more concerned than private collectors with such factors as quality, condition, and provenance, since they must justify their selection of each object by its excellence.

ATTRACTIVE FEATURES

Capital Gains

One benefit of investment in art is the enormous profit that can be gained. For example, a gilt-bronze figure of Loie Fuller by Raoul Larche (French, 1860–1912) fetched the German equivalent of $16,000 in 1979. During the slump in the Art Nouveau market (mid-1980s), the same model sold for $12,000. An excellent example of this figure recently sold at auction for $38,000, reflecting the strong interest again in this field. Such change in price can, of course, be dependent on currency fluctuations or inflation, but the primary cause in this case and in many similar instances is the increase in the number of buyers and the great current interest in this period of collecting. The market is international, with payments in a number of currencies over a period of time, and divided among several parties. Many galleries and dealers also will purchase objects for cash.

Extensive Market

An active trade in sculpture is conducted throughout the world, and the many buyers and sellers have driven up prices for works from numerous periods and geographical origins.

For those collecting Art Nouveau and Art Deco, the potential market is not limited to those with access to New York salesrooms. Dealers in Paris include fine Art Nouveau sculptures in their inventory, and London, Paris, Geneva, and Monaco offer outstanding sales of this period. The center of selling is developing in the United States, however. This is a result of market trends as well as favorable selling conditions; the U.S. government does not stop the export of any work of art, despite its possible historic or artistic importance.

The market for American sculpture is predominantly an American one. New York traditionally has been the center for both auctions and dealers, but considerable activity takes place in Washington, D.C., California, Texas, and elsewhere in the West. American sculpture can be viewed more often in salesroom catalogues than in galleries, however.

Physical Security

Sculpture requires little care in terms of physical security. It is more difficult to damage or steal than, say, paintings or jewelry, and small bronze sculptures could indeed be stolen, but most thieves are less impressed with their appearance than with that of objects made of more precious materials.

In addition, the physical appearance of sculpture changes little over extended periods of time. Those changes that do occur as part of the aging process will often enhance the object's value.

Intangible Benefits

As with all fields of art, sculpture investments are to some extent determined by aesthetic preference. Most collectors expect to enjoy as well as profit from their works of art. In the field of nineteenth- and twentieth-century sculpture, however, such considerations as prestige, interior decoration, and the hobbyist's enthusiasm for a particular subject (i.e., horses) often play a part in investment decisions.

POTENTIAL RISKS

Market Instability and Illiquidity

Although the art market is flexible as to manner and site of sale, including such alternatives as auction, dealers, and private sales, liquidity of capital is a problem. Often, it takes several months from time of consignment to payment. Sometimes, a market has gone soft at the moment that an investor must sell, and the profits that he has envisioned are wiped out in a short period. Some areas of collecting have been static in value for several years.

TAX CONSEQUENCES

Under federal tax law, profit from the sale of a sculpture held by an individual for more than one year is taxed as a capital gain. Under certain conditions, sculptures can be exchanged for others of equal or greater value in a tax-free transaction.

Museum collections in the United States do not have good inventories of Art Nouveau and Art Deco sculpture, and, because their purchase funds are usually intended for more "serious" works of art, they are unable to compete with the private buyers to supplement their holdings in a specific area. Therefore, it is possible for an individual to form a representative collection for eventual donation to a museum or university art gallery and to profit from the resultant tax benefits. Separate rules apply to those who are recognized as investors by the Internal Revenue Service. (See article on "Tax Considerations for Collector-Investors," elsewhere in this volume.) For complete guidance in these matters, readers are urged to consult a professional tax adviser.

REPRESENTATIVE TYPES OF INVESTORS

The sculpture market is of interest primarily to individual investors; virtually no corporate foundations are buying sculpture other than contemporary works, although many individual collectors do buy under a corporate name. Collectors of different types of sculpture fall into distinct categories.

Nineteenth- and Twentieth-Century Sculpture

Animalier. Most collectors are professionals or business people with an interest in a certain type of animal (e.g., horses) or sport (e.g., hunting or racing).

Academic/Salon. Most of the collectors in this field own many bronzes (usually more than thirty), which have been purchased over a number of years with a small capital investment. Typically, they are couples, buy large figures, tend to buy in quantity, and select figures to match their decor (e.g., Victorian furniture or paintings collection).

American. There is an older generation of American sculpture collectors who resemble the buyers of academic bronzes. The new collector-investor, who usually buys on the advice of an agent or dealer, is able to pay higher prices and is interested only in pieces over $25,000.

Medieval, Renaissance, and Baroque Sculpture

The few collectors in this field are not investment-oriented, but are avid students of the period, collecting all books and catalogues as well as the works themselves.

IMPORTANT FACTORS IN BUYING AND SELLING

Auction House vs. Gallery

Collectors faced with the choice of buying through the auction house or the gallery must compare quality, availability, and cost. Dealers have the advantage over the auction house in selection. Because of insurance, storage, shipping, and maintenance, a gallery must mark up the price of an object to a client for a specific price, whereas the auction house can only give a presale estimate with no guarantee of the actual price until after the sale. Often, an unsophisticated buyer will assume that he can purchase an object at auction for a fraction of the cost of a similar work in a dealer's shop. He will be bidding on that piece against other private collectors as well as dealers who must protect the asking price for the work in their shops. Certainly, a distinct difference exists between wholesale auction prices and retail trade prices, but with the educating of the private buyer and the rising popularity of the salesroom, the bargains at auction houses, with their enormous catalogue subscriptions, advertising budgets, and publicity, are absorbing too much of the market, and they are luring customers from the retail trade. The auction houses respond that, although the trade is necessary, there are too many brokers in each area.

Using an Agent

Another alternative for many serious investors is the agent. These can be either dealers or gallery owners but are usually authorities on the subject who own no stock. The investor will pay the agent a commission on any purchase, whether through auction or dealer, to obtain a trusted judgment and protection from publicity. These agents perform the actual bidding and arrange for payment and shipping.

Deciding How to Sell

Sellers as well as buyers of sculpture must choose their marketplace. The auction houses are an increasingly popular choice because they are able to handle a diverse collection (i.e., all categories of sculpture) and because their method is openly competitive with a very public process. As previously stated, auction houses will not make cash payments. The advantage of selecting a dealer or gallery is not only the method of payment but also the speed of the transaction. Dealers will also take goods in consignment, which allows them a percentage of the selling price (quite similar to the auction idea). The most appealing aspect of selling through a gallery or dealer is that a specific price is agreed on; this eliminates the uncertainty, risk, and speculation of an auction. On the other hand, many collectors feel that, at auction, they can often both obtain higher prices and reap a larger percentage of the profits.

Judging Quality of Nineteenth-Century Bronzes

The major problem in purchasing bronzes lies in the enormous quantity of fakes. It is quite simple to make a *sur-moulage* casting of any object (i.e., make a mold from a bronze). Most new investors have not seen enough period sculpture to be able to judge color of patina, quality of casing, crispness of signature, and method of facture. To them, any cast with a signature, foundry mark, and proof that the material is bronze is authentic. Many investors shy away from bronzes because they cannot tell these differences. The solution is either to buy from a reputable dealer or auction house that guarantees the authenticity of the work or to learn from looking at objects in museum exhibitions, asking experts, and viewing sales exhibits and gallery offerings until the fakes are obvious.

Checking Authenticity. The possibility of forgery is a major problem for collectors in this field. When buying an investment bronze, the investor will want to ascertain the answers to the following questions.

- Is the bronze epoxied to a marble base? If so, it is probably fake, as the foundry does not want the buyer to see the casting method or measurements (shrinkage results from *sur-moulage* casting).
- Is the signature crisp, or is there a ghost, as if it were rewritten? This is also a sign of *sur-moulage* casting.
- Is the patina (color) an even color, usually chocolate brown? Good nineteenth-century patinas were multicolored (reddish brown) and were rubbed on, not painted. If the color comes off with acetone or nail polish remover, or even chips with a touch of a finger, then it is not a nineteenth-century patina.
- Are there pimples and craters on the surface of the bronze, usually toward the bottom? Nineteenth-century casts were smoothed out before they were colored. The recasts do not have the same amount of handwork.
- Do the details, such as fingers and hair, merge with the bronze? Usually, on nineteenth-century casts, the foundry would chase (reinforce with an engraver's tool) certain details to add crispness and individuality to a cast. The recasts have no definition.

Number and Comparative Quality. Apart from the problem of forgeries, many investors also would like to know how many bronzes were made in an edition and which casting is better. The first question is usually unanswerable, as most foundry records have been lost. The second is one of aesthetic judgment, although certain details, such as shade of patina and amount of chasing, can help determine price.

A new investor in the field should have any bronze examined by an expert, either the auction cataloguers or one of the acknowledged authorities in the field. Museum experts do not have the time to authenticate every object in the market, nor are they allowed to comment on any piece's value, but many people in the trade, as well as scholars, can do so.

Judging Quality of Earlier Sculpture

Sculptures of the fourteenth through the eighteenth century are also judged for quality in terms of authenticity, rarity, and condition. Unlike nineteenth- and twentieth-century bronzes, which are usually in original condition, these works of art inevitably show signs of age. However, damage, extent of original color, as well as the quality of the cast very much determine the marketability of a given piece.

External factors such as provenance (history of ownership), exhibitions, literature, and comparison with similar works in museum collections are also important in judging both the quality and the price of a piece. For example, a sixteenth-century bronze sculpture depicting Nessus and Deianeira, after Giambologna, was sold in London this year for $720,000. A similar model, but seventeenth century, fetched $38,000 in a recent New York sale. The price reflects not only the difference in age but also the fact that the London piece had been mentioned by art historians in articles on the artist and was judged to be a rare and fine cast.

CUSTODIAL CARE

The incidental costs of sculpture ownership can be high. Insurance, warehousing, restoration, appraisals, and shipping are all expensive. As mentioned under *Attractive Features* earlier in this article, however, the sculpture itself requires little maintenance.

GLOSSARY

academic—Traditional and representational as opposed to abstract art.

animalier—The school of French nineteenth-century sculpture that specialized in naturalistic portrayals of animals.

Art Deco—Art produced from World War I until the mid-thirties, characterized by stylization and geometric form.

Art Nouveau—Turn of the century art characterized by exaggerated ornamental detail and a wide range of motifs.

casting—A foundry piece produced by pouring molten metal or a plaster into a mold.

edition—A limited number of castings made from the sculptor's original model.

foundry mark—An identifying inscription, stamp, or seal that can be found on a bronze.

patina—Color that is applied to a bronze (chemically or by brush) or that is acquired through age or use.

sur moulage—A casting made from a casting, not from the artist's original model—usually an unauthorized copy.

TRADE ORGANIZATIONS

Art and Antique Dealers League of America, New York, N.Y.

Art Dealers Association of America, New York, N.Y.

National Antique and Art Dealers Association of America, New York, N.Y.

LEADING DEALERS IN THE UNITED STATES

AMERICAN SCULPTURE

J.N. Bartfield Galleries, Inc., New York, N.Y.

Graham Galleries, New York, N.Y.

Hirschl and Adler, New York, N.Y.

Kennedy Galleries, New York, N.Y.

ART NOUVEAU AND ART DECO

Lillian Nassau, New York, N.Y.

Macklowe Gallery Ltd., New York, N.Y.

Trent Gallery, New York, N.Y.

BRONZES—ACADEMIC AND ANIMALIER

Bronzart Antiques, New York, N.Y.

F. Gorevic and Sons, New York, N.Y. (animalier only)

Graham Galleries, New York, N.Y.

Shepherd Gallery Associates, New York, N.Y.

MEDIEVAL, RENAISSANCE, AND BAROQUE

Blumka Gallery, New York, N.Y.

Michael Hall Fine Arts, New York, N.Y.

Ed Lubin, New York, N.Y.

Ellen Mitchell, New York, N.Y.

AUCTION HOUSES

Christie's, New York, N.Y.

Christie's, London, England

William Doyle Galleries, New York, N.Y.

Phillips, New York, N.Y.

Phillips, London, England

Sotheby Parke Bernet, New York, N.Y.

Sotheby's, London, England

SUGGESTED READING

PERIODICALS

Art and Auction. Published by The Auction Guild, New York, N.Y. Ten issues a year; good reporting about auctions and collecting trends.

Connoisseur. Published by National Magazine Company, Ltd., New York, N.Y. Monthly; scholarly articles and brief reviews of exhibitions.

REFERENCE BOOKS

Broder, P. *Bronzes of the American West*. New York: Abrams, 1974.

Catley, Bryan. *Art Deco and Other Figures*. London: Chancery House Publishing, 1978.

Duncan, J. Alastair. *Art Nouveau Sculpture*. London: Rizzoli, 1978.

______ . *American Art Deco*. New York: Abrams, 1987.

Fusco, Peter, and Janson, H.W. *The Romantics to Rodin*. Los Angeles: George Braziller, Inc., 1980.

Lami, S. *Dictionnaire des Sculpteurs de l'Ecole Francaise*. Reprint, Paris: Kraus, 1970.

Mackay, J. *The Dictionary of Western Sculpture in Bronze*. London: Collector's Club, 1977.

Payne, C. *Animals in Bronze*. London: Antique Collectors Club, 1986.

SPORTS MEMORABILIA

David S. Krause
George W. Kutner

BASIC CHARACTERISTICS

Interest in sports memorabilia, especially for those items related to baseball, has exploded in the United States since the late 1970s. Hobbyists, speculators and investors are estimated to have bought more than $1 billion of sports cards and other collectibles (e.g., jerseys, hats, and autographed baseballs) in 1987. To serve this market, there are more than 10,000 sports memorabilia dealers nationwide, including 3,500 retail shops. Nationally, at least 100 trade or swap shows are held weekly, and an extremely active and efficient mail order business for sports collectible items also exists.

Types of Sports Memorabilia

Nonpaper Items

Uniforms and Hats of Famous Players. For example, the 1937 Chicago White Sox uniform of Merve Shea sold for $3,500 in 1988, while a Pete Rose Philadelphia Phillies' baseball hat sold for $400.

Statues and Limited Edition Plates. Certain items, such as bobbin head dolls, Hartland baseball statues, and commemorative plates and glasses are highly coveted by collectors. For example, an early 1960s plastic statue of Mickey Mantle sold for more than $1,000 recently.

David S. Krause, MBA, is a Financial Consultant in Milwaukee, Wisconsin. George W. Kutner, Ph.D., is Assistant Professor of Finance, College of Business Administration, Marquette University, Milwaukee, Wis.

Autographed Items Such as Bats, Balls, and Hockey Sticks. A 1938 N.Y. Yankees baseball signed by Lou Gehrig sold for $500 in 1988, while a Wayne Gretzky autographed hockey stick commands $400.

Championship Pennants, Rings, and Press Pins. Items issued or sold at famous sporting events, such as the Rose Bowl, World Series, Super Bowl, Olympic games, and championship boxing matches, have sold for more than $500.

Paper Items

Autographed Photos. Autographs, especially those of deceased athletes, are avidly collected. For example, a signed 1934 Babe Ruth photo sold for $1,500 in 1988.

Programs and Yearbooks. A scored program of the 1956 World Series game in which Don Larsen pitched a no-hitter recently sold for $250, while a mint condition 1967 Super Bowl program commands a price of $1,000.

Sports Magazines and Books. Some older magazines, such as *Ring* and *Sport*, are considered to be valuable collectibles. For example, some recent *Sports Illustrated* swimsuit issues have sold for as much as $50.

Sports Cards. The most significant sports collectible item, in terms of volume and price, is the sports card. Older baseball cards are the most highly sought after sports memorabilia items.

Types of Sports Cards

Baseball. First issued during the nineteenth century and still marketed in mass quantity today, baseball cards are a clear reflection of the popularity of America's national sport. Cards depicting baseball players, as well as those of boxers, wrestlers, and other popular sports heroes, were originally issued as premiums and were intended to influence the buyer's choice of cigarettes. Over the years baseball cards became associated with children and were marketed by the gum and candy companies. Baseball cards are currently issued with bubble gum, candy, cookies, and cereal and as cards alone to both children and adults.

Recent research on baseball cards found that the compound average annual rate of return of all baseball cards issued by Topps Chewing Gum Company since 1952 has exceeded 25 percent during the 1980s. Further examination of the performance of famous players' rookie or first issue cards showed compound average annual returns in excess of forty percent during this same period.

Football. Cards of National Football League players were issued by cigarette and gum companies as far back as the 1930s and 1940s, but the Topps 1956 set is recognized by collectors as the first of the modern era. Since the 120-card set was issued, Topps has issued a set of professional football player cards annually. Even though the prices of older football cards are low in relation to baseball cards, their returns since 1980 have been impressive. On average, complete sets of football cards have increased in price 29 percent annually between 1978 and 1987. Similar to the performance of baseball cards, the rookie cards of famous football players rose dramatically in price during the 1980s.

Basketball. Basketball cards have usually been considered to be minor cards in the eyes of collectors. Topps issued an eighty-card set of National Basketball Association (NBA) cards in 1958. The complete set, which sold in 1988 for about $500 in mint condition, contains the cards of Bob Cousy, Tom Heinsohn, Bob Pettit, and Bill Russell. Because the basketball cards did not prove to be as popular as baseball and football cards, Topps did not issue another basketball card set until 1969. They continued to issue complete sets until 1981, when they again stopped printing basketball cards because of weak demand. Since then the Star and Fleer companies have issued complete sets of NBA cards annually.

Despite their lowly status, research indicates that the rookie cards of NBA stars have performed strongly during the 1980s. Not unlike the return performance of baseball and football cards, the results were impressive. The basketball cards of famous players rose in price, on average, by more than 47 percent annually since 1980.

Other. Other less popular sports cards include those of hockey players and professional wrestlers. Price guides for these collectible items are also available, and our research indicates that these collectibles rose in price by more than 20 percent annually during the 1980s.

HISTORY OF BASEBALL CARDS

An historical review of the baseball card market is instructive for prospective investors. Baseball cards were first issued during the 1880s by U.S. cigarette companies to promote business. Very few of those early issues remain in salable condition today, because most were printed on cheap cardboard and suffered from poor-quality photography. The extremely small supply and enormous demand for cards of that era make them highly valued. A 600-odd card set issued by Old Judge cigarettes in the late 1880s sold for $50,000 in 1988.

FIGURE 1. Hall-of-Famer Baseball Card

1955 Topps Henry Aaron

FIGURE 2. Baseball Rookie Cards

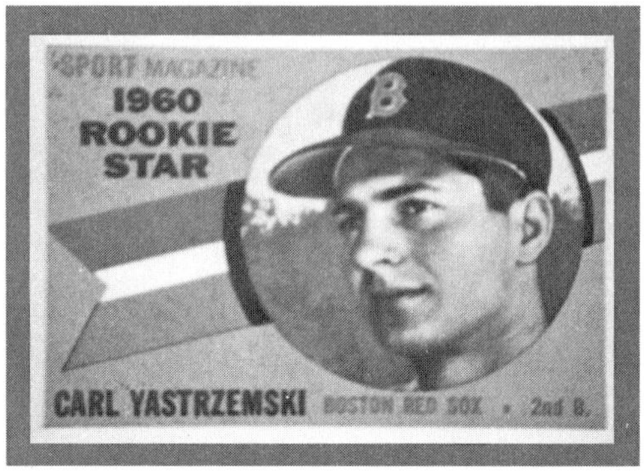

1960 Topps Carl Yastrzemski

1973 Topps Dave Winfield

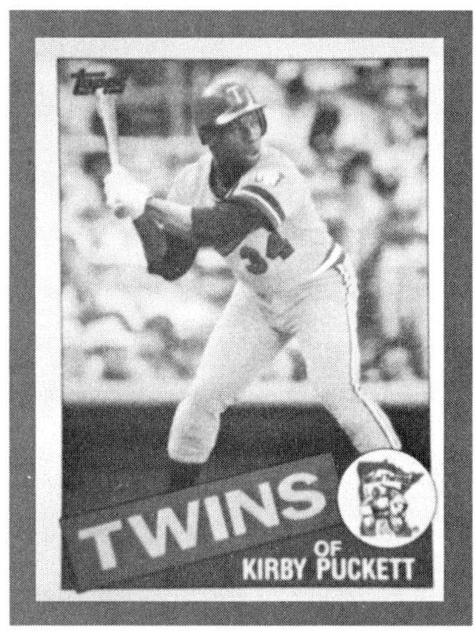

1985 Topps Kirby Puckett

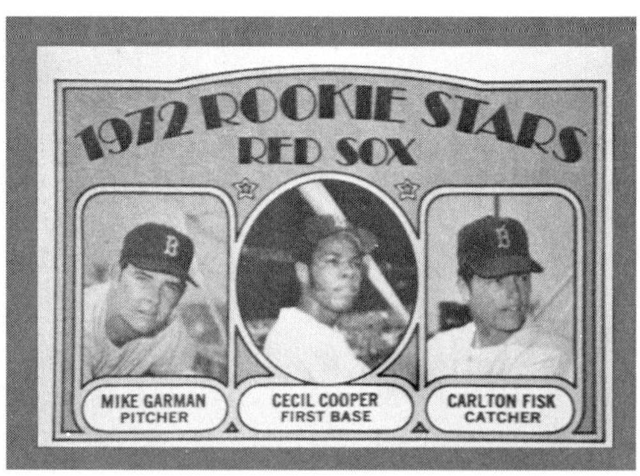

1972 Rookie Stars

FIGURE 3. Hockey and Football Sports Cards

Some vintage cards from this era sell for huge prices almost regardless of condition. For example, a T206 Honus Wagner card from a 1909–11 set, sold for a record $110,000 in 1988. Its price is a function of scarcity more than adoration of the Hall of Fame Pittsburgh Pirate shortstop nicknamed The Flying Dutchman. Fewer than 100 of the cards are known to be in existence. There are two possible reasons for this. One school holds that Wagner, an ardent nonsmoker; got an injunction prohibiting the card's manufacturer, the American Tobacco Company, from distributing it. Others maintain that Wagner had the cards recalled because he was never paid to appear on them.

When World War I led to raw material shortages, cigarette companies gave up the premiums. After the war, baseball cards were again printed and distributed in mass quantities, this time by candy and gum companies. The new cards were superior in quality to earlier ones and were issued in considerably greater quantity, typically tens of millions annually.

One of the most valuable complete sets of baseball cards is Goudey Gum Company's 240-card collection from 1933. The set includes Babe Ruth and Lou Gehrig and has reportedly sold for $20,000. The set also has one of the priciest individual player cards, that of Hall of Famer Napoleon Lajoie, which is valuable because its print order was small and was inadvertently delayed until 1934.

The second era of baseball card collecting faded during World War II when paper and rubber shortages limited card and gum production. Bowman Gum Company resumed the baseball card business in 1948, beginning the modern era of card collecting. Topps entered the industry in 1951 and has dominated the market ever since. The first complete Topps set, issued in 1952 with 407 cards, has sold for as much as $40,000. The set is highly prized by collectors largely because it contains the Topps rookie cards of Mickey Mantle and Willie Mays, two of baseball's most popular players.

For more than two decades after its 1956 acquisition of Bowman, Topps had a virtual monopoly on the card industry. Then in 1980, a U.S. district court ruled that Topps and the major leagues could not prevent other gum companies from issuing cards. A year later, Fleer and Donruss started competing. Sportflics followed in 1986, and Score began issuing cards in 1988.

ATTRACTIVE FEATURES

In general, sports collectible items are relatively easy to acquire and do not require the collector to possess any special level of expertise. They are also very attractive to display. Sports collectibles are colorful, historical, and interesting to examine. For example, not only does a sports card contain statistical information about the player depicted on the card, but it also contains an action photograph of the athlete.

Other sports memorabilia items, such as programs, baseballs, and uniforms, are also attractive display pieces. Collectors often decorate their dens or offices with their favorite collectible items, not to mention the countless thousands of children who line their bedroom walls with sports items of their favorite players and teams.

Buying sports collectible items is a more personal form of investment than buying bonds or gold bullion. Most sports memorabilia collectors are not in it for the investment alone. Nevertheless, these items have proved to be fine investment performers (see Table 1).

POTENTIAL RISKS

Although sports memorabilia have performed extremely well as investments in recent years, there are a number of risks of which the investor should be aware.

Quality Risk

Quality risk refers to the misrepresentation of the condition of the sports collectible. That is, condition grading is not uniform within the industry and is also subject to individual interpretation. Therefore, the investor should examine carefully any item before purchasing. Prices can vary significantly on the basis of condition. For example, a crease on a sports card can decrease its market value by as much as 95 percent.

In addition, after purchase it is important that the investor maintain the current condition of the item purchased. For many sports memorabilia collectors, this may not be an easy task. Sports cards, particularly older ones, can deteriorate from excessive pollution,

TABLE 1. Prices and Rates of Return of Famous Players' Rookie Cards and Complete Sets, 1979 to 1987

	1954		1952			1963	
End of Year	Aaron	Set	Mantle	Mays	Set	Rose	Set
1979	$185	$ 550	$2,500	$350	$10,000	$ 35	$ 350
1980	180	725	1,500	375	9,000	55	550
1981	125	600	1,000	250	6,900	90	500
1982	100	600	700	225	6,500	225	620
1983	140	800	1,250	275	7,500	300	725
1984	175	820	2,100	325	9,600	300	760
1985	225	1,100	2,900	450	15,000	450	975
1986	325	1,500	3,300	500	18,000	500	1,350
1987	450	2,300	4,500	650	24,000	500	1,750
Average rate of return	12%	20%	8%	8%	12%	39%	22%

Source: J. Beckett, *Sports Americana Baseball Card Price Guides,* 1979–1987. New York: Ballantine Books.

light, and moisture, because they are printed on a relatively cheap cardboard. Therefore, many investors seek appropriate safekeeping techniques to preserve card quality. Many dealers sell plastic cases for cards, which can help reduce their exposure to moisture and air and especially will protect them from rough handling.

Forgery Risk

As with any security or other collectible, sports memorabilia are subject to the risk of forgery. Most collectibles are not easily duplicated, and so the extent of forgeries in this market is relatively small. For example, sports cards printed in a variety of colors are difficult to duplicate.

In addition to outright duplication forgeries, there have been attempts to alter the condition of the collectible to enhance its value. Sometimes, corners of cards are clipped because bent corners reduce a card's value. Some dealers offer measuring devices that can determine if a card is of the proper size and, thus, identify any clipping. Clipping may also be done to center a picture on a card in order to increase its value. Although forgeries have been reported, they occur in extremely small numbers so as not to affect the market. However, an investor should be careful of forgery possibilities, especially for very expensive items where the incentive to alter is the highest.

Price Risk

Although price appreciation in the sports memorabilia market has been excellent, there still is significant price risk in these items. Price risk means the extent of variability in the market prices of these collectibles over time. The authors have examined the price risk of baseball cards over the period 1978 to 1987. Baseball cards were found to be about 30 percent more risky than the general stock market and less risky than many other commodities and collectibles. Financial theory suggests that investors assuming additional risk should be compensated with higher expected return. Baseball cards provided sufficient additional return for those investors deciding to bear the risk. However, given the additional inherent risk in these items, only investors less averse to risk should consider them for investment purposes.

Liquidity Risk

Liquidity risk refers to the ability of an investor to convert the investment into cash (market value) in a reasonable period of time. Since there is no formal trading facility where sports memorabilia can be traded, the items inherently have some liquidity risk. Finding a buyer through advertising and attending shows may take some time and effort. Ordinarily, the quickest way to liquidate an investment is to sell to a dealer. However, dealers generally pay significantly less than the current market value. They may pay as little as 25 percent or as much as 90 percent of the current market price. The amount they pay depends on many variables, such as market condition, price expectations, and dealer inventories.

REPRESENTATIVE TYPES OF INVESTORS

The market for sports memorabilia draws from a wide variety of individuals. Age groups range from the small child who is interested in sports to middle-aged and older individuals who probably collected cards and autographs when they were children. The market also attracts individuals from literally every profession, including doctors, lawyers, accountants, and plumbers. Individuals clearly dominate the market, with very few investment houses actively engaged in the market. Individual investors can be classified by their objectives as collectors, dealers, or speculators.

Collectors

The individual collector is one whose objective is primarily motivated by the desire to hold sports memorabilia. Many times this will be a person who actively collected sports cards and the like as a child; however, collectors new to the market also exist. The collector may be quite naive about the market or may be very informed about market conditions, price, quality, and other market aspects.

Many collectors focus their interest on particular types of sports memorabilia. For example, a collector may collect only baseball cards and, within this sector, may collect only the cards of certain players or teams. Some collectors may desire only the cards or autographs of Hall of Famers. Some collectors may focus only on older items, and some may collect only current complete sets of cards or autographs of current players. In general, collectible tastes vary widely.

Dealers

A major participant in the market is the dealer. The dealer's main objective is to buy and sell sports memorabilia while seeking a profit on the differential in prices. Most dealers will hold a large inventory of collectibles and may operate from their homes or in a small store. Within a major city, there will usually be a number of dealer-run operations. These dealers will usually participate in the various sports collectible shows and conventions that are held extensively throughout the country. Although motivated primarily by profit, many dealers usually have a strong interest in sports memorabilia, and many will have a private collection as well. Most dealers first have been exposed to the market as collectors. Dealers generally are very informed about the market and are well aware of changes and movements. Some dealers may specialize in particular items; however, most dealers attempt to provide a full range of products in order to attract as many investors as possible. Many dealers will advertise their prices to buy and sell memorabilia in the many trade periodicals (see *Suggested Reading*, at the end of this article) that are published weekly, monthly, and annually.

Speculators

The speculator is a collector who may have at most a passing interest in sports memorabilia as collectibles but is primarily motivated by the expectation of significant price appreciation over a short time span. Given the dramatic price increases that have been reported over the past decade, particularly for baseball items, the speculator has appeared in increasing numbers in recent years. Speculators are usually well informed about price conditions in these markets as well as their special nature with respect to liquidity, volume, and information. Usually, speculators are rather heavily capitalized relative to individual collectors and will seek out the higher priced items. A smaller number of higher priced items also reduces the safekeeping costs to these investors. This is particularly important to these investors since the condition of most items is critical to their keeping their investment value. Investment houses for the most part have not appeared in this market.

TAX CONSEQUENCES

Under federal tax law, profits from the sale of sports collectible items by an individual are taxable as capital gains or ordinary income, depending on the time held and whether sold by dealer or investor. (See article on "Tax Considerations for Collector-Investors," elsewhere in this volume.)

IMPORTANT FACTORS IN BUYING AND SELLING

Besides the potential risks and the types of investors mentioned previously, an investor should be aware of a number of additional factors.

The Market and Liquidity

The market for sports memorabilia has no particular place of exchange. Instead, most transactions come about through advertising in the many trade periodicals. The numerous conventions and trade shows that are held in cities across the country also offer the collector the ability to buy and sell. The thousands of dealers in this market also stand ready to buy and sell literally every type of sports memorabilia item. The dealer provides the individual investor with almost immediate liquidity in this market. That is, items may be bought or sold almost instantaneously; however, the prices at which dealers are willing to buy and sell can vary from 25 to 100 percent of market value. These bid-ask spreads are large in relation to most other investments, such as stocks and bonds. The investor, however, can circumvent the dealer by directly finding a buyer or seller in the mail order market. This can be costly and will take time, and significant liquidity can be lost.

Grading

The condition or grade of an item being bought or sold is extremely important for price considerations and demand for the item. Grading varies and is not uniform throughout the industry. Moreover, the assessment of condition is subject to a somewhat subjective evaluation. Grading can be partitioned into five or more different categories for most items. For example, baseball cards fall into five grade categories: mint, near mint, excellent, very good, and good. These grades depend on the condition, reflecting such factors as rounded corners, centering, clarity, and creases.

The importance of an item's condition cannot be overstated. Values can vary as much as 90 percent for the same item, depending on condition. Indeed, being below the first two categories may exclude the item from investment consideration in many cases. Since grading is somewhat subjective, an investor may do well to seek more than one opinion when the grade of a particular item is in doubt.

Price Information

Price information on most sports memorabilia is available on a regular basis. The Beckett price guides have been published annually since 1978 and provide current price information on almost all sports cards. In addition, Beckett publishes a monthly price guide for baseball cards. This is particularly important when prices rise during the summer months. Other publications, such as *Baseball Cards* magazine and *Sports Collectors Digest*, are published monthly and weekly and provide current price information on baseball cards. The investor should be aware of these publications in order to be current on existing market conditions.

Seasonality

Since professional sports such as baseball, football, basketball, and hockey are played during a particular period of the year, demand for memorabilia appears to vary during the year. The demand for baseball cards peaks during the summer months and reaches a low during the winter months. Likewise, dealer inventories may be lower during the winter months.

Given these fluctuations in demand, selling items during peak seasons may be more advantageous, particularly when attempting to sell to individuals rathers than dealers. Demand for items may increase during special events of the season. For example, during the World Series, there is a genuine increased interest from dealers in acquiring cards and other baseball collectible items.

CUSTODIAL CARE

Because the value of sports memorabilia is highly influenced by the physical condition of the items, it is important that these items be properly stored. Sports cards and other paper items should be stored in plastic containers to ensure that they do not become torn or soiled. It is also important to protect nonpaper items from moisture. For example, autographs on baseballs will disappear as ink dries up through time; it is therefore important to store items in airtight and moisture-proof display cases. Cloth items, such as hats and uniforms, should also be protected from moths and other vermin that could destroy these prized possessions.

GLOSSARY

Beckett—Dr. James Beckett has published numerous monthly and annual sports card price guides since 1978. Many people will use the word Beckett instead of price guide.

book value—The reported selling price of a card that has been determined by one of the various publications that specialize in sports cards. *Beckett's Baseball Card Monthly* and *Sports Collectors Digest* have the widest circulation. The reported values are determined by surveying dealers nationwide to obtain data concerning recent price increases or decreases.

Bowman—A card manufacturer from 1948 to 1955, which was acquired by Topps.

card show—A gathering of collectors, dealers, and investors with the purpose of buying, selling, or trading cards.

common card—A card of a player who has not or is not likely to reach star status. These cards carry the lowest book value of the cards found in a complete set.

complete set—One each of every card of the same type produced by a particular manufacturer during a single year. For 1988 Topps baseball cards, a complete numbered set consists of 792 cards.

Donruss—A card manufacturer since 1981. Based in Memphis, Tennessee, the parent company is located in Finland.

double print—A card in a series that is printed twice.

error cards—Cards with printing mistakes (i.e., wrong player, or name spelling). Some error cards are in short supply because very few were issued prior to the manufacturer detecting the error and correcting it.

Fleer—A manufacturer of sports cards from 1958 to 1961, 1963, and 1981 to present.

HOF—A sports card of a player that has been elected to the Hall of Fame.

rookie card—A player's first appearance on a card that is a regular issue from a major manufacturer. A regular issue card is one that is easily obtainable from the company's initial set for the year. Typically, rookie cards have the most appeal and carry the highest price.

Score—A card company that began distribution in 1988.

star card—A card of a popular player. The value of these cards is much greater than those of common cards for the same year.

Topps—The largest card manufacturer, located in Brooklyn, New York, which has distributed cards since 1951.

wax pack—A method of packaging cards for retail sale. The wrapper has a wax coating and a pack contains about fifteen cards.

SUGGESTED READING

ARTICLES

Dobritz, Pete. "Investing in Baseball Cards—What Lies Ahead?" *Sports Collectors Digest*, Sept. 30, 1988, pp. 64–70.

Geringer, Dan. "Mr. Mint, A Gallery of Good Investments," *Sports Illustrated*, Vol. 67, No. 1, July 4, 1988, pp. 78–86.

Haylar, John. "The Fine Art of Baseball Cards," *Wall Street Journal*, Oct. 23, 1985, p. 35.

Krause, David S. "Those Amazing Rookies: A Study of Baseball Cards," *AAII Journal*, Vol. X, No. 4, Apr. 1988, pp. 7–11.

______. "Baseball Cards Bat .425," *Money*, June 1988, pp. 140–147.

______. "The Benefits of Diversifying With Collectibles," *AAII Journal*, Vol. X, No. 9, Oct. 1988, pp. 7–11.

______, and Kutner, George W. "The Return Performance of Baseball Cards (1979–1986)," *Marquette University Working Paper*, pp. 88–103.

Lindley, Daniel. "Topp-Flight Investment," *Barrons*, Apr. 6, 1987, pp. 18, 75.

Weir, Tom. "Baseball Cards Can Be Diamonds," *USA Today*, Dec. 23, 1987, Pt. 4, pp. 1–2.

PERIODICALS

Baseball Cards. Published by Krause Publications, Inc., Iola, Wis. Monthly.

Beckett Baseball Card Monthly. Published by Statabase, Carrollton, Tex. Monthly price guide.

Current Card Prices. Current Card Prices, Inc., East Islip, N.Y. Monthly price guide.

The Old Judge. Published by Lewis Lipset, New York, N.Y. Bimonthly newsletter that focuses on older cards and memorabilia.

Sports Collectors Digest. Published by Krause Publications, Inc. Iola, Wis. Weekly tabloid with many advertisements.

BOOKS

Andrews, Todd. *The Collectors Guide to Baseball Cards 1948–1976*. Gas City, Ind.: L-W Promotions, 1977.

Beckett, James. *The Sports Americana Baseball Card Price Guide #11*. Cleveland: Edgewater Book Co., 1989.

Lipset, Lew. *The Encyclopedia of Baseball Cards, Vols. I, II, III*. New York: Lipset Publishing, 1986.

STAMPS

Peter M. Rexford

BASIC CHARACTERISTICS

In the past twenty years scarce and rare postage stamps and postal history collectibles have become accepted as a secure and viable investment alternative. Many individuals and financial planners recognize the advantage of a diversified investment portfolio that includes rare stamps.

The strength behind the rare-stamp market is due to the buying habits of more than 30 million U.S. collectors, a figure higher than that of any other hobby. This strong collector base has convinced many professional investment counselors to invest part of their assets in rare stamps, with notable success. This broad collector base assures them of consistent demand and high liquidity for quality pieces.

Investment-quality rare stamps can be found within a price range of $50 to $1 million. Regardless of the amount of money to be invested, a stamp portfolio should be well diversified. Generally, it should consist of five to twenty-five stamps. Their number, type, and quality should vary with the amount of money the individual wishes to invest and what is currently available on the market.

It is possible to invest the entire sum into one very rare issue; however, there is merit to a broad collection. By diversifying, the investor prepares for the possibility that interest in a particular issue may dwindle, thus assuring a ready market for other stamps that might continue to appreciate in value. Over the long run, however, the objective is appreciation for the entire portfolio.

Peter M. Rexford founded the first rare stamp and coin division for Newhard Cook, a New York Stock Exchange member firm. He currently writes a nationally syndicated newspaper column (The Stamp & Coin Exchange) on stamps and coins.

A good portfolio of stamps can be put together for as little as $500 and would consist of three or four excellent quality, early used stamps priced between $100 and $300. This plan allows some portfolio diversification while retaining the option of adding higher quality material at a later date.

To assemble a portfolio of high-quality mint examples of early U.S. issues, an investment of $5,000 to $10,000 would be advisable. The same rule of selective purchases should remain, with a maximum of five to ten items in the portfolio. These stamps would cost between $250 and $1,000 apiece.

A major benefit of purchasing stamps in the $1,000 range is that this is primarily the type of material sold on the major auction markets. (See *Stamp Auctions*, later in this article.) With a subscription to catalogs and prices-realized lists from a few selected auction houses, the investor will be able to keep a good record of prices that material of this type is bringing on a regular basis.

If an investor can spend more than $10,000, then true philatelic rarities can be included in his portfolio. Single stamps, classic rare covers, and plate blocks costing between $1,000 and $5,000 historically have done very well in appreciating in value. Many of the earlier classic issues in mint condition and nineteenth-century material in multiple blocks would be excellent additions. Airmail plate blocks and some of the rarer proofs have shown very good appreciation also.

If an investor wants to develop a portfolio worth up to $50,000, anywhere between ten to twenty-five stamps would be best. This allows for each stamp to be one of rarity, in excellent condition. Portfolios with an investment in the area of six figures may contain more stamps or sets but should still be based on the same guidelines of selective purchasing.

INVESTMENT CRITERIA

In determining the investment quality of a particular stamp, one must consider (1) its attractiveness to collectors; (2) its condition (e.g., centering, color, clarity); and (3) the quantity printed of that issue.

Collector Demand

The U.S. Post Office estimates that there are approximately 30 million stamp collectors in the United States. The supply-demand relationship for a stamp that may be purchased is gauged by this huge collection of individuals. If, for example, 10,000 individuals allocate a substantial amount of capital to rare stamps, and, of these, one fifth arc interested in a fine unused copy of the $5 stamp issued to commemorate the Columbian Exposition of 1893, of the 27,350 copies of this stamp originally printed, experts estimate that perhaps only several hundred examples would still be in unused superb condition. With the majority of these stamps in the hands of collectors, it is rare that a superb, defect-free copy of this stamp would appear at auction more than ten or twenty times a year. With a potential investment demand for 2,000 of these stamps and a limited supply available, this stamp would be considered a valuable candidate for acquisition under favorable supply-demand conditions. (A group of particularly illustrious stamps is shown in Figure 1.)

Condition of the Stamp

For the serious collector or investor of rare postage stamps, the stamp's condition is the most important factor in determining its selling price. The examination of a postage stamp

FIGURE 1. Four Stamps Especially Prized by Collectors

5-cent Benjamin Franklin—
the first regular postage stamp
officially issued by the U.S.
government, July 1, 1847

10-cent George Washington—
the second regular postage stamp
officially issued by the U.S.
government, July 1, 1847

90-cent Abraham Lincoln—
highest denomination of
the 1869 pictorial issue,
May 10, 1869

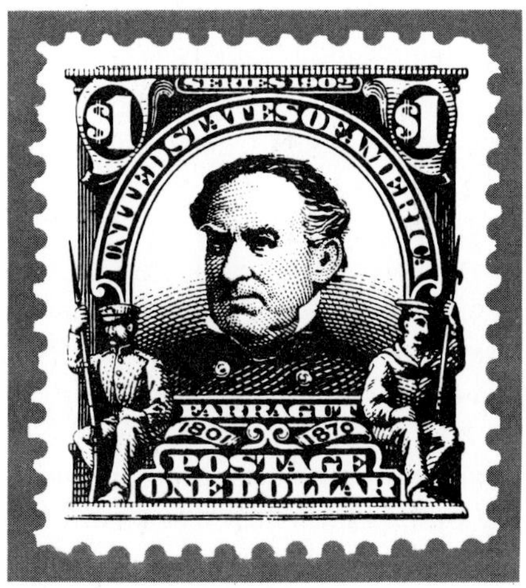

Admiral David G. Farragut
$1.00 denomination of the
1903 regular issue series,
June 5, 1903

has become akin to a science. High-powered microscopes, watermark fluids, ultraviolet lights, and other similar devices are used in determining a stamp's quality. While an investor need not set up a sophisticated laboratory to examine stamps, he should know what to consider in evaluating the investment characteristics of a stamp.

Centering. The centering of the design within the stamp's perforations or borders is one of the easiest key points to consider in judging a stamp's overall quality. It is mainly a matter of visually checking how the design of the stamp is spaced from its edges. Generally speaking, the more evenly the design is centered from the perforations of the stamp, the higher the price it will command. The following rankings of centering range from superb, where the design is equidistant from the edges, to space-filler, a stamp that a collector might purchase to fill space in an album:

- Superb—Design is clear of all perforations and borders of stamp are equal
- Extremely fine—Design is clear of all perforations but not quite perfectly centered
- Very fine—Design is clear of all perforations but slightly shifted, making borders partially unequal
- Fine—Design is close to, but clear of, perforations, and border may be very small on one or two sides
- Average—Perforations at one or more points cutting into the design
- Poor—A significant portion of the stamp's design is missing or affected by perforations in the design
- Space-filler—Poor perforations; in addition to being off-center, it will probably have other problems, such as a tear, a corner missing, or extensive thinning of the paper

In most cases, a centering rating of very fine for most stamps or fine for nineteenth-century varieties qualifies a stamp for an investment portfolio. Often a stamp in very fine condition can be purchased at perhaps 50 percent of the cost of one judged to be superb. Both stamps will have a good possibility for appreciation, but the investor must remember that the base of the stamp market is the collector who is more likely to spend less for a stamp that has only a fine appearance than an exorbitant sum for a perfectly centered one. A stamp graded at less than five should not be placed into an investment portfolio unless there are known to be very few copies in existence.

Color, Clarity, and Freshness. In both the Scott and Harris catalogs, a brief description is included of the ink colors used on each issue. (See *Philatelic Catalogs* at the end of this article.) On the majority of stamps issued after 1935, the exact name of the color is not absolutely essential to its value. When dealing with stamps from 1847 to the mid-1930s, however, the very slightest color variation can often mean the difference of hundreds or thousands of dollars.

The investor should make absolutely certain, when purchasing a stamp with an increased value due to its color variety, that the stamp is actually more valuable. The best way to accomplish this is to examine the stamp's certificate. If the stamp is not accompanied by a certificate, prior to purchase the buyer should arrange with the seller to secure one that guarantees its authenticity and color variety.

Just as a rare type of color variety can increase dramatically the value of a given stamp, the opposite is true for the condition of the color of a stamp. In other words, if purchasing a stamp that is described as dark carmine, that is exactly what it should be. With age and exposure to improper conditions, such as excessive sunlight, the color of a stamp can fade. As a result, although the stamp is completely genuine, its actual color might be light rose or just plain carmine. While this difference does not always affect the price of the stamp, it should be kept in mind when looking at a number of similar stamp choices.

The freshness of a stamp is entirely a matter of overall collector preference. A stamp that, when held with stamp tongs, seems to be just as fresh as it was when it was printed, is much more desirable than one that is limp and sags.

Even though the centering of a stamp may be extremely fine or superb, the actual value may be minimal if the perforations surrounding it are not as large as they were when the stamp was originally separated from the sheet. Occasionally, the perforations around a stamp will wear off from age or be torn off if mishandled. Although seemingly insignificant to the stamp as a whole, this too can decrease the stamp's value. This is one of the major reasons that investment stamps should be kept in protective holders. Often, the term nibbed perf will be used in describing a stamp in an auction catalog. This means that although some of the single perforation is still attached to the stamp, a small part is missing. The extent of the nibbed perf must be examined closely, for if the majority of the perforation is missing, its price will be substantially less. Although on rare occasions a stamp with a missing perf may be considered for an investment, it is better to pass it up and look for a better copy.

When purchasing a plate block or any combination of stamps still joined together by perforations, it is especially important to hold the stamps horizontally with tongs to ensure that the perforations attaching them are sound and will not separate accidentally. It is not uncommon to see a plate block of stamps listed in an auction catalog with a description including minor perf separations. Although only three or four of the perforations may have been torn apart, the price realized will still be lower than it would be for a plate block with all of the perforations intact.

Condition of the Gum. Undeniably, the condition of a stamp's gum has become one of the most disputed areas for both collectors and investors alike.

Hinged Versus Never Hinged. In the 1960s, collectors began to pay very careful attention to whether a stamp had ever been hinged, or whether the gum on the back was original. A hinge is a small piece of paper or glassine, with gum on one side, which is folded in half; one half is attached to the stamp, and the other half attached to the collector's album page. The hinge allows the collector to lift up the stamp to read what was printed on the album page underneath, usually the stamp's description or catalog number. Subsequent removal of the stamp from the album usually results in some damage to the gum of the stamp or the paper on which it was printed. Until the 1940s, the only way to mount stamps in an album was to hinge them; therefore, never-hinged copies of some issues often command a substantial premium over hinged copies. Very recently, however, the price gap seems to be narrowing slightly. If, at some point, more collectors and investors deemphasize the importance of gum, a gradual downswing in the never-hinged market is feasible.

Regumming. It is not unusual to find hinged stamps that have been regummed to give them the appearance of never having been hinged. Regumming a stamp is usually detectable. To thwart this practice, collectors began to look for hinge marks on the gum, since the intent of regumming was to remove any trace of a hinge. Soon the regummers became aware of this and lost no time in finding copies that had been heavily hinged, virtually beyond collector appeal. They would then remove the old adhesive and replace it with new gum. Then, to make them appear legitimate, they might place very light hinge marks on the regummed copies. The stamps were now in much better condition and still would be purchased by collectors at a premium. When news of this new method of stamp fraud became known, frustration among collectors grew. As a result, the experts responsible for detecting the regumming have a tremendous backlog of material to be examined and judged. (See organizations listed under *Certificate of Authenticity*, later in this article.)

As a general rule, lightly hinged material definitely should be considered as a solid investment; regummed material never should be considered unless every other facet of the stamp's condition makes the specimen unique. As mentioned earlier, never-hinged rarities will probably always bring premium prices. Equally as important, though, is the high initial price that this material currently demands. With the price gap between hinged versus nonhinged stamps closing, it would be hard for the investor to be wrong in acquiring lightly hinged stamps at more reasonable prices.

With this buying standard set, it is essential that the investor be able to discern the differences in the degree of severity of a stamp's hinging. Although every stamp is different and judging any point of its condition is relatively subjective, the extent of hinging for any given stamp can be broken down into four categories: (1) never hinged, (2) lightly hinged, (3) hinged, and (4) heavily hinged.

The safest way for the independent investor to guarantee that the gum on a stamp is original is to require that the seller furnish a written commitment or an accompanying certificate.

Reinforcement. When a block of stamps has been transferred from stamp album to stamp album over a period of many years, the perforations may become weak and begin to separate. As a result, collectors often reinforce the intersection of the perforations with a small portion of a hinge. Most reinforcements have been done skillfully and affect the stamp's valuc only minimally; however, other reinforcements have been made poorly and may affect the value of all of the stamps in the block. Although it is best to purchase only those multiples that have survived without the need for reinforcement, an investor should consider only those items with little or no hinge reinforcement.

Used vs. Mint. Most uninformed investors feel that used stamps do not have the investment potential of mint copies. This is a misconception, for a look through any major auction catalog will show the vast number of used stamps bringing record-breaking prices. For instance, the world's most valuable stamp, the one-cent British Guiana of 1856 that brought $850,000 at the 1980 Rarities of the World sale is a used stamp. Furthermore, since all of the known copies of the 1918 U.S. 24-cent inverted airmail stamp (#C3a) are unused, one found used and canceled on an envelope would easily bring at least double the price the mint copies command because it would be unique.[1] This is another example of such factors as collector demand and quantity issued (or availability) determining stamp prices.

In purchasing used stamps for an investment portfolio, the investor need not be concerned with original gum and hinging since any gum on a used stamp would have been soaked off when removed from the envelope.

Local Cancelations. An extremely specialized area of collecting is that of local cancelations. In the early days of the postal system, postmasters often designed their own types of cancelations. Interest in this area has never been greater, and new record prices are now being established.

Covers. The market for covers, or used envelopes, is tremendously active but very specialized. Also referred to as postal history, covers are most often purchased by collectors of a specific area (e.g., first day of issue, singular topic or event, and presidential address). A good-quality stamp on a cover will almost always realize a higher price than if it were not attached.

Historical covers and folded letters used prior to the issuance of postage stamps (pre-1845) are avidly sought after and realize high prices at auction. These are known as stampless covers.

MODERN RARITIES

Clearly, the most rapidly growing philatelic field of the past decade has been that of modern rarities. These are stamps that, although recently issued, contain a feature that makes them genuinely rare or unique and, therefore, attractive to collectors.

Modern rarities, often called errors, freaks, and oddities, are stamps that contain overt mistakes in the printing or perforating process. Easiest to spot are stamps that have been misperforated. These normally include those with the perforation holes running through or near the middle of the stamp's design, or are missing them altogether as a result of a sheet having been misfed into the perforating machine. Depending on the number of stamps found with misperforations, the value of the errors can range from a few dollars to many thousands.

Of even greater interest to collectors are stamps that are missing colors or those with the design inverted (Figure 2). This happens when a stamp of more than one color is run through the printing press on a second pass. On rare occasions, the printer will pull a sheet from the run to check it and then return it to the stack upside down. Consequently, when the second color is printed, it appears to be inverted on the sheet of stamps.

Such was the case with a sheet of 100 of the 1979 $1.00 railroad lantern stamps. Further intrigue and romance associated with the stamps stemmed from their sale to a Central Intelligence Agency (CIA) employee in northern Virginia. The employee, after the purchase, noticed the error and replaced the sheet with one with normal printing. Thus, the error stamps have become known as the CIA invert.

---

[1] The single known sheet of the 1918 24-cent inverted air mail was purchased by William T. Robey in Washington, D.C., for its face value of $24. In April 1981, a single copy of the stamp sold for $176,000 at auction in New York.

FIGURE 2. The Invert Candlestick Stamp

Note: This is the rarest U.S. error stamp since the 1918 Jenny airplane inverts.

Invert Regular

When first revealed, examples of the CIA invert sold for several thousand dollars. Within a few months, the price climbed to more than $17,000. Since the stamps are every bit as rare as the 1918 24-cent airmail invert, which can bring more than $100,000 at auction, the stamp's value may escalate even higher.

The return on the CIA stamp has been spectacular, but so has been the risk. Should one or more additional sheets of the invert error turn up, the supply would quickly close in on the collector demand and the price would drop. However, since the CIA invert has been on the market for so long a time, the appearance or discovery of more such stamps is highly unlikely.

Investing in error stamps can be compared to the more speculative, high-tech stocks. Appreciable research should be done in the field before investing in them. They also carry with them more risk and less immediate liquidity, but the prospects for a much greater and more rapid return on the investment hold a rare opportunity for investors.

ATTRACTIVE FEATURES

Collector Base of Millions

As mentioned earlier, the popularity of stamp collecting is international, especially for U.S. issues. This collector base continues to grow at an impressive rate. As more people enter the field of philately, vying for the finite supply of stamps in existence, prices will continue to appreciate.

Relatively High Liquidity

Liquidity for good quality philatelic material is strong, and there is a ready market of competitive buyers seeking investment material at any time, especially through auctions. Because of increased interest in purchasing rare stamps, dealers have been advertising aggressively (the number of advertisements has steadily increased over the past five years), and wholesale prices have increased concomitantly. Auctions frequently allow sellers to realize optimum prices and are a convenient outlet for selling their merchandise.

Portability

One of the most highly regarded characteristics of a rare-stamp portfolio is the ease of its portability and storage. Great amounts of wealth can be transported in a form that may be virtually undetected from city to city or from country to country. For the value, no other tangible can be stored or transported so conveniently and take up so little space.

POTENTIAL RISKS

Price Distortions

With the vast differences in stamp catalogs and stamp conditions, fair market pricing often becomes distorted, especially for the novice collector or investor. (The fair market price of a rare stamp can be defined as the amount that a buyer is willing to pay.) Both the buyer and seller should have a good enough knowledge of the market to determine a fair price for the very top-grade material. In most cases, the only route for purchasing investment-grade material at competitive prices is the major auction houses. Here, on a monthly basis, the items conforming to every investment category and in every conceivable condition are publicly bought and sold. It is in this market that, once the stamp is properly identified, the true forces of supply and demand prevail.

Volatility

In 1979, the price of a set of three 1930 graf zeppelin stamps rocketed in a matter of months from around $4,500 to $11,000 and more. This rapid price rise occurred when an article in a major East Coast newspaper mentioned that the set was scarce, historic, and popular with collectors. It also noted that the set had continually risen in value and might prove to be a lucrative investment for the future.

Panic buying of the zeppelin sets ensued nationwide. The major purchasers, however, were uninformed buyers who assumed that no matter how high the price, they were making the buy of a lifetime. To make matters worse, the truly uninformed were paying top prices for defective sets that were heavily hinged and had other problems.

When the buying rush began to diminish, and some of these purchasers decided to take a profit, they found that no one would pay anywhere near the inflated purchase price. Within a year the price plummeted to as low as $2,500; only in 1981 did the price return to a reasonable level of about $4,000. It is important to note, however, that although hundreds of people were caught in the zeppelin price disaster, there were many warning signs that should have alerted them to the impending danger.

False Scarcity

Anyone from a major dealer to a closet collector can create a false scarcity by mass purchasing of a single issue. Usually, an issue of low printing is selected that formerly had not been widely collected. Purchasing the material may take years, and the individual then must hold onto the purchase until demand for the issue begins. This may take many years, but after it becomes evident that the issue is in short supply, the price begins to rise, depending on what dealers and collectors are willing to pay. The initial purchaser then slowly releases the supply at a very large profit. False scarcities often can be detected in their early stages. The amount of time needed to track them is minimal and can prevent serious financial mistakes.

Physical Alteration

Reperforations. Reperforating the edges of some valuable stamps sometimes is attempted by unscrupulous collectors or dealers because stamps with perforations on all four sides are considered more valuable than those at the edge of a sheet with one or two nonperforated edges. Additionally, imperforated stamps that were printed for use in coil vending machines (which perforated the stamps automatically) have been reperforated to resemble rare, higher-value perforated issues. However, careful examination will reveal the vast majority of reperforations.

Camouflaged Defects. Stamps that have been mishandled may have defects that have been expertly repaired to deceive a purchaser as to its small faults. A stamp can be rebacked to complete some perforations that may have been torn off or to repair a tear in some small portion of the stamp's margin. A skilled artist might add a few strategic lines to a stamp's design to cover a scuff or, even worse, to make it appear to be a rarer variety.

Faulty Copies. An investor should avoid faulty copies of stamps. Their value will never appreciate in the same proportion as that of an extremely fine, sound copy. There are several kinds of natural defects that can occur on a stamp. A natural defect would be a design that is too far off-center, an easily seen crease in the stamp's paper or gum, or some foreign matter in the gum or paper (larger than the head of a pin) that was processed into the stamp at the time of manufacturing.

A thin area in a stamp's paper, which is visible when held to the light or dipped in watermark fluid, also is not acceptable.

It is important to note that all these potential alterations can be identified and avoided with the use of a certificate of authenticity (see discussion under *Certificate of Authenticity*, later in this article).

TAX CONSEQUENCES

Stamps held for investment purposes have been deemed capital assets by the Internal Revenue Service (IRS). If they are held for more than one year, any gain made on their sale is taxed at the capital gains rate.

Tax-Free Exchange

Stamps qualify under Section 1031 of the Internal Revenue Code as an investment asset suitable for like-kind exchange of property for which no gain or loss will be recognized at the time of the exchange.

This tax deferral gives an investor an opportunity to both consolidate a collection and diversify an investment portfolio with rare stamps. Therefore, an investor who has a collection of 100 stamps in mixed condition passed down to him may sell those stamps and reinvest the capital in a solid rare-stamp portfolio of perhaps five to ten pieces with excellent appreciation potential. (See article on "Tax Considerations for Collector-Investors," elsewhere in this volume.) For complete guidance in these matters, readers are urged to consult a professional tax advisor.

IMPORTANT FACTORS IN BUYING AND SELLING

Rare-Stamp Brokers

An investor who decides to diversify his or her investment portfolio with rare stamps should consider acquiring them through a qualified rare-stamp broker, who will assist the individual in purchasing a good-quality portfolio with the assurance of full disclosure as to a stamp's value, condition, and potential.

Rare-stamp brokers often offer other services in addition to acquisitions. Some will provide an annual updated valuation of the portfolios. Others may keep a close photographic record of each item to assist the investor in case the stamps are ever lost or stolen. An investor should always obtain instructions for the safe handling, care, and storage of a portfolio from these professionals.

Investment Services

Investment brokers who work on behalf of the investor emerged as a result of the relatively recent interest in rare-stamp investments and the lack of confidence in the average dealer who sells only from his own inventory. Investment brokers (sometimes referred to as agents) represent the safest method of purchasing stamps for the investor with a limited knowledge of the rare-stamp market. Most offer a wide range of services to accommodate many different types of investors. A few select agents in the United States are set up to operate strictly on a commission basis, which is usually fixed at 10 percent. Those agents who carry no inventory of stamps are best prepared to service a client by selecting only those items being sold on the open market to structure a portfolio suited to the client's needs.

Once the stamp agent or broker is given the investment capital, his goal is to assemble the highest quality portfolio possible, given what is then available on the market. Selecting the issues for the portfolio often may take one or two months, since some stamps may be available only at selected auctions.

Some investment houses will offer to buy back the stamps when the investor decides to sell. Other agents will act as liquidators in the sale. This service can be quite helpful to the investor. In most cases, the agents will charge a commission on the proceeds of the liquidation.

Selecting an Agent. When selecting an agent, not only should the investor be certain of the agent's reputation and credibility, but he must also determine whether the agent offers a guarantee regarding a stamp's authenticity. A guarantee that includes the replacement of any item that proves to be either counterfeit or misrepresented is preferable.

Stamp Auctions

For the investor who has done the required background research, investment-grade stamps may be purchased at competitive prices at stamp auctions held at major auction houses. Hundreds of auctions are held annually in the United States. Each house holds up to twenty auctions per year, many specializing in specific areas, including foreign issues. The smaller houses should not be discounted completely as, on occasion, it is possible to find good-quality items at moderate prices, although smaller houses may not describe the items being offered as fully as the larger ones do.

Bidding by Mail. Since the majority of the major auction houses are on the East or West Coasts, bidding by mail is an option for investors for whom the location of the house is inaccessible. By reviewing the auction catalog, the mail bidder is afforded most of the opportunities of the house bidder.

The specific rules for both floor and mail bidding are printed on the inside of most auction catalogs and should be read carefully by all bidders, as rules do differ from auction to auction. A few weeks after the auction, a list of the prices realized will be mailed to all catalog subscribers. It is essential that these lists be reviewed and kept, as they represent the prices currently being paid by dealers, collectors, and investors for the material offered.

Prior to the day of the auction, the house tabulates all the mail bids and selects the highest and second highest bid for each lot offered. When the lot comes up for sale, the floor bidding begins at one bid increment above the second highest mail bid. For example, on lot #1 , the highest mail bid may be $1,000. If the second highest mail bid is only $500, the bidding will start at $550. If no floor bids are received for this lot, the mail bidder of $1,000 will win the lot for $550, even though he was prepared to go to $1,000. This method allows the mail bidders the same benefits as those attending in person.

After the auction, the mail bidder will be notified that he has successfully bid on an item and, on receipt of the money, the auction house will mail the lot to him. If, after the mail bidder receives the lot, he discovers any defects or inconsistencies in the material that were not mentioned in the auction catalog's description, the stamp may then be returned on that basis. Return policies vary from auction to auction so mail bidders are advised to fully understand the conditions of the sale prior to placing bids.

Auction Fees. An auction house works strictly on a commission basis, usually 10 percent. However, this commission is added to both sides of the transaction, so most auctions receive from the seller, as well as from the purchaser, a total of 20 percent. This percentage fluctuates for some auctions, and with a few the buyer is not required to pay any commission on a purchase. For the vast majority of the major houses, however, an investor should expect to pay to the house 10 percent in addition to the price of the purchase.

As with any auctioned property, whether it be stamps, coins, fine art, or cars, shills may be used in the audience to bid up the prices on a number of items. Also, the owner of a lot may be able to bid up the price himself once he is on the floor. Although this activity occurs rarely, bidders should be aware of its existence.

Dealers

Dealer Integrity. One of the most effective ways for the investor to determine the integrity of a dealership is to check with an acquaintance who has done business with the dealer. A dealer's reputation, good or bad, can spread rapidly by word of mouth, so some discreet checking by the investor could be most profitable.

Furthermore, a self-regulatory body in the industry, the American Stamp Dealers Association (ASDA), protects the stamp buyer from some of the more unscrupulous dealers. It has established rules and regulations governing the activities of its members and takes whatever action is necessary against a member dealer if a record of impropriety is found.

Since the investor may be considering allocating a large sum of money for a rare-stamp portfolio, an inquiry with the local Better Business Bureau would also be appropriate.

Dealer Profit Margin. The profit margin for a dealer can range anywhere from 10 to 500 percent. More importantly, the dealer can place his profit anywhere within these percentages and still be dealing very honestly. For example, if a dealer had purchased 100 copies of a stamp in 1980 for $5 apiece and then resold them for $25 each in 1990, the percentage of profit would be great. If the fair market price for those stamps in 1990 was $27, then not only would the customer get a fair deal, but the dealer would still be making 500 percent on the investment. Doing research on a rare-stamp issue and its price is not too difficult and should be a prerequisite to any purchase.

Both large and small dealers often have some extremely desirable rare stamps available. For this reason, a local dealer should never be overlooked.

Catalogs. The most effective use of a stamp catalog is as a reference for background and approximate pricing. Most catalogs' pricing policy explains conditions that should be considered. Others list a number of different prices for various types of conditions.

On the whole, more common stamps sell for substantially less than the advertised price in a catalog. Conversely, rare issues in higher grades may sell for more than the catalog price. One important consideration concerning the accuracy of a catalog's stamp pricing should be whether the publishers have a vested interest in the stamp prices. In some instances, an order blank can be found at the back of the catalog. In these instances, the publishers of the catalog are ready to sell the stamps for the prices published because, in all probability, a high-price safety factor has been figured into the price of the listed stamp to compensate for many major price swings during the year of catalog distribution.

Certificate of Authenticity. As with other tangible investments, a certificate of authenticity is available for rare stamps. The certificate, in addition to verifying or disputing authenticity, will specify any noticeable defects within the stamp itself, such as thins, tears, stain, or condition of the gum. Any investment-quality stamp with an approved certificate from a recognized authority will bring more at auction that will an identical copy that does not have one.

The two primary organizations that offer the accepted certificates for stamps are the American Philatelic Society (State College, Pa.) and the Philatelic Foundation (New York, N.Y.). One wishing to submit material to them may obtain a mailing form from their offices. There is a minimum charge for their services and an additional fee, depending on the value of the stamp submitted and its authenticity.

CUSTODIAL CARE

Just as portability is a great asset to the collector, it can be an even greater asset to a thief. Unfortunately, it is no longer safe to keep a good stamp collection in the home to be enjoyed. If the collection has any value, it should be stored in a safe-deposit box in a bank vault with a reputable bank or trust company. To go one step further, it would be best to purchase a box located at eye level because bank vaults have been known to have a pipe break and flood. Also, banks monitor the temperature and humidity of their vaults, which helps protect a rare-stamp investment.

GLOSSARY

booklet pane—A small sheet of stamps especially printed and cut to be sold in booklets.

cancelation—A mark placed on a stamp by a postal authority to prevent its reuse.

certificates— A document with a scaled photograph attached; notarized if acquired from the American Philatelic Society or Philatelic Foundation.

coils—Stamps issued in rolls for use in affixing or vending machines.

commemorative—A stamp that honors anniversaries, important people, or special events.

cover—The entire wrapping or envelope in which a letter has been sent through the mail.

definitive—A regular issue of a stamp for denominated postal use.

essay—Design submitted for stamp use but not accepted for issuance.

imperforate—Stamps without perforations; collected in pairs for proof of authenticity.

pen cancel—A cancelation applied to the stamp with pen and ink; usually of less value than if handstamped.

plate block—The portion of the sheet of stamps that includes the plate printing number in the margin selvedge and a multiple of stamps attached. With earlier issues, along with the plate number, the label of the printing or engraving company may be present. The number of stamps included with the plate number varies with the type of printing and number of colors used on the stamps.

proof—Trial printing of a stamp made from the original die or plate.

stamp tongs—Tweezer-like instruments fashioned with tips that handle stamps safely, thus avoiding damage. The tips vary in shape from points to flat pads.

watermark— A design or pattern incorporated into the paper during its manufacture.

STAMP AUCTION HOUSES

This list of auction houses is included strictly as a guide to some of the larger firms. It is in no way complete or a recommendation of any specific auction company.

Auction houses with more than one location are marked with an asterisk (*).

Earl Apfelbaum, Inc., Philadelphia, Pa.

Central Suffolk Auctions, Inc., Farmingville, N.Y.

John A. Fox Auctions, Floral Park, N.J.

*Stanley Gibbons International, London, Eng.

*Harmers of New York, Inc., New York, N.Y.

Steve Ivy Philatelic Auctions, Inc., Dallas, Tex.

Peter Kenedi, Inc., Encino, Cal.

Greg Manning Auctions, Inc., Fairfield, N.J.

Metro Stamp Co., Inc., Middle Village, N.Y.

Robert A. Siegel Auction Galleries, Inc., New York, N.Y.

Simmy's Stamp Co., Inc., Boston, Mass.

J & H Stolow, Inc., New York, N.Y.

Richard Wolffers, Inc., San Francisco, Cal.

PHILATELIC SOURCES

TRADE ASSOCIATION

American Stamp Dealers Association, Lake Success, N.Y.

PHILATELIC CATALOGS

Brookman Price List for Stamps. Published by the Brookman Company, Fairfield, N.J. Annual.

Harris Postage Stamp Catalog. Published by H.E. Harris Co., Inc., Boston, Mass. Semiannual.

Scott Specialized Catalog of United States Stamps. Published by Scott Publishing Co., Sidney, Ohio. Annual.

SUGGESTED READING

PERIODICALS

The American Philatelist. Published by the American Philatelic Society, Pennsylvania State College, Pa. Monthly.

Linn's Stamp Newspaper. Published by Amos Press, Sidney, Ohio. Weekly.

Scott's Stamp Journal. Published by Scott Publishing Co., Sidney, Ohio. Monthly.

Stamp Collector. Published by Van Dahl Publications, Inc., Albany, Or. Weekly.

REFERENCE BOOKS

Armstrong, Martin A. *United States Coil Issues, 1906–1938*. Lawrenceville: Trenton Publishing Co., 1980.

______. *U.S. Definitive Series, 1922–1938*. Lawrenceville: Trenton Publishing Co., 1980.

______. *"Washington-Franklins" 1908–1921*. Lawrenceville: Trenton Publishing Co., 1980.

______. *Nassau Street*. Sunnyvale, Cal.: Western Philatelic Library, 1960.

Herst, Jr., Herman. *The Compleat Philatelist*. Florham Park, N.J.: The Washington Press, 1979.

Johl, Max. *United States Postage Stamps, 1902–1935*. Lawrence, Mass.: Quarterman Publications, 1976.

Luff, John N. *The Postage Stamps of the United States*. Lawrence, Mass.: Quarterman Publications, 1981.

Schmidt, Paul W. *How to Detect Damaged, Altered and Repaired Stamps*. Huntington: Palm Press, 1979.

Wagenheim, Kal. *Paper Gold*. New York: Wyden Books, 1976.

THEATRICAL PRODUCTIONS

Paul H. Epstein
Allan M. Shapiro
Alden W. Watson

BASIC CHARACTERISTICS

The legitimate theater represents an unusual investment opportunity in several respects. Financings are handled almost entirely by the principals involved, with no participation by brokers or other securities professionals. The productions to be financed rarely have any operating history and even the artistic form in which they will open to the public (especially musicals) may change drastically from what is envisioned during the period of financing. The investment is highly speculative, balancing a strong likelihood of total loss against a small chance of huge returns. Yet, it provides investors with the excitement of a creative adventure, a sense of artistic involvement, and a touch of the thrill of the theater that many investors find far more alluring than tax shelters or high price-earnings ratios.

Unusual Aspects

Over the years, the theater industry has developed traditional methods of doing business. The basic investment terms described in this article—some of which would be extraordinary in other contexts—have long been accepted by both producers and investors to be a fair allocation of risks and rewards. Similarly, the manner in which offerings are made reflects the peculiar nature of the theater industry. New York State, as the center of the American legitimate theater, has recognized the unique nature of these investments by enacting a special statute that governs only theatrical financings.

Paul H. Epstein, Esq., is a member of the firm of Proskauer Rose Goetz & Mendelsohn, New York; Allan M. Shapiro, Esq., is a member of the New York Bar; Alden W. Watson, Esq., who revised this article, is associated with Proskauer Rose Goetz & Mendelsohn.

Broadway productions are by far the major source of investment opportunities in terms both of numbers of shows and of dollars raised. The financing principles involved apply to Off-Broadway presentations as well, although there are likely to be some differences in the terms of the underlying agreements with the playwright and other creative personnel. Most other productions, such as those of regional theaters, are presented on a nonprofit basis and do not seek investment capital. This discussion deals principally with a Broadway theatrical production.

Initiating a Production. A theatrical production usually begins when a producer (who may be one person or corporation, or several acting together) obtains an option for a license from the playwright to produce specified stage productions of the work. The license expires after the last performance by the last company under the license agreement (subject to a right to reopen the play within a short period). A license for Broadway customarily includes certain additional rights to produce the play on a national tour and in the West End of London (England's equivalent of Broadway).

Financing Methods

In nearly all cases, the option is exercised by presenting at least one paid public performance of the play. To finance that production, the producer seeks money from investors, who customarily become limited partners in a limited partnership of which the producer is the general partner.

An investor who has made a major financial contribution may receive credit as an associate producer, although this billing is given, in most cases, to persons who are limited partners and have no responsibility or rights with respect to the management of the partnership.

The Investment Vehicle

Traditional Theatrical Limited Partnership. Traditionally, the entire financing of a theatrical limited partnership is contributed by the limited partners who receive, collectively, one half of any partnership net profits, divided in proportion to their respective investments. However, this allocation may vary; the limited partners are sometimes allocated up to 60 percent of the net profits and, at other times, as little as 40 percent. The remaining net profits are divided among the general partners as a group.

Assuming that the limited partners receive the usual 50 percent aggregate share, an investor must provide 2 percent of the capital (entitling him to 2 percent of the limited partners' 50 percent share) in order to receive a one percent participation in total net profits. Each limited partner is liable for a share of partnership losses in proportion to, and up to the amount of, the sum of his respective capital contribution and his share of net profits. Any partnership liabilities exceeding the sum of the limited partners' total contributions and net profits are the sole responsibility of the producer-general partner, unless the limited partners agree otherwise.

At times, the producer uses shares of net profits to compensate persons such as starring actors, directors, general managers, and important financial supporters. While third parties who participate in net profits because of financial support draw only from the general partner's share, creative or artistic participants are often paid off the top, that is, before allocation of the remaining net profits among the partners.

Definition of Terms. Generally, the term "net profits" is defined for all limited partnership purposes to be the excess of the partnership's gross receipts over the total of its production expenses, running expenses, and other expenses. While gross receipts include essentially all partnership revenues, as common usage suggests, the other terms have more technical meanings. Production expenses include all costs incurred prior to the official opening of the show. Somewhat surprisingly, operating losses arising from preview or out-of-town tryout performances are also carried as production expenses. Conversely, all costs incurred after opening are carried as running expenses, even if related to capital assets of the production, such as replacement costumes for new performers. (Percentages of gross weekly box-office receipts paid to the playwright, composer, director, theater, and others are included in this category.) The term "other expenses" includes any further costs, such as prosecution and defense of lawsuits, that fit neither of the first two categories.

Distribution of Partnership Revenues. Capital contributions of the limited partners are returned out of partnership funds after (1) payment of or provision for partnership liabilities and obligations, including weekly running expenses; (2) repayment of any loans; and (3) creation of one or more cash reserves. Normally, the partnership agreement requires funding of a so-called sinking fund of a specified dollar amount before any distribution is made to the limited partners.

The remaining partnership revenues are then distributed among the partners as net profits. When the partnership terminates, any assets remaining after provision for all partnership debts and liabilities and the return of capital contributions not previously returned are distributed among the limited and general partners in proportion to their respective rights to participate in partnership net profits.

Additional Payments to Producer. In addition to a share of the net profits, the producer-general partner often receives a fee of a few percentage points of the gross weekly box-office receipts as compensation for services in maintaining the production, such as the handling of cast replacements and advertising. He may also receive a modest weekly cash office charge, commonly a fixed dollar amount, to help defray the overhead and administrative costs. These additional payments reflect the fact that under the usual limited partnership agreement, the producer-general partner is entirely responsible for managing the partnership. He may elect, for example, to abandon or close the production at any time or to arrange for additional companies. Because the limited partner can expect to have no voice in these matters after investing, the integrity and experience of the producer-general partner are investment criteria at least as important as the commercial potential of the script.

Other General Partner Rights. The limited partnership agreement often gives the producer-general partner the right to demand an involuntary overcall (additional investment) from the limited partners—in some instances, up to 20 percent of their initial investments. In addition, the producer-general partner customarily has the right (rarely, if ever, exercised) to recall any net profits distributed to partners and any capital contributions repaid to the limited partners, if those amounts are required to meet later obligations of the partnership. The producer-general partner may be given discretion to retain as reserves for any proper preproduction or production purposes money otherwise distributable to the partners. Such reserves are most often established to mount additional productions of the play, such as touring or British companies or, in the case of a non-Broadway production, to transfer to Broadway.

Partnership Income and Assets. The capital of the partnership is the amount contributed by the limited partners, including any involuntary overcall. Most capital contributions are made in cash or, in some cases, by irrevocable letter of credit. On occasion, a limited partner may invest by supplying items required for the production or by assuming liabilities that otherwise would have been borne by the partnership (such as theater deposits or performance bonds posted with unions).

If the production requires more financing, as sometimes happens, the producer-general partner may make or obtain loans or may secure additional limited partners who receive net profits solely from the general partner's share. This additional capital will have a right of repayment equal or superior to that of the original limited partners because, without this infusion of funds, the entire initial investment would be lost.

Basic Source of Income. The basic source of partnership income is the box-office receipts from one or more companies presenting the play. A successful Broadway production may finance additional companies with its New York profits or with an additional offering, or it may license the rights to another producer for a fee and royalty (the normal arrangement for a London production). The rights of the original limited partners to approve or participate in these further presentations vary according to the particular partnership agreement.

Subsidiary Rights. The partners of a partnership also may earn income from the so-called subsidiary rights in the play—principally, the rights to produce motion picture and television versions, to license presentations by stock companies and amateur groups, and to record the original cast album of a musical. Less important subsidiary rights include radio versions; second-class touring performances; foreign language productions; condensed, tabloid, and concert tour versions; commercial uses; and grand opera rights. The revenues earned from the exploitation of these rights belong solely to the author, unless and until the partnership's production runs a qualifying number of performances. At that point, the production company generally becomes entitled to receive a share of the revenues the author derives from sales or licenses of those rights entered into during a specified period. This right of participation survives the closing of the partnership's production and may continue as a source of revenue—all of which is treated as normal partnership income—for an indefinite period. While this right can prove lucrative, it is likely to have significant value only when the production itself has been successful enough to create public interest in the play.

For most Broadway productions, the right of participation vests at a point between one performance (i.e., the official opening) and twenty-one performances in New York. Although Off-Broadway requirements are less uniform, the production's participation often begins on the twenty-first performance, including some limited number of previews.

For a Broadway production, the Dramatists Guild, Inc. Approved Production Contract allows the producer to choose from among three or four subsidiary rights participation programs. Those plans give the limited partnership a right of participation that varies among plans—from 50 percent for media productions and stock performances to 10 percent for amateur and ancillary performances. The producer also has the exclusive right to create or license others to manufacture "commercial use products" such as toys, games, and dolls that are connected with the play. The producer is paid the designated percentage earned from the disposition of the subsidiary rights according to the applicable rights participation program, pursuant to each contract entered into on or after the effective date of the Approved Production Contract, but prior to the expiration of the periods described in the rights participation program. Off-Broadway productions are classified as "Revival Performances" in which there is a 20 percent right of participation for fifty years.

Except for any continuing participation in subsidiary rights income, the investment represented by the theatrical production has virtually no value after the end of performances. Because the author rarely grants more than a production license, the production company retains no ownership of the script. Most physical elements, such as sets, costumes, and lights, if not rented, are likely to be so highly specialized in design that they have no residual value. Any goodwill or secondary meaning that has become attached to the production becomes worthless unless reflected in the value of the subsidiary rights.

Possibility of Total Loss. If the production fails totally, the limited partners receive, at best, the return of a small portion of their investment, representing unexpended capital reserves. More commonly, unrecoverable production costs exceed capital contributions, resulting in a total loss to the limited partners and additional losses borne by the producer-general partner. Even a production that enjoys a moderately long run may show little or no profit or may return only a portion of the investors' money. This paradox may result when royalty participants (such as the authors and director) waive or defer all or part of their weekly payments to avoid an operating loss when a production is close to its weekly break-even point. Under such conditions, a show may hover on the verge of operating profitability for more than a year.

Blind Pool Financing. In 1988, the New York State legislature amended Article 23 of the Arts and Cultural Affairs Law to provide for an entirely new method of financing theatrical productions, which has been used widely in the film industry. Under the new method, which took effect in December 1988, producers may establish "blind pool theatrical production companies," in which investors who may be limited partners can contribute funds to be used in any number of specified or unspecified productions. This new method contrasts with the former procedure under which a producer was able to raise money for only one specified production at a time. In addition, the blind pool allows a producer to establish cost efficiencies and enables investors to spread their risks over numerous productions. Because this method of financing has never been used for theatrical syndications, it is difficult to predict how effective it will be. Most likely, producers with good track records will initially be able to take advantage of blind pool financing more than those with less successful histories. However, drafters of the legislation believe that in five to ten years, the majority of theatrical productions will be financed this way.

Offering and Sale. The offering and sale of limited partnership interests are made under whatever provisions of federal and state securities laws are deemed most appropriate to the size and scope of the financing. The offering period customarily expires at the same time as the producer's option on the play. When contributions have been received for the full production budget (or, in some instances, a smaller alternative production budget), the limited partnership is assigned all of the producer's rights related to the show and begins to function as the production entity. Unless and until that occurs, all funds contributed by the proposed limited partners are held in escrow, to be refunded if the minimum capital is not raised. Preproduction expenses incurred by the producer-general partner are usually reimbursed as a charge against the production budget only at the time full capitalization is reached.

In some instances, an investor will authorize earlier use of all or part of his contribution. (Such funds may be needed to defray preproduction costs, such as theater deposits, advances to creative personnel, or, in some cases, actual rehearsal costs.) In this case, the investor either waives or reserves the right of refund if the financing fails. If his investment has been spent, the investor may be forced to look to the producer's personal assets to enforce a reserved right of refund.

Prior to a formal offering, an investor may advance preliminary funding, often termed "front money," to be used immediately by a producer to pay preproduction expenses, such as the cost of acquiring rights in the play, establishing a production budget, and preparing the offering documents. New York State law permits a producer to receive such investments from no more than four persons. These investors commonly receive up to one percent of the eventual partnership capitalization represented by the amount of their front money; if such an investment is converted to a limited partnership contribution, rather than repaid on full capitalization, the front-money investor receives a separate proportionate participation as an ordinary limited partner.

An investor who provides front money or who permits his investment to be used prior to the full technical formation of the partnership may risk unlimited liability with respect to expenses incurred prior to the formation of the limited partnership and might be legally classified as a general partner of the partnership until all legal requirements for the formation of the limited partnership have been satisfied. It is possible that such an investor may be held fully liable to creditors, even beyond his investment in the partnership, for all debts incurred during that earlier period. However, such liability has rarely, if ever, been asserted.

An investor rarely has the right to withdraw from the production, even before the full production capital has been raised. Although he may be allowed to assign the right to receive partnership distributions, the investor may not have another party substituted as limited partner, except by operation of law or with the prior written consent of the general partner. Applicable federal and state securities laws often impose additional limitations on transfer of partnership interests. Accordingly, an investment in a theatrical production is nearly always an irrevocable commitment to its success or failure.

ATTRACTIVE FEATURES

Certainly, the chance to earn huge returns entices many investors. Some backers are attracted by the magnitude of the risk involved. For others, the principal appeal is not an economic one, but the intangible benefit of being associated, however indirectly, with the production of an artistic work. There is a group of investors who will help finance what they consider to be important theater, regardless of its commercial potential. Others choose to invest simply because of the opportunity the investment may provide to participate in the glamour and excitement of the traditional Broadway opening-night parties held by some producers, at which backers may meet the stars of the play and share the anxiety of waiting for the reviews.

It is probably fair to say that the majority of investors in theatrical syndications have two common characteristics: First, backing shows gives them a thrill that other investments do not; second, they are fully prepared to lose whatever amount they invest.

POTENTIAL RISKS

Investing in a theatrical production is a highly speculative undertaking, the results of which cannot be predicted even by skilled and experienced producers. The fact that a major success can sometimes pay a large return on the investment offers many the possibility of sufficient reward to justify the risk. The potential investor for profit is likely to consider the number of performances given and awards won by other shows created by the people who created the production may have achieved under consideration. These are relevant facts, but easily overemphasized. A production may have achieved critical acclaim and run for months without accumulating profits and, in any case, prior success with other productions is an uncertain index of the commercial value of a subsequent production.

Ultimately, an investor must evaluate the worth of the play and its commercial appeal, as well as the quality of the production elements and the persons involved. The skill and integrity of the producer are critical considerations. Reviewing the profit and loss history of his previous productions will provide some indication of the producer's ability both to choose productions that will attract an audience and to manage them successfully. This information is contained in the offering circular required by the Securities and Exchange Commission (SEC) and the Office of the New York State Attorney General.

There are no investment advisors in this field, but various people connected with the theatrical business (such as general managers, publicists, and lawyers) can give their opinions as to the chances for the success of a production. Although their artistic opinions probably will vary, such people can help investigate a producer's business reputation.

By tradition, virtually all theatrical investments are sold directly by producers. As a result, there are no dealers in theatrical syndication interests. Furthermore, because such participations are generally nontransferable without the permission of the general partner, no secondary market exists.

TAX CONSEQUENCES

Generally, theatrical productions are financed solely with equity capital. There is no debt—either recourse or nonrecourse—to leverage the investment. Although losses incurred by theatrical partnerships are passed through to the investor, they do not generate net cash benefits to the investor. Theatrical limited-partnership investment participations are classified by the Tax Reform Act of 1986 as passive activities. Except as noted below, losses and credits generated from passive activities cannot be offset against income from active sources, such as a profession or a business carried on by the limited partner. Also, these losses or credits cannot be used to offset gains from portfolio income, such as interest and dividends. While the production is in progress, they may be offset only against gains from other passive activities. However, an indefinite passive loss carryforward is available which enables the limited partner to offset the loss against all of the limited partner's income when the entire interest in the activity is disposed of in a fully taxable transaction. At this time, the question of whether a theatrical production constitutes a single activity or more than one activity remains unanswered.

Accounting for theatrical partnerships is generally made on the basis of the calendar year. Prior to the Tax Reform Act of 1986, production costs were capitalized and were recovered under a so-called cost-recovery method. Under this method, no taxable income was reported until the net income from the operation of the production exceeded the production costs.

Currently, the income forecast method is used to recover production costs. Under this method, production costs must be capitalized and then deducted ratably over the anticipated income-producing life of the production. Thus, for a production that is expected to run longer than the end of its first accounting year, some income may be recognized for tax purposes even before production costs have been fully recovered.

It should also be noted that even if taxable revenues are held in partnership reserves, rather than distributed, a partner will still be subject to current taxation on such revenues.

REPRESENTATIVE TYPES OF INVESTORS

Individual investors, whether attracted by economic or artistic concerns, remain the principal source of production financing. However, various corporate entities in the entertainment industry may be significant investors in certain productions. It has not been uncommon for a motion picture company to contribute a substantial sum toward capitalization of a production in exchange for the right to acquire the motion picture rights for a predetermined price. Because of the unknown value of the play, the predetermined price usually has been lower than the price of rights in a proven success.

Record companies also may invest in musical plays in exchange for the right to record the cast album. With the advent of new television technologies, such as cable television and the numerous satellite-fed pay-television networks, the need for television programming is becoming increasingly important and may generate similar investments by programming services or independent producers for television. The significance of such sources as potential investors is not yet clear.

IMPORTANT FACTORS IN BUYING AND SELLING

Pursuant to provisions of the New York Arts and Cultural Affairs Law (the Law) that regulates theatrical syndication financing, the Attorney General of the State of New York has jurisdiction over any offering of any theatrical syndication interests made in or from the State of New York. The law and the regulations promulgated thereunder by the Attorney General require an offeror to provide detailed disclosure in the form of an offering circular that sets forth all the essential elements of the proposed production and to distribute detailed accounting statements to the investors.

The Law is a unique statute that reflects the actual practices and requirements of the legitimate theater and facilitates investment in theatrical syndications by New York State residents. It provides a system of regulation for these special securities that is separate from the regulation of other securities. However, offerings to and purchases by residents of other states must satisfy their local securities laws as well, and no statute similar to the Law exists in any other jurisdiction. In some states, the laws are interpreted and applied in such a way as to make it impossible, as a practical matter, to offer or sell theatrical syndication interests. The costs and complexities of compliance with such laws—laws that have not been shaped specifically to accommodate the peculiar needs of the theater industry—tend to discourage producers from taking the steps necessary to enable residents of other states to participate in theatrical syndications, no matter how eager to participate such potential investors may be.

The SEC regulates all interstate offerings of securities, including the sale of interests in theatrical syndications. The offering documents for most public offerings must be reviewed by the SEC before they may be used. If, in a particular offering, the total investment sought is less than $1.5 million, the producer may file his documents in accordance with the SEC's Regulation A, which relieves the producer of many of the more detailed disclosure requirements of Form S-1. Form S-18 can be used if the aggregate price of the offering does not exceed $7.5 million. The New York regional office of the SEC is experienced in the area of investments in theatrical syndications and, in cooperation with the Office of the New York State Attorney General, has compiled a standard form of offering circular that may be used for the offering of limited partnership interests in theatrical syndications. A packet containing this information may be obtained from the New York State Attorney General's Office.

If the offering is to be private (pursuant to Section 4(2) of the Securities Act of 1933, as amended, or Regulation D promulgated thereunder), the SEC form of offering circular need not be followed and the filing of full-disclosure documents with the SEC is unnecessary. Nevertheless, the Law requires a filing with the New York State Attorney General even when an offering relies on Regulation D for a federal exemption; it exempts private offerings from state filing only if the offer is made to fewer than thirty-six offerees and the producer-general partner complies with a stringent procedure requiring him to file certain documents, including a specified form of signed waiver from each investor.

MONITORING THE PRODUCTION

Generally, the only certificate representing an investor's contribution to a theatrical partnership is a conformed copy of the partnership agreement signed by the general partner and listing the names and percentage interests of each of the limited partners. This document is usually sent to each limited partner after the production is fully financed.

The investor can expect to be advised of the current status of the production by circulars from the producer, as well as by monthly accounting statements once paid performances begin. The financial statements set forth total gross weekly box-office receipts and unrecouped production costs, as well as other relevant information. In addition, the Attorney General of the State of New York requires other accounting reports, both prior to the opening and after the closing of the production. All reports must comply with the Attorney General's regulations for disclosure and accuracy. That office also handles investors' complaints and will investigate suspected malfeasance.

GLOSSARY

blind pool—A financing method established by statute in New York in 1988 that allows the formation of a theatrical production company in which investors contribute funds to be used for any number of specified or unspecified theatrical productions.

front money—Preliminary funding from a small number of investors (under New York State law, not more than four) raised by a producer for a particular production prior to the formal offering and commonly used to pay preproduction expenses.

general partner—In a theatrical limited partnership, a partner (usually a producer) responsible for the management of the partnership and directly liable for its debts in excess of the capital invested by the limited partners.

limited partner—In a theatrical limited partnership, an investor who puts at risk a limited amount of production capital and receives with the other limited partners a share of partnership net profits in proportion to his investment.

net profits—The excess of gross receipts of a theatrical limited partnership over the total of its production expenses, running expenses, and other expenses.

New York Arts and Cultural Affairs Law—The New York statute which, together with the regulations promulgated thereunder, governs any offering of interests in a theatrical syndication financing made in or from the State of New York.

other expenses—Expenses incurred for a theatrical production that are not production or running expenses.

producer—An individual or entity who has or shares final executive responsibility for the management of a theatrical production, in many cases including those initially acquiring the production rights from the author and acting as principals in the financing of the production.

production expenses—Expenses incurred for a theatrical production prior to its official opening.

running expenses—Expenses incurred for a theatrical production following its official opening.

subsidiary rights—Rights in a dramatic work other than the license acquired by the production company to present professional stage performances, the most important of which are for motion picture and television productions, presentations by stock companies and amateur groups, and the original cast album of a musical.

theatrical limited partnership—A limited partnership formed for the purpose of financing and presenting a theatrical production on the live stage, used as the traditional financing structure by the theatrical community.

TRADE ORGANIZATIONS

The League of American Theatres and Producers, Inc., New York, N.Y., is the leading trade organization for theatrical producers. This organization is very active in promoting the theater industry and supporting legislation favorable to the theatrical community.

LEADING PRODUCERS

Because of the large number of producers who are active at any time, any list of producers offered here would be necessarily incomplete. Moreover, even the most active producers have substantial periods between offerings.

The best approach is to contact a producer directly and to request the opportunity to consider participating in the financing of his next production. Although most producers would be receptive to such an inquiry, others prefer to allot participations to known investors who have a serious and continuing interest in their work. Furthermore, the acceptability of an investment from outside New York State will depend on the offering program and whether the producer deems it desirable to comply with applicable local and state regulations. Active producers can be identified by looking at the credits for shows in performance, or by contacting the League of American Theatres and Producers.

SUGGESTED READING

The most complete source of information on current theatrical productions is the *Theatrical Index*. *Variety*, an entertainment trade publication that is published daily and weekly, contains useful news also. Sources of more general information include the entertainment pages of *The New York Times*; in particular, the Sunday "Arts and Leisure" (second) section. For historical material, the annual volumes of *Theatre World* are invaluable.

U.S. TREASURY AND AGENCY SECURITIES

Jeffrey R. Leeds
Henry Engler

U.S. Treasury bills, notes, and bonds are direct obligations of the United States and comprise the marketable debt of the U.S. government. U.S. agency securities are generally less liquid than Treasury securities, with only a few agencies backed by the full faith and credit of the U.S. government. Bills are issued on a regular schedule with original maturities of three, six, and twelve months, in minimum amounts of $10,000 and multiples of $5,000 above the minimum. In contrast, Treasury notes and bonds have original maturities in excess of one year and often are sold in minimum denominations of $1,000 and $5,000. Although most agency securities conform to a regular auction schedule, a number are issued relatively infrequently. In addition, agency securities are sold in varying denominations.

U.S. TREASURY BILLS, NOTES, AND BONDS

BASIC CHARACTERISTICS

Primary Issuance

Bills are issued regularly by the U.S. Treasury at public auctions. Three- and six-month bills are auctioned weekly on Mondays. (If a holiday falls on a Monday, the auction is held the following Tuesday.) The bills are actually issued and payment collected the following Thursday. Twelve-month bills, called year bills, are auctioned every four weeks, usually on Thursdays, with settlement on the Thursday of the following week. All bill auctions are announced nearly a week in advance.

Jeffrey R. Leeds and Henry Engler are Managing Director and Vice-President, respectively, of the Capital Markets Group of Chemical Bank, New York, N.Y.

Participation in the auctions takes two forms. Small investors (buying up to $500,000 of bills) may submit a noncompetitive tender. In doing so, the investor agrees to pay the average price determined at the auction and is assured of receiving the entire amount applied for. Alternatively, the investor may submit a competitive tender. In this instance, the investor indicates the amount he is willing to purchase at a given price and yield. Depending on the other tenders submitted, the investor may be awarded all, part, or none of the bid-for securities.

The auction works as follows: The Treasury announces the bill auction, indicating the date of the auction and the total par amount of securities to be sold. Between the announcement and 1:30 P.M. (Eastern time) on the auction date, competitive and noncompetitive tenders are accepted at the U.S. Treasury and at all Federal Reserve Banks and their branches. After the auction is closed, the total of noncompetitive tenders is subtracted from the size of the issue. The remainder is allocated to the competitive tenders, beginning with the highest price (lowest yield) bid, until the entire amount is sold. The average of the prices actually paid is then computed, and the noncompetitive tenders are awarded in full at that price. On the day following the auction, a summary of the results is published in the financial sections of most newspapers, indicating the volume of tenders received; the high, low, and average prices accepted; and the amount of noncompetitive tenders awarded at the average and corresponding yields.

Physical Treasury bill securities are no longer issued. Record of ownership is maintained on a book-entry system, with the investor receiving a statement of account rather than a certificate.

The auction process for both notes and bonds is similar to bills, with the major differences being the frequency of the auctions. For instance, two-year notes are issued in the latter portion of each month, while three-year notes are issued only quarterly, along with ten-year notes and thirty-year bonds, in what is commonly referred to as the Treasury's quarterly refunding. (See Table 1.)

Secondary Market

An active secondary market for Treasury bills, notes, and bonds is part of the overall market for U.S. government securities. It is an over-the-counter market conducted by telephone. Participants include commercial banks, investment banking and brokerage firms, and a small number of specialized government securities trading firms. The nucleus of the market is a group of forty-four dealers recognized by the Federal Reserve Bank of New York. (See *Forty-Four Dealers Recognized by the Federal Reserve Bank of New York*, at the end of this article.) With foreign investors displaying an increasing appetite for U.S. securities in recent years, the number of recognized dealers has expanded to include non-U.S. firms. Smaller banks and brokerage firms have relationships with one or more of these recognized dealers, and small institutional or individual investors may obtain quotes or initiate a transaction with these firms. Closing quotations for all outstanding Treasury securities, identified by the date of maturity, are found in the financial sections of most newspapers.

Return on Treasury Bills, Notes, and Bonds

Treasury bills are discount instruments, that is, while par value is returned at maturity, the purchase price will be less than par by the amount of the discount. The interest or return on the investment, therefore, is equal to the discount and is received at maturity. In

TABLE 1. Normal Schedule of Treasury Security Auctions

Issue	Frequency	W.I. Period	Usual Auction Date	Usual Settlement Date
3- & 6-mo. bill	weekly, 4 P.M. Tuesday	9 days	Monday after Tuesday announcement	Thursday after Monday Auction
1-year bill	Every 4 weeks; 12 noon, Friday	13 days	Thursday after Friday announcement	Thursday, 1 week after Thursday auction
2-year note	Monthly, 3rd Wednesday of the month, 4 P.M., or 3rd Tuesday with quarterly 5-year or with quarterly 4- & 7-year	about 2 weeks i.e., from announcement date to settlement date	Wednesday, 1 week after Wednesday announcement or Tuesday if in the same week of 5-year or 4- & 7-year	last day of month or the 1st good business day after that
3-year refunding	Quarterly, 1st Wednesday of the 2nd month of the quarter, 4:30 P.M.	about 1 week	Tuesday after Wednesday announcement	15th of 2nd month of quarter or next good business day after that
10-year refunding	Quarterly, 1st Wednesday of the 2nd month of the quarter 4:30 P.M.	about 1 week	Wednesday, 1 week after Wednesday announcement	15th of 2nd month of quarter or next good business day after that
30-year refunding	Quarterly, 1st Wednesday of the 2nd month of the quarter, 4:30 P.M.	about 1 week	Thursday, 1 week after Wednesday announcement	15th of 2nd month of quarter or next good business day after that
4-year note	Quarterly, 3rd Wednesday of the 3rd month, 4 P.M.	about 1½ or 2 weeks	Tuesday, 1 week after Tuesday announcement	last day of quarter or next good business day after that
7-year note	Quarterly, 1st Wednesday of the 1st month, 4 P.M.	about 1½ or 2 weeks	Wednesday, 1 week after Wednesday announcement	15th of the month or next good business day after that
5-year note	Quarterly, 3rd Wednesday of 2nd month, 4 P.M.	about 2 weeks	Wednesday, 1 week after Wednesday announcement	1st business day of following month

contrast, most other money market investments are issued near par, and par plus interest is paid at maturity. In the case of Treasury notes and bonds, as well as other fixed-income securities with original maturity beyond one year, interest is paid on a regular schedule, usually semiannually, and par value is returned at maturity.

Pricing of Treasury Bills

The price of a Treasury bill, either at original issue or in the secondary market, is quoted in terms of the annualized discount rate. This annualized discount rate must then be converted to a dollar amount that is paid for the security. The formula for computing the actual price paid for a Treasury bill is as follows:

$$\text{Price} = \text{par} \times \left[1 - \frac{\text{discount rate}}{100} \times \frac{\text{number of days to maturity}}{360}\right]$$

For example, if \$100,000 worth of three-month Treasury bills are purchased, either at auction or in the secondary market, at a rate of 6.5 percent, the price paid which comes to \$98,356.94, would be computed by evaluating the formula:

$$\$98{,}356.94 = \$100{,}000 \times \left[1 - \frac{6.5\%}{100} \times \frac{91}{360}\right]$$

True Rate of Return on Treasury Bills

Although bills in the secondary market and at auctions are quoted in terms of the annualized discount rate, or discount, the true rate of return, or the yield on the investment, is higher. The yield is higher because less than par value is actually invested, and the discount is actually earned on that smaller amount. Thus, to determine the true investment yield of a Treasury bill, the following formula must be evaluated:

$$\text{True yield} = \frac{\text{par} - \text{price}}{\text{price}} \times \frac{365 \text{ (or } 366)}{\text{days to maturity}}$$

Using the example above, the true yield of a three-month Treasury bill quoted at 6.5 percent discount comes to 6.7 percent.

$$0.067 = \frac{(\$100{,}000 - \$98{,}356.94)}{\$98{,}356.94} \times \frac{365}{91}$$

Pricing of Treasury Notes and Bonds

The rate of interest on U.S. Treasury notes and bonds, often referred to as the coupon, is set at the time of issuance in line with rates that are prevailing in the secondary market. Unlike bills, which are discount securities, notes and bonds are priced equal or very close to their face amount, or par value. Both notes and bonds pay interest semiannually, with the full face amount redeemed at maturity.

Prices of notes and bonds are quoted in thirty-seconds per \$100 of face value. After the security is issued, the price generally fluctuates around par, influenced by a variety of factors, including the supply and demand for the security as well as economic conditions. For example, suppose an investor had purchased a two-year note at par with an 8.5 percent coupon, and the current price of the issue is quoted in the secondary market at $100^{16}/_{32}$, or \$100.50. By selling the security, the investor receives not only par plus the premium but also the interest accrued to date. The effective rate of return, which includes the capital gain (or loss) and the interest received, is normally referred to as the security's yield to maturity.

In order to calculate the yield to maturity based on the current price of a note or bond, the following formula is necessary:

$$y^1 = \frac{cy + 1 - p}{y - (1 - p)\frac{2y + 1}{4}}$$

where c = coupon rate
y = security's current maturity in years
p = current market price
y^1 = yield to maturity

To illustrate, suppose a four-year Treasury note issued on September 30, 1987, is due to mature on September 30, 1991, and its coupon is 8.5 percent. On November 1, 1988, the issue is traded at a price of 96-5, or 96⅟32. The first step in calculating the yield to maturity based on the current price is to determine y, the remaining life of the issue in years.

$$y = 2 + \frac{334}{365} = 2.915$$

By including the value for y in the formula, along with the current price, we get the following:

$$y^1 = \frac{0.085(2.915) + (1 - 0.96156)}{2.915 - (1 - 0.96156)\frac{2(2.915) + 1}{4}}$$

$$y^1 = 0.10045$$

$$y^1 = 10.05\%$$

Clearly, the illustration depicts an issue that is presently trading at a deep discount relative to par. Conversely, if the issue were trading at a premium (above par), the formula would result in a much lower yield to maturity. It is also important to note that the yield to maturity assumes that the investor will hold the security to maturity and be able to reinvest the interest payments at a constant rate. For example, a decline in the reinvestment rate will reduce the yield to maturity earned on an issue with a deep discount less than it will for an issue selling at par. The reason is that a larger percentage of the overall return for an issue with a deep discount comes in the form of capital appreciation. Therefore, a change in the reinvestment rate matters less than for an issue trading near par, where the total return is largely composed of interest, than it does for a deep discount issue.

Price Volatility

The degree to which a coupon security is subject to price risk is largely determined by two factors. First, given a change in interest rates, the price of issues with long current maturities will be affected more than those with short maturities. To better understand this feature, it is perhaps helpful to visualize capital gains (losses) as a stream of payments.

For example, if an investor purchases a security in the secondary market that is trading at a discount, the total return if held to maturity will include a capital gain (the face amount is redeemed at maturity) plus interest. If the current maturity of the issue is relatively short, the capital gains will be realized sooner and thus have greater value for the investor. As a result, the discount required to raise a security's yield to maturity by a given amount is greater the longer the maturity. The more slowly the gain is realized, the greater the differential in price for an equivalent change in interest rates.

A second factor affecting price risk is the security's coupon. Specifically, the higher the coupon, the less the percentage change in price will be if interest rates rise or fall. With a higher coupon, the overall return is influenced less by capital appreciation or depreciation. Conversely, a security with a low coupon will derive a greater proportion of its total return from changes in price (capital gains or losses). Therefore, from an investment standpoint, it is beneficial to own a low-coupon security when prices are rising and a high-coupon security when prices are falling.

The Value of an 01

The prices of notes and bonds are quoted in thirty-seconds per $100 of face value. Professional traders typically refer to 1⁄32 as an 01. The value of an 01 in terms of yield differs with respect to the maturity. Specifically, the longer the maturity, the less impact an 01 change in price will have on the yield of the security. The reasoning behind this is fairly straightforward: The value of an 01 is the discounted sum of remaining interest payments. A larger number of interest payments will diminish the value of an 01; in contrast, if the security is close to maturity, the value of an 01 increases accordingly. A simple formula used to determine the value of an 01 is the following:

$$\frac{1/32}{(1 + \frac{y}{2})^n}$$

where y = current yield
n = number of remaining coupon periods

Because the yield of 1⁄32 diminishes as the maturity of an issue lengthens, the price risk to which an investor is exposed increases. Consequently, an investor who holds a security that will mature shortly is less vulnerable to such price risk, as the yield value of an 01 is very small.

ATTRACTIVE FEATURES

Investment in U.S. Treasury securities offers a number of advantages.

Safety of Principal

Safety From Default. Since Treasury securities are the direct obligation of the U.S. Treasury, they are backed by the full faith and credit of the U.S. government. Under no circumstances will par value fail to be returned at maturity.

Safety From Market Risk. Although Treasury securities are safe from default, changes in interest rates can result in losses of principal. For example, if after purchasing the 6.5 percent bills described above, the discount rate on the three-month bill rose to 6.75 percent, the price, according to the formula, would be $98,293.75. Thus, a capital loss of $63.19 ($98,356.94 – $98,293.75) would be incurred. However, if the investor has a specific investment horizon, use of Treasury bills allows this capital or interest rate risk to be avoided. The frequency with which three-month and six-month bills are issued, and their availability in the secondary market, ensures obtaining a bill that will have a maturity near the investor's investment horizon. By holding the bill to maturity, one can avoid the risk to capital inherent in volatile interest rates. (See *Market Volatility*, later in this article.)

Liquidity

In terms of average trading volumes, the market in U.S. government securities is the largest securities market in the world. During 1987, an average of $109.8 billion worth of government securities changed hands each day. By comparison, average daily trading volume on the New York Stock Exchange amounted to only $7.4 billion per day. In terms of proportion, the average number of Treasury bills traded daily in 1987 amounted to $37.8 billion, while securities with maturities in excess of one year averaged $68.7 billion. Typically, trades of $5 million to $10 million can be effected without impact on overall prices, and a round lot is normally considered to be $1 million.

Scale of Investment

Despite the huge size of the Treasury securities market, the denominations required to purchase such securities are quite small compared to other money market instruments. Bills can be purchased in minimum amounts of $10,000 and in increments of $5,000 above the minimum. Coupon securities, meanwhile, are issued in minimum denominations of $1,000 and $5,000. In contrast, commercial paper is available in denominations no smaller than $25,000, and the minimum investment in bank-negotiable certificates of deposit is $100,000.

POTENTIAL RISKS

Market Volatility

Changes in interest rates can have an effect on the price at which an investment in Treasury securities can be liquidated. Evaluation of the formula presented in *Pricing of Treasury Bills*, earlier in this article, shows that each increase of 25 basis points (hundredths of one percent) results in a price decline, or capital loss, of $63.19 per $100,000 of three-month Treasury bills. For a thirty-year bond, the price risk would be even greater owing to the longer maturity.

During 1987, the average weekly change in the three-month bill discount rate (irrespective of direction of change) was 15 basis points. Thus, the average weekly price change experienced by investors in three-month bills was $37.91 per $100,000 invested. Of course, if the investor holds the security to maturity, no capital loss will be incurred. Since Treasury securities with a wide range of specific maturities are available at all times, the possibility of capital loss arises only when liquidation is forced unexpectedly or when the investment horizon and the security's maturity are intentionally mismatched, as described below.

Underperforming Issues

From time to time, certain Treasury securities tend to underperform the market by falling in price more than or rising in price less than securities with similar maturities. This underperformance may be the result of technical changes in the relative supply and demand for particular securities. In the case of bills, the Treasury periodically issues cash management bills to assist it in its debt management. These cash management bills may have the same maturity as the regular bills and thus add to the floating supply and depress the price relative to other bills. In the case of notes and bonds, certain maturities are eligible for delivery in the satisfaction of futures contracts on the Chicago Board of Trade. Technical changes in the supply and demand of specific securities are not always easy to predict in advance. As a consequence, the holders of affected securities, if forced to liquidate, may suffer a greater loss of value than if they had owned a security with a very similar maturity.

Illiquidity of Specific Issues

Although the Treasury market is the most liquid of securities markets because a price can nearly always be found for a significant-sized transaction, a particular security may only be salable at a discount to the values of other similar securities. Typically, the most actively traded securities are the most recently issued; as issues get older, the frequency of secondary market trading wanes. Thus, to buy or sell one of the less active issues may require considerable effort on the part of the investor and/or the dealer and may necessitate paying a somewhat higher purchase price or accepting a lower selling price.

As can be seen, all the potential market risks cited here involve selling a Treasury security prior to its maturity. Held to maturity, U.S. Treasury securities are the closest thing in the world to risk-free investment.

TAX CONSEQUENCES

Tax treatment of Treasury security returns is completely straightforward. The return is the difference between the price paid for the security and the price received either at maturity or when sold. In either case, the return is considered ordinary income and is taxed as such. Similarly, if yields rise and a Treasury security is sold at a price below its purchase price, the loss is considered an ordinary income loss and can offset only ordinary income, not capital gains. With Treasury bills, the income is considered earned in the period in which they are sold. Interest payments from notes and bonds, meanwhile, are simply applied to total interest income for each particular year and are taxed accordingly.

Income earned on Treasury securities is subject to federal income taxes, as well as federal and state estate and gift taxes. It is not subject to state and local income taxes.

REPRESENTATIVE TYPES OF INVESTORS

The safety and liquidity of U.S. Treasury securities makes them attractive for a wide variety of investors. Within the private sector, the most active participants include corporate pension trust funds, dealers and brokers, insurance companies, and commercial banks. In recent years, an increasing share of foreign investors have been attracted to Treasury securities. The decline of the U.S. dollar on world currency markets, together with the attractiveness of U.S. interest rates relative to those abroad, has made U.S. Treasury securities a worthwhile investment.

IMPORTANT FACTORS IN BUYING AND SELLING

Buying and selling Treasury securities in the market varies widely, depending on the size of the transaction, the particular investor involved, and the purpose of the purchase or sale. In general, transactions can be divided into two categories: those made directly with the Treasury via the regular auctions and those made through recognized dealers in Treasury securities.

Purchase at Auction

Direct participation in Treasury auctions typically is limited to very large, sophisticated investors and to very small, individual investors. For the former, the auction is the ultimate source of the newest and, at least initially, most actively traded Treasury securities. By submitting competitive tenders, the large investor can determine precisely the quantity of securities desired at a particular yield and price. The investor only receives the securities at a particular price if the securities are sold at that price.

The small, individual investor, by submitting a noncompetitive tender, can be assured of receiving the required securities at a fair price (the average of the auction determined by professional bidding) without any transaction costs. Moreover, by indicating on the tender, or by filling out a form, the investor automatically can replace, on the same day, maturing securities with the new securities issued.

A tender can be submitted either by completing a tender form available at any Federal Reserve Bank or branch or by letter, delivered in person or by mail to the nearest Federal Reserve Bank or branch of the U.S. Treasury. The letter should include the face amount of securities desired, the maturity (e.g., three months, two years, thirty years), whether the tender is competitive or noncompetitive (and, if competitive, the price), whether reinvestment is desired, and the tenderer's name, address, and Social Security and business telephone numbers. Payment in U.S. currency, certified personal check, cashier's check payable to the Federal Reserve Bank, or Treasury securities maturing on or before the issue date must accompany the tender form or the letter. Payment is made in the full face amount.

In the case of Treasury bills, when the discount is determined at the auction, a check is sent to the tenderer in the amount of the discount. With notes or bonds, a receipt outlining the actual par amount and price received will be detailed and sent to the tenderer. Unless reinvestment is specified, the U.S. Treasury automatically will issue and send a check for the face amount at maturity. Change in the reinvestment specifications or mailing address can be made up to twenty days prior to maturity by submitting Form PD4633-2, which will be sent after the tender is received and processed.

Transactions with a Dealer

Clearly, participation in an auction limits the investor to the specific maturities being issued, and it is impossible to sell Treasury securities at a Treasury auction. Additionally, it may be simpler to buy through a dealer than to fill out and submit a tender directly to the Treasury.

The market in Treasury securities is organized around a nucleus of primary dealers recognized by the Federal Reserve Bank of New York, which has general supervisory responsibility for the market. These dealers report their transactions to the Federal Reserve Bank of New York and most of them are cleared to make transactions with the Federal Reserve's

Open Market Account. (See *Forty-Four Dealers Recognized by the Federal Reserve Bank of New York,* at the end of this article.) In addition to this nucleus of primary dealers, most banks and brokerage firms conduct transactions in government securities for their customers.

The type of interaction with a dealer or dealers depends on the size and frequency of the investor's transactions. Small volume and infrequent contacts are handled as odd lots, bought on the bid side and sold at the offered side. Additionally, a transaction fee may be charged. Some dealers may waive or lower the transaction fee for regular customers. For example, large depositors may find lower transactions costs at their bank. In any case, it probably pays to shop around if transactions are frequent.

Large purchases and sales are treated quite differently. Recognized dealers and many other banks and brokerage firms make markets (provide bids and offerings) and stand ready to buy or sell at those prices. As indicated above, those quotations are made in terms of an annualized discount for bills, and in thirty-seconds for notes and bonds. At any time, different dealers may provide slightly different markets depending on their own circumstances and perceptions of supply and demand. Thus, large and frequent investors may have relationships with several dealers so that they can choose the most attractive price for a particular transaction. In addition to making markets on existing issues, dealers can and will submit either competitive or noncompetitive tenders on behalf of their customers.

U.S. AGENCY SECURITIES

BASIC CHARACTERISTICS

General Description

In an effort to support certain sectors of the economy, the U.S. government has created a number of federal agencies to regulate and finance specific economic groups. The two most popular of these groups have been homeowners and farmers. Thus, a good deal of federal agency financing involves issuing securities to aid these two economic groups.

Among the two interest groups are seven major federal agencies that issue securities in the open market. The agencies assisting the farming sector include the Federal Intermediate Credit Banks, the Federal Land Banks (FLBs), and the Bank for Cooperatives. The agencies assisting the housing sector include the Federal Home Loan Bank System, the Government National Mortgage Association, the Federal National Mortgage Association (FNMA), and the Federal Home Loan Mortgage Corporation.

All these agencies issue interest-bearing securities in the open market that typically yield slightly more than similarly dated U.S. Treasury securities. The reasons are twofold: (1) Although the agency market has grown considerably over the past ten years, it is still less liquid than the U.S. Treasury market and (2) only a few agencies are backed by the full faith and credit of the U.S. government. Although it is unlikely that the U.S. government would ever allow any particular agency to default on its securities, a risk premium nonetheless exists. Agency securities are generally issued as either short-term notes or long-term bonds, and have varying minimum denominations. For instance, the minimum denomination for a FLB bond is \$1,000, while the minimum for a Federal Home Loan Bank (FHLB) note is \$50,000. Moreover, the issuance of agency securities is at times erratic, dependent on the financing needs of each agency.

A further distinction between agency and Treasury securities revolves around the auction process. Agency securities are not offered directly to the public. Instead, each agency has a fiscal agent who offers the securities to a syndicate of dealers (essentially the same group of recognized primary dealers in Treasury securities) who distribute the securities to private investors. The dealers are paid a fee by each agency to market the securities and know well in advance the amount each agency will be issuing and when.

Short-term note maturities are typically less than one year, whereas bonds have maturities of more than one year. Interest on agency bonds are generally paid semiannually. At maturity, both principal and interest are payable at any Federal Reserve Bank, issuing agency, or the U.S. Treasury. Agency bonds are typically not callable.

Farm Credit Agencies

The Farm Credit Administration administers the activities of the Farm Credit System, which is similar in organization to the Federal Reserve System. Under this arrangement, the country is divided into twelve farm credit districts. Within each district there is a FLB, a Federal Intermediate Bank, and a Bank for Cooperatives.

FLBs are involved in making long-term mortgage loans on farm properties. The Federal Intermediate Banks are in the business of financing agricultural and livestock products, while the Bank for Cooperatives makes seasonal and term loans to farm cooperatives in the production of various agricultural products.

The securities issued by the Federal Reserve are consolidated among the various banks under the name of the Federal Farm Credit Bank (FFCB). The FFCB routinely issues short-term securities each month with maturities of three and six months. In addition, long-term bonds are issued several times a year. The minimum denomination for securities with maturities in excess of one year is $1,000, with $5,000 the minimum for shorter maturities.

The Federal Agricultural Mortgage Corporation, or Farmer Mac, enacted in 1988, seeks to create a secondary market for rural land mortgages. The program provides a government guarantee for loans made on farms and ranches. Thus, mortgage originators place the loan with a pooler who sells the pooled mortgages to investors. The program should function similarly to the FNMA program in housing.

Mortgage Credit Agencies

The most active issuers of mortgage-related debt include the FHLBs and the FNMA. Both agencies were developed for the purpose of assisting home buyers, either directly or through supporting thrift institutions active in the mortgage market.

FHLBs were created in 1932 to strengthen thrift institutions that were financially ravaged by the Great Depression. Similar to the Farm Credit System's organization, there are twelve geographic districts specified by the Federal Home Loan Bank Board (FHLBB). FHLBs assist savings and thrift institutions by providing funding in times of unusual seasonal credit demands.

In terms of issuance, FHLBs can be expected to issue new securities at least once a month. FHLBs issue short-term notes with maturities of less than one year and bonds with maturities of more than one year. The minimum denomination for both types of securities is $10,000, with increments of $5,000 thereafter.

The FNMA was originally created in 1938, with the purpose of creating a secondary market for federal housing-insured mortgages. Today, FNMA is essentially a privately owned corporation with common stock that is actively traded. Although it is privately owned, the federal government, through the auspices of the Housing and Urban Development Department, still keeps a watchful eye on the activities of the FNMA.

Simply put, FNMA buys government-insured or guaranteed mortgages when mortgage funds are in short supply and sells them when the supply of liquidity becomes more available. To finance its purchases, FNMA issues short-term notes and debentures. Short-term discount notes have a range of maturities anywhere from 30 to 360 days. The minimum purchase for short-term notes is $50,000, while a long-term bond requires $10,000, with increments of $5,000 thereafter.

Other Active Agencies

In recent years, the thrift industry has come under severe financial strain, as loans to certain sectors of the economy, in particular real estate, have proved to be unprofitable ventures. The regulatory body charged with rescuing such troubled institutions, the Federal Savings and Loan Insurance Corporation (FSLIC), in turn has suffered an enormous outflow of resources while aiding an ever-growing number of financially hampered thrifts.

In 1987, an effort to recapitalize FSLIC resulted in the formation of a mixed-ownership government corporation called the Financing Corporation (FICO). FICO and FSLIC operate under the supervision of the FHLBB. FICO is managed by a three-member directorate composed of the Director of the Office of Finance of the FHLBs and two presidents selected by the FHLBB. FICO is capitalized through investments by the FHLBs in the nonvoting capital stock of FICO. The FHLBB has the authority to prescribe the amounts and timing of FHLB investment in FICO capital stock.

In terms of actual financing, FICO is authorized to issue obligations solely for the purpose of purchasing FSLIC redeemable nonvoting capital stock and nonredeemable capital certificates and to retire previously issued obligations. The obligations are not obligations of, or guaranteed by, the United States, FHLBs, or the FSLIC. Since its inception in August of 1987, FICO has issued only thirty-year bonds, with a minimum denomination of $10,000. In addition, the timing of such issues has proven to be less predictable than that of other agency issues, since much is dependent on the financial conditions of ailing thrift institutions.

The Student Loan Marketing Association, commonly called Sallie Mae, has become the nation's leading financial intermediary to higher education and the largest single source of funds for insured education loans. It is a federally chartered and stockholder-owned corporation. Its principal activity is to provide a national secondary market for originators of guaranteed student loans—primarily banks and other financial institutions. By purchasing loans from financial institutions, Sallie Mae has funded about one in three of all guaranteed student loans. Additional activities include supplemental, privately insured education loans for students, college obligations issued to finance plant and equipment, and home equity loans for education purposes.

In terms of issuance, Sallie Mae regularly offers short-term floating rate notes that are priced in relation to the Treasury's three-month bill rate. Such issues are generally offered once a month, interspersed occasionally with longer-term issues.

ATTRACTIVE FEATURES

Safety of Principal

Although most agency issues are not explicitly backed by the full faith and credit of the U.S. government, the risk associated with such securities is very small or nonexistent. In the event that a particular agency runs into financial difficulty, the more than likely outcome is a federal government bailout. As a result, agency securities are nearly as risk free as U.S. Treasury obligations; their safety is most likely greater than other money market instruments.

Liquidity and Market Volatility

With regard to average trading volumes, the U.S. agency market is much smaller than the market for U.S. Treasury securities. For example, in 1987, an average of $18.9 billion worth of agency securities changed hands every day, compared with $109.8 billionin Treasury securities. The smaller size of the agency market is primarily why yields on agency securities are typically higher than for similarly dated Treasury obligations.

The direct consequence of a less liquid market is that prices of agency securities tend to be less volatile than those of Treasury securities. This characteristic may have particular advantages for the individual, who is generally more risk adverse than a large institutional investor.

The combination of low risk, attractive yields, and limited price volatility make U.S. agency obligations a valued investment for a wide category of investors.

POTENTIAL RISKS

Perhaps the single greatest risk in holding agency obligations relates to the financial difficulties that individual agencies may suffer periodically. Since the primary function of most agencies is aiding particular sectors of the U.S. economy, a severe economic downturn in any one sector can adversely affect the agency involved. To the extent an individual agency's resources become depleted from assisting a financially troubled area, the prices of its obligations may subsequently deteriorate relative to other agency securities. Therefore, an individual investor seeking to liquidate holdings before maturity may suffer a loss of value.

The most notable occurrence of such a development was the farm credit problem during 1984. Currently, attention is focused on the mounting difficulties of the nation's thrift industry.

TAX CONSEQUENCES

The tax treatment of U.S. agency returns is identical to that for Treasury securities: The return is considered ordinary income and taxed as such. The income earned on agency securities is subject to federal income taxes, as well as federal and state estate and gift taxes. Most agency securities are exempt from state and local income taxes, with the notable exception of the FNMA, which is a privately owned corporation.

GLOSSARY

average price—The average auction price among competitive bids received and accepted.

basis point—A pricing unit equivalent to 1/100 of one percent; a discount of 30 basis points is three tenths of one percent.

competitive tender—The investors bid to purchase securities at a certain price and yield, without assurance of receiving all or part of the securities.

discount—The amount by which par value is decreased in determining purchase price of the bill.

governments—The full range of negotiable U.S. Treasury securities.

noncompetitive tender—The investor's agreement to pay the average auction price for a Treasury bill, with assurance of receiving the entire amount applied for.

par—Face value of a bill.

primary dealers—Banks and brokerage firms, recognized by the Federal Reserve Bank of New York, that make a secondary market in Treasury securities.

secondary market—Over-the-counter market conducted by telephone for Treasury bills.

true rate of return—The true investment yield determined by applying the discount to the actual purchase price of the security.

FORTY-FOUR DEALERS RECOGNIZED BY THE FEDERAL RESERVE BANK OF NEW YORK

Bank of America NT & SA

Bankers Trust Co.

Bear, Stearns & Co., Inc.

Carroll McEntee & McGinley, Inc.

Chase Securities, Inc.

Chemical Bank

Citibank, N.A.

Continental Illinois National Bank and Trust Co. of Chicago

CRT Government Securities, Ltd.

Daiwa Securities America, Inc.

Dean Witter Reynolds, Inc.

Dillon, Read & Co., Inc.

Discount Corp. of New York

Donaldson, Lufkin & Jenrette Securities Corp.

Drexel Burnham Lambert Government Securities, Inc.

The First Boston Corp.

First National Bank of Chicago

Goldman, Sachs & Co.

Greenwich Capital Markets, Inc.

Harris Trust and Savings Bank

Irving Securities, Inc.

Kidder, Peabody & Co., Inc.

Kleinwort Benson Government Securities, Inc.

Aubrey G. Lanston & Co., Inc.

Lloyds Government Securities Corp.

Manufacturers Hanover Trust Co.

Merrill Lynch Government Securities, Inc.

Midland Montagu Securities, Inc.

J.P. Morgan Securities, Inc.

Morgan Stanley & Co., Inc.

The Nikko Securities Co., Inc.

Nomura Securities International, Inc.

Paine Webber, Inc.

Prudential-Bache Securities, Inc.

Salomon Brothers, Inc.

Sanwa-BGK Securities Co., L.P.

Security Pacific National Bank

Shearson Lehman Government Securities, Inc.

Smith Barney, Harris Upham & Co., Inc.

Thomson McKinnon Securities, Inc.

S.G. Warburg Securities, Inc.

Wertheim Schroder & Co., Inc.

Westpac Pollock Government Securities, Inc.

Yamaichi International, Inc.

SUGGESTED READING

PERIODICALS

Federal Reserve Bulletin. Published by the Board of Governors of the Federal Reserve System. Monthly; provides statistics and articles covering money and financial markets.

Treasury Bulletin. Published by the U.S. Treasury Department. Monthly; provides details of Treasury debt outstanding and the official results of all Treasury auctions; primarily statistical.

REFERENCE BOOKS

Fabozzi, Frank. *The Handbook of Treasury Securities*. Chicago: Probus Publishing, 1984.

Federal Reserve of Richmond. *Instruments of the Money Market*. Richmond, 1977.

First Boston Corporation. *Handbook of Securities of the United States Government and Federal Agencies*. New York, 1980.

Harris Bank. *The U.S. Government Securities Market*. Chicago, 1976.

Stigum, Marcia, in collaboration with John Mann. *Money Market Calculations: Yields Break-Evens and Arbitrage*. Homewood, Ill. Dow Jones-Irwin, 1981.

______. *The Money Market*. Homewood, Ill. Dow Jones-Irwin, 1983.

VENTURE CAPITAL

David G. Sparks

BASIC CHARACTERISTICS

Venture capital is the term used to describe a broad spectrum of business-financing opportunities, in which the investors providing the capital require a high return to compensate themselves for the high risk involved. Venture capital is high-risk, long-term capital; it is neither a liquid nor a passive investment.

The process of venture capital investing is the art of generating, evaluating, structuring, facilitating, and ultimately selling high-risk businesses and investments. Investors who participate in this process are known as venture capitalists; they typically seek capital gains from the sale of the securities in a successful business enterprise. Examples of the securities involved include private placements of common stock, preferred stocks, partnership interests, and debt financing coupled with warrants to acquire common stock of the business. Ultimately, these privately held securities may be registered for public trading. The range of venture capital investing extends from start-up businesses to leveraged buyouts of established companies.

Venture capitalists often limit their investment activities to certain industries or to companies at a certain stage of development. These limitations usually are established by the venture capitalists and are based on their own expertise and abilities in order to maximize the likelihood of earning the desired return from the risk taking. Stories of successful venture investments and leveraged buyouts have generated widespread interest among investors desiring to participate in these investment opportunities.

David G. Sparks is Vice-President of Lewis, Foote & Company, a private investment partnership located in Philadelphia, Pennsylvania.

Background

In the past, venture capital has been provided primarily by wealthy individuals and families and their related foundations, investment bankers, or a group of investors who have pooled their funds for the purpose of investing in a specific opportunity.

Complementing these activities, the Small Business Investment Company Act was enacted in 1958 to address the financing needs of small businesses. It provided for government incentives to encourage the formation of small business investment companies (SBICs). These incentives included supplementing the private capital of SBICs with low-interest government loans in order to increase the amount of SBIC funds available for qualified investment opportunities. The resulting investment activity by SBICs is now generally regarded as the first significant financial intermediation of venture capital.

In response to the burden of governmental regulations, an increasing demand for equity financing (SBICs generally provide debt), the historical preferential tax treatment accorded capital gains, and the growing interest in venture capital investing among wealthy individuals and institutional investors, private venture capital firms began to be organized and funded. Rather than investing in an SBIC, these venture firms formed funds to provide their investors with an attractive vehicle for participation in a portfolio of venture capital investments.

Venture Capital Today

Even though venture capital is not a new investment concept, the growth in the amount of capital committed to this arena through venture capital funds alone has been extraordinary (see Table 1).

Several related factors have contributed to the rapid growth of available venture capital. As the success stories of companies funded with venture capital became increasingly publicized, more interest was generated among investors desiring to participate. As the older venture capital funds matured, their successful performance allowed the general partners to raise larger pools of capital for their next funds. In addition, new firms were formed by departing principals of the matured funds who desired to establish and capitalize their own funds.

Another reason for the growth of available venture capital results from the fact that as technology continues to evolve at an ever-increasing rate, the opportunities to exploit these technological innovations commercially have also expanded. Furthermore, talented individuals continue to be willing to take the significant risks involved in establishing and creating businesses and providing the entrepreneurial and managerial leadership necessary for a venture-capital-backed company to be successful.

All the preceding factors have greatly spurred the growth of the venture capital industry. The growth of the industry, however, has created an interestingly competitive environment among venture capitalists. This competition has required the participants to become more sophisticated in their efforts. At least in theory, as more capital becomes available the competition among venture capitalists to participate in quality opportunities tends to lower the expected returns. Furthermore, the venture capitalist, whether an individual, a partnership fund, or a corporate entity, increasingly needs and expects to contribute more than capital, (often wishing to provide marketing, distribution, and important technological capabilities and expertise, including the recruiting of key personnel) to the companies in which the investment has been made (portfolio companies), in order to enhance the potential for success.

TABLE 1. Venture Capital Industry Estimated Fundings and Disbursements, 1969—1987

Year	New Capital Committed to Independent Private Venture Capital Firms Only	New New Capital Committed to All Venture Capital Firms*	Total Pool	Disbursements to Portfolio Companies
1987	$4,200	$4,900	$29,000	$3,900
1986	3,300	4,500	24,100	2,900
1985	2,300	3,300	19,600	2,600
1984	3,200	4,200	16,300	3,000
1983	3,400	4,500	12,100	2,800
1982	1,400	1,800	7,600	1,800
1981	867	1,300	5,800	1,400
1980	661	700	4,500	1,100
1979	170	300	3,800	1,000
1978	216	600	3,500	550
1977	—	39	2,500–3,000†	400
1976	—	50	—	300
1975	—	10	—	250
1974	—	57	—	350
1973	—	56	—	450
1972	—	62	—	425
1971	—	95	—	410
1970	—	97	—	350
1969	—	171	2,500–3,000	450

*Total new private capital less capital withdrawals.
†This pool remained static from 1969 through 1977 at some $2.5 to $3 billion, with new fundings more or less equal to withdrawals.

Note: Dollars in millions.

Source: Jane K. Morris, ed., *Venture Capital Yearbook*, Wellesley Hills, Mass.: Venture Economics, Inc., 1988

The Venture Capital Investment Process

The process of successful venture capital investing can be divided into several key areas: generating opportunities, evaluating opportunities, structuring the transaction, monitoring the business to assure that desired outcomes are attained, anticipating the need for subsequent investments in the business, and the sale of the investment in order to realize the return on the investment.

Generating Opportunities. The first step in the venture capital process is the generation of quality investment opportunities, known as deal flow. Deal flow, usually presented in the form of business plans, comes from many sources, including personal contacts, referrals from other venture capitalists, bankers, lawyers, accountants, and the venture capitalist's own persistence and intuition. As very few deals actually receive funding, generating deal flow in sufficient quality and volume and finding capable management to run the businesses are of great concern to the venture capitalist. In addition, venture capitalists have conceived their own deals, funded the proposed business in part with their firm's capital, and recruited the required management talent.

To support the generation of deal flow, the venture capitalist usually establishes a set of investment criteria to focus efforts, and those of outside sources, on situations mostly likely to meet investment objectives. The exercise of establishing these criteria is especially important because venture capital requires an investor to be active, rather than passive, and therefore able to contribute to the success of the business. A company that would satisfy the criteria of a venture capitalist is one that, at a desired stage of development,

- Possesses talented, proven management.
- Is competing or will compete in a rapidly growing or large market.
- Can demonstrate sustainable competitive advantages for its products and services that are salable to its customers.
- Will realize significant gross margins from the sale of its products.
- Competes in markets and uses technologies familiar to the venture capitalist.
- Is appropriately valued so that the investment potentially may generate the desired returns.
- Allows the venture capitalist, with the burden of financial risk, to protect the investment, if necessary.

Evaluating Opportunities. Once the venture capitalist identifies what appears to be an attractive investment opportunity, the due diligence phase begins. The importance of this process cannot be overemphasized. The venture capitalist must confirm the validity of the business by verifying the projected demand for the product or service, assure adequate planning of the business, and assess management's ability and integrity.

The venture capitalist evaluates every aspect of the opportunity against his investment criteria and, if he is to proceed with the transaction, resolves any shortcomings. During this process, the venture capitalist thoroughly studies and evaluates the company's business plan, including the industry, market, management, marketing plan, operating plan, financing plan, financial projections, and related assumptions and talks with customers and competitors. Throughout the investigation, the venture capitalist is also determining where he can, and needs to, contribute in nonmonetary ways to the business.

Some specific examples of the due diligence activities, which may be performed in part by the venture capitalist's outside advisors, include the following:

1. Management
    - Checking references
    - Checking credit
    - Interviewing customers and former associates and employers

- Constantly challenging management to see how pressure is handled
- Meeting key management's families
- Verifying the existence of noncompete, confidentiality, and nondisclosure agreements
- Exploring other conflicts of interest
- Reviewing management's financial contribution to the business

2. Market/product validity
   - Interviewing existing and anticipated customers
   - Verifying demonstrable price/performance improvement over competitive and alternative products
   - Evaluating distribution channels
   - Assessing the competition's strengths and weaknesses
   - Evaluating pricing strategies and gross margins
   - Interviewing the competition
3. Operating plans
   - Studying manufacturing methods
   - Reviewing control systems
   - Understanding staffing
   - Evaluating internal capabilities and support
4. Technological implications
   - Learning how technology is used in the business
   - Understanding the risk of technological obsolescence
   - Evaluating the ability to react to technological changes
   - Understanding ownership of and rights to the technology
5. History of the business
6. Existing and proposed capitalization
7. Regulatory, environmental, and other legal issues
8. Commitments and contingencies
9. Protection of proprietary assets

Throughout the due diligence process, the venture capitalist is formulating alternative structures under which he will agree to commit funds. During his due diligence, and until closing the transaction, the venture capitalist consistently challenges management personnel and their assumptions and maintains the necessary objectivity to walk away from a deal if an essential element is missing or if the required return is not attainable. This discipline is required because, even though venture capitalists expect all their deals to succeed, the reality of venture investing is that many investments do not perform as expected. It is the average of the home runs, doubles, and strikeouts in a portfolio that dictate its returns.

Structuring the Transaction

Often, more than one venture capitalist will invest in a financing, but only one or two venture capitalists will take the lead in negotiating and structuring the transaction with management or directors of the target company. If the lead venture capitalist negotiates an acceptable deal, the other venture capitalists, subject to their due diligence, may desire to (and be invited to) coinvest on the same terms. As a condition to organizing the investment group, the lead venture capitalist will probably require, at a minimum, representation on the board of directors.

In practice, venture capital is frequently structured last money in, first money out. Such priority in liquidation may often be accomplished by using a security that is senior to the investment of the early investors. The actual financial structures used are as varied as the particular deals. These structures include preferred stocks, common stock, voting trusts, convertible loans, and warrants issued in return for letters of credit or guarantees. Certain features, however, should always be considered in connection with an equity investment, including the following:

- Restrictions on the uses of the newly invested capital
- The investor's ability to step into the business to protect the investment, should performance falter
- Subordination of management's position to the investment group
- Restrictions on management's ability to sell or transfer its interest
- Staged funding of the investment, tied to certain financial and nonfinancial events (such as execution of a key contract, a successful testing of a product, or operation of a plant at a certain capacity and quality level)
- Appropriate antidilution provisions
- Demand and piggy-back registration rights to allow the venture capitalist to sell his interest in the company in the public market, based on some predetermined event
- Creation of significant incentives, in terms of both risk and reward, for key personnel
- Appropriate noncompete and nondisclosure agreements for key personnel
- Approval of certain key management decisions by the board of directors, or directly by the venture capitalist through either his security instrument (such as via loan covenants that evidence his investment in the company) or by a side agreement with the appropriate parties

The investee company's estimate of the amount of capital it requires is often less than the amount the company actually needs, and experience has proven that unexpected problems and growing pains occur in even the most successful business ventures. As both management and the venture capitalist want their investment in the company to appreciate in value, they need to ensure that adequate funding is provided, including a reasonable working capital reserve to survive interim crises, so that the company has the cash resources necessary for the business to progress to the next round of financing. Neither management nor the venture capitalist wants to raise additional financing from a position of weakness during an unforeseen cash crisis, although such a case may present an attractive opportunity for new investors.

In addition to the venture capitalist assessing the amount of capital needed by the company, he must estimate the future value of the business as well as additional funding to be provided in later rounds in order to determine the equity participation he needs to achieve the required return. To illustrate, a venture capitalist desiring an after-tax return of ten times his investment in five years (or approximately a 58 percent internal rate of return) would require an initial 86.8 percent equity interest, or a 34.72 percent equity interest on a fully diluted basis, in a potential portfolio company derived as follows:

Investment considered	$500,000
Estimated level of annual earnings before interest and taxes (EBIT) in five years	$4 million
Expected equity value of company in five years based on a multiple of five times EBIT	$20 million
Required after-tax proceeds realized in five years (ten times investment)	$5 million
After-tax share of proceeds from sale of the company stock (required after-tax proceeds divided by equity value)	25.00%
Share of before-tax proceeds at 28% capital gain tax rate (25% divided by 72%)	34.72%
Assumed dilution from management stock options and subsequent financings	60.00%
Equity interest required this round (34.72% divided by 40%, 1 minus dilution)	86.80%

If the company had 100,000 shares issued and outstanding, it would issue the venture capitalist securities equivalent to 657,575 shares of newly issued common stock (new stock) at $0.76 per share.

When a company issues new stock, the invested capital is infused into the company and is usually provided to grow the business. If the invested capital is used to repay debt, the investor may require an incremental ownership or control premium for cleaning up the situation.

In the event the venture capitalist was acquiring an existing operating business in a leveraged buyout, a reasonable rule of thumb is to pay five times historical operating cash flow before interest and taxes, but after deducting annual capital expenditures. This starting price may be adjusted depending on any net excess assets or liabilities acquired or assumed in the transaction. Note that this rule of thumb price is based on historical cash flow, not projected future results. The buyer of a business should not pay the seller for improved performance resulting from the buyer's successful efforts.

Monitoring and Operating the Business. Every venture capitalist expects to be involved in his investments by providing input into strategy, planning, marketing, financing, and key personnel issues. A portfolio company should be able to rely on the venture capitalist's experience in these matters, and it is not uncommon that, as a condition to investing in a company, a venture capitalist will require that he be involved significantly.

A primary reason for the venture capitalist's close monitoring of his portfolio companies is that since the investments are illiquid, he usually waits several years to realize a return on his investment. Accordingly, the venture capitalist must maintain close contact with the business and management if he is to make sure that the business stays on track and that he will be in a position to correct problems in a timely manner. However, as the venture capitalist often has a portfolio of investments for which he is responsible, he is not usually involved in the day-to-day details that are the responsibility of management.

Primary areas of concern for the venture capitalist are the company's earnings growth, cash flow, and cash reserves, and management's ongoing decision making and implementation of the business. If the company is to prosper, its operating cash flows are going to be reinvested in the business or to retire debt, in the case of a leveraged buyout. Because management will be faced with making decisions under extreme pressure, the venture capitalist's involvement provides an additional objective, rational decision-making perspective consistent with the goal of maximizing the value of the business.

An involved venture capitalist must judge whether management is growing the business as expected. If management attains the operating, financial, and other performance targets projected in the business plan that the venture capitalist relied on for investing in the business, no changes are likely. However, if management fails to reach its targets, the venture capitalist may need to step in and make any necessary changes.

Follow-On Investments. A growing business will always need to raise additional capital to finance its growth. When structuring his investment, the venture capitalist must anticipate the need for this additional capital and the resulting dilution of his interest, and factor that dilution into the price he is willing to pay in order to realize the desired return. In addition, the venture capitalist should anticipate the opportunity for participating in subsequent rounds of financing. Accordingly, the venture capitalist should maintain some reserve for appropriate follow-on investments in portfolio companies.

The degree to which follow-on investments are required depends on the stage of the business's development. The level of risk and the demand for the venture capitalist's involvement are greatest for early-stage financings, as compared to later-stage financings for more established companies. The different stages of financing and the typical use of the funds in each stage can be characterized as follows:

1. Early-stage financing (establishment of a business)
    - *Seed financing:* Capital required to explore the feasibility of a product or a concept.
    - *Start-up financing:* Capital required to develop products and test the products under real-world situations.
    - *Initial, or first-round, financing:* Capital required to commercialize the business after successful test results, including establishment of marketing, distribution, and support of the business's products or services.
2. Expansion-stage financing (growth of a business)
    - *Second-round financing:* Capital required to finance working capital until the business is profitable or at least breaking even.
    - *Subsequent rounds of financing:* Capital provided to allow a proven company to expand into new markets, develop new products, and establish or expand its facilities.

3. Mezzanine financing is later-round financing that may be provided to a more established business in connection with, or in lieu of, traditional debt and equity financing. This financing may provide for both a current yield, in the form of interest on a subordinated loan or dividend on a preferred stock, and an equity kicker in the form of warrants to purchase common stock or some other conversion feature.

4. Acquisition, leveraged, or management buyout financing is capital used to acquire an existing business by pledging the business assets and cash flow as collateral. This may involve straight debt, straight equity, and mezzanine financing to acquire the assets, or stock, and provide working capital.

Exit Plan. Finally, when making the decision to invest, the venture capitalist must anticipate the most likely method and timing of selling his ownership in the company in order to realize his return. The venture capitalist's return from an investment can be realized in one or more of the following ways:

- Acquisition or merger
- Sale via a public offering
- Management buyout
- Distribution of corporate profits
- Liquidation

The venture capitalist will groom the business to enhance the appeal of the company based on the desired exit avenue. The actual exit, however, is dependent on the performance of the company and external variables, especially the then existing economic, tax, and regulatory climate, the stock market, the availability of financing, and the industry in which the business competes.

Method of Participating in Venture Capital Investments

An investor can participate in venture capital investments in two ways. He can invest directly in the securities of a portfolio company, or he may invest in the equity or debt securities indirectly through a venture capital fund, partnership, syndicate, or other intermediary. The important difference is the degree to which the investor will participate in the venture capital process. In other words, an investor seeking venture capital opportunities will either generate his own deal flow and effectively become a venture capitalist, or he will rely on others by investing in a partnership or other entity in which the general partners or officers perform the functions of the venture capitalist.

Direct Participation. An investor who desires to invest his capital in venture capital opportunities will execute the steps of the venture capital process outlined above. A venture capitalist will typically not provide the entire capital for a given deal, but will seek other venture capitalists to coinvest. This deal sharing allows a venture capitalist to confirm his analysis, will likely result in his being asked to coinvest in the other venture capitalists' deals, and allows him to maintain a balanced portfolio by not overallocating his resources to any single deal.

The lead venture capitalist takes responsibility for the deal. Not all venture capitalists have the desire or capability to take the lead role. Who the lead venture capitalist is, or colead venture capitalists are, depends on the parties involved and the particulars of the situation.

Most venture capitalists, but especially the lead investor, provide nonmonetary value to their portfolio companies. As a result, a lead investor, such as the general partner of a venture capital fund, usually has had significant related experience or contacts that can benefit the company. These experiences and contacts may have developed from previous business and venture investing experience.

Indirect Participation. If an investor desiring to participate in venture capital opportunities is neither prepared to fulfill the responsibilities of a lead investor nor possessed of sufficient capital to invest in several deals at a meaningful level, then investing in a venture capital fund may be the most effective manner in which to participate in the venture arena. Blind pools and some private placements of identified, designated investments are indirect investment vehicles for the investor and require him to rely on others to perform the duties of the venture capitalist. However, when relying on others, an investor should at least perform his own very thorough due diligence on those on whom he is relying and to whom he is entrusting his funds.

ATTRACTIVE FEATURES

In deciding whether the most efficient and effective manner to participate in venture capital is through a venture capital fund, several items are important to consider.

Benefits of Investing in a Venture Capital Fund

There are three primary benefits available for an investor participating in a venture capital fund. First, the investor can rely on venture capitalists who are experienced in the execution of the venture capital process, who possess knowledge of the businesses and markets being explored, and who are keenly aware of management and personnel issues vital in successful venture capital investing.

Second, qualified venture capitalists enjoy quality deal flow not otherwise available to those not in the business on a full-time basis.

Third, a venture capital fund internally provides for a diversified portfolio of venture capital investments. As mentioned previously, many investments do not perform as expected. It is hoped, however, that some investments will be so successful that a superior return over the entire portfolio will be realized.

Costs of Investing in a Venture Capital Fund

The general partner of a venture capital partnership is provided significant incentives for successfully investing the partnership's capital. These general partner incentives will not, however, prohibit the limited partners from receiving a superior return from their investment should the fund prove successful. The primary incentive for the general partner is through participation in the net profits of the partnership in excess of the general partner's partnership interest. For example, the general partner may have contributed 1 percent of the partnership's capital but receive 20 percent of the partnership's portfolio profits. The limited partners bear the cost of this incentive, as they may have provided 99 percent of the partnership's capital but receive 80 percent of the profits. Some funds, however, provide the limited partners with a preference in the net profits of the partnership in an amount equal to an accrued priority return, roughly equivalent to interest imputed on the limited partners' capital contributions, with the general partner's incentive participation applied to any remaining net profits.

Second, the general partner may charge an annual fee to the partnership for his overhead. An annual management fee equal to 2.5 percent of the value of the partnership assets is common and is paid out of the partnership's cash.

A third cost to the investor results if capital is contributed to the partnership in advance of investments being identified. In these blind pools, the investor incurs an imputed cost equal to the lost opportunity to invest his funds elsewhere until needed by the partnership. However, many valid reasons exist for requiring the limited partners to contribute capital in advance of the partnership's formation or at other predetermined funding dates, such as enhancing the partnership's credibility by demonstrating the amount of capital available and avoiding the burden of making capital calls on a when-needed, transactional basis. The venture capitalist invests the idle funds in money market securities until needed to fund particular venture capital investments, the earnings on which may cover all or part of the general partner's management fee. Finally, a portion of the contributed capital often is used to pay the organizational and start-up costs of the fund.

Other Factors to Consider

When evaluating a potential investment in a venture capital fund, an investor should determine the expected life of the fund and how distributions are to be made. Most investments are expected to take three to seven years to mature, and it may take three or more years for the fund to become fully invested. Accordingly, the fund may make distributions intermittently and make the final payout of its investment portfolio in kind by issuing to each limited partner his pro rata share of the remaining portfolio investments. Some funds provide for the ability to reinvest the original cost of matured investments, but distribute profits in an amount at least equal to the tax liabilities of its partners resulting from those profits.

Also, the general partner of a fund may experience several conflicts of interest. It is not unusual for a general partner to be involved in more than one fund at a time. However, the specific funds are usually at different stages of maturity; some may be fully invested or may just be starting. In such cases, the general partner must decide how each different fund will participate in an attractive investment opportunity, and otherwise explicitly provide for the resolution of conflicts.

POTENTIAL RISKS

The process of venture capital investing has many risks. By their nature, the portfolio companies of venture capitalists have limited operating histories or are highly leveraged. Accordingly, investing in venture capital opportunities should not exceed an individual's ability to absorb the loss of his entire investment, as many specific investments ultimately fail or do not perform as expected.

On an operating level, venture-capital-backed companies face intense competition from companies having far greater financial resources and more established marketing, distribution, manufacturing, managerial, and technical capabilities. As a result, a portfolio company may incur substantial losses and eventually become insolvent.

Venture capital investments are illiquid and require the investor to carry his investment until an appropriate exit is available, often without current returns (such as interest or dividends). In addition, follow-on investments may be required and may not be forthcoming from current investors, thereby requiring the portfolio company to seek new investors. Even if the company goes public, the venture capitalist may be prohibited from selling stock for various reasons, including not qualifying under the Securities and Exchange Commission's (SEC) Rule 144 and underwriters' restrictions.

Investors in venture capital funds organized as limited partnerships are typically restricted from selling or transferring their limited partnership interests for reasons necessary to preserve the partnership status of the fund for income tax purposes (and avoid double taxation of profits) and to comply with applicable federal and state securities laws; however, the general partner may, and usually will, approve such sales and transfers. This transferability restriction precludes a public market for most limited partnership interests of venture capital funds.

Regardless of the specific investment, contingent liabilities, lawsuits, and environmental problems can cripple a business. Every effort to structure a transaction to avoid the exposure to contingent liabilities, known and unknown, should be made. For example, if an established business is to be acquired, an asset purchase, as opposed to a stock purchase, usually enables the buyer of the business to avoid the assumption of liabilities not explicitly assumed. An important prescript is that if indemnifcations, representations, and warranties are sought in connection with a transaction, efforts should be made to confirm that those parties providing said assurances can in fact make good on their promises and that sufficient, realizable remedies are available.

TAX CONSEQUENCES

In general, the purchase and sale of securities are capital transactions and result in capital gains and losses. If interest income or dividend income is a feature of an investment, that income is taxed as ordinary income.

Depending on the specific tax situation of an investor, items of gain, income, loss, or deduction may be recognized in different tax periods from when those items are actually received or paid. The reasons for these potential timing differences lie in the accounting methods used for income tax purposes, classification of income or loss as passive, portfolio or investment income or loss, limitations on interest deductions, imputation of interest income and interest expense based on original issue discount rules, limitation of deductions to the amount an investor is at risk, and limitation of the deduction for net capital losses. In addition, the alternative minimum tax, state taxes, and estate and gift taxes all should be considered when making venture capital investments.

In the case where the venture capitalist desires to purchase a business, the purchase should be structured so that asset values can be written up for depreciation purposes and so that any acquisition debt can be placed inside the surviving business entity, thereby avoiding limitations on the deductibility of interest expense. In addition to avoiding contingent liabilities, an asset purchase is one effective way to accomplish this outcome. Another reason to write up asset values is that if certain assets of the acquired business need to be sold to pay down the acquisition debt, the potential tax liability from a sale of the assets, whose income tax basis carried over from previous ownership as a result of a stock sale, may severely impair the investor's ability to generate the desired amount of cash after paying any associated taxes.

Although virtually all venture capital financings are structured to avoid double taxation on gains recognized from the sale of investments, including the use of partnerships that allow taxable events to flow through to the partners, the tax laws have become increasingly complex and have changed significantly in recent years. To avoid unpleasant surprises, advice from a competent tax advisor should be obtained in connection with a contemplated investment.

REPRESENTATIVE TYPES OF INVESTORS

Venture capital investors are able to allocate a portion of their investment capital for risky investment opportunities. Although their expectations are for superior returns, these investors can absorb the losses resulting from the failure of one or more investments. To improve the likelihood of generating a superior return, the typical venture capital investor desires a portfolio of investments rather than being overexposed to, or overinvested in, a few situations.

In addition, venture capital investors typically have substantial liquid resources and therefore can carry an illiquid investment for many years. Table 2 reflects the recent sources of capital provided to venture capital funds.

Historically, because of either self-imposed or regulatory investment restrictions, large financial institutions have indirectly participated in venture capital investing via venture capital partnerships. However, many of the financial institutions providing capital to venture funds selectively coinvest with the fund by also directly investing in the securities of a portfolio company. In these cases, the institution usually relies on the general partner of a partnership it has invested in to provide the lead.

IMPORTANT FACTORS IN BUYING AND SELLING

Some of the most important elements that influence venture capital investments deal with external events beyond the control of the venture capitalist or management of portfolio

TABLE 2. Sources of Capital Commitments

	1983	1984	1985	1986	1987
Pension funds	31%	34%	33%	50%	39%
Insurance companies	12	13	11	10	15
Foreign investors	16	18	23	11	13
Individuals and families	21	15	13	12	12
Corporations	12	14	12	11	11
Endowments and foundations	8	6	8	6	10
Total	100%	100%	100%	100%	100%

Note: Institutionally backed independent private funds only, does not include capital committed to SBICs, family groups, or corporate affiliates.

Source: Jane K. Morris, ed., *Venture Capital Yearbook*, Wellesley Hills, Mass.: Venture Economics, Inc. 1988

companies. The stock market, the economic and regulatory climate, changes in tax rates or treatment of capital gains, availability of financing, and other dynamic events that occur in a competitive, free market society, may enhance or diminish the venture capitalist's investment and exit opportunities.

Because venture capital is the risk capital that is provided to companies on a negotiated, private-transaction basis, the venture capitalist is in a position to negotiate a tailor-made security designed to satisfy his investment objectives and provide the portfolio company with its needed capital. Although these objectives may initially push in opposite directions, a careful analysis of the situation allows for the creation of a security that in the final analysis mutually satisfies the parties' objectives.

Since securities are involved in the venture capital investment process, federal and state securities laws and registration requirements must be followed. Those persons or entities investing in venture-capital-related securities may have to meet certain suitability standards in order to be allowed to invest. Specifically, a venture capital fund must comply with applicable securities laws that regulate the issuance of the fund's securities, such as units of limited partnership interest and common or preferred stock, and the securities of its portfolio companies.

In the absence of an exemption from registration, federal and state securities laws generally require the registration of securities before any offers to sell or actual sales are made. In addition, certain states restrict or regulate the type of information that may be provided to prospective investors, particularly information concerning financial projections or projected returns to investors. Although certain sales and offers to sell may be exempt from the registration requirements of applicable federal or state securities laws, the antifraud provisions of such laws will still apply to the disclosure of information to prospective investors. In addition to federal securities laws, the securities laws of certain states must be reviewed and complied with prior to making any offer: those of the state of incorporation, formation, or principal place of business of the issuing entity; those of the state of the place of residence or principal place of business of each prospective offeree; and those of any state where the issuer intends actually to make the offer or sale. Attorneys knowledgeable in securities law should be consulted prior to making any offers to sell securities.

The resale of the fund's securities or those of its portfolio companies must comply with the applicable securities laws. Many state securities laws that exempt certain private placements from the registration requirements require that investors hold the securities they purchase for a certain period of time prior to reselling the securities.

Securities laws may also affect the venture capitalist's exit from an investment, especially if the company goes public. Furthermore, underwriters of a public offering may require insiders to hold their stock for a specified period of time beyond the registration in order to establish an orderly market for the company's securities.

Finally, venture capitalists should address the maximum extent to which they are willing to commit their capital to any single deal or portfolio company. Venture capitalists often will limit their investment in any one company, including anticipated follow-on investments, to 10 percent of the total capital designated for investing in venture capital transactions. The reasons for such a restriction are to ensure that sufficient funds are available for other attractive investments and to make certain that the portfolio of investments is not overexposed to the performance of any one specific investment.

GLOSSARY

asset purchase—Where the buyer of a business acquires specific assets and assumes specific liabilities of the business, usually resulting in increased depreciation deductions and avoidance of contingent liabilities.

demand registration rights—Ability to require a company to register securities for a public offering, usually based on some set of events such as the issuer's previous initial public offering.

dilution—An investor may experience dilution, a reduction of his ownership interest in a business, as a consequence of either a subsequent financing round requiring the portfolio company to sell addtional equity securities or making an investment where he pays a price per share in excess of the book value per share of the company.

due diligence—The complete review and investigation of all aspects of an investment or business opportunity in order to support an investment decision.

financing round—A series of events, activities or project(s) that identifies a specific capital-raising effort undertaken by a company seeking financing at a particular point in time at a particular stage of the company's development.

piggyback registration rights—Refers to the ability of an investor to register, for sale in public markets, securities he owns when the insuer or other investors register securities for a public offering.

portfolio companies—The group of specific businesses that a venture capitalist holds an interest in as a result of his venture capital investing activity (i.e., his portfolio of investments).

private placement—The sale of securities under federal and state securities laws to a small number of investors who meet certain suitability requirements, without the use of public solicitation, advertising, or marketing.

stock purchase—Where the buyer of a business acquires the stock of an entity and owns the assets of the business, subject to all of the business's liabilities, by virtue of the buyer's stock ownership.

syndicate—An associtiion of a group of persons or entities or both formed to conduct a specific business transaction, usually for arranging the sale or placement of securities.

VENTURE CAPITAL GROUPS

Owing to the hands-on nature of venture capital investing, venture capitalists prefer investments in businesses that are located close by. As a result, although several national organizations exist, venture capital trade groups are largely regional in nature. Accounting firms, attorneys, bankers, chambers of commerce, and governments in your area are aware of how to contact local venture capital companies and trade groups. Some of the sources listed in the *Suggested Reading*, as well as other reference materials available from your local library, provide lists of venture capitalists and trade organizations.

PERIODICALS

Morris, Jane K., ed. *Venture Capital Journal.* Wellesley Hills, Mass.: Venture Economics, Inc. Monthly.

______, ed. *Venture Capital Yearbook.* Wellesley Hills, Mass.: Venture Economics, Inc. Annual.

Pratt, Stanley E., and Morris, Jane K. *Pratt's Guide to Venture Capital Sources.* Wellesley Hills, Mass.: Venture Economics, Inc. Annual.

SUGGESTED READING

REFERENCE BOOKS

Lipper III, Arthur, with Ryan, George. *Venture's Guide to Investing in Private Companies.* Homewood, Ill.: Dow Jones-Irwin, 1984.

WARRANTS AND RIGHTS

Allan E. Young

BASIC CHARACTERISTICS

Description

Warrants are securities that derive their value as the result of their interrelationship with a related common stock. Although a warrant holder does not have the same rights as a common-stock holder (e.g., a claim on earnings and assets; the right to vote for corporate board members, changes in the corporate charter, bylaws, or other corporate matters, such as certain resolutions; and the right to receive dividends when declared and paid), a warrant holder has the ability to obtain these rights by converting the warrant into common stock.

Conversion Option. By owning a warrant, an investor has the option of converting that security into common stock (usually on a one-for-one basis) by paying the issuing company a specified sum. However, in the vast preponderance of cases, the warrant holder must make the request for conversion of the security into common stock before a specified expiration date.

Exercise Price. The amount paid to convert a warrant into common stock, or the exercise price, is usually above the market price of the common stock at the time of the issuance of the warrant. The exercise price frequently changes at stated times during the life of a warrant. Most warrants are protected from dilution of value arising from stock

Allan E. Young is Professor of Finance in the School of Management at Syracuse University.

dividends and stock splits and may, in unusual cases, be protected from abnormally large cash dividends as well.

Expiration Date. European warrants can be exercised only on their expiration dates. American warrants can be exercised at any time during the length of their lives. The vast preponderance of warrants have finite lives, which are specified in their terms of issue. There are some warrants, however, such as those issued by Atlas Corporation, and Tri-Continental Corporation, which have an indefinite length of life and are known as perpetual warrants. Some warrants (sometimes called CD warrants) give their holders the option to purchase common stock either with the payment of cash (as with other warrants) or with the surrender, at par, of a stipulated amount of the company's debentures. If these debentures can be acquired by a warrant holder at a discount from their par value, the effective exercise price of the warrant is thereby reduced by an equal percentage.

Starting in 1919, warrants could not be listed on the New York Stock Exchange (NYSE) because they were considered highly speculative instruments. Thus, trading in these securities took place on the American Stock Exchange, the regional stock exchanges, and in the over-the-counter market. However, in 1970, American Telephone and Telegraph Company (AT&T) issued a warrant as part of a bond offering. This issue became a landmark offering in many respects, particularly because it led to the eventual listing of the warrant on the NYSE. In subsequent years, a number of additional warrants have been listed on the NYSE; as of fall 1988, a total of seventeen listings could be found.

The AT&T warrant gave its holder the right to exchange this security for common stock on a one-for-one basis with the payment of a stated sum (exercise price) to the company. However, warrant holders were to have this right only until five years from the date of issue (expiration date). After that date, the security would be worthless. For about a year prior to the expiration of its warrant, there was some speculation that AT&T might extend its life. On the one hand, by securing exercise of the warrant, the company could, in effect, obtain equity financing. On the other hand, since its common stock was selling below the exercise price, it seemed that the company could extend the life of the warrant and thus make it more likely that its common stock would reach this level before expiration. The common stock did, in fact, increase to just about the exercise price in the last few days of the life of the warrant. Relatively few warrants were exercised (slightly more than 10 percent of the number originally issued), and the company did not attempt to extend the expiration date to increase the number of warrants exercised. Nevertheless, companies have been known to extend the lives of their expiring warrants in spite of the damage this caused to those who were short the warrants and despite the legal ambiguities of the procedure. Thus far, the procedure of extending the lives of expiring warrants has not been legally tested.

Other Securities—Similarities and Differences

Call Option. The security most similar to a warrant is a call option. The holder of a call option also has the right to convert that security into common stock with the payment of a specified sum. Additionally, as in the case of a warrant, this conversion right on the part of the owner of a call option must be exercised within a specified period (by the expiration date) or the right will lapse and the security becomes worthless. An exercise of the conversion right of both call options and warrants will occur only if the common stock price rises above the exercise price (in the case of call options, this is normally referred to as the striking price) sometime before the expiration date of the security.

However, call options and warrants differ in a number of important respects.

Time Period. Calls are normally written for rather brief periods, most commonly between three and six months. On the other hand, recent warrants have been issued with expiration dates as long as five to ten years away.

Issuing Party. Calls are issued (the more common term in the case of options is "written,") by an investor, individual, or institution. Warrants are issued as a financing mechanism by a corporation seeking funds. Thus, if and when either security is exercised (converted into common stock), the party receiving payment is different. In the case of exercise of a call option, the holder pays the writer of the option (who is also an investor) an amount equal to the striking price and receives the common stock from this party. Alternatively, on exercising the conversion right, the holder of a warrant pays the exercise price to the issuing company and is given common stock in return by the firm.

Convertible Bonds and Preferred Stock. The conversion feature of a warrant makes it comparable to convertible bonds and convertible preferred stock. However, unlike these latter securities, the holders of warrants receive no current income, as the issuing firm pays warrant holders neither interest (as in the case of convertible bonds) nor dividends (as in the case of convertible preferred stock).

Stock Rights. Finally, warrants are similar to stock rights, which also give the holder the opportunity to purchase common stock with cash and surrender of the instrument. However, stock rights are issued by corporations with expiration dates far shorter than those of warrants.

Basic Determinants of Value

The primary determinants of the value of a warrant are similar to those of a call option because of the similarity between these two securities.

Relationship Between Exercise Price and Market Price. One of the most significant factors in determining value is the relationship between the exercise price of the warrant and the current market price of the related common stock. Obviously, the value of a warrant will be far greater if the current market price of the related common stock is far in excess of the exercise price of the warrant than if the exercise price is considerably above the current market price of the common stock. In effect, since a warrant can be exercised at any time prior to expiration, when the price of the common stock is in excess of the exercise price of the warrant, the value of the warrant can never be less than the difference between these two prices. (This, of course, ignores transaction costs.) For example, if a warrant is exercisable at $30 (the investor submits $30 and the warrant to the issuing firm in order to receive a share of its common stock), and the current market price of the common stock is $40, the value of the warrant cannot be less than $10. Should the price of such a warrant fall below $10, traders would buy this warrant, sell short the common stock for $40, convert the warrant into common stock to cover their short position by paying the issuing firm $30, and make a sure profit.

However, the value of a warrant that is about to expire (after expiration, the value of all warrants is zero under any circumstance) will be zero if the exercise price of the warrant is above the current market price of the common stock. For example, if the warrant just discussed is about to expire and the current market price of the common stock is $30 or less, the value of the warrant must be zero, since the common stock can be bought more cheaply without the warrant. As discussed below, however, certain warrant hedging strategies require that warrants be sold short, a position that is often covered by purchases of warrants on their expiration date even if their exercise price is below the market price of the common stock. Transactions such as these give such warrants a small trading value on their expiration date.

Time Remaining Before Expiration. Another important determinant of value is the period before expiration of the conversion right of the warrant. Warrants have a speculative appeal in that the owner of the warrant may profit if the price of the underlying common stock rises before the conversion right of the warrant expires. When a warrant is about to expire, its speculative appeal is zero. Therefore, other things being equal, warrants with a greater amount of time before expiration will have a greater value than warrants with less time before expiration.

Degree of Leverage. Since warrants normally trade at prices far lower than the price of the underlying common stock, and since the price of the common stock is an important determinant of the price of the warrant, greater percentage returns can be achieved from favorable movements in the price of the warrant than from similar movements in the common stock. The extent of this leverage difference between a warrant and its related common stock is determined by the relative prices of the two securities. The greater the price of the common stock relative to the price of the warrant, the greater the degree of leverage from purchase of the warrant as opposed to the common stock. Since warrants are rather speculative instruments and the potential for leverage enhances their speculative appeal, other things being equal, the greater the degree of the leverage in a warrant relative to its common stock, the greater the value of the warrant.

Volatility of the Common Stock. As previously mentioned, warrants are largely speculative instruments and derive a good part of their value from the speculative potential of a rise in the price of the common stock. Other things being equal, the warrants that relate to volatile stocks with a greater potential for larger favorable price movements can be expected to have a greater value than the warrants of stable stocks because they have a greater speculative appeal.

A related concern is the degree of speculative interest in the general stock market at any particular point in time. Since warrants are largely speculative instruments, their appeal is enhanced by a greater speculative fervor on the part of investors in general.

Other Considerations. Two final considerations are the time value of funds to investors and the extent of the dividend paid on the common stock. As the time value of funds to investors increases, the price of the warrant falls, making it increasingly more attractive relative to the common stock. Further, the greater the dividend paid on the common stock, the relatively less attractive the warrant vis-à-vis the common stock.

In sum, then, the value of the warrant is determined by the period before expiration and the relationship between the market price of the underlying common stock and the exercise price of the warrant. The value of warrants that are about to expire is determined by the extent to which the market price of the common stock exceeds the exercise price of the warrant. However, for warrants that still have time before expiration, the extent of this period and the relationship between the market price of the common stock and the exercise price of the warrant are of primary relevance in determining the value of the warrant. Also of consideration is the degree of leverage in the warrant relative to the underlying common stock, the degree of volatility of the common stock, the degree of speculative interest in securities in general, the time value of funds to investors, and the dividend paid on the common stock. In no case, however, can the value of a warrant ever be greater than the price of its underlying common stock.

ATTRACTIVE FEATURES

Leverage

One of the primary advantages of the use of warrants is the leverage they offer over the purchase of common stocks. Warrants normally sell for prices far lower than their related common stocks. Further, as long as a common stock is selling above the exercise price of the warrant, a given dollar increase in the price of the common stock must bring about at least an equal dollar increase in the price of the warrant. If, for example, a warrant is exercisable at $30 and the related common stock is selling for $40, arbitrage will assure that the warrant will not sell for less than $10. If the common stock increases by $10 to $50, arbitrage also assures that the warrant will increase by at least $10 to $20. A 25 percent increase in the price of the common stock will bring about a 100 percent increase in the price of the warrant. With warrants selling at prices lower than the related common stock and offering at least equal dollar increases (when the common stock is selling above the exercise price of the warrant), the warrant holder has a potentially greater return for a given dollar investment than does the common-stock holder. A greater percentage return to the warrant holder implies a leverage advantage over the common-stock holder. Even warrants whose common stock is selling below their exercise price have a leverage advantage over the related common stock. The normally low price of such warrants offers great percentage returns should the common stock move favorably.

Thus, if a common stock goes up, its warrant will go up faster on a percentage basis; the leverage thereby provided can turn a few hundred dollars invested in warrants into a call on many thousands of dollars worth of common stock. This leverage factor inherent in warrants is valuable and frequently results in a warrant selling at a considerable premium above its minimum value. In cases where the warrant is about to expire or where the common stock is greatly in excess of the exercise price, the warrant will sell at little or no premium, since there is either little time or little leverage left. However, when there is an extensive time before expiration, or the common stock is much below the exercise price, the premium can be considerable. Further, as the premium on a warrant is a measure of the speculative value attached to the instrument, warrant premiums tend to decline in bear markets and rise in market rallies.

Warrant Premlums. Since warrants selling at greater premiums are encumbered with a greater downside risk in the event of a market fall, it is appropriate at this point to define the premium on a warrant more precisely.

Warrant premiums are expressed as a percent of the common stock price and are defined as the excess cost of a share of common stock acquired through exercise of a warrant as opposed to a direct purchase of the common stock in the market. In percentage terms, the premium on a warrant is best expressed by subtracting from the warrant price the excess of the common stock price less the exercise price, and dividing the result by the price of the common stock. For example, if the price of a common stock is \$25, and its related warrant, which carries an exercise price of \$20, is selling for \$8, the premium is 12 percent:

$$\frac{8 - (25 - 20)}{25} = 12\%$$

Thus, common stock obtained through purchase and exercise of the warrant costs 12 percent more than common stock purchased directly in the stock market.

However, should the common stock fall below the exercise price of the warrant, the premium on the warrant would most likely rise considerably. If, in the preceding example, the common stock were to fall to \$10 and the warrant sold at \$2, the premium would be 120 percent:

$$\frac{2 - (10 - 20)}{10} = 120\%$$

In this instance, the common stock purchased by an investor through purchase and exercise of the warrants costs 120 percent more than the market price of the stock. Or, stated differently, the common stock in this case must advance by 120 percent in order for the intrinsic worth of the warrant to be equal to its market price.

Use of Warrants in Hedging

Hedging strategies employing warrants can be a fruitful investment technique for certain categories of investors. (For an expanded discussion of certain warrant hedging strategies, see *Hedging With Warrants,* later in this article.)

POTENTIAL RISKS

Risk of Total Loss

One of the major disadvantages of a long position in warrants is that a warrant to purchase shares of common stock will be worthless on the expiration date if the exercise price of the warrant is above the market price of the common stock. Holders of such warrants will then incur a total loss—in other words, they will lose an amount equal to their entire investment).

No Current Income

For investors who desire a current return, the absence of either interest or dividends from the ownership of warrants can represent a considerable disadvantage. Although warrants may be exchanged ultimately for common stocks (which may pay dividends), payment must be made for the common stock at the exercise price before dividends can be received.

Greater Volatility Than Common Stock

Another important disadvantage of warrants is that they are normally far more volatile than their related common stocks. This greater volatility stems from several sources.

The dividends on a security normally fluctuate far less than the price of the security and constitute the more stable segment of total return. (The total return equals the price change plus the dividends received.) Since warrants pay no current income, all the total return on the instrument is made up of price changes.

Warrants have an expiration date at which time, unless converted, will be worthless to their holders. Not only does the loss of value, in itself, produce volatility, but the inexorable movement to this condition as time passes further diminishes the warrant's stability.

While warrants have a leverage advantage over common stock, the presence of greater leverage for a security works in both directions and makes it more volatile and, in turn, more risky.

Removal of Conversion Rights

A final disadvantage to the ownership of warrants is the risk that the right to convert the warrant into common stock will be removed prior to its normal expiration date. This situation has occurred, for example, when the firm issuing the warrant is acquired by another company.

Warrant agreements (complex legal documents setting forth a warrant's terms and the conditions under which these terms may be altered) frequently indicate that, in the event of a liquidation, dissolution, or winding up of the affairs of the issuing corporation, the right to purchase its stock contained in the warrant will cease to exist. Certain companies, prior to their acquisition by other firms, have interpreted their acquisition as tantamount to a liquidation for purposes of determining the rights of their warrant holders. Under this interpretation of the warrant agreement, all warrants that were not converted into common stock were extinguished. Warrant holders in this situation do have the option to convert to common stock with the payment of the exercise price. However, in the case of an impending acquisition, this option must be exercised immediately and is worthless if the exercise price is above the market price of the common stock. Thus, although warrant holders must be notified of an impending extinguishment of their conversion rights, they may suddenly find their security without value.

TAX CONSEQUENCES

There are no real differences between the taxation of investments in common stocks or call options and the taxation of warrant holdings. However, because of the unique properties of warrants, certain tax consequences of an investment in warrants should be explained.

Warrants pay no current income (dividends or interest); therefore, all returns from warrants are capital transactions and are short or long term, depending on the length of the holding period. A gain or loss is calculated by comparing the purchase and sale prices of the warrant.

Further, it should be noted, one of the hedging strategies analyzed later in the article requires selling warrants short. Also, as in the case of common stock, short positions normally give rise to gains or losses that are short term, regardless of the period for which such positions are maintained.

The exercise of a warrant is not a taxable transaction. However, the worthless expiration of a warrant results in a capital loss that is long or short term, depending on the holding period.

Finally, when a warrant is exercised and converted into common stock by the payment of a given sum, that sum, plus the original purchase price of the warrant, becomes the basis for computing any gain or loss on the subsequent sale of that common stock. The period used to determine whether the transaction is long or short term depends on when the warrant was exercised. If the time from the exercise of the warrant to the final disposition of the common stock is sufficient to qualify for long-term treatment, then the transaction is viewed as long term for tax purposes.

REPRESENTATIVE TYPES OF INVESTORS

Institutional Investors

Warrants are attractive to institutional investors, such as certain investment companies and hedge funds, that are seeking large returns and are able to assume considerable risk. The leverage warrants offer vis-à-vis common stock may make warrants particularly appropriate for these investors.

Warrants are not recommended, on the other hand, for institutional investors, such as college endowment funds or income-oriented investment companies that require current income. For these investors, the lack of either interest or dividend income accruing to the holders of warrants makes them inappropriate investment vehicles. Moreover, some institutions are prohibited from taking short positions and thus are unable to avail themselves of the kind of hedge transactions that involve short positions. Their own charters and state laws prevent certain institutional investors from holding warrants, and therefore, for them, the instrument is inappropriate.

Individual Investors

Individuals, like institutional investors, who are highly averse to risk or who desire current income will find the holding of warrants inconsistent with their investment goals. However, warrants may be very attractive to those speculative individual investors who seek substantial percentage returns and who are willing to assume considerable risk to do so. Such individuals would normally be in high tax brackets and in a position to withstand the total loss that sometimes occurs if the market price of the underlying common stock does not exceed the exercise price prior to the warrant's expiration date.

Investors Who Benefit From Hedging

Although warrants are highly speculative when held as a long position, the use of such instruments in hedge transactions can often result in a highly conservative transaction. Thus, unlike the simple holding of warrants, the employment of the security in certain hedging strategies may be inappropriate for risk-taking speculative individual and institutional investors seeking high returns, but highly valuable for most categories of conservative risk-averse investors seeking current income and secure returns. Certain warrant hedging procedures reduce risk and increase the likelihood of a moderate to considerable return. By the same token, they may reduce the probability of loss while at the same time limiting the maximum level of returns.

HEDGING WITH WARRANTS

Procedures of Warrant Hedging

A hedge is a transaction that enables an investor to limit losses. In warrant hedging, the limiting of losses is in terms of the market price of the underlying common stock. In one type of warrant hedge, the investor is assured of avoiding a loss (or of making a profit) as long as the market price of the common stock remains within specified boundaries until the expiration of the warrant. In another variety of warrant hedge, a profit will result at expiration of the warrant as long as the common stock has moved beyond another set of boundaries, either on the upside or the downside.

An investor might employ a warrant hedge with any security that is convertible into common stock, such as convertible bonds or convertible preferred stock. However, for simplicity, this article is concerned only with hedge transactions that relate a warrant to its underlying common stock.

Warrant Hedging vs. Reverse Warrant Hedging. The procedures for the two types of warrant-hedging transactions discussed here are fairly simple. Briefly stated, for the first kind of warrant hedge, sometimes referred to as a reverse warrant hedge, the investor simply sells a warrant short and establishes a long position in the underlying common stock. The second type, referred to simply as a warrant hedge, requires precisely the opposite procedure, buying warrants and selling the underlying common stock short. By employing the reverse warrant hedge, the investor collects dividends on his long position and profits from all upward movements in the price of the common stock. Of course, he also incurs a reduction in profits from all downward movements in the price of the common stock. Additionally, downward movements in the price of the warrant increase his returns, while upward movements in the price of the warrant reduce returns. The opposite procedure (shorting the stock and buying the warrants), of course, produces precisely the opposite results.

Advantages and Disadvantages of Hedging Procedures

While taking a long position in warrants constitutes a rather risky endeavor (offering the possibility of both total loss on the commitment and substantial percentage returns), using warrants in a hedging or reverse-hedging strategy represents just the opposite kind of investment situation. By hedging or reverse hedging with warrants, an investor can limit (in some cases rather rigidly) his chance of loss and his dollar exposure. However, in so doing, the investor may also have to place limits on potential gain or on the price boundaries under which a gain will occur. In this sense, warrant hedging or reverse warrant hedging represents a conservative investment strategy. However, the historical returns from reverse warrant hedging have not only exceeded those on the Standard and Poor's 500 Composite Stock Index, but have also proved more favorable than a simple buy-and-hold strategy for the common stocks that underlie most of the warrants in question.[1]

Using a warrant hedge (buying the warrant and selling the common stock short) limits the maximum dollar loss that can occur. However, in such a transaction, gains do not

[1] See Kim, Moon K., and Young, Allan E. "Rewards and Risks From Warrant Hedging." *The Journal of Portfolio Management*. Summer 1980, pages 65–68.

occur unless a considerable movement has taken place in the price of the common stock. Alternatively, in the case of a reverse warrant hedge (shorting the warrants and buying the common stock), the opposite will prevail; a gain will result unless the common stock incurs a substantial movement in either direction. Additionally, the potential gain, at least theoretically, on a warrant hedge is unlimited. However, for a reverse warrant hedge, the maximum gain is limited. Thus, at least for reverse warrant hedging, the investor need not accurately predict the movements of the securities that compose his portfolio in order to profit. An investor can find a reverse warrant hedge quite profitable even if the price of the common stock that underlies the warrant remains roughly unchanged over the life of the hedge transaction. The common stock can even move moderately in an unfavorable direction and still provide the investor with a considerable return. Only if a substantial movement in the price of the common stock occurs can a loss result from a reverse-warrant- hedging strategy.

Illustration of Warrant-Hedging Strategies. The following examples illustrate the two warrant-hedging strategies. By relating a warrant to its underlying common stock, what is seen is not only what the prospective rates of return might have been for various price movements, but also what the actual rate of return would have turned out to be for investors using these strategies and employing the hedge ratio shown. The hedge ratio refers to the number of warrants sold short for each share of common stock purchased (a reverse warrant hedge) and/or the number of warrants purchased for each share of common stock sold short (a warrant hedge).[2]

Assume, for example, that approximately three years prior to its scheduled expiration, a warrant is selling for $7. At that time, the underlying common stock is selling for $42. The warrant is exercisable at $52. To be determined are the rates of return that will result from various terminal prices for the common stock (on the expiration date of the warrant) and a hedge ratio of, say, 2:1 (two warrants sold short for each common share purchased for a reverse warrant hedge, and two warrants purchased for each share of common stock sold short for a warrant hedge). It is assumed that transaction costs are 1.5 percent on each of the buy and sell sides. Finally, for the reverse warrant hedge, a full cash payment for the common stock will adequately margin the short sale of the warrants. For simplicity, it is also assumed that for the warrant hedge, Treasury bills already in an investor's portfolio are used to satisfy any margin requirements beyond a full cash purchase of the warrants. For each hedge strategy, a rate of return can now be calculated, based on the assumption of no more cash required than that needed for a full cash purchase of the long position.

If a reverse warrant hedge were undertaken and if the common stock stood at the original purchase price of $42 on the expiration date of the warrant, neither a gain nor a loss would have resulted from the long position. However, the warrants would have expired worthless, resulting in a gain of $14 ($7 × 2), and the investor would have received dividends that are assumed to average $3 a year over the three-year period until expiration of the warrant. Alternatively, if a warrant hedge were employed, the warrants would have expired worthless, resulting in a loss of $14 ($7 × 2). Neither a gain nor a loss would have resulted from the short position in the common stock. However, dividends of $3 per share of short position would have to be paid. Assuming a 1,000 share position in the stock (either long or

---

[2] For the determination of the optimal hedge ratio, see Kim and Young, supra note 1.

TABLE 1. Warrant Hedging Strategies: No Change in Stock Prices

From a Reverse Warrant Hedge		From Warrant Hedge	
On the Common Stock		**On the Common Stock**	
Buy for	$42,000	Buy (cover) for	$42,000
Sell for	$42,000	Sell short for	$42,000
Gain or (loss)	0	Gain or (loss)	0
On the Warrants		**On the Warrants**	
Buy (cover) for	$ 0	Buy for	$14,000
(As mentioned above, practically speaking, warrants would sell for a small fraction)			
Sell short for	14,000	Sell for	
Gain or (loss)	$14,000	Gain or (loss)	($14,000)
Dividends	9,000	Dividends	(9,000)
Transaction costs		Transaction costs	
([$42,000 + $42,000 + $14,000] ÷ 0.015)	(1,470)	([$42,000 + $42,000 + $14,000] × 0.015)	(1,470)
Net gain or (loss)	$21,530	Net gain or (loss)	($24,470)
Rate of return over three years or total dollar (loss) if negative ($21,530 ÷ $42,000)	51.3%	Rate of return over three years or total dollar (loss) if negative	($24,470)
Approximate rate of return annualized for one year (51.3% ÷ 3)	17.1%		

short), the rate of return can be approximated as shown in Table 1. On the reverse warrant hedge, 17.1 percent represents a rather handsome rate of return in a situation where the common stock in question moves neither favorably nor unfavorably. However, a rather considerable loss resulted from the warrant hedge.

Now, it might be asked, How far down can the stock go before a loss occurs for the reverse warrant hedge or a profit results from the warrant hedge? The answer is to approximately $20 for a reverse warrant hedge and $18 for a warrant hedge, as illustrated in Table 2.

After consideration of dividends, therefore, a profit results from a reverse warrant hedge when the terminal price for the common stock falls to between $20 and $42. However, a profit does not begin to occur for a warrant hedge until the price goes below $18. But what about movements on the up side for the common stock? When will a loss result from an upward movement in the price of the security for a reverse warrant hedge and a profit occur for a warrant hedge? As shown in Table 3, a loss will occur for a reverse warrant hedge if the price of the common stock goes above $82 on the expiration date of the warrant. Only when the price of the common stock rises above $88 can a profit result from a warrant hedge.

TABLE 2. Warrant Hedging Strategies: Losses in Stock Price

From a Reverse Warrant Hedge		From a Warrant Hedge	
On the Common Stock		**On the Common Stock**	
Buy for	$42,000	Buy (cover) for	$18,000
Sell for	20,000	Sell short for	$42,000
Gain or (loss)	($22,000)	Gain or (loss)	$24,000
On the Warrants		**On the Warrants**	
Buy (cover) for	$ 0	Buy for	$14,000
Sell short for	14,000	Sell for	0
Gain or (loss)	$14,000	Gain or (loss)	($14,000)
Dividends	9,000	Dividends	(9,000)
Transaction costs		Transaction costs	
([$42,000 + $20,000 + $14,000] × 0.015)	(1,140)	([$42,000 + $18,000 + $14,000] × 0.015)	(1,110)
Net gain or (loss)	($ 140)	Net gain or (loss)	($ 110)

TABLE 3. Warrant Hedging Strategies: Rise in Stock Price

From a Reverse Warrant Hedge		From a Warrant Hedge	
On the Common Stock		**On the Common Stock**	
Buy for	$42,000	Buy (cover) for	$88,000
Sell for	$82,000	Sell short for	42,000
Gain or (loss)	$40,000	Gain or (loss)	($46,000)
On the Warrants		**On the Warrants**	
Buy (cover) for		Buy for	$14,000
([$82 − $52] × 2,000)	$60,000	Sell for	
Sell short for	14,000	([$88 − $52] × 2,000)	72,000
Gain or (loss)	($46,000)	Gain or (loss)	$58,000
Dividends	9,000	Dividends	(9,000)
Transaction costs		Transaction costs	
([$42,000 + $82,000 + $60,000 + $14,000] × 0.015)	(2,970)	([$88,000 + $42,000 + $14,000 + $72,000)] × 0.015)	(3,240)
Net gain or (loss)	$ 30	Net gain or (loss)	($ 240)

For all prices between \$20 and \$82, therefore, a profit must result from the reverse-warrant-hedge strategy; thus, there is a band of profitability of from \$20 to \$82 from such a strategy. Any terminal price for the common stock within this range must result in a profit. However, a profit could only result from a warrant hedge if the common stock would go either below \$18 or above \$88 within the period in question.

Another question concerns the maximum rate of return to be earned on a reverse warrant hedge. This always occurs at the exercise price of the warrant (\$52 in this case), computed as shown in Table 4. The table shows that \$52 also represents the maximum loss from the warrant hedge strategy.

Dangers and Pitfalls

The principal danger involved in reverse warrant hedging is not the risk of loss resulting from the common stock moving beyond the bounds of profitability. Such boundaries can often be made broad enough (as in the preceding example) that the chance of the common stock moving beyond those limits is quite small.

Risk of a Buy-In: Reverse Warrant Hedging. Rather, the principal danger in a reverse warrant hedge is that the investor may not be able to retain a short position in the warrants until the expiration date. Short positions can only be maintained as long as the security in question can be borrowed. If the broker handling the transaction is unable to continue to borrow the warrants, he may have to buy them in and close out the short

TABLE 4. Warrant Hedging Strategies: Maximum Rate of Return

Maximum Gain		Maximum Loss	
On the Common Stock		**On the Common Stock**	
Buy for	\$42,000	Buy (cover) for	\$42,000
Sell for	52,000	Sell short for	\$42,000
Gain or (loss)	\$10,000	Gain or (loss)	(\$10,000)
On the Warrants		**On the Warrants**	
Buy (cover) for	\$ 0	Buy for	\$14,000
Sell short for	14,000	Sell for	0
Gain or (loss)	\$14,000	Gain or (loss)	(\$14,000)
Dividends	9,000	Dividends	(9,000)
Transaction costs ([\$42,000 + \$52,000 + \$14,000] × 0.015)	(1,620)	Transaction costs ([\$52,000 + \$42,000 + \$14,000] × 0.015)	(1,620)
Net gain or (loss)	\$31,380	Total dollar (loss)	(\$34,620)
Rate of return over three years $= \frac{\text{Net gain or (loss)}}{\text{Amount invested}} = \frac{\$31,380}{\$42,000}$	74.7%		
Approximate rate of return annualized for one year (74.7% ÷ 3)	24.9%		

position prior to the expiration date. In this event, of course, the investor need not incur a loss on the entire reverse warrant hedge, but it is harder to predict the pricing relationship between the warrant and the common stock prior to the expiration date than it is on the expiration date.

To increase the likelihood that the short position can be maintained until the expiration date, the investor should maintain a good relationship with his broker and secure the broker's assurances that a buy-in will be unlikely. He can also decrease the chance of a buy-in by choosing a reverse warrant hedge in a security whose short interest is relatively small in relation to the number of warrants outstanding and the floating supply of such warrants.

As can be seen on a reverse warrant hedge, there is a band of profitability, with a maximum at the exercise price of the warrant. Returns are then scaled downward toward the bounds of profitability, the range of which resembles a triangle. On the other hand, for warrant hedging undertaken when the common stock is below the exercise price of the warrant, the maximum loss occurs when the common stock rises, on the expiration date, to the exercise price of the warrant.

Risk of a Buy-In: Warrant Hedging. The foregoing discussion is also relevant to the danger of a buy-in of common stock in a warrant hedge. A warrant hedge will only be profitable if the common stock moves considerably in either direction from the exercise price of the warrant. Such a movement may take some time to develop. However, if the common stock is bought in before this movement can occur, a hedge that is potentially profitable may not prove to be so. Nevertheless, as there are normally more common shares than warrants outstanding, a buy-in of common stock in the face of a warrant hedge is less likely to occur than a buy-in of warrants relative to a reverse warrant hedge.

Risk of Warrant Extension. Another danger involved in reverse warrant hedging is that the corporation might extend the life of warrants that have been sold short. Aside from maintaining the position longer than had been originally contemplated, the reverse warrant hedger can lose through extension of the life of the warrant as the result of its likely increase in value. (As has been stated, reverse warrant hedging requires a short position in warrants, and their increase in value is detrimental to the reverse warrant hedger.)

One obvious precaution that the investor can take to mitigate the effects of a warrant extension is to cover the short position as expiration is about to take place rather than waiting to see if the company extends the lives of the warrants. The investor should also try to ascertain, at the time the hedge is originally contemplated, whether a particular warrant is likely to be extended. A company's practices in the past with respect to its expiring warrants might be of assistance in this respect. Also, a company that wants its stockholders to purchase its new equity issues would not wish to alienate them and possibly violate their preemptive rights by extending the life of its warrants. Finally, reverse warrant hedgers should avoid employing their strategy with respect to real estate investment trusts and other stock groups that frequently extend the lives of their warrants.

As was evident from the preceding examples, reverse warrant hedging generally is the better strategy when the common stock has a relatively high dividend yield and the investor expects only moderate movements in either direction for the security. Alternatively, a warrant hedge is the more appropriate strategy when the yield on the common stock is relatively low and considerable movements in either direction are anticipated for the common stock.

Limited Use of Reverse Warrant Hedging

The reasons that reverse warrant hedging is not employed more generally can only be speculated on. (More frequent use of the strategy by investors would reduce some of its profitability.) However, in some cases, it would seem as though the limits to institutional short sales and their dealing in warrants would account for some of the lack of the use of reverse warrant hedging. Further, the fact that there is an absolute limit to the returns that can be earned may inhibit some speculative investors desirous of achieving very high returns. (Alternatively, for warrant hedging, there is no limit to returns, at least on the upside.) Most reverse warrant hedges are best employed over a period from three to four years prior to the expiration date until the expiration date. Some investors may not wish to maintain a position for this long a period.

GLOSSARY

call—The right to purchase the underlying stock. Similar to a warrant.

exercise price—The amount of money that must be given by the holder of a warrant (along with the warrant itself) to the issuing corporation in order to exchange the warrant for common stock. For options, it is the stated price at which the option holder may purchase or sell the underlying security.

expiration date—The date at which the right to convert the warrant into common stock ceases. A warrant may be exercised (converted into common stock through the payment of the exercise price) at any time prior to the expiration date. For options, it is the date at which the terms of the option contract become void.

hedge—A means of limiting losses. Hedging with securities is normally accomplished by trading in opposite directions with similar or related securities (i.e., buying one while selling the other short).

hedge ratio—The relationship between the number of warrants sold short (or purchased) and the number of shares of common stock purchased (or sold short) in a reverse warrant hedge (or a warrant hedge).

optimal hedge ratio—The hedge ratio that maximizes the probability of obtaining returns on a warrant hedge or reverse warrant hedge, which is in excess of a required rate of return or a rate stipulated by the investor.

perpetual warrant—A warrant with an infinite life and, thus, no expiration date.

put—The right to sell the underlying stock.

reverse spread—Refers to option contracts. One put and one call where the exercise price of the put is above the exercise price of the call.

reverse warrant hedging—Buying warrants and selling the underlying common stock short.

strip—Refers to option contracts. Two puts and one call.

strap—Refers to option contracts. Two calls and one put.

straddle—Refers to option contracts. One put and one call.

spread—Refers to option contracts. One put and one call where the exercise price of the put is below the exercise price of the call.

warrant—A security issued by a corporation, which gives its holder the right to purchase shares of the issuing corporation's common stock at a stipulated price.

warrant agreements—Rather complex legal documents setting forth a warrant's terms and the conditions under which these terms may be altered.

warrant hedging—Operating on opposite sides of the market between a warrant and its related common stock (i.e., buying the warrant while selling the common stock short).

warrant premium—The excess of the cost of a share of common stock acquired through purchase and exercise of a warrant, as opposed to a direct purchase of the common stock in the market. This is usually expressed in terms of a percentage of the current market price of the common stock. The warrant premium is found by subtracting the excess of the common stock price from the warrant price, less the exercise price, and dividing the result by the price of the common stock. (See *Warrant Premiums* in this article for examples of this calculation.)

SUGGESTED READING

Bernstein, S. "Wising Up on Warrants: Do Your Homework and Find a Safe Speculation." *Canadian Business*, Nov. 1984.

Bierman, Harold, Jr. "The Cost of Warrants." *Journal of Financial and Quantitative Analysis*, June 1973, pages 499–504.

Chen, Andrew H. Y. *A Dynamic Programming Approach to the Valuation of Warrants*. Unpublished Ph.D. Dissertation, Graduate School of Business Administration, University of California, Berkeley, 1969.

______ . "A Model of Warrant Pricing in a Dynamic Market." *Journal of Finance*, Dec. 1970, pages 1041–1059.

Ferri, M.G., et al. "Investor Expectations About Warrants; Evidence Seems to Show That Investors Price Warrants Expecting Them to Be Called." *Journal of Portfolio Management*, Spring 1988, pages 84–87.

Hilliard, Jimmy E., and Leitch, Robert A. "Analysis of the Warrant Hedge in a Stable Paretian Market." *Journal of Financial and Quantitative Analysis*, Mar. 1977, pages 85–103.

Kim, Moon K., and Young, Allan E. "Rewards and Risks From Warrant Hedging." *The Journal of Portfolio Management*, Summer 1980, pages 65–68.

Leabo, Dick A., and Rogalski, Richard J. "Warrant Price Movements and the Efficient Market Hypothesis." *Journal of Finance*, Mar. 1975, pages 163–177.

Lee, P., and Crabbe, M. "The Wonderful World of Warrants." *Euromoney*, Aug. 1987, pages 29–44.

Madrick, Jeffrey. "Inside Wall Street: Safety First With a Very Cheap Warrant." *Business Week*, Feb. 9, 1976, page 75.

Miller, Jerry D. "Effects of Longevity on Values of Stock Purchase Warrants." *Financial Analysts Journal*, Nov.–Dec. 1971, pages 78–85.

Moscovitz, S.D. "They Warrant a Look; How Warrants Work as Hedging Devices." *Barron's*, Dec. 1987, pages 28–29.

Polks, W.R., Jr., and Ferri, M.G. Equity Linked Cross-Currency International Financial Instruments: A Study of the Pricing of Euro-Warrants." *Managerial Finance*, Spring 1987, pages 23–27.

Rogalski, Richard J. "Trading in Warrants by Mechanical Systems." *Journal of Finance*, Mar. 1977, pages 87–101.

Sacher, Laura. "Less Speculation, More Leverage (Warrants)." *Financial World*, Feb. 1987.

Samuelson, Paul A. "Rational Theory of Warrant Pricing." *Industrial Management Review*, Spring 1965, pages 13–39.

______ , and Merton, Robert C. "A Complete Model of Warrant Pricing That Maximizes Utility." *Industrial Management Review*, Winter 1969, pages 17–46.

Schwartz, William. "The Advantage Warrants Have—Leverage Prospects." *The Commercial and Financial Chronicle*. Mar. 5, 1970, pages 18–20.

Sinkey, J.F., and Miles, J.A. "The Use of Warrants in the Bail Out of First Pennsylvanian Bank; An Application of Option Pricing." *Financial Management*, Autumn 1982, pages 27–32.

Sisson, James R. "The Evaluation of Employee Stock Options: An Inquiry Into the Use of Warrant Pricing Models." *Akron Business and Economic Review*, Fall 1987, pages 25–48.

Spatt, C., and Sterbenz, F.P. "Warrant Exercise, Dividends and Reinvestment Policy." *Journal of Finance*, June 1988, pages 483–497.

Stanton, Thomas C., and Maxwell, Philip H. "Warrants: A Cost of Capital Perspective." *Financial Executive,* Sept. 1980, pages 27–31.

Stone, Bernell K. "Warrant Betas and the Effect of Warrant Financing on Systematic Risk." *Cornell University Working Paper,* 1980.

———. "Warrant Financing." *Journal of Financial and Quantitative Analysis,* Mar. 1976, pages 143–153.

Turov, Daniel. "Beyond Maturity: More Companies Are Extending the Life of Their Warrants." *Barron's,* July 22, 1974, pages 11–12.

———. "Dividend Paying Stocks and Their Warrants." *Financial Analysts Journal,* Mar.–Apr. 1973, pages 76–78.

———. "Trampled Rights: Warrant-Holders Have Become an Oppressed Minority." *Barron's,* Mar. 19, 1973, pages 11, 25.

Van Horne, James C. "Warrant Valuation in Relation to Volatility and Opportunity Costs." *Industrial Management Review.* Spring 1969, Pages 19–32.

Yeasting, Kenneth. "CD Warrants." *Financial Analysts Journal,* Mar.–Apr. 1970, pages 44–47.

WINES

George M. Schofield

Historically, wine has been an article of commerce and a versatile consumer product. Wine has served as a food beverage and has played important roles in religious liturgy, feasts, and commemorations and celebrations of every sort.

When he left the ark after the flood, Noah is reported to have planted a vineyard and consumed the wine. Will Durant, in his monumental work *The Story of Civilization*, claims that in the early first century in Italy, "Vineyards were everywhere, beautifully terraced on the slopes. Italy produced 50 famous kinds of wine and [the inhabitants of] Rome alone drank 25,000,000 gallons per year."

Although civilized people have purchased and consumed wines since time immemorial, significant interest in wine as an investment is still in its infancy. Until recently, the unique nature of wine has posed serious problems for the conventional acceptance of wine as a long-term investment vehicle.

BASIC CHARACTERISTICS

Vintage

Wine is produced from the juice of grapes, an annual agricultural product. Production of grapes and wine varies, often significantly, in quantity and quality from year to year. Once annual production is completed, vintage wine is unique and irreplaceable.

George M. Schofield is President of the George M. Schofield Co., which specializes in Financial and Economic Planning, St. Helena, Cal. He has a Bachelor of Science degree from Fordham University and a Masters in Business Administration from Harvard University and is a Certified Public Accountant.

Kinds of Wine

The selection process for wine investment focuses initially on those few categories of wines whose quality and related values will substantially improve over time. Experience has established that the better, long-lived red Bordeaux, red Burgundy, and vintage Port wines are the dominant groups in this classification. The best vintages of the top producers of the sweet and elegant botrytis wines (see glossary) from Sauternes and Germany also present some investment opportunities. Similarly, a few of the better long-lived sparkling wines and Italian red wines are increasingly gaining recognition for investment potential.

The newest group of wines to achieve recognition as an investment vehicle is California Cabernet Sauvignon, made from the same grape variety as most red Bordeaux appellation wines. Over the past 20 years, the California Cabernet Sauvignon wines have established quality credentials that place them among the fine wines of the world. Leaning more on scientific technology and research than on pure tradition, vintners such as Andre Tchelistcheff, Robert Mondavi, Warren Winiarski, and Bernard Portet have demonstrated in international competition that the New World now presents some exciting wine investment alternatives.

In a book called *Liquid Assets*, William Sokolin extensively treats the selection process and strategy for investing in wines. Most noteworthy is his concept and definition of investment grade wines.

Alcohol Content

Yeast cells cause the sugar content of grape juice to be converted into alcohol and carbon dioxide. This process occurs naturally but is induced and controlled in modern winemaking. Generally, the fermented alcohol content of most wines ranges from 9 to 14 percent by volume. Through fortification with previously fermented alcohol, certain dessert wines, such as port and sherry, are raised in alcohol content to a range of 15 to 20 percent.

Governments have attempted to regulate, control, and tax every aspect of wine production and sale, primarily with the justification that alcoholic beverages are potentially subject to substance abuse. In particular, excise taxes have become a significant source of government revenue and an instrument of social policy.

Consumer Product

Wine is a beverage primarily consumed by adults during meals. Most individuals that purchase wine assume it is ready for immediate consumption. Unfortunately, cash flow considerations rather than wine maturity too often dictate the timing of sale by premium wineries. As a result, many of the better, long-lived wines are consumed far too young and never survive to peak quality or investment value. This significant, untimely reduction of available supply of irreplaceable vintage wines contributes to the upward investment potential as scarcity and demand increase in later years.

Liquid

As a fluid, wine needs a safe container and tight but removable closure for storage and transportation. The occurrence of spillage, leakage, and breakage are real risks at every stage of existence, from initial pressing of grapes to drinking from a glass. Wine is also easily blended and absorbs additives readily. Hence, the integrity and reputation of the producer is a major marketing factor.

Perishable

Although some wines improve in quality over time, all wines are eventually subject to natural deterioration. Exposure to air, light, and biological and chemical contamination will inevitably cause wine to suffer early maturity, if not mortality. However, technological developments in every phase of winemaking, from fermentation through bottling and storage, have accelerated to the point that fine wines can be aged many years to ideal maturity without inordinate difficulties. Oxygen-free processing, packaging, and temperature- and humidity-controlled storage have contributed to the success of long-term storage.

Improvement With Age

When stored under proper conditions, certain wines improve in quality over time, sometimes for up to fifty years. The vast majority of wines are made for the pleasure of short-term consumption. However, the taste and aroma of a small percentage of wines improve substantially in quality when they are aged under proper conditions.

ATTRACTIVE FEATURES

Two centuries ago, the British explicitly realized the attractive features of fine wines in their approach to the Bordeaux trade. On release of the better Bordeaux wines, British wine merchants took a major financial position. Within a year or two, they sold enough of the wines to recover their entire investment. Two or three years later, another portion of the original inventory sold at a handsome profit. A final portion of wine inventory was kept for the personal consumption and enjoyment of the merchants, their family, and friends.

Salability

As a desired consumer product, wine can be converted to currency or used in official and unofficial barter arrangements. However, government regulations and difficulties in ascertaining a market price on a daily basis impose some limitations.

Pleasure

The joy of sharing a fine bottle of wine with family, friends, or business associates is a multidimensional pleasure. The collection of a personal cellar of fine wines is also a source of pride and personal achievement for many people.

Divisibility

The initial investment unit for fine wines is most often a case that, depending on size, normally contains six, twelve, or twenty-four identical bottles. Hence, considerable flexibility exists for tasting, partial sale, and retention.

Potential Appreciation

Constant reduction of supply through consumption, and improvement by aging, afford certain wines a unique set of factors spurring upward valuation over time.

Dr. Orley Ashenfelter, professor of economics at Princeton University, provides a broad insight into the historic appreciation of international fine wines. His semiannual publication, *Liquid Assets*, tracks and analyzes wine auction prices throughout the world. The Liquid Assets Index of Finest Wines, as measured in pounds sterling, rose threefold during the thirteen-year period 1972 to 1985, representing a 9 percent compounded annual return. When measured in U.S. dollars, the index rose almost sixfold versus a two-fold increase in the Dow Jones stock index. Moreover, the index of prices of slightly less prestigious wines increased far more than the finest wine price index, leading to this conclusion by Dr. Ashenfelter: "Returns have been absolutely staggering for investors and collectors who have put their money into the best wines that are priced just below the very top".[1] Analysis of Dr. Ashenfelter's thirteen-year data does reveal periods of unfavorable market movements, which suggest that timing and pricing of purchases are factors critical to wine investment success.

POTENTIAL RISKS

Timing

Specific wines are an investment that may appreciate significantly but not predictably or indefinitely. From both a quality and financial viewpoint, difficulty arises in determining when a wine may have reached its peak value or passed its best point of drinkability.

Besides annual variation between vintages, the wine market is also subject to cyclical variations. The cumulative effect of a series of similar vintages can cause trends in wine prices lasting several years. Fluctuations in disposable personal income, interest rates, foreign exchange ratios, and other economic factors have had repercussions that exaggerate or moderate the intra-industry volatility of wine prices. Accordingly, the timing of wine purchases and sales can be a crucial factor. Careful review of vintage reports, monitoring of economic trends, and astute pricing analysis may be prerequisites for optimizing returns.

Another timing issue relates to the age at which a given wine might be purchased. Commonly, purchase occurs through wine merchants shortly after the initial release of bottled wine by the producer. Alternatively, acquisitions are made through wine auctions some years later. The gap in availability that frequently occurs reflects the preference of auction houses to sell red wines that are at least ten years old.

Availability and Futures Contracts

For some small, highly regarded wine producers, availability may be a problem from the outset. The traditional practice of Bordeaux producers who sell a portion of their wines under futures contracts has recently spread to California as a means of coping with wine allocation difficulties. Consumers and investors willing to pay one to two years in advance of release can thus assure themselves of supply. Some wineries, appreciating the accelerated cash flow benefits, have extended the concept into one primarily involving a discounting of prices. Investors should be alert to distinguish the facts and to assure themselves that the futures price reflects a differential commensurate with the financial risk. Caution also ought to be exercised concerning the financial viability of the wine merchant and winery from and through whom the wine futures are obtained. Until delivery occurs, the purchaser may be in the unfavorable position of unsecured creditor.

[1] *Liquid Assets*, No. 1, Fall 1986, p. 12.

Overpricing

Surges in demand, imperfectly functioning markets, and inadequate information can cause wines to be overpriced. Certain wines or vintages may not live up to initial evaluations or quality expectations. Losses in the long run are not common, but some wines may not appreciate above purchase price for long periods or significantly enough to offset storage and insurance costs. Young wines, generously priced by historic standards for similarly regarded vintages, are particularly risky. The emerging practice of buying unbottled wines under future delivery contracts can lead to opportunities either to profit significantly or to experience the disappointment of a lower subsequent price.

Resale Restrictions

The twenty-first amendment to the U.S. Constitution did not simply repeal prohibition. The regulation of alcoholic beverages, unlike any other product, was relegated to individual states. With this opportunity and with a tax revenue incentive, alcoholic beverages have been subjected to a plethora of different regulations by each of the fifty states. Who may sell alcoholic beverages and how they can be sold are strictly prescribed. As a result, in many jurisdictions, the resale of wine by private, unlicensed individuals is a crime subject to harsh penalties.

The states of California and Illinois have relaxed their statutes, allowing individuals to resell wine through wine auctions and to retailers under conditions mainly related to the age of the wines. As a result, even wines from other states can, in most circumstances, be sold through auctions in Chicago and San Francisco. Taking into consideration the opportunities also afforded by international auctions, investors should be wary, but not totally intimidated, by potential resale restrictions.

TAX CONSEQUENCES

Investors not in the trade or business of selling alcoholic beverages generally treat the sale of wine as the sale of a capital asset subject to capital gains taxation. Federal tax legislation effective after 1986 equated capital gains and ordinary income tax rates. Hence, at least temporarily, the favorable capital gains tax advantage of wine has disappeared; however, long-term appreciation would be untaxed until sold or traded. The untaxed compounding of gross investment appreciation versus a taxed periodic sale and reinvestment affords a real tax advantage. This benefit grows in significance as the appreciation rate, tax rate, and holding periods increase.

State and local sales taxation, often in ranges of 5 to 8 percent, can be a hidden cost to investors. An investor not in the trade or business would not have a resale exemption permit and, on purchase, would be subject to any applicable sales tax. Ultimate sale to another investor may trigger another sales tax. Although the investor would not be liable for sales tax as a seller, an indirect depressing effect on realization may occur. When combined with other transaction costs, such as auction commissions, the cumulative impact may be considerable.

Wine shipped from one state jurisdiction into another for the purpose of sale or consumption will probably be levied with additional taxes by the destination state. However, such taxes are likely to be a small factor relative to the value of wines held for investment purposes.

REPRESENTATIVE TYPES OF INVESTORS

Individual wine consumers and connoisseurs represent the largest group of investors. Most are hobbyists with personal wine cellars of no more than 1,000 bottles with a valuation of under $50,000. A smaller group of more serious, wealthier investors have larger collections, often including several cases of specific wines and some very rare and expensive individual bottles or cases. This group is in the highest one percent income bracket and may have wine cellars of well over $100,000 in value.

A separate category of investors are the professionals, restaurant owners, retailers, vineyard owners, and others who are directly or indirectly involved in the wine trade on at least a part-time or investment basis. Because of the coincidence of their personal and occupational interests, and with the resources of a business to assist in the financing and disposal of their investments, such individuals may have cellars valued at $250,000 and, occasionally, $1 million or more.

A relatively new wine investing phenomenon is the collective investor. Syndications and partnerships have been formed to gain leverage and expertise in purchasing as well as to facilitate financing. Such organizations can also advantageously handle the licensing, compliance, excise tax, and logistical aspects of purchasing, aging, and selling wine. Individual investors in wine syndicates, however, often have little say in the selection of wines and may participate primarily on a financial basis. Examples of two California-based ventures are the Wine Futures Exchange, Inc., and Unique Wines, Inc., the latter controlled by the author. Both ventures have been in existence only a few years. Because of the long aging period of the wines purchased, neither has yet completed the wine sales cycle nor demonstrated financial results.

IMPORTANT FACTORS IN BUYING AND SELLING

Appreciation Potential

A critical factor for buyers is not to confuse personal preferences with investment objectives. For the investor, the foremost quality should be long-term value appreciation. Unfortunately, the most acclaimed wines of a vintage or decade often are priced so high that relatively little appreciation potential exists. An example is found in the 1982 "first growth" Bordeaux wines, currently priced in the range of $85 to $100+ per bottle. Similarly, entire vintages, such as 1986 Bordeaux, can be touted so highly at an early age by the trade and media that initial pricing threatens reasonable investment expectations.

Ironically, despite the premise that older wines are better than comparable vintage younger wines, new vintage wines frequently outprice older wines. From a consumption and investment viewpoint, the mature wines may represent attractive acquisitions; conversely, in such situations, the younger wines may be speculative and risky investments.

A related investment dilemma exists with the reserve or vineyard appellation Cabernet Sauvignon wines of some California producers. Some wines may well be slightly better from a taste or quality viewpoint than the related nondesignated "regular" wines. However, the initial pricing of $20 to $35 per bottle for the appellation wines versus the $10 to $15 for the regular wines tends to bias the investment economics in the opposite direction. In research done in four consecutive years by Robert Murray, an associate of the author, the nonreserve category wines have generally yielded 1 to 3 percentage points higher compounded annual rate of appreciation than the more heralded reserve wines, as shown in

TABLE 1. California Cabernet Sauvignon Wine Pricing Survey

	Average Annual Compounded Appreciation Rates			
	1985	1986	1987	1988
All wines	25.7%	20.3%	18.7%	16.9%
Reserve style wines	24.2	22.0	19.8	15.7
Nonreserve wines	27.7	23.1	20.9	18.1

Table 1. Accordingly, to optimize return, an investor may have to use value analysis as well as sensory and media input.

Condition of the Wine

Prudent investors are diligent concerning the condition of the wine they purchase. Pretasting is a normal practice, but is not always possible or totally reliable. Inspection of wine for telltale indications of problems before purchase and/or acceptance is another important precaution, since value on resale may be limited by preexisting defects, whether real or cosmetic. Among the signs that may cause concern are:

- Soiled bottle labels or case cartons
- Labels separated from the bottles
- Indication of cork leakage
- Abnormal bottle fill levels
- Heavy sedimentation
- Browning of wine color

Written records of storage history provide major comfort in assuring the condition of wine. A continuous log of proper storage back to winery release is an advantage to any wine seller. Accordingly, an investor should not only provide the wine investment with good aging facilities, but keep written documentation of such. Depending on the volume and quality control specifications, adequate storage may cost from $1 to $6 per case per year.

Use of Expert Opinion

Wine experts, although most useful, have helped make wine an intimidating product to purchase. In reality, wine is a product of simple pleasures: aroma, taste, and appearance. The role experts can best play is to screen the large number of possibilities down to a manageable decision level. In a negative sense, experts can also help to avoid making costly mistakes. Perhaps the most critical factor in making use of expert opinion—whether from a wine merchant, a wine writer, or a wine maker—is to employ one whose tastes and value objectives are in harmony with those of the purchaser.

FIGURE 1. Rate of Return Profile

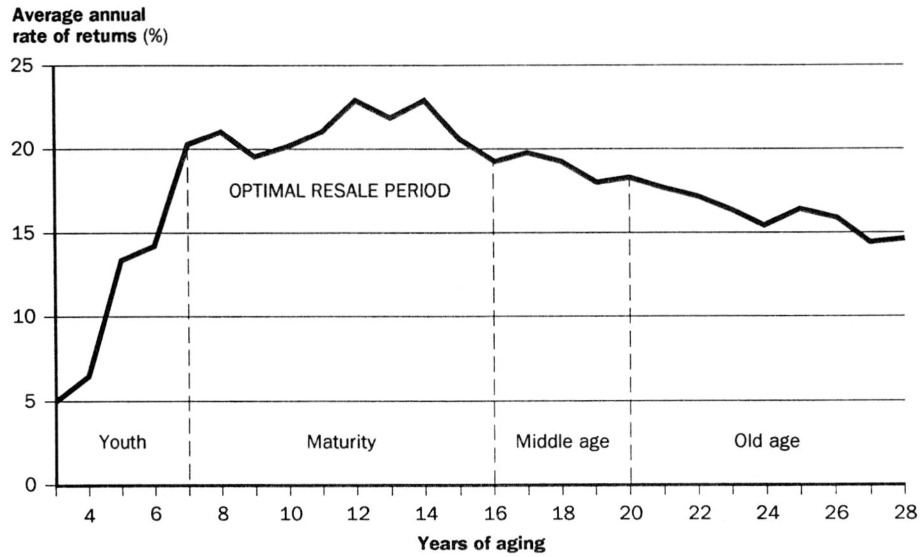

Timing the Sale of Wine

The upward appreciation of wine value is typically an S-shape curve rather than a straight line. Little appreciation can be expected in the first few years after commercial release. As wines gradually mature and resurface in wine auction markets, valuations generally escalate rapidly. For the long-lived wines, this process may occur around the fifth or sixth year after production and continue for a ten-year or longer period, when some slowing of the growth rate may occur (see Figure 1). Optimization of investment realization may involve correlation of this general pattern with the cyclical trend in the wine market and the overall economic outlook.

Resale Channels

Primitive regulations in many U.S. jurisdictions restrict resale options. Barter and sale to friends and trade contacts do occur. However, the most practical resale alternative may now be domestic and international wine auctions. The rise in wine auction market activity internationally since late 1966, and within the U.S. since 1980, has substantially increased the ease with which wine is sold. Major auction houses and organizations conduct auction activity mostly on a spring and fall calendar, as shown in Table 2.

In a May 31, 1988, cover story, the *Wine Spectator*, the leading industry newspaper, estimated 1987 wine auction sales to be $20 million in London, with an additional $6 million in the United States. With the major transaction channel for aged wines accounting for only $26 million of sales auctions in 1987, international wine investment activity, although growing rapidly, must be deemed to be in its infancy.

An investor considering the auction channel for acquisition or sales should realize that

TABLE 2. Locations of Wine Auctions

	Butterfield	Chicago Wine Co.	Christie's	Int'l Wine Auction	Sotheby's
Amsterdam			X		X
Bordeaux			X		
Geneva			X		X
London			X	X	X
Chicago		X	X		
San Francisco	X				
Los Angeles	X				

the commission structure generally totals a cumulative 25 percent on buyer and seller combined. The exact percentages vary among the auction houses, but the typical arrangement involves a 15 percent charge to the seller and a 10 percent charge to the buyer. Despite the transaction costs, auction houses provide an efficient and effective service as well as a useful adjunct to the normal retail channels. As wine investing moves into adolescence, the frequency and locations of auctions are bound to increase dramatically. As a result, volume and competition will improve the efficiency of the market and the ability to convert wine investments into cash. This, in turn, will have a most beneficial effect on the attractiveness of fine wine as an investment alternative.

CUSTODIAL CARE

Wine Loss

As a liquid stored in glass, wine is subject to loss from breakage. Accordingly, wine must be carefully handled and stored. The shipping containers, labels, and wine itself are also subject to fire, smoke, and water damage. Insurance can normally be obtained against such risks. The valuation for both insurance premium and claim purposes should be predicated on estimated current market value rather than original costs. Earthquake coverage may also be available in public storage facilities, although high premium costs and deductible loss may make such coverage unattractive.

Unless spoilage results from an insurable calamity, such as fire, the risk of quality deterioration generally rests with the owner. Ideally, wines should be stored in cool temperatures (50° to 60° F.), and in the absence of light, vibrations, and humidity. It is more important that conditions remain constant than that they are precisely ideal.

GLOSSARY

appellation—Geographic, vineyard, grape varietal, or vintage designations used to distinguish wines. Generally, wines using these designations must conform to specified requirements to be eligible to use the specific appellation. Local and national governments generally legislate and control appellation usage.

botrytis—Generally refers to wines made from shriveled grapes affected by the botrytis cineria mold, commonly called noble rot. Because of their highly concentrated sugar content, such grapes produce very sweet, nectar-like wines.

dessert wines—Wines such as sherry and port, which exceed 14 percent in alcohol content, generally have a relatively high residual sugar. Such wines are fortified to specific alcoholic content by the addition of alcohol.

dry—Refers to wines that have been fermented to a nondetectable level of residual sugar. In wines, the threshold of sugar recognition by taste is normally in the range of 0.5 percent to 1.0 percent volume content.

fortification—The process of adding distilled spirits to raise the alcohol content level of a beverage. Wine fortification regulations generally require the source of the distilled spirits to be grapes.

growths—Refers to a prestigious classification, created in 1855, of 62 red Bordeaux wines, in five categories of *cru vigneron*, or growths. The first growth, or top classification, originally included four producers. The only changes to the original classification were a regional expansion to include three other producers in 1955 and the elevation of Chateau Mouton-Rothschild from a second growth to a first growth in 1973.

reserve—A designation used particularly by California vintners to distinguish a small portion of the annual production of a given wine. Generally, reserve wine represents the best grapes, often specially processed, and frequently barrel and bottle aged for longer periods.

table wines—In the United States, refers to an excise tax classification of wines under 14 percent in alcohol content. Generally, table wines are dry in style, with far less residual sugar than dessert wines. In Europe, table wine also has a connotation of lower quality.

vintage—Appellation designation used to distinguish wines from a specific grape harvest year. In Europe, especially for Port wines, vintage declaration does not occur each year. When proclaimed, it is a clear indication of high quality by the shipper and producer.

SUGGESTED READING

PERIODICALS

Liquid Assets. Published by Dr. Orley Ashenfelter (Professor of Economics at Princeton University); 169 Nassau Street, Princeton, N.J. 08542. $30 for two issues per year. This biannual publication tracks the prices of fine wines in international auctions and contains current market advice on what to buy and sell. A special feature is vintage advice based on detailed analysis of the weather.

Wine Spectator. Published by M. Shanken Communications Inc., 387 Park Avenue South, New York, N.Y. 10016. $35 per year. This semimonthly publication contains background articles on individual wineries, wines, and vintners.

Wine Advocate. Published by R.M. Parker, Jr., P.O. Box 311, Monkton, Md. 21111. $30 per year. This bimonthly publication contains critical wine quality reviews and recently has become most influential in rating of Bordeaux and California Cabernet Sauvignon wines.

The Finigan Wine Letter. Published by Counterpoint Publishing Inc., P.O. Box 2021, Canal Street Station, New York, N.Y. 10013. $45 per year. This bimonthly publication is one of the oldest U.S. wine review letters. Stylistically, *Finigan* tends to favor the lighter, more elegant wines, while Parker is more inclined toward the more intense and heavily structured wines.

REFERENCE BOOKS

Broadbent, Michael. *The Great Vintage Wine Book*. New York: Alfred A. Knopf, 1980.

Gold, Richard. *How and Why to Build a Wine Cellar*, 2nd ed. Amherst, Mass.: Sundhill Publishing Company, 1985.

Lichine, Alexis. *Alexis Lichine's New Encyclopedia of Wines and Spirits*, 3rd ed. New York: Alfred A. Knopf, 1984.

Sokolin, William. *Liquid Assets*. New York: Macmillan Publishing Company, 1987.

Sutcliff, Serene. *Andre Simon's Wines of the World*, 2nd ed. New York: McGraw-Hill Book Company, 1981.

ZERO COUPON BONDS

Perry L. Burns
Jan L. Dillow

BASIC CHARACTERISTICS

Zero coupon bonds pay no interest to the holder. Does this sound like a loan to your brother-in-law or a ne'er-do-well friend? Not so! Zero coupon bonds offer unique and valuable investment characteristics to various types of buyers. Their main attraction is that they mature on a specified date at par, usually $1,000 per bond. Zeros are issued at substantial discounts to par. They trade in the secondary, or resale, market at prices that appreciate gradually as maturity nears. The structure is similar to two well-known, time-honored investment vehicles—U.S. Treasury bills and U.S. Savings bonds. Neither make periodic interest payments. The investor receives his return at maturity. Names synonymous to zeros are "capital accumulation bonds," "deferred interest bonds," and "money multipliers."

Normal bonds, by comparison, have a stated interest rate and maturity date. A bond with a 9 percent coupon rate pays $45 semiannually for a total of $90 each year per $1,000 principal amount. Additionally, principal is repaid at maturity. Bond buyers concern themselves with current yield and yield to maturity. Current yield at par (or $1,000 per bond) is 9.00 percent. At $900 per bond (90 percent of par or "90" in trade vernacular), current yield is 10 percent ($90/$900 = 10 percent).

Yield to maturity is a more complicated calculation. (See article on "Municipal Securities," elsewhere in this volume for the exact formula.) Bondholders receive their coupon annually *plus* an annual appreciation toward par. A 9 percent bond due in twelve years has

Perry L. Burns and Jan L. Dillow are Executive Vice-President and Vice-President, respectively, of Shearson Lehman Hutton, Inc.

a 10.48 percent yield to maturity when purchased at 90. It is important to note that yield-to-maturity calculations implicity assume that the bondholder can invest every semiannual interest payment at the same coupon rate and with the same maturity as the bond held. However, this is highly theoretical!

Zero coupon bonds have no current yield. They trade only on a yield to maturity basis. Normal semiannual payments are reinvested automatically. In contrast to the example in the previous paragraph, a twelve-year bond priced to yield 10.48 percent to maturity would cost $293.45. The price is calculated as follows:

$$\text{Price} = 1{,}000 \times \left(1 + \frac{i}{m}\right)^{mn}$$

where i = interest rate, n = number of years to maturity, and m = number of compounding periods per year.

$$\$293.45 = \$1{,}000 \times \left(1 + \frac{.1048}{2}\right)^{2 \times 12}$$

This formula eliminates problems of reinvestment. A true yield to maturity is locked in. The investor has only two questions: Will I get my principal back? Will I get it on time?

Two important caveats exist for buyers. Tax consequences vary considerably, depending on the bond purchased. Credit analysis of the issuer is critical because creditworthiness can change dramatically over a long period.

Securities Backed by U.S. Treasury Bonds

Our federal government has issued zero coupon bonds known as STRIPS (separate trading of interest and principal of securities). Billions of additional zeros are available that are backed by U.S. Treasury securities. These bonds were created by financial intermediaries, such as major brokerage firms and government bond dealers. The intermediaries bought normal Treasury bonds which pay interest semiannually, "stripped" the bonds of their coupon payments, and repackaged them into series that pay no interest, only par at maturity. An independent trustee, usually a major bank, is the conduit between the U.S. government and the investor. These securities are known by colorful acronyms, the most popular of which are CATS (Certificates of Accrual on Treasury Securities), COUGARS (Certificates of Government Receipts), and TIGRS (Treasury Investment Growth Receipts).

These conduits differ mainly in the actual security delivered to the buyer. CATS, for instance, are a receipt-type instrument. The buyer physically gets a receipt as proof of ownership from the custodian bank. STRIPS, on the other hand, are held in book-entry form only at the Federal Reserve Bank registered in the name of the holder. No physical certificate is available. In both cases, the buyer receives a confirmation of purchase from his agent, bank, or brokerage house.

Treasury-backed zeros are the most attractive vehicles for the individual investor. They are the safest and the most liquid. Billions of dollars have been issued, and millions trade every day. They are easy to buy and easy to sell should investment objectives change. They are visible. CATS, COUGARS, and TIGRS all trade on the New York Stock Exchange (NYSE). A multitude of maturities exist from a few months to thirty years in duration. Commissions paid to buy and sell are small fractions of their principal amount. They may be exempt from state and local income taxes. (See *Tax Consequences*, discussed later in this article.)

Federal Agency Zeros

A few agencies of the federal government have issued zero coupon bonds. These issuers are Federal National Mortgage Association (Fannie Mae), Federal Home Loan Mortgage Corporation (Freddie Mac), and Student Loan Marketing Association (Sallie Mae). Whereas these bonds are not guaranteed by the U.S. government, their safety is only slightly inferior to those that are. Outstanding issues are large and marketable and trade in volume on the NYSE and over-the-counter markets (markets made in the offices of broker/dealers). Another attraction is their lengthy maturity and, therefore, deep discount from par. Freddie Mac and Sallie Mae have zeros that mature in 2022 and that trade at $46.00 per $1,000 bond. Long maturities have appeal to both the investor and the speculator.

Corporate Bond Zeros

Corporate America has been a prolific issuer of zeros since 1982. Included in this discussion are two noncorporate credits—International Bank for Reconstruction & Development (World Bank) and Kingdom of Sweden—because they trade similarly to corporate bonds. The appeal of corporate zeros is that they yield more to maturity than do CATS, the accepted standard bearer.

Yields to Maturities

Current yields to maturities as of August 1988 are shown in Table 1. Yields fluctuate with the general level of interest rates, but yield spreads between CATS and corporates remain relatively constant. It should be noted that yields correspond inversely to quality ratings assigned by the two leading bond agencies, Moody's Investors Service and Standard & Poor's Corporation. Allied Corp's bonds are rated A2/A by M/S&P, PepsiCo, Inc. is rated Aa3/AA–, Kingdom of Sweden is rated Aaa/AAA, and World Bank is rated Aaa/AAA.

TABLE 1. Yields to Maturities

	CATS due 8/15	Allied Corp. due 8/1	PepsiCo, Inc. due 4/1	Sweden due 4/1	World Bank due 2/15
1990	8.80%	9.30%	9.20%	9.20%	9.10%
1992	9.20	9.60	9.50	9.50	9.40
1994	9.45	9.85	9.75	9.75	9.65
1996	9.55	10.00	9.90	9.90	9.80
1998	9.60	10.25	10.15	10.15	10.05
2000	9.67	10.25	10.15	10.15	10.05
2002	9.75	10.25	10.15	10.15	10.05
2004	9.78	10.25	10.15	10.15	10.05

(See article on "Municipal Securities," elsewhere in this volume, for definitions of assigned ratings.) The better the rating, the lower the yield.

Tax-Free Municipal Zeros

State and other municipalities issue zero coupon obligations, too, although less frequently. The buyer/holder pays no federal taxes on interest theoretically received. These investments are usually tax-free in the state and municipality of issuance but are usually taxable in other states and local jurisdictions. If bonds are held until maturity, the investor will not be subject to capital gains taxes provided that the bonds were purchased at or above the original compounded accreted value. (See *Tax Consequences*, later in this article.)

ATTRACTIVE FEATURES

Safety

Zero coupon Treasuries represent ownership of future interest and principal payments on U.S. Treasury obligations. Government agency issues are slightly less risk-free. Buyers of corporate and municipal bonds get more yield in exchange for less safety. They should rely on ongoing rating reviews by Moody's Investors Service and Standard & Poor's Corporation.

Capital Accumulation

Zeros are priced at a substantial discount from their maturity value. A relatively small investment grows automatically to a significant future amount. The current value of a $1,000 bond is shown in Table 2; values given should be used as approximations.

Assured Rate of Return

A true compounded yield to maturity exists because there are no interest payments to reinvest. The small investor need not worry about reinvesting a small coupon payment. The large investor does not have to find a certain coupon and maturity. Future change in interest rates is not a concern.

Choice of Maturities

A wide variety of maturities is available. Zero coupon Treasuries, for instance, mature quarterly every year for thirty years out. Some agency and corporate bonds have even longer maturities.

High Yield

Zeros offer attractive and competitive yields when compared to coupon-paying instruments of similar rating and maturity. Higher yields are available if the investor is willing to assume higher credit risks.

Liquidity

There is a large and active secondary market for most Treasury and agency zeros. Corporate and municipal zeros are usually less marketable. Investors who might want, or have to, sell prior to maturity should restrict their purchases to Treasury-backed zeros.

TABLE 2. Current Value of a $1,000 Bond*

Years to Maturity	Yield to Maturity 7.5%	8%	8.5%	9%	9.5%	10%	10.5%	11%
30	$ 110	$ 95	$ 82	$ 71	$ 62	$ 54	$ 46	$ 40
29	114	103	89	78	68	59	51	45
28	127	111	97	85	74	65	57	50
27	137	120	106	93	82	72	63	56
26	147	130	115	101	90	79	70	62
25	159	141	125	111	98	87	77	69
24	171	152	136	121	108	96	86	77
23	184	165	147	132	118	106	95	85
22	198	178	160	144	130	117	105	95
21	213	193	174	157	142	129	117	106
20	229	208	189	172	156	142	129	117
19	247	225	206	188	171	157	143	131
18	266	244	223	205	188	173	159	146
17	287	264	243	224	206	190	176	162
16	308	285	264	245	227	210	194	180
15	332	308	287	267	249	231	215	201
14	357	333	312	292	273	255	239	223
13	384	361	339	318	299	281	264	249
12	414	390	368	348	328	310	293	277
11	445	422	400	380	360	342	324	308
10	480	456	435	415	395	377	359	343
9	516	494	473	453	434	416	398	381
8	555	534	514	494	476	458	441	425
7	597	577	558	540	522	505	489	473
6	643	625	607	590	573	557	541	526
5	692	676	660	644	629	614	600	585
4	745	731	717	703	690	677	664	652
3	802	790	779	768	757	746	736	725
2	863	855	847	839	831	823	815	807
1	930	925	920	916	911	907	903	899
0	1,000	1,000	1,000	1,000	1,000	1,000	1,000	1,000

*These values should be used as approximations.

Note: The current value of a $1,000 bond is at the intersection of its years to maturity and its yield to maturity.

Market and Credit Plays

Zeros appreciate faster in a bull bond market than do coupon paying bonds. Of course, the opposite is true in a bear market. The chart in Figure 1 traces price differences between the overall market (SECT 899)[1] and Treasury zeros due Nov. 15, 2012. The price ratio is almost similar in the spring of 1987 and fall of 1988 (despite a 5 percent decline in the overall market). An investor could have bought nine zero coupon bonds for every one overall unit. Note, however, interim swings in the price ratio. At the end of the bear bond market in October 1987, zeros had declined in price to the point where the investor could have purchased zeros on a 12.5 to 1 ratio. Subsequently, a sharp rally reduced the ratio to 8 to 1 by March 1988. Put another way, a 100 basis point reduction in yield (one percent) results in twice the appreciation for a twenty-year zero.

Similarly, changes in creditworthiness have a more volatile effect on price movement of zeros. Figure 2 traces the price ratio of BankAmerica Corp. zeros due June 22, 1993 versus the overall market (SECT 899). At the height of that bank's credit problems in May 1987, bond buyers could have bought 1.95 bonds for every one overall unit. Now, these zeros have appreciated such that the ratio is 1.56 to 1.00. Market and credit plays appeal to the sophisticated investor.

FIGURE 1. Shearson Price Ratio History Statistics for Treasury Zeros Due 2012

Source: Prepared by Shearson Lehman Hutton—Maps System

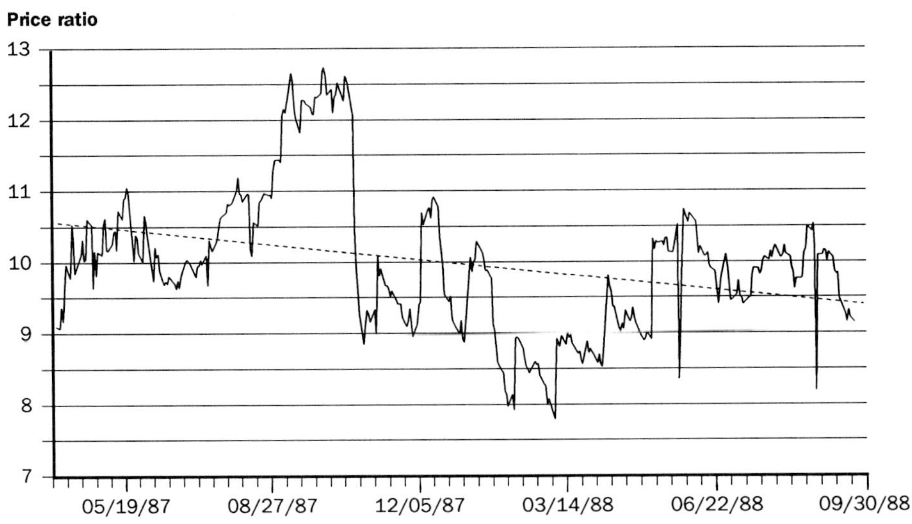

Ratio history: April 2, 1987 to September 12, 1988 (366 business days)

[1] SECT 899 refers to a selection by Shearson Lehman Hutton of taxable, investment grade bonds with average coupons, maturities and quality intended to replicate the general level of prices and yields.

FIGURE 2. Shearson Price Ratio History Statistics for Bank America Zeros Due 1993

Source: Prepared by Shearson Lehman Hutton—Maps System

Ratio history: April 2, 1987 to September 12, 1988 (366 business days)

POTENTIAL RISKS

Conservative investors should limit purchases to Treasury-backed zeros. Creditworthiness of corporate issuers can change dramatically before a long-term bond matures. In 1975, for instance, bonds of Beatrice Foods and Federated Department Stores received highest ratings possible (Aaa by Moody's and AAA by Standard & Poor's). Now, both companies receive speculative, below investment grade, ratings (Ba3/BB and B2/B).

Buyers of corporate zeros can mitigate effects of deterioration by owning senior debt of the issuer. Avoid junior debt or subordinated debentures. Another protective feature should be ascertained. Indentures of most corporate zeros contain a provision that in the event of default, the trustee may declare due and payable an amount equal to the sum of the initial public offering price plus the aggregate of the portions of the original issue discount accrued ratably since the date of issue. The underlying value of such zeros appreciates toward par, too.

Call Price

Most zeros are noncallable until maturity by the issuer, an attractive feature to the holder if interest rates fall sharply. However, some zeros are callable at their compound accreted value (CAV). (See *Tax Consequences*, later in this article, for discussion of CAV.) Buyers should not pay a price for a zero in excess of its call price.

TAX CONSEQUENCES

Taxable Bonds

For the vast majority of originally issued zero coupon bonds and stripped securities, the holder is taxed on interest income that accrues each year even though payment will not be received until maturity. Colloquially, this is termed "taxing phantom income." It results in a negative cash flow up to the point of sale or maturity. This tax aspect of zero coupon bonds makes these obligations attractive primarily to tax-qualified pension funds, including individual retirement accounts (IRAs) and Keogh accounts, that are neither subject to current income taxation nor concerned with current income.

The general rules for individual investors relating to original issue discount (OID) for obligations with a fixed maturity of greater than one year are discussed in this section. For many taxable bonds purchased at original issuance, an explanation of how to compute taxable OID can generally be found in IRS Publication 1212. In any regard, income tax laws and computations are complex. For specific information, your tax advisor should be consulted.

Stripped Taxable Bonds

Stripped bonds and stripped coupons include zero coupon instruments available either through the Department of the Treasury's STRIPS programs or through brokerage houses in the form of CATS, TIGRS, or stripped corporate bonds. For most taxpayers, the annual accreted (unpaid) discount on zero coupon strips must be reported as ordinary income each year. Total taxable income generated by a strip is the excess of the state redemption price at maturity over its purchase price. Taxable income is allocated between years using the constant interest method. Under this method, taxable income is equal to the holder's tax basis multiplied by the yield to maturity at the time of purchase. (It should be noted that the yield to maturity for bonds purchased prior to January 1, 1985 should be computed based on annual compounding. For bonds purchased after January 1, 1985, yield to maturity should be computed using semiannual compounding. To determine the appropriate yield to maturity, a broker should be consulted. A bondholder's original tax basis is the purchase price. It increases each year by the amount of previous accrued discount. The steps are shown below. For the sake of simplicity, annual compounding is assumed. The variations needed for semiannual compounding are shown in the next section.

1. *Taxable income (discount) in purchase year:*

   Purchase price × Yield to maturity × Number of days owned/365 = Income (discount) recognized in first year

Taxable income on all taxable zeros must be prorated based on the number of days or, in some cases, months owned during the taxable year.

2. *New tax basis computed on anniversary or purchase:*

   Purchase price + Income (discount) recognized in first year = New tax basis

3. *Taxable income in subsequent years:*

   (Old tax basis × Yield to maturity × Number of days to anniversary/365) + (New tax basis × Yield to maturity × Number of days from anniversary to year-end/365) = Taxable income in subsequent years

As an example, suppose an investor purchased a stripped U.S. Treasury bond for $350 on May 15, 1984. Assuming a redemption value of $1,000 on May 15, 1994, the annual yield to maturity is 11.069 percent. In the first year of ownership, the taxable income would be $24.52 ($350 × 11.069 percent × 231/365). In the second year of ownership, the taxable income would be $41.46 [($350 × 11.069% × 134/365)+ ($388.74 × 11.069% × 231/365)]. It should be noted that as the obligation matures, the compounding effect produces an increasing recognition of taxable income liability.

Original Issue Zeros

Corporate bonds originally issued as zero coupons and held in a taxable account receive different tax treatment based on the date of original issuance and whether the bond was purchased at original issuance or subsquently in secondary market trading. OID equals the excess of the stated redemption price over the original issue price. It may be split between one or more subsequent purchasers over the life of the bond. For bonds issued on or after July 2, 1982, the same method used in the computation of accrued interest for stripped zeros applies. However, in this incarnation of the constant interest method, the original issue yield to maturity replaces the purchaser's yield to maturity and the CAV, or adjusted issue price, replaces the holder's tax basis. CAV is the sum of the original issue price plus accrued OID for each year the investment has been outstanding.

The steps to follow for the constant interest method for annual compounding are presented in the previous section on strips. Slight adjustments should be made for semiannual compounding. (The yield to maturity for bonds issued prior to January 1, 1985 should be computed based on annual compounding. For bonds issued on or after January 1, 1985, compute the yield to maturity by using seminannual compounding.) To use the equation, simply replace the purchase yield to maturity with the original issue yield to maturity, the tax basis with the CAV, and the purchase anniversary date with the issuance anniversary date.

As an example, assume Acme Corporation issued a zero coupon bond priced at $376.89 to yield 10 percent (on a semiannual basis) on July 1, 1985. The redemption price of $1,000 will be paid on maturity on July 1, 1995. For original issue purchasers, 1985 taxable income is $18.84 ($376.89 × 10%/2 × 184/184). When using seminannual compounding, the CAV is adjusted on the six-month anniversary of issuance. The six-month compounding periods are measured in actual days. The new CAV on January 1, 1986 is $395.73 ($376.89 + 18.84). For the same bondholder, 1986 taxable income would be $40.56 ($395.73 × 10%/2 × 181/181) + ($415.52 × 10%/2 × 184/184). Again, taxable income increases with proximity to maturity.

If bonds issued on or after July 2, 1982 are purchased before July 18, 1984 at a premium to CAV, an acquisition premium, taxable income as computed under the **constant interest** method would be decreased by the premium allocated ratably among the accrual periods. If purchased at a premium on or after July 18, 1984, taxable income in future years would be reduced by the proportion of the premium paid to the amount of original issue discount remaining at the time of purchase. If bonds are purchased at the CAV, taxable income remains the same as computed under the original issue scenario.

Assume the same facts as in the previous example, except that the bonds were purchased on January 1, 1986 at $500, a premium of $104.27 to CAV. Recall that the OID is the redemption price ($1,000) less the original issue price ($376.89), or $623.11, and that

OID of $18.84 was realized in 1985. For the new bondholder, 1986 taxable income would be reduced by 17.26 percent ($104.27/(623.11 − $18.84)). This quantity represents current amortization of acquisition premium. Thus, 1986 taxable income would be $33.56 ($40.56 × (1 − 17.26%)).

If bonds issued prior to July 19, 1984 are purchased at a discount to CAV, the investor need not accrue this market discount, although OID income as computed under the original issue scenario must still be computed. Upon the bonds reaching maturity, the investor would recognize a capital gain equal to the market discount. If bonds issued subsequent to July 19, 1984 are purchased at a market discount, the investor may either defer recognition of market discount until redemption or disposition or accrue market discount, computed under constant interest method annually. Under the constant interest method, the investor amortizes the difference between the stated redemption price and the purchase price (OID and market discount) based on the yield to maturity at purchase. For bonds issued subsequent to July 19, 1984, market discount is treated as ordinary income at redemption or disposition.

The *straight-line method* is used for zero coupon bonds issued prior to July 2, 1982. Under this method, simply prorate the OID over the number of months from issuance to maturity using the following equation:

$$\text{OID} = \text{Number of months from issuance to maturity} \times \text{Number of months owned in taxable year}$$

Under this method, taxable income will be the same every year except for the years of issuance and sale or maturity.

As an example, assume Acme Corporation issued a zero coupon bond priced at $400 on January 1, 1982. The redemption value is $1,000 at maturity on January 1, 1992. The OID is $600 ($1,000 − $400), and 1987 taxable income for bondholders who purchased the bonds at original issue and held the bond for the entire year would be $60 ($600/120 × 12).

If bonds issued before July 2, 1982 are purchased at a premium to CAV, taxable income in future years as computed under the straight-line method will be decreased by a pro rata portion of the premium paid. If these bonds are purchased at the CAV or at a discount to CAV, taxable income remains the same as computed under the original issue scenario.

Assume the same facts as in the previous example, except that the bonds were purchased on January 1, 1987 at $800, a premium of $100 to CAV. (CAV is computed as the original issue price of $400 plus the sum of OID accruals to the date of purchase, or $300 (60 months × $60/12).) Taxable income in 1987 would be $40 ($60/12 − $100/60 months to maturity × 12 months).

Exceptions

There are a few exceptions to the general rule of taxing phantom income. For zero coupon bonds issued from 1954 to May 27, 1969, the holder pays no tax on accumulating interest until the year the instrument is sold, exchanged, or redeemed. As with all zero coupon bonds, including strips, if a gain on sale results, the portion attributable to interest is taxed as ordinary income to the seller. The balance of the gain is a capital gain to the seller, long or short term, based on the holding period. If proceeds from final disposition are less than the sum of the purchase price plus previously recognized OID, a loss may be recognized. For more details and legal opinions on any public debt issues, please refer to the prospectuses. Finally, if zero coupon bonds are held in a tax-deferred account, such as an IRA or Keogh, there is no tax liability until withdrawal.

REPRESENTATIVE TYPES OF INVESTORS

Individuals

Anyone wishing to build wealth for the future should consider investing in zero coupon bonds. An IRA, Keogh plan, or IRA rollover account is tax-deferred. Neither income nor principal is taxed until withdrawal. For most investors, withdrawal begins after the age 59½, when they are in a lower tax bracket.

Tax-Free Buyers

Individuals in high income brackets and high tax areas like New York State and New York City should consider municipal zeros, especially if they are additionally exempt from local taxes. Multiply available taxable yield by 100 percent less the effective marginal tax rate to see if a tax-free yield is attractive.

$$9.00\% \times (100\% - 30\%) = 6.30\%$$

Also, tax-free zeros are more appealing than most tax-deferred retirement vehicles, such as IRAs, which require tax payments upon distribution.

Custodial Accounts

Calculated amounts can be set aside for anticipated needs, such as college tuition, weddings, anniversaries, and retirement. The 1986 Tax Reform Act made this vehicle less attractive. Most income of a minor fourteen years old or younger is taxed at the parent's tax rate. Choose between taxable and tax-free zeros accordingly.

Insurance Companies

Portfolio managers use zeros to lock in yields versus liabilities of long duration. Policies with distant, lump-sum payments—single premium annuities, universal life, or whole life—can be met even if interest rates fall in the interim.

Pension and Profit-Sharing Accounts

This is another type of tax-advantage account. If beneficiaries prefer lump-sum distributions on specific future dates to current income, zeros are ideal.

IMPORTANT FACTORS IN BUYING AND SELLING

Diversification

Buy bonds of different issuers to spread credit risk. Buy bonds of different maturities in case a premature sale is necessary. Even small IRA investments of $2,000 per year can be spread over a number of sequential years.

Check Markets and Yields

Zeros are quoted daily in the financial pages of major newspapers under New York Exchange Bonds. Allied Corp. zeros are abbreviated to "AlldC zr92" in the *Wall Street Journal*, for example. Buyers should not pay higher prices than those established by this auction market. Often, bonds are available through brokers and dealer banks at cheaper prices. Shop around to get the best ratings at the lowest price.

GLOSSARY

acquisition premium—The excess of the purchase price over the issue price plus the portion of accrued OID for each year the investment has been outstanding.

call features—A provision in the bond indenture under which the issuing firm or governmental entity retains the right to retire the debt, fully or partially, before the scheduled maturity.

Certificates of Accrual on Treasury Securities (CATS)—U.S. Treasury obligations stripped of coupon and principal payments and packaged into bonds, generally by securities firms.

Certificates of Government Receipts (COUGARS)—Similar to Certificates of Accrual on Treasury Securities (CATS).

compound accreted value (CAV)—The sum of original issue price plus the portion of accrued OID for each year the investment has been outstanding.

issue price—When issued for cash the issue price is the initial offering price to the public. When not issued for cash, the issue price is the fair market value of property exchanged.

market discount—The excess of the issue price plus accreted income over the purchase price.

original issue discount (OID)—The excess of the stated redemption price at maturity over the issue price.

par value—The principal amount of a security that is to be repaid at maturity, generally $1,000.

separate trading of interest and principal of securities (STRIPS)—Obligations backed by U.S. Treasury bonds that are issued by the U.S. federal government.

Treasury Investment Growth Receipts (TIGRS)—Similar to Certificates of Accrual on Treasury Securities (CATS).

SUGGESTED READING

Douglas, Livingston G. *Yield Curve Analysis: The Fundamentals of Risk and Return*. New York: Simon & Schuster, Inc., 1988.

Internal Revenue Code, Sections 1221(1), 1232A(a)(6), 1272(a)(7)(B).

Internal Revenue Service Publication 1212.

Moody's Bond Record, page 1, published by Moody's Investors Service. Monthly

Panich, Richard L., and Purvis, S.E.C. "Amortization of Premium, Acquisition Premium and Market Discount," *The Tax Advisor*, Jan. 1988, p. 54.

Tax Reform Act of 1984, Sections 44(i)(1), 44(i)(2).

INVESTMENT STRATEGY

MODERN PORTFOLIO THEORY

Marshall E. Blume

The primary reason for saving and investing is to provide for future obligations or desires. A husband and wife may invest funds to provide for their retirement or their children's education, or a corporation may set up a pension fund to provide for the payments of its future pension obligations.

In addition, some investments, such as housing and collectibles, provide not only potential monetary gains but also services that are of value to an investor. This article is primarily concerned with the construction of desirable portfolios in terms of potential monetary gains. Most of the material was prepared under the assumption that a dollar of return from one asset is just as valuable as a dollar of return from any other asset.

Portfolio theory deals with ways of combining assets into portfolios so as to provide for one's future obligations in the best possible way. Any portfolio has associated with it an expected return as well as the potential risk of not realizing this expectation. The section *Rewards and Risks* describes the concept and measurement of expected returns and risk, and demonstrates that the risk characteristics of a portfolio as a whole can differ substantially from the risk characteristics of the component assets. Specifically, a portfolio can be of very low risk even though each component asset, judged by itself, is of very high risk.

Currently, it is in vogue to associate principles of portfolio theory with the term "modern portfolio theory" (MPT), as if there is a substantive difference between portfolio theory of old and of new. In fact, the basic principles of constructing portfolios are not new. What is new is that, following the theoretical contributions of Harry Markowitz in

---

Marshall E. Blume is Howard Butcher Professor of Finance at the Wharton School, University of Pennsylvania, Philadelphia.

the early 1950s, it has been possible to model the process of selecting a portfolio into a very precise mathematical form.

This ability to mathematically model the portfolio selection process has led, at the theoretical level, to a much better understanding of the relationship of expected returns of individual assets to their underlying risks and, at the practical level, to the development of new quantitative techniques for investment analysis. Perhaps the most widely known tool developed from MPT is the beta coefficient for individual assets. Beta coefficients, risk measures for individual assets, are widely available to the investing public, at least for common stocks, through such publications as *Value Line*. Beta coefficients measure the relative contribution of different assets to the risk of a well-diversified portfolio. The greater the beta coefficient of an asset, the more the asset will contribute to the overall risk of a well-diversified portfolio.

This article applies the basic principles of MPT to the practical problem of how to allocate one's wealth over the available assets, using the portfolio optimization procedures developed by the Rodney L. White Center of Financial Research at the Wharton School. These procedures were developed by a joint effort of the Center and several of its corporate members. This analysis documents the trade-off for optimal portfolios between expected returns and the level of risk and explores the factors that should be weighed in determining the specific level of risk.

Along with an intuitive but fairly thorough discussion of portfolio theory and its implications for optimal investment strategies, there is a brief examination of what investors actually do. Although many portfolios are constructed in substantial conformity to the precepts of MPT, a large number of portfolios probably expose investors to unnecessary or undesirable risks. As is true in many endeavors, theory and practice are not always the same.

REWARDS AND RISKS

The primary reason for investing is to provide for future obligations or desires over a long period of time. Nonetheless, MPT generally concentrates on results over the short term, such as a year or even a month. Under certain assumptions that are appropriate for many investors, such a concentration on near-term results is warranted. However, for some investors, such as life insurance companies, the investment process is considerably more complicated, and such investors are concerned with more than just short-term results. Investors with a heavy commitment to real estate and, perhaps, collectibles may face a problem that is conceptually similar to that faced by life insurance companies.

Measuring Risk

The usual applications of MPT assume that risk can be measured over the short term, by volatility, typically measured over a one- to twelve-month period. This concentration on the short term is often compatible with a long-term or multi-year investment horizon, because the long term is nothing more than a series of short terms.

However, the specific level of short-term volatility to which an investor exposes himself is dictated by long-term considerations. Thus, an investor who is saving for retirement and wants to be fairly certain of reaching his goals would generally expose himself to a fairly low level of volatility in the near term. He wants no unpleasant surprises. In contrast, an investor who has little current wealth but wishes to accumulate a large amount of wealth may be willing to assume substantial short-term risks. Substantial short-term risks generally imply substantial long-term risks of not meeting one's goals.

A Common Misconception

There is a misconception, most frequently espoused in booming markets, that an investor with a long-term horizon should invest in portfolios with higher short-term expected returns (so-called growth portfolios), even though such portfolios entail greater short-term volatility. The logic underlying this misconception is that short-term fluctuations in the value of a portfolio will somehow wash out in the long term. Nothing could be further from the truth. A study of all stocks on the New York Stock Exchange from July 1928 through June 1968 found that the stocks with the greatest increase in value over these forty years were those with moderate risk in the short term and that both the lowest-risk and highest-risk stocks had lesser increases in value.[1] This finding is consistent with expectations for the lowest-risk stocks, but not consistent with those for the highest-risk stocks.

Besides this empirical evidence, there is a strong theoretical presumption that, if a portfolio with greater expected short-term rates of return has greater short-term volatility, this same portfolio will also have greater long-term volatility. Assume for the moment that this is not the case, so that an investor could be assured of a greater level of wealth in the long term, say ten to twenty years, by investing in a portfolio of assets with greater short-term volatility as well as greater expected returns. What would happen? Because most investments are made to satisfy long-term obligations or desires, there would be an immediate stampede toward the purchase of those assets with greater short-term volatility, in view of the certainty of greater rewards in the long term. Such purchases presumably would be financed by the sale of assets with lesser short-term volatility. The immediate effect would be to drive up the prices of those assets with the greater short-term volatility, thereby reducing their future expected returns. Similarly, as investors sold assets with lesser volatility, the prices of these latter assets would drop, thereby increasing their future expected returns. This process would continue until there was no longer certainty that growth portfolios would out-return other portfolios in the long term.

If there is a positive relation between short-term volatility and short-term expected returns, one would expect a similar relation in the long term, but there is no guarantee that expectations will be realized. Indeed, the differences between expectations and realizations are sometimes large.

In sum, the long term is nothing more than a series of short terms. An investor who does well in each short-term period automatically will do well in the long term. For instance, consider two bond managers who are each given $10 million to invest. Assume that the first manager judges long-term interest rates to be at their peak and thus commits the entire $10 million to long-term bonds. Assume further that the second manager feels that long-term interest rates will be at their peak in a year and thus commits the money to one-year governments.

If the second manager is correct, his portfolio will realize a greater return over the year than the portfolio of the first manager. To be concrete, assume that the portfolio of the second manager, with re-investment of interest, is worth $11.5 million at the end of the year and that of the first manager is worth $10 million—a difference of 15 percent. If, at

1 Marshall E. Blume and Irwin Friend, "Risk, Investment Strategy and the Long-Run Rates of Return," *The Review of Economics and Statistics*, Vol. 56, No. 3, Aug. 1974. 259–269.

the end of the year, the second manager, invests the appreciated portfolio in the same kind of long-term bonds as the first, the subsequent returns of both managers will be similar. For purposes of argument, assume that their subsequent returns are the same. No matter how many years the two managers are retained, the value of the portfolio of the second manager will always be 15 percent greater than that of the first manager's portfolio.[2]

Investors With Long-Term Horizons

Despite this argument, it is sometimes felt that for an investor with a long-term horizon bonds are not risky, even though the market value of a bond does fluctuate over its life. If interest rates increase, the market price of a long-term bond will drop; nonetheless, the price ultimately will increase as the bond approaches maturity. If a bond's return in the first part of its life is less than expected, the return in the second part will be greater than expected as the market price of the bond increases to its redemption value.

There is no empirical evidence that stocks have this property. The fact that a stock has not performed up to expectations in one year has virtually no bearing on how it will perform in the following year.

This trait of a bond of "remembering," where its price has been and where its price must go by maturity may be extremely important to a life insurance company, but is probably not very important to most other types of investors. A primary difference between a life insurance company and a typical investor is that a life insurance company deals in nominal dollars, whereas the typical investor is more concerned with real dollars. In other words, the life insurance company is concerned with the number of dollars available to it and not what they will buy; a typical investor is interested in what the dollars will buy.

A life insurance company may be able to estimate with a high degree of accuracy the total number of policyholders who will die in a given year and thus the dollar amount of its liability. By buying an appropriate portfolio of bonds, the insurance company can be certain of having this estimated number of dollars at a designated point in the future. In the terminology of the investment world, such portfolios are "immunized." A life insurance company may be willing to trade off some degree of immunization in order to obtain a greater expected short-term return; the degree to which a life insurance company deviates from a fully immunized strategy hinges on regulatory considerations, the competitive market for life insurance policies, and the risk tolerance of the company relative to its other goals.

The Nature of the Investor's Liabilities

The key to the difference between a life insurance company and the more typical investor lies in the nature of the investor's liabilities and goals. Those investors whose liabilities are in nominal dollars will be concerned with more than just short-term volatility and short-term expected returns. Such investors will also have to consider the potential for an asset to "remember" that it has to have good returns following poor returns.

In contrast, the liabilities of most investors, including most corporations with defined-benefit pension plans, are more closely tied to real dollars. The certainty of receiving a fixed-dollar amount at some point in the future is not really relevant to these more usual

[2] The annual compounded rates of return for the two portfolios will approach each other, but the second portfolio manager's annual compounded rate of return will always be sufficiently greater than that of the first to produce a difference in wealth of 15 percent.

types of investors. By the time the payment will be received, the liability may well have changed. The best way for an investor to discharge such a changing liability is to concentrate on doing the best job possible in each short-term period.

If, however, there are assets available that pay an amount fixed in real terms at some future date, short-term volatility will no longer be an adequate measure of risk to the usual investor whose liabilities are in real dollars. Such assets provide a hedge if inflation turns out to be greater than anticipated. Are there assets available to the typical investor that would provide such a hedge? Bonds and stocks are not good hedges if inflation turns out to be greater than anticipated. In fact, bonds behave opposite to what one would want in a hedge, and the returns on stocks, at least in the United States, have shown little relationship to inflation. If there is any relationship, it is an almost negligible, negative one.

There is evidence that private residential real estate has been a hedge against the unanticipated increases in inflation rates, but even so its realized returns have sometimes differed by large amounts from what would be anticipated from inflation.[3] In the late 1970s, a period of rapid inflation, private residential real estate in some parts of the country had spectacular returns. In the 1980s, the returns on private residential real estate nationwide just kept pace with inflation, but with wide regional differences. In view of the diverse returns in different parts of the country, only part of the returns on real estate are attributable to inflation, with local conditions playing a major role. If an investor is considering a substantial commitment to real estate, he has to take into account not only the short-term expected returns and risks, but also the capability of the portfolio to hedge against realized inflation rates.

Portfolios

A portfolio of assets has characteristics quite different from those of the individual assets. To visualize the potential metamorphosis of a portfolio, commonly called diversification, consider the following stylized example: Asset A has a 50 percent probability of returning 40 percent on the original investment and a 50 percent probability of losing 10 percent. Thus, on a flip of a coin, the return on asset A will be either 40 percent or -10 percent. Because roughly half of the time, the return on the asset will be 40 percent and, the other half, the return, -10 percent, the return expected on average would be 0.5×40 percent $+ 0.5 \times -10$ percent, or 15 percent. Asset B has a 50 percent probability of returning 40 percent and a 50 percent probability of returning -10 percent. The expected return is 15 percent, the same as that of asset A.

Although most investors probably do not conceive of an asset or a portfolio of assets as a lottery, an investment is actually just that. For a fixed amount of money, an investor buys the right to potential returns, to each of which he could assign a probability. By viewing investments as lotteries, it becomes easier to separate the uncertainty, or risk, from the expected return. An investment in a U.S. Treasury bill has no risk attached to it if one holds it to maturity and is concerned only with nominal dollars. Likewise, an investment in the Pennsylvania State Lottery has very little risk attached to it. The potential risk is almost certainly -100 percent, which removes most of the uncertainty associated with

[3] Eugene F. Fama, and G. William Schwert, "Asset Returns and Inflation," *Journal of Financial Economics*, Vol. 5, No. 2, Nov. 1977, pp. 115–146. This is the seminal study. A more recent study is Joseph Gyourko and Peter Linneman, "Owner-Occupied Homes, Income-Producing Properties, and REITs as Inflation Hedges: Empirical Findings," *Journal of Real Estate Finance and Economics*, Vol. 1, 1988, pp. 347–372.

such an investment. Of course, most investors, given the choice of a state lottery or a government bill, will choose the bill because it has a greater expected (and, in this case, certain) return.

Now let's form a portfolio of assets A and B, with an equal amount invested in each. The expected return will be the average of the expected return on each of the two assets, or 15 percent. The uncertainty of return, or volatility, will hinge on the correlation of the returns of the two assets and will be smaller, the smaller the correlation.

Correlation of One

Consider that whenever asset A has a return of 40 percent, asset B has a return of 40 percent; and whenever asset A has a return of − 10 percent, asset B has a return of − 10 percent. In this case, the returns on assets A and B are said to be perfectly positively correlated; the correlation coefficient is 1.0. In this scenario, the possible outcomes associated with the portfolio of these two assets are as follows:

	Return		
Probability	A	B	Portfolio Return
50%	40%	40%	40%
50	− 10	− 10	− 10

The distribution of the returns of the portfolio is identical to the distribution of the returns of either asset. Thus, the expected return will still be 15 percent and the level of volatility unchanged. This example illustrates the general proposition that diversification among assets whose returns are perfectly correlated does not reduce the volatility of the portfolio.

Correlation of Zero

If, however, returns are not perfectly correlated, diversification will generally reduce volatility. Consider, for instance, the case in which there is no relationship between the returns on assets A and B. Even if the return on asset A is 40 percent, there is an equal probability of obtaining either 40 percent or − 10 percent on asset B. In this case, the returns on the two assets are said to be uncorrelated; the correlation coefficient is 0.

The possible outcomes with the corresponding probabilities would be as follows:

	Return		
Probability	A	B	Portfolio Return
25%	40%	40%	40%
25	40	− 10	15
25	− 10	40	15
25	− 10	− 10	10

Under the assumed lack of correlation, each possible combination of returns on assets A and B is equally likely, implying a probability of 25 percent for each combination. The expected return is 15 percent, given as the sum of 0.25 × 40 percent + 0.50 × 15 percent + 0.25 × − 10 percent.

A comparison of the case of zero correlation with the prior case of perfect positive correlation discloses that the expected return on the two portfolios is unchanged, indicating that the magnitude of the correlation between the returns on the two assets has no effect on the portfolio's expected return. This property holds for any level of correlation and will be generalized subsequently to the case in which the two assets have different expected returns.

However, the uncertainty, or volatility, of the portfolio has changed drastically. In the case of perfect positive correlation, the volatility of the portfolio was unchanged from the volatility of the individual assets. In the case of zero correlation, the volatility of the portfolio is less than the volatility of either asset alone. There is now only a 25 percent probability of losing 10 percent, in contrast to the 50 percent probability for each asset. Unfortunately, the probability of making 40 percent has also been reduced. In general, diversification, through the formation of a portfolio, reduces the probability of obtaining extreme values—both favorable and unfavorable.

Correlation of Minus One

Finally, consider the case in which, whenever the return on asset A is 40 percent, the return on asset B is −10 percent, and whenever the return on asset A is −10 percent, the return on asset B is 40 percent. In this case, the returns on assets A and B are said to be perfectly negatively correlated; the correlation coefficient is −1.0.

The possible outcomes with the corresponding probabilities would be as follows:

	Return		
Probability	A	B	Portfolio Return
50%	40%	10%	15%
50	− 10	40	15

The portfolio has a certain return of 15 percent, which in a trivial sense is also the expected return. The loss on one of the assets is always fully offset by the gain on the other. In this extreme case, diversification has transformed two volatile assets into a risk-free asset.

Although this example is highly stylized, it does contain the essence of how the volatility of a portfolio can be substantially different from the volatility of the component assets. What is happening is that there is an averaging effect, except for the case of perfect positive correlation. A poor return on one asset is not always associated with a poor return on another asset, and, in the case of perfect negative correlation, the poor return on one asset is exactly offset by the favorable return on the other.[4]

[4] The case of perfect negative correlation plays a critical role in the Black-Scholes option formula. The basic assumption underlying this formula in the case of calls is that the return on the option in an instantaneous period is perfectly positively correlated with the return on the underlying security in the same period. If the price of the underlying security rises, so will the option. In a short position, because the sign of the return is the opposite of the return on the long position, Black and Scholes have observed that in an instantaneous period, the correlation between the return from a short position in a call option and the return from a long position in the underlying stock would be −1. They then determine appropriate investment weights for the short position and the long position such that the returns on the short position that are greater than or less than expected are exactly offset by the returns on the long position. Thus, they have created a risk-free asset whose returns must be the same as the risk-free rate to prevent arbitrage. Using this equality, they derive their option pricing formula.

Standard Deviation

The previous examples illustrate the role of the correlation coefficient in determining the volatility of a portfolio of two assets. These examples are highly stylized in that the expected return and volatility of the individual assets are the same. In practice, the equality of these two statistics across assets would be most unusual. The purpose of this section is to examine the more realistic case in which these two characteristics are not identical.

To accomplish this purpose, it is necessary to propose an explicit measure of volatility. Although there are numerous measures of short-term volatility, MPT usually utilizes the standard deviation of return, which is frequently designated by the lowercase Greek letter σ. Sometimes to refer to a specific portfolio or asset, A, for example, the letter is subscripted by A, as σ_A.

An Interpretation

If returns on assets or portfolios are approximately distributed by a normal distribution, the standard deviation has a very useful interpretation. Most people are familiar with a normal distribution, although perhaps not by that name. The bell-shaped curve that educators sometimes use to curve test scores around a C is approximately a normal curve. The number of B grades is the same as the number of D grades and less than the number of C grades. In turn, the number of A grades is the same as the number of F grades and less than the number of B or D grades.

Although returns of assets or portfolios are not exactly described by a normal distribution, the approximation is probably good enough to permit the following interpretation of the standard deviation within the context of this distribution: The interval formed by adding and subtracting one standard deviation from the expected return will bracket roughly two-thirds of the possible outcomes. Thus, if the standard deviation is on an annual basis, 15 percent, and the expected return is 10 percent, it would be anticipated that on average, in two out of every three years, the actual return would be between -5 percent and 25 percent. A fair bet that the actual return next year will be between -5 percent and 25 percent will have odds of 1 to 2. The odds are 5 to 1 that the return will be in excess of 25 percent and also 5 to 1 that the return will be less than -5 percent. These odds are approximate but close enough to be useful in evaluating the uncertainty associated with different possible portfolios.

Bracketing the expected return by two standard deviations results in an interval that covers approximately 95 percent of the possible outcomes. Thus, there is a 95 percent chance that the actual return next year will be between -20 percent and 40 percent.

The figures in Table 1 are annualized standard deviations for well-diversified portfolios of different kinds of common stocks and high-grade corporate bonds. These numbers were estimated over two different time periods. To interpret these numbers, consider high-grade long-term corporate bonds with a standard deviation of 12.6 percent for the 1945 to 1987 period. If a return of 10 percent on such bonds were expected, there is roughly a two-thirds probability that the actual return fell in the interval -2.6 percent to 22.6 percent, 10 percent ± 12.6

General Conclusions

Some general conclusions can be made about the relationship between the expected return and the standard deviation of return of a portfolio of assets and the expected returns

TABLE 1. Standard Deviations of Annual Returns for Selected Portfolios

Asset	Estimation Period	
	1945–1987	1978–1987
S&P index	17.6	17.7
Low capitalization NYSE stocks	29.6	30.4
High-grade long-term corporate bonds	12.6	21.2

and standard deviations of the component assets. If short sales are not permitted, the following two statements are true:

1. The expected return on a portfolio of assets is the weighted average of the expected returns on the individual assets, where each weight is the proportion of wealth invested in each asset.

2. The standard deviation of return on a portfolio of assets is equal to or less than the weighted average of the standard deviations of the individual assets, where the weights are the proportions of wealth invested in each asset. The portfolio standard deviation will be strictly less than the weighted average of the individual standard deviations in the usual case in which the correlation between any pair of assets is less than one and non-zero investments are made in each asset.

As an example, if an investor places one third of his wealth in a portfolio with an expected return of 9 percent and a standard deviation of 10 percent, and two thirds of his wealth in a portfolio with an expected return of 12 percent and a standard deviation of 20 percent, the investor's portfolio will have an expected return of 11 percent and a standard deviation of, at most, 16.6 percent. The expected return of 11 percent is given by the sum of one third of 9 percent and two thirds of 12 percent. The maximum standard deviation of 16.6 percent is given by the sum of one third of 10 percent and two thirds of 20 percent. The smaller the correlation coefficient between the two assets or portfolios, the smaller the standard deviation of the portfolio return for fixed levels of investment in each asset.

THE BASIC PRINCIPLES OF PORTFOLIO THEORY

The use of MPT to select an optimal portfolio of assets entails two steps of analysis. The first step is to determine the set of portfolios of risky assets that, for a given risk, maximize the expected return and, for a given expected return, minimize risk. Risky assets are any assets whose returns in the short term are uncertain, such as stocks or long-term bonds. This set of portfolios is called the efficient set of risky assets. The second step is to select one of these risky portfolios to be held in conjunction with an investment in risk-free assets. Risk-free assets are short-term, readily marketable securities of the highest grade. U.S. Treasury bills are one obvious candidate, although some investors might be willing to consider certificates of deposit of the most stable commercial banks, commercial paper of prime grade, or certain, but not all, money market funds as risk-free. In describing these two steps, it is assumed that the investor is willing to utilize the standard deviation of annual returns as the measure of risk.

The Efficient Set of Risky Assets

To simplify the exposition, consider an investor who has already selected a bond portfolio and a stock portfolio for possible investment, but has not yet determined how much to invest in each. Although highly simplifed, this example parallels the decision process of many investors with substantial assets. In investing its pension fund, a corporation may have interviewed a group of bond managers and a group of stock managers and, based on these interviews, selected a bond manager and a stock manager without determining exactly how much money to invest with each.

Although this procedure is more often followed by large investors, it is not a bad procedure for small investors. Thus, a small investor might select for potential investment a mutual fund specializing in bonds and one specializing in common stocks. If feasible, the investor might select several mutual funds of each type in order to diversify management styles.

Moreover, although this text refers to bond and stocks these categories are in fact much more general than may appear at first sight. A mortgage participation is really a bond in disguise, and an equity participation is in some ways similar to stock. Thus, the essential difference between the two funds to be examined here is that one must be of relatively low risk and the other of relatively high risk, so as to cover assets of all types of risk.

Assume that the bond fund is of moderate maturity and that its expected annual return is one percent greater than the rate on risk-free assets and that its standard deviation is 7 percent. Thus, if risk-free assets are returning 7 percent, the expected return on the bond fund is 8 percent. Further assume that the expected return on the stock fund is 6 percent greater than the rate on risk-free assets and that the standard deviation of the stock fund is 21 percent.

Investing in Bonds and Stocks

The bond fund and the stock fund have been plotted in the expected return-standard deviation space in Figure 1. The stock fund is plotted upward and to the right of the bond fund, reflecting both its greater expected return and its greater standard deviation.

Now consider a portfolio consisting of investments in both the bond and the stock funds. Specifically, let 80 percent of the available funds be invested in the bond fund and the remaining 20 percent in the stock fund. As already pointed out, the expected return on the combined portfolio will be a weighted average of the expected return on the bond fund and the expected return on the stock fund. The combined portfolio will have an expected return of 2 percent in excess of the risk-free rate, given as the result of 0.8×1 percent $+0.2 \times 6$ percent.

The standard deviation of the return on the combined portfolio will depend on the correlation between the returns on the bond fund and the returns on the stock fund. If the returns are perfectly positively correlated with a correlation of 1.0, the standard deviation of the return on the combined portfolio will be a weighted average of the standard deviation of the component portfolios, 0.8×7 percent $+0.2 \times 21$ percent, or 9.8 percent. The reason the standard deviation is a weighted average is that, with perfect positive

FIGURE 1. Bond and Stock Portfolios and Combination Portfolios

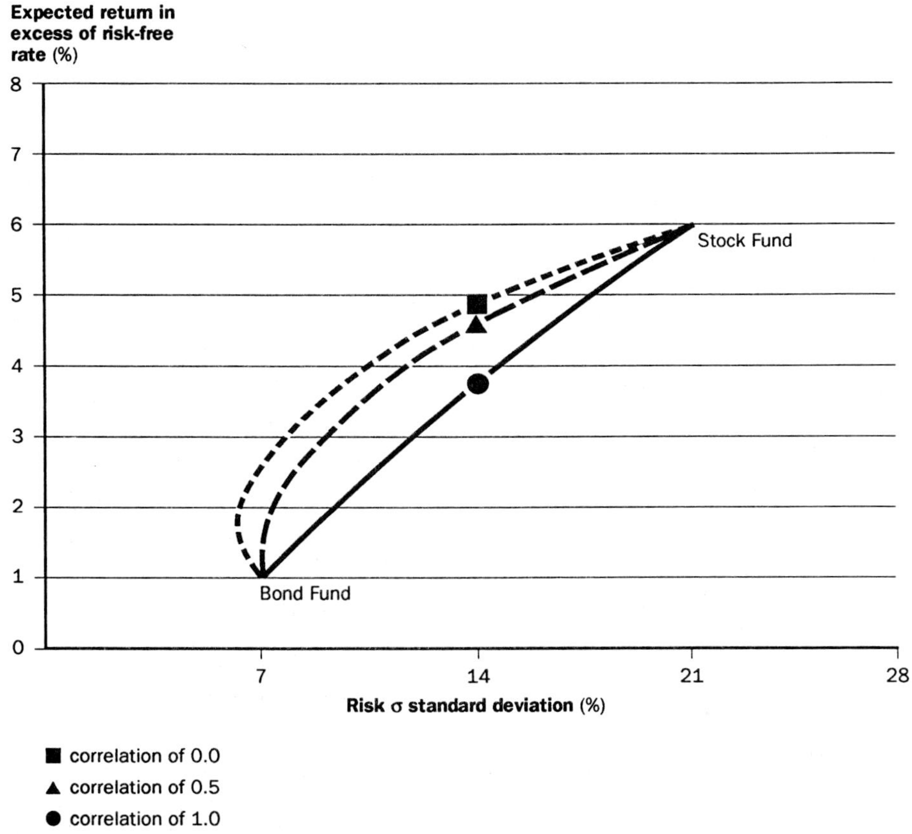

correlation, there is no averaging or diversification effect. When one portfolio does poorly, the other portfolio also does poorly.

If the correlation between the returns of the two portfolios is smaller than 1.0, the portfolio return will reflect some averaging or diversification effects. A poor return on one portfolio may be partially offset by a favorable return on the other. The smaller the correlation, the more likely the averaging effect. Figure 1 contains two examples of correlations smaller than 1.0. If 80 percent is placed in the bond portfolio, the expected return will always be 2 percent in excess of the risk-free rate, regardless of the correlation.

More generally, if the correlation is 0.5, a positive but weak correlation, an investor who initially had 100 percent invested in bonds and who then began to switch into stocks would first see the expected return increase at a faster rate than the increase in standard deviation. At some point in this process, the increase in expected return would be at a rate slower than the increase in standard deviation.

If the correlation is 0, as the investment in bonds decreased from 100 percent, an investor would initially see the expected return increase; at the same time, the standard deviation would actually decrease from 7 percent. The averaging or diversification effect is so strong that it overcomes the inherent volatility of the component funds. At some point in this process, the standard deviation of the combined portfolio will increase from the minimum possible value as the volatility of the stock portfolio outweighs the diversification effect.

In this last case, note that an investor would never want to hold just the bond fund. By combining the bond fund with the stock fund, the investor can obtain a greater expected return at the same risk as the bond fund. Thus, if the correlation is 0, the investor would not want to hold a portfolio with 100 percent in bonds.

"Efficient Portfolio" Defined

Portfolios of risky assets that no investor would want to hold constitute the inefficient set of portfolios of risky assets. The set of portfolios that some investors may want to hold is termed the efficient set. Portfolios in the efficient set have the property that, for a given standard deviation, the expected return is maximized and, for a given level of expected return, the standard deviation is minimized.

Frequently, an investor considers more than just a single bond fund and a single stock fund as components of his risky portfolio. Figure 2 illustrates this more general case, assuming that no two assets are perfectly correlated. The edges and the shaded area represent every feasible portfolio, but the efficient set would consist only of those portfolios on the heavy line. No investor would want to hold a portfolio off this line.

Although calculating the efficient set requires a computer, except in the simplest cases, the concept of the efficient set has an important implication for money management. An investment advisor does not need to know the objectives of his clients in order to construct desirable portfolios of risky assets. Basically, for any given level of risk, he wants to maximize expected return. The goals of the client enter into determining which efficient portfolio to hold.

This concept of the efficient set underlies the marketing strategy of families of mutual funds or of bank commingled funds. For mutual funds, a family might have a growth, a growth-income, an income-growth, and an income fund. The growth fund is presumably the most risky; the growth-income, the next risky; the income-growth, the next risky; and the income, the least risky. The investment advisor would try to obtain the greatest level of expected return for each of these risks. The goals of the client help determine which fund or combination of funds should be held.

Thus, investments do not have to be managed separately to satisfy the goals of an investor. This observation is important for an investor who is considering whether his funds should be managed in separate accounts, in a mutual fund, or in a bank commingled fund. The critical question in solving this problem is: Which approach promises the greatest expected return for a given level of risk?

The Role of the Risk-Free Asset

Investments in a risk-free asset play a central role in MPT. Such investments permit an investor to modify the risk of a risky portfolio to the level of risk with which he is comfortable. Particularly for investors who do not wish to bear a great amount of risk, the judicious use of an investment in the risk-free asset can frequently lead to a substantial increase in expected return with no increase in overall risk. This point is examined below.

FIGURE 2. The Efficient Set of Risky Assets

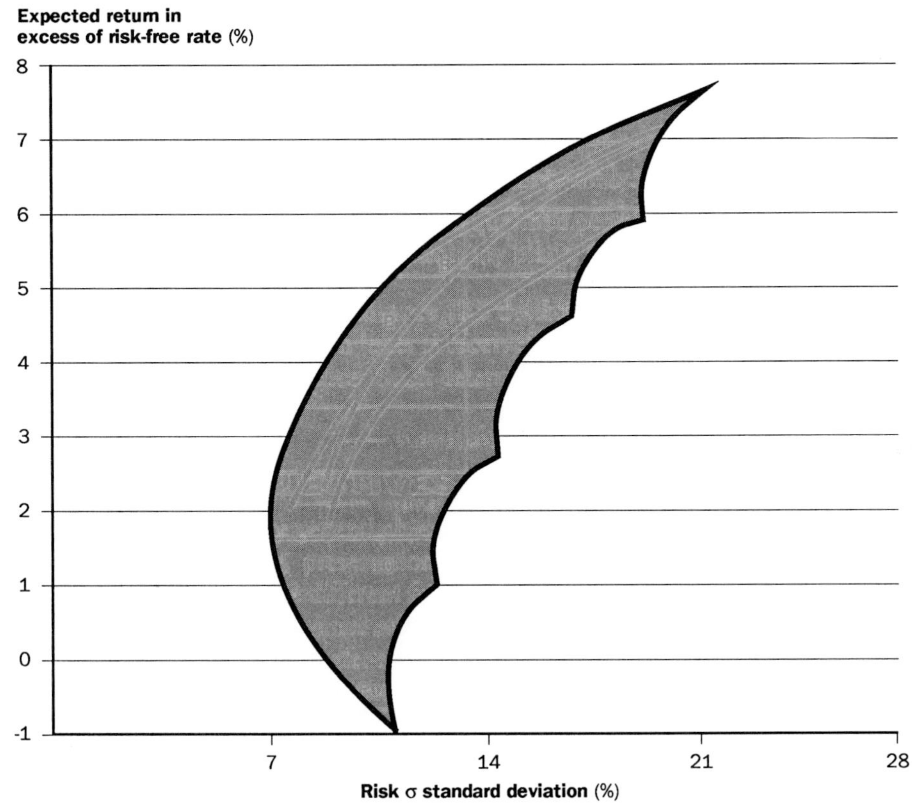

Illustrative Example

Consider asset A, which above was assumed to have an equal probability of realizing 40 percent or losing 10 percent. An investor might well judge the expected return of 15 percent quite attractive relative to the volatility or uncertainty associated with the investment, but at the same time feel that the risk is too great for his particular situation.

By placing a portion of the money in asset A and the remainder in the risk-free asset, the investor could obtain a portfolio with an overall level of risk lower than that of asset A alone. If the risk-free rate is 10 percent and the investor places 60 percent of his wealth in asset A with the remaining 40 percent in the risk-free asset, he would obtain the following possible outcomes, each equally likely:

Probability	Return A	Portfolio Return
50%	40%	0.6(40) + 0.4(10) = 28%
50%	− 10%	0.60 (−10) + 0.4(10) = − 2%

The expected return is 13 percent, given by the sum of 0.05 × 28 percent + 0.50 × −2 percent. The maximum loss is now 2 percent instead of 10 percent.

Although the range of outcomes is not as satisfactory a measure of risk as the standard deviation for types of investments encountered in real life, it is a reasonable measure for lotteries with two outcomes, each having the same probability. The range of returns for asset A is 50 percentage points, and the range for the combined portfolio is 30 percentage points.

The expected return of 13 percent is 60 percent of the difference between 10 percent and 15 percent, or 10 percent plus 60 percent of the difference between 15 and 10 percent. Likewise, the range of 30 percent is 60 percent of the range of asset A. If standard deviations are calculated, the standard deviation of the combined portfolio would likewise be 60 percent of the standard deviation of asset A. These linear relationships are not an accident and will occur when any risky asset or portfolio is combined with an investment in the risk-free asset. An investment in a risk-free asset in conjunction with an investment in a risky portfolio provides no averaging or diversification effects, only a straightforward risk-reduction effect.

This linear relationship between expected returns and standard deviations is illustrated in Figure 3. The risky asset or portfolio is taken to be the stock fund used in the last section with an assumed expected return in excess of the risk-free rate of 6 percent and a standard deviation of 21 percent. If an investor wants a portfolio with two thirds of the volatility of the stock fund, he can invest two thirds of his assets in the stock fund and one third in the risk-free asset. The resulting standard deviation is 14 percent, and the expected return in excess of the risk-free rate, 4 percent. This portfolio is designated *b* in Figure 3.

If the investor feels that such an expected return is not great enough to justify assuming a standard deviation of 14 percent, he might further reduce the risk of his overall portfolio by placing only one third of the assets in the risky portfolio. Such a portfolio, designated by point *a* in Figure 3, has a standard deviation of 7 percent and an expected return in excess of the risk-free rate of 2 percent.

Although most institutional investors are usually concerned with reducing the overall risk, some investors increase the risk of their overall portfolios in pursuit of a greater expected return. Individuals who have margin accounts are effectively utilizing a short position in a risk-free asset to lever their risky portfolios. A short position in a risk-free asset is equivalent to borrowing at the risk-free rate. If the borrowing and lending rates are the same, an investor can move a portfolio up the dotted line in Figure 3. At point *c* in Figure 3, the investor's overall portfolio has a standard deviation of 31.5 percent and an expected return in excess of the risk-free rate of 9 percent. Assuming a net worth of $100, to obtain portfolio *c*, an investor borrows $50 and, combined with the initial $100, then invests $150 in the risky portfolio. As long as the realized return of the risky portfolio is greater than the risk-free rate, this leverage increases his total realized return; but, if the realized return is less this leverage decreases his total realized return.

The assumption in Figure 3 is that the risk-free borrowing and lending rates are identical. In fact, the borrowing rate is usually in excess of the lending rate. The effect is to reduce the increase in expected return from leveraging a portfolio. However, there is no effect on the standard deviation of the levered portfolio. Thus, the investor with a net worth of $100 who borrows at, say, 3 percentage points above the risk-free lending rate to finance an investment of $150 in the stock portfolio has an expected return in excess of the risk-free rate of 7.5 percent and a standard deviation of 31.5 percent. Such a portfolio is

FIGURE 3. The Use of the Risk-Free Rate to Alter Risk

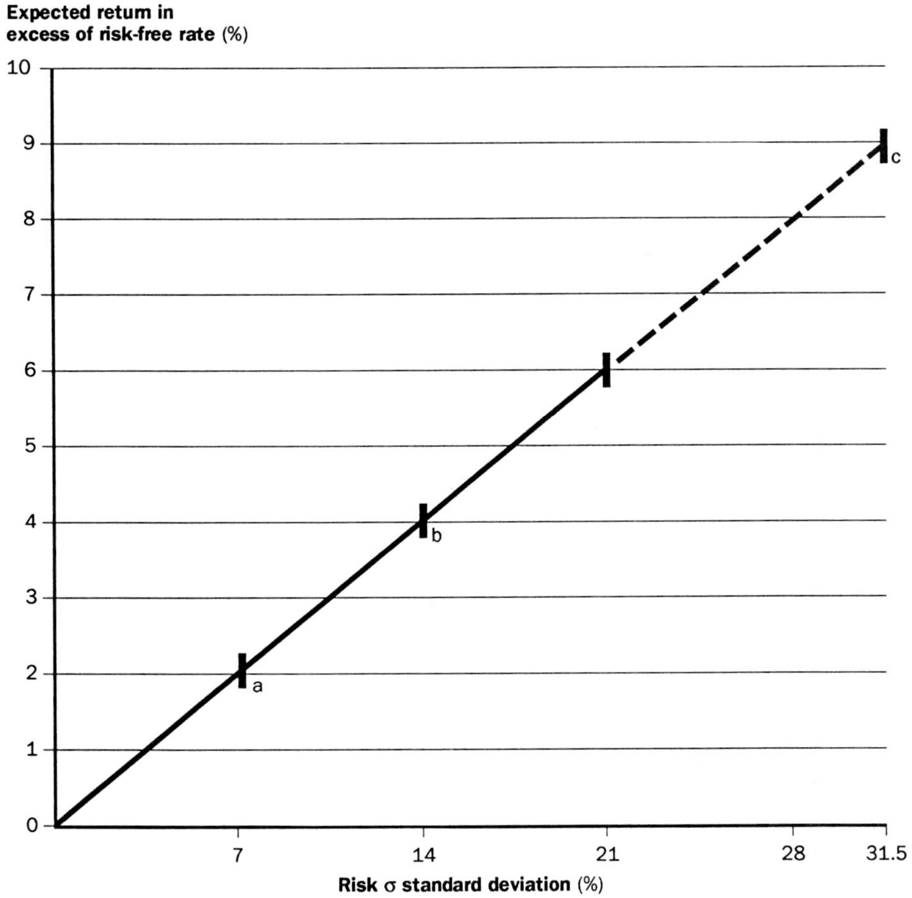

indicated by the point *c* in Figure 4. Differences in borrowing and lending rates introduce a kink in the straight line.

Adjusting the Risk of a Portfolio

Besides merely understanding the geometry of combining a risk-free position with a risky portfolio, the reader should note that by varying the investment in the risk-free asset an investor can obtain any risk level with which he is comfortable, regardless of the original risk of the portfolio. Thus, a conservative investor, who typically does not want to assume much risk could invest in a highly speculative but well-managed venture. By placing a substantial portion of his net worth in risk-free assets, the investor can obtain an overall conservative portfolio, but with an expected return greater than that possible by investing directly in conservative assets.

In short, an investor, regardless of goals, should be open to any type of investment. Just because the portfolio has risk characteristics that are unsuitable for a particular investor is

FIGURE 4. Unequal Borrowing and Lending Rates With One Risky Portfolio

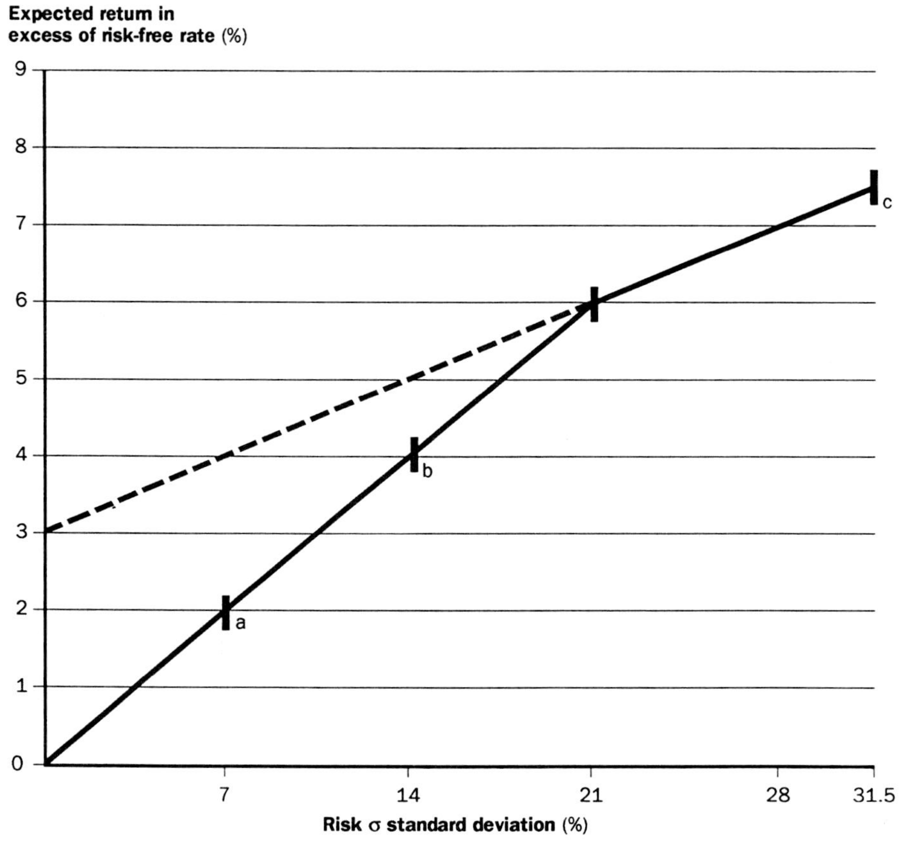

no reason to discard it. The overall risk characteristics of a portfolio can be modified easily.

Determining the Optimal Portfolio

MPT uses the risk-free asset in conjunction with the efficient set of risky assets to determine the optimal set of portfolios that, at each level of risk, promise the greatest expected return. Consider an investor who wants to invest in bonds, stocks, and risk-free or cash-equivalent investments. Although other types of assets might be included, these three represent the bulk of institutional holdings and are the major holdings of many individual investors of substantial means. As previously mentioned, if bonds are interpreted more generally as long-term fixed-interest obligations, and stocks as equity investments, this classification is broader than it may appear on the surface.

Assume that the investor is responsible for a profit-sharing plan whose participants are risk-averse. They are willing to assume only modest risk in the expectation of receiving a return somewhat in excess of the return on the risk-free asset. Specifically, the participants will be satisfied in terms of expected return and standard deviation with a high-grade long-term bond portfolio. The question is whether some combination of investments in these bonds, stocks, and risk-free assets would lead to an increase in expected return with no increase in overall risk.

On the basis of the same assumptions as before, the bond fund would have an expected return in excess of the risk-free rate of one percent and a standard deviation of 7 percent. The stock fund would have an expected return in excess of the risk-free rate of 6 percent and a standard deviation of 21 percent. Assume that the correlation between the returns on these two funds is 0.3, a weak but positive correlation.

Indeed, the investor in this example could improve the portfolio's expected return without increasing the risk level from that implicit in the bond fund by exploiting the geometry of the efficient set. The approach is as follows: The investor who currently holds a portfolio of bonds only should sell some bonds and invest the proceeds in common stock. Thus, the portfolio will move up the efficient set of risky assets in the direction indicated in Figure 5. He could continue to do this until reaching the portfolio designated in Figure 5 as the "optimal risky portfolio." It will soon be clear why this is the optimal risky portfolio. Because this portfolio contains more risk than the investor wants, he should then reduce the risk to which he is exposed by reducing his position in this optimal risky portfolio and investing the proceeds in the risk-free asset until the overall portfolio has a standard deviation of 7 percent.

Step One. The optimal risky portfolio is determined by drawing a line or ray from the risk-free rate (the origin in Figure 5) to that efficient portfolio of risky assets that maximizes the slope of the ray. Because the efficient set is, in general, curved and a ray is a straight line, the efficient portfolio that maximizes this slope will be at the tangent of the ray and the efficient set. Drawing the ray to any other efficient portfolio of risky assets will produce a lesser slope and thus create a lesser expected return for a given risk than that possible with the optimal risky portfolio.

For the assumed values of the expected returns and standard deviations, the optimal long-term portfolio will have 41.4 percent in the bond fund and 58.6 percent in the stock fund. This allocation to bonds and stocks was determined by a computer algorithm developed at the Rodney L. White Center for Financial Research. Because most of the readers of this article will probably not have such computer algorithms available to them, some examples of optimal risky portfolios for various scenarios are presented here.

Step Two. In this example, the optimal long-term portfolio has an expected return in excess of the risk-free rate of 3.93 percent and a standard deviation of 13.47 percent. Because the investor wants a standard deviation of only 7 percent, he should expose 7 ÷ 13.47, or 52 percent of his assets to this optimal long-term portfolio and place the remaining funds, or 48 percent, in the risk-free asset. The resulting portfolio will have a standard deviation of 7 percent, and the expected return in excess of the risk-free rate will be 2.04 percent, for a gain of 1.04 percentage points with no additional risk. As a rough rule of thumb, a one-percentage-point increase in expected return will permit a reduction of 10 to 20 percent in contributions to a defined benefit plan. Thus, a gain of one percentage point is significant.

FIGURE 5. Determining the Optimal Portfolio

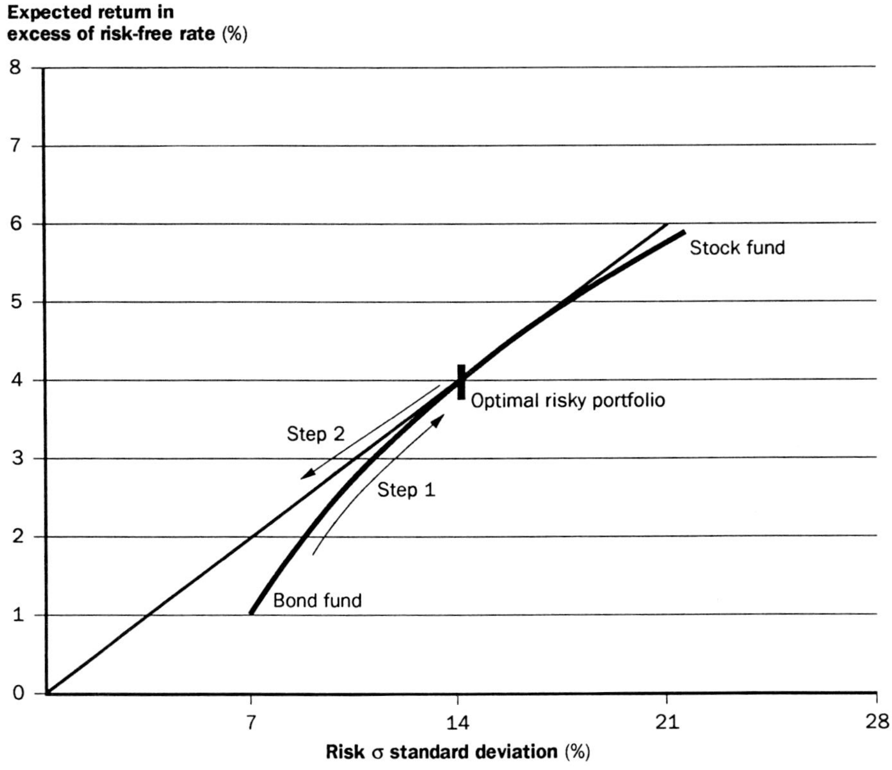

The actual proportions to hold in the three types of asset for each $100 of wealth is determined as follows:

$48 risk-free	$ 48.00 risk-free
$52 optimal risky portfolio	
41.4%	21.50 bonds
58.6%	30.50 stocks
	$100.00

Although many investors probably would not intuitively construct a portfolio of moderate risk in this way, it is clear why such a portfolio has only a moderate level of risk. The high-risk component, represented by the common stock fund, has been offset by the zero risk of the risk-free asset. By holding a portfolio with both bonds and stocks, the investor has received some benefit from the diversification effect, a benefit that would not be present with an investment in only one kind of asset.

More generally, all investors who hold the same judgments as to the expected returns and risks of the bond and stock funds should hold the same optimal portfolio of risky assets.

The investor's risk preferences should not affect the composition of this optimal long-term portfolio of risky assets. The investor's risk preferences determine how he should allocate his wealth between the optimal portfolio of risky assets and the risk-free asset. If an investor wants a risk greater than 7 percent, he would invest less in the risk-free asset than would the investor in the above example. If he wants a risk greater than 13.46 percent and can borrow and lend at the same risk-free rate, he should borrow and lever the optimal portfolio as discussed above.

If the investor is prohibited as some are, from borrowing to lever a portfolio, the only way to increase the expected return from that of the optimal portfolio is to hold only risky assets and increase the proportion in equities from that implicit in the optimal portfolio of risky assets. As can be seen in Figure 5, the differences in expected returns from this latter strategy and the leverage strategy are not great. The efficient set of risky assets is relatively flat in its upper part.

Although a computer can give the optimal proportions in the risky funds to any apparent degree of accuracy, the real accuracy of the calculated proportions depends critically on the forecasted values of the expected returns and risks. If these are grossly in error, the proportions given by a computer will also be in error. Nonetheless, an examination of the geometry in Figure 5 indicates that if one is close to the optimal weights in the risky portfolio, the expected return on the overall portfolio with an appropriate position in the risk-free asset will be close to the maximum observable expected return. Thus, if the optimal proportion in bonds is 50 percent, but the actual percentage is 40 percent, an investor can obtain an expected return for a given level of risk almost as great as before.[5] Because the proportion held in bonds is less and the proportion in stocks is more than the optimal proportions, the portfolio of risky assets actually held is more risky than the optimal portfolio. To maintain the same level of overall risk, the investor has to take a greater position in risk-free assets than otherwise.

Use of Optimizing Procedures

Only a limited number of investors currently undertake the formal optimization process implicit in MPT. This limited number generally would have substantial sums to invest and a technical staff to perform the analysis. Nonetheless, the typical investor who would not undertake this formal process still can utilize some of the implications of MPT to obtain an overall portfolio that, though not optimal, is probably close to optimal.

Under normal circumstances, an investor should first construct a portfolio of risky assets, including assets of all types of risk, from the lowest risks to the greatest risks. In constructing this portfolio, the investor should make sure that it is well diversified to obtain the fullest possible benefits of diversification. He should not worry about the riskiness of the resulting portfolio in terms of his own goals. With an appropriate investment in a risk-free asset, an investor can modify the overall risk.

A risky portfolio consisting only of bonds or mortgages is generally inconsistent with this principle of covering a broad range of risk. Likewise, a portfolio of a single stock is almost always dominated by a well-diversified portfolio of different types of assets. It is sometimes alleged that an investor of modest means must of necessity hold a poorly diversified portfolio: An investor with, say, $4,000 can realistically hold only one or two stocks. This last

[5] The ray connecting the risk-free asset to the suboptimal portfolio would be close to the best obtainable.

statement is nonsense. Such an investor can most certainly hold two or three mutual funds, such as a bond fund and one or two stock funds.

Now that the investor has a well-diversified portfolio of assets spanning the entire range of risk, he should determine his position in risk-free assets. According to surveys undertaken by the New York Stock Exchange (NYSE) and the Rodney L. White Center for Financial Research, most individual investors are highly risk-averse. Likewise, many pension plans and most profit-sharing plans do not want to expose their investments to extreme risk. For these investors, the usual question is how much to invest in risk-free assets. A very risk-averse investor might, for instance, place 75 percent of his wealth in risk-free assets and the remaining 25 percent in a well-diversified portfolio of risky assets. A less risk-averse investor might only place one third to one half of an overall portfolio in risk-free assets.

An investor who wants to assume an extreme amount of risk in hopes of realizing substantial returns should lever the portfolio through borrowings. The usual mechanism is a margin account at a brokerage house. Alternatively, the investor can tilt a well-diversified portfolio of risky assets toward the more risky assets in the portfolio.

Despite the logic of this two-step approach, the reader is cautioned that this approach may have to be modified for legal reasons in the case of personal trusts and certain other types of trusts. For such trusts, the trustee may be responsible for determining not only the appropriateness of the overall portfolio but also, in some sense, the appropriateness or suitability of each asset in the portfolio. In contrast, MPT evaluates a portfolio only in terms of the expected returns and risks of the total returns on the overall portfolio, whereas in managing a personal trust, the investor also may have to evaluate each asset on its own. As with any legal question, the investor is well advised to obtain expert legal advice.

Portfolio Selection: Two-Step Summary

MPT implies that an investor should select a portfolio in two steps:

1. The investor shall select a portfolio of risky assets that is well diversified over all types of risks. In this step, the investor should not consider the appropriateness of the expected returns and risks of the selected portfolio.
2. If the risk level of the selected portfolio of risky assets is too risky relative to the expected return, as is often the case, the investor should put a portion of the wealth in this risky portfolio and the remainder in a risk-free asset. If the risk level is too low, the investor should lever the portfolio with, for instance, a margin account, or tilt the portfolio toward the more risky components of the risky portfolio.

SELECTION OF A SPECIFIC PORTFOLIO

The use of MPT to select a specific portfolio involves two steps: First, determine the optimal portfolio of risky assets and, second, combine this portfolio with a position in the risk-free asset. The first part of this section contains some numerical examples of this process. The purpose of these examples is to give the reader an intuitive feel for the composition of optimal portfolios at a low risk level and at a moderate risk level.

The second part of this section contains an analysis of the long-term implications of various short-term strategies. Most investors probably should view the investment decision in a short-term perspective by trying to obtain the best possible return each month or each year for the level of risk that has been assumed. However, the level of risk that an investor is willing to assume in the short term is dictated by long-term considerations.

Optimal Allocations

The first step in using MPT to obtain an optimal portfolio is to identify those assets that an investor would consider and then to assess the expected returns and risks attached to these assets. Assume that the assets under consideration are a bond fund, a stock fund, and a risk-free asset. For many investors, particularly those of substantial means, these three types of assets represent the bulk of their holdings. If bonds and stocks are interpreted more generally as long-term fixed-interest obligations and equity participations, respectively, real estate investments can be included in these categories.

Potential Risks

The specific allocations, shown in Table 2, are based on the following assumptions: The standard deviation of the annual rate of return on the stock fund is 20 percent. The standard deviation of the annual rate of return on the bond fund is 10 percent. Thus, if an investor expects a return of 9 percent on bonds, there is roughly a two-thirds probability that the realized return in the next year will be between -1 and 19 percent—9 percent $\pm$ 10 percent. The returns on the bond fund and the stock fund are assumed to have a correlation coefficient of 0.5. This correlation coefficient is virtually identical to its historical value in the post-World War II period, from 1945 to 1987.

By comparison, during the 1945 to 1987 period, the standard deviation of annual returns for the Standard & Poor's (S&P) Composite Index of 500 stocks was 17.6, and for low capitalization stocks, 29.6. The standard deviation of annual returns on a portfolio of high-grade industrial bonds managed so as to have a constant maturity of twenty years was 12.6.[6] Thus, the assumed standard deviation for the stock fund is between that of the S&P 500 and that of small stocks, while the assumed standard deviation for the bond fund is somewhat less than its historical value and corresponds to a bond portfolio of slightly shorter maturity.

Investors can be relatively confident in the estimates of the historical risk levels for stocks and bonds.[7] It does not take an investor long to learn that prices of stocks have fluctuated by amounts considerably greater than those of the prices of bonds. Unless an investor has some explicit reason to believe that these relationships have changed, he should probably assume that in the future, the risks associated with common stocks will be much greater than the risks associated with bonds.

Expected Returns

Unlike risks, an investor should be cautious in extrapolating the past to assess future expected returns. In view of the greater risks attached to stocks, an investor is probably warranted in assuming that the marketplace expects a greater return on stocks than bonds, although there is no certainty that stocks will out-return bonds. It is probably also true that the marketplace expects a greater return on bonds than on risk-free assets.

---

[6] These estimates were made by the Rodney L. White Center for Financial Research at the Wharton School, University of Pennsylvania.

[7] Robert C. Merton, "On Estimating the Expected Return on the Market: An Exploratory Investigation," *Journal of Financial Economics*, Vol. 8, No. 4, Dec. 1980, pp. 323–362.

TABLE 2. Optimal Portfolios of Bonds, Stocks, and Risk-Free Assets

Expected Annual Return in Excess of Risk-Free Rate		Optimal Portfolios of Risky Assets				Portfolio With 5% Standard Deviation				Portfolio with 10% Standard Deviation			
		Allocation		Expected Excess Return	Standard Deviation	Allocation			Expected Excess Return	Allocation			Expected Excess Return
Bonds	Stocks	Bonds	Stocks			Risk-Free	Bonds	Stocks		Risk-Free	Bonds	Stocks	
1.0%	1.0%	100.0%	0.0%	1.00%	10.00%	50.0%	50.0%	0.0%	0.50%	0.0%	100.0%	0.0%	1.00%
1.0	2.0	66.7	33.3	1.33	11.55	56.7	28.9	14.4	0.58	13.4	57.7	28.9	1.15
1.0	3.0	33.3	66.7	2.33	15.28	67.3	10.9	21.8	0.76	34.5	21.8	43.6	1.53
1.0	4.0	0.0	100.0	4.00	20.00	75.0	0.0	25.0	1.00	50.0	0.0	50.0	2.00
2.0	2.0	100.0	0.0	2.00	10.00	50.0	50.0	0.0	1.00	0.0	100.0	0.0	2.00
2.0	3.0	83.3	16.7	2.17	10.41	52.0	40.0	8.0	1.04	3.9	80.1	16.0	2.08
2.0	4.0	66.7	33.3	2.67	11.55	56.7	28.9	14.4	1.15	13.4	57.7	28.9	2.31
2.0	5.0	50.0	50.0	3.50	13.23	62.2	18.9	18.9	1.32	24.4	37.8	37.8	2.65
2.0	6.0	33.3	66.7	4.67	15.28	67.3	10.9	21.8	1.53	34.5	21.8	43.6	3.06
2.0	7.0	16.7	83.3	6.17	17.56	71.5	4.7	23.7	1.76	43.1	9.5	47.5	3.51
2.0	8.0	0.0	100.0	8.00	20.00	75.0	0.0	25.0	2.00	50.0	0.0	50.0	4.00
3.0	3.0	100.0	0.0	3.00	10.00	50.0	50.0	0.0	1.50	0.0	100.0	0.0	3.00
3.0	4.0	88.9	11.1	3.11	10.18	50.9	43.6	5.5	1.53	1.8	87.3	10.9	3.06
3.0	5.0	77.8	22.2	3.44	10.72	53.3	36.3	10.4	1.61	6.7	72.6	20.7	3.21
3.0	6.0	66.7	33.3	4.00	11.55	56.7	28.9	14.4	1.73	13.4	57.7	28.9	3.46
3.0	7.0	55.6	44.4	4.78	12.62	60.4	22.0	17.6	1.89	20.8	44.0	35.2	3.79
3.0	8.0	44.4	55.6	5.78	13.88	64.0	16.0	20.0	2.08	27.9	32.0	40.0	4.16
3.0	9.0	33.3	66.7	7.00	15.28	67.3	10.9	21.8	2.29	34.5	21.8	43.6	4.58

The difficulty in assessing expected returns is that the historical evidence is so variable. Depending on the period analyzed, it is found that the average return on long-term bonds is 1.0 to 3.0 percentage points in excess of the risk-free rate and that the average return on a composite index of stocks is from 3 to 8 percentage points greater than the average return on bonds.

Assume that the expected return of bonds is from 1 to 3 percent more than risk-free assets and that stocks are expected to return 0 to 6 percent more than bonds. Because of the uncertainty attached to these expectations and, further, to allow the interested reader to adjust for taxes and other factors, optimal allocations have been determined for a large number of alternative assumptions. In the case of bonds, the example assumes an expected return in excess of the risk-free rate of 1 to 3 percent, and in the case of stocks, an expected return in excess of the risk-free rate of 0 to 7 percent.

The optimal allocations are shown in Table 2 under various assumptions. All returns that have been measured in excess of the risk-free rate are called excess returns. These optimal allocations are affected only by the returns expected in excess of the risk-free rate, not by the level of the risk-free rate itself. The numbers in Table 2 are valid regardless of the risk-free return.

Specific Allocations

Table 2 contains a large amount of information and should be used as a reference table. For example, if an excess return on bonds of one percent and an excess return on stocks of 3 percent is expected, go to the appropriate row as indicated by the first two columns of figures. The next four columns reveal that the optimal portfolio of risky assets has 33.3 percent in bonds and 66.7 percent in stocks. The expected excess return on this portfolio is 2.33 percent, and the standard deviation, 15.28 percent. If the risk-free rate is 8 percent, the total expected return is 10.33 percent.

If the investor wants a portfolio with a risk level of 5 percent, which is a fairly low risk, the next four columns show that he should place 67.3 percent in the risk-free asset and the remainder in the optimal portfolio of risky assets resulting in 10.9 percent in bonds and 21.8 percent in stocks. The expected excess return would be 0.76 percent. If the investor wants a portfolio with a risk level of 10 percent, a moderate risk level, the last four columns show that he should invest 34.5 percent in the risk-free asset, 21.8 percent in bonds, and 43.6 percent in stocks, for an expected excess return of 1.53 percent.

Depending on the assumed values for the expected excess returns on bonds and stocks, the expected excess returns on an optimally constructed portfolio with a standard deviation of 5 percent range from roughly 0.5 to slightly more than 2 percent. The expected excess returns on an optimally constructed portfolio with a standard deviation of 10 percent range from one percent to slightly less than 5 percent. The next part of this article explores the long-term implications of different combinations of expected returns and standard deviations of annual returns.

Long-Term Implications

Although investment decisions are usually short-term in nature, the exposure to overall risk should be dictated by long-term considerations. In setting the risk level for the short term, the investor should consider the implied probabilities of meeting long-term goals. These probabilities will be related to the level of short-term risk to which an investor is exposed as well as the expected return associated with that level of risk.

By definition, for optimal portfolios, there will be a positive relationship between risks in the short term and expected returns in the short term. This statement does not imply that all investors will face the same trade-off. Some investors may be better able than others to find assets whose expected returns are greater than warranted by their underlying risks.

CONCLUSION

The basic idea underlying MPT is that an investor wants the greatest possible expected return for the risk to which he is exposed. For many investors, including most individual investors, it is possible to measure risk by the short-term volatility of a portfolio, even though most investors have a multiyear horizon. The greater the short-term volatility, the greater the long-term volatility. The level of risk to which an investor will expose himself in the short term is directly related to long-term considerations.

At the cost of oversimplifying, any risky asset can be viewed as having three characteristics: (1) its expected return; (2) its volatility; and (3) its diversification potential. Portfolio theory is concerned with the balancing of these three characteristics in conjunction with a position in a risk-free asset, such as a U.S. Treasury bill, to obtain the greatest expected return for a given level of risk. As several examples showed, the diversification effect can be powerful. It is possible for a portfolio to be of very low risk even though each of the component assets is extremely volatile.

The role of the risk-free asset in this process is not generally well understood. However, if properly used, a position in a risk-free asset in conjunction with an investment in a risky portfolio can lead to significant gains in expected returns at no increase in risk, particularly for portfolios of low to moderate risk. As an example, under normal market conditions, an investor who is satisfied with the risk and expected returns of a high-grade bond portfolio and currently holds such a portfolio could obtain a greater expected return at no increase in risk. Specifically, the investor can buy some stock for diversification reasons and then shift some of his assets into risk-free assets to reduce the overall risk of the portfolio. The gain in expected return can be up to one percent per year. When compounded, a difference of one percent per year is substantial.

Although computer algorithms are available to determine optimal portfolios, given an investor's judgments of the future, most investors, particularly those of modest means, do not have the resources to utilize these algorithms. However, an investor can realize many of the potential diversification effects merely by holding a portfolio of a large number of different types of assets without too much invested in any one asset. A surprising number of individual investors hold poorly diversified portfolios. According to one survey of stockholders,[8] the median number of issues held by a stockholding family, exclusive of mutual funds and personal trusts, was fewer than four, with 34 percent owning only one or two issues. Such poorly diversified portfolios impose unnecessary risks on investors, and it is not surprising that many of these investors reported that their performance was worse than the market's.

In conclusion, one of the principal lessons of portfolio theory is that there are benefits in diversification. An undiversified portfolio does not increase expected returns; it only exposes an investor to unnecessary and avoidable risks.

---

[8] Id.

HISTORICAL RETURNS ON PRINCIPAL INVESTMENTS

Roger G. Ibbotson
Laurence B. Siegel
Marvin B. Waring

INTRODUCTION

The twentieth century has been a remarkable variety of world events, which have been reflected in capital market returns. The Great Depression, for example, was associated with an 84 percent decline in the value of common stocks, while the long growth era of 1948 to 1965 showed an thirteen-fold gain in the value of stocks with dividends reinvested. Dramatic events have also occurred more recently. After suffering for decades, bondholders in the 1980s enjoyed spectacular returns, as did stockholders until the crash of October 1987 wiped out more than 20 percent of equity value in one day.

These short- and intermediate-term ups and downs of the various capital markets are interesting to the observer and exciting to the investor. They are, however, only part of the long-term picture. Given a long enough period of study, the capital markets' enduring relationships, masked by the noise of short-period data, can be discerned.

Perhaps the easiest relationship to observe is that between return and risk. Investors are risk-averse, which means that given two assets that have the same expected return and all other things being equal, investors will buy the less risky one. A corollary of this observation is that investors expect higher returns for taking risk. Although there is no guarantee that these expectations will be realized, the set of common stocks, called the Standard and Poor's (S&P) 500, outperformed riskless U.S. Treasury bills by an average margin of

---

Roger G. Ibbotson is Professor in Practice of Finance at Yale School of Management, New Haven, Conn., and President of Ibbotson Associates, Inc., Chicago. Laurence B. Siegel and Marvin B. Waring are both Managing Directors of Ibbotson Associates, Inc., Chicago.

8.5 percentage points per year in the period 1926 to 1987.[1] This extra return, called a risk premium, may be interpreted as the price paid to investors for bearing the risk of stock ownership.

Scope of This Study

This article presents the historical returns on a broad range of world assets for long periods. First, the major asset classes of the U.S. capital market are studied over the period 1960 to 1987. Then S&P stocks, small stocks, U.S. government bonds and bills, corporate bonds, and inflation are studied for the very long period 1926 to 1987. World assets, including world stock and bond markets, U.S. real estate, and gold and silver, are studied over the period 1860 to 1987. Additionally, sections of this discussion focus on specific asset classes.

The Measurement of Risk

For most asset categories, the relationship between return and risk is shown by displaying the standard deviation of returns as well as the mean return. Standard deviation is a statistical measure of the volatility of returns. The standard deviation is calculated in such a way that, for a normal or bell-shaped distribution, two thirds of the observations (returns) fall within (plus or minus) one standard deviation of the mean, and 95 percent fall within two standard deviations of the mean.

For example, in Table 1, the standard deviation of the New York Stock Exchange total return is given as 16.3 percent, and the arithmetic mean return as 10.7 percent. These numbers indicate that two thirds of the outcomes were within 16.3 percentage points (plus or minus) of 10.7 percent, that is, between minus 5.6 and plus 27.0 percent. Likewise, 95 percent of the observations were within two standard deviations (32.6 percentage points) of 10.7 percent. While the standard deviation of returns is not a flawless measure of risk, it is a useful estimate. During most historical periods, higher standard deviations of returns have been associated with higher returns.

Other Factors in Determining Asset Returns

Numerous factors influence the return on an investment in equilibrium. These include marketability, taxation, and management costs. Risk itself occurs across different dimensions: economy or beta risk; inflation or interest rate risk; residual risk; and other possible risks. The various assets discussed in this article are priced by the market according to the desirability of all their attributes. Thus, expected returns on a wide variety of assets are not determined solely by risk characteristics.

The Market Value of Asset Classes

The aggregate market value of an asset category is another characteristic of interest to investors, who may want to study aggregate value out of general curiosity or because they want to hold assets in the approximate proportions in which they exist in the market. For example, U.S. government bonds have been falling as a percentage of total investment

[1] The average excess return referred to is the arithmetic mean, or simple average, of the differences between S&P and Treasury bill returns. The geometric mean, or compound annual rate, of the series differences is 6.4 percent. The arithmetic mean of a variable series is always greater than the geometric mean.

TABLE 1. U.S. Capital Market Total Annual Returns, 1960–1987

	Geometric Mean	Arithmetic Mean	Standard Deviation
Common Stocks			
NYSE stocks	9.44%	10.68%	16.33%
AMEX stocks	7.32	9.75	22.80
OTC stocks	11.51	13.78	22.16
Total	9.46	10.79	16.86
Fixed Income Corporate Securities			
Preferred stocks	5.82	6.67	14.10
Long-term corporate bonds	6.42	6.98	11.55
Intermediate corporate bonds	7.09	7.42	8.72
Commercial paper	7.04	7.08	3.09
Total	6.80	7.03	7.28
Real Estate			
Farms	9.31	9.68	9.27
Residential housing	9.82	9.88	3.70
Business real estate	8.86	8.97	4.99
Total	9.69	9.75	3.90
U.S. Government Securities			
Long term (20 years)	5.92	6.44	11.23
Intermediate (5 years)	7.24	7.44	6.77
Short term (1 year)	7.40	7.46	3.55
Bills (30 days)	6.27	6.31	3.00
Agencies	7.38	7.57	6.57
Total	6.85	6.98	5.44
Municipal (State and Local) Bonds			
Long-term	3.78	4.62	13.94
Short-term	3.91	3.92	1.72
Total	3.84	4.58	13.13
Inflation (CPI)	5.01	5.07	3.57

Source: The Asset Allocation Inputs module of Ibbotson Associates' I/IDEAS software and data package. Returns and market values of most of these assets are backdated to 1947 in Roger G. Ibbotson and Carol L. Fall, "The United States Market Wealth Portfolio," *Journal of Portfolio Management* (Fall 1979). Reproduction or use of these data requires prior written permission of Ibbotson Associates.

assets for most of the last thirty years. This fact is surprising in view of the growth of government debt in that period, but it reflects the even greater growth of the stock and real estate markets. Summary data on aggregate market values are presented here to highlight such trends.

FIGURE 1. Cumulative Wealth Indexes of Capital Market Security Groups (year-end 1959 = $1.00)

Source: The Asset Allocation Inputs module of Ibbotson Associates' I/IDEAS software and data package. Reproduction or use of these data requires prior written permission of Ibbotson Associates.

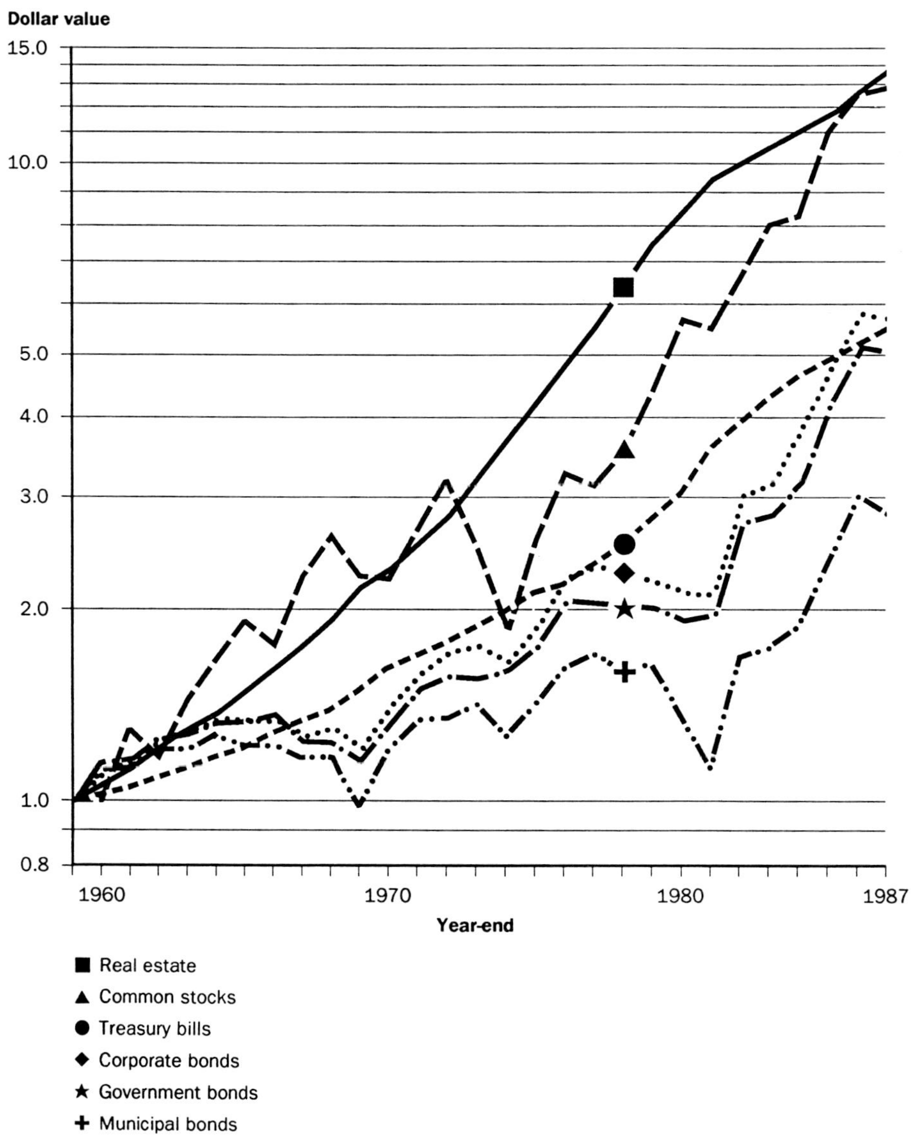

Using History to Forecast the Future

In this article, the historical risk-return relationship is not used to forecast the future. Such forecasts, however, have been made for stocks and bonds with considerable success. The underlying assumption of these forecasts is that the return paid to investors for taking risk is relatively constant over time and can be deduced from historical results, while the return paid to investors as compensation for inflation varies with the inflation rate. In addition, investors receive a real riskless rate of interest that has varied considerably over short periods but that has averaged scarcely more than zero over the long term. The sum of the inflation return, the real riskless rate of interest, and the return provided as compensation for the risk of an asset is the expected return for that asset. For example of the use of this method of forecasting is found in *Stocks, Bonds, Bills, and Inflation.*[2]

RETURNS ON A BROAD SPECTRUM OF U.S. ASSETS

We studied the returns and market values (amounts outstanding) of stocks, bonds and bills, real estate, and other assets over the period 1960 to 1987.[3] Figure 1 shows the growth (with income reinvested) of one dollar invested in each of these assets on December 31, 1959. Clearly, common stocks and real estate were the winners over the twenty-eight-year period, while fixed-income securities barely outpaced inflation. (Municipal bonds, which have lower yields because income from them is exempt from federal personal income tax, did not even match the inflation rate.)

As shown in Table 1, over-the-counter (OTC) stocks were the highest-returning asset over the period. A dollar invested in 1959 in these stocks would have grown to $21.15 by year-end 1987. Real estate investors also did exceptionally well, in part because of leverage. The returns reported in Table 1 reflect returns on unleveraged investments. Most real estate investors bought leveraged real estate and had even higher (although more variable) returns.

Table 2 shows the returns on the various assets in five-year increments. Returns are portrayed in compound annual form. As in Table 1, the inflation rate is shown for comparison with asset returns.

The market value of each asset category as a percentage of the total of all of the assets is graphed year by year in Figure 2. This graph shows that real estate is the largest component of the market. Common stock maintained its proportion of total wealth over most of the period, while fixed-income corporate securities declined. The municipal bond category has had a stable share of the U.S. capital market, while U.S. government debt dropped in terms of relative wealth until the decade of the 1980s.

As noted earlier, risk is as important a characteristic of an investment as is its return. As measured by the standard deviation of returns in Table 1, stocks were the riskiest category of asset to hold, followed by various kinds of long-term bonds. Real estate appeared to have low risk and high return—the investor's dream. But it pays to look at the risk of real estate more critically. Real estate price series are often produced using an appraisal method that artificially smooths price changes. Thus, while it is justified to conclude that real estate

---

[2] Roger G. Ibbotson and Rex A. Sinquefield, *Stocks, Bonds, Bills, and Inflation: The Past and The Future* (Charlottesville, Va.: Institute of Chartered Financial Analysts, 1982), updated each year in the year-end forecast edition of Ibbotson Associates' *Stocks, Bonds, Bills, and Inflation: Quarterly Market Report*.

[3] Figures and tables refer to various Ibbotson Associates software and data packages as sources.

TABLE 2. Compound Total Annual Rates of Return on U.S. Asset Classes Over Five-Year Holding Periods From 1963 to 1987

	1963–1967	1968–1972	1973–1977	1978–1982	1982–1987
Common Stocks					
NYSE stocks	13.24%	7.05%	0.13%	14.95	15.34
AMEX stocks	15.18	−1.39	−3.15	18.99	8.66
OTC stocks	23.43	10.87	−0.17	20.66	9.20
Fixed Income Corporate Securities					
Preferred stocks	−1.88	3.79	6.50	4.19	15.26
Long-term corporate bonds	0.30	5.85	6.29	5.84	13.78
Intermediate corporate bonds	0.76	6.48	7.81	7.15	14.35
Commercial paper	4.51	6.24	7.04	11.73	8.04
Real Estate					
Farms	10.49	10.79	20.62	9.77	−2.67
Residential housing	7.23	9.71	13.94	12.99	7.97
Business real estate	4.52	10.31	7.86	16.16	9.51
U.S. Government Securities					
Long term (20 years)	−0.14	4.90	5.50	6.04	13.01
Intermediate (5 years)	2.47	6.75	6.41	9.60	11.79
Short term (1 year)	4.43	6.86	6.98	11.46	9.24
Bills (30 days)	3.91	5.30	6.18	10.78	7.59
Agencies	3.21	6.80	7.47	8.79	11.35
Municipal (State and Local) Bonds					
Long-term	−0.61	2.95	4.56	−0.01	11.00
Short-term	2.46	3.63	3.48	6.10	5.06
Other Assets and Inflation					
Gold	NA	NA	20.50	22.60	1.26
Venture capital	NA	NA	8.05	38.18	9.86
Inflation	2.23	4.61	7.89	9.46	3.40

NA = Not available.

Source: The Asset Allocation Inputs module of Ibbotson Associates' I/IDEAS software and data package. Reproduction or use of these data requires prior written permission of Ibbotson Associates.

was a very good performer over the period 1960 to 1987, it cannot be concluded that the standard deviations reported in Table 1 are evidence of low risk in real estate.

Real property has characteristics that distinguish it from stocks and bonds. Real estate, directly held, not only may be hard to sell; it requires management effort by the owner. Thus, it has some of the attributes of buying a business rather than just investing money. Real estate limited partnerships and investment trusts have arisen in response to investors' needs for a management-free investment vehicle in real estate.

FIGURE 2. Value of Capital Market Security Groups as a Percentage of the Total

Source: The Asset Allocation inputs module of Ibbotson Associates' I/IDEAS software and data package. Reproduction or use of these data requires prior written permission of Ibbotson Associates.

A SIXTY-TWO-YEAR HISTORY OF STOCKS, BONDS, BILLS, AND INFLATION

A long-period study can uncover relationships hidden in short-period data. The Ibbotson and Sinquefield book, cited earlier, plus updates cover the sixty-two years from 1926 to 1987, which included many types of events: a major depression, a world war, various periods of boom and bust, and low and high inflation and interest rates. Although there is no way of knowing what events will occur in the future, it is resasonable to assume that the historical events of a sixty-two-year period are representative of the types of events that can occur. Thus, the relationships derived from this examination of capital market returns may be useful in predicting future returns.

This article presents total returns on six asset categories: common stocks, represented by the S&P 500 common stock index; small company stocks;[4] U.S. government bonds, both long-term (twenty years to maturity) and intermediate-term (five years); long-term corporate bonds; and thirty-day Treasury bills. Returns are calculated assuming no taxes or transactions costs.[5] In addition, similar data for the general price level (inflation) are presented. While the price level itself cannot be purchased, it represents a market basket of goods and services that can be purchased and that serves as a benchmark for asset returns.

Figure 3 shows the growth of one dollar invested on December 31, 1925 in four of the assets previously described. Stocks were the winner by a very large margin, with small company stocks growing to $1,202.97 by the end of 1987 (with dividends reinvested) and S&P 500 stocks growing to $347.96. This phenomenal growth was not without considerable risk. Returns on S&P 500 stocks for individual years ranged from plus 54 percent (1933) to minus 43 precent (1931), and short holding periods for stocks variously showed large gains and losses. For example, the 21.5 percent decline in the S&P for October 1987 was only the fifth worse monthly return over the period. The worst was minus 29.7 percent in September 1931.

Total return indices of corporate bonds and long- and intermediate-term government bonds stood at $19.78, $13.35, and $17.89 respectively, at the end of 1987. A substantial fraction of these bond returns occurred in two years, 1982 and 1985, in which long-term government bond total returns were roughly 40 and 31 percent, respectively. (These returns include both bond income and the capital gains arising from the sharp drop in yields in these two years.) The U.S. Treasury bill index rose by approximately a factor of eight over the period 1926 to 1987, and consumer prices (inflation) rose by a factor of six.

The graph in Figure 3 can be examined to reveal some specific market facts. The Great Crash period of 1929 to 1932 cut the value of stocks drastically but, with dividends reinvested, the 1929 high was exceeded as soon as 1936 and was passed for the last time in 1943. Likewise, the so-called second great crash of 1973 to 1974, which was larger than any other decline since the Great Crash, was followed by a recovery that, in 1976, passed

---

[4] Over the period 1926 to 1981, small company stocks are defined as the one fifth of the NYSE-listed stocks that rank as the smallest in terms of market value (price per share times number of shares outstanding). Over the period 1982 to 1987, returns on the Dimensional Fund Advisors (Santa Monica, Cal.) Small Company Fund are used; this fund is a portfolio of the smallest quintile of NYSE stocks and American Stock Exchange and over-the-counter stocks with similar market values.

[5] Total returns on small company stocks over the period 1982 to 1987 represent the performance of an actual fund and are thus net of transaction costs.

FIGURE 3. Wealth Indices of Investments in Stocks, Bonds, Bills, and Inflation, 1926–1987 (Year-End 1925 = 1.0)

Source: Ibbotson Associates' SBBI/PC software and data package. Reproduction or use of these data requires prior written permission of Ibbotson Associates.

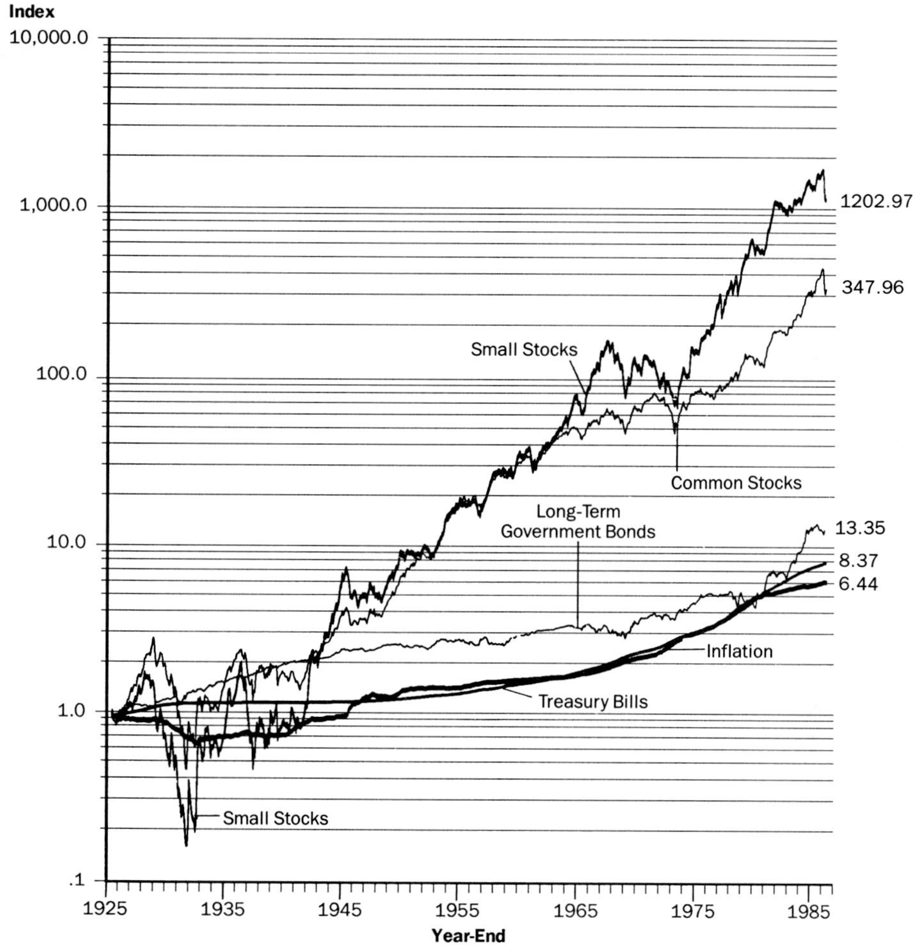

the previous peak. The crash of October 1987 was not as severe in total return terms as the others, but since most of the crash occurred in one day, this event broke totally new ground in terms of daily volatility. The volatility of common stock returns is depicted and compared with that of long-term government bond returns in Figure 4.

The common stock returns appear to divide into four periods: the Great Depression and first part of World War II, in which returns were poor and highly volatile; a long period of growth from the early 1940s to the late 1960s, in which returns were high and stable; a period of "stagflation" generally associated with the 1970s, but actually extending to 1982;

FIGURE 4. Month-by-Month Returns on Stocks and Bonds, 1926—1987

Source: Ibbotson Associates' SBBI/PC software and data package. Reproduction or use of these data requires prior written permission of Ibbotson Associates.

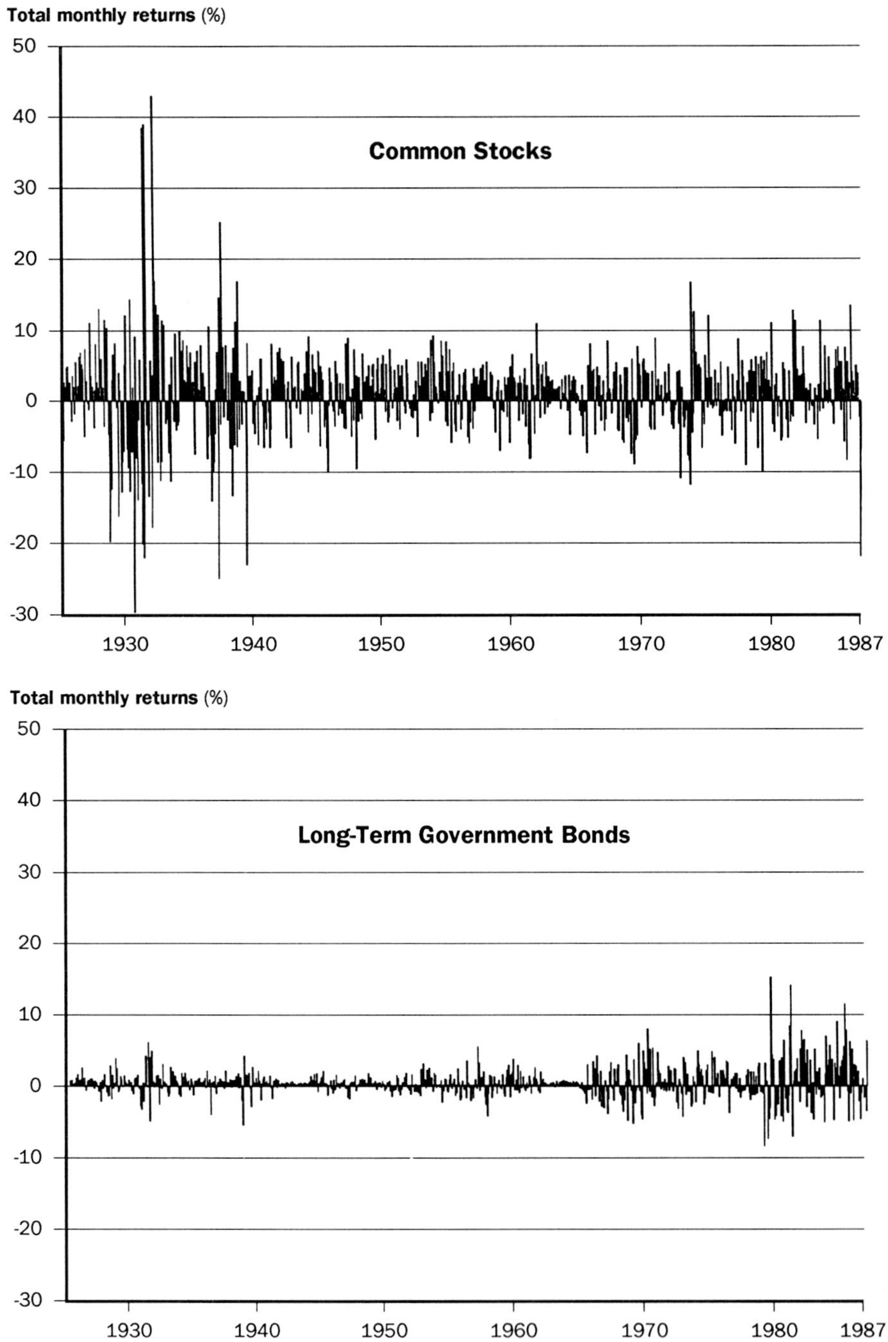

and the 1982 to 1987 bull market. It is not clear whether a new period began with the events of October 1987.

The rise of 1982 to 1987, incidentally, is often referred to as the greatest bull market in history. A historical perspective shows that this is only partially true. While the compound annual rate of return from trough (July 1982) to peak (August 1987) was 30.1 percent—a speed of ascent unmatched in any other period of similar length—other bull markets rose farther. Specifically, the rise of 1949 to 1961, while punctuated with occasional corrections, accounted for a nearly ninefold increase in investor wealth, compared with a nearly fourfold increase over mid-1982 to mid-1987.

S&P 500 stock returns were positive in more than two thirds of the years (forty-three out of sixty-two years). The longest period over which a year-end investor in the S&P 500 total return index would have earned a negative return was the fourteen-year period 1929 to 1942. A month-end investor would have earned negative returns for an additional three months, from the beginning of December 1928 to February 1943.

The longest period for which an investor would have earned a negative return in real terms was more recent. It covers eighteen years and three months, from the beginning of July 1964 through the end of September 1982. In nominal terms, the investor would have more than tripled his investment over that same period.

As shown by the inflation series in Figure 3, the first seven years of the study period were deflationary. This is one of the many deflationary periods in history; in fact, until after World War II, alternating periods of inflation and deflation were the rule in the United States. In the postwar period, deflation has been rare, with only two deflationary years (1949 and 1954). More recently, there were deflationary months in 1982, 1983, and 1987. The high and persistent inflation rates of the 1970s and the beginning of the 1980s were an aberration, not the rule, when viewed in long-term perspective.

The high inflation and interest rates of 1966 to 1981 hurt the bond markets badly, and the spectacular bond market recovery of 1982 to 1986 recouped only a part of investors' long-term capital losses. At the end of 1965, a year-end 1925 one-dollar investment in long-term government bonds had grown to $3.46 (including reinvestment of coupons) compared with $1.78 for the consumer price index (CPI). By the end of 1981, the gap had closed, with long-term government bonds at $5.16 and the CPI return index at $5.24. The eighties bond rally boosted the bond index to $13.35 and the CPI to only $6.44. Thus, investors in bonds earned all of their real (inflation-adjusted) return in the recent disinflationary years. Without reinvestment of coupons, a dollar invested in bonds in 1925 would have shrunk to 66 cents.

Figure 5 presents the geometric mean (compound annual) and arithmetic mean returns on the asset categories, along with standard deviations. In geometric mean terms, common stocks outperformed riskless U.S. Treasury bills by 6.4 percent per year. This may be thought of as the risk premium paid to investors for taking the investment risk of stocks rather than buying riskless securities. From the standard deviations and the distribution histograms, it is clear that the more risky assets (with wider distributions) are more highly rewarded, in terms of return, than the safer assets. It is thus appropriate that stocks return more than Treasury bills; if they do not, no one would buy stocks.

Bonds are less risky than stocks on average because of their seniority in a firm's capital structure, and they do not command as high a risk premium. (Although there have been recent periods when interest rate fluctuations caused bonds to be as risky as stocks, the

FIGURE 5. Summary Statistics of Total Annual Returns on Stocks, Bonds, Bills, and Inflation, 1926–1987

Source: Ibbotson Associates' SBBI/PC software and data package. Reproduction or use of these data requires prior written permission of Ibbotson Associates.

Series	Geometric Mean	Arithmetic Mean	Standard Deviation	Distribution (%)
Common stocks	9.9%	12.0%	21.1%	
Small company stocks	12.1	17.7	35.9	
Long-term corporate bonds	4.9	5.2	8.5	
Long-term government bonds	4.3	4.6	8.5	
Intermediate-term government bonds	4.8	4.9	5.5	
U.S. Treasury bills	3.5	3.5	3.4	
Inflation rates	3.0	3.2	4.8	

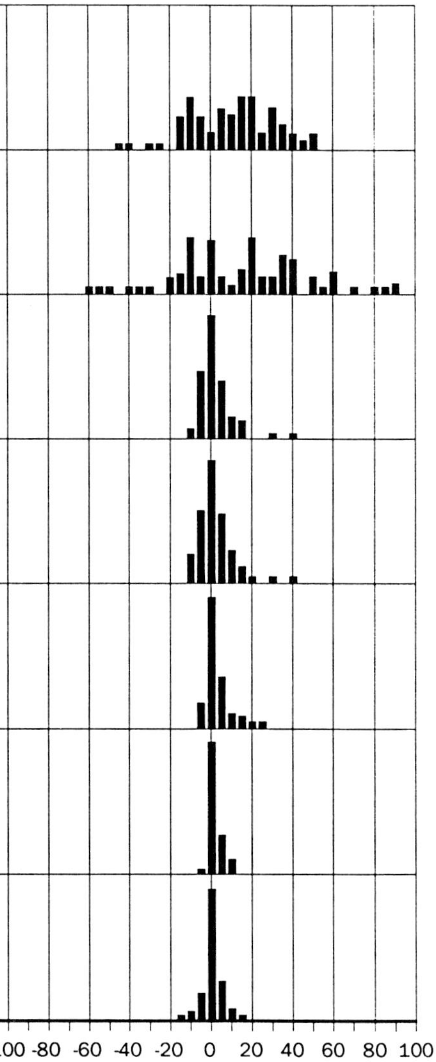

histogram in Figure 5 clearly shows that bonds were less risky over the period 1926 to 1987.) Long-term corporate bonds have outperformed government bonds of similar maturity by 0.6 percent per year over the study period. This excess return may be regarded as a default premium for the default risk of corporate bonds. (Investors do not get to keep all of the default premium, since part of it goes to pay the defaults that occasionally occur in a corporate bond portfolio.)

TABLE 3. Compound Total Annual Rates of Return on Stocks, Bonds, Bills, and Inflation Over Five-Year Holding Periods From 1963 to 1987

Period	Common (S&P 500) Stocks	Small Company Stocks	Long-Term Corp. Bonds	Long-Term Gov't. Bonds	Intermediate Term Gov't. Bonds	U.S. Treasury Bills	Inflation
1928–1932	−12.47%	−27.54%	4.52%	3.69%	3.94%	2.48%	−5.42%
1933–1937	14.29	23.96	8.60	4.46	4.45	0.22	1.96
1938–1942	4.62	10.70	3.76	4.32	3.21	0.07	3.21
1943–1947	14.86	35.00	2.17	2.48	1.74	0.37	6.77
1948–1952	19.37	12.55	2.05	1.37	1.37	1.25	2.65
1953–1957	13.58	10.01	2.10	2.15	2.49	1.97	1.27
1958–1962	13.31	16.65	3.63	2.42	3.39	2.40	1.33
1963–1967	12.39	29.86	0.30	−0.14	2.47	3.91	2.23
1968–1972	7.53	0.47	5.85	4.90	6.75	5.30	4.61
1973–1977	−0.21	10.77	6.29	5.50	6.41	6.18	7.89
1978–1982	14.05	29.28	5.84	6.04	9.60	10.78	9.46
1983–1987	16.49	9.51	13.78	13.01	11.79	7.59	3.41

Source: Ibbotson Associates' SBBI/PC software and data package. Reproduction or use of these data requires prior written permission of Ibbotson Associates.

Long-term government bonds, which are virtually default-free, returned a 0.8 percent increment over short-term U.S. Treasury bills. This excess return may be thought of as a horizon premium. Since a premium is realized for long-term bonds, we may conclude that on average, investors regard long-term bonds as riskier than short-term bills. Of course, investors with long-time horizons may take the opposite view.

Table 3 displays the return on large (S&P) and small stocks, three categories of bonds, bills, and inflation in five-year increments: 1928 to 1932, 1933 to 1937, and so forth through the most recent five years, 1983 to 1987. Returns are shown in compound annual form. While only total returns (including reinvestment of income) are shown, it is instructive to see what would have happened if dividends and coupons were consumed instead. While a $1.00 investment in common stocks at year-end 1925 would have grown to almost $350 by year-end 1987 with income reinvested, capital appreciation alone would have raised the value of the same investment to less than $20. This fact illustrates the remarkable power of compounding over the long term.[6]

In real (inflation-adjusted) terms, a dollar invested in common stock at year-end 1925 would have grown to $54.05 by year-end 1987. (Such a hypothetical inflation-adjusted dollar is also referred to as a constant dollar.) In contrast, a constant dollar invested in long-term government bonds would have grown to $2.07, and in Treasury bills to $1.30, over the sixty-two-year period.

[6] Albert Einstein, when asked what he thought was the greatest discovery of mankind, is said to have replied, "compound interest."

TABLE 4. Summary Statistics of NYSE Stocks Sorted Into Deciles by Market Capitalization, 1926–1987

	Returns			Recent Market Capitalization Bounds of Portfolio*	
Portfolio	Geometric Mean	Arithmetic Mean	Standard Deviation	Upper	Lower
Decile 1 (largest)	9.13%	10.96%	19.43%	$72,710.76	$3,530.26
Decile 2	10.58	13.05	22.75	3,504.93	1,723.87
Decile 3	10.08	12.91	24.50	1,719.70	982.48
Decile 4	11.74	15.19	28.26	978.96	607.10
Decile 5	11.65	15.47	29.33	604.09	357.03
Decile 6	11.56	15.36	28.97	356.54	227.32
Decile 7	12.11	16.80	32.70	226.38	147.43
Decile 8	11.71	16.81	33.69	146.90	96.98
Decile 9	13.23	19.04	36.74	95.94	54.64
Decile 10 (smallest)	14.98	22.87	46.03	54.44	3.73

*Market capitalization of largest and smallest stock in portfolio as of January 1987, in millions of dollars.

Source: The Market Capitalization module of Ibbotson Associates' I/IDEAS software and data package. Reproduction or use of these data requires prior written permission of Ibbotson Associates.

FOCUS ON STOCKS: THE RELATIONSHIP BETWEEN COMPANY SIZE AND RETURN

It is now relatively well-known that small stocks (ranked by their market capitalizations, or price per share times number of shares outstanding) outperform large stocks over the long run. Furthermore, according to Rolf Banz, who discovered this phenomenon,[7] the higher betas of small stocks do not fully explain their higher returns. Thus, it would have frequently been preferable to hold small stocks.

Returns on one measure of small stocks are provided in Table 3 and Figure 3 in the foregoing section. There, small stocks are defined as the bottom two deciles of the stocks on the New York Stock Exchange (NYSE) ranked by market capitalization, plus (starting in 1982) the stocks on the American Stock Exchange (AMEX) and NASDAQ National Market with similar upper and lower bounds of size.

Unlike large stocks, whose price movements are close to a random walk, small stocks follow definite trends. From 1926 to 1931, the compound annual rate of return for the small stock premium (small minus large stock return) was minus 17.0 percent, and the

[7] Rolf W. Banz, "The Relationship Between Return and Market Value of Common Stocks," *Journal of Financial Economics,* Vol. 9, No. 1, Mar. 1981.

premium was negative in every year. From 1932 to 1945, the premium had a compound annual return of 16.6 percent and was positive in twelve of the fourteen years. From 1946 to 1957, the premium compound annual return was minus 4.4 percent, and the premium was negative in nine of the twelve years. Subsequently, the small stock premium returned 7.8 percent per year from 1958 to 1983. Most of the 1958 to 1983 gain occurred from 1975 to 1979, with an astonishing compound rate of return of 23.2 percent in that five-year subperiod. The 1984 to 1987 compound annual small stock premium was minus 10.4 percent, one of the more pronounced periods of relative small stock decline. In the very recent past, small stock returns have been more favorable.

To further investigate the size-related behavior of return, all NYSE stocks were sorted into deciles, and the value-weighted returns were calculated on these ten portfolios from 1926 to 1987. Table 4 reports the summary statistics of returns on the ten deciles of stocks, along with recent (January 1987) bounds of the market capitalizations of stocks in each decile. Table 5 provides the returns for each decile in five-year increments from 1928 to 1932 through 1983 to 1987.

The patterns that can be discerned from Tables 4 and 5 are quite remarkable. Over the 1926 to 1987 period, both risk and return increase with decreasing firm size, almost without exception. Looking at five-year subperiods, smaller stocks outperform larger stocks across all or nearly all of the deciles in 1933 to 1937, 1943 to 1947, 1963 to 1967, and the ten-year period 1973 to 1982. The poorest performance by smaller stocks is observed in the Great Crash period of 1928 to 1932, although there have been other periods of poor performance more recently. It is especially noteworthy that the small stock effect is visible in the middle-range deciles as well as the smallest deciles of the NYSE.

FOCUS ON CORPORATE BONDS

A sample of corporate bonds covering the period 1926 to 1987 were sorted by industrial sector, Moody's Investors Service rating, and maturity. Summary statistics from this study are shown in Table 6. The composite portfolio of all corporate bonds achieved a 5.03 percent compound annual return over the period, far lower than the return earned by stocks and just slightly higher than the inflation rate.

Looking at the industrial sectors covering sixty-two years of data, industrials had the highest return and utility bonds, including telephones, had the lowest return. Risk differed little among the sectors. Returns were also tightly clustered: A dollar invested at year-end 1925 would have grown to $22.37 by 1987 if invested in industrial bonds, and to $18.74 if invested in utility bonds. Financial company bonds were studied over a shorter (thirty-eight year) period.

As expected, issues rated highest by Moody's had the lowest returns. The differences between Aaa-rated and below-Baa-rated issues is dramatic. A dollar invested in Aaa issues at year-end 1925 would have grown to only $13.60 by 1987, while the same dollar invested in the riskier below-Baa issues would have grown to $36.42—a vivid illustration of the principle that investors have been rewarded for taking risk.

Results are displayed for three maturity categories: 1 to 4.99 years, 5 to 14.99 years, and 15 years and more to maturity. Of the three categories, intermediate-term bonds (5 to 14.99 years) had the highest returns. A dollar invested in intermediate-term bonds at year-end 1925 would have grown to $32.03 by 1987, compared with $27.97 for short issues and $17.87 for long-term bonds. This result illustrates the extent to which long-term issues

TABLE 5. Compound Total Annual Rates of Return on NYSE Stocks Sorted Into Deciles by Market Capitalization Over Five-Year Holding Periods From 1926 to 1987

	Capitalization Decile									
Period	1	2	3	4	5	6	7	8	9	10
1928–1932	−13.29	−15.07	−20.38	−18.47	−20.32	−21.12	−25.95	−27.53	−25.12	−23.98
1933–1937	14.29	17.74	16.67	23.01	25.60	21.93	28.62	24.64	31.50	37.23
1938–1942	4.01	5.50	6.36	7.64	8.11	10.10	8.48	7.30	8.46	3.81
1943–1947	13.29	19.42	17.62	23.40	24.87	24.23	26.09	30.75	36.11	43.19
1948–1952	17.02	19.18	15.51	16.15	15.83	15.02	15.22	15.15	12.81	16.51
1953–1957	13.30	13.33	11.58	11.87	11.83	12.16	11.35	10.04	11.08	10.99
1958–1962	12.73	15.01	15.94	16.00	14.79	13.78	16.75	18.38	17.04	17.35
1963–1967	11.12	14.23	16.63	18.81	19.89	20.02	25.74	25.64	27.96	29.39
1968–1972	7.99	5.32	7.77	5.58	4.69	5.47	4.68	2.78	2.80	6.54
1973–1977	− 1.73	1.90	3.44	5.82	5.82	7.47	8.34	9.33	9.84	11.93
1978–1982	12.11	16.83	20.05	20.05	22.81	24.28	26.54	26.83	29.47	27.82
1983–1987	17.51	15.98	14.20	14.87	14.25	13.15	11.49	11.77	13.46	12.72

Source: The Market Capitalization module of Ibbotson Associates' I/IDEAS software and data package. Reproduction or use of these data requires prior written permission of Ibbotson Associates.

TABLE 6. Annual Percentage Returns in the Corporate Bond Market, 1926–1987

Portfolio	Total Returns: Geometric Mean	Total Returns: Arithmetic Mean	Total Returns: Standard Deviation	Return in Excess of Yield: Geometric Mean	Return in Excess of Yield: Arithmetic Mean
Composite	5.03%	5.33%	8.04%	− 1.33%	− 1.09%
Industry					
Utility	4.84	5.13	8.04	− 1.39	− 1.16
Industrial	5.14	5.44	8.13	− 1.15	− 0.91
Financial [1]	5.95	6.20	7.58	− 1.68	− 1.50
Transportation	5.01	5.41	9.20	− 1.51	− 1.15
Moody's rating					
Aaa	4.30	4.53	7.22	− 1.14	− 0.96
Aa	4.23	4.48	7.40	− 1.46	− 1.27
A	4.47	4.83	8.76	− 1.66	− 1.37
Baa	5.08	5.46	8.90	− 1.66	− 1.34
Below Baa [2]	5.97	6.69	12.11	− 2.28	− 1.59
Maturity					
1 to 4.99 years	5.52	5.67	5.63	− 1.29	− 1.16
5 to 14.99 years	5.75	5.99	7.33	− 0.63	− 0.44
15 years or more	4.76	5.17	9.37	− 1.61	− 1.27

[1] Data for financial category is for 1950–1987.
[2] Includes bonds not rated by Moody's.

Source: The Corporate Bond module of Ibbotson Associates' I/IDEAS software and data package. Reproduction or use of these data requires prior written permission of Ibbotson Associates.

were hurt by rising inflation rates and, consequently, interest rates over the period; intermediate issues nevertheless beat short-term bonds because of the intermediates' higher yields.

The columns headed *Return in Excess of Yield* in Table 6 show the direction of the market. A negative return in excess of yield means that the attained return was, on average, less than the market-anticipated return (i.e., the yield to maturity). Over the 1926 to 1987 period, the negative returns in excess of yield show that the bond market went down; that is, bond yields rose. The price trend was upward (bond yields went down) from 1926 to 1945; then prices fell sharply (and yields rose to unprecedented levels) from 1946 to 1981. Recently, bond prices have risen dramatically.

Interestingly, return in excess of yield was lower for the riskier, lower-rated bonds, because higher yields to maturity were subtracted from the total returns to arrive at the excess return measures. Thus, more than all of the higher returns experienced by lower-rated bonds was due to their higher yields.

THE INTERNATIONAL VIEW—STOCK MARKET RETURNS IN EIGHTEEN COUNTRIES

The U.S. stock market constitutes less than half of the world's common equities. The market capitalization of Japan's equity market is larger than that of the United States, and the countries of Western Europe have important and active markets. Smaller markets are present in still other countries. From 1960 to 1987, and especially in the last three years of that period, foreign stocks were very desirable for a U.S. investor to hold. Over the entire period, the stocks of twelve out of fifteen foreign countries studied outperformed the U.S.

TABLE 7. Summary Statistics of Annual Total Returns on Equities in Eighteen Countries, 1960—1987

	Geometric Mean	Arithmetic Mean	Standard Deviation
Pacific Basin			
Australia	8.77%	11.52%	24.98%
Hong Kong*	15.86	28.64	56.65
Japan	19.34	22.84	32.17
Singapore*	16.39	28.89	63.94
Europe			
Austria	10.17	13.53	33.47
Belgium	12.55	14.45	22.46
Denmark	11.75	14.54	28.60
France	8.18	11.47	29.49
Germany	10.33	13.49	30.18
Italy	6.07	11.94	41.94
Netherlands	12.25	14.04	21.11
Norway	10.16	16.87	47.15
Spain	13.12	16.80	31.76
Sweden	11.68	13.70	21.72
Switzerland	10.61	13.59	27.97
United Kingdom	11.83	15.78	31.26
North America			
Canada	9.94	11.18	16.86
United States	9.79	11.13	16.94

*1970–1987

Note: Returns are expressed as percentages based on conversion to U.S. dollars.

Source: The World Asset Returns module of Ibbotson Associates' I/IDEAS software and data package. Returns and market values of most of these assets are backdated to 1947 in Roger G. Ibbotson and Carol L. Fall, "The United States Market Wealth Portfolio," *Journal of Portfolio Management* (Fall 1979). Reproduction or use of these data requires prior written permission of Ibbotson Associates.

stock market. This was partly because the foreign stock markets did well in their home currencies and partly because foreign currencies appreciated in relation to the dollar.

An investment in stocks traded in a foreign currency is a bet on that currency as well as on the return in the foreign market. While it is possible to hedge the currency bet by transacting in the currency forward or futures markets, the study shows the results from unhedged portfolios.

Table 7 shows average annual returns for the 1960 to 1987 period for the United States and seventeen foreign countries, grouped by continental areas. The Pacific Basin countries had the highest returns. Japan had the highest compound annual return over the entire period (19.3 percent); a dollar invested in Japanese stocks at year-end 1959 grew to an astonishing $141.22 in twenty-eight years. This return far exceeded the retun on U.S. equities over any historical twenty-eight-year period.

European countries varied widely in their stock market performance. Spain led the group, with a compound annual return of 13.1 percent. Much of this gain was achieved very recently. The other countries of Europe had returns that fell between 9 and 13 percent per year, except for France and Italy, which lagged behind. Despite a dramatic rally in the mid-1980s, a dollar invested in Italian stocks grew to only $5.21 over the twenty-eight-year period, a compound return of 6.1 percent.

The North American region consists of the United States and Canada. Canadian stocks edged out U.S. stocks, returning 9.9 percent per year. The United States, represented by a value-weighted portfolio of NYSE, AMEX, and OTC stocks, returned 9.8 percent per year over the twenty-eight-year period.

These results show the gains from international diversification over the past three decades. The United States was only a middling performer, and an investor who diversified out of the domestic market would have greatly increased his or her wealth relative to the U.S. domestic equity investor.

THE INTERNATIONAL VIEW—RETURNS ON NONDOLLAR BONDS

The foreign fixed-income market is larger than either the U.S. or foreign equity market, or the U.S. fixed-income market. From a market capitalization point of view, then, non-U.S. bonds merit study. In addition, they have been high performers in the recent past, motivating many U.S. investors to hold them.

This study of foreign bonds focuses on those denominated in currencies other than U.S. dollars. As with stocks, an investment with nondollar-denominated bonds is a bet on the currency held. While this bet may be hedged, we study unhedged returns only.

Table 8 presents summary statistics of returns for the bonds of ten countries. Total returns include capital gain or loss, coupon income, and currency appreciation or depreciation. The bonds studied are generally government issues or issues with similar credit standing, and have a very low probability of default. Intermediate-term (generally ten-year) issues were used to construct the returns.

Returns were highest in Japan and lowest in New Zealand. While Japanese inflation and interest rates rose in the 1960s and 1970s, they began to fall earlier and fell farther than in other countries. Japanese interest rates are now among the world's lowest. Germany, the Netherlands, and Switzerland, which were relatively successful in limiting inflation, also had high bond returns. Many countries, including the U.S., had poor bond

TABLE 8. Summary Statistics of Annual Total Returns on Intermediate-Term Bonds in Ten Countries, 1960—1987

Country	Geometric Mean	Arithmetic Mean	Standard Deviation
Australia	4.44%	5.06%	11.69%
Canada	6.23	6.55	8.76
France	7.20	8.27	16.00
Germany	11.53	12.36	14.07
Japan	13.32	14.48	16.57
Netherlands	11.06	11.99	14.97
New Zealand	3.17	5.00	19.61
Switzerland	10.54	11.66	16.30
United Kingdom	7.16	9.04	21.72
United States	5.92	6.44	11.23

Note: Returns are expressed as percentages based on conversion to U.S. dollars.

Source: Ibbotson Associates' Benchmark Plus software and data package. The set of major credit markets is covered. An extended set is covered in the World Asset Returns module of I/IDEAS. Reproduction or use of these data requires prior written permission of Ibbotson Associates.

returns over the greater part of the period, then rallied in the 1980s. Australia and New Zealand bonds, while poor performers historically, are popular today because of their high yields.

In U.S. dollar-converted terms, bond returns were much more volatile in the 1970s and 1980s when exchange rates floated, than in earlier years when exchange rates were fixed. Exchange rate movement was not the only reason for this increased volatility; bond returns in local currencies were also volatile in the turbulent 1970s and 1980s.

WORLD WEALTH: INVESTING IN DIVERSIFIED MARKETS

A market wealth portfolio of the principal world assets that are investable by a U.S. institution or individual has been constructed. These assets include U.S. and foreign equities, bonds, cash; real estate in the U.S. only (since foreign real estate is difficult for the U.S. investor to hold); and gold and silver. The returns that are accessible to the investor who chooses to diversify to the greatest extent reasonable are also identified. In the Capital Asset Pricing Model theory, the market portfolio is represented not just by the stock market and not just by one country's capital markets, but by the entire opportunity set of asset classes.[8]

Table 9 presents summary statistics of returns on the principal world asset classes.

[8] A more extensive discussion of the world portfolio is found in Roger G. Ibbotson, Laurence B. Siegel, and Kathryn S. Love, "World Wealth: Market Values and Returns," *Journal of Portfolio Management*, Fall 1985.

TABLE 9. Summary Statistics of Annual Total Returns on World Asset Classes, 1960—1987

Asset Class	Geometric Mean	Arithmetic Mean	Standard Deviation
Equities			
United States	9.79%	11.13%	16.94%
Foreign			
Europe	10.61	12.31	20.68
Pacific Basin	18.66	22.39	33.23
Foreign total equities [1]	13.22	14.82	19.83
World total equities	11.40	12.70	16.92
Bonds			
United States	6.57	6.83	7.76
Foreign			
Europe	9.13	9.68	11.57
Foreign total bonds [1]	8.69	9.11	10.14
World total bonds	8.01	8.28	7.97
Cash Equivalents			
United States	6.50	6.54	3.11
Foreign	7.94	8.33	9.52
World total cash	8.01	8.28	7.97
U.S. Real Estate [2]	9.59	9.65	3.87
Monetary Metals [3]			
Gold	16.27	22.31	41.46
Silver	10.33	27.61	94.27
World total metals	16.18	22.31	42.08
Market Wealth Portfolios			
U.S. market wealth	8.84	8.95	5.02
Foreign market wealth	10.00	10.62	12.37
World market wealth (excluding metals)	9.26	9.44	6.32
World market wealth (including metals)	9.74	9.96	6.99

[1] Foreign portfolios include countries (e.g., Canada) other than those in the Pacific Basin and Europe.
[2] See Table 1 for components of the U.S. real estate portfolio.
[3] Statistics for gold, silver, and the monetary metals portfolio (gold plus silver) cover 1972 to 1987.

Note: Returns are expressed as percentages based on conversion to U.S. dollars.

Source: The World Asset Returns module of Ibbotson Associates' I/IDEAS software and data package.

TABLE 10. Compound Total Annual Rates of Return on World Asset Classes Over Five-Year Holding Periods From 1963 to 1987

	1963–1967	1968–1972	1973–1977	1978–1982	1982–1987
Equities					
United States	14.12%	6.93%	−0.26%	16.29	−15.58
Foreign					
Europe	4.01	13.08	2.79	8.88	27.26
Pacific Basin	8.73	41.48	1.40	13.50	40.60
Foreign total equities [1]	5.51	18.79	2.33	11.89	33.04
World total equities	11.49	10.21	0.59	14.11	25.16
Bonds					
United States	0.56	5.43	6.55	7.99	14.35
Foreign					
Europe	3.29	7.41	12.32	4.92	20.57
Foreign total bonds	3.75	8.05	11.67	5.82	18.97
World total bonds	2.54	7.02	10.10	6.99	17.17
Cash Equivalents					
United States	4.02	5.59	6.46	11.23	7.71
Foreign	3.62	8.55	11.45	5.76	15.19
World total cash	3.96	6.10	7.33	10.12	10.73
U.S. Real Estate [2]	7.63	9.98	14.41	12.43	6.61
Monetary Metals [3]					
Gold	NA	NA	20.50	22.60	1.26
Silver	NA	NA	18.54	17.92	9.40
World total metals	NA	NA	20.46	22.48	1.13
Market Wealth Portfolios					
U.S. market wealth	8.09	8.05	7.66	12.37	10.18
Foreign market wealth	4.43	12.38	7.57	7.95	23.75
World market wealth (excluding metals)	7.07	9.11	7.69	10.98	15.06
World market wealth (including metals)	7.07	9.16	8.22	12.04	13.40

NA = Not available.

[1] Foreign portfolios include countries (e.g., Canada) other than those in the Pacific Basin and Europe.
[2] See Table 1 for components of the U.S. real estate portfolio.
[3] Statistics for gold, silver, and the monetary metals portfolio (gold plus silver) cover 1972 to 1987.

Note: Returns are expressed as percentages based on conversion to U.S. dollars.

Source: The World Wealth module of Ibbotson Associates' I/IDEAS software and data package. Reproduction or use of these data requires prior written permission of Ibbotson Associates.

Pacific Basin equities, dominated by Japan, had the highest returns. Gold also had a high return over the subperiod (1970 to 1987) for which returns were available, although the return on gold was quite volatile. As expected in a world where risk-taking is rewarded, most categories of equities outperformed bonds, and bonds typically outperformed cash. Real estate had high returns as well as a moderate level of risk.[9] Within the asset classes, foreign assets tended to outperform their U.S. counterparts.

The size of the markets themselves is worth noting. As of 1987, the investable wealth of the world amounted to more than $20 trillion. For comparison, the U.S. equity market has a market capitalization of about $3 trillion. Of course, such estimates are only approximate.

Returns for four aggregated portfolios were estimated: the U.S. and foreign market wealth portfolios, and the world market portfolio, both excluding and including monetary metals. Of these four, the foreign market wealth portfolio had the highest return, with a dollar invested at year-end 1959 growing to $14.41 by the end of 1987. The U.S. portfolio had a lower return, and was (or appeared to be) substantially less risky, in large part because of the high proportion of real estate in the portfolio. The world portfolios had a return nearly as high as that of the foreign markets, but with less risk, and would probably have been the most desirable portfolios to hold.

Comparing the world portfolios with and without metals, returns and risks were both higher when metals were included. In some portions of the period studied, gold and silver have had a powerful diversifying effect, because they tend to move counter to other assets and serve as a kind of risk-reducing "insurance asset class." Although holding monetary metals did not reduce risk over the entire period 1960 to 1987, these assets did provide gains from diversification. Table 10 shows the returns on the various world asset classes and portfolios in five-year increments. Shorter-period effects, such as the gain from holding real estate in the 1970s, gold in various inflationary episodes, and foreign stocks in the last few years, become apparent when Table 10 is examined.

CONCLUSIONS

In examining the behavior of most asset categories that investors hold, it can be seen that over long periods, capital at risk in business—common stock—earns higher returns than less risky assets. Real estate, which is the most widely held tangible asset, also fares well. Bonds have low returns, and short-term money market instruments, such as U.S. Treasury bills, track inflation.

Over short periods, any specific asset class can outperform any other asset class. While it is interesting to compare realized returns on assets over any period, it seems that the most reliable inferences are drawn from results over long periods.

Investors should buy and hold assets according to their needs and investment goals, and they should diversify their holdings to include more than one type of asset. An investor should not hold only those assets that went up the most in some past time. It is very useful, however, for the investor to have access to historical return data in order to understand fundamental risk-return relationships and make intelligent investment decisions.

---

[9] As noted earlier, some of the apparent low risk of real estate is due to the fact that real estate returns are estimated using appraisal data.

TAX CONSIDERATIONS FOR COLLECTOR-INVESTORS

Eugene M. Krader

INTRODUCTION

Collectors of the tangibles dealt with in this volume (books, collectibles, coins, gemstones, paintings, furniture, porcelain, rugs, sculpture, sports memorabilia, stamps, and wine) should be aware of the tax benefits and limitations that may attach to the disposition of a piece or an entire collection, depending on such factors as timing, nature of disposition, and status of the collector as perceived by the tax authorities.

ESSENTIAL DISTINCTION BETWEEN COLLECTORS AND INVESTORS

From the tax standpoint, there is a significant difference between an object bought primarily as an investment and one bought for personal pleasure. Taxation rules for the art investor differ from those for the art collector. Either can make a charitable gift or sell an object at a profit and incur the same tax treatment. However, on a sale below cost, the investor can deduct his loss; the noninvestor cannot. If the object is bought primarily for investment, many expenses are deductible, including the cost of insurance, restoration, cleaning, storage, and the installation of a home security system. Otherwise, these are simply nondeductible personal expenses.

The investor must prove a profit motive. On audit, the Internal Revenue Service (IRS) will look for evidence of investment, such as turnover rate through sales and exchanges, as

Eugene M. Krader is a Managing Editor of tax periodicals at Warren, Gorham & Lamont, Inc., New York.

well as financial position. The IRS position may be interpreted to mean that the poorer a person is, the more likely he is to buy art for investment. Other important indications of investment purpose would be the routine hiring of experts when buying and selling, enrollment in educational programs relating to collectibles, the loan of works to museums, good business records, and financing through borrowing.

GOVERNING INCOME TAX ASPECTS

Fair Market Value

The concept of fair market value is a fluid one: what a willing buyer would pay a willing seller, neither being under any compulsion to buy or to sell and both having reasonable knowledge of relevant facts. This leaves a wide latitude to the owner who may want to maximize or minimize the value of his collection, depending on the situation. If he is selling, he wants the highest price; if he is giving to charity, he wants the highest deduction. On the other hand, in the estate and gift tax area, he will want the lowest possible value attached to his collection. It is an issue of some importance and delicacy in the areas in which the IRS may become involved. Among the relevant factors to be considered by collectors of the tangibles dealt with here are whether the price for the type of work involved is trending upward, and the quality, condition, and provenance of the particular piece.

Charitable Contributions

An attractive tax aspect for the collector is the availability of deductions for income tax purposes on donations to charitable institutions. The basic rule, which is subject to certain limitations and complications, is that a taxpayer is allowed a deduction for the full fair market value of the property contributed at the time of the contribution. This is subject to a deduction ceiling of 50 percent of the taxpayer's adjusted gross income.

Nature of Donee. The taxpayer must choose his charitable recipient carefully. This is because only certain organizations qualify for deductions of up to 50 percent of the donor's contribution base. In general, the 50 percent ceiling applies to contributions made to publicly supported charities and to certain types of private foundations. This ceiling is consistent with the general purpose of the law, which favors contributions to recognized public charities but frowns on gifts to certain private organizations.

The 50 percent ceiling applies to the familiar charities, such as churches, schools, hospitals, publicly supported organizations (Red Cross, community museums, and libraries), and government units. The ceiling also applies to certain types of private foundations referred to as operating foundations, pass-through foundations, and pooled-fund foundations. Private foundations that qualify for the 50 percent ceiling are defined so that gifts received by these qualifying private foundations will soon be used for the benefit of 50 percent ceiling public charity organizations.

Thirty Percent Ceiling Organizations. A charitable deduction of up to 30 percent of an individual's contribution base (adjusted gross income) is permitted for contributions to qualifying organizations that are not 50 percent organizations. Generally, these organizations include the usual type of private foundations that do not pass their contributions through to qualified charities within specified time limits.

When there are contributions to both 50 percent organizations and to 30 percent organizations, there may be an additional reduction affecting the 30 percent limitation. This is because there is an overall 50 percent annual limitation for all charitable contributions of which no more than 30 percent may consist of contributions to 30 percent organizations. Contributions to 30 percent organizations suffer, since such contributions are taken into account only after deductions for contributions to 50 percent organizations. Excess 30 percent contributions are not allowed to be carried over as deductions to succeeding taxable years. Therefore, careful tax planning of contributions to 30 percent organizations is recommended; otherwise such deductions may be lost forever.

Compatability of Gift With Donee Organization. To qualify for the full deduction, the gift must relate to the exempt purpose or function of the institution. An allowable deduction will be drastically reduced if, for example, a work of art is donated to a hospital rather than a museum; while the function of a museum is the ownership and display of works of art, a hospital has a function unrelated to art. The deduction for a donation of a collectible to a hospital will be its fair market value at the time of contribution reduced by 40 percent.

The objective is to reduce the deduction for the collectible, which the hospital is generally expected to sell, rather than retain. Since the application of this rule depends on the use made of the contributed property, it is important to ascertain what use will be made of the donated property by the charity.

Since very few museums have sufficient space to exhibit all the collectibles in their possession at one time, the fact that a donor can anticipate that his gift may be placed in storage part or even most of the time will not cause the value of the gift to be reduced.

There are still unanswered questions concerning what is a related use. For example, it has been established that a gift of a painting to an art museum is related to the museum's exempt purpose. On the other hand, the same painting donated to a hospital generally will not be considered related to its exempt purpose; therefore, the amount of the contribution deduction must be reduced by 40 percent, as previously noted. If the same painting is donated to a university, it will be considered related to the university's exempt function if the painting is placed in the library for display and study by art students. If the university sells the painting and uses the proceeds to further its exempt purpose, then the use of the property is an unrelated use. What position would the IRS take if the painting were placed outside the library for artistic display? This question and similar potential challenges still remain unanswered.

Property Appreciation. Another limitation applies where the property has appreciated in value. Here it is important to distinguish between ordinary income property (dealer property) and capital gain property (investment property). In the former case, the charitable contribution is limited to the taxpayer's basis, that is, the amount he originally paid for the object. In the case of capital gain property held for over one year (more than six months for property acquired after June 22, 1984, and before 1988), the deduction is the full fair market value subject to the 50 percent deduction ceiling, as previously discussed. Parenthetically, it should be noted that net capital gains are no longer subject to a special (lower) tax rate. The structure for capital gains has been retained in the statute to facilitate reinstatement of the capital gains rate differential should there be a future tax rate increase for ordinary income.

If the fair market value is lower than the price originally paid, no loss deduction is allowed. Where a taxpayer has established himself as an investor as opposed to a collector, he could sell the object, realize the loss for tax purposes, and then make a gift of the proceeds.

Corporate Donor. In the case of a corporate giver, the contribution deduction is limited to 5 percent of its taxable income before deducting the amount of the contribution. At the same time, the corporation is giving a significant boost to its public image. Many corporations have their own foundations to house their works of art.

In view of the obvious possibilities of exploitation, valuation of art objects is sometimes subject to Treasury scrutiny. Although only a small percentage of tax returns are actually audited because of the obvious possibilities of exploitation, the possibility of an audit must always be considered.

Tax-Free Exchanges

The tax law provides that if a property is held for investment and is exchanged for another property of like kind, no gain is recognized. Just what constitutes an investment in a collectible is still an open question, a matter that tax courts have addressed but not finally settled. Similarly, when it comes to collectibles, the meaning of "like kind" is up in the air. The words "like kind" refer to the nature or character of the property, not to its grade or quality. One kind or class of property may not, under Section 1031(a) of the Internal Revenue Code, be exchanged for property of a different kind or class. The purpose of the like-kind requirement is to extend tax-free treatment only to exchanges in which the taxpayer's position remains basically unaltered.

For exchanges of real property, the courts have been liberal in their interpretation of what constitutes like-kind property. In the area of certain types of tangible personal property, on the other hand, the cases and rulings have taken a more constricted view of what constitutes a like-kind exchange. Whether a Gainsborough oil painting may be exchanged tax-free for a modern sculpture or antique furniture is an open question. In such circumstances, an advance ruling from the IRS is strongly recommended. Several cases and rulings bear on this question in the foreign money area.

In Revenue Ruling 76-214, 1976-1 CB 218, the IRS held that an exchange of Mexican 50-peso gold coins for Austrian 100-corona bullion-type gold coins was a like-kind exchange and qualified for nonrecognition of gain treatment. The gold coins were restrikes and were not circulating mediums of exchange in their respective countries and, therefore, were not currency or money. It follows that in Revenue Ruling 82-96, 1982-1 CB 113, the exchange of gold bullion for Canadian Maple Leaf gold coins was likewise deemed to qualify for nonrecognition treatment because it was a like-kind exchange.

On the other hand, Revenue Ruling 79-143, 1979-1 CB 264, held that the exchange of U.S. $20 gold (numismatic) coins for South African Krugerrand gold (bullion) coins does not qualify for nonrecognition of gain because numismatic and bullion coins are not property of like-kind. The value of numismatic coins is determined by their age, number minted, history, art and aesthetics, condition, and metal content, while the value of bullion coins is determined solely on the basis of their metal content. In this ruling, the IRS viewed the numismatic and bullion coins as representing totally different types of underlying investments and therefore not of the same nature or character. Similarly, in California

Federal Life Insurance Co. v. Commissioner (680 F2d 85 (1982)), the Ninth Circuit held that an exchange of circulating Swiss francs for numismatic U.S. gold coins was not a like-kind exchange.

Exchanges for Boot. If a collector exchanges an investment property for a combination of like-kind items and cash ("boot"), the gain will be taxable to the extent of the cash only. For example, assume that an investor has a chair originally purchased for $5,000, which is then exchanged for another piece of furniture appraised to be worth $6,000 plus $2,000 in cash. The actual gain is $3,000, but the taxable gain is only $2,000 (the amount of boot involved). If the $5,000 chair had been exchanged for a like-kind item appraised to be worth $8,000, the $3,000 gain would not be taxable.

As a result of this rule, a collector of tangibles could go through life trading up his like-kind investments without ever selling anything and thus would never have to pay any capital gains tax. If the property were held until death, the estate's basis for computing gains on the eventual sale of the property would be the valuation placed at death. Thus, tax on the appreciation of the collectibles owned during the collector's lifetime would be eliminated. However, this whole area clearly shows the need for careful record keeping. If something obtained from a series of exchanges through the years is eventually sold, the burden of showing tax base cost is on the collector. If it cannot be shown, the collector risks having it assigned a value of zero and having to pay the maximum tax.

Depreciation

Generally, collectibles are not depreciable. The position of the IRS regarding depreciation of one type of collectible — a work of art — is set forth in Revenue Ruling 68-232:

> A valuable and treasured art piece does not have a determinable useful life. While the actual physical condition of the property may influence the value placed on the object, it will not ordinarily limit or determine the useful life. Accordingly, depreciation of works of art generally is not allowable.

Collectibles held for personal use and enjoyment or for investment are nondepreciable. For collectibles used in a trade or business to be depreciable, they must have a determinable useful life. Thus, the first step in attempting to depreciate a collectible is to show that it should be considered a business asset owing to its use in the owner's trade or business. Office and restaurant decorations qualify as business assets, and the IRS will accept such a classification.

Once business use is established, a determinable useful life and salvage value, if any, must be proved. The useful life of property is a question of fact, to be determined on the basis of all the facts and circumstances reasonably known or anticipated at the end of the year for which depreciation is taken. In determining useful life, wear and tear and decay from natural causes must be considered. If the property is not subject to wear and tear and decay from natural causes, depreciation is not allowable.

Because of the longevity of collectibles and the fact that many collectibles actually increase in value over time, it is difficult to claim a depreciation deduction for them. However, a collectible for which depreciation is claimed must be one that will actually physically decay or be subject to wear and tear or become obsolete within a foreseeable period.

Deductions for Theft or Fire Losses

Many collectors take comfort in the idea that theft and fire losses not covered by insurance are fully tax-deductible. In fact, nothing could be farther from the truth. Such deductions are limited to tax cost or current value, whichever is less. Unless the market for a collectible takes a dramatic plunge, tax cost will nearly always be less than current value. Thus, if a collector paid $200 for a painting that is worth $2,000 on the open market, when it is lost by fire or theft, he will get a deduction of only $200. For the individual in a 33 percent tax bracket, this saves only $66 in taxes. In other words, the IRS is one's co-insurer for only 3.3 percent of replacement cost. Even this understates the loss, since the first $100 of any such loss is nondeductible. Needless to say, this loss would pay for many years of insurance premiums on a sizeable collection.

In this example, if the theft or fire loss even on the basis of cost is so large as to reduce taxable income to below the 33 percent bracket, then the government bears even less than 3.3 percent of the loss in most cases. However, if the loss exceeds the collector's income for the entire year, it can be carried back against income for up to the preceding three years, starting with the immediately preceding tax year. If even this does not absorb the taxpayer's loss, he can carry the excess forward for up to the succeeding fifteen years starting with the immediately succeeding year. The taxpaying collector can also elect to waive the three-year carryback and carry losses forward if doing so would yield greater tax benefits.

More important, the collector should never lose sight of the fact that deductions are based on cost or market value, whichever is less.

Deducting Expenses of Collecting

Deducting expenses attributable to collecting is not easily accomplished by the individual collector. In Wrightsman v. United States (428 F2d 1316 (1970)), the leading case in this area, the Court of Claims, despite the recommendation of the fact-finding commissioner to rule otherwise, disallowed a loss on the sale of art objects where it found personal pleasure, not investment, to be the primary purpose for the taxpayer's having gotten involved in collecting. With personal pleasure found to be the motivating factor, the transaction was not entered into for profit, a critical factor for an individual's obtaining a deduction in this area.

To get around the *Wrightsman* case, the individual collector must establish an investment purpose. This can best be accomplished by the collector's comporting himself in a businesslike manner and by keeping careful records. Good record keeping includes establishing the basis of the collectibles (original cost, expenses, and buildup costs when an item is traded), having the pieces photographed (preferably from more than one angle), and obtaining periodic appraisals to establish current market value. Acting in a businesslike manner entails carrying full insurance on the collectibles and making provision for their disposition after the collector's death. This type of documentation and comportment in connection with his activities is essential for the taxpayer to convince the IRS that acquiring and trading the collectibles is something more than an avocation.

ROLE OF TANGIBLES IN AN INVESTMENT PORTFOLIO

James R. Webb
Jack H. Rubens

Tangibles, or real assets, as they are sometimes called, are some of the most interesting and intrinsically pleasing investments available. Many, such as antique furniture and antique silver, can be used on a day-to-day basis, while still retaining their investment potential. Many investment analysts argue that a large part of the return from owning tangibles is simply the aesthetic pleasure they bring to the owner. Each area of tangible investment requires in-depth specialized knowledge in order to avoid the buying and collecting of worthless junk or overpaying for items. As people educate themselves about how a specific tangible was made and its cultural heritage, they gain a respect for the expertise involved in creating an item and begin to appreciate its historical significance. The collecting mentality is legendary. Supposedly, true collectors may occasionally trade but will never sell items in their collection. Although not unheard of, this attitude is much rarer with stocks and bonds.

The collecting or purchase of tangibles as investments is much more common in Europe than it is in the United States. This phenomenon is at least partially the result of the different characteristics of the financial market catastrophes experienced in the two regions earlier in this century. In the 1920s, Europe experienced hyperinflation, which destroyed the value of paper money and bonds, while tangibles maintained their relative values and appreciated rapidly. In the early 1930s, the United States experienced

---

James R. Webb is Professor and Chairman, Department of Finance, James J. Nance College of Business, at Cleveland State University, Ohio. Jack H. Rubens is Assistant Professor, Department of Finance, James. J. Nance College of Business, at Cleveland State University, Ohio.

deflation, which meant that paper money became more valuable; a dollar in 1933 bought more than it did in 1928. Since tangible assets are known in the investment world as hedges to protect against inflation, they generally are of little interest during deflationary periods.

In the United States in the 1970s, high relative rates of inflation revived the interest of many people in tangible investments. Companies began promoting everything from rare coins to diamond dust as hedges against the continuing annual double-digit inflation that many people expected. Inflation did not continue at these high rates, but many people expect double-digit inflation to return some day and thus have become investor-collectors of various tangibles. An investor's interest in tangibles, once activated for whatever reason, usually persists for many years.

ECONOMIC FUNDAMENTALS

To be sure, tangibles are affected by the basic economic valuation factors of supply and demand. If the supply decreases or the demand increases, prices rise. Conversely, if supply increases or demand decreases, prices decline. Although the supply of gold, silver, and diamonds can readily increase, the supply of such items as Old Master paintings and Chinese ceramics is virtually fixed, unless new discoveries occur.

In addition, the price movements of tangibles affect the demand. During inflationary times when prices are increasing for tangibles, the demand for them is also usually increasing. If the supply is fixed, prices often will appreciate faster than inflation. The reverse is also true. If inflation is low or deflation is present and tangible prices are rising slowly or declining, demand often also is declining. The changes in demand often significantly increase the underlying price trend.

Tangibles are similar to stocks and bonds in terms of fashion. Different types of tangibles and different subgroups of tangibles within major types (e.g., Morgan dollars within U.S. coins) become fashionable at certain times. Demand increases as a result of this factor, and prices rise quickly for short to intermediate periods. When a specific tangible goes out of fashion, prices decline quickly, as happens with certain types of common stock; the rapid price increases and decreases for high technology stocks, as they become and then stop being fashionable, are an example.

Investment Hype

Many of the tangible groups have their own special groups of dealers who hype and promote them. Two good examples are gold and U.S. coins. Advertisements to induce buying either gold or U.S. coins for investment purposes are extremely common in print, as well as on television. At the opposite end of the spectrum are such tangibles as Chinese ceramics or Old Master paintings, which are not marketed by means of mass advertising or special inducements. Only rarely does an individual tangible dealer promote a balanced portfolio approach; most promote only the particular tangible they sell.

To invest a large portion of funds in a single asset class or subgroup of an asset class is very risky and, therefore, not wise. Diversification within a portfolio generally reduces risk and, therefore, should be the approach used by investors who wish to minimize risk. A portfolio consists of numerous assets. A well-diversified portfolio should contain cash equivalents, stocks, bonds, and real estate, as well as tangibles.

Nonmonetary Returns

For the true collector of certain types of tangibles, many of the benefits are nonmonetary. Much of the return for owning stamps, nonbullion coins, Chinese ceramics or Old Master paintings is the aesthetic pleasure of seeing them, handling them, and having them in close proximity. These types of return are not experienced by the noncollector or person interested only in financial returns. People who buy gold or silver bullion and keep it in an account where they never see it seek only financial returns. They treat gold and silver like a stock or bond.

This article adopts the same point of view. In order to compare tangibles with other types of asset, only their financial returns are considered. Therefore, the investment conclusions drawn in this chapter should be tempered by those who are collectors and thus derive nonmonetary returns from their tangible investments.

PORTFOLIOS

A portfolio can consist of two or hundreds of assets in one or numerous asset classes. Examples of asset classes are cash and cash equivalents (such as money market funds and certificates of deposit), bonds (corporate and municipal), common stock, real estate (residential, business, or farmland), and tangibles. Most portfolios consist of all of these asset classes in various combinations. However, some people concentrate their assets in just one or two asset classes, which either lowers their expected returns or increases their risk in comparison to a well-diversified portfolio. In general, investors try to maximize their returns at a given risk level or to minimize their risk at a given level of returns.

Investments in any asset class are made for the future. In other words, investments are made based on an expectation of future returns and risks. Historical data are used to form the expectations, but the future is the relevant time frame. Since what we expect to happen is rarely exactly what happens, diversification is important. Some investments perform worse than expected, while others perform better. When the better-and-worse-than expected investment results are contained in a well-diversified portfolio, the net result is often close to our expectation for all the assets together.

PORTFOLIO SIMULATION

Portfolio studies historically have used only two or three types of assets. Usually common stocks and cash are included; sometimes bonds are also included.

Recently, portfolio studies have begun to include other assets. The one major asset usually included in these studies is real estate, which takes various forms. Residential real estate, business or commercial real estate, and farmland are the three types most commonly referenced. Some studies use only one type. Brueggeman, Chen, and Thibodeau use business real estate while Kaplan uses farmland. Eun and Curcio use farmland and residential, while Webb and Rubens use all three types. In addition to real estate, gold has been used in portfolio studies. However, with the exception of gold and real estate, all other real assets and most tangibles have been omitted from portfolio studies thus far. Many of these tangibles, sometimes referred to as collectibles, gained substantial recognition and following during the late 1970s, when they were perceived as inflation hedges by many investors.

For this analysis, a mixed-asset portfolio has been constructed that includes the traditional stocks and bonds as well as real estate (three types) and seven types of tangibles. Unfortunately, not all the tangibles described in this book could be analyzed. Unfortunately, not all the tangibles described in this book could be analyzed. The portfolio includes the following:

- Common stocks
- Corporate bonds
- Small stocks
- Residential real estate
- Business real estate
- Farmland
- Gold
- Silver
- U.S. stamps
- U.S. coins
- Diamonds
- Old Master paintings
- Chinese ceramics

In order to examine the effects of combining these assets into an after-tax portfolio, after-tax rates of return were obtained for all asset types. Data for the common stocks, corporate bonds, and small stocks were obtained from Ibbotson and Sinquefield and from updates. Data for the residential real estate, business real estate, and farmland were obtained from Ibbotson and Siegel and from Ibbotson, Siegel, and Love. Data for gold, silver, U.S. stamps, U.S. coins, diamonds, Old Masters, and Chinese ceramics were derived from the annual Salomon Brothers *Investment Policy Report on Tangible Assets*. Information on the portion of returns from appreciation and income were obtained directly from R. G. Ibbotson Associates, Inc. (real estate), Dimensional Fund Advisors, Inc. (small stocks), and the *Stocks, Bonds, Bills, and Inflation 1985 Yearbook* from R. G. Ibbotson Associates, Inc. The data were obtained for the period 1969 to 1984. In addition, six marginal tax bracket investors were assumed: 0 percent, 10 percent, 20 percent, 30 percent, 40 percent, and 50 percent.

Using this return data, the Elton, Gruber, and Padberg model for obtaining optimal portfolios, and a constructed market index, the optimal asset proportion for each asset was calculated for the period 1969 to 1979 (a decade of increasing inflation), 1974 to 1984 (which includes the moderation of inflation in the last few years), and 1969 to 1984 (the entire period) for each of the six tax brackets. Keep in mind that some researchers believe that the variance of the returns (risk) is understated for everything but stocks and bonds. The mean returns and standard deviations of the various investment media for all time periods are shown in Tables 1 through 3. The returns for each asset for each year are shown in Table 4. Transaction costs were included as a reduction of return in the year incurred (Table 5). Transaction costs are a major expense for tangibles, including real estate.

For the inclusion of tangible assets in mixed-asset portfolios to be beneficial, their returns must not be perfectly correlated with the common stock (New York Stock Exchange (NYSE)), bonds, small stocks, residential real estate, business real estate, or farmland already in the portfolio. The lower the interinvestment correlations, the more beneficial is diversification using nontraditional tangible assets. That is, the lower the interinvestment correlations, the greater the risk reduction of the portfolio. For a detailed explanation, see article on "Modern Portfolio Theory," by Marshall Blume, elsewhere in this volume.

TABLE 1. Mean Returns and Standard Deviations for 1969 to 1979 (Values expressed as percentages)

Investment Type	0% Bracket		10% Bracket		20% Bracket		30% Bracket		40% Bracket		50% Bracket	
	Mean Return	Standard Deviation	Mean Return	Standard Deviation	Mean Return	Standard Deviation	Mean Return	Standard Deviation	Mean Return	Standard Deviation	Mean Return	Standard Deviation
Common stock	5.78	18.88	5.30	17.98	4.83	17.09	4.36	16.19	3.88	15.30	3.41	14.41
Corporate bonds	4.98	9.62	4.50	9.03	4.03	8.45	3.56	7.87	3.08	7.30	2.61	6.73
Small stocks	11.56	31.98	10.99	30.37	10.43	28.76	9.87	27.15	9.31	25.54	8.74	23.94
Residential real estate	10.40	2.90	9.74	2.79	9.07	2.68	8.41	2.57	7.75	2.46	7.09	2.36
Business real estate	9.01	2.94	8.28	2.82	7.55	2.71	6.82	2.60	6.09	2.50	5.35	2.41
Farmland	16.17	8.01	15.37	7.63	14.56	7.24	13.75	6.85	12.95	6.46	12.14	6.07
Gold	23.65	33.13	22.58	31.61	21.51	30.08	20.45	28.56	19.38	27.04	18.32	25.52
Silver	20.77	29.10	19.86	27.75	18.94	26.40	18.02	25.05	17.11	23.71	16.19	22.36
U.S. stamps	18.00	13.05	17.20	12.51	16.40	11.97	15.60	11.43	14.80	10.89	14.00	10.36
U.S. coins	12.27	12.55	11.70	11.91	11.14	11.27	10.88	10.63	10.01	9.99	9.45	9.36
Diamonds	11.76	12.27	11.23	11.67	10.70	11.08	10.18	10.49	9.65	9.90	9.12	9.31
Old Masters	12.88	8.80	12.29	8.35	11.69	7.89	11.10	7.44	10.51	6.98	9.92	6.53
Chinese ceramics	32.95	33.66	31.39	31.88	29.83	30.10	28.27	28.32	26.71	26.54	25.15	24.77

TABLE 4. Total Returns of Various Assets (Returns expressed as percentages)

Year	Common Stock	Corporate Bonds	Residential Real Estate	Business Farmland	Small Real Estate	Chinese Stocks	Ceramics	Gold	Silver	Diamonds	Stamps	Coins	Old Masters
1969	−8.50	−8.09	10.53	7.24	6.10	−25.05	−12.52	−3.86	−8.60	2.00	16.20	2.98	3.50
1970	4.01	18.37	11.69	7.77	10.00	−17.43	19.37	0.31	−7.23	1.93	13.89	2.95	3.07
1971	14.31	11.01	7.69	11.70	15.50	16.50	66.27	27.68	−2.20	8.41	10.23	2.34	12.28
1972	18.98	7.26	6.34	18.94	9.50	4.43	89.39	54.95	29.75	28.61	17.85	1.97	24.03
1973	−14.66	1.14	6.56	35.27	7.40	−30.90	36.04	65.65	67.76	22.70	16.70	8.92	16.54
1974	−26.47	−3.06	13.21	19.80	8.10	−19.95	2.40	32.36	39.26	2.26	10.20	22.96	8.63
1975	37.20	14.64	13.02	18.52	8.86	52.85	45.94	−10.72	−3.92	4.41	16.71	33.70	18.81
1976	23.84	18.65	7.31	19.54	8.02	57.38	75.42	−20.34	2.46	19.99	21.00	28.39	20.92
1977	−7.18	1.71	11.38	11.20	8.99	25.38	14.95	0.98	8.76	29.92	17.84	18.61	16.00
1978	6.56	−0.07	14.22	18.18	12.17	23.46	23.09	37.60	36.81	14.65	37.69	14.48	18.03
1979	18.44	−4.18	18.92	19.70	14.52	43.46	22.10	79.50	69.65	14.50	52.05	17.65	19.75
1980	32.42	−2.62	14.46	10.47	11.42	39.88	24.80	45.05	25.10	12.50	30.60	8.65	20.15
1981	−4.91	−0.96	4.32	1.07	13.46	13.95	18.22	10.05	−35.55	0.00	7.50	−17.90	0.45
1982	21.41	43.79	10.62	−4.38	10.38	28.01	−0.03	31.30	−32.25	0.00	−4.60	−5.50	−10.15
1983	22.52	4.70	6.75	−0.31	16.00	36.67	1.50	12.30	42.15	0.00	−5.20	9.10	8.00
1984	6.27	16.39	5.62	19.27	9.99	−6.67	4.45	−12.15	−29.75	0.00	−6.80	9.15	13.95

TABLE 3. Mean Returns and Standard Deviations for 1969 to 1984 (Values expressed as percentages)

Investment Type	0% Bracket		10% Bracket		20% Bracket		30% Bracket		40% Bracket		50% Bracket	
	Mean Return	Standard Deviation	Mean Return	Standard Deviation	Mean Return	Standard Deviation	Mean Return	Standard Deviation	Mean Return	Standard Deviation	Mean Return	Standard Deviation
Common stock	8.83	17.89	8.24	17.08	7.65	16.28	7.07	15.48	6.48	14.68	5.89	13.89
Corporate bonds	7.25	12.99	6.67	12.39	6.08	11.79	5.50	11.20	4.91	10.62	4.33	10.04
Small stocks	14.94	28.56	14.23	27.17	13.52	25.77	12.81	24.38	12.10	22.99	11.39	21.61
Residential real estate	9.76	4.76	9.13	4.59	8.49	4.42	7.86	4.24	7.23	4.07	6.60	3.90
Business real estate	10.02	4.00	9.21	3.82	8.40	3.65	7.59	3.48	6.78	3.32	5.97	3.16
Farmland	12.75	9.76	12.12	9.29	11.50	8.83	10.87	8.36	10.25	7.90	9.63	7.44
Gold	21.67	29.88	20.72	28.53	19.77	27.18	18.82	25.84	17.87	24.49	16.92	23.15
Silver	12.39	33.42	11.83	31.96	11.28	30.50	10.72	29.04	10.17	27.58	9.62	26.13
U.S. stamps	13.72	17.36	13.11	16.64	12.51	15.92	11.91	15.20	11.30	14.49	10.70	13.77
U.S. coins	8.70	15.56	8.30	12.92	7.90	12.28	7.50	11.64	7.11	11.00	6.71	10.36
Diamonds	8.87	12.15	8.47	11.59	8.08	11.02	7.68	10.46	7.29	9.89	6.89	9.33
Old Masters	10.88	10.29	10.39	9.81	9.90	9.33	9.41	8.85	8.93	8.37	8.44	7.90
Chinese ceramics	25.70	30.58	24.50	29.00	23.30	27.42	22.11	25.84	20.92	24.25	19.72	22.68

TABLE 2. Mean Returns and Standard Deviations for 1974 to 1984 (Values expressed as percentages)

	0% Bracket		10% Bracket		20% Bracket		30% Bracket		40% Bracket		50% Bracket	
Investment Type	Mean Return	Standard Deviation	Mean Return	Standard Deviation	Mean Return	Standard Deviation	Mean Return	Standard Deviation	Mean Return	Standard Deviation	Mean Return	Standard Deviation
Common stock	11.55	19.40	10.84	18.55	10.13	17.71	9.42	16.86	8.70	16.01	7.99	15.17
Corporate bonds	7.85	14.51	7.23	13.90	6.60	13.29	5.98	12.68	5.35	12.09	4.73	11.50
Small stocks	26.49	24.27	25.22	23.13	23.95	21.98	22.68	20.84	21.41	19.71	20.14	18.57
Residential real estate	10.30	5.54	9.67	5.34	9.03	5.14	8.40	4.95	7.76	4.75	7.12	4.56
Business real estate	10.17	4.32	9.29	4.14	8.42	3.96	7.55	3.78	6.67	3.61	5.80	3.43
Farmland	11.19	8.95	10.67	8.53	10.15	8.12	9.63	7.71	9.11	7.30	8.59	6.89
Gold	18.36	29.90	17.62	28.66	16.89	27.41	16.16	26.17	15.42	24.92	14.69	23.68
Silver	10.79	34.83	10.33	33.41	9.86	31.98	9.40	30.56	8.94	29.14	8.47	27.72
U.S. stamps	14.27	20.62	13.67	19.78	13.06	18.95	12.46	18.12	11.85	17.29	11.25	16.45
U.S. coins	10.91	14.67	10.40	14.00	9.90	13.32	9.40	12.65	8.89	11.98	8.39	11.31
Diamonds	7.11	12.24	6.81	11.72	6.51	11.21	6.21	10.69	5.91	10.17	5.61	9.65
Old Masters	10.41	10.77	9.96	10.31	9.51	9.84	9.06	9.37	8.61	8.91	8.16	8.44
Chinese ceramics	19.32	24.44	18.45	23.23	17.57	22.02	16.70	20.82	15.82	19.61	14.94	18.40

TABLE 5. Assumed Transaction Costs

	In	Out
Common stocks	1.5%	1.5%
Corporate bonds	1	1
Small stocks	1.5	1.5
Residential real estate	0.5	6.5
Business real estate	0	10
Farmland	0	10
Gold	2	2
Silver	2	2
U.S. stamps	10	10
U.S. coins	10	10
Diamonds	2	2
Old Masters	10	10
Chinese cermamics	10	10

The potential risk reduction resulting from diversification using nontraditional tangible assets can quickly be estimated by observing a correlation matrix of the various asset returns. There are eighteen correlation matrices for this study (three time periods, with six different tax brackets). None of these has been included in this article, but all are available from the authors. Observation of the correlation matrices indicates that significant after-tax benefits can be derived by including the tangible assets in a portfolio.

A market index was constructed that includes the thirteen assets used in this study. Using the process enumerated by Elton and Gruber and Elton, Gruber, and Padberg, the optimal portfolio was then calculated for each time period (1969 to 1979, 1974 to 1984, and 1969 to 1984). This process assumes use of a single-index model. Elton, Gruber, and Padberg have shown that once the single-index model is assumed, the desirability of an asset from the viewpoint of selecting the optimal portfolio can be readily measured by the asset's excess-return-to-market-risk ratio. They have shown further that any asset will be included in the optimal portfolio if and only if the asset's desirability index (DI) exceeds a certain cutoff rate. The DI is defined as an asset's excess return to market risk. Only assets whose desirability index exceeds the cutoff rate will be included in the optimal portfolio. Since this technique relies on the estimate of market risk for a constructed market index, all the assumptions and associated problems discussed by Roll should be remembered when reviewing the results. A summary of the optimal portfolio composition for all time periods using the standard calculated variance is shown in Tables 6, 7, and 8.

RESULTS

For the 1969 to 1979 period of increasing inflation (Table 6), tangibles, as a group, make up a substantial part of the optimal portfolio. For the 0 percent, 10 percent, 20 percent, 30 percent, 40 percent, and 50 percent tax brackets with normal variance, the proportion of

TABLE 6. Optimal Portfolio Composition at Various Tax Rates With Normal Variance, for 1969 to 1979

Asset	Tax Bracket 0%	10%	20%	30%	40%	50%
Common stock	—	—	—	—	—	—
Corporate bonds	—	—	—	—	—	—
Small stocks	.02	.02	.03	.02	.03	.02
Residential real estate	.18	.21	.19	.28	.26	.25
Business real estate	.26	.21	.18	.09	—	—
Farmland	.09	.09	.09	.09	.09	.09
Gold	.12	.13	.14	.14	.17	.18
Silver	.10	.09	.10	.11	.13	.14
U.S. stamps	.03	.03	.04	.04	.05	.05
U.S. coins	.07	.07	.07	.07	.08	.08
Diamonds	.03	.03	.03	.03	.03	.03
Old Masters	.01	.01	.01	.01	.02	.01
Chinese ceramics	.10	.11	.12	.12	.15	.14

TABLE 7. Optimal Portfolio Composition at Various Tax Rates With Normal Variance, for 1974 to 1984

Asset	Tax Bracket 0%	10%	20%	30%	40%	50%
Common stock	.05	.04	.03	.02	—	—
Corporate bonds	—	—	—	—	—	—
Small stocks	.19	.20	.21	.24	.25	.27
Residential real estate	.02	.01	—	—	—	—
Business real estate	.04	.02	—	—	—	—
Farmland	.08	.07	.06	.04	.02	—
Gold	.30	.30	.34	.38	.42	.44
Silver	.03	.03	.03	.02	.01	—
U.S. stamps	.05	.06	.06	.06	.06	.05
U.S. coins	.04	.03	.05	.02	.01	—
Diamonds	—	—	—	—	—	—
Old Masters	.02	.02	.01	—	—	—
Chinese ceramics	.19	.20	.21	.23	.23	.24

TABLE 8. Optimal Portfolio Composition at Various Tax Rates With Normal Variance, for 1969 to 1984

	Tax Bracket					
Asset	**0%**	**10%**	**20%**	**30%**	**40%**	**50%**
Common stock	.02	.01	—	—	—	—
Corporate bonds	—	—	—	—	—	—
Small stocks	.12	.13	.14	.14	.14	.14
Residential real estate	.06	.04	.02	—	—	—
Business real estate	.06	.04	.02	—	—	—
Farmland	.11	.11	.11	.11	.10	.08
Gold	.24	.26	.30	.31	.32	.34
Silver	.07	.07	.07	.07	.06	.06
U.S. stamps	.06	.07	.05	.07	.07	.07
U.S. coins	.02	.01	—	—	—	—
Diamonds	.01	.01	—	—	—	—
Old Masters	.03	.03	.03	.02	.02	.01
Chinese ceramics	.20	.23	.26	.28	.29	.30

TABLE 9. Optimal After-Tax Portfolio Characteristics: Standard Variance

	Tax Rate					
	0%	**10%**	**20%**	**30%**	**40%**	**50%**
1969 to 1979						
Mean return ($\bar{R}p$)	16.68	16.00	15.66	14.97	15.52	14.41
Standard deviation (σp)	9.39	9.09	9.41	9.01	10.13	9.75
1974 to 1984						
Mean return ($\bar{R}p$)	18.35	17.49	17.41	17.46	16.85	16.34
Standard deviation (σp)	14.08	13.67	13.91	14.08	13.86	13.46
1969 to 1984						
Mean return ($\bar{R}p$)	17.44	17.25	17.08	16.79	16.09	15.45
Standard deviation (σp)	15.11	15.29	15.40	15.37	14.65	14.16

tangibles in the portfolio are 46 percent, 47 percent, 51 percent, 52 percent, 63 percent, and 63 percent, respectively.

For individual tangibles, the portfolio proportions for gold, silver, and Chinese ceramics were the highest. Allocations for gold went up to 17 to 18 percent of the portfolio in higher tax brackets. The allocation for U.S. coins hovered around 7 percent for all tax brackets, while the allocation for U.S. stamps stayed around 4 percent. The allocation for diamonds was a steady 3 percent, whereas for Old Master paintings it was an inconsequential 1 percent. The allocations for U.S. stamps and U.S. coins are undoubtedly lower than many people who collect these tangibles hold in their portfolios. The portion for gold and silver together as precious metals is probably much higher than the portion many people hold in their portfolios. However, this was a period of increasing inflation, which has the effect of increasing tangible prices at an increasing rate.

For the 1974 to 1984 period when inflation peaked and started to decline, tangibles, as a group, increased as a proportion of the portfolio (Table 7). For the 0 percent, 10 percent, 20 percent, 30 percent, 40 percent, and 50 percent tax brackets with normal variance, the proportion of tangibles in the portfolio are 63 percent, 64 percent, 70 percent, 71 percent, 73 percent, and 73 percent, respectively.

Gold and Chinese ceramics far outpaced the other tangibles in their allocation to the portfolio. The allocation for gold ranged from 30 to 44 percent, depending on the tax bracket. The allocation for Chinese ceramics varied from 19 to 24 percent, depending on the tax bracket. Diamonds disappeared from the portfolio entirely, while Old Masters were still an insignificant 1 to 2 percent. Silver declined to 0 to 3 percent of the portfolio. The portfolio allocations for U.S. coins and U.S. stamps were small, ranging from 0 to 4 percent and 5 to 6 percent, respectively.

For the combined period 1969 to 1984, tangibles, as a group, increased as a proportion of the portfolio for both subperiods (1969 to 1979 and 1974 to 1984). Tangibles, as a group, in the portfolio with normal variance are 64 percent, 68 percent, 70 percent, 75 percent, 76 percent, and 78 percent for the 0 percent, 10 percent, 20 percent, 30 percent, 40 percent, and 50 percent tax brackets, respectively.

Again, gold and Chinese ceramics far outpaced the other collectibles. Gold ranged from 24 to 34 percent, depending on the tax bracket, while Chinese ceramics ranged from 20 to 30 percent, depending on the tax bracket. The high allocations for gold and Chinese ceramics did not leave much of the portfolio for the other tangibles. Old Masters increased slightly, but still ranged from only 1 to 3 percent. Diamonds virtually did not enter the portfolio. One surprise is that U.S. coins almost disappeared from all portfolios except for the zero percent tax bracket. The allocation for U.S. stamps ranged from 5 to 7 percent of the total portfolio while silver ranged from 6 to 7 percent of the portfolio.

CONCLUSION

Although portfolio simulations indicated a high allocation for tangibles as a group, the variation for specific tangibles was very high. In general, the highest allocations were for gold, which got as high as 44 percent of the portfolio for one instance (50 percent tax bracket, 1974 to 1984 period) and Chinese ceramics, which got as high as 30 percent of the portfolio for one instance (50 percent tax bracket, 1969 to 1984 period). At the other end were allocations of zero for diamonds, U.S. coins, and Old Masters for various periods and tax brackets. This indicates that, in a real-life mixed-asset portfolio context, all tangibles are not equally beneficial. When examined individually, many tangibles undoubtedly appear to offer much more promise than when examined in a portfolio context.

Since investing in many types of tangibles requires a substantial amount of specialized knowledge and it is not possible for most people to be expert in even the small number of tangibles discussed in this article, substitution probably occurs. That is, an investor who knows about gold and U.S. stamps may buy increased amounts of them to substitute for other tangibles about which he knows very little or nothing. Nevertheless, these simulations would indicate that, using purely financial considerations (ignoring the nonmonetary returns), knowledge about some tangibles would be better than knowledge about certain others. Knowledge about precious metals, especially gold, would be especially worthwhile.

SUGGESTED READING

Brueggeman, W.B., Chen, A.H., and Thibodeau, T.G. "Real Estate Investment Funds: Performance and Portfolio Considerations," *AREUEA Journal*, Fall 1984, pp. 333–354.

Elton, E.J., Gruber, M.J., and Padberg, M.W. "Simple Criteria for Optimal Portfolio Selection," *Journal of Finance*, Dec. 1976.

Elton, E.J., and Gruber, M.J. *Modern Portfolio Theory and Investment Analysis*. New York: John Wiley & Sons, 1981.

Eun, Charles S., and Curcio, Richard J. "Diversification Gains from Including Real Estate in Mixed-Asset Portfolios." Paper presented at the 1983 annual meeting of the Financial Management Association, Atlanta, Georgia.

Fogler, H. Russell, Granito, Michael R., and Smith, Laurence R. "The Role of Real Estate in Portfolio Diversification." Paper presented at the 1984 Allied Social Science Annual Meeting, Dallas, Texas.

Friedman, H.C. "Real Estate Investment and Portfolio Theory," *Journal of Financial and Quantitative Analysis*, Mar. 1971, pp. 861–874.

Ibbotson, Roger G., and Siegel, Laurence B. "Real Estate Returns: A Comparison with Other Investments," *AREUEA Journal*, Fall 1984, pp. 219–242.

Ibbotson, Roger G., Siegel, Laurence B., and Love, Kathryn S. "World Wealth: U.S. and Foreign Market Values and Returns," *The Journal of Portfolio Management*, Nov. 1985.

Ibbotson, Roger G., and Sinquefield, Rex A. *Stocks, Bonds, Bills and Inflation: The Past and the Future*. Financial Analysts Research Foundation, 1982.

Kaplan, Howard. "Farm Land Investment." Paper presented at the 1984 Allied Social Science Annual Meeting, Dallas, Texas.

Roll, R. "A Critique of the Asset Pricing Theory's Tests. Part I: On Past and Potential Testability of the Theory," *Journal of Financial Economics*, Mar. 1977, pp. 129–176.

Salomon, R.S., Jr. *Investment Policy Report on Tangible Assets*. Reports, various issues. New York: Salomon Brothers Inc.

Sherman, Eugene. "The Application of Modern Portfolio Theory to Gold, 1974–1983." Paper presented at the 1984 Allied Social Science Annual Meeting, Dallas, Texas.

Webb, James R., and Rubens, Jack H. "Portfolio Considerations in the Valuation of Real Estate," *AREUEA Journal*, 1984.

DIVERSIFICATION THROUGH INTERNATIONAL MONEY MARKETS

Adrian F. Lee

The world's fixed-income markets totaled $9,400 billion publicly issued securities at the end of 1987. Table 1 shows a breakdown by country and issuer. These large, liquid markets generally comprise government or government agency bonds. Fixed-income markets have offered, and should continue to offer, opportunities to U.S. investors for returns and diversification outside the U.S. domestic market.

The case for diversification into these markets by a U.S. investor is significantly enhanced by considering the benefits of diversification on a currency-hedged basis. The purchase of a foreign security represents an investment in the asset purchased and also in the currency in which this asset is denominated. This currency exposure can be reduced by separately selling the currency exposure forward for the base currency. When the full exposure is sold forward, a fully hedged foreign asset is created. Fully hedged foreign returns are made up of the local market returns plus the forward premiums.

Hedged international fixed income overcomes some of the traditional drawbacks associated with international fixed-income investment, such as currency risk and duplication with international equity investment. In doing so, it provides the investor with the following benefits:

- Return opportunities beyond domestic fixed income
- Volatility reduction in overall fixed-income portfolios
- Diversification versus all domestic assets as well as international equities

Adrian F. Lee is Vice-President in charge of International Capital Markets Research and New Product Development at J.P. Morgan Investment Management, Inc., New York.

TABLE 1. Breakdown of World Bond Markets

Bond Market	Total Publicly Issued	As % of Issues in All Markets	Central Gov't	Central Gov't Agency and Gov't Guarantee	State and Local Gov't	Corp.	Other Domestic Publicly Issued	International Bonds: Foreign Bonds	International Bonds: Euro Bonds	Private Placement and Unclassified
U.S. dollar	$4,165.7	44.3%	$1,335.2	$945.1	$778.3	$658.5	$ 16.0	$ 55.1	$379.5	$364.8
Japanese yen	2,120.6	22.6	1,236.2	153.5	54.0	157.3	412.7	41.0	65.9	346.9
deutschemark	811.5	8.6	191.7	34.6	23.6	1.6	458.0	104.0		328.4
Italian lira	540.1	5.7	415.5	24.6	—	5.4	91.3	1.8	1.5	—
French franc	336.8	3.6	98.9	160.5	3.6	62.8	—	3.1	7.9	—
U.K. sterling	332.7	3.5	258.6	—	0.2	19.4	—	6.6	47.9	—
Belgian franc	196.8	2.1	97.0	60.4	—	7.6	27.0	4.4	0.4	—
Canadian dollar	192.9	2.1	78.4	0.1	63.4	31.3	0.7	0.8	18.2	—
Swiss franc	171.7	1.8	9.1	—	10.5	35.2	38.4	80.5	—	58.1
Danish krone	171.2	1.8	49.8	—	—	—	117.9	—	3.5	—
Swedish krona	160.6	1.7	68.7	—	2.4	12.8	76.8	—	0.1	—
Dutch guilder	128.4	1.4	77.3	—	3.9	29.8	—	12.1	5.3	92.2
Australian dollar	73.6	0.8	28.5	13.8	—	12.9	—	—	18.4	25.9
Total	$9,402.6		$3,944.9	$1,392.6	$937.9	$1,034.6	$1,234.6	$858.0		$1,216.3
Sector as a percent of public issues in all markets		100.0%	42.0%	14.8%	10.0%	11.0%	13.1%	9.1%		

Note: Size of major bond markets at year-end 1987 (nominal value outstanding in billions of U.S. dollars equivalent).

Source: *How Big Is the World Bond Market?—1988 Update*, Salomon Brothers, Inc.

Hedged international fixed income is an attractive diversifying asset class, providing long asset returns with a risk level that has historically been only marginally greater than that of U.S. Treasury bills. Fundamentally, hedged international fixed income diversifies the exposure of fixed-income assets to changes in fiscal and monetary policies across many different governments and economies.

This discussion of the benefits of hedged international fixed income refers to the long run, or strategic benefits, of such a hedging policy. This point of view in no way reduces the role or need for active currency management on a tactical basis. Hedged investment simply suggests that the neutral currency exposure for tactical purposes should be considered as zero or 100 percent in the base currency. This approach can be contrasted with the more traditional one, which used the market capitalization of the foreign markets as the neutral currency exposure. In many ways, the role of tactical currency management is even more crucial in an environment in which international investment is defined on a fully hedged basis.

HISTORICAL BENEFITS OF HEDGED INTERNATIONAL FIXED INCOME

Opportunity for Return

The return to a U.S. investor from a fully hedged foreign bond investment is equal to the local market return plus the forward premium. The forward premium is equal to the interest rate differential between deposits in each market, with maturity equal to the length of the hedge contract.

Using monthly hedges rolled over, Figure 1 shows the returns to hedged and unhedged fixed-income investments (ten-year government bonds) in the major markets over the last ten years. It is assumed that any market appreciation during the month was known and hedged at the beginning of the month. This residual, which in practice cannot be hedged, was and can be expected to be insignificant over extended periods.

The unhedged non-U.S. fixed-income market significantly outperformed the U.S. market over the last five years, but underperformed it over the previous five years. The hedged non-U.S. markets slightly underperformed the U.S. market over the last five years, but significantly outperformed it over the previous five. Figure 1 shows the opportunity for outperformance versus the U.S. markets in individual markets and in the aggregate, but also shows the possibility of underperformance for extended periods.

Volatility Reduction in Fixed-Income Portfolios

Figure 2 shows the historical volatility, or risk, of hedged investment in each of the major fixed-income markets. Each individual foreign market has been less risky than the U.S. alone; in the aggregate, non-U.S. markets had a risk of 5 percent over the last five years and 5.4 percent over the previous 5 years. This situation can be contrasted with the higher risk levels on an unhedged basis.

However, the key benefit of non-U.S. fixed-income investment is the risk reduction or diversification it provides a U.S. fixed-income portfolio. A world portfolio of U.S. and hedged non-U.S. bonds was consistently less risky than the U.S. market over the period 1978 to 1987. A world portfolio was weighted approximately 50 percent U.S. and 50 percent non-U.S.

FIGURE 1. International Fixed-Income Markets—Compound Returns

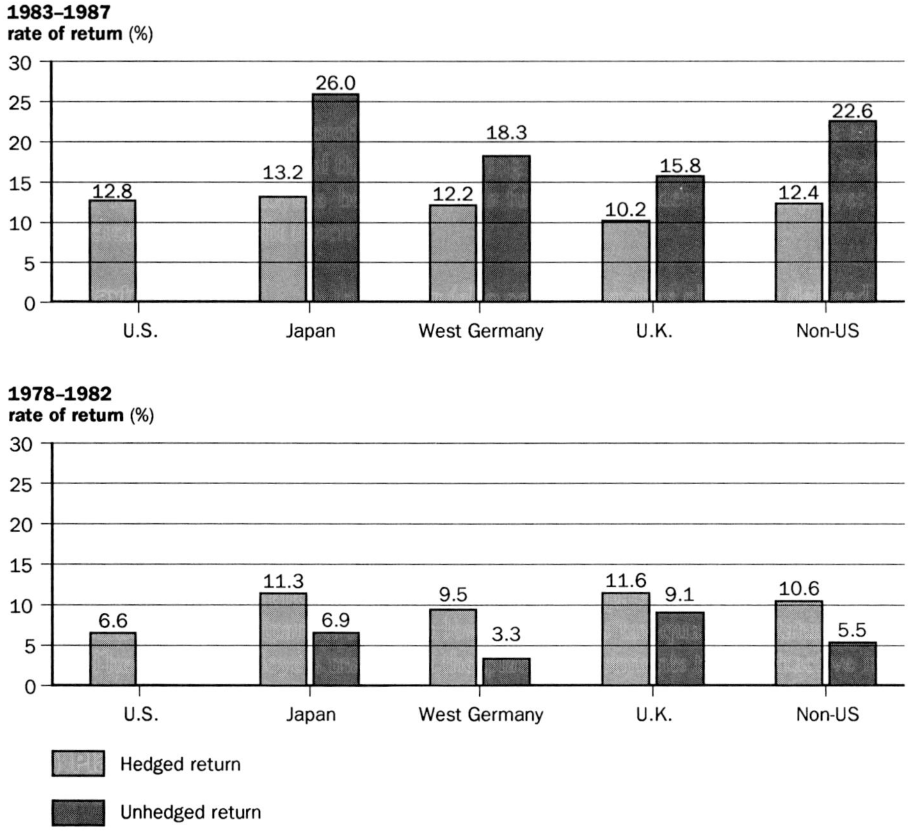

The fixed-income diversification benefits over various combinations of U.S. and non-U.S. markets on a hedged and unhedged basis are plotted in Figure 3. It can be observed that any size allocation to non-U.S. bonds reduced total fixed-income risk consistently over the period 1978 to 1987. For example, for the period 1983–1987, a 25 percent allocation to non-U.S. bonds (hedged) reduced the total portfolio risk from approximately 10 percent to 8 percent per year.

Historically, this risk reduction has been due in part to the fact that the non-U.S. markets have in themselves been less risky individually; more significantly, they are the result of the diversification effect across many markets. While it may not be reasonable to expect each individual non-U.S. market to be less risky than the U.S. market, it is reasonable to expect that any diversified portfolio of markets will be less risky than any individual one.

The risk benefits of hedged international fixed income can be contrasted with those available from unhedged international fixed income, the latter providing some diversification benefits for allocations of up to approximately 30 percent.

FIGURE 2. International Fixed-Income Markets—Standard Deviation of Return

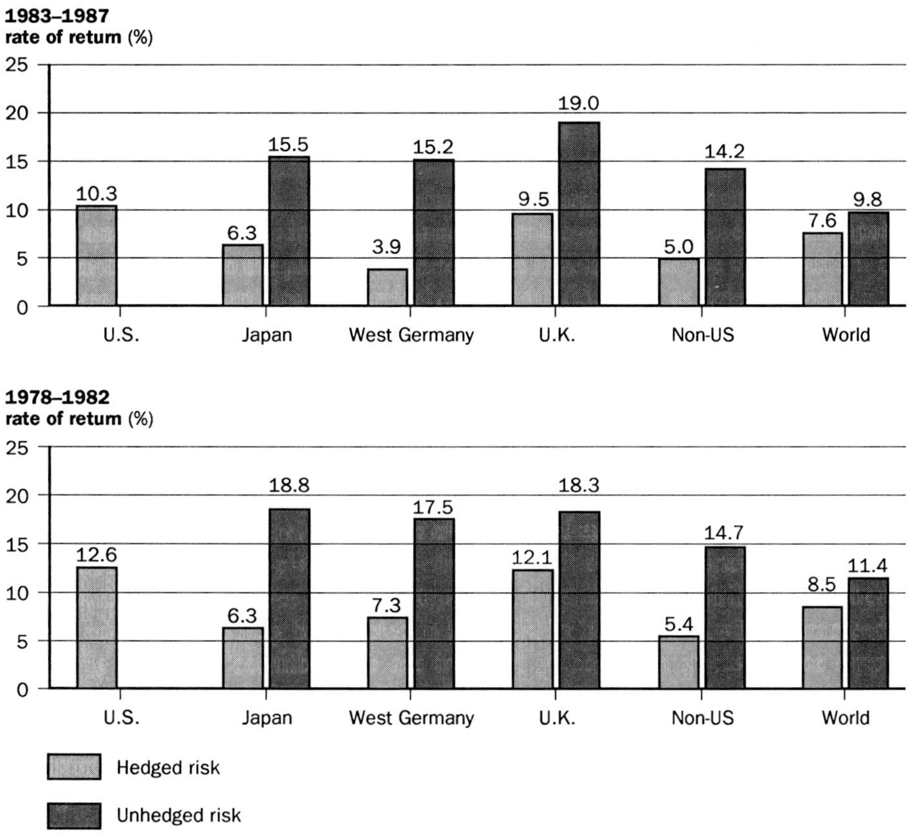

Total Portfolio Diversification

Hedged international fixed income offers diversification in the context of the total portfolio. Diversification benefits in general are measured by the correlation or, more precisely, lack of correlation between different asset categories.

These correlations over the last ten years are highlighted in Figure 4. These data indicate that historically hedged international fixed income has had low correlations with U.S. stocks (.12), U.S. bonds (.54), and, more important, non-U.S. stocks (.39). This correlation of .39 between non-U.S. stocks and non-U.S. bonds (hedged) can be contrasted with the equivalent correlation with non-U.S. bonds (unhedged), which was .66. This relatively high correlation is due in part to the duplicated currency exposure of international stocks and bonds. Hedging reduces this duplication and thereby improves diversification.

The shaded area in Figure 4 represents the historical improvement in terms of total portfolio risk and returns to a U.S. investor who, already invested in U.S. stocks, U.S. bonds, and non-U.S. stocks, considers the inclusion of hedged international fixed income.

FIGURE 3. Fixed-Income Diversification Benefits, 1978—1987 (U.S. dollars)

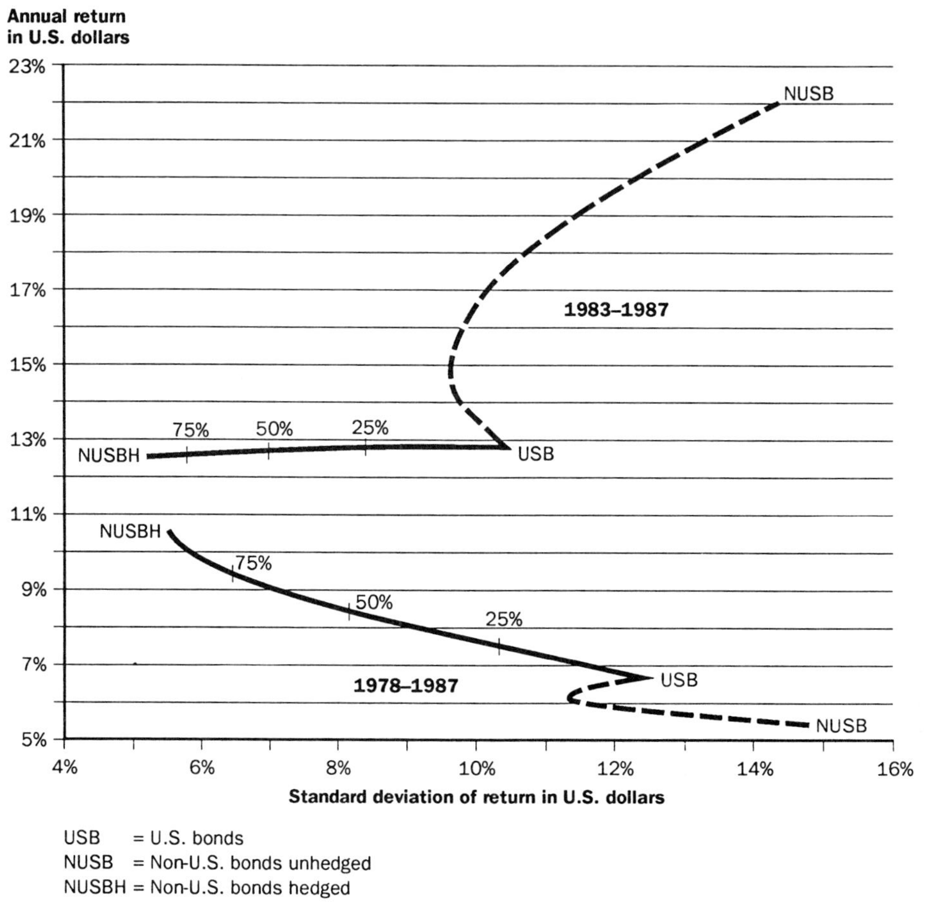

OPTIMAL ASSET ALLOCATION

This section provides a framework within which investors can identify appropriate asset allocation strategies for the future. Asset allocation is appropriately based on the investor's expectations for returns, risk, and covariance. These expectations should reflect relationships that are anticipated to hold over an extended period of time. An illustration of one such set of equilibrium expectations is shown in Table 2. The table shows the expected benefits or value added from the inclusion of each separate asset class in an unconstrained and then in a constrained environment. It also examines the sensitivity of these benefits to changes in expectations for returns.

The equilibrium assumptions in Table 2 imply a number of expectations:

- U.S. stocks will outperform U.S. bonds, but with higher risk.
- International stocks will slightly outperform U.S. stocks with a marginally higher risk.

FIGURE 4. Total Portfolio Diversification Benefits, 1978–1987 (U.S. dollars)

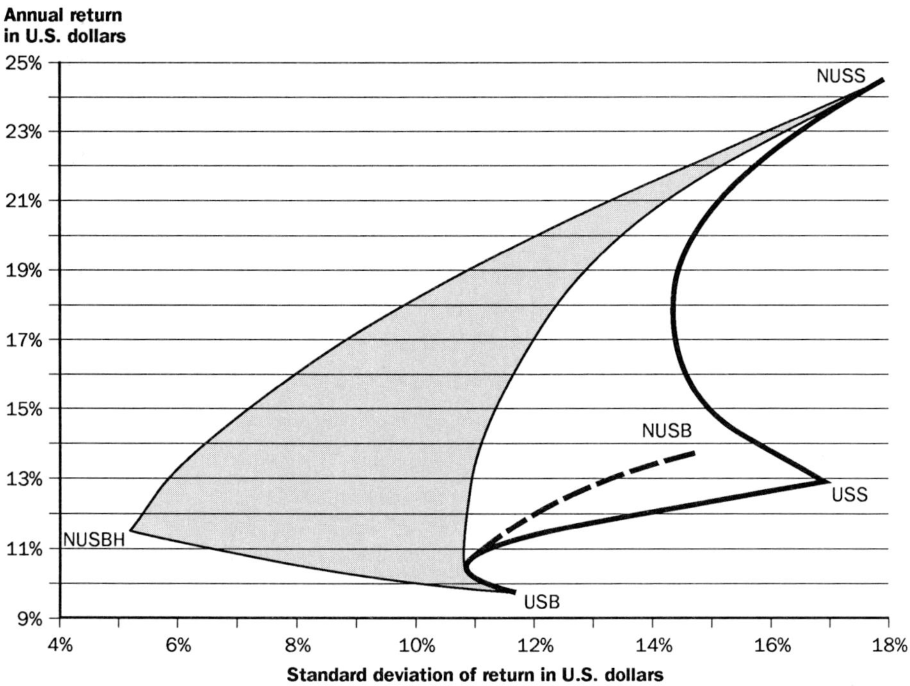

Correlations

U.S. stocks (USS)	1				
U.S. bonds (USB)	.28	1			
Non-U.S. stocks (NUSS)	.39	.25	1		
Non-U.S. bonds (NUSB)	.02	.41	.66	1	
Non-U.S. bonds hedged (NUSBH)	.12	.54	.39	.68	1

TABLE 2. Illustrative Equilibrium Assumptions—U.S. Investor

	Annual Return	Annual Standard Deviation	Correlation of Return				
U.S. equities	10.5%	18.0%	1.00				
U.S. bonds	7.5	9.0	.30	1.00			
Non-U.S. equities	11.0	20.0	.40	.25	1.00		
Non-U.S. bonds	7.5	11.0	.00	.40	.65	1.00	
Non-U.S. bonds–hedged	7.5	4.5	.10	.55	.40	.65	1.00

- Non-U.S. bonds will perform in line with U.S. bonds but with a higher risk due to currency exposure.
- Hedged non-U.S. bonds will perform in line with unhedged non-U.S. bonds but with less risk.
- The approximate interrelationships of the past between these asset classes will hold into the future.

There is considerable historical and theoretical evidence to support expectations that broadly reflect these relationships. In particular, there are four justifications for hedged and unhedged expected returns being equal over the long run.

1. The rational expectation that forward exchange markets cannot be surprised continuously in one direction
2. The expectation that purchasing power parity should hold in the long run and that short-term real rates are expected to be equal across markets, again in the long run
3. The lack of significant theoretical or empirical evidence that there is a systematic reward associated with bearing currency risk
4. The theoretical contradiction associated with simultaneously rewarding a U.S. investor for bearing currency risk and a foreign investor for bearing U.S. dollar risk (theory suggests that currency should be expected to be a zero sum game)

It is worth stressing that equilibrium assumptions, by definition, are highly likely not to be realized over short or even extended periods. For example, hedged and unhedged returns differed by more than 10 percent per year over the five years ending December 1987. Ultimately, investors must identify, explicitly or implicitly, expectations with which they feel comfortable. These assumptions are presented for illustrative purposes only.

On the basis of these expectations and quadratic optimization techniques that minimize risk and maximize returns, the marginal benefits of the inclusion of each asset class separately into the investor's opportunity set can be examined. Figure 5 illustrates the results of this analysis.

The line "U.S. bonds/U.S. stocks" represents the return and risk opportunity range available to the investor who considers U.S. bonds and stocks only. For example, Portfolio A on this line is 45 percent U.S. bonds and 55 percent U.S. stocks. If the investor is also allowed to include international equities in his portfolio, then the available opportunity set is shifted to the line marked "International Equity." Here, Portfolio B has the same risk as Portfolio A, but higher expected return. Portfolio B is made up of 30 percent U.S. bonds, 35 percent U.S. stocks, and 35 percent international equity.

The added inclusion of international bonds, as represented by the shift to the line "International Bonds," has an insignificant impact on return and risk opportunities, because of the relatively high correlation between international bonds and international equities and the significant allocations to international equities. This result suggests that in the presence of existing international equity allocations, the international fixed-income diversification has limited impact except at the lowest levels of risk.

FIGURE 5. Return/Risk Opportunity Set Under No Constraints

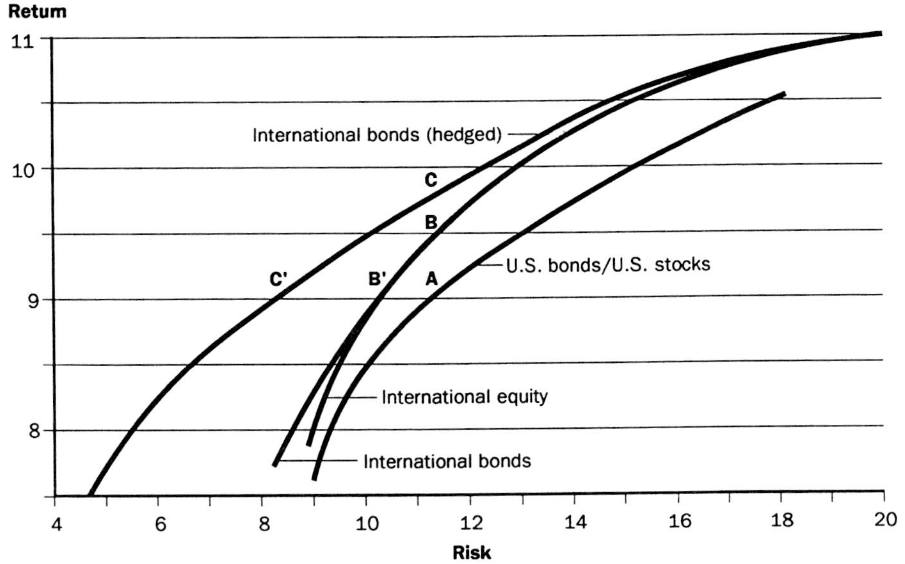

Assets	A	B	B'	C	C'
	Portfolio composition (%)				
U.S. bonds	45	30	50	—	—
U.S. stocks	55	35	25	40	30
International equity	—	35	25	35	25
International bonds	—	—	—	—	—
International bonds (hedged)	—	—	—	25	45

If, however, international bonds (hedged) are included in the universe of available assets, then the return/risk opportunity set is significantly enhanced, as represented by the shift to the line "International Bonds (hedged)." Here, Portfolio C, which is comprised of 40 percent U.S. stocks, 35 percent international equities, and 25 percent international bonds (hedged), has the same risk as Portfolio A., but significantly higher return.

It appears that the value added from hedged international fixed income is significant, particularly at moderate to lower levels of risk.

Figure 6 presents the results of these optimizations in a constrained environment, where international assets in total must not exceed 30 percent of the portfolio. In this environment, the allocation to international fixed income (hedged) appears to be inversely related to the overall risk level of the portfolio, but is still desirable in portfolios in which the domestic stock/bond ratio is as high as 2:1 (Risk Level III).

FIGURE 6. International Assets Constrained to 30 percent Maximum

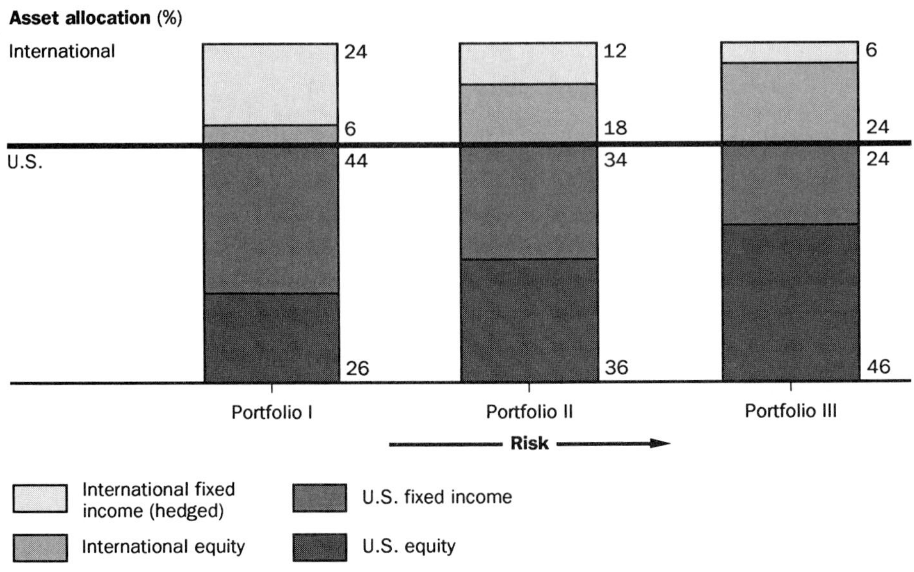

FIGURE 7. Impact of Change in Expected Return of Hedged International Fixed Income

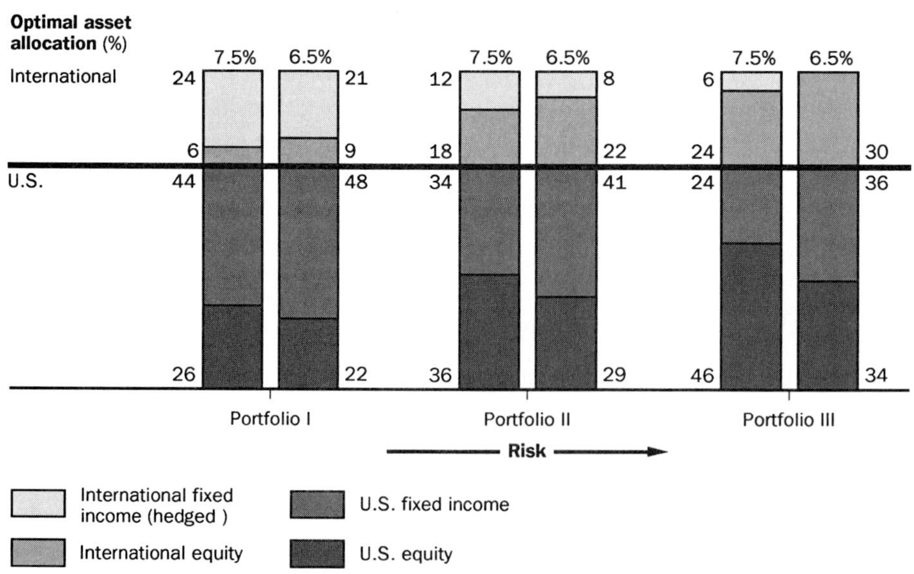

Sensitivity Analysis

It is important to be aware of the sensitivity of the role of hedged international fixed income to a reduction in the long-run expected return from international fixed income and the impact of a positive long-run return to currency exposure. Figure 7 shows how the optimal long-run allocations to the various asset classes alter, if the expected return to hedged international fixed income is reduced by one percent. The results vary by risk level. At risk level I, the optimal allocation to hedged international fixed income is reduced from 24 percent to 21 percent. At risk level III, international fixed income is replaced by international equity. Figure 7 suggests that the case for hedged international fixed income is more sensitive to changes in expected return for high-risk investors than for low-risk investors.

If currencies are expected to appreciate over the long run in excess of what is implied by the forward premium, then the expected currency surprise is defined as being greater than zero. Figure 8 shows the role of hedged versus unhedged international fixed income for varying levels of currency surprise, for a given level of risk. For example, if the currency surprise is expected to be 2 percent per year, then the international portfolio should be structured as 45 percent equity, 40 percent hedged international fixed income, and 15 percent international fixed income (unhedged). It is not until the currency surprise is as high as 6 percent per year that hedged international fixed income appears to be dominated by unhedged international fixed income. These results are dependent to some extent on the

FIGURE 8. Impact of Currency Surprise

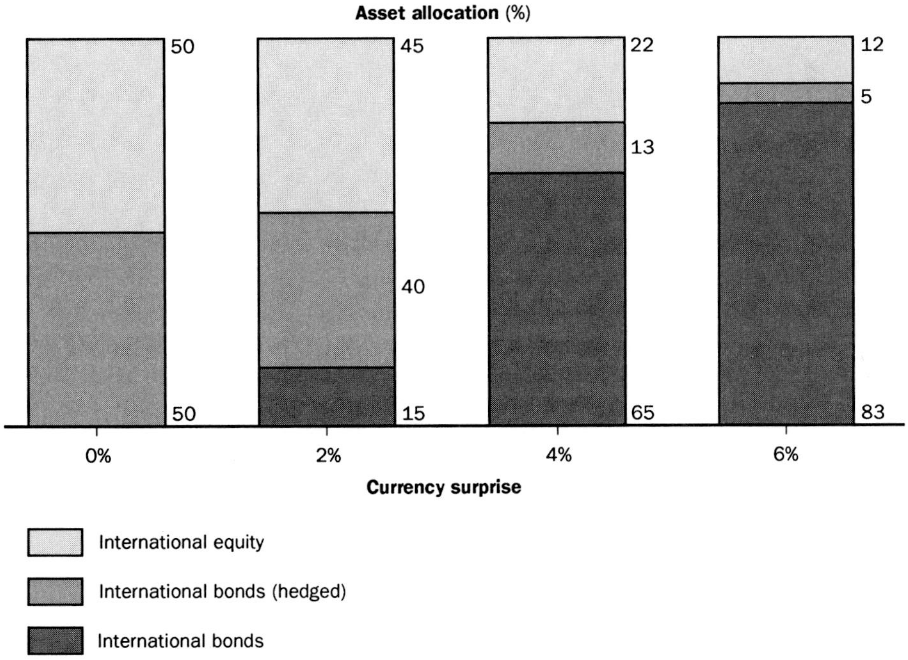

risk level chosen as well as the fact that international equity is unhedged; but overall, they appear to indicate that one requires quite optimistic expectations for foreign currencies to justify a fully unhedged international fixed-income investment.

SUMMARY

On the basis of past evidence and equilibrium expectations, hedged international fixed income offers an investor several benefits, including the opportunity for enhanced return, reduced volatility in the fixed income portfolio, and diversification. Hedged international fixed income can be an attractive diversifying separate asset class.

ESTATE PLANNING FOR INVESTORS

D. Larry Crumbley
Edward E. Milam

In these days of inflation, investments grow in value more rapidly than ever before. Many investors are surprised to find that they have problems with a tax that they have never heard of before: the estate tax. The federal government imposes a tax on the fair market value of all assets, less liabilities, held by a person when he dies. This amount includes life insurance (even though paid to someone else) and property owned jointly with someone else. The first \$600,000 of a deceased person's estate is not taxable (\$1.2 million in a community property state). The law is written so that the first \$192,800 of estate taxes is not paid, which converts into a taxable estate of about \$600,000. Thereafter, the tax graduates from 32 percent up to an eventual 50 percent in the highest bracket.

Many state governments also impose inheritance taxes on the amounts received by the individual heirs. Here again, there is usually an exemption for a certain amount of property, depending on the relationship of the heir to the person who died. However, there are many instances where the federal and state death taxes consumed a major portion of the decedent's estate where there was inadequate tax planning. For example, the late Howard Hunt left an estate of about \$460 million. The death taxes on his estate were 77 percent because he died in 1976 without a will.

D. Larry Crumbley, Ph.D., CPA, is Shelton Taxation Professor at Texas A&M University and editor of the Handbook of Estate Planning, *published by Dow Jones-Irwin. Edward E. Milam, Ph.D., CPA, is Professor of Accounting at the University of Mississippi.*

DEATH TAXES

Gift taxes and estate taxes are excise taxes imposed on the transfer of taxable amount of property during life or on death. They are also called succession taxes and transfer taxes. On transfers during life, the primary liability for payment of any resulting gift tax is on the donor. If he does not pay it, the donee has secondary liability. The estate tax is imposed on the aggregate value of all property left by a decedent after reduction by deductions and credits, and is payable by the estate's executor or administrator out of that property. The degree of kinship, if any, of heirs to the decedent is immaterial.

An estate tax differs from an inheritance tax. An inheritance tax, which is imposed by most states, is based on the value of property passing to each particular heir. The exempt amounts and tax rates depend on the degree of kinship of the heir to the decedent and the value of the property passing to the particular heir. The primary liability for payment is on the heir, but decedents' wills frequently provide for payment of state inheritance taxes out of the residuary estate. A few states also have an estate tax. Less than a handful impose a gift tax. Estate planning, therefore, is essential for all investors.

THE NEED FOR ESTATE PLANNING

Estate planning has been defined as the art of designing a program for the effective enjoyment, management, and disposition of property at the minimum possible tax cost. It is more than just planning for death. Estate planning tries to encourage a wealth-building approach for investors. It looks at the income tax, fiduciary tax, estate tax, and gift tax to minimize the overall tax burden of the family unit. Building an estate throughout life should be part of estate planning.

Anyone with income, property, and investments must be concerned with estate planning. It may be even more important to the owner of a medium-sized estate than to the owner of a large estate, because the waste of a single asset in such an estate could prevent the accomplishment of objectives and bring hardship to the family unit. In other words, everyone who owns assets needs an estate plan. The estate plan might be reflected by a simple will or by a complex arrangement consisting of several of the estate planning devices or tools available to the estate owner.

Implementing and Reviewing the Plan

Before the estate plan becomes effective, the appropriate legal documents must be executed. The necessity for careful planning and execution of the legal documents cannot be overemphasized, for faulty execution is a sure way of invalidating the entire efforts of any estate plan. Thus, these legal instruments must be drafted by a competent attorney who is well versed in estate planning techniques.

These documents must be reviewed periodically to ascertain that they continue to express the objectives of the estate owner. A periodic review of the financial status and family relationships should be conducted to determine if there have been any changes that necessitate a revision of the estate plan. For example, a divorce would necessitate a change in an investor's will. Also, the plan should be reviewed in the light of any changes or potential changes in the relevant legal or tax aspects. Such a review could bring about a modification in the plan that would produce significant benefits to the estate owner, while the neglect of such a review could be very costly.

As can be seen from the preceding discussion of the estate planning process, many professional skills are required to effectively perform such a service. Usually, a team effort is used during the process. The attorney, the accountant (CPA), the trust officer, and the life insurance underwriter are the professionals most often associated with the team.

Estate Planning Team

By virtue of a tendency toward salesmanship, the life insurance underwriter may be the prime motivator to interest prospects in an estate plan that will eventually involve the orchestration of the other members of the estate planning team. Unlike the lawyer and the accountant, the insurance salesperson has a license to sell and has a special skill to seek out and solicit new insurance business. Often, the life insurance underwriter uncovers situations in which only a properly executed estate plan can save a taxpayer's estate from erosion. Also, the insurance underwriter has a specialized knowledge of the many forms of life insurance and knows what various policies can and cannot do.

The attorney's participation is essential in determining the legal and tax consequences of every phase in the process of developing an estate plan. The lawyer must determine whether certain recommendations and phases in the formulation of the plan have legal substance and merit. Only a competent attorney can draft the legal documents that provide the framework for the execution of an effective estate plan.

Estate planning is the trust officer's prime concern and constitutes the bulk of the trust department's activities. The trust officer, who is essentially an instrument of estate conservation and management, can lend advice on the practicalities of the plan and play a major role in the administration of the estate. Under a specific agreement, the trust officer accepts custody of the property, manages and invests it, and distributes it to the beneficiaries according to the stipulations of the trust instrument.

Normally, the accountant is considered to be the member of the estate planning team who is intimately acquainted with the financial affairs of the taxpayer and is knowledgeable about income and estate tax laws. In addition, the CPA is to advise on valuation problems and to determine the existing and potential earning power of a business. Otherwise, the accountant's role as a member of the estate planning team is not so easily ascertained or clearly defined as the roles of the other members; but because accountants know their client's affairs, they should recognize each client's need for estate planning services. Therefore, the accountant is often the person on the team who has the responsibility to initiate the estate process.

Estate Administration

A number of players are involved in estate administration (see Figure 1). The estate planning team participates in the final estate administration. The county or state probate court is also an important participant. The functions of the probate court are to oversee the executor, conserve the decedent's assets, interpret the will, and, if there is no will, apply the laws of intestate succession.

The will designates an executor or executrix (quite often the surviving spouse) to manage the assets and liabilites of the decedent. It is not an easy task and may be time-consuming. The major roles of the executor are to search for all the assets, publish notices to creditors in local newspapers, file appropriate estate and income tax returns, pay expenses and liabilities, and distribute the remaining assets to the beneficiaries. The executor will

FIGURE 1. The Players in Estate Administration
Source: *Federal Reserve Bulletin*

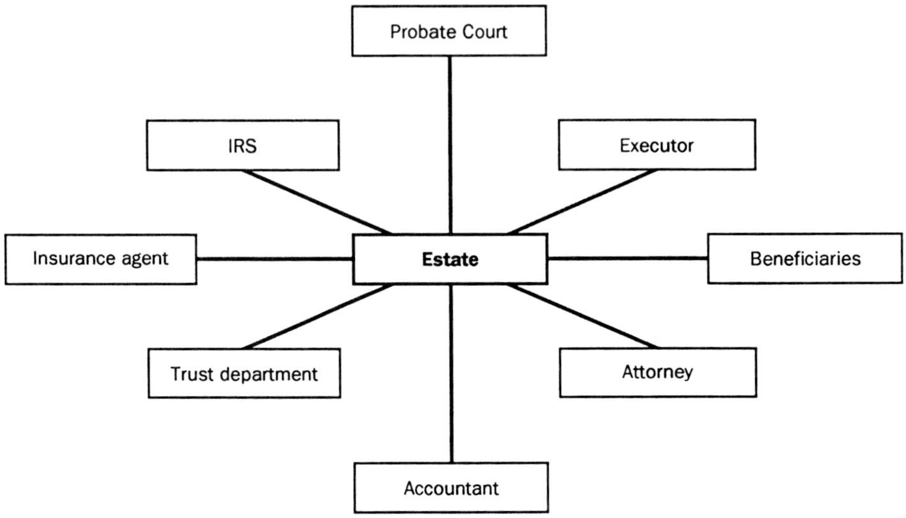

control only the probate assets. There are often assets in the gross estate that do not go through probate (e.g., jointly held property, life insurance proceeds, and trust assets).

Obviously, the Internal Revenue Service (IRS) is an interested participant. The income tax return (Form 1040), the estate tax return (Form 706), and the estate income tax return (Form 1041) may be required. Proper estate planning, however, will help minimize the overall impact of these death taxes.

The Estate Owner's Will

The will is a key vehicle of transfer, and its preparation is often the first step taken by investors in planning the disposition of their estates. Everybody needs a will. Stories are legion about the disastrous consequences of dying intestate, which refers to dying without a will. In such a situation, the state laws specify how the assets will be distributed, thus providing a will by default. The county or state probate court will appoint an administrator (who may or may not be qualified to manage the estate). Most intestate succession laws favor the surviving spouse, child, or grandchildren. However, assets might also be assigned to children of a previous marriage, to distant nephews and nieces, or even to enemies. The estate process can drag on for many years because of conflicting claims and so forth. The lawyers may get the bulk of the estate assets.

Without a will, an estate owner in effect agrees to allow the state to draft his will. Most state laws assume that family members (and not friends) are the natural objects of one's bounty. For the nearly two million unmarried couples living together, dying without a will can have catastrophic consequences. Most state laws do not recognize a living-together relationship. Certainly, the law on intestate succession is especially problematic for homosexuals. Young people do not necessarily live to old age.

Wills and estate plans become outdated and must be reviewed and revised. People outgrow their initial wills, and new laws make revision of wills essential. Thus, estate planning is a lifelong process.

If a person runs a business, mention should be made in the will concerning operation of the business after death. In some states, an executor cannot lawfully continue a business without a specific authorization. The business operation may come to a halt, buildings may deteriorate, or the business may have to liquidate if proper authority is not given.

The will is used to designate heirs, identify the property they are to receive, indicate the person (or institution) who will act as executor or executrix of the estate, and clarify similar details. Some useful provisions attached to the will are the marital deduction and the marital deduction trusts. The basic advantage of using the marital deduction concerns the favorable tax consequences. The cost of this tax savings, however, may be the compromise of the estate owner's objectives, the possible deferred increase in transfer costs, or the loss of control of an asset.

Under certain conditions and limitations, the estates of citizens and residents of the United States are allowed an unlimited marital deduction. The purpose of the marital deduction is to eliminate the tax advantages held by those persons domiciled in community property states. These statutes provide all taxpayers with the same tax treatment as was previously available only to residents of community property states.

Trusts

Trusts are another means of orderly estate transfer. Inter vivos and testamentary, revocable and irrevocable, and funded and unfunded trusts may be used by the estate planner. Some of the important advantages of trusts are that they are based on the concepts of property arrangement and property settlement. The main purpose of the trust device is to serve as a means of preserving and administering property for the benefit of the beneficiaries.

Because it permits considerable flexibility in the disposition of property, the trust is one of the most valuable tools used in estate planning. It provides the flexibility needed to achieve nontax objectives, such as relieving other family members of responsibility, obtaining competent management of the property, providing discretion in income and principal distributions, and many others. Also advantageous, and perhaps equally significant in many instances, are the income and estate tax economies obtainable through the use of trusts.

Trusts are formed for many purposes. A trust may be created to achieve any desired objective, as long as the objective is not illegal or contrary to any policy or rule of law. Some of the more common types of trusts, classified as to purpose, include insurance trusts, educational trusts, support trusts, charitable trusts, exemption-equivalent trusts, and marital-deduction trusts.

When a trust is created, it is only natural and proper that the grantor and the estate planning team should construct it in a way that maximizes the use of the available favorable tax provisions. However, the purpose of a trust's establishment is ordinarily not just to save taxes. The saving of taxes is one reason for the creation of trusts, but the process of carrying out an orderly and sensible disposition of the trust property according to the desires of the estate owner should be the primary reason for its establishment. The generation-skipping tax must be considered when a trust is established, however.

Many estate owners dislike the fact that the amount of their estate and the way in which they provide for their families become public record. All property subject to probate or to court disposition becomes public record and thus is open to public scrutiny. The sure way to avoid this public scrutiny is to avoid probate.

In a smaller estate, probate can be avoided by holding property jointly between spouses. On the death of the first spouse, all the property goes to the surviving spouse outside of probate, and administration expenses are reduced. Such jointly held property may be exempt from state inheritance taxes along with disclosure and reporting requirements.

Estate owners also can avoid probate by placing their investment properties in a revocable trust for the benefit of their survivors (the so-called living trust). The trust becomes irrevocable on the grantor's death. The fact is that property left in trust is not subject to probate; neither does it become part of the basis from which the executor and attorney fees are determined. Thus, by placing investment property in trust, the estate owner avoids the public scrutiny and reduces the amount of the executor fees that the estate has to pay. Also, disgruntled relatives are more prone to attack the capacity of estate owners to make a will than the right of the estate owner to establish an inter vivos trust.

Life Insurance

Another means of transfer is life insurance, which is often the only practical way of guaranteeing that sufficient cash will be available to meet the financial cost of death. Life insurance has many advantages. In many states, its use provides savings in estate taxes. Also, insurance proceeds can be removed from the probate estate (by giving up all incidents of ownership), thus reducing probate and administrative costs. It many instances, the greatest advantage of life insurance in estate planning is that it can satisfy the obligations of the estate and thus prevent the forced sale of income-producing assets. In essence, whether to include life insurance in the estate plan should be determined by the needs for liquidity, flexibility, tax minimization, investment, and family income.

As with other devices of transfer, estate owners and their advisors should carefully consider the tax consequences of the use of life insurance, which provides many tax advantages.

Annuities

Private annuities represent another important vehicle of transfer. However, careful consideration must be given to the risks involved. In such a contract, the annuitant transfers property other than cash to the obligor in return for the obligor's unsecured promise to make periodic payments of money to the annuitant for a specific period of time. The period is usually for the life of the annuitant. Thus, the major risk to the annuitant is the obligor's failure to make the required payments.

Fortunately, the private annuity offers several tax advantages. First, since this is a valid sales contract, the property is removed from the estate of the obligor. Second, Section 72 of the Internal Revenue Code governs the income taxability of the annuity payments. Thus, each annuity payment is broken into three portions: an excluded portion, an ordinary income portion, and a capital gain or loss portion. This gives the annuitant the additional advantage of spreading any gain from the sale of such property over a period of several years for income tax purposes. In essence, it gives the annuitant a deferment for payment of income taxes associated with the transfer.

A set of 10 percent actuarial tables is used in valuation of annuities and life estates. These tables require higher payments to be made in retained-income transactions and generate interest income to the annuitant, with a nondeductible basis to the obligor. Thus, an alternative to a private annuity is a self-canceling installment note (SCIN). Essentially, the SCIN works as follows: A person sells an asset to someone (such as a relative) and receives an installment note. The installment note is paid in full over the actuarial life expectancy of the seller. Since the installment note is canceled automatically in the event of the seller's death, a risk premium is added to the sale price of the asset to compensate the seller for a possible early death. The SCIN may be superior to a private annuity.

Lifetime Gifts

Another effective vehicle of transfer in estate planning is the lifetime gift, which eliminates all probate and administration expenses on the property transferred. Gifts may reduce estate taxes because the gift plus income that would have accumulated from the property is removed from the transferor's gross estate. Often, the use of a gift provides savings in income taxes because the income is shifted from the high tax bracket of the transferor into the low tax bracket of the transferee. Of course, the use of gifts produces many advantages other than taxes. They may be used to continue control of a business within the family or to serve specific desires the estate owner has for his children. Gifts, like all other devices, have their costs; the most significant cost of making a gift is the complete loss of control of the asset. Of course, with the unified tax structure, the use of gifts as an estate planning tool has lost some of its glamour. Furthermore, the new kiddie tax on unearned income of children under age 14 is calculated at the custodial parent's marginal (highest) tax rate.

Since making gifts is an obvious method of avoiding the estate tax at death, the government imposes a tax on gift transfers to partially plug this escape route. However, gifts can still be made without incurring this tax. Tax-free gifts of $10,000 can be made to each person during each year, plus unified credit at any time during lifetime. Further, if spouses consent on the gift tax return to split their gifts, all gifts to third parties are considered as having been made one-half by each spouse. It may be advantageous to make gifts as time goes by.

A combination of the annual exclusion, the specific exemption, and the gift-splitting election allows a donor to transfer a great deal of property to family members and thereby escape the federal estate tax. For example, a husband and wife could transfer $2.4 million of tax-free gifts to their three sons and their wives over a ten-year period (if they die in 1987 and thereafter). The calculation of this tax-free amount is as follows:

$20,000 annual exclusion × 6	$ 120,000 per year
	× 10 years
	$1,200,000
Husband's equivalent exemption	600,000
Wife's equivalent exemption	600,000
Total tax-free amount	$2,400,000

This example demonstrates the advantages of planned and systematic inter vivos giving.

A transfer under the Gifts of Securities to Minors Act should also be considered. In a typical situation, the donor irrevocably transfers assets to a minor by registering the property in the name of a custodian designated by the donor. To be sure the property will not be included in the donor's estate, the donor should not be the custodian. The donor should make the spouse or someone else the custodian.

The donor must be able to prove that gifts are in fact made. For example, one father wished to leave several of his ivory figurines to each of his minor children. He identified the figurines by clearly labeling each child's initials under various figurines contained in his collection. But all the figurines remained in his safe-deposit box. In this case, the IRS refused to agree that the gifts had in fact been made.

Before making lifetime gifts, it must be remembered that, under certain circumstances, the gift property may later be included in the donor's gross estate along with a gross-up of the gift taxes, even though they were made during the donor's lifetime. Without adequate and full consideration of this tax risk, any transfers of certain types of property made by the decedent within three years of each are interpreted as having been made in contemplation of death; thus, such property and gift tax gross-ups are included in the donor's gross estate. Likewise, the relinquishment of a power over property transferred during lifetime, or the exercise or release of a power of appointment, within three years before death is deemed to have been made in contemplation of death.

As people become older and the value of their assets increases, a program of lifetime gifts may be beneficial. Let us assume that a wealthy married man in a high tax bracket plans to leave a portion of his estate to his children. If the father's estate surpasses the exemption-equivalent level, it may be advantageous for him to make gifts while he is still living. If the children who receive the gifts are in a low tax bracket, the taxpayer may both obtain savings in income tax and also use his unified credit early by giving a portion of the assets to them. Since the children will eventually receive the assets anyway, it makes sense for the father to distribute them in the most advantageous manner. Although it is usually beneficial to make gifts, many people do not use this valuable tax-planning tool. Findings indicate that ignorance of potential tax savings and other nontax factors are the major reasons.

The vehicles of transfer discussed in the preceding paragraphs are only some of those available to the estate owner. During the designing and before the implementation of an estate plan, the members of the estate planning team must evaluate the advantages and disadvantages of these methods of transfer. The vehicles that aid in the accomplishment of the estate owner's objectives should be incorporated into the estate plan.

Kiddie Tax

Shifting property to children may result in tax savings. However, if the child is age 13 or under, the $1,000 of dividends (unearned income) will be taxed to the child at the parent's top rate (effective maximum rate of 33 percent). Beginning in 1987, *all* unearned income of more than $1,000 received by a child under age 14 is *taxed to the child* at the parent's rate. This procedure will apply to income received after 1986 even if the property was transferred to the child before 1987 or the property was transferred to the child by someone other than the parents. However, if the child is over age 13, there can be a modest savings—the first $1,000 is not taxed and the remainder taxed at the child's (possibly lower) rate.

For children under age 14, parents (or grandparents) may wish to transfer the following items:

1. *Growth stock.* Such stock will pay little dividends, and the child can sell the stock after reaching age 14 and pay tax on any gain at the child's low rate.
2. *U.S. Savings bonds.* Series EE U.S. Savings bond can be selected to postpone interest accruals at maturity.

3. *Deep-discount municipal bonds*. Here, the bond interest is tax-free to the child, and the discount (face value less cost basis) is taxed when the bonds are redeemed at maturity.

4. *Appreciating collectible assets*.

INVENTORY OF INVESTMENT ASSETS

A danger facing many investors and traders is that on their death, no one in their family will have sufficient knowledge of which investments are valuable and which are not. This hazard is especially common where the decedent has a vast collection (e.g., coins, stamps, antiques, gems, sculptures, and art). Often, the other family members have no interest in the collection. Thus, the collector must keep a complete inventory of all investments at all times. Make certain the spouse or other family member knows where the inventory list is in case something should unexpectedly happen. There have been many valuable collections destroyed due to ignorance of their value.

DETERMINATION OF TAXABLE ESTATE AND ESTATE TAX

The taxable gross estate consists of much more than the probate estate (that is, in general, property actually and fully owned at the moment of death). Property deemed to be owned, primarily through an interest in a trust or as a depositor in a bank account, is also included. In some estates, a major part of the gross estate consists of life insurance proceeds, whether payble to named beneficiaries or to the estate, provided that the decedent was not only the insured but also the owner of the policies. If the decedent made any gifts after 1976 and within three years before his death that were not split gifts, their gross amount (valued at date of death) less his applicable annual exclusions, plus the gift taxes he or his estate paid on them, may be includable.

If the gifts were split gifts, quite technical consequences ensue. If any gifts were made before 1977 and the decedent dies within three years thereafter, the date of death being after 1976 and before 1980, such gifts may be held to have been made "in contemplation of death" and, accordingly, may be includable in the gross estate. However, the entire amount is excludable if the prior gift did not require a gift tax return to be filed (except for insurance policies). There are special problems concerning jointly owned property, and these are discussed later.

From the gross estate there are deducted (1) indebtedness such as mortgages and loans owed by the decedent; (2) expenses incurred and paid during administration, such as attorney fees and court costs; (3) taxes, principally income taxes and property taxes, during administration (not federal estate and gift taxes and not state death taxes); and (4) casualty losses incurred during administration of the estate. The result is the amount of the adjusted gross estate. The sole object of the calculation of the amount of the adjusted gross estate is to determine the amount, if any, of a marital deduction. Then, any marital deduction and any charitable contributions are deducted, resulting in the taxable estate.

Next, there must be added to the amount of the taxable estate any taxable gifts made in 1977 and later years, but not gifts in contemplation of death. These are called adjusted taxable gifts. Values used are those of the dates of the gifts, and the amounts of gift taxes paid are ignored. At this point, the tentative tax base is reached.

To the amount of the tentative tax base (taxable estate plus adjusted taxable gifts), the unified tax rate table is applied. The result is the amount of the tentative estate tax. The next deduction is for gift taxes paid on gifts made after 1976 (including gift taxes paid by decedent's spouse for split gifts if decedent was the donor and the gifts were includable in the decedent's gross estate). The resulting amount is called the tax before unified credit. The unified credit is then deducted.

From the balance, the following credits for any of the following taxes that were paid are deducted:

1. State death taxes
2. Gift taxes paid on gifts made before 1977 where the subject of the gift is included in the gross estate, such as a gift made in contemplation of death that occurs after 1976 but within three years after the gift
3. Foreign death taxes
4. Estate taxes on prior transfers to decedent from a transferor decedent who dies within ten years before, or within two years after, this decedent's death

The resulting balance is the estate tax payable. The return and a check for the tax are due within nine months after death.

Marital Deduction

Investment assets and other property left by a decedent to a surviving spouse qualify for a marital deduction. The interest bequeathed must be a nonterminable one (except for a qualified terminable interest trust). In other words, suppose the wife is the survivor. If she dies before all installments of an obligation are paid to her, the balance must go to her heirs or as she otherwise directs. If the survivor's interest is only a life estate, it does not qualify. If the interest is as a beneficiary of a trust, she must have a general power of appointment so that she can take out any or all of the cash and property at any time and for any reason. Further, she must be able, under her will, to bequeath any trust corpus not distributed to her during her lifetime to her estate or any entity she wishes.

For a decedent dying on or after January 1, 1982, an unlimited estate tax marital deduction is available for property passing to a surviving spouse (including community property). Keep in mind that if all the assets are left to the surviving spouse, the survivor may be pushed into a very high estate tax bracket. Of course, as long as the surviving spouse marries young and then dies first, a new generation-skipping technique may develop. Theoretically, as long as each surviving spouse marries young, dies first, and there are no simultaneous deaths, assets may escape the estate tax indefinitely.

A major exception to the terminable interest rule is a qualified terminable interest property trust (Q-TIP). After 1981, a Q-TIP qualifies for both marital deductions. Where a spouse receives certain life estates, at the election of the executor (or donor), such property is deemed to pass to the spouse without a tax. The election is irrevocable. However, the spouse (or spouse's estate) is subject later to a tax at the earliest of (1) the time of disposal, or (2) death. A Q-TIP may be appropriate when an individual has married a second spouse and would like to be assured that certain property will pass to children of the first marriage.

From a tax standpoint, many advisors believe it frequently is not prudent to use the full marital deduction. The needs of a surviving spouse can be met by a trust providing income for life accompanied by a discretionary power on the part of the trustee to invade corpus for the surviving spouse's welfare; on death, the remainder can go to their children.

STEP-UP IN BASIS

When an estate is settled, the heirs receive the estate assets at a stepped-up basis. Thus, the appreciation in any estate assets escape the federal income tax. For example, assume that a decedent dies in 1989 owning an antique round oak table valued at $8,000. The decedent had purchased the table for $50. The table would be included in the estate at $8,000 for federal estate tax purposes, and the heir would receive a stepped-up basis of $8,000 in the table. In other words, the $7,950 appreciation would escape the federal income tax. If the heir later sells the table for $8,500, he would recognize only a $500 gain.

Since substantial income tax savings may result, any assets that have increased in value (especially if the taxpayer is elderly) should be retained until death so that the heirs will receive the step-up in basis.

VALUATION OF ASSETS

In general, all assets are valued at their fair market value at the date of death or on an alternative valuation date six months later. In certain situations, a special use valuation is available for property used for farming purposes or closely held businesses.

Fair market value is the price at which the asset would change hands between a willing seller and willing buyer, neither being under any compulsion to sell or buy and both having reasonable knowledge of relevant facts. The amount is not to be determined by a forced-sale price. Also, fair market value is not to be determined by the sale price of the item in a market other than that in which such item is most commonly sold to the public. For example, the includable value of an automobile is the price for which that automobile could be purchased by a consumer, not the price purchased by a dealer.

The value of collectibles are arrived at by appraisers usually appointed by the court. For example, suppose an estate has a large antique collection. The administrator of an estate may hire a professional antique appraiser if the amount involved justifies the expenditure of his fee. The final appraisal figure will be based on the amount that the estate or heirs could fairly expect to receive if they were to offer the antiques for sale on the open market. That is, fair market value is the price at which the antiques would change hands between a willing buyer and a willing seller. Thus, fair market value is the price at which the antiques could be sold at retail rather than dealers' prices. However, if the executor has to sell the antiques for less than fair market value, part of this difference may be deducted.

An executor may elect to value an estate as of the date six months from the date of death. Such an election applies to all the assets of the gross estate. Where property is distributed, sold, exchanged, or otherwise disposed of within the six-month period after the decedent's death, such assets must be valued on the disposition date.

In determining the fair market value of any item of property, all the relevant facts and elements of value of the valuation date must be considered.

Stocks and Bonds

Stocks and bonds are included in the decedent's gross estate at their fair market value per share or per bond on the valuation date. This fair market value is the mean value between the highest and lowest selling prices on the date of valuation. When there are sales on dates within a reasonable period both before and after the valuation date but no sale on the valuation date, the fair market value is the weighted average of the means between the highest and lowest sales on the nearest dates both before and after the valuation date. This average should be weighted inversely by the respective numbers of trading days between the valuation date and the nearest selling date. If there are no actual sales within a reasonable period of the valuation date, then the fair market value is considered to be the mean between the bona fide bid-and-asked prices on the date of valuation.

If it can be established that the value of such stocks and bonds determined on the basis of selling prices or on bid-and-asked prices does not reflect the fair market value, then other relevant facts and elements must be considered in determining the fair market value. For example, if a block of stock was so large in relation to actual sales on the existing market that it could not be liquidated within a reasonable time without depressing the market, or if the block represents a controlling interest, then the price at which other lots change hands may have little relation to the true market value.

An argument can be made for a marketability discount. That is, to the extent a prospective buyer will have difficulty reselling shares of stock in a corporation, such purchaser will pay less than he would if given a convenient method of disposing of the shares. The discount for lack of marketability ranges from 10 to 30 percent.

A minority-interest discount reflects the inability of a minority shareholder to have any influence on the decision-making process of a corporation. Thus, in theory, the minority interest is worth less than the proportionate share of the underlying assets in the corporation. The IRS will often fight both the minority-interest discount and the marketability discount.

If no actual sales prices or bona fide bid-and-asked prices exist, then other factors must be considered in determining the fair market value. In the case of bonds, the soundness of the security, the interest yield, the date of maturity, and other relevant factors must be considered. The factors to consider in the case of share of stock are the company's net worth, prospective earnings, dividend-paying capacity, and other relevant factors. Some of the other relevant factors are goodwill of the business, the economic outlook of the industry, the company's position within the industry, and, of course, its management capability.

There is no theoretical standard or general formula for valuing stock of closely held corporations of any other unlisted stock. A hypothetical marketplace must be established, but the IRS admits that valuation is not an exact science. IRS instructions to appeals officers indicate that they should not expect an appraiser to arrive at the same valuation conclusion as the appeals officer.

The factors to be considered in determining the value of such stock vary with the particular facts involved. The weight to be given to any factor depends on the specific circumstances of that case. The following fundamental factors should receive careful analysis in every case:

1. The nature of the business and the history of the enterprise from its inception
2. The economic outlook in general, and the condition and outlook of the specific industry in particular
3. The book value of the stock and the financial condition of the business
4. The earning capacity of the company
5. The dividend-paying capacity

6. Whether or not the enterprise has goodwill or other intangible value

7. Sales of the stock and the size of the block to be valued

8. The market price of stocks of corporations engaged in the same or a similar line of business and having their stocks actively traded in a free and open market, either as an exchange or over the counter

Business Interests

The fair market value of a decedent's interest in any business is the net amount that a willing buyer would pay a willing seller for such interest, neither being under any compulsion to buy or to sell, and both having reasonable knowledge of all the facts. A fair appraisal should be made of the earning capacity of the business and of all its assets, including goodwill. These elements should be considered in determining its net value. However, the value of a business interest may be fixed by a mutual buy-and-sell agreement. For such an agreement to be effective for estate tax purposes, it must bind the estate to sell, either by giving the survivors an option or by binding all parties, and the price must not be so grossly inadequate as to make the agreement a mere gratuitous promise.

Cash Accounts

All cash belongings to the decedent, including that in the possession of others and that deposited in banks, is included in the gross estate. The bank account may be reduced by valued and bona fide checks that are outstanding on the date of death, but that are subsequently honored by the bank. The fair market value of any secured or unsecured note held by the decedent is presumed to be the principal face amount of the note plus interest accrued to the date of death. Under certain circumstances, the executor may establish that the value of the note is something less or even worthless.

Personal Property

Generally, the fair market value of the decedent's household and personal effects is considered to be the price that a willing buyer would pay to a willing seller. There should be a room-by-room itemization of these articles. A separate value should be listed for each item; however, all articles in a room worth \$100 or less may be grouped together. Instead of making such an itemized list, the executor may, under the risk of penalties of perjury, submit a written statement containing the aggregate value of the property as appraised by a competent appraiser. But if there are included among these household and personal effects any articles having an artistic or intrinsic value of more than \$3,000, the appraisal of an expert must be filed with the estate tax return. Before the executor may sell or distribute any of the household or personal effects in advance of an investigation by an officer of the IRS, he must give the district director notice of such action. This notice must be accompanied by an appraisal of such property.

Real Property

Real property is to be valued under Reg. 20.2031-1 at its "highest and best use." This phrase means the most profitable use to which the property might logically and probably be put. The one exception is the special use valuation method under Section 2032A.

The three generally recognized methods used to value real property are:

1. Comparable sales approach
2. Income capitalization method
3. Replacement cost approach

The comparable sales approach involves comparing the property being valued with similar properties that have been sold recently in arm's length transactions. Rev. Proc. 79-24, 1979-1 CB 565, give guidelines for the comparable-sales approach in appraising unimproved real property. This approach is used often for valuation of unimproved real estate.

The income capitalization method is based on a projection of the real property's net income over its reasonable economic life which is capitalized to convert the income stream into a market value. The income capitalization approach is used often for valuation of industrial and commercial property.

The replacement cost approach is subject to the greatest risk of error. This valuation method is based on the construction cost, less depreciation, of replacing property similar to the property being valued.

Annuities, Insurance, and Other Term Contracts

The fair market value of annuities, life estates, terms for years, remainders, and reversions is their present value. The regulations provide tables to be used in calculating the present value of these assets. The value of a contract for the payment of an annuity or an insurance policy on the life of another person is the price for which such a contract could be acquired on the date of the decedent's death from a company regularly engaged in selling contracts of that nature. If further premiums are to be paid on a life insurance policy on the life of another person, the value of such a policy may be approximated by adding to the interpolated terminal reserve at the date of the decedent's death the proportionate part of the gross premium that was last paid before the decedent's death and that covers the period extending beyond that date.

Alternative Valuation

Although all property belonging to the decedent on the date of death is included in the gross estate and is generally appraised at its fair market value, the executor may elect to value the estate either at the date of the decedent's death or as of the date six months (not 180 days) after the decedent's date of death. This later date is referred to as the alternative valuation date (AVD).

If the AVD is to be used, the executor must make that election on the estate tax return. In no case may such an election be made or a previous election be changed after the date of the tax return. When the AVD is elected, it is applied to all property of the gross estate and is valued according to the following rules:

1. Any property distributed, sold, exchanged, or otherwise disposed of within six months after the decedent's death must be valued as of the date on which it is disposed of.

2. Any property not distributed, sold, exchanged, or otherwise disposed of within six months after the decedent's death must be valued as of the date six months after the decedent's death.

3. Any property, interest, or estate that is affected by a mere lapse of time must be valued as of the date of the decedent's death. However, it must be adjusted for any change in value not due to a mere lapse of time within six months after the decedent's death or as of the date of its disposition, whichever occurs first.

Of course the purpose of the alternative valuation date is to permit a reduction in estate taxes whenever there is a shrinkage in the aggregate value of the estate property. However, there are some interrelated income tax consequences that should be evaluated before selecting the most advantageous valuation date, especially since the AVD may not be elected unless the valuation amount decreases both the value of the gross estate and the estate tax liability of the estate.

For example, a decedent's gross estate at the date of death is $480,000 in 1989, but its value six months later is $520,000. There would not be an estate tax whether or not the alternative valuation date election were made because the threshold filing requirement for the year is $600,000. Thus, for purposes of a possible stepped-up basis, the executor could not elect AVD.

THE FINANCIAL PLANNING INDUSTRY

Maria Crawford Scott

Financial planning is a nebulous term to many investors. Financial planners include accountants, brokers, and insurance salesmen, not to mention those who simply refer to themselves as financial planners.

Like investing, much of this work can be done by individuals who have the time, understanding, and access to information regarding the process. The financial planning industry is booming; many individuals are using financial planners, so there must be a perceived need. Exactly what financial planning is will be presented here.

RESPONSIBILITIES OF THE FINANCIAL PLANNER

Financial planning encompasses an evaluation of an individual's current financial situation, an identification of the individual's financial goals, and the presentation of a plan to achieve those goals. The financial planning industry stresses that planners are not substitutes for tax preparers, accountants, and estate attorneys. Instead, the planner delineates a plan with a specified goal; with that basis, the planner can then coordinate the others, if needed, so that everyone is working toward the same goal.

A typical financial plan includes the following:

- A balance sheet and analysis—this is an overall financial picture of the individual's assets, income, insurance, taxes, business interests and wills, and

Maria Crawford Scott is Editor of the AAII Journal, a publication of the American Association of Individual Investors, Chicago, Ill.

includes an asset allocation breakdown that relates to the risk preferences and needs of the individual

- Projection of income taxes
- Projection of cash flow
- Long-term accumulation plans—this includes planning for children's education, retirement, and so forth as well as a statement of the individual's goals
- Insurance analysis
- Estate and tax planning

In addition, the plan should identify weaknesses in the individual's financial picture, such as inadequate cash flow, unnecessary tax payments, and the wrong kind of insurance or investments, and it should recommend specific improvements. Finally, the plan should include recommendations for implementing the program.

NEEDS FOR FINANCIAL PLANNING

Financial planners list a number of reasons individuals go to them for help, including:

- Lack of knowledge even in relatively basic areas
- Specific problem that arises and the individual is not sure of the overall ramifications (e.g., a profit-sharing distribution)
- Complex financial picture with the need for a single source to sort it out
- Lack of time or desire to do it
- Need for a third-party observer to objectively review a plan and help determine if the assumptions and goals are reasonable

The question of whether an individual needs a planner comes down to practical considerations. If an individual understands most of his financial problems and has the time to devote to them, he doesn't need a planner. Most individuals with incomes under $50,000 can easily gain the education they need to plan their own finances, although some people simply do not understand even the basics. On the other hand, individuals making over $50,000 will tend to have net worths of some substance. While they can get the education needed, they may not have the necessary time to commit.

CHOOSING A FINANCIAL PLANNER

The checklist provided here is mentioned in most guides to picking a financial planner and is based primarily on common sense. However, one item that is stressed by planners themselves is the type of client a particular planner serves. Most planners specialize in types of clients with similar goals and life-styles. For instance, one planner's clients may be primarily physicians, another's may be yuppies, and another's may be older executives. Most individuals within such as group will have similar financial concerns, goals, and life-styles, all of which are critical elements in the financial planning process.

Most individuals should schedule a short meeting with several planners before one is actually chosen. This allows both parties to determine how well they get along, and how they will work together.

Other steps in the selection process include the following:

- Individuals can request from various professional associations lists of planners in a specific area; in some instances, the planners must pass certain requirements to be listed (see Figure 1).
- Individuals should review a planner's background and credentials (e.g., education and professional experience). Experts recommend at least a four-year college degree in a financially related field, such as accounting, economics, business administration, or finance. Related degrees and designations are presented in Figure 1.
- It is helpful for planners to provide references, including clients and professionals (e.g., bankers and lawyers) with whom the planner has worked.
- Individuals want to know the areas in which a planner is knowledgeable, such as investments, insurance, and tax strategies. However, the planner should also be working with other professionals, including accountants and tax attorneys.
- Planners should explain exactly what the financial planning service includes. This should be comprehensive and should include a written analysis of the client's financial situation and the planner's recommendations.
- Planners should provide a sample plan—one that is similar to the client's.
- It should be clear that the plan is individualized; the planner should not rely on a uniform plan applied to everyone.
- It should be clear to the client who does the work; that is, who will actually be working on the plan?
- Individuals should understand how investment solutions are researched. Is it independent analysis or does the planner depend on some other company?
- The planner should explain how he charges—whether he is fee only or compensated fully or partially through commissions. Fees should be discussed during the first visit, as well as whether the firm is affiliated with a broker/dealer.
- Finally, the planner who receives commissions should explain what products those commissions are primarily generated from.

FEES AND COSTS

Financial planners charge clients in one of three ways: on a fee-only basis, on a fee-and-commission basis, or on a commission basis.

Fee-only planners charge clients either by the hour or based on the value of the client's assets or income. Commission planners make their money from the purchase of products necessary to implement the financial plan; the client is not charged for the plan design itself. Fee-and-commission planners use a combination of the two, with the fee-to-commission ratio varying from planner to planner.

It is important to realize that the cost to the individual is not necessarily dependent on the method of compensation. Planners that are compensated somewhat or entirely through commissions can charge less for the basic plan. However, they will steer clients toward the purchase of commission-based products. Fee-only planners, on the other hand, will charge

FIGURE 1. The Financial Planning Industry

EDUCATIONAL INSTITUTIONS

The following educational institutions provide designations or degrees specifically in financial planning. Many also offer adult education courses on financial planning for nonprofessionals.

College for Financial Planning: *9725 East Hampden Ave., Denver, Colo. 80231; (303) 755-7101.* Offers the Certified Financial Planner Professional Education Program. The college also sponsors continuing education programs. Courses are available through self-study or through classroom study offered by affiliated colleges, universities, and an independent adjunct faculty.

The American College: *270 Bryn Mawr Ave., Bryn Mawr, Penn.; (215) 526-1000.* Offers the Chartered Financial Consultant program that leads to the ChFC designation. It also offers a program leading to the Chartered Life Underwriter (CLU) designation; programs leading to master's degrees in financial services and mananagement; and continuing education.

PROFESSIONAL ORGANIZATIONS

International Association for Financial Planning: *2 Concourse Parkway, Suite 800, Atlanta, Ga. 30328; (404) 395-1605.* Has 22,000 members who must be actively involved in the financial services industry and subscribe to its code of ethics. Has reached an agreement in principle to establish formal links with the ICFP.

Referrals: On request, the IAFP will provide names and addresses of financial planners in a specified location who are listed in The Registry, which has qualification requirements.

The Institute of Certified Financial Planners: *10065 E. Harvard Ave., Suite 320, Denver, Colo. 80231; (303) 751-7600.* Has 8,000 members and associate members. Full members are CFPs while associate members include CFP candidates and instructors, CPAs, JDs, CLUs, and ChFCs. Full members must complete 60 hours of continuing education every two years, must declare practitioner status in financial planning, and must subscribe to the group's code of ethics. Has reached an agreement in principal to establish formal links with the IAFP.

Referrals: On request, the ICEP will send a list of five financial planners in a specified location who are CFPs and declare financial planning as their primary activity. The list includes the planner's name, address, telephone number, educational background, degrees, designations, membership in professional organizations, and compensation.

The National Association of Personal Financial Advisors: *1130 Lake Cook Road, Suite 105, Buffalo Grove, Ill. 60089; (312) 537-7722.* Has about 180 members who are fee-only financial planners. Members must be practicing financial planners, their compensation must be fee-only, and they must have certain educational designations or equivalent job experience. NAPFA will also provide a disclosure form to assist individuals when interviewing a prospective planner.

Referrals: For $1, the association will send a list of members in a state. There is no screening process other than the membership requirement.

PROFESSIONAL DESIGNATIONS

CFP: Certified Financial Planner, conferred by the International Board of Standards and Practices for Certified Financial Planners after completion of a registered financial planning education program and after passing the six-part national IBCFP certification examination series.

ChFC: Chartered Financial Consultant, conferred by the American College after passing all courses offered in the ChFC program, and providing the applicant has three years related business experience.

more for the basic plan but steer clients toward commission-free products, such as no-load mutual funds and no-load life insurance, which are considerably cheaper. When comparing planners with different fee structures, individuals should consider the total cost of implementing the plan.

The actual costs of financial plans vary. The International Association for Financial Planning (IAFP) estimates custom-developed plans at $750 to $2,000. Another financial planning industry official put the customized plan cost at about $2,000 to $5,000 for a typical plan for an individual with an income of from $75,000 to $200,000 and a portfolio of about $250,000 and up. Hourly charges for fee-only planners typically range from $75 to $150. In general, the simpler the plan, the lower the cost. A simple plan for an individual with a salary of $25,000 can cost as low as $500.

The typical computer-generated plan, offered by such firms as American Express and Merrill Lynch, costs about $250. Individuals fill out detailed financial statements, the results of which are run through a computer and compared with a model plan. However, these plans draw low ratings from professional financial planners.

The various methods of compensation have caused considerable controversy within the financial planning industry itself. Most planners have commission compensation arrangements. This, however, has raised conflict of interest questions: Can a planner who has part or all of his income based on the sale of a product be truly objective in devising a financial plan? The two major organizations, the IAFP and the Institute of Certified Financial Planners (ICFP), have not taken any position as to whether financial planners should be fee-only. Both have large numbers of commission and fee-and-commission financial planners as members. However, both organizations insist that clients should know in advance how the planner will be compensated.

Some financial planners have organized around smaller groups that promote fee-only planning. The National Association of Personal Financial Advisors (NAPFA) is a group composed of fee-only planners. The group feels strongly that the industry will not be truly professionalized unless it moves to eliminate compensation arrangements that may compromise a planner's objectivity.

INDUSTRY WATCHDOGS

Currently, there are no industry watchdogs: No state or federal regulations define any qualifications for financial planners. Industry groups say, however, that it is only a matter of time, and the major financial planning organizations are pushing for some form of state licensing. Many states currently have bills pending that would regulate the financial planning industry. These range from capital requirements for financial planning firms, to definitions as to who can call themselves financial planners, to various forms of disclosure and registration. No bills have yet passed, however, and there is no consensus on what kind of regulation would be appropriate. The IAFP has adopted a two-track approach, seeking uniform federal regulation and, at the same time, attempting to assure uniform and effective regulation in the states. The IAFP federal proposal seeks the establishment of an independent self-regulatory organization for investment advisors and financial planners.

The Securities and Exchange Commission (SEC) has stated that financial planners should register as financial advisors. Individuals should be aware, however, that SEC registration means only that the proper forms have been filed and the proper fees paid; the SEC does not pass judgment on competence or training. On the other hand, SEC rules do require that registered planners inform clients, in writing, of their education and experience, of the type of work they do, and how they are paid.

PROFESSIONAL DESIGNATIONS

Two industry organizations accredit planners who have completed certain educational and professional requirements: The International Board of Standards and Practices for Certified Financial Planners (IBCFP) confers the Certified Financial Planner (CFP) designation, and the American College confers the Chartered Financial Consultant (ChFC) designation.

The designation processes are similar to those used to confer the Certified Public Accountant (CPA) and Chartered Financial Analyst (CFA) designations, although they have been criticized as not being as rigorous as either the CPA or CFA. In addition, the ChFC has been criticized as being tied too closely to the insurance industry. The American College opened in 1927 with a program in the life insurance field services and management that offers the Chartered Life Underwriter (CLU) designation. The American College later expanded its program and began offering the ChFC designation in 1981.

The CFP program was started in 1972 by the College for Financial Planning (the College), which currently provides the educational program. The CFP designation, however, is conferred by the IBCFP, which oversees the examination process. The CFP program has a number of requirements. To be eligible for the program, individuals must have at least a high school diploma or GED. The CFP program is two-year, six-part curriculum covering insurance, investments, tax planning and management, retirement planning, employee benefits, and estate planning. The program is available through self-study or classroom study. Classroom study is available through seventy affiliate colleges and universities throughout the U.S. under a license agreement with the College. In addition, an independent adjunct faculty approved by the College teaches courses in most major metropolitan areas. Successful completion of courses and a final examination leads to a certificate of completion from the College. The College also offers courses that qualify for continuing education credit hours to meet requirements for the IAFP, IBCFP, and ICFP.

To qualify for CFP designation, individuals must complete a financial planning education program that has been registered with the IBCFP, and they must pass the six-part national IBCFP certification examination series.

The ChFC program has a ten-course curriculum covering the environment (three courses, encompassing the economic, tax, and regulatory environment; identification of client needs and objectives; the role of various financial institutions; and concepts in professionalism and ethics), "products tools and techniques" (three courses), and planning concepts and applications (four courses). Each course has a two-hour examination. Requirements for the ChFC designation are as follows:

- Must pass all courses
- Must have three years of related business experience, including twelve months just prior to the award of the designation
- Must meet established ethical standards
- Must be over age 21

Since there are no comprehensive regulations governing the field, financial planners do not necessarily have any of these designations. Many financial planners come from related fields, such as accounting, law, real estate and insurance, each of which has its own designations.

PROFESSIONAL ORGANIZATIONS

Two major professional organizations cover the financial services industry: the International Association for Financial Planning and the Institute of Certified Financial Planners. The latter organization's educational arm is the College for Financial Planning, which confers the CFP designation. In mid-1988, these two organizations agreed in principle to link, forming one professional organization and an industry organization: The agreement is designed to lead to a more formalized connection between the two groups.

The IAFP currently has about 22,000 members. The association requires that members be actively involved in the financial services industry and subscribe to its code of ethics. Membership can be withdrawn as a result of disciplinary action. The IAFP says its purpose is to provide a continuing education program, to build an unified approach to financial planning, and to maintain high ethical standards. The group also serves to promote the industry.

The IAFP has a referral service known as The Registry of Financial Planning Practitioners. Since IAFP membership has no specific educational or professional requirements, minimum standards were established for listing in The Registry. These include conferment of an accepted degree in the area of financial planning or a related field, three years of professional experience, direct involvement in all defined steps of the planning process, and completion of a written examination. On request, the IAFP will supply names of financial planners in a specific location that are listed in The Registry. Local chapters of the IAFP will also provide lists of area financial planners, although they provide no screening process. The Registry will continue to exist despite the formalized tie with the ICFP. Under the linkage agreement, current members of the Registry will be grandfathered, but the IAFP will support the CFP designation as the financial planning industry designation.

The ICEP has about 8,000 members who are CFPs (designated by its sister educational organization—the College) and associate members. Full members also must complete sixty hours of continuing education every two years, must be full-time planners, and subscribe to the group's code of ethics. Membership can be withdrawn through disciplinary action. The ICFP says its purpose is to establish and maintain professionalism in financial planning. Policies for financial planning procedures as well as ethics enforcement are maintained by the IBCFP. This board is similar to the accounting industry's FASB.

On request, the ICFP will send a list of financial planners in a specified location. The list consists of CFP members in good standing, and includes the planner's name, address, phone number, educational background, licenses, and other organization memberships, and how the planner is compensated.

NAPFA is a much smaller organization of about 180 financial planners that was started in 1983 to advance the practice of fee-only financial planning. Members must be practicing financial planners, their compensation must be fee only and they must have certain educational designations or equivalent job experience. The association will, on request, send a list of members in a specific location, but it does not have any screening process other than the membership requirement. The organization will also, on request, send a financial planner disclosure form, which includes a list of questions the organization feels all clients should be informed of before selecting a planner.

INDEX

• A •

• C •

• E •

• **F** •

• G •

• H •

• I •

• J •

• K •

• L •

• M •

• P •

• Q •

• R •

• S •

• W •

• Y •

• Z •